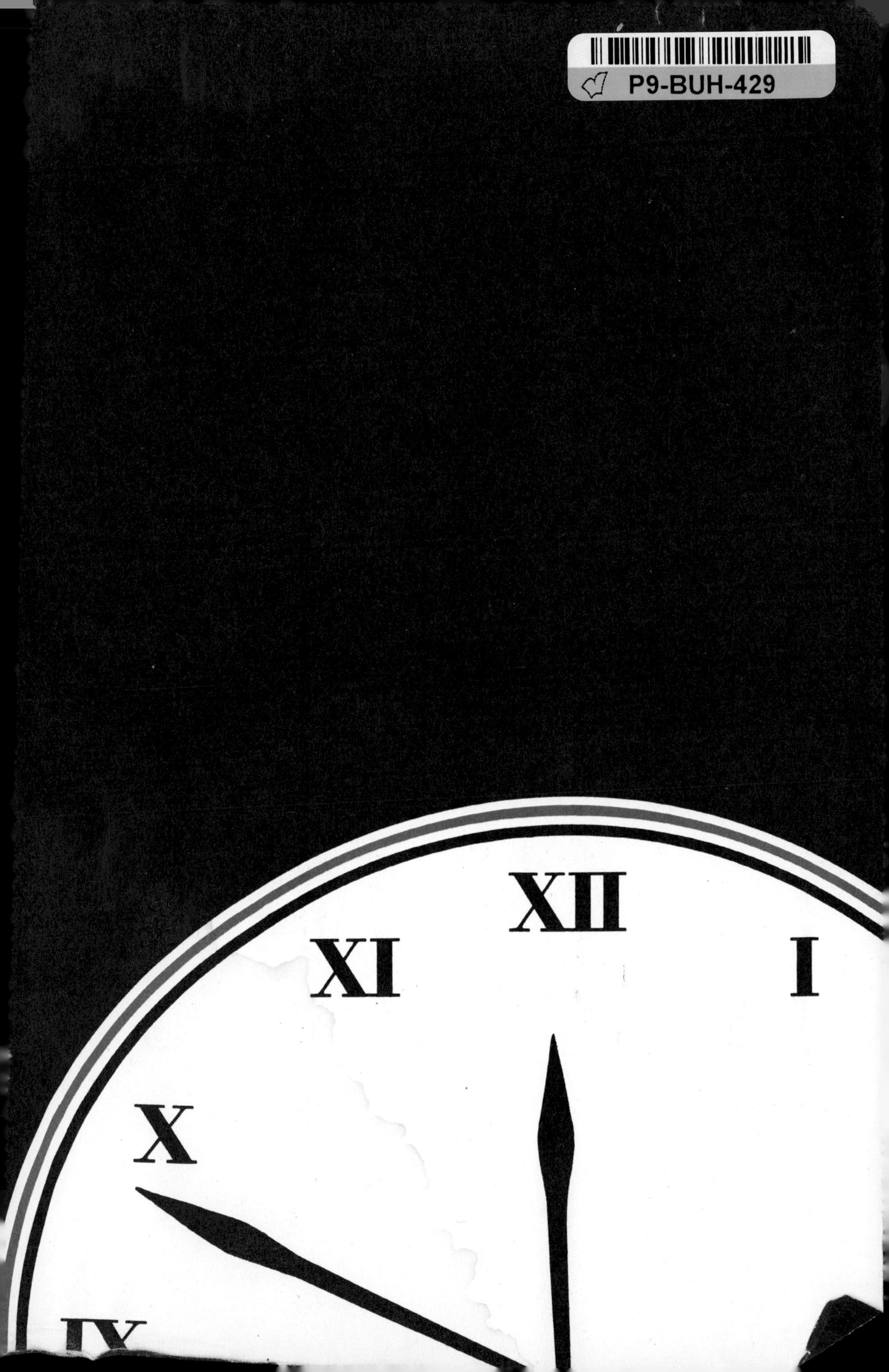
XII
XI
I
X

ALAN MOORE
writer

DAVE GIBBONS
illustrator/letterer

JOHN HIGGINS
colorist

Watchmen created by
Alan Moore and
Dave Gibbons

LEN WEIN & BARBARA RANDALL
Editors — Original Series

JEB WOODARD
Group Editor — Collected Editions

PETER HAMBOUSSI
Editor — Collected Edition

RACHEL PINNELAS
Assistant Editor — Collected Edition

STEVE COOK
Design Director — Books

LOUIS PRANDI
Publication Design

BOB HARRAS
Senior VP — Editor-in-Chief, DC Comics

PAT McCALLUM
Executive Editor, DC Comics

DAN DiDIO
Publisher

JIM LEE
Publisher & Chief Creative Officer

BOBBIE CHASE
VP — New Publishing Initiatives & Talent Development

DON FALLETTI
VP— Manufacturing Operations & Workflow Management

LAWRENCE GANEM
VP — Talent Services

ALISON GILL
Senior VP — Manufacturing & Operations

HANK KANALZ
Senior VP — Publishing Strategy & Support Services

DAN MIRON
VP — Publishing Operations

NICK J. NAPOLITANO
VP — Manufacturing Administration & Design

NANCY SPEARS
VP — Sales

MICHELE R. WELLS
VP & Executive Editor, Young Reader

WATCHMEN (NEW EDITION)

DC COMICS, 2900 W. ALAMEDA AVENUE, BURBANK, CA 91505
PRINTED BY LSC COMMUNICATIONS, OWENSVILLE, MO, USA. 5/10/19.
FIRST PRINTING. ISBN: 978-1-7795-0112-7

LIBRARY OF CONGRESS CATALOGING-IN-PUBLICATION DATA

MOORE, ALAN, 1953- AUTHOR.
  WATCHMEN : NEW EDITION / ALAN MOORE, DAVE GIBBONS.
    PAGES CM
  "ORIGINALLY PUBLISHED IN SINGLE MAGAZINE FORM IN WATCHMEN
  1-12."
  ISBN 978-1-4012-4525-2
  1. GRAPHIC NOVELS. I. GIBBONS, DAVE, 1949- ILLUSTRATOR. II. TITLE.
  PN6737.M66W39 2013
  741.5'942–DC23
                                    20130
03992

ORIGINAL COLOR: 1986; ADDITIONAL COLORING &
DIGITAL FINISHING 2005 BY JOHN HIGGINS.

ART RECONSTRUCTION BY HANK MANFRA, AARON TAPPEN,
EMILY RYAN LERNER AND COREY BREEN.

COLOR RECONSTRUCTION BY WILDSTORM FX: CARRIE STRACHAN,
RANDY MAYOR, DARLENE ROYER AND DAVID RODRIGUEZ.

With special thanks to
Neil Gaiman, Mike Lake,
Pat Mills, and Joe Orlando.

It began with Bob Dylan.

For me, a couplet from his 1966 masterpiece Desolation Row was the spark that would one day ignite WATCHMEN.

At Midnight all the agents
and the superhuman crew

Come out and round up
everyone who knows more
than they do.

It was a glimpse, a mere fragment of something; something ominous, paranoid and threatening. But something that showed that comics, like poetry or rock and roll or Bob Dylan himself, might feasibly become part of the greater cultural continuum. The lines must have also lodged in Alan's consciousness for, nearly twenty years later, Dylan's words eventually provided the title of the first issue of our comic book series WATCHMEN.

Another twenty years on from then, in collected form, WATCHMEN itself would become a widely heralded cultural touchstone. Way, way back in the sixties, however, comics still lay on the dim margins of culture. Emasculated in the witch-hunts of the previous decade, they were largely saccharine and censored, harmless juvenile reading fodder at best.

There were signs to be glimpsed though, hints of what might lie ahead. A brief mention of a superhero in a newspaper here, a slim volume of comics history there or a fragment of a comic book page appropriated as "pop art" in a gallery. By the middle of the decade, the anarchic glee of underground comics seemed no more odd than the absurd Batman TV series. The times they were a-changin', indeed.

We comics fans were partly pleased, partly disappointed, that our medium, for so long overlooked, had been spotted by the wider world. Like so many offbeat obsessions, comics might lose their exclusive, secretive allure if everyone noticed and dragged them into the full light of day.

More than any other, the comic book medium is founded on the evocative glimpse. Indeed, the very fabric, the mechanism, of comics is essentially a series of static snapshot panels magically given continuity by the reader's attention.

The cover of a comic is typically a tight little promise of pleasure, crafted to lure the eye, excite the curiosity and, that done, hook the reader into buying. Once inside the comic, the true fan needs but a few panels depicting some prior continuity or an incarnation of a character published decades earlier to open up vast suggested histories of wonder.

Such is the power of the glimpse, the magpie lure of a promising hint.

Often, in their actual content, comics would show these promises to be lies. But sometimes, just sometimes, they would prove to be truly memorable fictional realities. Such a thing was possible for comics; such a thing could be aspired to.

The particular qualities of the form aside, there is nothing that fundamentally separates comics from other storytelling media. The same considerations, essential to a satisfying narrative, apply here as elsewhere in the realms of fiction.

Whether tales are told by the light of a campfire or by the glow of a screen, the prime decision for the teller has always been what to reveal and what to withhold. Whether in words alone or with images, the narrator must be clear about what is to be shown and what is to be hidden.

Relating the entirety of experience is too full, too unmediated and sprawling to appeal, too much like the mundane existence it approximates. It is for the storyteller to offer the tantalizing glimpse and for the audience to supply the closure which it suggests.

It was in this knowledge that we approached WATCHMEN.

Although Alan knew the broad strokes of the story from the beginning, the precise narrative decisions were made only as we talked and pondered, sifting possibilities, waiting for the flash of gold in the stream of conversation and ideas. Waited for the glimpse of something valuable.

The story in this volume is the aggregation of what we gathered, what we thought would best tell our tale. The rest, discarded, washed downstream and vanished from view.

In truth, for all its breadth and detail, actual and implied, WATCHMEN is finite, as closed and complete as a varnished oil painting or, perhaps, a delicate clock mechanism.

We crafted it as carefully as we could and, concentrated and intense though it was, enjoyed every moment of its creation. There really is nothing left to add other than to cordially invite the reader to enjoy bringing their own closure to the work.

In the end, Bob Dylan probably put it best, in another of his masterpieces, Gates of Eden:

> At dawn my lover comes to me
> and tells me of her dreams,
>
> With no attempts to shovel the
> glimpse
>
> Into the ditch of what each one
> means.

Dave Gibbons
March 2013

CHAPTER I

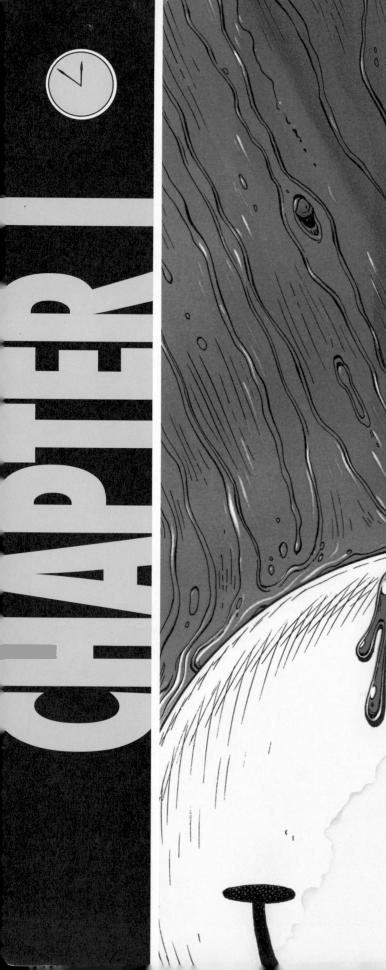

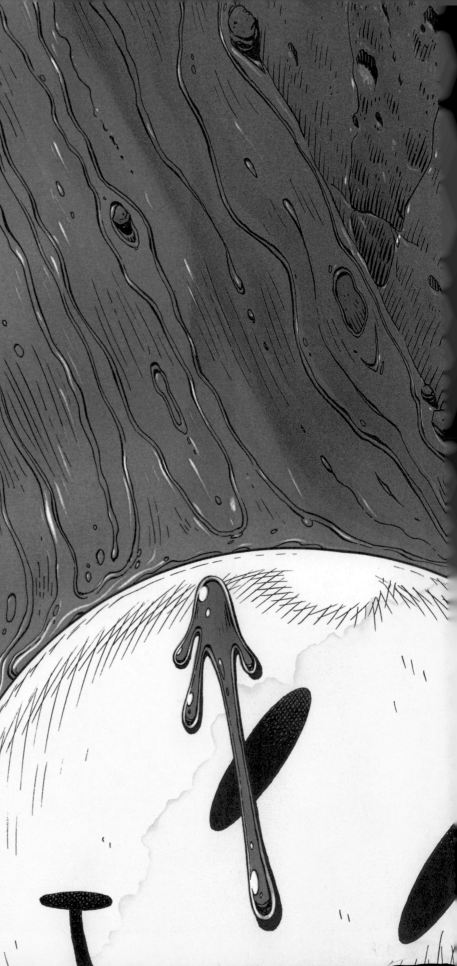

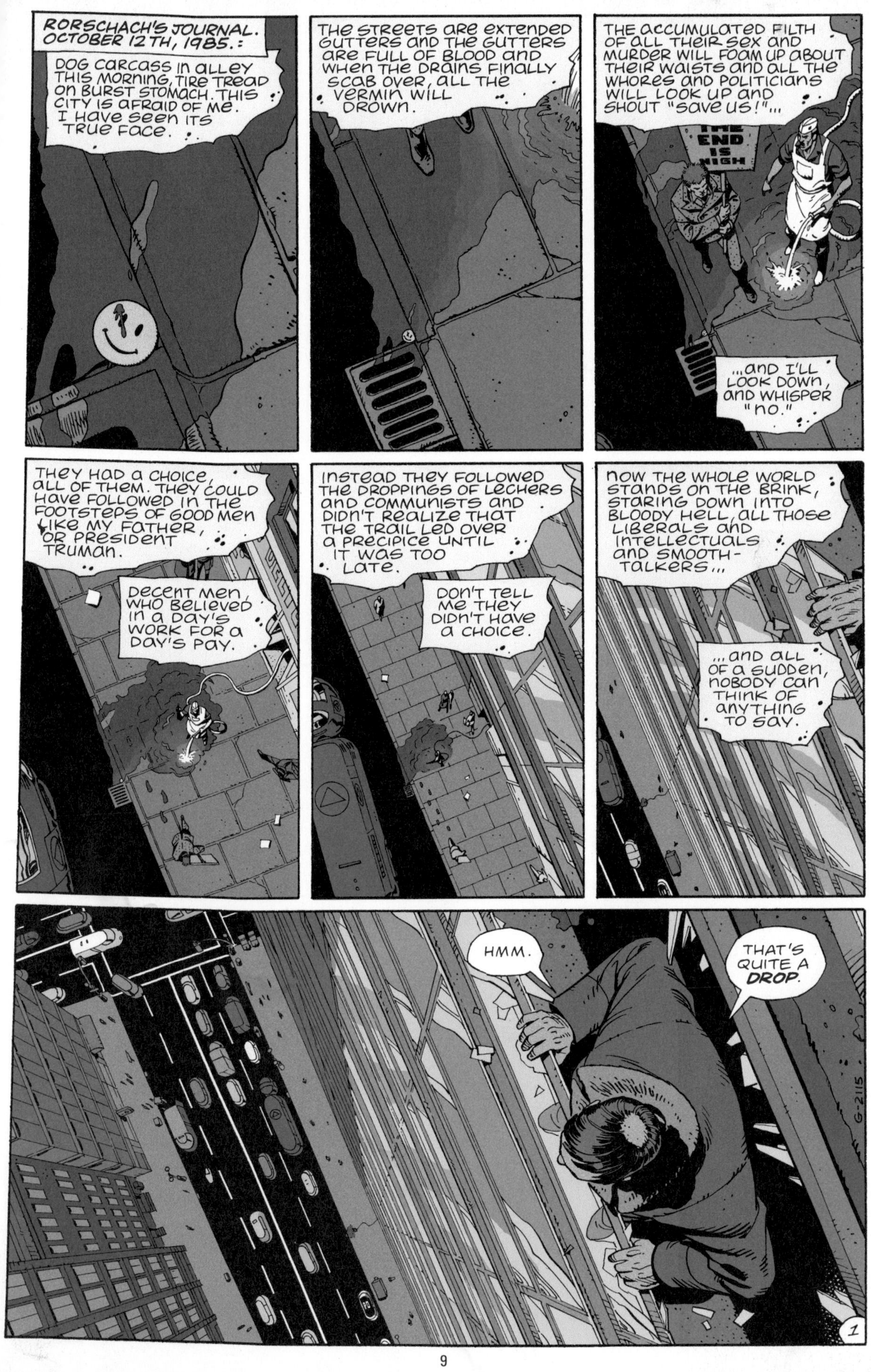
RORSCHACH'S JOURNAL. OCTOBER 12TH, 1985.:
DOG CARCASS IN ALLEY THIS MORNING, TIRE TREAD ON BURST STOMACH. THIS CITY IS AFRAID OF ME. I HAVE SEEN ITS TRUE FACE.
THE STREETS ARE EXTENDED GUTTERS AND THE GUTTERS ARE FULL OF BLOOD AND WHEN THE DRAINS FINALLY SCAB OVER, ALL THE VERMIN WILL DROWN.
THE ACCUMULATED FILTH OF ALL THEIR SEX AND MURDER WILL FOAM UP ABOUT THEIR WAISTS AND ALL THE WHORES AND POLITICIANS WILL LOOK UP AND SHOUT "SAVE US!"...
...AND I'LL LOOK DOWN, AND WHISPER "NO."
THEY HAD A CHOICE, ALL OF THEM. THEY COULD HAVE FOLLOWED IN THE FOOTSTEPS OF GOOD MEN LIKE MY FATHER, OR PRESIDENT TRUMAN.
DECENT MEN, WHO BELIEVED IN A DAY'S WORK FOR A DAY'S PAY.
INSTEAD THEY FOLLOWED THE DROPPINGS OF LECHERS AND COMMUNISTS AND DIDN'T REALIZE THAT THE TRAIL LED OVER A PRECIPICE UNTIL IT WAS TOO LATE.
DON'T TELL ME THEY DIDN'T HAVE A CHOICE.
NOW THE WHOLE WORLD STANDS ON THE BRINK, STARING DOWN INTO BLOODY HELL, ALL THOSE LIBERALS AND INTELLECTUALS AND SMOOTH-TALKERS...
...AND ALL OF A SUDDEN, NOBODY CAN THINK OF ANYTHING TO SAY.
HMM.
THAT'S QUITE A DROP.
1

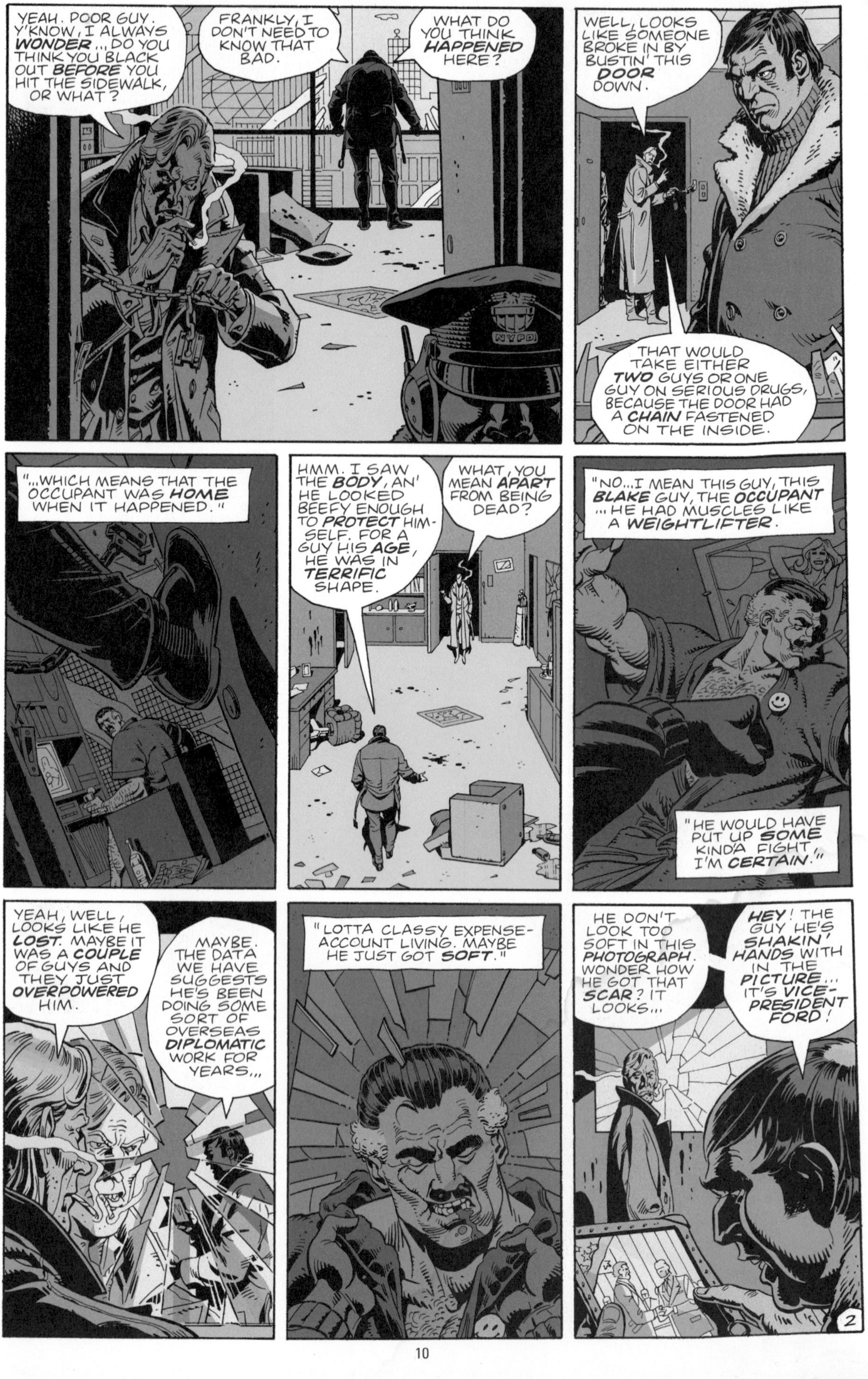
YEAH. POOR GUY. Y'KNOW, I ALWAYS WONDER ... DO YOU THINK YOU BLACK OUT BEFORE YOU HIT THE SIDEWALK, OR WHAT?
FRANKLY, I DON'T NEED TO KNOW THAT BAD.
WHAT DO YOU THINK HAPPENED HERE?
NYPD
WELL, LOOKS LIKE SOMEONE BROKE IN BY BUSTIN' THIS DOOR DOWN.
THAT WOULD TAKE EITHER TWO GUYS OR ONE GUY ON SERIOUS DRUGS, BECAUSE THE DOOR HAD A CHAIN FASTENED ON THE INSIDE.
"...WHICH MEANS THAT THE OCCUPANT WAS HOME WHEN IT HAPPENED."
HMM. I SAW THE BODY, AN' HE LOOKED BEEFY ENOUGH TO PROTECT HIMSELF. FOR A GUY HIS AGE, HE WAS IN TERRIFIC SHAPE.
WHAT, YOU MEAN APART FROM BEING DEAD?
"NO...I MEAN THIS GUY, THIS BLAKE GUY, THE OCCUPANT ... HE HAD MUSCLES LIKE A WEIGHTLIFTER.
"HE WOULD HAVE PUT UP SOME KIND'A FIGHT, I'M CERTAIN."
YEAH, WELL, LOOKS LIKE HE LOST. MAYBE IT WAS A COUPLE OF GUYS AND THEY JUST OVERPOWERED HIM.
MAYBE. THE DATA WE HAVE SUGGESTS HE'S BEEN DOING SOME SORT OF OVERSEAS DIPLOMATIC WORK FOR YEARS...
"LOTTA CLASSY EXPENSE-ACCOUNT LIVING. MAYBE HE JUST GOT SOFT."
HE DON'T LOOK TOO SOFT IN THIS PHOTOGRAPH. WONDER HOW HE GOT THAT SCAR? IT LOOKS...
HEY! THE GUY HE'S SHAKIN' HANDS WITH IN THE PICTURE... IT'S VICE-PRESIDENT FORD!
2

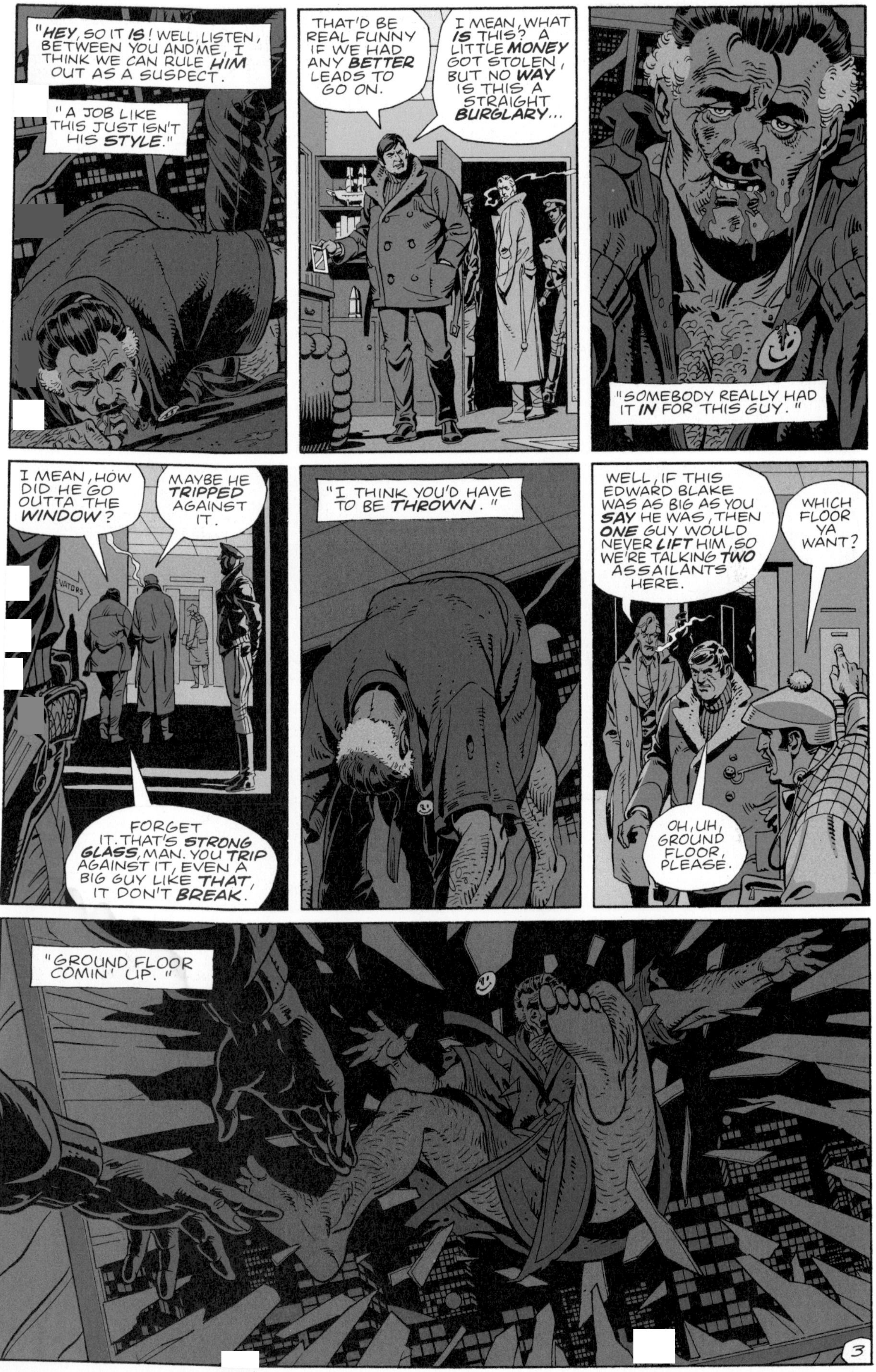
"HEY, SO IT IS! WELL, LISTEN, BETWEEN YOU AND ME, I THINK WE CAN RULE HIM OUT AS A SUSPECT.
"A JOB LIKE THIS JUST ISN'T HIS STYLE."
THAT'D BE REAL FUNNY IF WE HAD ANY BETTER LEADS TO GO ON.
I MEAN, WHAT IS THIS? A LITTLE MONEY GOT STOLEN, BUT NO WAY IS THIS A STRAIGHT BURGLARY...
"SOMEBODY REALLY HAD IT IN FOR THIS GUY."
I MEAN, HOW DID HE GO OUTTA THE WINDOW?
MAYBE HE TRIPPED AGAINST IT.
FORGET IT. THAT'S STRONG GLASS, MAN. YOU TRIP AGAINST IT, EVEN A BIG GUY LIKE THAT, IT DON'T BREAK.
"I THINK YOU'D HAVE TO BE THROWN."
WELL, IF THIS EDWARD BLAKE WAS AS BIG AS YOU SAY HE WAS, THEN ONE GUY WOULD NEVER LIFT HIM, SO WE'RE TALKING TWO ASSAILANTS HERE.
WHICH FLOOR YA WANT?
OH, UH, GROUND FLOOR, PLEASE.
"GROUND FLOOR COMIN' UP."
3

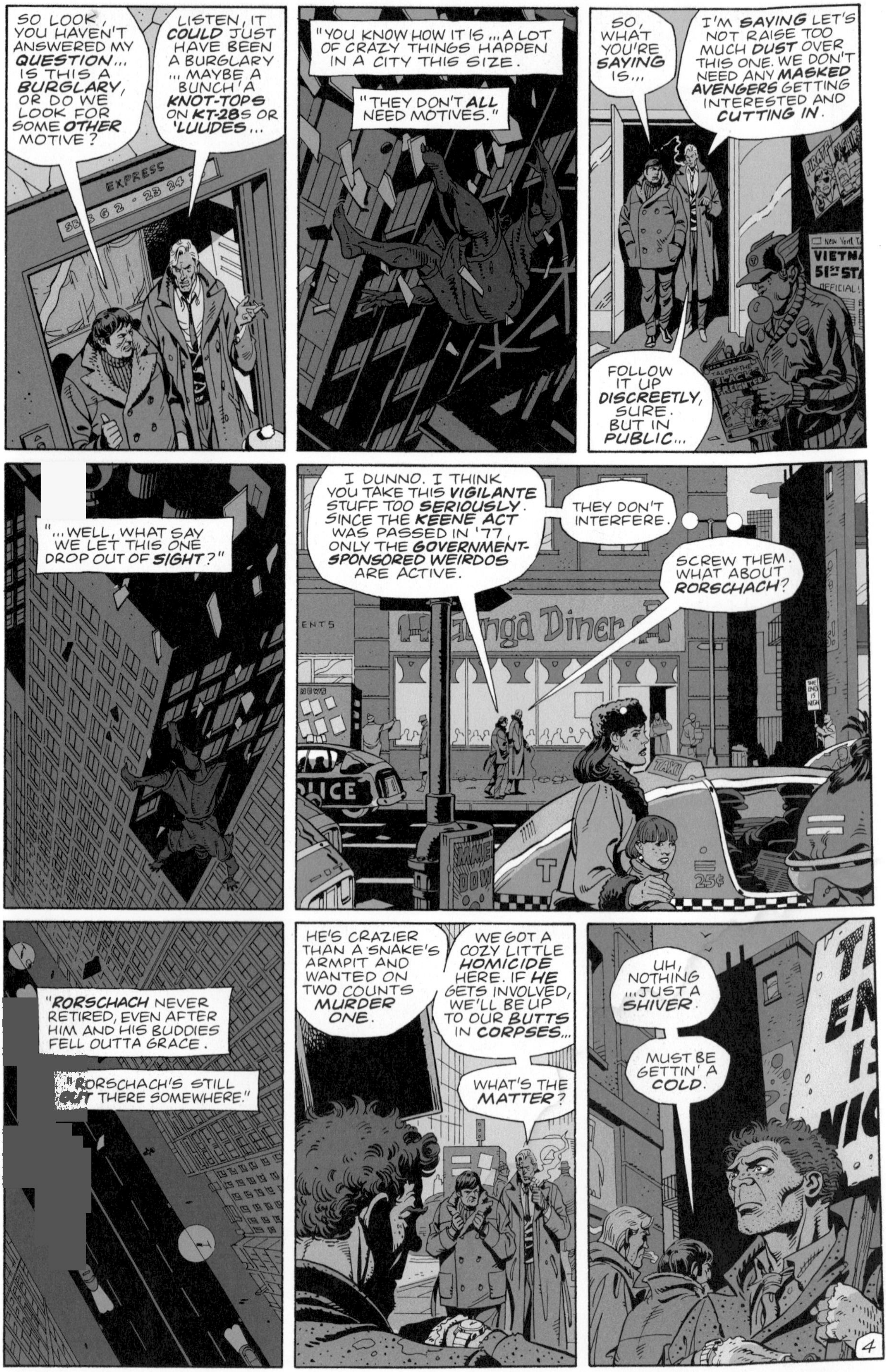
SO LOOK, YOU HAVEN'T ANSWERED MY QUESTION... IS THIS A BURGLARY, OR DO WE LOOK FOR SOME OTHER MOTIVE?
LISTEN, IT COULD JUST HAVE BEEN A BURGLARY ...MAYBE A BUNCH 'A KNOT-TOPS ON KT-28S OR 'LUUDES...
EXPRESS
"YOU KNOW HOW IT IS ...A LOT OF CRAZY THINGS HAPPEN IN A CITY THIS SIZE.
"THEY DON'T ALL NEED MOTIVES."
SO, WHAT YOU'RE SAYING IS...
I'M SAYING LET'S NOT RAISE TOO MUCH DUST OVER THIS ONE. WE DON'T NEED ANY MASKED AVENGERS GETTING INTERESTED AND CUTTING IN.
FOLLOW IT UP DISCREETLY, SURE. BUT IN PUBLIC...
"...WELL, WHAT SAY WE LET THIS ONE DROP OUT OF SIGHT?"
I DUNNO. I THINK YOU TAKE THIS VIGILANTE STUFF TOO SERIOUSLY. SINCE THE KEENE ACT WAS PASSED IN '77, ONLY THE GOVERNMENT-SPONSORED WEIRDOS ARE ACTIVE.
THEY DON'T INTERFERE.
SCREW THEM. WHAT ABOUT RORSCHACH?
Gunga Diner
"RORSCHACH NEVER RETIRED, EVEN AFTER HIM AND HIS BUDDIES FELL OUTTA GRACE.
"RORSCHACH'S STILL OUT THERE SOMEWHERE."
HE'S CRAZIER THAN A SNAKE'S ARMPIT AND WANTED ON TWO COUNTS MURDER ONE.
WE GOT A COZY LITTLE HOMICIDE HERE. IF HE GETS INVOLVED, WE'LL BE UP TO OUR BUTTS IN CORPSES...
WHAT'S THE MATTER?
UH, NOTHING ...JUST A SHIVER.
MUST BE GETTIN' A COLD.
4

mmeltdowns!

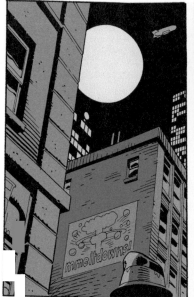

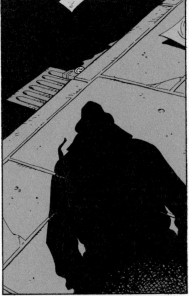

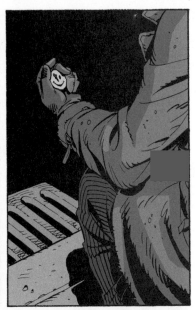

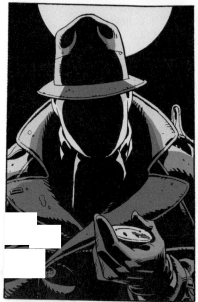

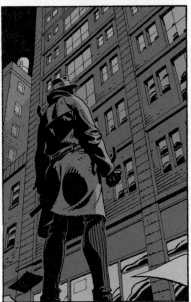

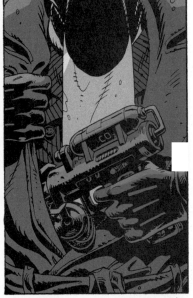

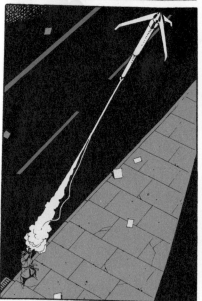

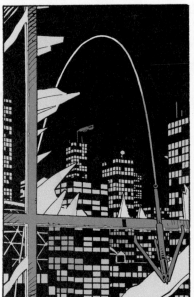

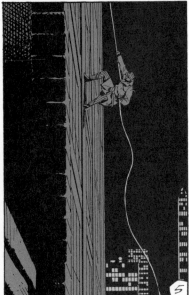

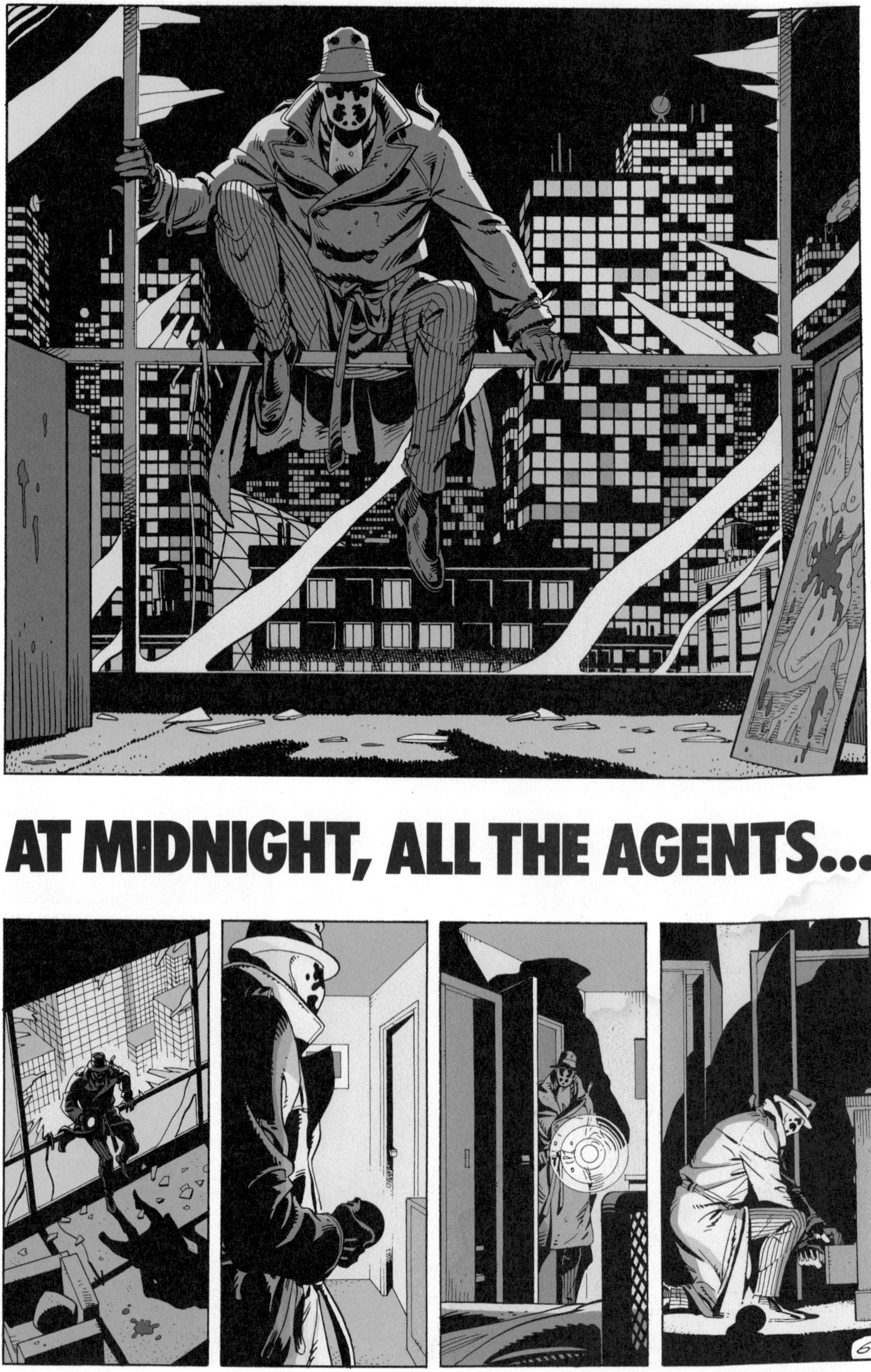
AT MIDNIGHT, ALL THE AGENTS...
6

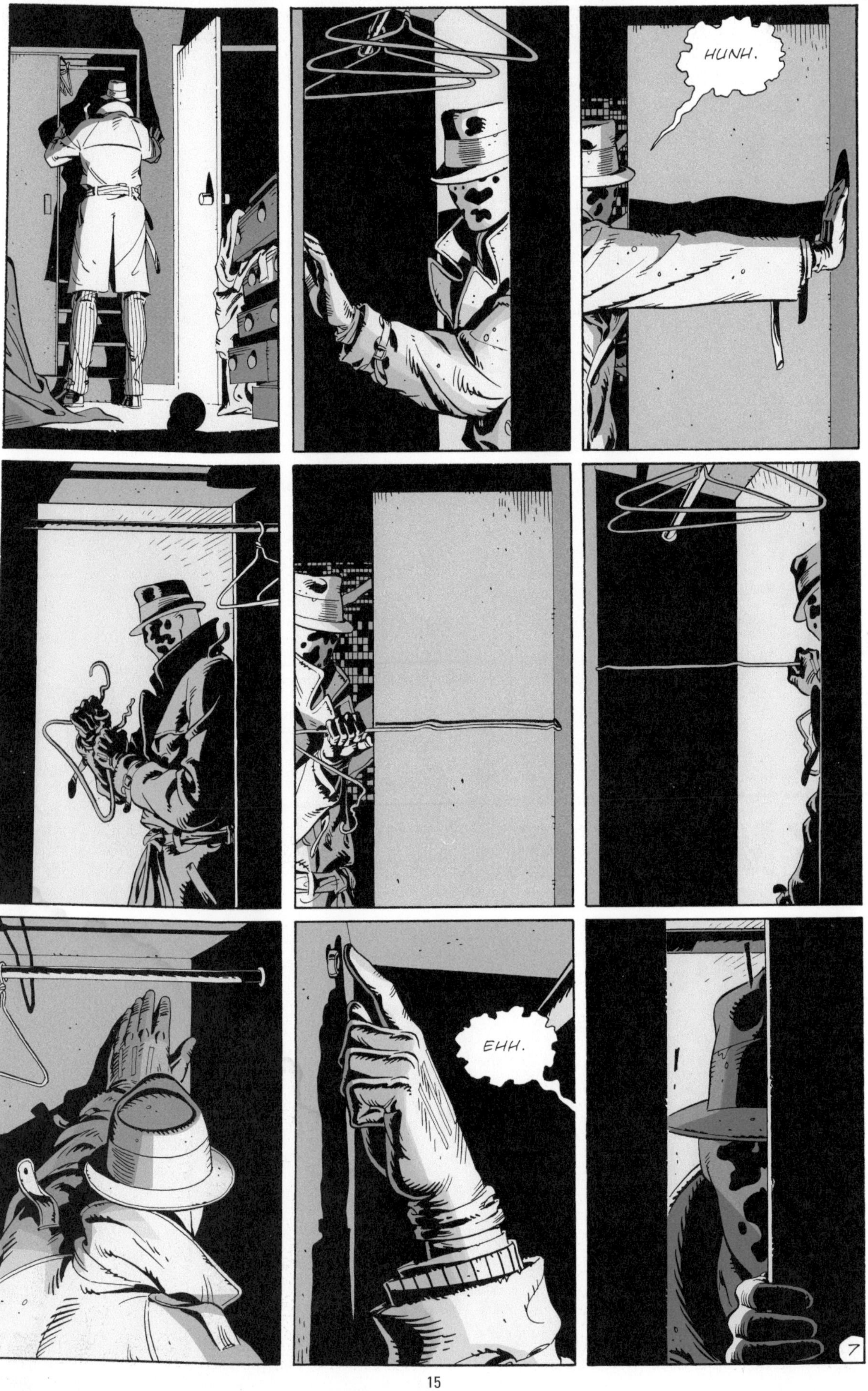
HUNH.
EHH.
7

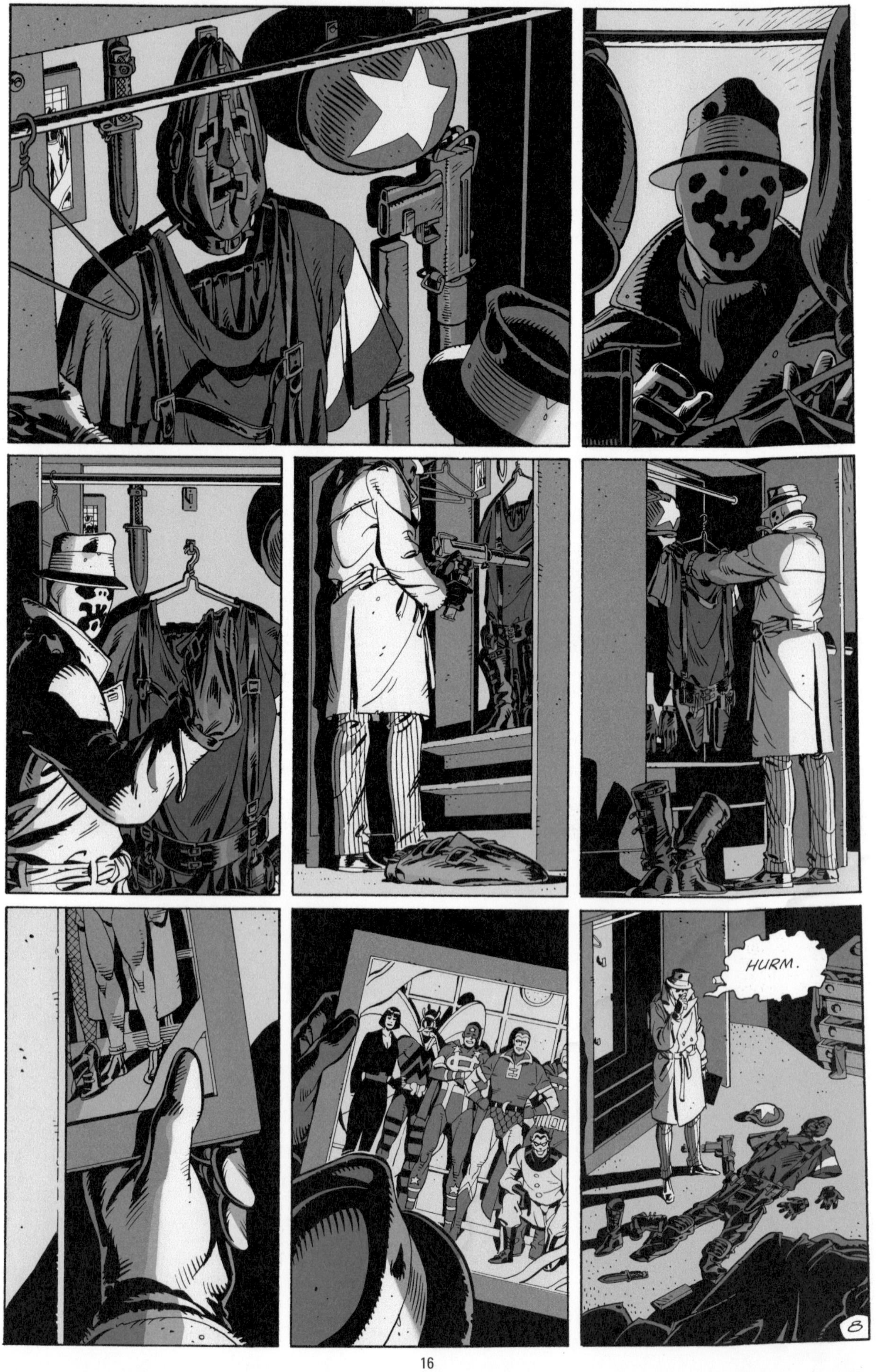
HURM.
8

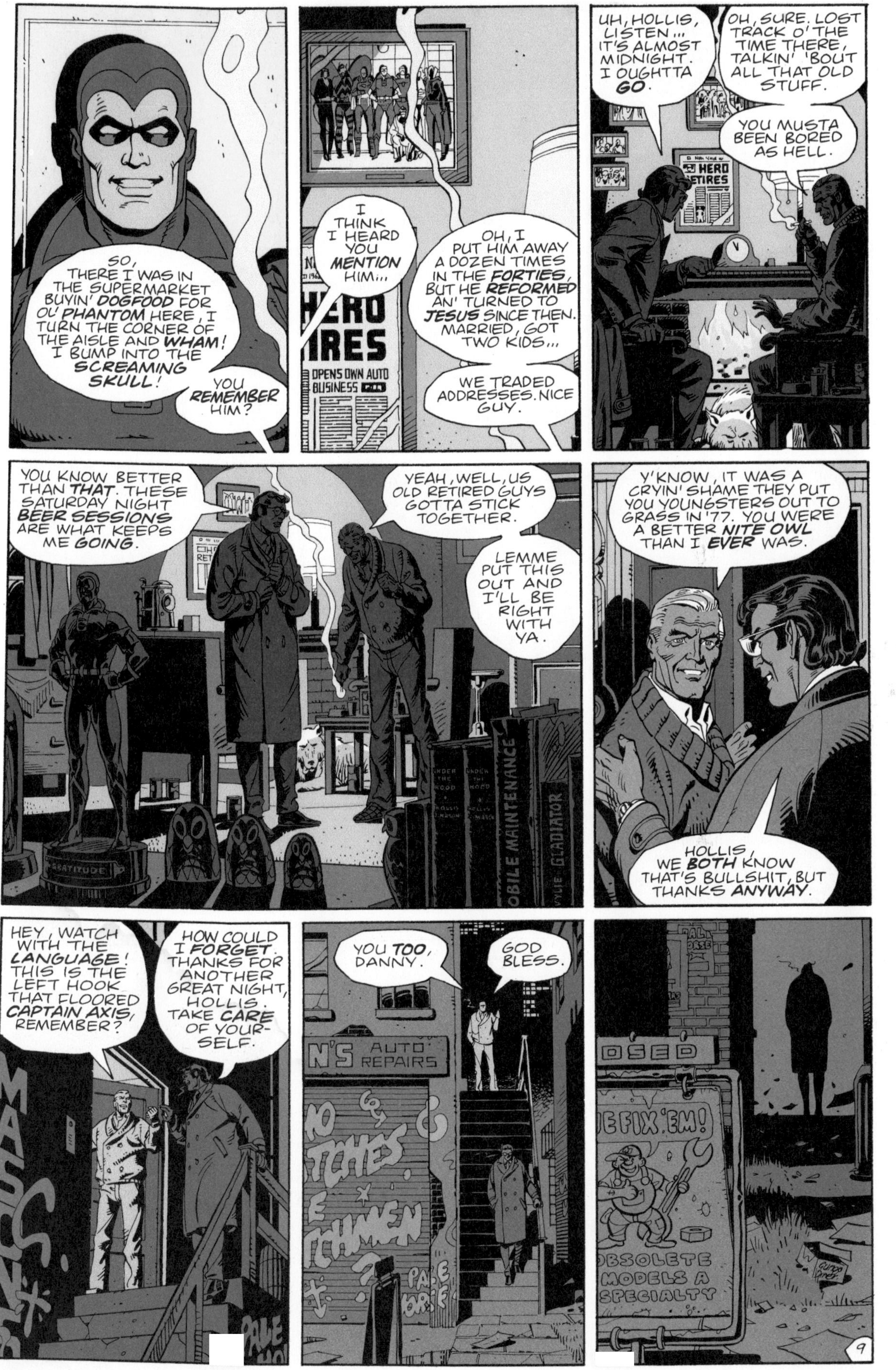

SO, THERE I WAS IN THE SUPERMARKET BUYIN' DOGFOOD FOR OL' PHANTOM HERE, I TURN THE CORNER OF THE AISLE AND WHAM! I BUMP INTO THE SCREAMING SKULL!
YOU REMEMBER HIM?
I THINK I HEARD YOU MENTION HIM...
OH, I PUT HIM AWAY A DOZEN TIMES IN THE FORTIES, BUT HE REFORMED AN' TURNED TO JESUS SINCE THEN. MARRIED, GOT TWO KIDS...
WE TRADED ADDRESSES. NICE GUY.
HERO
IRES
OPENS OWN AUTO BUSINESS
UH, HOLLIS, LISTEN... IT'S ALMOST MIDNIGHT. I OUGHTTA GO.
OH, SURE. LOST TRACK O' THE TIME THERE, TALKIN' 'BOUT ALL THAT OLD STUFF.
YOU MUSTA BEEN BORED AS HELL.
HERO
RETIRES
YOU KNOW BETTER THAN THAT. THESE SATURDAY NIGHT BEER SESSIONS ARE WHAT KEEPS ME GOING.
YEAH, WELL, US OLD RETIRED GUYS GOTTA STICK TOGETHER.
LEMME PUT THIS OUT AND I'LL BE RIGHT WITH YA.
GRATITUDE
UNDER THE HOOD
HOLLIS J. MASON
OBILE MAINTENANCE
GLADIATOR
Y'KNOW, IT WAS A CRYIN' SHAME THEY PUT YOU YOUNGSTERS OUT TO GRASS IN '77. YOU WERE A BETTER NITE OWL THAN I EVER WAS.
HOLLIS, WE BOTH KNOW THAT'S BULLSHIT, BUT THANKS ANYWAY.
HEY, WATCH WITH THE LANGUAGE! THIS IS THE LEFT HOOK THAT FLOORED CAPTAIN AXIS, REMEMBER?
HOW COULD I FORGET. THANKS FOR ANOTHER GREAT NIGHT, HOLLIS. TAKE CARE OF YOURSELF.
YOU TOO, DANNY.
GOD BLESS.
N'S AUTO REPAIRS
OSED
E FIX 'EM!
OBSOLETE MODELS A SPECIALTY
9

...LOOK DOWN YOUR BACK STAIRS, BUDDY, SOMEBODY'S LIVING THERE AN' THEY DON'T REALLY FEEL THE WEATHER...

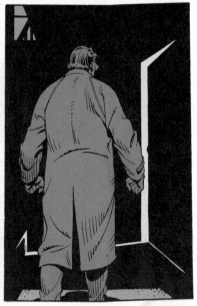

CHLOP.

THLUP.

SHORP.

LEP.

HELLO, DANIEL.

GOT HUNGRY WAITING. HELPED MYSELF TO SOME BEANS.

HOPE YOU DON'T MIND.

RORSCHACH..?

18

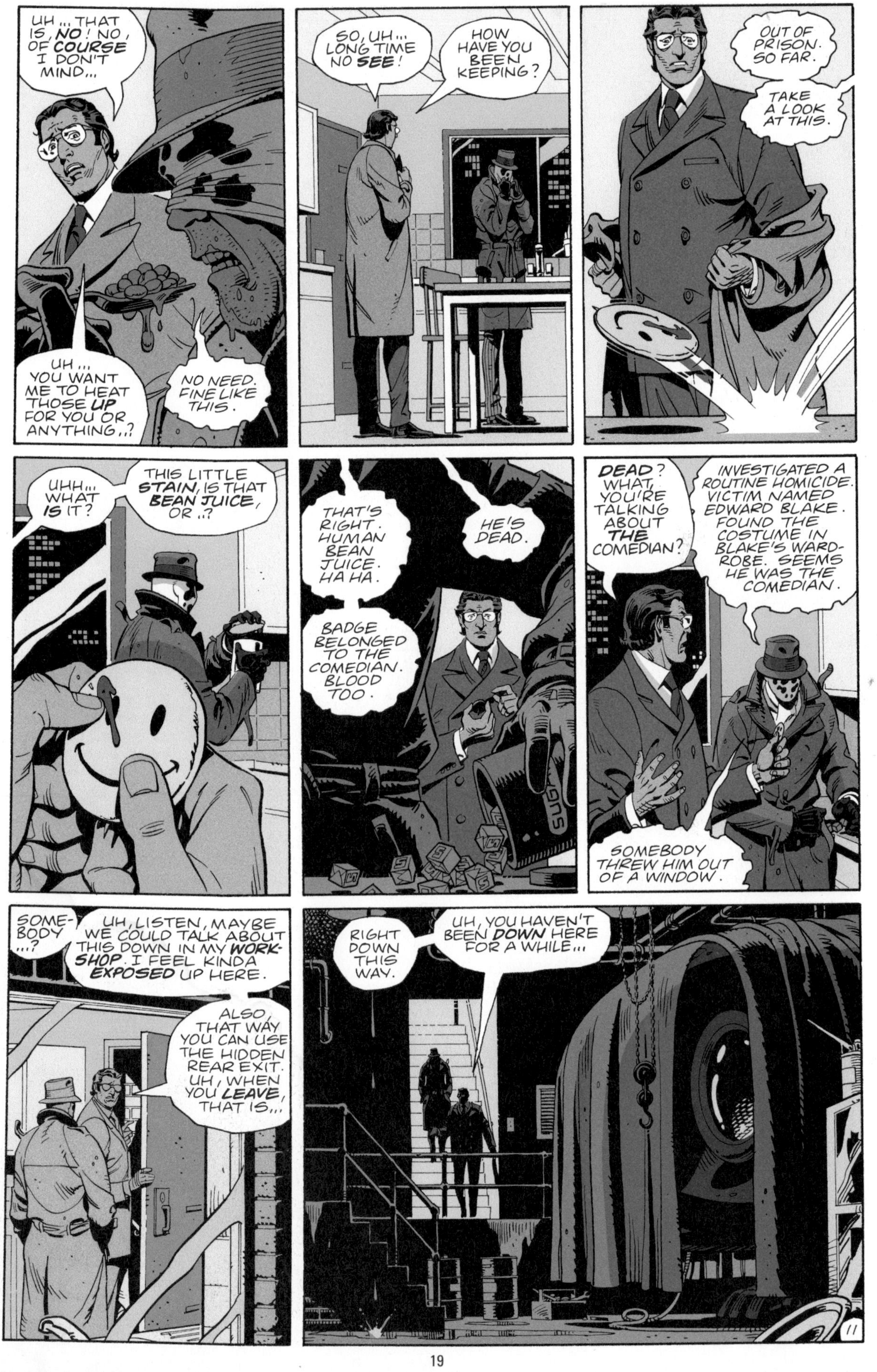
UH... THAT IS, NO! NO, OF COURSE I DON'T MIND...
UH... YOU WANT ME TO HEAT THOSE UP FOR YOU OR ANYTHING..?
NO NEED. FINE LIKE THIS.
SO, UH... LONG TIME NO SEE!
HOW HAVE YOU BEEN KEEPING?
OUT OF PRISON. SO FAR.
TAKE A LOOK AT THIS.
UHH... WHAT IS IT?
THIS LITTLE STAIN, IS THAT BEAN JUICE, OR ..?
THAT'S RIGHT. HUMAN BEAN JUICE. HA HA.
HE'S DEAD.
BADGE BELONGED TO THE COMEDIAN. BLOOD TOO.
DEAD? WHAT, YOU'RE TALKING ABOUT THE COMEDIAN?
INVESTIGATED A ROUTINE HOMICIDE. VICTIM NAMED EDWARD BLAKE. FOUND THE COSTUME IN BLAKE'S WARD-ROBE. SEEMS HE WAS THE COMEDIAN.
SOMEBODY THREW HIM OUT OF A WINDOW.
SOME-BODY ...?
UH, LISTEN, MAYBE WE COULD TALK ABOUT THIS DOWN IN MY WORK-SHOP. I FEEL KINDA EXPOSED UP HERE.
ALSO, THAT WAY YOU CAN USE THE HIDDEN REAR EXIT. UH, WHEN YOU LEAVE, THAT IS...
RIGHT DOWN THIS WAY.
UH, YOU HAVEN'T BEEN DOWN HERE FOR A WHILE...
11

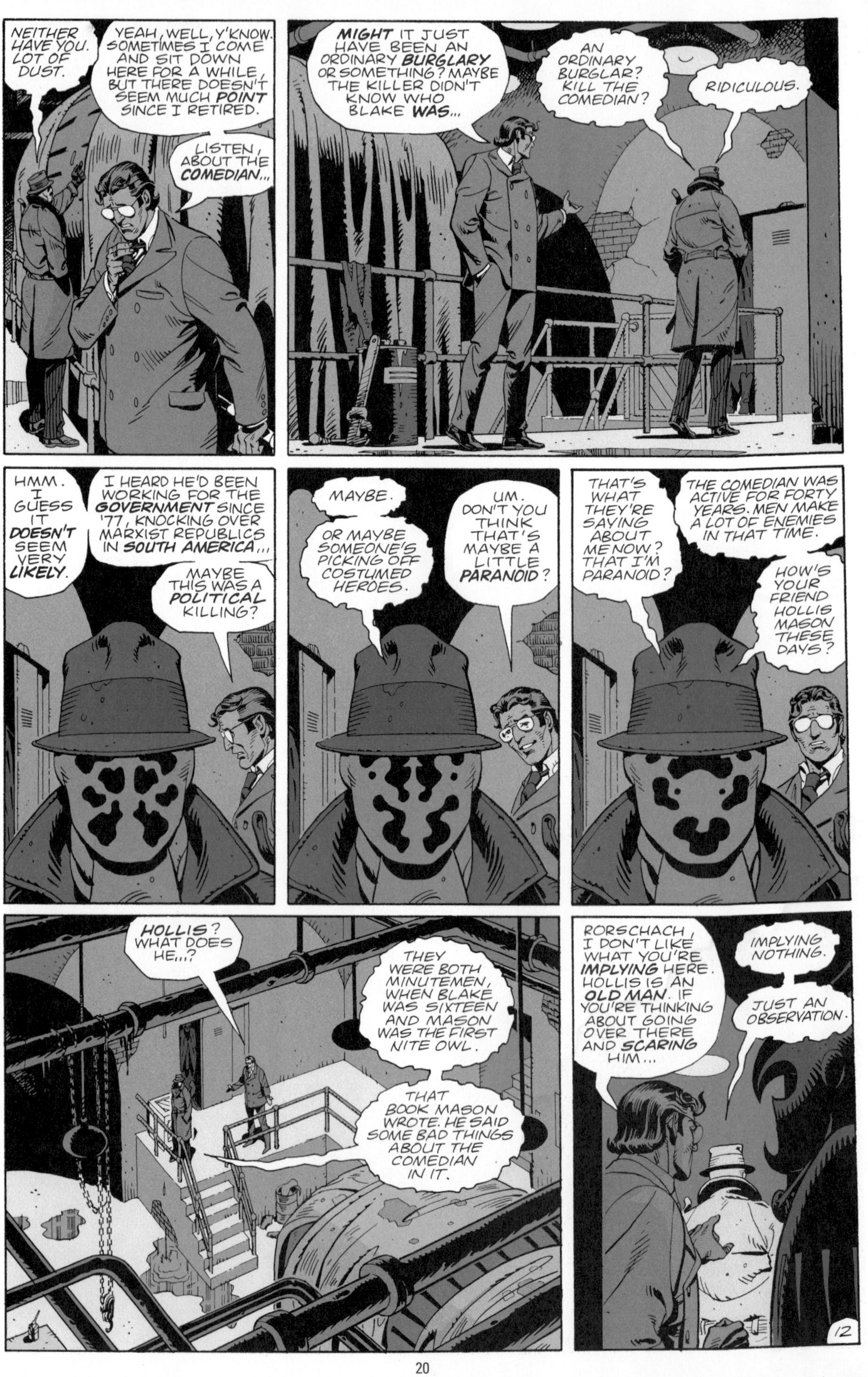

NEITHER HAVE YOU. LOT OF DUST.
YEAH, WELL, Y'KNOW. SOMETIMES I COME AND SIT DOWN HERE FOR A WHILE, BUT THERE DOESN'T SEEM MUCH POINT SINCE I RETIRED.
LISTEN, ABOUT THE COMEDIAN...
MIGHT IT JUST HAVE BEEN AN ORDINARY BURGLARY OR SOMETHING? MAYBE THE KILLER DIDN'T KNOW WHO BLAKE WAS...
AN ORDINARY BURGLAR? KILL THE COMEDIAN?
RIDICULOUS.
HMM. I GUESS IT DOESN'T SEEM VERY LIKELY.
I HEARD HE'D BEEN WORKING FOR THE GOVERNMENT SINCE '77, KNOCKING OVER MARXIST REPUBLICS IN SOUTH AMERICA...
MAYBE THIS WAS A POLITICAL KILLING?
MAYBE.
OR MAYBE SOMEONE'S PICKING OFF COSTUMED HEROES.
UM. DON'T YOU THINK THAT'S MAYBE A LITTLE PARANOID?
THAT'S WHAT THEY'RE SAYING ABOUT ME NOW? THAT I'M PARANOID?
THE COMEDIAN WAS ACTIVE FOR FORTY YEARS. MEN MAKE A LOT OF ENEMIES IN THAT TIME.
HOW'S YOUR FRIEND HOLLIS MASON THESE DAYS?
HOLLIS? WHAT DOES HE...?
THEY WERE BOTH MINUTEMEN, WHEN BLAKE WAS SIXTEEN AND MASON WAS THE FIRST NITE OWL.
THAT BOOK MASON WROTE. HE SAID SOME BAD THINGS ABOUT THE COMEDIAN IN IT.
RORSCHACH, I DON'T LIKE WHAT YOU'RE IMPLYING HERE. HOLLIS IS AN OLD MAN. IF YOU'RE THINKING ABOUT GOING OVER THERE AND SCARING HIM...
IMPLYING NOTHING.
JUST AN OBSERVATION.
12

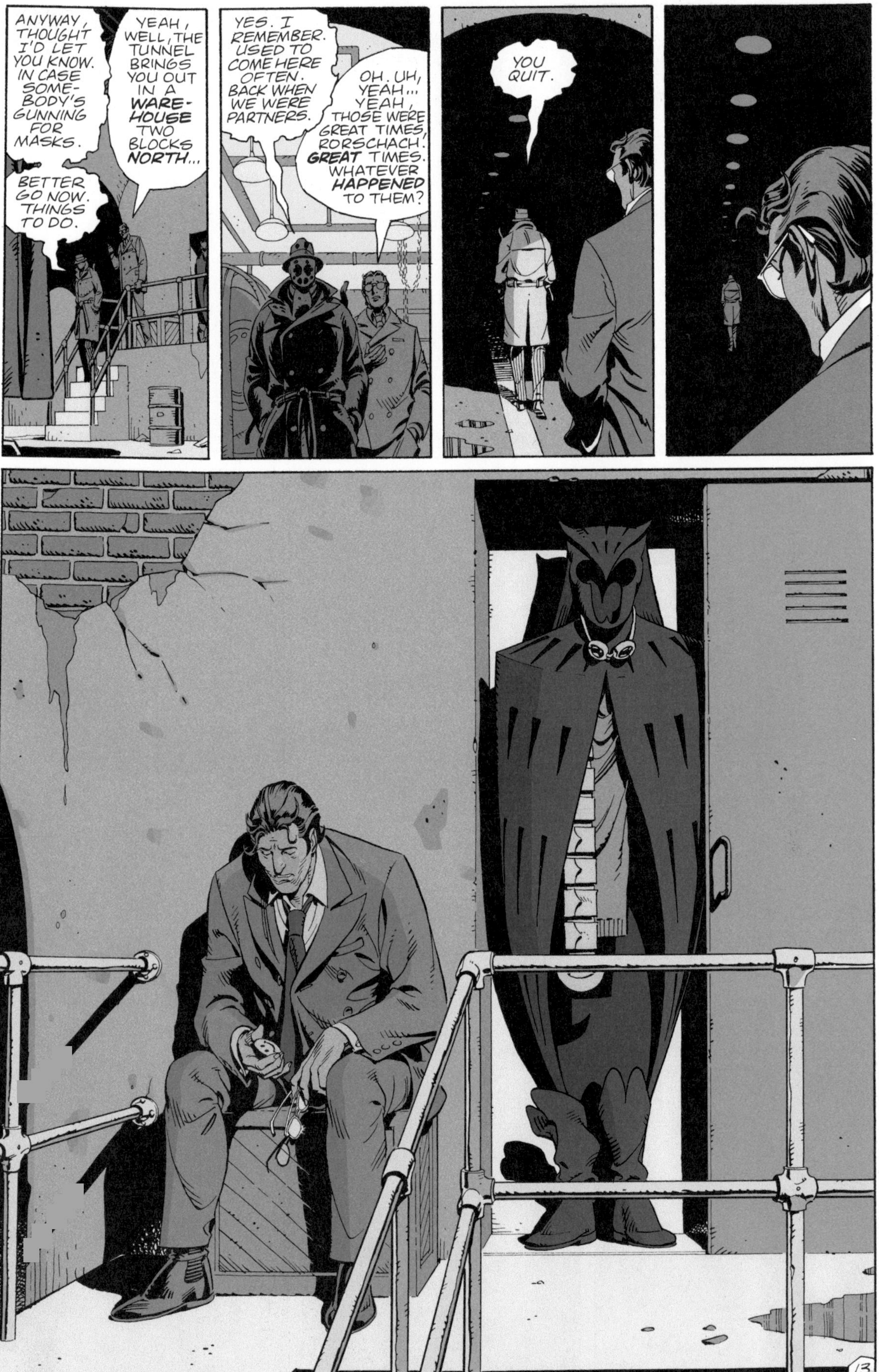
ANYWAY, THOUGHT I'D LET YOU KNOW. IN CASE SOMEBODY'S GUNNING FOR MASKS.
YEAH, WELL, THE TUNNEL BRINGS YOU OUT IN A **WAREHOUSE** TWO BLOCKS **NORTH**...
BETTER GO NOW. THINGS TO DO.
YES. I REMEMBER. USED TO COME HERE OFTEN. BACK WHEN WE WERE PARTNERS.
OH. UH, YEAH... YEAH, THOSE WERE GREAT TIMES, RORSCHACH! **GREAT** TIMES. WHATEVER **HAPPENED** TO THEM?
YOU QUIT.
13

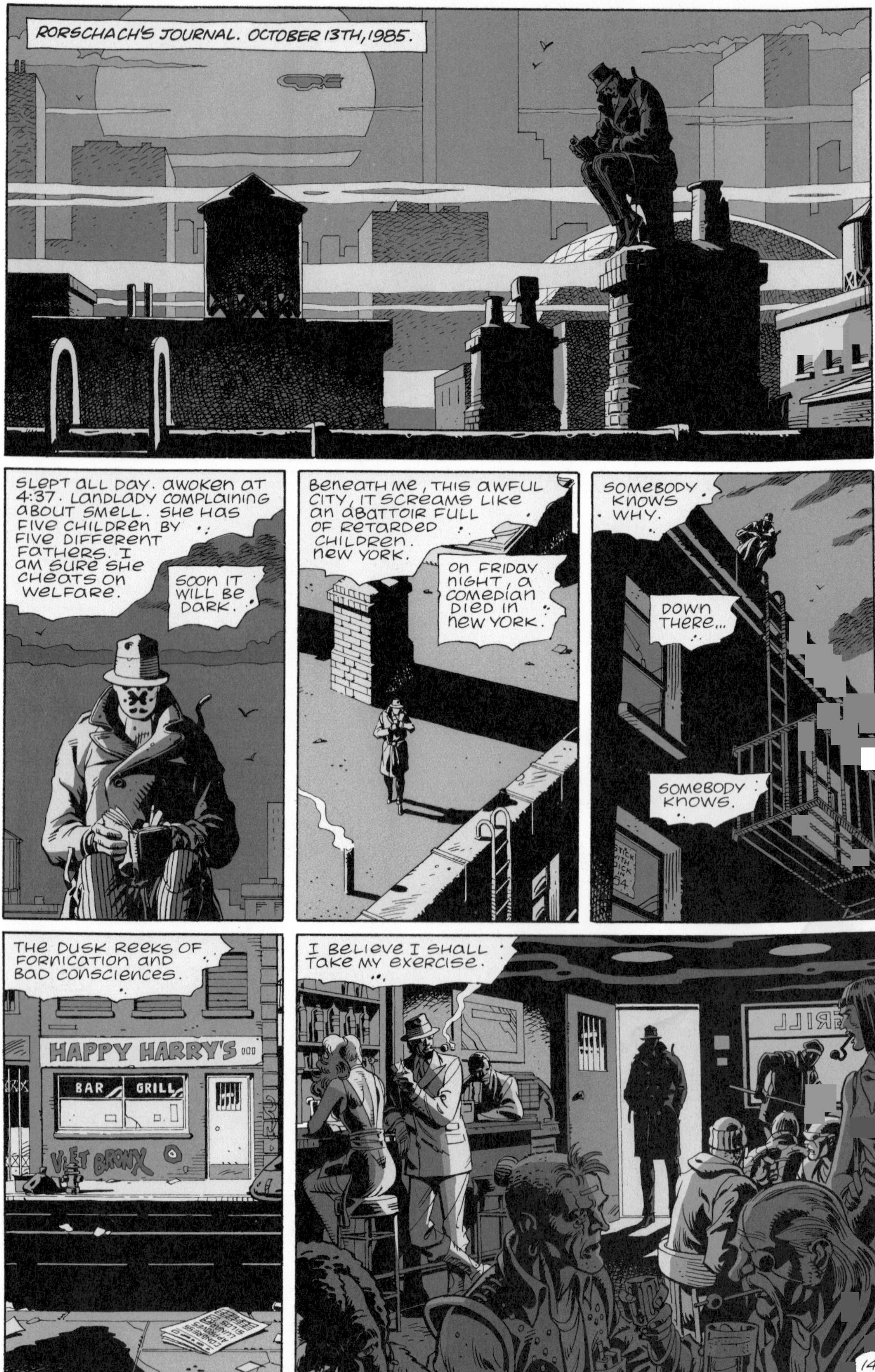
RORSCHACH'S JOURNAL. OCTOBER 13TH, 1985.
SLEPT ALL DAY. AWOKEN AT 4:37. LANDLADY COMPLAINING ABOUT SMELL. SHE HAS FIVE CHILDREN BY FIVE DIFFERENT FATHERS. I AM SURE SHE CHEATS ON WELFARE.
SOON IT WILL BE DARK.
BENEATH ME, THIS AWFUL CITY, IT SCREAMS LIKE AN ABATTOIR FULL OF RETARDED CHILDREN. NEW YORK.
ON FRIDAY NIGHT, A COMEDIAN DIED IN NEW YORK.
SOMEBODY KNOWS WHY.
DOWN THERE...
SOMEBODY KNOWS.
THE DUSK REEKS OF FORNICATION AND BAD CONSCIENCES.
HAPPY HARRY'S
BAR GRILL
I BELIEVE I SHALL TAKE MY EXERCISE.
14

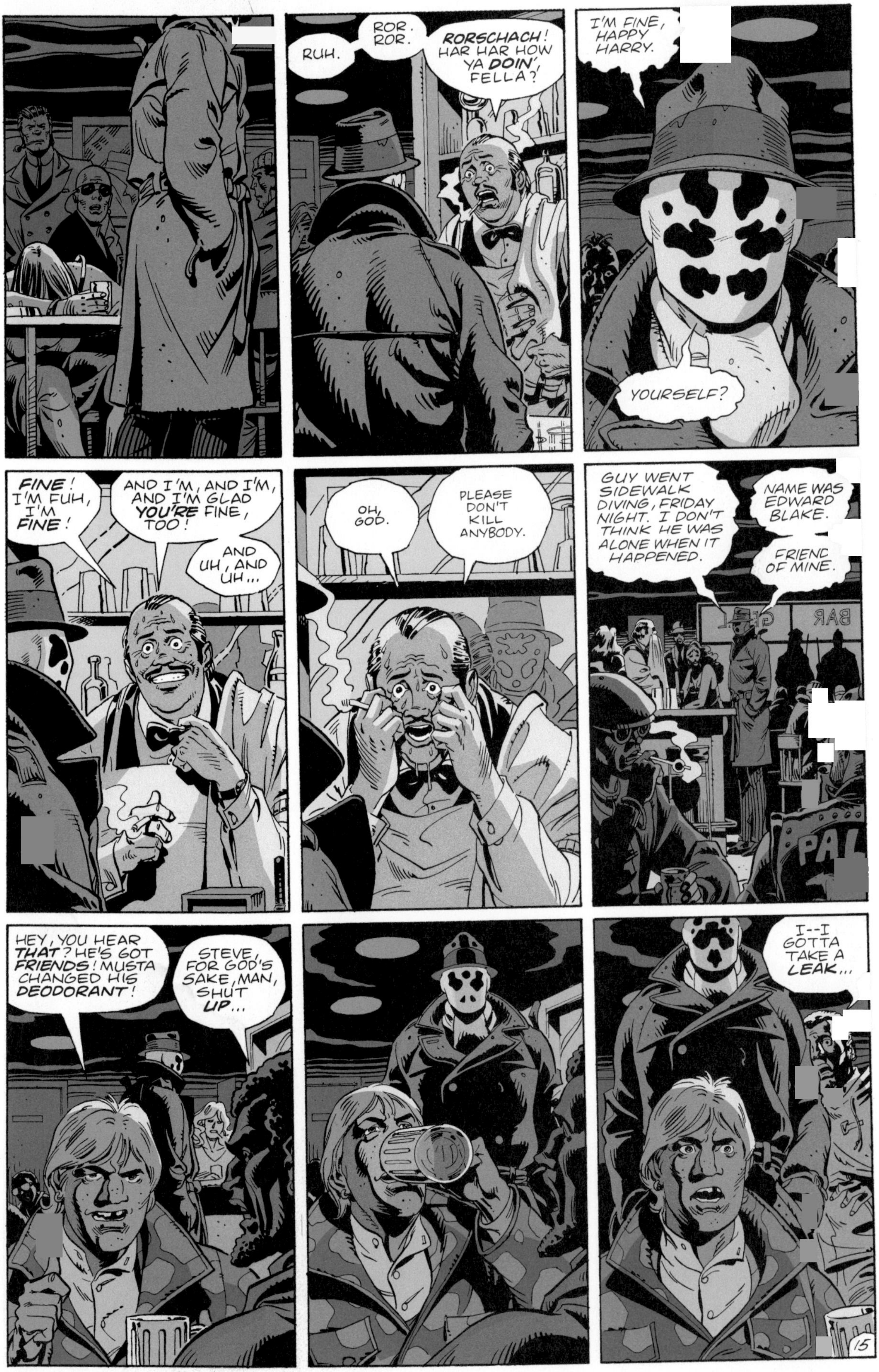
RUH.
ROR. ROR.
RORSCHACH! HAR HAR HOW YA DOIN', FELLA?
I'M FINE, HAPPY HARRY.
YOURSELF?
FINE! I'M FUH, I'M FINE!
AND I'M, AND I'M, AND I'M GLAD YOU'RE FINE, TOO!
AND UH, AND UH...
OH, GOD.
PLEASE DON'T KILL ANYBODY.
GUY WENT SIDEWALK DIVING, FRIDAY NIGHT. I DON'T THINK HE WAS ALONE WHEN IT HAPPENED.
NAME WAS EDWARD BLAKE.
FRIEND OF MINE.
HEY, YOU HEAR THAT? HE'S GOT FRIENDS! MUSTA CHANGED HIS DEODORANT!
STEVE, FOR GOD'S SAKE, MAN, SHUT UP...
I--I GOTTA TAKE A LEAK...
15

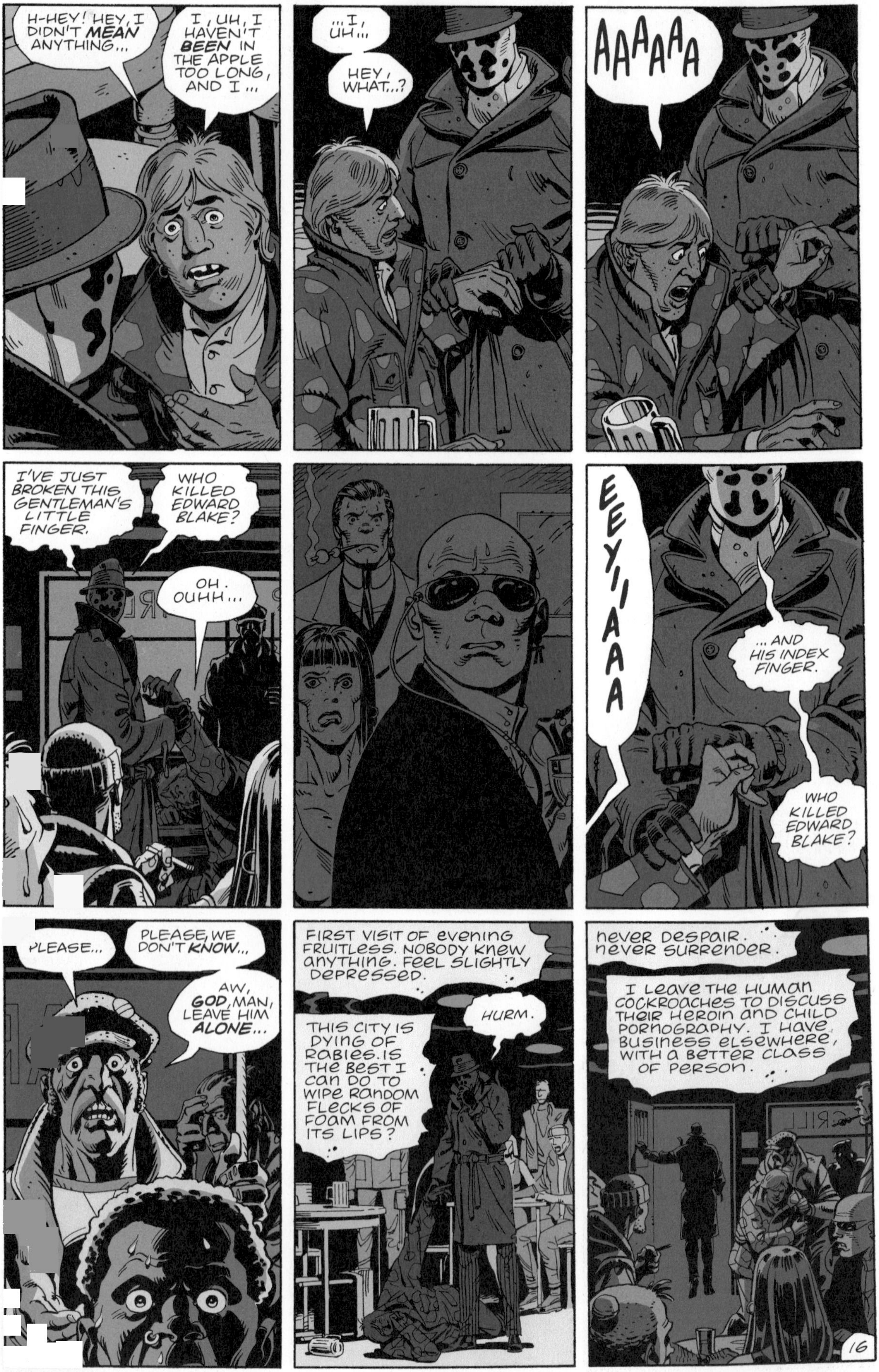

H-HEY! HEY, I DIDN'T MEAN ANYTHING...
I, UH, I HAVEN'T BEEN IN THE APPLE TOO LONG, AND I...
...I, UH...
HEY, WHAT...?
AAAAAA
I'VE JUST BROKEN THIS GENTLEMAN'S LITTLE FINGER.
WHO KILLED EDWARD BLAKE?
OH. OUHH...
EEYIIIAAA
...AND HIS INDEX FINGER.
WHO KILLED EDWARD BLAKE?
PLEASE...
PLEASE, WE DON'T KNOW...
AW, GOD, MAN, LEAVE HIM ALONE...
FIRST VISIT OF EVENING FRUITLESS. NOBODY KNEW ANYTHING. FEEL SLIGHTLY DEPRESSED.
HURM.
THIS CITY IS DYING OF RABIES. IS THE BEST I CAN DO TO WIPE RANDOM FLECKS OF FOAM FROM ITS LIPS?
NEVER DESPAIR. NEVER SURRENDER.
I LEAVE THE HUMAN COCKROACHES TO DISCUSS THEIR HEROIN AND CHILD PORNOGRAPHY. I HAVE BUSINESS ELSEWHERE, WITH A BETTER CLASS OF PERSON.
16

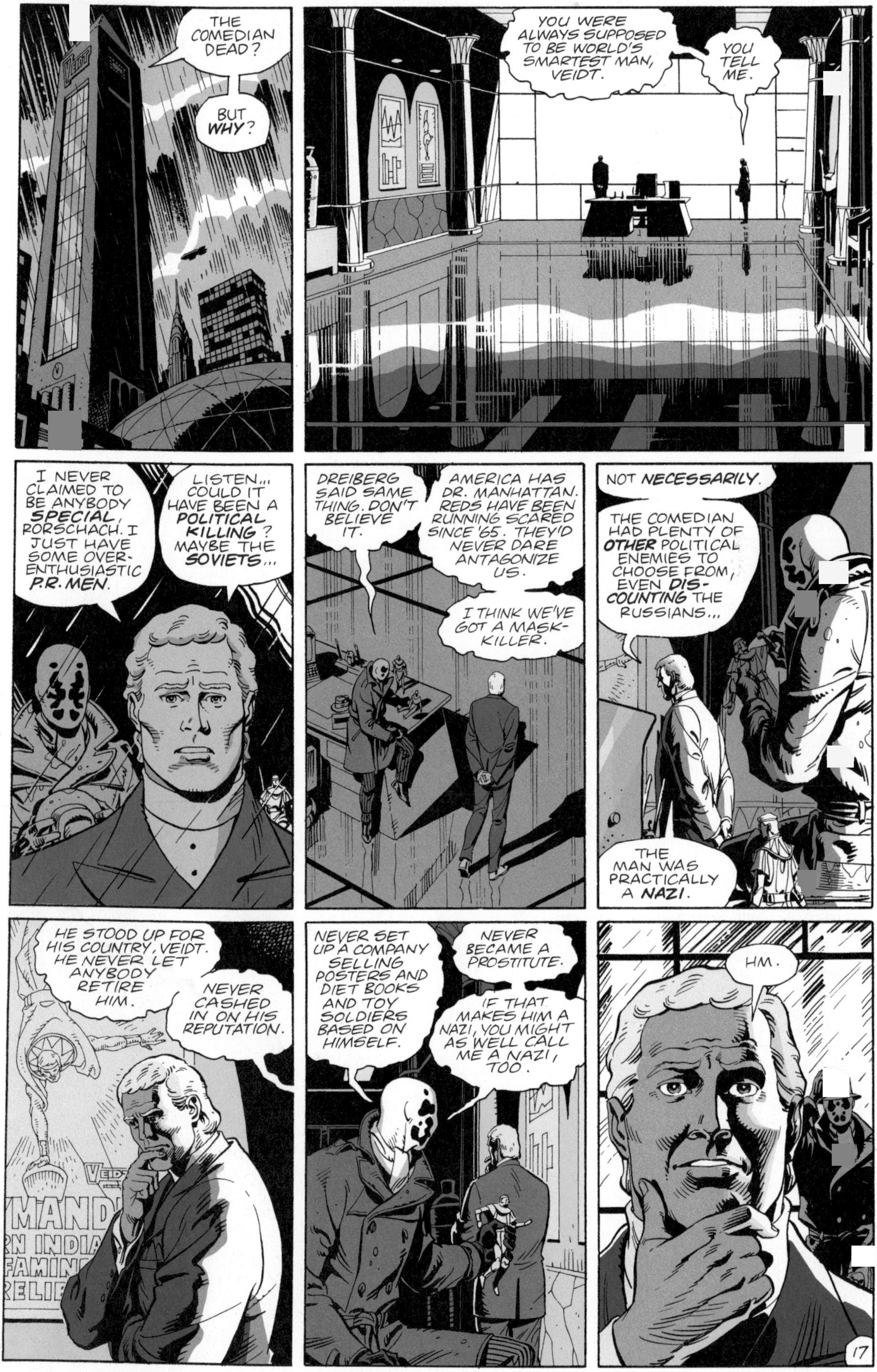
THE COMEDIAN DEAD?
BUT WHY?
YOU WERE ALWAYS SUPPOSED TO BE WORLD'S SMARTEST MAN, VEIDT.
YOU TELL ME.
I NEVER CLAIMED TO BE ANYBODY SPECIAL, RORSCHACH. I JUST HAVE SOME OVER-ENTHUSIASTIC P.R. MEN.
LISTEN... COULD IT HAVE BEEN A POLITICAL KILLING? MAYBE THE SOVIETS...
DREIBERG SAID SAME THING. DON'T BELIEVE IT.
AMERICA HAS DR. MANHATTAN. REDS HAVE BEEN RUNNING SCARED SINCE '65. THEY'D NEVER DARE ANTAGONIZE US.
I THINK WE'VE GOT A MASK-KILLER.
NOT NECESSARILY.
THE COMEDIAN HAD PLENTY OF OTHER POLITICAL ENEMIES TO CHOOSE FROM, EVEN DIS-COUNTING THE RUSSIANS...
THE MAN WAS PRACTICALLY A NAZI.
HE STOOD UP FOR HIS COUNTRY, VEIDT. HE NEVER LET ANYBODY RETIRE HIM.
NEVER CASHED IN ON HIS REPUTATION.
NEVER SET UP A COMPANY SELLING POSTERS AND DIET BOOKS AND TOY SOLDIERS BASED ON HIMSELF.
NEVER BECAME A PROSTITUTE.
IF THAT MAKES HIM A NAZI, YOU MIGHT AS WELL CALL ME A NAZI, TOO.
HM.
17

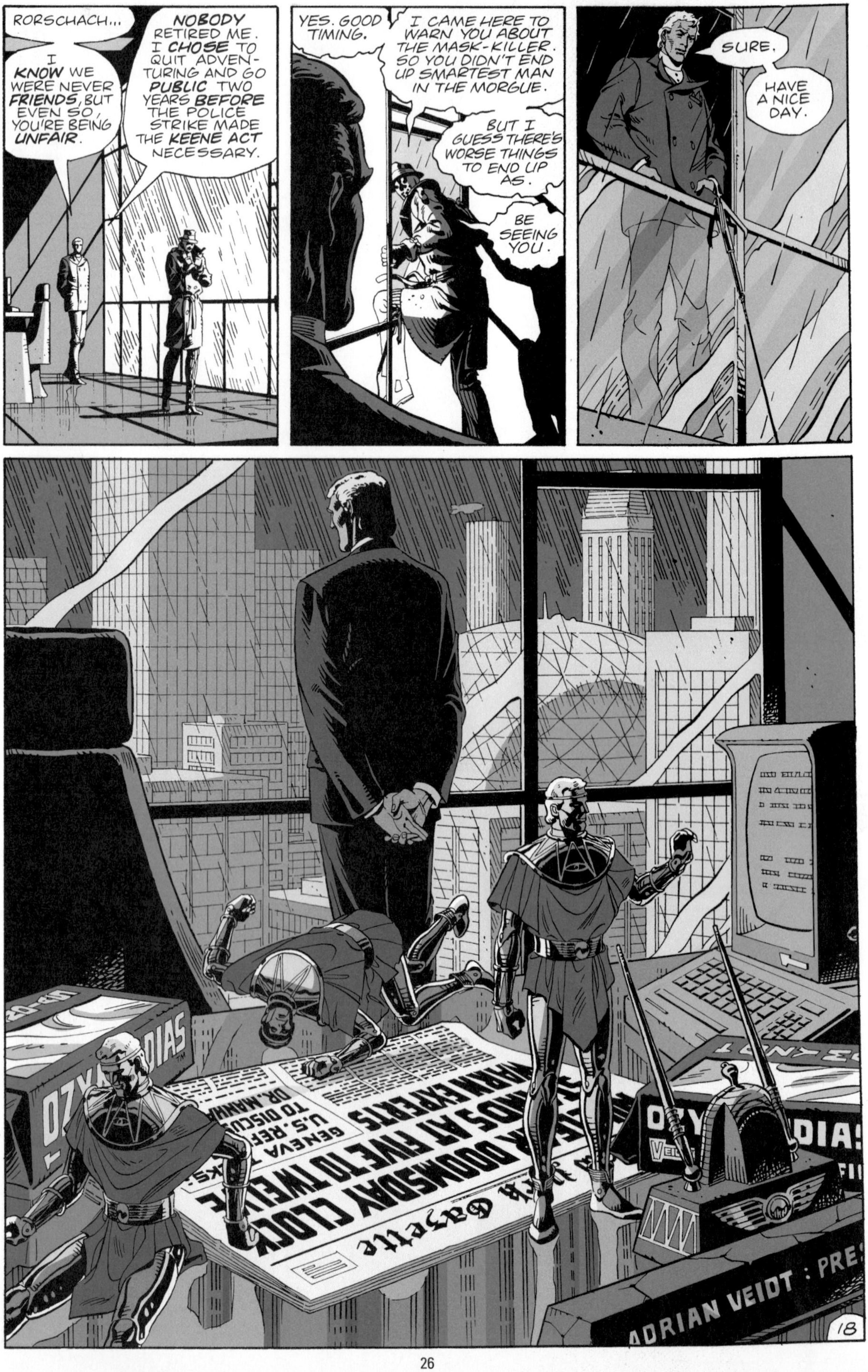
RORSCHACH... I KNOW WE WERE NEVER FRIENDS, BUT EVEN SO, YOU'RE BEING UNFAIR.
NOBODY RETIRED ME. I CHOSE TO QUIT ADVENTURING AND GO PUBLIC TWO YEARS BEFORE THE POLICE STRIKE MADE THE KEENE ACT NECESSARY.
YES. GOOD TIMING.
I CAME HERE TO WARN YOU ABOUT THE MASK-KILLER. SO YOU DIDN'T END UP SMARTEST MAN IN THE MORGUE.
BUT I GUESS THERE'S WORSE THINGS TO END UP AS.
BE SEEING YOU.
SURE.
HAVE A NICE DAY.
18

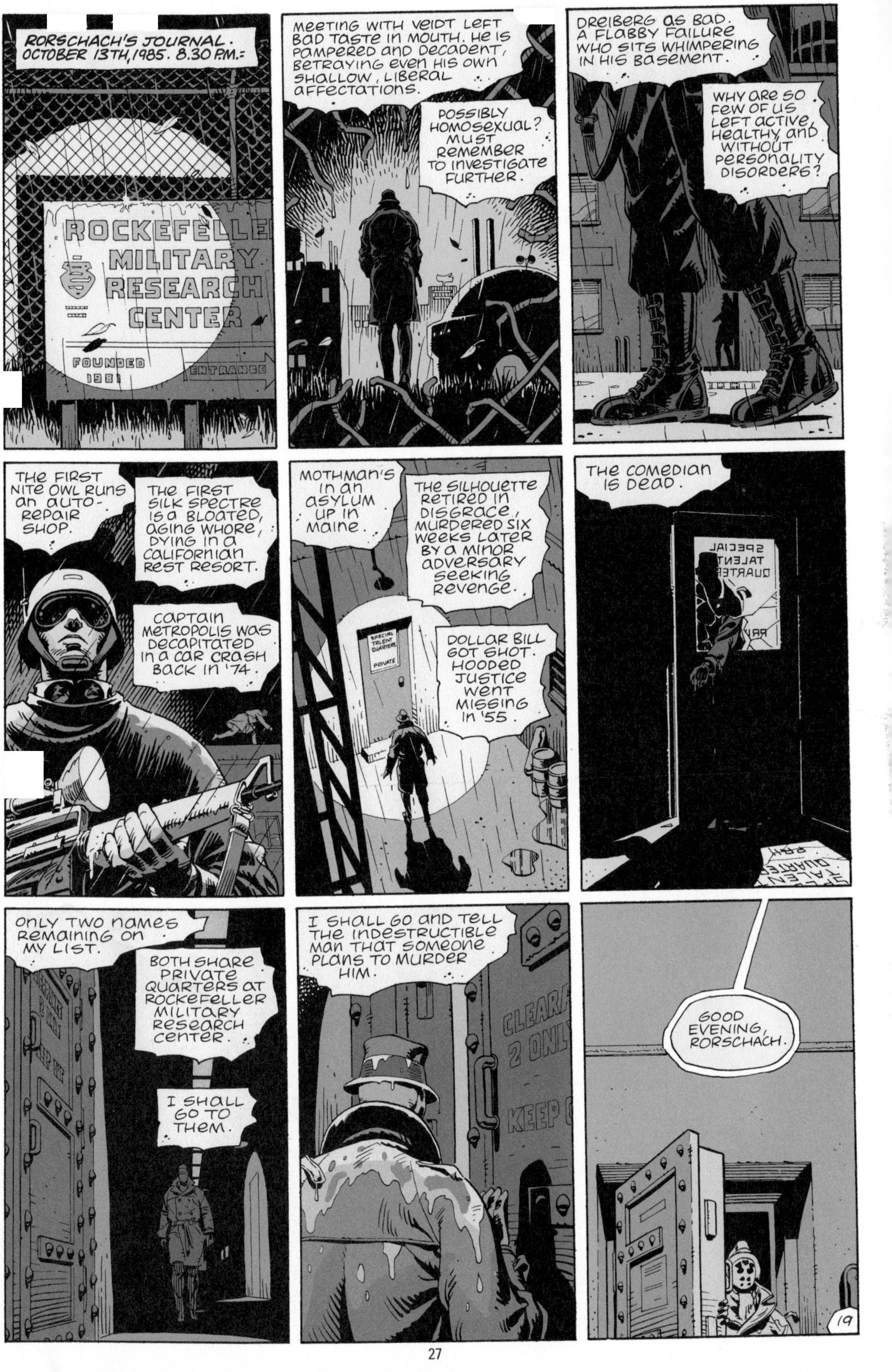
RORSCHACH'S JOURNAL. OCTOBER 13TH, 1985. 8.30 P.M.:
ROCKEFELLER MILITARY RESEARCH CENTER
FOUNDED 1981
ENTRANCE
MEETING WITH VEIDT LEFT BAD TASTE IN MOUTH. HE IS PAMPERED AND DECADENT, BETRAYING EVEN HIS OWN SHALLOW, LIBERAL AFFECTATIONS.
POSSIBLY HOMOSEXUAL? MUST REMEMBER TO INVESTIGATE FURTHER.
DREIBERG AS BAD. A FLABBY FAILURE WHO SITS WHIMPERING IN HIS BASEMENT.
WHY ARE SO FEW OF US LEFT ACTIVE, HEALTHY, AND WITHOUT PERSONALITY DISORDERS?
THE FIRST NITE OWL RUNS AN AUTO-REPAIR SHOP.
THE FIRST SILK SPECTRE IS A BLOATED, AGING WHORE, DYING IN A CALIFORNIAN REST RESORT.
CAPTAIN METROPOLIS WAS DECAPITATED IN A CAR CRASH BACK IN '74.
MOTHMAN'S IN AN ASYLUM UP IN MAINE.
THE SILHOUETTE RETIRED IN DISGRACE, MURDERED SIX WEEKS LATER BY A MINOR ADVERSARY SEEKING REVENGE.
SPECIAL TALENT QUARTERS
PRIVATE
DOLLAR BILL GOT SHOT. HOODED JUSTICE WENT MISSING IN '55.
THE COMEDIAN IS DEAD.
ONLY TWO NAMES REMAINING ON MY LIST.
BOTH SHARE PRIVATE QUARTERS AT ROCKEFELLER MILITARY RESEARCH CENTER.
I SHALL GO TO THEM.
I SHALL GO AND TELL THE INDESTRUCTIBLE MAN THAT SOMEONE PLANS TO MURDER HIM.
CLEARA
2 ONLY
KEEP
GOOD EVENING, RORSCHACH.
19

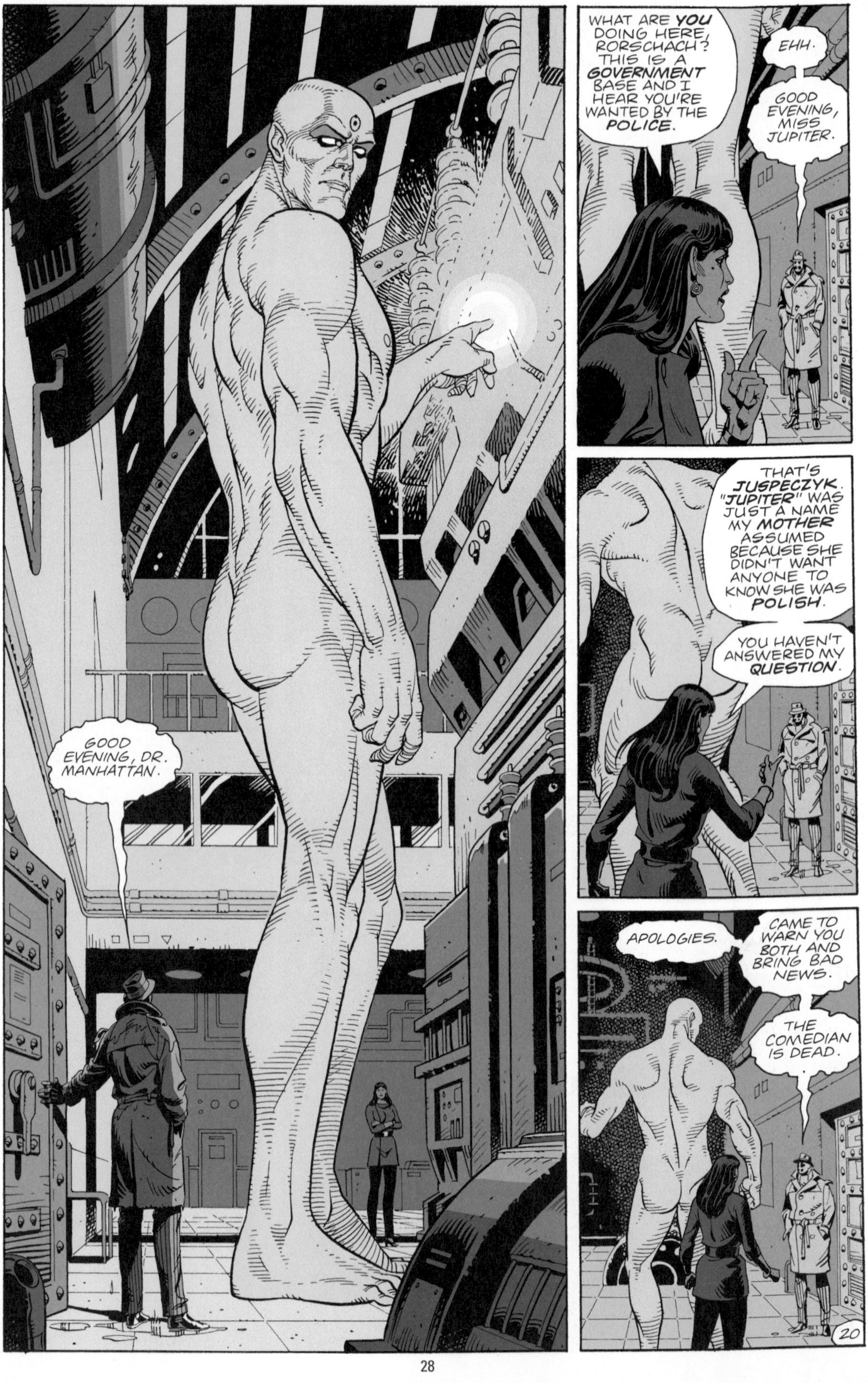
GOOD EVENING, DR. MANHATTAN.
WHAT ARE YOU DOING HERE, RORSCHACH? THIS IS A GOVERNMENT BASE AND I HEAR YOU'RE WANTED BY THE POLICE.
EHH.
GOOD EVENING, MISS JUPITER.
THAT'S JUSPECZYK. "JUPITER" WAS JUST A NAME MY MOTHER ASSUMED BECAUSE SHE DIDN'T WANT ANYONE TO KNOW SHE WAS POLISH.
YOU HAVEN'T ANSWERED MY QUESTION.
APOLOGIES.
CAME TO WARN YOU BOTH AND BRING BAD NEWS.
THE COMEDIAN IS DEAD.
20

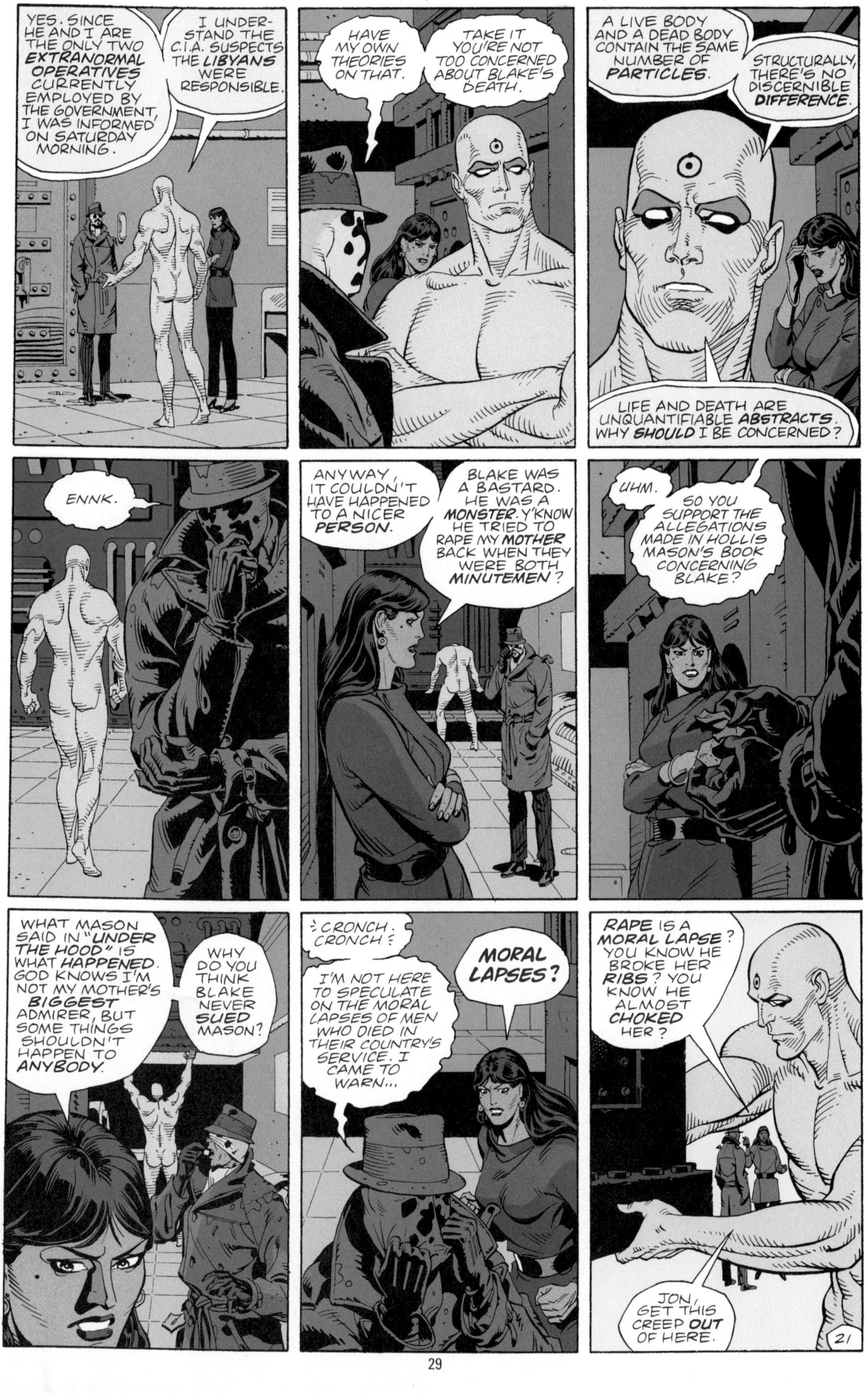
YES. SINCE HE AND I ARE THE ONLY TWO **EXTRANORMAL OPERATIVES** CURRENTLY EMPLOYED BY THE GOVERNMENT, I WAS INFORMED ON SATURDAY MORNING.
I UNDERSTAND THE C.I.A. SUSPECTS THE **LIBYANS** WERE RESPONSIBLE.
HAVE MY OWN THEORIES ON THAT.
TAKE IT YOU'RE NOT TOO CONCERNED ABOUT BLAKE'S DEATH.
A LIVE BODY AND A DEAD BODY CONTAIN THE SAME NUMBER OF **PARTICLES**.
STRUCTURALLY, THERE'S NO DISCERNIBLE **DIFFERENCE**.
LIFE AND DEATH ARE UNQUANTIFIABLE **ABSTRACTS**. WHY **SHOULD** I BE CONCERNED?
ENNK.
ANYWAY, IT COULDN'T HAVE HAPPENED TO A NICER **PERSON**.
BLAKE WAS A BASTARD. HE WAS A **MONSTER**. Y'KNOW HE TRIED TO RAPE MY **MOTHER** BACK WHEN THEY WERE BOTH **MINUTEMEN**?
UHM.
SO YOU SUPPORT THE ALLEGATIONS MADE IN HOLLIS MASON'S BOOK CONCERNING BLAKE?
WHAT MASON SAID IN "**UNDER THE HOOD**" IS WHAT **HAPPENED**. GOD KNOWS I'M NOT MY MOTHER'S **BIGGEST** ADMIRER, BUT SOME THINGS SHOULDN'T HAPPEN TO **ANYBODY**.
WHY DO YOU THINK BLAKE NEVER **SUED** MASON?
CRONCH. CRONCH
I'M NOT HERE TO SPECULATE ON THE MORAL LAPSES OF MEN WHO DIED IN THEIR COUNTRY'S SERVICE. I CAME TO WARN...
MORAL LAPSES?
RAPE IS A **MORAL LAPSE**? YOU KNOW HE BROKE HER **RIBS**? YOU KNOW HE ALMOST **CHOKED** HER?
JON, GET THIS CREEP **OUT** OF HERE.
21

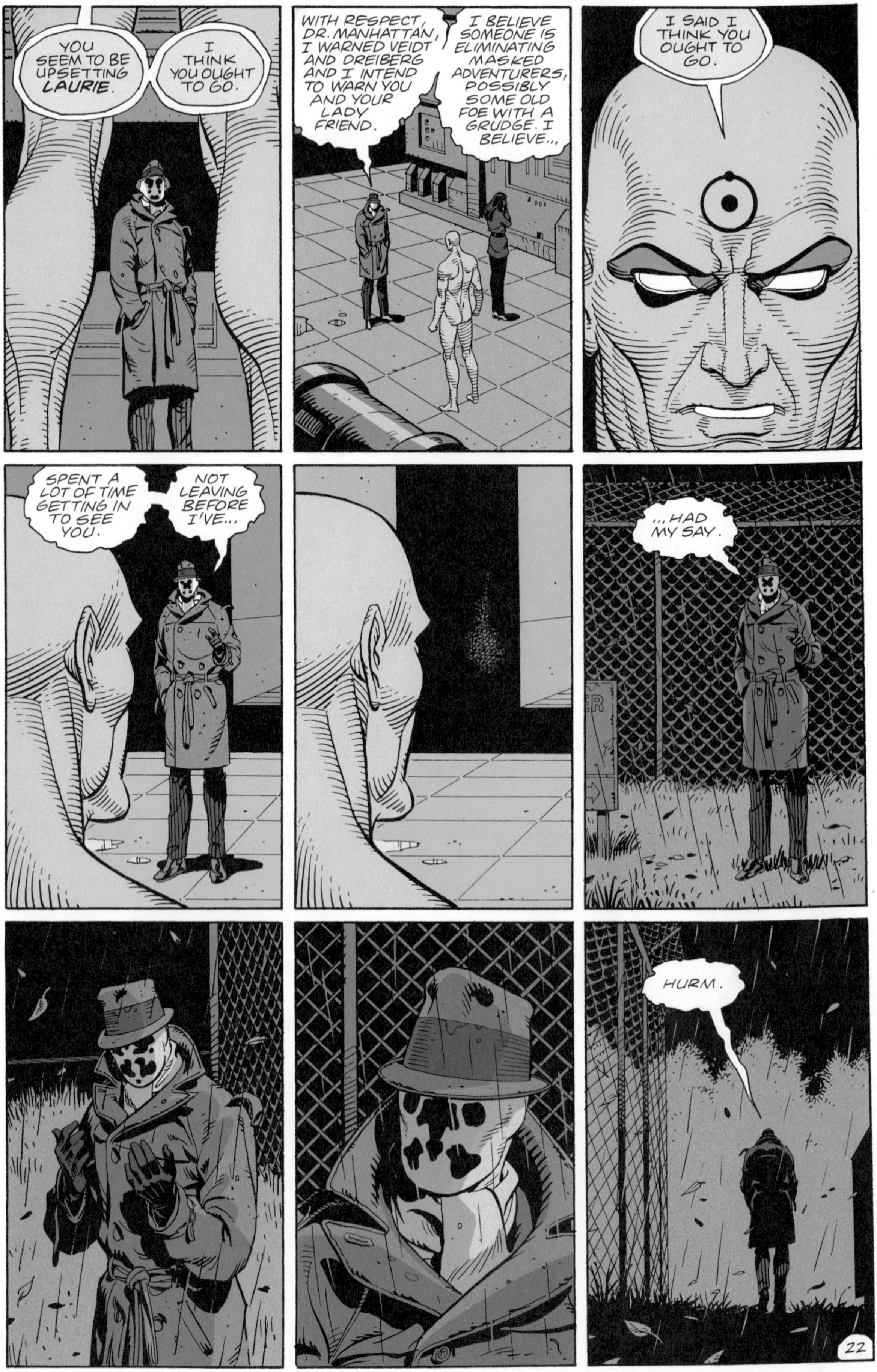
YOU SEEM TO BE UPSETTING LAURIE.
I THINK YOU OUGHT TO GO.
WITH RESPECT, DR. MANHATTAN, I WARNED VEIDT AND DREIBERG AND I INTEND TO WARN YOU AND YOUR LADY FRIEND.
I BELIEVE SOMEONE IS ELIMINATING MASKED ADVENTURERS, POSSIBLY SOME OLD FOE WITH A GRUDGE. I BELIEVE...
I SAID I THINK YOU OUGHT TO GO.
SPENT A LOT OF TIME GETTING IN TO SEE YOU.
NOT LEAVING BEFORE I'VE...
...HAD MY SAY.
HURM.
22

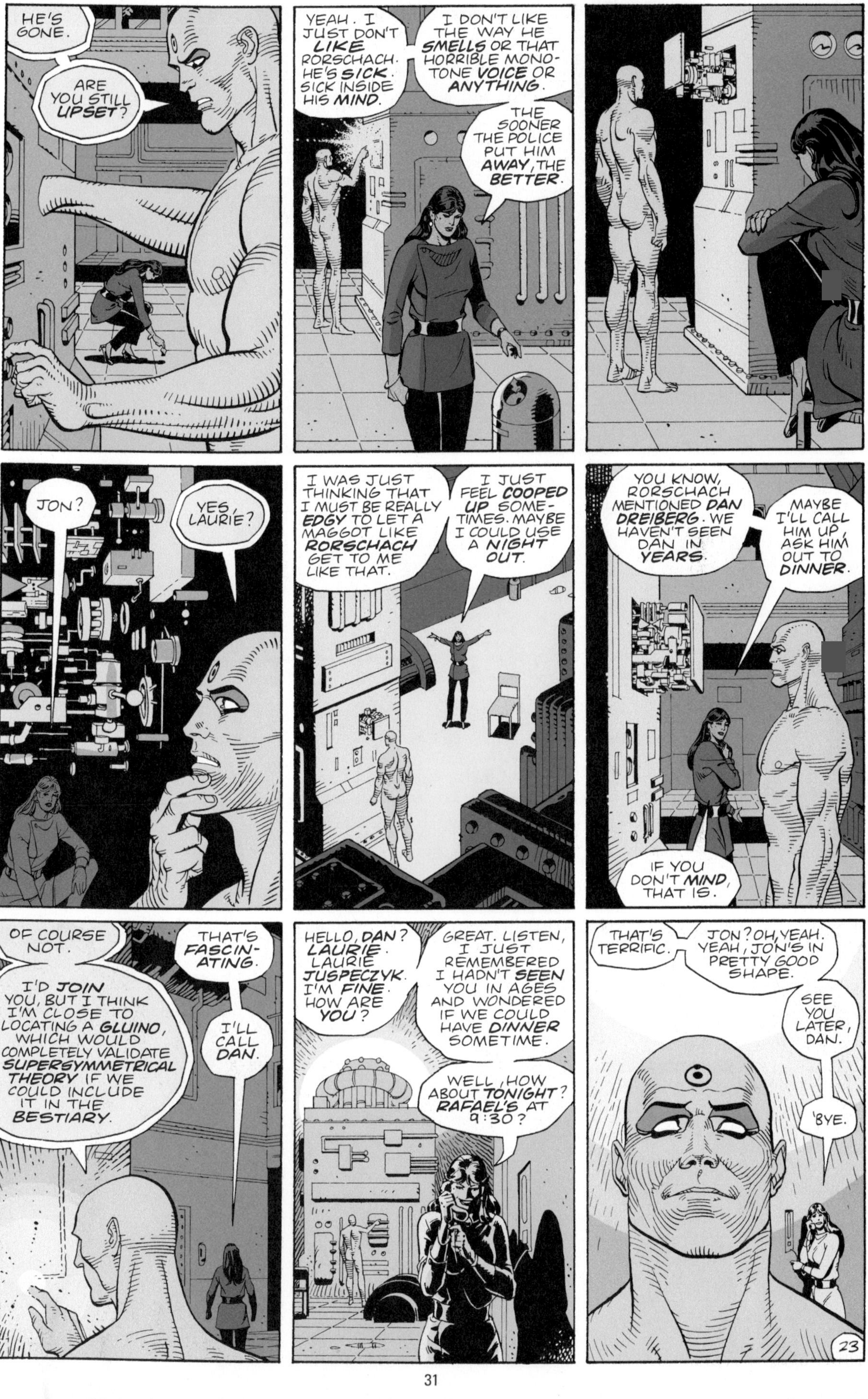
HE'S GONE.
ARE YOU STILL UPSET?
YEAH. I JUST DON'T LIKE RORSCHACH. HE'S SICK. SICK INSIDE HIS MIND.
I DON'T LIKE THE WAY HE SMELLS OR THAT HORRIBLE MONOTONE VOICE OR ANYTHING.
THE SOONER THE POLICE PUT HIM AWAY, THE BETTER.
JON?
YES, LAURIE?
I WAS JUST THINKING THAT I MUST BE REALLY EDGY TO LET A MAGGOT LIKE RORSCHACH GET TO ME LIKE THAT.
I JUST FEEL COOPED UP SOMETIMES. MAYBE I COULD USE A NIGHT OUT.
YOU KNOW, RORSCHACH MENTIONED DAN DREIBERG. WE HAVEN'T SEEN DAN IN YEARS.
MAYBE I'LL CALL HIM UP, ASK HIM OUT TO DINNER.
IF YOU DON'T MIND, THAT IS.
OF COURSE NOT.
I'D JOIN YOU, BUT I THINK I'M CLOSE TO LOCATING A GLUINO, WHICH WOULD COMPLETELY VALIDATE SUPERSYMMETRICAL THEORY IF WE COULD INCLUDE IT IN THE BESTIARY.
THAT'S FASCINATING.
I'LL CALL DAN.
HELLO, DAN? LAURIE. LAURIE JUSPECZYK. I'M FINE. HOW ARE YOU?
GREAT. LISTEN, I JUST REMEMBERED I HADN'T SEEN YOU IN AGES AND WONDERED IF WE COULD HAVE DINNER SOMETIME.
WELL, HOW ABOUT TONIGHT? RAFAEL'S AT 9:30?
THAT'S TERRIFIC.
JON? OH, YEAH. YEAH, JON'S IN PRETTY GOOD SHAPE.
SEE YOU LATER, DAN.
'BYE.
23

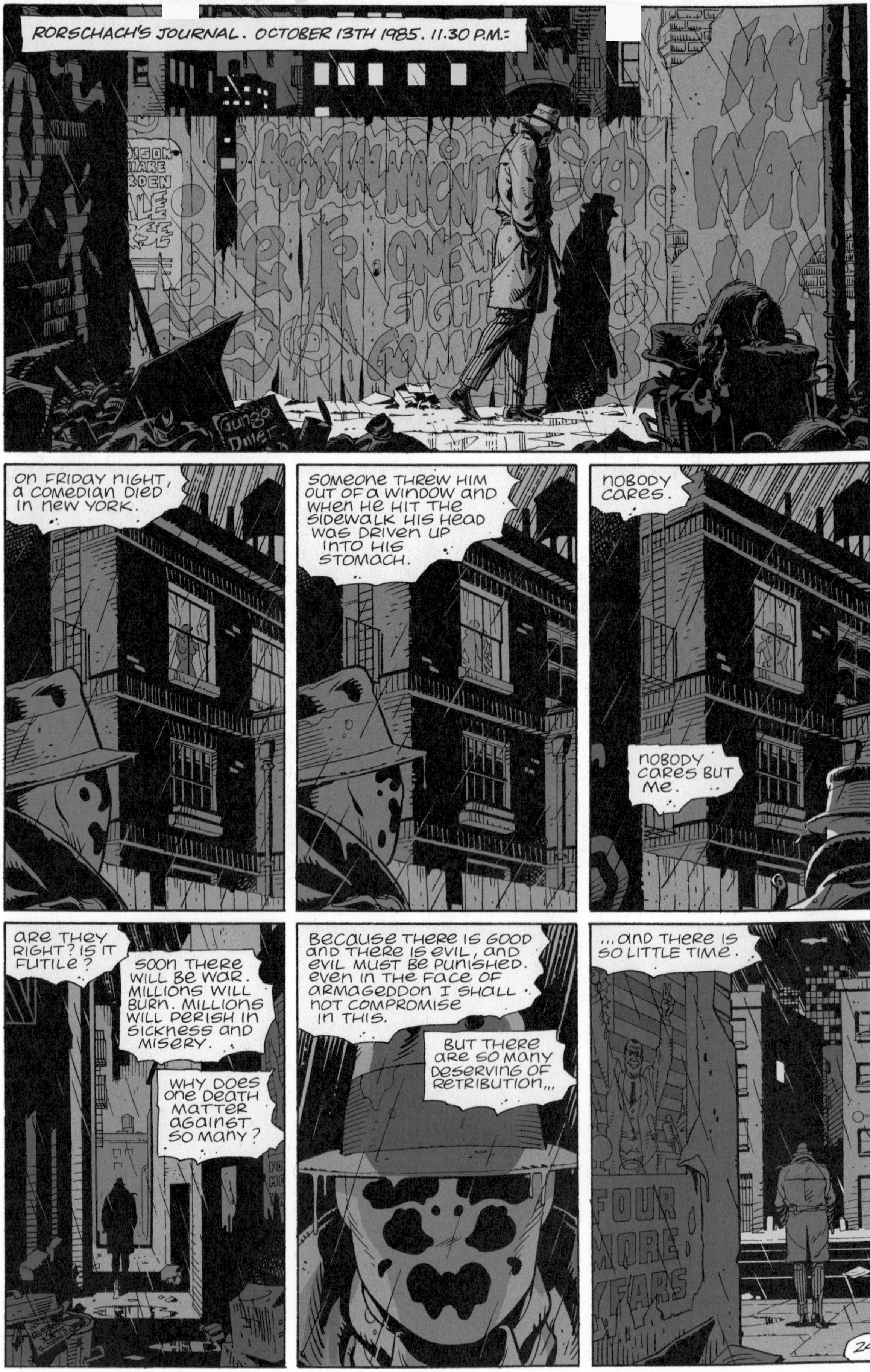
RORSCHACH'S JOURNAL. OCTOBER 13TH 1985. 11.30 P.M.:
ON FRIDAY NIGHT, A COMEDIAN DIED IN NEW YORK.
SOMEONE THREW HIM OUT OF A WINDOW AND WHEN HE HIT THE SIDEWALK HIS HEAD WAS DRIVEN UP INTO HIS STOMACH.
NOBODY CARES.
NOBODY CARES BUT ME.
ARE THEY RIGHT? IS IT FUTILE?
SOON THERE WILL BE WAR. MILLIONS WILL BURN. MILLIONS WILL PERISH IN SICKNESS AND MISERY.
WHY DOES ONE DEATH MATTER AGAINST SO MANY?
BECAUSE THERE IS GOOD AND THERE IS EVIL, AND EVIL MUST BE PUNISHED. EVEN IN THE FACE OF ARMAGEDDON I SHALL NOT COMPROMISE IN THIS.
BUT THERE ARE SO MANY DESERVING OF RETRIBUTION...
...AND THERE IS SO LITTLE TIME.
FOUR MORE YEARS
24

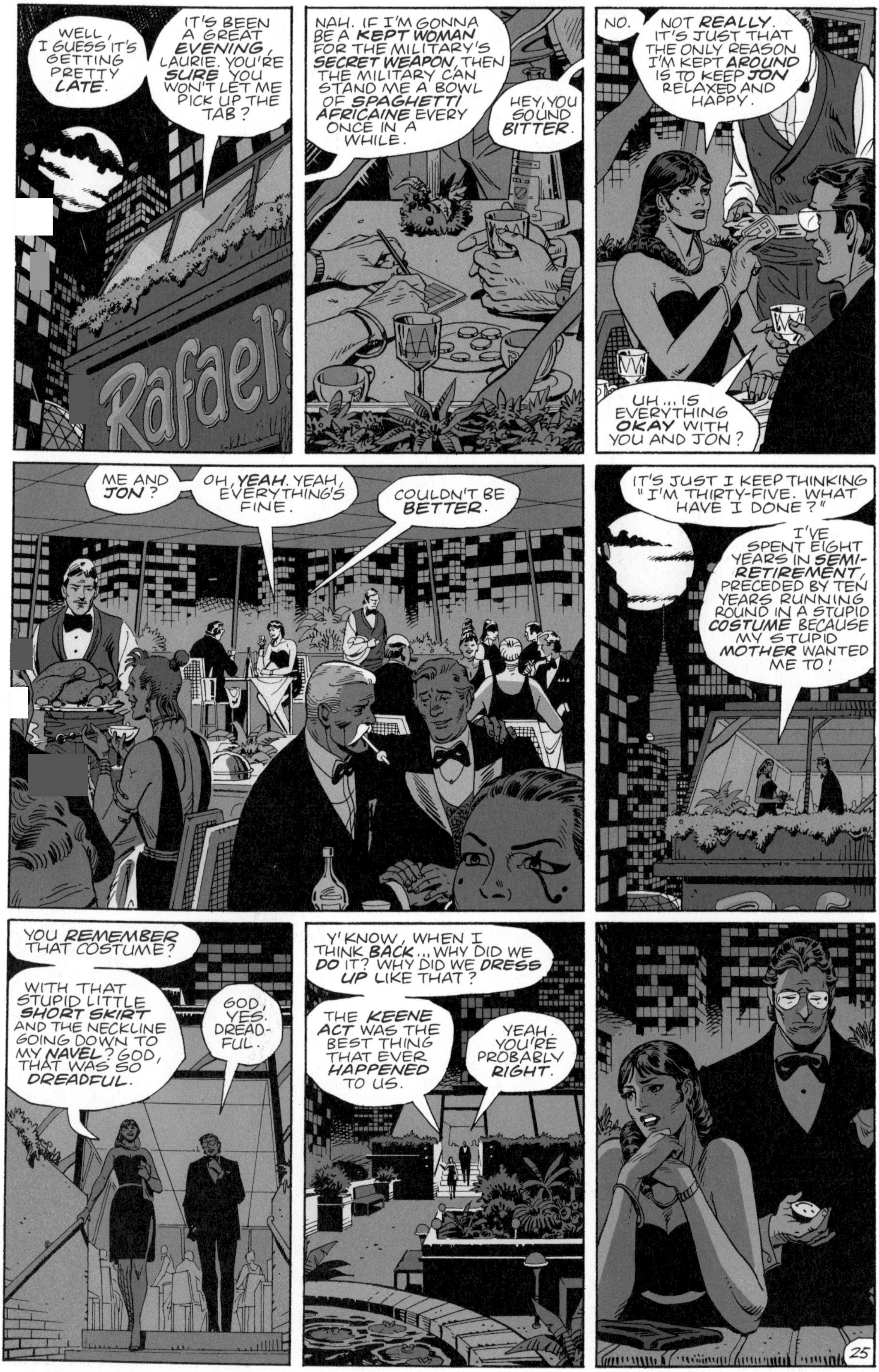
WELL, I GUESS IT'S GETTING PRETTY LATE.
IT'S BEEN A GREAT EVENING, LAURIE. YOU'RE SURE YOU WON'T LET ME PICK UP THE TAB?
Rafael's
NAH. IF I'M GONNA BE A KEPT WOMAN FOR THE MILITARY'S SECRET WEAPON, THEN THE MILITARY CAN STAND ME A BOWL OF SPAGHETTI AFRICAINE EVERY ONCE IN A WHILE.
HEY, YOU SOUND BITTER.
NO.
NOT REALLY. IT'S JUST THAT THE ONLY REASON I'M KEPT AROUND IS TO KEEP JON RELAXED AND HAPPY.
UH... IS EVERYTHING OKAY WITH YOU AND JON?
ME AND JON?
OH, YEAH. YEAH, EVERYTHING'S FINE.
COULDN'T BE BETTER.
IT'S JUST I KEEP THINKING "I'M THIRTY-FIVE. WHAT HAVE I DONE?"
I'VE SPENT EIGHT YEARS IN SEMI-RETIREMENT, PRECEDED BY TEN YEARS RUNNING ROUND IN A STUPID COSTUME BECAUSE MY STUPID MOTHER WANTED ME TO!
YOU REMEMBER THAT COSTUME?
WITH THAT STUPID LITTLE SHORT SKIRT AND THE NECKLINE GOING DOWN TO MY NAVEL? GOD, THAT WAS SO DREADFUL.
GOD, YES. DREADFUL.
Y'KNOW, WHEN I THINK BACK... WHY DID WE DO IT? WHY DID WE DRESS UP LIKE THAT?
THE KEENE ACT WAS THE BEST THING THAT EVER HAPPENED TO US.
YEAH. YOU'RE PROBABLY RIGHT.
25

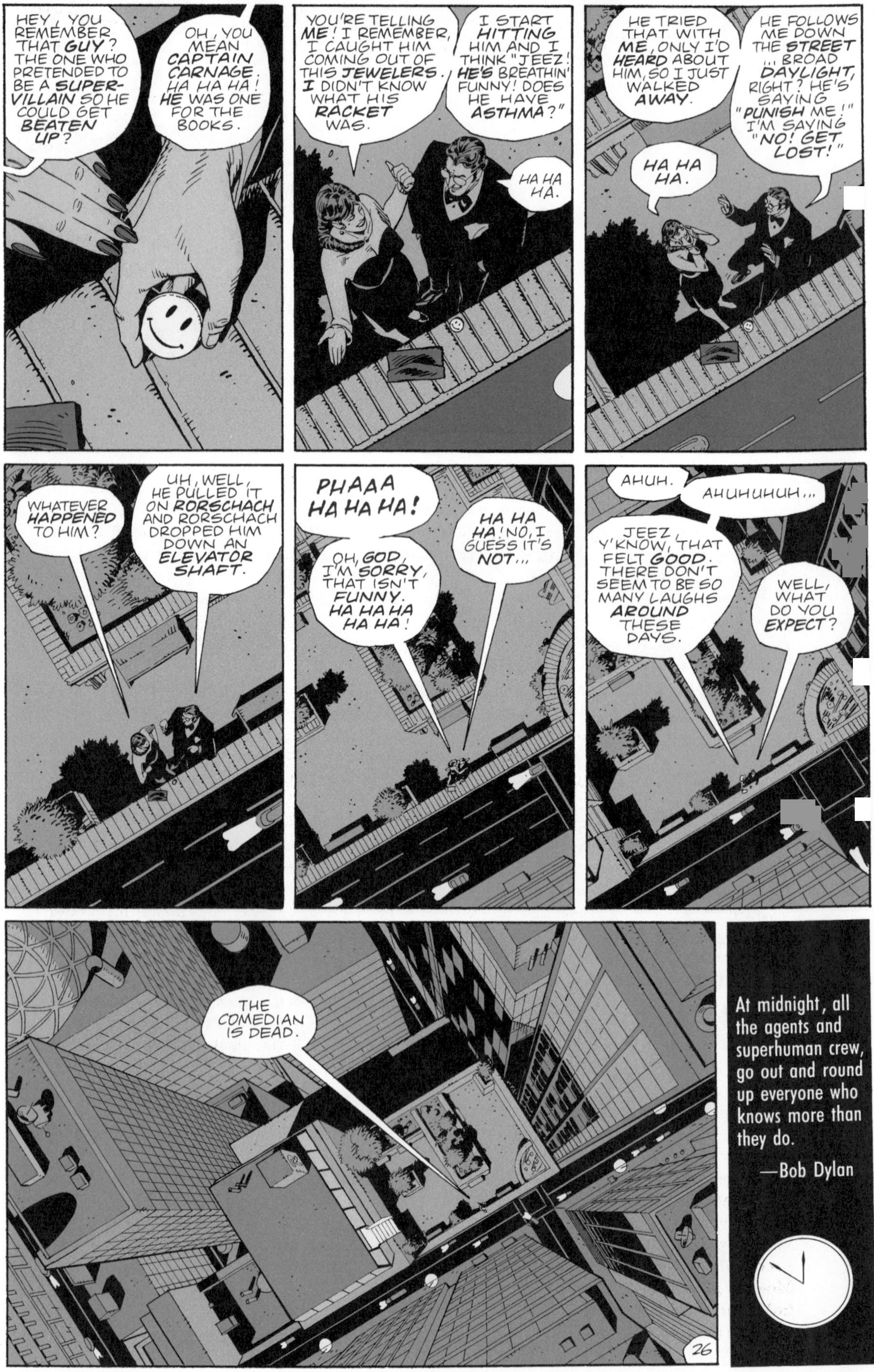
HEY, YOU REMEMBER THAT GUY? THE ONE WHO PRETENDED TO BE A SUPER-VILLAIN SO HE COULD GET BEATEN UP?
OH, YOU MEAN CAPTAIN CARNAGE. HA HA HA! HE WAS ONE FOR THE BOOKS.
YOU'RE TELLING ME! I REMEMBER, I CAUGHT HIM COMING OUT OF THIS JEWELERS. I DIDN'T KNOW WHAT HIS RACKET WAS.
I START HITTING HIM AND I THINK "JEEZ! HE'S BREATHIN' FUNNY! DOES HE HAVE ASTHMA?"
HA HA HA.
HE TRIED THAT WITH ME, ONLY I'D HEARD ABOUT HIM, SO I JUST WALKED AWAY.
HE FOLLOWS ME DOWN THE STREET ... BROAD DAYLIGHT, RIGHT? HE'S SAYING "PUNISH ME!" I'M SAYING "NO! GET LOST!"
HA HA HA.
WHATEVER HAPPENED TO HIM?
UH, WELL, HE PULLED IT ON RORSCHACH AND RORSCHACH DROPPED HIM DOWN AN ELEVATOR SHAFT.
PHAAA HA HA HA!
OH, GOD, I'M SORRY, THAT ISN'T FUNNY. HA HA HA HA HA!
HA HA HA! NO, I GUESS IT'S NOT...
AHUH.
AHUHUHUH...
JEEZ, Y'KNOW, THAT FELT GOOD. THERE DON'T SEEM TO BE SO MANY LAUGHS AROUND THESE DAYS.
WELL, WHAT DO YOU EXPECT?
THE COMEDIAN IS DEAD.
26
At midnight, all the agents and superhuman crew, go out and round up everyone who knows more than they do.
—Bob Dylan

UNDER THE HOOD

We present here excerpts from Hollis Mason's autobiography, UNDER THE HOOD, leading up to the time when he became the masked adventurer, Nite Owl. Reprinted with permission of the author.

I.

The lady who works in the grocery store at the corner of my block is called Denise, and she's one of America's great unpublished novelists. Over the years she's written *forty-two* romantic novels, none of which have ever reached the bookstores. I, however, have been fortunate enough to hear the plots of the last twenty-seven of these recounted in installments by the authoress herself every time I drop by the store for a jar of coffee or can of beans, and my respect for Denise's literary prowess knows no bounds. So, naturally enough, when I found myself faced with the daunting task of actually starting the book you now hold in your hands, it was Denise I turned to for advice.

"Listen," I said. "I don't know from writing a book. I have all this stuff in my head that I want to get down, but what do I write about first? Where do I begin?"

Without looking up from the boxes of detergent to which she was fixing price tags, Denise graciously delivered up a pearl of her accumulated wisdom in a voice of bored but benign condescension.

"Start off with the saddest thing you can think of and get the audience's sympathies on your side. After that, believe me, it's a walk."

Thank you, Denise. This book is dedicated to you, because I don't know how to choose between all the other people I should be dedicating it to

The saddest thing I can think of is "The Ride of the Valkyries." Every time I hear it I get depressed and start wondering about the lot of humanity and the unfairness of life and all those other things that you think about at three in the morning when your digestion won't let you sleep. Now, I realize that nobody else on the planet has to brush away a tear when they hear that particular stirring refrain, but that's because they don't know about Moe Vernon.

When my father upped and left my Granddad's farm in Montana to bring his family to New York, Moe Vernon was the man he worked for. Vernon's Auto Repairs was just off Seventh Avenue, and although it was only 1928 when Dad started working there, there was just about enough trade for his wages to keep me and Mom and my sister Liantha in food and clothing. Dad was always really keen and enthusiastic about his work, and I used to think it was just because he had a thing about cars. Looking back, I can see it was more than that. It must have meant so much to him, just to have a job and be able to support his family. He'd had a lot of arguments with his father about coming east rather than taking over the farm, like the old man had planned for him, and most of the rows had ended with my grandfather predicting poverty and moral ruination for my dad and mom if they so much as set foot in New York. To be living the life that he himself had chosen and keeping his family above the poverty line in spite of his father's warnings must have meant more to my dad than anything in the world, but that's something I only understand now, with hindsight. Back then, I just thought he was crazy for crankshafts.

Anyway, I was twelve years old when we left Montana, so during those next few years in the big city I was just the age to appreciate the occasional trips to the auto shop with my dad, which is where I first set eyes on Moe Vernon, his employer.

Moe Vernon was a man around fifty-five or so, and he had one of those old New York faces that you don't see anymore. It's funny, but certain faces seem to go in and out of style. You look at old photographs and everybody has a certain look to them, almost as if they're related. Look at pictures from ten years later and you can see that there's a new kind of face starting to predominate, and that the old faces are fading away and vanishing, never to be seen again. Moe Vernon's face was like that: three thins, a wiseacre cynical curl to his lower lip, a certain hollowness around the eyes, hair retreating back across his head, attempting a rendezvous with the label on his shirt collar.

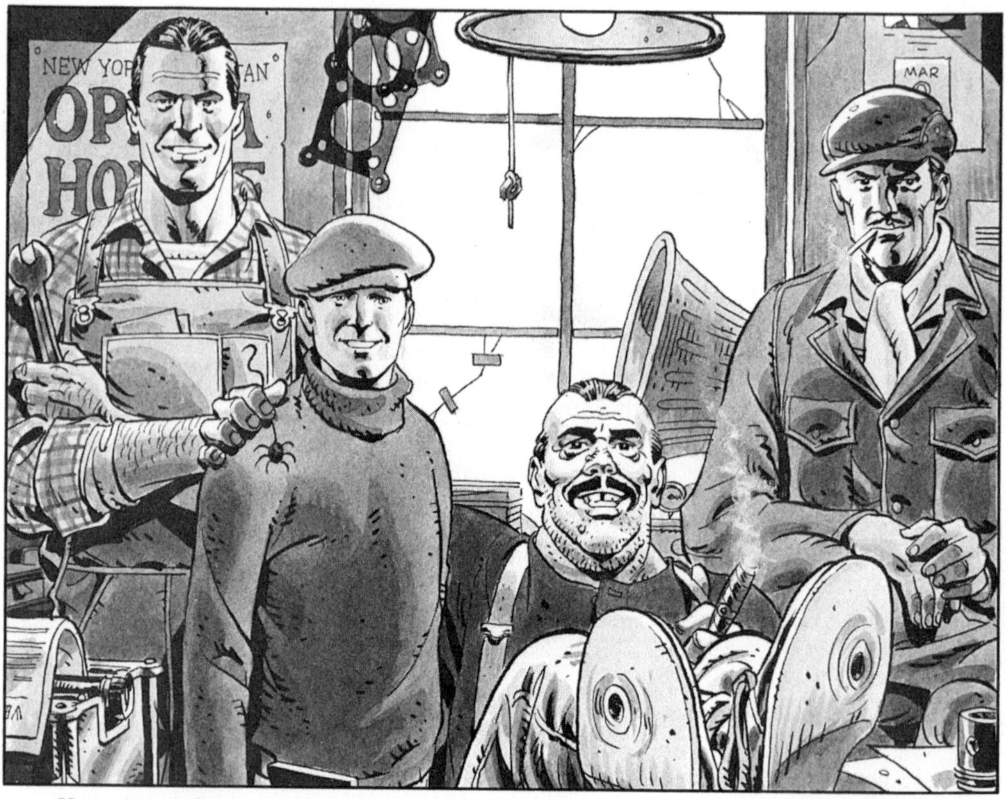
NEW YOR
AN
OP
HO
MAR

Vernon's Auto Repair c. 1928. (left to right) My father; myself, age 12; Moe Vernon; Fred Motz.

I'd go into the shop with my dad and Moe would be sitting there in his office, which had glass sides so he could watch the men working. Sometimes, if my father wanted to check something out with Moe before going ahead with his work, he'd send me over to the office to do it for him, which meant that I got to see the insides of Moe's inner sanctum. Or rather, I got to hear them.

You see, Moe was an opera buff. He had one of the new gramophones over in the corner of his office and all day he used to play scratchy old seventy-eight recordings of his favorites just as loud as he could manage. By today's standard, "as loud as he could manage" didn't amount to a whole lot of noise, but it sounded pretty cacophonous back in 1930, when things were generally quieter.

The other thing that was peculiar about Moe was his sense of humor, as represented by all the stuff he used to keep in the top right side drawer of his desk.

In that drawer, amongst a mess of rubber bands and paper clips and receipts and stuff, Moe had one of the largest collections of tasteless novelty items that I had seen up until that point or have seen at any time since. They were all risqué little toys and gadgets that Moe had picked up from gag shops or on visits to Coney Island, but it was the sheer range of them that was overwhelming: every cheap blue gimmick that you can remember your dad bringing home when he'd been out drinking with the boys and embarrassing your mom with; every ballpoint pen with a girl on the side whose swimsuit vanished when you turned it upside down; every salt and pepper crewet set shaped like a woman's breasts; every plastic dog mess. Moe had the works. Every time anybody went into his office he'd try to startle them by displaying his latest plaything. Actually, it used to shock my dad more than it did me. I don't think he liked the idea of his son being exposed to that kind of stuff, probably because of all the moral warnings my grandfather had impressed upon him. For my part, I wasn't offended and I even found it kind of funny. Not the things themselves . . . even by then I was too old to get much amusement out of stuff like that. What I found funny was that for no apparent reason, a grown man should have a desk drawer full of such ludicrous devices.

Anyway, one day in 1933, a little after my seventeenth birthday, I was over at Vernon's Auto Repairs with Dad, helping him poke around in the oily innards of a busted-up Ford. Moe was in his office, and although we didn't find out till later, he was sitting wearing an artificial foam rubber set of realistically painted lady's bosoms, with which he hoped to get a few laughs from the guy who brought him the morning mail through from the front office when it arrived. While he waited, he was listening to Wagner.

The mail arrived in due course, and the guy handing it over managed to raise a dutiful chuckle at Moe's generous cleavage before leaving him to open and peruse the morning's missives. Amongst these (again, as we found out later) there was a letter from Moe's wife Beatrice, informing him that for the past two years she'd been sleeping with Fred Motz, the senior and most trusted mechanic employed at Vernon's Auto Repairs, who, unusually, hadn't shown up for work on that particular morning. This, according to the concluding paragraphs of the letter, was because Beatrice had taken all the money out of the joint account she shared with her husband and had departed with Fred for Tijuana.

The first anyone in the workshop knew about this was when the door of Moe's office slammed open and the startlingly loud and crackling rendition of "Ride of the Valkyries" blasted out from within. Framed in the doorway with tears in his eyes and the crumpled letter in his hand, Moe stood dramatically with all eyes turned towards him. He was still wearing the set of artificial breasts. Almost inaudible above the rising strains of Wagner swelling behind him, he spoke, with so much hurt and outrage and offended dignity fighting for possession of his voice that the end result was almost toneless.

"Fred Motz has had carnal knowledge of my wife Beatrice for the past two years."

He stood there in the wake of his announcement, the tears rolling down over his multiple chins to soak into the pink foam rubber of his bosom, making tiny sounds in his chest and throat that were trampled under the hooves of the Valkyries and lost forever.

And everybody started laughing.

I don't know what it was. We could see he was crying, but it was just something in the toneless way he'd said it, standing there wearing a pair of false breasts with all that crashing, triumphant music soaring all around him. None of us could help it, laughing at him like that. My dad and I were both doubled up and the other guys slaving over the nearby cars were wiping tears from their eyes and smearing their faces with oil in the process. Moe just looked at us all for a minute and then went back into his office and closed the door. A moment or two later the Wagner stopped with an ugly scraping noise as Moe snatched the needle from the groove of the gramophone record, and after that there was silence.

About half an hour passed before someone went in to apologize on behalf of everybody and to see if Moe was all right. Moe accepted the apology and said that he was fine. Apparently he was sitting there at his desk, breasts now discarded, getting on with normal routine paperwork as if nothing had happened.

I graduate from Police Academy (1938)

That night, he sent everybody home early. Then, running a tube from the exhaust of one of the shop's more operational vehicles in through the car's window, he started up the engine and drifted off into a final, bitter sleep amongst the carbon monoxide fumes. His brother took over the business and even eventually reemployed Fred Motz as chief mechanic.

And that's why "The Ride of the Valkyries" is the saddest thing I can think of, even though it's somebody else's tragedy rather than my own. I was there and I laughed along with all the rest and I guess that makes it part of my story too.

Now, if Denise's theory is correct, I should have your full sympathy and the rest will be a walk. So maybe it's safe to tell you about all the stuff you probably bought this book to read about. Maybe it's safe to tell you why I'm crazier than Moe Vernon ever was. I didn't have a drawer full of erotic novelties, but I guess I had my own individual quirks. And although I've never worn a set of false bosoms in my life, I've stood there dressed in something just as strange, with tears in my eyes while people died laughing.

II.

By 1939 I was twenty-three years old and had taken a job on the New York City police force. I've never really examined until now just why I should have chosen that particular career, but I guess it came as a result of a number of things. Foremost amongst these was probably my grandfather.

Even though I resented the old man for the amount of guilt and pressure and recrimination he'd subjected my dad to, I suppose that the simple fact of spending the first twelve years of my life living in my grandfather's proximity had indelibly stamped a certain set of moral values and conditions upon me. I was never so extreme in my beliefs concerning God, the family, and the flag as my father's father was, but if I look at myself today I can see basic notions of decency that were passed down direct from him to me. His name was Hollis Wordsworth Mason, and perhaps because my parents had flattered the old man by naming me after him, he always took a special concern over my upbringing and moral instruction. One of the things that he took great pains to impress upon me was that country folk were morally healthier than city folk and that cities were just cesspools into which all the world's dishonesty and greed and lust and godlessness drained and was left to fester unhindered. Obviously, as I got older and came to realize just how much drunkenness and domestic violence and child abuse was hidden behind the neighborly facade of some of these lonely Montana farmhouses, I understood that my grandfather's appraisal had been a little one-sided. Nevertheless, some of the things that I saw in the city during my first few years here filled me with a sort of ethical revulsion that I couldn't shake off. To some degree, I still can't.

The pimps, the pornographers, the protection artists. The landlords who set dogs on their elderly tenants when they wanted them out to make way for more lucrative custom. The old men who touched little children and the callous young rapists who were barely old enough to shave. I saw these people all around me and I'd feel sick in my gut at the world and what it was becoming. Worse, there were times when I'd upset my dad and mom by loudly wishing I was back in Montana. Despite everything, I wished no such thing, but sometimes I'd be mad at them and it seemed like the best way to hurt them, to reawaken all those old doubts and worries and sleeping dogs of guilt. I'm sorry I did it now, and I wish I could have told them that while they were alive. I wish I could have told them that they were right in bringing me to the city, that they did the right thing by me. I wish I could have let them know that. Their lives would have been so much easier.

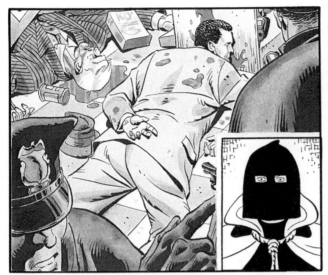

Masked adventurers make the front page. (New York Gazette, October 14th, 1938) Note artist's impression of "The Hooded Vigilante."

When the gap between the world of the city and the world my grandfather had presented to me as right and good became too wide and depressing to tolerate, I'd turn to my other great love, which was pulp adventure fiction. Despite the fact that Hollis Mason Senior would have had nothing but scorn and loathing for all of those violent and garish magazines, there was a sort of prevailing morality in them that I'm sure he would have responded to. The world of Doc Savage and The Shadow was one of absolute values, where what was good was never in the slightest doubt and where what was evil inevitably suffered some fitting punishment. The notion of good and justice espoused by Lamont Cranston with his slouch hat and blazing automatics seemed a long way from that of the fierce and taciturn old man I remembered sitting up alone into the Montana night with no company save his bible, but I can't help feeling that if the two had ever met they'd have found something to talk about. For my part, all those brilliant and resourceful sleuths and heroes offered a glimpse of a perfect world where morality worked the way it was *meant* to. Nobody in Doc Savage's world ever killed themselves except thwarted kamikaze assassins or enemy spies with cyanide capsules. Which world would you rather live in, if you had the choice?

Answering that question, I suppose, was what led me to become a cop. It was also what led me to later become something more than a cop. Bear that in mind and I think the rest of this narrative will be easier to swallow. I know people always have trouble understanding just what brings a person to behave the way that I and people like me behave, what makes us do the sort of things we do. I can't answer for anybody else, and I suspect that all our answers would be different anyway, but in my case it's fairly straightforward: I like the idea of adventure, and I feel bad unless I'm doing good. I've heard all the psychologists' theories, and I've heard all the jokes and the rumors and the innuendo, but what it comes down to for me is that I dressed up like an owl and fought crime because it was fun and because it needed doing and because I goddam felt like it.

Okay. There it is. I've said it. I dressed up. As an owl. And fought crime. Perhaps you begin to see why I half expect this summary of my career to raise more laughs than poor cuckolded Moe Vernon with his foam teats and his Wagner could ever hope to have done.

For me, it all started in 1938, the year when they invented the super-hero. I was too old for comic books when the first issue of ACTION COMICS came out, or at least too old to read them in public without souring my promotion chances, but I noticed a lot of the little kids on my beat reading it and couldn't resist asking one of them if I could glance through it. I figured if anybody saw me I could put it all down to keeping a good relationship with the youth of the community.

There was a lot of stuff in that first issue. There were detective yarns and stories about magicians whose names I can't remember, but from the moment I set eyes on it I only had eyes for the Superman story. Here was something that presented the basic morality of the pulps without all their darkness and ambiguity. The atmosphere of the horrific and faintly sinister that hung around the Shadow was nowhere to be seen in the bright primary colors of Superman's world, and there was no hint of the repressed sex-urge which had sometimes been apparent in the pulps, to my discomfort and embarrassment. I'd never been entirely sure what Lamont Cranston was up to with Margo Lane, but I'd bet it was nowhere near as innocent and wholesome as Clark Kent's relationship with her namesake Lois. Of course, all of these old characters are gone and forgotten now, but I'm willing to bet that there are at least a few older readers out there who will remember enough to know what I'm talking about. Anyway, suffice it to say that I read that story through about eight times before giving it back to the complaining kid that I'd snitched it from.

It set off a lot of things I'd forgotten about, deep inside me, and kicked all those old fantasies that I'd had when I was thirteen or fourteen back into gear: The prettiest girl in the class would be attacked by bullies, and I'd be there to beat them off, but when she offered to kiss me as a reward, I'd refuse. Gangsters would kidnap my math teacher, Miss Albertine, and I'd track them down and kill them one by one until she was free, and then she'd break off her engagement with my sarcastic English teacher, Mr. Richardson, because she'd fallen hopelessly in love with her grim-faced and silent fourteen-year-old savior. All of this stuff came flooding back as I stood there gawking at the hijacked comic book, and even though I laughed at myself for having entertained such transparent juvenile fantasies, I didn't laugh as hard as I might have done. Not half as hard as I'd laughed at Moe Vernon, for example.

Anyway, although I'd occasionally manage to trick some unsuspecting tyke into lending me his most recent issue of the funnybook in question and then spend the rest of the day leaping tall buildings inside my head, my fantasies were to remain as fantasies until I opened a newspaper in the autumn of that same year and found that the super-heroes had escaped from their four-color world and invaded the plain, factual black and white of the headlines.

The first news story was simple and unpresupposing enough, but it shared enough elements with those fictions that were closest to my heart to make me notice it and file it in my memory for future reference. It concerned an attempted assault and robbery that had taken place in Queens, New York. A man and his girlfriend, walking home after a night at the theater, had been set upon by a gang of three men armed with guns. After relieving the couple of their valuables, the gang has started to beat and physically abuse the young man while threatening to indecently assault his girlfriend. At this point, the crime had been interrupted by a figure "Who dropped into the alleyway from above with something over his face" and proceeded to disarm the three attackers before beating them with such severity that all three required hospital treatment and that one subsequently lost the use of both legs as a result of a spinal injury. The witnesses' recounting of the event was confused and contradictory, but there was still something in the story that gave me a tingle of recognition. And then, a week later, it happened again.

Reportage on this second instance was more detailed. A supermarket stick-up had been prevented thanks to the intervention of "A tall man, built like a wrestler, who wore a black hood and cape and also wore a noose around his neck." This extraordinary being had crashed in through the window of the supermarket while the robbery was in progress and attacked the man responsible with such intensity and savagery that those not disabled immediately were only too willing to drop their guns and surrender. Connecting this incidence of masked intervention with its predecessor, the papers ran the story under a headline that read simply "Hooded Justice." The first masked adventurer outside comic books had been given his name.

Reading and rereading that news item, I knew that I had to be the second. I'd found my vocation.

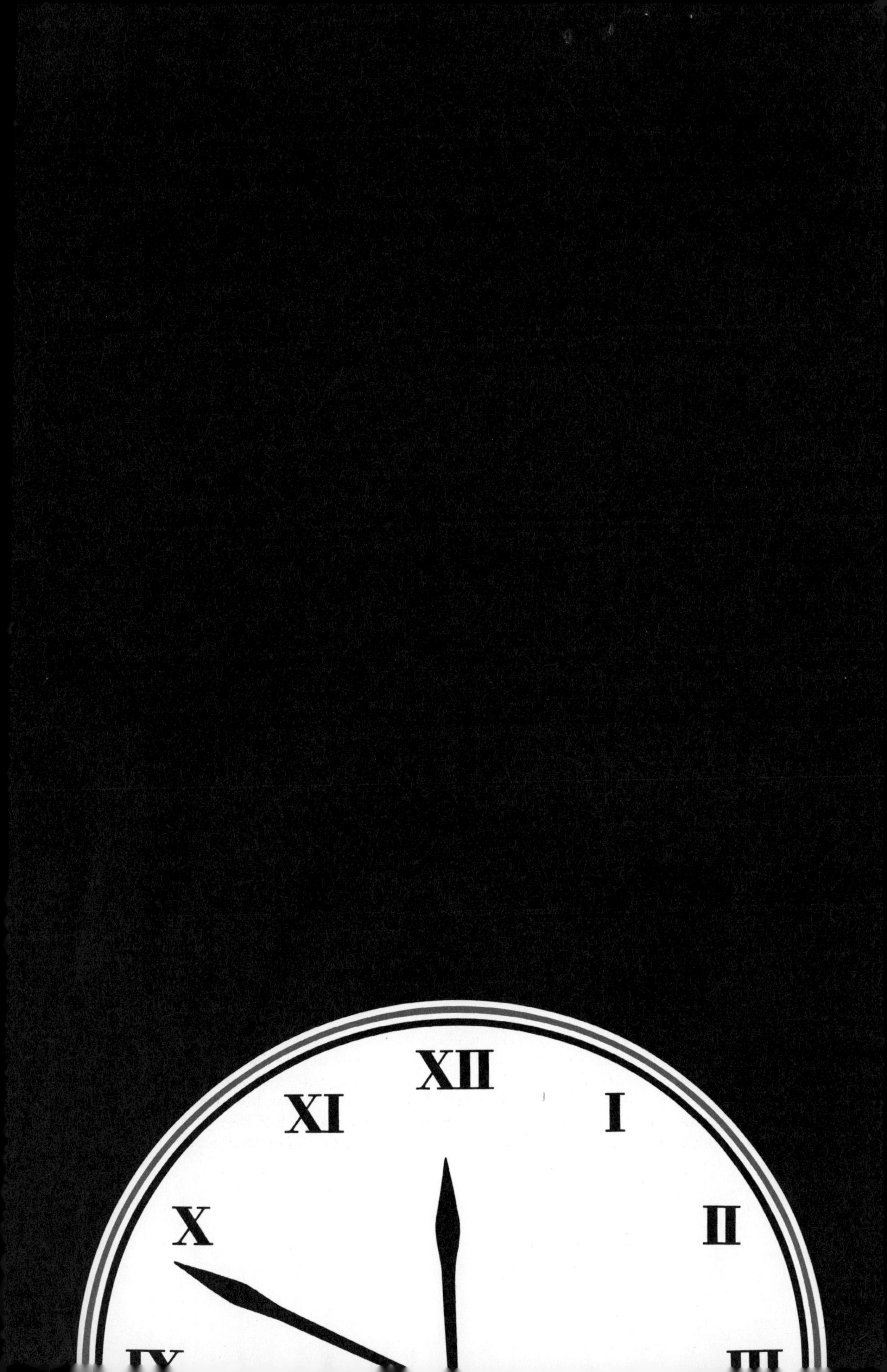
XII
XI
I
X
II

CHAPTER

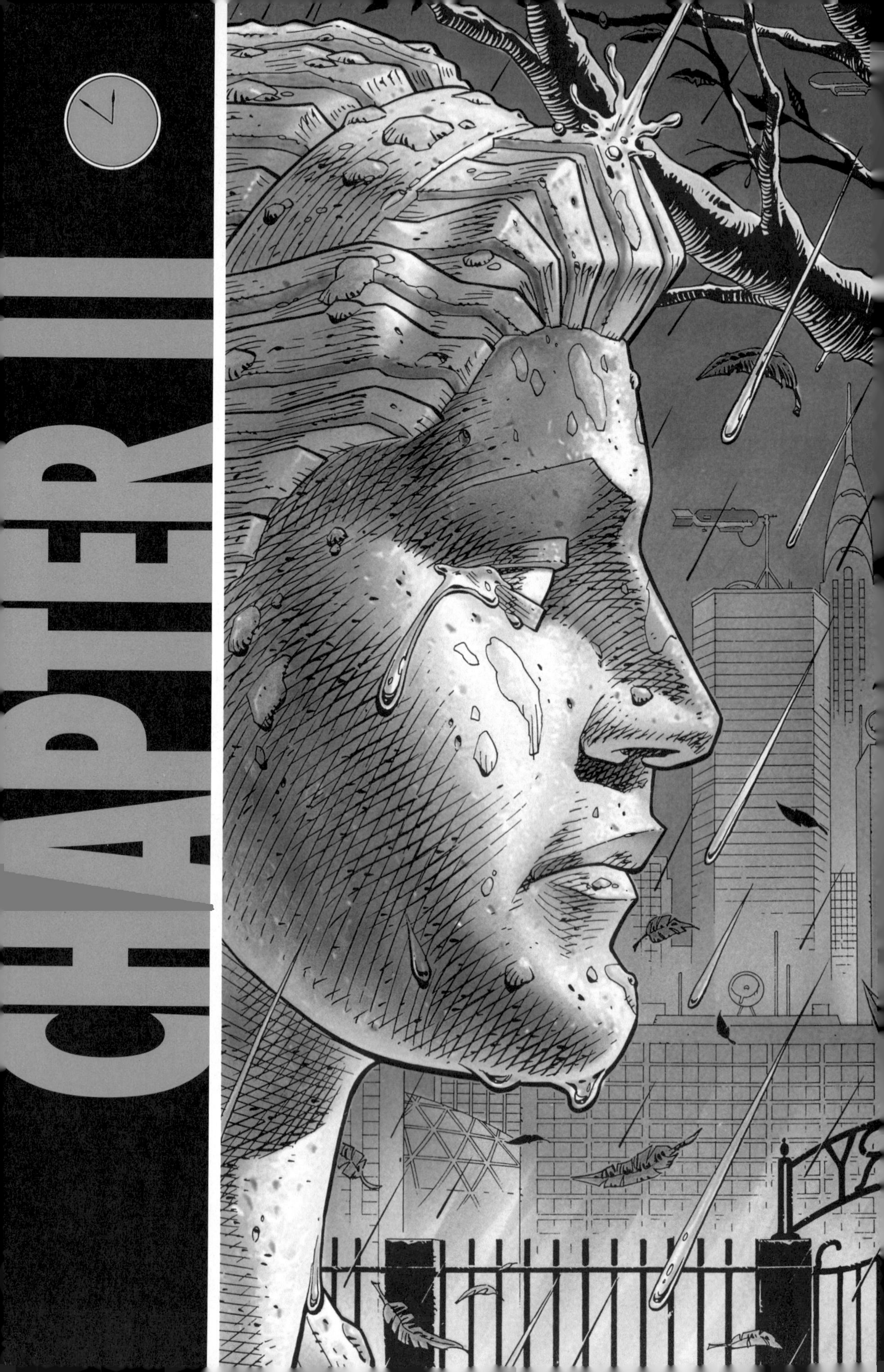

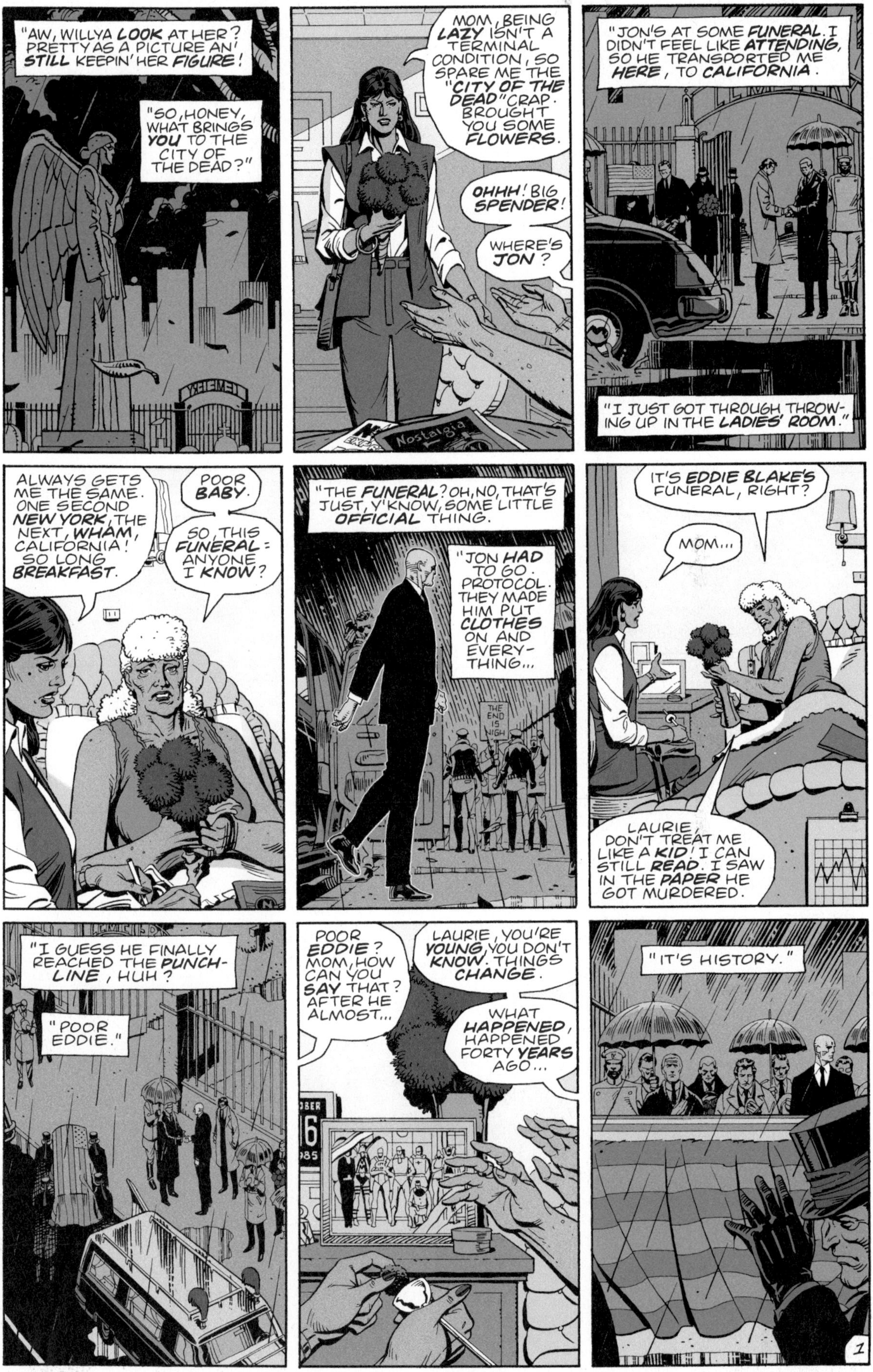
"AW, WILLYA LOOK AT HER? PRETTY AS A PICTURE AN' STILL KEEPIN' HER FIGURE!
"SO, HONEY, WHAT BRINGS YOU TO THE CITY OF THE DEAD?"
MOM, BEING LAZY ISN'T A TERMINAL CONDITION, SO SPARE ME THE "CITY OF THE DEAD" CRAP. BROUGHT YOU SOME FLOWERS.
OHHH! BIG SPENDER!
WHERE'S JON?
Nostalgia
"JON'S AT SOME FUNERAL. I DIDN'T FEEL LIKE ATTENDING, SO HE TRANSPORTED ME HERE, TO CALIFORNIA.
"I JUST GOT THROUGH THROWING UP IN THE LADIES' ROOM."
ALWAYS GETS ME THE SAME. ONE SECOND NEW YORK, THE NEXT, WHAM, CALIFORNIA! SO LONG BREAKFAST.
POOR BABY.
SO, THIS FUNERAL: ANYONE I KNOW?
"THE FUNERAL? OH, NO, THAT'S JUST, Y'KNOW, SOME LITTLE OFFICIAL THING.
"JON HAD TO GO. PROTOCOL. THEY MADE HIM PUT CLOTHES ON AND EVERYTHING...
THE END IS NIGH
IT'S EDDIE BLAKE'S FUNERAL, RIGHT?
MOM...
LAURIE, DON'T TREAT ME LIKE A KID! I CAN STILL READ. I SAW IN THE PAPER HE GOT MURDERED.
"I GUESS HE FINALLY REACHED THE PUNCHLINE, HUH?
"POOR EDDIE."
POOR EDDIE? MOM, HOW CAN YOU SAY THAT? AFTER HE ALMOST...
LAURIE, YOU'RE YOUNG, YOU DON'T KNOW. THINGS CHANGE.
WHAT HAPPENED, HAPPENED FORTY YEARS AGO...
"IT'S HISTORY."
1

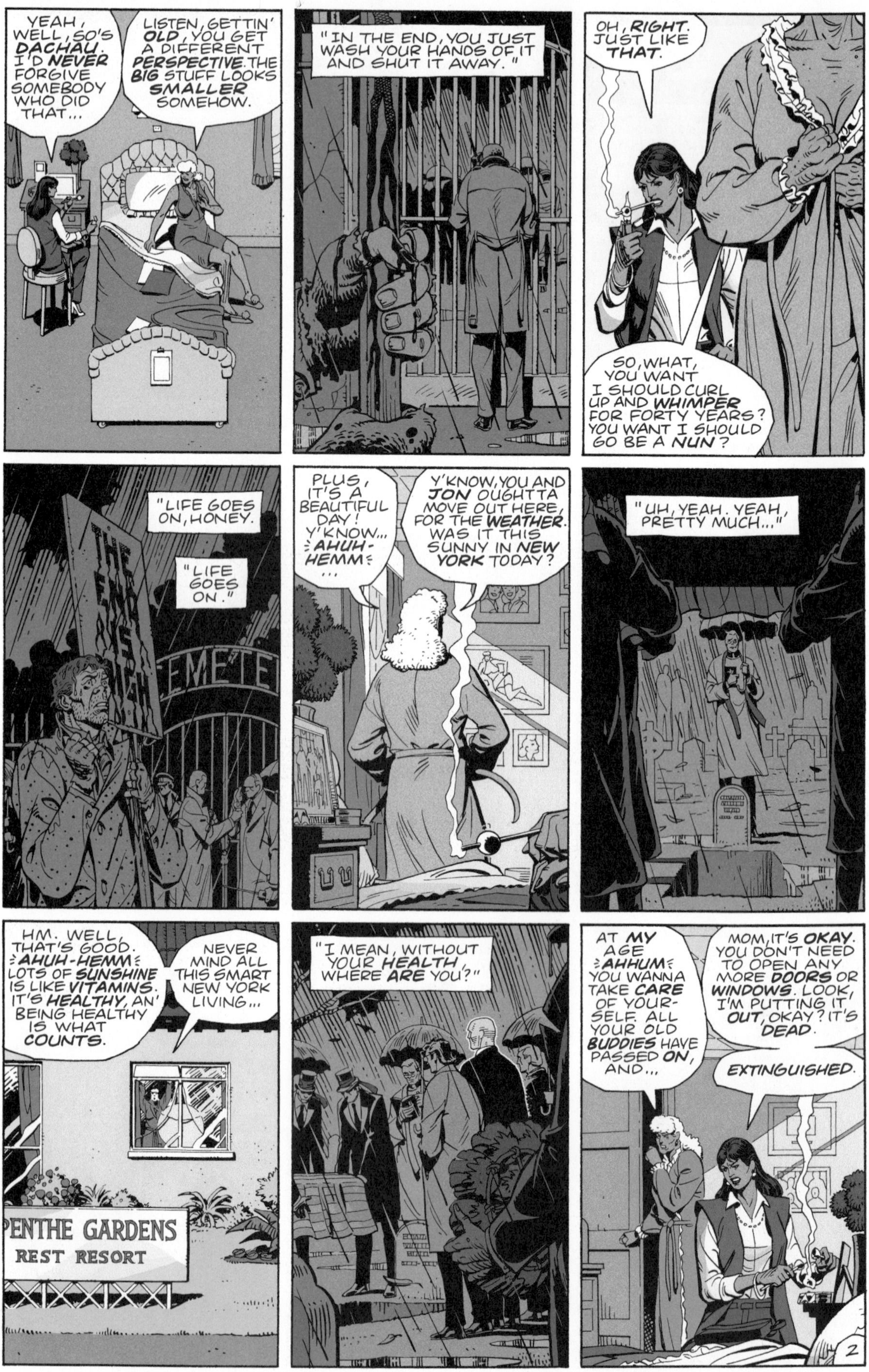
YEAH, WELL, SO'S DACHAU. I'D NEVER FORGIVE SOMEBODY WHO DID THAT...
LISTEN, GETTIN' OLD, YOU GET A DIFFERENT PERSPECTIVE. THE BIG STUFF LOOKS SMALLER SOMEHOW.
"IN THE END, YOU JUST WASH YOUR HANDS OF IT AND SHUT IT AWAY."
OH, RIGHT. JUST LIKE THAT.
SO, WHAT, YOU WANT I SHOULD CURL UP AND WHIMPER FOR FORTY YEARS? YOU WANT I SHOULD GO BE A NUN?
"LIFE GOES ON, HONEY.
"LIFE GOES ON."
PLUS, IT'S A BEAUTIFUL DAY! Y'KNOW... AHUH-HEMM ...
Y'KNOW, YOU AND JON OUGHTTA MOVE OUT HERE, FOR THE WEATHER. WAS IT THIS SUNNY IN NEW YORK TODAY?
"UH, YEAH. YEAH, PRETTY MUCH..."
HM. WELL, THAT'S GOOD. AHUH-HEMM LOTS OF SUNSHINE IS LIKE VITAMINS. IT'S HEALTHY, AN' BEING HEALTHY IS WHAT COUNTS.
NEVER MIND ALL THIS SMART NEW YORK LIVING...
PENTHE GARDENS
REST RESORT
"I MEAN, WITHOUT YOUR HEALTH, WHERE ARE YOU?"
AT MY AGE AHHUM YOU WANNA TAKE CARE OF YOURSELF. ALL YOUR OLD BUDDIES HAVE PASSED ON, AND...
MOM, IT'S OKAY. YOU DON'T NEED TO OPEN ANY MORE DOORS OR WINDOWS. LOOK, I'M PUTTING IT OUT, OKAY? IT'S DEAD.
EXTINGUISHED.
2

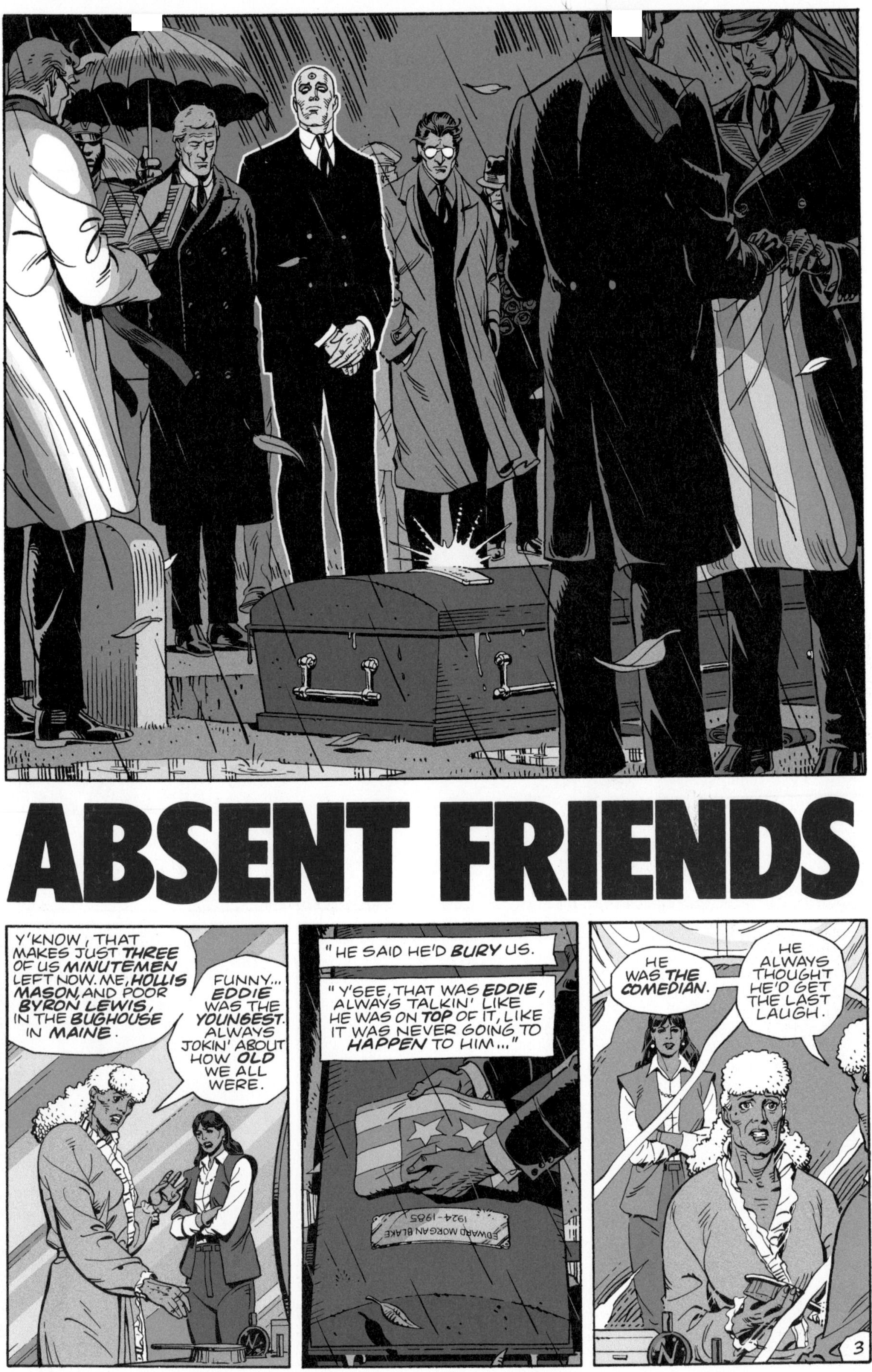
ABSENT FRIENDS
Y'KNOW, THAT MAKES JUST **THREE** OF US **MINUTEMEN** LEFT NOW. ME, **HOLLIS MASON**, AND POOR **BYRON LEWIS**, IN THE **BUGHOUSE** IN **MAINE**.
FUNNY... **EDDIE** WAS THE **YOUNGEST**. ALWAYS JOKIN' ABOUT HOW **OLD** WE ALL WERE.
"HE SAID HE'D **BURY** US.
"Y'SEE, THAT WAS **EDDIE**, ALWAYS TALKIN' LIKE HE WAS ON **TOP** OF IT, LIKE IT WAS NEVER GOING TO **HAPPEN** TO HIM..."
EDWARD MORGAN BLAKE
1924-1985
HE WAS **THE COMEDIAN**.
HE ALWAYS THOUGHT HE'D GET THE LAST LAUGH.
3

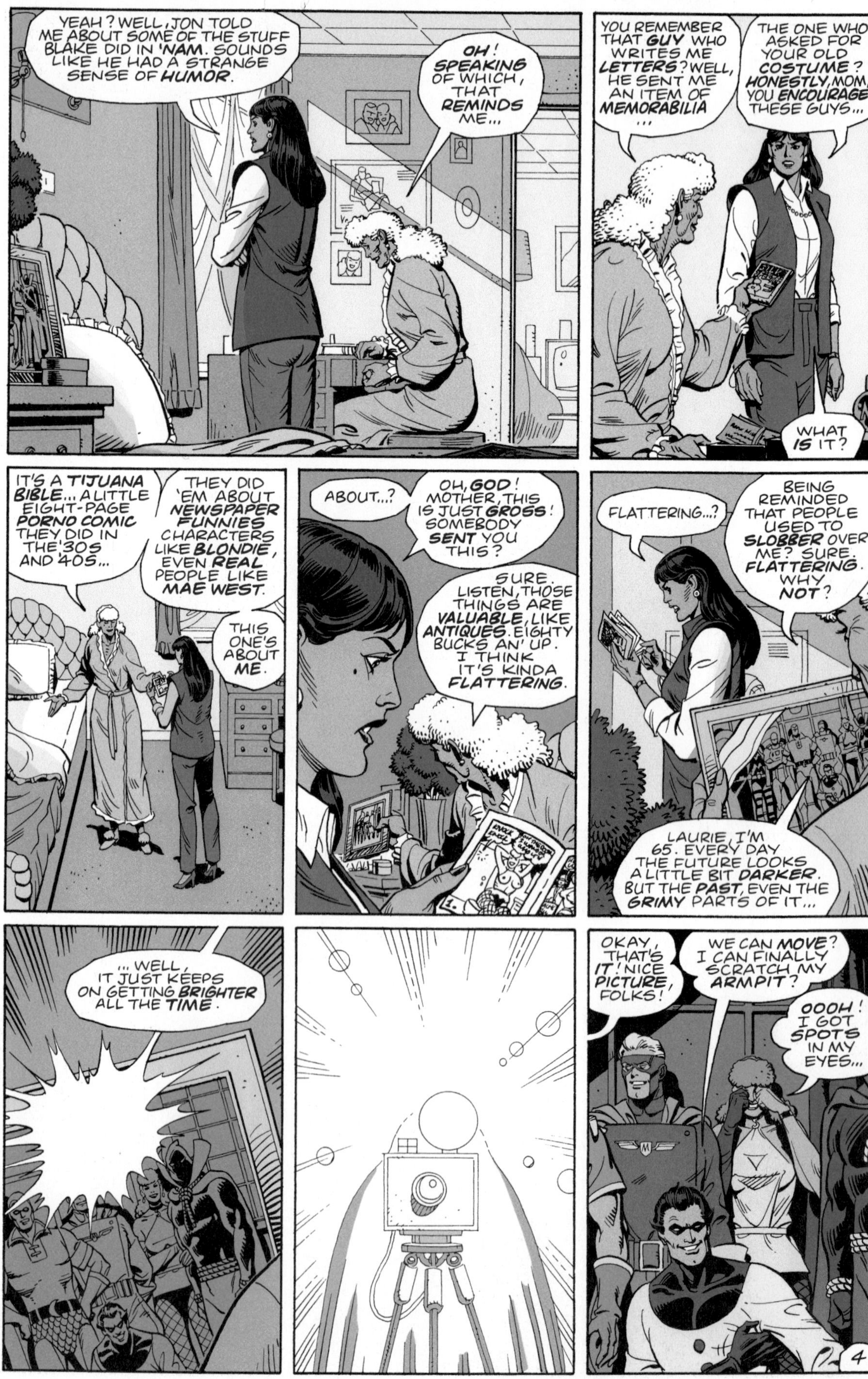
YEAH? WELL, JON TOLD ME ABOUT SOME OF THE STUFF BLAKE DID IN 'NAM. SOUNDS LIKE HE HAD A STRANGE SENSE OF HUMOR.
OH! SPEAKING OF WHICH, THAT REMINDS ME...
YOU REMEMBER THAT GUY WHO WRITES ME LETTERS? WELL, HE SENT ME AN ITEM OF MEMORABILIA...
THE ONE WHO ASKED FOR YOUR OLD COSTUME? HONESTLY, MOM, YOU ENCOURAGE THESE GUYS...
WHAT IS IT?
IT'S A TIJUANA BIBLE... A LITTLE EIGHT-PAGE PORNO COMIC THEY DID IN THE '30S AND '40S...
THEY DID 'EM ABOUT NEWSPAPER FUNNIES CHARACTERS LIKE BLONDIE, EVEN REAL PEOPLE LIKE MAE WEST.
THIS ONE'S ABOUT ME.
ABOUT...?
OH, GOD! MOTHER, THIS IS JUST GROSS! SOMEBODY SENT YOU THIS?
SURE. LISTEN, THOSE THINGS ARE VALUABLE, LIKE ANTIQUES. EIGHTY BUCKS AN' UP. I THINK IT'S KINDA FLATTERING.
FLATTERING...?
BEING REMINDED THAT PEOPLE USED TO SLOBBER OVER ME? SURE. FLATTERING. WHY NOT?
LAURIE, I'M 65. EVERY DAY THE FUTURE LOOKS A LITTLE BIT DARKER. BUT THE PAST, EVEN THE GRIMY PARTS OF IT...
...WELL, IT JUST KEEPS ON GETTING BRIGHTER ALL THE TIME.
OKAY, THAT'S IT! NICE PICTURE, FOLKS!
WE CAN MOVE? I CAN FINALLY SCRATCH MY ARMPIT?
OOOH! I GOT SPOTS IN MY EYES...
4

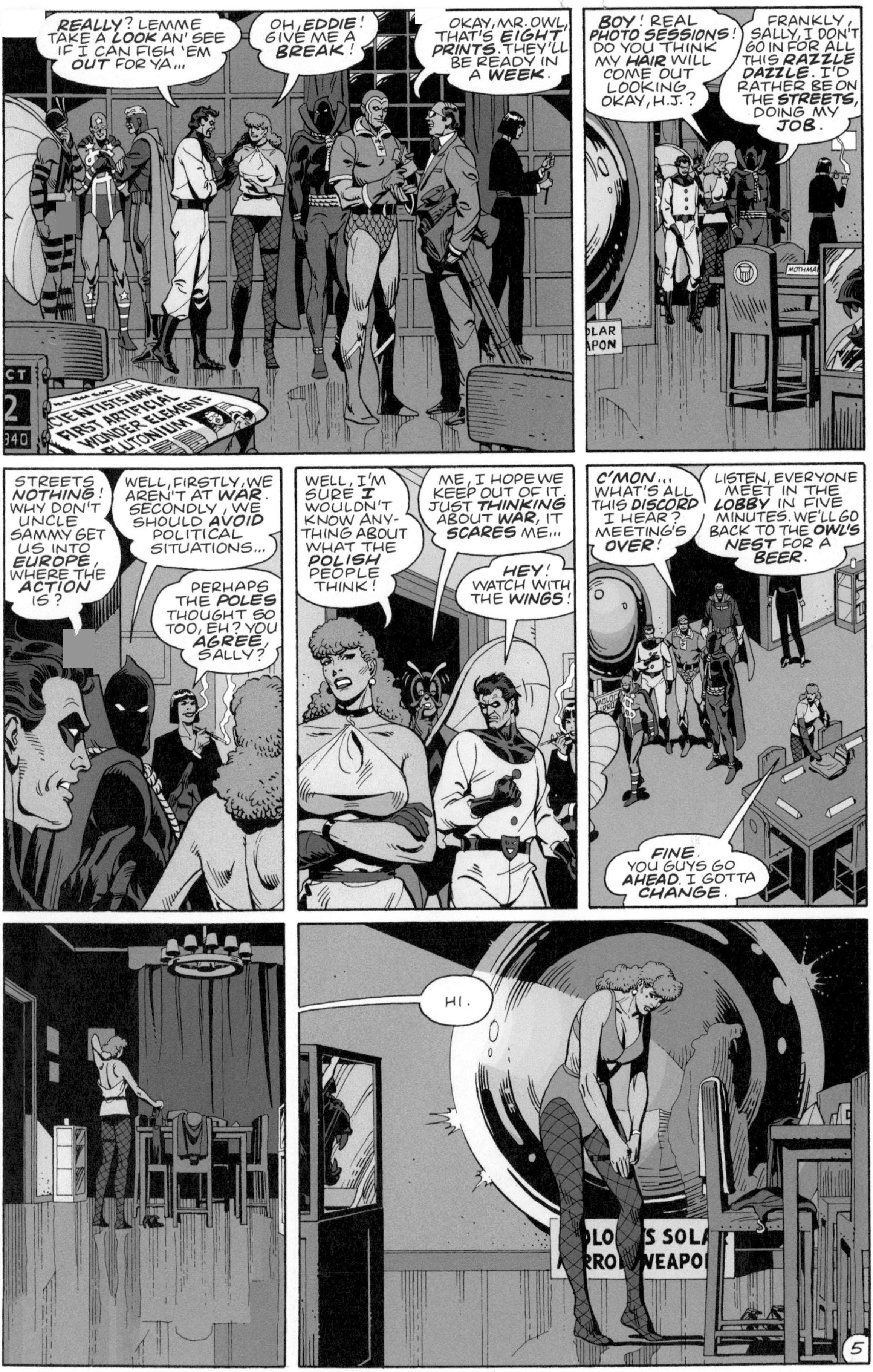
REALLY? LEMME TAKE A LOOK AN' SEE IF I CAN FISH 'EM OUT FOR YA...
OH, EDDIE! GIVE ME A BREAK!
OKAY, MR. OWL, THAT'S EIGHT PRINTS. THEY'LL BE READY IN A WEEK.
FIRST ARTIFICIAL WONDER ELEMENT: PLUTONIUM
BOY! REAL PHOTO SESSIONS! DO YOU THINK MY HAIR WILL COME OUT LOOKING OKAY, H.J.?
FRANKLY, SALLY, I DON'T GO IN FOR ALL THIS RAZZLE DAZZLE. I'D RATHER BE ON THE STREETS, DOING MY JOB.
STREETS NOTHING! WHY DON'T UNCLE SAMMY GET US INTO EUROPE, WHERE THE ACTION IS?
WELL, FIRSTLY, WE AREN'T AT WAR. SECONDLY, WE SHOULD AVOID POLITICAL SITUATIONS...
PERHAPS THE POLES THOUGHT SO TOO, EH? YOU AGREE, SALLY?
WELL, I'M SURE I WOULDN'T KNOW ANYTHING ABOUT WHAT THE POLISH PEOPLE THINK!
ME, I HOPE WE KEEP OUT OF IT. JUST THINKING ABOUT WAR, IT SCARES ME...
HEY! WATCH WITH THE WINGS!
C'MON... WHAT'S ALL THIS DISCORD I HEAR? MEETING'S OVER!
LISTEN, EVERYONE MEET IN THE LOBBY IN FIVE MINUTES. WE'LL GO BACK TO THE OWL'S NEST FOR A BEER.
FINE. YOU GUYS GO AHEAD. I GOTTA CHANGE.
HI.
5

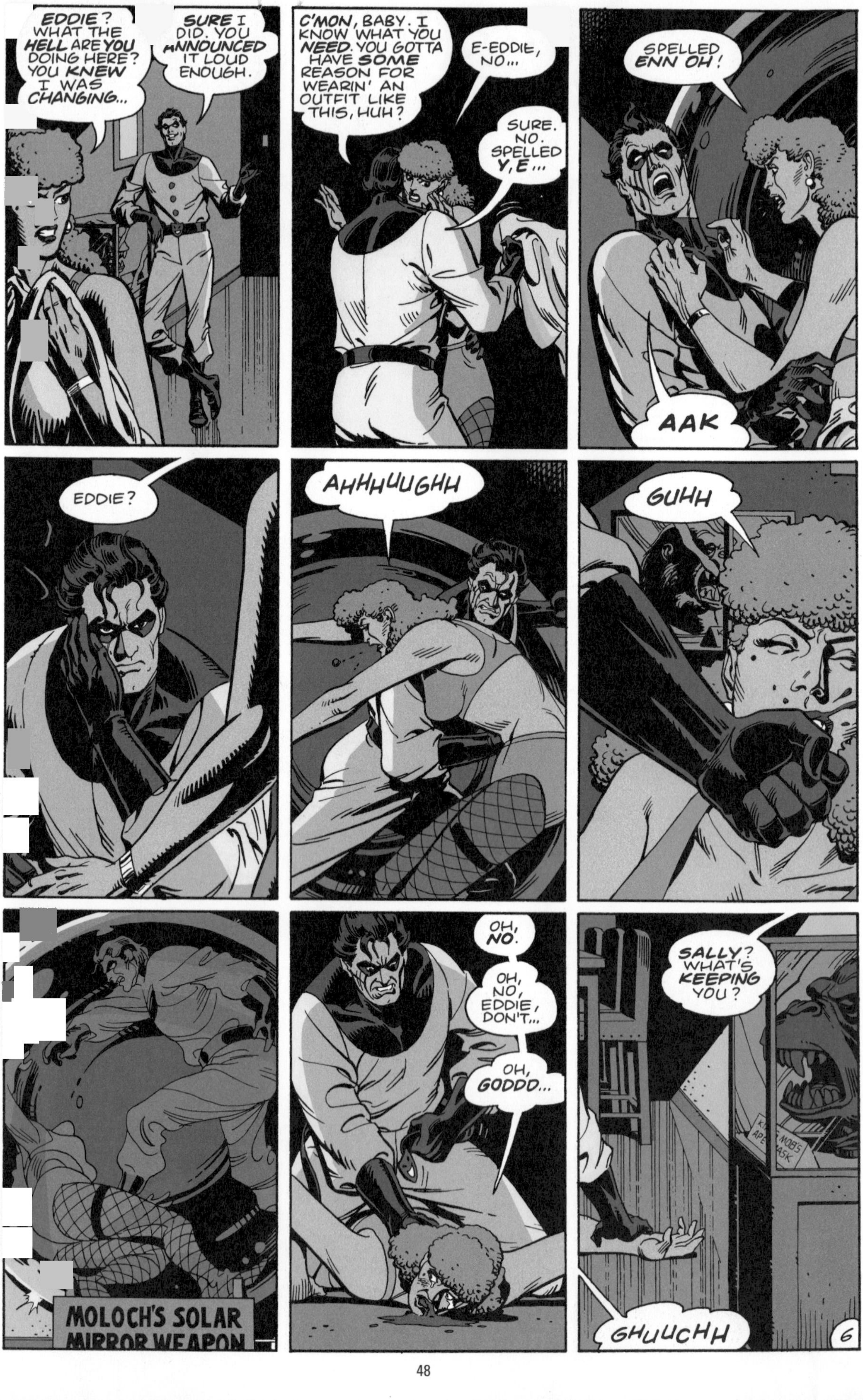
EDDIE? WHAT THE HELL ARE YOU DOING HERE? YOU KNEW I WAS CHANGING...
SURE I DID. YOU ANNOUNCED IT LOUD ENOUGH.
C'MON, BABY. I KNOW WHAT YOU NEED. YOU GOTTA HAVE SOME REASON FOR WEARIN' AN OUTFIT LIKE THIS, HUH?
E-EDDIE, NO...
SURE. NO. SPELLED Y, E...
SPELLED ENN OH!
AAK
EDDIE?
AHHHUUGHH
GUHH
MOLOCH'S SOLAR MIRROR WEAPON
OH, NO.
OH, NO, EDDIE, DON'T...
OH, GODDD...
SALLY? WHAT'S KEEPING YOU?
GHUUCHH
6

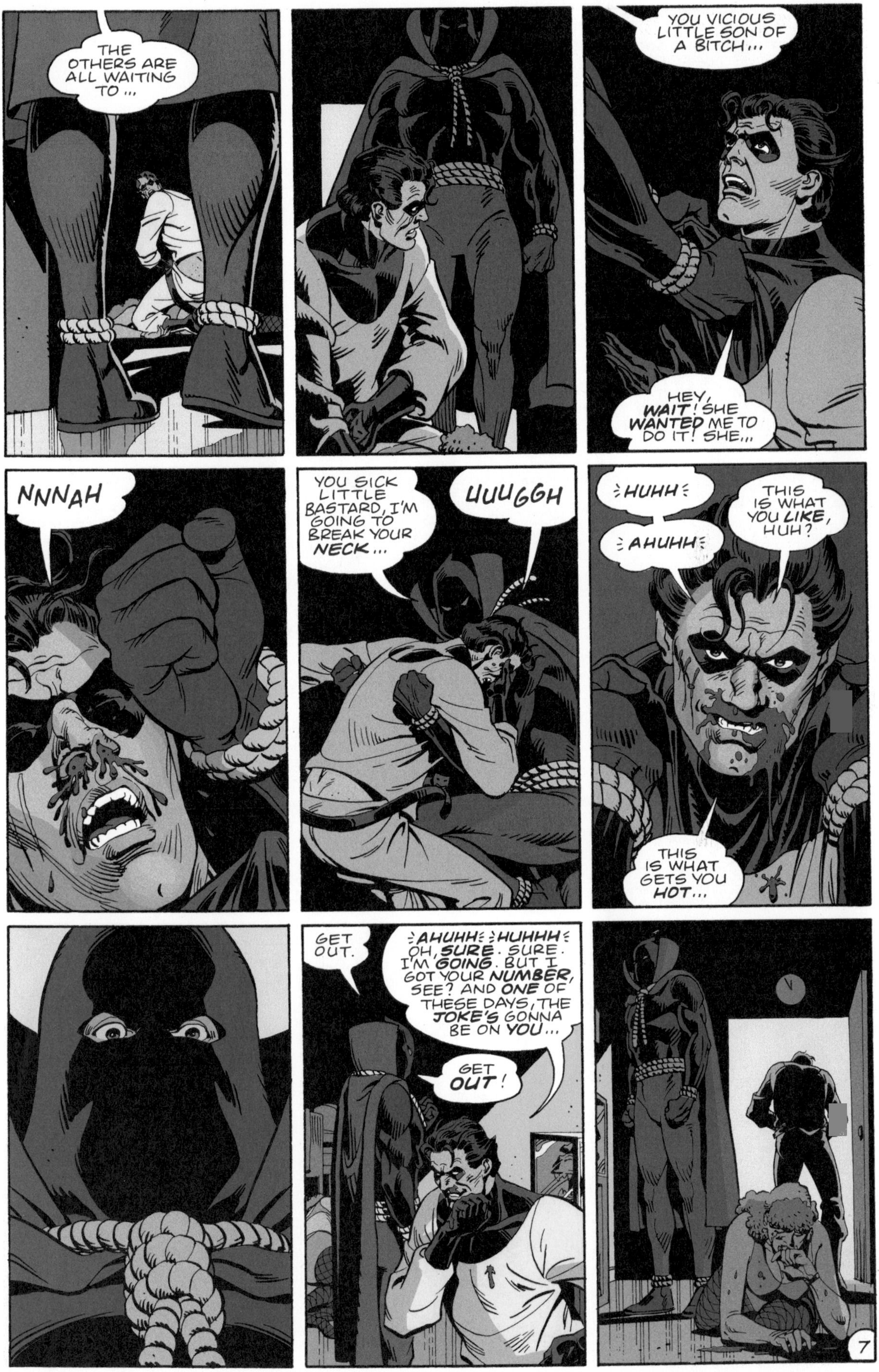

THE OTHERS ARE ALL WAITING TO...
YOU VICIOUS LITTLE SON OF A BITCH...
HEY, WAIT! SHE WANTED ME TO DO IT! SHE...
NNNAH
YOU SICK LITTLE BASTARD, I'M GOING TO BREAK YOUR NECK...
UUUGGH
HUHH
AHUHH
THIS IS WHAT YOU LIKE, HUH?
THIS IS WHAT GETS YOU HOT...
GET OUT.
AHUHH HUHHH OH, SURE. SURE. I'M GOING. BUT I GOT YOUR NUMBER, SEE? AND ONE OF THESE DAYS, THE JOKE'S GONNA BE ON YOU...
GET OUT!
7

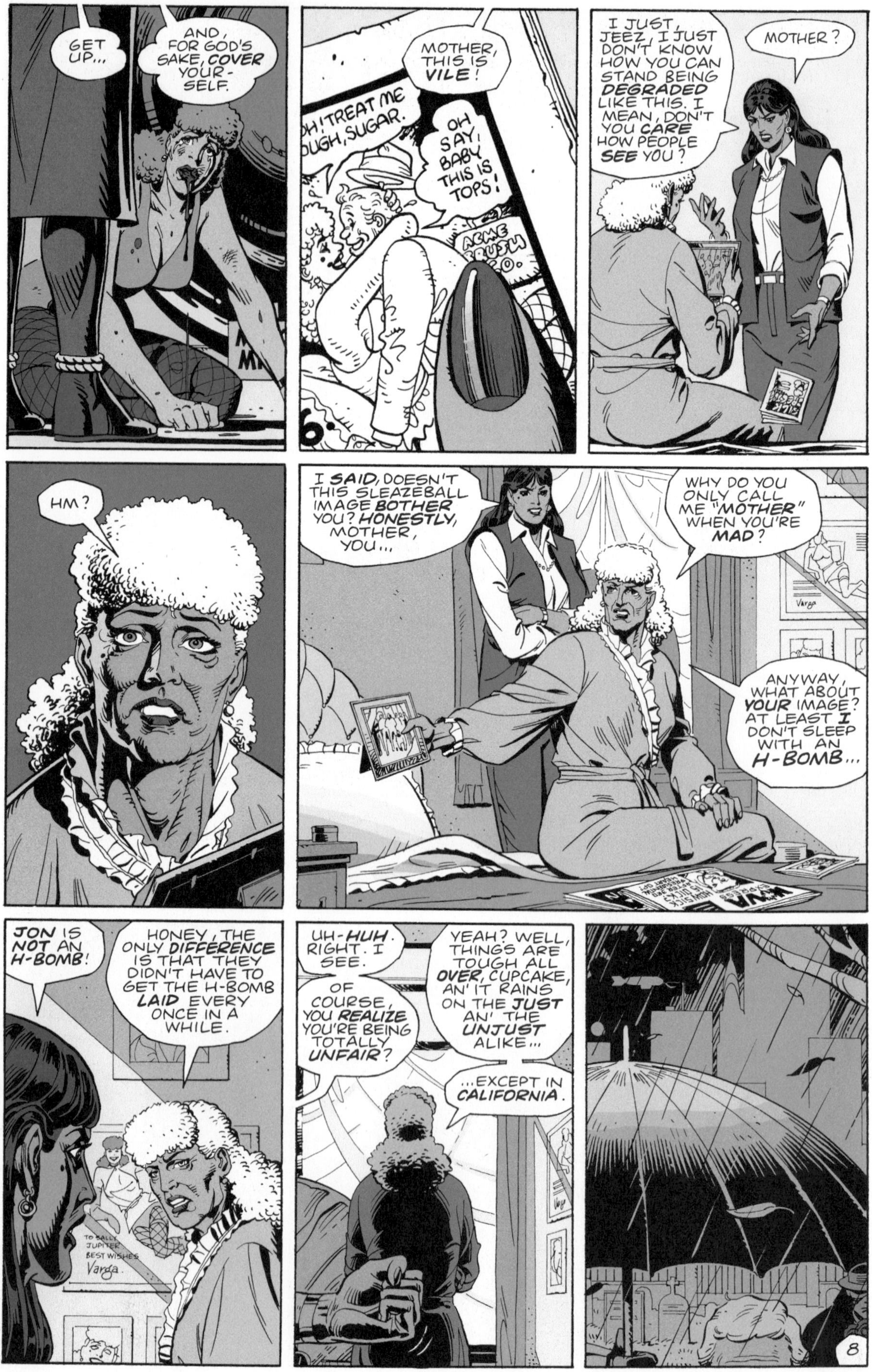

GET UP...
AND, FOR GOD'S SAKE, COVER YOURSELF.
MOTHER, THIS IS VILE!
OH, TREAT ME ROUGH, SUGAR.
OH SAY, BABY, THIS IS TOPS!
ACME BRUSH CO.
I JUST, JEEZ, I JUST DON'T KNOW HOW YOU CAN STAND BEING DEGRADED LIKE THIS. I MEAN, DON'T YOU CARE HOW PEOPLE SEE YOU?
MOTHER?
HM?
I SAID, DOESN'T THIS SLEAZEBALL IMAGE BOTHER YOU? HONESTLY, MOTHER, YOU...
WHY DO YOU ONLY CALL ME "MOTHER" WHEN YOU'RE MAD?
Varga
ANYWAY, WHAT ABOUT YOUR IMAGE? AT LEAST I DON'T SLEEP WITH AN H-BOMB...
JON IS NOT AN H-BOMB!
HONEY, THE ONLY DIFFERENCE IS THAT THEY DIDN'T HAVE TO GET THE H-BOMB LAID EVERY ONCE IN A WHILE.
TO SALLY JUPITER BEST WISHES Varga.
UH-HUH. RIGHT. I SEE.
OF COURSE, YOU REALIZE YOU'RE BEING TOTALLY UNFAIR?
YEAH? WELL, THINGS ARE TOUGH ALL OVER, CUPCAKE, AN' IT RAINS ON THE JUST AN' THE UNJUST ALIKE...
...EXCEPT IN CALIFORNIA.
8

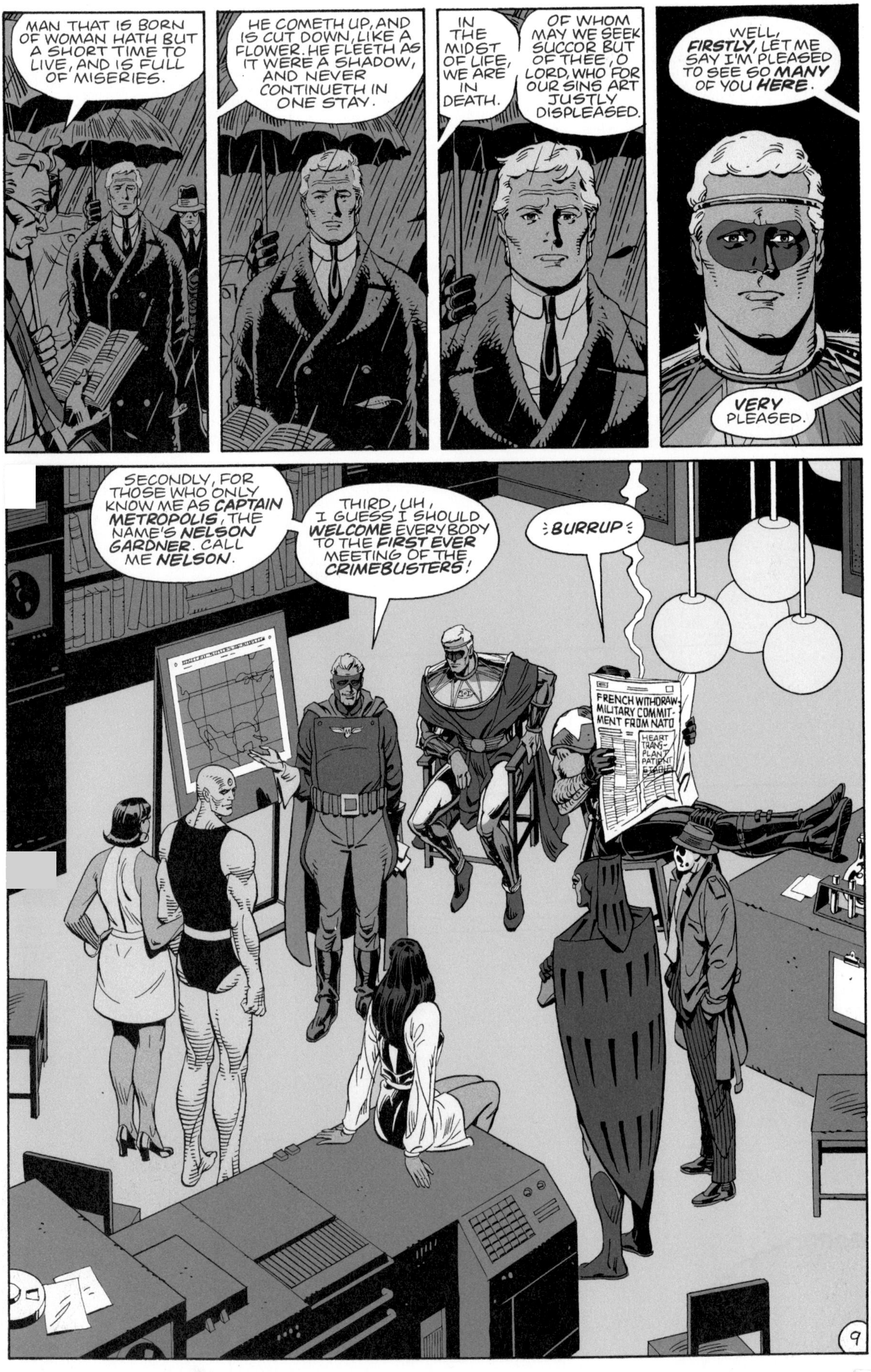
MAN THAT IS BORN OF WOMAN HATH BUT A SHORT TIME TO LIVE, AND IS FULL OF MISERIES.
HE COMETH UP, AND IS CUT DOWN, LIKE A FLOWER. HE FLEETH AS IT WERE A SHADOW, AND NEVER CONTINUETH IN ONE STAY.
IN THE MIDST OF LIFE, WE ARE IN DEATH.
OF WHOM MAY WE SEEK SUCCOR BUT OF THEE, O LORD, WHO FOR OUR SINS ART JUSTLY DISPLEASED.
WELL, FIRSTLY, LET ME SAY I'M PLEASED TO SEE SO MANY OF YOU HERE.
VERY PLEASED.
SECONDLY, FOR THOSE WHO ONLY KNOW ME AS CAPTAIN METROPOLIS, THE NAME'S NELSON GARDNER. CALL ME NELSON.
THIRD, UH, I GUESS I SHOULD WELCOME EVERYBODY TO THE FIRST EVER MEETING OF THE CRIMEBUSTERS!
BURRUP
FRENCH WITHDRAW MILITARY COMMITMENT FROM NATO
HEART TRANSPLANT PATIENT STABLE
9

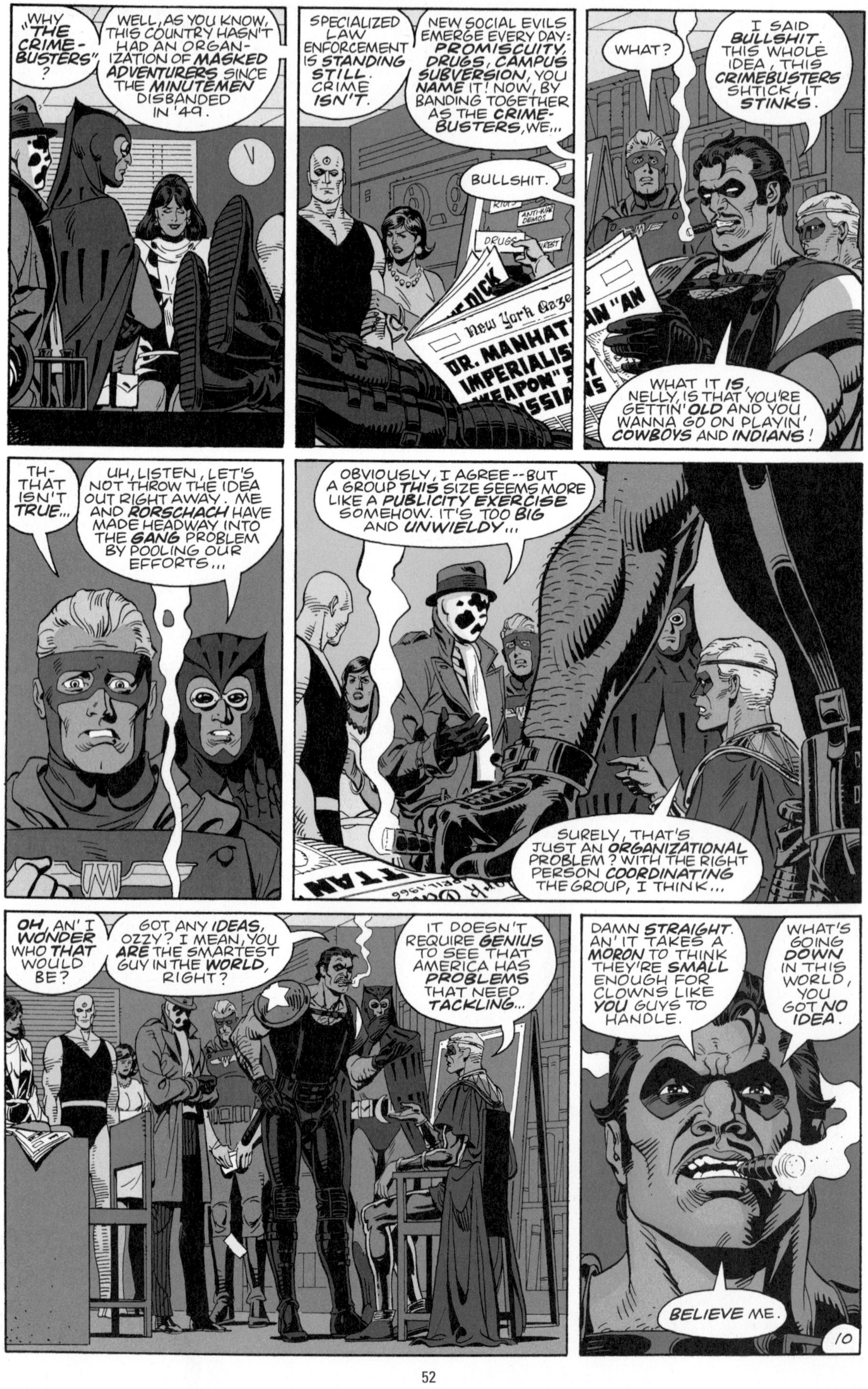
WHY "THE CRIME-BUSTERS"?
WELL, AS YOU KNOW, THIS COUNTRY HASN'T HAD AN ORGAN-IZATION OF MASKED ADVENTURERS SINCE THE MINUTEMEN DISBANDED IN '49.
SPECIALIZED LAW ENFORCEMENT IS STANDING STILL. CRIME ISN'T.
NEW SOCIAL EVILS EMERGE EVERY DAY: PROMISCUITY, DRUGS, CAMPUS SUBVERSION, YOU NAME IT! NOW, BY BANDING TOGETHER AS THE CRIME-BUSTERS, WE...
BULLSHIT.
ANTI-WAR DEMOS
DRUGS
New York Gaze
WHAT?
I SAID BULLSHIT. THIS WHOLE IDEA, THIS CRIMEBUSTERS SHTICK, IT STINKS.
WHAT IT IS, NELLY, IS THAT YOU'RE GETTIN' OLD AND YOU WANNA GO ON PLAYIN' COWBOYS AND INDIANS!
TH-THAT ISN'T TRUE...
UH, LISTEN, LET'S NOT THROW THE IDEA OUT RIGHT AWAY. ME AND RORSCHACH HAVE MADE HEADWAY INTO THE GANG PROBLEM BY POOLING OUR EFFORTS...
OBVIOUSLY, I AGREE--BUT A GROUP THIS SIZE SEEMS MORE LIKE A PUBLICITY EXERCISE SOMEHOW. IT'S TOO BIG AND UNWIELDY...
SURELY, THAT'S JUST AN ORGANIZATIONAL PROBLEM? WITH THE RIGHT PERSON COORDINATING THE GROUP, I THINK...
OH, AN' I WONDER WHO THAT WOULD BE?
GOT ANY IDEAS, OZZY? I MEAN, YOU ARE THE SMARTEST GUY IN THE WORLD, RIGHT?
IT DOESN'T REQUIRE GENIUS TO SEE THAT AMERICA HAS PROBLEMS THAT NEED TACKLING...
DAMN STRAIGHT. AN' IT TAKES A MORON TO THINK THEY'RE SMALL ENOUGH FOR CLOWNS LIKE YOU GUYS TO HANDLE.
WHAT'S GOING DOWN IN THIS WORLD, YOU GOT NO IDEA.
BELIEVE ME.
10

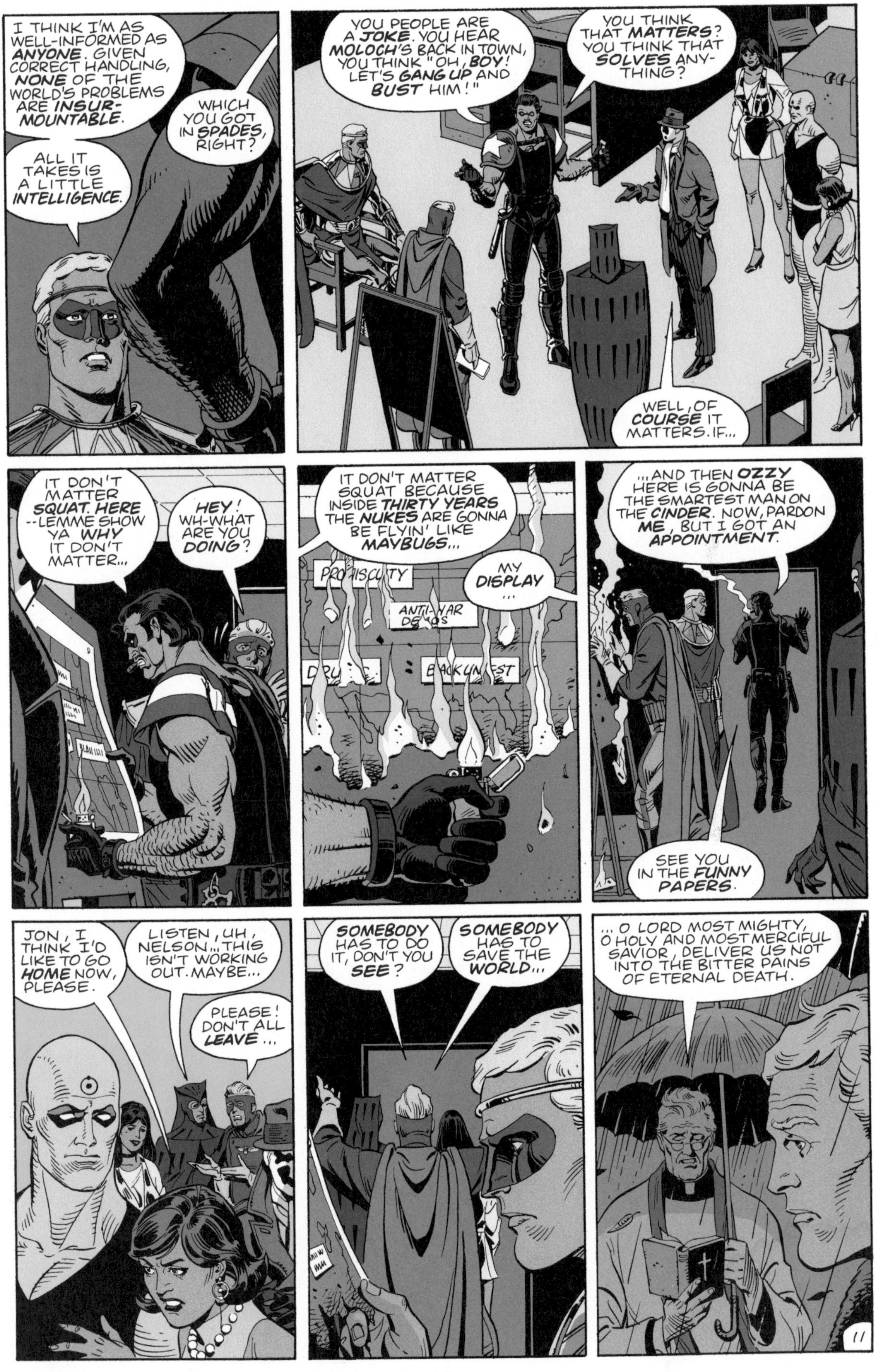

I THINK I'M AS WELL-INFORMED AS ANYONE. GIVEN CORRECT HANDLING, NONE OF THE WORLD'S PROBLEMS ARE INSURMOUNTABLE.
WHICH YOU GOT IN SPADES, RIGHT?
ALL IT TAKES IS A LITTLE INTELLIGENCE.
YOU PEOPLE ARE A JOKE. YOU HEAR MOLOCH'S BACK IN TOWN, YOU THINK "OH, BOY! LET'S GANG UP AND BUST HIM!"
YOU THINK THAT MATTERS? YOU THINK THAT SOLVES ANYTHING?
WELL, OF COURSE IT MATTERS. IF...
IT DON'T MATTER SQUAT. HERE --LEMME SHOW YA WHY IT DON'T MATTER...
HEY! WH-WHAT ARE YOU DOING?
IT DON'T MATTER SQUAT BECAUSE INSIDE THIRTY YEARS THE NUKES ARE GONNA BE FLYIN' LIKE MAYBUGS...
MY DISPLAY ...
...AND THEN OZZY HERE IS GONNA BE THE SMARTEST MAN ON THE CINDER. NOW, PARDON ME, BUT I GOT AN APPOINTMENT.
SEE YOU IN THE FUNNY PAPERS.
JON, I THINK I'D LIKE TO GO HOME NOW, PLEASE.
LISTEN, UH, NELSON... THIS ISN'T WORKING OUT. MAYBE...
PLEASE! DON'T ALL LEAVE...
SOMEBODY HAS TO DO IT, DON'T YOU SEE?
SOMEBODY HAS TO SAVE THE WORLD...
... O LORD MOST MIGHTY, O HOLY AND MOST MERCIFUL SAVIOR, DELIVER US NOT INTO THE BITTER PAINS OF ETERNAL DEATH.
11

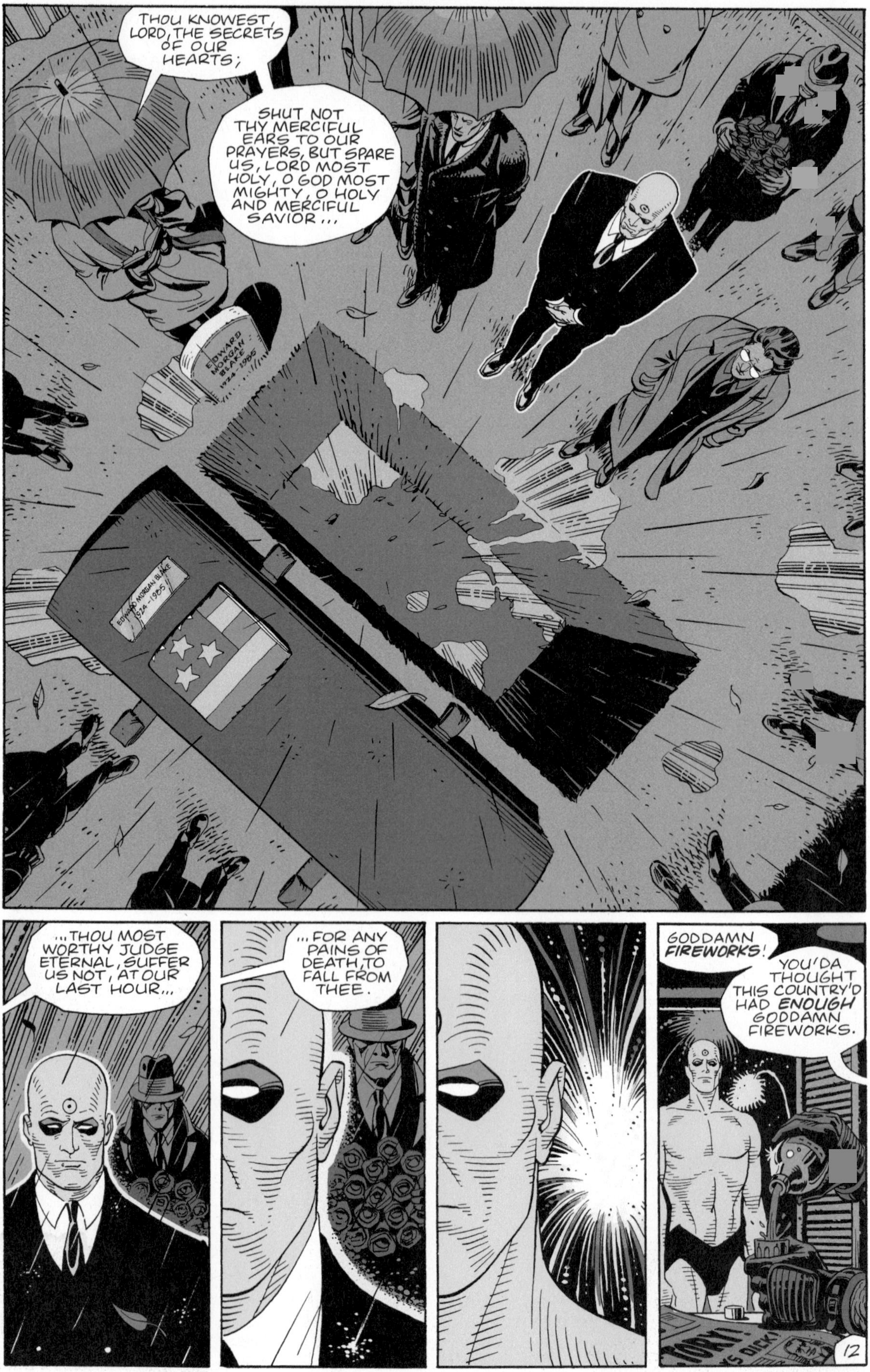
THOU KNOWEST, LORD, THE SECRETS OF OUR HEARTS;
SHUT NOT THY MERCIFUL EARS TO OUR PRAYERS, BUT SPARE US, LORD MOST HOLY, O GOD MOST MIGHTY, O HOLY AND MERCIFUL SAVIOR...
EDWARD MORGAN BLAKE 1924-1985
...THOU MOST WORTHY JUDGE ETERNAL, SUFFER US NOT, AT OUR LAST HOUR...
...FOR ANY PAINS OF DEATH, TO FALL FROM THEE.
GODDAMN **FIREWORKS**!
YOU'DA THOUGHT THIS COUNTRY'D HAD **ENOUGH** GODDAMN FIREWORKS.
12

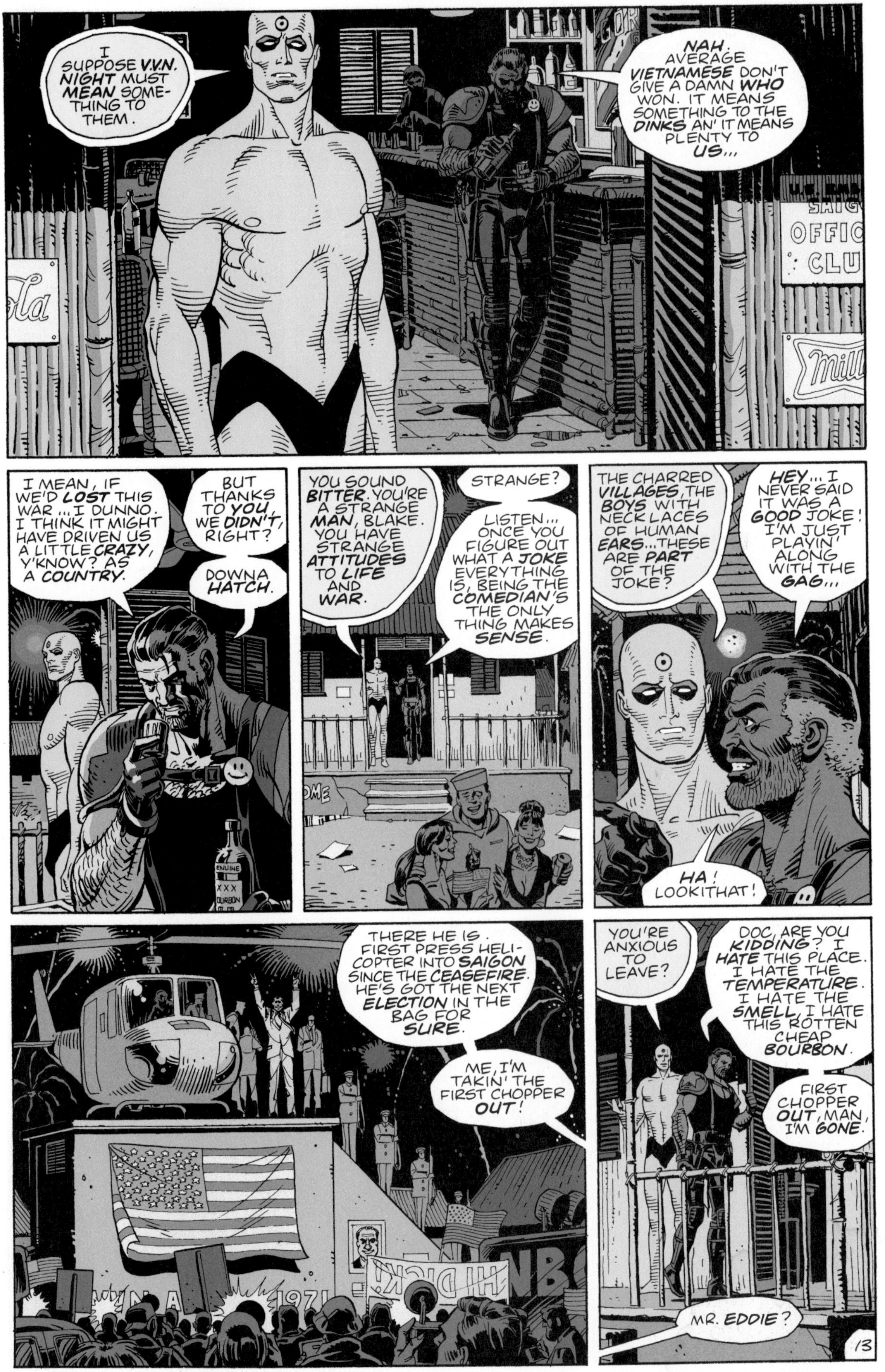
I SUPPOSE V.V.N. NIGHT MUST MEAN SOMETHING TO THEM.
NAH. AVERAGE VIETNAMESE DON'T GIVE A DAMN WHO WON. IT MEANS SOMETHING TO THE DINKS AN' IT MEANS PLENTY TO US...
SAIG
OFFIC
CLU
ola
Mill
I MEAN, IF WE'D LOST THIS WAR... I DUNNO. I THINK IT MIGHT HAVE DRIVEN US A LITTLE CRAZY, Y'KNOW? AS A COUNTRY.
BUT THANKS TO YOU, WE DIDN'T, RIGHT?
DOWNA HATCH.
ENUINE
XXX
OURBON
YOU SOUND BITTER. YOU'RE A STRANGE MAN, BLAKE. YOU HAVE STRANGE ATTITUDES TO LIFE AND WAR.
STRANGE?
LISTEN... ONCE YOU FIGURE OUT WHAT A JOKE EVERYTHING IS, BEING THE COMEDIAN'S THE ONLY THING MAKES SENSE.
OME
THE CHARRED VILLAGES, THE BOYS WITH NECKLACES OF HUMAN EARS...THESE ARE PART OF THE JOKE?
HEY... I NEVER SAID IT WAS A GOOD JOKE! I'M JUST PLAYIN' ALONG WITH THE GAG...
HA! LOOKITHAT!
THERE HE IS. FIRST PRESS HELICOPTER INTO SAIGON SINCE THE CEASEFIRE. HE'S GOT THE NEXT ELECTION IN THE BAG FOR SURE.
ME, I'M TAKIN' THE FIRST CHOPPER OUT!
HI DICK!
NB
1971
YOU'RE ANXIOUS TO LEAVE?
DOC, ARE YOU KIDDING? I HATE THIS PLACE. I HATE THE TEMPERATURE. I HATE THE SMELL, I HATE THIS ROTTEN CHEAP BOURBON.
FIRST CHOPPER OUT, MAN, I'M GONE.
MR. EDDIE?
13

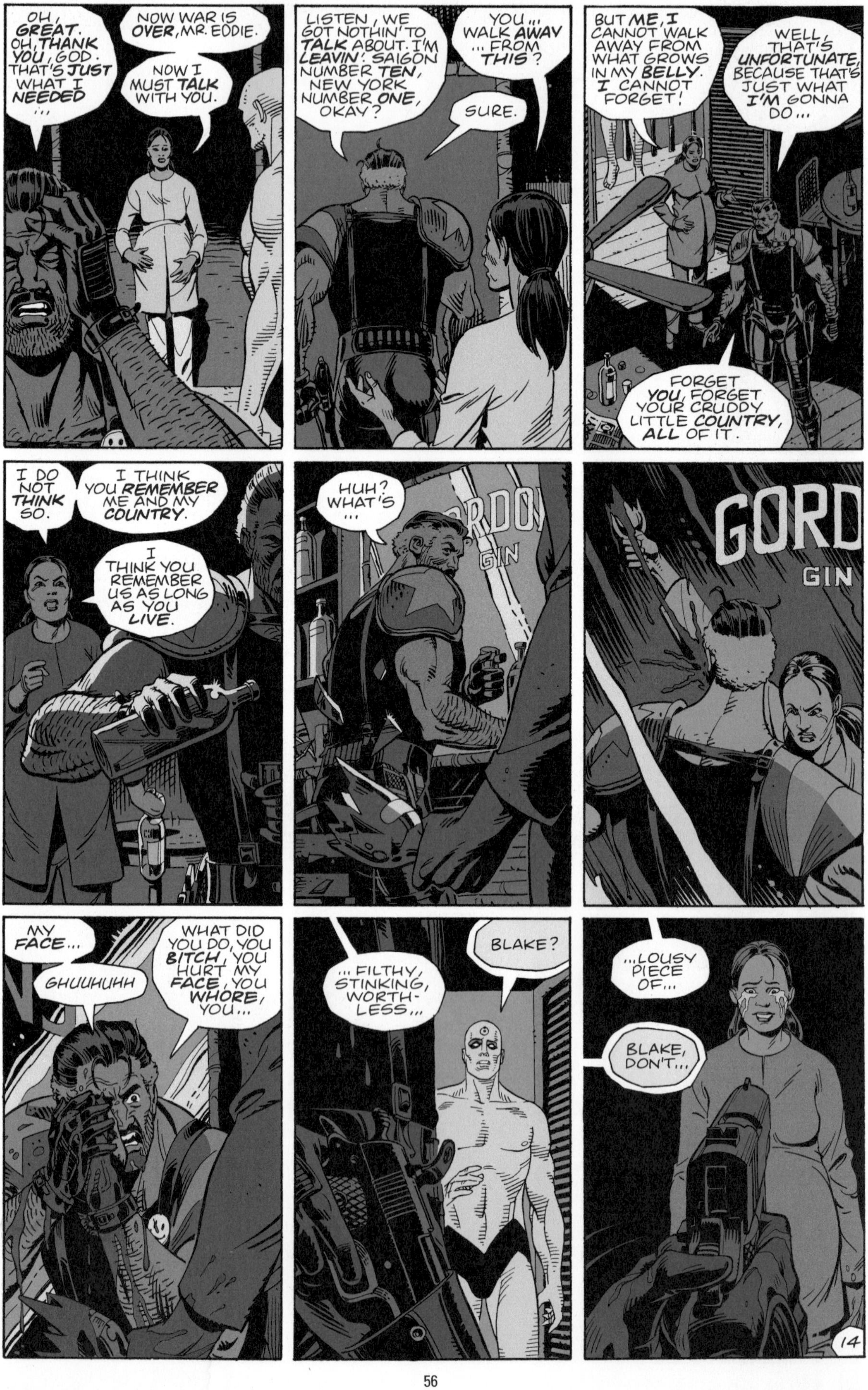
OH, GREAT. OH, THANK YOU, GOD. THAT'S JUST WHAT I NEEDED...
NOW WAR IS OVER, MR. EDDIE.
NOW I MUST TALK WITH YOU.
LISTEN, WE GOT NOTHIN' TO TALK ABOUT. I'M LEAVIN'. SAIGON NUMBER TEN, NEW YORK NUMBER ONE, OKAY?
YOU... WALK AWAY ... FROM THIS?
SURE.
BUT ME, I CANNOT WALK AWAY FROM WHAT GROWS IN MY BELLY. I CANNOT FORGET!
WELL, THAT'S UNFORTUNATE, BECAUSE THAT'S JUST WHAT I'M GONNA DO...
FORGET YOU, FORGET YOUR CRUDDY LITTLE COUNTRY, ALL OF IT.
I DO NOT THINK SO.
I THINK YOU REMEMBER ME AND MY COUNTRY.
I THINK YOU REMEMBER US AS LONG AS YOU LIVE.
HUH? WHAT'S ...
GORDON
GIN
GORD
GIN
MY FACE...
GHUUHUHH
WHAT DID YOU DO, YOU BITCH, YOU HURT MY FACE, YOU WHORE, YOU...
... FILTHY, STINKING, WORTH-LESS...
BLAKE?
...LOUSY PIECE OF...
BLAKE, DON'T...
14

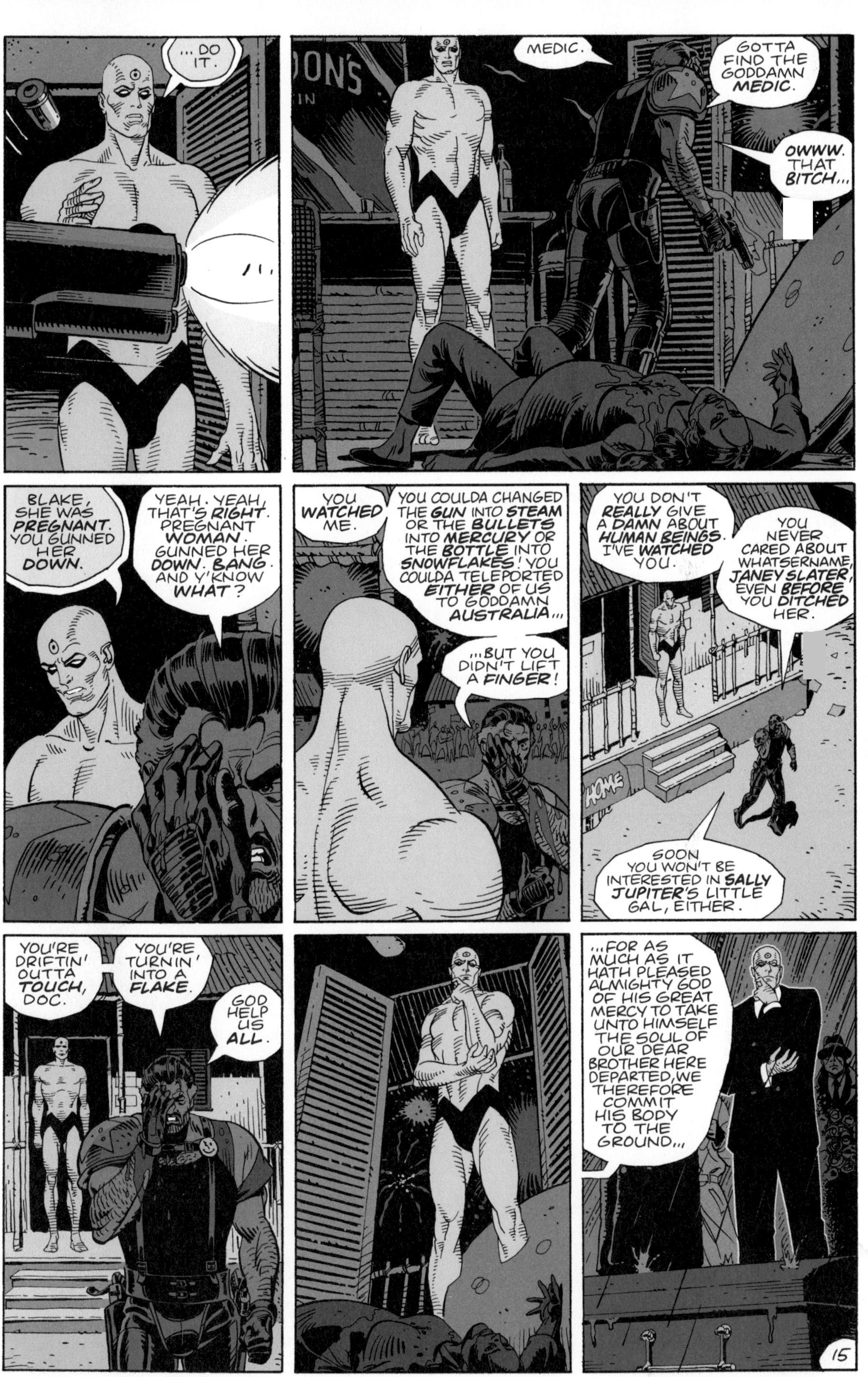
...DO IT.
MEDIC.
GOTTA FIND THE GODDAMN MEDIC.
OWWW. THAT BITCH...
BLAKE, SHE WAS PREGNANT. YOU GUNNED HER DOWN.
YEAH. YEAH, THAT'S RIGHT. PREGNANT WOMAN. GUNNED HER DOWN. BANG. AND Y'KNOW WHAT?
YOU WATCHED ME.
YOU COULDA CHANGED THE GUN INTO STEAM OR THE BULLETS INTO MERCURY OR THE BOTTLE INTO SNOWFLAKES! YOU COULDA TELEPORTED EITHER OF US TO GODDAMN AUSTRALIA...
...BUT YOU DIDN'T LIFT A FINGER!
YOU DON'T REALLY GIVE A DAMN ABOUT HUMAN BEINGS. I'VE WATCHED YOU.
YOU NEVER CARED ABOUT WHATSERNAME, JANEY SLATER, EVEN BEFORE YOU DITCHED HER.
HOME
SOON YOU WON'T BE INTERESTED IN SALLY JUPITER'S LITTLE GAL, EITHER.
YOU'RE DRIFTIN' OUTTA TOUCH, DOC.
YOU'RE TURNIN' INTO A FLAKE.
GOD HELP US ALL.
...FOR AS MUCH AS IT HATH PLEASED ALMIGHTY GOD OF HIS GREAT MERCY TO TAKE UNTO HIMSELF THE SOUL OF OUR DEAR BROTHER HERE DEPARTED, WE THEREFORE COMMIT HIS BODY TO THE GROUND...
15

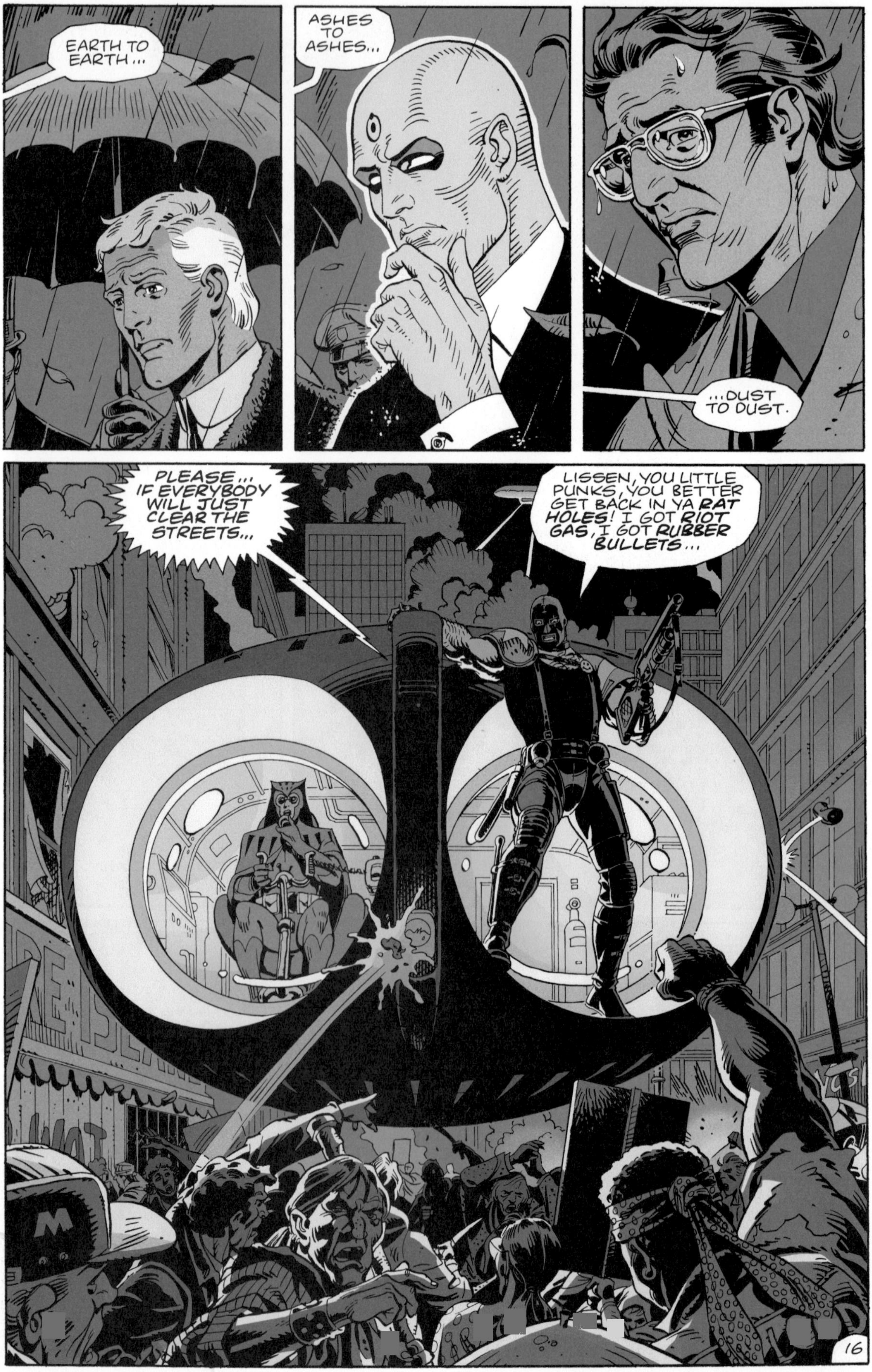
EARTH TO EARTH...
ASHES TO ASHES...
...DUST TO DUST.
PLEASE... IF EVERYBODY WILL JUST CLEAR THE STREETS...
LISSEN, YOU LITTLE PUNKS, YOU BETTER GET BACK IN YA RAT HOLES! I GOT RIOT GAS, I GOT RUBBER BULLETS...
16

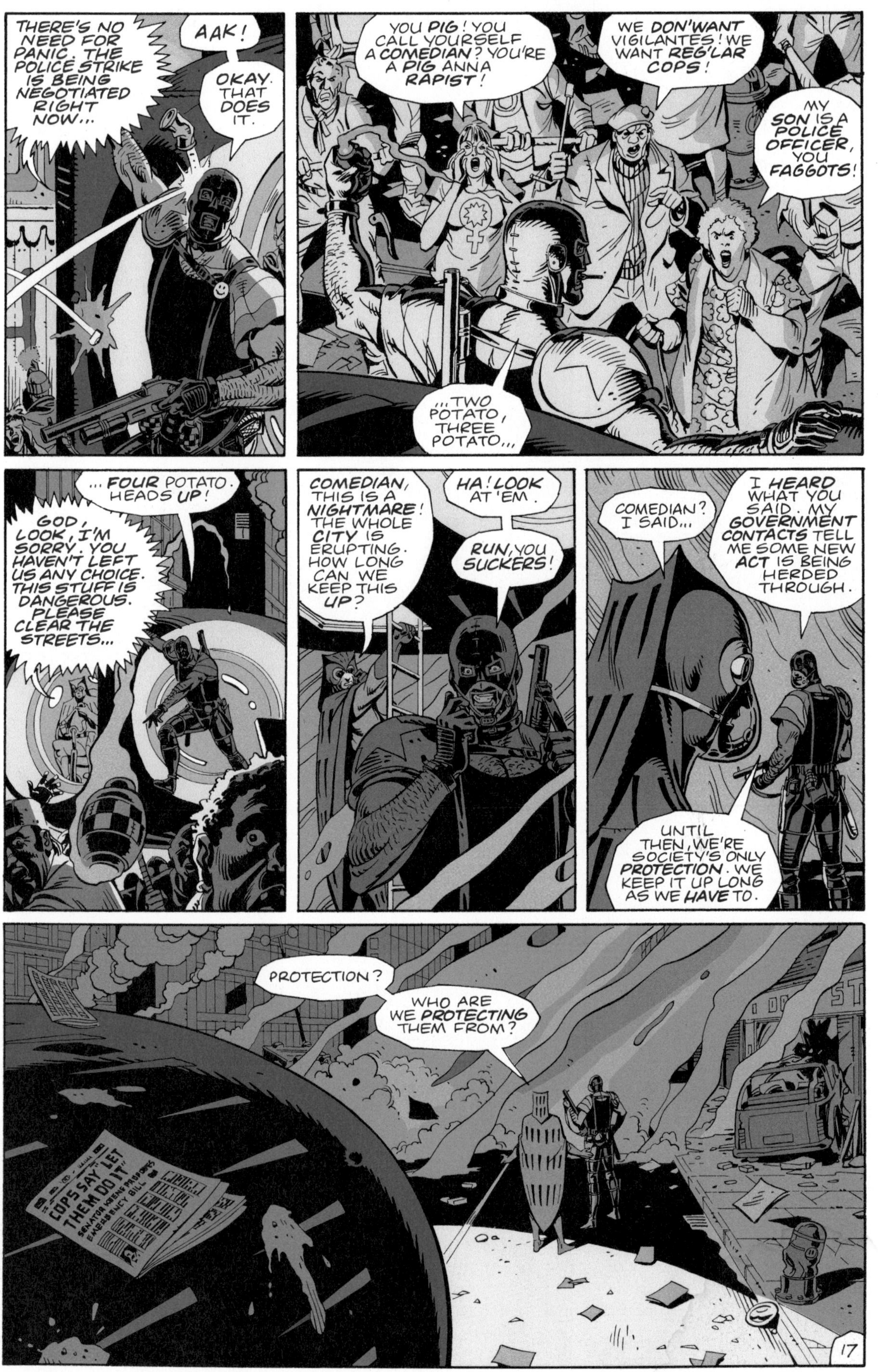

THERE'S NO NEED FOR PANIC. THE POLICE STRIKE IS BEING NEGOTIATED RIGHT NOW...
AAK!
OKAY. THAT DOES IT.
YOU PIG! YOU CALL YOURSELF A COMEDIAN? YOU'RE A PIG ANNA RAPIST!
WE DON'WANT VIGILANTES! WE WANT REG'LAR COPS!
MY SON IS A POLICE OFFICER, YOU FAGGOTS!
...TWO POTATO, THREE POTATO...
...FOUR POTATO. HEADS UP!
GOD, LOOK, I'M SORRY. YOU HAVEN'T LEFT US ANY CHOICE. THIS STUFF IS DANGEROUS. PLEASE CLEAR THE STREETS...
COMEDIAN, THIS IS A NIGHTMARE! THE WHOLE CITY IS ERUPTING. HOW LONG CAN WE KEEP THIS UP?
HA! LOOK AT 'EM.
RUN, YOU SUCKERS!
COMEDIAN? I SAID...
I HEARD WHAT YOU SAID. MY GOVERNMENT CONTACTS TELL ME SOME NEW ACT IS BEING HERDED THROUGH.
UNTIL THEN, WE'RE SOCIETY'S ONLY PROTECTION. WE KEEP IT UP LONG AS WE HAVE TO.
PROTECTION?
WHO ARE WE PROTECTING THEM FROM?
COPS SAY "LET THEM DO IT"
SENATOR KEENE PROPOSES EMERGENCY BILL
17

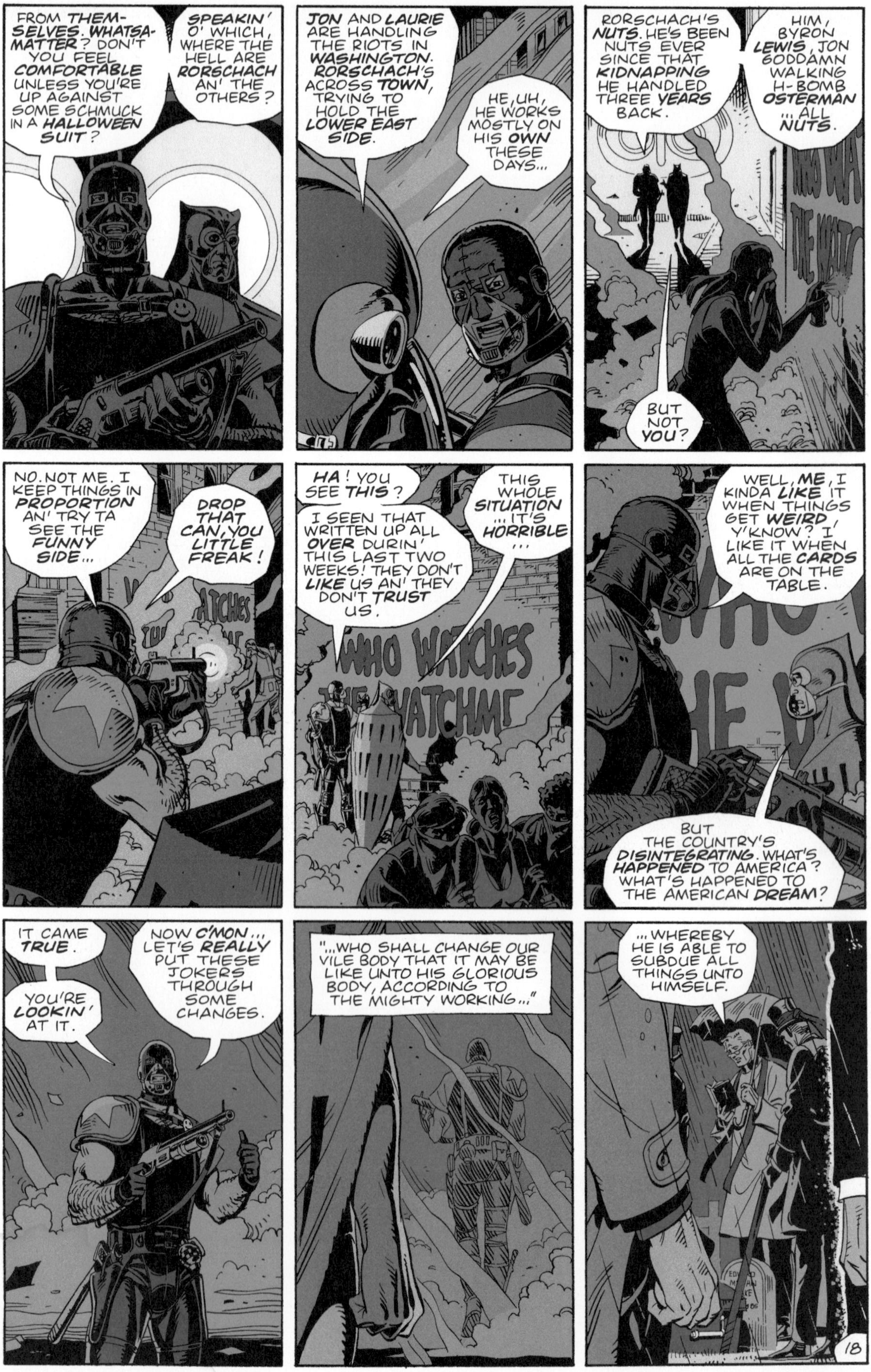
FROM THEM-SELVES. WHATSA-MATTER? DON'T YOU FEEL COMFORTABLE UNLESS YOU'RE UP AGAINST SOME SCHMUCK IN A HALLOWEEN SUIT?
SPEAKIN' O' WHICH, WHERE THE HELL ARE RORSCHACH AN' THE OTHERS?
JON AND LAURIE ARE HANDLING THE RIOTS IN WASHINGTON. RORSCHACH'S ACROSS TOWN, TRYING TO HOLD THE LOWER EAST SIDE.
HE, UH, HE WORKS MOSTLY ON HIS OWN THESE DAYS...
RORSCHACH'S NUTS. HE'S BEEN NUTS EVER SINCE THAT KIDNAPPING HE HANDLED THREE YEARS BACK.
HIM, BYRON LEWIS, JON GODDAMN WALKING H-BOMB OSTERMAN... ALL NUTS.
BUT NOT YOU?
NO. NOT ME. I KEEP THINGS IN PROPORTION AN' TRY TA SEE THE FUNNY SIDE...
DROP THAT CAN, YOU LITTLE FREAK!
HA! YOU SEE THIS?
I SEEN THAT WRITTEN UP ALL OVER DURIN' THIS LAST TWO WEEKS! THEY DON'T LIKE US AN' THEY DON'T TRUST US.
THIS WHOLE SITUATION... IT'S HORRIBLE...
WHO WATCHES THE WATCHMEN
WELL, ME, I KINDA LIKE IT WHEN THINGS GET WEIRD, Y'KNOW? I LIKE IT WHEN ALL THE CARDS ARE ON THE TABLE.
BUT THE COUNTRY'S DISINTEGRATING. WHAT'S HAPPENED TO AMERICA? WHAT'S HAPPENED TO THE AMERICAN DREAM?
IT CAME TRUE.
YOU'RE LOOKIN' AT IT.
NOW C'MON... LET'S REALLY PUT THESE JOKERS THROUGH SOME CHANGES.
"...WHO SHALL CHANGE OUR VILE BODY THAT IT MAY BE LIKE UNTO HIS GLORIOUS BODY, ACCORDING TO THE MIGHTY WORKING..."
...WHEREBY HE IS ABLE TO SUBDUE ALL THINGS UNTO HIMSELF.
18

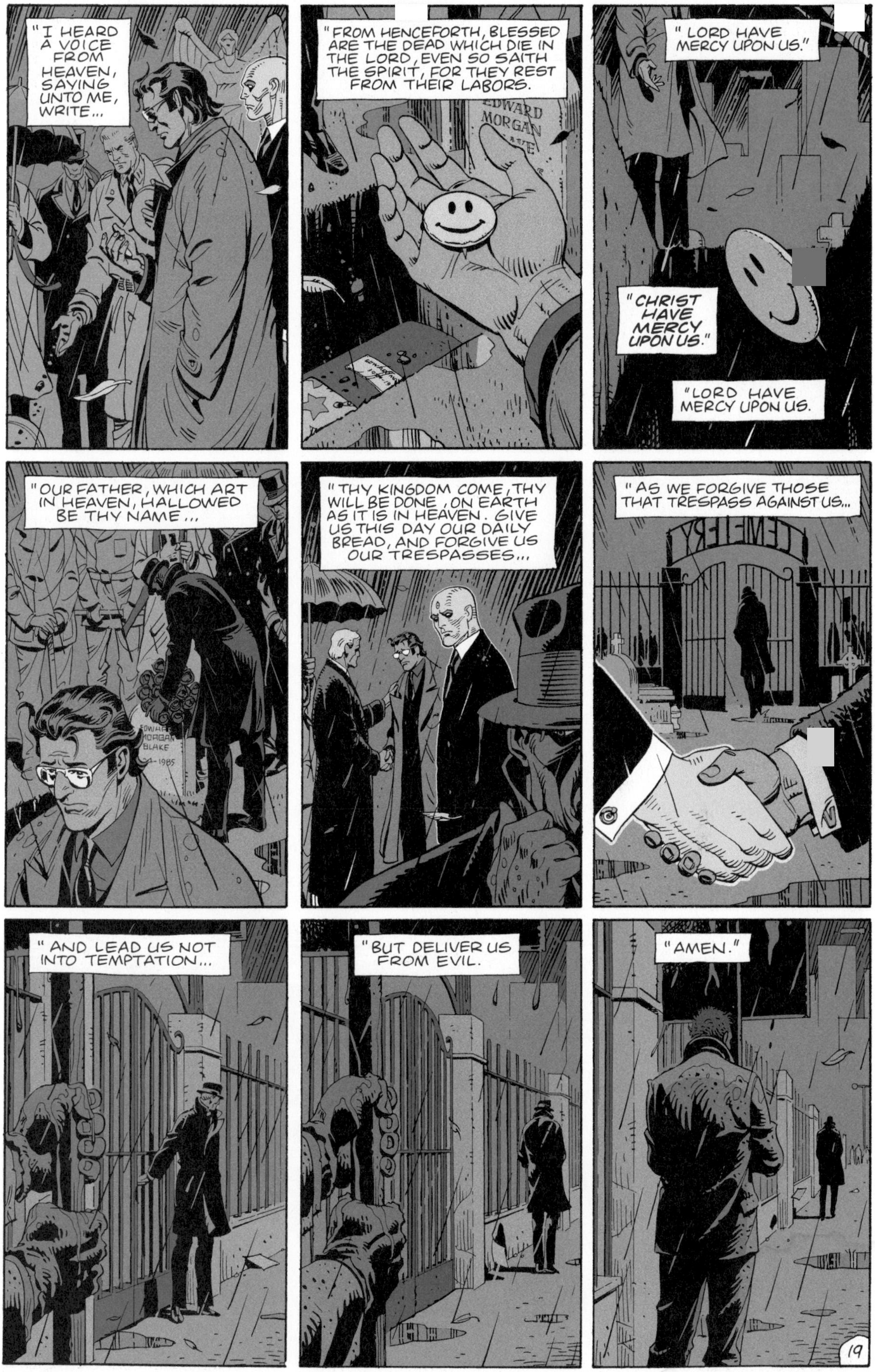
"I HEARD A VOICE FROM HEAVEN, SAYING UNTO ME, WRITE...
"FROM HENCEFORTH, BLESSED ARE THE DEAD WHICH DIE IN THE LORD, EVEN SO SAITH THE SPIRIT, FOR THEY REST FROM THEIR LABORS.
EDWARD MORGAN
"LORD HAVE MERCY UPON US."
"CHRIST HAVE MERCY UPON US."
"LORD HAVE MERCY UPON US.
"OUR FATHER, WHICH ART IN HEAVEN, HALLOWED BE THY NAME...
"THY KINGDOM COME, THY WILL BE DONE, ON EARTH AS IT IS IN HEAVEN. GIVE US THIS DAY OUR DAILY BREAD, AND FORGIVE US OUR TRESPASSES...
"AS WE FORGIVE THOSE THAT TRESPASS AGAINST US...
CEMETERY
"AND LEAD US NOT INTO TEMPTATION...
"BUT DELIVER US FROM EVIL.
"AMEN."
19

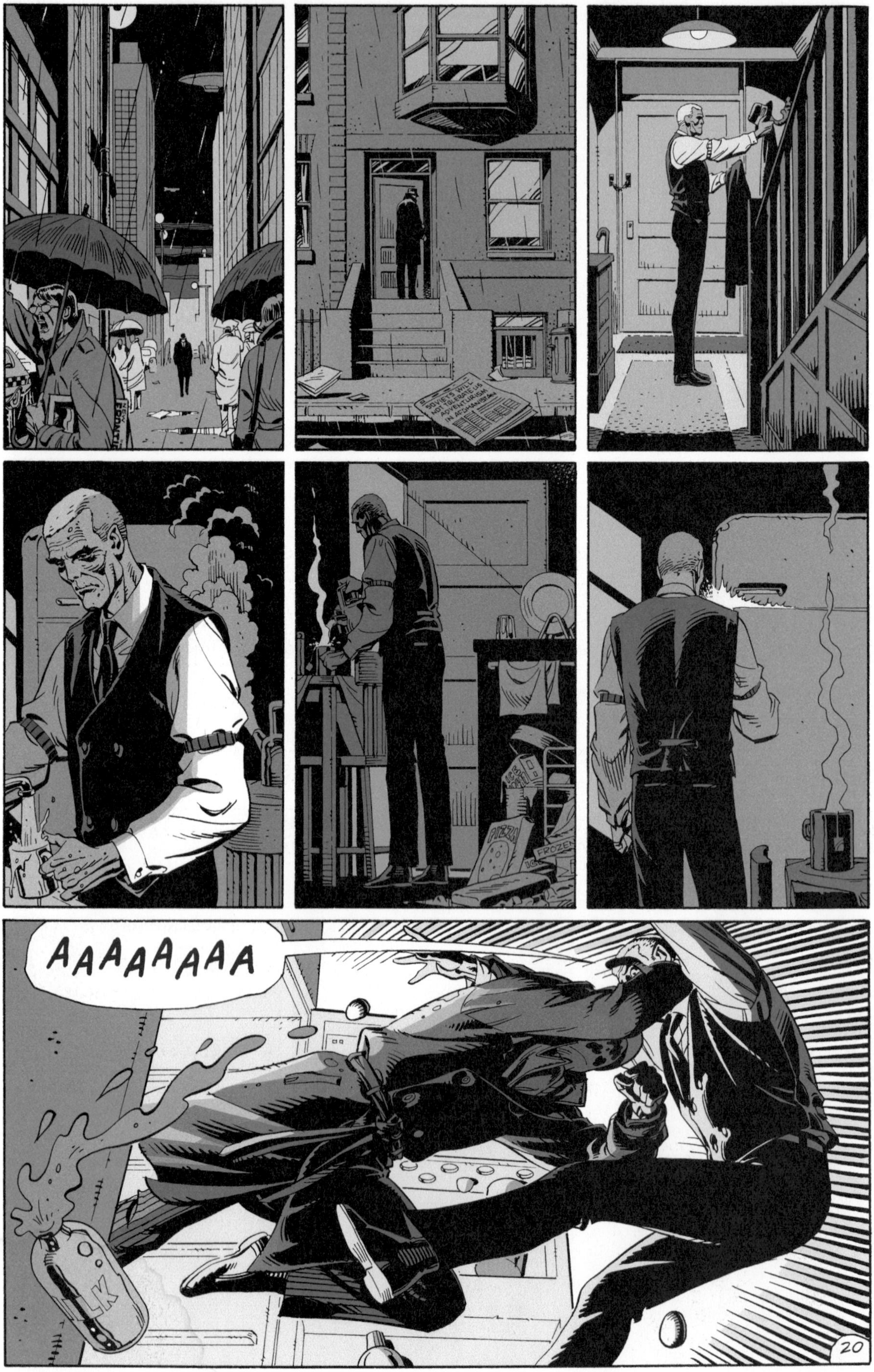
SOVIETS WILL NOT TOLERATE US ADVENTURISM IN AFGHANISTAN
PIZZA
FROZEN
AAAAAAAA
20

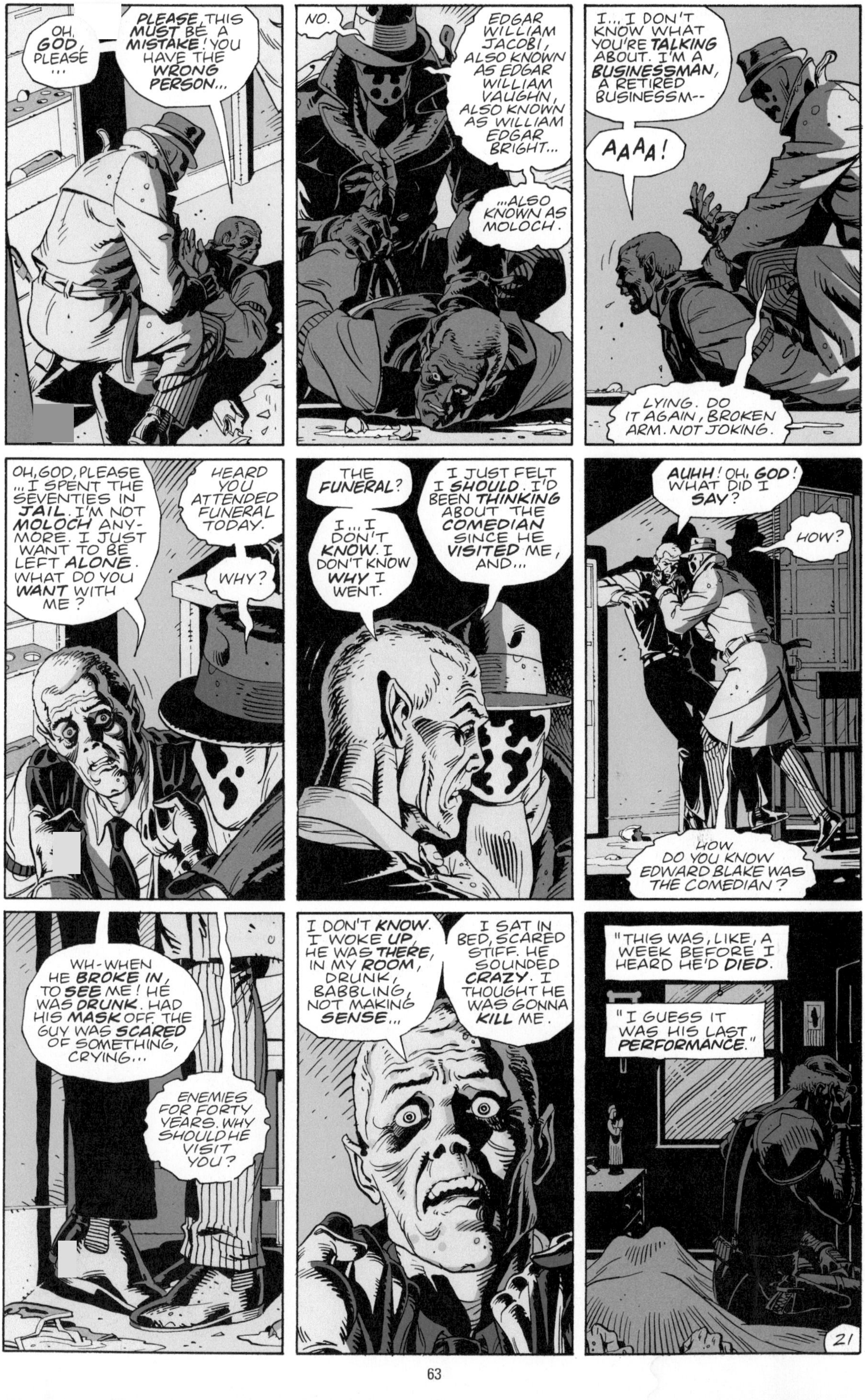

OH, GOD, PLEASE ...
PLEASE, THIS MUST BE A MISTAKE! YOU HAVE THE WRONG PERSON...
NO.
EDGAR WILLIAM JACOBI, ALSO KNOWN AS EDGAR WILLIAM VAUGHN, ALSO KNOWN AS WILLIAM EDGAR BRIGHT...
...ALSO KNOWN AS MOLOCH.
I... I DON'T KNOW WHAT YOU'RE TALKING ABOUT. I'M A BUSINESSMAN, A RETIRED BUSINESSM--
AAAA!
LYING. DO IT AGAIN, BROKEN ARM. NOT JOKING.
OH, GOD, PLEASE ...I SPENT THE SEVENTIES IN JAIL. I'M NOT MOLOCH ANY-MORE. I JUST WANT TO BE LEFT ALONE. WHAT DO YOU WANT WITH ME?
HEARD YOU ATTENDED FUNERAL TODAY.
WHY?
THE FUNERAL?
I... I DON'T KNOW. I DON'T KNOW WHY I WENT.
I JUST FELT I SHOULD. I'D BEEN THINKING ABOUT THE COMEDIAN SINCE HE VISITED ME, AND...
AUHH! OH, GOD! WHAT DID I SAY?
HOW?
HOW DO YOU KNOW EDWARD BLAKE WAS THE COMEDIAN?
WH-WHEN HE BROKE IN, TO SEE ME! HE WAS DRUNK. HAD HIS MASK OFF. THE GUY WAS SCARED OF SOMETHING, CRYING...
ENEMIES FOR FORTY YEARS. WHY SHOULD HE VISIT YOU?
I DON'T KNOW. I WOKE UP, HE WAS THERE, IN MY ROOM, DRUNK, BABBLING, NOT MAKING SENSE...
I SAT IN BED, SCARED STIFF. HE SOUNDED CRAZY. I THOUGHT HE WAS GONNA KILL ME.
"THIS WAS, LIKE, A WEEK BEFORE I HEARD HE'D DIED.
"I GUESS IT WAS HIS LAST PERFORMANCE."
21

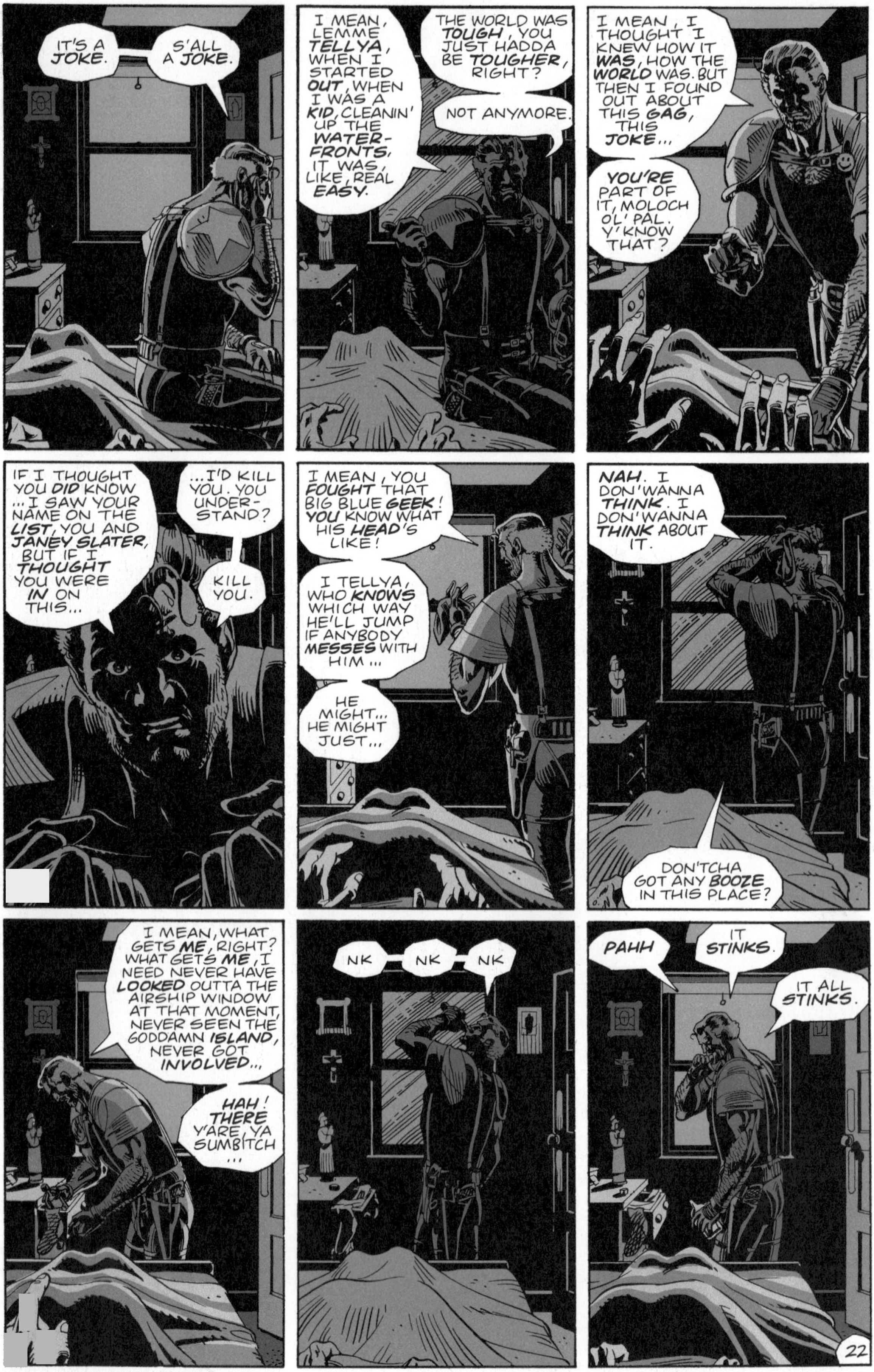
IT'S A JOKE.
S'ALL A JOKE.
I MEAN, LEMME TELLYA, WHEN I STARTED OUT, WHEN I WAS A KID, CLEANIN' UP THE WATER-FRONTS, IT WAS, LIKE, REAL EASY.
THE WORLD WAS TOUGH, YOU JUST HADDA BE TOUGHER, RIGHT?
NOT ANYMORE.
I MEAN, I THOUGHT I KNEW HOW IT WAS, HOW THE WORLD WAS. BUT THEN I FOUND OUT ABOUT THIS GAG, THIS JOKE...
YOU'RE PART OF IT, MOLOCH OL' PAL. Y'KNOW THAT?
IF I THOUGHT YOU DID KNOW ...I SAW YOUR NAME ON THE LIST, YOU AND JANEY SLATER, BUT IF I THOUGHT YOU WERE IN ON THIS...
...I'D KILL YOU. YOU UNDER-STAND?
KILL YOU.
I MEAN, YOU FOUGHT THAT BIG BLUE GEEK! YOU KNOW WHAT HIS HEAD'S LIKE!
I TELLYA, WHO KNOWS WHICH WAY HE'LL JUMP IF ANYBODY MESSES WITH HIM...
HE MIGHT... HE MIGHT JUST...
NAH. I DON'WANNA THINK. I DON'WANNA THINK ABOUT IT.
DON'TCHA GOT ANY BOOZE IN THIS PLACE?
I MEAN, WHAT GETS ME, RIGHT? WHAT GETS ME, I NEED NEVER HAVE LOOKED OUTTA THE AIRSHIP WINDOW AT THAT MOMENT, NEVER SEEN THE GODDAMN ISLAND, NEVER GOT INVOLVED...
HAH! THERE Y'ARE, YA SUMBITCH...
NK
NK
NK
PAHH
IT STINKS.
IT ALL STINKS.
22

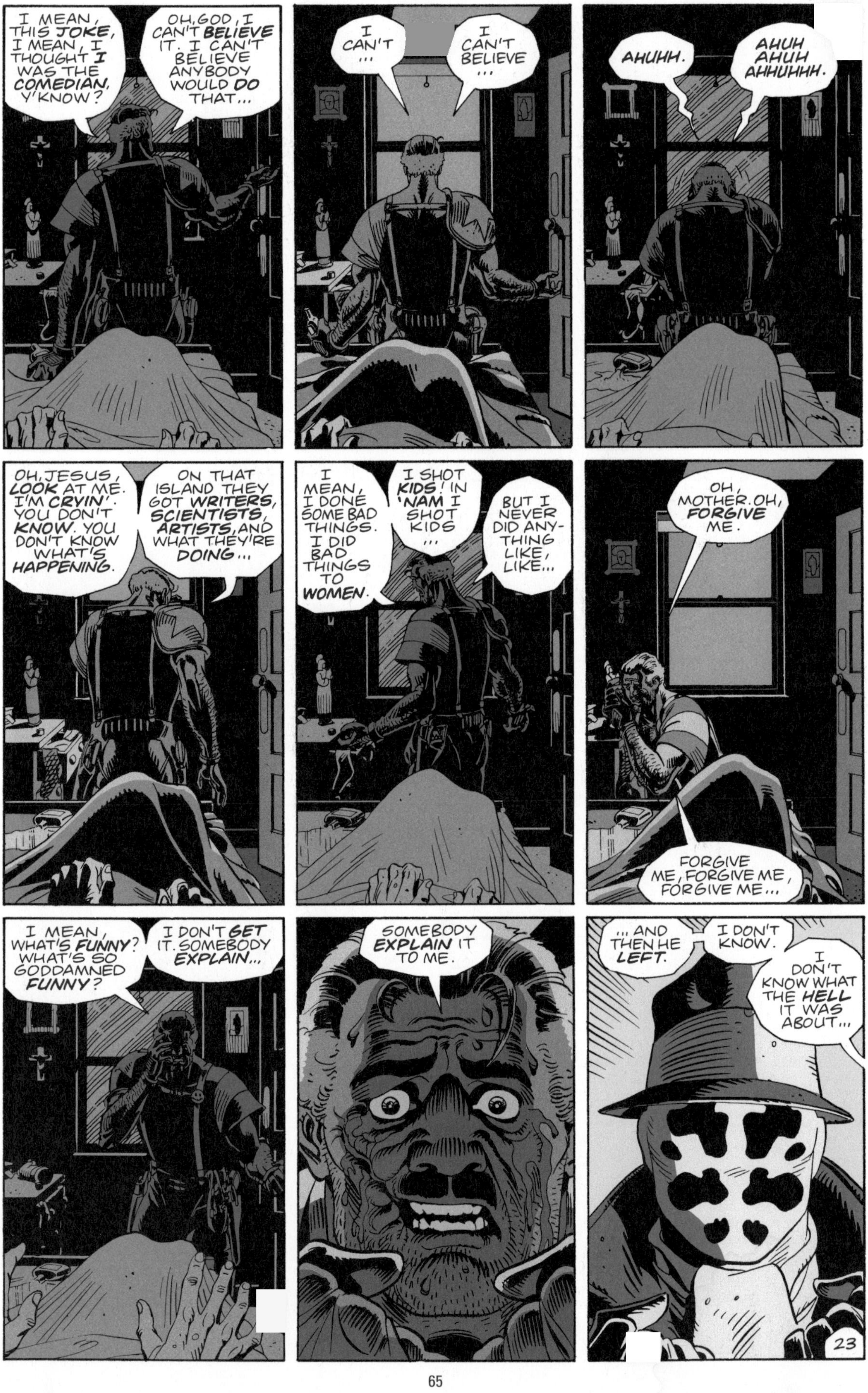

I MEAN, THIS JOKE, I MEAN, I THOUGHT I WAS THE COMEDIAN, Y'KNOW?
OH, GOD, I CAN'T BELIEVE IT. I CAN'T BELIEVE ANYBODY WOULD DO THAT...
I CAN'T ...
I CAN'T BELIEVE ...
AHUHH.
AHUH AHUH AHHUHHH.
OH, JESUS, LOOK AT ME. I'M CRYIN'. YOU DON'T KNOW. YOU DON'T KNOW WHAT'S HAPPENING.
ON THAT ISLAND THEY GOT WRITERS, SCIENTISTS, ARTISTS, AND WHAT THEY'RE DOING...
I MEAN, I DONE SOME BAD THINGS. I DID BAD THINGS TO WOMEN.
I SHOT KIDS! IN 'NAM I SHOT KIDS ...
BUT I NEVER DID ANYTHING LIKE, LIKE...
OH, MOTHER. OH, FORGIVE ME.
FORGIVE ME, FORGIVE ME, FORGIVE ME...
I MEAN, WHAT'S FUNNY? WHAT'S SO GODDAMNED FUNNY?
I DON'T GET IT. SOMEBODY EXPLAIN...
SOMEBODY EXPLAIN IT TO ME.
... AND THEN HE LEFT.
I DON'T KNOW.
I DON'T KNOW WHAT THE HELL IT WAS ABOUT...
23

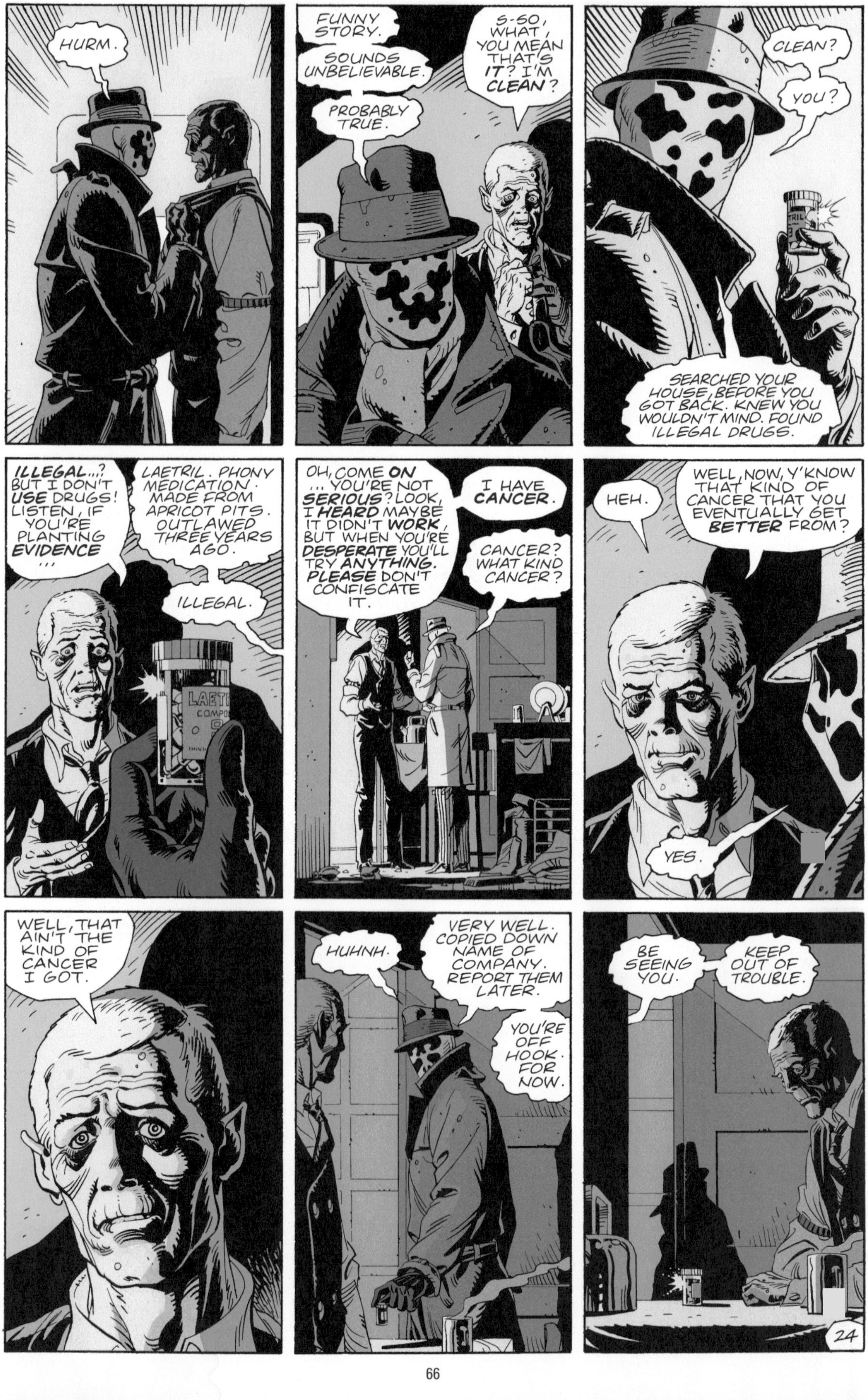
HURM.
FUNNY STORY.
SOUNDS UNBELIEVABLE.
PROBABLY TRUE.
S-SO, WHAT, YOU MEAN THAT'S IT? I'M CLEAN?
CLEAN?
YOU?
SEARCHED YOUR HOUSE, BEFORE YOU GOT BACK. KNEW YOU WOULDN'T MIND. FOUND ILLEGAL DRUGS.
ILLEGAL...? BUT I DON'T USE DRUGS! LISTEN, IF YOU'RE PLANTING EVIDENCE ...
LAETRIL. PHONY MEDICATION. MADE FROM APRICOT PITS. OUTLAWED THREE YEARS AGO.
ILLEGAL.
OH, COME ON ... YOU'RE NOT SERIOUS? LOOK, I HEARD MAYBE IT DIDN'T WORK, BUT WHEN YOU'RE DESPERATE YOU'LL TRY ANYTHING. PLEASE DON'T CONFISCATE IT.
I HAVE CANCER.
CANCER? WHAT KIND CANCER?
HEH.
WELL, NOW, Y'KNOW THAT KIND OF CANCER THAT YOU EVENTUALLY GET BETTER FROM?
YES.
WELL, THAT AIN'T THE KIND OF CANCER I GOT.
HUHNH.
VERY WELL. COPIED DOWN NAME OF COMPANY. REPORT THEM LATER.
YOU'RE OFF HOOK. FOR NOW.
BE SEEING YOU.
KEEP OUT OF TROUBLE.
24

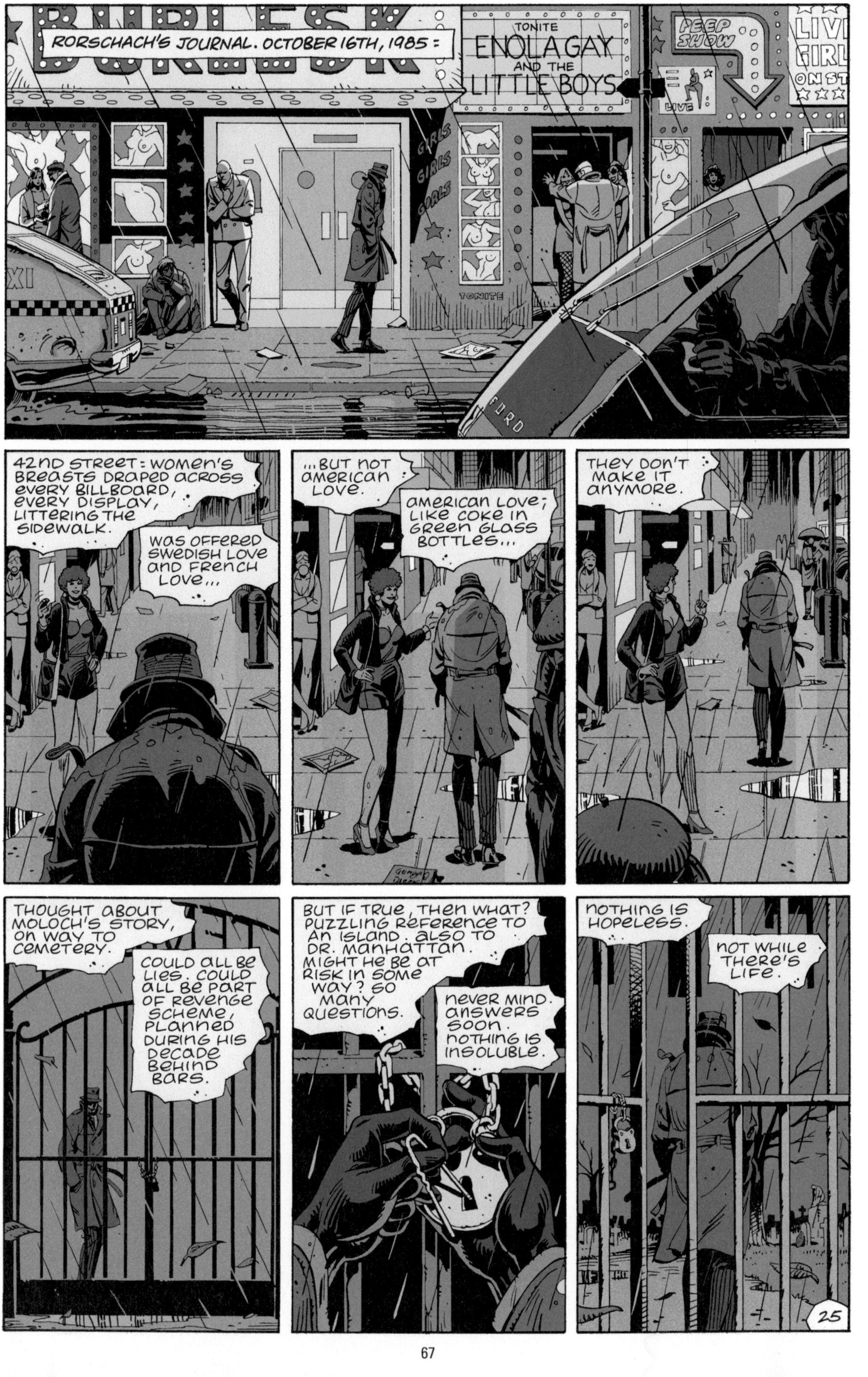
BURLESK
RORSCHACH'S JOURNAL. OCTOBER 16TH, 1985:
TONITE
ENOLA GAY
AND THE
LITTLE BOYS
PEEP SHOW
LIVE GIRLS
GIRLS
GIRLS
GIRLS
TONITE
FORD
42ND STREET: WOMEN'S BREASTS DRAPED ACROSS EVERY BILLBOARD, EVERY DISPLAY, LITTERING THE SIDEWALK.
WAS OFFERED SWEDISH LOVE AND FRENCH LOVE...
...BUT NOT AMERICAN LOVE.
AMERICAN LOVE; LIKE COKE IN GREEN GLASS BOTTLES...
THEY DON'T MAKE IT ANYMORE.
THOUGHT ABOUT MOLOCH'S STORY, ON WAY TO CEMETERY.
COULD ALL BE LIES. COULD ALL BE PART OF REVENGE SCHEME, PLANNED DURING HIS DECADE BEHIND BARS.
BUT IF TRUE, THEN WHAT? PUZZLING REFERENCE TO AN ISLAND. ALSO TO DR. MANHATTAN. MIGHT HE BE AT RISK IN SOME WAY? SO MANY QUESTIONS.
NEVER MIND. ANSWERS SOON. NOTHING IS INSOLUBLE.
NOTHING IS HOPELESS.
NOT WHILE THERE'S LIFE.
25

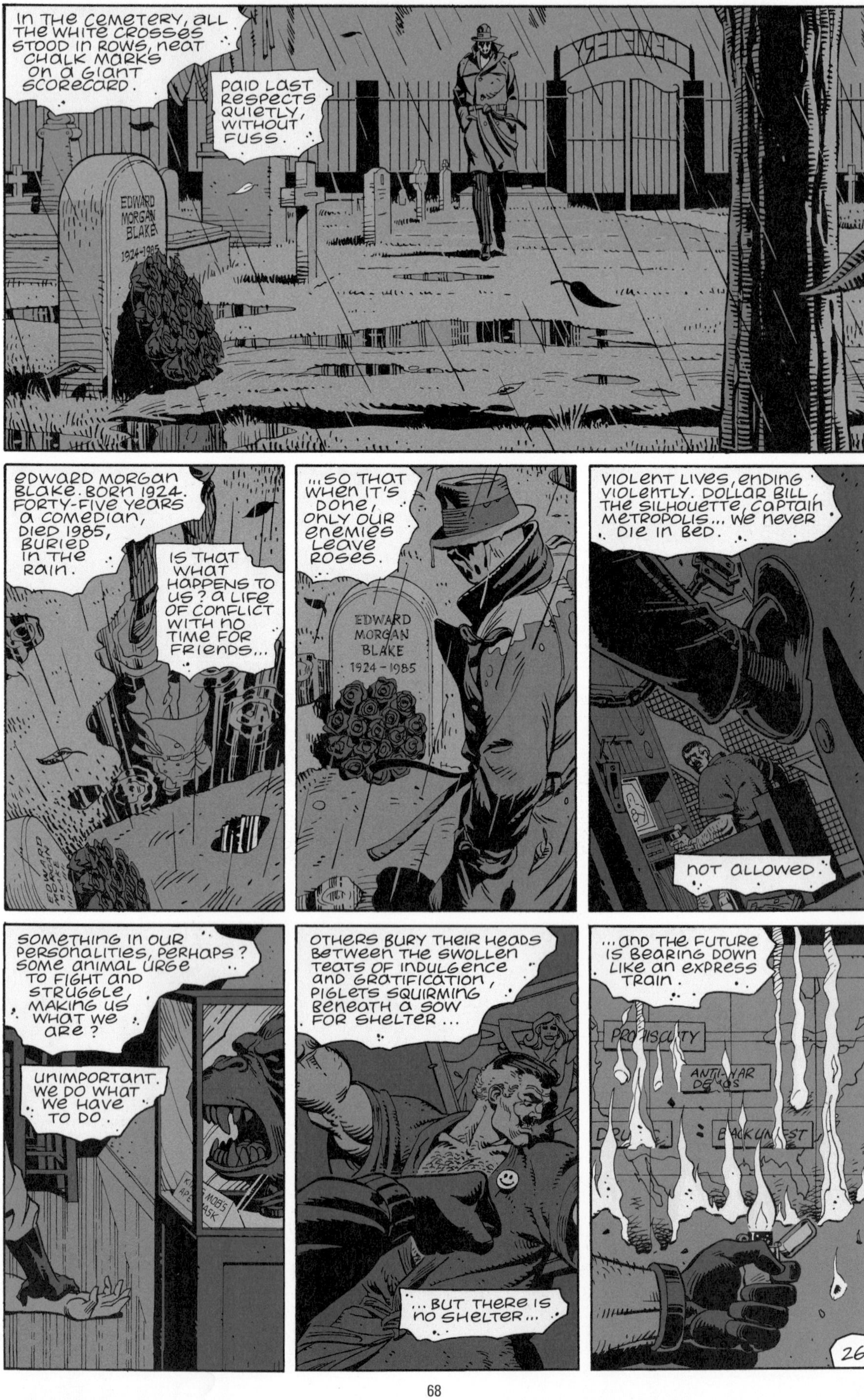
In the cemetery, all the white crosses stood in rows, neat chalk marks on a giant scorecard.
Paid last respects quietly, without fuss.
EDWARD MORGAN BLAKE 1924-1985
Edward Morgan Blake. Born 1924. Forty-five years a comedian, died 1985, buried in the rain.
Is that what happens to us? A life of conflict with no time for friends...
...so that when it's done, only our enemies leave roses.
EDWARD MORGAN BLAKE 1924-1985
Violent lives, ending violently. Dollar Bill, the Silhouette, Captain Metropolis... we never die in bed.
Not allowed.
Something in our personalities, perhaps? Some animal urge to fight and struggle, making us what we are?
Unimportant. We do what we have to do.
Others bury their heads between the swollen teats of indulgence and gratification, piglets squirming beneath a sow for shelter...
...but there is no shelter...
...and the future is bearing down like an express train.
26

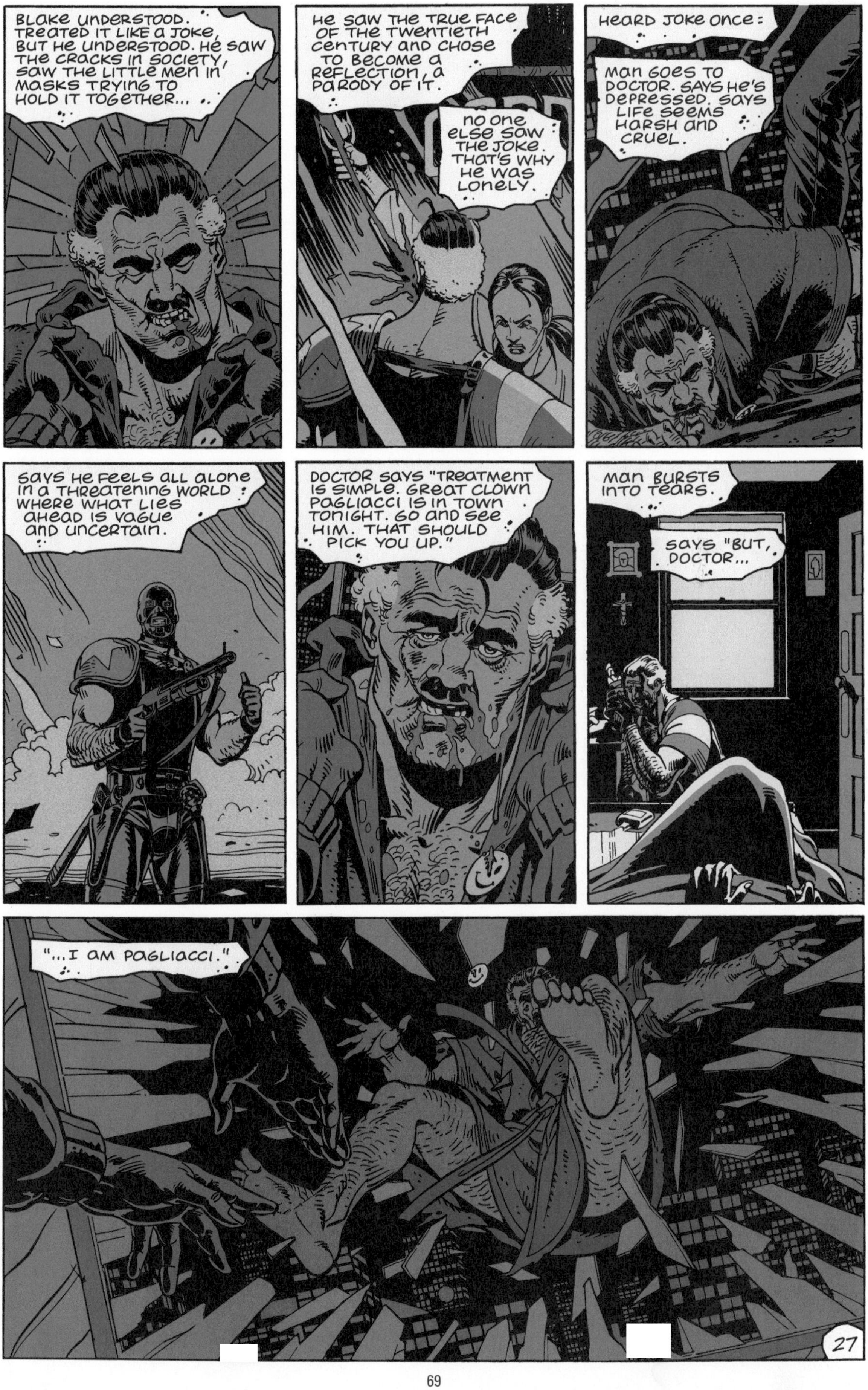
BLAKE UNDERSTOOD. TREATED IT LIKE A JOKE, BUT HE UNDERSTOOD. HE SAW THE CRACKS IN SOCIETY, SAW THE LITTLE MEN IN MASKS TRYING TO HOLD IT TOGETHER...
HE SAW THE TRUE FACE OF THE TWENTIETH CENTURY AND CHOSE TO BECOME A REFLECTION, A PARODY OF IT.
NO ONE ELSE SAW THE JOKE. THAT'S WHY HE WAS LONELY.
HEARD JOKE ONCE:
MAN GOES TO DOCTOR. SAYS HE'S DEPRESSED. SAYS LIFE SEEMS HARSH AND CRUEL.
SAYS HE FEELS ALL ALONE IN A THREATENING WORLD WHERE WHAT LIES AHEAD IS VAGUE AND UNCERTAIN.
DOCTOR SAYS "TREATMENT IS SIMPLE. GREAT CLOWN PAGLIACCI IS IN TOWN TONIGHT. GO AND SEE HIM. THAT SHOULD PICK YOU UP."
MAN BURSTS INTO TEARS.
SAYS "BUT, DOCTOR...
"...I AM PAGLIACCI."
27

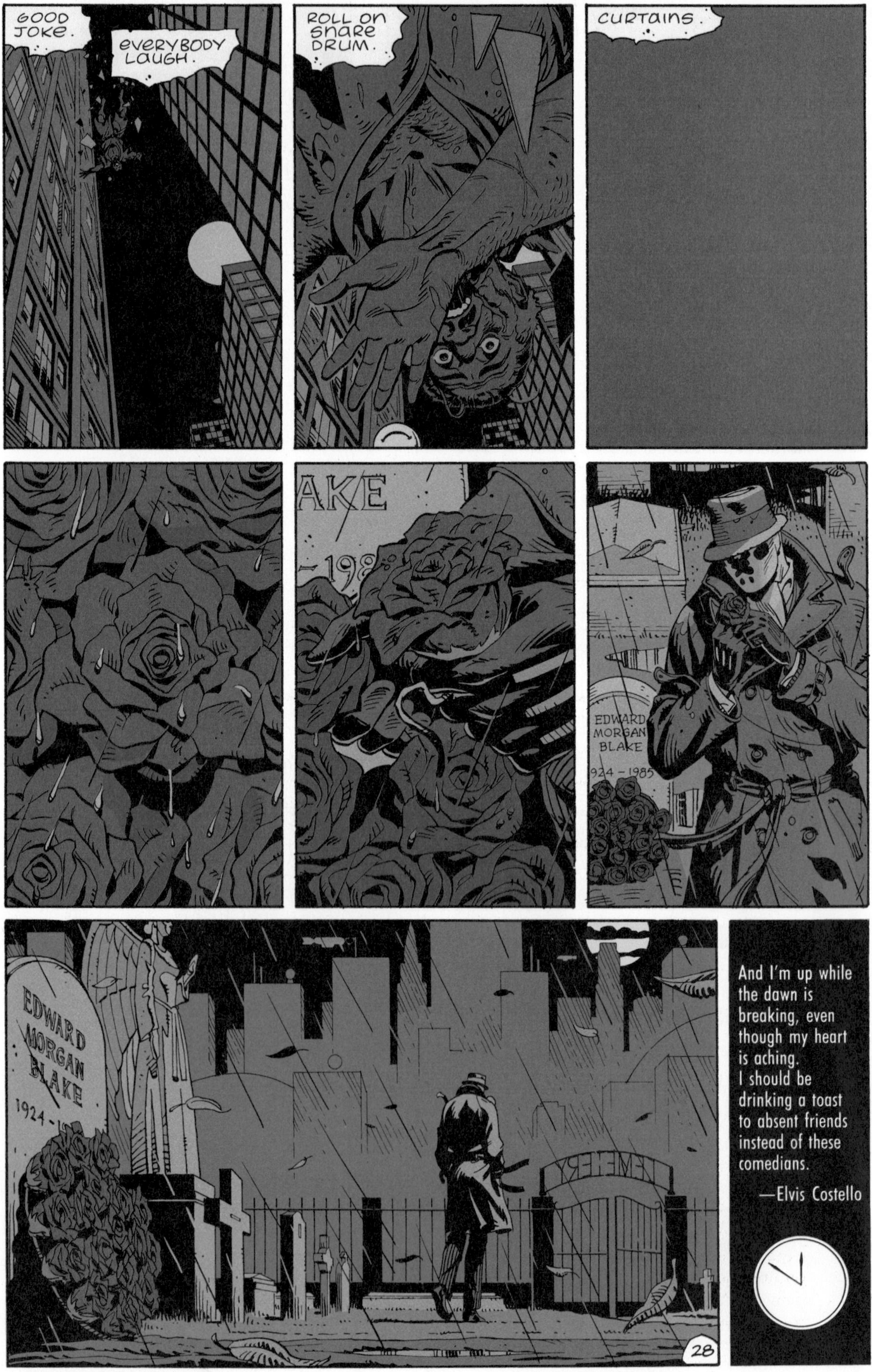
GOOD JOKE.
EVERYBODY LAUGH.
ROLL ON SNARE DRUM.
CURTAINS.
EDWARD MORGAN BLAKE 1924 – 1985
EDWARD MORGAN BLAKE
28
And I'm up while the dawn is breaking, even though my heart is aching. I should be drinking a toast to absent friends instead of these comedians.
—Elvis Costello

UNDER THE HOOD

III.

Presented here are the excerpts from UNDER THE HOOD. In these next chapters Hollis Mason discusses the formation of the Minutemen. Reprinted with permission of the author.

From the moment that I decided somewhere deep inside myself that I wanted to try my hand at being a costumed adventurer, to the moment I first stepped out into the night with a mask on my face and the wind on my bare legs, took about three months. Three months of self-doubt and self-ridicule. Three months of self-conscious training down at the Police Gymnasium. Three months figuring out how the hell I was going to make myself a costume.

The costume was difficult, because I couldn't start designing it until I'd thought of a name. This stumped me for a couple of weeks, because every name I came up with sounded stupid, and what I really wanted was something with the same sense of drama and excitement as "Hooded Justice."

Eventually, a suitable handle was provided inadvertently by one of the other cops that I worked with down at the station house. He'd invited me out for a beer after work two or three times only to be turned down because I wanted to spend as much of my evenings working out in the Police Gymnasiums as possible, after which I'd usually go to bed around nine o'clock and sleep through until five the next morning, when I'd get up and put in a couple of hours workout before donning my badge and uniform in readiness for my day job. After having his offer of beer and relaxation turned down yet again by reason of me wanting to be in bed early, he finally gave up asking and took to calling me "Nite Owl" out of sarcasm until he finally found somebody else to drink with.

"Nite Owl." I liked it. Now all I had to come up with was the costume.

A masked adventurer's costume is one of those things that nobody really thinks about. Should it have a cape, or no cape? Should it be thick and armored to protect you from harm, or flexible and lightweight to allow maneuverability? What sort of mask should it have? Do bright colors make you more of a target than dark ones? All of these were things that I had to consider.

Eventually, I opted for a design that left the arms and legs as free as possible, while protecting my body and head with a tough leather tunic, light chainmail briefs, and a layer of leather-over-chainmail protecting my head. I experimented with a cloak, remembering how the Shadow would use his cloak to misguide enemy bullets, leading them to shoot at parts of the swirling black mass where his body didn't happen to be. In practice, however, I found it too unwieldy. I was always tripping over it or getting it caught in things, and so I abandoned it for an outfit that was as streamlined as I could make it.

With the mail and leather headpiece hiding my hair, I found I only really needed a small domino mask to conceal my identity, but even this presented problems that weren't obvious at first glance. My first mask was attached to my face by the simple expediency of a string, but this nearly got me killed during my first ever outing in full costume, when a drunk with a knife hooked his fingers into the eyeholes of the domino and pulled it down so that I could only see out of one eye. If I'd been less fit and alert or he'd been less drunk my career might well have ended then. As it was I was able to tear off the mask completely and then disarm him, trusting that the alcohol would fog any clear recollection of my face. After that, I dispensed with the string and stuck the mask to my face using spirit gum, such as actors use to attach false beards or mustaches.

I first became Nite Owl during the early months of 1939, and although my first few exploits were largely unspectacular, they aroused a lot of media interest simply because by 1939, dressing up in costume and protecting your neighborhood had become something of a fad, with the whole of America at least briefly interested in its development. A month after I made my debut, a young woman who called herself The Silhouette broke into the headlines by exposing the activities of a crooked publisher trafficking in child pornography, delivering a punitive beating to the entrepreneur and his two chief cameramen in the process. A little after that, the first reports of a man dressed like a moth who could glide through the air started to come in from Connecticut, and a particularly vicious and brutal young man in a gaudy yellow boiler suit started cleaning up the city's waterfronts under the name of The Comedian. Within twelve months of Hooded Justice's dramatic entrance into the public consciousness, there were at least seven other costumed vigilantes operating on or around America's West Coast.

There was Captain Metropolis, who brought a knowledge of military technique and strategy to his attempt at eradicating organized crime in the inner urban areas, and who is still active to this day.

There was The Silk Spectre, now retired and living with her daughter after an unsuccessful early marriage, who in retrospect was probably the first of us ever to realize that there could be commercial benefits in being a masked adventurer. The Silk Spectre used her reputation as a crimefighter primarily to make the front pages and receive exposure for her lucrative modeling career, but I think all of us who knew her loved her a little bit and we certainly didn't begrudge her a living. I think we were all too unsure of our own motives to cast aspersions upon anybody else.

There was Dollar Bill, originally a star college athlete from Kansas who was actually employed as an in-house super-hero by one of the major national banks, when they realized that the masked man fad made being able to brag about having a hero of your own to protect your customer's money a very interesting publicity prospect. Dollar Bill was one of the nicest and most straightforward men I have ever met, and the fact that he died so tragically young is something that still upsets me whenever I think about it. While attempting to stop a raid upon one of his employer's banks, his cloak became entangled in the bank's revolving door and he was shot dead at point-blank range before he could free it. Designers employed by the bank had designed his costume for maximum publicity appeal. If he'd designed it himself he might have left out that damned stupid cloak and still be alive today.

There was Mothman and The Silhouette and The Comedian and there was me, all of us choosing to dress up in gaudy opera costumes and express the notion of good and evil in simple, childish terms, while over in Europe they were turning human beings into soap and lampshades. We were sometimes respected, sometimes analyzed, and most often laughed at, and in spite of all the musings above, I don't think that those of us still surviving today are any closer to understanding just why we *really* did it all. Some of us did it because we were hired to and some of us did it to gain publicity. Some of us did it out of a sense of childish excitement and some of us, I think, did it for a kind of excitement that was altogether more adult if perhaps less healthy. They've called us fascists and they've called us perverts and while there's an element of truth in both those accusations, neither of them are big enough to take in the whole picture.

Yes, some of us were politically extreme. Before Pearl Harbor, I heard Hooded Justice openly expressing approval for the activities of Hitler's Third Reich, and Captain Metropolis has gone on record as making statements about black and Hispanic Americans that have been viewed as both racially prejudiced and inflammatory, charges that it is difficult to argue or deny.

Yes, I daresay some of us did have our sexual hang-ups. Everybody knows what eventually became of the Silhouette and although it would be tasteless to rehash the events surrounding her death in this current volume, it provides proof for those who need it that for some people, dressing up in a costume did have its more libidinous elements.

Yes, some of us were unstable and neurotic. Only a week ago as of this writing, I received word that the man behind the mask and wings of Mothman, whose true identity I am not at liberty to divulge, has been committed to a mental institution after a long bout of alcoholism and a complete mental breakdown.

Yes, we were crazy, we were kinky, we were Nazis, all those things that people say. We were also doing something because we believed in it. We were attempting, through our personal efforts, to make our country a safer and better place to live in. Individually, working on our separate patches of turf, we did too much good in our respective communities to be written off as mere aberration, whether social or sexual or psychological.

It was only when we got together that the problems really started. I sometimes think without the Minutemen we might all have given up and called it quits pretty soon. The costumed adventurer might have become quietly and simply extinct.

And the world might not be in the mess it's in today.

IV.

There's no mystery behind how the Minutemen first got together. Captain Metropolis had written to Sally Jupiter care of her agent, suggesting that they might meet with a view to forming a group of masked adventurers who could pool their resources and experience to combat crime. The Captain has always had a strategic approach to crimefighting, so I can see why the idea would appeal to him, although back then I was surprised that he'd made an effort to get in touch with Sally. He was so polite and reserved that Sally's drinking, swearing and mode of dress were guaranteed to shock him speechless. Later, I realized that Sally was simply the only costumed vigilante forethoughtful enough to have an agent whose address was in the phone book.

Sally's agent (and, much later, her husband) was an extremely shrewd individual named Laurence Schexnayder. He realized that without the occasional gimmick to revitalize flagging public interest, the fad for long underwear heroes would eventually fade, reducing his girl Sally's chances of media exposure as The Silk Spectre to zero. Thus it was Schexnayder, in mid-1939, who suggested placing a large ad in the Gazette asking other mystery men to come forward.

One by one we came, over the next few weeks. We were introduced to Sally, to Captain Metropolis, to each other and to Laurence Schexnayder. He was very organized and professional, and although only in his mid-thirties he seemed very mature and respectable to us back then. Maybe that was just because he'd be the only person in the room not wearing their boxer shorts over their pants. By the fall of '39 he'd arranged all the publicity and the Minutemen were finally born.

The *real* mystery is how the hell we managed to *stay* together.

Dressing up in a costume takes a very extreme personality, and the chances of eight such personalities getting along together were about seventy-eleven million to one against. This isn't to say that some of us didn't get along, of course. Sally attached herself pretty swiftly to Hooded Justice, who was one of the biggest men I've ever seen. I never found out his real name, but I'd be willing to bet that those early news reports weren't far off in comparing him to a wrestler. Strangely enough, even though Sally would always be hanging onto his arm, he never seemed very interested in *her*. I don't think I ever saw him kiss her, although maybe that was just because of his mask. Anyway, they started going out together, sort of, after the first Minutemen Christmas Party in 1939, which is the last time I can remember us all having a real good time together. After that, things went bad. We had worms in the apple, eating it from inside.

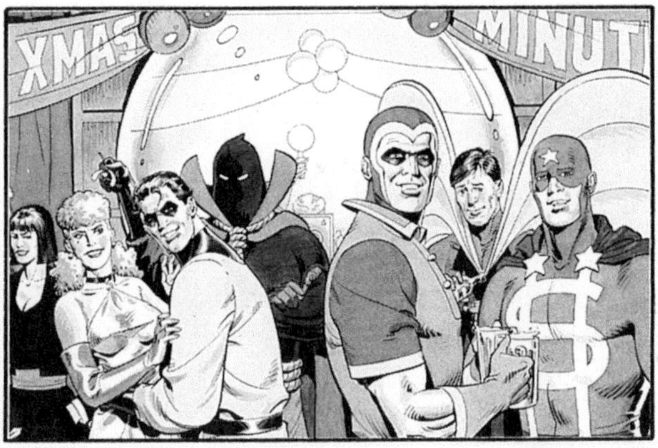
XMAS
MINUT

The first Minutemen Christmas party, 1939 (from left to right) The Silhouette, Silk Spectre, Comedian, Hooded Justice, Captain Metropolis (in mirror), Nite Owl, Mothman, Dollar Bill

The worst of these was the Comedian. I'm aware that he's still active today and even respected in some quarters, but I know what I know, and that man is a disgrace to our profession. In 1940 he attempted to sexually assault Sally Jupiter in the Minutemen trophy room after a meeting. He left the group shortly thereafter by mutual consent and with a minimum of publicity. Schexnayder had persuaded Sally not to press charges against the Comedian for the good of the group's image, and she complied. The Comedian went his way unscathed...even though he was badly wounded in an unconnected stabbing incident about a year later. This is what made him decide to change his flimsy yellow costume for the leather armor he wears at present. He went on to make a name for himself as a war hero in the Pacific, but all I can think of is the bruises along Sally Jupiter's ribcage and hope to God that America can find itself a better class of hero than *that*.

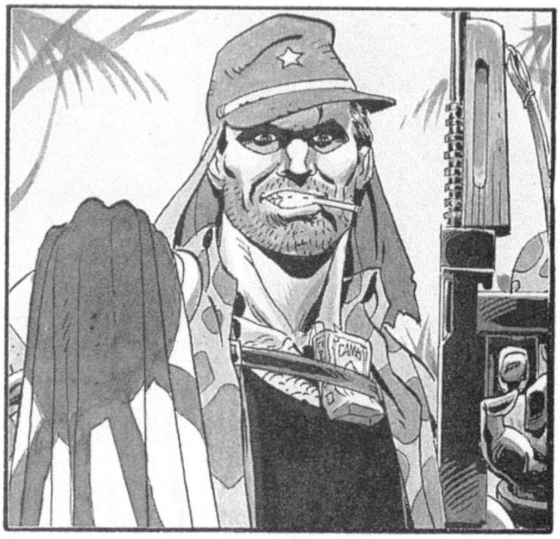

Newsreel footage of the Comedian in the South Pacific, 1942

After that, things deteriorated. In 1946, the papers revealed that the Silhouette was living with another woman in a lesbian relationship. Schexnayder persuaded us to expel her from the group, and six weeks later she was murdered, along with her lover, by one of her former enemies. Dollar Bill was shot dead, and in 1947 the group was dealt its most serious blow when Sally quit crimefighting to marry her agent. We always thought she might come back, but in 1949 she had a daughter, so that clinched that. Eventually, those of us who were left didn't even fight crime anymore. It wasn't interesting. The villains we'd fought with were either in prison or had moved on to less glamorous activities. Moloch, for example, who had started out aged seventeen as a stage magician, evolving into an ingenious and flamboyant criminal mastermind through underworld contacts made in his world of nightclubs, had moved into impersonal crime like drugs, financial fraud and vice clubs by the late '40s. Eventually, there was just me, Mothman, Hooded Justice and Captain Metropolis sitting around in a meeting hall that smelled like a locker room now that there weren't any women in the group. There was nobody interesting left to fight, nothing notable to talk about. In 1949, we called it a day. By then, however, we'd been around long enough to somehow inspire younger people, God help them, to follow in our footsteps.

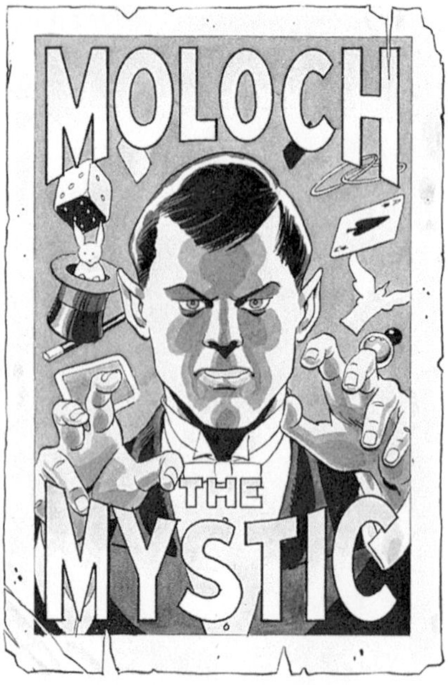
MOLOCH
THE
MYSTIC

Early publicity poster of Moloch, 1937

The Minutemen were finished, but it didn't matter. The damage had already been done.

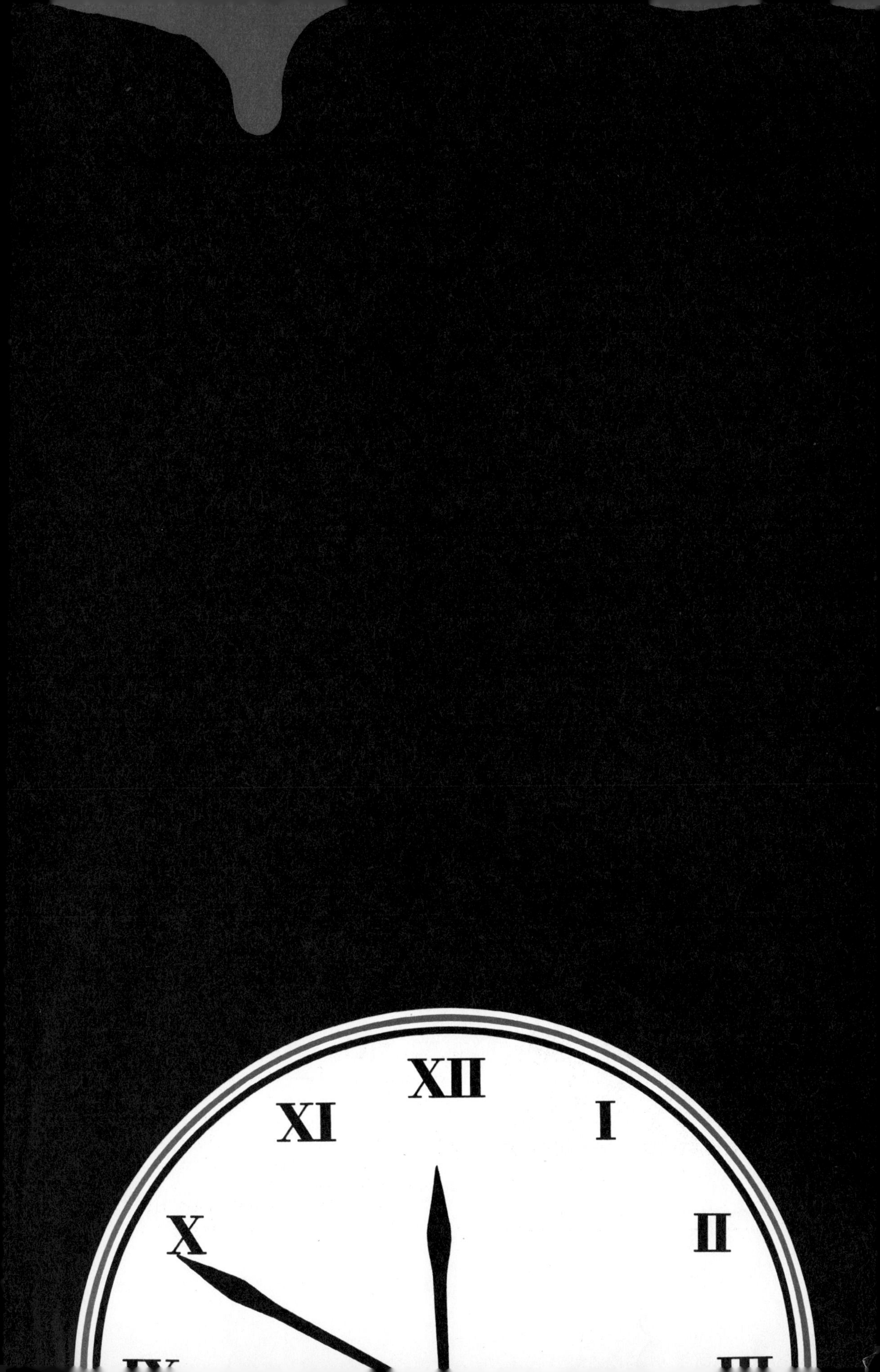

XII
XI
I
X
II

CHAPTER III

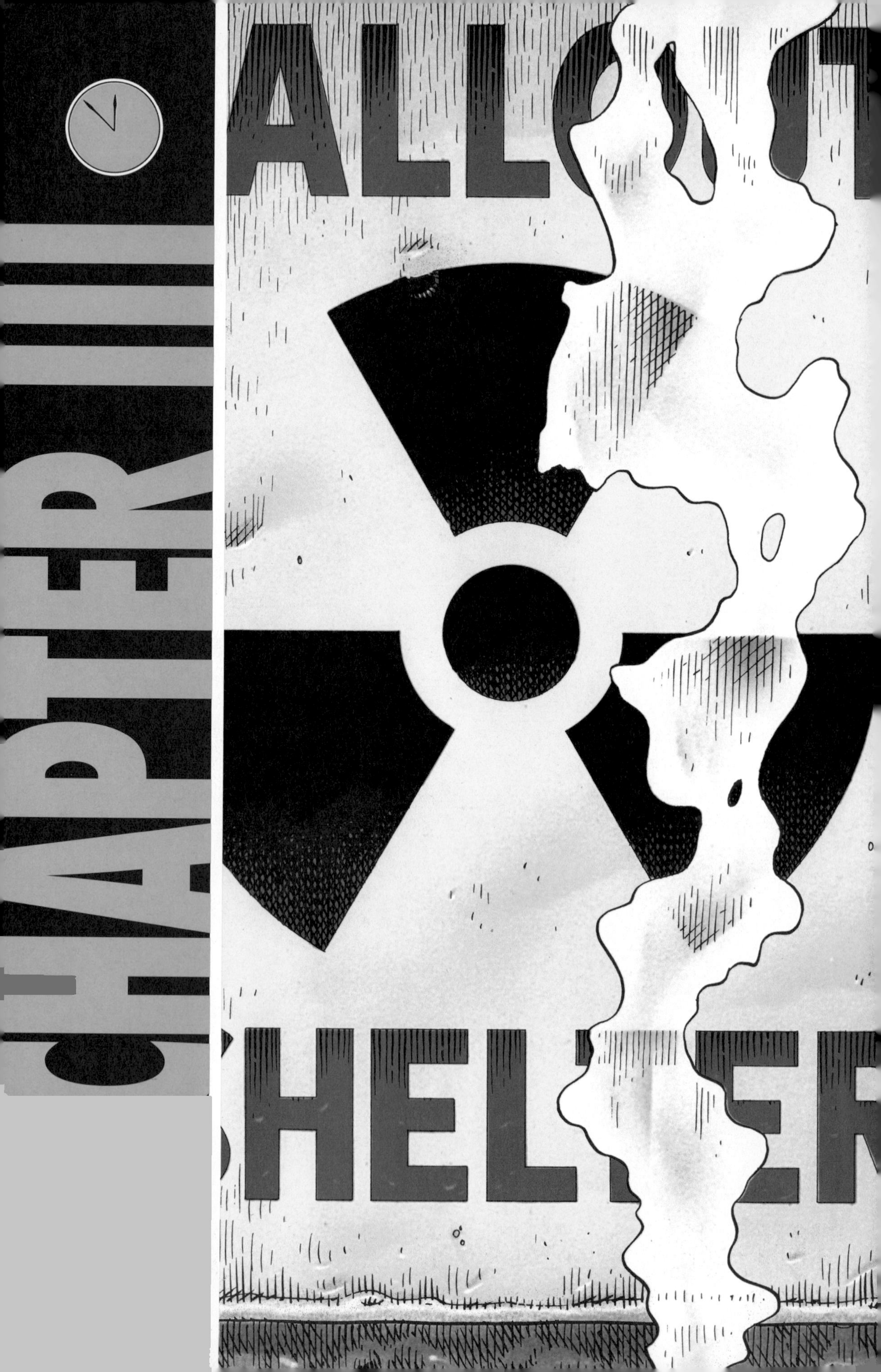
ALL
HEL

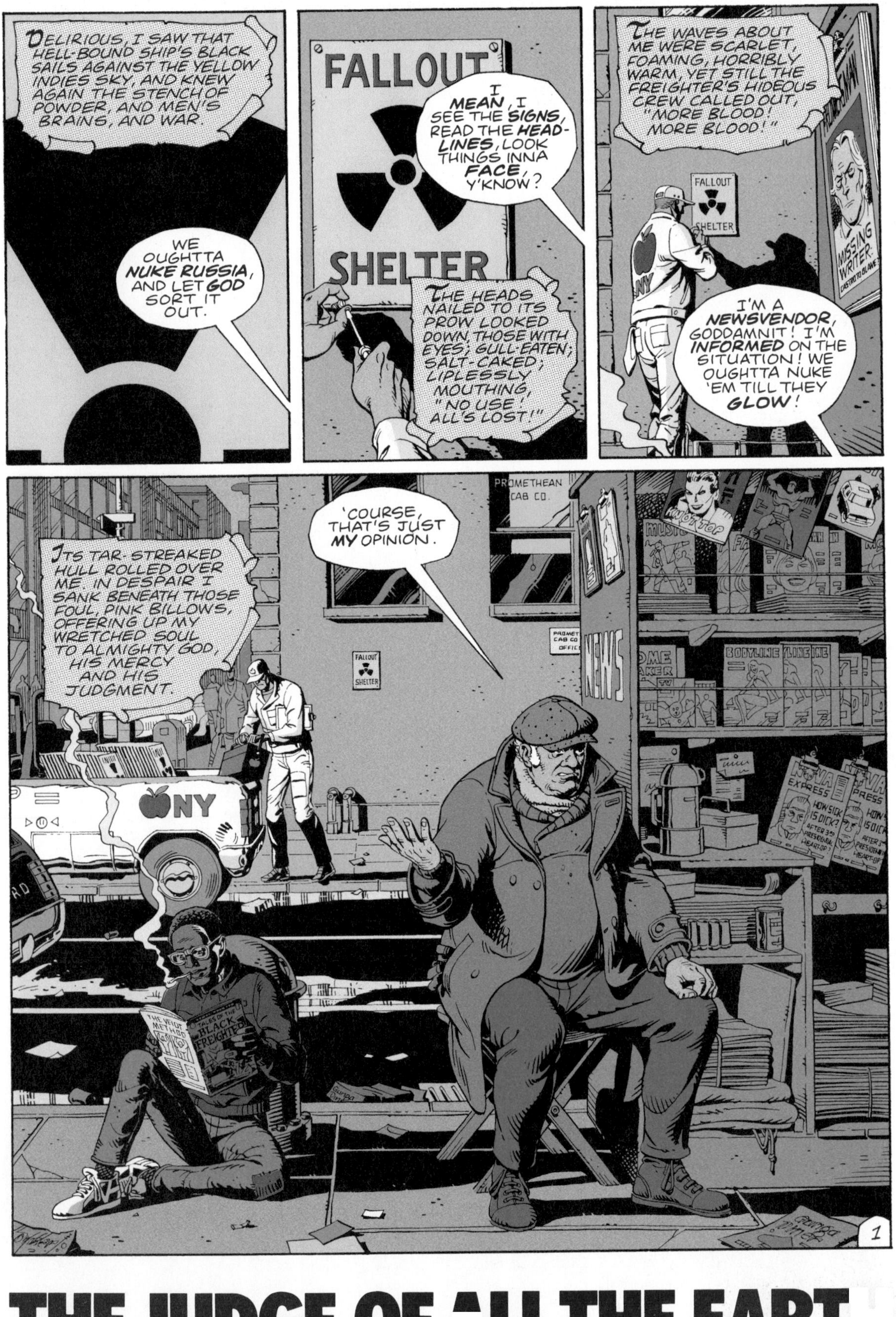
DELIRIOUS, I SAW THAT HELL-BOUND SHIP'S BLACK SAILS AGAINST THE YELLOW INDIES SKY, AND KNEW AGAIN THE STENCH OF POWDER, AND MEN'S BRAINS, AND WAR.
WE OUGHTTA NUKE RUSSIA, AND LET GOD SORT IT OUT.
FALLOUT SHELTER
I MEAN, I SEE THE SIGNS, READ THE HEADLINES, LOOK THINGS INNA FACE, Y'KNOW?
THE HEADS NAILED TO ITS PROW LOOKED DOWN, THOSE WITH EYES; GULL-EATEN; SALT-CAKED; LIPLESSLY MOUTHING, "NO USE! ALL'S LOST!"
THE WAVES ABOUT ME WERE SCARLET, FOAMING, HORRIBLY WARM, YET STILL THE FREIGHTER'S HIDEOUS CREW CALLED OUT, "MORE BLOOD! MORE BLOOD!"
FALLOUT SHELTER
MISSING WRITER
I'M A NEWSVENDOR, GODDAMNIT! I'M INFORMED ON THE SITUATION! WE OUGHTTA NUKE 'EM TILL THEY GLOW!
ITS TAR-STREAKED HULL ROLLED OVER ME. IN DESPAIR I SANK BENEATH THOSE FOUL, PINK BILLOWS, OFFERING UP MY WRETCHED SOUL TO ALMIGHTY GOD, HIS MERCY AND HIS JUDGMENT.
PROMETHEAN CAB CO.
'COURSE, THAT'S JUST MY OPINION.
FALLOUT SHELTER
NEWS
NY
TALES OF THE BLACK FREIGHTER
NOVA EXPRESS
HOW SICK IS DICK?
1

THE JUDGE OF ALL THE EARTH

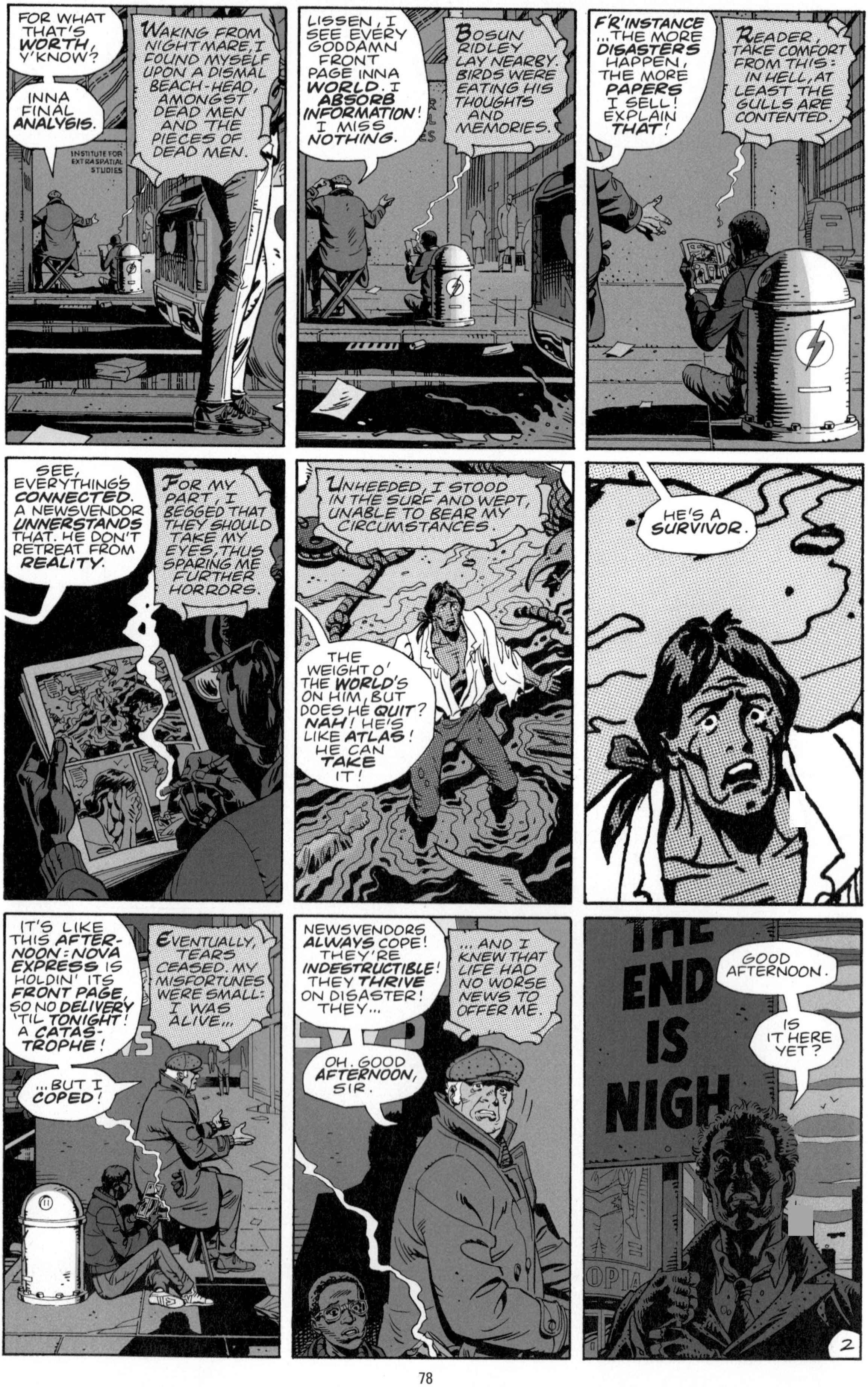
FOR WHAT THAT'S WORTH, Y'KNOW?
INNA FINAL ANALYSIS.
WAKING FROM NIGHTMARE, I FOUND MYSELF UPON A DISMAL BEACH-HEAD, AMONGST DEAD MEN AND THE PIECES OF DEAD MEN.
INSTITUTE FOR EXTRASPATIAL STUDIES
LISSEN, I SEE EVERY GODDAMN FRONT PAGE INNA WORLD. I ABSORB INFORMATION! I MISS NOTHING.
BOSUN RIDLEY LAY NEARBY. BIRDS WERE EATING HIS THOUGHTS AND MEMORIES.
F'R'INSTANCE ...THE MORE DISASTERS HAPPEN, THE MORE PAPERS I SELL! EXPLAIN THAT!
READER, TAKE COMFORT FROM THIS: IN HELL, AT LEAST THE GULLS ARE CONTENTED.
SEE, EVERYTHING'S CONNECTED. A NEWSVENDOR UNNERSTANDS THAT. HE DON'T RETREAT FROM REALITY.
FOR MY PART, I BEGGED THAT THEY SHOULD TAKE MY EYES, THUS SPARING ME FURTHER HORRORS.
UNHEEDED, I STOOD IN THE SURF AND WEPT, UNABLE TO BEAR MY CIRCUMSTANCES.
THE WEIGHT O' THE WORLD'S ON HIM, BUT DOES HE QUIT? NAH! HE'S LIKE ATLAS! HE CAN TAKE IT!
HE'S A SURVIVOR.
IT'S LIKE THIS AFTERNOON: NOVA EXPRESS IS HOLDIN' ITS FRONT PAGE, SO NO DELIVERY 'TIL TONIGHT! A CATASTROPHE!
EVENTUALLY, TEARS CEASED. MY MISFORTUNES WERE SMALL: I WAS ALIVE...
...BUT I COPED!
NEWSVENDORS ALWAYS COPE! THEY'RE INDESTRUCTIBLE! THEY THRIVE ON DISASTER! THEY...
...AND I KNEW THAT LIFE HAD NO WORSE NEWS TO OFFER ME.
OH. GOOD AFTERNOON, SIR.
THE END IS NIGH
GOOD AFTERNOON.
IS IT HERE YET?
2

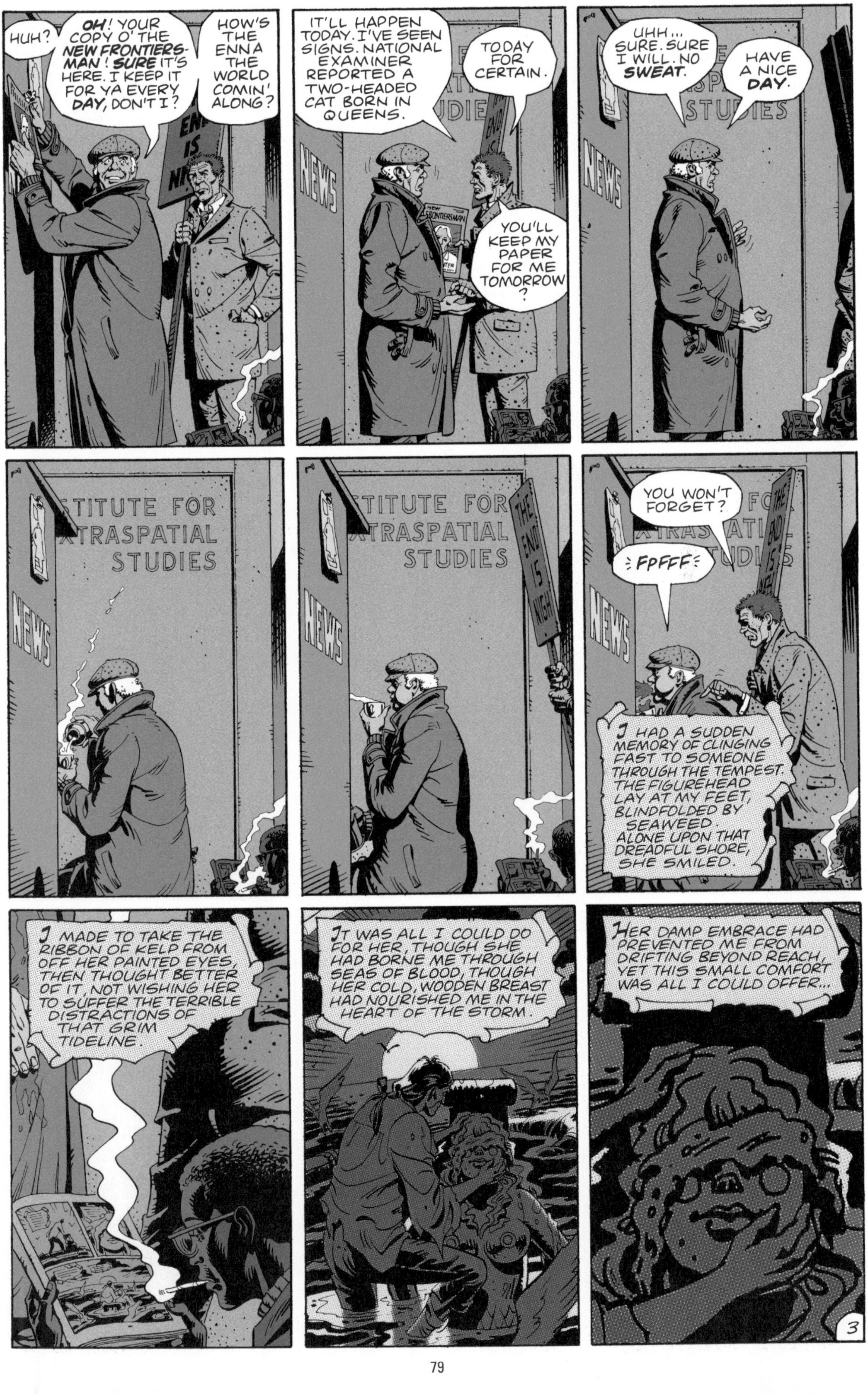
HUH?
OH! YOUR COPY O' THE NEW FRONTIERSMAN! SURE IT'S HERE. I KEEP IT FOR YA EVERY DAY, DON'T I?
HOW'S THE ENNA THE WORLD COMIN' ALONG?
IT'LL HAPPEN TODAY. I'VE SEEN SIGNS. NATIONAL EXAMINER REPORTED A TWO-HEADED CAT BORN IN QUEENS.
TODAY FOR CERTAIN.
YOU'LL KEEP MY PAPER FOR ME TOMORROW?
UHH... SURE. SURE I WILL. NO SWEAT.
HAVE A NICE DAY.
NEWS
STITUTE FOR XTRASPATIAL STUDIES
THE END IS NIGH
YOU WON'T FORGET?
FPFFF
I HAD A SUDDEN MEMORY OF CLINGING FAST TO SOMEONE THROUGH THE TEMPEST. THE FIGUREHEAD LAY AT MY FEET, BLINDFOLDED BY SEAWEED. ALONE UPON THAT DREADFUL SHORE, SHE SMILED.
I MADE TO TAKE THE RIBBON OF KELP FROM OFF HER PAINTED EYES, THEN THOUGHT BETTER OF IT, NOT WISHING HER TO SUFFER THE TERRIBLE DISTRACTIONS OF THAT GRIM TIDELINE.
IT WAS ALL I COULD DO FOR HER, THOUGH SHE HAD BORNE ME THROUGH SEAS OF BLOOD, THOUGH HER COLD, WOODEN BREAST HAD NOURISHED ME IN THE HEART OF THE STORM.
HER DAMP EMBRACE HAD PREVENTED ME FROM DRIFTING BEYOND REACH, YET THIS SMALL COMFORT WAS ALL I COULD OFFER...
3

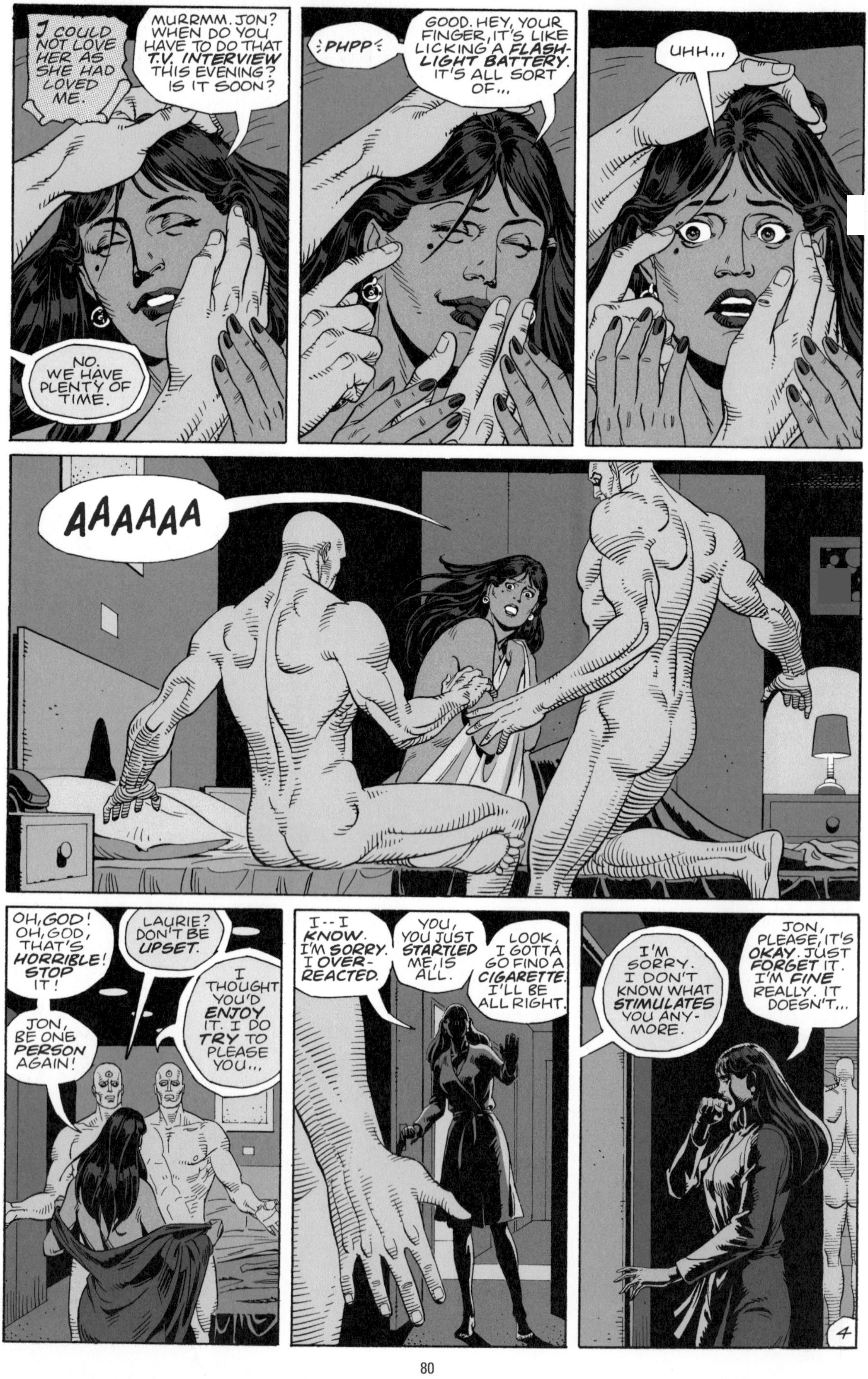

I COULD NOT LOVE HER AS SHE HAD LOVED ME.
MURRMM. JON? WHEN DO YOU HAVE TO DO THAT T.V. INTERVIEW THIS EVENING? IS IT SOON?
NO. WE HAVE PLENTY OF TIME.
PHPP
GOOD. HEY, YOUR FINGER, IT'S LIKE LICKING A FLASHLIGHT BATTERY. IT'S ALL SORT OF...
UHH...
AAAAAA
OH, GOD! OH, GOD, THAT'S HORRIBLE! STOP IT!
LAURIE? DON'T BE UPSET.
I THOUGHT YOU'D ENJOY IT. I DO TRY TO PLEASE YOU...
JON, BE ONE PERSON AGAIN!
I--I KNOW. I'M SORRY. I OVER-REACTED.
YOU, YOU JUST STARTLED ME, IS ALL.
LOOK, I GOTTA GO FIND A CIGARETTE. I'LL BE ALL RIGHT.
I'M SORRY. I DON'T KNOW WHAT STIMULATES YOU ANY-MORE.
JON, PLEASE, IT'S OKAY. JUST FORGET IT. I'M FINE REALLY. IT DOESN'T...
4

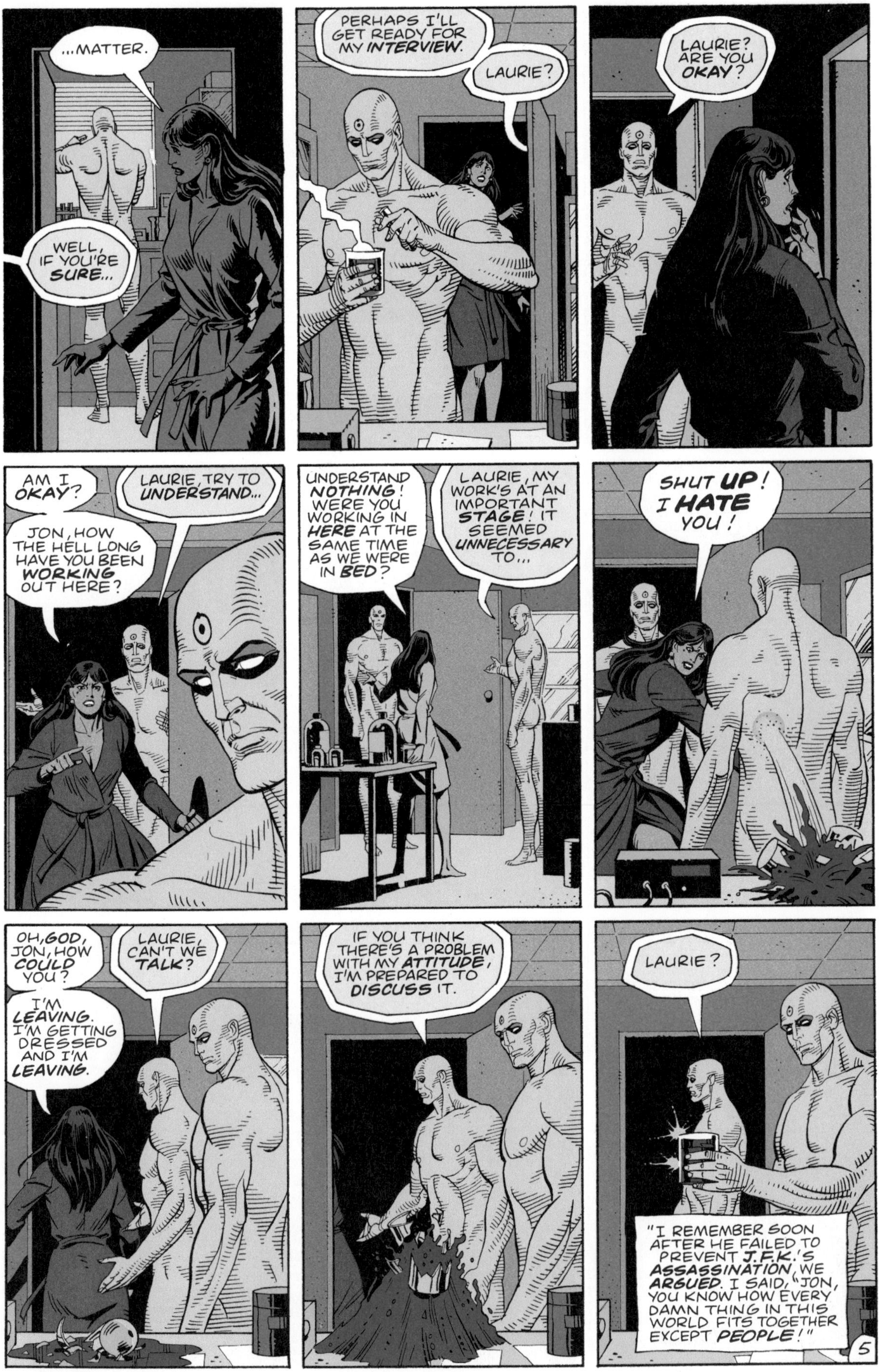
...MATTER.
WELL, IF YOU'RE SURE...
PERHAPS I'LL GET READY FOR MY INTERVIEW.
LAURIE?
LAURIE? ARE YOU OKAY?
AM I OKAY?
JON, HOW THE HELL LONG HAVE YOU BEEN WORKING OUT HERE?
LAURIE, TRY TO UNDERSTAND...
UNDERSTAND NOTHING! WERE YOU WORKING IN HERE AT THE SAME TIME AS WE WERE IN BED?
LAURIE, MY WORK'S AT AN IMPORTANT STAGE! IT SEEMED UNNECESSARY TO...
SHUT UP! I HATE YOU!
OH, GOD, JON, HOW COULD YOU?
I'M LEAVING. I'M GETTING DRESSED AND I'M LEAVING.
LAURIE, CAN'T WE TALK?
IF YOU THINK THERE'S A PROBLEM WITH MY ATTITUDE, I'M PREPARED TO DISCUSS IT.
LAURIE?
"I REMEMBER SOON AFTER HE FAILED TO PREVENT J.F.K.'S ASSASSINATION, WE ARGUED. I SAID, "JON, YOU KNOW HOW EVERY DAMN THING IN THIS WORLD FITS TOGETHER EXCEPT PEOPLE!"
5

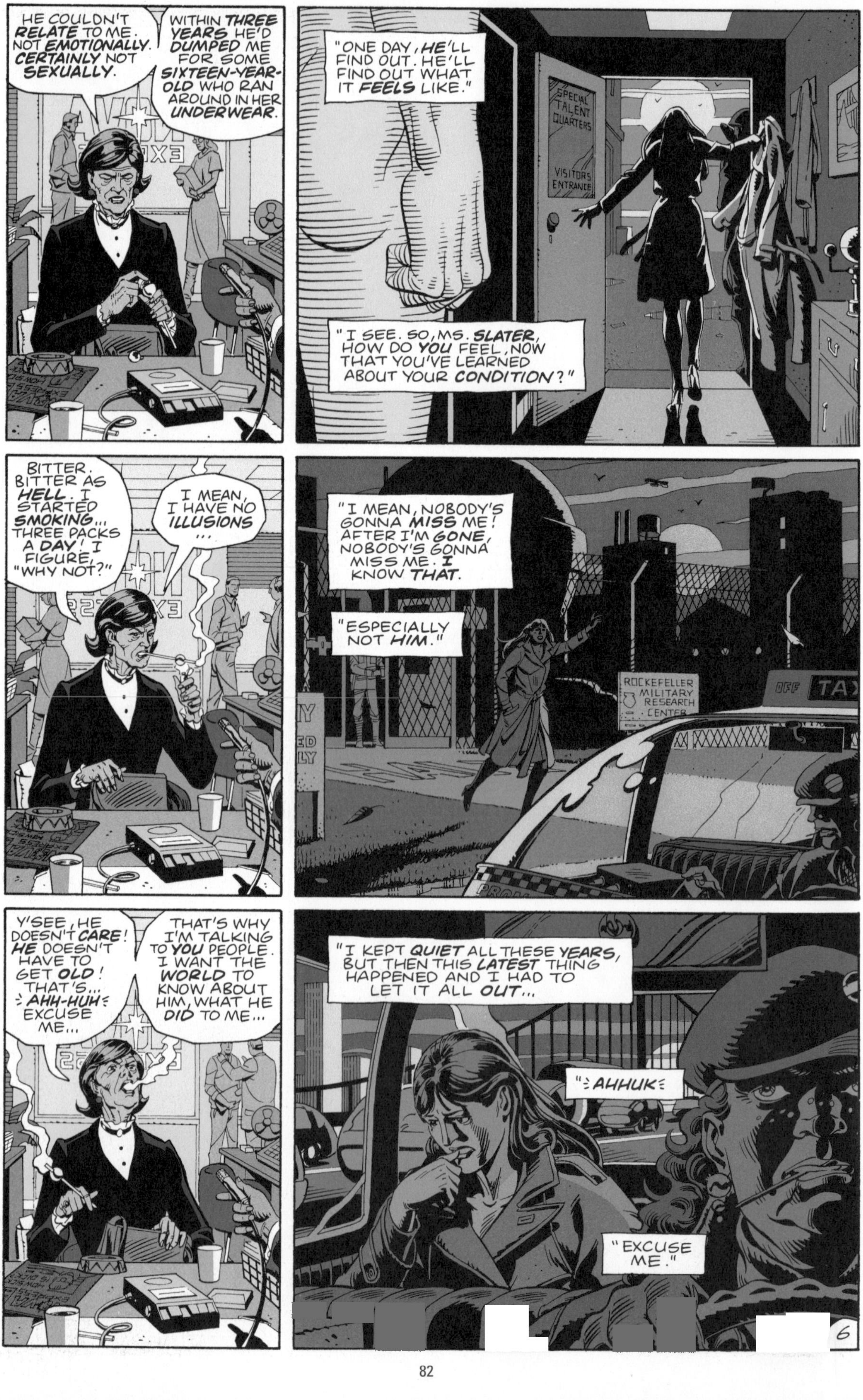
HE COULDN'T RELATE TO ME. NOT EMOTIONALLY. CERTAINLY NOT SEXUALLY.
WITHIN THREE YEARS HE'D DUMPED ME FOR SOME SIXTEEN-YEAR-OLD WHO RAN AROUND IN HER UNDERWEAR.
"ONE DAY, HE'LL FIND OUT. HE'LL FIND OUT WHAT IT FEELS LIKE."
SPECIAL TALENT QUARTERS
VISITORS ENTRANCE
"I SEE. SO, MS. SLATER, HOW DO YOU FEEL, NOW THAT YOU'VE LEARNED ABOUT YOUR CONDITION?"
BITTER. BITTER AS HELL. I STARTED SMOKING... THREE PACKS A DAY! I FIGURE, "WHY NOT?"
I MEAN, I HAVE NO ILLUSIONS...
"I MEAN, NOBODY'S GONNA MISS ME! AFTER I'M GONE, NOBODY'S GONNA MISS ME. I KNOW THAT.
"ESPECIALLY NOT HIM."
ROCKEFELLER MILITARY RESEARCH CENTER
OFF
Y'SEE, HE DOESN'T CARE! HE DOESN'T HAVE TO GET OLD! THAT'S... AHH-HUH EXCUSE ME...
THAT'S WHY I'M TALKING TO YOU PEOPLE. I WANT THE WORLD TO KNOW ABOUT HIM, WHAT HE DID TO ME...
"I KEPT QUIET ALL THESE YEARS, BUT THEN THIS LATEST THING HAPPENED AND I HAD TO LET IT ALL OUT...
"AHHUK
"EXCUSE ME."
6

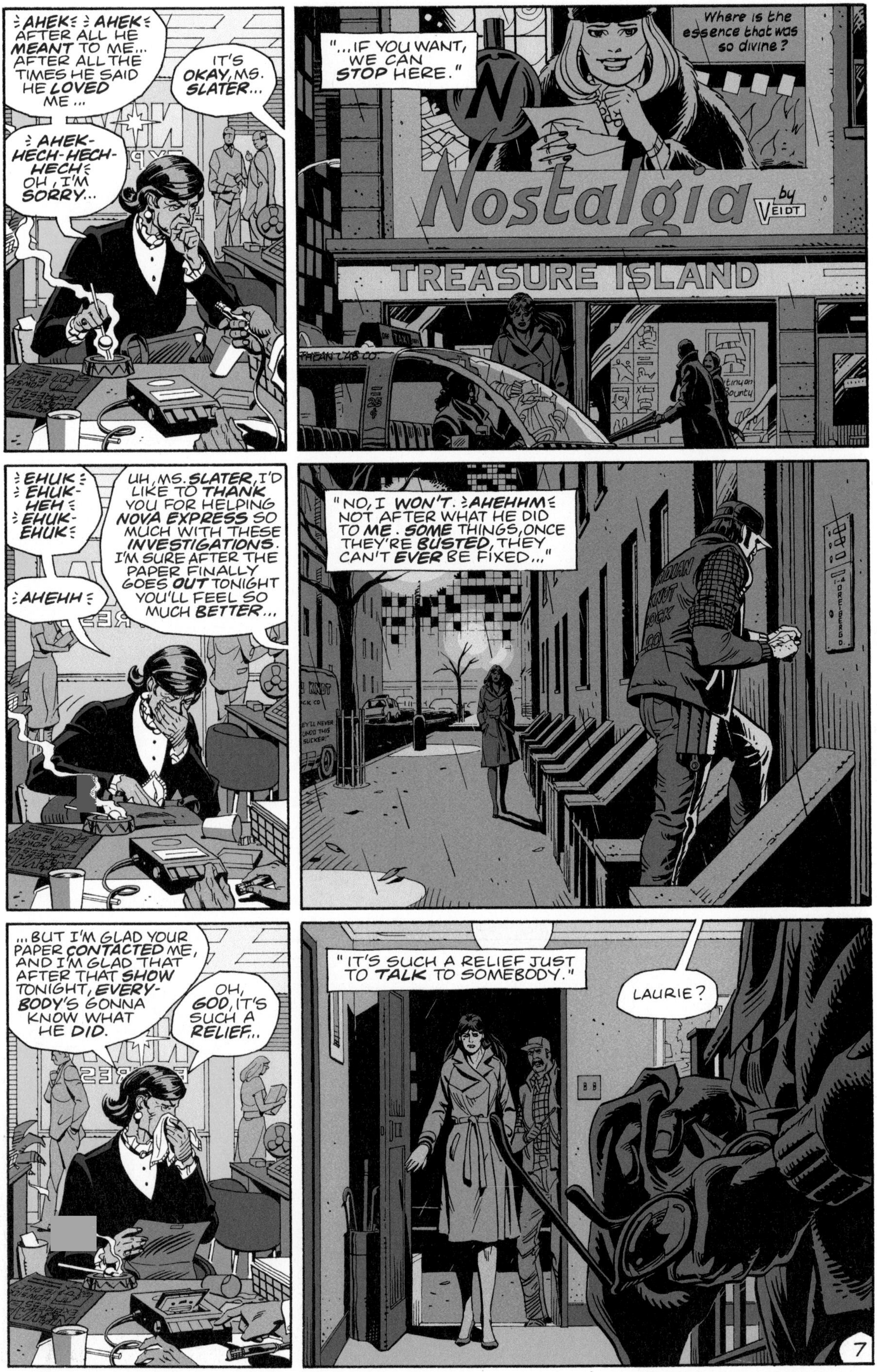
AHEK AHEK AFTER ALL HE MEANT TO ME... AFTER ALL THE TIMES HE SAID HE LOVED ME...
IT'S OKAY, MS. SLATER...
AHEK-HECH-HECH-HECH OH, I'M SORRY...
"...IF YOU WANT, WE CAN STOP HERE."
Where is the essence that was so divine?
Nostalgia by VEIDT
TREASURE ISLAND
EHUK EHUK-HEH EHUK-EHUK
UH, MS. SLATER, I'D LIKE TO THANK YOU FOR HELPING NOVA EXPRESS SO MUCH WITH THESE INVESTIGATIONS. I'M SURE AFTER THE PAPER FINALLY GOES OUT TONIGHT YOU'LL FEEL SO MUCH BETTER...
AHEHH
"NO, I WON'T. AHEHHM NOT AFTER WHAT HE DID TO ME. SOME THINGS, ONCE THEY'RE BUSTED, THEY CAN'T EVER BE FIXED..."
...BUT I'M GLAD YOUR PAPER CONTACTED ME, AND I'M GLAD THAT AFTER THAT SHOW TONIGHT, EVERYBODY'S GONNA KNOW WHAT HE DID.
OH, GOD, IT'S SUCH A RELIEF...
"IT'S SUCH A RELIEF JUST TO TALK TO SOMEBODY."
LAURIE?
7

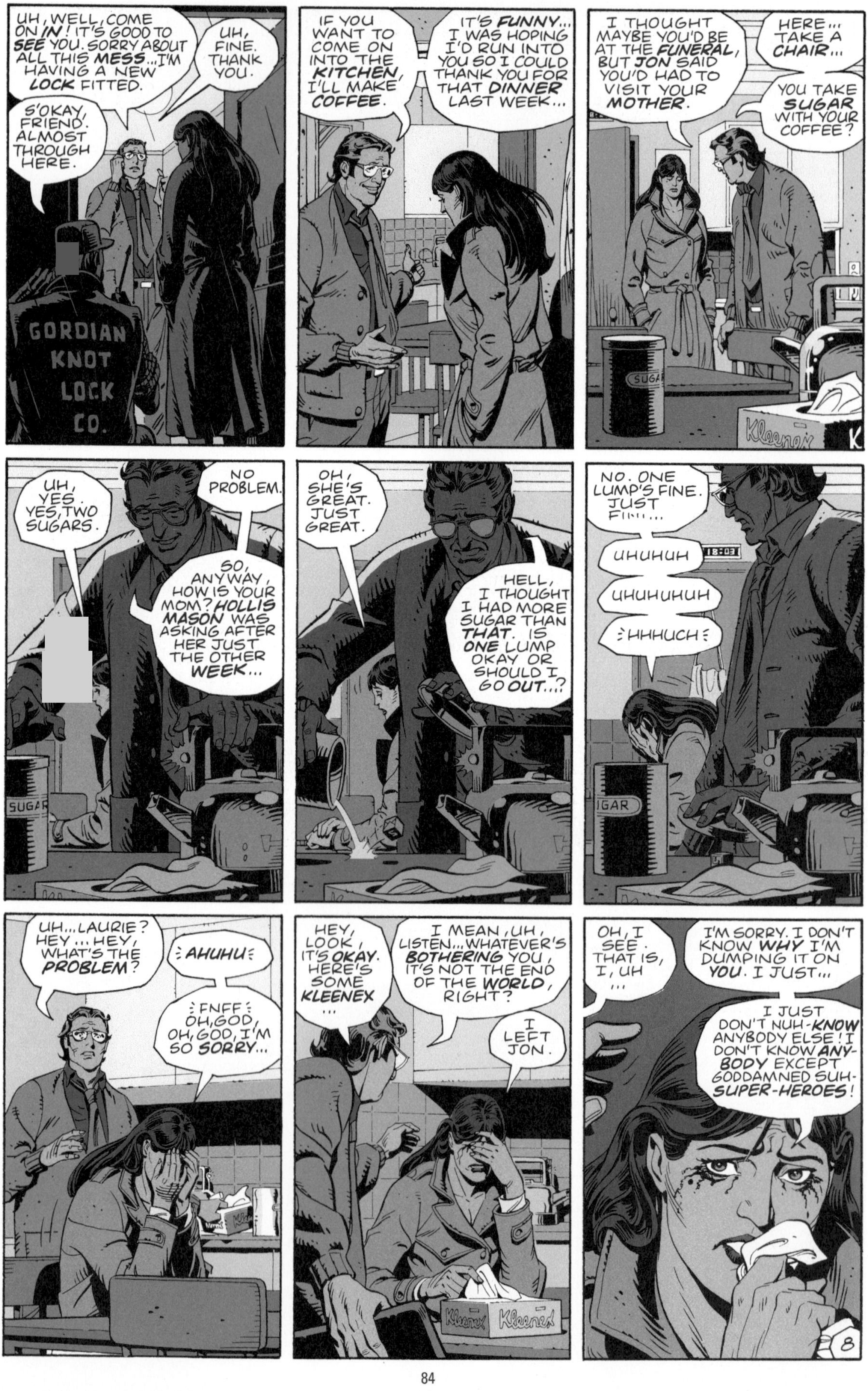
UH, WELL, COME ON IN! IT'S GOOD TO SEE YOU. SORRY ABOUT ALL THIS MESS...I'M HAVING A NEW LOCK FITTED.
UH, FINE. THANK YOU.
S'OKAY, FRIEND. ALMOST THROUGH HERE.
GORDIAN KNOT LOCK CO.
IF YOU WANT TO COME ON INTO THE KITCHEN, I'LL MAKE COFFEE.
IT'S FUNNY... I WAS HOPING I'D RUN INTO YOU SO I COULD THANK YOU FOR THAT DINNER LAST WEEK...
I THOUGHT MAYBE YOU'D BE AT THE FUNERAL, BUT JON SAID YOU'D HAD TO VISIT YOUR MOTHER.
HERE... TAKE A CHAIR...
YOU TAKE SUGAR WITH YOUR COFFEE?
SUGAR
Kleenex
UH, YES. YES, TWO SUGARS.
NO PROBLEM.
SO, ANYWAY, HOW IS YOUR MOM? HOLLIS MASON WAS ASKING AFTER HER JUST THE OTHER WEEK...
SUGAR
OH, SHE'S GREAT. JUST GREAT.
HELL, I THOUGHT I HAD MORE SUGAR THAN THAT. IS ONE LUMP OKAY OR SHOULD I GO OUT...?
NO. ONE LUMP'S FINE. JUST FI...
UHUHUH
UHUHUHUH
HHHUCH
18:03
GAR
UH...LAURIE? HEY...HEY, WHAT'S THE PROBLEM?
AHUHU
FNFF OH, GOD, OH, GOD, I'M SO SORRY...
HEY, LOOK, IT'S OKAY. HERE'S SOME KLEENEX...
I MEAN, UH, LISTEN...WHATEVER'S BOTHERING YOU, IT'S NOT THE END OF THE WORLD, RIGHT?
I LEFT JON.
Kleenex Kleenex
OH, I SEE. THAT IS, I, UH...
I'M SORRY. I DON'T KNOW WHY I'M DUMPING IT ON YOU. I JUST...
I JUST DON'T NUH-KNOW ANYBODY ELSE! I DON'T KNOW ANYBODY EXCEPT GODDAMNED SUH-SUPER-HEROES!
8

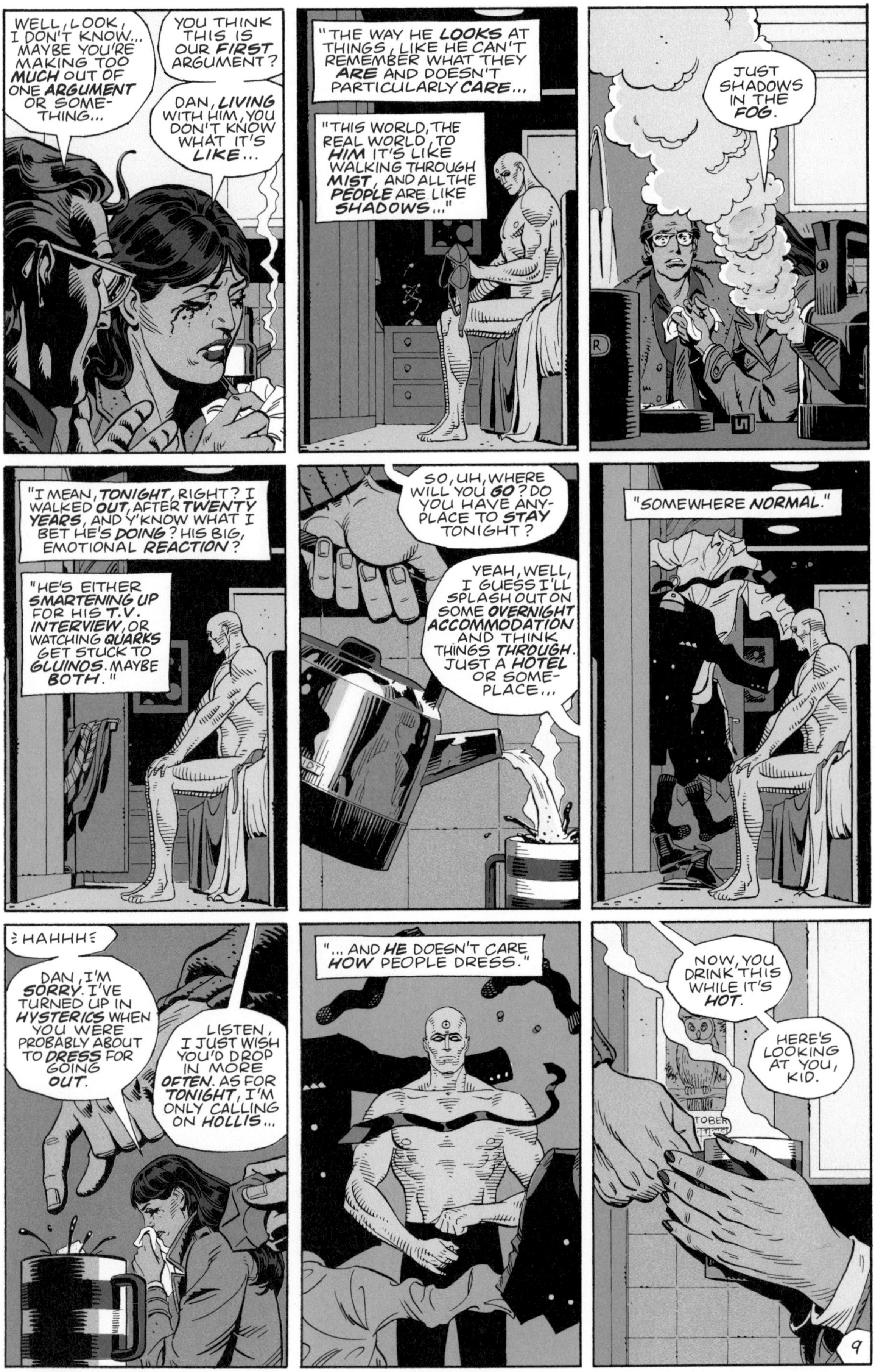
WELL, LOOK, I DON'T KNOW... MAYBE YOU'RE MAKING TOO MUCH OUT OF ONE ARGUMENT OR SOME-THING...
YOU THINK THIS IS OUR FIRST ARGUMENT?
DAN, LIVING WITH HIM, YOU DON'T KNOW WHAT IT'S LIKE...
"THE WAY HE LOOKS AT THINGS, LIKE HE CAN'T REMEMBER WHAT THEY ARE AND DOESN'T PARTICULARLY CARE...
"THIS WORLD, THE REAL WORLD, TO HIM IT'S LIKE WALKING THROUGH MIST, AND ALL THE PEOPLE ARE LIKE SHADOWS..."
JUST SHADOWS IN THE FOG.
"I MEAN, TONIGHT, RIGHT? I WALKED OUT, AFTER TWENTY YEARS, AND Y'KNOW WHAT I BET HE'S DOING? HIS BIG, EMOTIONAL REACTION?
"HE'S EITHER SMARTENING UP FOR HIS T.V. INTERVIEW, OR WATCHING QUARKS GET STUCK TO GLUINOS. MAYBE BOTH."
SO, UH, WHERE WILL YOU GO? DO YOU HAVE ANY-PLACE TO STAY TONIGHT?
YEAH, WELL, I GUESS I'LL SPLASH OUT ON SOME OVERNIGHT ACCOMMODATION AND THINK THINGS THROUGH. JUST A HOTEL OR SOME-PLACE...
"SOMEWHERE NORMAL."
HAHHH
DAN, I'M SORRY. I'VE TURNED UP IN HYSTERICS WHEN YOU WERE PROBABLY ABOUT TO DRESS FOR GOING OUT.
LISTEN, I JUST WISH YOU'D DROP IN MORE OFTEN. AS FOR TONIGHT, I'M ONLY CALLING ON HOLLIS...
"...AND HE DOESN'T CARE HOW PEOPLE DRESS."
NOW, YOU DRINK THIS WHILE IT'S HOT.
HERE'S LOOKING AT YOU, KID.
9

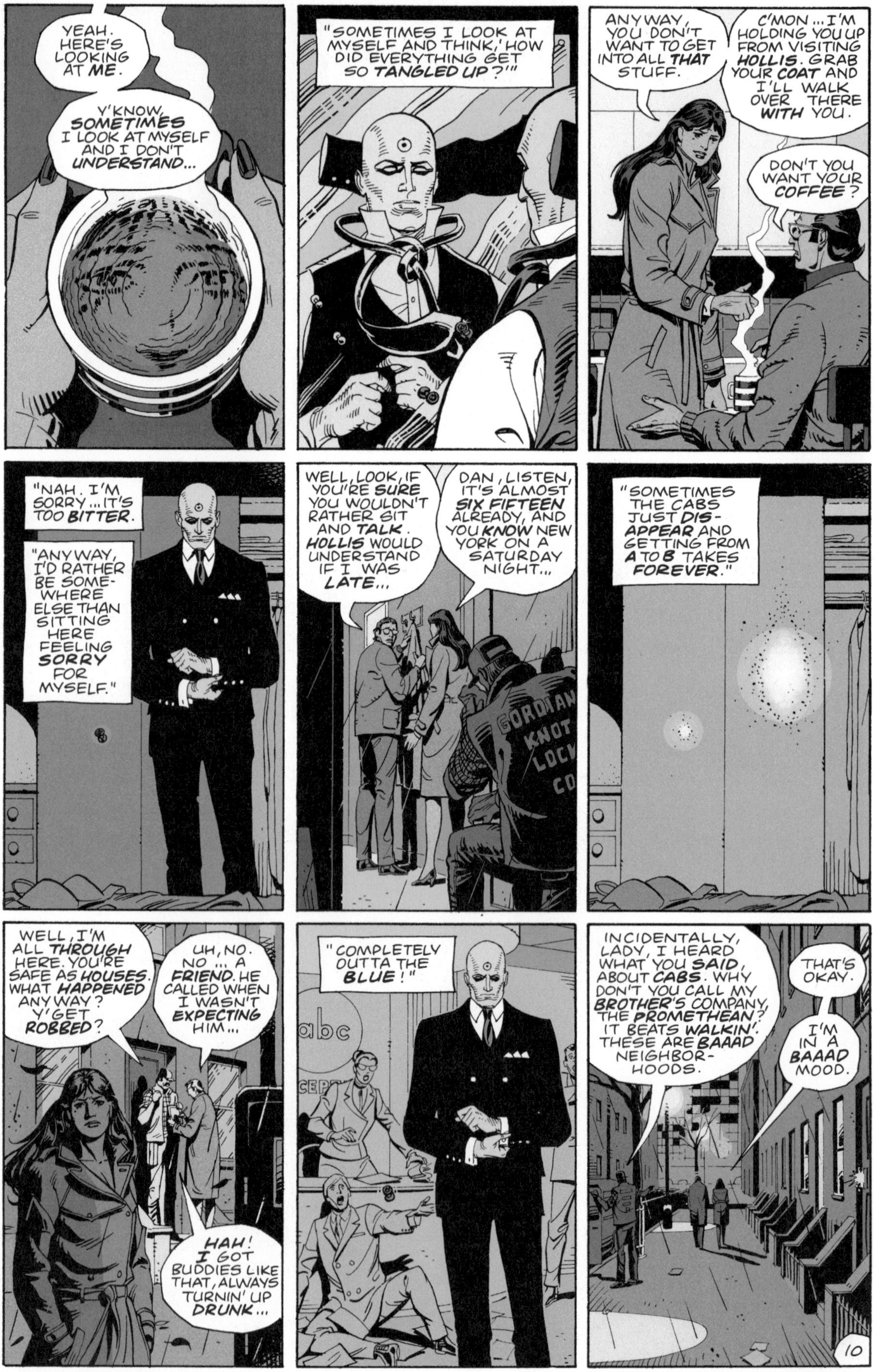
YEAH. HERE'S LOOKING AT ME.
Y'KNOW, SOMETIMES I LOOK AT MYSELF AND I DON'T UNDERSTAND...
"SOMETIMES I LOOK AT MYSELF AND THINK, 'HOW DID EVERYTHING GET SO TANGLED UP?'"
ANYWAY, YOU DON'T WANT TO GET INTO ALL THAT STUFF.
C'MON... I'M HOLDING YOU UP FROM VISITING HOLLIS. GRAB YOUR COAT AND I'LL WALK OVER THERE WITH YOU.
DON'T YOU WANT YOUR COFFEE?
"NAH. I'M SORRY... IT'S TOO BITTER.
"ANYWAY, I'D RATHER BE SOMEWHERE ELSE THAN SITTING HERE FEELING SORRY FOR MYSELF."
WELL, LOOK, IF YOU'RE SURE YOU WOULDN'T RATHER SIT AND TALK. HOLLIS WOULD UNDERSTAND IF I WAS LATE...
DAN, LISTEN, IT'S ALMOST SIX FIFTEEN ALREADY, AND YOU KNOW NEW YORK ON A SATURDAY NIGHT...
GORDIAN KNOT LOCK CO
"SOMETIMES THE CABS JUST DISAPPEAR AND GETTING FROM A TO B TAKES FOREVER."
WELL, I'M ALL THROUGH HERE. YOU'RE SAFE AS HOUSES. WHAT HAPPENED ANYWAY? Y'GET ROBBED?
UH, NO. NO... A FRIEND. HE CALLED WHEN I WASN'T EXPECTING HIM...
HAH! I GOT BUDDIES LIKE THAT, ALWAYS TURNIN' UP DRUNK...
"COMPLETELY OUTTA THE BLUE!"
abc
INCIDENTALLY, LADY, I HEARD WHAT YOU SAID, ABOUT CABS. WHY DON'T YOU CALL MY BROTHER'S COMPANY, THE PROMETHEAN? IT BEATS WALKIN'. THESE ARE BAAAD NEIGHBORHOODS.
THAT'S OKAY.
I'M IN A BAAAD MOOD.
10

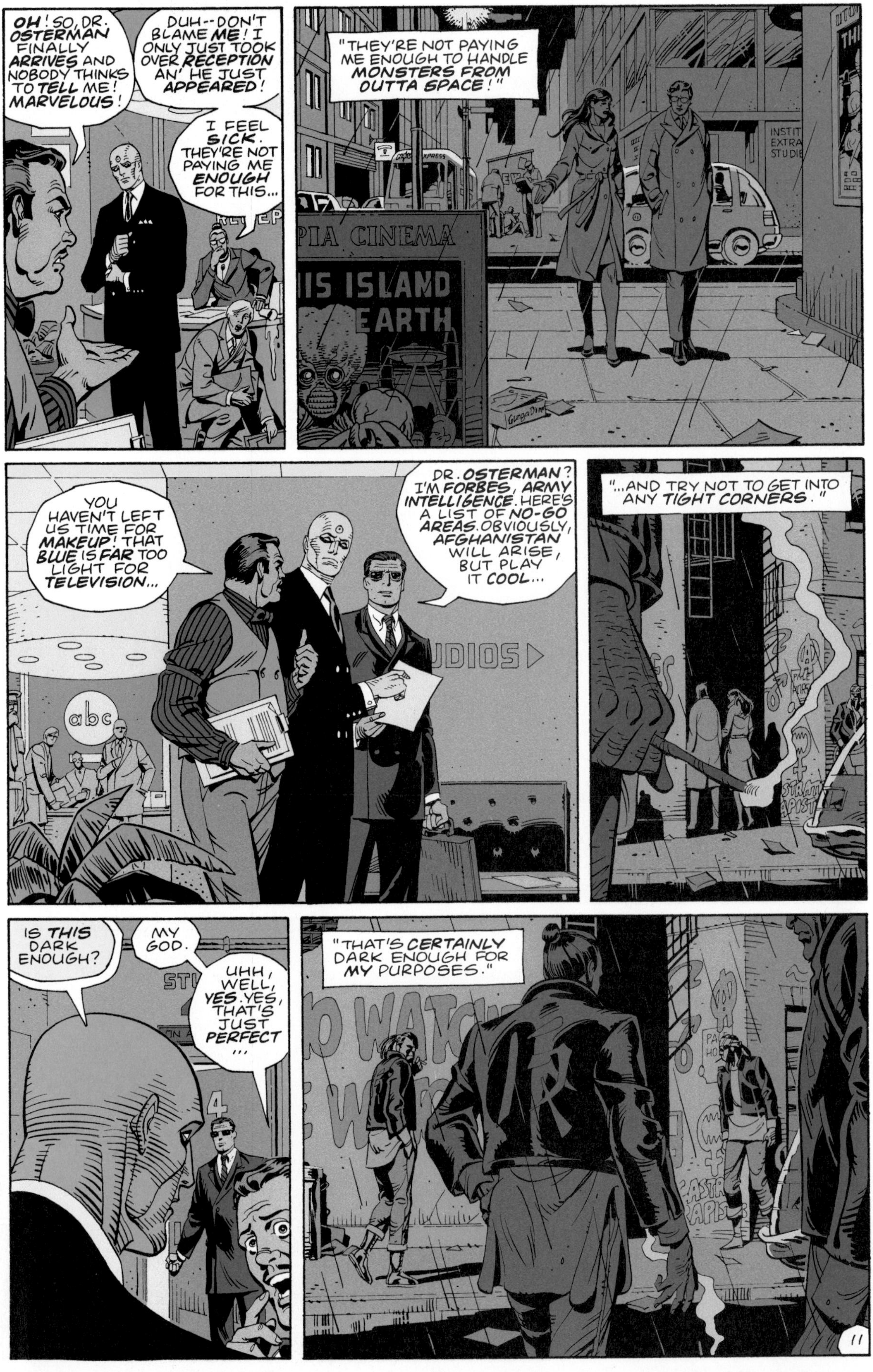
OH! SO, DR. OSTERMAN FINALLY ARRIVES AND NOBODY THINKS TO TELL ME! MARVELOUS!
DUH--DON'T BLAME ME! I ONLY JUST TOOK OVER RECEPTION AN' HE JUST APPEARED!
I FEEL SICK. THEY'RE NOT PAYING ME ENOUGH FOR THIS...
"THEY'RE NOT PAYING ME ENOUGH TO HANDLE MONSTERS FROM OUTTA SPACE!"
PIA CINEMA
IS ISLAND
EARTH
YOU HAVEN'T LEFT US TIME FOR MAKEUP! THAT BLUE IS FAR TOO LIGHT FOR TELEVISION...
DR. OSTERMAN? I'M FORBES, ARMY INTELLIGENCE. HERE'S A LIST OF NO-GO AREAS. OBVIOUSLY, AFGHANISTAN WILL ARISE, BUT PLAY IT COOL...
abc
UDIOS
"...AND TRY NOT TO GET INTO ANY TIGHT CORNERS."
IS THIS DARK ENOUGH?
MY GOD.
UHH, WELL, YES. YES, THAT'S JUST PERFECT...
"THAT'S CERTAINLY DARK ENOUGH FOR MY PURPOSES."
11

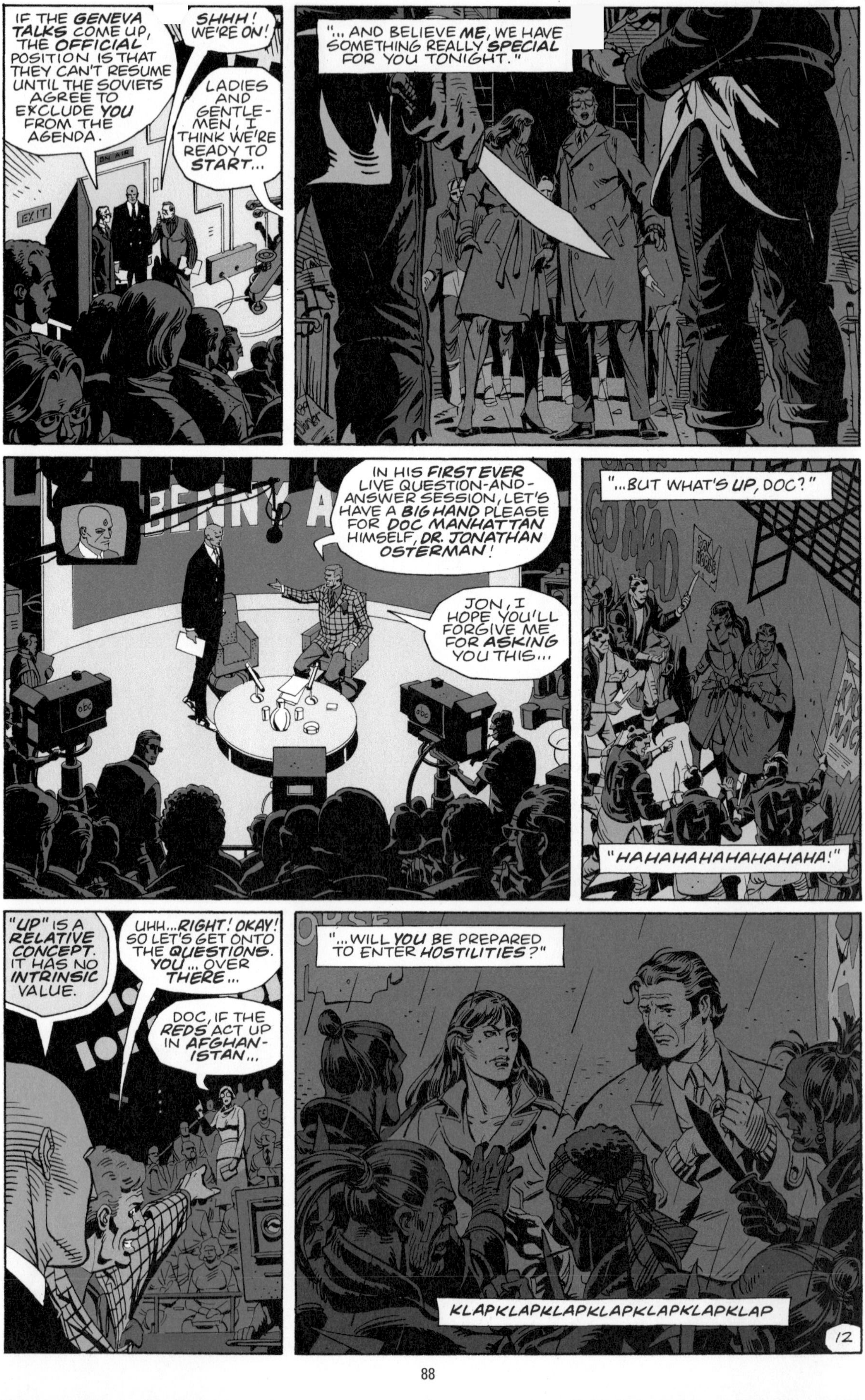
IF THE GENEVA TALKS COME UP, THE OFFICIAL POSITION IS THAT THEY CAN'T RESUME UNTIL THE SOVIETS AGREE TO EXCLUDE YOU FROM THE AGENDA.
SHHH! WE'RE ON!
LADIES AND GENTLE-MEN, I THINK WE'RE READY TO START...
ON AIR
EXIT
"... AND BELIEVE ME, WE HAVE SOMETHING REALLY SPECIAL FOR YOU TONIGHT."
IN HIS FIRST EVER LIVE QUESTION-AND-ANSWER SESSION, LET'S HAVE A BIG HAND PLEASE FOR DOC MANHATTAN HIMSELF, DR. JONATHAN OSTERMAN!
JON, I HOPE YOU'LL FORGIVE ME FOR ASKING YOU THIS...
"...BUT WHAT'S UP, DOC?"
"HAHAHAHAHAHAHAHAHA!"
"UP" IS A RELATIVE CONCEPT. IT HAS NO INTRINSIC VALUE.
UHH...RIGHT! OKAY! SO LET'S GET ONTO THE QUESTIONS. YOU... OVER THERE...
DOC, IF THE REDS ACT UP IN AFGHAN-ISTAN...
"...WILL YOU BE PREPARED TO ENTER HOSTILITIES?"
KLAPKLAPKLAPKLAPKLAPKLAPKLAP
12

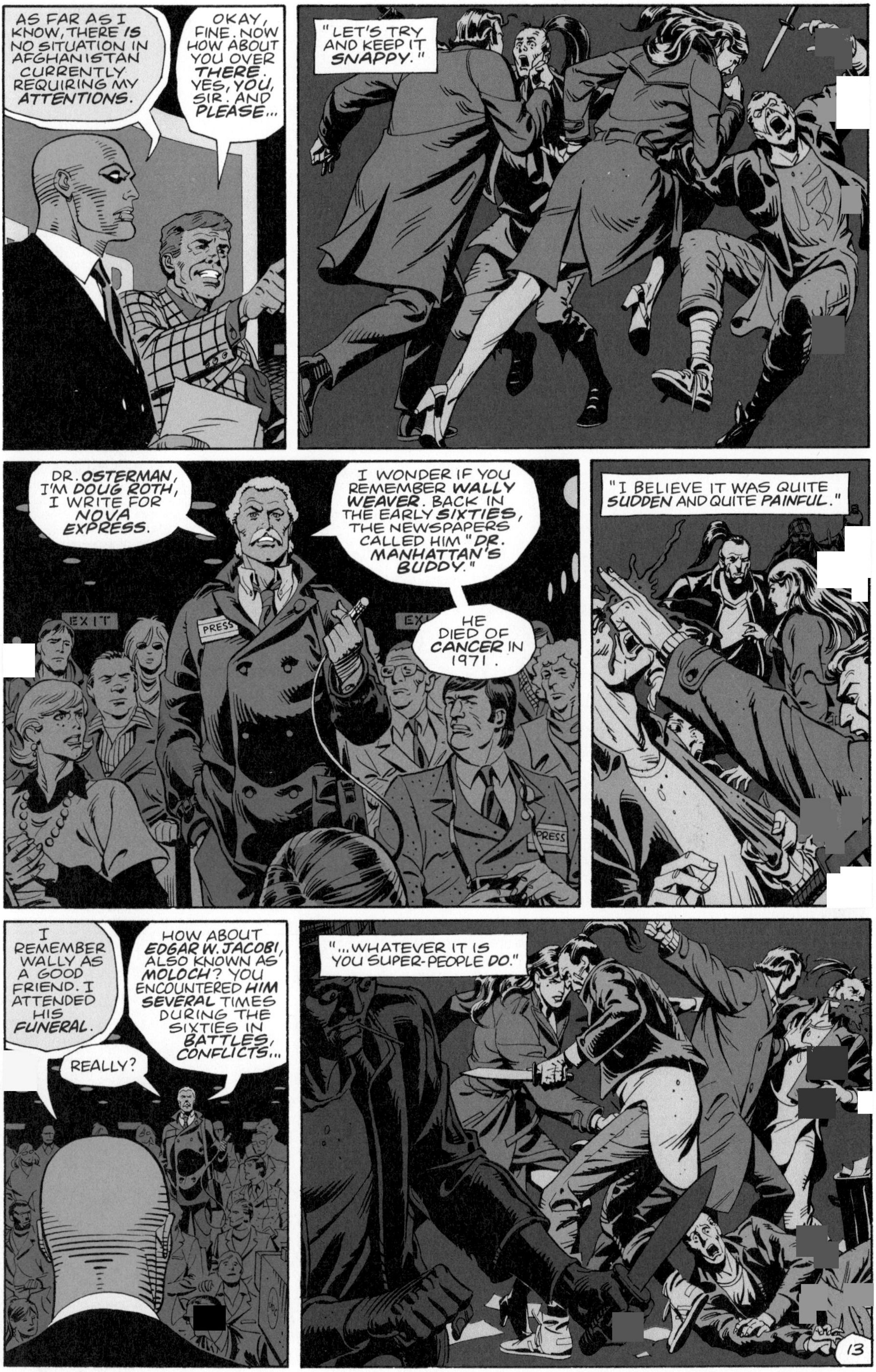
AS FAR AS I KNOW, THERE IS NO SITUATION IN AFGHANISTAN CURRENTLY REQUIRING MY ATTENTIONS.
OKAY, FINE. NOW HOW ABOUT YOU OVER THERE. YES, YOU, SIR. AND PLEASE...
"LET'S TRY AND KEEP IT SNAPPY."
DR. OSTERMAN, I'M DOUG ROTH, I WRITE FOR NOVA EXPRESS.
I WONDER IF YOU REMEMBER WALLY WEAVER. BACK IN THE EARLY SIXTIES, THE NEWSPAPERS CALLED HIM "DR. MANHATTAN'S BUDDY."
HE DIED OF CANCER IN 1971.
EXIT
PRESS
"I BELIEVE IT WAS QUITE SUDDEN AND QUITE PAINFUL."
I REMEMBER WALLY AS A GOOD FRIEND. I ATTENDED HIS FUNERAL.
HOW ABOUT EDGAR W. JACOBI, ALSO KNOWN AS MOLOCH? YOU ENCOUNTERED HIM SEVERAL TIMES DURING THE SIXTIES IN BATTLES, CONFLICTS...
REALLY?
"...WHATEVER IT IS YOU SUPER-PEOPLE DO."
13

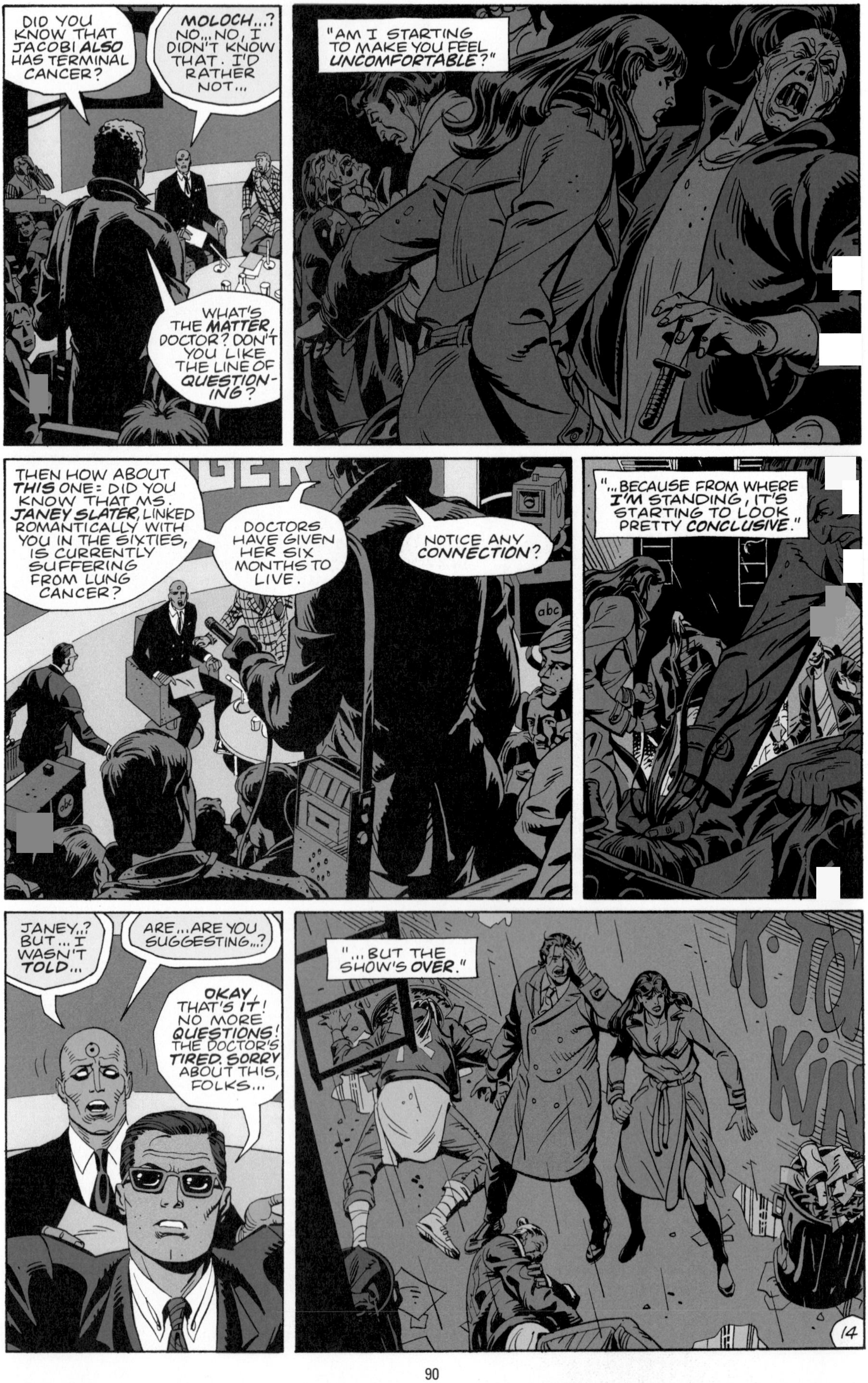
DID YOU KNOW THAT JACOBI ALSO HAS TERMINAL CANCER?
MOLOCH...? NO... NO, I DIDN'T KNOW THAT. I'D RATHER NOT...
WHAT'S THE MATTER, DOCTOR? DON'T YOU LIKE THE LINE OF QUESTIONING?
"AM I STARTING TO MAKE YOU FEEL UNCOMFORTABLE?"
THEN HOW ABOUT THIS ONE: DID YOU KNOW THAT MS. JANEY SLATER, LINKED ROMANTICALLY WITH YOU IN THE SIXTIES, IS CURRENTLY SUFFERING FROM LUNG CANCER?
DOCTORS HAVE GIVEN HER SIX MONTHS TO LIVE.
NOTICE ANY CONNECTION?
"...BECAUSE FROM WHERE I'M STANDING, IT'S STARTING TO LOOK PRETTY CONCLUSIVE."
JANEY..? BUT... I WASN'T TOLD...
ARE... ARE YOU SUGGESTING...?
OKAY, THAT'S IT! NO MORE QUESTIONS! THE DOCTOR'S TIRED. SORRY ABOUT THIS, FOLKS...
"...BUT THE SHOW'S OVER."
14

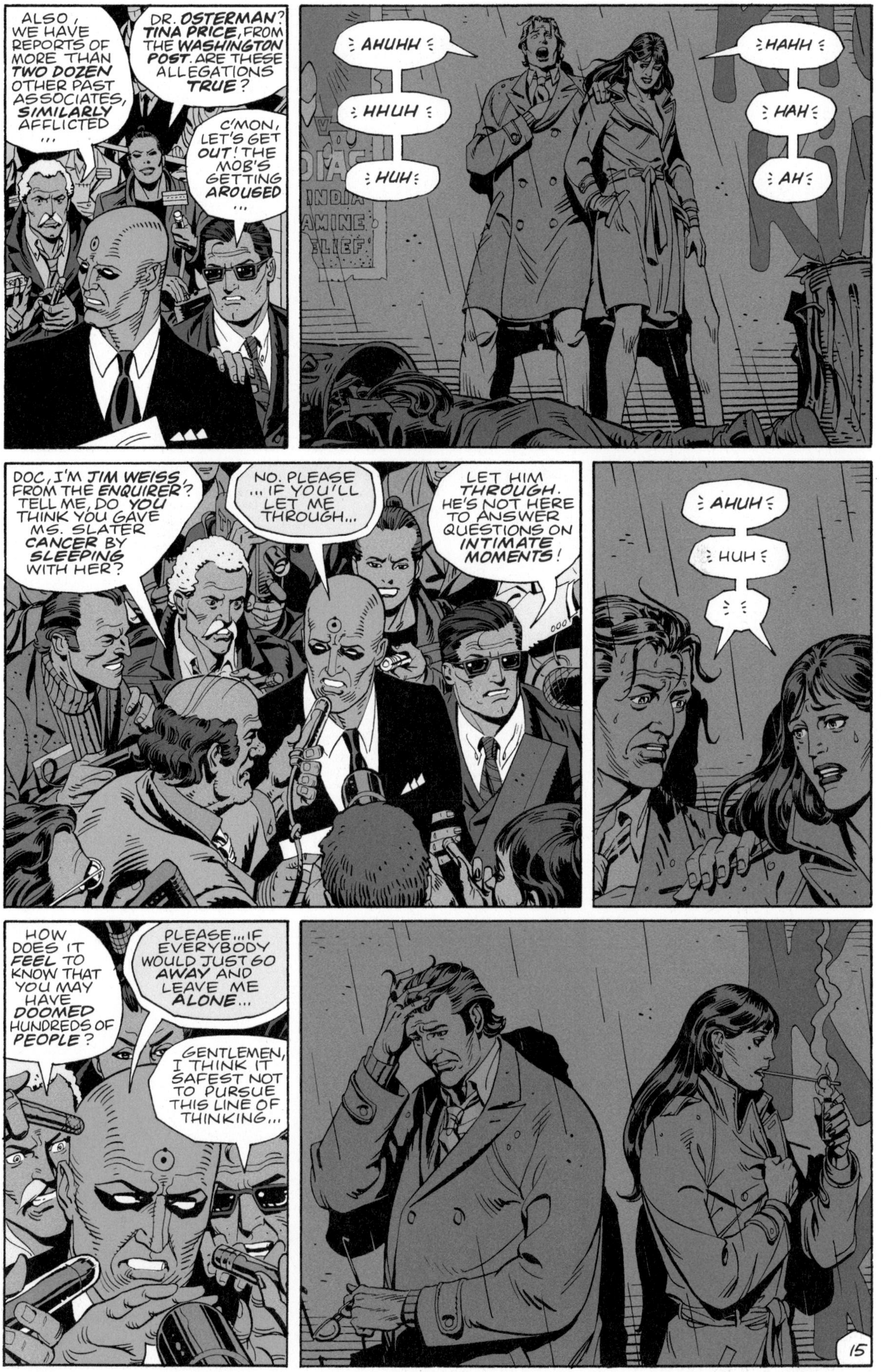

ALSO, WE HAVE REPORTS OF MORE THAN TWO DOZEN OTHER PAST ASSOCIATES, SIMILARLY AFFLICTED ...
DR. OSTERMAN? TINA PRICE, FROM THE WASHINGTON POST. ARE THESE ALLEGATIONS TRUE?
C'MON, LET'S GET OUT! THE MOB'S GETTING AROUSED ...
AHUHH
HHUH
HUH
HAHH
HAH
AH
DOC, I'M JIM WEISS, FROM THE ENQUIRER? TELL ME, DO YOU THINK YOU GAVE MS. SLATER CANCER BY SLEEPING WITH HER?
NO. PLEASE ... IF YOU'LL LET ME THROUGH...
LET HIM THROUGH. HE'S NOT HERE TO ANSWER QUESTIONS ON INTIMATE MOMENTS!
AHUH
HUH
HOW DOES IT FEEL TO KNOW THAT YOU MAY HAVE DOOMED HUNDREDS OF PEOPLE?
PLEASE... IF EVERYBODY WOULD JUST GO AWAY AND LEAVE ME ALONE...
GENTLEMEN, I THINK IT SAFEST NOT TO PURSUE THIS LINE OF THINKING...
15

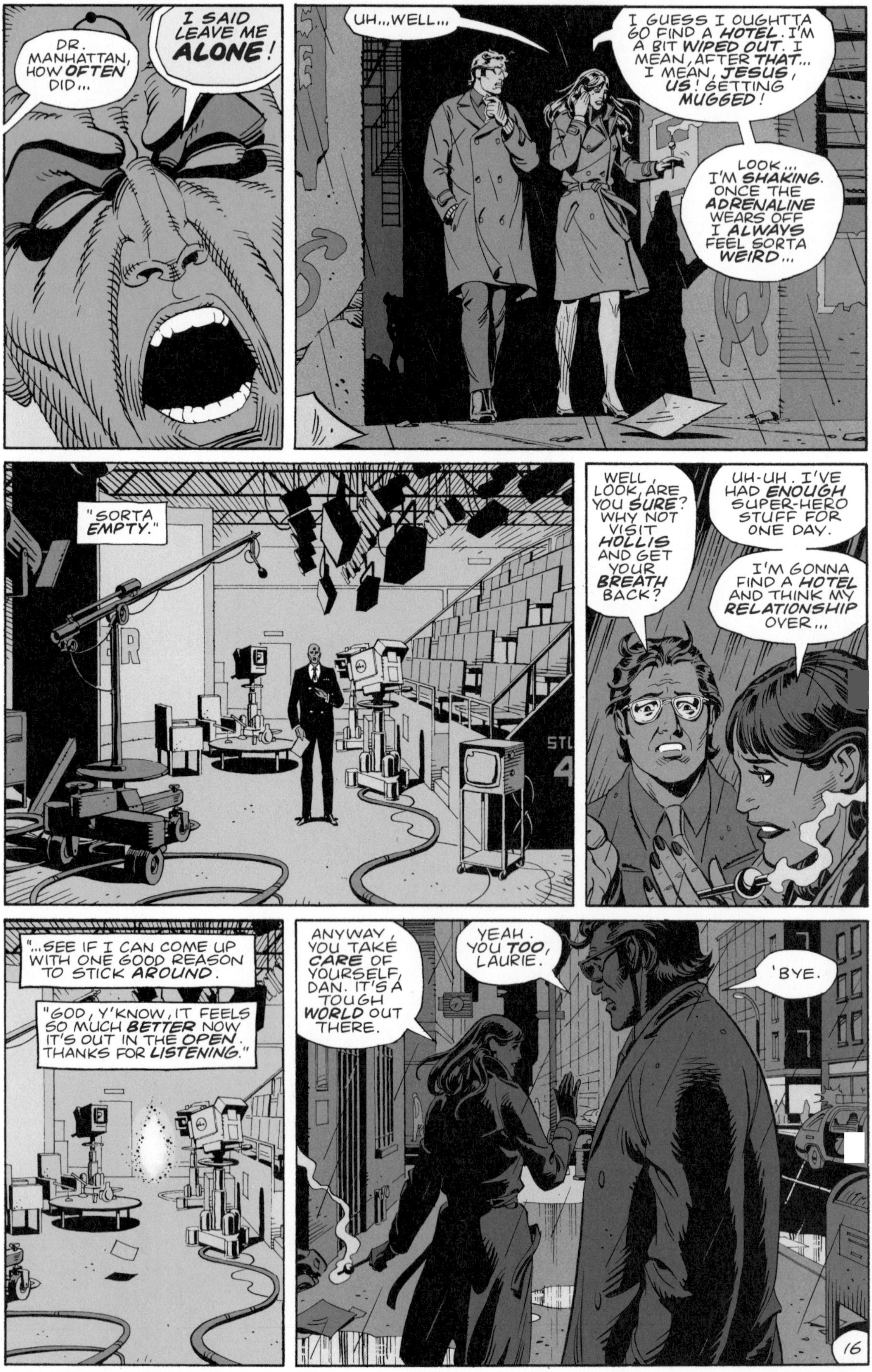

DR. MANHATTAN, HOW OFTEN DID...
I SAID LEAVE ME ALONE!
UH...WELL...
I GUESS I OUGHTTA GO FIND A HOTEL. I'M A BIT WIPED OUT. I MEAN, AFTER THAT... I MEAN, JESUS, US! GETTING MUGGED!
LOOK... I'M SHAKING. ONCE THE ADRENALINE WEARS OFF I ALWAYS FEEL SORTA WEIRD...
"SORTA EMPTY."
WELL, LOOK, ARE YOU SURE? WHY NOT VISIT HOLLIS AND GET YOUR BREATH BACK?
UH-UH. I'VE HAD ENOUGH SUPER-HERO STUFF FOR ONE DAY.
I'M GONNA FIND A HOTEL AND THINK MY RELATIONSHIP OVER...
"...SEE IF I CAN COME UP WITH ONE GOOD REASON TO STICK AROUND.
"GOD, Y'KNOW, IT FEELS SO MUCH BETTER NOW IT'S OUT IN THE OPEN. THANKS FOR LISTENING."
ANYWAY, YOU TAKE CARE OF YOURSELF, DAN. IT'S A TOUGH WORLD OUT THERE.
YEAH. YOU TOO, LAURIE.
'BYE.
16

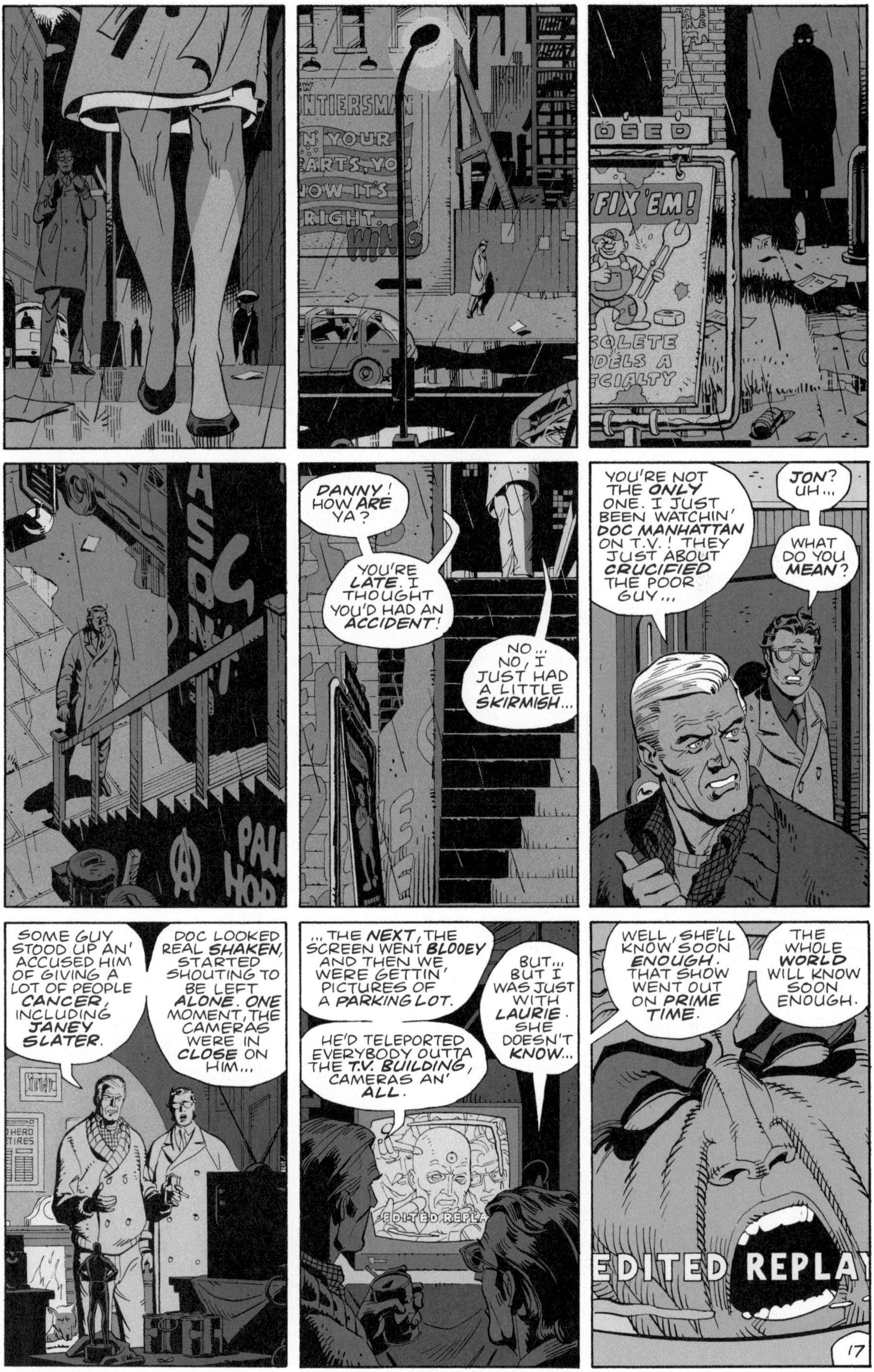
FIX 'EM!
DANNY! HOW ARE YA?
YOU'RE LATE. I THOUGHT YOU'D HAD AN ACCIDENT!
NO... NO, I JUST HAD A LITTLE SKIRMISH...
YOU'RE NOT THE ONLY ONE. I JUST BEEN WATCHIN' DOC MANHATTAN ON T.V.! THEY JUST ABOUT CRUCIFIED THE POOR GUY...
JON? UH...
WHAT DO YOU MEAN?
SOME GUY STOOD UP AN' ACCUSED HIM OF GIVING A LOT OF PEOPLE CANCER, INCLUDING JANEY SLATER.
DOC LOOKED REAL SHAKEN, STARTED SHOUTING TO BE LEFT ALONE. ONE MOMENT, THE CAMERAS WERE IN CLOSE ON HIM...
...THE NEXT, THE SCREEN WENT BLOOEY AND THEN WE WERE GETTIN' PICTURES OF A PARKING LOT.
HE'D TELEPORTED EVERYBODY OUTTA THE T.V. BUILDING, CAMERAS AN' ALL.
BUT... BUT I WAS JUST WITH LAURIE. SHE DOESN'T KNOW...
WELL, SHE'LL KNOW SOON ENOUGH. THAT SHOW WENT OUT ON PRIME TIME.
THE WHOLE WORLD WILL KNOW SOON ENOUGH.
17

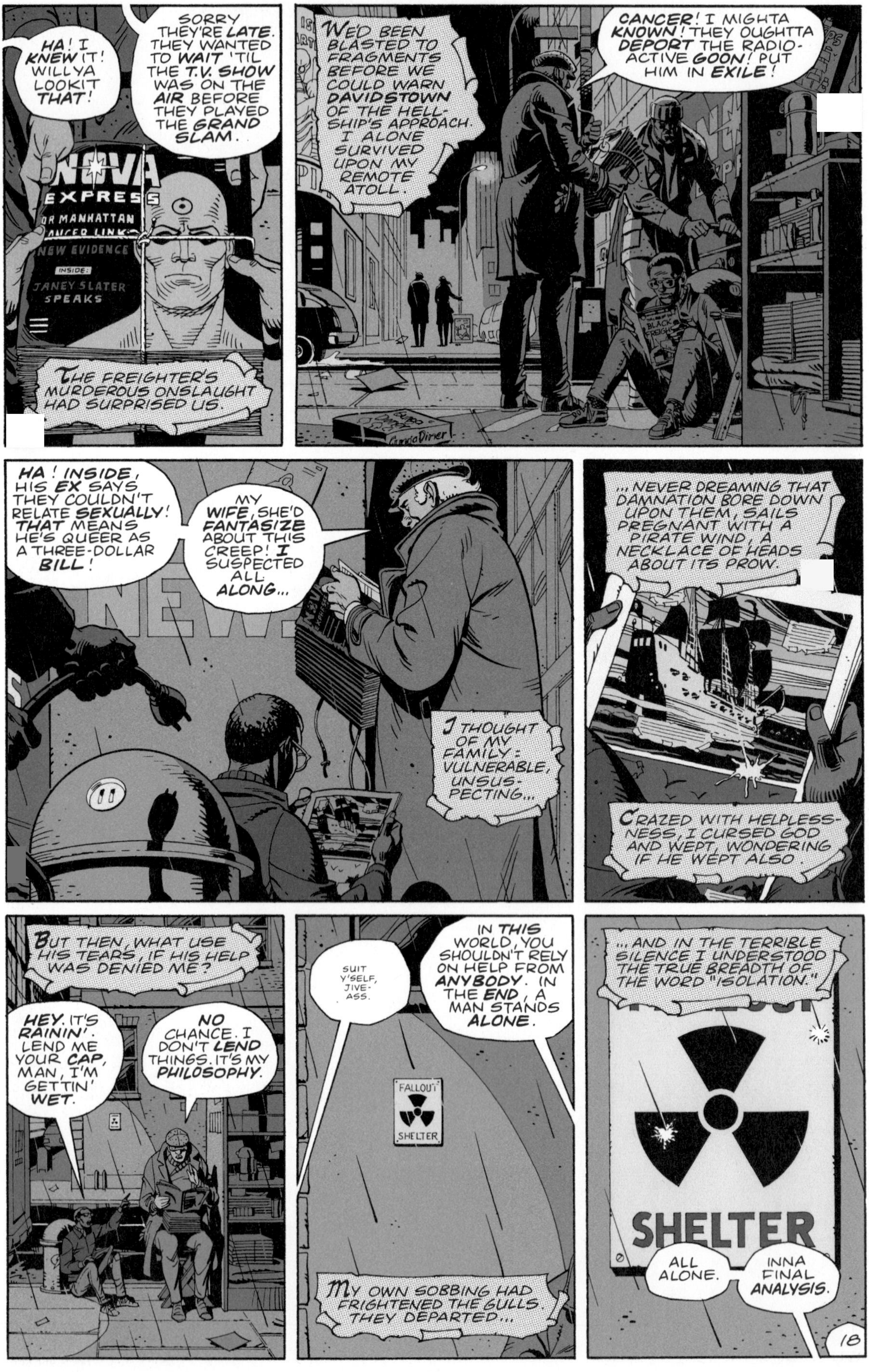
HA! I KNEW IT! WILLYA LOOKIT THAT!
SORRY THEY'RE LATE. THEY WANTED TO WAIT 'TIL THE T.V. SHOW WAS ON THE AIR BEFORE THEY PLAYED THE GRAND SLAM.
NOVA EXPRESS
DR MANHATTAN CANCER LINK: NEW EVIDENCE
INSIDE: JANEY SLATER SPEAKS
THE FREIGHTER'S MURDEROUS ONSLAUGHT HAD SURPRISED US.
WE'D BEEN BLASTED TO FRAGMENTS BEFORE WE COULD WARN DAVIDSTOWN OF THE HELL-SHIP'S APPROACH. I ALONE SURVIVED UPON MY REMOTE ATOLL.
CANCER! I MIGHTA KNOWN! THEY OUGHTTA DEPORT THE RADIO-ACTIVE GOON! PUT HIM IN EXILE!
HA! INSIDE, HIS EX SAYS THEY COULDN'T RELATE SEXUALLY! THAT MEANS HE'S QUEER AS A THREE-DOLLAR BILL!
MY WIFE, SHE'D FANTASIZE ABOUT THIS CREEP! I SUSPECTED ALL ALONG...
NEWS
I THOUGHT OF MY FAMILY: VULNERABLE, UNSUSPECTING...
...NEVER DREAMING THAT DAMNATION BORE DOWN UPON THEM, SAILS PREGNANT WITH A PIRATE WIND, A NECKLACE OF HEADS ABOUT ITS PROW.
CRAZED WITH HELPLESSNESS, I CURSED GOD AND WEPT, WONDERING IF HE WEPT ALSO.
BUT THEN, WHAT USE HIS TEARS, IF HIS HELP WAS DENIED ME?
HEY. IT'S RAININ'. LEND ME YOUR CAP, MAN, I'M GETTIN' WET.
NO CHANCE. I DON'T LEND THINGS. IT'S MY PHILOSOPHY.
SUIT Y'SELF, JIVE-ASS.
IN THIS WORLD, YOU SHOULDN'T RELY ON HELP FROM ANYBODY. IN THE END, A MAN STANDS ALONE.
FALLOUT SHELTER
MY OWN SOBBING HAD FRIGHTENED THE GULLS. THEY DEPARTED...
...AND IN THE TERRIBLE SILENCE I UNDERSTOOD THE TRUE BREADTH OF THE WORD "ISOLATION."
SHELTER
ALL ALONE.
INNA FINAL ANALYSIS.
18

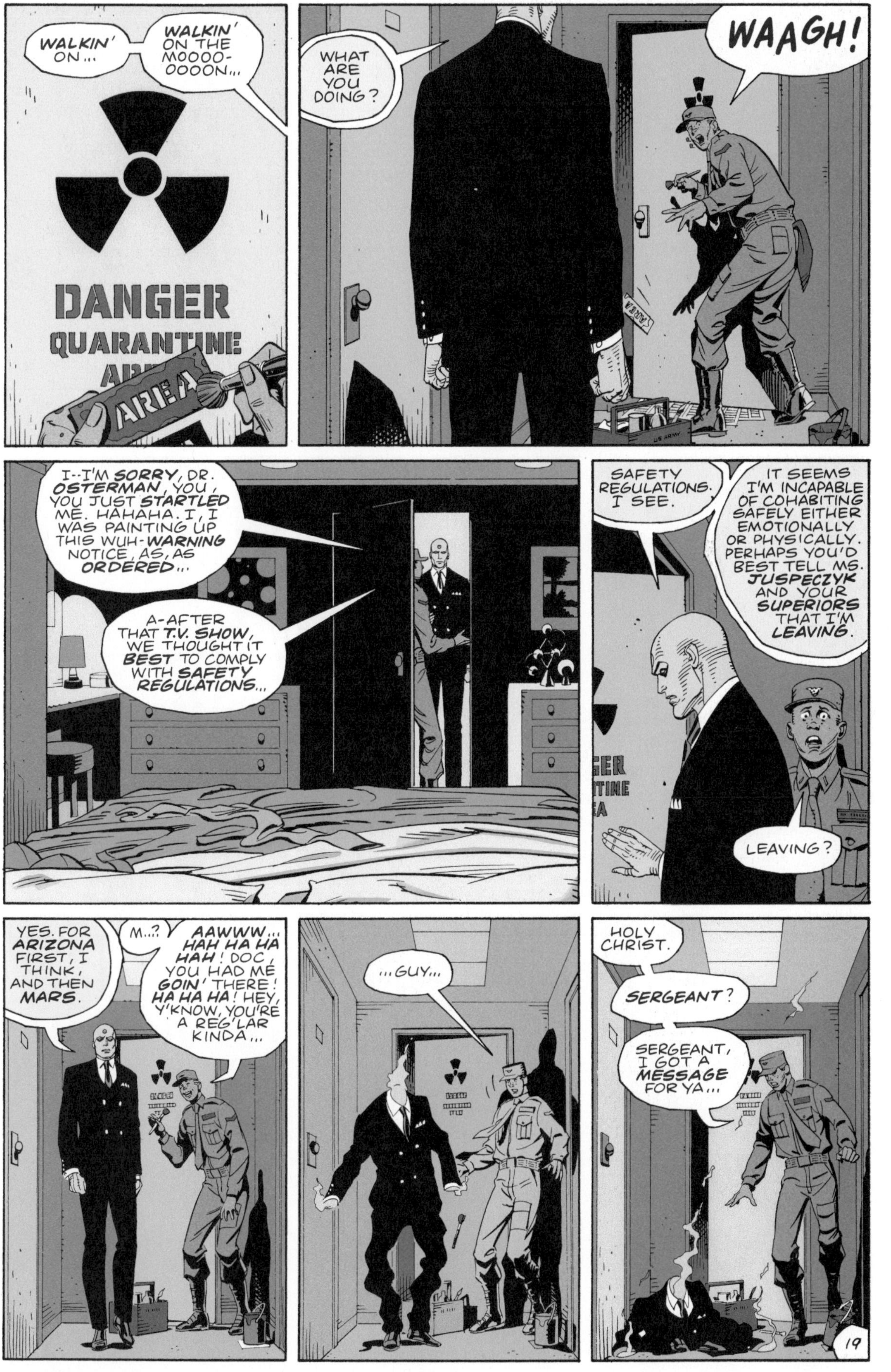
WALKIN' ON...
WALKIN' ON THE MOOOO-OOOON...
DANGER
QUARANTINE
AREA
WHAT ARE YOU DOING?
WAAGH!
U.S. ARMY
I--I'M SORRY, DR. OSTERMAN, YOU, YOU JUST STARTLED ME. HAHAHA. I, I WAS PAINTING UP THIS WUH-WARNING NOTICE, AS, AS ORDERED...
A-AFTER THAT T.V. SHOW, WE THOUGHT IT BEST TO COMPLY WITH SAFETY REGULATIONS...
SAFETY REGULATIONS. I SEE.
IT SEEMS I'M INCAPABLE OF COHABITING SAFELY EITHER EMOTIONALLY OR PHYSICALLY. PERHAPS YOU'D BEST TELL MS. JUSPECZYK AND YOUR SUPERIORS THAT I'M LEAVING.
LEAVING?
YES. FOR ARIZONA FIRST, I THINK, AND THEN MARS.
M...?
AAWWW... HAH HA HA HAH! DOC, YOU HAD ME GOIN' THERE! HA HA HA! HEY, Y'KNOW, YOU'RE A REG'LAR KINDA...
...GUY...
HOLY CHRIST.
SERGEANT?
SERGEANT, I GOT A MESSAGE FOR YA...
19

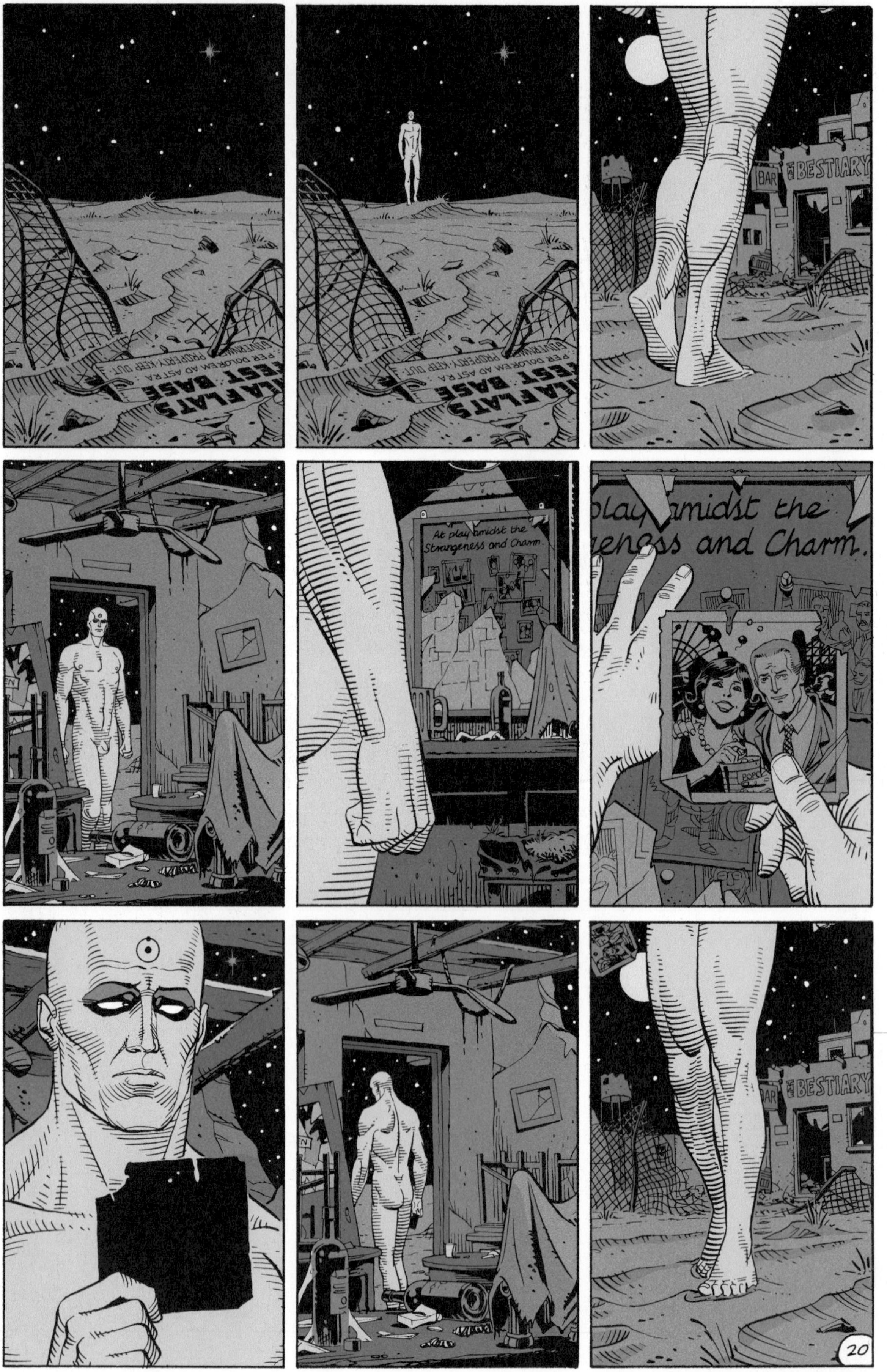
PER DOLOREM AD ASTRA
PROPERTY-KEEP OUT
BAR
BESTIARY
At play amidst the Strangeness and Charm.
20

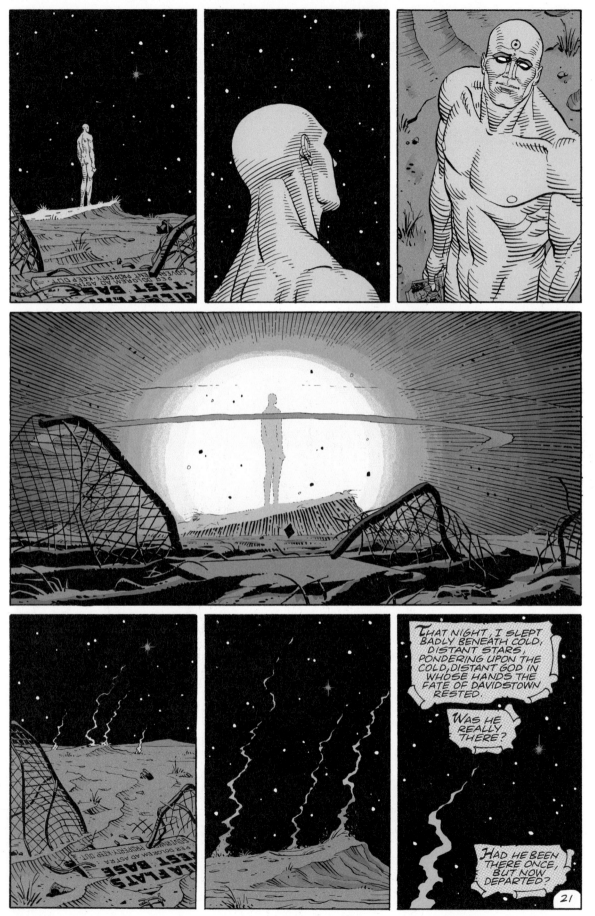

THAT NIGHT, I SLEPT BADLY BENEATH COLD, DISTANT STARS, PONDERING UPON THE COLD, DISTANT GOD IN WHOSE HANDS THE FATE OF DAVIDSTOWN RESTED.

WAS HE REALLY THERE?

HAD HE BEEN THERE ONCE, BUT NOW DEPARTED?

21

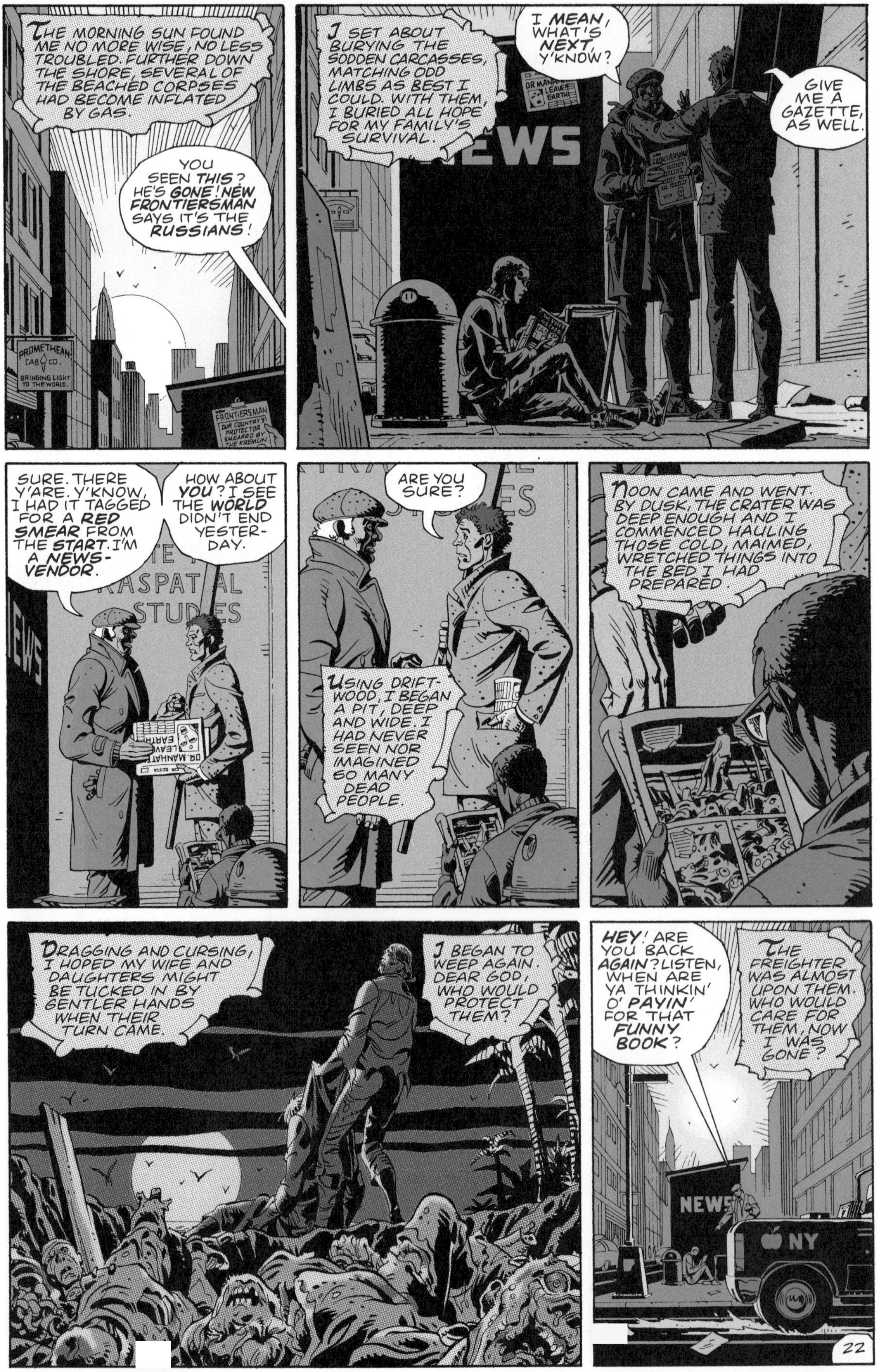
THE MORNING SUN FOUND ME NO MORE WISE, NO LESS TROUBLED. FURTHER DOWN THE SHORE, SEVERAL OF THE BEACHED CORPSES HAD BECOME INFLATED BY GAS.
YOU SEEN THIS? HE'S GONE! NEW FRONTIERSMAN SAYS IT'S THE RUSSIANS!
PROMETHEAN CAB CO. BRINGING LIGHT TO THE WORLD.
NEW FRONTIERSMAN OUR COUNTRY'S PROTECTOR SMEARED BY THE KREMLIN.
I SET ABOUT BURYING THE SODDEN CARCASSES, MATCHING ODD LIMBS AS BEST I COULD. WITH THEM, I BURIED ALL HOPE FOR MY FAMILY'S SURVIVAL.
I MEAN, WHAT'S NEXT, Y'KNOW?
GIVE ME A GAZETTE, AS WELL.
NEWS
SURE. THERE Y'ARE. Y'KNOW, I HAD IT TAGGED FOR A RED SMEAR FROM THE START. I'M A NEWS-VENDOR.
HOW ABOUT YOU? I SEE THE WORLD DIDN'T END YESTER-DAY.
ARE YOU SURE?
USING DRIFT-WOOD, I BEGAN A PIT, DEEP AND WIDE. I HAD NEVER SEEN NOR IMAGINED SO MANY DEAD PEOPLE.
NOON CAME AND WENT. BY DUSK, THE CRATER WAS DEEP ENOUGH AND I COMMENCED HAULING THOSE COLD, MAIMED, WRETCHED THINGS INTO THE BED I HAD PREPARED.
DRAGGING AND CURSING, I HOPED MY WIFE AND DAUGHTERS MIGHT BE TUCKED IN BY GENTLER HANDS WHEN THEIR TURN CAME.
I BEGAN TO WEEP AGAIN. DEAR GOD, WHO WOULD PROTECT THEM?
HEY! ARE YOU BACK AGAIN? LISTEN, WHEN ARE YA THINKIN' O' PAYIN' FOR THAT FUNNY BOOK?
THE FREIGHTER WAS ALMOST UPON THEM. WHO WOULD CARE FOR THEM, NOW I WAS GONE?
NEWS
NY
22

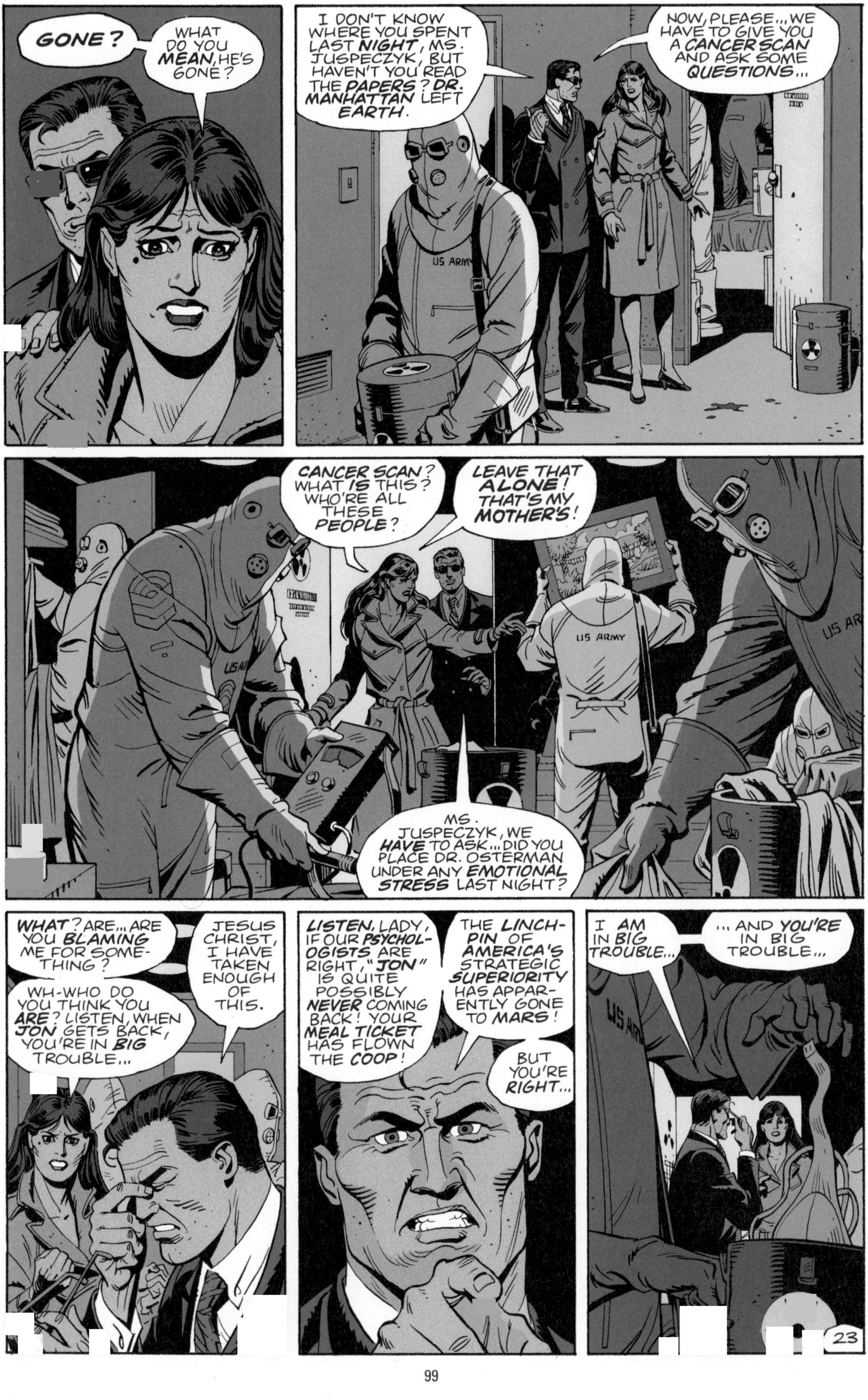
GONE?
WHAT DO YOU MEAN, HE'S GONE?
I DON'T KNOW WHERE YOU SPENT LAST NIGHT, MS. JUSPECZYK, BUT HAVEN'T YOU READ THE PAPERS? DR. MANHATTAN LEFT EARTH.
NOW, PLEASE... WE HAVE TO GIVE YOU A CANCER SCAN AND ASK SOME QUESTIONS...
US ARMY
CANCER SCAN? WHAT IS THIS? WHO'RE ALL THESE PEOPLE?
LEAVE THAT ALONE! THAT'S MY MOTHER'S!
US ARMY
MS. JUSPECZYK, WE HAVE TO ASK... DID YOU PLACE DR. OSTERMAN UNDER ANY EMOTIONAL STRESS LAST NIGHT?
WHAT? ARE... ARE YOU BLAMING ME FOR SOMETHING?
WH-WHO DO YOU THINK YOU ARE? LISTEN, WHEN JON GETS BACK, YOU'RE IN BIG TROUBLE...
JESUS CHRIST, I HAVE TAKEN ENOUGH OF THIS.
LISTEN, LADY, IF OUR PSYCHOLOGISTS ARE RIGHT, "JON" IS QUITE POSSIBLY NEVER COMING BACK! YOUR MEAL TICKET HAS FLOWN THE COOP!
THE LINCHPIN OF AMERICA'S STRATEGIC SUPERIORITY HAS APPARENTLY GONE TO MARS!
BUT YOU'RE RIGHT...
I AM IN BIG TROUBLE...
...AND YOU'RE IN BIG TROUBLE...
23

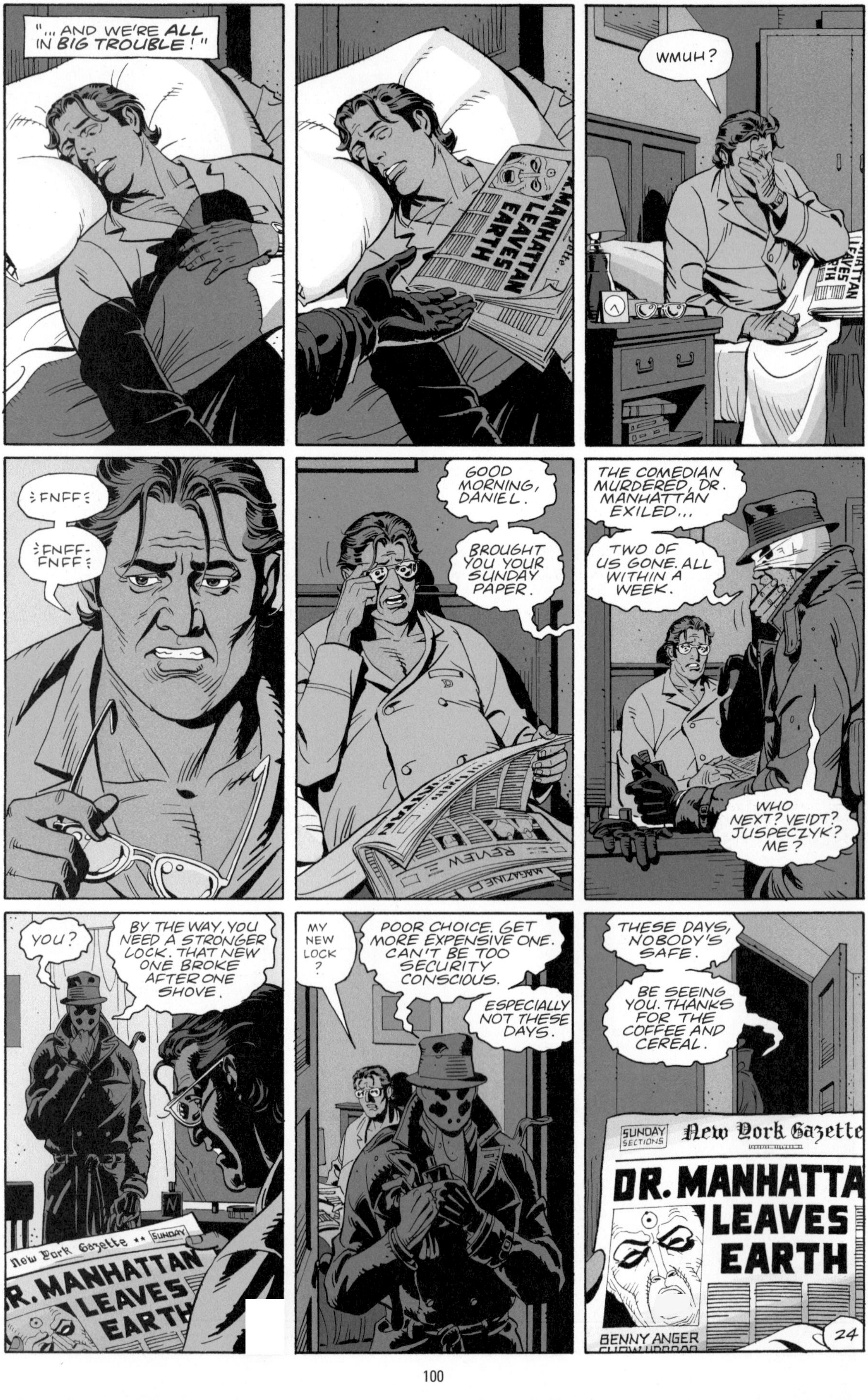
"... AND WE'RE ALL IN BIG TROUBLE!"
DR. MANHATTAN LEAVES EARTH
WMUH?
FNFF
FNFF-FNFF
GOOD MORNING, DANIEL.
BROUGHT YOU YOUR SUNDAY PAPER.
REVIEW
MAGAZINE
THE COMEDIAN MURDERED, DR. MANHATTAN EXILED...
TWO OF US GONE. ALL WITHIN A WEEK.
WHO NEXT? VEIDT? JUSPECZYK? ME?
YOU?
BY THE WAY, YOU NEED A STRONGER LOCK. THAT NEW ONE BROKE AFTER ONE SHOVE.
New York Gazette
SUNDAY
DR. MANHATTAN LEAVES EARTH
MY NEW LOCK?
POOR CHOICE. GET MORE EXPENSIVE ONE. CAN'T BE TOO SECURITY CONSCIOUS.
ESPECIALLY NOT THESE DAYS.
THESE DAYS, NOBODY'S SAFE.
BE SEEING YOU. THANKS FOR THE COFFEE AND CEREAL.
SUNDAY SECTIONS
New York Gazette
DR. MANHATTA
LEAVES EARTH
BENNY ANGER
24

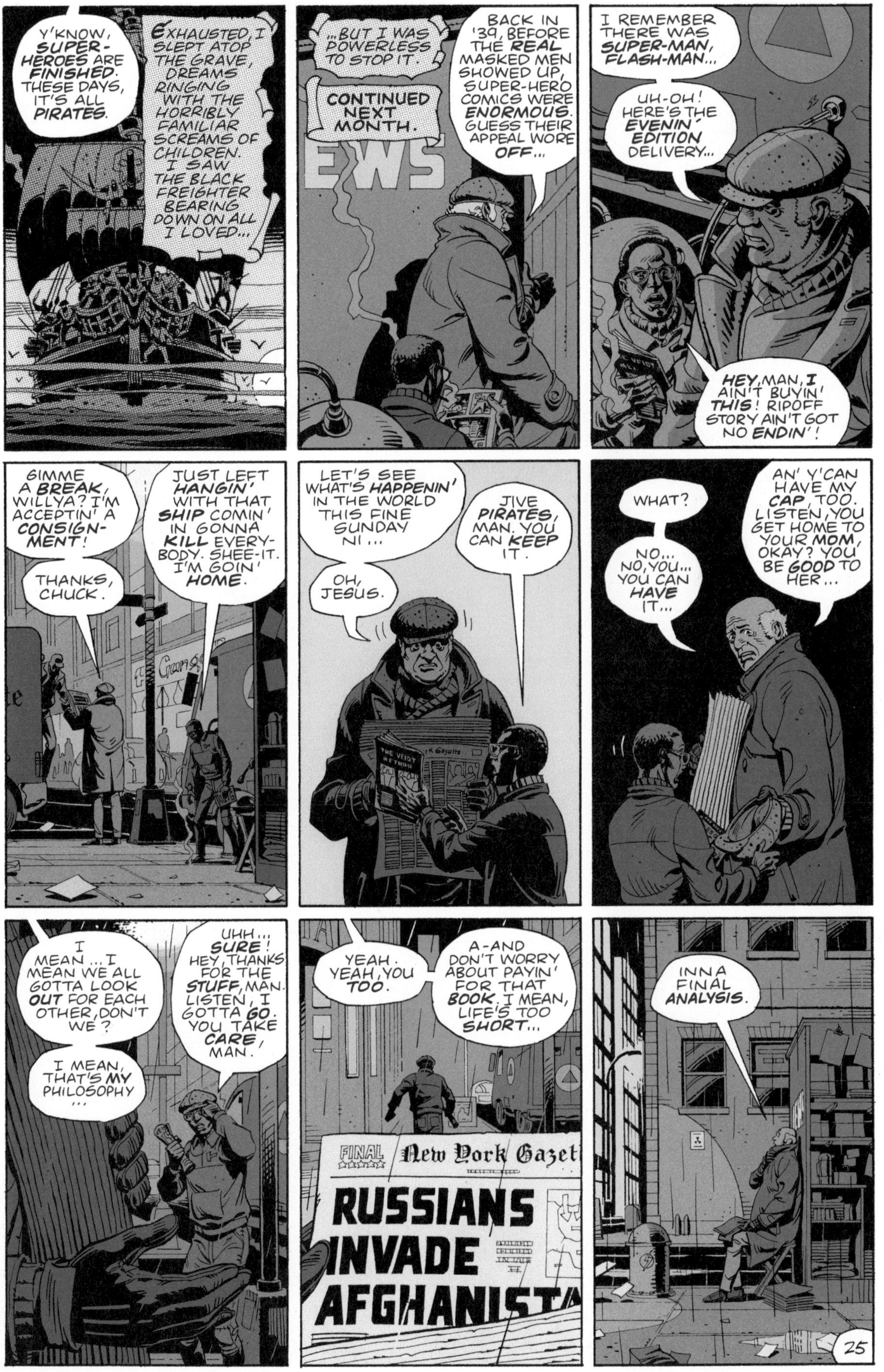
Y'KNOW, SUPER-HEROES ARE FINISHED. THESE DAYS, IT'S ALL PIRATES.
EXHAUSTED, I SLEPT ATOP THE GRAVE, DREAMS RINGING WITH THE HORRIBLY FAMILIAR SCREAMS OF CHILDREN. I SAW THE BLACK FREIGHTER BEARING DOWN ON ALL I LOVED...
...BUT I WAS POWERLESS TO STOP IT.
CONTINUED NEXT MONTH.
BACK IN '39, BEFORE THE REAL MASKED MEN SHOWED UP, SUPER-HERO COMICS WERE ENORMOUS. GUESS THEIR APPEAL WORE OFF...
EWS
I REMEMBER THERE WAS SUPER-MAN, FLASH-MAN...
UH-OH! HERE'S THE EVENIN' EDITION DELIVERY...
HEY, MAN, I AIN'T BUYIN' THIS! RIPOFF STORY AIN'T GOT NO ENDIN'!
GIMME A BREAK, WILLYA? I'M ACCEPTIN' A CONSIGNMENT!
THANKS, CHUCK.
JUST LEFT HANGIN' WITH THAT SHIP COMIN' IN GONNA KILL EVERY-BODY. SHEE-IT. I'M GOIN' HOME.
LET'S SEE WHAT'S HAPPENIN' IN THE WORLD THIS FINE SUNDAY NI...
OH, JESUS.
JIVE PIRATES, MAN. YOU CAN KEEP IT.
THE VEIDT METHOD
WHAT?
NO... NO, YOU... YOU CAN HAVE IT...
AN' Y'CAN HAVE MY CAP, TOO. LISTEN, YOU GET HOME TO YOUR MOM, OKAY? YOU BE GOOD TO HER...
I MEAN... I MEAN WE ALL GOTTA LOOK OUT FOR EACH OTHER, DON'T WE?
I MEAN, THAT'S MY PHILOSOPHY...
UHH... SURE! HEY, THANKS FOR THE STUFF, MAN. LISTEN, I GOTTA GO. YOU TAKE CARE, MAN.
YEAH. YEAH, YOU TOO.
A-AND DON'T WORRY ABOUT PAYIN' FOR THAT BOOK. I MEAN, LIFE'S TOO SHORT...
FINAL
New York Gazet
RUSSIANS INVADE AFGHANISTA
INNA FINAL ANALYSIS.
25

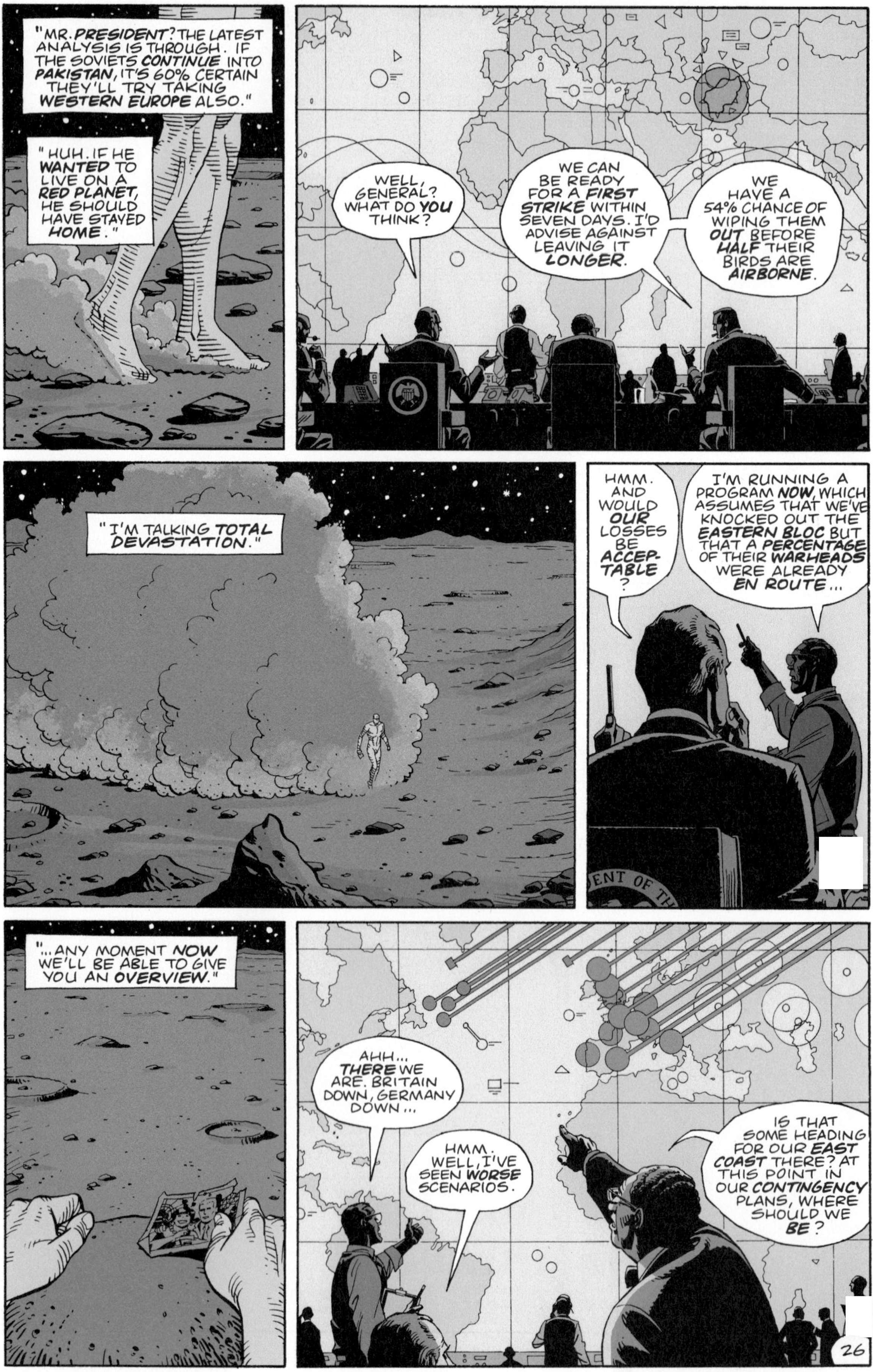
"MR. PRESIDENT? THE LATEST ANALYSIS IS THROUGH. IF THE SOVIETS CONTINUE INTO PAKISTAN, IT'S 60% CERTAIN THEY'LL TRY TAKING WESTERN EUROPE ALSO."
"HUH. IF HE WANTED TO LIVE ON A RED PLANET, HE SHOULD HAVE STAYED HOME."
WELL, GENERAL? WHAT DO YOU THINK?
WE CAN BE READY FOR A FIRST STRIKE WITHIN SEVEN DAYS. I'D ADVISE AGAINST LEAVING IT LONGER.
WE HAVE A 54% CHANCE OF WIPING THEM OUT BEFORE HALF THEIR BIRDS ARE AIRBORNE.
"I'M TALKING TOTAL DEVASTATION."
HMM. AND WOULD OUR LOSSES BE ACCEP-TABLE?
I'M RUNNING A PROGRAM NOW, WHICH ASSUMES THAT WE'VE KNOCKED OUT THE EASTERN BLOC BUT THAT A PERCENTAGE OF THEIR WARHEADS WERE ALREADY EN ROUTE...
"...ANY MOMENT NOW WE'LL BE ABLE TO GIVE YOU AN OVERVIEW."
AHH... THERE WE ARE. BRITAIN DOWN, GERMANY DOWN...
HMM. WELL, I'VE SEEN WORSE SCENARIOS.
IS THAT SOME HEADING FOR OUR EAST COAST THERE? AT THIS POINT IN OUR CONTINGENCY PLANS, WHERE SHOULD WE BE?
26

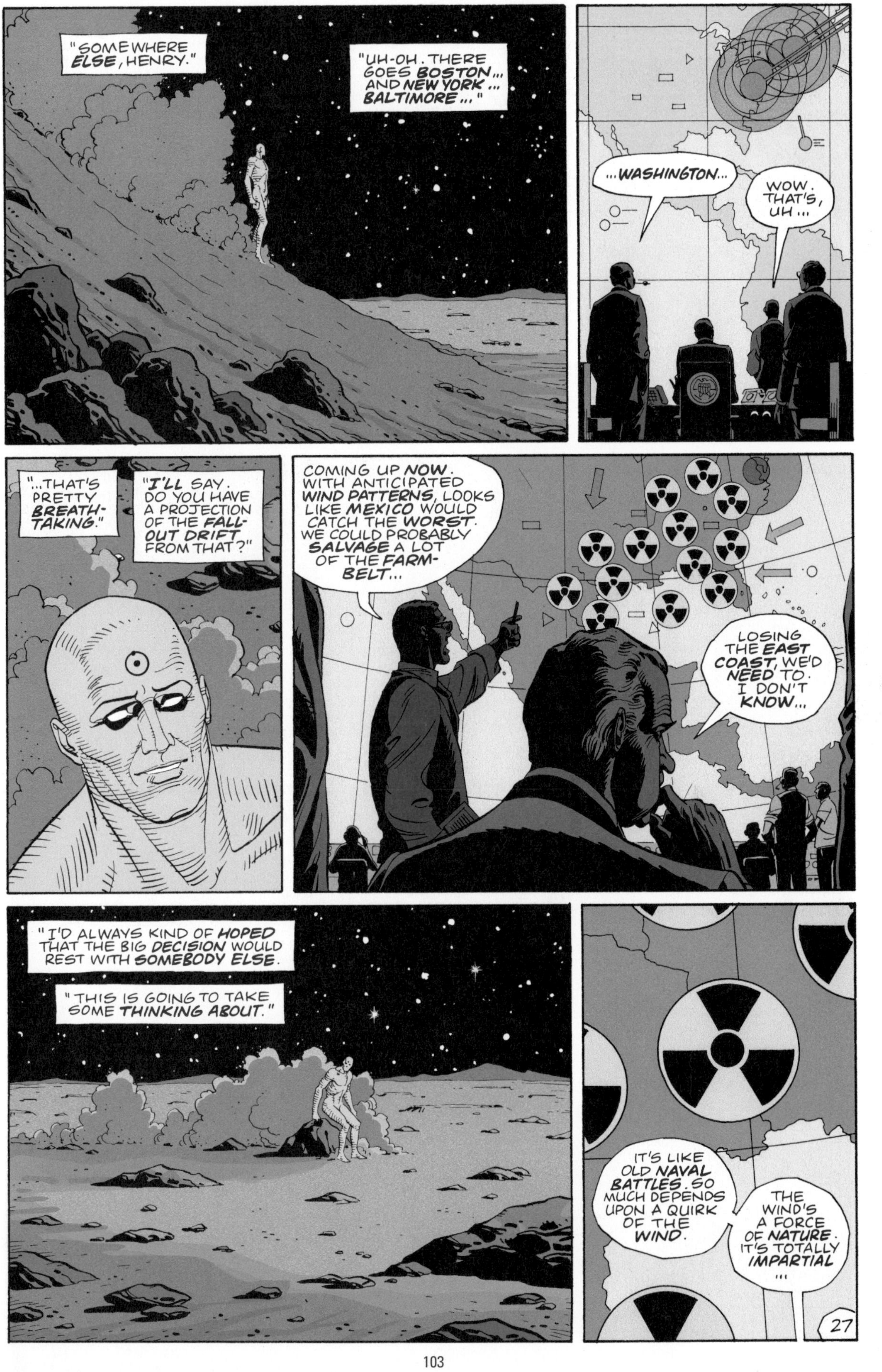
"SOMEWHERE ELSE, HENRY."
"UH-OH. THERE GOES BOSTON... AND NEW YORK... BALTIMORE..."
...WASHINGTON...
WOW. THAT'S, UH...
"...THAT'S PRETTY BREATH-TAKING."
"I'LL SAY. DO YOU HAVE A PROJECTION OF THE FALL-OUT DRIFT FROM THAT?"
COMING UP NOW. WITH ANTICIPATED WIND PATTERNS, LOOKS LIKE MEXICO WOULD CATCH THE WORST. WE COULD PROBABLY SALVAGE A LOT OF THE FARM-BELT...
LOSING THE EAST COAST, WE'D NEED TO. I DON'T KNOW...
"I'D ALWAYS KIND OF HOPED THAT THE BIG DECISION WOULD REST WITH SOMEBODY ELSE.
"THIS IS GOING TO TAKE SOME THINKING ABOUT."
IT'S LIKE OLD NAVAL BATTLES. SO MUCH DEPENDS UPON A QUIRK OF THE WIND.
THE WIND'S A FORCE OF NATURE. IT'S TOTALLY IMPARTIAL...
27

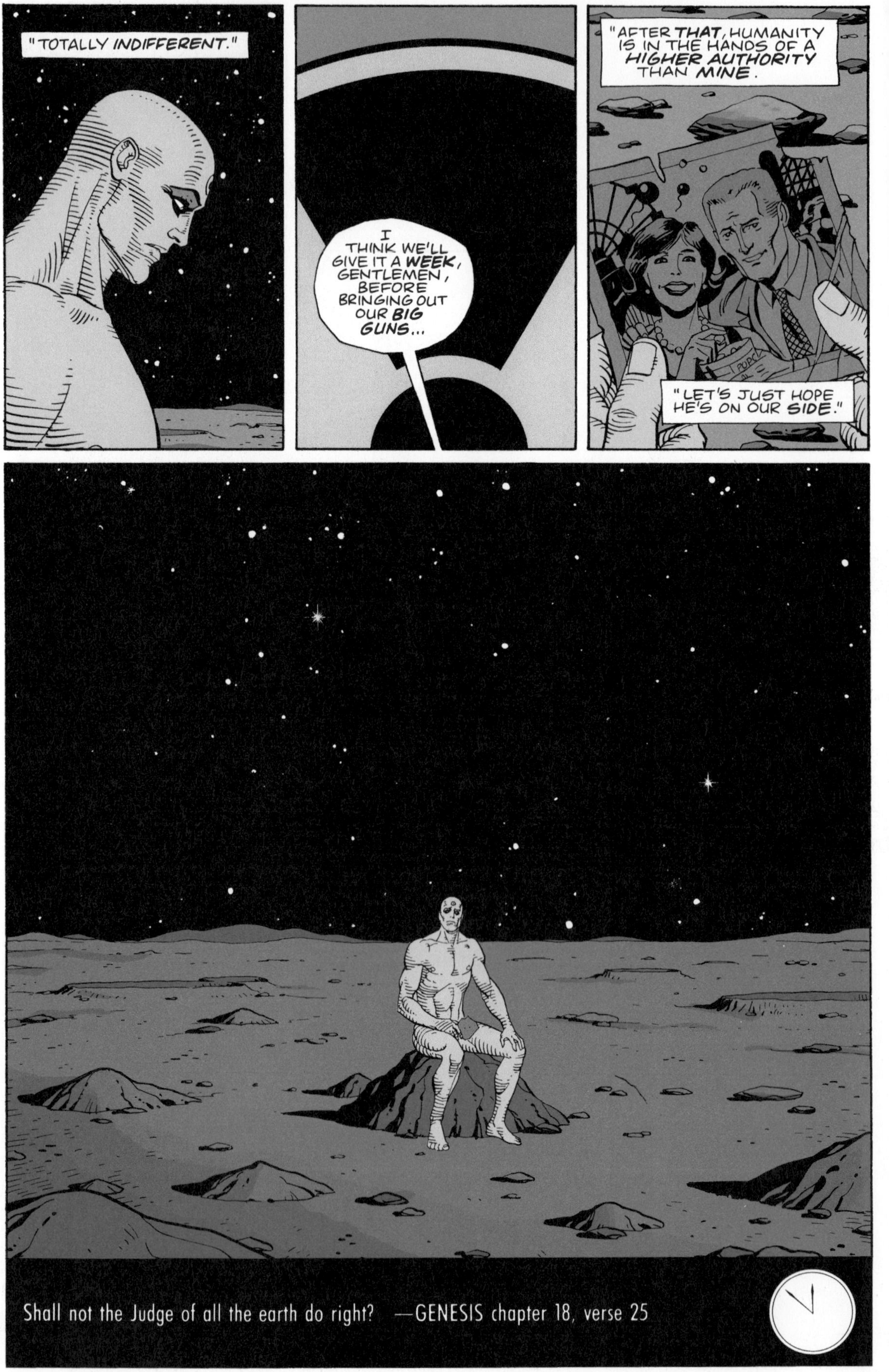
"TOTALLY INDIFFERENT."
I THINK WE'LL GIVE IT A WEEK, GENTLEMEN, BEFORE BRINGING OUT OUR BIG GUNS...
"AFTER THAT, HUMANITY IS IN THE HANDS OF A HIGHER AUTHORITY THAN MINE.
"LET'S JUST HOPE HE'S ON OUR SIDE."
Shall not the Judge of all the earth do right? —GENESIS chapter 18, verse 25

UNDER THE HOOD

Presented here are the excerpts from UNDER THE HOOD. In this next chapter Hollis Mason discusses the traumas of the 1950s and the emergence of the new super-heroes. Reprinted with permission of the author.

V.

The Minutemen didn't get to usher in the 1950s with a Christmas celebration the way we'd ushered in the '40s, and perhaps that's appropriate. The decade following the disbanding of the group was cold and bleak, both for me in particular and for masked adventurers in general. Plus, it seemed to go on forever.

I think the worst thing was the belated realization of just how much a fad we'd always been, something to fill the dead columns of the newspapers right alongside the Hula Hoop and the Jitterbug. Ever since Sally Jupiter married her manager, his tireless, shrewd efforts as a publicist had been noticeably absent. He'd recognized that the day of the costumed hero was over — even though we hadn't — and he'd gotten out while the getting was good. Consequently, we found our exploits being reported less and less frequently. When they were reported, the tone

1947: Sally Jupiter marries Laurence Schexnayder. Can you spot the famous faces in the crowd?

was often derisive. I can remember a lot of hooded vigilante jokes coming into circulation during the early fifties. The mildest was one that suggested we were called The Minutemen due to our performance in the bedroom. There were an awful lot of bright blue gags about Sally Jupiter. I know, because she told me most of them herself the last time I saw her.

Sally had a baby girl named Laurel Jane in 1949, and it seemed to be right about then that her marital problems started. These were widely discussed, so I don't think I need repeat them here. Suffice it to say that the marriage ended in 1956, and since then Sally has done a first rate job of bringing her daughter up into a bright, spunky youngster that any mother could be proud of.

The thing about that particular decade is that things first started getting *serious* then. I remember thinking at the time that it was funny how the more serious things got, the better the Comedian seemed to do. Out of the whole bunch of us, he was the only one who was still right up there on the front pages, still making the occasional headline. On the strength of his military work he had good government connections, and it often seemed as if he was being groomed into some sort of patriotic symbol. At the height of the McCarthy era, nobody had any doubts about where the Comedian's feet were planted politically.

That was more than could be said for the rest of us. We all had to testify before the House UnAmerican Activities Committee, and were all forced to reveal our true identities to one of its representatives. Galling though this was, it didn't present any immediate problems for most of us. With Captain Metropolis having such an outstanding military record and with my own service in the police force, we both were more or less cleared of suspicion right away. Mothman met with more difficulty, mostly because of some left-wing friends he'd cultivated during his student days. He was eventually cleared, but the investigations were both lengthy and ruthless, and I think that the pressure he was under at that time prompted the beginnings of the drinking problem that has contributed so much to his later mental ill-health.

Only Hooded Justice refused to testify, on the grounds that he was not prepared to reveal his true identity to anyone. When pressed, he simply vanished...or at least that's how it seemed. Vanishing is no big problem when you're a costumed hero — you just take your costume off. It seemed quite likely that Hooded Justice had simply chosen to retire rather than reveal his identity, which the authorities seemed perfectly happy with.

The only detail concerning the disappearance of America's first masked adventurer that still nags at me was trivial, and maybe not even connected at all; it was brought up in an article that appeared in *The New Frontiersman*, almost a year after Hooded Justice vanished. The author mentioned the disappearance of a well known circus strongman of the day named Rolf Müller, who had quit his job at the height of the Senate Subcommittee hearings. Three months later, a badly decomposed body that was tentatively identified as Müller's was pulled from the sea after being washed up on the coast of Boston. Müller, assuming the

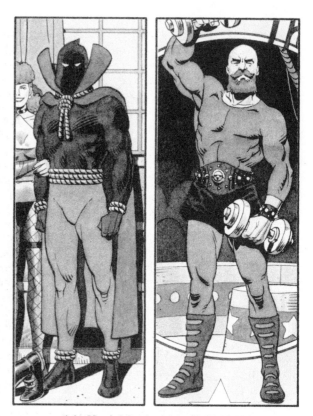

*(left) Hooded Justice (right) Rolf Müller.
Were they the same man?*

body actually was that of the renowned weightlifter, had been shot through the head. The inference of the article was that Müller, whose family was East German, had gone on the run for fear of being uncovered while the Communist witch hunts were at their most feverish. The piece also implied that Müller had probably been executed by his own Red superiors.

I always wondered about that. Müller disappeared at almost exactly the same time as Hooded Justice was last seen, and the two men had corresponding builds. Whether the body washed up on that Boston shoreline belonged to Müller or not, neither he nor Hooded Justice were ever seen or heard from again. Were they the same man? If they were, were they really dead? If they were dead, who killed them? Was Hooded Justice really working for the Reds? I don't know. Real life is messy, inconsistent, and it's seldom when anything ever really gets resolved. It's taken me a long time to realize that.

One of the big problems that faced costumed heroes at the time was the absence of costumed criminals of any real note. I don't think any of us realized how much we needed those goons until they started to thin out. You see, if you're the only one who'd bothered to turn up for a free-for-all in costume, you tended to look kind of stupid. If the bad guys joined in as well, it wasn't so bad, but without them it was always sort of embarrassing. There had never been as many costumed criminals as heroes, but with the end of the 1940s the trend grew much more pronounced.

Most of the crooks turned in their costumes along with their criminal careers, but some just opted for a less extroverted and more profitable approach. The new breed of villains, despite their often colorful names, were mostly ordinary men in business suits who ran drug and prostitution rackets. That's not to say they didn't cause as much trouble...far from it; I just mean that they weren't as much fun to fight. All the cases I ended up investigating during the '50s seemed sordid and depressing and quite often blood-chillingly horrible. I don't know what it was...there just seemed to be a sort of bleak, uneasy feeling in the air. It was as if some essential element of our lives, of all our lives, was vanishing before we knew entirely what it was. I don't think I could really describe it completely except maybe to somebody who remembered the terrific elation we all felt after the war: we felt that we'd taken the worst that the 20th century could throw at us and stood our ground. We felt as if we'd really won a hard-earned age of peace and prosperity that would see us well into the year 2000. This optimism lasted all through the '40s and the early '50s, but by the middle of that latter decade it was starting to wear thin, and there was a sort of ominous feeling in the air.

Partly it was the beatniks, the jazz musicians and the poets openly condemning American values whenever they opened their mouths. Partly it was Elvis Presley and the whole Rock 'n' Roll boom. Had we fought a war for our country so that our daughters could scream and swoon over young men who looked like *this*, who sounded like *that?* With all these sudden social upheavals just when we thought we'd gotten everything straight, it was impossible to live through the 1950s without a sense of impending catastrophe bearing implacably down upon the whole country, the whole world. Some people thought it was war and others thought it was flying saucers, but those things weren't really what was bearing down upon us. What was bearing down upon us was the 1960s.

The '60s, along with the mini-skirt and the Beatles, brought one thing to the world that was significant above all others — its name was Dr. Manhattan. The arrival of Dr. Manhattan would make the terms "masked hero" and "costumed adventurer" as obsolete as the persons they described. A new phrase had entered the American language, just as a new and almost terrifying concept had entered its consciousness. It was the dawn of the Super-Hero.

Manhattan's existence was announced to the world in the March of 1960, and I don't think there can have been anybody on the planet who didn't feel that same strange jumble of emotions when they heard the news. Foremost amongst this assortment of sensations was disbelief. The idea of a being who could walk through walls, move from one place to another without covering the intervening distance and re-arrange things completely with a single thought was flat-out impossible. On the other hand, the people presenting this news to us were our own government. The notion that they might simply have made it up was equally improbable, and in the face of this contradiction, it became gradually easier to accept the dream-like unreality of those first newsreel images: a blue man melting a tank with a wave of his hand; the fragments of a disassembled rifle floating there eerily in the air with nobody touching them. Once accepted as reality, however, such things became no easier to digest. If you accept that floating rifle parts are real you also have to somehow accept that everything you've ever known to be a fact is probably untrue. That peculiar unease is something that most of us have learned to live with over the years, but it's still there.

The other emotions that accompanied the announcement were perhaps harder to identify and pin down. There was a certain elation...it felt as if Santa Claus had suddenly turned out to be real after all. Coupled with and complementary to this was a terrible and uneven sense of fear and uncertainty. While this was hard to define precisely, if I had to boil it down into three words, those words would be, "We've been replaced." I'm not just talking about the non-powered costumed hero fraternity here, you understand, although Dr. Manhattan's appearance was certainly one of the factors that led to my own increased feelings of obsolescence and my eventual decision to quit the hero business altogether. You see, while masked vigilantes had certainly been made obsolete, so in a sense had every other living organism upon the planet. I don't think that society has fully realized yet just exactly what Dr. Manhattan's arrival means; how much it's likely to change every detail of our lives.

Although Dr. Manhattan was the most prominent by far of the 'New Breed' of costumed heroes, he wasn't quite the first nor by any means the last. In the closing months of 1958, the papers mentioned that a major opium and heroin smuggling racket had been busted by a young adventurer named Ozymandias, who seemed to have quickly gained a reputation amongst the criminal fraternity for his boundless and implacable intelligence, not to mention a large degree of athletic prowess.

I met both Dr. Manhattan and Ozymandias for the first time at a charity event in the June of 1960. Ozymandias seemed to be a nice young fellow, although I personally found Dr. Manhattan to be a little distant. Maybe that was more my fault than his, though, since I found it very difficult to feel easy around the guy, even once I'd got used to the shock of his physical presence. It's a strange feeling...the first time you meet him your brain wants to scream, blow a fuse and shut itself down immediately, refusing to accept that he exists. This lasts for a couple of minutes, at which time he's still there and hasn't gone away, and in the end you just accept him because he's standing there and talking to you and after a while it almost seems normal.

Almost.

Anyway, at that charity event...I think it was Red Cross relief for the ongoing famine in India...a lot of things became apparent to me. Looking around at the other adventurers there, I wasn't happy with what I saw: The Comedian was there, imposing his overbearing personality and his obnoxious cigar smoke upon anyone within reach. Mothman was there, a glass in one hand, slurring his words and letting his sentences trail off into incoherence. Captain Metropolis was there, his paunch starting to show despite a strict regimen of Canadian Air Force Exercises. Finally, leaving the two younger heroes aside for a moment, there was me: Forty-six years old and starting to feel it, still trying to cut it in the company of guys who could level a mountain by snapping their fingers. I think it was when that moment of self insight hit me that I first decided to finally hang up my mask and get myself a proper job. I'd been about due to retire from the police force for some time, and I started wondering about what I wanted to do now that the thrill of adventure had finally started to pale. Looking back over my life, I tried to work out what I'd been doing during my existence's happier stretches, in order to form a basis for my future contentment.

After much deliberation, I concluded that I'd never been happier than when helping my dad beat some sense into an obstinate engine down at Moe Vernon's yard. After a life of crime-fighting, no notion seemed sweeter to me than that of spending my autumn years contentedly making dead vehicles run again in the confines of my own auto repair shop.

In the May of this year, 1962, that's exactly what I opted to do.

I retired. To mend cars. Probably for the rest of my life. As I see it, part of the art of being a hero is knowing when you don't need to be one anymore, realizing that the game has changed and that the stakes are different and that there isn't necessarily a place for you in this strange new pantheon of extraordinary people. The world has moved on, and I'm content to watch it from my armchair with a beer by my side and the smell of fresh oil still on my fingers.

Part of my contentment comes from knowing that there have maybe been some overall consequence of my twenty-three years behind the mask. This knowledge came to me in the shape of a letter from a young man whose name I'm not at liberty to reveal. He told me of his great admiration for my efforts as Nite Owl and proposed that since I'd retired and would no longer be using the name, perhaps he could borrow it since he intended to follow my example and become a crime-fighter. I've visited his home since then and seen some of the fabulous technology he intends to bring to bear on the war against crime. I was certainly far too impressed to refuse him the use of what I'd always thought was a dumb name to begin with, so by the time this sees print there may well be a new Nite Owl patrolling the streets of New York. Also, Sally Jupiter tells me that as soon as little Laurie's old enough she wants to be a super-heroine just like her mom, so who knows? It seems as if from being a novelty nine-day wonder, the super-hero has become a part of American life. It's here to stay.

For better, or for worse.

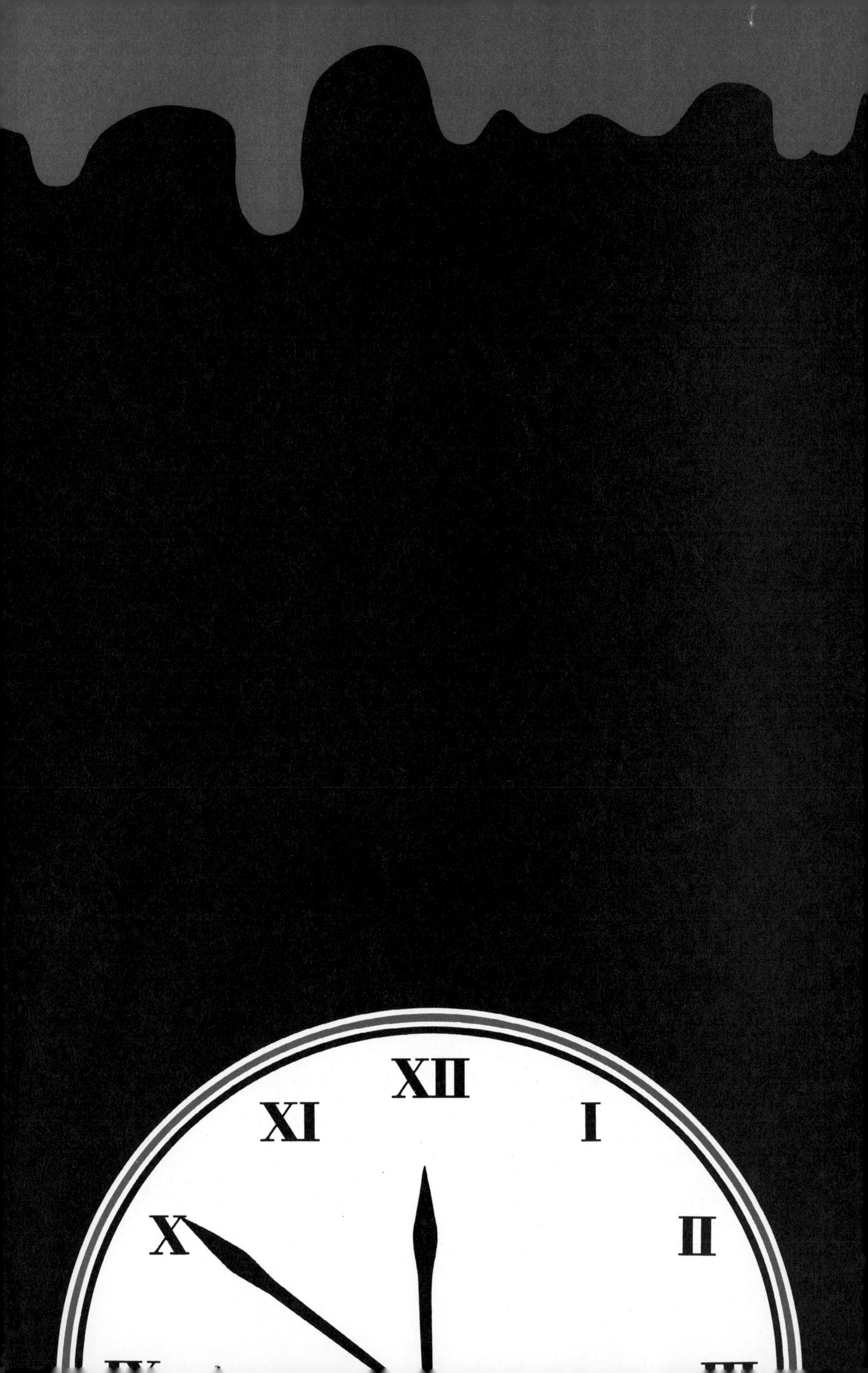
XII
XI
I
X
II

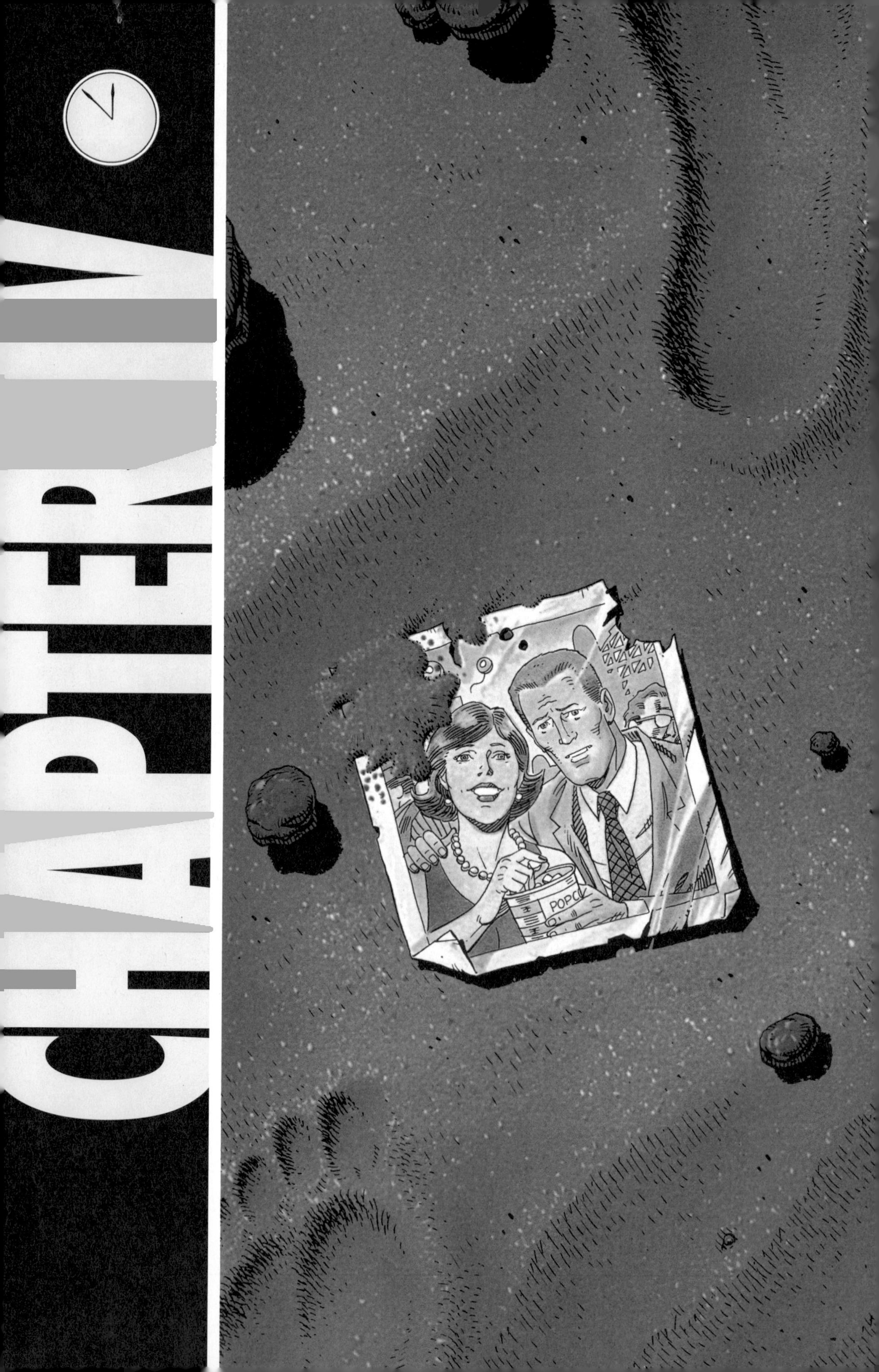
CHAPTER IV
POPC

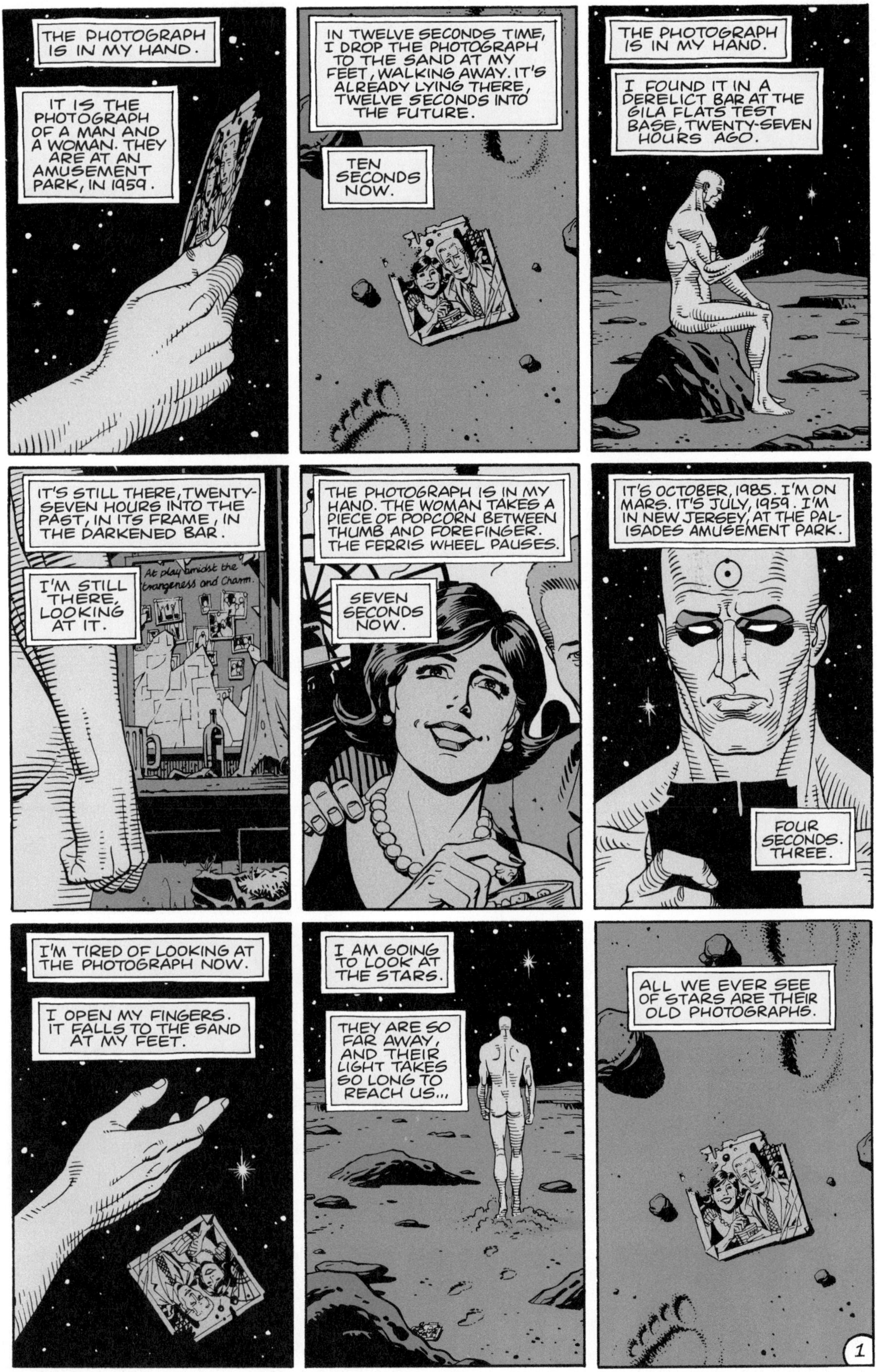
THE PHOTOGRAPH IS IN MY HAND.
IT IS THE PHOTOGRAPH OF A MAN AND A WOMAN. THEY ARE AT AN AMUSEMENT PARK, IN 1959.
IN TWELVE SECONDS TIME, I DROP THE PHOTOGRAPH TO THE SAND AT MY FEET, WALKING AWAY. IT'S ALREADY LYING THERE, TWELVE SECONDS INTO THE FUTURE.
TEN SECONDS NOW.
THE PHOTOGRAPH IS IN MY HAND.
I FOUND IT IN A DERELICT BAR AT THE GILA FLATS TEST BASE, TWENTY-SEVEN HOURS AGO.
IT'S STILL THERE, TWENTY-SEVEN HOURS INTO THE PAST, IN ITS FRAME, IN THE DARKENED BAR.
At play amidst the
trangeness and Charm.
I'M STILL THERE, LOOKING AT IT.
THE PHOTOGRAPH IS IN MY HAND. THE WOMAN TAKES A PIECE OF POPCORN BETWEEN THUMB AND FOREFINGER. THE FERRIS WHEEL PAUSES.
SEVEN SECONDS NOW.
IT'S OCTOBER, 1985. I'M ON MARS. IT'S JULY, 1959. I'M IN NEW JERSEY, AT THE PALISADES AMUSEMENT PARK.
FOUR SECONDS. THREE.
I'M TIRED OF LOOKING AT THE PHOTOGRAPH NOW.
I OPEN MY FINGERS. IT FALLS TO THE SAND AT MY FEET.
I AM GOING TO LOOK AT THE STARS.
THEY ARE SO FAR AWAY, AND THEIR LIGHT TAKES SO LONG TO REACH US...
ALL WE EVER SEE OF STARS ARE THEIR OLD PHOTOGRAPHS.
1

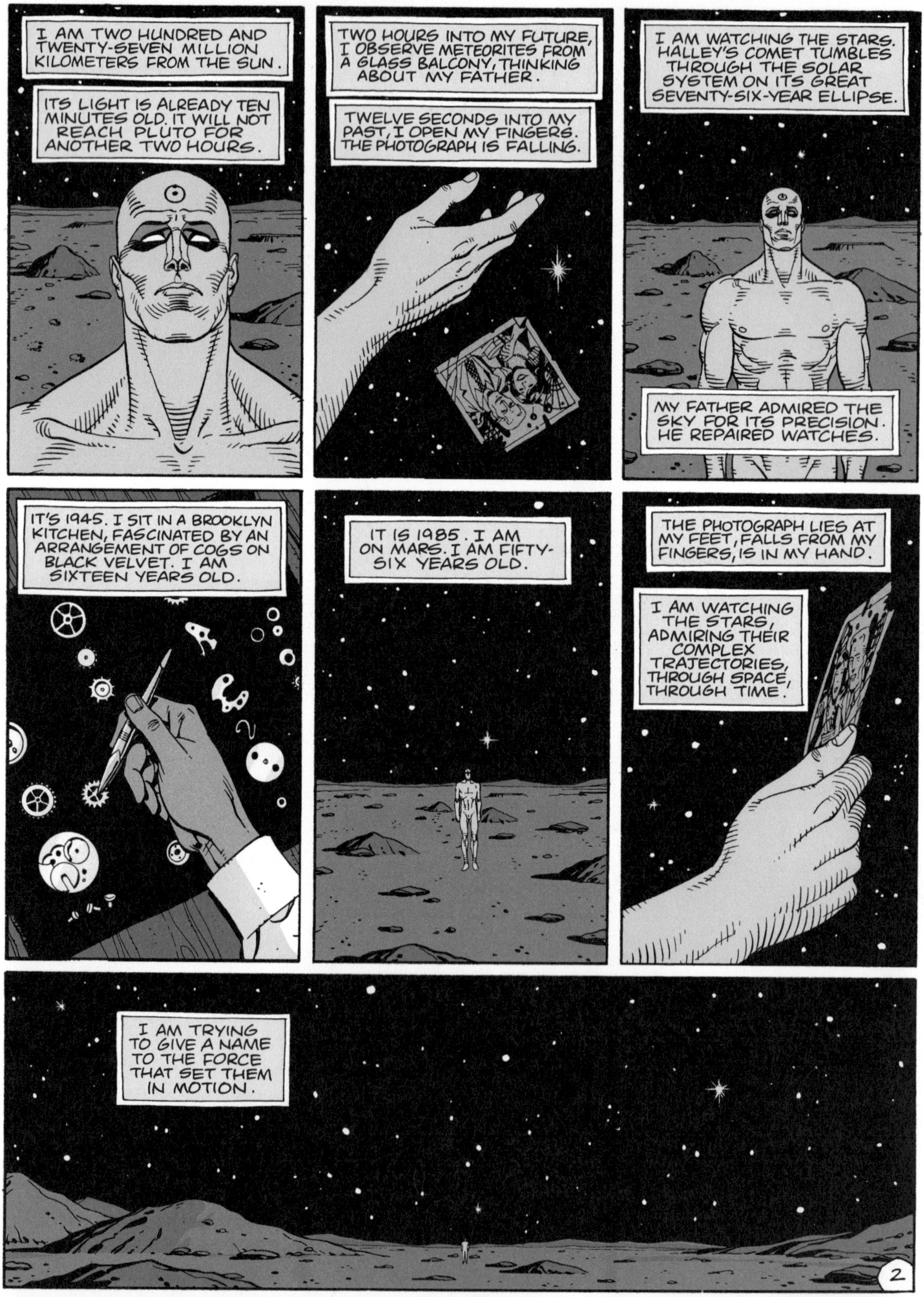
I AM TWO HUNDRED AND TWENTY-SEVEN MILLION KILOMETERS FROM THE SUN.
ITS LIGHT IS ALREADY TEN MINUTES OLD. IT WILL NOT REACH PLUTO FOR ANOTHER TWO HOURS.
TWO HOURS INTO MY FUTURE, I OBSERVE METEORITES FROM A GLASS BALCONY, THINKING ABOUT MY FATHER.
TWELVE SECONDS INTO MY PAST, I OPEN MY FINGERS. THE PHOTOGRAPH IS FALLING.
I AM WATCHING THE STARS. HALLEY'S COMET TUMBLES THROUGH THE SOLAR SYSTEM ON ITS GREAT SEVENTY-SIX-YEAR ELLIPSE.
MY FATHER ADMIRED THE SKY FOR ITS PRECISION. HE REPAIRED WATCHES.
IT'S 1945. I SIT IN A BROOKLYN KITCHEN, FASCINATED BY AN ARRANGEMENT OF COGS ON BLACK VELVET. I AM SIXTEEN YEARS OLD.
IT IS 1985. I AM ON MARS. I AM FIFTY-SIX YEARS OLD.
THE PHOTOGRAPH LIES AT MY FEET, FALLS FROM MY FINGERS, IS IN MY HAND.
I AM WATCHING THE STARS, ADMIRING THEIR COMPLEX TRAJECTORIES, THROUGH SPACE, THROUGH TIME.
I AM TRYING TO GIVE A NAME TO THE FORCE THAT SET THEM IN MOTION.
2

WATCHMAKER

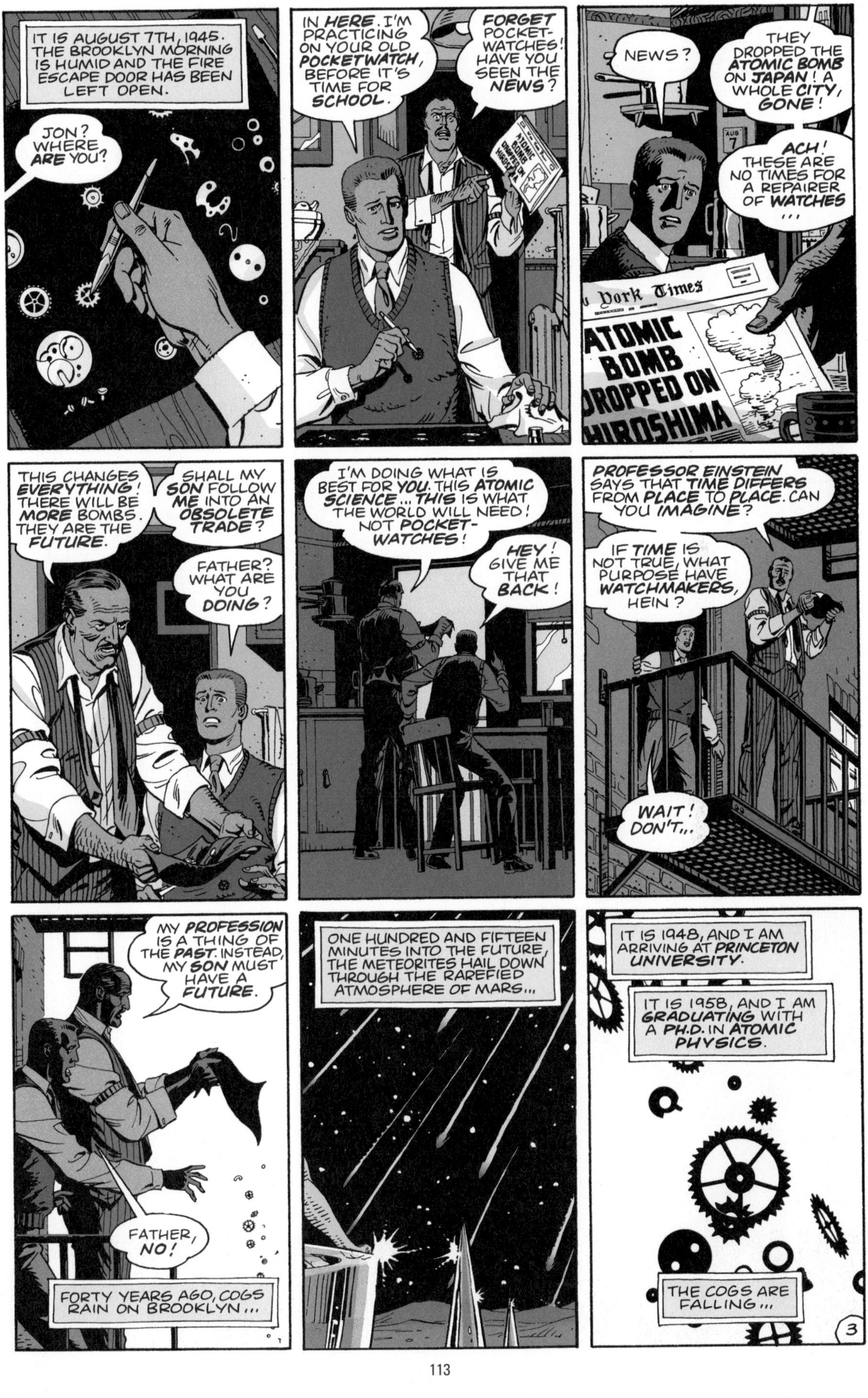
IT IS AUGUST 7TH, 1945. THE BROOKLYN MORNING IS HUMID AND THE FIRE ESCAPE DOOR HAS BEEN LEFT OPEN.
JON? WHERE ARE YOU?
IN HERE. I'M PRACTICING ON YOUR OLD POCKETWATCH, BEFORE IT'S TIME FOR SCHOOL.
FORGET POCKET-WATCHES! HAVE YOU SEEN THE NEWS?
NEWS?
THEY DROPPED THE ATOMIC BOMB ON JAPAN! A WHOLE CITY, GONE!
ACH! THESE ARE NO TIMES FOR A REPAIRER OF WATCHES...
ATOMIC BOMB DROPPED ON HIROSHIMA
THIS CHANGES EVERYTHING! THERE WILL BE MORE BOMBS. THEY ARE THE FUTURE.
SHALL MY SON FOLLOW ME INTO AN OBSOLETE TRADE?
FATHER? WHAT ARE YOU DOING?
I'M DOING WHAT IS BEST FOR YOU. THIS ATOMIC SCIENCE... THIS IS WHAT THE WORLD WILL NEED! NOT POCKET-WATCHES!
HEY! GIVE ME THAT BACK!
PROFESSOR EINSTEIN SAYS THAT TIME DIFFERS FROM PLACE TO PLACE. CAN YOU IMAGINE?
IF TIME IS NOT TRUE, WHAT PURPOSE HAVE WATCHMAKERS, HEIN?
WAIT! DON'T...
MY PROFESSION IS A THING OF THE PAST. INSTEAD, MY SON MUST HAVE A FUTURE.
FATHER, NO!
FORTY YEARS AGO, COGS RAIN ON BROOKLYN...
ONE HUNDRED AND FIFTEEN MINUTES INTO THE FUTURE, THE METEORITES HAIL DOWN THROUGH THE RAREFIED ATMOSPHERE OF MARS...
IT IS 1948, AND I AM ARRIVING AT PRINCETON UNIVERSITY.
IT IS 1958, AND I AM GRADUATING WITH A PH.D. IN ATOMIC PHYSICS.
THE COGS ARE FALLING...
3

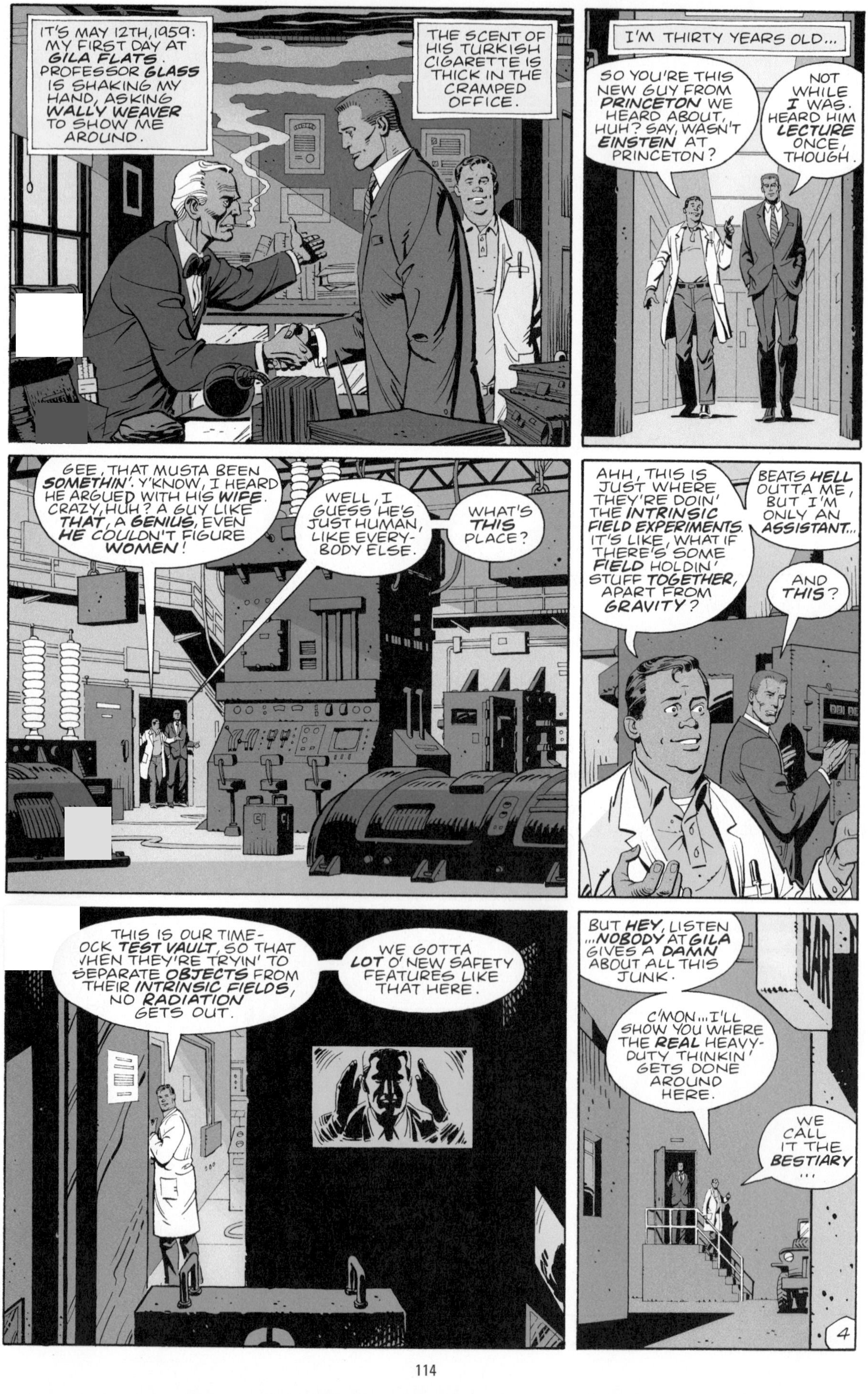

IT'S MAY 12TH, 1959: MY FIRST DAY AT GILA FLATS. PROFESSOR GLASS IS SHAKING MY HAND, ASKING WALLY WEAVER TO SHOW ME AROUND.
THE SCENT OF HIS TURKISH CIGARETTE IS THICK IN THE CRAMPED OFFICE.
I'M THIRTY YEARS OLD...
SO YOU'RE THIS NEW GUY FROM PRINCETON WE HEARD ABOUT, HUH? SAY, WASN'T EINSTEIN AT PRINCETON?
NOT WHILE I WAS. HEARD HIM LECTURE ONCE, THOUGH.
GEE, THAT MUSTA BEEN SOMETHIN'. Y'KNOW, I HEARD HE ARGUED WITH HIS WIFE. CRAZY, HUH? A GUY LIKE THAT, A GENIUS, EVEN HE COULDN'T FIGURE WOMEN!
WELL, I GUESS HE'S JUST HUMAN, LIKE EVERYBODY ELSE.
WHAT'S THIS PLACE?
AHH, THIS IS JUST WHERE THEY'RE DOIN' THE INTRINSIC FIELD EXPERIMENTS. IT'S LIKE, WHAT IF THERE'S SOME FIELD HOLDIN' STUFF TOGETHER, APART FROM GRAVITY?
BEATS HELL OUTTA ME, BUT I'M ONLY AN ASSISTANT...
AND THIS?
THIS IS OUR TIME-OCK TEST VAULT, SO THAT VHEN THEY'RE TRYIN' TO SEPARATE OBJECTS FROM THEIR INTRINSIC FIELDS, NO RADIATION GETS OUT.
WE GOTTA LOT O' NEW SAFETY FEATURES LIKE THAT HERE.
BUT HEY, LISTEN ...NOBODY AT GILA GIVES A DAMN ABOUT ALL THIS JUNK.
C'MON...I'LL SHOW YOU WHERE THE REAL HEAVY-DUTY THINKIN' GETS DONE AROUND HERE.
WE CALL IT THE BESTIARY...
4

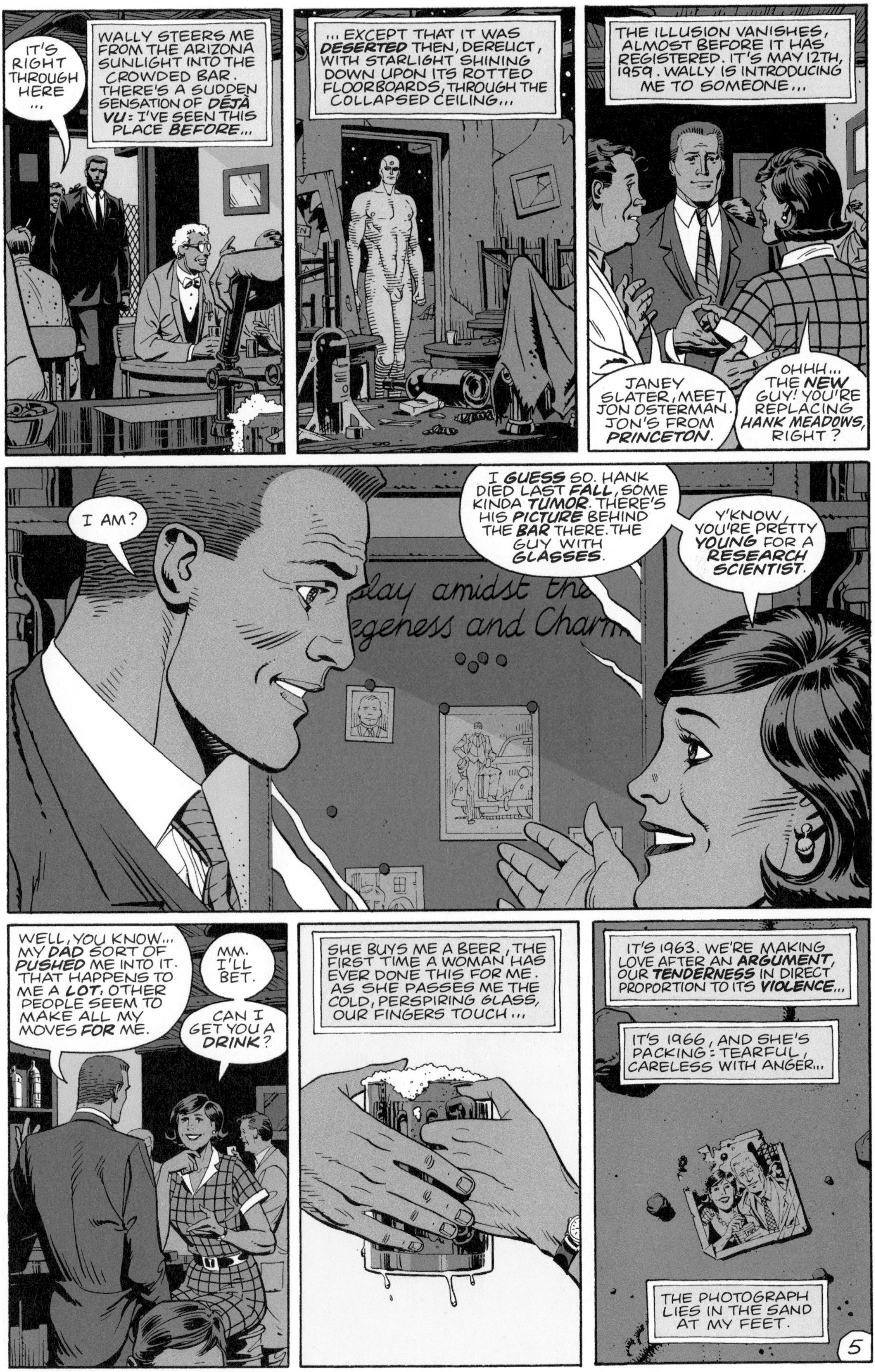
IT'S RIGHT THROUGH HERE ...
WALLY STEERS ME FROM THE ARIZONA SUNLIGHT INTO THE CROWDED BAR. THERE'S A SUDDEN SENSATION OF DÉJÀ VU: I'VE SEEN THIS PLACE BEFORE...
... EXCEPT THAT IT WAS DESERTED THEN, DERELICT, WITH STARLIGHT SHINING DOWN UPON ITS ROTTED FLOORBOARDS, THROUGH THE COLLAPSED CEILING...
THE ILLUSION VANISHES, ALMOST BEFORE IT HAS REGISTERED. IT'S MAY 12TH, 1959. WALLY IS INTRODUCING ME TO SOMEONE...
JANEY SLATER, MEET JON OSTERMAN. JON'S FROM PRINCETON.
OHHH... THE NEW GUY! YOU'RE REPLACING HANK MEADOWS, RIGHT?
I AM?
I GUESS SO. HANK DIED LAST FALL, SOME KINDA TUMOR. THERE'S HIS PICTURE BEHIND THE BAR THERE. THE GUY WITH GLASSES.
Y'KNOW, YOU'RE PRETTY YOUNG FOR A RESEARCH SCIENTIST.
WELL, YOU KNOW... MY DAD SORT OF PUSHED ME INTO IT. THAT HAPPENS TO ME A LOT: OTHER PEOPLE SEEM TO MAKE ALL MY MOVES FOR ME.
MM. I'LL BET.
CAN I GET YOU A DRINK?
SHE BUYS ME A BEER, THE FIRST TIME A WOMAN HAS EVER DONE THIS FOR ME. AS SHE PASSES ME THE COLD, PERSPIRING GLASS, OUR FINGERS TOUCH...
IT'S 1963. WE'RE MAKING LOVE AFTER AN ARGUMENT, OUR TENDERNESS IN DIRECT PROPORTION TO ITS VIOLENCE...
IT'S 1966, AND SHE'S PACKING: TEARFUL, CARELESS WITH ANGER...
THE PHOTOGRAPH LIES IN THE SAND AT MY FEET.
5

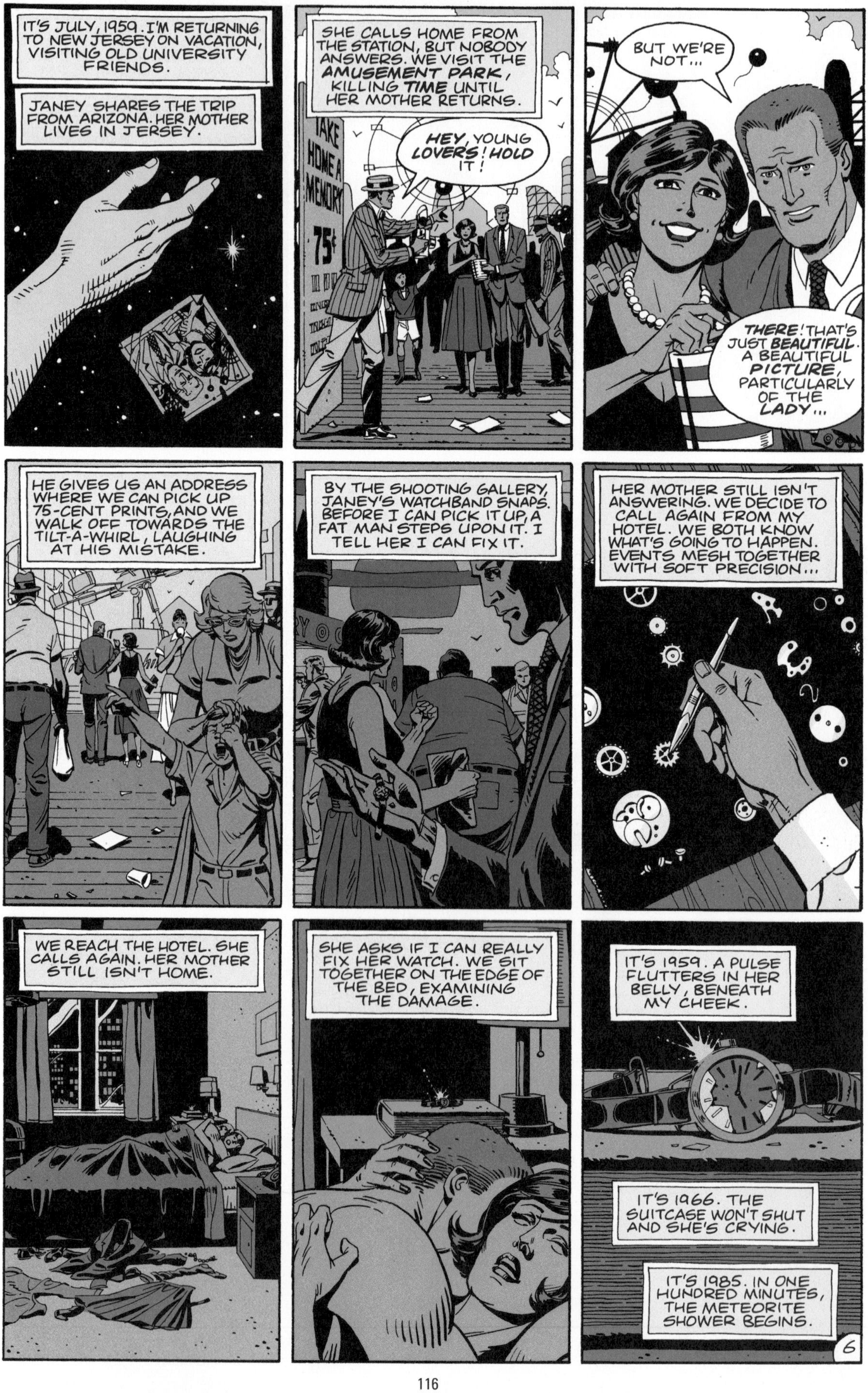
IT'S JULY, 1959. I'M RETURNING TO NEW JERSEY ON VACATION, VISITING OLD UNIVERSITY FRIENDS.
JANEY SHARES THE TRIP FROM ARIZONA. HER MOTHER LIVES IN JERSEY.
SHE CALLS HOME FROM THE STATION, BUT NOBODY ANSWERS. WE VISIT THE AMUSEMENT PARK, KILLING TIME UNTIL HER MOTHER RETURNS.
TAKE HOME A MEMORY
75¢
HEY, YOUNG LOVERS! HOLD IT!
BUT WE'RE NOT...
THERE! THAT'S JUST BEAUTIFUL. A BEAUTIFUL PICTURE, PARTICULARLY OF THE LADY...
HE GIVES US AN ADDRESS WHERE WE CAN PICK UP 75-CENT PRINTS, AND WE WALK OFF TOWARDS THE TILT-A-WHIRL, LAUGHING AT HIS MISTAKE.
BY THE SHOOTING GALLERY, JANEY'S WATCHBAND SNAPS. BEFORE I CAN PICK IT UP, A FAT MAN STEPS UPON IT. I TELL HER I CAN FIX IT.
HER MOTHER STILL ISN'T ANSWERING. WE DECIDE TO CALL AGAIN FROM MY HOTEL. WE BOTH KNOW WHAT'S GOING TO HAPPEN. EVENTS MESH TOGETHER WITH SOFT PRECISION...
WE REACH THE HOTEL. SHE CALLS AGAIN. HER MOTHER STILL ISN'T HOME.
SHE ASKS IF I CAN REALLY FIX HER WATCH. WE SIT TOGETHER ON THE EDGE OF THE BED, EXAMINING THE DAMAGE.
IT'S 1959. A PULSE FLUTTERS IN HER BELLY, BENEATH MY CHEEK.
IT'S 1966. THE SUITCASE WON'T SHUT AND SHE'S CRYING.
IT'S 1985. IN ONE HUNDRED MINUTES, THE METEORITE SHOWER BEGINS.
6

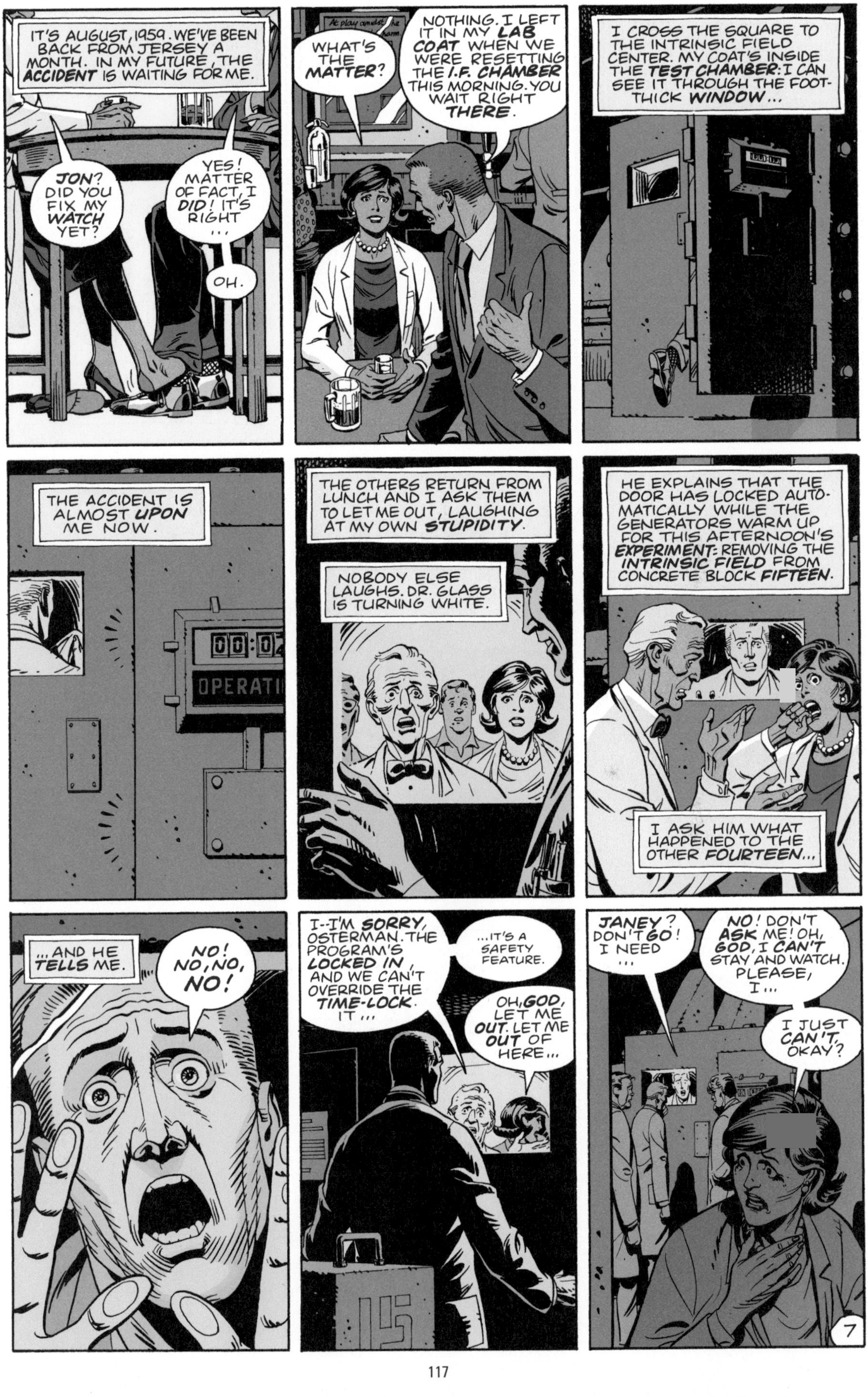

IT'S AUGUST, 1959. WE'VE BEEN BACK FROM JERSEY A MONTH. IN MY FUTURE, THE ACCIDENT IS WAITING FOR ME.
JON? DID YOU FIX MY WATCH YET?
YES! MATTER OF FACT, I DID! IT'S RIGHT ...
OH.
WHAT'S THE MATTER?
NOTHING. I LEFT IT IN MY LAB COAT WHEN WE WERE RESETTING THE I.F. CHAMBER THIS MORNING. YOU WAIT RIGHT THERE.
I CROSS THE SQUARE TO THE INTRINSIC FIELD CENTER. MY COAT'S INSIDE THE TEST CHAMBER: I CAN SEE IT THROUGH THE FOOT-THICK WINDOW...
THE ACCIDENT IS ALMOST UPON ME NOW.
OPERATI
THE OTHERS RETURN FROM LUNCH AND I ASK THEM TO LET ME OUT, LAUGHING AT MY OWN STUPIDITY.
NOBODY ELSE LAUGHS. DR. GLASS IS TURNING WHITE.
HE EXPLAINS THAT THE DOOR HAS LOCKED AUTOMATICALLY WHILE THE GENERATORS WARM UP FOR THIS AFTERNOON'S EXPERIMENT: REMOVING THE INTRINSIC FIELD FROM CONCRETE BLOCK FIFTEEN.
I ASK HIM WHAT HAPPENED TO THE OTHER FOURTEEN...
...AND HE TELLS ME.
NO! NO, NO, NO!
I--I'M SORRY, OSTERMAN. THE PROGRAM'S LOCKED IN, AND WE CAN'T OVERRIDE THE TIME-LOCK. IT ...
...IT'S A SAFETY FEATURE.
OH, GOD, LET ME OUT. LET ME OUT OF HERE...
JANEY? DON'T GO! I NEED ...
NO! DON'T ASK ME! OH, GOD, I CAN'T STAY AND WATCH. PLEASE, I...
I JUST CAN'T, OKAY?
7

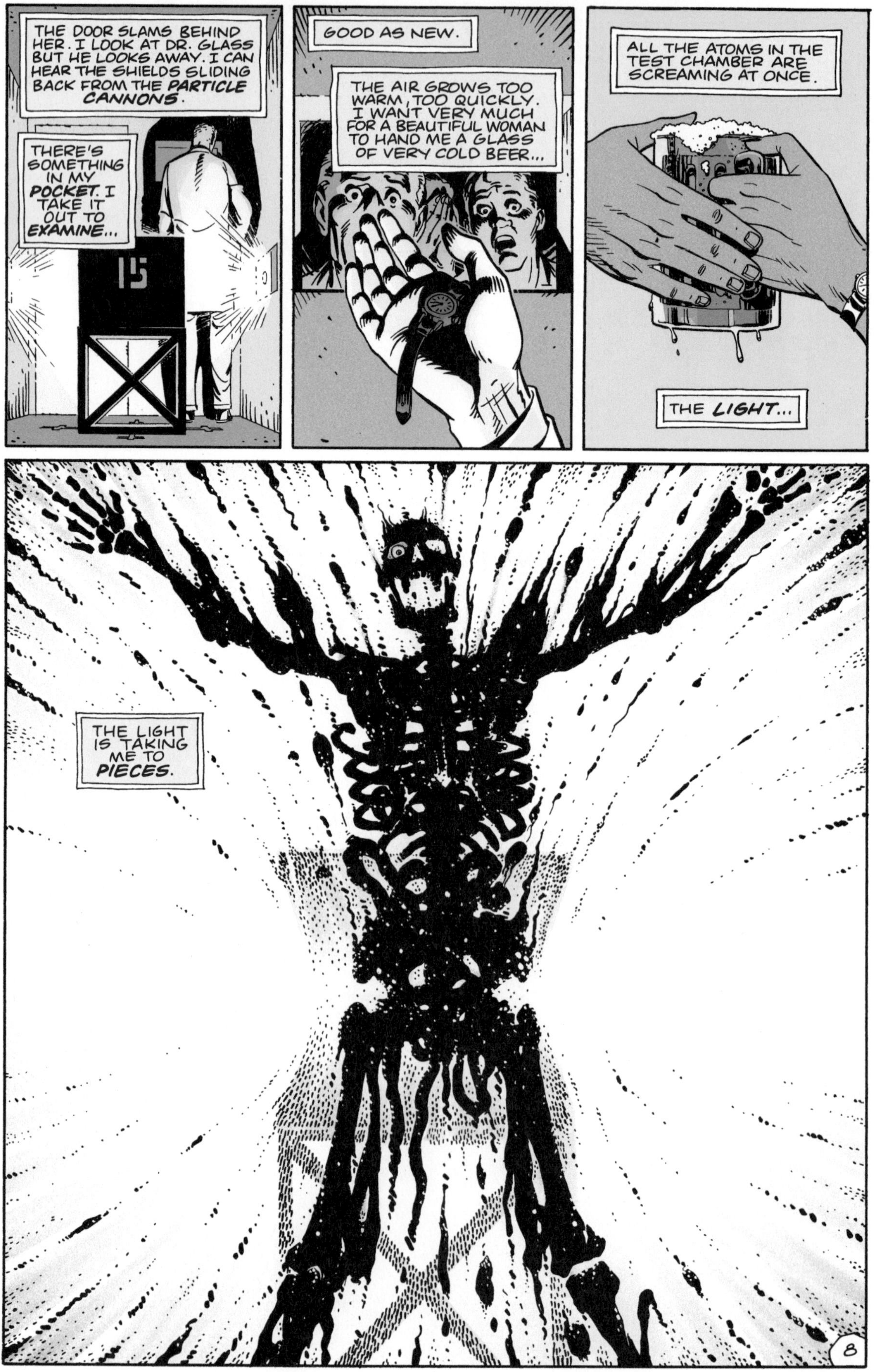
THE DOOR SLAMS BEHIND HER. I LOOK AT DR. GLASS BUT HE LOOKS AWAY. I CAN HEAR THE SHIELDS SLIDING BACK FROM THE PARTICLE CANNONS.
THERE'S SOMETHING IN MY POCKET. I TAKE IT OUT TO EXAMINE...
15
GOOD AS NEW.
THE AIR GROWS TOO WARM, TOO QUICKLY. I WANT VERY MUCH FOR A BEAUTIFUL WOMAN TO HAND ME A GLASS OF VERY COLD BEER...
ALL THE ATOMS IN THE TEST CHAMBER ARE SCREAMING AT ONCE.
THE LIGHT...
THE LIGHT IS TAKING ME TO PIECES.
8

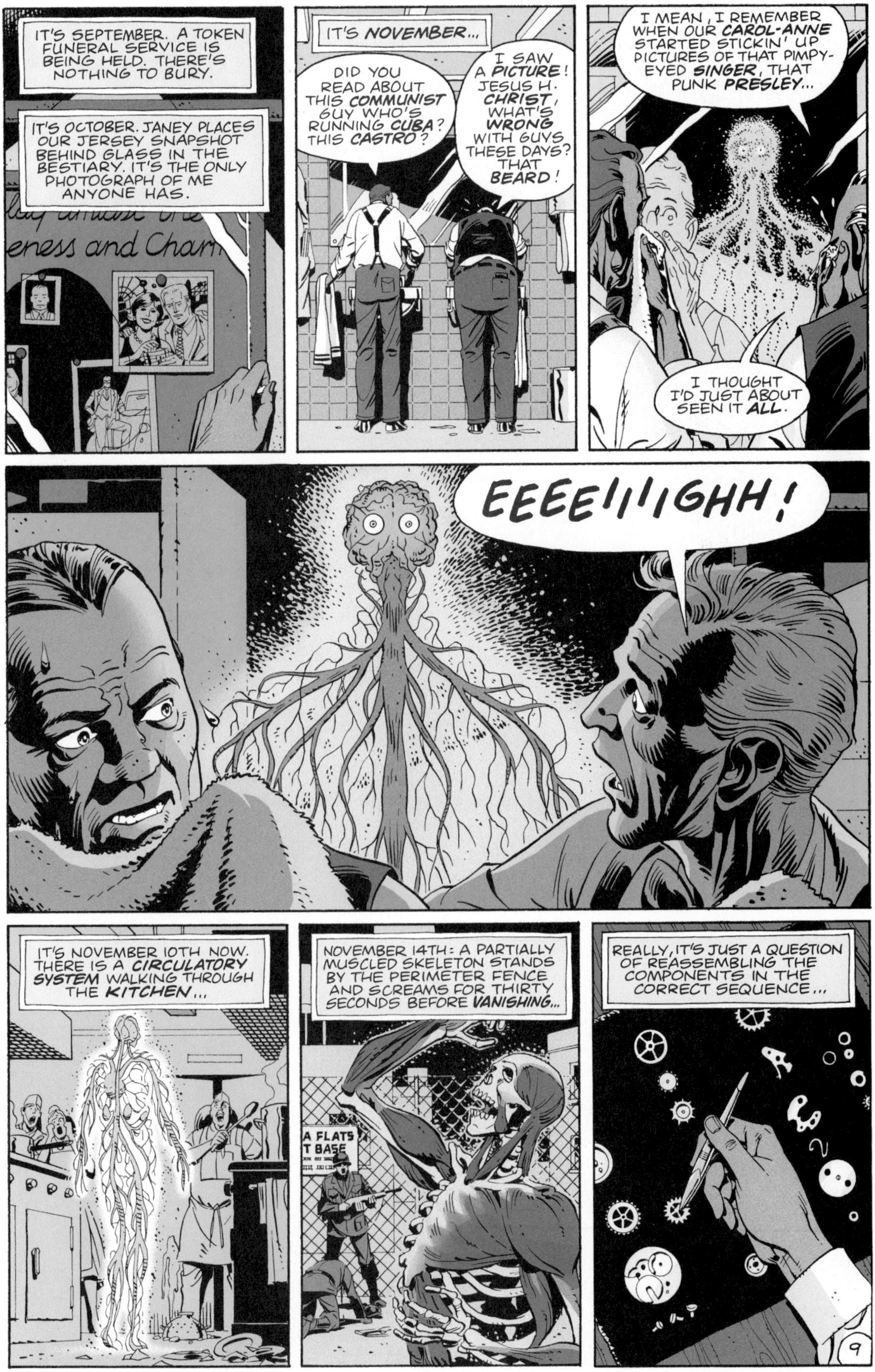
IT'S SEPTEMBER. A TOKEN FUNERAL SERVICE IS BEING HELD. THERE'S NOTHING TO BURY.
IT'S OCTOBER. JANEY PLACES OUR JERSEY SNAPSHOT BEHIND GLASS IN THE BESTIARY. IT'S THE ONLY PHOTOGRAPH OF ME ANYONE HAS.
eness and Charm
IT'S NOVEMBER...
DID YOU READ ABOUT THIS COMMUNIST GUY WHO'S RUNNING CUBA? THIS CASTRO?
I SAW A PICTURE! JESUS H. CHRIST, WHAT'S WRONG WITH GUYS THESE DAYS? THAT BEARD!
I MEAN, I REMEMBER WHEN OUR CAROL-ANNE STARTED STICKIN' UP PICTURES OF THAT PIMPY-EYED SINGER, THAT PUNK PRESLEY...
I THOUGHT I'D JUST ABOUT SEEN IT ALL.
EEEEIIIIGHH!
IT'S NOVEMBER 10TH NOW. THERE IS A CIRCULATORY SYSTEM WALKING THROUGH THE KITCHEN...
NOVEMBER 14TH: A PARTIALLY MUSCLED SKELETON STANDS BY THE PERIMETER FENCE AND SCREAMS FOR THIRTY SECONDS BEFORE VANISHING...
A FLATS
T BASE
REALLY, IT'S JUST A QUESTION OF REASSEMBLING THE COMPONENTS IN THE CORRECT SEQUENCE...
9

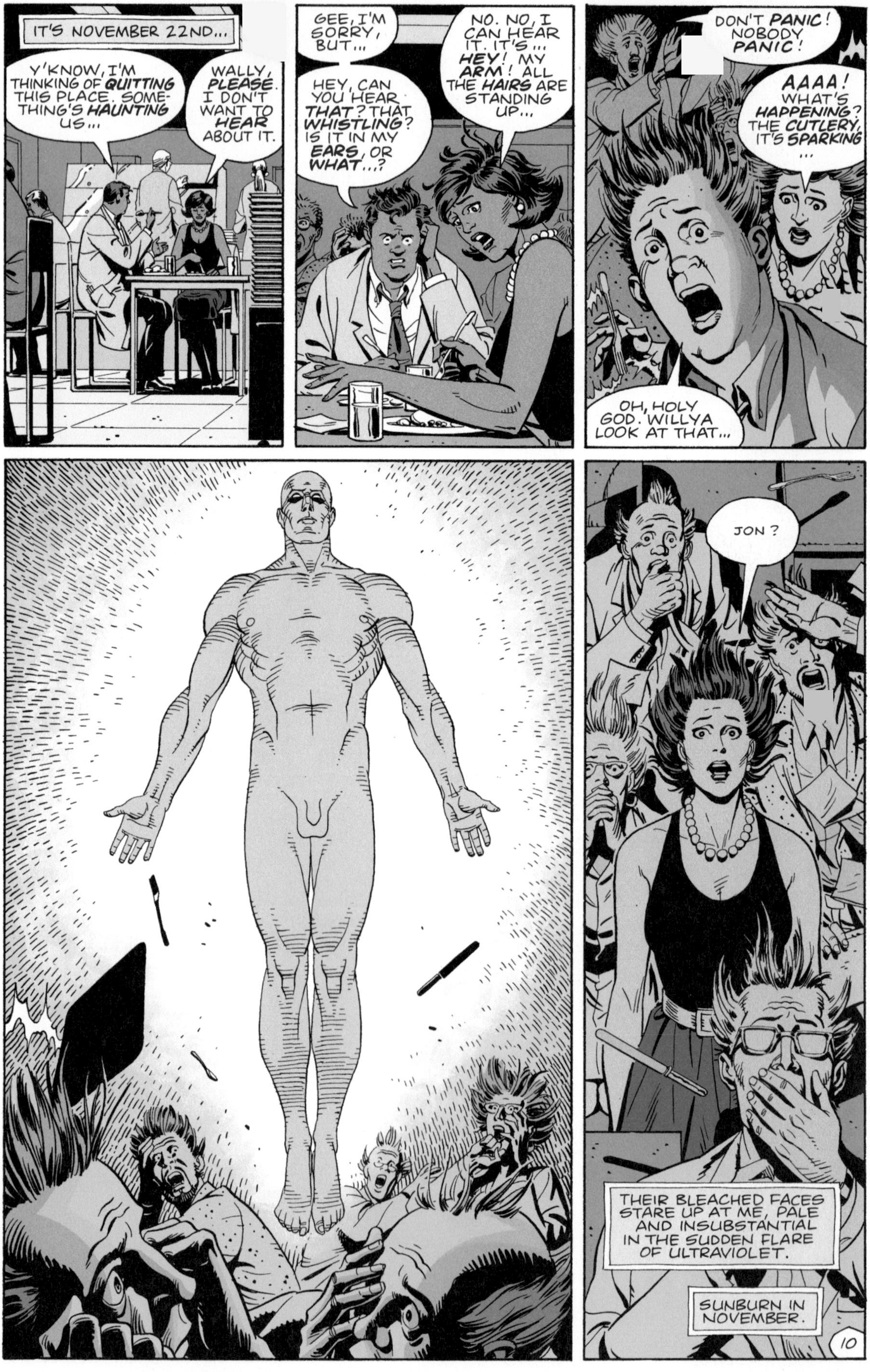

IT'S NOVEMBER 22ND...
Y'KNOW, I'M THINKING OF QUITTING THIS PLACE. SOMETHING'S HAUNTING US...
WALLY, PLEASE. I DON'T WANT TO HEAR ABOUT IT.
GEE, I'M SORRY, BUT...
HEY, CAN YOU HEAR THAT? THAT WHISTLING? IS IT IN MY EARS, OR WHAT...?
NO. NO, I CAN HEAR IT. IT'S... HEY! MY ARM! ALL THE HAIRS ARE STANDING UP...
DON'T PANIC! NOBODY PANIC!
AAAA! WHAT'S HAPPENING? THE CUTLERY, IT'S SPARKING...
OH, HOLY GOD. WILLYA LOOK AT THAT...
JON?
THEIR BLEACHED FACES STARE UP AT ME, PALE AND INSUBSTANTIAL IN THE SUDDEN FLARE OF ULTRAVIOLET.
SUNBURN IN NOVEMBER.
10

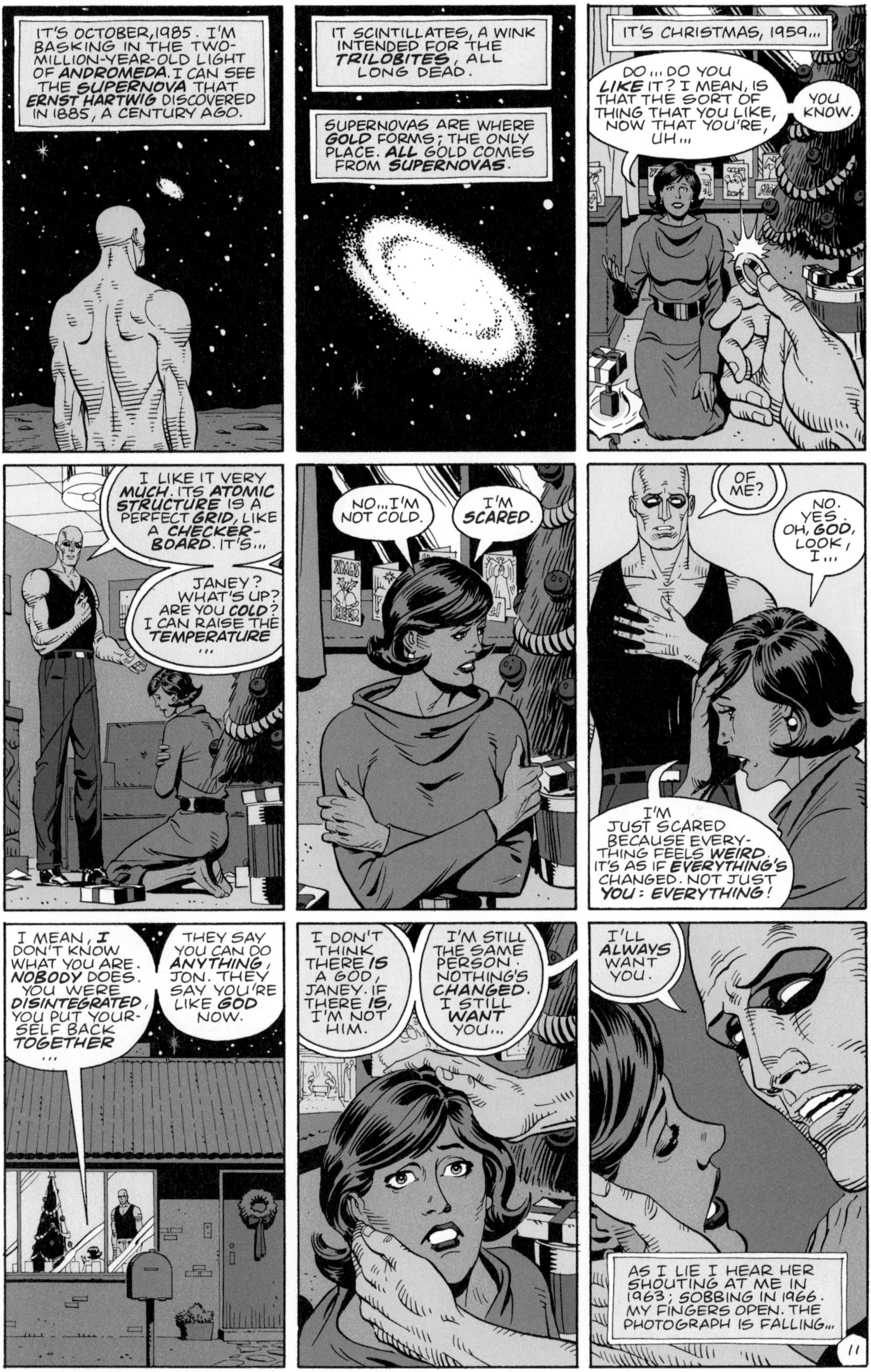
IT'S OCTOBER, 1985. I'M BASKING IN THE TWO-MILLION-YEAR-OLD LIGHT OF ANDROMEDA. I CAN SEE THE SUPERNOVA THAT ERNST HARTWIG DISCOVERED IN 1885, A CENTURY AGO.
IT SCINTILLATES, A WINK INTENDED FOR THE TRILOBITES, ALL LONG DEAD.
SUPERNOVAS ARE WHERE GOLD FORMS; THE ONLY PLACE. ALL GOLD COMES FROM SUPERNOVAS.
IT'S CHRISTMAS, 1959...
DO... DO YOU LIKE IT? I MEAN, IS THAT THE SORT OF THING THAT YOU LIKE, NOW THAT YOU'RE, UH...
YOU KNOW.
I LIKE IT VERY MUCH. ITS ATOMIC STRUCTURE IS A PERFECT GRID, LIKE A CHECKER-BOARD. IT'S...
JANEY? WHAT'S UP? ARE YOU COLD? I CAN RAISE THE TEMPERATURE ...
NO... I'M NOT COLD.
I'M SCARED.
OF ME?
NO. YES. OH, GOD, LOOK, I...
I'M JUST SCARED BECAUSE EVERY-THING FEELS WEIRD. IT'S AS IF EVERYTHING'S CHANGED. NOT JUST YOU: EVERYTHING!
I MEAN, I DON'T KNOW WHAT YOU ARE. NOBODY DOES. YOU WERE DISINTEGRATED, YOU PUT YOUR-SELF BACK TOGETHER ...
THEY SAY YOU CAN DO ANYTHING, JON. THEY SAY YOU'RE LIKE GOD NOW.
I DON'T THINK THERE IS A GOD, JANEY. IF THERE IS, I'M NOT HIM.
I'M STILL THE SAME PERSON. NOTHING'S CHANGED. I STILL WANT YOU...
I'LL ALWAYS WANT YOU.
AS I LIE I HEAR HER SHOUTING AT ME IN 1963; SOBBING IN 1966. MY FINGERS OPEN. THE PHOTOGRAPH IS FALLING...
11

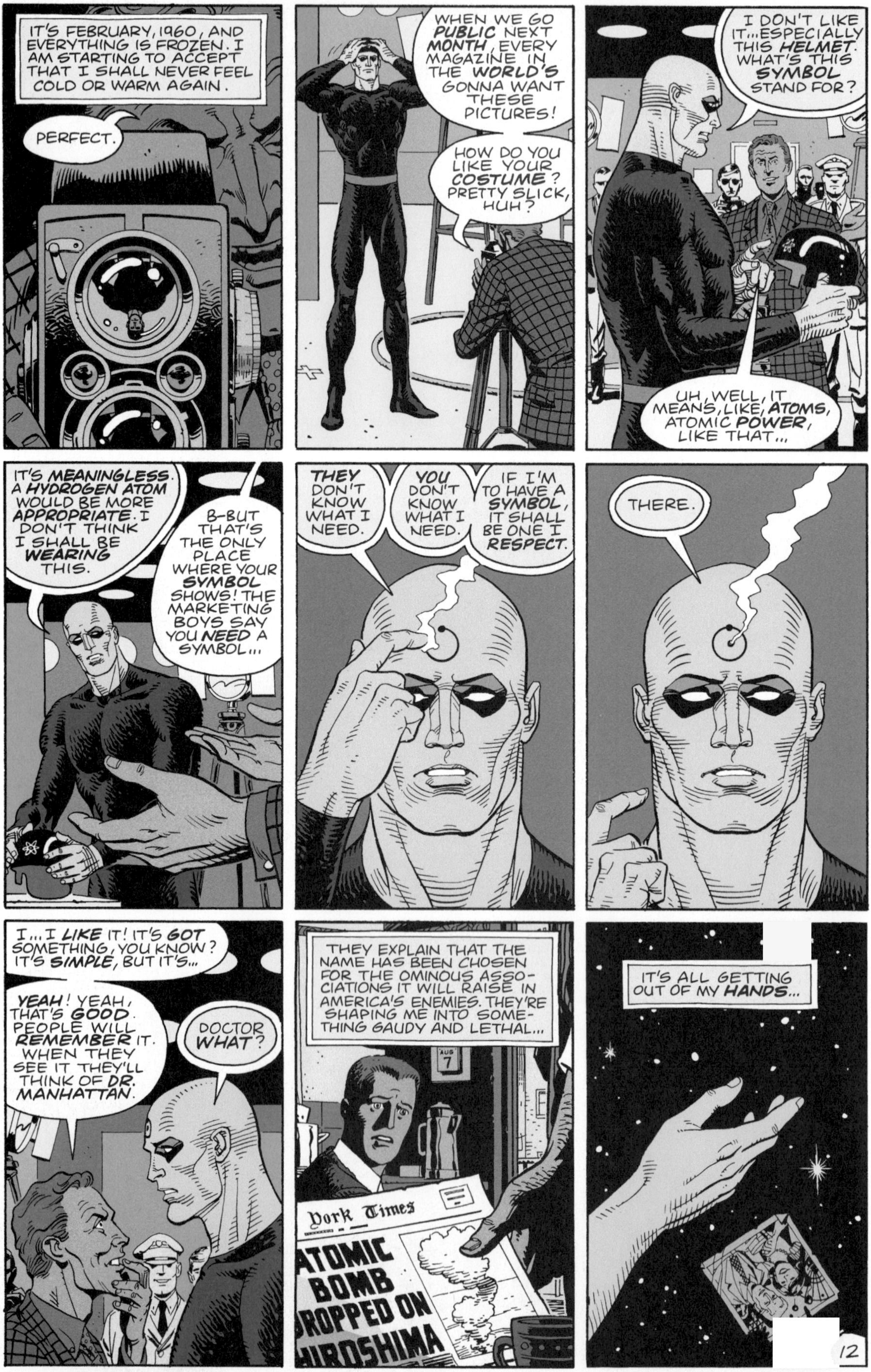
IT'S FEBRUARY, 1960, AND EVERYTHING IS FROZEN. I AM STARTING TO ACCEPT THAT I SHALL NEVER FEEL COLD OR WARM AGAIN.
PERFECT.
WHEN WE GO PUBLIC NEXT MONTH, EVERY MAGAZINE IN THE WORLD'S GONNA WANT THESE PICTURES!
HOW DO YOU LIKE YOUR COSTUME? PRETTY SLICK, HUH?
I DON'T LIKE IT...ESPECIALLY THIS HELMET. WHAT'S THIS SYMBOL STAND FOR?
UH, WELL, IT MEANS, LIKE, ATOMS, ATOMIC POWER, LIKE THAT...
IT'S MEANINGLESS. A HYDROGEN ATOM WOULD BE MORE APPROPRIATE. I DON'T THINK I SHALL BE WEARING THIS.
B-BUT THAT'S THE ONLY PLACE WHERE YOUR SYMBOL SHOWS! THE MARKETING BOYS SAY YOU NEED A SYMBOL...
THEY DON'T KNOW WHAT I NEED.
YOU DON'T KNOW WHAT I NEED.
IF I'M TO HAVE A SYMBOL, IT SHALL BE ONE I RESPECT.
THERE.
I... I LIKE IT! IT'S GOT SOMETHING, YOU KNOW? IT'S SIMPLE, BUT IT'S...
YEAH! YEAH, THAT'S GOOD. PEOPLE WILL REMEMBER IT. WHEN THEY SEE IT THEY'LL THINK OF DR. MANHATTAN.
DOCTOR WHAT?
THEY EXPLAIN THAT THE NAME HAS BEEN CHOSEN FOR THE OMINOUS ASSOCIATIONS IT WILL RAISE IN AMERICA'S ENEMIES. THEY'RE SHAPING ME INTO SOMETHING GAUDY AND LETHAL...
AUG 7
York Times
ATOMIC BOMB DROPPED ON HIROSHIMA
IT'S ALL GETTING OUT OF MY HANDS...
12

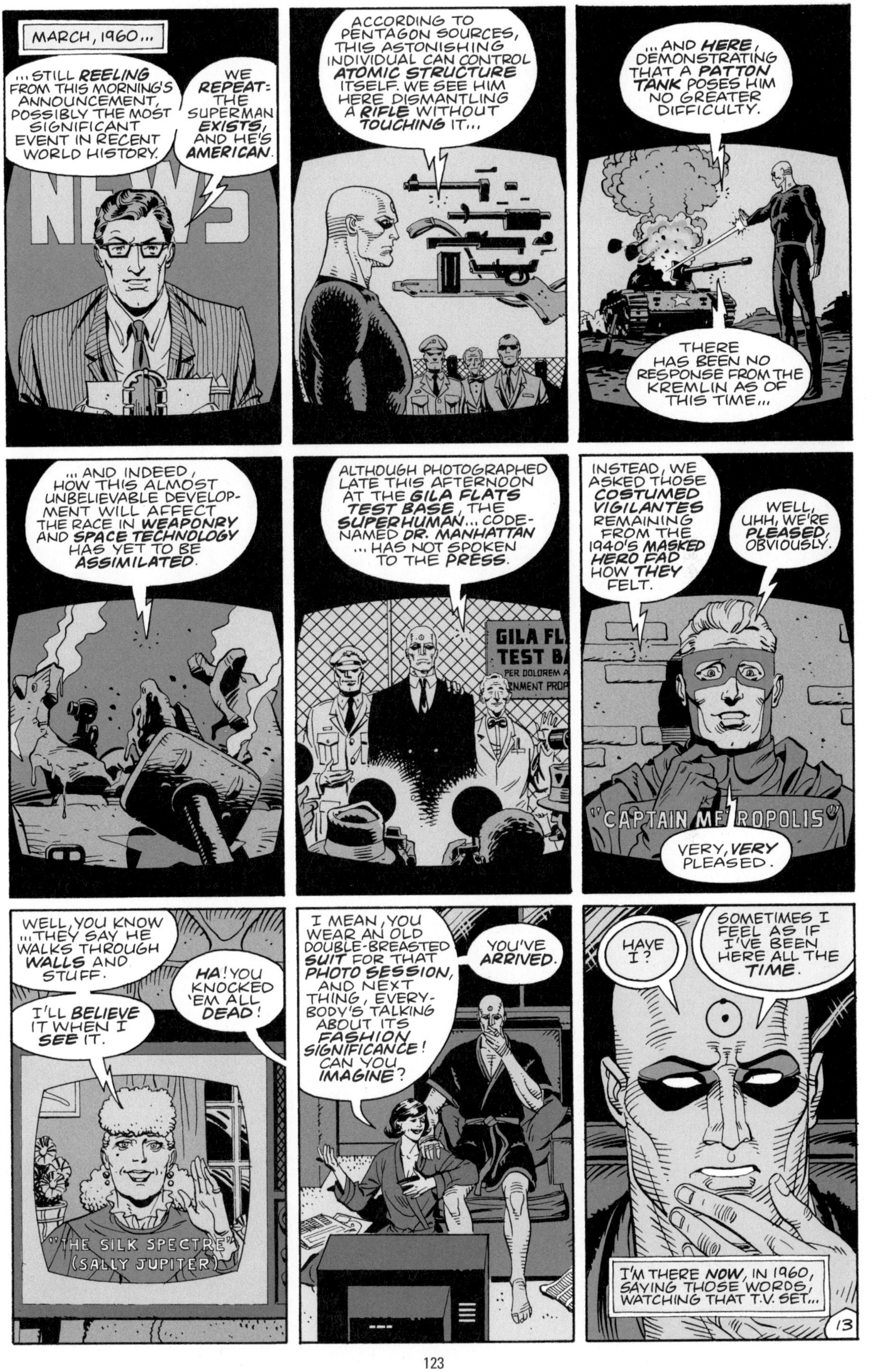
MARCH, 1960...
...STILL REELING FROM THIS MORNING'S ANNOUNCEMENT, POSSIBLY THE MOST SIGNIFICANT EVENT IN RECENT WORLD HISTORY.
WE REPEAT: THE SUPERMAN EXISTS, AND HE'S AMERICAN.
NEWS
ACCORDING TO PENTAGON SOURCES, THIS ASTONISHING INDIVIDUAL CAN CONTROL ATOMIC STRUCTURE ITSELF. WE SEE HIM HERE DISMANTLING A RIFLE WITHOUT TOUCHING IT...
...AND HERE, DEMONSTRATING THAT A PATTON TANK POSES HIM NO GREATER DIFFICULTY.
THERE HAS BEEN NO RESPONSE FROM THE KREMLIN AS OF THIS TIME...
...AND INDEED, HOW THIS ALMOST UNBELIEVABLE DEVELOPMENT WILL AFFECT THE RACE IN WEAPONRY AND SPACE TECHNOLOGY HAS YET TO BE ASSIMILATED.
ALTHOUGH PHOTOGRAPHED LATE THIS AFTERNOON AT THE GILA FLATS TEST BASE, THE SUPERHUMAN... CODE-NAMED DR. MANHATTAN ...HAS NOT SPOKEN TO THE PRESS.
GILA FL
TEST BA
PER DOLOREM A
RNMENT PROP
INSTEAD, WE ASKED THOSE COSTUMED VIGILANTES REMAINING FROM THE 1940'S MASKED HERO FAD HOW THEY FELT.
WELL, UHH, WE'RE PLEASED, OBVIOUSLY.
"CAPTAIN METROPOLIS"
VERY, VERY PLEASED.
WELL, YOU KNOW ...THEY SAY HE WALKS THROUGH WALLS AND STUFF.
I'LL BELIEVE IT WHEN I SEE IT.
HA! YOU KNOCKED 'EM ALL DEAD!
"THE SILK SPECTRE" (SALLY JUPITER)
I MEAN, YOU WEAR AN OLD DOUBLE-BREASTED SUIT FOR THAT PHOTO SESSION, AND NEXT THING, EVERYBODY'S TALKING ABOUT ITS FASHION SIGNIFICANCE! CAN YOU IMAGINE?
YOU'VE ARRIVED.
HAVE I?
SOMETIMES I FEEL AS IF I'VE BEEN HERE ALL THE TIME.
I'M THERE NOW, IN 1960, SAYING THOSE WORDS, WATCHING THAT T.V. SET...
13

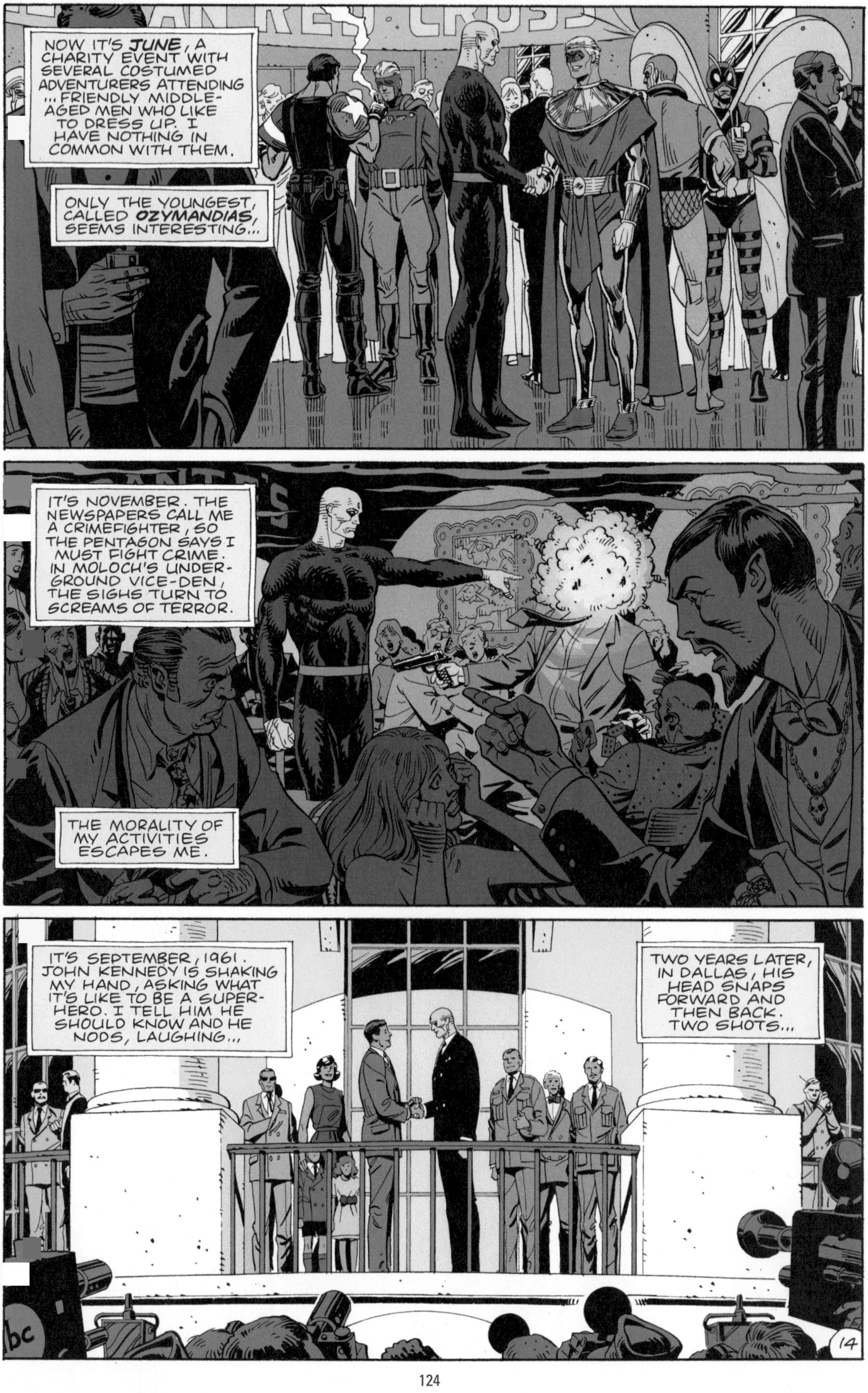
NOW IT'S JUNE, A CHARITY EVENT WITH SEVERAL COSTUMED ADVENTURERS ATTENDING ...FRIENDLY MIDDLE-AGED MEN WHO LIKE TO DRESS UP. I HAVE NOTHING IN COMMON WITH THEM.
ONLY THE YOUNGEST, CALLED OZYMANDIAS, SEEMS INTERESTING...
IT'S NOVEMBER. THE NEWSPAPERS CALL ME A CRIMEFIGHTER, SO THE PENTAGON SAYS I MUST FIGHT CRIME. IN MOLOCH'S UNDERGROUND VICE-DEN, THE SIGHS TURN TO SCREAMS OF TERROR.
THE MORALITY OF MY ACTIVITIES ESCAPES ME.
IT'S SEPTEMBER, 1961. JOHN KENNEDY IS SHAKING MY HAND, ASKING WHAT IT'S LIKE TO BE A SUPERHERO. I TELL HIM HE SHOULD KNOW AND HE NODS, LAUGHING...
TWO YEARS LATER, IN DALLAS, HIS HEAD SNAPS FORWARD AND THEN BACK. TWO SHOTS...
abc
14

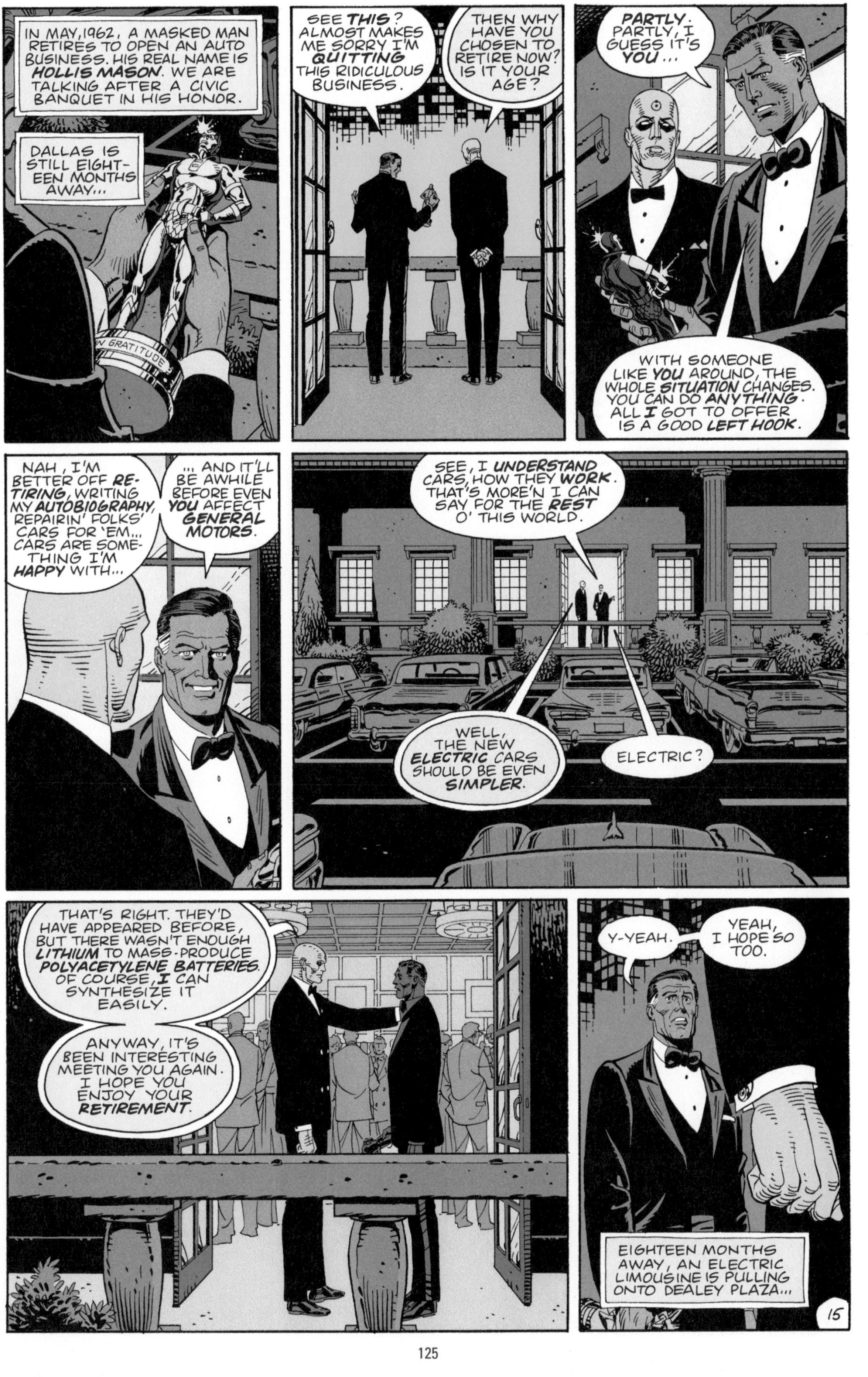

IN MAY, 1962, A MASKED MAN RETIRES TO OPEN AN AUTO BUSINESS. HIS REAL NAME IS HOLLIS MASON. WE ARE TALKING AFTER A CIVIC BANQUET IN HIS HONOR.
DALLAS IS STILL EIGHTEEN MONTHS AWAY...
IN GRATITUDE
SEE THIS? ALMOST MAKES ME SORRY I'M QUITTING THIS RIDICULOUS BUSINESS.
THEN WHY HAVE YOU CHOSEN TO RETIRE NOW? IS IT YOUR AGE?
PARTLY. PARTLY, I GUESS IT'S YOU...
WITH SOMEONE LIKE YOU AROUND, THE WHOLE SITUATION CHANGES. YOU CAN DO ANYTHING. ALL I GOT TO OFFER IS A GOOD LEFT HOOK.
NAH, I'M BETTER OFF RETIRING, WRITING MY AUTOBIOGRAPHY, REPAIRIN' FOLKS' CARS FOR 'EM... CARS ARE SOMETHING I'M HAPPY WITH...
... AND IT'LL BE AWHILE BEFORE EVEN YOU AFFECT GENERAL MOTORS.
SEE, I UNDERSTAND CARS, HOW THEY WORK. THAT'S MORE'N I CAN SAY FOR THE REST O' THIS WORLD.
WELL, THE NEW ELECTRIC CARS SHOULD BE EVEN SIMPLER.
ELECTRIC?
THAT'S RIGHT. THEY'D HAVE APPEARED BEFORE, BUT THERE WASN'T ENOUGH LITHIUM TO MASS-PRODUCE POLYACETYLENE BATTERIES. OF COURSE, I CAN SYNTHESIZE IT EASILY.
ANYWAY, IT'S BEEN INTERESTING MEETING YOU AGAIN. I HOPE YOU ENJOY YOUR RETIREMENT.
Y-YEAH.
YEAH, I HOPE SO TOO.
EIGHTEEN MONTHS AWAY, AN ELECTRIC LIMOUSINE IS PULLING ONTO DEALEY PLAZA...
15

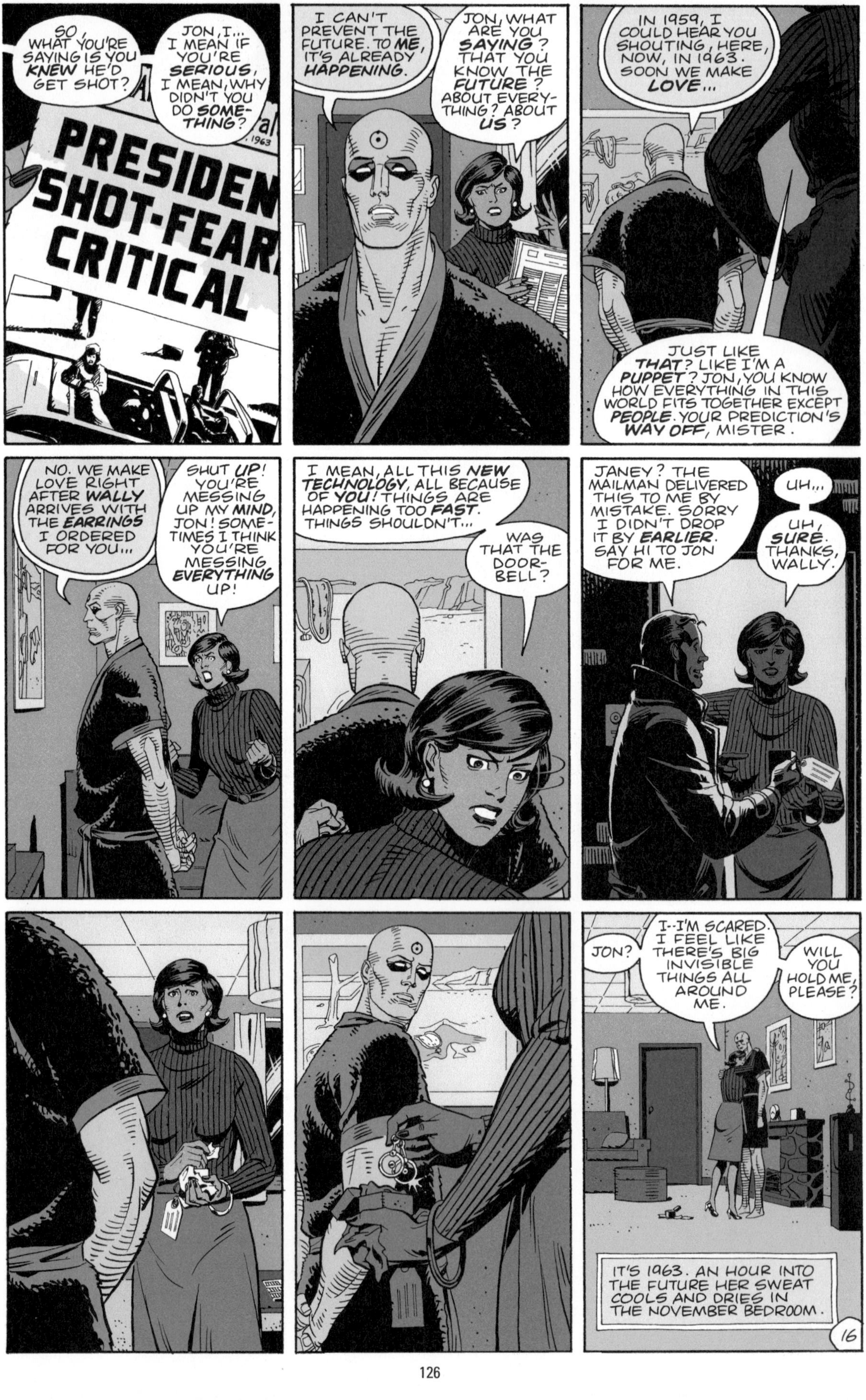
SO, WHAT YOU'RE SAYING IS YOU KNEW HE'D GET SHOT?
JON, I... I MEAN IF YOU'RE SERIOUS, I MEAN, WHY DIDN'T YOU DO SOMETHING?
PRESIDEN
SHOT-FEAR
CRITICAL
1963
I CAN'T PREVENT THE FUTURE. TO ME, IT'S ALREADY HAPPENING.
JON, WHAT ARE YOU SAYING? THAT YOU KNOW THE FUTURE? ABOUT EVERYTHING? ABOUT US?
IN 1959, I COULD HEAR YOU SHOUTING, HERE, NOW, IN 1963. SOON WE MAKE LOVE...
JUST LIKE THAT? LIKE I'M A PUPPET? JON, YOU KNOW HOW EVERYTHING IN THIS WORLD FITS TOGETHER EXCEPT PEOPLE. YOUR PREDICTION'S WAY OFF, MISTER.
NO. WE MAKE LOVE RIGHT AFTER WALLY ARRIVES WITH THE EARRINGS I ORDERED FOR YOU...
SHUT UP! YOU'RE MESSING UP MY MIND, JON! SOMETIMES I THINK YOU'RE MESSING EVERYTHING UP!
I MEAN, ALL THIS NEW TECHNOLOGY, ALL BECAUSE OF YOU! THINGS ARE HAPPENING TOO FAST. THINGS SHOULDN'T...
WAS THAT THE DOORBELL?
JANEY? THE MAILMAN DELIVERED THIS TO ME BY MISTAKE. SORRY I DIDN'T DROP IT BY EARLIER. SAY HI TO JON FOR ME.
UH...
UH, SURE. THANKS, WALLY.
JON?
I--I'M SCARED. I FEEL LIKE THERE'S BIG INVISIBLE THINGS ALL AROUND ME.
WILL YOU HOLD ME, PLEASE?
IT'S 1963. AN HOUR INTO THE FUTURE HER SWEAT COOLS AND DRIES IN THE NOVEMBER BEDROOM.
16

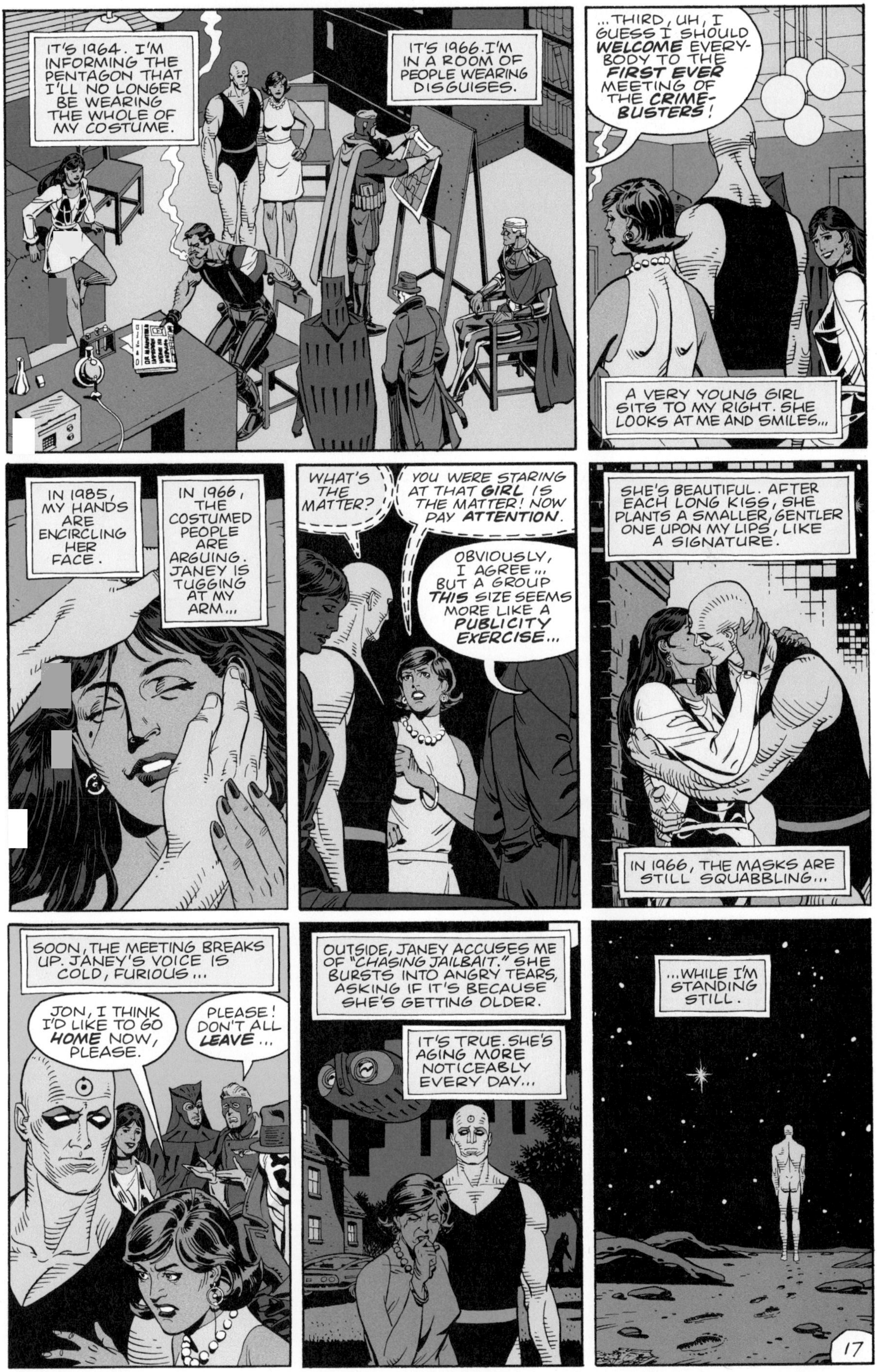
IT'S 1964. I'M INFORMING THE PENTAGON THAT I'LL NO LONGER BE WEARING THE WHOLE OF MY COSTUME.
IT'S 1966. I'M IN A ROOM OF PEOPLE WEARING DISGUISES.
...THIRD, UH, I GUESS I SHOULD WELCOME EVERYBODY TO THE FIRST EVER MEETING OF THE CRIME-BUSTERS!
A VERY YOUNG GIRL SITS TO MY RIGHT. SHE LOOKS AT ME AND SMILES...
IN 1985, MY HANDS ARE ENCIRCLING HER FACE.
IN 1966, THE COSTUMED PEOPLE ARE ARGUING. JANEY IS TUGGING AT MY ARM...
WHAT'S THE MATTER?
YOU WERE STARING AT THAT GIRL IS THE MATTER! NOW PAY ATTENTION.
OBVIOUSLY, I AGREE... BUT A GROUP THIS SIZE SEEMS MORE LIKE A PUBLICITY EXERCISE...
SHE'S BEAUTIFUL. AFTER EACH LONG KISS, SHE PLANTS A SMALLER, GENTLER ONE UPON MY LIPS, LIKE A SIGNATURE.
IN 1966, THE MASKS ARE STILL SQUABBLING...
SOON, THE MEETING BREAKS UP. JANEY'S VOICE IS COLD, FURIOUS...
JON, I THINK I'D LIKE TO GO HOME NOW, PLEASE.
PLEASE! DON'T ALL LEAVE...
OUTSIDE, JANEY ACCUSES ME OF "CHASING JAILBAIT." SHE BURSTS INTO ANGRY TEARS, ASKING IF IT'S BECAUSE SHE'S GETTING OLDER.
IT'S TRUE. SHE'S AGING MORE NOTICEABLY EVERY DAY...
...WHILE I'M STANDING STILL.
17

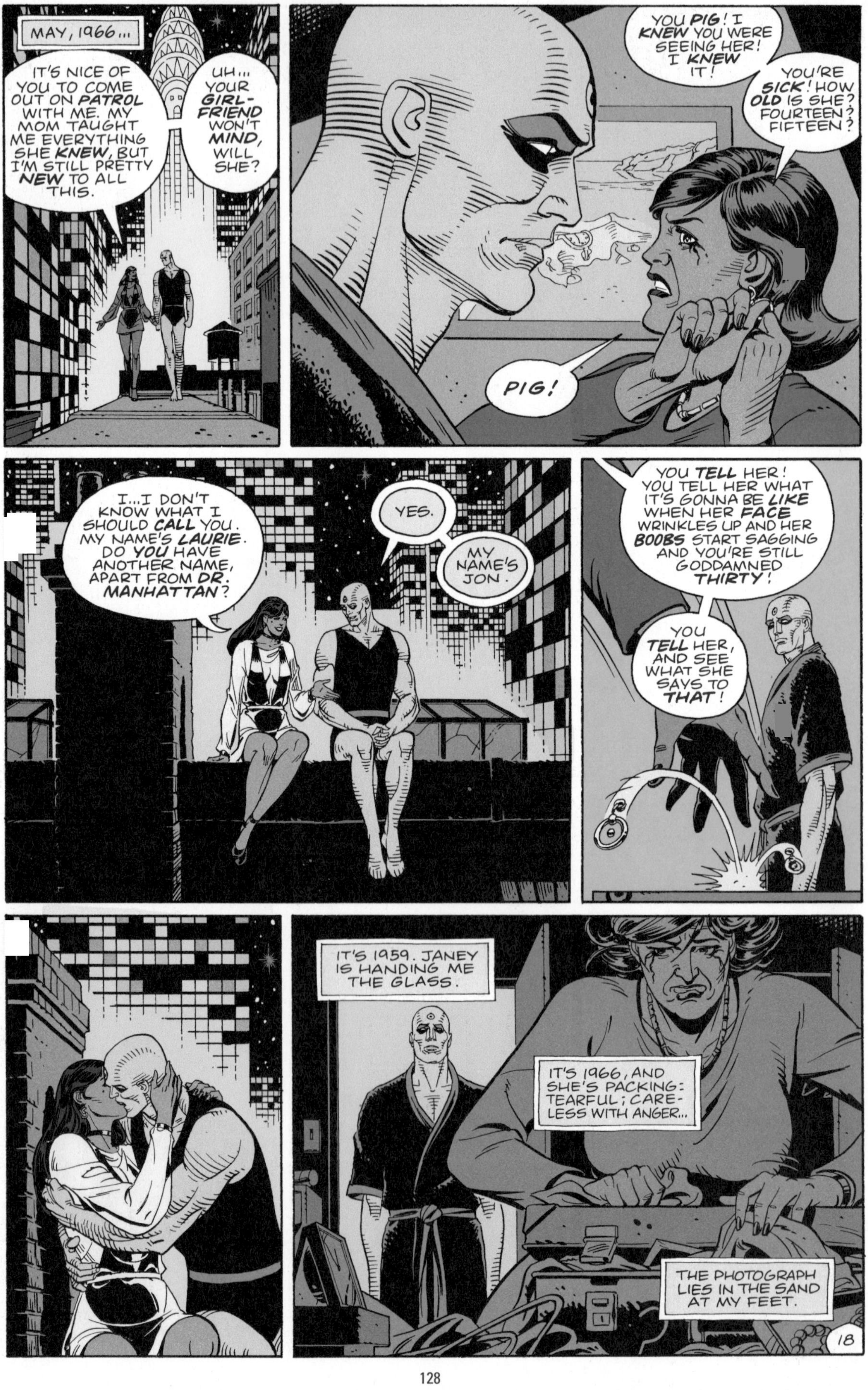

MAY, 1966...
IT'S NICE OF YOU TO COME OUT ON PATROL WITH ME. MY MOM TAUGHT ME EVERYTHING SHE KNEW, BUT I'M STILL PRETTY NEW TO ALL THIS.
UH... YOUR GIRLFRIEND WON'T MIND, WILL SHE?
YOU PIG! I KNEW YOU WERE SEEING HER! I KNEW IT!
YOU'RE SICK! HOW OLD IS SHE? FOURTEEN? FIFTEEN?
PIG!
I...I DON'T KNOW WHAT I SHOULD CALL YOU. MY NAME'S LAURIE. DO YOU HAVE ANOTHER NAME, APART FROM DR. MANHATTAN?
YES.
MY NAME'S JON.
YOU TELL HER! YOU TELL HER WHAT IT'S GONNA BE LIKE WHEN HER FACE WRINKLES UP AND HER BOOBS START SAGGING AND YOU'RE STILL GODDAMNED THIRTY!
YOU TELL HER, AND SEE WHAT SHE SAYS TO THAT!
IT'S 1959. JANEY IS HANDING ME THE GLASS.
IT'S 1966, AND SHE'S PACKING: TEARFUL; CARELESS WITH ANGER...
THE PHOTOGRAPH LIES IN THE SAND AT MY FEET.
18

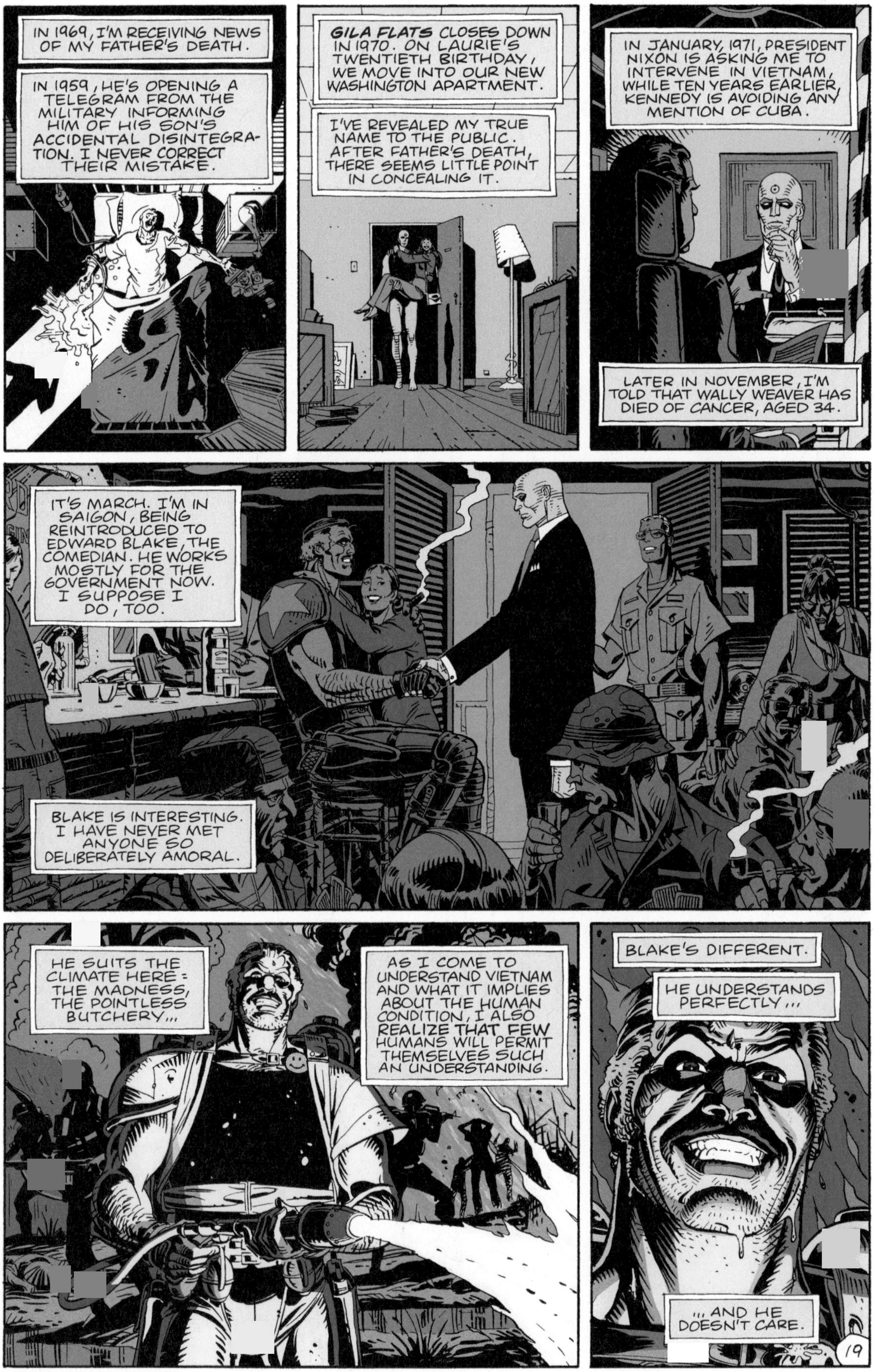

IN 1969, I'M RECEIVING NEWS OF MY FATHER'S DEATH.
IN 1959, HE'S OPENING A TELEGRAM FROM THE MILITARY INFORMING HIM OF HIS SON'S ACCIDENTAL DISINTEGRATION. I NEVER CORRECT THEIR MISTAKE.
GILA FLATS CLOSES DOWN IN 1970. ON LAURIE'S TWENTIETH BIRTHDAY, WE MOVE INTO OUR NEW WASHINGTON APARTMENT.
I'VE REVEALED MY TRUE NAME TO THE PUBLIC. AFTER FATHER'S DEATH, THERE SEEMS LITTLE POINT IN CONCEALING IT.
IN JANUARY, 1971, PRESIDENT NIXON IS ASKING ME TO INTERVENE IN VIETNAM, WHILE TEN YEARS EARLIER, KENNEDY IS AVOIDING ANY MENTION OF CUBA.
LATER IN NOVEMBER, I'M TOLD THAT WALLY WEAVER HAS DIED OF CANCER, AGED 34.
IT'S MARCH. I'M IN SAIGON, BEING REINTRODUCED TO EDWARD BLAKE, THE COMEDIAN. HE WORKS MOSTLY FOR THE GOVERNMENT NOW. I SUPPOSE I DO, TOO.
BLAKE IS INTERESTING. I HAVE NEVER MET ANYONE SO DELIBERATELY AMORAL.
HE SUITS THE CLIMATE HERE: THE MADNESS, THE POINTLESS BUTCHERY...
AS I COME TO UNDERSTAND VIETNAM AND WHAT IT IMPLIES ABOUT THE HUMAN CONDITION, I ALSO REALIZE THAT FEW HUMANS WILL PERMIT THEMSELVES SUCH AN UNDERSTANDING.
BLAKE'S DIFFERENT.
HE UNDERSTANDS PERFECTLY...
...AND HE DOESN'T CARE.
19

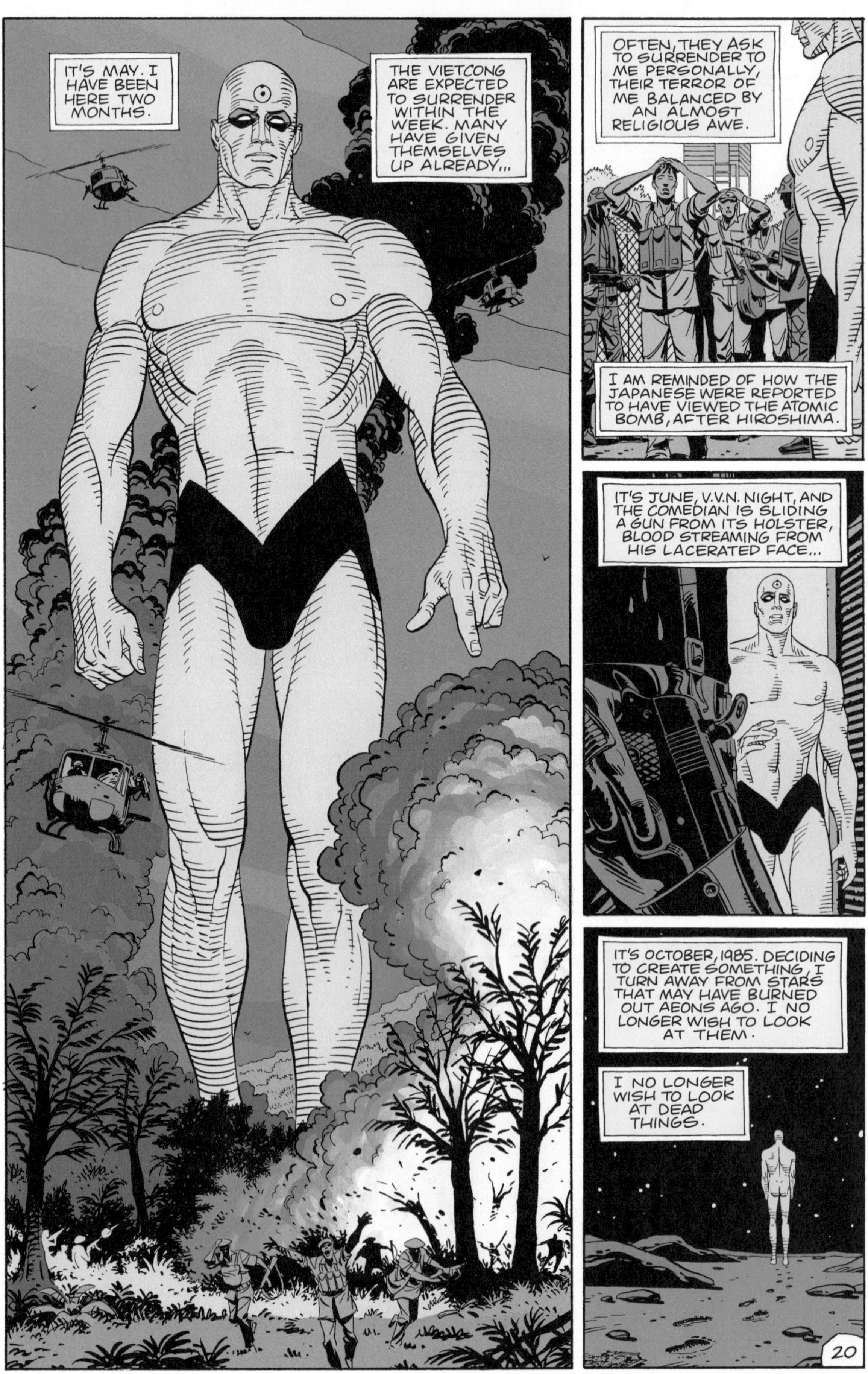
IT'S MAY. I HAVE BEEN HERE TWO MONTHS.
THE VIETCONG ARE EXPECTED TO SURRENDER WITHIN THE WEEK. MANY HAVE GIVEN THEMSELVES UP ALREADY...
OFTEN, THEY ASK TO SURRENDER TO ME PERSONALLY, THEIR TERROR OF ME BALANCED BY AN ALMOST RELIGIOUS AWE.
I AM REMINDED OF HOW THE JAPANESE WERE REPORTED TO HAVE VIEWED THE ATOMIC BOMB, AFTER HIROSHIMA.
IT'S JUNE, V.V.N. NIGHT, AND THE COMEDIAN IS SLIDING A GUN FROM ITS HOLSTER, BLOOD STREAMING FROM HIS LACERATED FACE...
IT'S OCTOBER, 1985. DECIDING TO CREATE SOMETHING, I TURN AWAY FROM STARS THAT MAY HAVE BURNED OUT AEONS AGO. I NO LONGER WISH TO LOOK AT THEM.
I NO LONGER WISH TO LOOK AT DEAD THINGS.
20

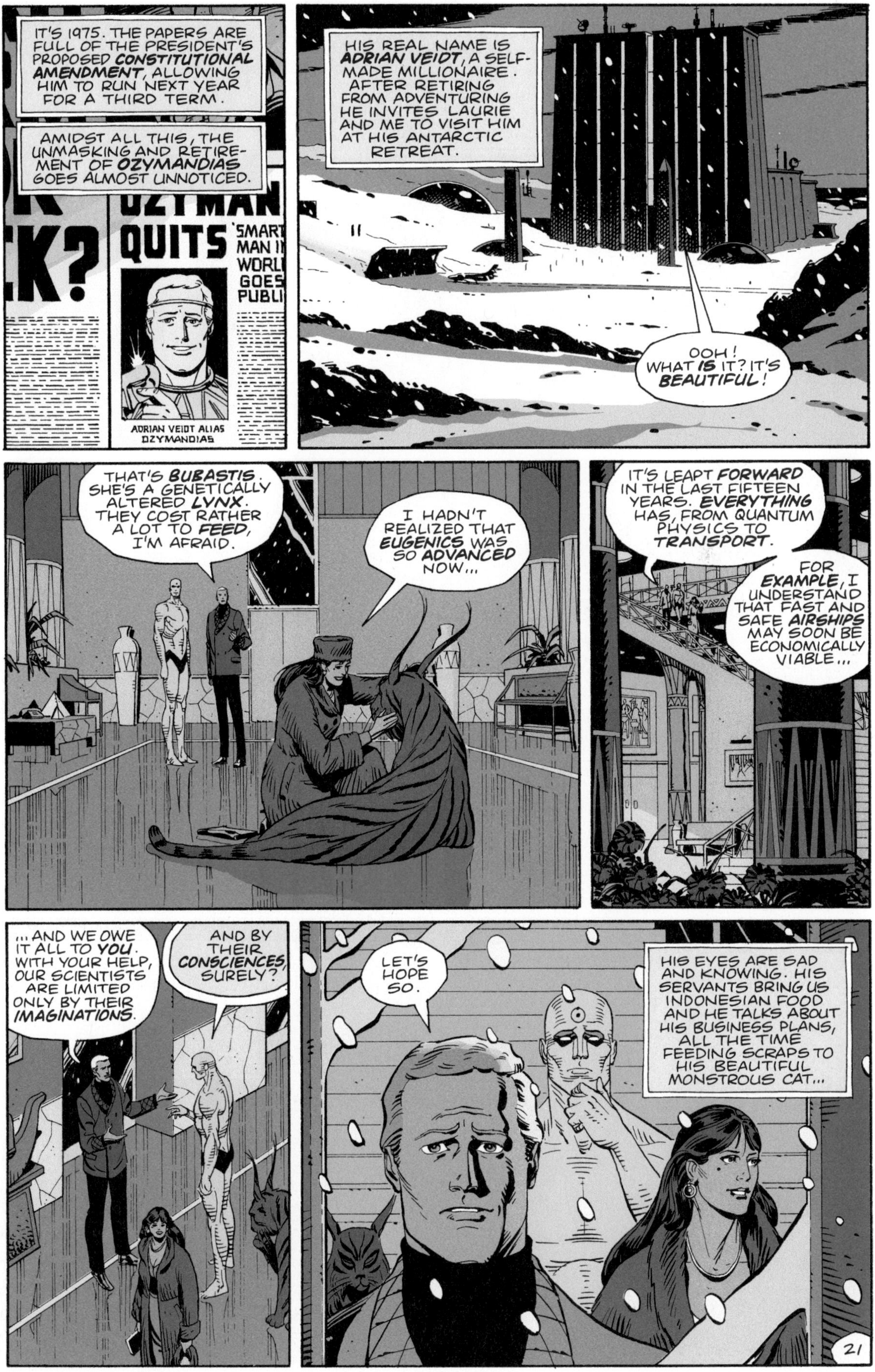
IT'S 1975. THE PAPERS ARE FULL OF THE PRESIDENT'S PROPOSED CONSTITUTIONAL AMENDMENT, ALLOWING HIM TO RUN NEXT YEAR FOR A THIRD TERM.
AMIDST ALL THIS, THE UNMASKING AND RETIREMENT OF OZYMANDIAS GOES ALMOST UNNOTICED.
OZYMAN
QUITS
'SMART MAN IN WORLD GOES PUBLI
ADRIAN VEIDT ALIAS OZYMANDIAS
HIS REAL NAME IS ADRIAN VEIDT, A SELF-MADE MILLIONAIRE. AFTER RETIRING FROM ADVENTURING HE INVITES LAURIE AND ME TO VISIT HIM AT HIS ANTARCTIC RETREAT.
OOH! WHAT IS IT? IT'S BEAUTIFUL!
THAT'S BUBASTIS. SHE'S A GENETICALLY ALTERED LYNX. THEY COST RATHER A LOT TO FEED, I'M AFRAID.
I HADN'T REALIZED THAT EUGENICS WAS SO ADVANCED NOW...
IT'S LEAPT FORWARD IN THE LAST FIFTEEN YEARS. EVERYTHING HAS, FROM QUANTUM PHYSICS TO TRANSPORT.
FOR EXAMPLE, I UNDERSTAND THAT FAST AND SAFE AIRSHIPS MAY SOON BE ECONOMICALLY VIABLE...
...AND WE OWE IT ALL TO YOU. WITH YOUR HELP, OUR SCIENTISTS ARE LIMITED ONLY BY THEIR IMAGINATIONS.
AND BY THEIR CONSCIENCES, SURELY?
LET'S HOPE SO.
HIS EYES ARE SAD AND KNOWING. HIS SERVANTS BRING US INDONESIAN FOOD AND HE TALKS ABOUT HIS BUSINESS PLANS, ALL THE TIME FEEDING SCRAPS TO HIS BEAUTIFUL MONSTROUS CAT...
21

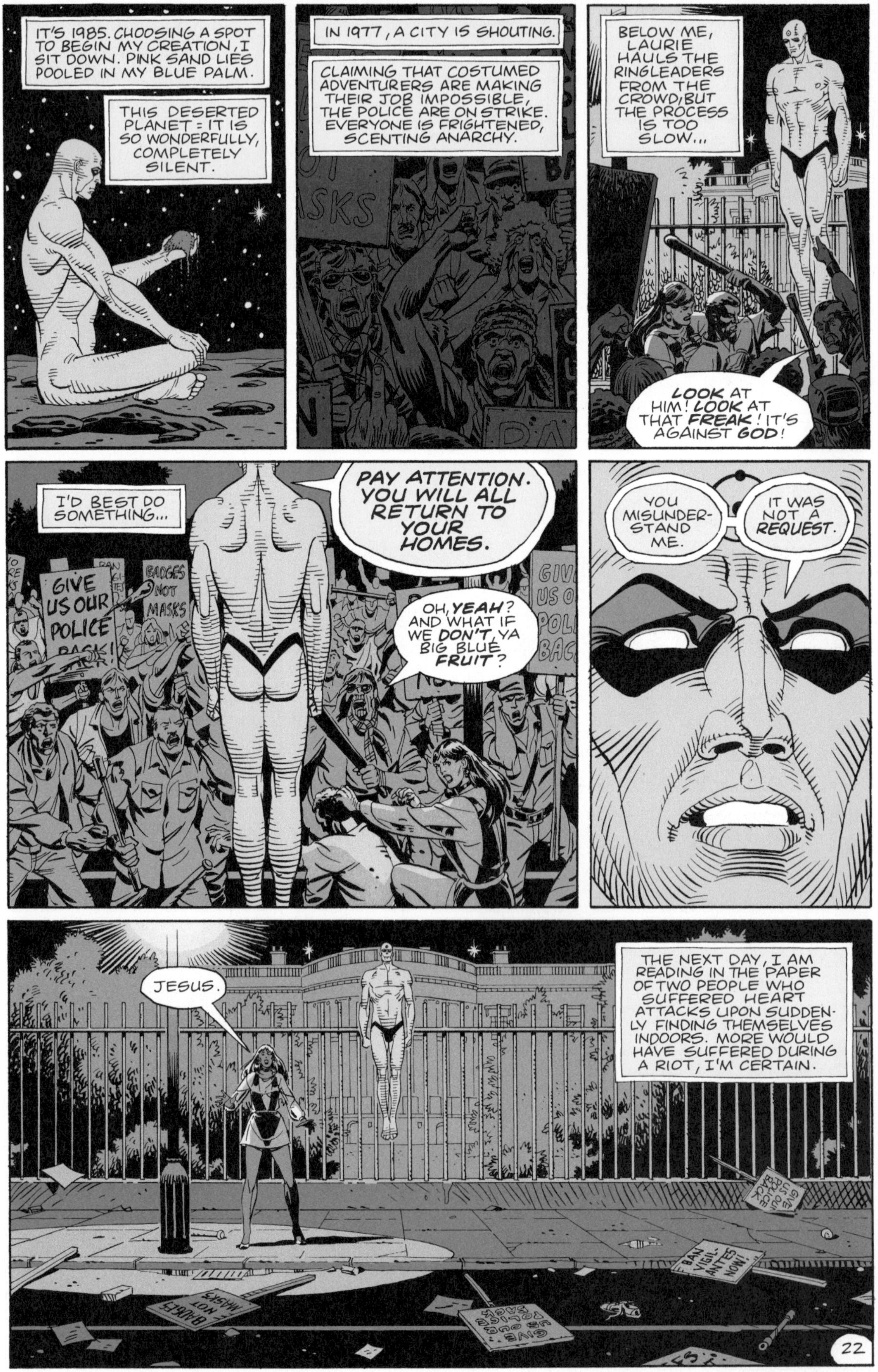
IT'S 1985. CHOOSING A SPOT TO BEGIN MY CREATION, I SIT DOWN. PINK SAND LIES POOLED IN MY BLUE PALM.
THIS DESERTED PLANET: IT IS SO WONDERFULLY, COMPLETELY SILENT.
IN 1977, A CITY IS SHOUTING.
CLAIMING THAT COSTUMED ADVENTURERS ARE MAKING THEIR JOB IMPOSSIBLE, THE POLICE ARE ON STRIKE. EVERYONE IS FRIGHTENED, SCENTING ANARCHY.
BELOW ME, LAURIE HAULS THE RINGLEADERS FROM THE CROWD, BUT THE PROCESS IS TOO SLOW...
LOOK AT HIM! LOOK AT THAT FREAK! IT'S AGAINST GOD!
I'D BEST DO SOMETHING...
PAY ATTENTION. YOU WILL ALL RETURN TO YOUR HOMES.
GIVE US OUR POLICE
BADGES NOT MASKS
OH, YEAH? AND WHAT IF WE DON'T, YA BIG BLUE FRUIT?
YOU MISUNDERSTAND ME.
IT WAS NOT A REQUEST.
JESUS.
THE NEXT DAY, I AM READING IN THE PAPER OF TWO PEOPLE WHO SUFFERED HEART ATTACKS UPON SUDDENLY FINDING THEMSELVES INDOORS. MORE WOULD HAVE SUFFERED DURING A RIOT, I'M CERTAIN.
BAN VIGILANTES NOW!
22

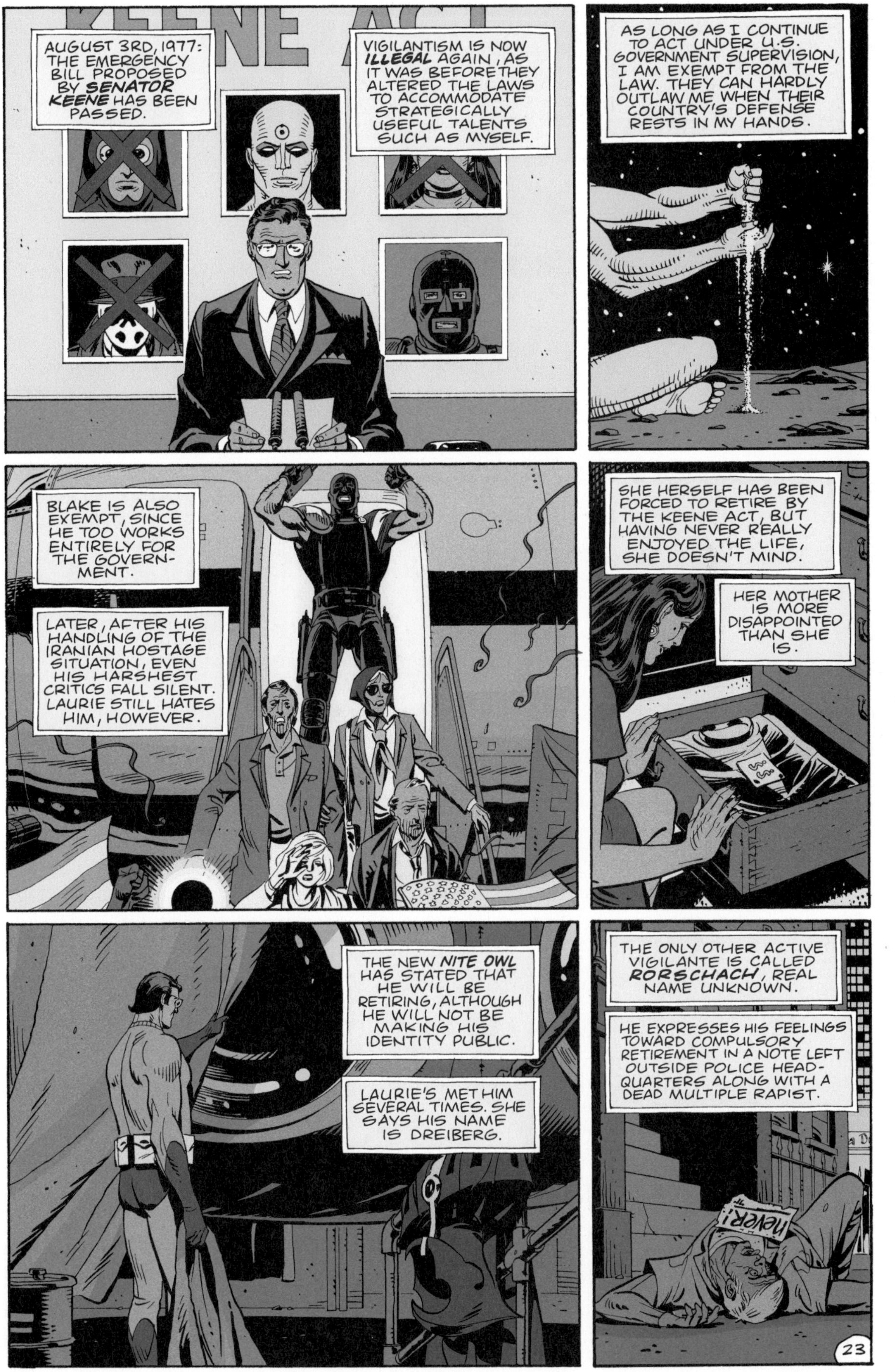
AUGUST 3RD, 1977: THE EMERGENCY BILL PROPOSED BY SENATOR KEENE HAS BEEN PASSED.
VIGILANTISM IS NOW ILLEGAL AGAIN, AS IT WAS BEFORE THEY ALTERED THE LAWS TO ACCOMMODATE STRATEGICALLY USEFUL TALENTS SUCH AS MYSELF.
AS LONG AS I CONTINUE TO ACT UNDER U.S. GOVERNMENT SUPERVISION, I AM EXEMPT FROM THE LAW. THEY CAN HARDLY OUTLAW ME WHEN THEIR COUNTRY'S DEFENSE RESTS IN MY HANDS.
BLAKE IS ALSO EXEMPT, SINCE HE TOO WORKS ENTIRELY FOR THE GOVERNMENT.
LATER, AFTER HIS HANDLING OF THE IRANIAN HOSTAGE SITUATION, EVEN HIS HARSHEST CRITICS FALL SILENT. LAURIE STILL HATES HIM, HOWEVER.
SHE HERSELF HAS BEEN FORCED TO RETIRE BY THE KEENE ACT, BUT HAVING NEVER REALLY ENJOYED THE LIFE, SHE DOESN'T MIND.
HER MOTHER IS MORE DISAPPOINTED THAN SHE IS.
THE NEW NITE OWL HAS STATED THAT HE WILL BE RETIRING, ALTHOUGH HE WILL NOT BE MAKING HIS IDENTITY PUBLIC.
LAURIE'S MET HIM SEVERAL TIMES. SHE SAYS HIS NAME IS DREIBERG.
THE ONLY OTHER ACTIVE VIGILANTE IS CALLED RORSCHACH, REAL NAME UNKNOWN.
HE EXPRESSES HIS FEELINGS TOWARD COMPULSORY RETIREMENT IN A NOTE LEFT OUTSIDE POLICE HEADQUARTERS ALONG WITH A DEAD MULTIPLE RAPIST.
never!
23

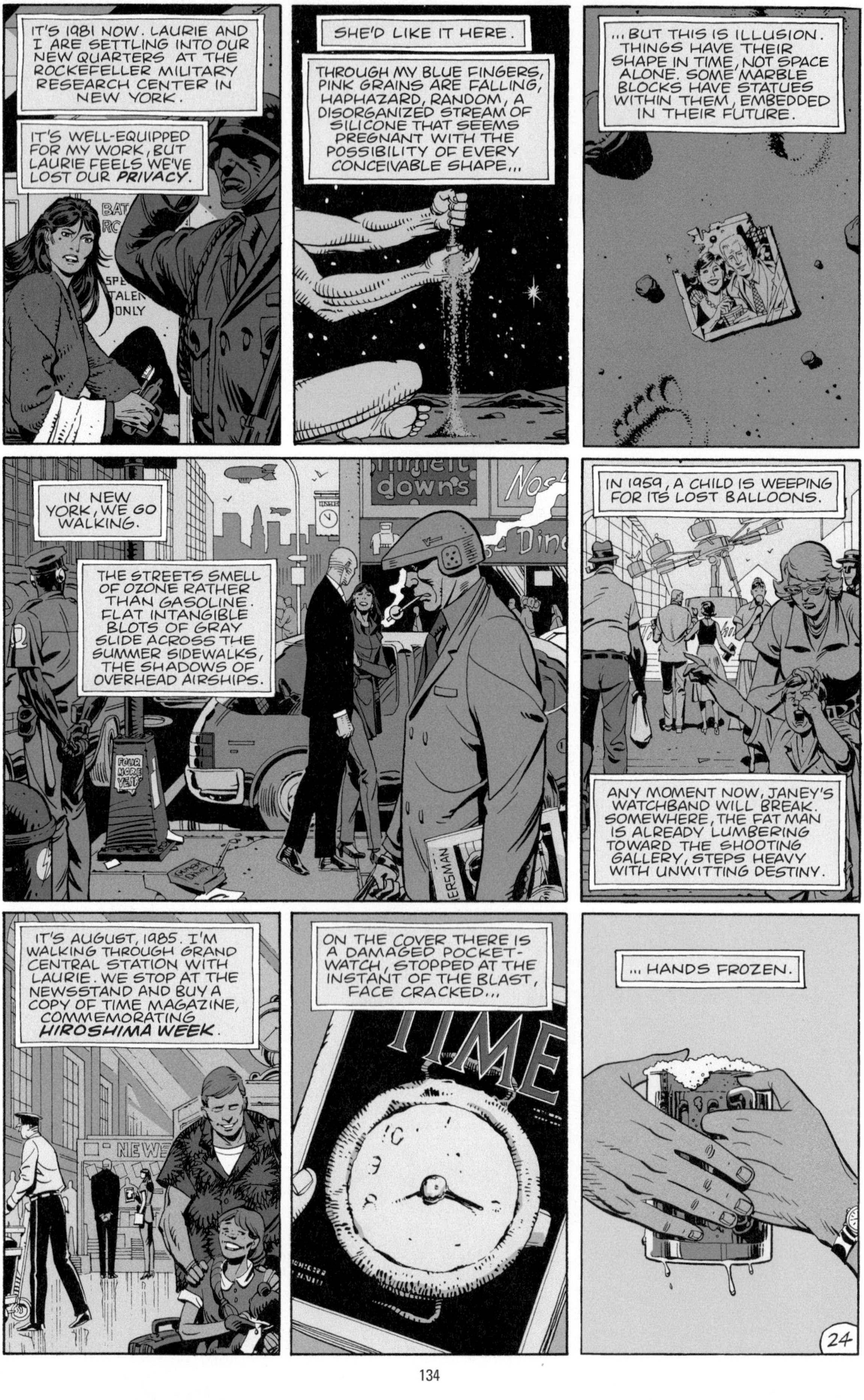
IT'S 1981 NOW. LAURIE AND I ARE SETTLING INTO OUR NEW QUARTERS AT THE ROCKEFELLER MILITARY RESEARCH CENTER IN NEW YORK.
IT'S WELL-EQUIPPED FOR MY WORK, BUT LAURIE FEELS WE'VE LOST OUR *PRIVACY*.
SHE'D LIKE IT HERE.
THROUGH MY BLUE FINGERS, PINK GRAINS ARE FALLING, HAPHAZARD, RANDOM, A DISORGANIZED STREAM OF SILICONE THAT SEEMS PREGNANT WITH THE POSSIBILITY OF EVERY CONCEIVABLE SHAPE...
...BUT THIS IS ILLUSION. THINGS HAVE THEIR SHAPE IN TIME, NOT SPACE ALONE. SOME MARBLE BLOCKS HAVE STATUES WITHIN THEM, EMBEDDED IN THEIR FUTURE.
IN NEW YORK, WE GO WALKING.
THE STREETS SMELL OF OZONE RATHER THAN GASOLINE. FLAT INTANGIBLE BLOTS OF GRAY SLIDE ACROSS THE SUMMER SIDEWALKS, THE SHADOWS OF OVERHEAD AIRSHIPS.
IN 1959, A CHILD IS WEEPING FOR ITS LOST BALLOONS.
ANY MOMENT NOW, JANEY'S WATCHBAND WILL BREAK. SOMEWHERE, THE FAT MAN IS ALREADY LUMBERING TOWARD THE SHOOTING GALLERY, STEPS HEAVY WITH UNWITTING DESTINY.
IT'S AUGUST, 1985. I'M WALKING THROUGH GRAND CENTRAL STATION WITH LAURIE. WE STOP AT THE NEWSSTAND AND BUY A COPY OF TIME MAGAZINE, COMMEMORATING **HIROSHIMA WEEK**.
ON THE COVER THERE IS A DAMAGED POCKET-WATCH, STOPPED AT THE INSTANT OF THE BLAST, FACE CRACKED...
TIME
...HANDS FROZEN.
24

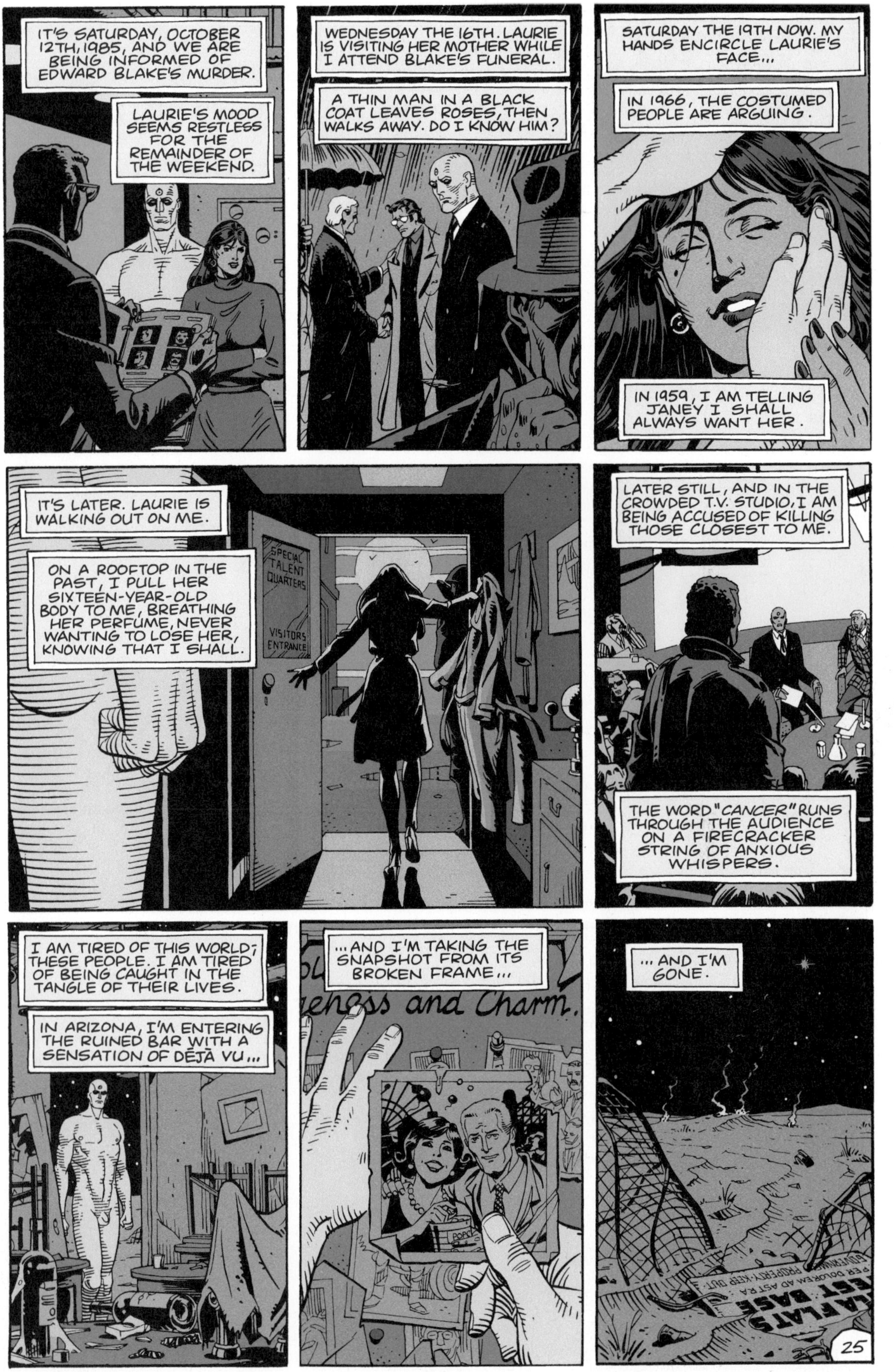
IT'S SATURDAY, OCTOBER 12TH, 1985, AND WE ARE BEING INFORMED OF EDWARD BLAKE'S MURDER.
LAURIE'S MOOD SEEMS RESTLESS FOR THE REMAINDER OF THE WEEKEND.
WEDNESDAY THE 16TH. LAURIE IS VISITING HER MOTHER WHILE I ATTEND BLAKE'S FUNERAL.
A THIN MAN IN A BLACK COAT LEAVES ROSES, THEN WALKS AWAY. DO I KNOW HIM?
SATURDAY THE 19TH NOW. MY HANDS ENCIRCLE LAURIE'S FACE...
IN 1966, THE COSTUMED PEOPLE ARE ARGUING.
IN 1959, I AM TELLING JANEY I SHALL ALWAYS WANT HER.
IT'S LATER. LAURIE IS WALKING OUT ON ME.
ON A ROOFTOP IN THE PAST, I PULL HER SIXTEEN-YEAR-OLD BODY TO ME, BREATHING HER PERFUME, NEVER WANTING TO LOSE HER, KNOWING THAT I SHALL.
SPECIAL TALENT QUARTERS
VISITORS ENTRANCE
LATER STILL, AND IN THE CROWDED T.V. STUDIO, I AM BEING ACCUSED OF KILLING THOSE CLOSEST TO ME.
THE WORD "CANCER" RUNS THROUGH THE AUDIENCE ON A FIRECRACKER STRING OF ANXIOUS WHISPERS.
I AM TIRED OF THIS WORLD; THESE PEOPLE. I AM TIRED OF BEING CAUGHT IN THE TANGLE OF THEIR LIVES.
IN ARIZONA, I'M ENTERING THE RUINED BAR WITH A SENSATION OF DÉJÀ VU...
...AND I'M TAKING THE SNAPSHOT FROM ITS BROKEN FRAME...
...AND I'M GONE.
25

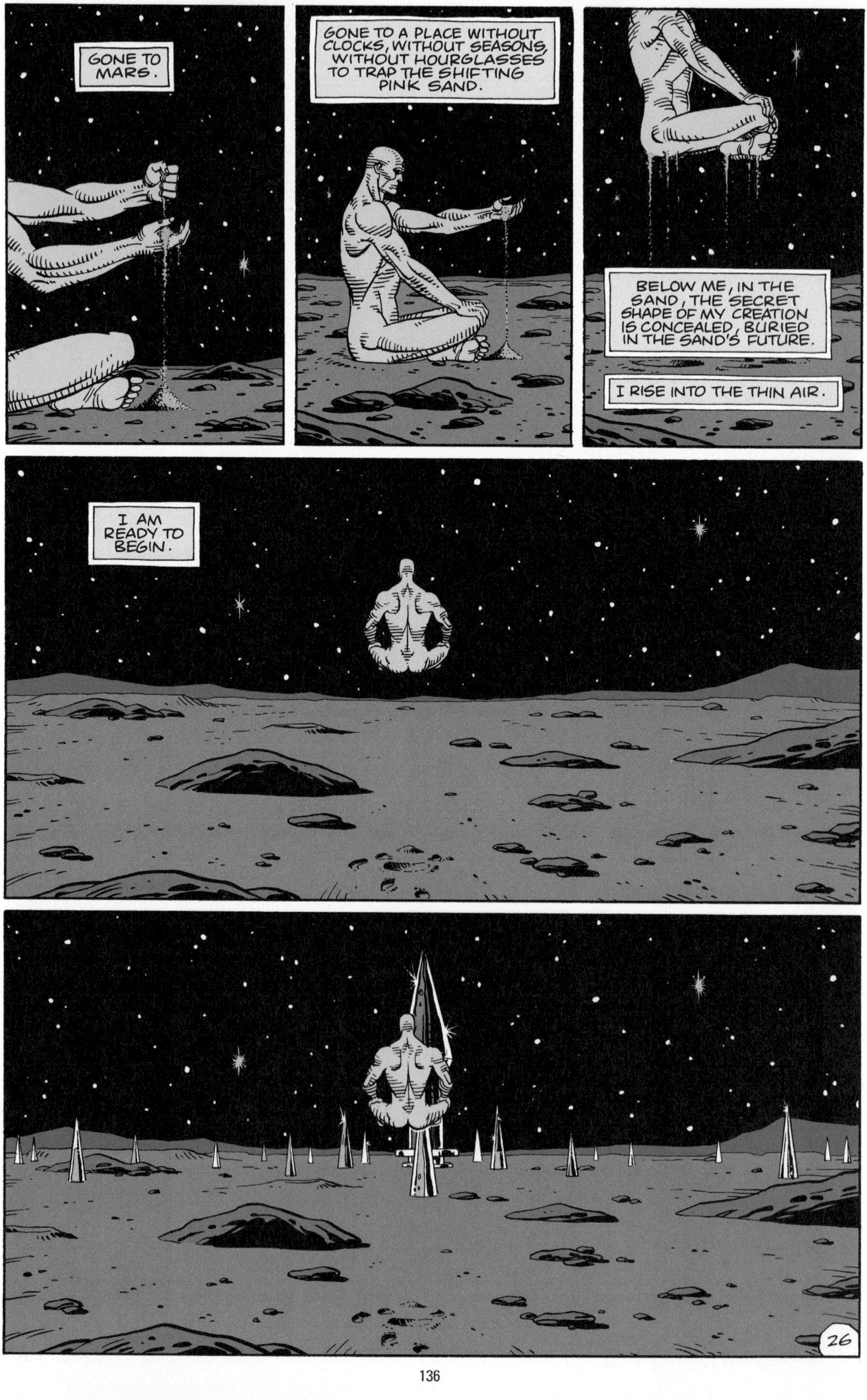
GONE TO MARS.
GONE TO A PLACE WITHOUT CLOCKS, WITHOUT SEASONS, WITHOUT HOURGLASSES TO TRAP THE SHIFTING PINK SAND.
BELOW ME, IN THE SAND, THE SECRET SHAPE OF MY CREATION IS CONCEALED, BURIED IN THE SAND'S FUTURE.
I RISE INTO THE THIN AIR.
I AM READY TO BEGIN.
26

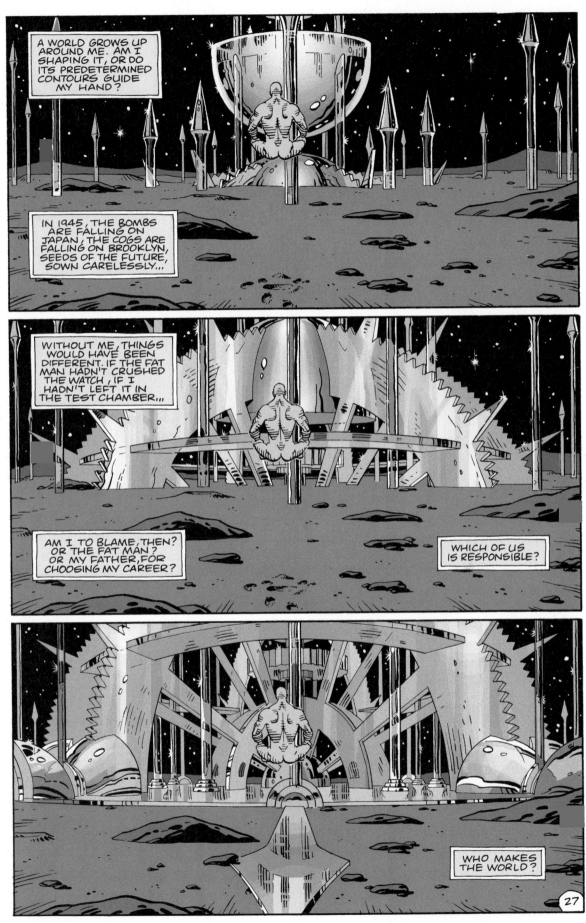

A WORLD GROWS UP AROUND ME. AM I SHAPING IT, OR DO ITS PREDETERMINED CONTOURS GUIDE MY HAND?

IN 1945, THE BOMBS ARE FALLING ON JAPAN, THE COGS ARE FALLING ON BROOKLYN, SEEDS OF THE FUTURE, SOWN CARELESSLY...

WITHOUT ME, THINGS WOULD HAVE BEEN DIFFERENT. IF THE FAT MAN HADN'T CRUSHED THE WATCH, IF I HADN'T LEFT IT IN THE TEST CHAMBER...

AM I TO BLAME, THEN? OR THE FAT MAN? OR MY FATHER, FOR CHOOSING MY CAREER?

WHICH OF US IS RESPONSIBLE?

WHO MAKES THE WORLD?

27

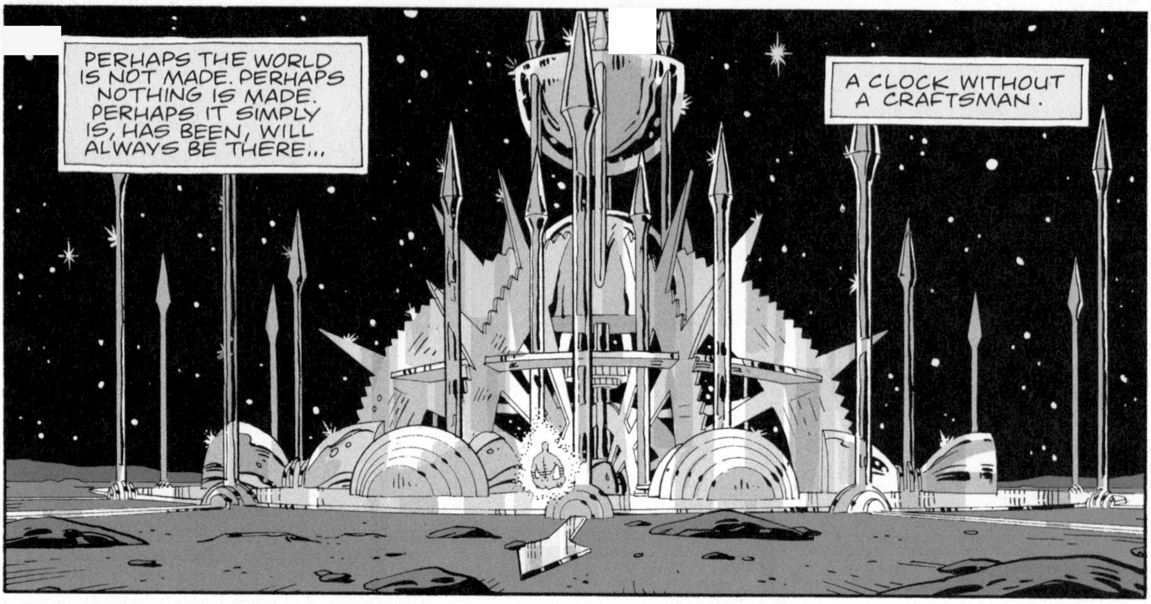
PERHAPS THE WORLD IS NOT MADE. PERHAPS NOTHING IS MADE. PERHAPS IT SIMPLY IS, HAS BEEN, WILL ALWAYS BE THERE...
A CLOCK WITHOUT A CRAFTSMAN.

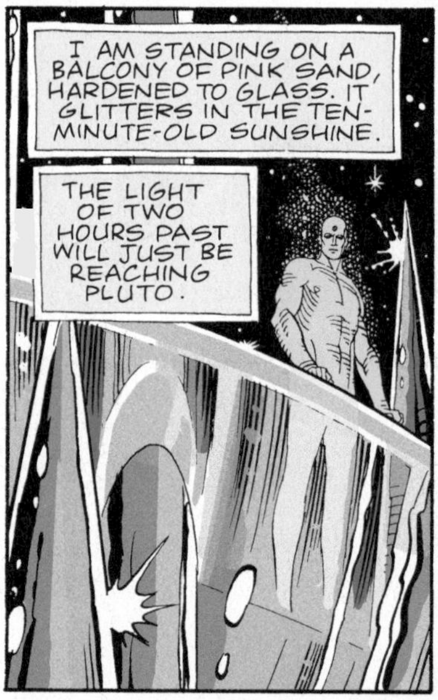
I AM STANDING ON A BALCONY OF PINK SAND, HARDENED TO GLASS. IT GLITTERS IN THE TEN-MINUTE-OLD SUNSHINE.
THE LIGHT OF TWO HOURS PAST WILL JUST BE REACHING PLUTO.

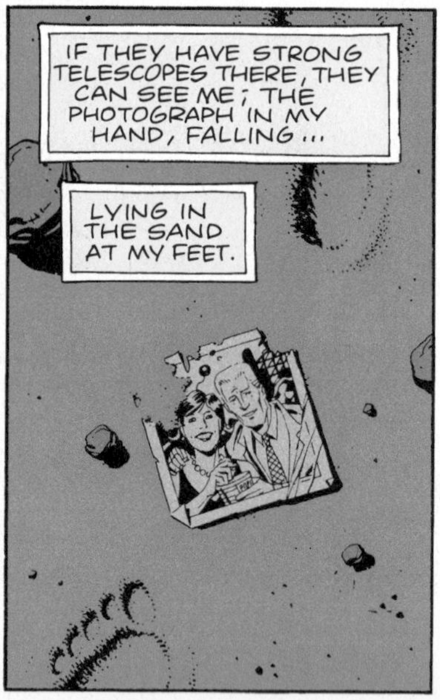
IF THEY HAVE STRONG TELESCOPES THERE, THEY CAN SEE ME; THE PHOTOGRAPH IN MY HAND, FALLING...
LYING IN THE SAND AT MY FEET.

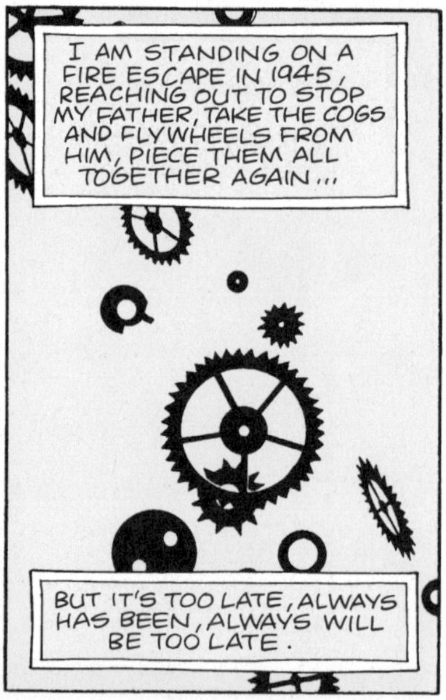
I AM STANDING ON A FIRE ESCAPE IN 1945, REACHING OUT TO STOP MY FATHER, TAKE THE COGS AND FLYWHEELS FROM HIM, PIECE THEM ALL TOGETHER AGAIN...
BUT IT'S TOO LATE, ALWAYS HAS BEEN, ALWAYS WILL BE TOO LATE.

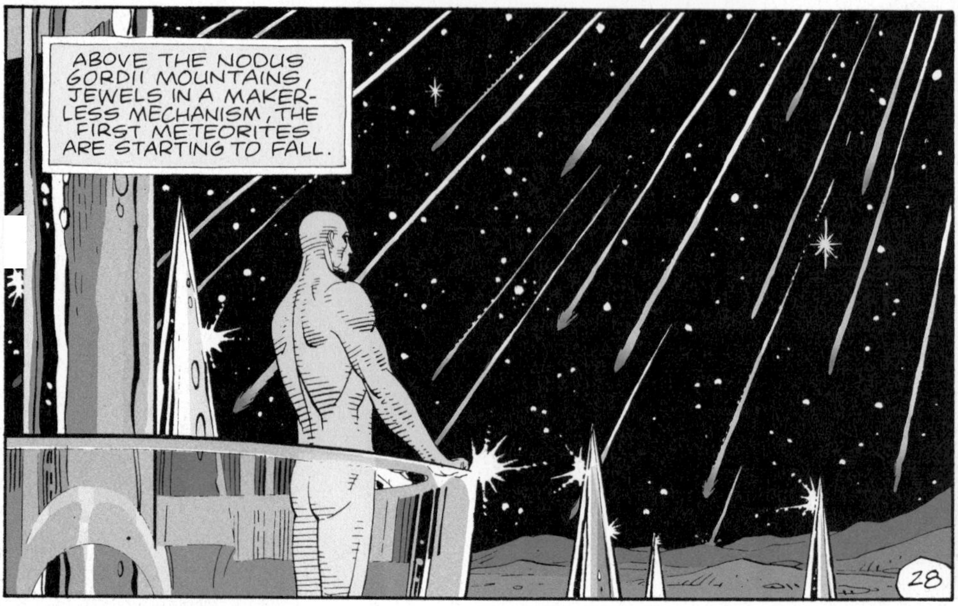
ABOVE THE NODUS GORDII MOUNTAINS, JEWELS IN A MAKER-LESS MECHANISM, THE FIRST METEORITES ARE STARTING TO FALL.
28

The release of atom power has changed everything except our way of thinking... The solution to this problem lies in the heart of mankind. If only I had known, I should have become a watchmaker.
—Albert Einstein

DR. MANHATTAN: SUPER-POWERS AND THE SUPERPOWERS

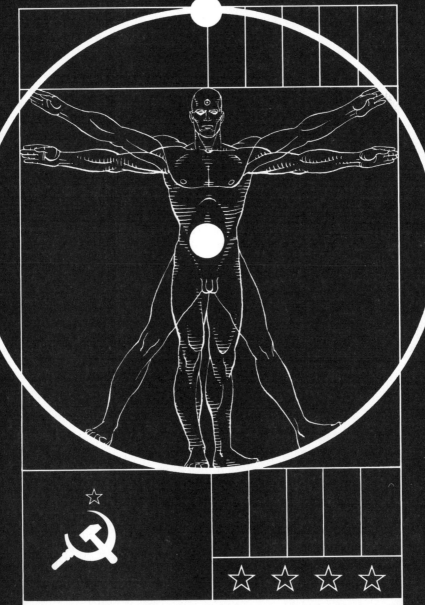

BY PROFESSOR MILTON GLASS

Introduction

For those of us who delight in such things, the twentieth century has, in its unfolding, presented mankind with an array of behavioral paradoxes and moral conundrums hitherto unimagined and perhaps unimaginable. Science, traditional enemy of mysticism and religion, has taken on a growing understanding that the model of the universe suggested by quantum physics differs very little from the universe that Taoists and other mystics have existed in for centuries. Large numbers of young people, raised in rigidly structured and industrially oriented cultures, violently reject industrialism and seek instead some modified version of the agricultural lifestyle that their forebears (debatably) enjoyed, including extended communal families and in some instances a barter economy in miniature. Children starve while boots costing many thousands of dollars leave their mark upon the surface of the moon. We have labored long to build a heaven, only to find it populated with horrors.

It is the oldest ironies that are still the most satisfying: man, when preparing for bloody war, will orate loudly and most eloquently in the name of peace. This dichotomy is not an invention of the twentieth century, yet it is in this century that the most striking examples of the phenomena have appeared. Never before has man pursued global harmony more vocally while amassing stockpiles of weapons so devastating in their effect. The second world war—we were told—was The War To End Wars. The development of the atomic bomb is the Weapon To End Wars.

And yet wars continue. Currently, no nation on this planet is not involved in some form of armed struggle, if not against its neighbors then against internal forces. Furthermore, as ever-escalating amounts of money are poured into the pursuit of the specific weapon or conflict that will bring lasting peace, the drain on our economies creates a run-down urban landscape where crime flourishes and people are concerned less with national security than with the simple personal security needed to stop at the store late at night for a quart of milk without being mugged. The places we struggled so viciously to keep safe are becoming increasingly dangerous. The wars to end wars, the weapons to end wars, these things have failed us.

Now we have a man to end wars.

Since my association with Dr. Jonathan Osterman and the being he eventually became are well documented elsewhere, I feel I need only recap them briefly here. In 1959, in an accident that was certainly unplanned and just as certainly unrepeatable, a young American man was completely disintegrated, at least in a physical sense. Despite the absence of a body, a form of electromagnetic pattern resembling consciousness survived, and was able, in time, to rebuild an approximation of the body it had lost.

DR. MANHATTAN:

Perhaps in the process of reconstructing its corporeal form, this new and wholly original entity achieved a complete mastery of all matter; able to shape reality by the manipulation of its basic building blocks. When news of this being's phenomenal genesis was first released to the world, a certain phrase was used that has—at varying times—been attributed both to me and to others. On the newsflashes coming over our tvs on that fateful night, one sentence was repeated over and over again: 'The superman exists and he's American.'

I never said that, although I do recall saying something similar to a persistent reporter who would not leave without a quote. I presume the remark was edited or toned down so as not to offend public sensibilities; in any event, I never said 'The superman exists and he's American'. What I said was '*God* exists and he's American'. If that statement starts to chill you after a couple of moments' consideration, then don't be alarmed. A feeling of intense and crushing religious terror at the concept indicates only that you are still sane.

Since the mid-1960s, when the dazed and numbed mass consciousness first began to comprehend the significance of this new life form in humanity's midst, the political balance has changed drastically. Many people in this country feel that this is for the best. America's unquestioned military supremacy has also provided us with a certain economic leverage where we can dictate the economic policies of the western world and direct them to our advantage. There is little wonder, then, that the idea of a world run by an omnipotent God-King owing allegiance to the United States seems eminently desirable. By placing our superhuman benefactor in the position of a walking nuclear deterrent, it is assumed we have finally guaranteed lasting peace on earth. It is with this last contention that my most serious point of issue lies: I do not believe that we have a man to end wars.

I believe that we have made a man to end worlds.

The assumption that America's opponents are powerless before Dr. Manhattan, while comforting, begins to fail before closer examination. As I understand current Pentagon thinking, the conventional wisdom suggests that when faced with an insoluble problem, the Soviet Union will have no other option than acceptance of a loss of world influence culminating in its eventual defeat. It has been demonstrated, at least in well-supported theoretical terms, that Dr. Manhattan could at any time destroy large areas of Soviet territory instantly. It has been similarly theoretically demonstrated that, were a full scale nuclear assault to be launched upon America from Soviet bases in the U.S.S.R. and Europe, Dr. Manhattan would be able to deflect or disarm at least sixty percent of all incoming missiles before they had reached their targets. Against odds like that, it is argued, Russia would never risk instigating a full-scale global conflict. Since it is not in America's interests to promote such a conflict, does that mean that global peace is once and finally assured? No. It does not.

For one thing, it is an assumption based upon the belief that American psychology and its Soviet counterpart are interchangeable. To understand the Russian attitude to the possibility of a third world war one must first understand their attitude to the second. In WWII, none of the allied powers fought so bitterly or sustained such losses as did the Russians. It was Hitler's lack of success in his assault upon the

Soviet heartland that assured his eventual defeat, and though it was paid for mostly by Soviet lives, the entire world reaped the benefits. In time, the Russian contribution to the war effort has been downplayed and dismissed—most noticeably as our political differences became wider—as we glorified our own contribution while forgetting that of our estranged former allies. The Russians, however, have not forgotten. There are still those who remember the horror of a war fought on their soil, and almost certainly there are members of the Politburo in that category. From my reading of various pronouncements made by the Russian high command over the years, I am convinced that they will never again permit their nation to be threatened in a similar manner, *no matter what the cost.*

The presence of a deterrent such as Dr. Manhattan has doubtless curbed Soviet adventurism, as there have been numerous occasions when the U.S.S.R. has had to step down over some issue rather than risk escalation into a war it certainly could not win. Often, these reversals have been humiliating, and this has perhaps fostered the illusion that the Soviets will suffer such indignities endlessly. This is a misconception, for there is indeed another option available.

That option is Mutually Assured Destruction. Stated simply, Dr. Manhattan cannot stop all the Soviet warheads from reaching American soil, even a greatly reduced percentage would still be more than enough to effectively end the organic life in the northern hemisphere. The suggestion that the presence of a superhuman has inclined the world more towards peace is refudiated by the sharp increase in both Russian and American nuclear stockpiles since the advent of Dr. Manhattan. Infinite destruction divided by two or ten or twenty is still infinite destruction. If threatened with eventual domination, would the Soviets pursue this unquestionably suicidal course? Yes. Given their history and their view of the world, I believe that they would.

Our current administration believes otherwise. They continually push their unearned advantage until American influence comes uncomfortably close to key areas of Soviet interest. It is as if—with a real live Deity on their side—our leaders have become intoxicated with a heady draught of Omnipotence-by-Association, without realizing just how his very existence has deformed the lives of every living creature on the face of this planet.

This is true in a domestic sense as well as a broader, international one. The technology that Dr. Manhattan has made possible has changed the way we think about our clothes, our food, our travel. We drive in electric cars and travel in leisure and comfort in clean, economical airships. Our entire culture has had to contort itself to accommodate the presence of something more than human, and we have all felt the results of this. The evidence surrounds us, in our everyday lives and on the front pages of the newspapers we read. One single being has been allowed to change the entire world, pushing it closer to its eventual destruction in the process. The Gods now walk amongst us, affecting the lives of every man, woman and child on the planet in a direct way rather than through mythology and the reassurances of faith. The safety of a whole world rests in the hands of a being far beyond what we understand to be human.

We are all of us living in the shadow of Manhattan.

DR. MANHATTAN:

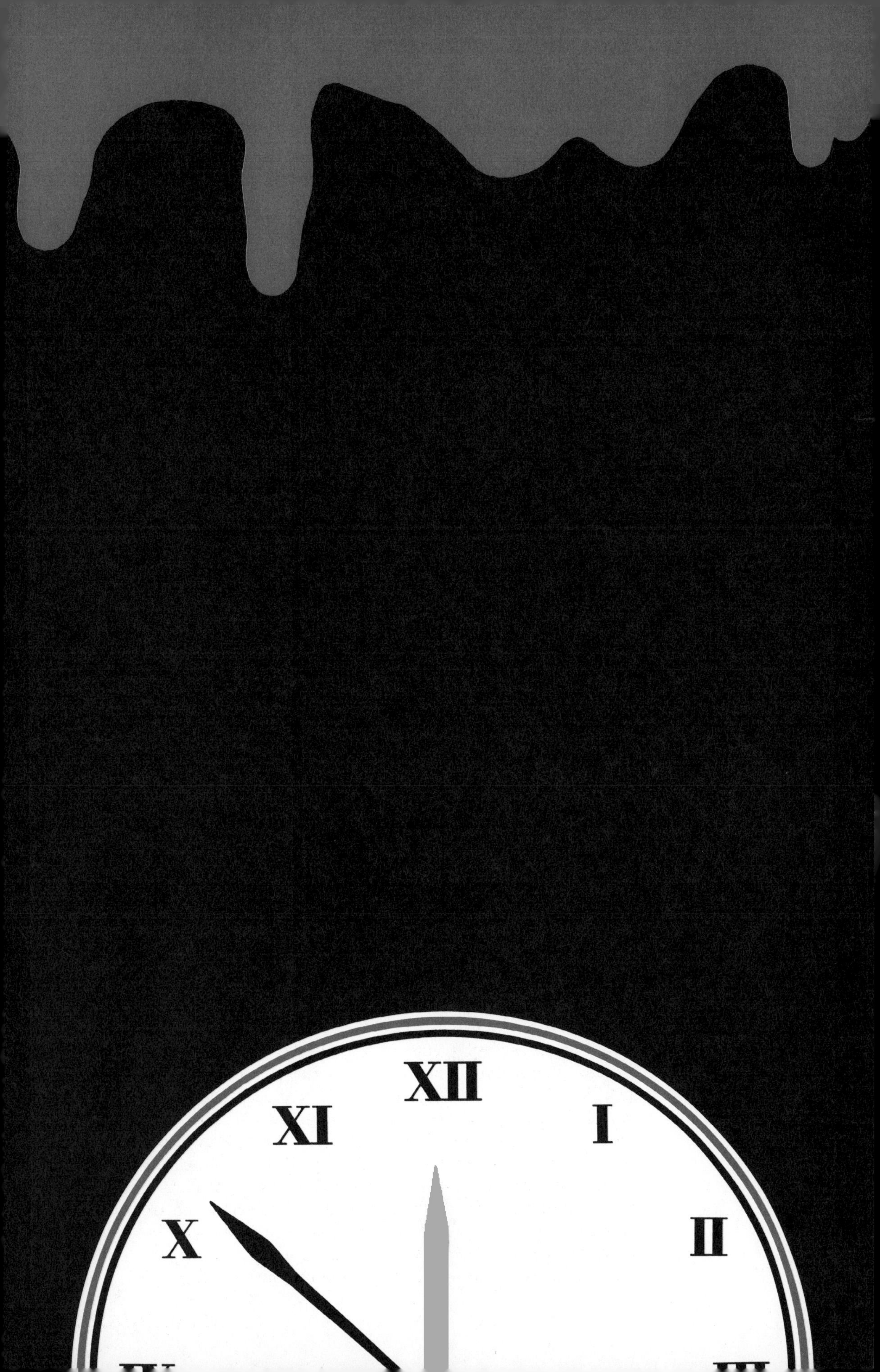
XII
XI
I
X
II

CHAPTER V

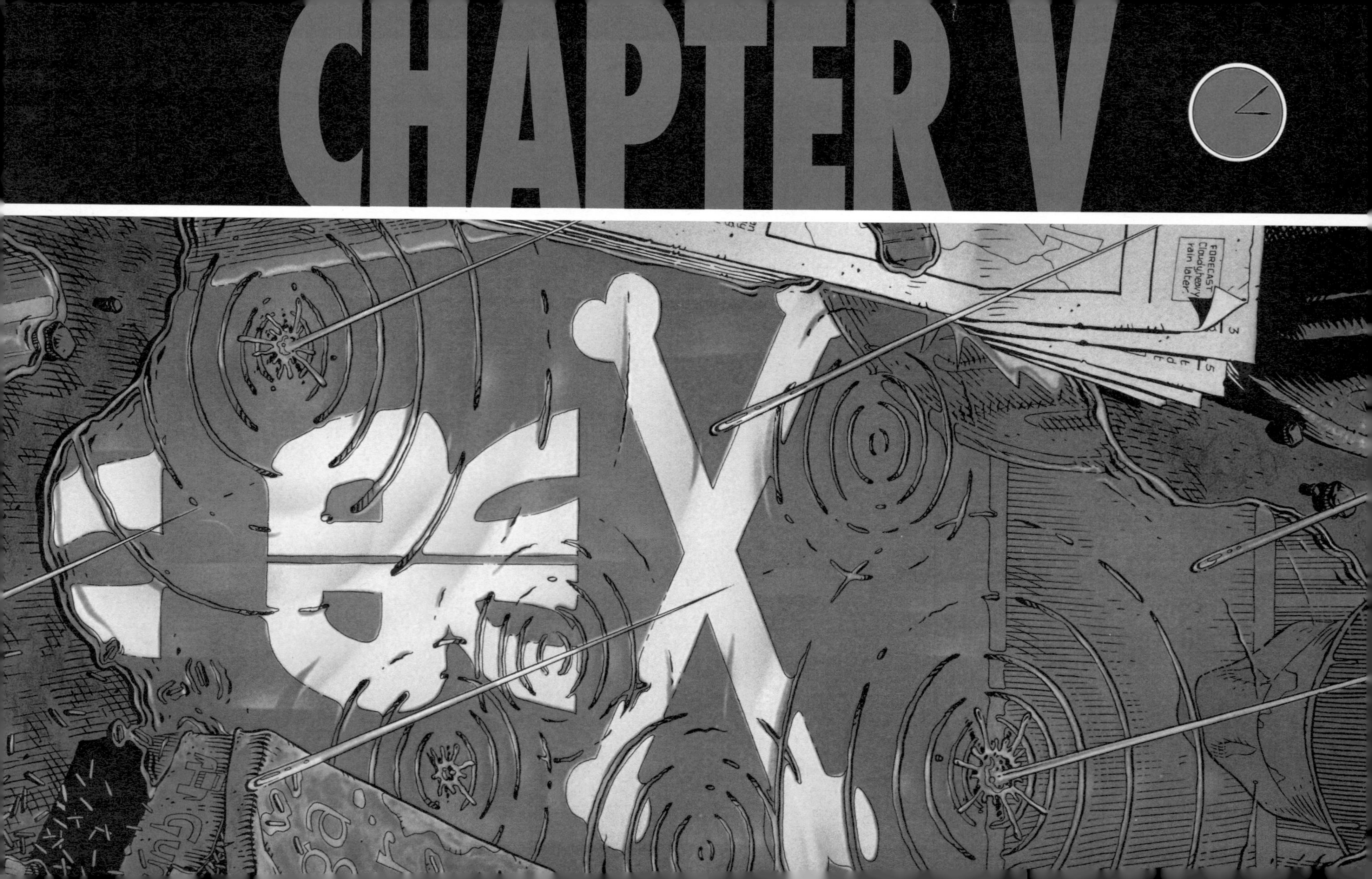
FORECAST
Cloudy,heavy
rain later.

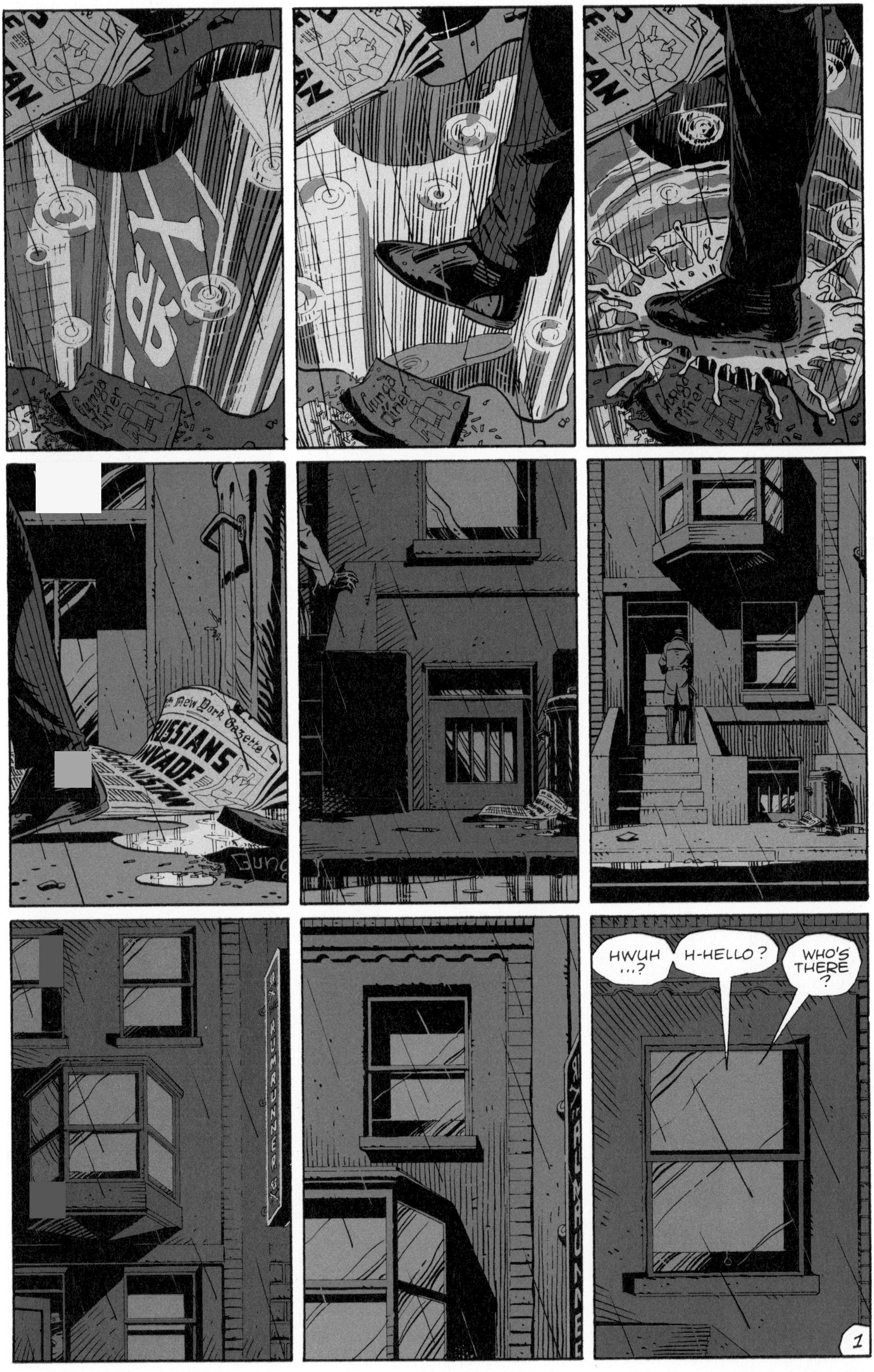

Gunga Diner
New York Gazette
RUSSIANS
RUMRUNNER
HWUH ...?
H-HELLO?
WHO'S THERE?
1

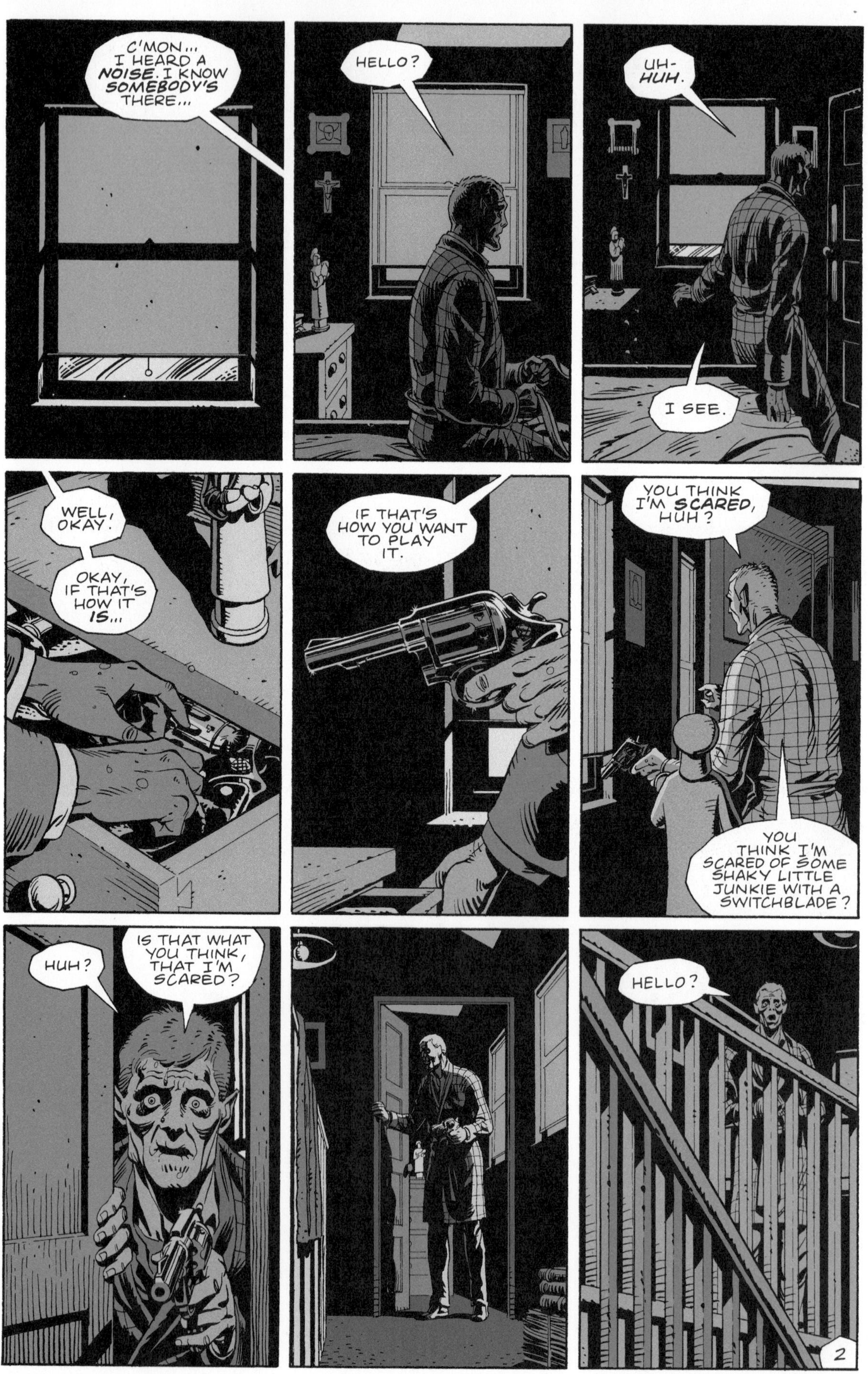
C'MON... I HEARD A NOISE. I KNOW SOMEBODY'S THERE...
HELLO?
UH-HUH.
I SEE.
WELL, OKAY.
OKAY, IF THAT'S HOW IT IS...
IF THAT'S HOW YOU WANT TO PLAY IT.
YOU THINK I'M SCARED, HUH?
YOU THINK I'M SCARED OF SOME SHAKY LITTLE JUNKIE WITH A SWITCHBLADE?
HUH?
IS THAT WHAT YOU THINK, THAT I'M SCARED?
HELLO?
2

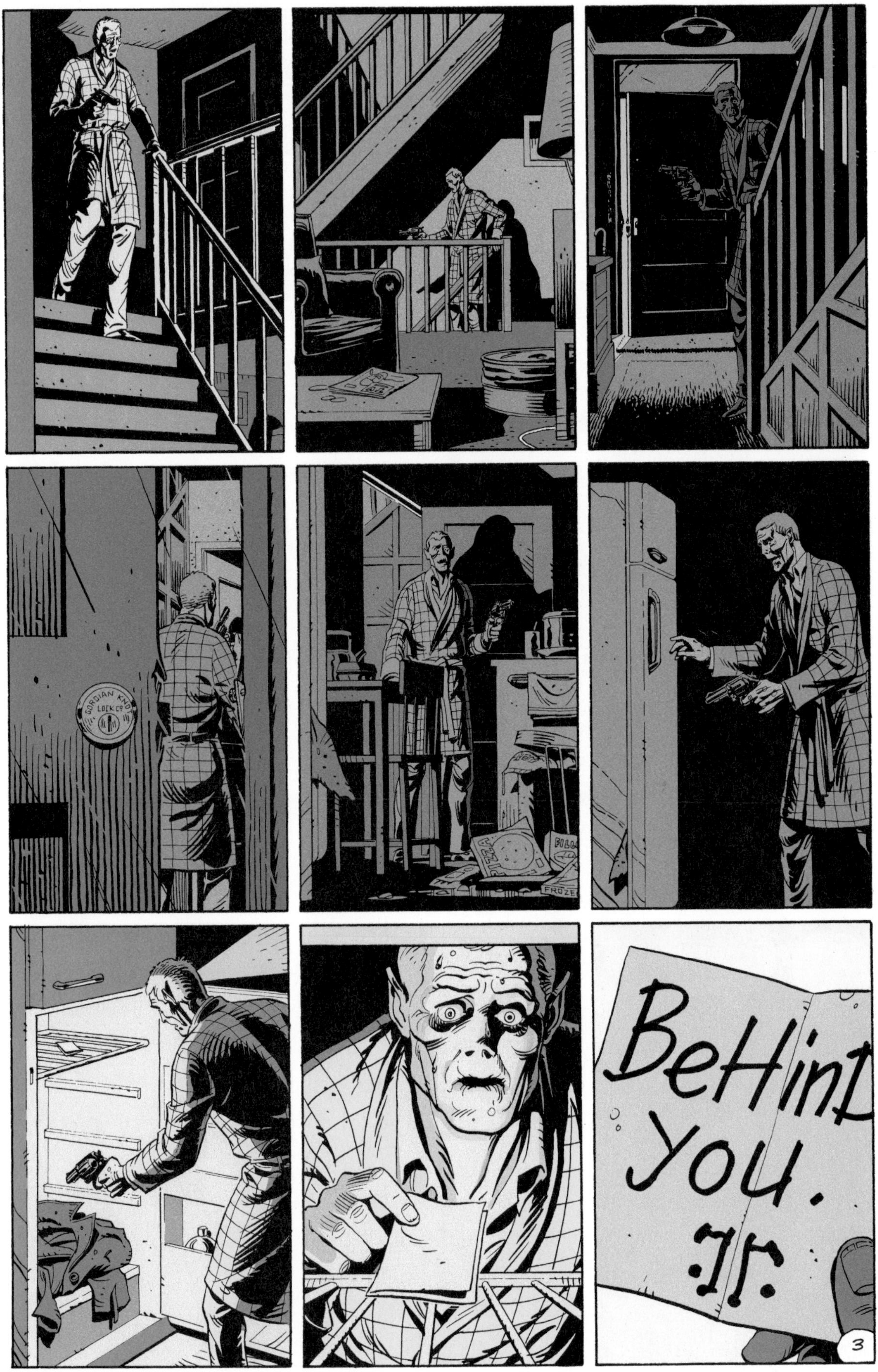
GORDIAN KNOT LOCK CO
PIZZA
BeHinD you.
3

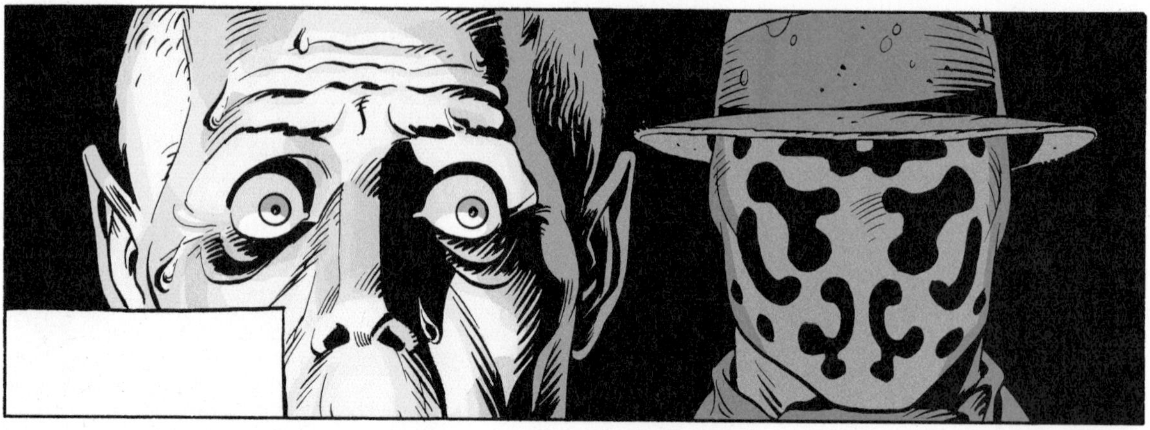

FEARFUL SYMMETRY

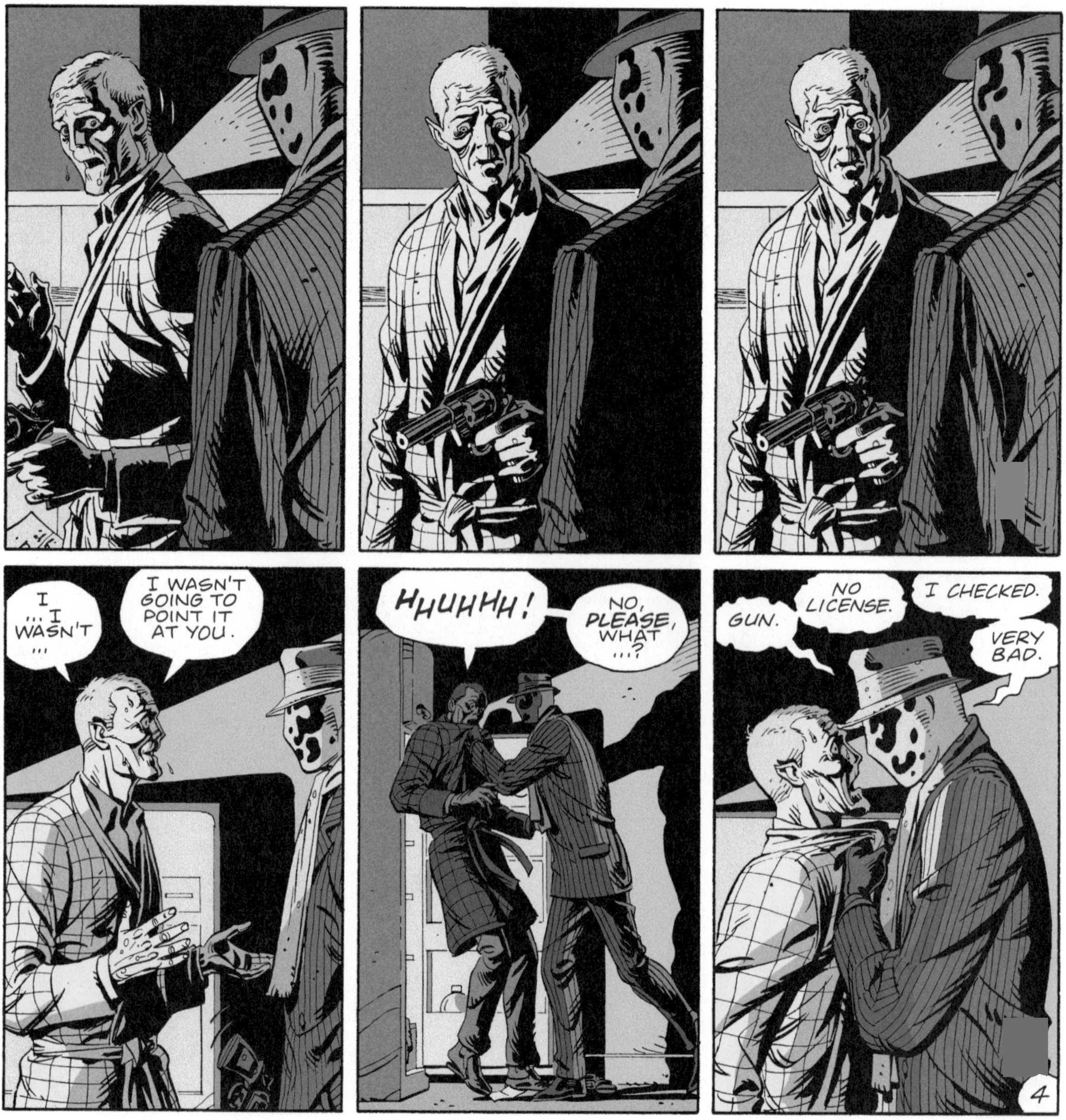

I ... I WASN'T ...
I WASN'T GOING TO POINT IT AT YOU.
HHUHHH!
NO, PLEASE, WHAT ...?
GUN.
NO LICENSE.
I CHECKED.
VERY BAD.
4

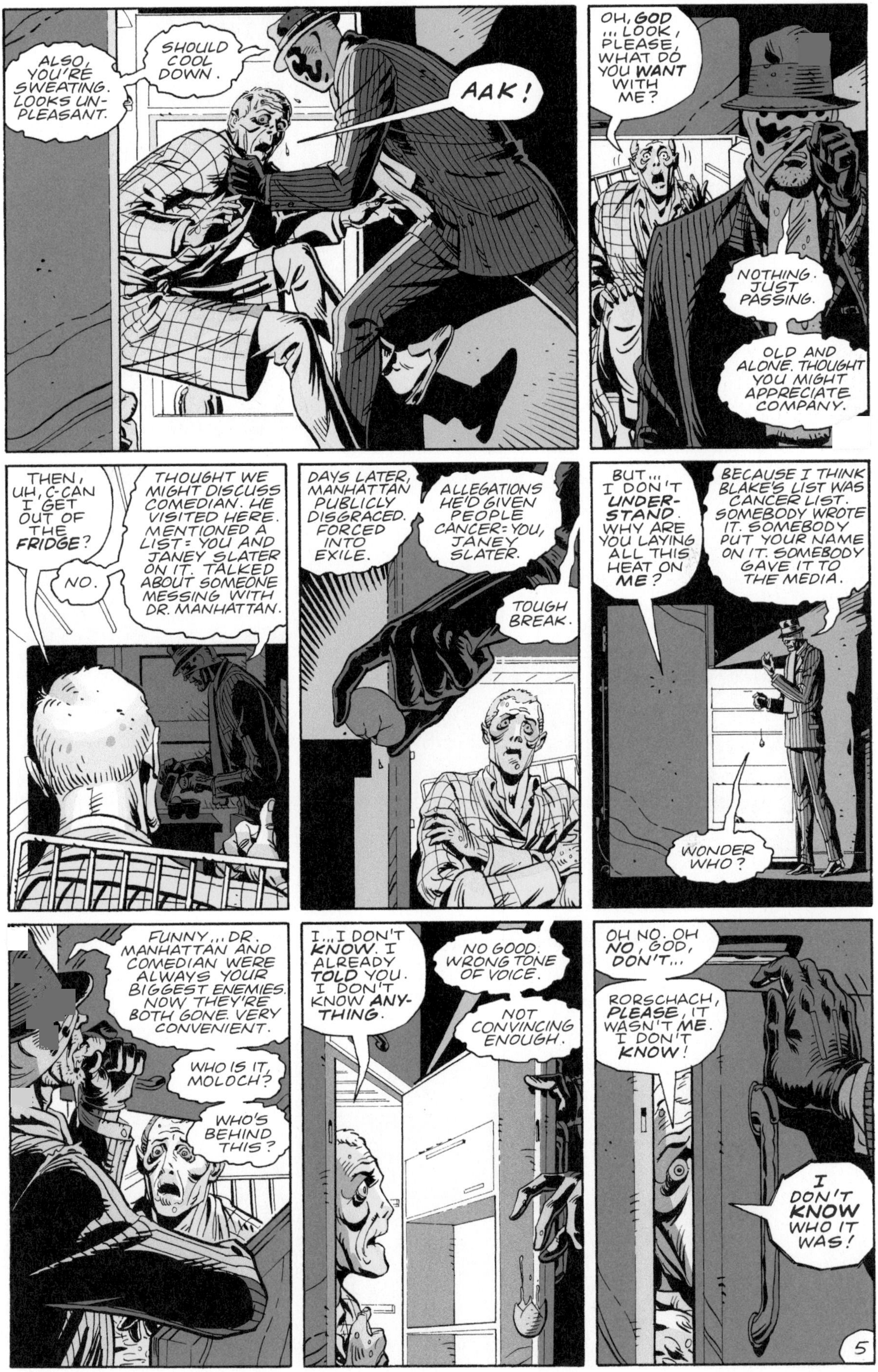

ALSO, YOU'RE SWEATING. LOOKS UN-PLEASANT.
SHOULD COOL DOWN.
AAK!
OH, GOD ... LOOK, PLEASE, WHAT DO YOU WANT WITH ME?
NOTHING. JUST PASSING.
OLD AND ALONE. THOUGHT YOU MIGHT APPRECIATE COMPANY.
THEN, UH, C-CAN I GET OUT OF THE FRIDGE?
NO.
THOUGHT WE MIGHT DISCUSS COMEDIAN. HE VISITED HERE. MENTIONED A LIST: YOU AND JANEY SLATER ON IT. TALKED ABOUT SOMEONE MESSING WITH DR. MANHATTAN.
DAYS LATER, MANHATTAN PUBLICLY DISGRACED. FORCED INTO EXILE.
ALLEGATIONS HE'D GIVEN PEOPLE CANCER: YOU, JANEY SLATER.
TOUGH BREAK.
BUT ... I DON'T UNDER-STAND. WHY ARE YOU LAYING ALL THIS HEAT ON ME?
BECAUSE I THINK BLAKE'S LIST WAS CANCER LIST. SOMEBODY WROTE IT. SOMEBODY PUT YOUR NAME ON IT. SOMEBODY GAVE IT TO THE MEDIA.
WONDER WHO?
FUNNY ... DR. MANHATTAN AND COMEDIAN WERE ALWAYS YOUR BIGGEST ENEMIES. NOW THEY'RE BOTH GONE. VERY CONVENIENT.
WHO IS IT, MOLOCH?
WHO'S BEHIND THIS?
I ... I DON'T KNOW. I ALREADY TOLD YOU. I DON'T KNOW ANY-THING.
NO GOOD. WRONG TONE OF VOICE.
NOT CONVINCING ENOUGH.
OH NO. OH NO, GOD, DON'T...
RORSCHACH, PLEASE, IT WASN'T ME. I DON'T KNOW!
I DON'T KNOW WHO IT WAS!
5

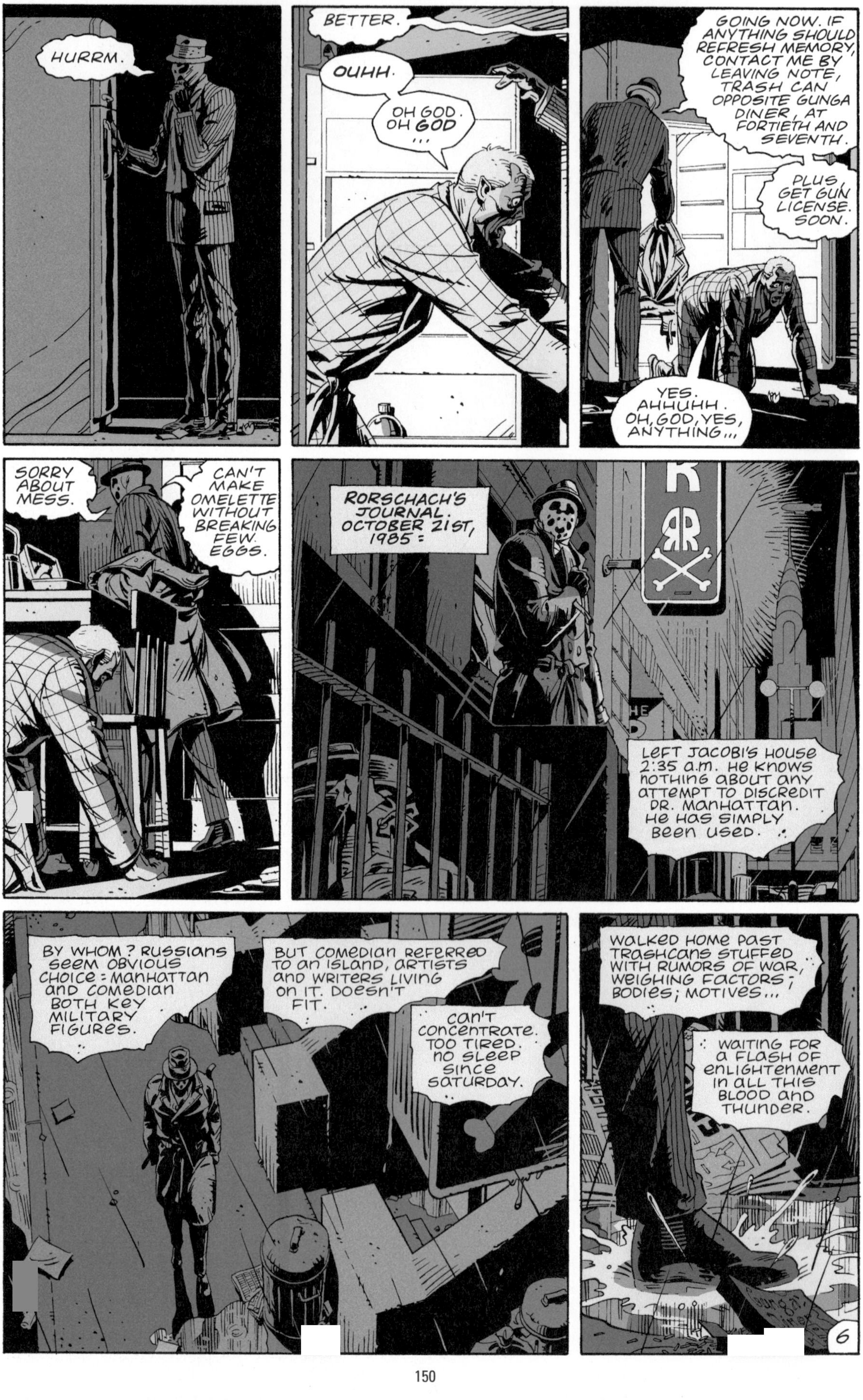
HURRM.
BETTER.
OUHH.
OH GOD. OH GOD...
GOING NOW. IF ANYTHING SHOULD REFRESH MEMORY, CONTACT ME BY LEAVING NOTE, TRASH CAN OPPOSITE GUNGA DINER, AT FORTIETH AND SEVENTH.
PLUS, GET GUN LICENSE. SOON.
YES. AHHUHH. OH, GOD, YES, ANYTHING...
SORRY ABOUT MESS.
CAN'T MAKE OMELETTE WITHOUT BREAKING FEW EGGS.
RORSCHACH'S JOURNAL. OCTOBER 21ST, 1985:
LEFT JACOBI'S HOUSE 2:35 a.m. HE KNOWS NOTHING ABOUT ANY ATTEMPT TO DISCREDIT DR. MANHATTAN. HE HAS SIMPLY BEEN USED.
BY WHOM? RUSSIANS SEEM OBVIOUS CHOICE: MANHATTAN AND COMEDIAN BOTH KEY MILITARY FIGURES.
BUT COMEDIAN REFERRED TO AN ISLAND, ARTISTS AND WRITERS LIVING ON IT. DOESN'T FIT.
CAN'T CONCENTRATE. TOO TIRED. NO SLEEP SINCE SATURDAY.
WALKED HOME PAST TRASHCANS STUFFED WITH RUMORS OF WAR, WEIGHING FACTORS; BODIES; MOTIVES...
WAITING FOR A FLASH OF ENLIGHTENMENT IN ALL THIS BLOOD AND THUNDER.
6

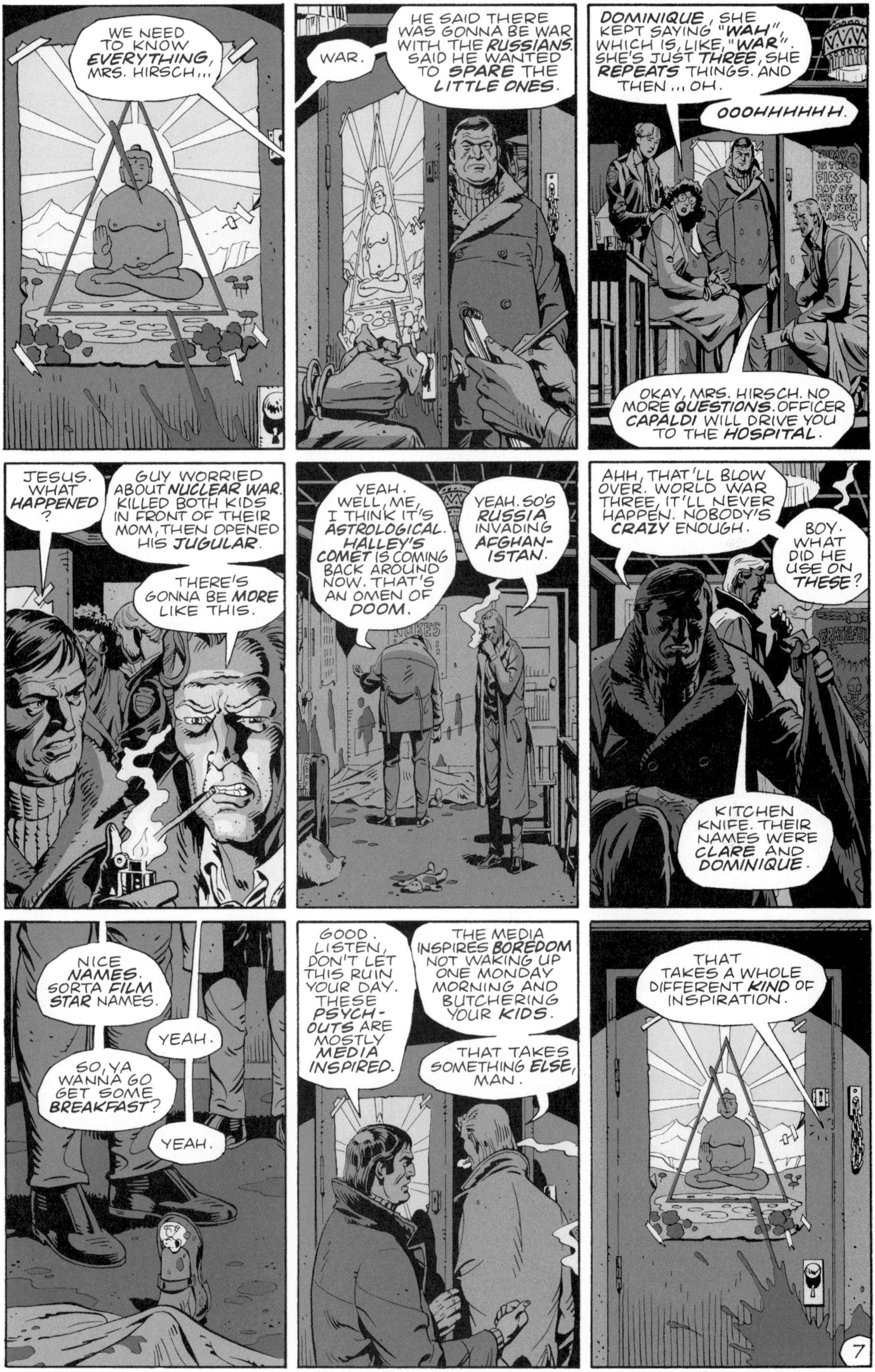

WE NEED TO KNOW EVERYTHING, MRS. HIRSCH...
WAR.
HE SAID THERE WAS GONNA BE WAR WITH THE RUSSIANS. SAID HE WANTED TO SPARE THE LITTLE ONES.
DOMINIQUE, SHE KEPT SAYING "WAH", WHICH IS, LIKE, "WAR". SHE'S JUST THREE, SHE REPEATS THINGS. AND THEN ... OH.
OOOHHHHHH.
TODAY IS THE FIRST DAY OF THE REST OF YOUR LIFE
OKAY, MRS. HIRSCH. NO MORE QUESTIONS. OFFICER CAPALDI WILL DRIVE YOU TO THE HOSPITAL.
JESUS. WHAT HAPPENED?
GUY WORRIED ABOUT NUCLEAR WAR. KILLED BOTH KIDS IN FRONT OF THEIR MOM, THEN OPENED HIS JUGULAR.
THERE'S GONNA BE MORE LIKE THIS.
YEAH. WELL, ME, I THINK IT'S ASTROLOGICAL. HALLEY'S COMET IS COMING BACK AROUND NOW. THAT'S AN OMEN OF DOOM.
YEAH. SO'S RUSSIA INVADING AFGHANISTAN.
AHH, THAT'LL BLOW OVER. WORLD WAR THREE, IT'LL NEVER HAPPEN. NOBODY'S CRAZY ENOUGH.
BOY. WHAT DID HE USE ON THESE?
KITCHEN KNIFE. THEIR NAMES WERE CLARE AND DOMINIQUE.
NICE NAMES. SORTA FILM STAR NAMES.
YEAH.
SO, YA WANNA GO GET SOME BREAKFAST?
YEAH.
GOOD. LISTEN, DON'T LET THIS RUIN YOUR DAY. THESE PSYCH-OUTS ARE MOSTLY MEDIA INSPIRED.
THE MEDIA INSPIRES BOREDOM NOT WAKING UP ONE MONDAY MORNING AND BUTCHERING YOUR KIDS.
THAT TAKES SOMETHING ELSE, MAN.
THAT TAKES A WHOLE DIFFERENT KIND OF INSPIRATION.
7

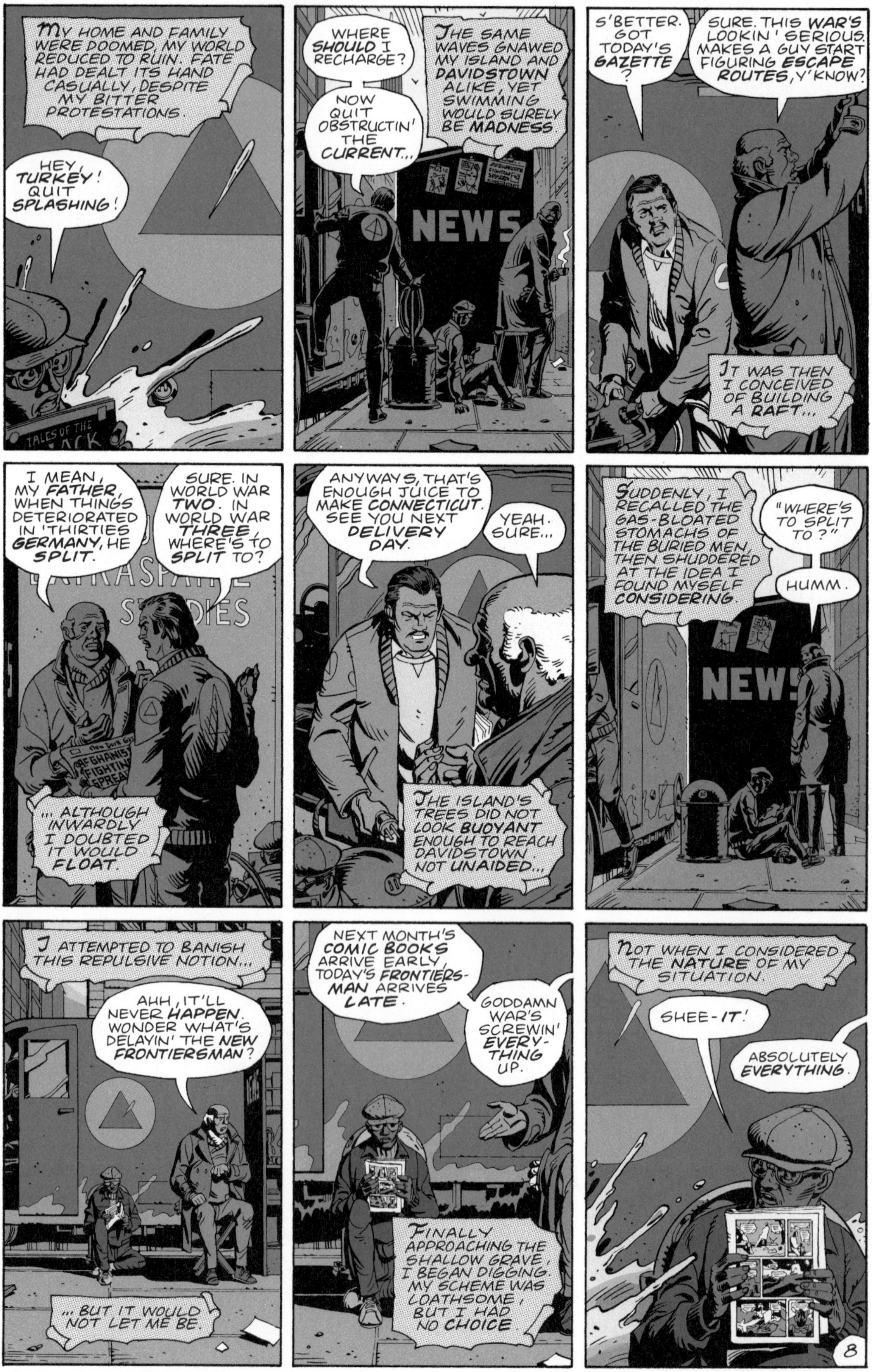
MY HOME AND FAMILY WERE DOOMED, MY WORLD REDUCED TO RUIN. FATE HAD DEALT ITS HAND CASUALLY, DESPITE MY BITTER PROTESTATIONS.
HEY, TURKEY! QUIT SPLASHING!
WHERE SHOULD I RECHARGE?
NOW QUIT OBSTRUCTIN' THE CURRENT...
THE SAME WAVES GNAWED MY ISLAND AND DAVIDSTOWN ALIKE, YET SWIMMING WOULD SURELY BE MADNESS.
NEWS
S'BETTER. GOT TODAY'S GAZETTE?
SURE. THIS WAR'S LOOKIN' SERIOUS. MAKES A GUY START FIGURING ESCAPE ROUTES, Y'KNOW?
IT WAS THEN I CONCEIVED OF BUILDING A RAFT...
I MEAN, MY FATHER, WHEN THINGS DETERIORATED IN 'THIRTIES GERMANY, HE SPLIT.
SURE. IN WORLD WAR TWO. IN WORLD WAR THREE, WHERE'S TO SPLIT TO?
...ALTHOUGH INWARDLY I DOUBTED IT WOULD FLOAT.
ANYWAYS, THAT'S ENOUGH JUICE TO MAKE CONNECTICUT. SEE YOU NEXT DELIVERY DAY.
YEAH. SURE...
THE ISLAND'S TREES DID NOT LOOK BUOYANT ENOUGH TO REACH DAVIDSTOWN NOT UNAIDED...
SUDDENLY, I RECALLED THE GAS-BLOATED STOMACHS OF THE BURIED MEN, THEN SHUDDERED AT THE IDEA I FOUND MYSELF CONSIDERING.
"WHERE'S TO SPLIT TO?"
HUMM.
NEWS
I ATTEMPTED TO BANISH THIS REPULSIVE NOTION...
AHH, IT'LL NEVER HAPPEN. WONDER WHAT'S DELAYIN' THE NEW FRONTIERSMAN?
...BUT IT WOULD NOT LET ME BE.
NEXT MONTH'S COMIC BOOKS ARRIVE EARLY, TODAY'S FRONTIERSMAN ARRIVES LATE.
GODDAMN WAR'S SCREWIN' EVERYTHING UP.
FINALLY APPROACHING THE SHALLOW GRAVE, I BEGAN DIGGING. MY SCHEME WAS LOATHSOME, BUT I HAD NO CHOICE.
NOT WHEN I CONSIDERED THE NATURE OF MY SITUATION.
SHEE-IT!
ABSOLUTELY EVERYTHING.
8

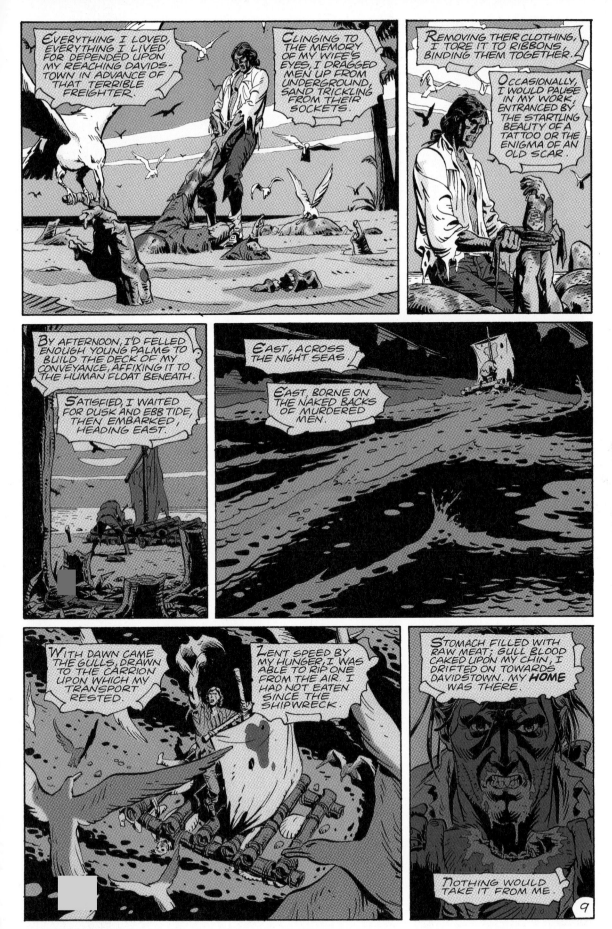

EVERYTHING I LOVED, EVERYTHING I LIVED FOR DEPENDED UPON MY REACHING DAVIDS-TOWN IN ADVANCE OF THAT TERRIBLE FREIGHTER.

CLINGING TO THE MEMORY OF MY WIFE'S EYES, I DRAGGED MEN UP FROM UNDERGROUND, SAND TRICKLING FROM THEIR SOCKETS.

REMOVING THEIR CLOTHING, I TORE IT TO RIBBONS, BINDING THEM TOGETHER.

OCCASIONALLY, I WOULD PAUSE IN MY WORK, ENTRANCED BY THE STARTLING BEAUTY OF A TATTOO OR THE ENIGMA OF AN OLD SCAR.

BY AFTERNOON, I'D FELLED ENOUGH YOUNG PALMS TO BUILD THE DECK OF MY CONVEYANCE, AFFIXING IT TO THE HUMAN FLOAT BENEATH.

SATISFIED, I WAITED FOR DUSK AND EBB TIDE, THEN EMBARKED, HEADING EAST.

EAST, ACROSS THE NIGHT SEAS!

EAST, BORNE ON THE NAKED BACKS OF MURDERED MEN.

WITH DAWN CAME THE GULLS, DRAWN TO THE CARRION UPON WHICH MY TRANSPORT RESTED.

LENT SPEED BY MY HUNGER, I WAS ABLE TO RIP ONE FROM THE AIR. I HAD NOT EATEN SINCE THE SHIPWRECK.

STOMACH FILLED WITH RAW MEAT; GULL BLOOD CAKED UPON MY CHIN, I DRIFTED ON TOWARDS DAVIDSTOWN. MY **HOME** WAS THERE.

NOTHING WOULD TAKE IT FROM ME.

9

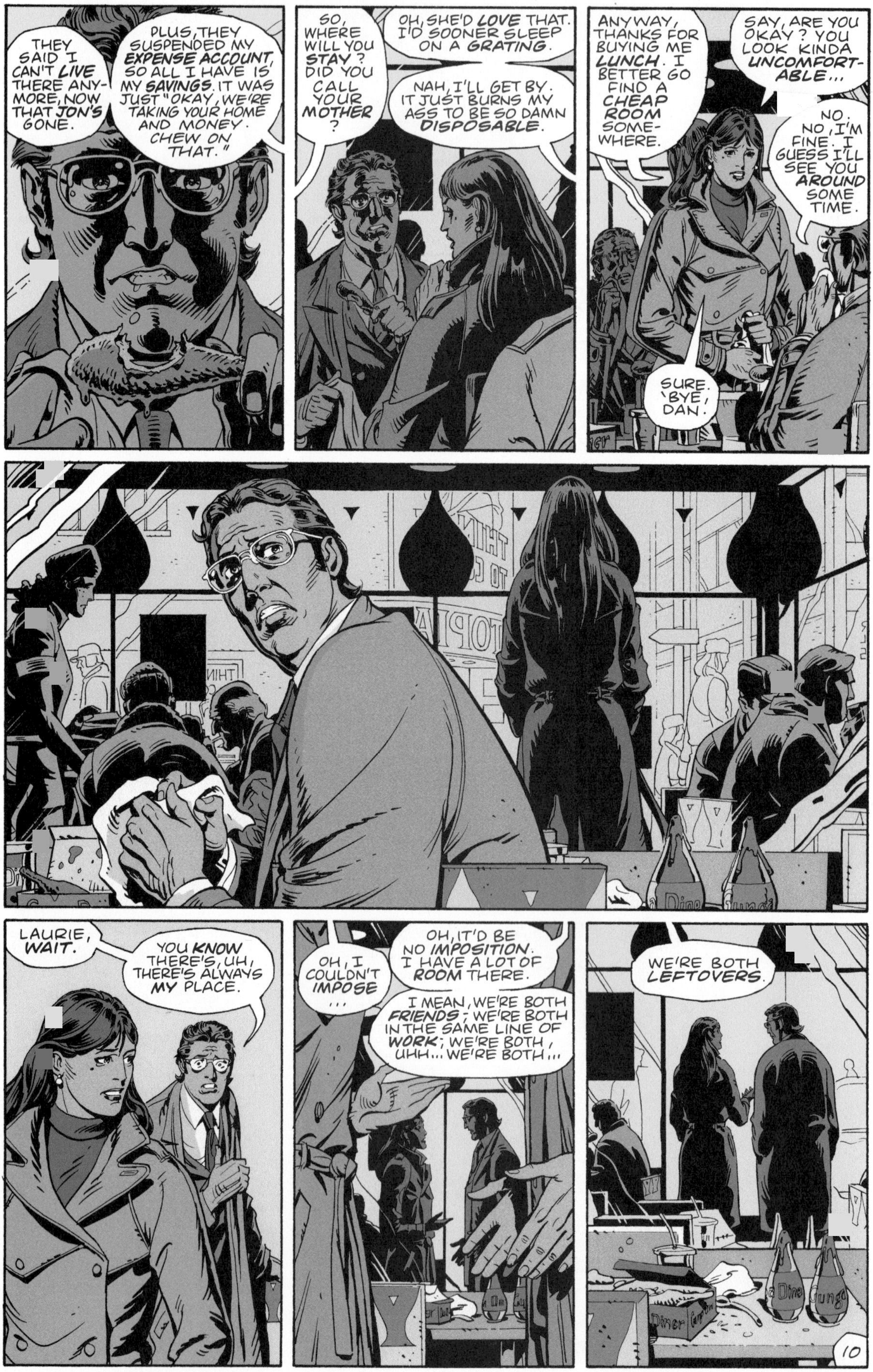
THEY SAID I CAN'T LIVE THERE ANYMORE, NOW THAT JON'S GONE.
PLUS, THEY SUSPENDED MY EXPENSE ACCOUNT, SO ALL I HAVE IS MY SAVINGS. IT WAS JUST "OKAY, WE'RE TAKING YOUR HOME AND MONEY. CHEW ON THAT."
SO, WHERE WILL YOU STAY? DID YOU CALL YOUR MOTHER?
OH, SHE'D LOVE THAT. I'D SOONER SLEEP ON A GRATING.
NAH, I'LL GET BY. IT JUST BURNS MY ASS TO BE SO DAMN DISPOSABLE.
ANYWAY, THANKS FOR BUYING ME LUNCH. I BETTER GO FIND A CHEAP ROOM SOMEWHERE.
SAY, ARE YOU OKAY? YOU LOOK KINDA UNCOMFORTABLE...
NO. NO, I'M FINE. I GUESS I'LL SEE YOU AROUND SOME TIME.
SURE. 'BYE, DAN.
LAURIE, WAIT.
YOU KNOW THERE'S, UH, THERE'S ALWAYS MY PLACE.
OH, I COULDN'T IMPOSE...
OH, IT'D BE NO IMPOSITION. I HAVE A LOT OF ROOM THERE.
I MEAN, WE'RE BOTH FRIENDS - WE'RE BOTH IN THE SAME LINE OF WORK; WE'RE BOTH, UHH... WE'RE BOTH...
WE'RE BOTH LEFTOVERS.
10

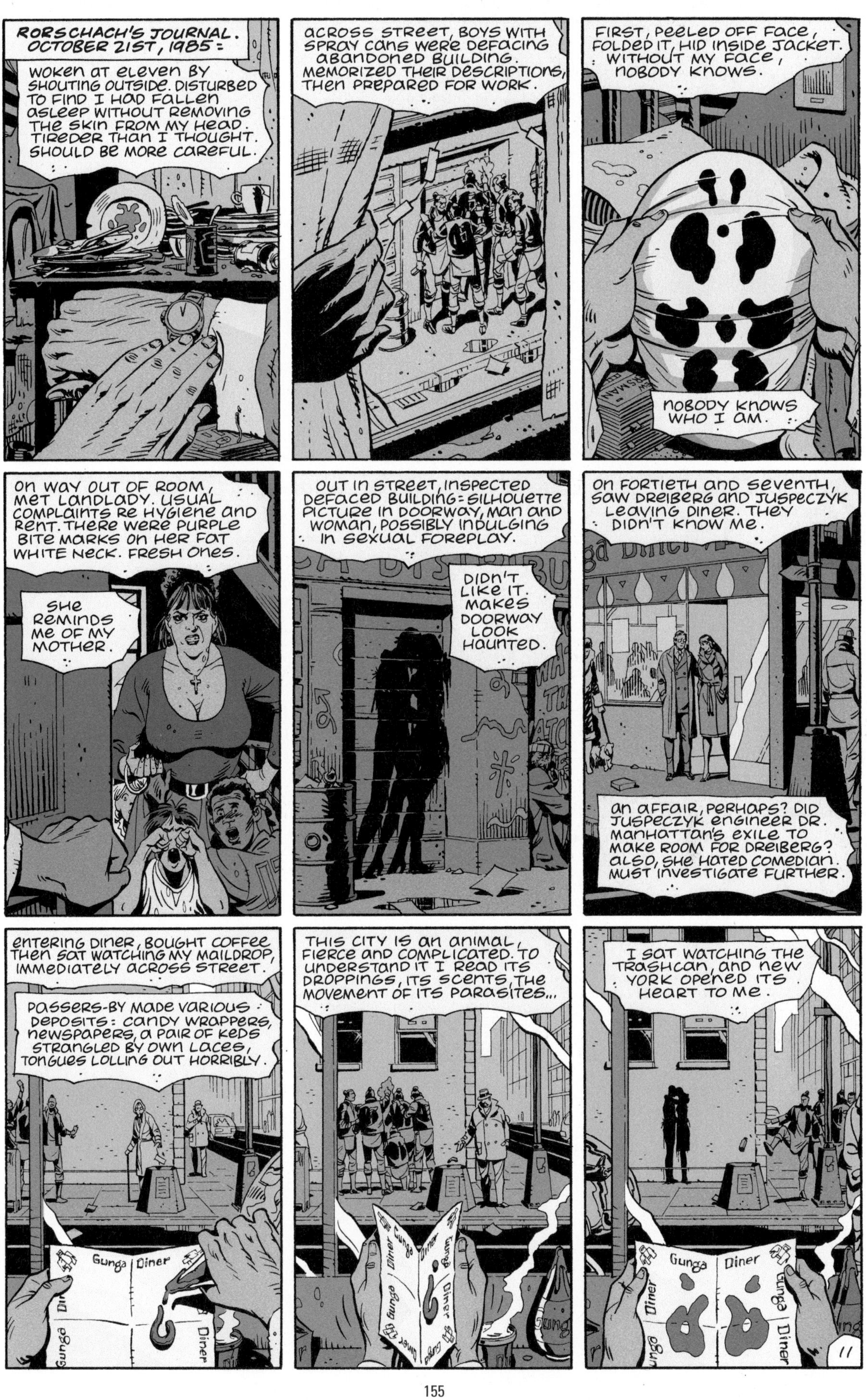
RORSCHACH'S JOURNAL. OCTOBER 21ST, 1985:
WOKEN AT ELEVEN BY SHOUTING OUTSIDE. DISTURBED TO FIND I HAD FALLEN ASLEEP WITHOUT REMOVING THE SKIN FROM MY HEAD. TIREDER THAN I THOUGHT. SHOULD BE MORE CAREFUL.
ACROSS STREET, BOYS WITH SPRAY CANS WERE DEFACING ABANDONED BUILDING. MEMORIZED THEIR DESCRIPTIONS, THEN PREPARED FOR WORK.
FIRST, PEELED OFF FACE, FOLDED IT, HID INSIDE JACKET. WITHOUT MY FACE, NOBODY KNOWS.
NOBODY KNOWS WHO I AM.
ON WAY OUT OF ROOM, MET LANDLADY. USUAL COMPLAINTS RE HYGIENE AND RENT. THERE WERE PURPLE BITE MARKS ON HER FAT WHITE NECK. FRESH ONES.
SHE REMINDS ME OF MY MOTHER.
OUT IN STREET, INSPECTED DEFACED BUILDING: SILHOUETTE PICTURE IN DOORWAY, MAN AND WOMAN, POSSIBLY INDULGING IN SEXUAL FOREPLAY.
DIDN'T LIKE IT. MAKES DOORWAY LOOK HAUNTED.
ON FORTIETH AND SEVENTH, SAW DREIBERG AND JUSPECZYK LEAVING DINER. THEY DIDN'T KNOW ME.
AN AFFAIR, PERHAPS? DID JUSPECZYK ENGINEER DR. MANHATTAN'S EXILE TO MAKE ROOM FOR DREIBERG? ALSO, SHE HATED COMEDIAN. MUST INVESTIGATE FURTHER.
ENTERING DINER, BOUGHT COFFEE THEN SAT WATCHING MY MAILDROP, IMMEDIATELY ACROSS STREET.
PASSERS-BY MADE VARIOUS DEPOSITS: CANDY WRAPPERS, NEWSPAPERS, A PAIR OF KEDS STRANGLED BY OWN LACES, TONGUES LOLLING OUT HORRIBLY.
Gunga Diner
THIS CITY IS AN ANIMAL, FIERCE AND COMPLICATED. TO UNDERSTAND IT I READ ITS DROPPINGS, ITS SCENTS, THE MOVEMENT OF ITS PARASITES...
Gunga Diner
I SAT WATCHING THE TRASHCAN, AND NEW YORK OPENED ITS HEART TO ME.
Gunga Diner
11

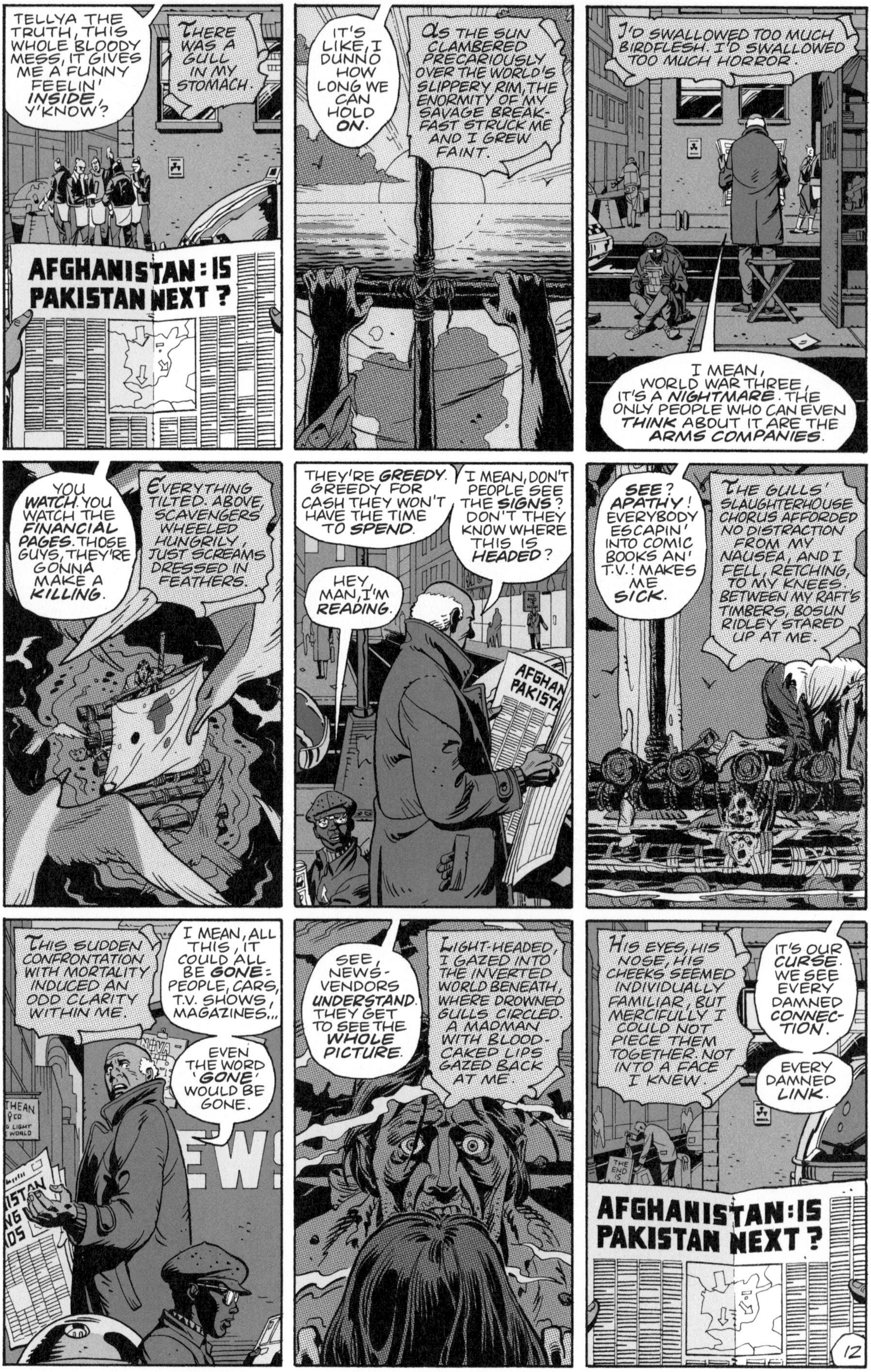
TELLYA THE TRUTH, THIS WHOLE BLOODY MESS, IT GIVES ME A FUNNY FEELIN' INSIDE, Y'KNOW?
THERE WAS A GULL IN MY STOMACH.
AFGHANISTAN: IS PAKISTAN NEXT?
IT'S LIKE, I DUNNO HOW LONG WE CAN HOLD ON.
AS THE SUN CLAMBERED PRECARIOUSLY OVER THE WORLD'S SLIPPERY RIM, THE ENORMITY OF MY SAVAGE BREAKFAST STRUCK ME AND I GREW FAINT.
I'D SWALLOWED TOO MUCH BIRDFLESH. I'D SWALLOWED TOO MUCH HORROR.
I MEAN, WORLD WAR THREE, IT'S A NIGHTMARE. THE ONLY PEOPLE WHO CAN EVEN THINK ABOUT IT ARE THE ARMS COMPANIES.
YOU WATCH. YOU WATCH THE FINANCIAL PAGES. THOSE GUYS, THEY'RE GONNA MAKE A KILLING.
EVERYTHING TILTED. ABOVE, SCAVENGERS WHEELED HUNGRILY, JUST SCREAMS DRESSED IN FEATHERS.
THEY'RE GREEDY. GREEDY FOR CASH THEY WON'T HAVE THE TIME TO SPEND.
I MEAN, DON'T PEOPLE SEE THE SIGNS? DON'T THEY KNOW WHERE THIS IS HEADED?
HEY, MAN, I'M READING.
AFGHAN PAKISTA
SEE? APATHY! EVERYBODY ESCAPIN' INTO COMIC BOOKS AN' T.V.! MAKES ME SICK.
THE GULLS' SLAUGHTERHOUSE CHORUS AFFORDED NO DISTRACTION FROM MY NAUSEA, AND I FELL, RETCHING, TO MY KNEES. BETWEEN MY RAFT'S TIMBERS, BOSUN RIDLEY STARED UP AT ME.
THIS SUDDEN CONFRONTATION WITH MORTALITY INDUCED AN ODD CLARITY WITHIN ME.
I MEAN, ALL THIS, IT COULD ALL BE GONE: PEOPLE, CARS, T.V. SHOWS, MAGAZINES...
EVEN THE WORD 'GONE' WOULD BE GONE.
EWS
SEE, NEWS-VENDORS UNDERSTAND. THEY GET TO SEE THE WHOLE PICTURE.
LIGHT-HEADED, I GAZED INTO THE INVERTED WORLD BENEATH, WHERE DROWNED GULLS CIRCLED. A MADMAN WITH BLOOD-CAKED LIPS GAZED BACK AT ME.
HIS EYES, HIS NOSE, HIS CHEEKS SEEMED INDIVIDUALLY FAMILIAR, BUT MERCIFULLY I COULD NOT PIECE THEM TOGETHER. NOT INTO A FACE I KNEW.
IT'S OUR CURSE. WE SEE EVERY DAMNED CONNECTION.
EVERY DAMNED LINK.
THE END IS
AFGHANISTAN: IS PAKISTAN NEXT?
12

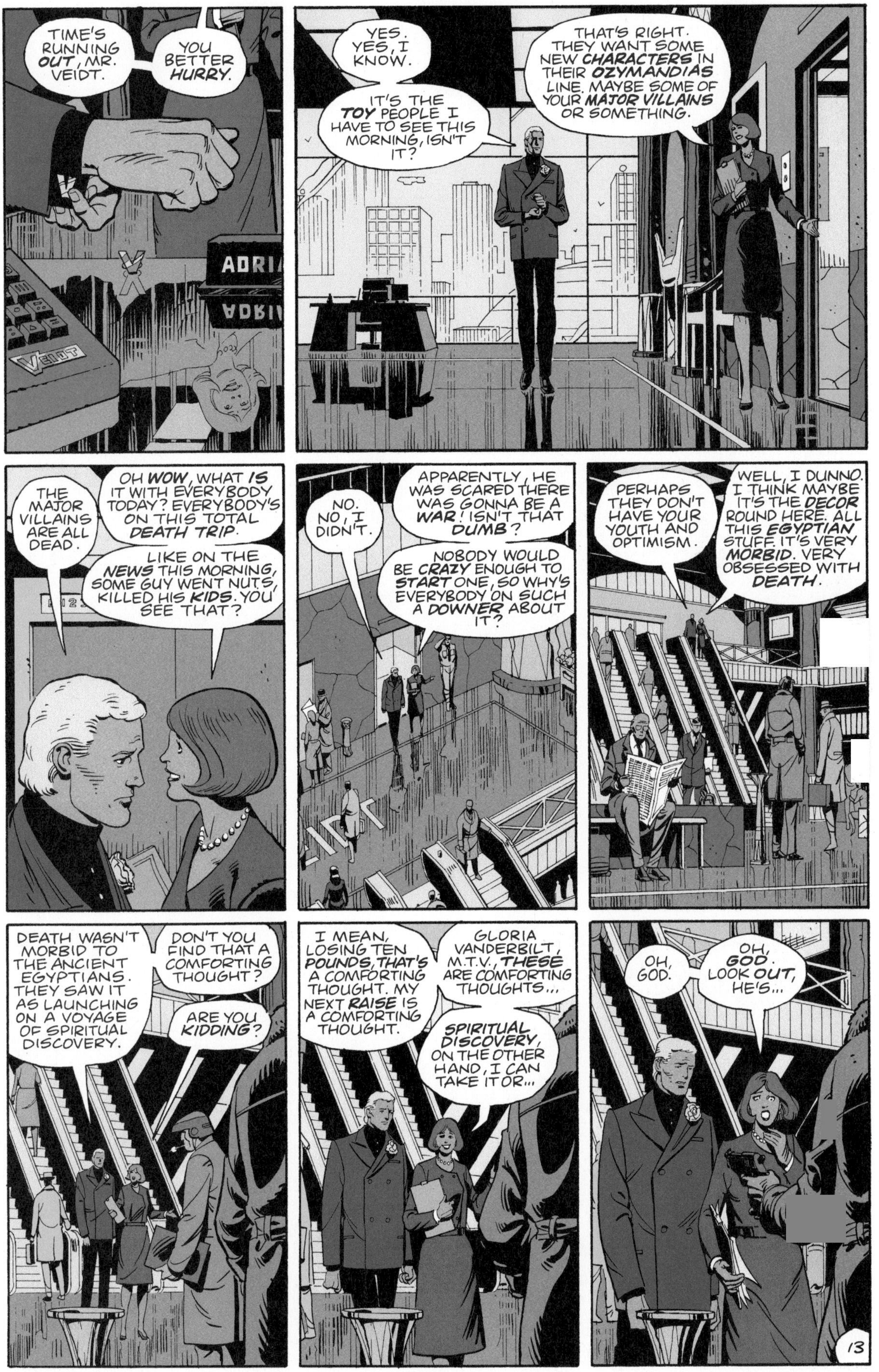
TIME'S RUNNING OUT, MR. VEIDT.
YOU BETTER HURRY.
ADRIA
VEIDT
YES. YES, I KNOW.
IT'S THE TOY PEOPLE I HAVE TO SEE THIS MORNING, ISN'T IT?
THAT'S RIGHT. THEY WANT SOME NEW CHARACTERS IN THEIR OZYMANDIAS LINE. MAYBE SOME OF YOUR MAJOR VILLAINS OR SOMETHING.
THE MAJOR VILLAINS ARE ALL DEAD.
OH WOW, WHAT IS IT WITH EVERYBODY TODAY? EVERYBODY'S ON THIS TOTAL DEATH TRIP.
LIKE ON THE NEWS THIS MORNING, SOME GUY WENT NUTS, KILLED HIS KIDS. YOU SEE THAT?
NO. NO, I DIDN'T.
APPARENTLY, HE WAS SCARED THERE WAS GONNA BE A WAR! ISN'T THAT DUMB?
NOBODY WOULD BE CRAZY ENOUGH TO START ONE, SO WHY'S EVERYBODY ON SUCH A DOWNER ABOUT IT?
PERHAPS THEY DON'T HAVE YOUR YOUTH AND OPTIMISM.
WELL, I DUNNO. I THINK MAYBE IT'S THE DECOR ROUND HERE. ALL THIS EGYPTIAN STUFF. IT'S VERY MORBID. VERY OBSESSED WITH DEATH.
DEATH WASN'T MORBID TO THE ANCIENT EGYPTIANS. THEY SAW IT AS LAUNCHING ON A VOYAGE OF SPIRITUAL DISCOVERY.
DON'T YOU FIND THAT A COMFORTING THOUGHT?
ARE YOU KIDDING?
I MEAN, LOSING TEN POUNDS, THAT'S A COMFORTING THOUGHT. MY NEXT RAISE IS A COMFORTING THOUGHT.
GLORIA VANDERBILT, M.T.V., THESE ARE COMFORTING THOUGHTS...
SPIRITUAL DISCOVERY, ON THE OTHER HAND, I CAN TAKE IT OR...
OH, GOD.
OH, GOD. LOOK OUT, HE'S...
13

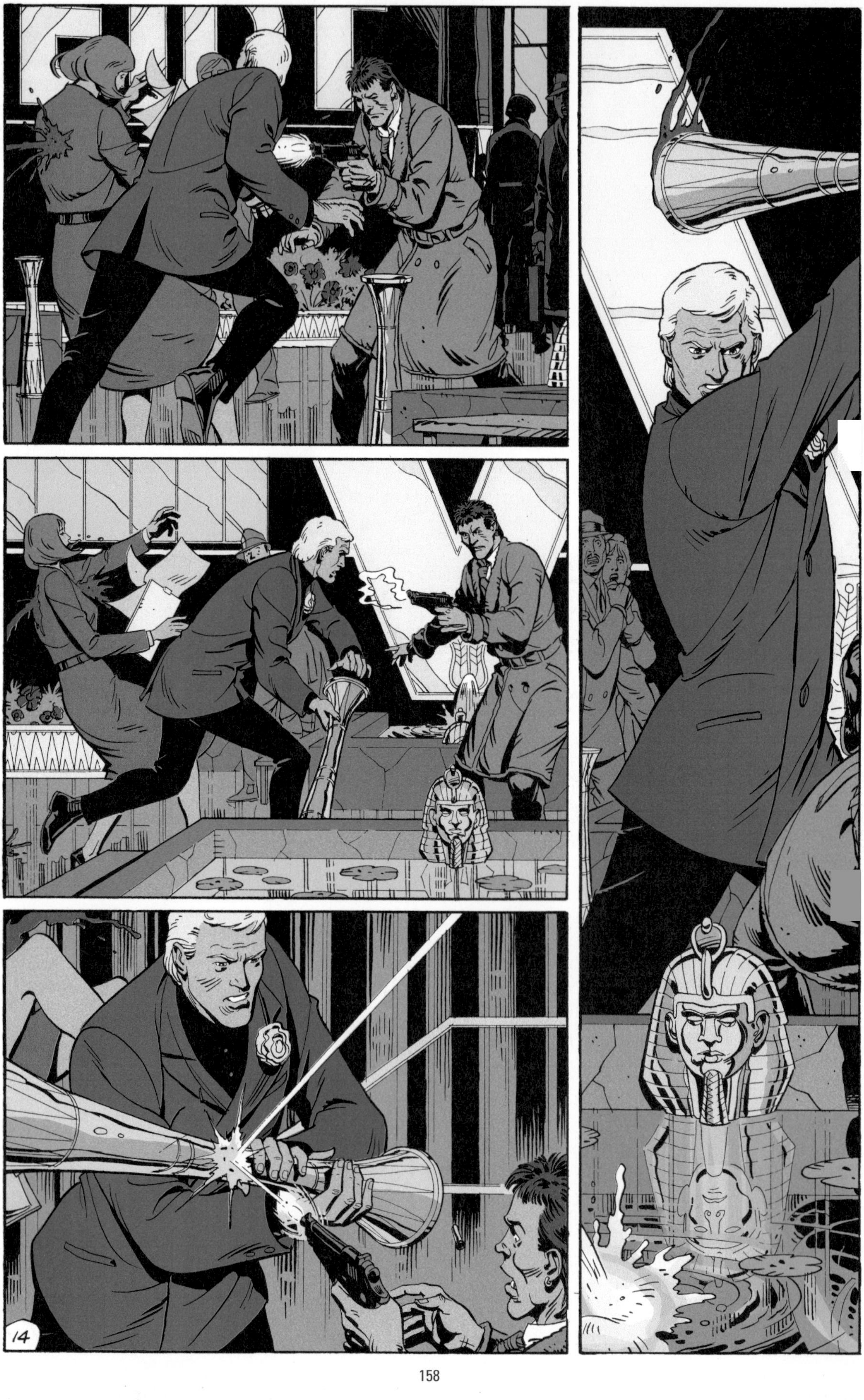
14

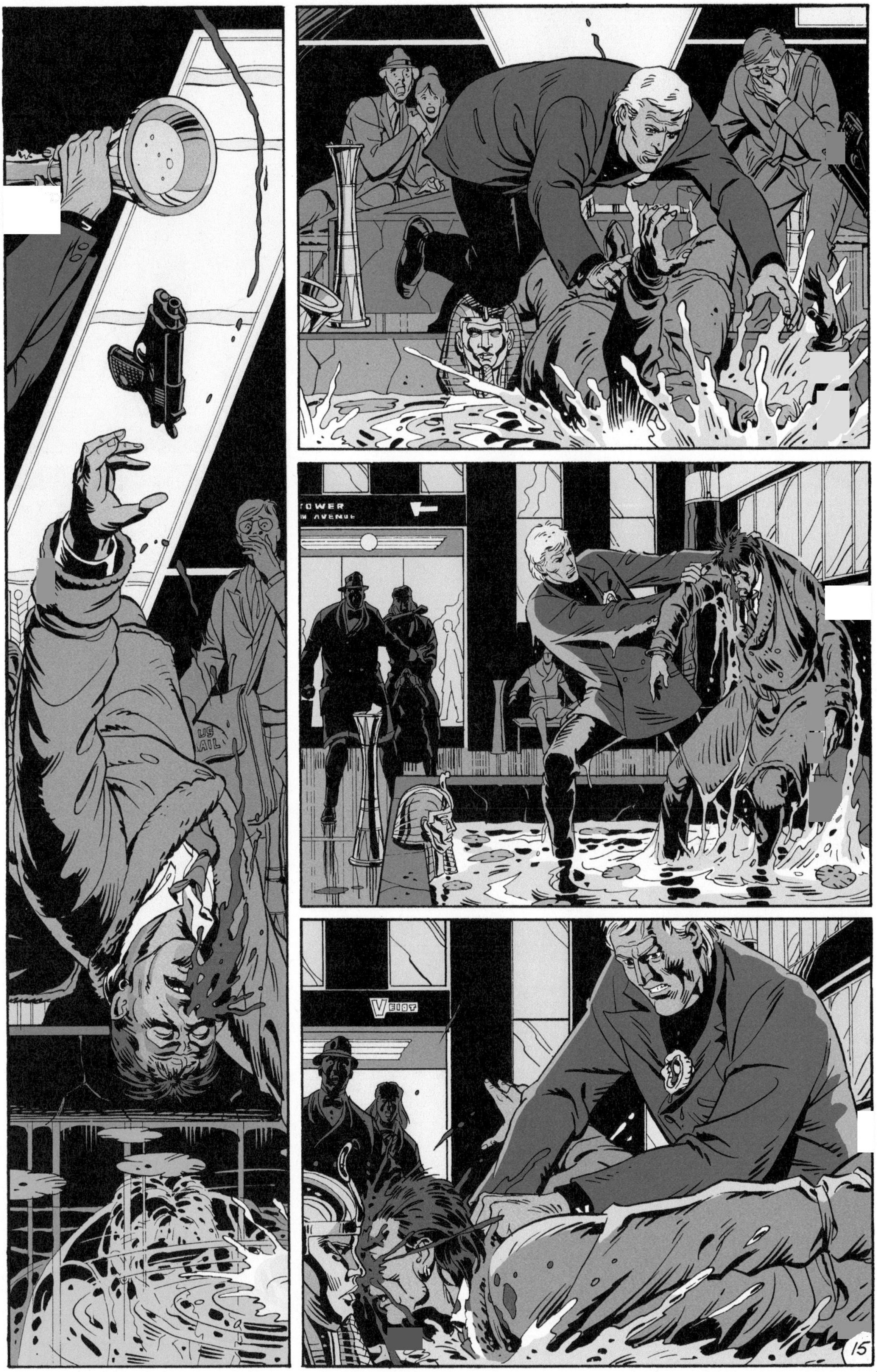
TOWER
AVENUE
US
VEIDT
15

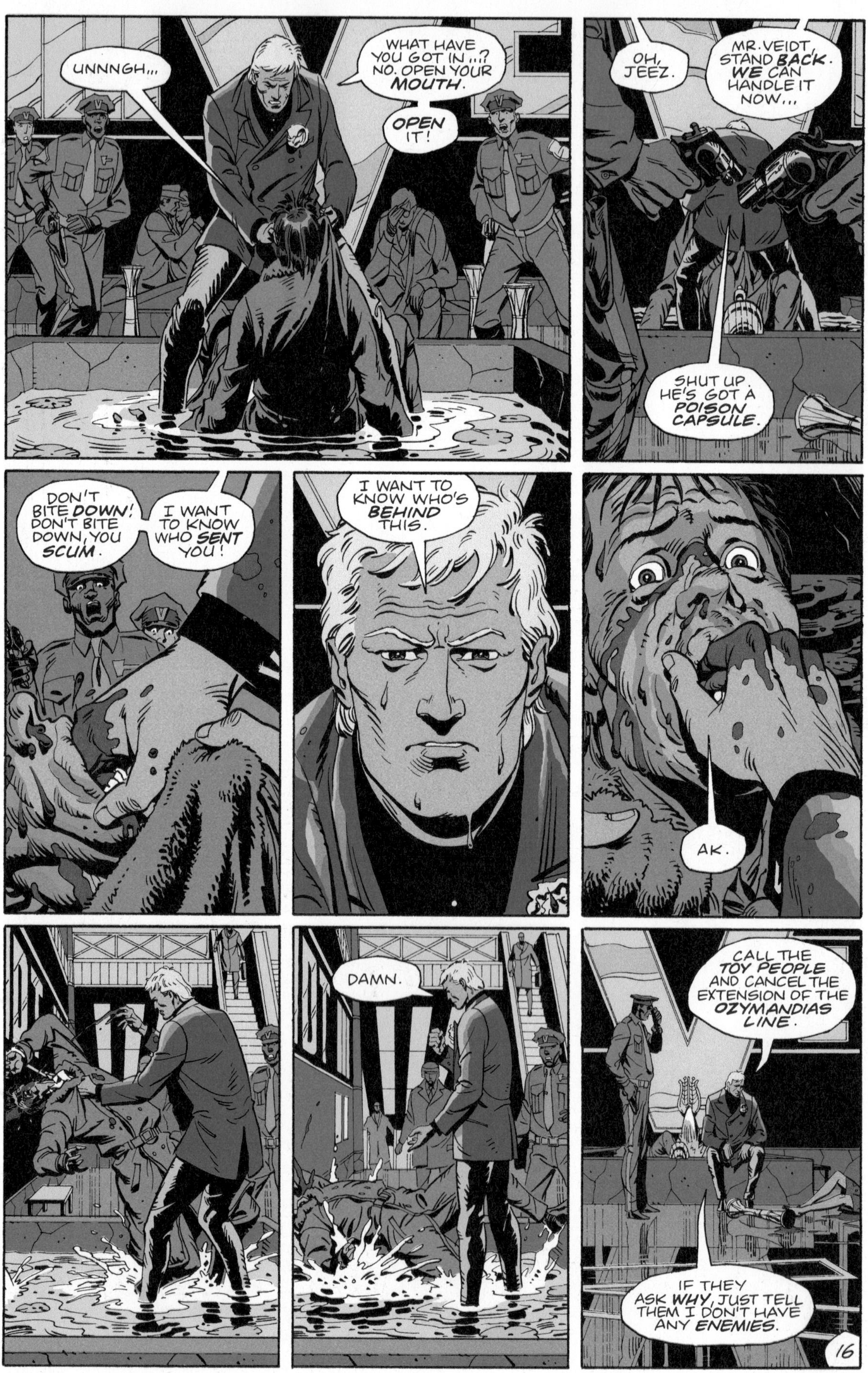
UNNNGH...
WHAT HAVE YOU GOT IN...? NO. OPEN YOUR MOUTH.
OPEN IT!
OH, JEEZ.
MR. VEIDT, STAND BACK. WE CAN HANDLE IT NOW...
SHUT UP. HE'S GOT A POISON CAPSULE.
DON'T BITE DOWN! DON'T BITE DOWN, YOU SCUM.
I WANT TO KNOW WHO SENT YOU!
I WANT TO KNOW WHO'S BEHIND THIS.
AK.
DAMN.
CALL THE TOY PEOPLE AND CANCEL THE EXTENSION OF THE OZYMANDIAS LINE.
IF THEY ASK WHY, JUST TELL THEM I DON'T HAVE ANY ENEMIES.
16

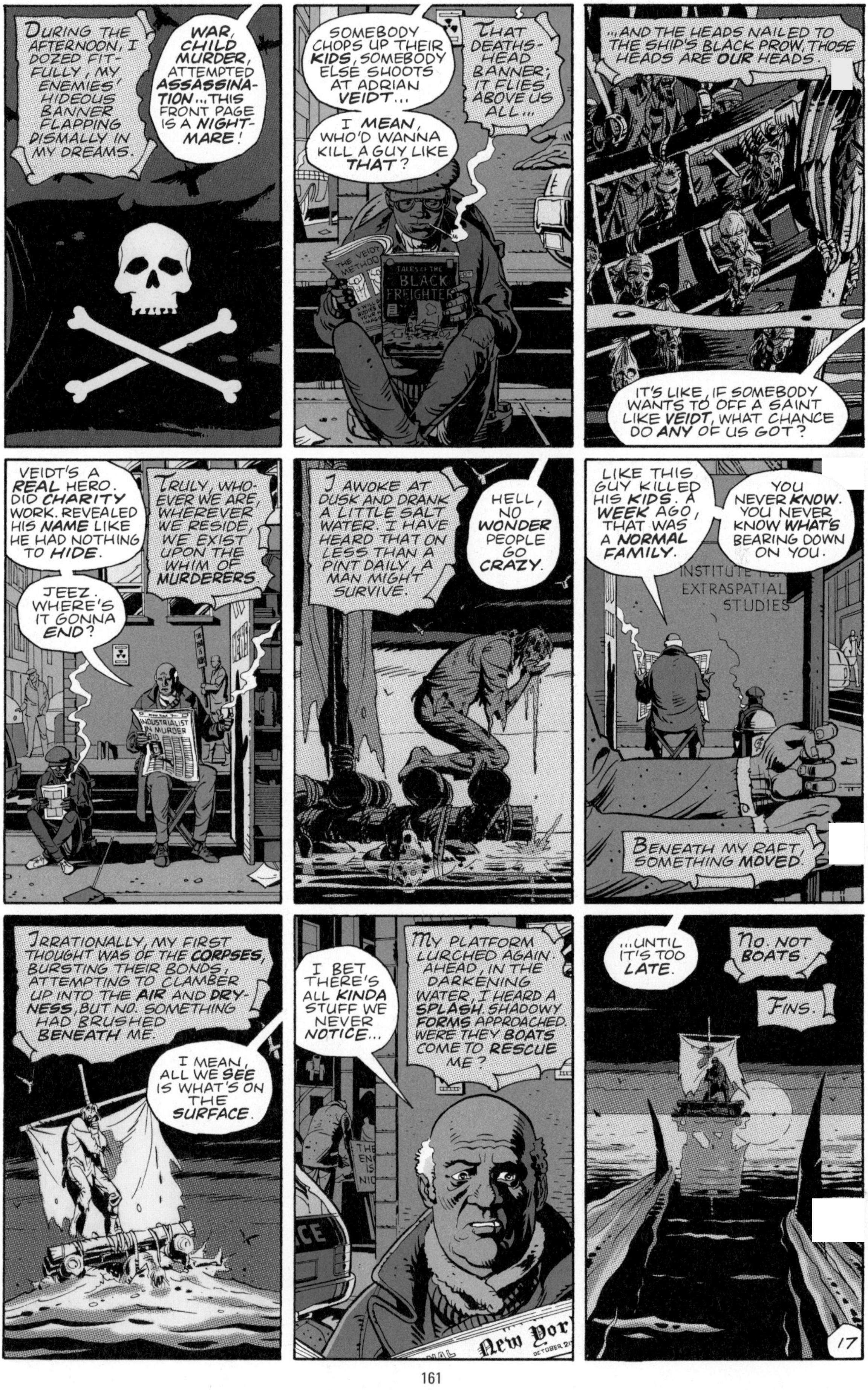
During the afternoon, I dozed fitfully, my enemies' hideous banner flapping dismally in my dreams.
WAR, CHILD MURDER, ATTEMPTED ASSASSINATION... THIS FRONT PAGE IS A NIGHTMARE!
SOMEBODY CHOPS UP THEIR KIDS, SOMEBODY ELSE SHOOTS AT ADRIAN VEIDT...
I MEAN, WHO'D WANNA KILL A GUY LIKE THAT?
That deaths-head banner; it flies above us all...
THE VEIDT METHOD
TALES OF THE BLACK FREIGHTER
...and the heads nailed to the ship's black prow, those heads are our heads.
IT'S LIKE, IF SOMEBODY WANTS TO OFF A SAINT LIKE VEIDT, WHAT CHANCE DO ANY OF US GOT?
VEIDT'S A REAL HERO. DID CHARITY WORK. REVEALED HIS NAME LIKE HE HAD NOTHING TO HIDE.
Truly, whoever we are, wherever we reside, we exist upon the whim of murderers.
JEEZ. WHERE'S IT GONNA END?
INDUSTRIALIST IN MURDER
I awoke at dusk and drank a little salt water. I have heard that on less than a pint daily, a man might survive.
HELL, NO WONDER PEOPLE GO CRAZY.
LIKE THIS GUY KILLED HIS KIDS. A WEEK AGO, THAT WAS A NORMAL FAMILY.
YOU NEVER KNOW. YOU NEVER KNOW WHAT'S BEARING DOWN ON YOU.
INSTITUTE FOR EXTRASPATIAL STUDIES
Beneath my raft, something moved.
Irrationally, my first thought was of the corpses, bursting their bonds, attempting to clamber up into the air and dryness. But no. Something had brushed beneath me.
I MEAN, ALL WE SEE IS WHAT'S ON THE SURFACE.
I BET THERE'S ALL KINDA STUFF WE NEVER NOTICE...
My platform lurched again. Ahead, in the darkening water, I heard a splash. Shadowy forms approached. Were they boats come to rescue me?
New York
...UNTIL IT'S TOO LATE.
No. Not boats.
Fins.
17

RORSCHACH'S JOURNAL. OCTOBER 21ST, 1985 =

SOMEONE TRIED TO KILL VEIDT. PROVES 'MASK KILLER' THEORY. MURDERER IS CLOSING IN.

CHECKED MAILDROP. MESSAGE FROM MOLOCH. CONNECTED PERHAPS?

R-
Call tonight, 11:30 p.m.
Have information.
URGENT.
—Jacobi

NEXT, WENT TO RETRIEVE FACE FROM ALLEY. OUTSIDE UTOPIA, POLICE RESTRAINED A YOUTH ON KT-28S.

HE WAS SCREAMING SOMETHING ABOUT PRESIDENT NIXON. SOMETHING ABOUT BOMBS.

UTOPIA C
THINGS
TO COM

IS EVERYONE BUT ME GOING MAD? OVER 40TH STREET, AN ELEPHANT WAS DRIFTING.

Gunga Diner

BEYOND THAT, UNSEEN, SPY SATELLITES. IF THEY SO MUCH AS NARROW THEIR GLASS EYES, WE SHALL ALL BE DEAD.

THIS RELENTLESS WORLD = THERE IS ONLY ONE SANE RESPONSE TO IT.

THE ALLEYWAY WAS COLD AND DESERTED.

MY THINGS WERE WHERE I'D LEFT THEM.

WAITING FOR ME.

PUTTING THEM ON, I ABANDONED MY DISGUISE AND BECAME MYSELF, FREE FROM FEAR OR WEAKNESS OR LUST.

Oh, how the ghost of you clings...

MY COAT, MY SHOES, MY SPOTLESS GLOVES.

MY FACE.

HAD THREE HOURS BEFORE CALLING ON MOLOCH.

AWAY DOWN ALLEY, HEARD WOMAN SCREAM, FIRST BUBBLING NOTE OF CITY'S EVENING CHORUS.

APPROACHED DISTURBANCE. AN ATTEMPTED RAPE / MUGGING / BOTH.

CLEARED THROAT. THE MAN TURNED AND THERE WAS SOMETHING REWARDING IN HIS EYES.

SOMETIMES, THE NIGHT IS GENEROUS TO ME.

18

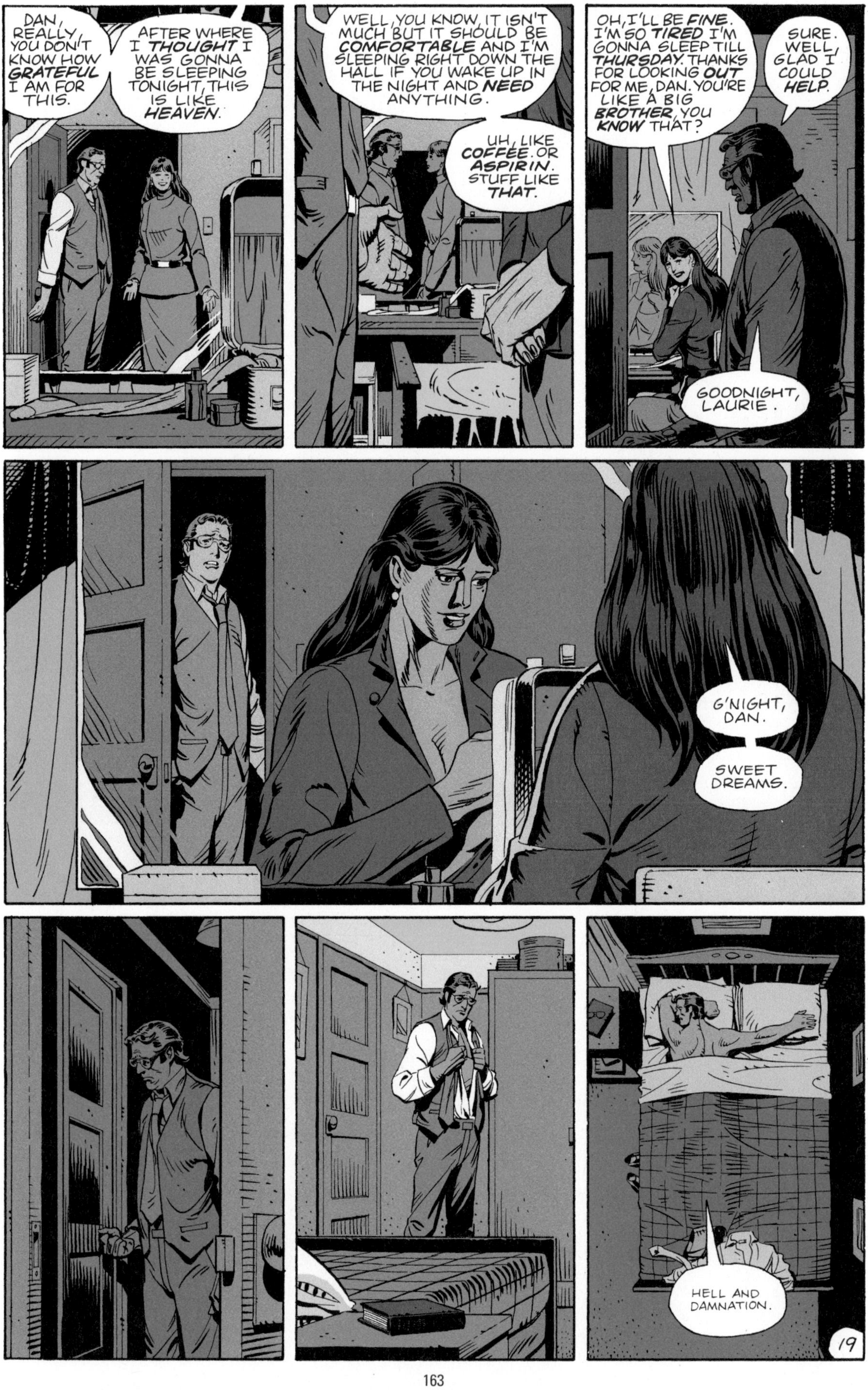
DAN, REALLY, YOU DON'T KNOW HOW GRATEFUL I AM FOR THIS.
AFTER WHERE I THOUGHT I WAS GONNA BE SLEEPING TONIGHT, THIS IS LIKE HEAVEN.
WELL, YOU KNOW, IT ISN'T MUCH BUT IT SHOULD BE COMFORTABLE AND I'M SLEEPING RIGHT DOWN THE HALL IF YOU WAKE UP IN THE NIGHT AND NEED ANYTHING.
UH, LIKE COFFEE. OR ASPIRIN. STUFF LIKE THAT.
OH, I'LL BE FINE. I'M SO TIRED I'M GONNA SLEEP TILL THURSDAY. THANKS FOR LOOKING OUT FOR ME, DAN. YOU'RE LIKE A BIG BROTHER, YOU KNOW THAT?
SURE. WELL, GLAD I COULD HELP.
GOODNIGHT, LAURIE.
G'NIGHT, DAN.
SWEET DREAMS.
HELL AND DAMNATION.
19

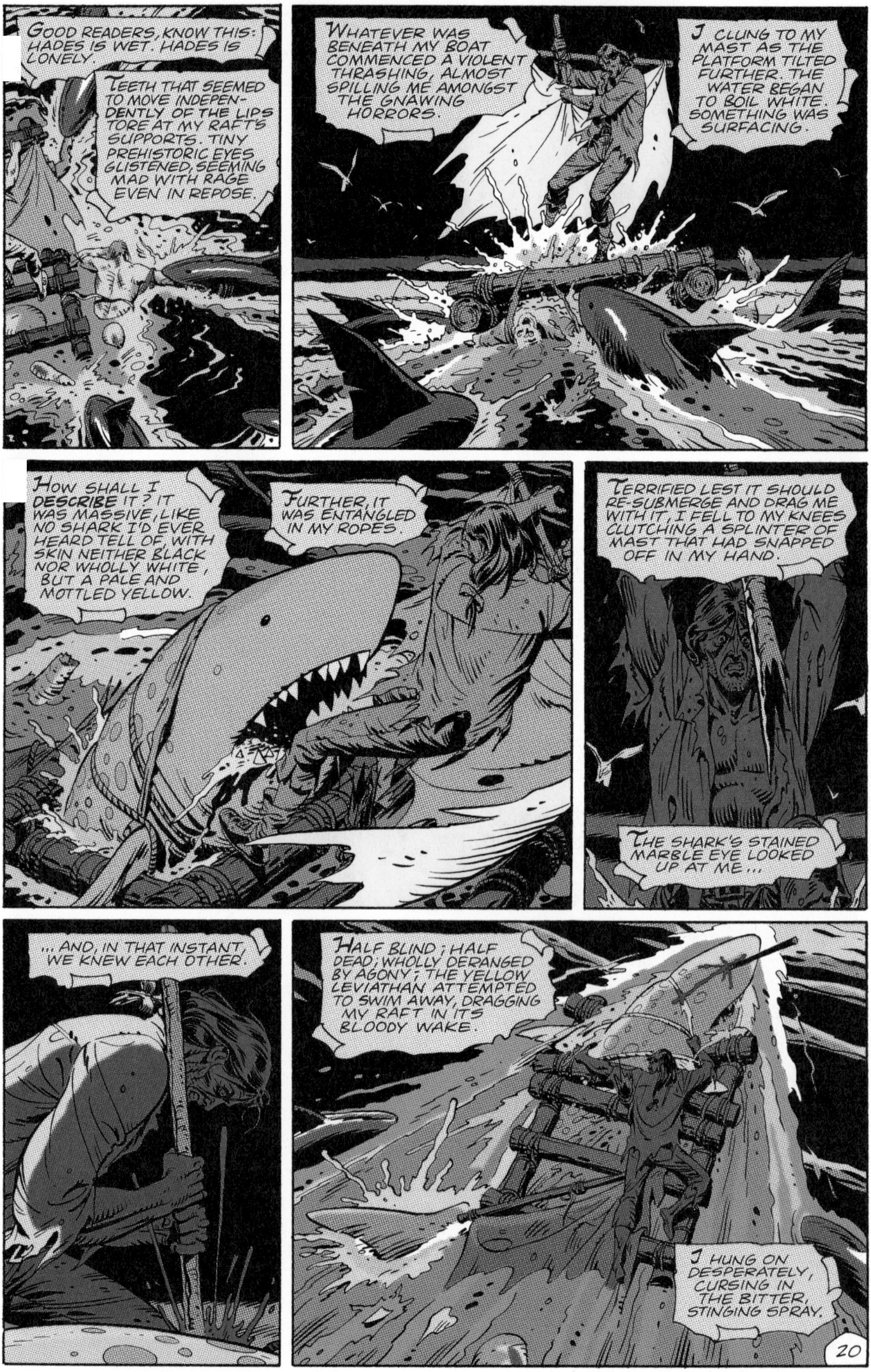
GOOD READERS, KNOW THIS: HADES IS WET. HADES IS LONELY.
TEETH THAT SEEMED TO MOVE INDEPENDENTLY OF THE LIPS TORE AT MY RAFT'S SUPPORTS. TINY PREHISTORIC EYES GLISTENED, SEEMING MAD WITH RAGE EVEN IN REPOSE.
WHATEVER WAS BENEATH MY BOAT COMMENCED A VIOLENT THRASHING, ALMOST SPILLING ME AMONGST THE GNAWING HORRORS.
I CLUNG TO MY MAST AS THE PLATFORM TILTED FURTHER. THE WATER BEGAN TO BOIL WHITE. SOMETHING WAS SURFACING.
HOW SHALL I DESCRIBE IT? IT WAS MASSIVE, LIKE NO SHARK I'D EVER HEARD TELL OF, WITH SKIN NEITHER BLACK NOR WHOLLY WHITE, BUT A PALE AND MOTTLED YELLOW.
FURTHER, IT WAS ENTANGLED IN MY ROPES.
TERRIFIED LEST IT SHOULD RE-SUBMERGE AND DRAG ME WITH IT, I FELL TO MY KNEES CLUTCHING A SPLINTER OF MAST THAT HAD SNAPPED OFF IN MY HAND.
THE SHARK'S STAINED MARBLE EYE LOOKED UP AT ME...
...AND, IN THAT INSTANT, WE KNEW EACH OTHER.
HALF BLIND; HALF DEAD; WHOLLY DERANGED BY AGONY; THE YELLOW LEVIATHAN ATTEMPTED TO SWIM AWAY, DRAGGING MY RAFT IN ITS BLOODY WAKE.
I HUNG ON DESPERATELY, CURSING IN THE BITTER, STINGING SPRAY.
20

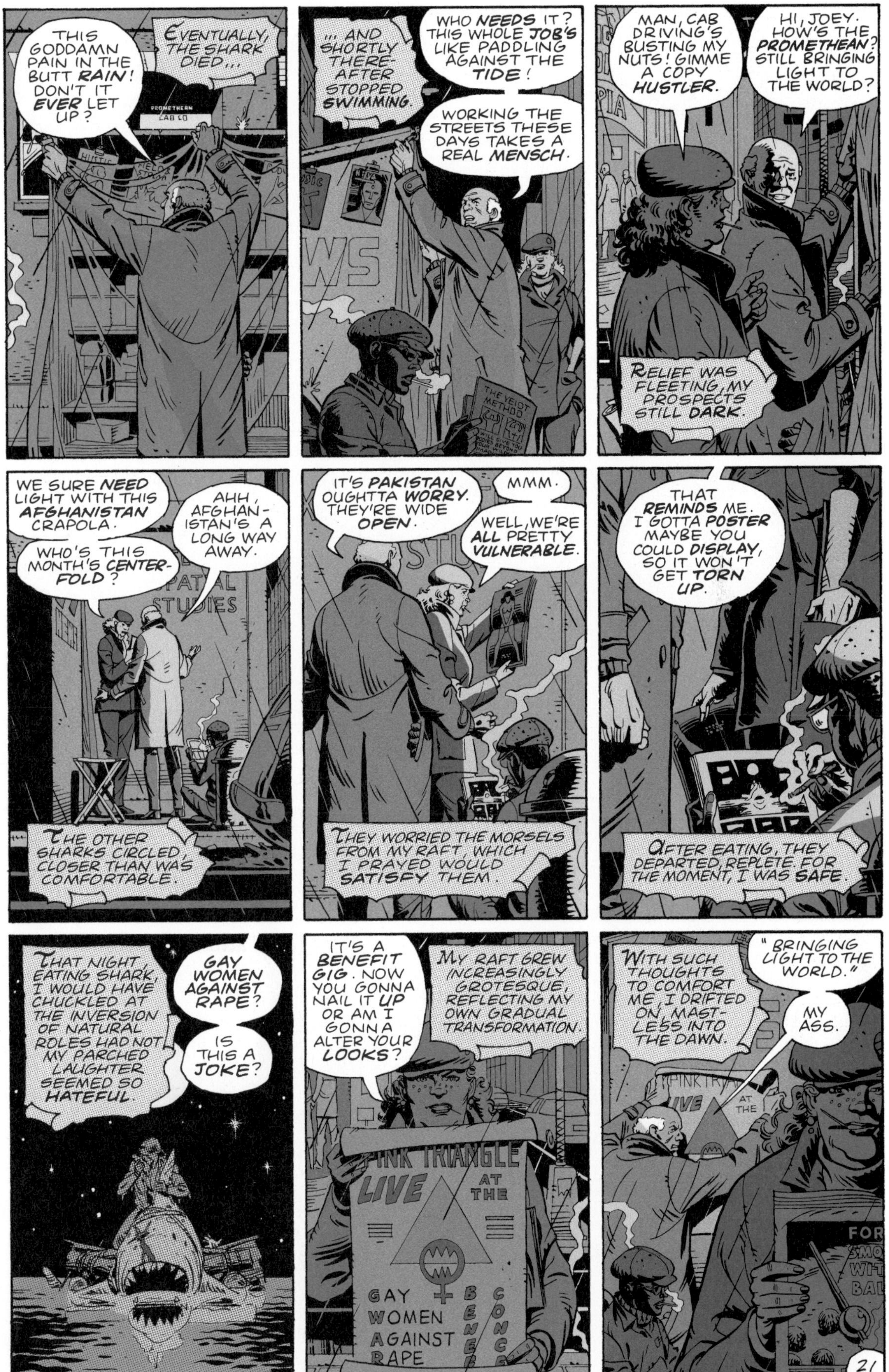
THIS GODDAMN PAIN IN THE BUTT RAIN! DON'T IT EVER LET UP?
EVENTUALLY, THE SHARK DIED...
PROMETHEAN CAB CO
...AND SHORTLY THEREAFTER STOPPED SWIMMING.
WHO NEEDS IT? THIS WHOLE JOB'S LIKE PADDLING AGAINST THE TIDE!
WORKING THE STREETS THESE DAYS TAKES A REAL MENSCH.
THE VEIDT METHOD
MAN, CAB DRIVING'S BUSTING MY NUTS! GIMME A COPY HUSTLER.
HI, JOEY. HOW'S THE PROMETHEAN? STILL BRINGING LIGHT TO THE WORLD?
RELIEF WAS FLEETING, MY PROSPECTS STILL DARK.
WE SURE NEED LIGHT WITH THIS AFGHANISTAN CRAPOLA.
AHH, AFGHANISTAN'S A LONG WAY AWAY.
WHO'S THIS MONTH'S CENTERFOLD?
THE OTHER SHARKS CIRCLED, CLOSER THAN WAS COMFORTABLE.
IT'S PAKISTAN OUGHTTA WORRY. THEY'RE WIDE OPEN.
MMM.
WELL, WE'RE ALL PRETTY VULNERABLE.
THEY WORRIED THE MORSELS FROM MY RAFT, WHICH I PRAYED WOULD SATISFY THEM.
THAT REMINDS ME. I GOTTA POSTER MAYBE YOU COULD DISPLAY, SO IT WON'T GET TORN UP.
AFTER EATING, THEY DEPARTED, REPLETE. FOR THE MOMENT, I WAS SAFE.
THAT NIGHT, EATING SHARK, I WOULD HAVE CHUCKLED AT THE INVERSION OF NATURAL ROLES HAD NOT MY PARCHED LAUGHTER SEEMED SO HATEFUL.
GAY WOMEN AGAINST RAPE?
IS THIS A JOKE?
IT'S A BENEFIT GIG. NOW YOU GONNA NAIL IT UP OR AM I GONNA ALTER YOUR LOOKS?
MY RAFT GREW INCREASINGLY GROTESQUE, REFLECTING MY OWN GRADUAL TRANSFORMATION.
PINK TRIANGLE LIVE AT THE
GAY WOMEN AGAINST RAPE
WITH SUCH THOUGHTS TO COMFORT ME, I DRIFTED ON, MASTLESS INTO THE DAWN.
"BRINGING LIGHT TO THE WORLD."
MY ASS.
21

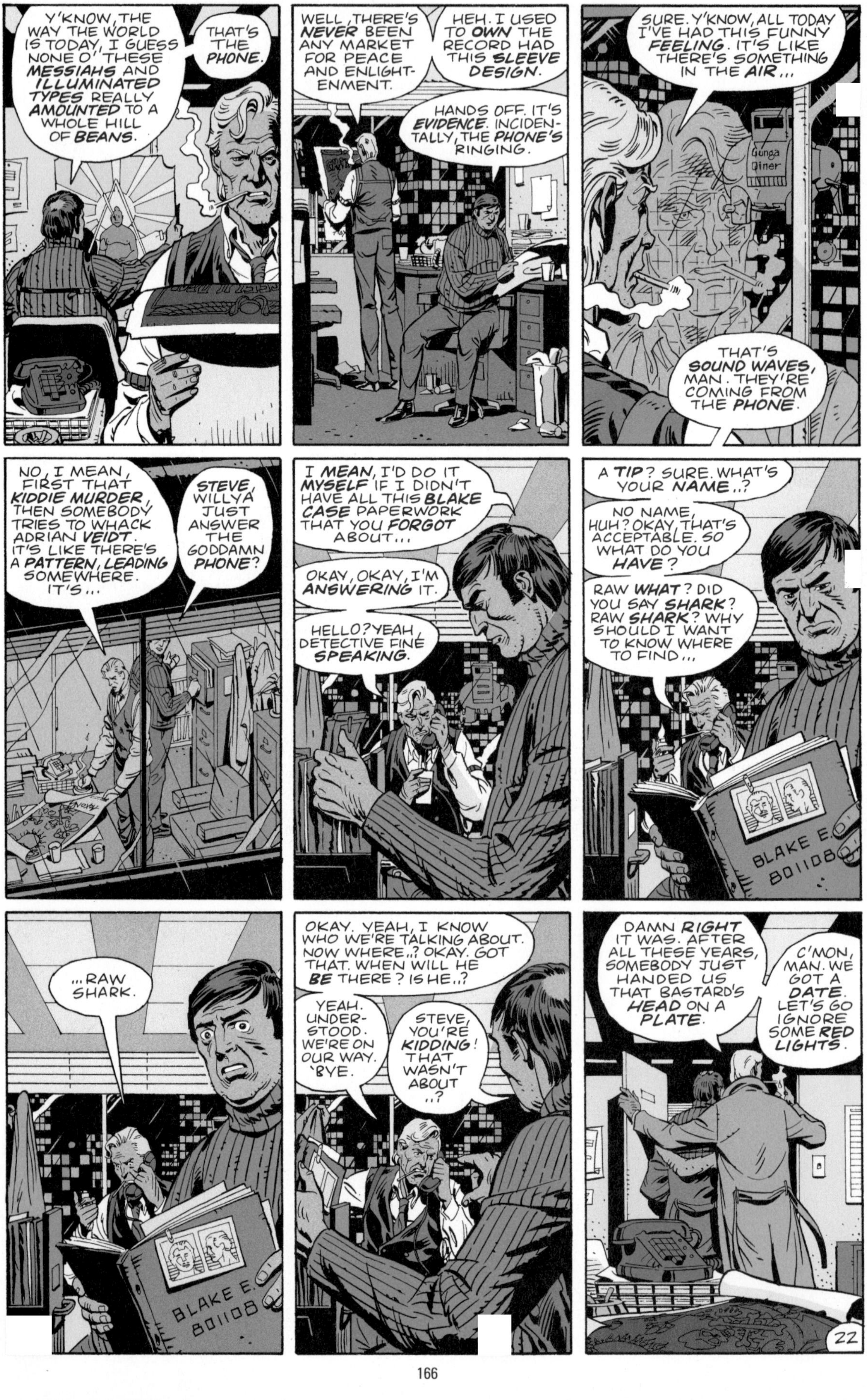
Y'KNOW, THE WAY THE WORLD IS TODAY, I GUESS NONE O' THESE MESSIAHS AND ILLUMINATED TYPES REALLY AMOUNTED TO A WHOLE HILL OF BEANS.
THAT'S THE PHONE.
WELL, THERE'S NEVER BEEN ANY MARKET FOR PEACE AND ENLIGHTENMENT.
HEH. I USED TO OWN THE RECORD HAD THIS SLEEVE DESIGN.
HANDS OFF. IT'S EVIDENCE. INCIDENTALLY, THE PHONE'S RINGING.
SURE. Y'KNOW, ALL TODAY I'VE HAD THIS FUNNY FEELING. IT'S LIKE THERE'S SOMETHING IN THE AIR...
Gunga Diner
THAT'S SOUND WAVES, MAN. THEY'RE COMING FROM THE PHONE.
NO, I MEAN, FIRST THAT KIDDIE MURDER, THEN SOMEBODY TRIES TO WHACK ADRIAN VEIDT. IT'S LIKE THERE'S A PATTERN, LEADING SOMEWHERE. IT'S...
STEVE, WILLYA JUST ANSWER THE GODDAMN PHONE?
I MEAN, I'D DO IT MYSELF IF I DIDN'T HAVE ALL THIS BLAKE CASE PAPERWORK THAT YOU FORGOT ABOUT...
OKAY, OKAY, I'M ANSWERING IT.
HELLO? YEAH, DETECTIVE FINE SPEAKING.
A TIP? SURE. WHAT'S YOUR NAME..?
NO NAME, HUH? OKAY, THAT'S ACCEPTABLE. SO WHAT DO YOU HAVE?
RAW WHAT? DID YOU SAY SHARK? RAW SHARK? WHY SHOULD I WANT TO KNOW WHERE TO FIND...
BLAKE E. 801108
...RAW SHARK.
BLAKE E. 801108
OKAY. YEAH, I KNOW WHO WE'RE TALKING ABOUT. NOW WHERE..? OKAY. GOT THAT. WHEN WILL HE BE THERE? IS HE..?
YEAH. UNDERSTOOD. WE'RE ON OUR WAY. 'BYE.
STEVE, YOU'RE KIDDING! THAT WASN'T ABOUT ..?
DAMN RIGHT IT WAS. AFTER ALL THESE YEARS, SOMEBODY JUST HANDED US THAT BASTARD'S HEAD ON A PLATE.
C'MON, MAN. WE GOT A DATE. LET'S GO IGNORE SOME RED LIGHTS.
22

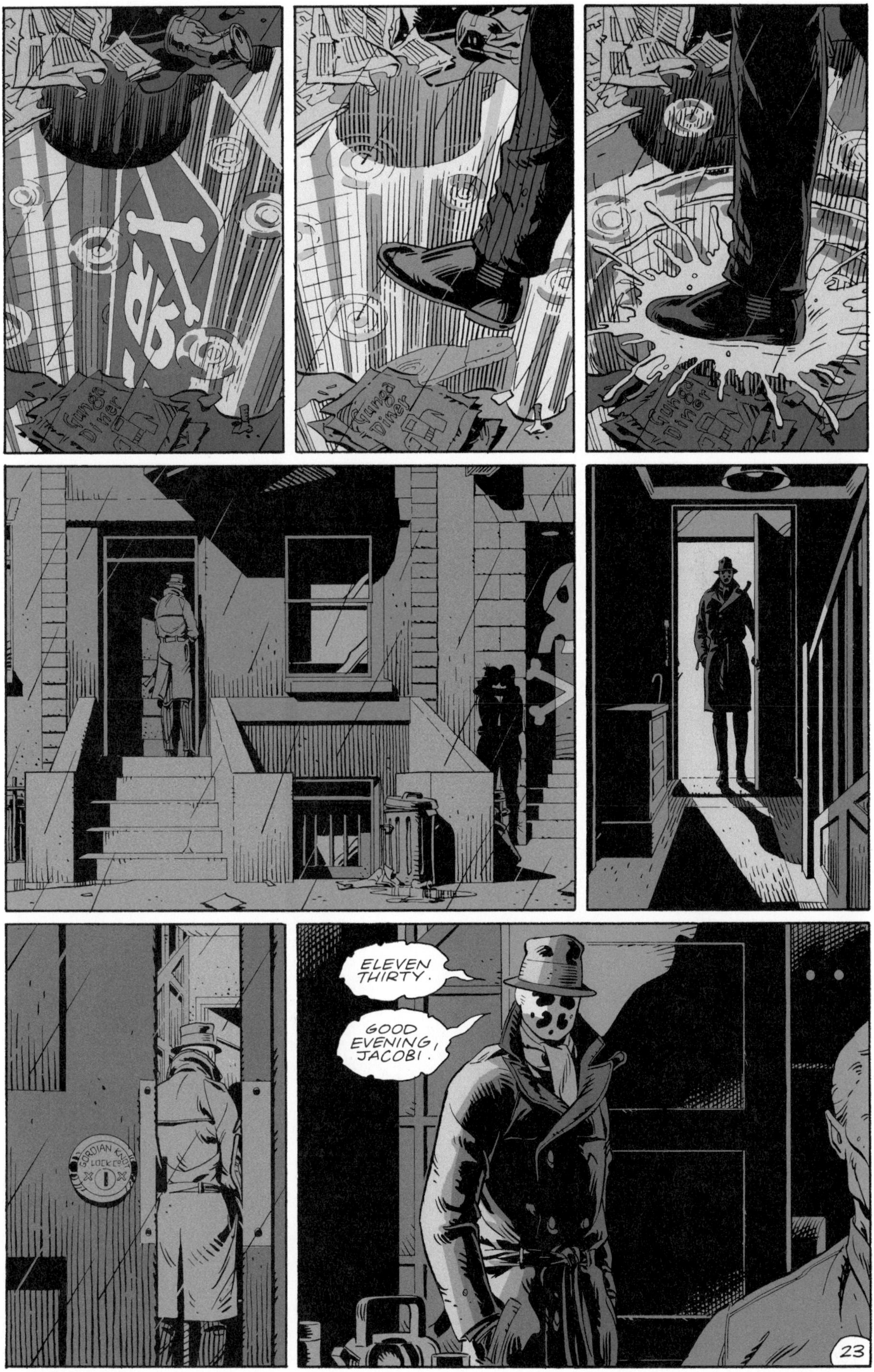
Gunga Diner
Gunga Diner
Gunga Diner
GORDIAN KNOT LOCK Co.
ELEVEN THIRTY.
GOOD EVENING, JACOBI.
23

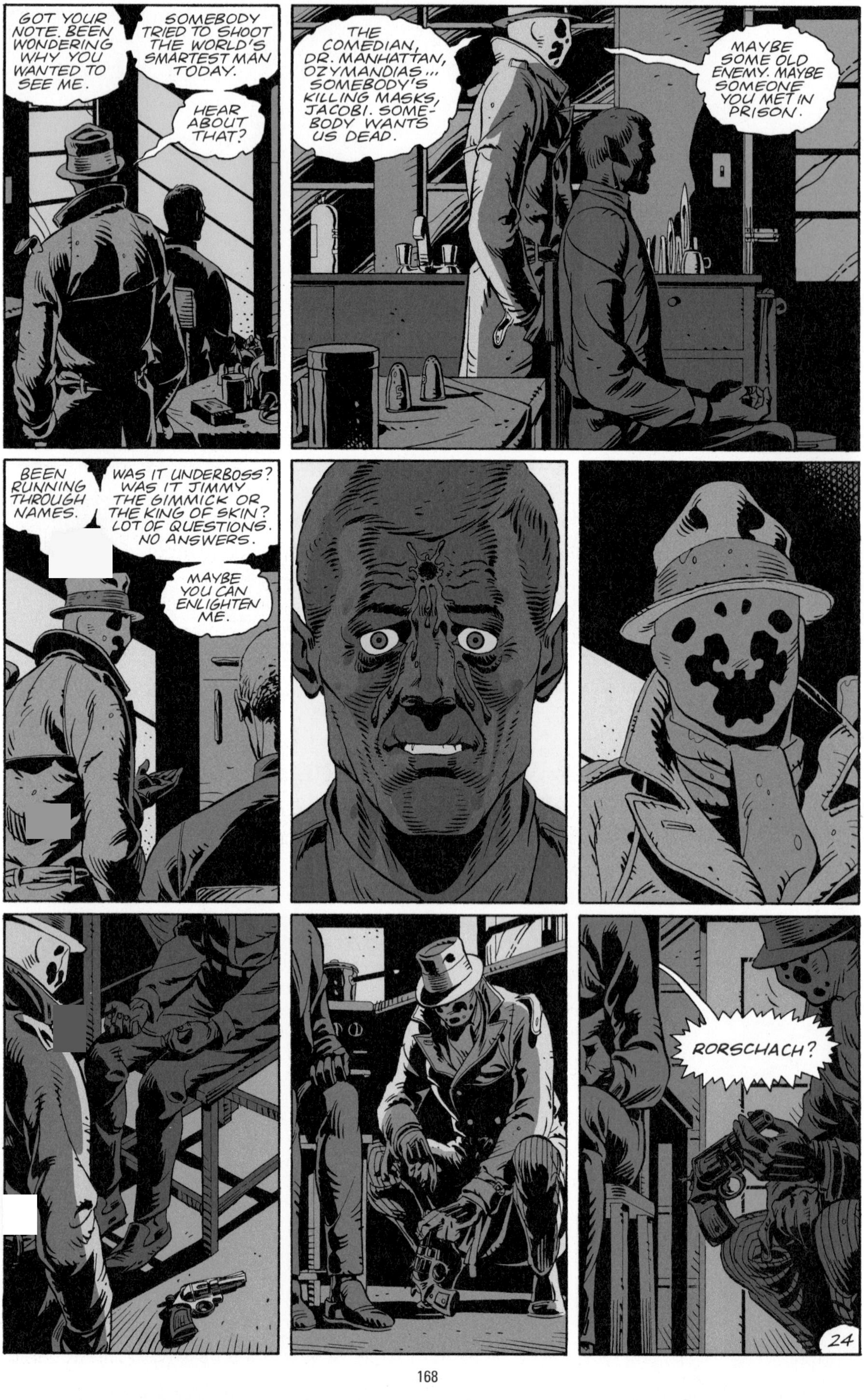
GOT YOUR NOTE. BEEN WONDERING WHY YOU WANTED TO SEE ME.
SOMEBODY TRIED TO SHOOT THE WORLD'S SMARTEST MAN TODAY.
HEAR ABOUT THAT?
THE COMEDIAN, DR. MANHATTAN, OZYMANDIAS... SOMEBODY'S KILLING MASKS, JACOBI. SOMEBODY WANTS US DEAD.
MAYBE SOME OLD ENEMY. MAYBE SOMEONE YOU MET IN PRISON.
BEEN RUNNING THROUGH NAMES.
WAS IT UNDERBOSS? WAS IT JIMMY THE GIMMICK OR THE KING OF SKIN? LOT OF QUESTIONS. NO ANSWERS.
MAYBE YOU CAN ENLIGHTEN ME.
RORSCHACH?
24

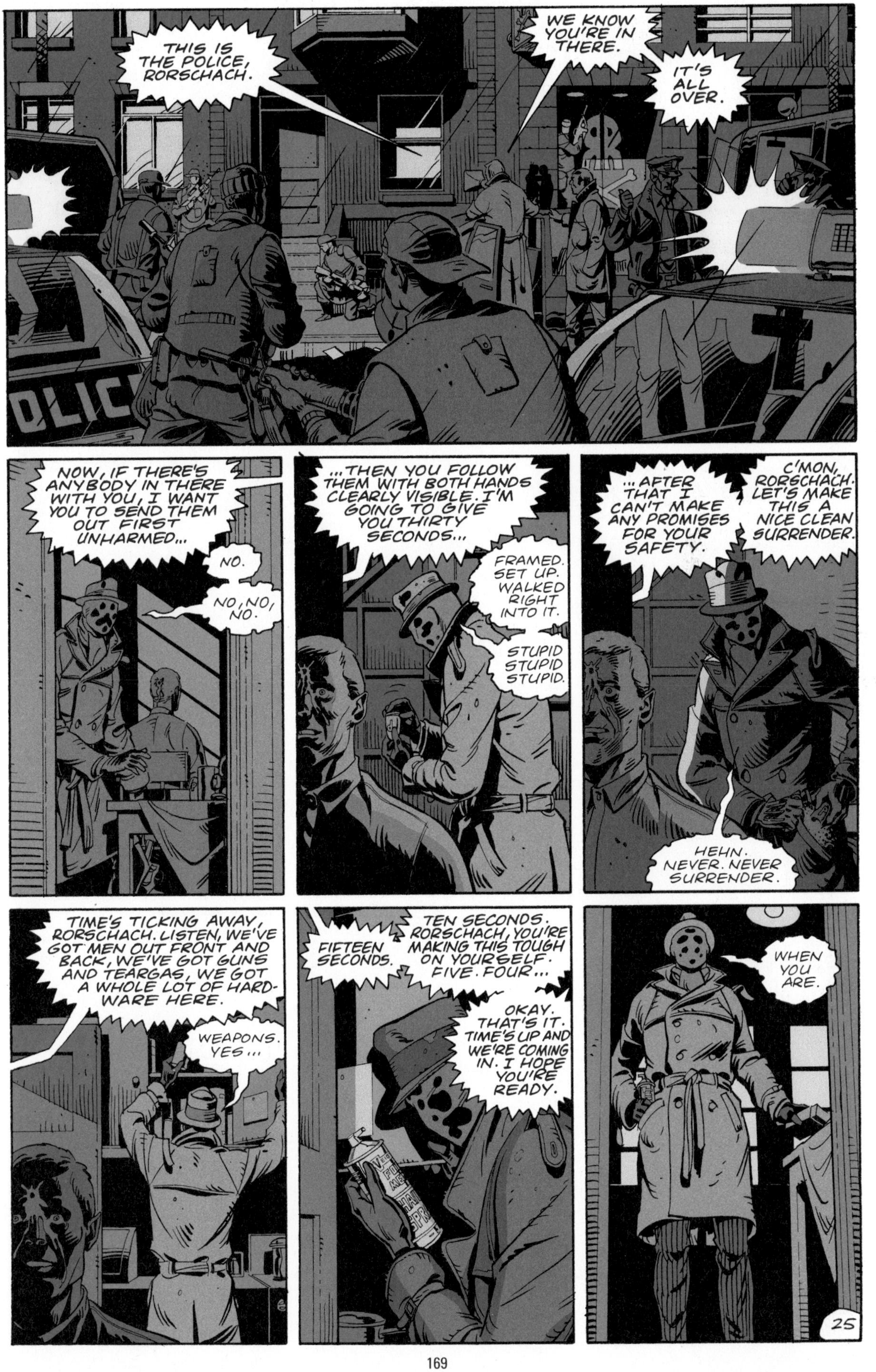
THIS IS THE POLICE, RORSCHACH.
WE KNOW YOU'RE IN THERE.
IT'S ALL OVER.
POLIC
NOW, IF THERE'S ANYBODY IN THERE WITH YOU, I WANT YOU TO SEND THEM OUT FIRST UNHARMED...
NO.
NO, NO, NO.
...THEN YOU FOLLOW THEM WITH BOTH HANDS CLEARLY VISIBLE. I'M GOING TO GIVE YOU THIRTY SECONDS...
FRAMED. SET UP. WALKED RIGHT INTO IT.
STUPID STUPID STUPID.
...AFTER THAT I CAN'T MAKE ANY PROMISES FOR YOUR SAFETY.
C'MON, RORSCHACH. LET'S MAKE THIS A NICE CLEAN SURRENDER.
HEHN. NEVER. NEVER SURRENDER.
TIME'S TICKING AWAY, RORSCHACH. LISTEN, WE'VE GOT MEN OUT FRONT AND BACK, WE'VE GOT GUNS AND TEARGAS, WE GOT A WHOLE LOT OF HARDWARE HERE.
WEAPONS. YES...
FIFTEEN SECONDS.
TEN SECONDS. RORSCHACH, YOU'RE MAKING THIS TOUGH ON YOURSELF. FIVE. FOUR...
OKAY. THAT'S IT. TIME'S UP AND WE'RE COMING IN. I HOPE YOU'RE READY.
WHEN YOU ARE.
25

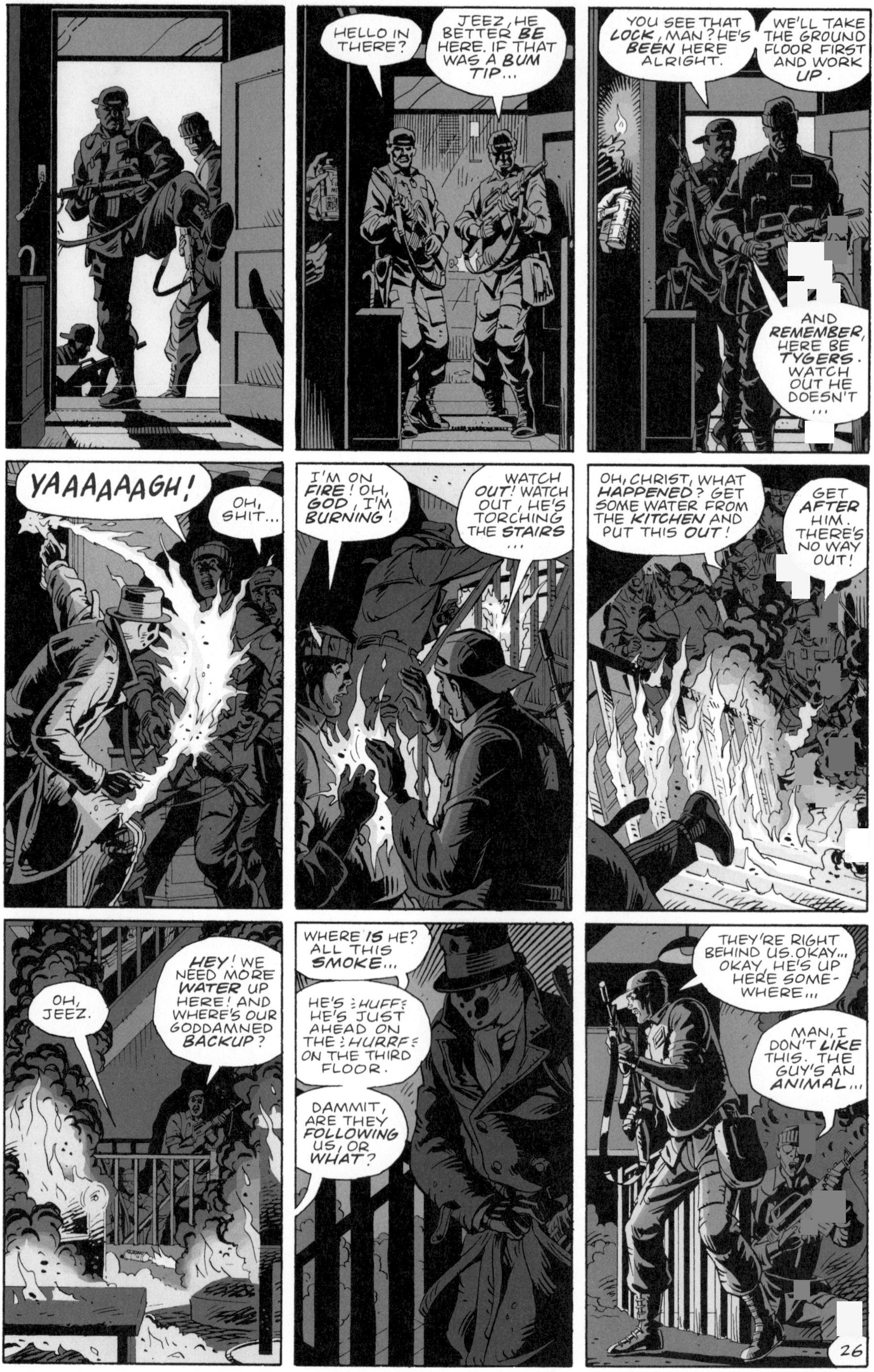
HELLO IN THERE?
JEEZ, HE BETTER BE HERE. IF THAT WAS A BUM TIP...
YOU SEE THAT LOCK, MAN? HE'S BEEN HERE ALRIGHT.
WE'LL TAKE THE GROUND FLOOR FIRST AND WORK UP.
AND REMEMBER, HERE BE TYGERS. WATCH OUT HE DOESN'T ...
YAAAAAAAGH!
OH, SHIT...
I'M ON FIRE! OH, GOD, I'M BURNING!
WATCH OUT! WATCH OUT, HE'S TORCHING THE STAIRS ...
OH, CHRIST, WHAT HAPPENED? GET SOME WATER FROM THE KITCHEN AND PUT THIS OUT!
GET AFTER HIM. THERE'S NO WAY OUT!
OH, JEEZ.
HEY! WE NEED MORE WATER UP HERE! AND WHERE'S OUR GODDAMNED BACKUP?
WHERE IS HE? ALL THIS SMOKE...
HE'S HUFF HE'S JUST AHEAD ON THE HURRF ON THE THIRD FLOOR.
DAMMIT, ARE THEY FOLLOWING US, OR WHAT?
THEY'RE RIGHT BEHIND US. OKAY... OKAY, HE'S UP HERE SOME-WHERE...
MAN, I DON'T LIKE THIS. THE GUY'S AN ANIMAL...
26

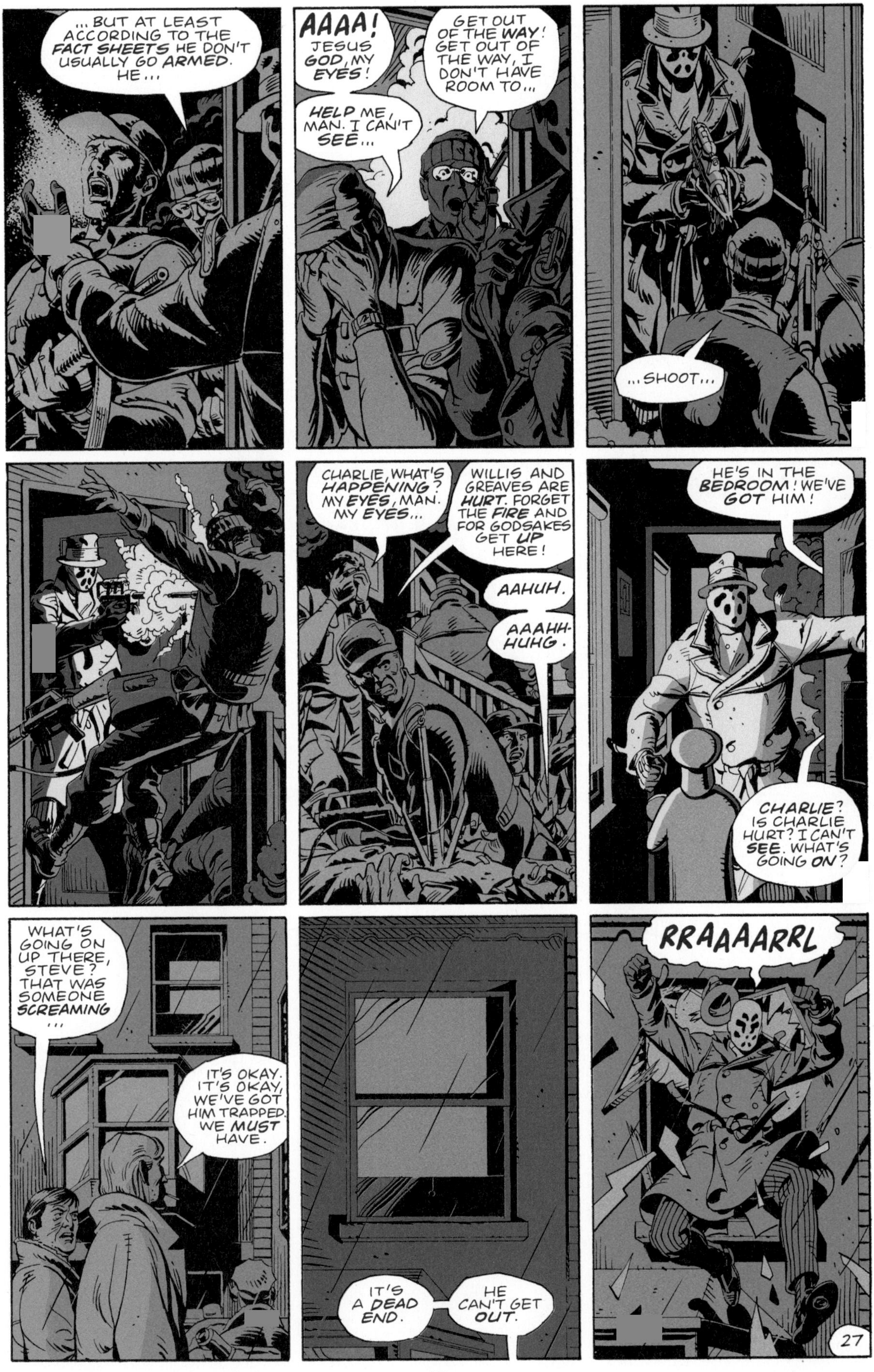
...BUT AT LEAST ACCORDING TO THE FACT SHEETS HE DON'T USUALLY GO ARMED. HE...
AAAA! JESUS GOD, MY EYES!
GET OUT OF THE WAY! GET OUT OF THE WAY, I DON'T HAVE ROOM TO...
HELP ME, MAN. I CAN'T SEE...
...SHOOT...
CHARLIE, WHAT'S HAPPENING? MY EYES, MAN. MY EYES...
WILLIS AND GREAVES ARE HURT. FORGET THE FIRE AND FOR GODSAKES GET UP HERE!
AAHUH.
AAAHH-HUHG.
HE'S IN THE BEDROOM! WE'VE GOT HIM!
CHARLIE? IS CHARLIE HURT? I CAN'T SEE. WHAT'S GOING ON?
WHAT'S GOING ON UP THERE, STEVE? THAT WAS SOMEONE SCREAMING...
IT'S OKAY. IT'S OKAY, WE'VE GOT HIM TRAPPED. WE MUST HAVE.
IT'S A DEAD END.
HE CAN'T GET OUT.
RRAAAARRL
27

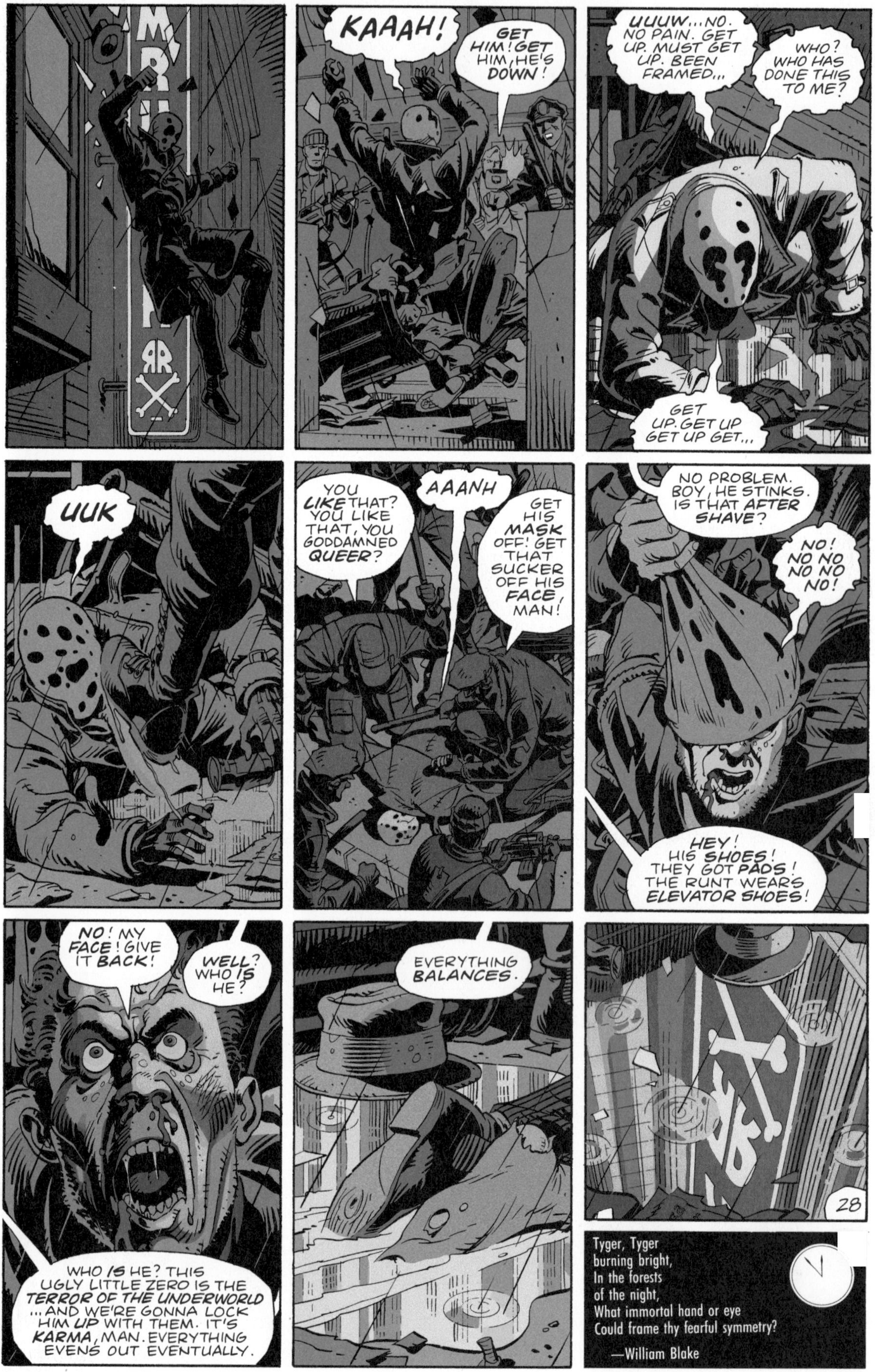

KAAAH!
GET HIM! GET HIM, HE'S DOWN!
UUUW... NO. NO PAIN. GET UP. MUST GET UP. BEEN FRAMED...
WHO? WHO HAS DONE THIS TO ME?
GET UP. GET UP GET UP GET...
UUK
YOU LIKE THAT? YOU LIKE THAT, YOU GODDAMNED QUEER?
AAANH
GET HIS MASK OFF! GET THAT SUCKER OFF HIS FACE, MAN!
NO PROBLEM. BOY, HE STINKS. IS THAT AFTER SHAVE?
NO! NO NO NO NO NO!
HEY! HIS SHOES! THEY GOT PADS! THE RUNT WEARS ELEVATOR SHOES!
NO! MY FACE! GIVE IT BACK!
WELL? WHO IS HE?
WHO IS HE? THIS UGLY LITTLE ZERO IS THE TERROR OF THE UNDERWORLD ... AND WE'RE GONNA LOCK HIM UP WITH THEM. IT'S KARMA, MAN. EVERYTHING EVENS OUT EVENTUALLY.
EVERYTHING BALANCES.
28

Tyger, Tyger
burning bright,
In the forests
of the night,
What immortal hand or eye
Could frame thy fearful symmetry?

—William Blake

TREASURE ISLAND TREASURY OF COMICS

The following is reprinted from chapter five of the Treasure Island Treasury Of Comics (Flint Editions, New York, 1984) with permission of the author and publishers.

A MAN ON FIFTEEN DEAD MEN'S CHESTS

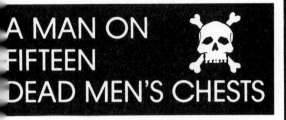

As discussed in our last chapter, the close of the 1950s saw E.C.'s line of Pirate titles dominating the marketplace from a near unassailable position. The brief surge of anti-comic book sentiment in the mid-fifties, while it could conceivably have damaged E.C. as a company, had instead come to nothing and left them stronger as a result. With the government of the day coming down squarely on the side of comic books in an effort to protect the image of certain comic book-inspired agents in their employ, it was as if the comic industry had suddenly been given the blessing of Uncle Sam himself—or at least J. Edgar Hoover. Unsurprisingly, as one of the few companies to anticipate the coming massive boom in pirate-related material, E.C. flourished and their hold upon the field remained unchallenged.

Until May, 1960. That date saw the first publication of an extraordinary new title from National Comics, now DC. The book was called 'Tales of the Black Freighter', and while its sales never quite topped those of the E.C. giants such as PIRACY and BUCCANEERS, in terms of critical acclaim and influence upon later books of the same type, TALES OF THE BLACK FREIGHTER made an impression upon the comic book landscape that remains to this day. Indeed, with DC comics currently reprinting the first classic thirty issues of the title and apparently meeting with considerable success, it would seem that its impact remains undiluted despite the quarter century that has elapsed since the original publication.

What exactly was it that made TALES OF THE BLACK FREIGHTER so special? Despite the fact that nowadays most people are attracted by the controversy surrounding the later issues of the book, it should be remembered that this title was very popular from the outset. So: What was it that fascinated all those thousands of readers in the first place?

Well, to begin with, it was almost certainly the artwork of Joe Orlando, who drew the entire book from its first issue through issue nine, with the exception of GALAPAGOS JONES, a rather insipid back-up feature that lasted until issue six. Orlando, having been successfully tempted away from his well-received run of 'SARGASSO SEA STORIES' in E.C.'s PIRACY by National editor Julius Schwartz, was regarded as a star amongst pirate artists, and a prize catch. Having adapted more smoothly from science fiction and horror to the different atmospheric demands of pirate stories than many of his E.C. contemporaries, he was perhaps the best respected artist in a rapidly burgeoning field, and fans awaited the first issue of TALES OF THE BLACK FREIGHTER with relish.

Nor were they disappointed. The first issue is classic Orlando. The script—by then-newcomer Max Shea—while sturdy enough, is cliched and predictable in comparison with the work that Shea did later, and in that first issue was easily outshone by the darkly compelling majesty of Orlando's textures, shadows and faces.

The story served as an introduction to the vessel that lent the book its title, and which was itself apparently borrowed from a ship referred to in Brecht and Weill's 'THREEPENNY OPERA'. In that first story, three men with different paths through life have all been led to the same dockside tavern in search of work. The place is deserted save for a shadowy innkeeper who serves them ale in silence and the large, dark figure of a sea captain who sits at the next table and listens to them recount their stories to each other.

The stories are recounted as small, self-contained tales within the larger narrative that frames them, and are all effective if predictable twist-ending yarns that reveal the various tellers to be utterly unprincipled and worthless creatures capable of almost any act of treachery. Overhearing their stories, the sea captain says he is impressed and offers them passage upon his ship. By the time the men are aboard the ship and have noticed the dreadful, deathly smell that seems to exude from the ship's timbers, it is too late. The three hapless sailors learn that the ship is a vessel from Hell itself to take on board the souls of evil men so that they may walk its blood-stained decks for all eternity.

The identity of the captain is never made clear—is he meant to be Satan, or is he himself a victim of the ship? But this scarcely matters when confronted with Orlando's breathtaking rendition. From the marvelous scene in the first man's story where two ghouls fight to the death with shovels in the worm-infested tunnels beneath a churchyard, right through the haunting and evocative final shots of the horrible black ship drifting away into the white mist, the art is breathtaking, conveying a tangible sense of doom and evil even in those places where the writing fails to do so.

With the issues that followed, Orlando's art continued to shine while the scripts supplied by Shea

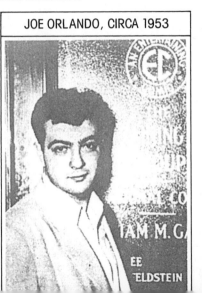

JOE ORLANDO, CIRCA 1953

also began to gradually improve in quality as the writer became used to the medium. With rapidly increasing confidence, Shea began attempting ideas for stories which at the time seemed wildly radical and innovative. The third issue's story, "Between Breaths", is told from the viewpoint of a man who is drowning, alternating between memories of his past life as they flash before his bulging eyes and horrific descriptions of what it is like to drown. Even read today, the story induces an almost tangible sense of suffocation, so that finishing the story and putting the book down is actually a relief. The closing images, with a multitude of dead and drowned men walking across the ocean bed towards the anchor rope of the Black Freighter which they climb to take their rightful positions on board the ship, remain some of Orlando's most haunting work on the series.

By issue five, reader reaction was obviously in favor of the title, and the praise seemed to be divided equally between Orlando and Shea. According to insiders, receiving fan mail for the first time in his life had an adverse effect upon the writer, who began to see himself as the driving force of the book, becoming increasingly resentful of Orlando's clearly important role and harassing the artist with impossibly detailed panel descriptions and endless carping requests for revisions of artwork already drawn.

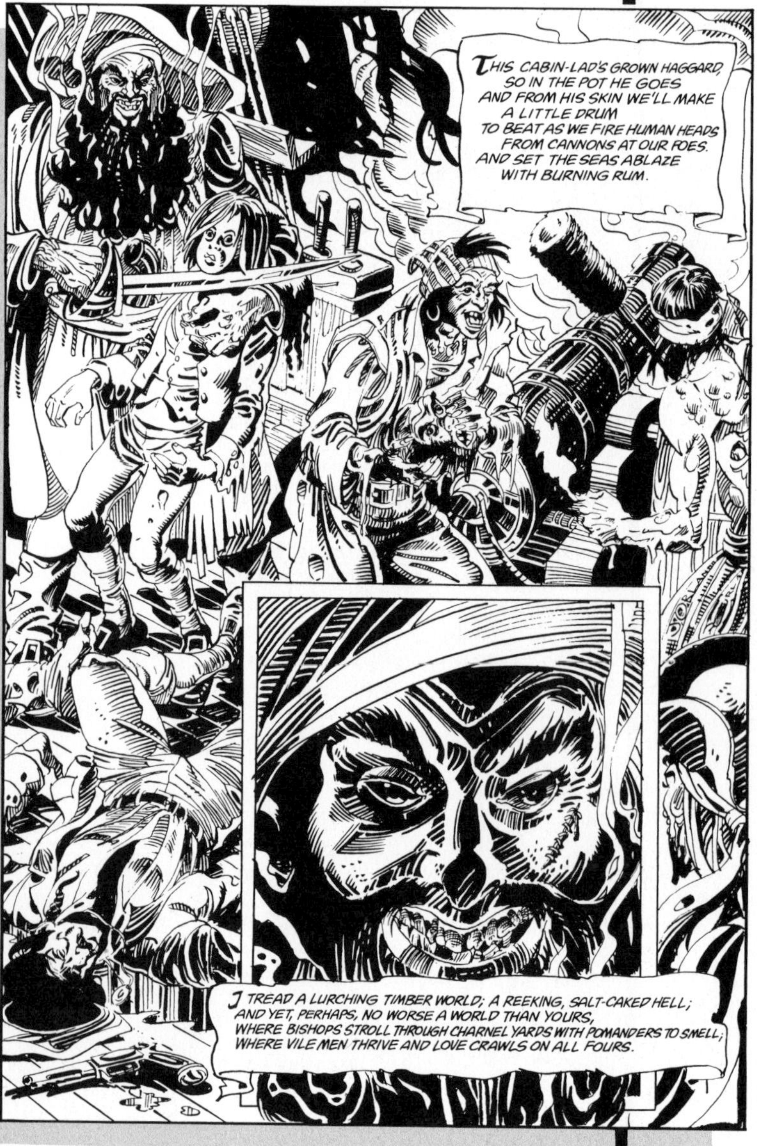
THIS CABIN-LAD'S GROWN HAGGARD, SO IN THE POT HE GOES AND FROM HIS SKIN WE'LL MAKE A LITTLE DRUM TO BEAT AS WE FIRE HUMAN HEADS FROM CANNONS AT OUR FOES. AND SET THE SEAS ABLAZE WITH BURNING RUM.
I TREAD A LURCHING TIMBER WORLD; A REEKING, SALT-CAKED HELL; AND YET, PERHAPS, NO WORSE A WORLD THAN YOURS, WHERE BISHOPS STROLL THROUGH CHARNEL YARDS WITH POMANDERS TO SMELL; WHERE VILE MEN THRIVE AND LOVE CRAWLS ON ALL FOURS.

Despite growing friction within the creative team, both lasted on TALES OF THE BLACK FREIGHTER until the ninth issue, when Orlando asked Schwartz to take him off the book, citing the ego of the writer as being the major factor in his decision. During those nine issues they crafted many memorable stories together, including the most famous of all, "The Shanty of Edward Teach", in issue seven. In this story, narrated in rhyme by the dead pirate Edward Teach (otherwise known as Blackbeard), we first begin to see the dark and pessimistic moral sensibilities showing that were later to form most of Shea's work on the series. These are more than adequately matched by Orlando's artwork, and there can be few readers of that period who will forget the heart-stopping close-up shot of Blackbeard, portrayed as violent and leering evil incarnate, in which he seems to look out at the reader and remind them that their own position is perhaps no more noble than Teach's own: "I tread a lurching timber world, a reeking salt-caked hell; and yet, perhaps, no worse a world than yours, where bishops stroll through charnel yards with pomanders to smell; where vile men thrive and love crawls on all fours."

After Orlando's departure, the art for the series was taken over by a relatively unknown but supremely capable artist named Walt Feinberg, previously best known for his work upon numerous western titles where he would often provide excellent fill-in issues that nevertheless seemed

EAST, ACROSS THE NIGHT SEAS.

EAST, BORNE ON THE NAKED BACKS OF MURDERED MEN.

to go unnoticed when slotted in between the work of great western comic artists such as Gil Kane and Alex Toth. Despite having Orlando's early work on the series to live up to, on TALES OF THE BLACK FREIGHTER, Feinberg was finally given a chance to shine. For some reason, there are few incidents on record relating friction between Feinberg and Shea, and indeed the two of them continued to work together on the book until issue thirty-one, at which point Shea quit (perhaps the moody and temperamental writer was making a deliberate effort to control his behavior, having been taught an expensive lesson by Orlando's departure).

In any event the next twenty or so issues of the book became every bit as much instant classics as the Orlando issues had, a fact not hindered by Shea's gradually developing skill as a writer.

The stories that came from his pen in this period are uniformly dark and sinister, balancing metaphysical terrors against an unnerving sense of reality, particularly when applied to matters of mortality or sexuality. Readers who came to the series expecting a good rousing tale of swashbuckling were either repulsed or fascinated by what were often perverse and blackly lingering comments upon the human condition. Tales such as ''The Figurehead'', which deal unflinchingly with male homosexuality, and the harrowing ''Marooned'' spring most readily to mind.

In ''Marooned'', a two-part story occupying issues twenty-three and twenty-four of the book's run, we see Feinberg and Shea at their blood-freezing best. Unusual in that it is a one-character story narrated mostly in captions, ''Marooned'' tells the story of a young mariner whose vessel is wrecked by the Black Freighter before it can return to its hometown and warn it of the hell-ship's approach. Cast adrift on an uninhabited island with only his dead shipmates for company, we experience the frantic mariner's torment at the knowledge that while he is trapped on his island, the bestial crew of the Freighter are surely bearing down upon his town, his home, his wife and his children. Driven by his burning desire to avert this calamity, we see the mariner finally

escape from the island by what may be one of the most striking and horrific devices thus far in pirate comic books: digging up the recently buried and gas-bloated corpses of his shipmates, the mariner lashes them together and uses them as the floats on an improvised raft on which he hopes to reach the mainland (hence the title of this chapter.) On reaching the mainland safely

upon his horrific craft we see the increasingly distraught and dishevelled mariner trying desperately to reach his home, even resorting to murder to acquire a horse for himself. In the final scenes, thanks to the skillful interplay of text and pictures, we see that the mariner, though he has escaped from his island, is in the end marooned from the rest of humanity in a much more terrible fashion.

Problems set in for the book around issue twenty-five, when Shea began his controversial

TALES OF THE BLACK FREIGHTER

run of issues based around the contents of plundered books in the library of the Freighter's captain, including banned tomes supposedly originally headed for eternal suppression within the vaults of Vatican city when stolen en route by the pirates. Described as 'blatantly pornographic', four of the projected five stories were rejected by DC, which brought about the argument in which Shea quit the book and comics as well, going on to write such classic novels as the twice-filmed FOGDANCING.

At the time of this writing, Shea's whereabouts are unknown. In circumstances as strange as those in any of his stories, the writer apparently vanished from his home one morning and has not been seen since, although police are continuing their inquiries. In his wake he leaves not only a string of excellent novels and screenplays, but also an exemplary run of pirate stories which today fetch mint prices of almost a thousand dollars according to the Overstreet Guide. Stories there to be rediscovered and reexamined, like so many of the fascinating sunken treasures lurking just beneath the surface of this fabulous and compelling genre.

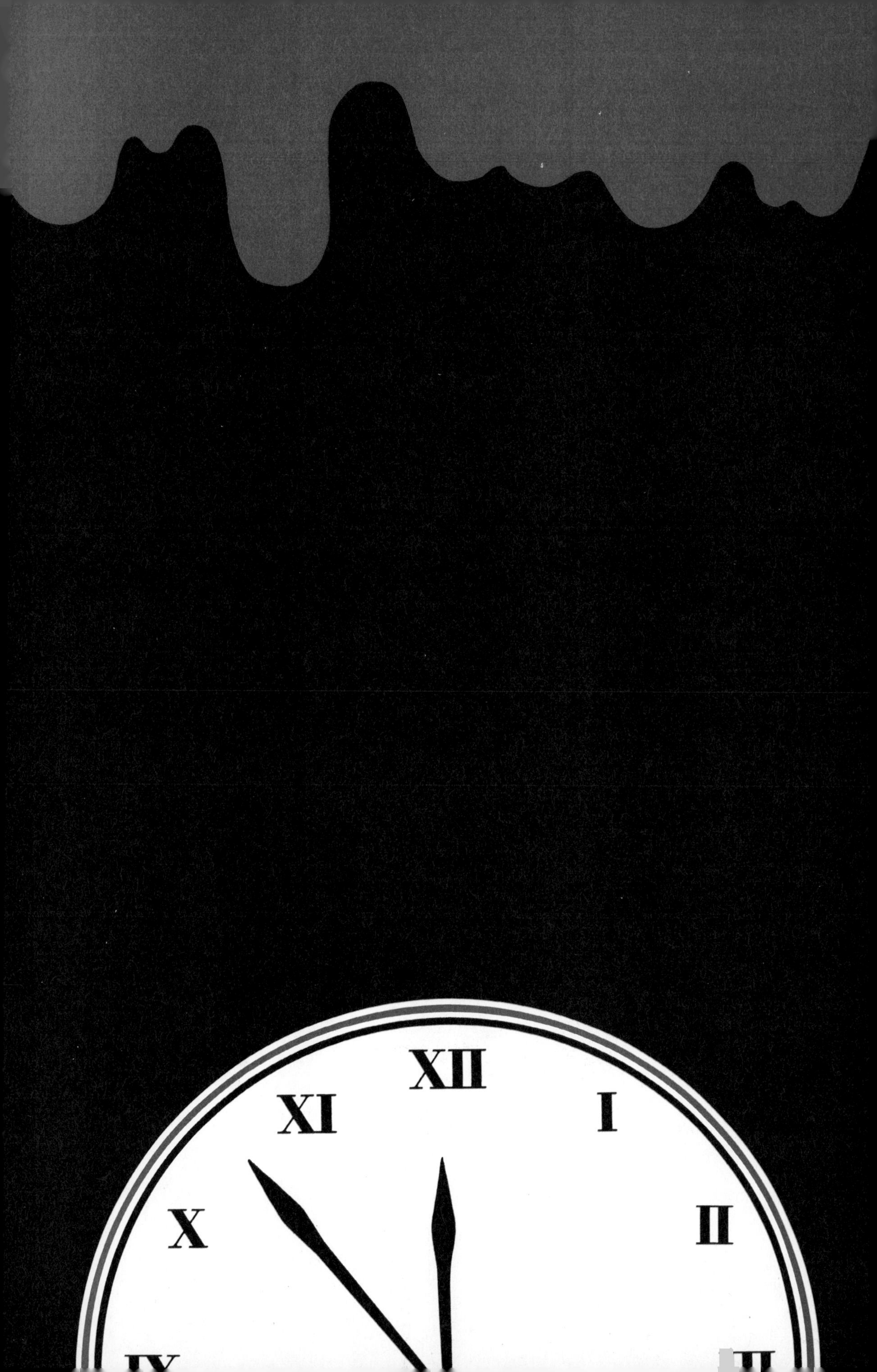
XII
XI
I
X
II

CHAPTER VI

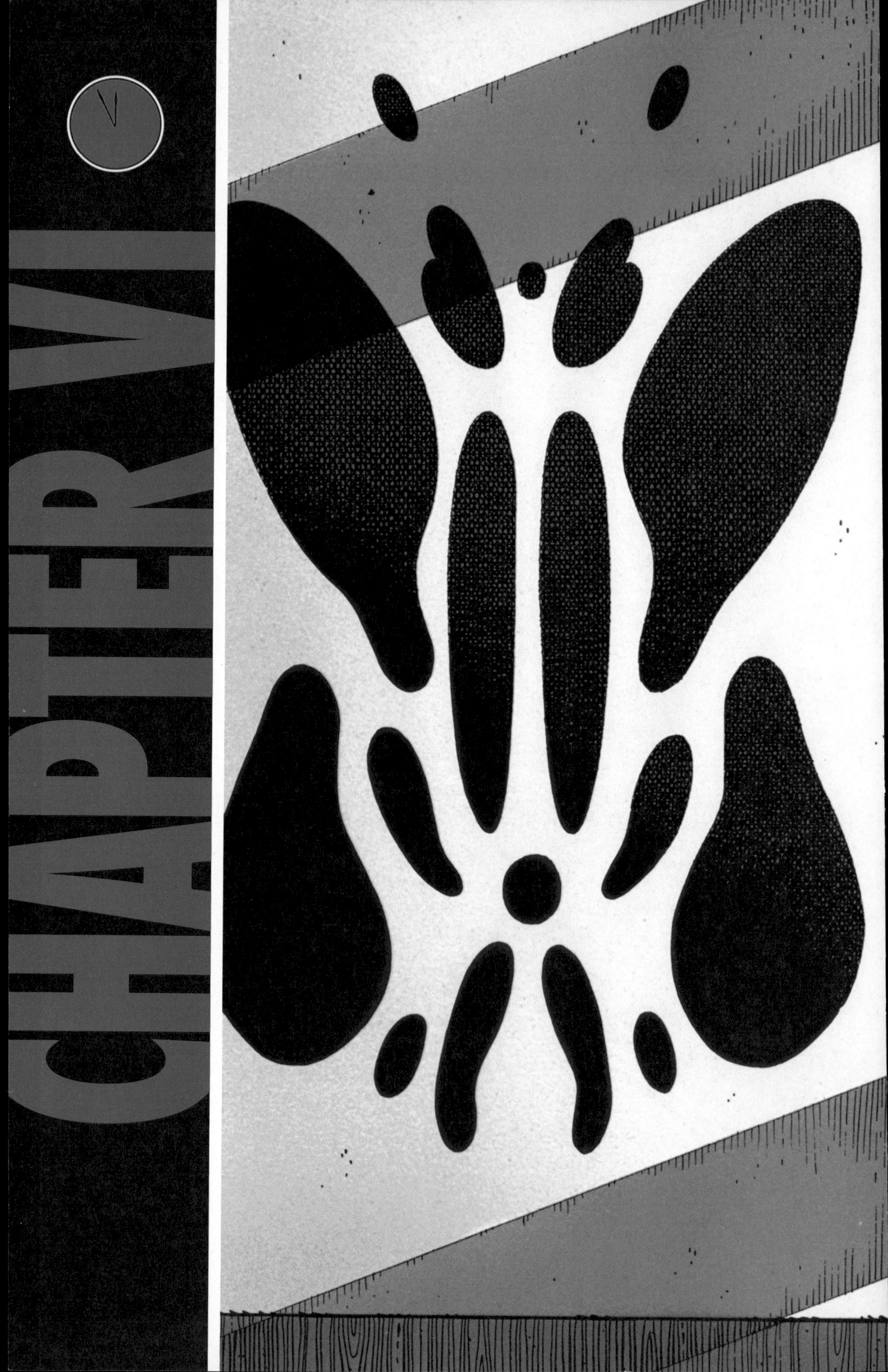

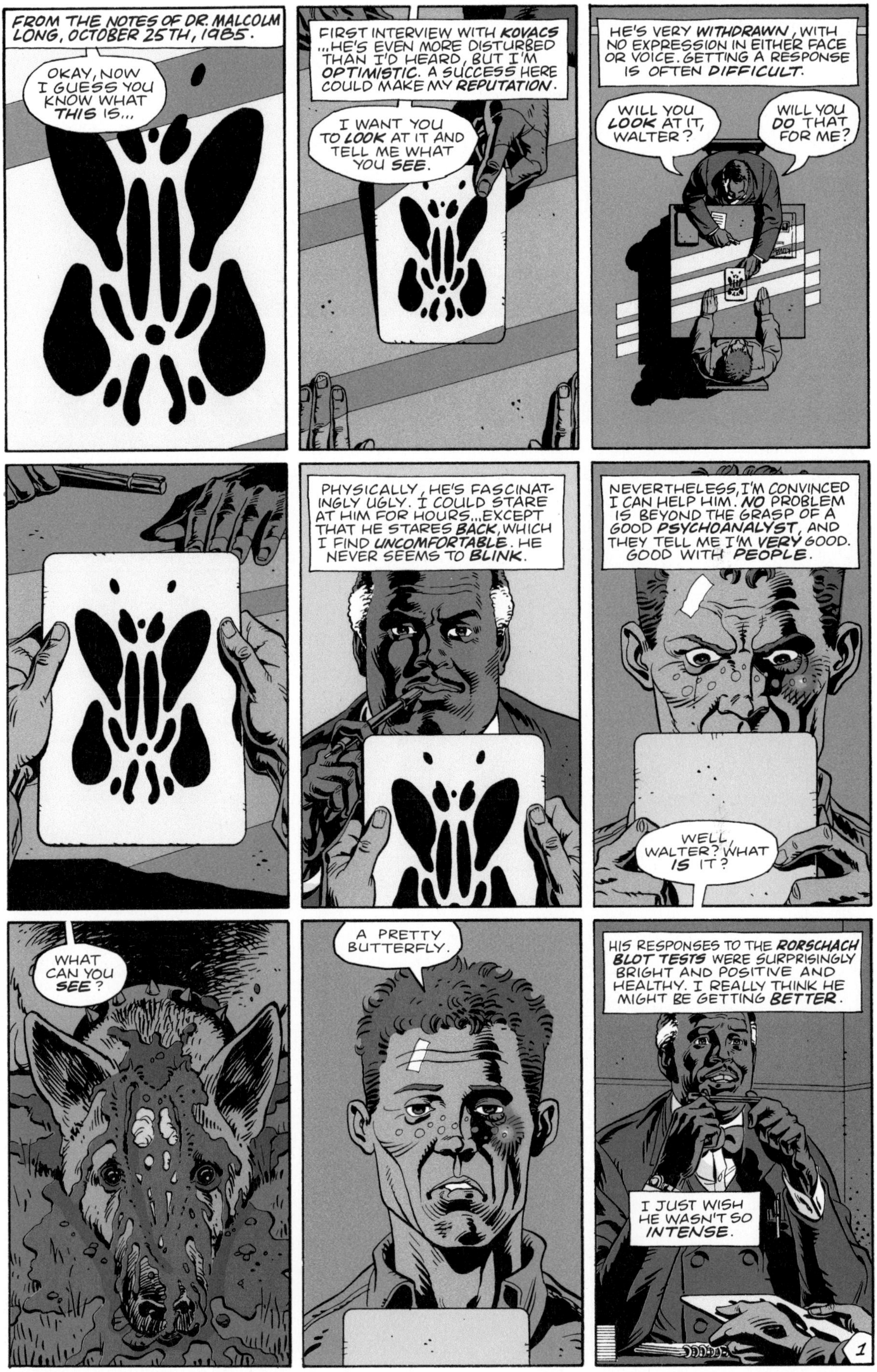
FROM THE NOTES OF DR. MALCOLM LONG, OCTOBER 25TH, 1985.
OKAY, NOW I GUESS YOU KNOW WHAT THIS IS...
FIRST INTERVIEW WITH KOVACS ...HE'S EVEN MORE DISTURBED THAN I'D HEARD, BUT I'M OPTIMISTIC. A SUCCESS HERE COULD MAKE MY REPUTATION.
I WANT YOU TO LOOK AT IT AND TELL ME WHAT YOU SEE.
HE'S VERY WITHDRAWN, WITH NO EXPRESSION IN EITHER FACE OR VOICE. GETTING A RESPONSE IS OFTEN DIFFICULT.
WILL YOU LOOK AT IT, WALTER?
WILL YOU DO THAT FOR ME?
PHYSICALLY, HE'S FASCINATINGLY UGLY. I COULD STARE AT HIM FOR HOURS...EXCEPT THAT HE STARES BACK, WHICH I FIND UNCOMFORTABLE. HE NEVER SEEMS TO BLINK.
NEVERTHELESS, I'M CONVINCED I CAN HELP HIM. NO PROBLEM IS BEYOND THE GRASP OF A GOOD PSYCHOANALYST, AND THEY TELL ME I'M VERY GOOD. GOOD WITH PEOPLE.
WELL, WALTER? WHAT IS IT?
WHAT CAN YOU SEE?
A PRETTY BUTTERFLY.
HIS RESPONSES TO THE RORSCHACH BLOT TESTS WERE SURPRISINGLY BRIGHT AND POSITIVE AND HEALTHY. I REALLY THINK HE MIGHT BE GETTING BETTER.
I JUST WISH HE WASN'T SO INTENSE.
1

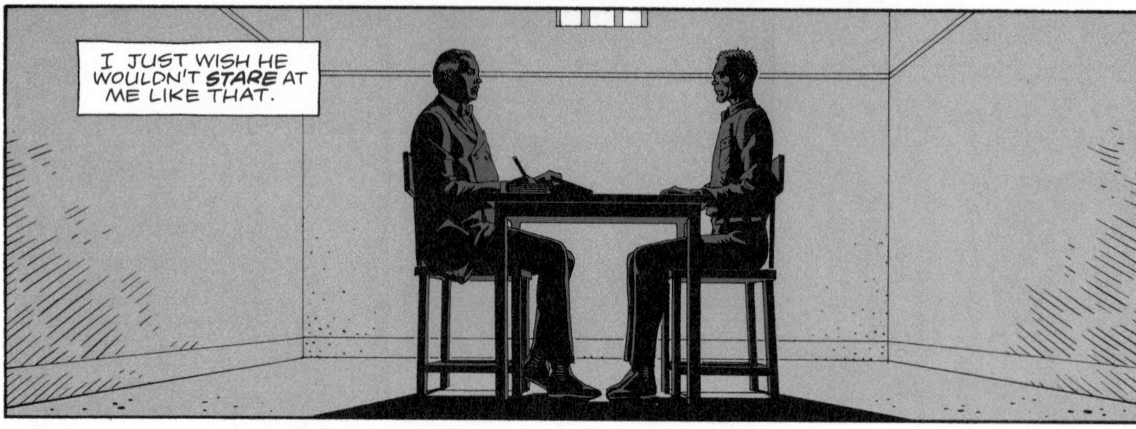
I JUST WISH HE WOULDN'T STARE AT ME LIKE THAT.

THE ABYSS GAZES ALSO

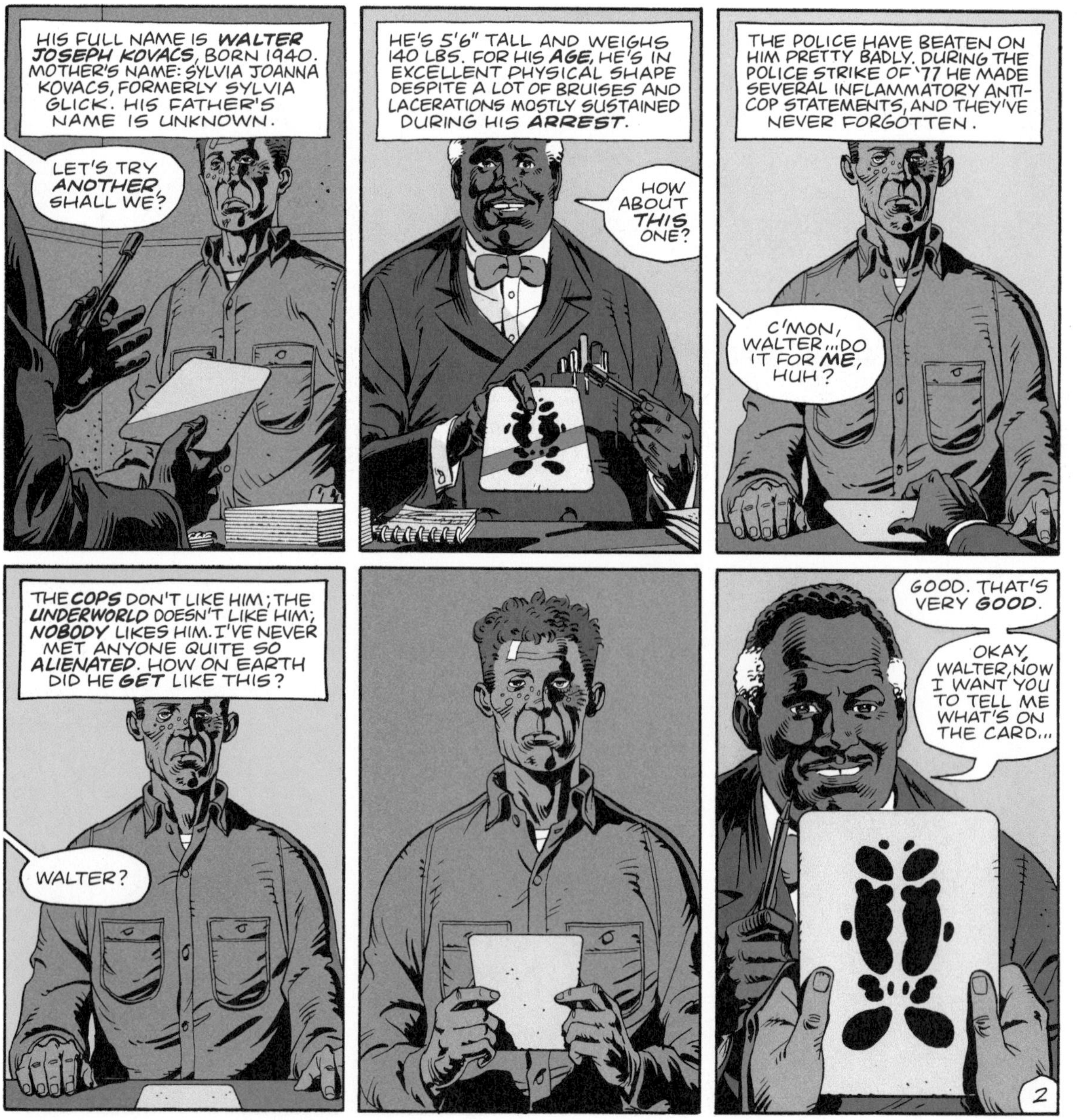
HIS FULL NAME IS WALTER JOSEPH KOVACS, BORN 1940. MOTHER'S NAME: SYLVIA JOANNA KOVACS, FORMERLY SYLVIA GLICK. HIS FATHER'S NAME IS UNKNOWN.
LET'S TRY ANOTHER, SHALL WE?
HE'S 5'6" TALL AND WEIGHS 140 LBS. FOR HIS AGE, HE'S IN EXCELLENT PHYSICAL SHAPE DESPITE A LOT OF BRUISES AND LACERATIONS MOSTLY SUSTAINED DURING HIS ARREST.
HOW ABOUT THIS ONE?
THE POLICE HAVE BEATEN ON HIM PRETTY BADLY. DURING THE POLICE STRIKE OF '77 HE MADE SEVERAL INFLAMMATORY ANTI-COP STATEMENTS, AND THEY'VE NEVER FORGOTTEN.
C'MON, WALTER...DO IT FOR ME, HUH?
THE COPS DON'T LIKE HIM; THE UNDERWORLD DOESN'T LIKE HIM; NOBODY LIKES HIM. I'VE NEVER MET ANYONE QUITE SO ALIENATED. HOW ON EARTH DID HE GET LIKE THIS?
WALTER?
GOOD. THAT'S VERY GOOD.
OKAY, WALTER, NOW I WANT YOU TO TELL ME WHAT'S ON THE CARD...
2

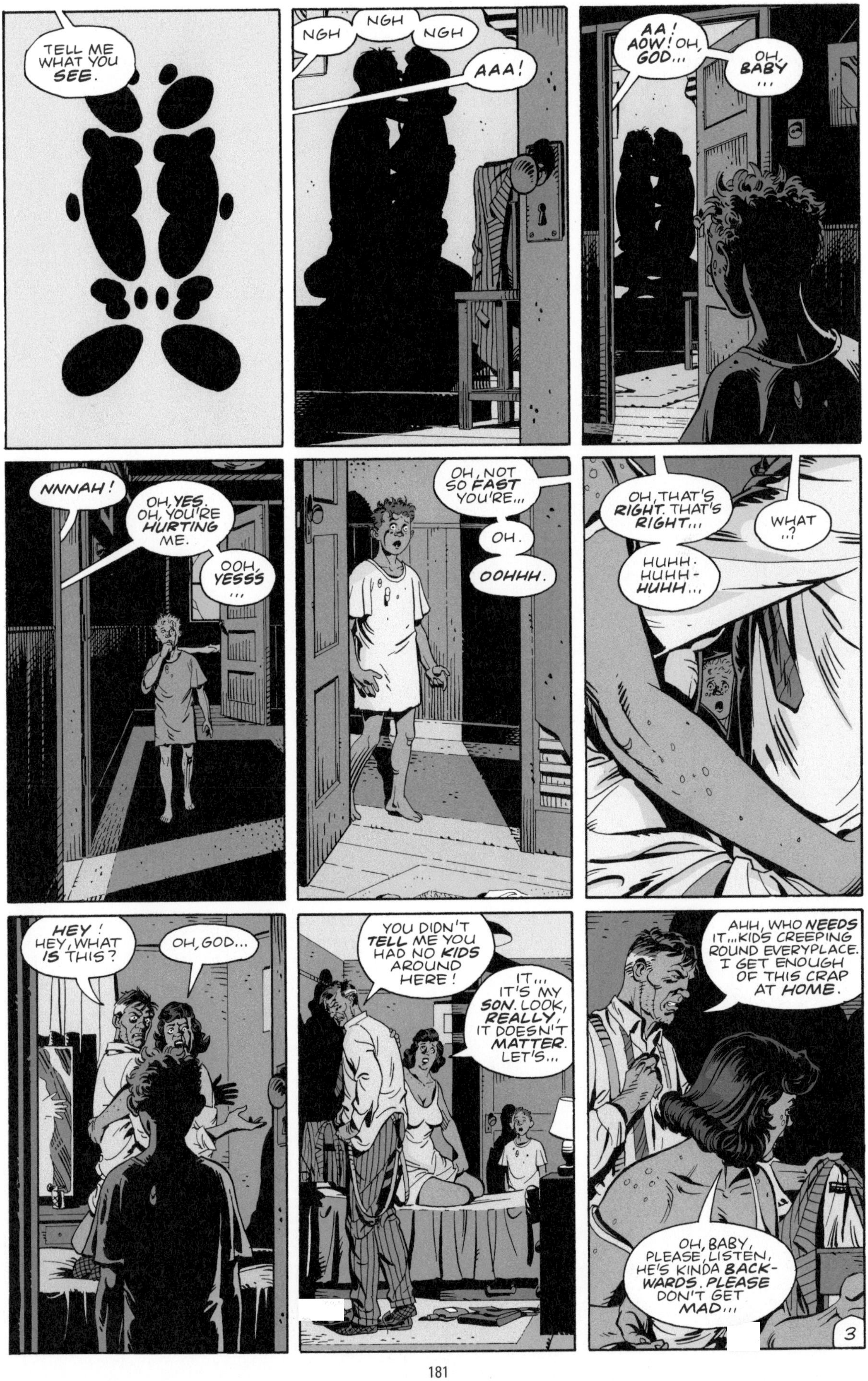
TELL ME WHAT YOU SEE.
NGH
NGH
NGH
AAA!
AA! AOW! OH, GOD...
OH, BABY...
NNNAH!
OH, YES. OH, YOU'RE HURTING ME.
OOH, YESSS...
OH, NOT SO FAST YOU'RE...
OH.
OOHHH.
OH, THAT'S RIGHT. THAT'S RIGHT...
HUHH. HUHH-HUHH...
WHAT..?
HEY! HEY, WHAT IS THIS?
OH, GOD...
YOU DIDN'T TELL ME YOU HAD NO KIDS AROUND HERE!
IT... IT'S MY SON. LOOK, REALLY, IT DOESN'T MATTER. LET'S...
AHH, WHO NEEDS IT...KIDS CREEPING ROUND EVERYPLACE. I GET ENOUGH OF THIS CRAP AT HOME.
OH, BABY, PLEASE, LISTEN. HE'S KINDA BACK-WARDS. PLEASE DON'T GET MAD...
3

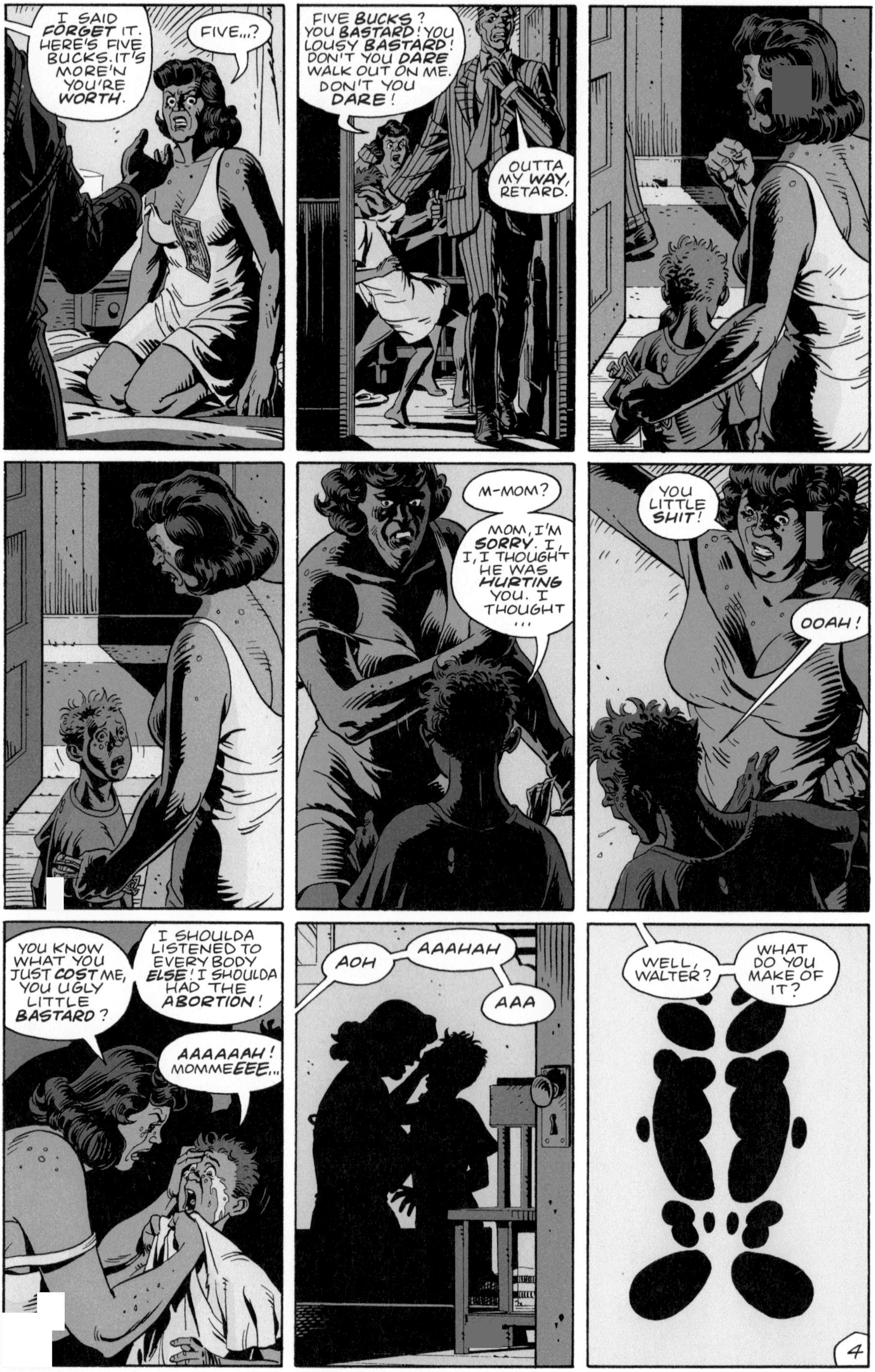
I SAID FORGET IT. HERE'S FIVE BUCKS. IT'S MORE'N YOU'RE WORTH.
FIVE...?
FIVE BUCKS? YOU BASTARD! YOU LOUSY BASTARD! DON'T YOU DARE WALK OUT ON ME. DON'T YOU DARE!
OUTTA MY WAY, RETARD.
M-MOM?
MOM, I'M SORRY. I, I, I THOUGHT HE WAS HURTING YOU. I THOUGHT ...
YOU LITTLE SHIT!
OOAH!
YOU KNOW WHAT YOU JUST COST ME, YOU UGLY LITTLE BASTARD?
I SHOULDA LISTENED TO EVERYBODY ELSE! I SHOULDA HAD THE ABORTION!
AAAAAAH! MOMMEEEE...
AOH
AAAHAH
AAA
WELL, WALTER?
WHAT DO YOU MAKE OF IT?
4

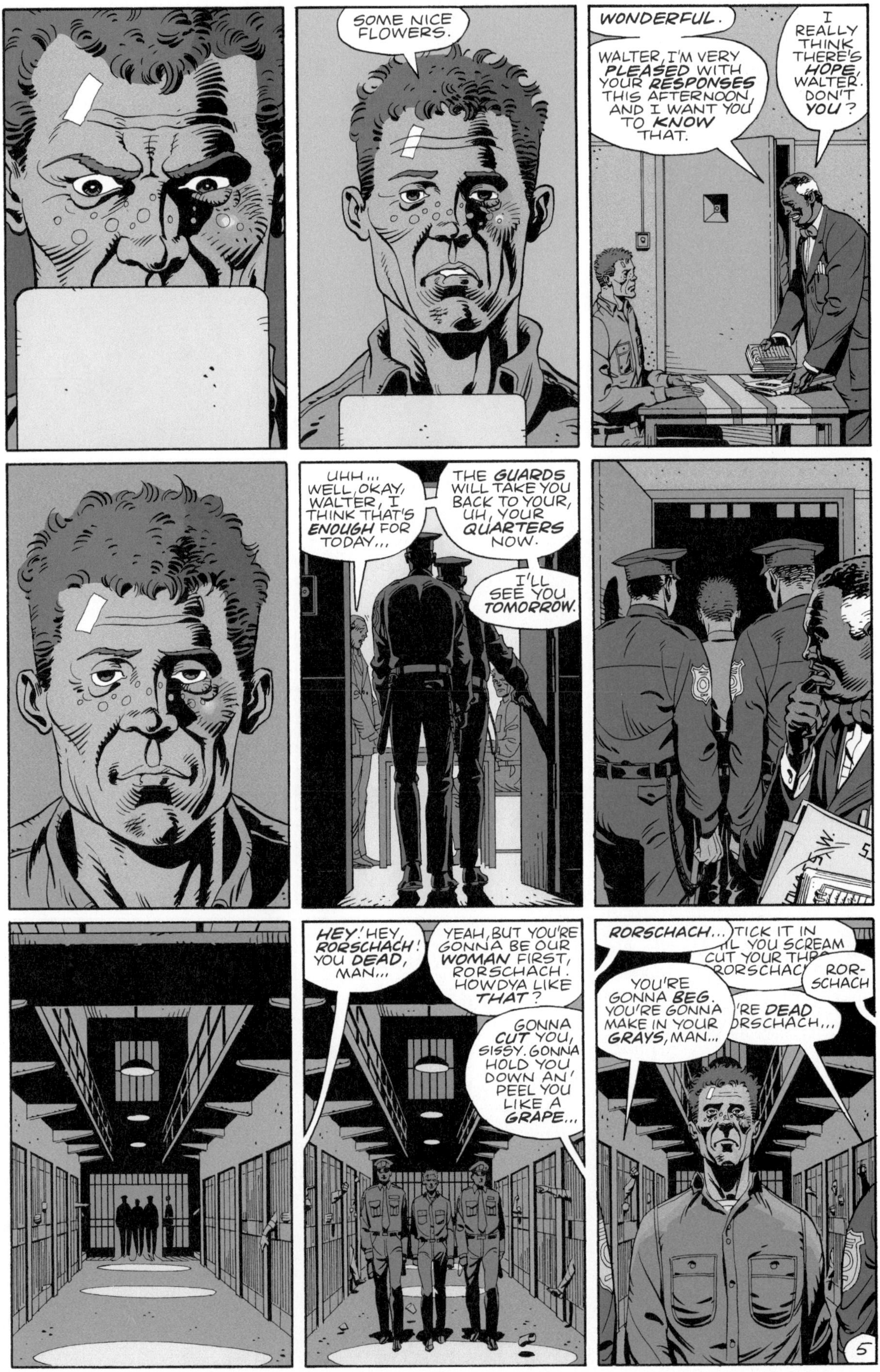
SOME NICE FLOWERS.
WONDERFUL.
WALTER, I'M VERY PLEASED WITH YOUR RESPONSES THIS AFTERNOON, AND I WANT YOU TO KNOW THAT.
I REALLY THINK THERE'S HOPE, WALTER. DON'T YOU?
UHH... WELL, OKAY, WALTER, I THINK THAT'S ENOUGH FOR TODAY...
THE GUARDS WILL TAKE YOU BACK TO YOUR, UH, YOUR QUARTERS NOW.
I'LL SEE YOU TOMORROW.
HEY! HEY, RORSCHACH! YOU DEAD, MAN...
YEAH, BUT YOU'RE GONNA BE OUR WOMAN FIRST, RORSCHACH. HOWDYA LIKE THAT?
GONNA CUT YOU, SISSY. GONNA HOLD YOU DOWN AN' PEEL YOU LIKE A GRAPE...
RORSCHACH...
TICK IT IN
IL YOU SCREAM
CUT YOUR THR
RORSCHAC
RORSCHACH
YOU'RE GONNA BEG. YOU'RE GONNA MAKE IN YOUR GRAYS, MAN...
'RE DEAD
RSCHACH...
5

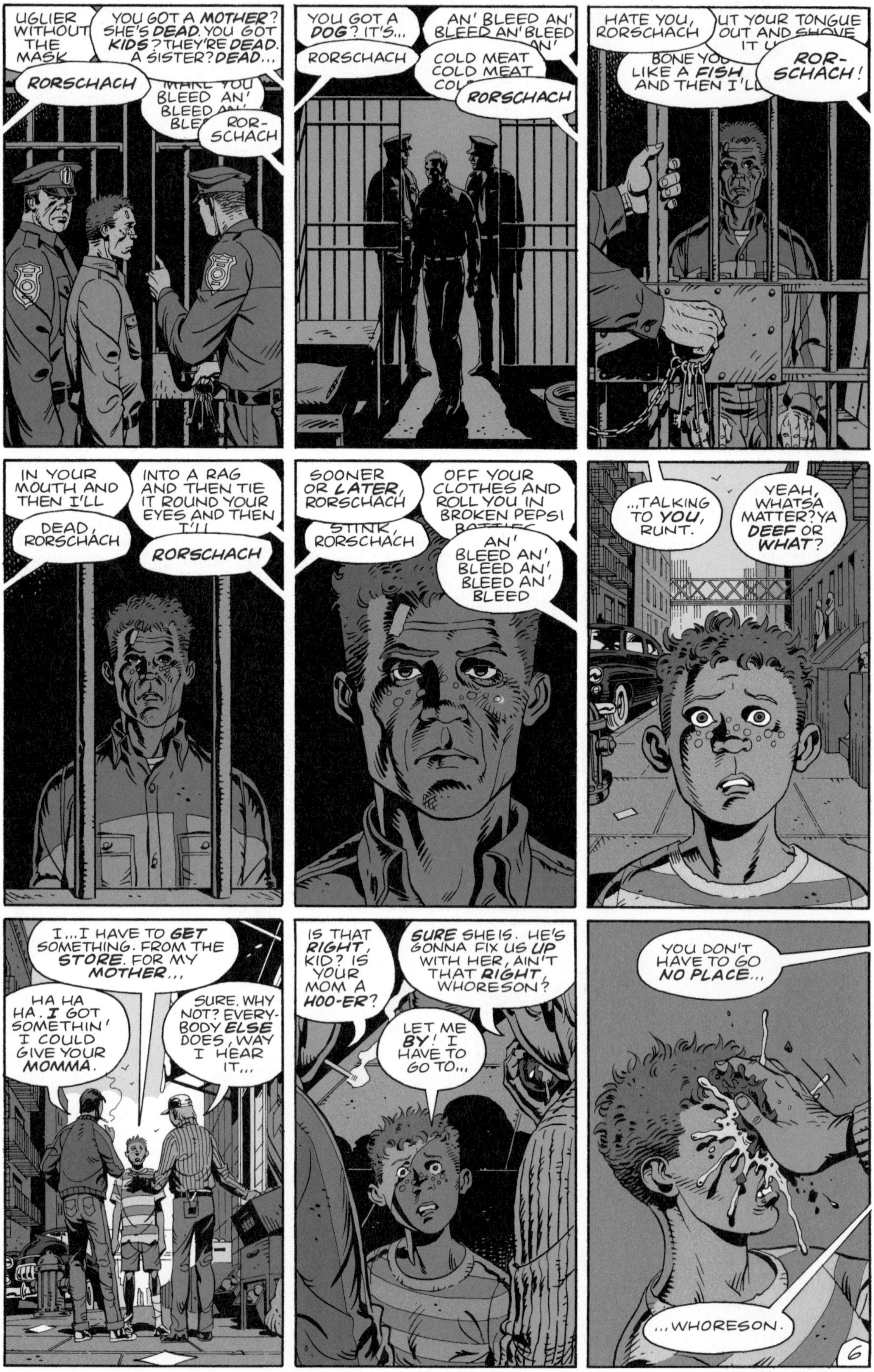
UGLIER WITHOUT THE MASK
YOU GOT A MOTHER? SHE'S DEAD. YOU GOT KIDS? THEY'RE DEAD. A SISTER? DEAD...
RORSCHACH
BLEED AN' BLEED AN'
ROR-SCHACH
YOU GOT A DOG? IT'S...
AN' BLEED AN' BLEED AN' BLEED
RORSCHACH
COLD MEAT COLD MEAT
RORSCHACH
HATE YOU, RORSCHACH
UT YOUR TONGUE OUT AND
BONE YOU LIKE A FISH AND THEN I'LL
ROR-SCHACH!
IN YOUR MOUTH AND THEN I'LL
INTO A RAG AND THEN TIE IT ROUND YOUR EYES AND THEN
DEAD, RORSCHACH
RORSCHACH
SOONER OR LATER, RORSCHACH
OFF YOUR CLOTHES AND ROLL YOU IN BROKEN PEPSI
RORSCHACH
AN' BLEED AN' BLEED AN' BLEED AN' BLEED
...TALKING TO YOU, RUNT.
YEAH, WHATSA MATTER? YA DEEF OR WHAT?
I...I HAVE TO GET SOMETHING. FROM THE STORE. FOR MY MOTHER...
HA HA HA. I GOT SOMETHIN' I COULD GIVE YOUR MOMMA.
SURE. WHY NOT? EVERYBODY ELSE DOES, WAY I HEAR IT...
IS THAT RIGHT, KID? IS YOUR MOM A HOO-ER?
SURE SHE IS. HE'S GONNA FIX US UP WITH HER, AIN'T THAT RIGHT, WHORESON?
LET ME BY! I HAVE TO GO TO...
YOU DON'T HAVE TO GO NO PLACE...
...WHORESON.
6

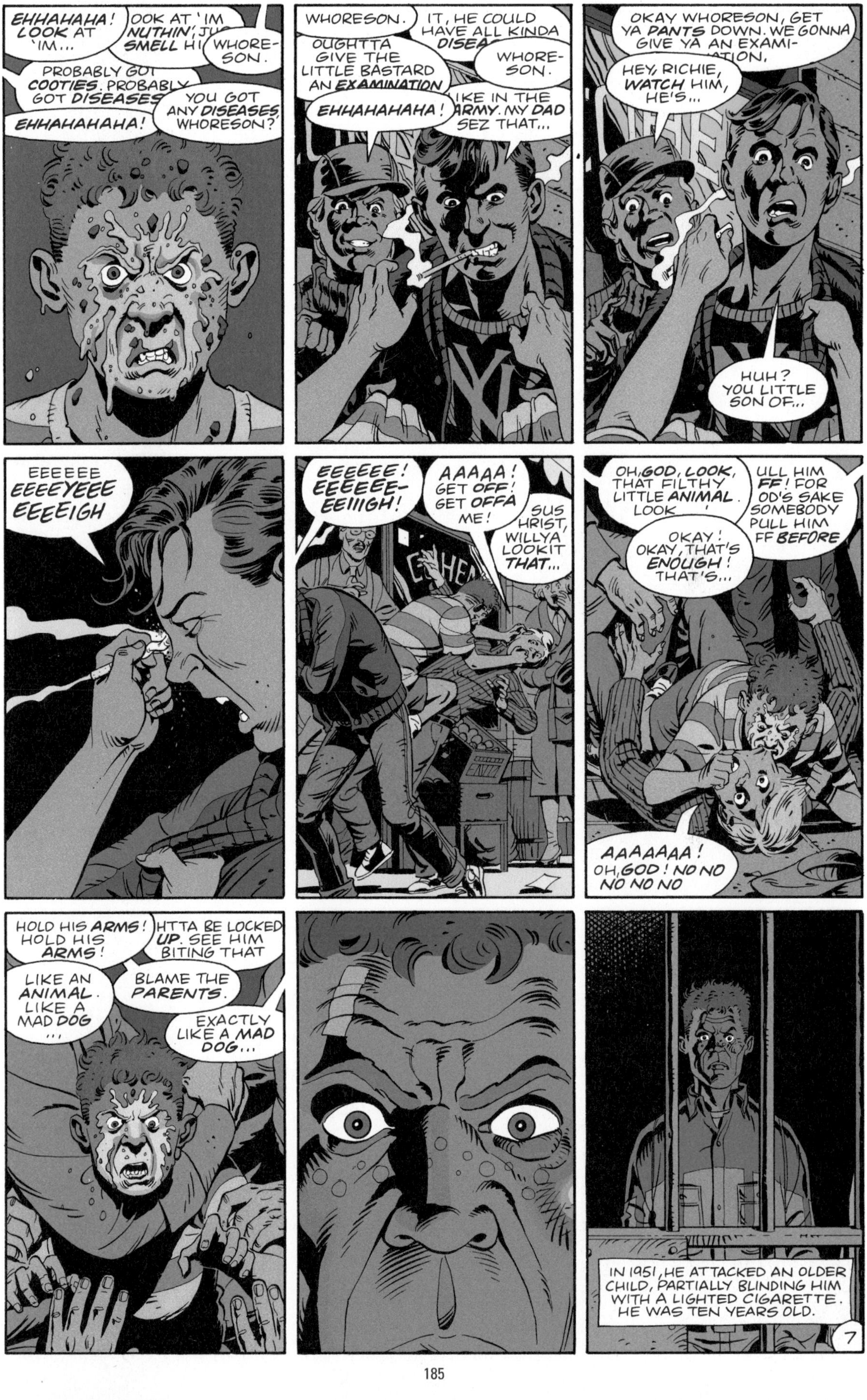
EHHAHAHA! LOOK AT 'IM...
OOK AT 'IM NUTHIN', JU SMELL HI
WHORE-SON.
PROBABLY GOT COOTIES. PROBABLY GOT DISEASES
EHHAHAHAHA!
YOU GOT ANY DISEASES, WHORESON?
WHORESON.
OUGHTTA GIVE THE LITTLE BASTARD AN EXAMINATION
IT, HE COULD HAVE ALL KINDA DISEA
WHORE-SON.
EHHAHAHAHA!
IKE IN THE ARMY. MY DAD SEZ THAT...
OKAY WHORESON, GET YA PANTS DOWN. WE GONNA GIVE YA AN EXAMI- ATION,
HEY, RICHIE, WATCH HIM, HE'S...
HUH? YOU LITTLE SON OF...
EEEEEE EEEEYEEE EEEEIGH
EEEEEE! EEEEEE-EEIIIGH!
AAAAA! GET OFF! GET OFFA ME!
SUS HRIST, WILLYA LOOKIT THAT...
OH, GOD, LOOK, THAT FILTHY LITTLE ANIMAL. LOOK
ULL HIM FF! FOR OD'S SAKE SOMEBODY PULL HIM FF BEFORE
OKAY! OKAY, THAT'S ENOUGH! THAT'S...
AAAAAAA! OH, GOD! NO NO NO NO NO
HOLD HIS ARMS! HOLD HIS ARMS!
HTTA BE LOCKED UP. SEE HIM BITING THAT
LIKE AN ANIMAL. LIKE A MAD DOG ...
BLAME THE PARENTS.
EXACTLY LIKE A MAD DOG...
IN 1951, HE ATTACKED AN OLDER CHILD, PARTIALLY BLINDING HIM WITH A LIGHTED CIGARETTE. HE WAS TEN YEARS OLD.
7

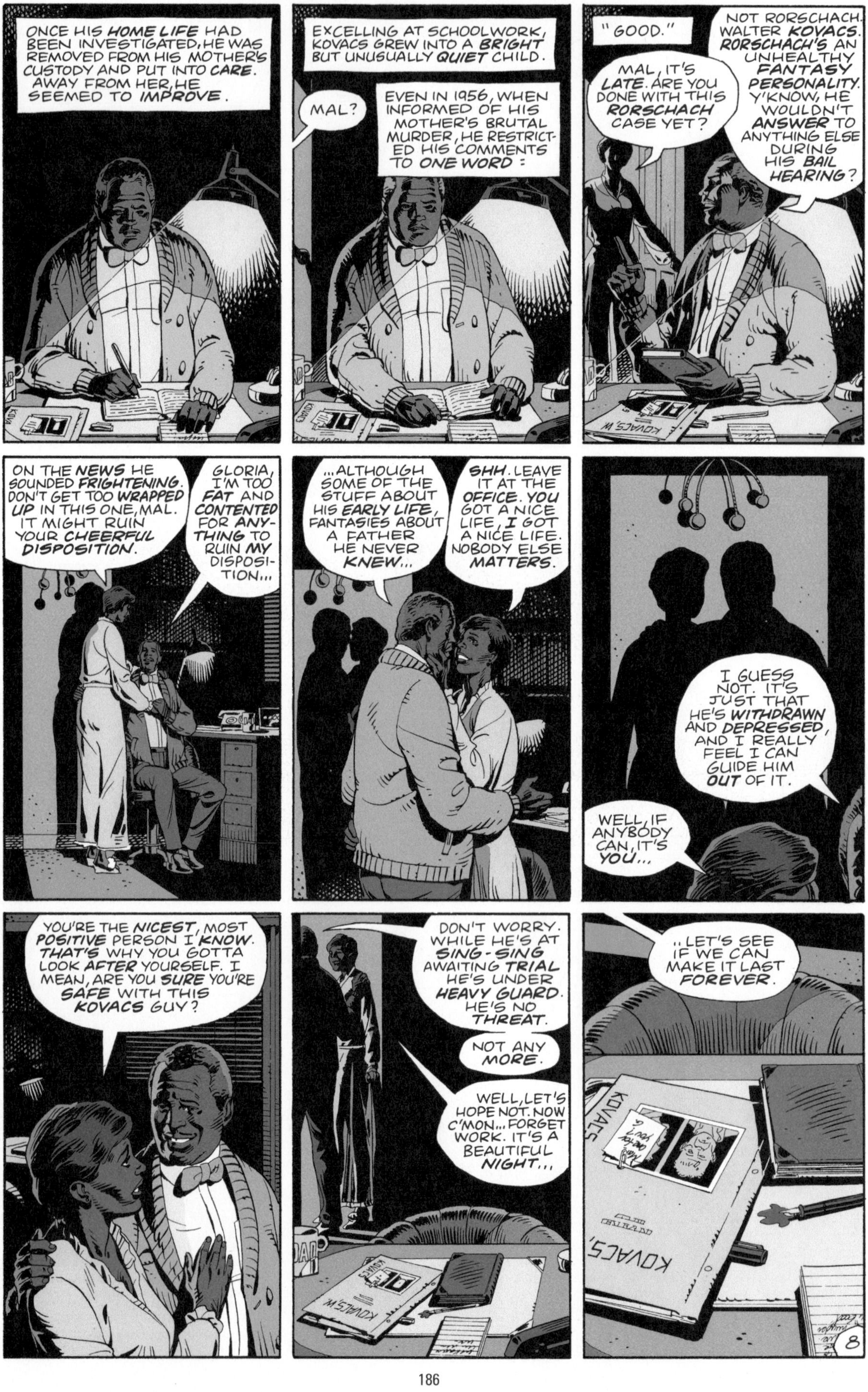
ONCE HIS HOME LIFE HAD BEEN INVESTIGATED, HE WAS REMOVED FROM HIS MOTHER'S CUSTODY AND PUT INTO CARE. AWAY FROM HER, HE SEEMED TO IMPROVE.
EXCELLING AT SCHOOLWORK, KOVACS GREW INTO A BRIGHT BUT UNUSUALLY QUIET CHILD.
MAL?
EVEN IN 1956, WHEN INFORMED OF HIS MOTHER'S BRUTAL MURDER, HE RESTRICTED HIS COMMENTS TO ONE WORD:
"GOOD."
MAL, IT'S LATE. ARE YOU DONE WITH THIS RORSCHACH CASE YET?
NOT RORSCHACH. WALTER KOVACS. RORSCHACH'S AN UNHEALTHY FANTASY PERSONALITY. Y'KNOW, HE WOULDN'T ANSWER TO ANYTHING ELSE DURING HIS BAIL HEARING?
ON THE NEWS HE SOUNDED FRIGHTENING. DON'T GET TOO WRAPPED UP IN THIS ONE, MAL. IT MIGHT RUIN YOUR CHEERFUL DISPOSITION.
GLORIA, I'M TOO FAT AND CONTENTED FOR ANYTHING TO RUIN MY DISPOSITION...
...ALTHOUGH SOME OF THE STUFF ABOUT HIS EARLY LIFE, FANTASIES ABOUT A FATHER HE NEVER KNEW...
SHH. LEAVE IT AT THE OFFICE. YOU GOT A NICE LIFE, I GOT A NICE LIFE. NOBODY ELSE MATTERS.
I GUESS NOT. IT'S JUST THAT HE'S WITHDRAWN AND DEPRESSED, AND I REALLY FEEL I CAN GUIDE HIM OUT OF IT.
WELL, IF ANYBODY CAN, IT'S YOU...
YOU'RE THE NICEST, MOST POSITIVE PERSON I KNOW. THAT'S WHY YOU GOTTA LOOK AFTER YOURSELF. I MEAN, ARE YOU SURE YOU'RE SAFE WITH THIS KOVACS GUY?
DON'T WORRY. WHILE HE'S AT SING-SING AWAITING TRIAL HE'S UNDER HEAVY GUARD. HE'S NO THREAT.
NOT ANY MORE.
WELL, LET'S HOPE NOT. NOW C'MON... FORGET WORK. IT'S A BEAUTIFUL NIGHT...
..LET'S SEE IF WE CAN MAKE IT LAST FOREVER.
KOVACS
KOVACS,
8

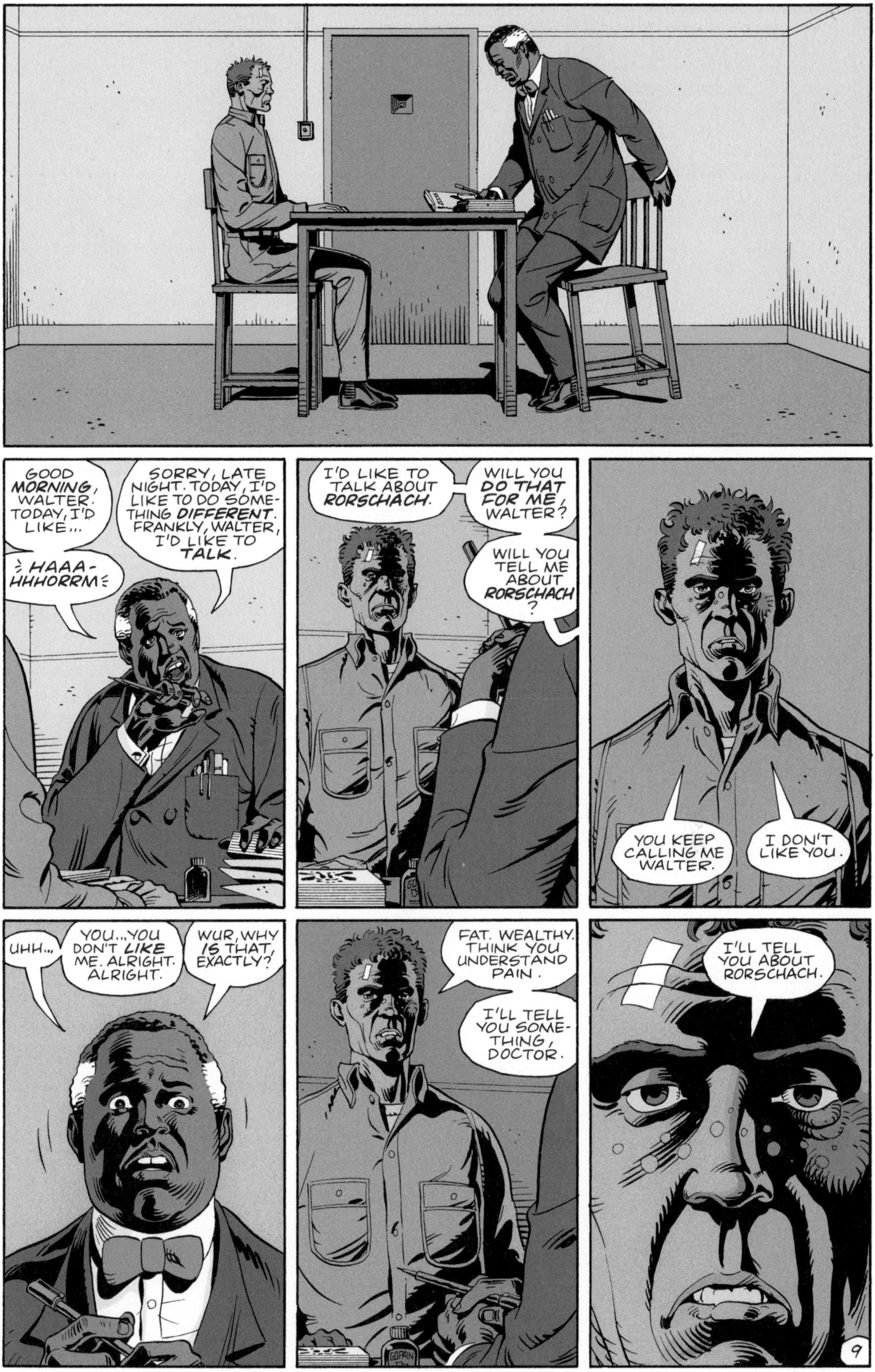
GOOD MORNING, WALTER. TODAY, I'D LIKE...
≡HAAA-HHHORRM≡
SORRY, LATE NIGHT. TODAY, I'D LIKE TO DO SOMETHING DIFFERENT. FRANKLY, WALTER, I'D LIKE TO TALK.
I'D LIKE TO TALK ABOUT RORSCHACH.
WILL YOU DO THAT FOR ME, WALTER?
WILL YOU TELL ME ABOUT RORSCHACH?
YOU KEEP CALLING ME WALTER.
I DON'T LIKE YOU.
UHH...
YOU...YOU DON'T LIKE ME. ALRIGHT. ALRIGHT.
WUR, WHY IS THAT, EXACTLY?
FAT. WEALTHY. THINK YOU UNDERSTAND PAIN.
I'LL TELL YOU SOMETHING, DOCTOR.
I'LL TELL YOU ABOUT RORSCHACH.
9

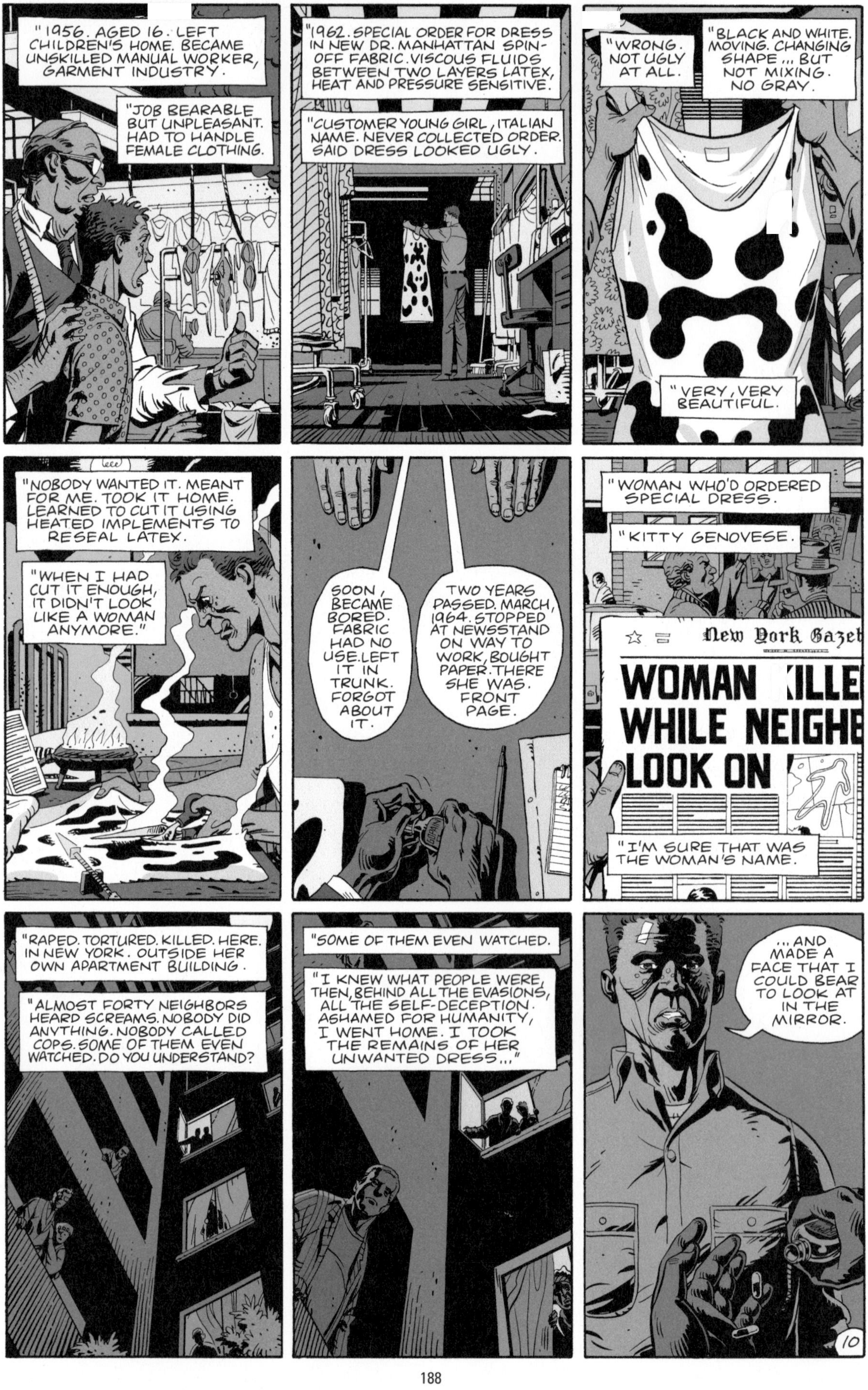
"1956. AGED 16. LEFT CHILDREN'S HOME. BECAME UNSKILLED MANUAL WORKER, GARMENT INDUSTRY.
"JOB BEARABLE BUT UNPLEASANT. HAD TO HANDLE FEMALE CLOTHING.
"1962. SPECIAL ORDER FOR DRESS IN NEW DR. MANHATTAN SPIN-OFF FABRIC. VISCOUS FLUIDS BETWEEN TWO LAYERS LATEX, HEAT AND PRESSURE SENSITIVE.
"CUSTOMER YOUNG GIRL, ITALIAN NAME. NEVER COLLECTED ORDER. SAID DRESS LOOKED UGLY.
"WRONG. NOT UGLY AT ALL.
"BLACK AND WHITE. MOVING. CHANGING SHAPE... BUT NOT MIXING. NO GRAY.
"VERY, VERY BEAUTIFUL.
"NOBODY WANTED IT. MEANT FOR ME. TOOK IT HOME. LEARNED TO CUT IT USING HEATED IMPLEMENTS TO RESEAL LATEX.
"WHEN I HAD CUT IT ENOUGH, IT DIDN'T LOOK LIKE A WOMAN ANYMORE."
SOON, BECAME BORED. FABRIC HAD NO USE. LEFT IT IN TRUNK. FORGOT ABOUT IT.
TWO YEARS PASSED. MARCH, 1964. STOPPED AT NEWSSTAND ON WAY TO WORK, BOUGHT PAPER. THERE SHE WAS. FRONT PAGE.
"WOMAN WHO'D ORDERED SPECIAL DRESS.
"KITTY GENOVESE.
New York Gazet
WOMAN KILLE
WHILE NEIGHB
LOOK ON
"I'M SURE THAT WAS THE WOMAN'S NAME.
"RAPED. TORTURED. KILLED. HERE. IN NEW YORK. OUTSIDE HER OWN APARTMENT BUILDING.
"ALMOST FORTY NEIGHBORS HEARD SCREAMS. NOBODY DID ANYTHING. NOBODY CALLED COPS. SOME OF THEM EVEN WATCHED. DO YOU UNDERSTAND?
"SOME OF THEM EVEN WATCHED.
"I KNEW WHAT PEOPLE WERE, THEN, BEHIND ALL THE EVASIONS, ALL THE SELF-DECEPTION. ASHAMED FOR HUMANITY, I WENT HOME. I TOOK THE REMAINS OF HER UNWANTED DRESS..."
...AND MADE A FACE THAT I COULD BEAR TO LOOK AT IN THE MIRROR.
10

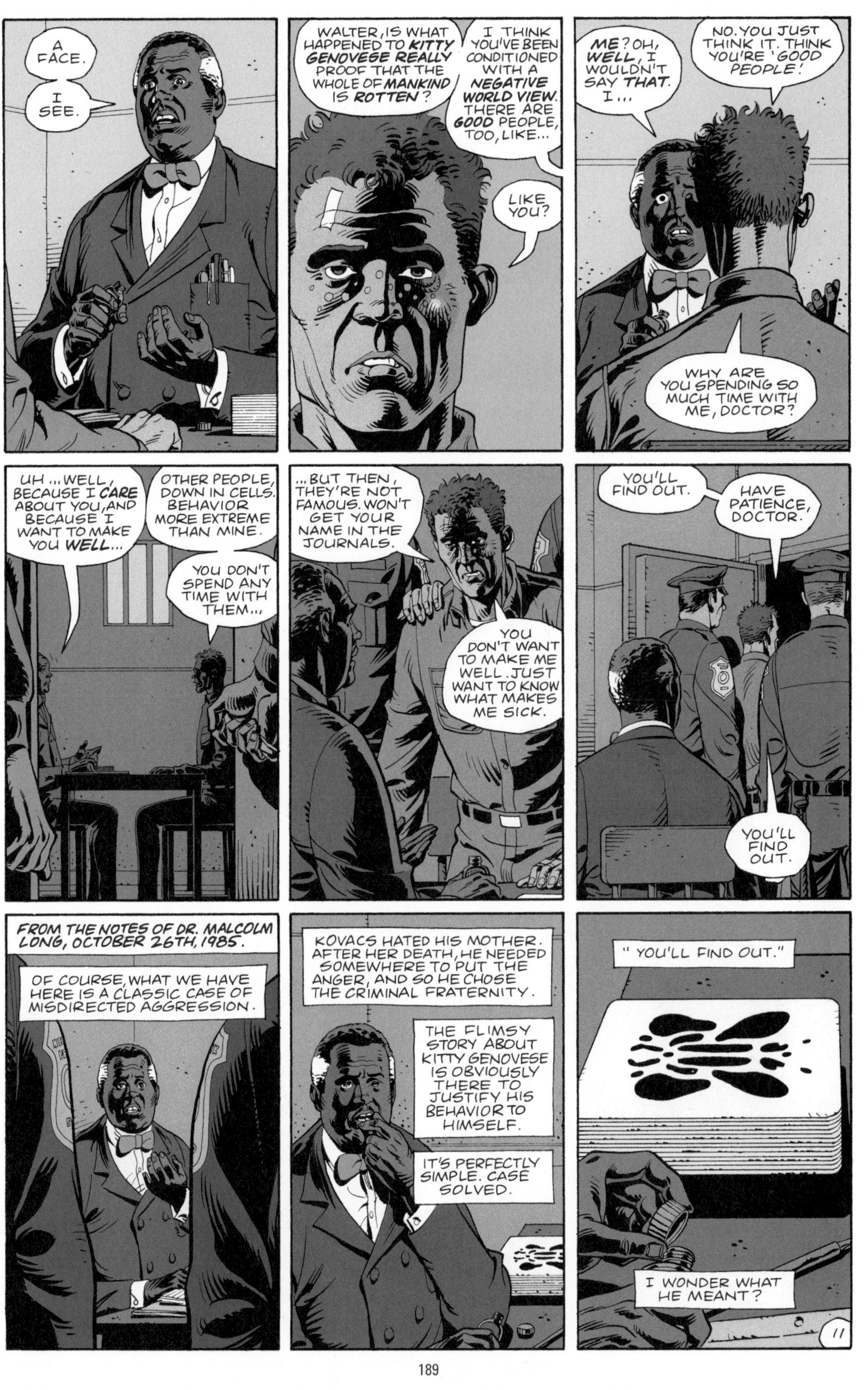
A FACE.
I SEE.
WALTER, IS WHAT HAPPENED TO KITTY GENOVESE REALLY PROOF THAT THE WHOLE OF MANKIND IS ROTTEN?
I THINK YOU'VE BEEN CONDITIONED WITH A NEGATIVE WORLD VIEW. THERE ARE GOOD PEOPLE, TOO, LIKE...
LIKE YOU?
ME? OH, WELL, I WOULDN'T SAY THAT. I...
NO. YOU JUST THINK IT. THINK YOU'RE 'GOOD PEOPLE'.
WHY ARE YOU SPENDING SO MUCH TIME WITH ME, DOCTOR?
UH... WELL, BECAUSE I CARE ABOUT YOU, AND BECAUSE I WANT TO MAKE YOU WELL...
OTHER PEOPLE, DOWN IN CELLS. BEHAVIOR MORE EXTREME THAN MINE.
YOU DON'T SPEND ANY TIME WITH THEM...,
...BUT THEN, THEY'RE NOT FAMOUS. WON'T GET YOUR NAME IN THE JOURNALS.
YOU DON'T WANT TO MAKE ME WELL. JUST WANT TO KNOW WHAT MAKES ME SICK.
YOU'LL FIND OUT.
HAVE PATIENCE, DOCTOR.
YOU'LL FIND OUT.
FROM THE NOTES OF DR. MALCOLM LONG, OCTOBER 26TH, 1985.
OF COURSE, WHAT WE HAVE HERE IS A CLASSIC CASE OF MISDIRECTED AGGRESSION.
KOVACS HATED HIS MOTHER. AFTER HER DEATH, HE NEEDED SOMEWHERE TO PUT THE ANGER, AND SO HE CHOSE THE CRIMINAL FRATERNITY.
THE FLIMSY STORY ABOUT KITTY GENOVESE IS OBVIOUSLY THERE TO JUSTIFY HIS BEHAVIOR TO HIMSELF.
IT'S PERFECTLY SIMPLE. CASE SOLVED.
" YOU'LL FIND OUT."
I WONDER WHAT HE MEANT?
11

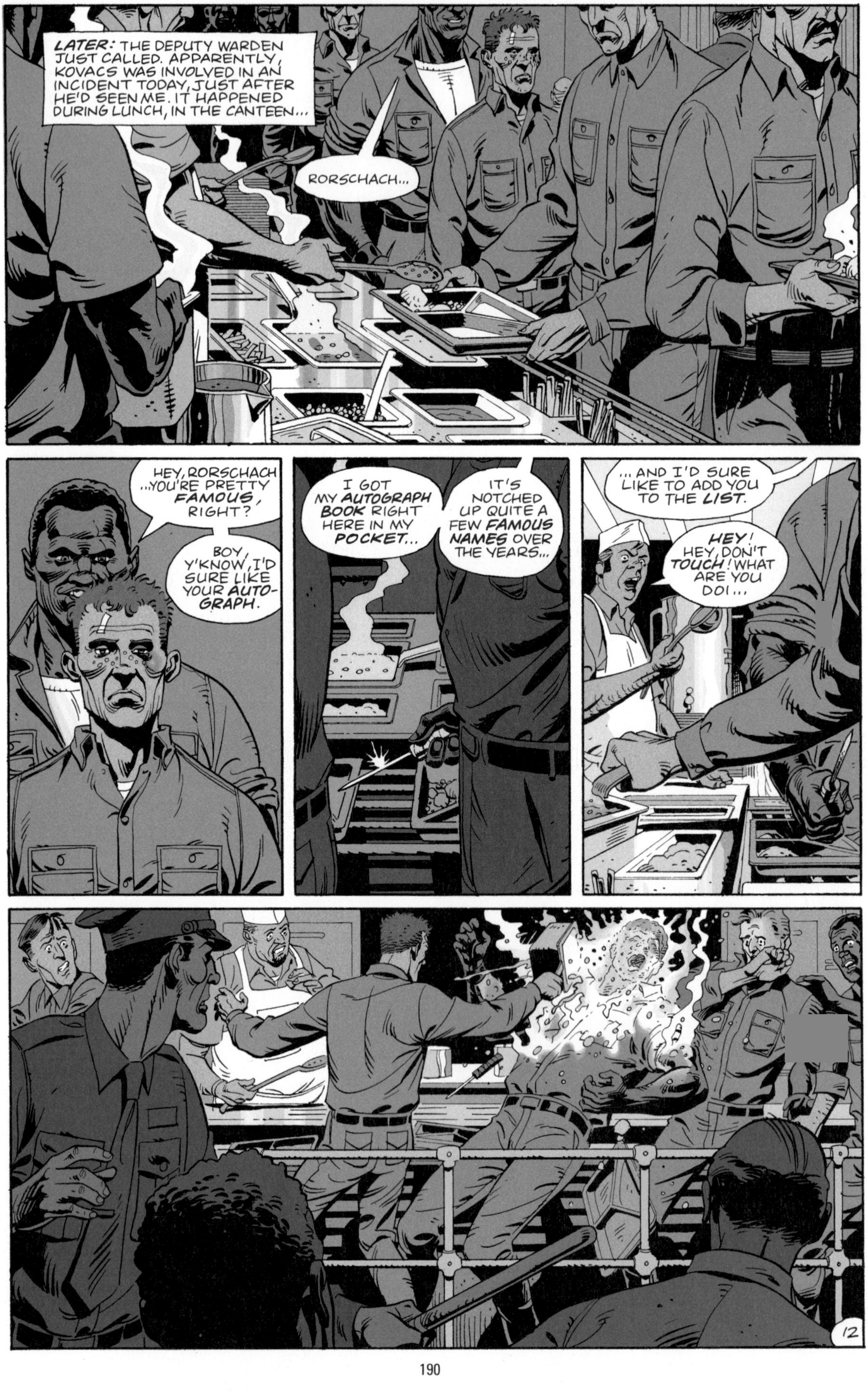
LATER: THE DEPUTY WARDEN JUST CALLED. APPARENTLY, KOVACS WAS INVOLVED IN AN INCIDENT TODAY, JUST AFTER HE'D SEEN ME. IT HAPPENED DURING LUNCH, IN THE CANTEEN...
RORSCHACH...
HEY, RORSCHACH ...YOU'RE PRETTY FAMOUS, RIGHT?
BOY, Y'KNOW, I'D SURE LIKE YOUR AUTOGRAPH.
I GOT MY AUTOGRAPH BOOK RIGHT HERE IN MY POCKET...
IT'S NOTCHED UP QUITE A FEW FAMOUS NAMES OVER THE YEARS...
...AND I'D SURE LIKE TO ADD YOU TO THE LIST.
HEY! HEY, DON'T TOUCH! WHAT ARE YOU DOI...
12

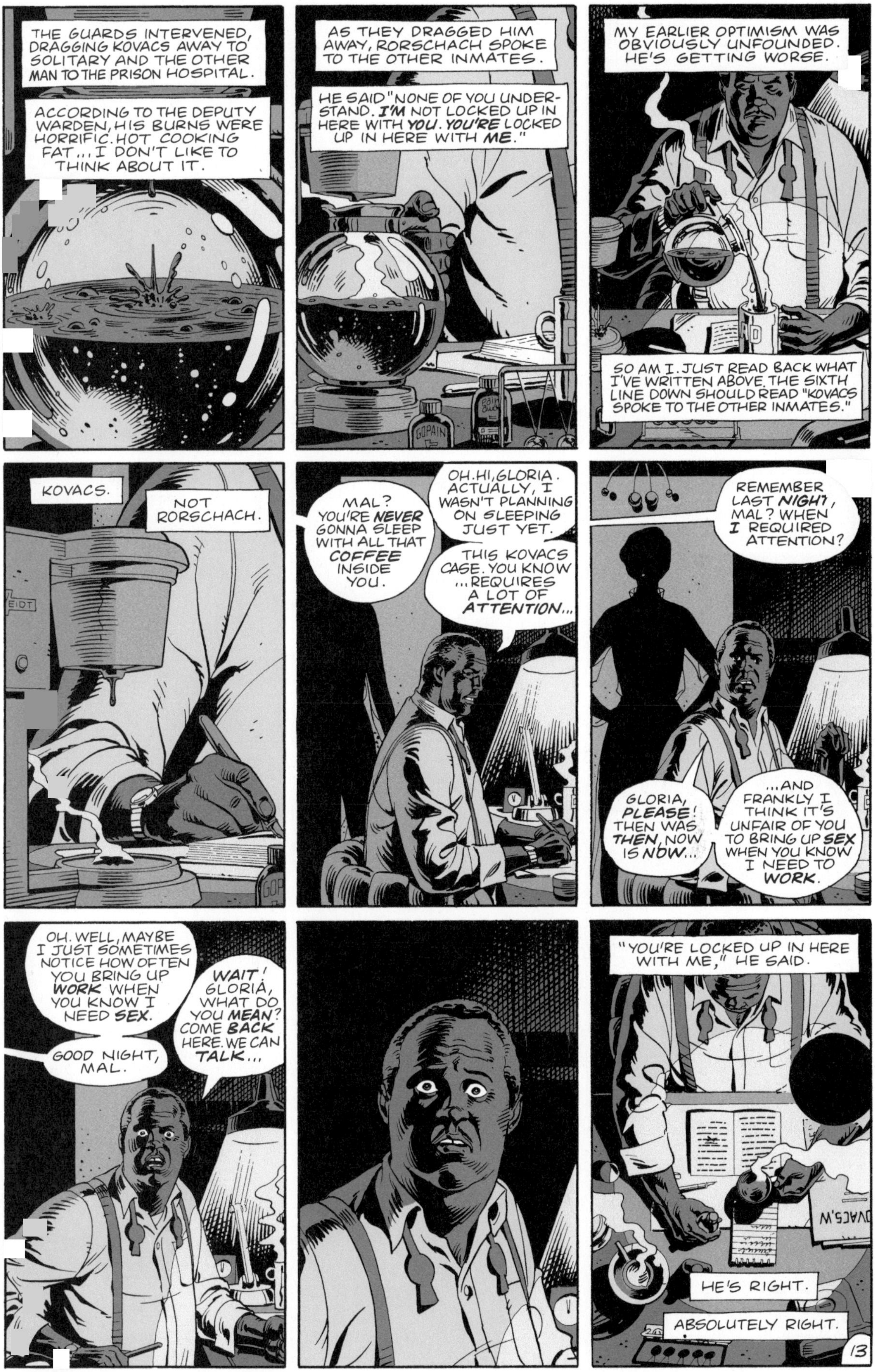
THE GUARDS INTERVENED, DRAGGING KOVACS AWAY TO SOLITARY AND THE OTHER MAN TO THE PRISON HOSPITAL.
ACCORDING TO THE DEPUTY WARDEN, HIS BURNS WERE HORRIFIC. HOT COOKING FAT... I DON'T LIKE TO THINK ABOUT IT.
AS THEY DRAGGED HIM AWAY, RORSCHACH SPOKE TO THE OTHER INMATES.
HE SAID "NONE OF YOU UNDERSTAND. I'M NOT LOCKED UP IN HERE WITH YOU. YOU'RE LOCKED UP IN HERE WITH ME."
MY EARLIER OPTIMISM WAS OBVIOUSLY UNFOUNDED. HE'S GETTING WORSE.
SO AM I. JUST READ BACK WHAT I'VE WRITTEN ABOVE. THE SIXTH LINE DOWN SHOULD READ "KOVACS SPOKE TO THE OTHER INMATES."
KOVACS.
NOT RORSCHACH.
MAL? YOU'RE NEVER GONNA SLEEP WITH ALL THAT COFFEE INSIDE YOU.
OH. HI, GLORIA. ACTUALLY, I WASN'T PLANNING ON SLEEPING JUST YET.
THIS KOVACS CASE. YOU KNOW ...REQUIRES A LOT OF ATTENTION...
REMEMBER LAST NIGHT, MAL? WHEN I REQUIRED ATTENTION?
GLORIA, PLEASE! THEN WAS THEN, NOW IS NOW...
...AND FRANKLY I THINK IT'S UNFAIR OF YOU TO BRING UP SEX WHEN YOU KNOW I NEED TO WORK.
OH. WELL, MAYBE I JUST SOMETIMES NOTICE HOW OFTEN YOU BRING UP WORK WHEN YOU KNOW I NEED SEX.
GOOD NIGHT, MAL.
WAIT! GLORIA, WHAT DO YOU MEAN? COME BACK HERE. WE CAN TALK...
"YOU'RE LOCKED UP IN HERE WITH ME," HE SAID.
HE'S RIGHT.
ABSOLUTELY RIGHT.
13

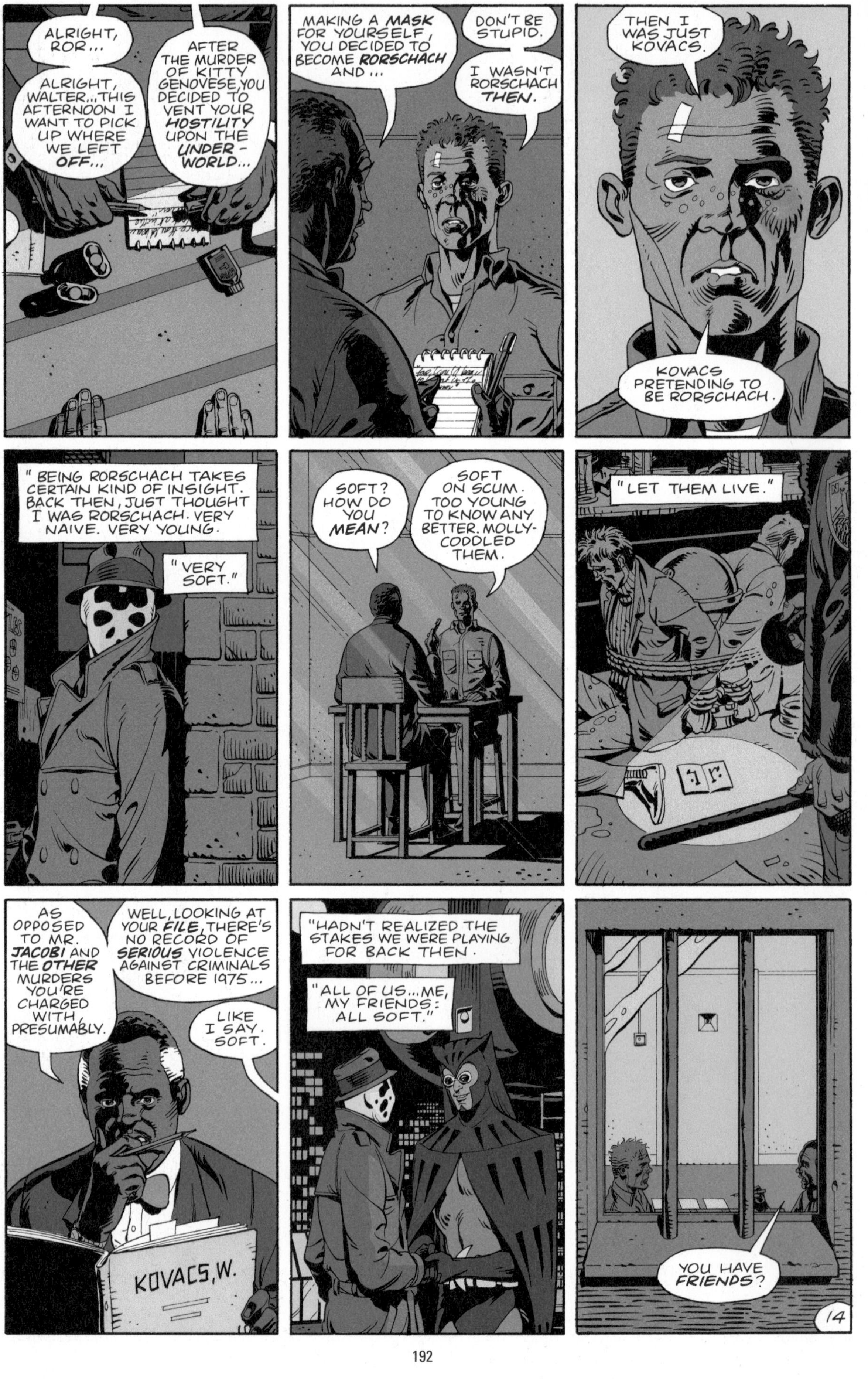

ALRIGHT, ROR...
ALRIGHT, WALTER... THIS AFTERNOON I WANT TO PICK UP WHERE WE LEFT OFF...
AFTER THE MURDER OF KITTY GENOVESE, YOU DECIDED TO VENT YOUR HOSTILITY UPON THE UNDER-WORLD...
MAKING A MASK FOR YOURSELF, YOU DECIDED TO BECOME RORSCHACH AND...
DON'T BE STUPID.
I WASN'T RORSCHACH THEN.
THEN I WAS JUST KOVACS.
KOVACS PRETENDING TO BE RORSCHACH.
"BEING RORSCHACH TAKES CERTAIN KIND OF INSIGHT. BACK THEN, JUST THOUGHT I WAS RORSCHACH. VERY NAIVE. VERY YOUNG.
"VERY SOFT."
SOFT? HOW DO YOU MEAN?
SOFT ON SCUM. TOO YOUNG TO KNOW ANY BETTER. MOLLY-CODDLED THEM.
"LET THEM LIVE."
AS OPPOSED TO MR. JACOBI AND THE OTHER MURDERS YOU'RE CHARGED WITH, PRESUMABLY.
WELL, LOOKING AT YOUR FILE, THERE'S NO RECORD OF SERIOUS VIOLENCE AGAINST CRIMINALS BEFORE 1975...
LIKE I SAY. SOFT.
KOVACS, W.
"HADN'T REALIZED THE STAKES WE WERE PLAYING FOR BACK THEN.
"ALL OF US... ME, MY FRIENDS: ALL SOFT."
YOU HAVE FRIENDS?
14

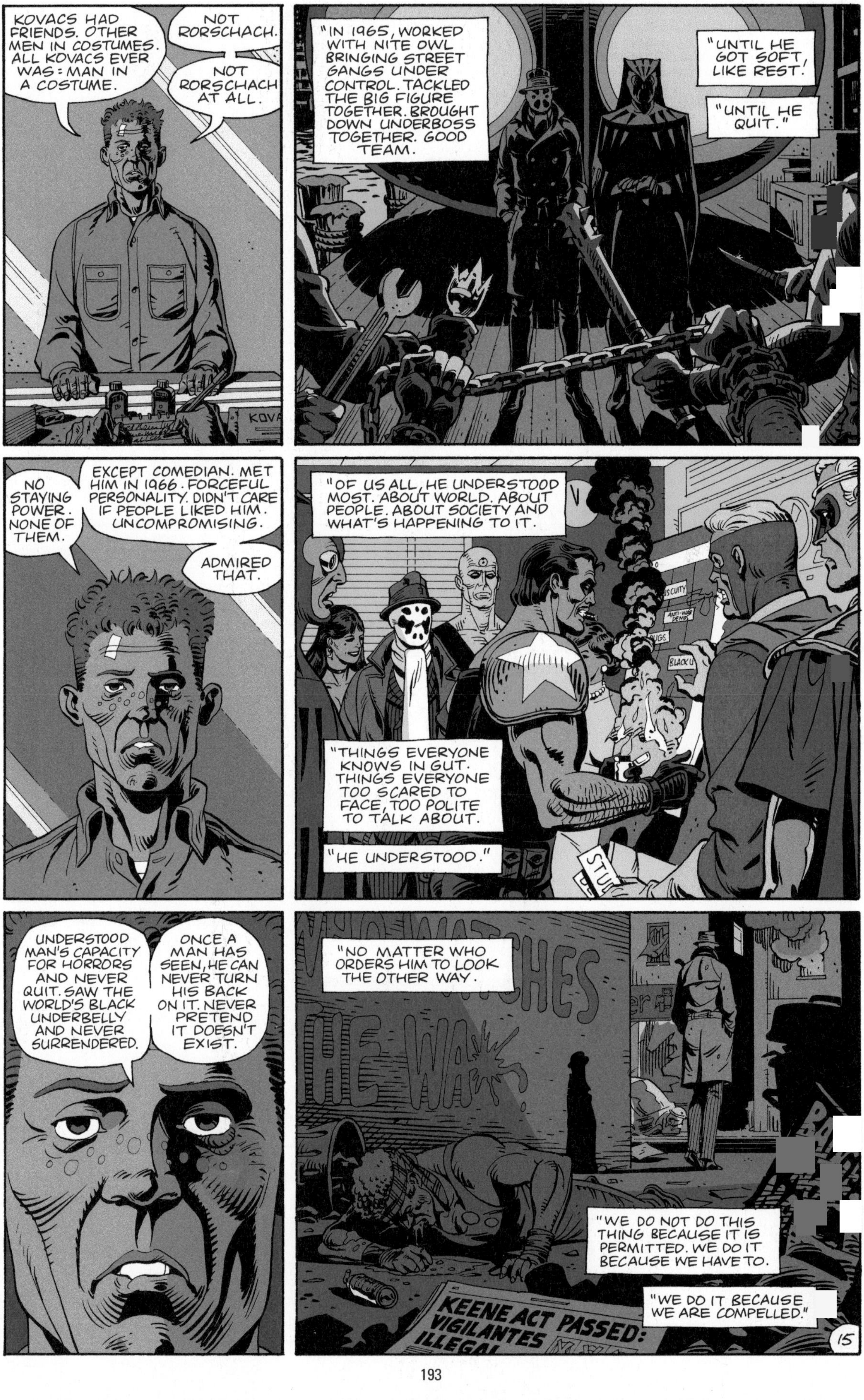
KOVACS HAD FRIENDS. OTHER MEN IN COSTUMES. ALL KOVACS EVER WAS: MAN IN A COSTUME.
NOT RORSCHACH.
NOT RORSCHACH AT ALL.
"IN 1965, WORKED WITH NITE OWL BRINGING STREET GANGS UNDER CONTROL. TACKLED THE BIG FIGURE TOGETHER. BROUGHT DOWN UNDERBOSS TOGETHER. GOOD TEAM.
"UNTIL HE GOT SOFT, LIKE REST!
"UNTIL HE QUIT."
NO STAYING POWER. NONE OF THEM.
EXCEPT COMEDIAN. MET HIM IN 1966. FORCEFUL PERSONALITY. DIDN'T CARE IF PEOPLE LIKED HIM. UNCOMPROMISING.
ADMIRED THAT.
"OF US ALL, HE UNDERSTOOD MOST. ABOUT WORLD. ABOUT PEOPLE. ABOUT SOCIETY AND WHAT'S HAPPENING TO IT.
"THINGS EVERYONE KNOWS IN GUT. THINGS EVERYONE TOO SCARED TO FACE, TOO POLITE TO TALK ABOUT.
"HE UNDERSTOOD."
UNDERSTOOD MAN'S CAPACITY FOR HORRORS AND NEVER QUIT. SAW THE WORLD'S BLACK UNDERBELLY AND NEVER SURRENDERED.
ONCE A MAN HAS SEEN, HE CAN NEVER TURN HIS BACK ON IT. NEVER PRETEND IT DOESN'T EXIST.
"NO MATTER WHO ORDERS HIM TO LOOK THE OTHER WAY.
"WE DO NOT DO THIS THING BECAUSE IT IS PERMITTED. WE DO IT BECAUSE WE HAVE TO.
"WE DO IT BECAUSE WE ARE COMPELLED."
KEENE ACT PASSED: VIGILANTES ILLEGAL
15

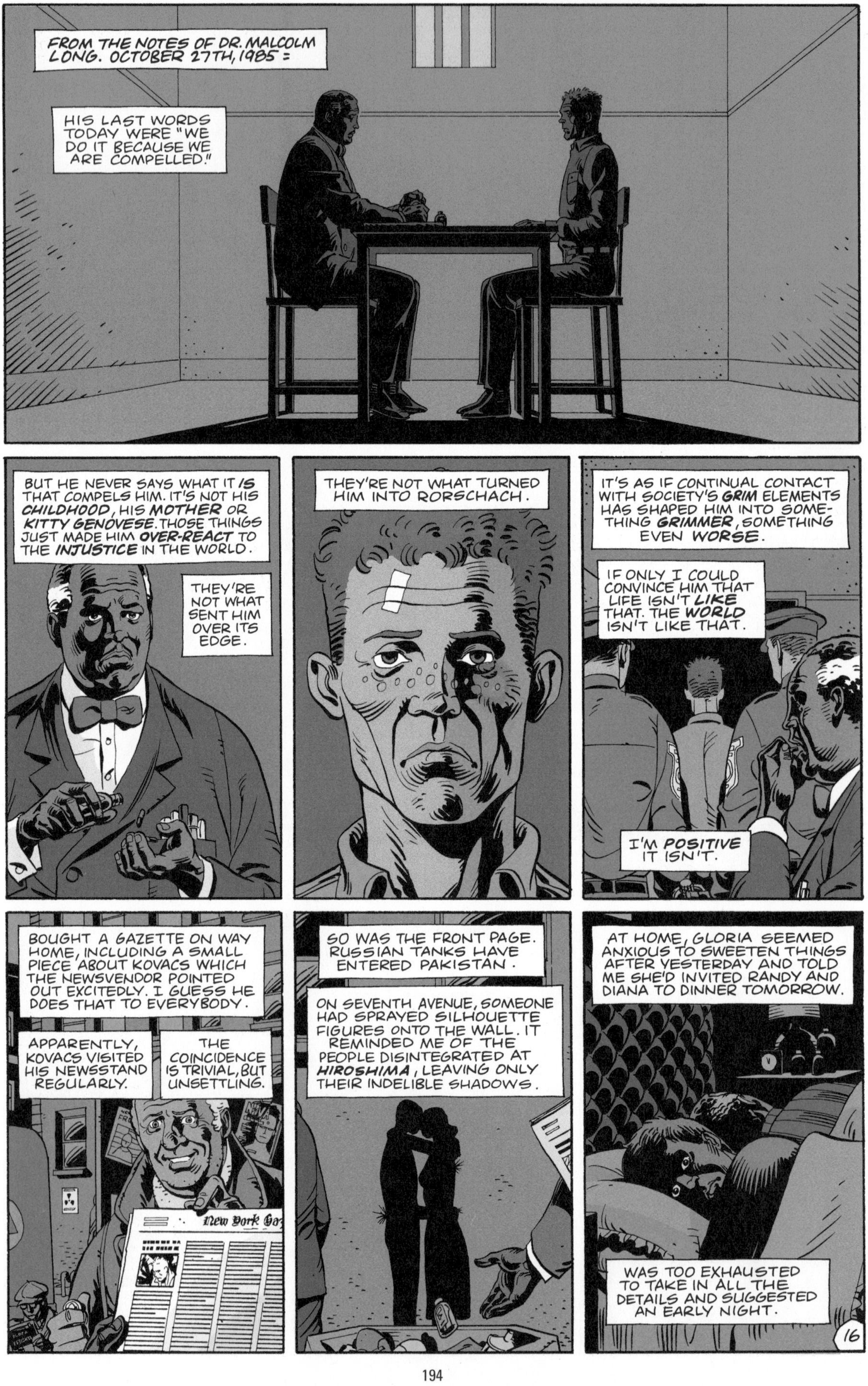
FROM THE NOTES OF DR. MALCOLM LONG. OCTOBER 27TH, 1985 =
HIS LAST WORDS TODAY WERE "WE DO IT BECAUSE WE ARE COMPELLED."
BUT HE NEVER SAYS WHAT IT IS THAT COMPELS HIM. IT'S NOT HIS CHILDHOOD, HIS MOTHER OR KITTY GENOVESE. THOSE THINGS JUST MADE HIM OVER-REACT TO THE INJUSTICE IN THE WORLD.
THEY'RE NOT WHAT SENT HIM OVER ITS EDGE.
THEY'RE NOT WHAT TURNED HIM INTO RORSCHACH.
IT'S AS IF CONTINUAL CONTACT WITH SOCIETY'S GRIM ELEMENTS HAS SHAPED HIM INTO SOMETHING GRIMMER, SOMETHING EVEN WORSE.
IF ONLY I COULD CONVINCE HIM THAT LIFE ISN'T LIKE THAT. THE WORLD ISN'T LIKE THAT.
I'M POSITIVE IT ISN'T.
BOUGHT A GAZETTE ON WAY HOME, INCLUDING A SMALL PIECE ABOUT KOVACS WHICH THE NEWSVENDOR POINTED OUT EXCITEDLY. I GUESS HE DOES THAT TO EVERYBODY.
APPARENTLY, KOVACS VISITED HIS NEWSSTAND REGULARLY.
THE COINCIDENCE IS TRIVIAL, BUT UNSETTLING.
New York Ga
SO WAS THE FRONT PAGE. RUSSIAN TANKS HAVE ENTERED PAKISTAN.
ON SEVENTH AVENUE, SOMEONE HAD SPRAYED SILHOUETTE FIGURES ONTO THE WALL. IT REMINDED ME OF THE PEOPLE DISINTEGRATED AT HIROSHIMA, LEAVING ONLY THEIR INDELIBLE SHADOWS.
AT HOME, GLORIA SEEMED ANXIOUS TO SWEETEN THINGS AFTER YESTERDAY AND TOLD ME SHE'D INVITED RANDY AND DIANA TO DINNER TOMORROW.
WAS TOO EXHAUSTED TO TAKE IN ALL THE DETAILS AND SUGGESTED AN EARLY NIGHT.
16

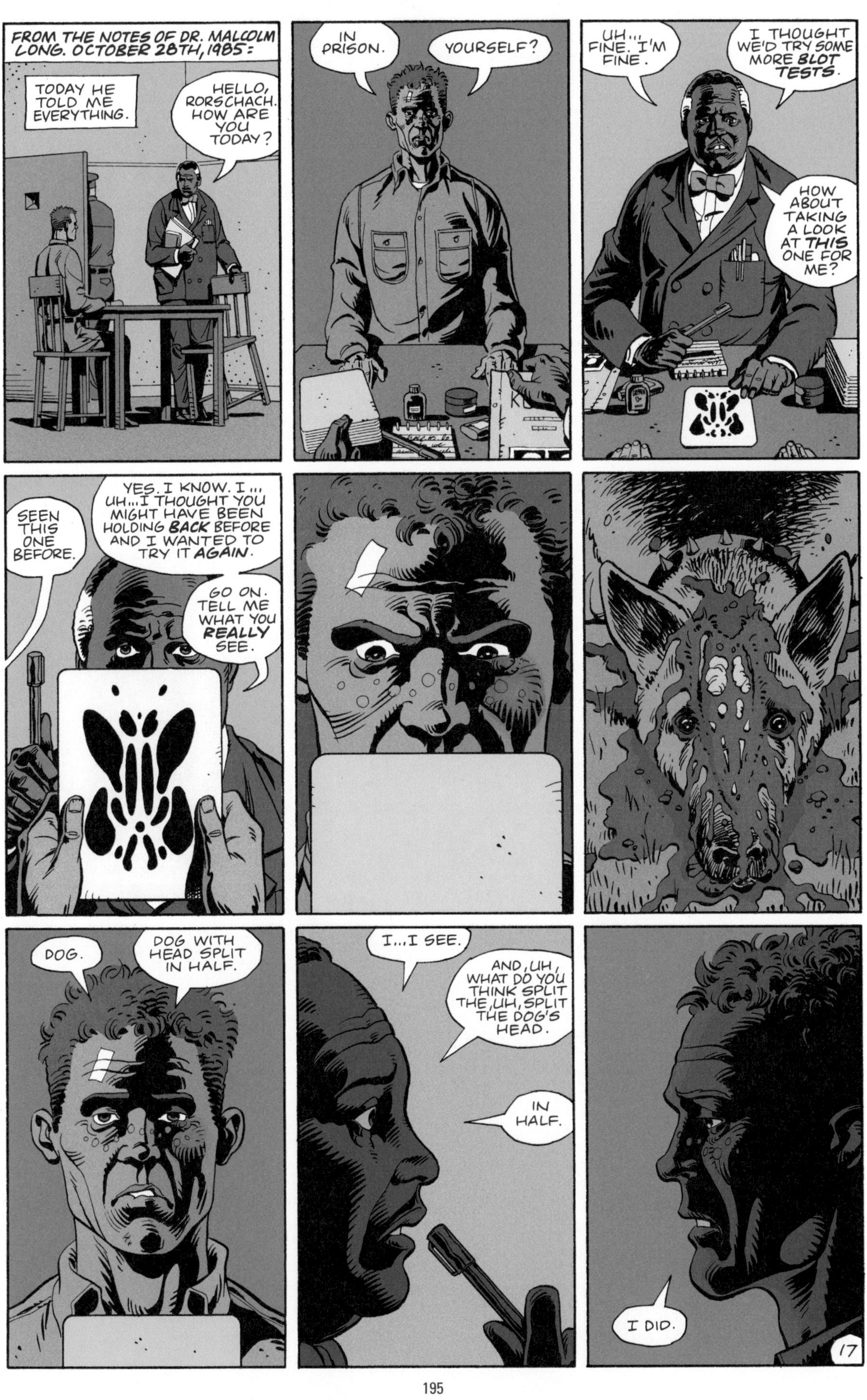
FROM THE NOTES OF DR. MALCOLM LONG. OCTOBER 28TH, 1985:
TODAY HE TOLD ME EVERYTHING.
HELLO, RORSCHACH. HOW ARE YOU TODAY?
IN PRISON.
YOURSELF?
UH... FINE. I'M FINE.
I THOUGHT WE'D TRY SOME MORE BLOT TESTS.
HOW ABOUT TAKING A LOOK AT THIS ONE FOR ME?
SEEN THIS ONE BEFORE.
YES. I KNOW. I... UH...I THOUGHT YOU MIGHT HAVE BEEN HOLDING BACK BEFORE AND I WANTED TO TRY IT AGAIN.
GO ON. TELL ME WHAT YOU REALLY SEE.
DOG.
DOG WITH HEAD SPLIT IN HALF.
I...I SEE.
AND, UH, WHAT DO YOU THINK SPLIT THE, UH, SPLIT THE DOG'S HEAD.
IN HALF.
I DID.
17

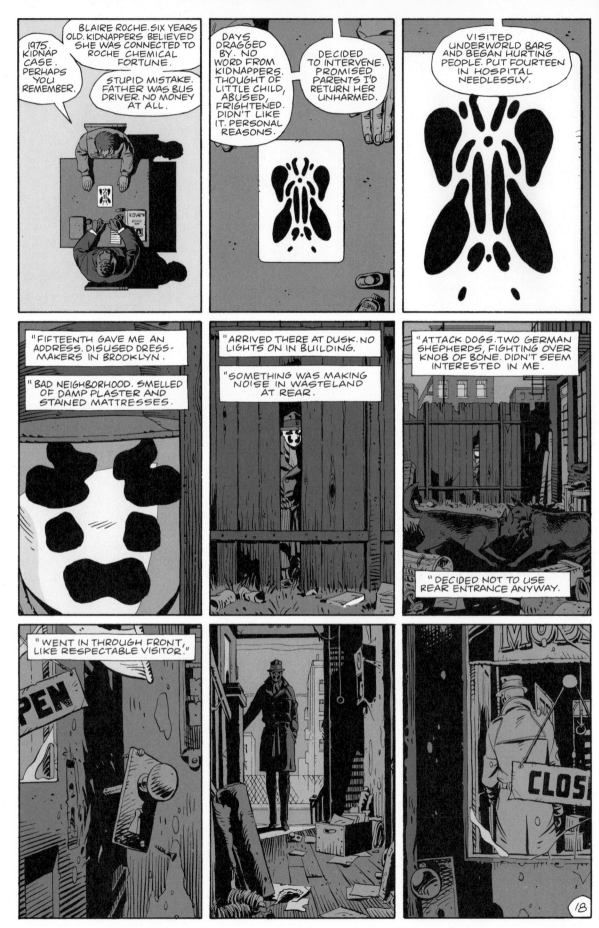

1975. KIDNAP CASE. PERHAPS YOU REMEMBER.

BLAIRE ROCHE. SIX YEARS OLD. KIDNAPPERS BELIEVED SHE WAS CONNECTED TO ROCHE CHEMICAL FORTUNE.

STUPID MISTAKE. FATHER WAS BUS DRIVER. NO MONEY AT ALL.

DAYS DRAGGED BY. NO WORD FROM KIDNAPPERS. THOUGHT OF LITTLE CHILD, ABUSED, FRIGHTENED. DIDN'T LIKE IT. PERSONAL REASONS.

DECIDED TO INTERVENE. PROMISED PARENTS I'D RETURN HER UNHARMED.

VISITED UNDERWORLD BARS AND BEGAN HURTING PEOPLE. PUT FOURTEEN IN HOSPITAL NEEDLESSLY.

"FIFTEENTH GAVE ME AN ADDRESS. DISUSED DRESS-MAKERS IN BROOKLYN."

"BAD NEIGHBORHOOD. SMELLED OF DAMP PLASTER AND STAINED MATTRESSES."

"ARRIVED THERE AT DUSK. NO LIGHTS ON IN BUILDING."

"SOMETHING WAS MAKING NOISE IN WASTELAND AT REAR."

"ATTACK DOGS. TWO GERMAN SHEPHERDS, FIGHTING OVER KNOB OF BONE. DIDN'T SEEM INTERESTED IN ME."

"DECIDED NOT TO USE REAR ENTRANCE ANYWAY."

"WENT IN THROUGH FRONT, LIKE RESPECTABLE VISITOR.'"

18

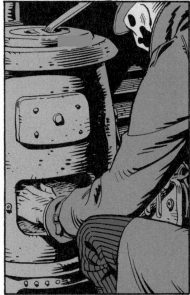

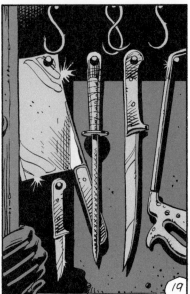

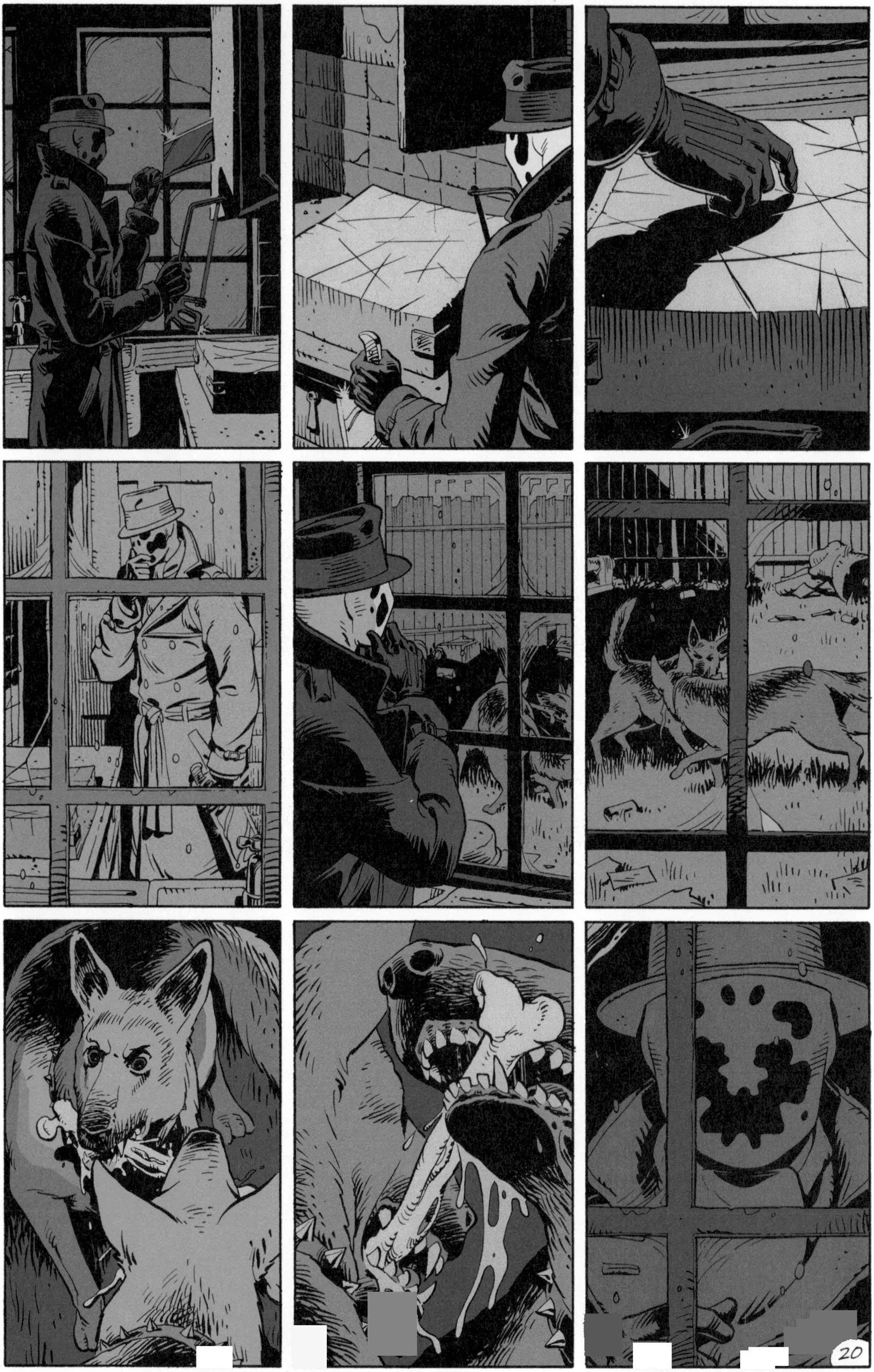
20

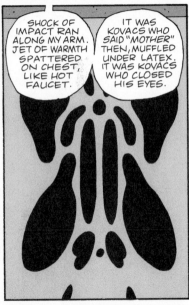

SHOCK OF IMPACT RAN ALONG MY ARM. JET OF WARMTH SPATTERED ON CHEST, LIKE HOT FAUCET.

IT WAS KOVACS WHO SAID "MOTHER" THEN, MUFFLED UNDER LATEX. IT WAS KOVACS WHO CLOSED HIS EYES.

IT WAS RORSCHACH WHO OPENED THEM AGAIN.

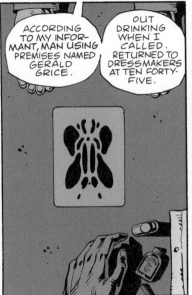

ACCORDING TO MY INFORMANT, MAN USING PREMISES NAMED GERALD GRICE.

OUT DRINKING WHEN I CALLED. RETURNED TO DRESSMAKERS AT TEN FORTY-FIVE.

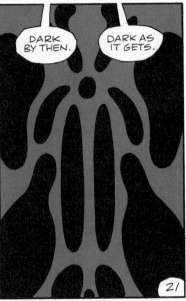

DARK BY THEN.

DARK AS IT GETS.

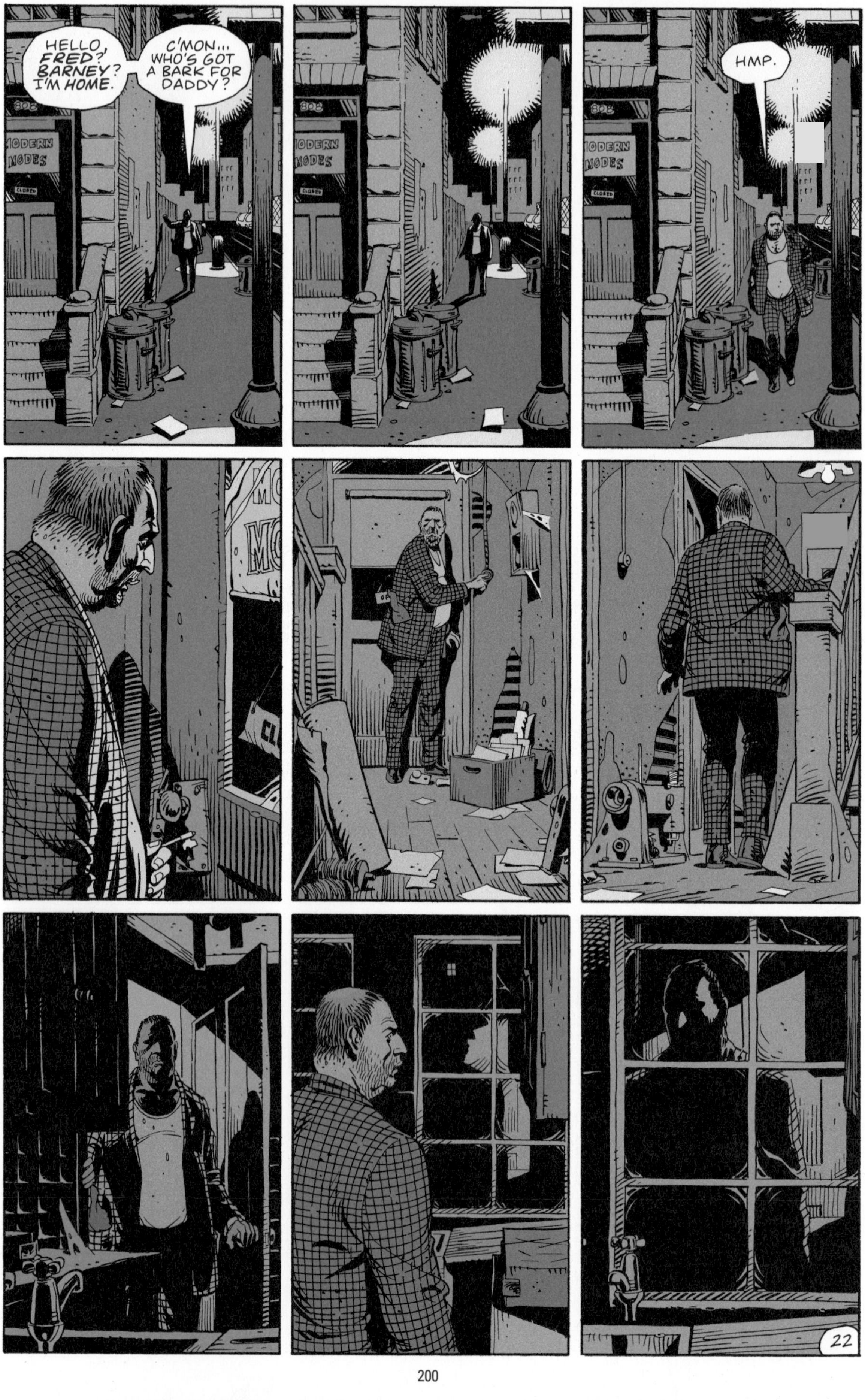
HELLO, FRED? BARNEY? I'M HOME.
C'MON... WHO'S GOT A BARK FOR DADDY?
808
MODERN MODES
CLOSED
HMP.
22

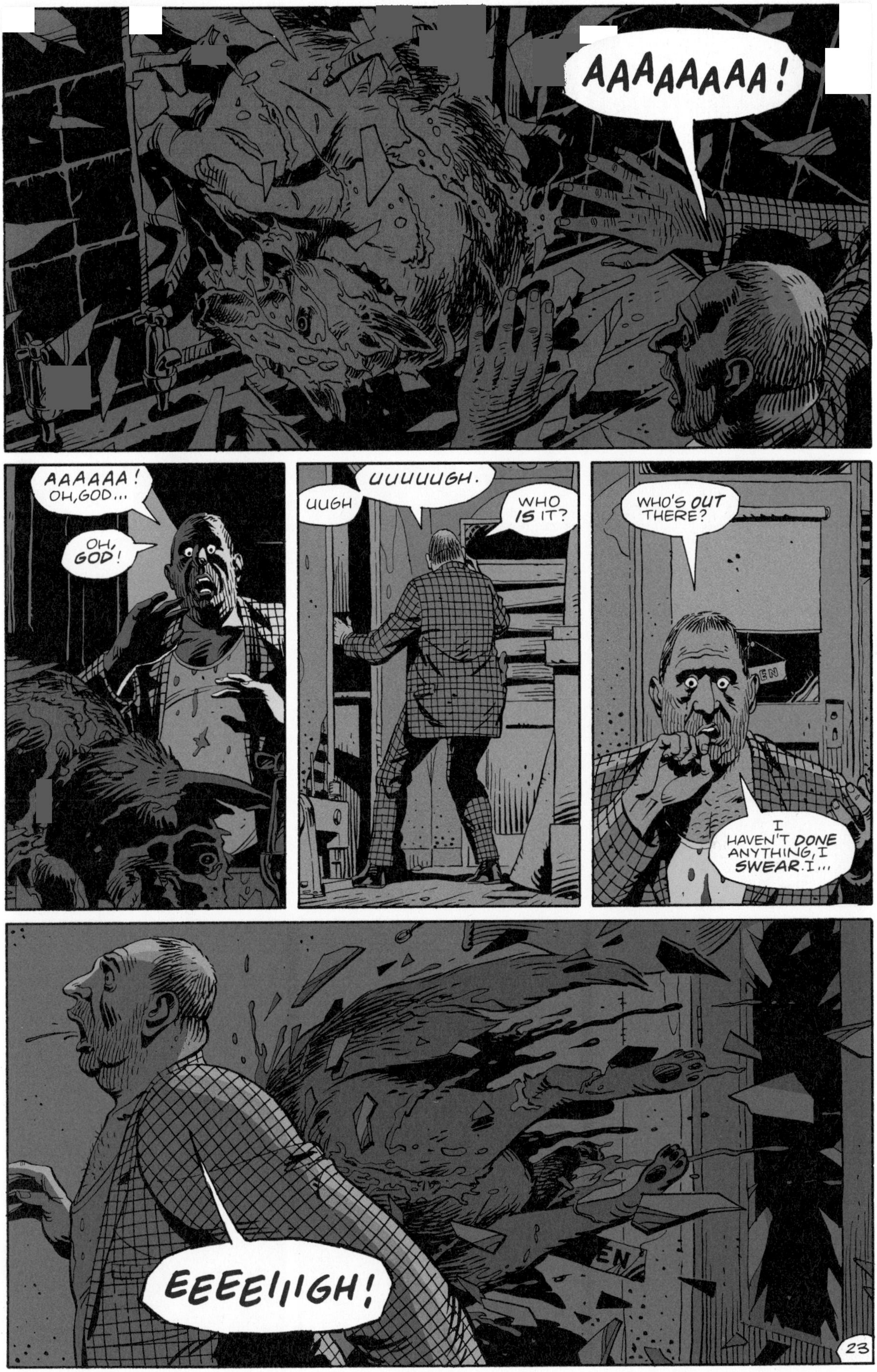

AAAAAAAA!
AAAAAA! OH, GOD...
OH, GOD!
UUUUUGH.
UUGH
WHO IS IT?
WHO'S OUT THERE?
I HAVEN'T DONE ANYTHING, I SWEAR. I...
EEEEIIIGH!
23

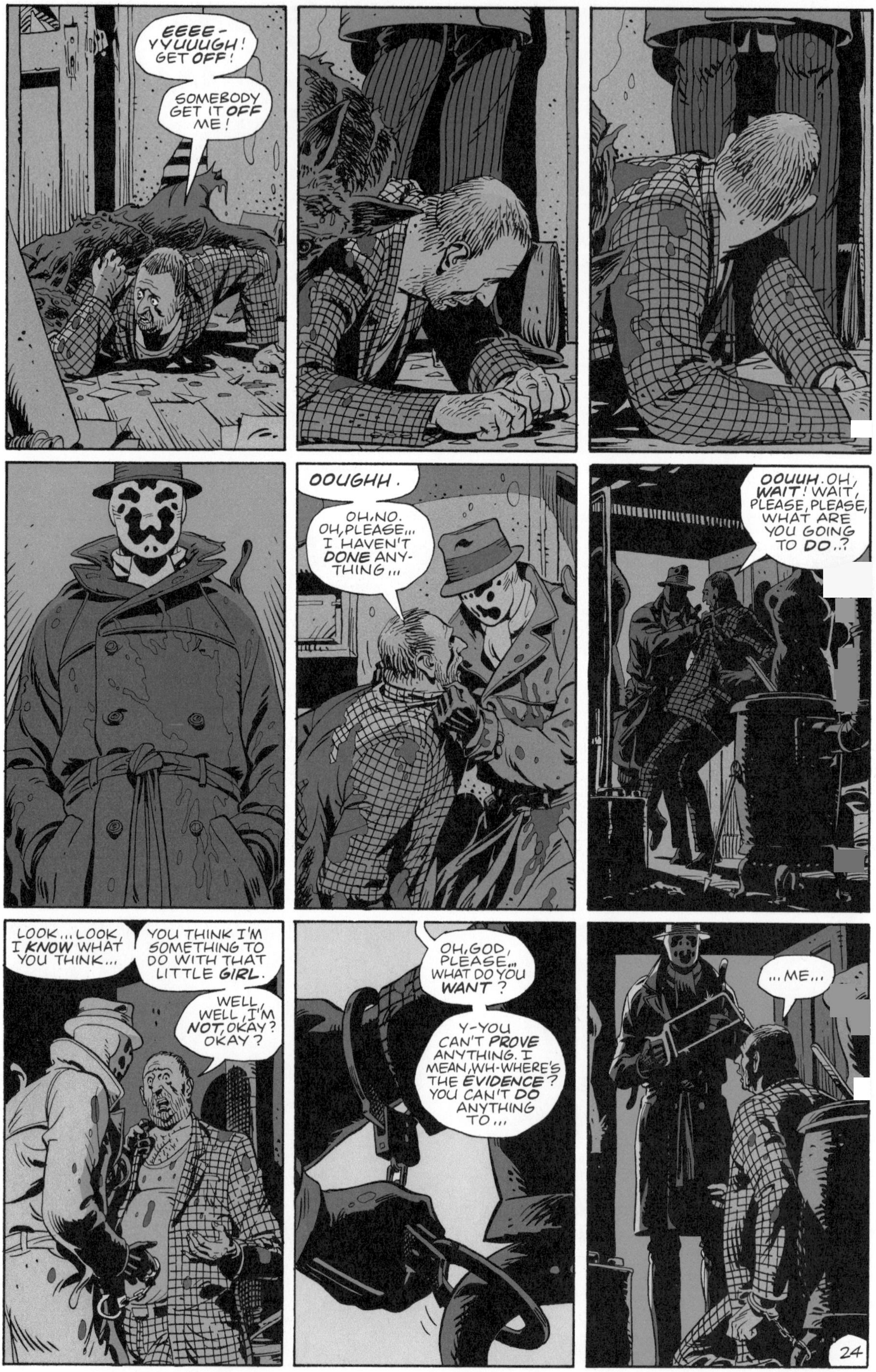
EEEE-YYUUUGH! GET OFF!
SOMEBODY GET IT OFF ME!
OOUGHH.
OH, NO. OH, PLEASE... I HAVEN'T DONE ANYTHING...
OOUUH. OH, WAIT! WAIT, PLEASE, PLEASE, WHAT ARE YOU GOING TO DO..?
LOOK... LOOK, I KNOW WHAT YOU THINK...
YOU THINK I'M SOMETHING TO DO WITH THAT LITTLE GIRL.
WELL, WELL, I'M NOT, OKAY? OKAY?
OH, GOD, PLEASE... WHAT DO YOU WANT?
Y-YOU CAN'T PROVE ANYTHING. I MEAN, WH-WHERE'S THE EVIDENCE? YOU CAN'T DO ANYTHING TO...
...ME...
24

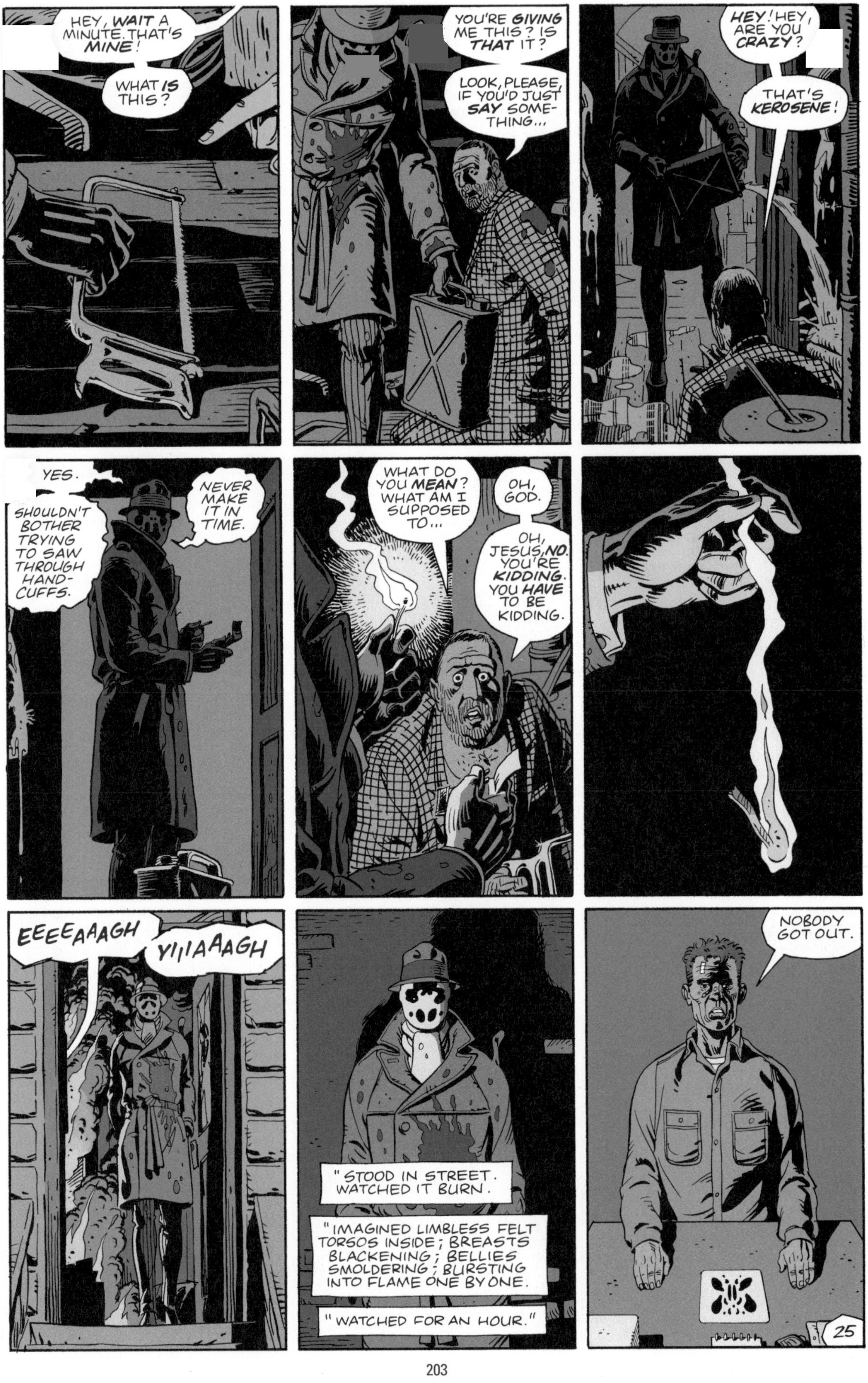
HEY, WAIT A MINUTE. THAT'S MINE!
WHAT IS THIS?
YOU'RE GIVING ME THIS? IS THAT IT?
LOOK, PLEASE, IF YOU'D JUST SAY SOMETHING...
HEY! HEY, ARE YOU CRAZY?
THAT'S KEROSENE!
YES.
SHOULDN'T BOTHER TRYING TO SAW THROUGH HANDCUFFS.
NEVER MAKE IT IN TIME.
WHAT DO YOU MEAN? WHAT AM I SUPPOSED TO...
OH, GOD.
OH, JESUS, NO. YOU'RE KIDDING. YOU HAVE TO BE KIDDING.
EEEEAAAGH
YIIIAAAGH
"STOOD IN STREET. WATCHED IT BURN.
"IMAGINED LIMBLESS FELT TORSOS INSIDE; BREASTS BLACKENING; BELLIES SMOLDERING; BURSTING INTO FLAME ONE BY ONE.
"WATCHED FOR AN HOUR."
NOBODY GOT OUT.
25

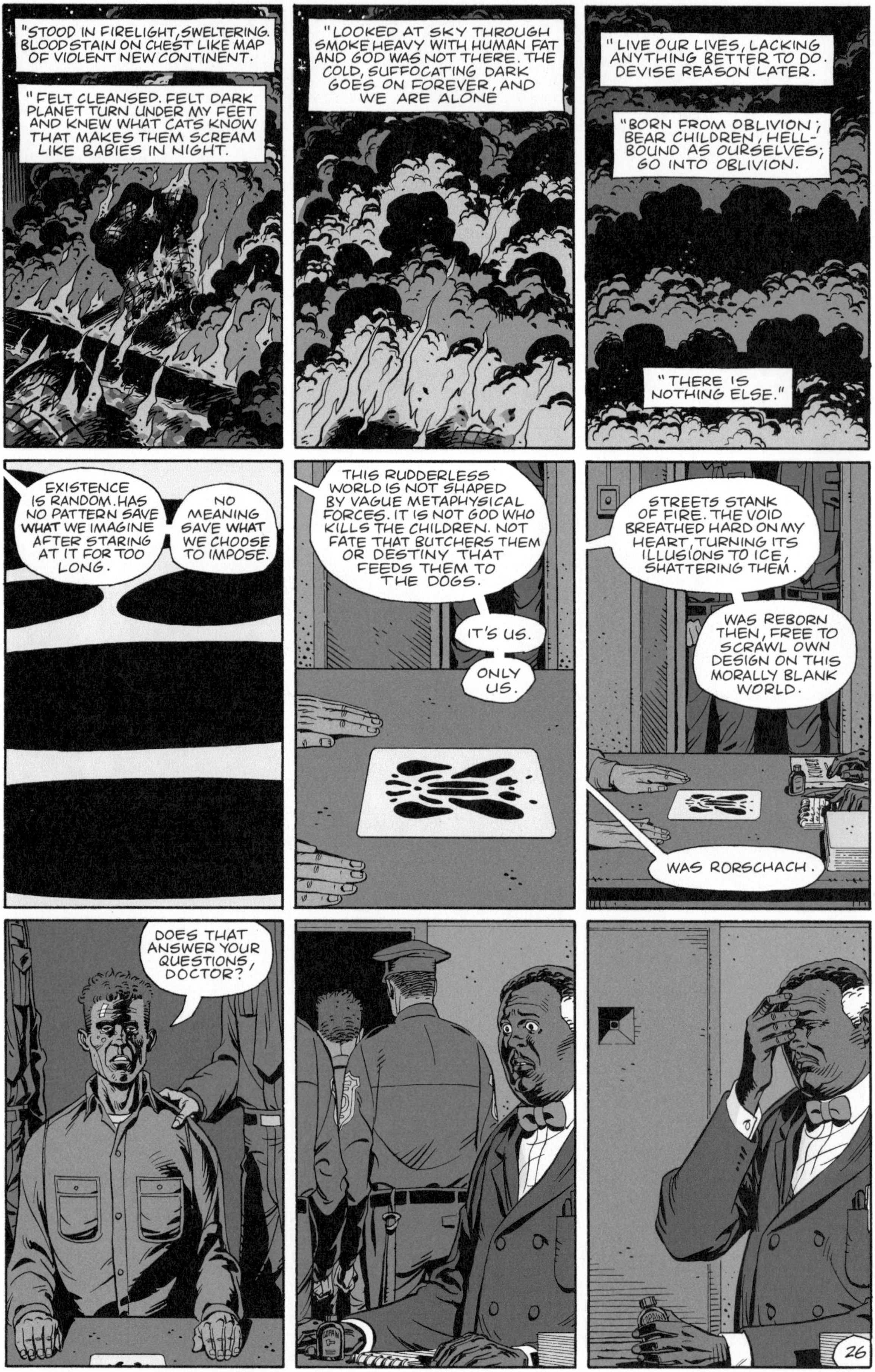
"STOOD IN FIRELIGHT, SWELTERING. BLOODSTAIN ON CHEST LIKE MAP OF VIOLENT NEW CONTINENT.
"FELT CLEANSED. FELT DARK PLANET TURN UNDER MY FEET AND KNEW WHAT CATS KNOW THAT MAKES THEM SCREAM LIKE BABIES IN NIGHT.
"LOOKED AT SKY THROUGH SMOKE HEAVY WITH HUMAN FAT AND GOD WAS NOT THERE. THE COLD, SUFFOCATING DARK GOES ON FOREVER, AND WE ARE ALONE
"LIVE OUR LIVES, LACKING ANYTHING BETTER TO DO. DEVISE REASON LATER.
"BORN FROM OBLIVION; BEAR CHILDREN, HELL-BOUND AS OURSELVES; GO INTO OBLIVION.
"THERE IS NOTHING ELSE."
EXISTENCE IS RANDOM. HAS NO PATTERN SAVE WHAT WE IMAGINE AFTER STARING AT IT FOR TOO LONG.
NO MEANING SAVE WHAT WE CHOOSE TO IMPOSE.
THIS RUDDERLESS WORLD IS NOT SHAPED BY VAGUE METAPHYSICAL FORCES. IT IS NOT GOD WHO KILLS THE CHILDREN. NOT FATE THAT BUTCHERS THEM OR DESTINY THAT FEEDS THEM TO THE DOGS.
IT'S US.
ONLY US.
STREETS STANK OF FIRE. THE VOID BREATHED HARD ON MY HEART, TURNING ITS ILLUSIONS TO ICE, SHATTERING THEM.
WAS REBORN THEN, FREE TO SCRAWL OWN DESIGN ON THIS MORALLY BLANK WORLD.
WAS RORSCHACH.
DOES THAT ANSWER YOUR QUESTIONS, DOCTOR?
26

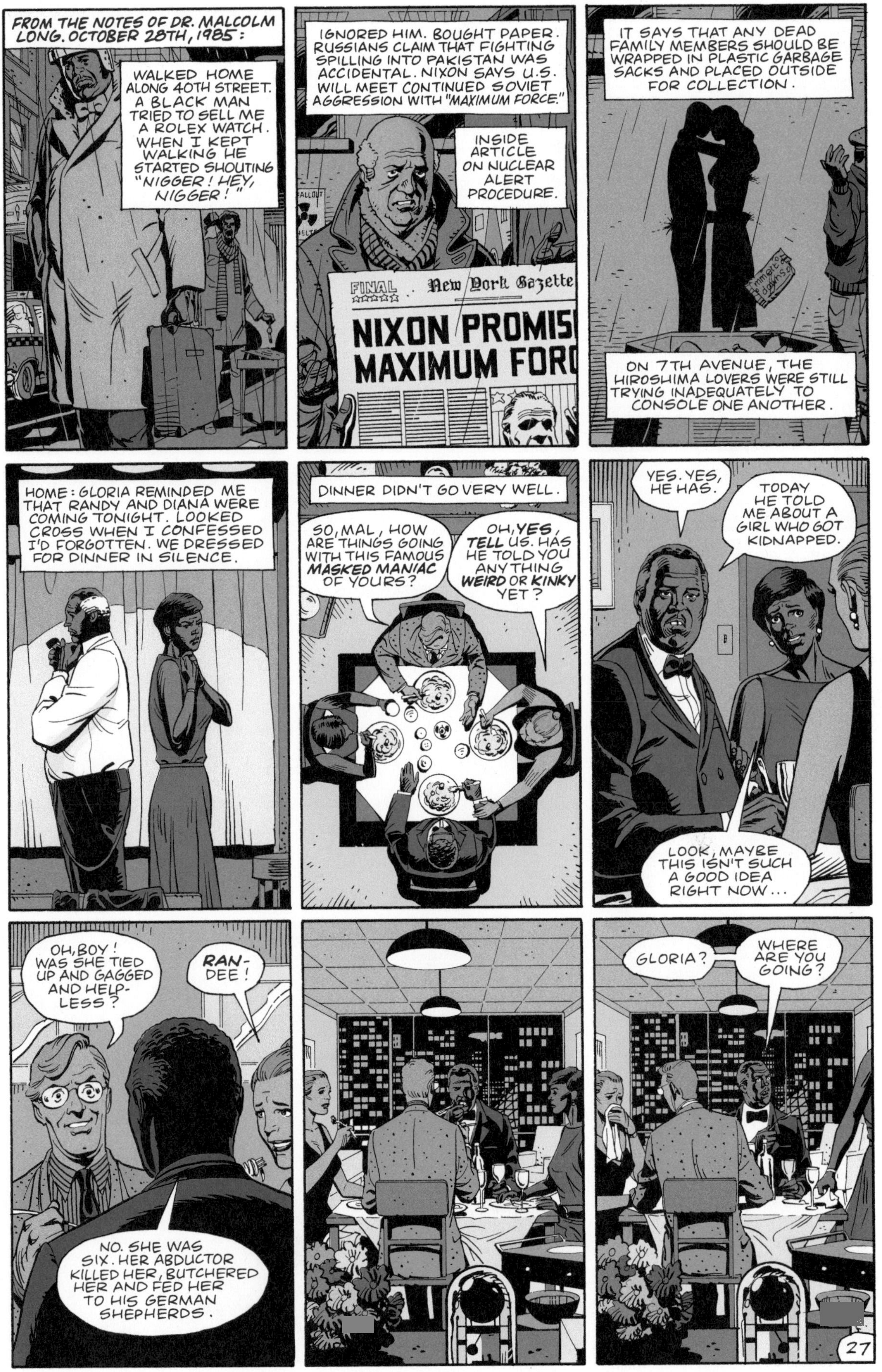
FROM THE NOTES OF DR. MALCOLM LONG. OCTOBER 28TH, 1985:
WALKED HOME ALONG 40TH STREET. A BLACK MAN TRIED TO SELL ME A ROLEX WATCH. WHEN I KEPT WALKING HE STARTED SHOUTING "NIGGER! HEY, NIGGER!"
IGNORED HIM. BOUGHT PAPER. RUSSIANS CLAIM THAT FIGHTING SPILLING INTO PAKISTAN WAS ACCIDENTAL. NIXON SAYS U.S. WILL MEET CONTINUED SOVIET AGGRESSION WITH "MAXIMUM FORCE."
INSIDE ARTICLE ON NUCLEAR ALERT PROCEDURE.
FINAL
New York Gazette
NIXON PROMIS
MAXIMUM FOR
IT SAYS THAT ANY DEAD FAMILY MEMBERS SHOULD BE WRAPPED IN PLASTIC GARBAGE SACKS AND PLACED OUTSIDE FOR COLLECTION.
ON 7TH AVENUE, THE HIROSHIMA LOVERS WERE STILL TRYING INADEQUATELY TO CONSOLE ONE ANOTHER.
HOME: GLORIA REMINDED ME THAT RANDY AND DIANA WERE COMING TONIGHT. LOOKED CROSS WHEN I CONFESSED I'D FORGOTTEN. WE DRESSED FOR DINNER IN SILENCE.
DINNER DIDN'T GO VERY WELL.
SO, MAL, HOW ARE THINGS GOING WITH THIS FAMOUS MASKED MANIAC OF YOURS?
OH, YES, TELL US. HAS HE TOLD YOU ANYTHING WEIRD OR KINKY YET?
YES. YES, HE HAS.
TODAY HE TOLD ME ABOUT A GIRL WHO GOT KIDNAPPED.
LOOK, MAYBE THIS ISN'T SUCH A GOOD IDEA RIGHT NOW...
OH, BOY! WAS SHE TIED UP AND GAGGED AND HELP-LESS?
RAN-DEE!
NO. SHE WAS SIX. HER ABDUCTOR KILLED HER, BUTCHERED HER AND FED HER TO HIS GERMAN SHEPHERDS.
GLORIA?
WHERE ARE YOU GOING?
27

DIANA REMEMBERED THAT THEIR BABYSITTER HAD TO BE HOME EARLY AND THEY LEFT SOON AFTER DINNER.

GLORIA WENT INTO THE BEDROOM. I FOLLOWED HER. SHE WALKED OUT AGAIN, INTO THE HALL.

I SAT ON THE BED.

SHE CAME IN, WEARING HER COAT, SUBJECTED ME TO A LOT OF CRUDE SEXUAL INSULTS, WENT OUT. THE FRONT DOOR SLAMMED.

WHY DO WE ARGUE? LIFE'S SO FRAGILE, A SUCCESSFUL VIRUS CLINGING TO A SPECK OF MUD, SUSPENDED IN ENDLESS NOTHING.

CAUTION
DO NOT EXCEED STATED DOSE

ALE
YOU HEAR TH
SIREN W
OUTDOOR

RUN TO THE
NEAREST BUIL
IF THERE ARE
NO NEAR

OBEY T

NEXT WEEK, I COULD BE PUTTING HER INTO A GARBAGE SACK, PLACING HER OUTSIDE FOR COLLECTION.

I SAT ON THE BED. I LOOKED AT THE RORSCHACH BLOT.

I TRIED TO PRETEND IT LOOKED LIKE A SPREADING TREE, SHADOWS POOLED BENEATH IT, BUT IT DIDN'T.

IT LOOKED MORE LIKE A DEAD CAT I ONCE FOUND, THE FAT, GLISTENING GRUBS WRITHING BLINDLY, SQUIRMING OVER EACH OTHER, FRANTICALLY TUNNELING AWAY FROM THE LIGHT.

BUT EVEN THAT IS AVOIDING THE REAL HORROR.

THE HORROR IS THIS: IN THE END, IT IS SIMPLY A PICTURE OF EMPTY MEANINGLESS BLACKNESS.

WE ARE ALONE.

THERE IS NOTHING ELSE.

Battle not with monsters, lest ye become a monster,

and if you gaze into the abyss, the abyss gazes also into you.

—Friedrich Wilhelm Nietzsche

28

WALTER J. KOVACS

Form 2-18

New York Police Department
MANHATTAN

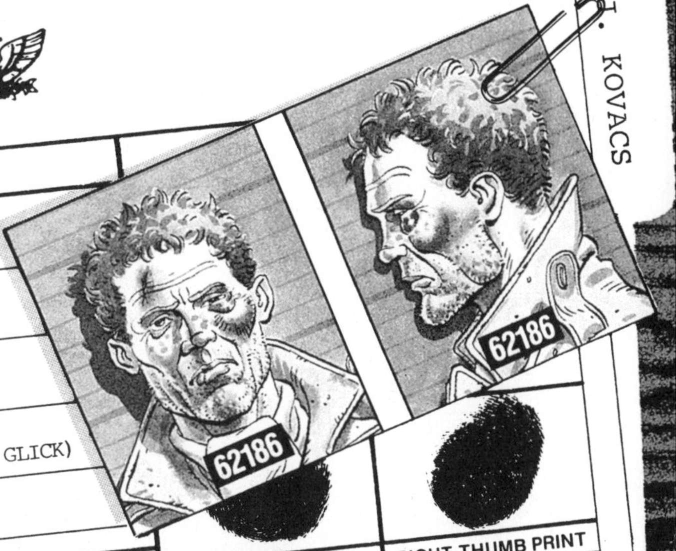
62186
62186

LEFT THUMB PRINT

RIGHT THUMB PRINT

FOR INTER-DEPARTMENTAL USE ONLY

(Please type or print clearly)

Name KOVACS, Walter Joseph

Address TRANSIENT

Born 3/21/40

Mothers name KOVACS, Sylvia Joanna (née GLICK)

Fathers name Unknown

DETAILS OF ARREST | **COPIES:**

Walter Joseph Kovacs, A.K.A. RORSCHACH, was arrested on the night of Monday, October 21st when a squadron of police officers led by Detectives FINE and BOURQUIN surrounded the house of EDGAR WILLIAM JACOBI, A.K.A. EDGAR WILLIAM VAUGHN, A.K.A. WILLIAM EDGAR BRIGHT, A.K.A. MOLOCH, following an anonymous tip: Kovacs, who was on the premises at the time, injured two police officers while resisting arrest. Officer SHAW was admitted to the hospital with minor burns, while Officer Greaves, who was shot at point blank range with a gas-powered grappling gun, has a shattered sternum and is still on the hospital's critical list as of this writing (10/22/85).

When the house was explored, the body of Edgar Jacobi was discovered in the kitchen, shot through the head. The murder weapon was found less than two feet away, and although there were no fingerprints on the gun it should be remembered that since Kovacs was wearing gloves when arrested, this lack of prints is hardly remarkable. Although Kovacs has denied the murder of Jacobi, given his previous history of violence against other criminals and his location in the murder house at the time, few other conclusions seem possible. Curiously, Kovacs has not denied the two other murders attributed to him, those of GERALD ANTHONY GRICE, unemployed, in the summer of 1975, and of wanted multiple rapist HARVEY CHARLES FURNISS two years later in the summer of 1977, immediately following the passage of the Keene Act into law.

At the time of his arrest, the contents of Kovacs' pockets were as follows: 1 battery powered flashlight; 5 individually wrapped cubes 'Sweet Chariot' chewing sugar; 1 map New York underground and subway system, dated 1968 with recent alterations drawn in with a red ballpoint pen; withered remains one red rose; one dollar fifty-nine cents in assorted loose change; one pencil; one notebook, pages filled with what is either an elaborate cypher or handwriting too cramped and eccentric to be legible; one broken bottle 'Nostalgia' cologne for men, possibly broken during leap from Jacobi's second story window during arrest; a residue of ground black pepper.

(If second sheet is needed refer to Form 6-2)

New York State Psychiatric Hospital
West Branch

EARLY HISTORY: A SUMMARY:

Sylvia Kovacs came to New York from Ohio in the spring of 1935 with her husband, Peter Joseph Kovacs, whom she divorced in 1937 amidst mutual accusations of adultery and mental cruelty. After the divorce she had no further contact with her former husband, and for the next three years, she lived in a number of low-rent apartments, both alone and with a number of male acquaintances. Exactly when she drifted into prostitution as a means of meeting her mounting debts is uncertain, but it seems likely that her last semi-permanent relationship was with the true father of Walter Kovacs, who left her two months before the baby was born. Mrs. Kovacs was either unable or unwilling to provide any details concerning him other than that his name was 'Charlie'. Sicne shortly after the birth of her son we see Mrs. Kovacs' first arrest on charges of prostitution, we can perhaps assume that the additional cost of keeping an infant child may have been what necessitated this new occupation, and perhaps also speculate as to whether the above factors were the cause of the resentment and cruelty which Sylvia Kovacs showed to her son as he grew older.

In the July of 1951, the boy was admitted into care after viciously attacking two older boys in the street, partially blinding one of them. When questioned, Kovacs refused to talk about what had caused him to attack the boys, so it must be presumed that it was an unprovoked assault. Nerertheless, investigation of the circumstances the boy lived in revealed that he was regularly beaten and exposed to the worst excesses of a prostitutes lifestyle, and it was decide to place the child under care. He was admitted to the Lillian Charlton Home for Problem Children in New Jersey, where he remained until 1956, when it was decided that he was intelligent and stable enough to function in normal society. During his time at hte home, removed from his mother's negative influence, Kovacs did very well at schoolwork, excelling particularly in the fields of literature and religious educscation as well as possessing an impressive skill in the areas of gymnastics and amateur boxing. While quiet and shy, especially with women, Kovacs was capable of long and well-reasoned conversations with hi classmates and instructors, and struck most peo as a serious but likeable child who was merely a bit withdrawn.

This aside, it is clear that his loathin of his mother remained undiminished. Shortly before Kovacs left the Charlton home in 1956, news was received that his mother, who had never made any attempt to contact her child and who ha continued to become further involved in the worl of small-time vice, had been murdered. Her body had been found in a back alleyway in the South Bronx, the cause of death being the forced ing estion of Drano cleaning fluid.A man named George Paterson, Mrs. Kovacs' pimp, was later charged

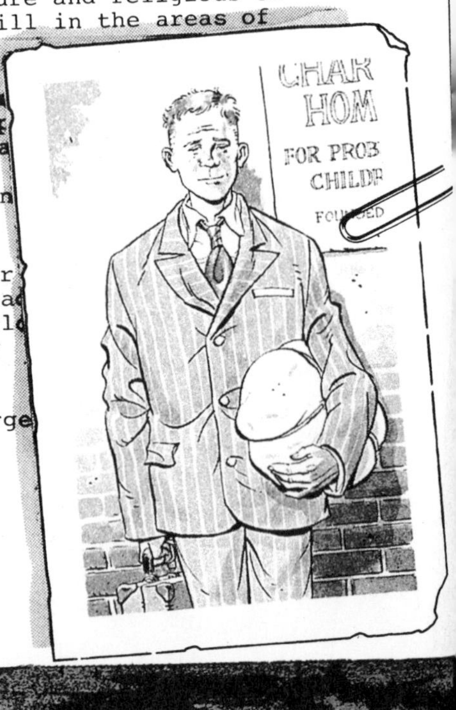
CHAR
HOM
FOR PROB

New York State Psychiatric Hospital
West Branch

with her murder. When the news was broken to Walter Kovacs, then aged sixteen, his only comment was 'Good.' Shor tly after this , Kovacs left the home to take up residence in the first of a series of small apartments and also take up full employment in a menial capacity within the garment industry, an occupation he apparently remained in up until the mid-seventies, maintaining a dual life between his daytime employment and his nocturnal activities in the guise of 'Rorschach'.

Very little physical evidence existsthat gives a clear insight into the psychology of this troubled man. Some police officers have tentatively identified hima s a prophet-of-doom sandwich-board man seen locally over the last several years, but as Kovacs refuses to divulge his current address, if any, this is not provable at such an early stage in the investigation. Similarly, material relating to his early years is scarce, although I have been able to obtain photocopies of two pieces written by Kovacs during his stay at the Charlton Home, one being an essay written on the set topic of 'My Parents' when Kovacs was eleven, the other being a transcription of Kovacs' verbal recounting of a nightmare he suffered when he was thirteen.

CONFIDENTIAL

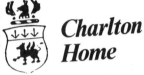

Charlton Home

by Walter Kovacs

My Parents

I have two parents, although actually, I don't have any. I never see my mom, but that's okay, although I would like to see my dad sometimes. I have never met my dad and I would sure like to. He had to leave our house when I wasn't even born, I guess because he couldn't get along with my mother. I would of done the same if I was him.

I used to ask my mom about my dad, but she doesn't talk much about him. His name was charlie, which is short for Charles although it has the same number of letters. She says she doesn't know his second name although how can you live with somebodt if you don't know who they are? It is just stupid.

My mom told me she threw my dad out because he was always getting into political arguments with her because he liked President Truman and she didn't. I think perhaps my dad was some sort of aide to President Truman, because he liked him so much. Most probably he was out of the country during the war when I was growing up on some sort of mission. I think he was the kind of guy who would fight for his country and what was right. Maybe he got killed fighting the Nazis and he's with God now and that's how come he never managed to find me.

I like President Truman, the way Dad would of wanted me to. He dropped the atom bomb on Japan and saved millions of lives because if he hadn't of, then there would of been a lot more war than there was and more people would of been killed. I think it was a good thing to drop the atomic bomb on Japan.

That is all I have to say about my parents.

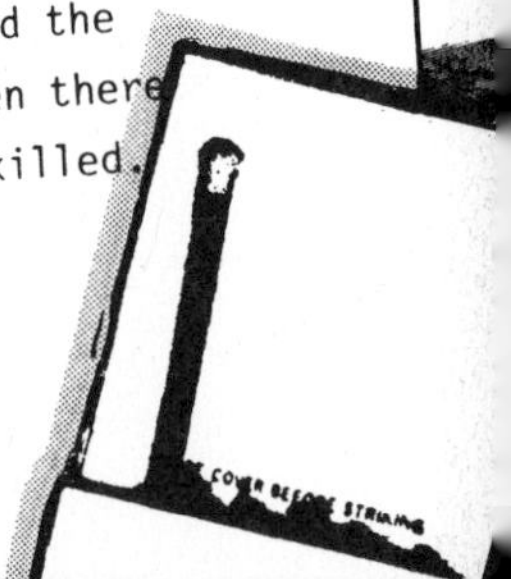

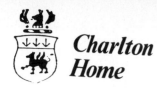

Charlton Home

CONFIDENTIAL

DREAM, 5/27/63

" A man was in my old house, with my mom. They were eating some stuff like raw dough, and my mom choked on a piece. The guy with her tried to fish it out of her throat. He got his whole hand in her mouth and then it was like he had his whole arm down her throat. He told me to get a doctor, so I ran out of the room but the house was all different and there wasn't any doctor there anyway, so I went back to find mom. I was walking down this sort of hallway, and it was dark and I saw what looked like my mom and this guy dancing, old fashioned dancing at the other end of the room, and they didn't have any clothes on. They were sort of clopping around like a horse in a pantomine with two guys in a suit. When they got nearer, I saw they weren't dancing at all, they were squashed together like siamese twins, joined at the face and chest and stomach. They didn't have any face, you could only see their ears, two on either side of the head facing towards each other. Their hands were growing into each other as well, but they had all four legs free and they were sort of dancing sideways towards me down the dark hall like a crab, and there was something tripping 'em up, wrapped around their feet, and I looked down and I saw it was trousers and underwear and stuff. They were coming towards me, and then I woke up. I had feelings when I woke up. Dirty feelings, thoughts and stuff. The dream it sort of upset me, physically. I couldn't help it. I feel bad just talking about it."

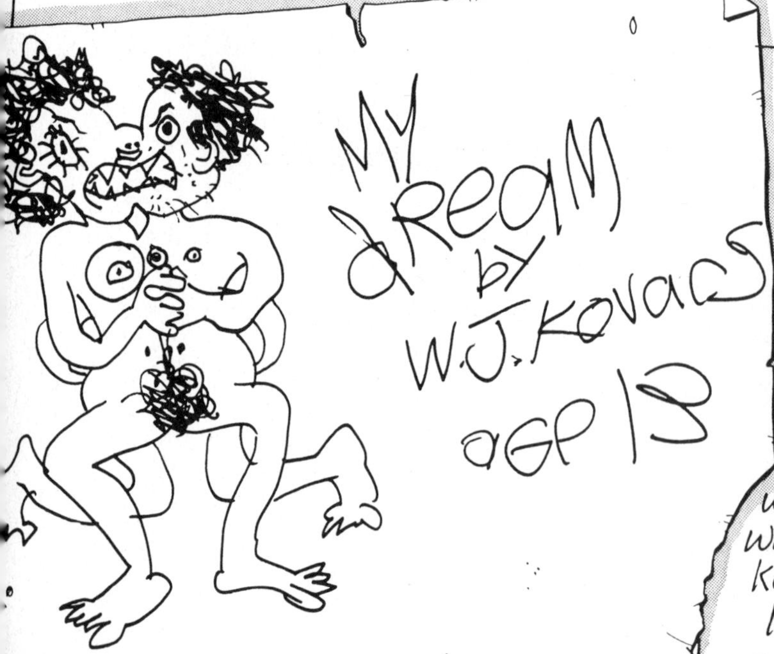
MY DREAM
BY
W.J. KOVACS
AGE 13

From the desk of: Dr. Malcol

10

Walter Joseph Kovacs promises to
a complex case, especially in
of the extreme nature of hi
vigilante activities. It may b
possible to identify a new
syndrome that will help us
understand those other people
who have in the past shared
Kovacs masked vigilante activi
In any event, keep notes
with an eye to possible
future publication.
First interview with Kovacs
is Friday afternoon. Looking
forward to it.

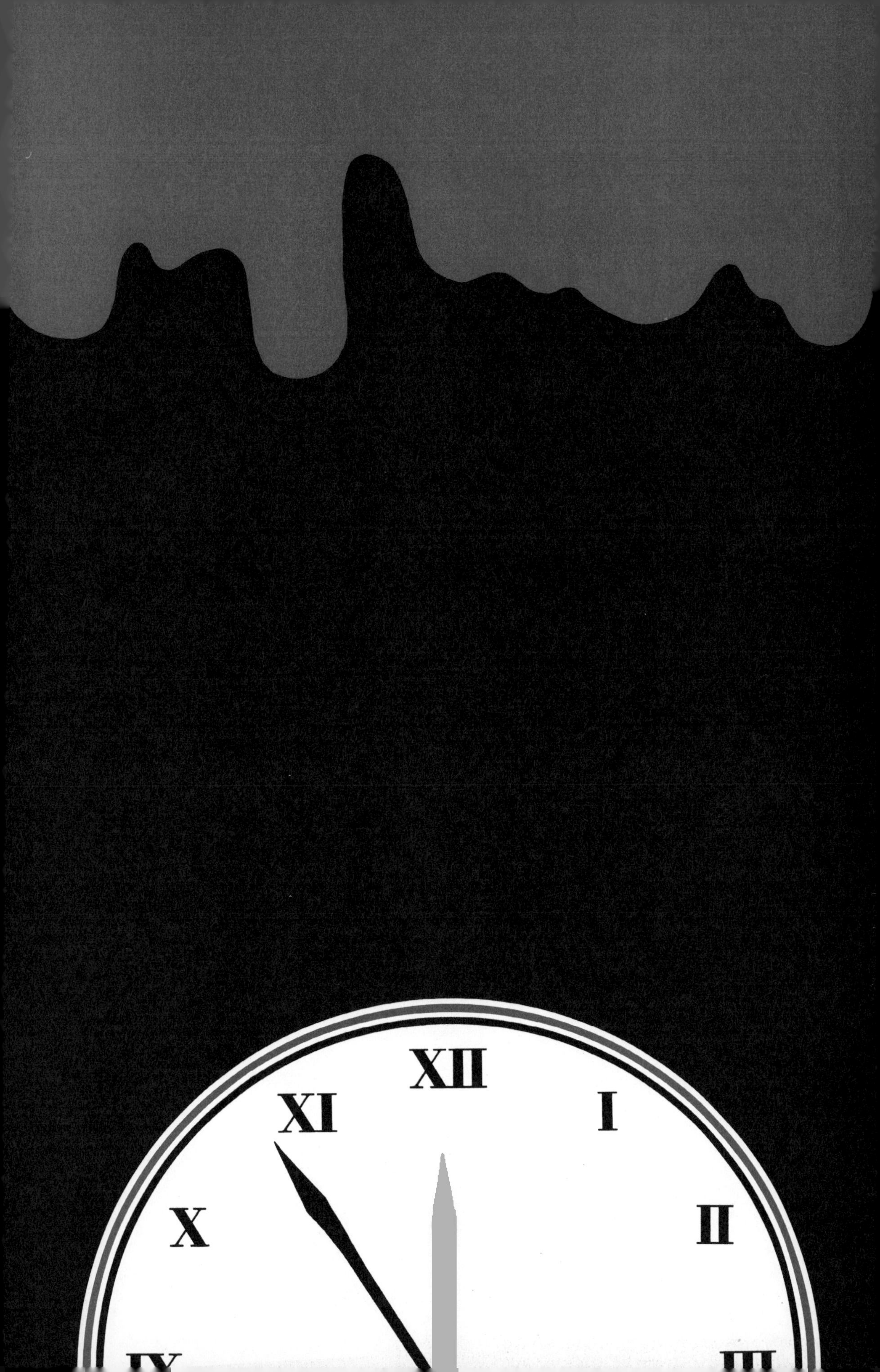
XII
XI
I
X
II

CHAPTER VII

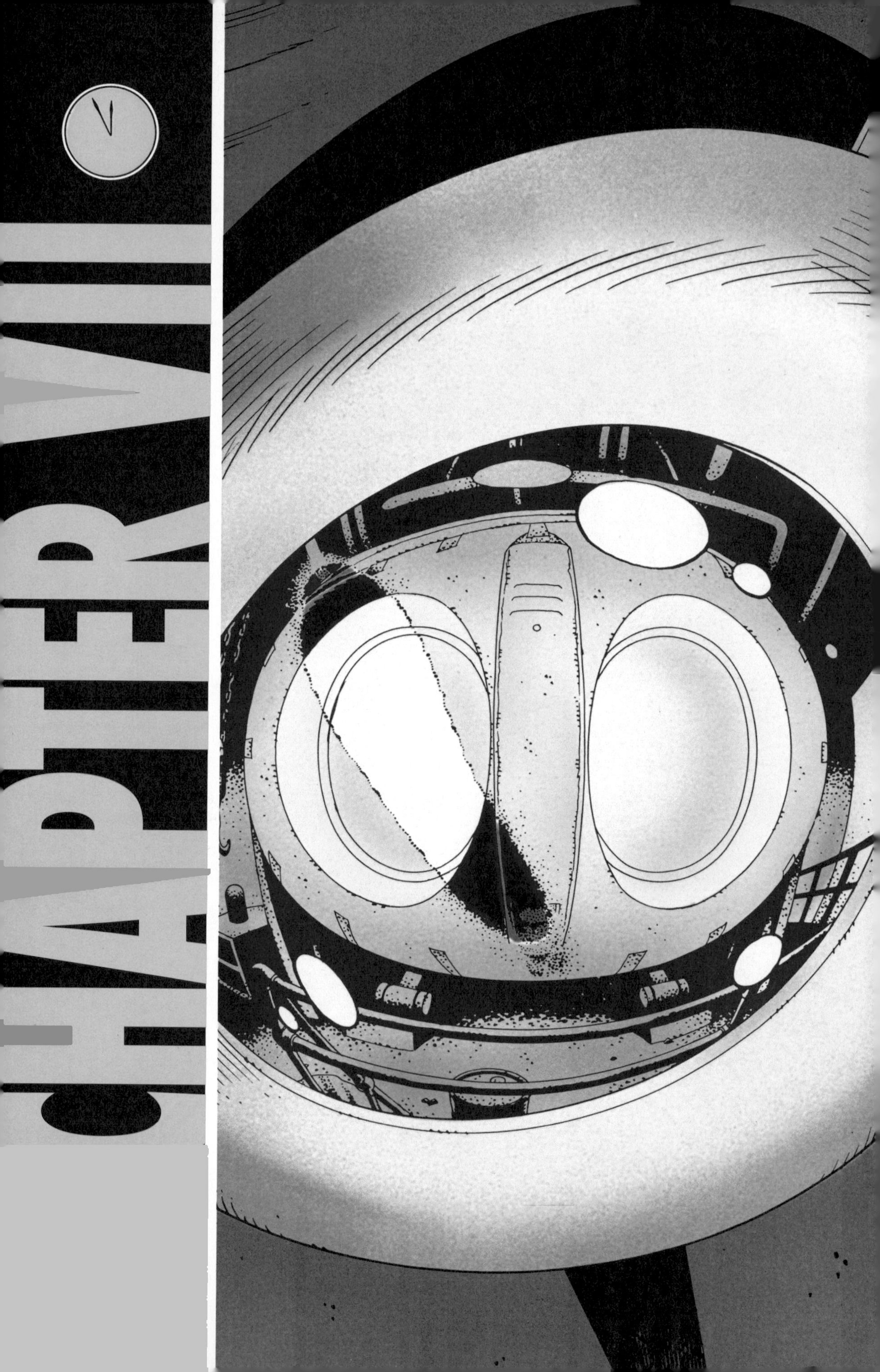

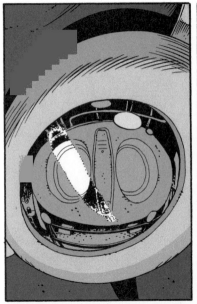

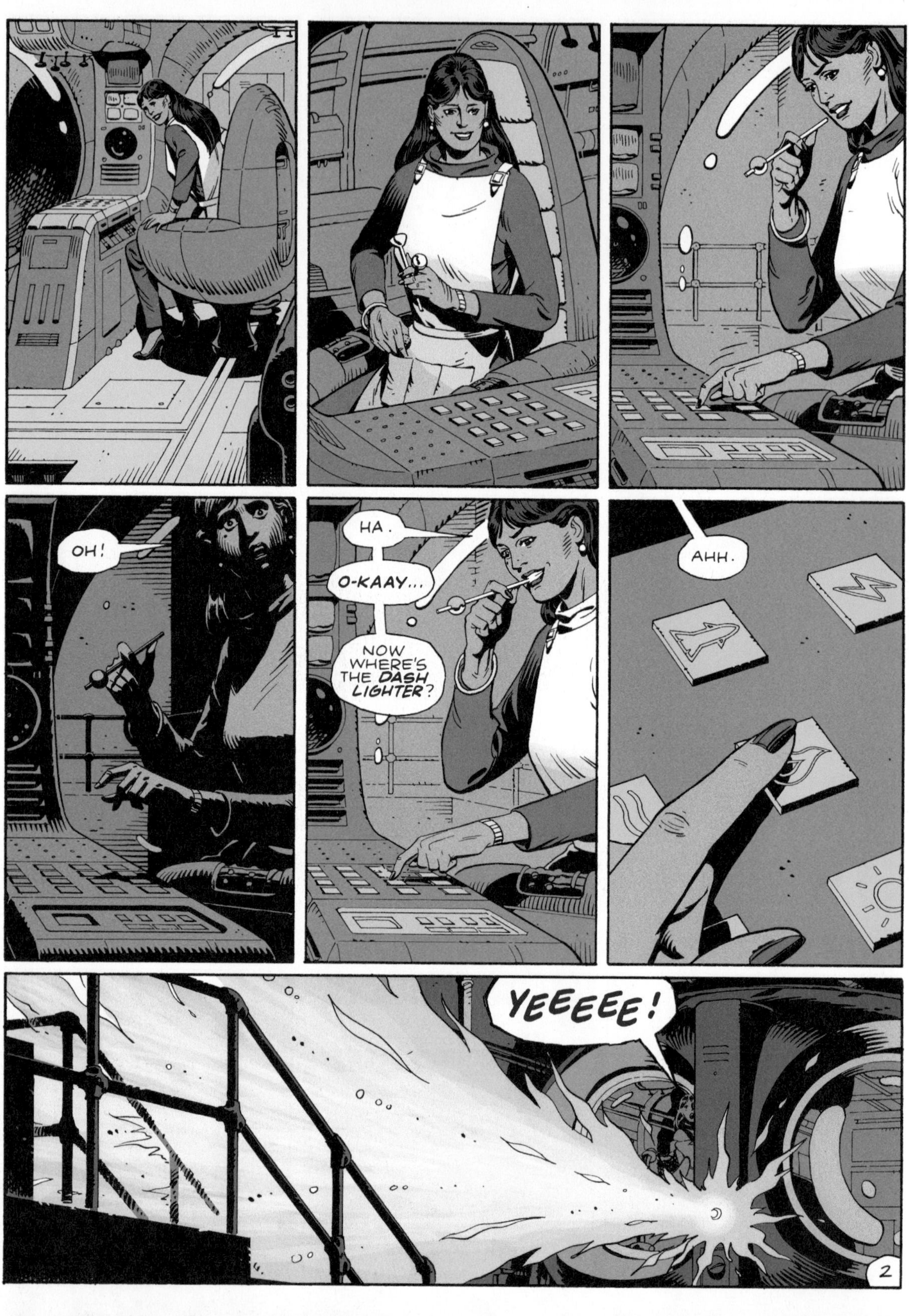
OH!
HA.
O-KAAY...
NOW WHERE'S THE DASH LIGHTER?
AHH.
YEEEEE!
2

A BROTHER TO DRAGONS

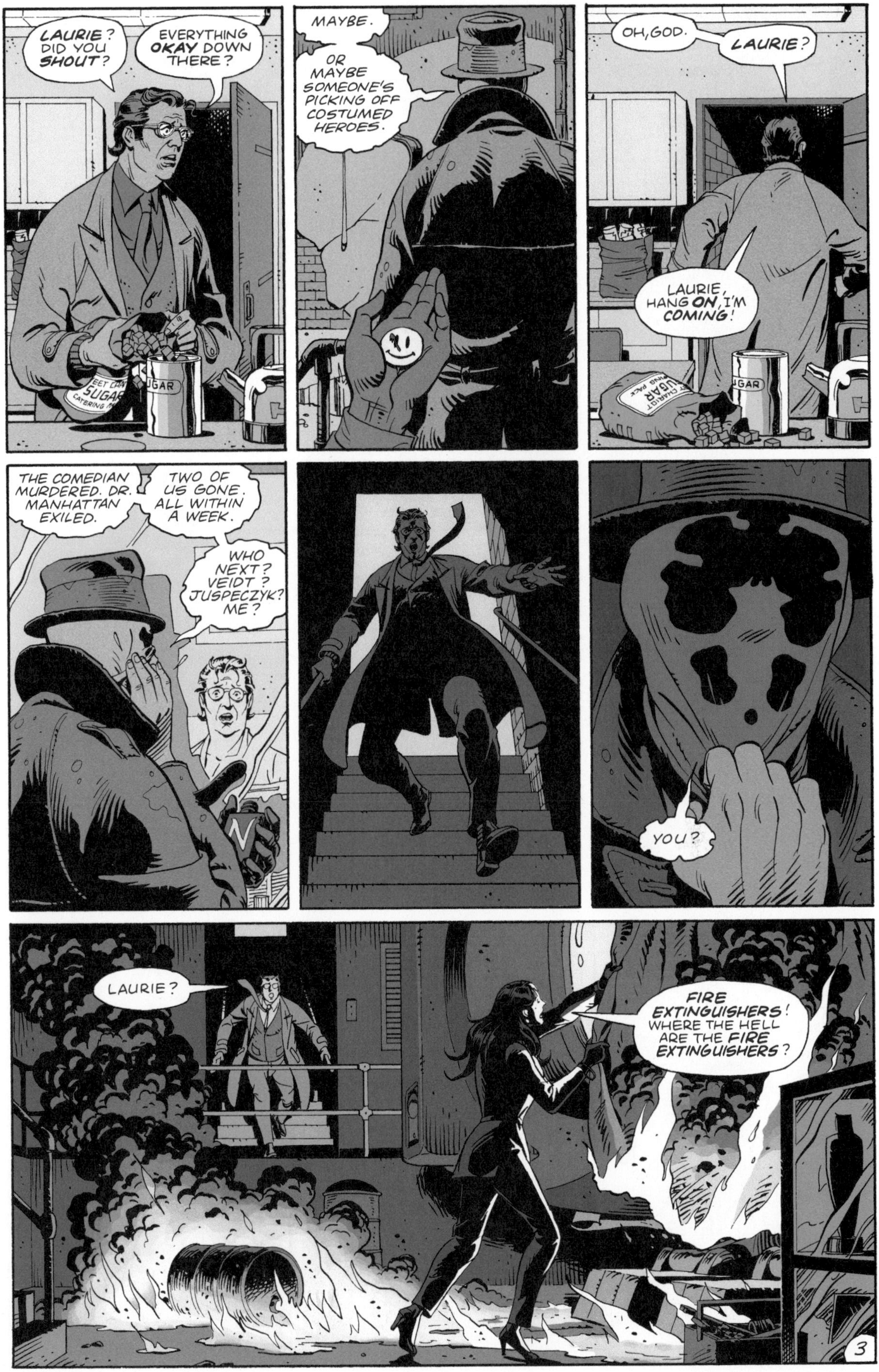
LAURIE? DID YOU SHOUT?
EVERYTHING OKAY DOWN THERE?
SWEET CANE SUGAR CATERING PACK
SUGAR
MAYBE.
OR MAYBE SOMEONE'S PICKING OFF COSTUMED HEROES.
OH, GOD.
LAURIE?
LAURIE, HANG ON, I'M COMING!
SUGAR
THE COMEDIAN MURDERED. DR. MANHATTAN EXILED.
TWO OF US GONE. ALL WITHIN A WEEK.
WHO NEXT? VEIDT? JUSPECZYK? ME?
YOU?
LAURIE?
FIRE EXTINGUISHERS! WHERE THE HELL ARE THE FIRE EXTINGUISHERS?
3

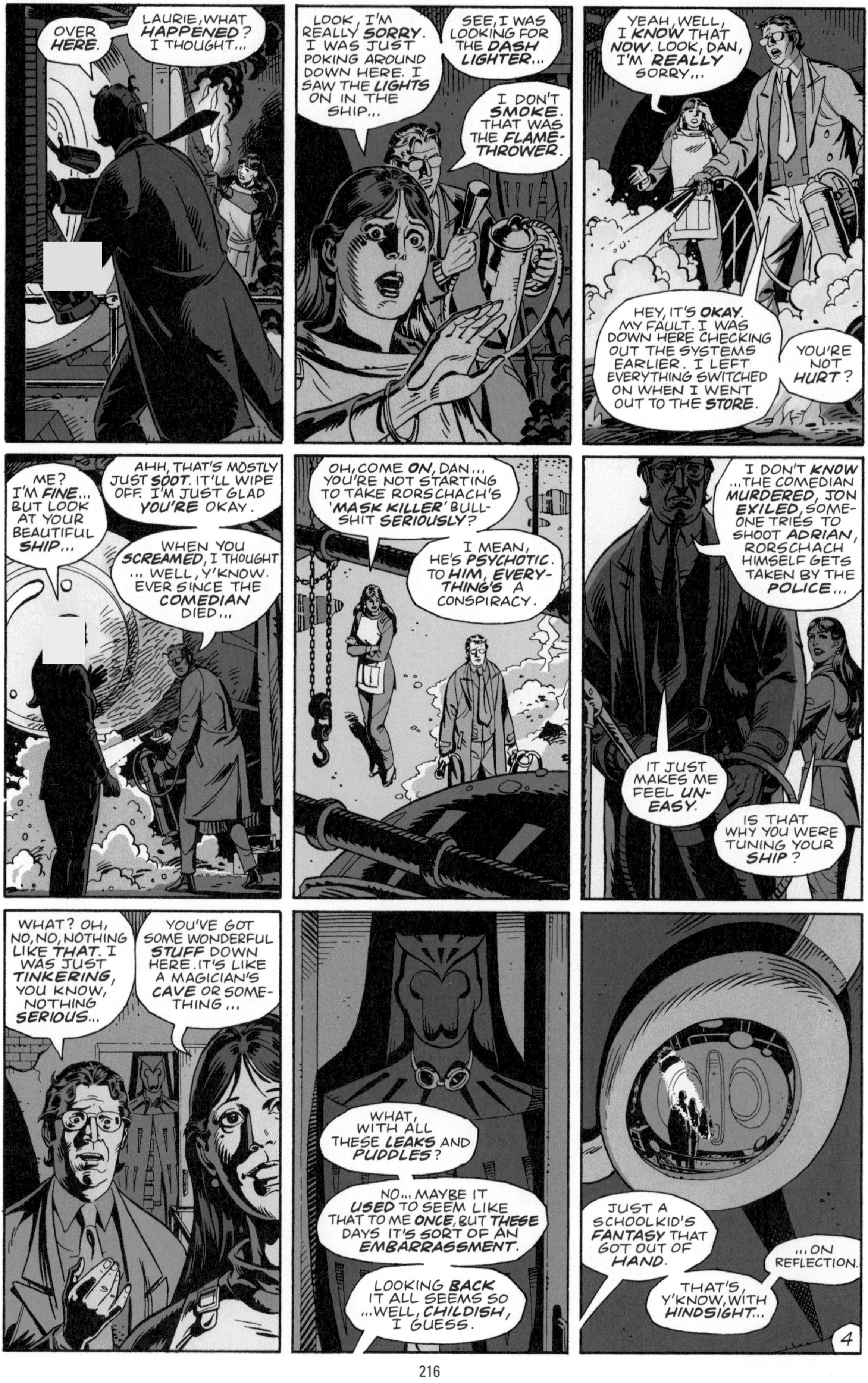

OVER HERE.
LAURIE, WHAT HAPPENED? I THOUGHT...
LOOK, I'M REALLY SORRY. I WAS JUST POKING AROUND DOWN HERE. I SAW THE LIGHTS ON IN THE SHIP...
SEE, I WAS LOOKING FOR THE DASH LIGHTER...
I DON'T SMOKE. THAT WAS THE FLAME-THROWER.
YEAH, WELL, I KNOW THAT NOW. LOOK, DAN, I'M REALLY SORRY...
HEY, IT'S OKAY. MY FAULT. I WAS DOWN HERE CHECKING OUT THE SYSTEMS EARLIER. I LEFT EVERYTHING SWITCHED ON WHEN I WENT OUT TO THE STORE.
YOU'RE NOT HURT?
ME? I'M FINE... BUT LOOK AT YOUR BEAUTIFUL SHIP...
AHH, THAT'S MOSTLY JUST SOOT. IT'LL WIPE OFF. I'M JUST GLAD YOU'RE OKAY.
WHEN YOU SCREAMED, I THOUGHT ... WELL, Y'KNOW. EVER SINCE THE COMEDIAN DIED...
OH, COME ON, DAN... YOU'RE NOT STARTING TO TAKE RORSCHACH'S 'MASK KILLER' BULL-SHIT SERIOUSLY?
I MEAN, HE'S PSYCHOTIC. TO HIM, EVERY-THING'S A CONSPIRACY.
I DON'T KNOW ...THE COMEDIAN MURDERED, JON EXILED, SOME-ONE TRIES TO SHOOT ADRIAN, RORSCHACH HIMSELF GETS TAKEN BY THE POLICE...
IT JUST MAKES ME FEEL UN-EASY.
IS THAT WHY YOU WERE TUNING YOUR SHIP?
WHAT? OH, NO, NO, NOTHING LIKE THAT. I WAS JUST TINKERING, YOU KNOW, NOTHING SERIOUS...
YOU'VE GOT SOME WONDERFUL STUFF DOWN HERE. IT'S LIKE A MAGICIAN'S CAVE OR SOME-THING...
WHAT, WITH ALL THESE LEAKS AND PUDDLES?
NO... MAYBE IT USED TO SEEM LIKE THAT TO ME ONCE, BUT THESE DAYS IT'S SORT OF AN EMBARRASSMENT.
LOOKING BACK IT ALL SEEMS SO ...WELL, CHILDISH, I GUESS.
JUST A SCHOOLKID'S FANTASY THAT GOT OUT OF HAND.
THAT'S, Y'KNOW, WITH HINDSIGHT...
...ON REFLECTION.
4

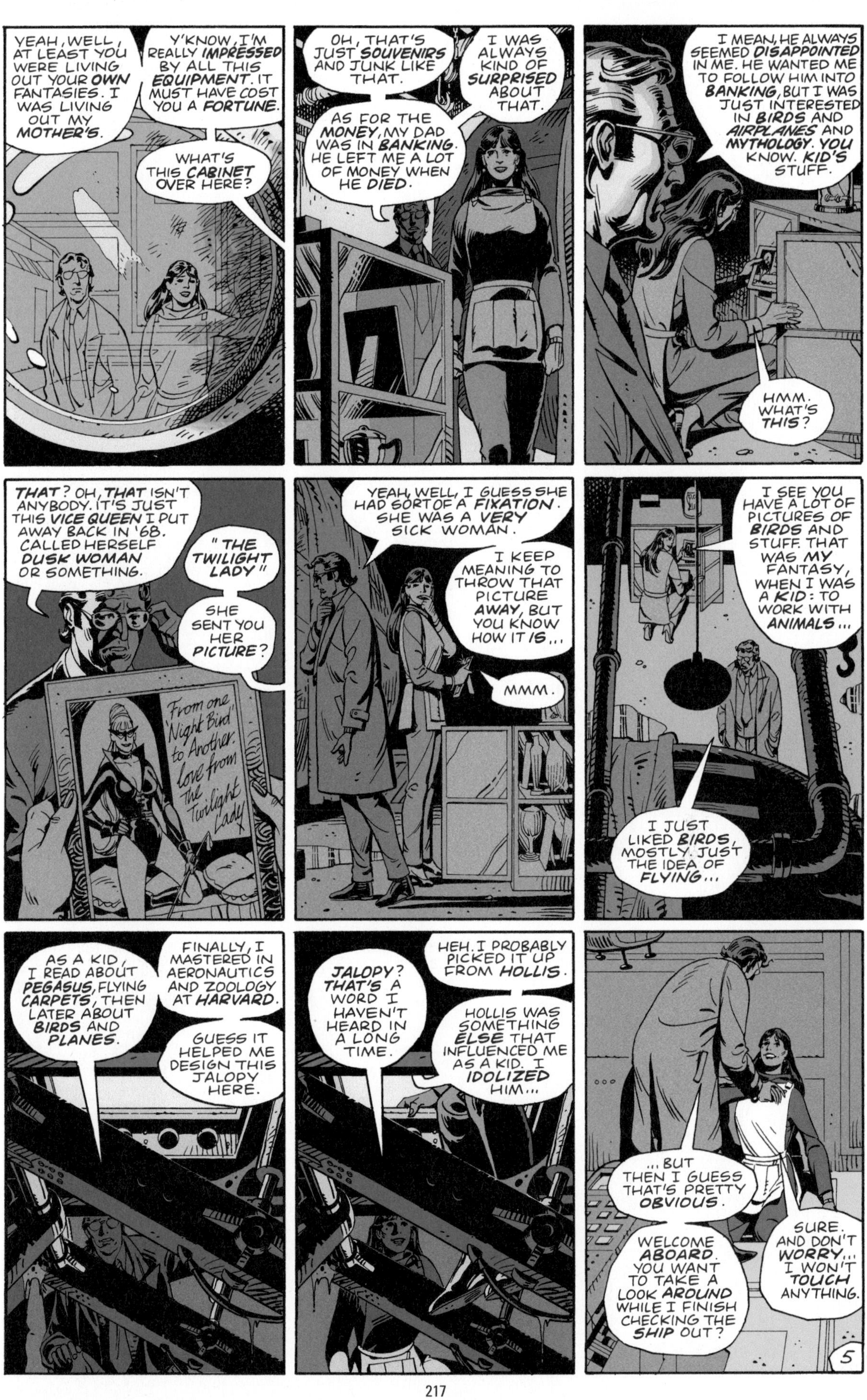

YEAH, WELL, AT LEAST YOU WERE LIVING OUT YOUR OWN FANTASIES. I WAS LIVING OUT MY MOTHER'S.
Y'KNOW, I'M REALLY IMPRESSED BY ALL THIS EQUIPMENT. IT MUST HAVE COST YOU A FORTUNE.
WHAT'S THIS CABINET OVER HERE?
OH, THAT'S JUST SOUVENIRS AND JUNK LIKE THAT.
AS FOR THE MONEY, MY DAD WAS IN BANKING. HE LEFT ME A LOT OF MONEY WHEN HE DIED.
I WAS ALWAYS KIND OF SURPRISED ABOUT THAT.
I MEAN, HE ALWAYS SEEMED DISAPPOINTED IN ME. HE WANTED ME TO FOLLOW HIM INTO BANKING, BUT I WAS JUST INTERESTED IN BIRDS AND AIRPLANES AND MYTHOLOGY. YOU KNOW. KID'S STUFF.
HMM. WHAT'S THIS?
THAT? OH, THAT ISN'T ANYBODY. IT'S JUST THIS VICE QUEEN I PUT AWAY BACK IN '68. CALLED HERSELF DUSK WOMAN OR SOMETHING.
"THE TWILIGHT LADY"
SHE SENT YOU HER PICTURE?
From one 'Night Bird' to Another. love from The Twilight Lady
YEAH, WELL, I GUESS SHE HAD SORT OF A FIXATION. SHE WAS A VERY SICK WOMAN.
I KEEP MEANING TO THROW THAT PICTURE AWAY, BUT YOU KNOW HOW IT IS...
MMM.
I SEE YOU HAVE A LOT OF PICTURES OF BIRDS AND STUFF. THAT WAS MY FANTASY, WHEN I WAS A KID: TO WORK WITH ANIMALS...
I JUST LIKED BIRDS, MOSTLY. JUST THE IDEA OF FLYING...
AS A KID, I READ ABOUT PEGASUS, FLYING CARPETS, THEN LATER ABOUT BIRDS AND PLANES.
FINALLY, I MASTERED IN AERONAUTICS AND ZOOLOGY AT HARVARD.
GUESS IT HELPED ME DESIGN THIS JALOPY HERE.
JALOPY? THAT'S A WORD I HAVEN'T HEARD IN A LONG TIME.
HEH. I PROBABLY PICKED IT UP FROM HOLLIS.
HOLLIS WAS SOMETHING ELSE THAT INFLUENCED ME AS A KID. I IDOLIZED HIM...
...BUT THEN I GUESS THAT'S PRETTY OBVIOUS.
WELCOME ABOARD. YOU WANT TO TAKE A LOOK AROUND WHILE I FINISH CHECKING THE SHIP OUT?
SURE. AND DON'T WORRY... I WON'T TOUCH ANYTHING.
5

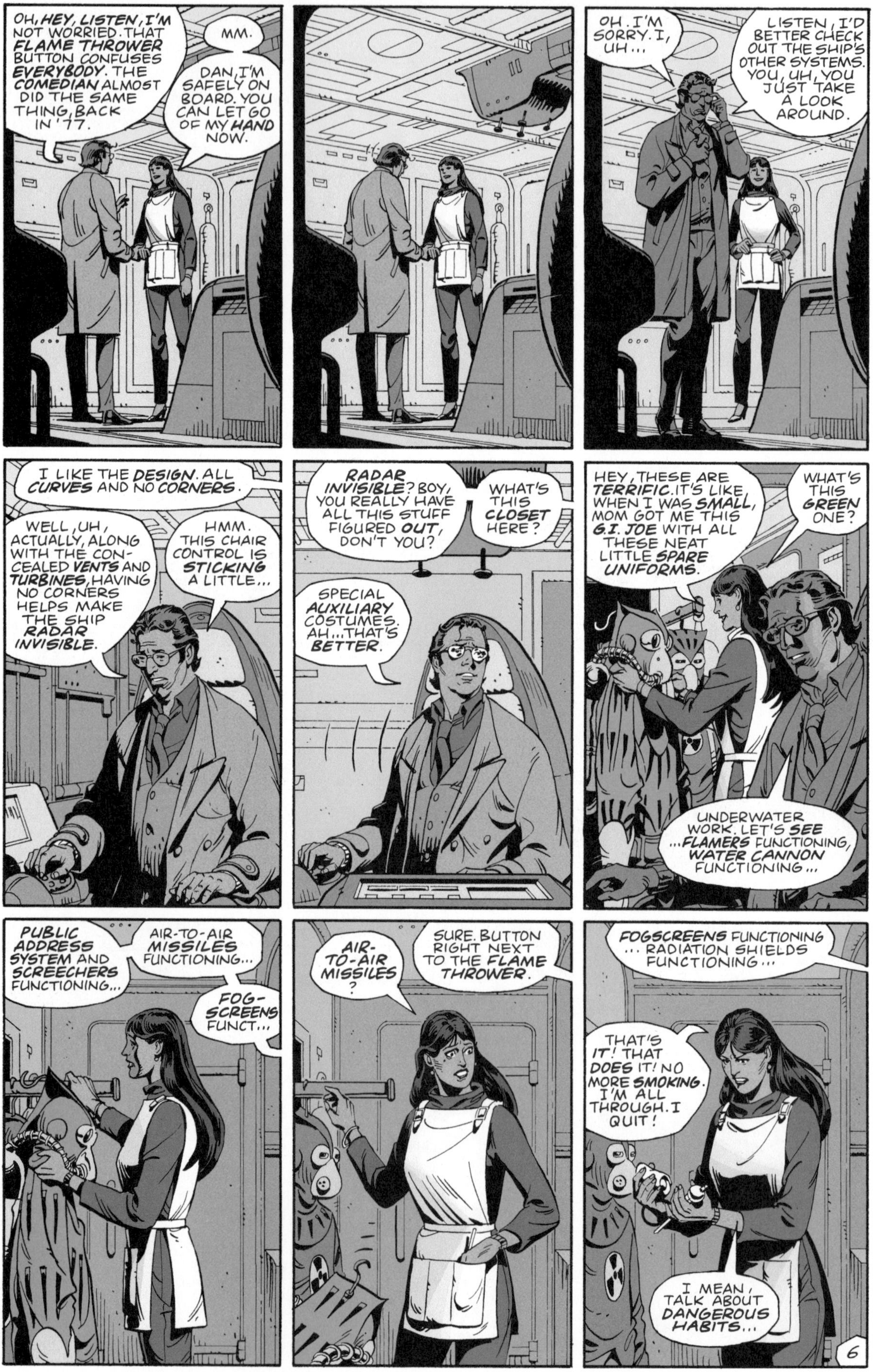
OH, HEY, LISTEN, I'M NOT WORRIED. THAT FLAME THROWER BUTTON CONFUSES EVERYBODY. THE COMEDIAN ALMOST DID THE SAME THING, BACK IN '77.
MM.
DAN, I'M SAFELY ON BOARD. YOU CAN LET GO OF MY HAND NOW.
OH. I'M SORRY. I, UH...
LISTEN, I'D BETTER CHECK OUT THE SHIP'S OTHER SYSTEMS. YOU, UH, YOU JUST TAKE A LOOK AROUND.
I LIKE THE DESIGN. ALL CURVES AND NO CORNERS.
WELL, UH, ACTUALLY, ALONG WITH THE CONCEALED VENTS AND TURBINES, HAVING NO CORNERS HELPS MAKE THE SHIP RADAR INVISIBLE.
HMM. THIS CHAIR CONTROL IS STICKING A LITTLE...
RADAR INVISIBLE? BOY, YOU REALLY HAVE ALL THIS STUFF FIGURED OUT, DON'T YOU?
WHAT'S THIS CLOSET HERE?
SPECIAL AUXILIARY COSTUMES. AH... THAT'S BETTER.
HEY, THESE ARE TERRIFIC. IT'S LIKE, WHEN I WAS SMALL, MOM GOT ME THIS G.I. JOE WITH ALL THESE NEAT LITTLE SPARE UNIFORMS.
WHAT'S THIS GREEN ONE?
UNDERWATER WORK. LET'S SEE ...FLAMERS FUNCTIONING, WATER CANNON FUNCTIONING...
PUBLIC ADDRESS SYSTEM AND SCREECHERS FUNCTIONING...
AIR-TO-AIR MISSILES FUNCTIONING...
FOG-SCREENS FUNCT...
AIR-TO-AIR MISSILES?
SURE. BUTTON RIGHT NEXT TO THE FLAME THROWER.
FOGSCREENS FUNCTIONING ... RADIATION SHIELDS FUNCTIONING...
THAT'S IT! THAT DOES IT! NO MORE SMOKING. I'M ALL THROUGH. I QUIT!
I MEAN, TALK ABOUT DANGEROUS HABITS...
6

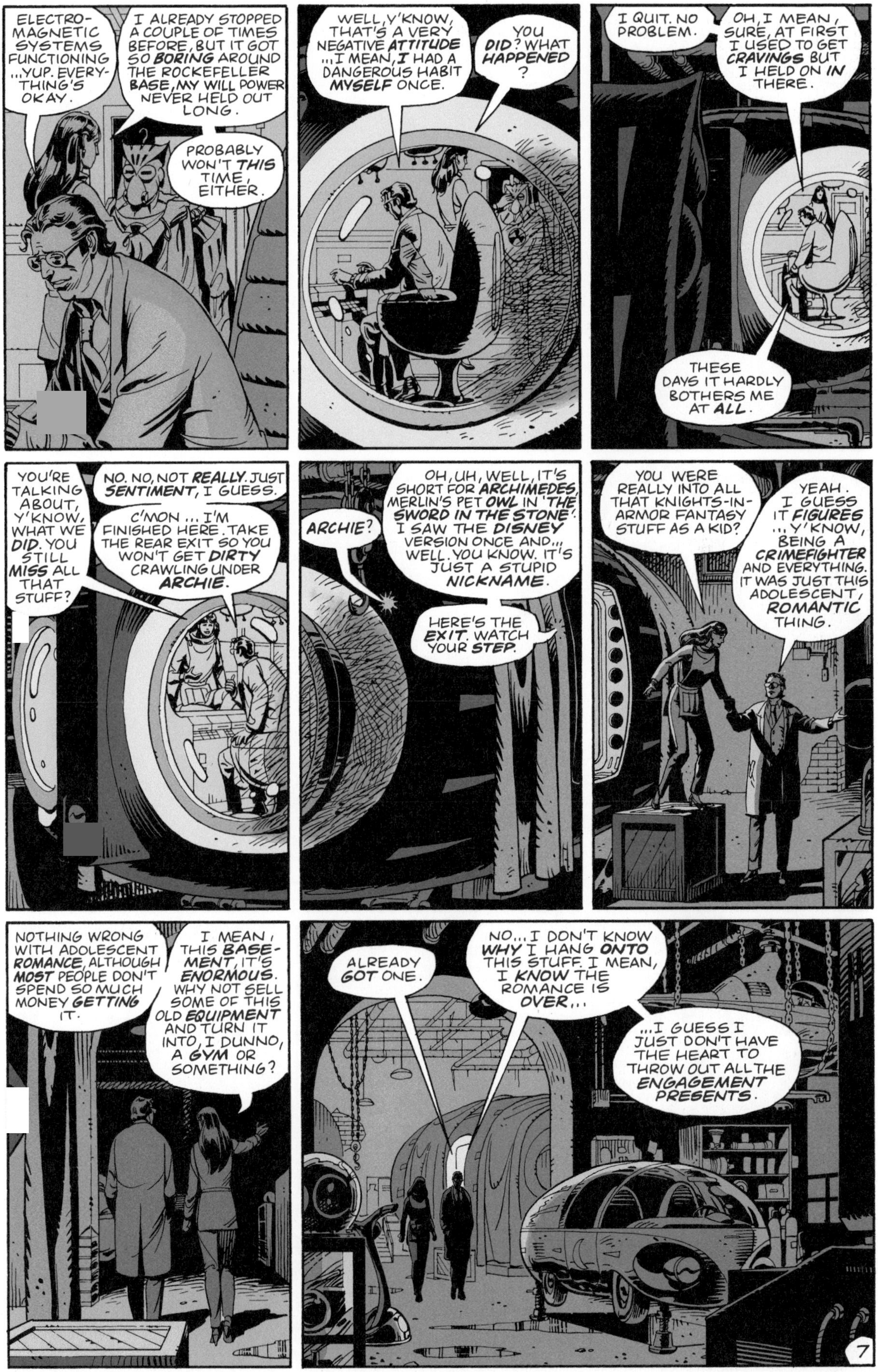
ELECTRO-MAGNETIC SYSTEMS FUNCTIONING ...YUP. EVERY-THING'S OKAY.
I ALREADY STOPPED A COUPLE OF TIMES BEFORE, BUT IT GOT SO BORING AROUND THE ROCKEFELLER BASE, MY WILL POWER NEVER HELD OUT LONG.
PROBABLY WON'T THIS TIME, EITHER.
WELL, Y'KNOW, THAT'S A VERY NEGATIVE ATTITUDE ...I MEAN, I HAD A DANGEROUS HABIT MYSELF ONCE.
YOU DID? WHAT HAPPENED ?
I QUIT. NO PROBLEM.
OH, I MEAN, SURE, AT FIRST I USED TO GET CRAVINGS BUT I HELD ON IN THERE.
THESE DAYS IT HARDLY BOTHERS ME AT ALL.
YOU'RE TALKING ABOUT, Y'KNOW, WHAT WE DID. YOU STILL MISS ALL THAT STUFF?
NO. NO, NOT REALLY. JUST SENTIMENT, I GUESS.
C'MON ... I'M FINISHED HERE. TAKE THE REAR EXIT SO YOU WON'T GET DIRTY CRAWLING UNDER ARCHIE.
ARCHIE?
OH, UH, WELL, IT'S SHORT FOR ARCHIMEDES, MERLIN'S PET OWL IN 'THE SWORD IN THE STONE'. I SAW THE DISNEY VERSION ONCE AND... WELL. YOU KNOW. IT'S JUST A STUPID NICKNAME.
HERE'S THE EXIT. WATCH YOUR STEP.
YOU WERE REALLY INTO ALL THAT KNIGHTS-IN-ARMOR FANTASY STUFF AS A KID?
YEAH. I GUESS IT FIGURES ...Y'KNOW, BEING A CRIMEFIGHTER AND EVERYTHING. IT WAS JUST THIS ADOLESCENT, ROMANTIC THING.
NOTHING WRONG WITH ADOLESCENT ROMANCE, ALTHOUGH MOST PEOPLE DON'T SPEND SO MUCH MONEY GETTING IT.
I MEAN, THIS BASEMENT, IT'S ENORMOUS. WHY NOT SELL SOME OF THIS OLD EQUIPMENT AND TURN IT INTO, I DUNNO, A GYM OR SOMETHING?
ALREADY GOT ONE.
NO... I DON'T KNOW WHY I HANG ONTO THIS STUFF. I MEAN, I KNOW THE ROMANCE IS OVER...
...I GUESS I JUST DON'T HAVE THE HEART TO THROW OUT ALL THE ENGAGEMENT PRESENTS.
7

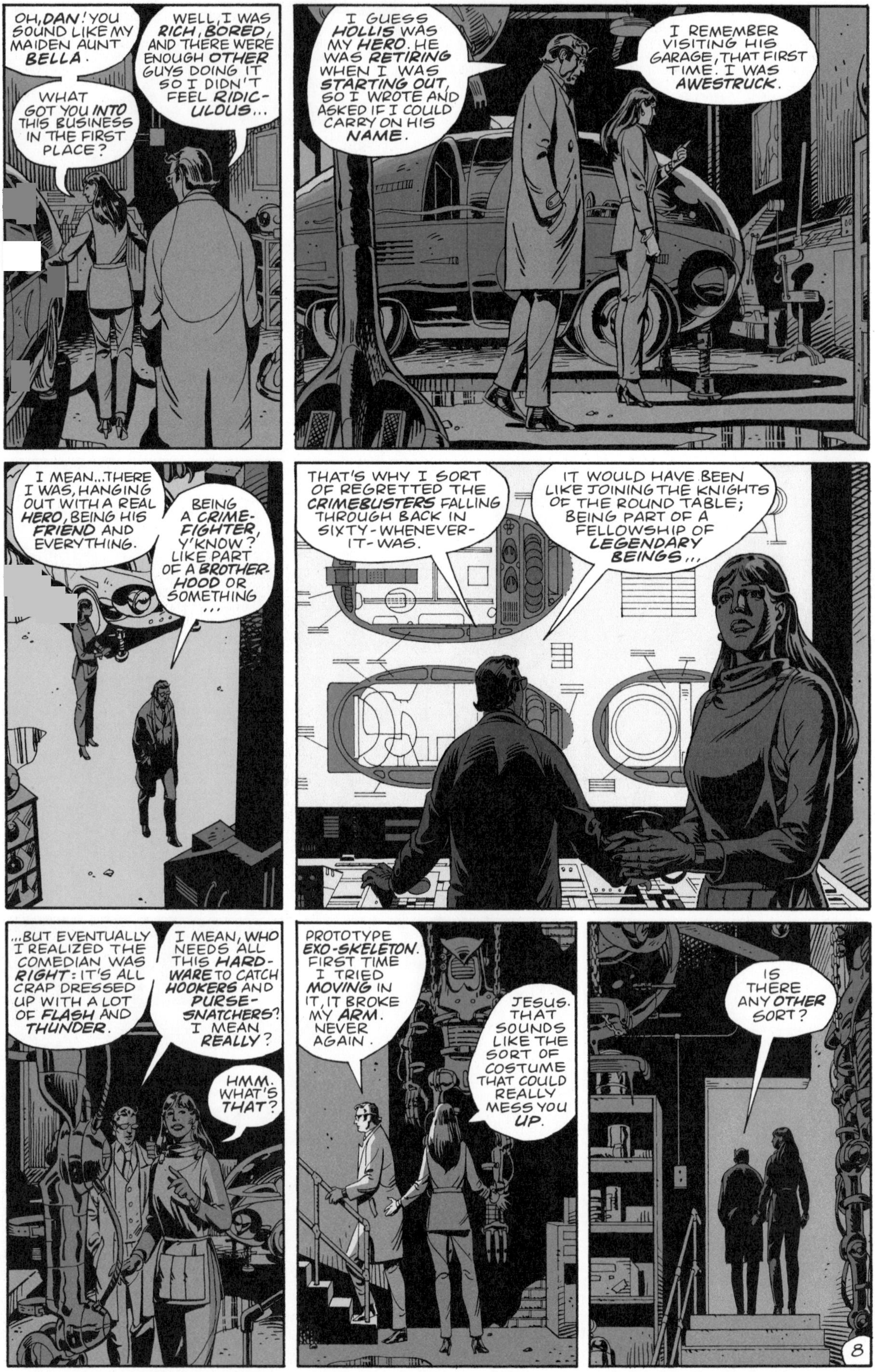

OH, DAN! YOU SOUND LIKE MY MAIDEN AUNT BELLA.
WHAT GOT YOU INTO THIS BUSINESS IN THE FIRST PLACE?
WELL, I WAS RICH, BORED, AND THERE WERE ENOUGH OTHER GUYS DOING IT SO I DIDN'T FEEL RIDICULOUS...
I GUESS HOLLIS WAS MY HERO. HE WAS RETIRING WHEN I WAS STARTING OUT, SO I WROTE AND ASKED IF I COULD CARRY ON HIS NAME.
I REMEMBER VISITING HIS GARAGE, THAT FIRST TIME. I WAS AWESTRUCK.
I MEAN...THERE I WAS, HANGING OUT WITH A REAL HERO, BEING HIS FRIEND AND EVERYTHING.
BEING A CRIME-FIGHTER, Y'KNOW? LIKE PART OF A BROTHERHOOD OR SOMETHING...
THAT'S WHY I SORT OF REGRETTED THE CRIMEBUSTERS FALLING THROUGH BACK IN SIXTY-WHENEVER-IT-WAS.
IT WOULD HAVE BEEN LIKE JOINING THE KNIGHTS OF THE ROUND TABLE; BEING PART OF A FELLOWSHIP OF LEGENDARY BEINGS...
...BUT EVENTUALLY I REALIZED THE COMEDIAN WAS RIGHT: IT'S ALL CRAP DRESSED UP WITH A LOT OF FLASH AND THUNDER.
I MEAN, WHO NEEDS ALL THIS HARDWARE TO CATCH HOOKERS AND PURSE-SNATCHERS? I MEAN REALLY?
HMM. WHAT'S THAT?
PROTOTYPE EXO-SKELETON. FIRST TIME I TRIED MOVING IN IT, IT BROKE MY ARM. NEVER AGAIN.
JESUS. THAT SOUNDS LIKE THE SORT OF COSTUME THAT COULD REALLY MESS YOU UP.
IS THERE ANY OTHER SORT?
8

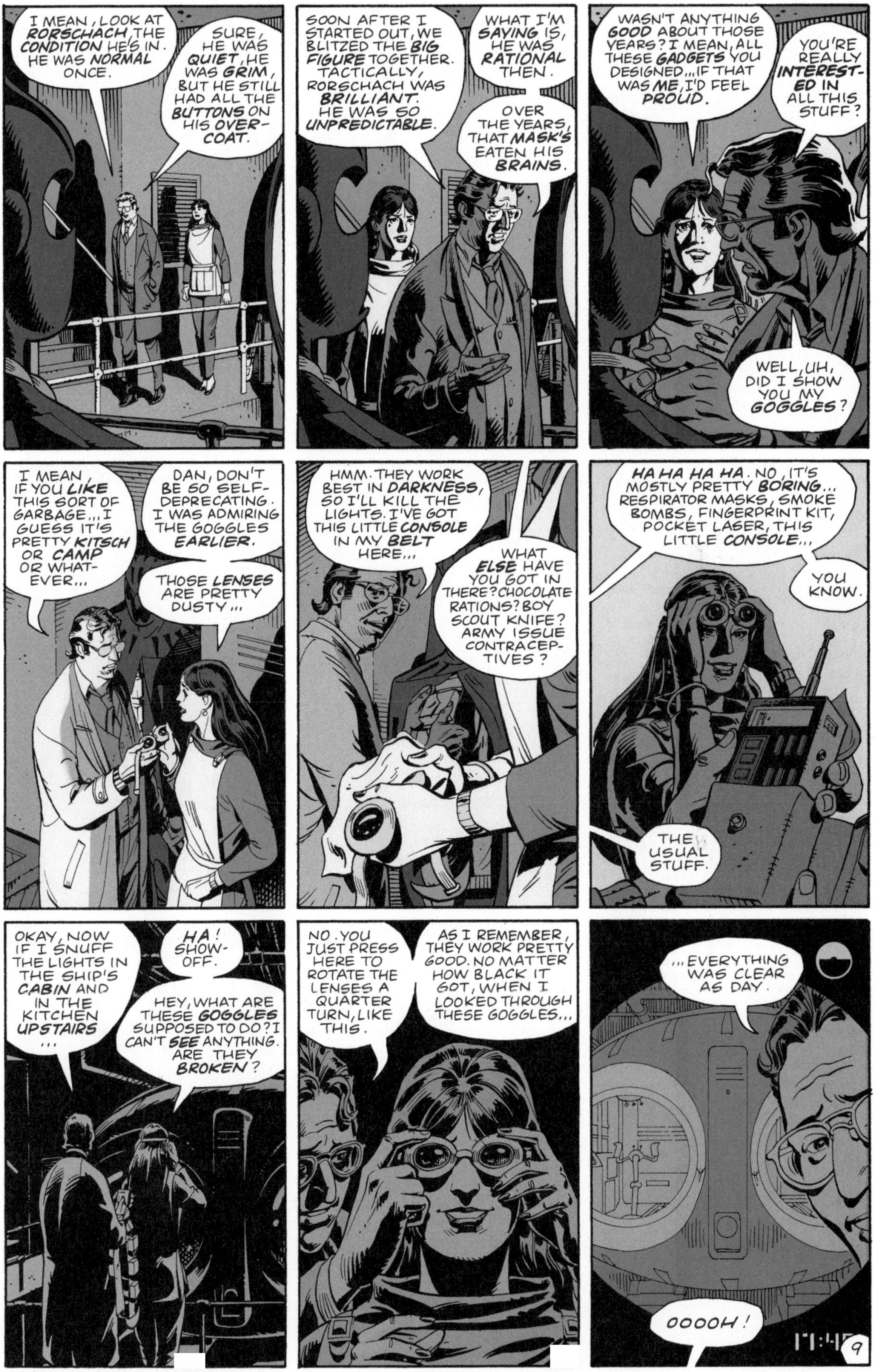
I MEAN, LOOK AT RORSCHACH, THE CONDITION HE'S IN. HE WAS NORMAL ONCE.
SURE, HE WAS QUIET, HE WAS GRIM, BUT HE STILL HAD ALL THE BUTTONS ON HIS OVERCOAT.
SOON AFTER I STARTED OUT, WE BLITZED THE BIG FIGURE TOGETHER. TACTICALLY, RORSCHACH WAS BRILLIANT. HE WAS SO UNPREDICTABLE.
WHAT I'M SAYING IS, HE WAS RATIONAL THEN.
OVER THE YEARS, THAT MASK'S EATEN HIS BRAINS.
WASN'T ANYTHING GOOD ABOUT THOSE YEARS? I MEAN, ALL THESE GADGETS YOU DESIGNED... IF THAT WAS ME, I'D FEEL PROUD.
YOU'RE REALLY INTERESTED IN ALL THIS STUFF?
WELL, UH, DID I SHOW YOU MY GOGGLES?
I MEAN, IF YOU LIKE THIS SORT OF GARBAGE... I GUESS IT'S PRETTY KITSCH OR CAMP OR WHATEVER...
DAN, DON'T BE SO SELF-DEPRECATING. I WAS ADMIRING THE GOGGLES EARLIER.
THOSE LENSES ARE PRETTY DUSTY...
HMM. THEY WORK BEST IN DARKNESS, SO I'LL KILL THE LIGHTS. I'VE GOT THIS LITTLE CONSOLE IN MY BELT HERE...
WHAT ELSE HAVE YOU GOT IN THERE? CHOCOLATE RATIONS? BOY SCOUT KNIFE? ARMY ISSUE CONTRACEPTIVES?
HA HA HA HA. NO, IT'S MOSTLY PRETTY BORING... RESPIRATOR MASKS, SMOKE BOMBS, FINGERPRINT KIT, POCKET LASER, THIS LITTLE CONSOLE...
YOU KNOW.
THE USUAL STUFF.
OKAY, NOW IF I SNUFF THE LIGHTS IN THE SHIP'S CABIN AND IN THE KITCHEN UPSTAIRS...
HA! SHOW-OFF.
HEY, WHAT ARE THESE GOGGLES SUPPOSED TO DO? I CAN'T SEE ANYTHING. ARE THEY BROKEN?
NO. YOU JUST PRESS HERE TO ROTATE THE LENSES A QUARTER TURN, LIKE THIS.
AS I REMEMBER, THEY WORK PRETTY GOOD. NO MATTER HOW BLACK IT GOT, WHEN I LOOKED THROUGH THESE GOGGLES...
...EVERYTHING WAS CLEAR AS DAY.
OOOOH!
11:45
9

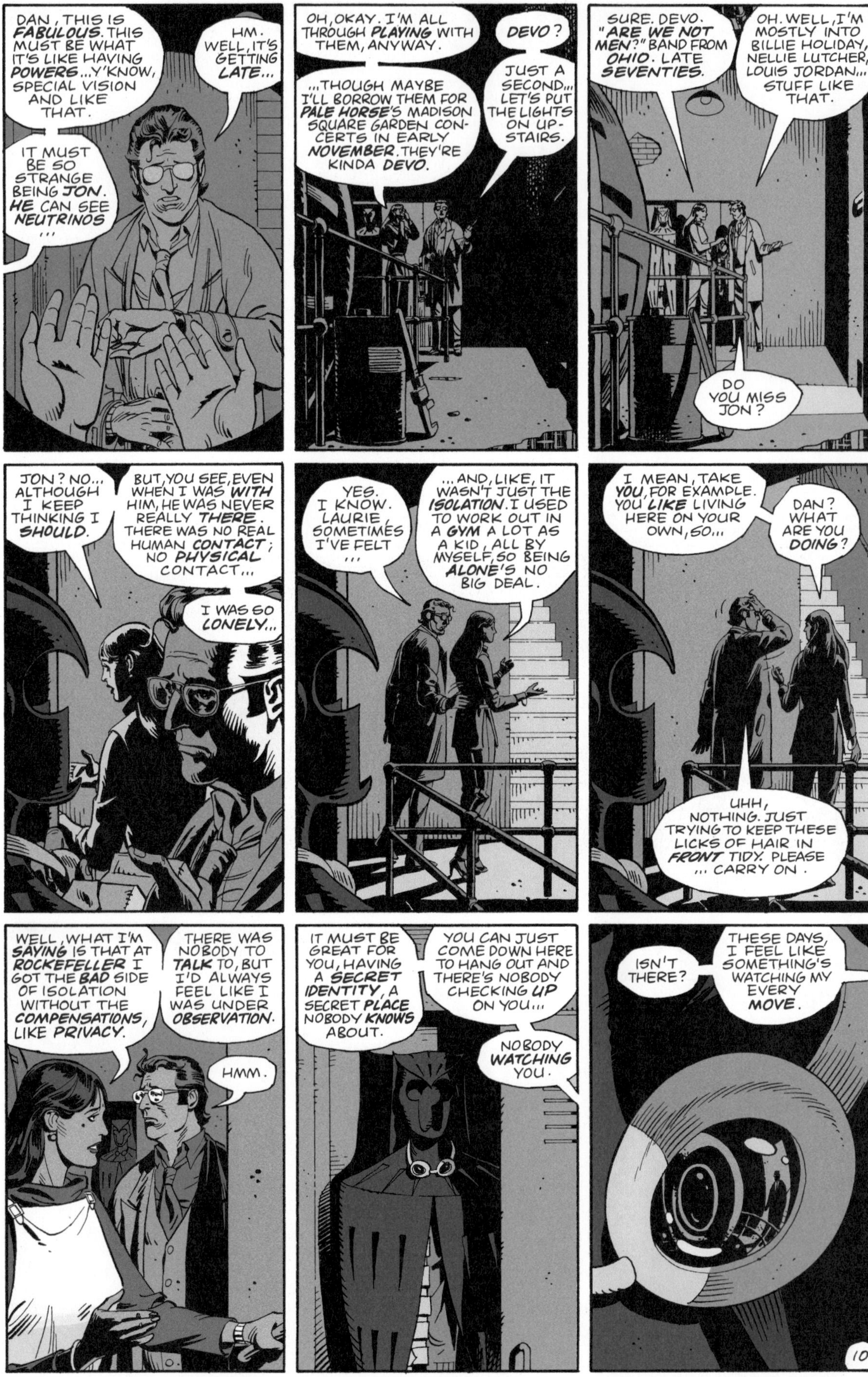
DAN, THIS IS FABULOUS. THIS MUST BE WHAT IT'S LIKE HAVING POWERS... Y'KNOW, SPECIAL VISION AND LIKE THAT.
HM. WELL, IT'S GETTING LATE...
IT MUST BE SO STRANGE BEING JON. HE CAN SEE NEUTRINOS ...
OH, OKAY. I'M ALL THROUGH PLAYING WITH THEM, ANYWAY.
...THOUGH MAYBE I'LL BORROW THEM FOR PALE HORSE'S MADISON SQUARE GARDEN CONCERTS IN EARLY NOVEMBER. THEY'RE KINDA DEVO.
DEVO?
JUST A SECOND... LET'S PUT THE LIGHTS ON UPSTAIRS.
SURE. DEVO. "ARE WE NOT MEN?" BAND FROM OHIO. LATE SEVENTIES.
OH. WELL, I'M MOSTLY INTO BILLIE HOLIDAY, NELLIE LUTCHER, LOUIS JORDAN... STUFF LIKE THAT.
DO YOU MISS JON?
JON? NO... ALTHOUGH I KEEP THINKING I SHOULD.
BUT, YOU SEE, EVEN WHEN I WAS WITH HIM, HE WAS NEVER REALLY THERE. THERE WAS NO REAL HUMAN CONTACT; NO PHYSICAL CONTACT...
I WAS SO LONELY...
YES. I KNOW. LAURIE, SOMETIMES I'VE FELT ...
... AND, LIKE, IT WASN'T JUST THE ISOLATION. I USED TO WORK OUT IN A GYM A LOT AS A KID, ALL BY MYSELF, SO BEING ALONE'S NO BIG DEAL.
I MEAN, TAKE YOU, FOR EXAMPLE. YOU LIKE LIVING HERE ON YOUR OWN, SO...
DAN? WHAT ARE YOU DOING?
UHH, NOTHING. JUST TRYING TO KEEP THESE LICKS OF HAIR IN FRONT TIDY. PLEASE ... CARRY ON.
WELL, WHAT I'M SAYING IS THAT AT ROCKEFELLER I GOT THE BAD SIDE OF ISOLATION WITHOUT THE COMPENSATIONS, LIKE PRIVACY.
THERE WAS NOBODY TO TALK TO, BUT I'D ALWAYS FEEL LIKE I WAS UNDER OBSERVATION.
HMM.
IT MUST BE GREAT FOR YOU, HAVING A SECRET IDENTITY, A SECRET PLACE NOBODY KNOWS ABOUT.
YOU CAN JUST COME DOWN HERE TO HANG OUT AND THERE'S NOBODY CHECKING UP ON YOU...
NOBODY WATCHING YOU.
THESE DAYS, I FEEL LIKE SOMETHING'S WATCHING MY EVERY MOVE.
ISN'T THERE?
10

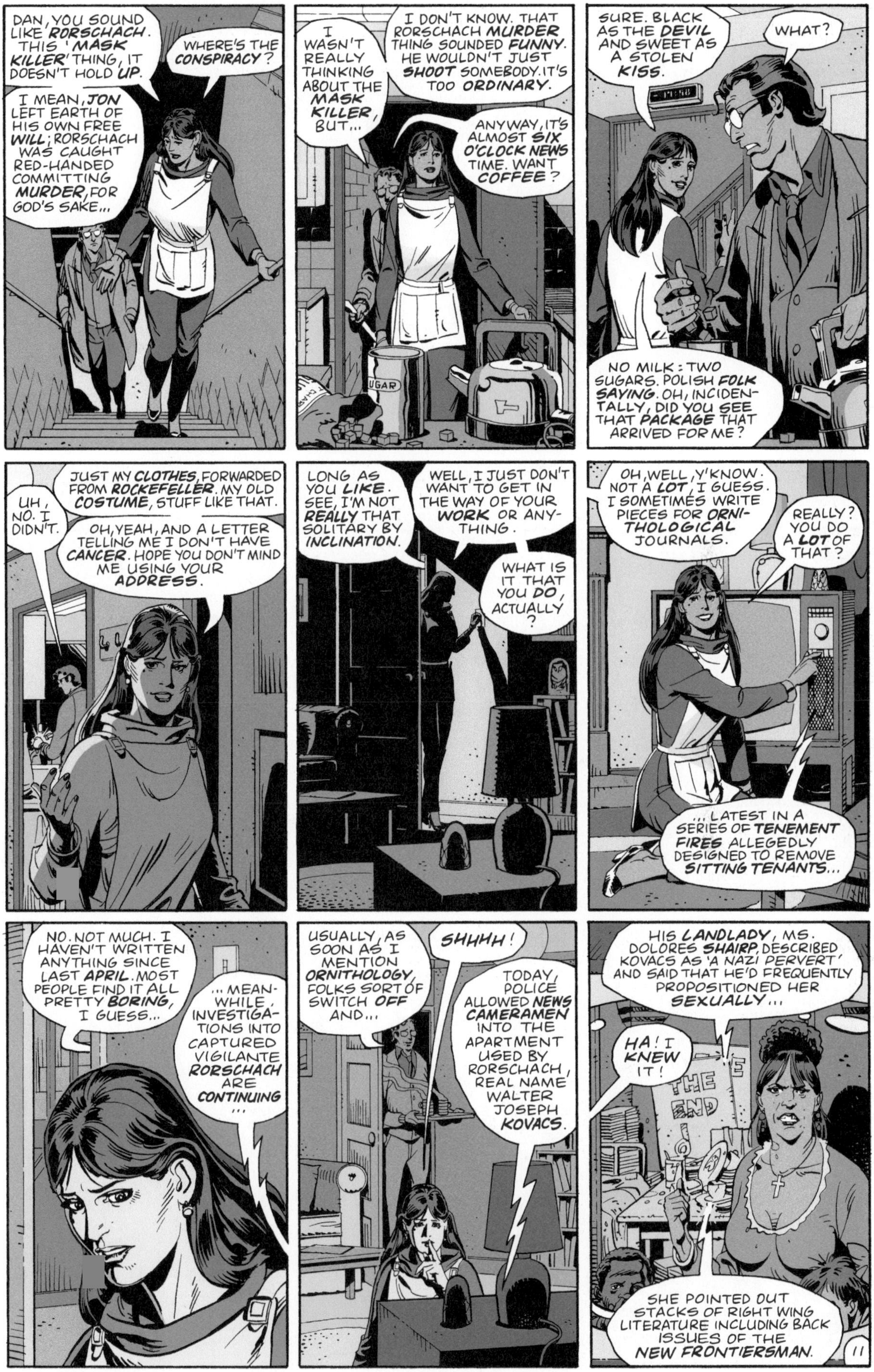
DAN, YOU SOUND LIKE RORSCHACH. THIS 'MASK KILLER' THING, IT DOESN'T HOLD UP.
WHERE'S THE CONSPIRACY?
I MEAN, JON LEFT EARTH OF HIS OWN FREE WILL; RORSCHACH WAS CAUGHT RED-HANDED COMMITTING MURDER, FOR GOD'S SAKE...
I WASN'T REALLY THINKING ABOUT THE MASK KILLER, BUT...
I DON'T KNOW. THAT RORSCHACH MURDER THING SOUNDED FUNNY. HE WOULDN'T JUST SHOOT SOMEBODY. IT'S TOO ORDINARY.
ANYWAY, IT'S ALMOST SIX O'CLOCK NEWS TIME. WANT COFFEE?
SUGAR
SURE. BLACK AS THE DEVIL AND SWEET AS A STOLEN KISS.
WHAT?
NO MILK: TWO SUGARS. POLISH FOLK SAYING. OH, INCIDENTALLY, DID YOU SEE THAT PACKAGE THAT ARRIVED FOR ME?
UH, NO. I DIDN'T.
JUST MY CLOTHES, FORWARDED FROM ROCKEFELLER. MY OLD COSTUME, STUFF LIKE THAT.
OH, YEAH, AND A LETTER TELLING ME I DON'T HAVE CANCER. HOPE YOU DON'T MIND ME USING YOUR ADDRESS.
LONG AS YOU LIKE. SEE, I'M NOT REALLY THAT SOLITARY BY INCLINATION.
WELL, I JUST DON'T WANT TO GET IN THE WAY OF YOUR WORK OR ANYTHING.
WHAT IS IT THAT YOU DO, ACTUALLY?
OH, WELL, Y'KNOW. NOT A LOT, I GUESS. I SOMETIMES WRITE PIECES FOR ORNITHOLOGICAL JOURNALS.
REALLY? YOU DO A LOT OF THAT?
...LATEST IN A SERIES OF TENEMENT FIRES ALLEGEDLY DESIGNED TO REMOVE SITTING TENANTS...
NO. NOT MUCH. I HAVEN'T WRITTEN ANYTHING SINCE LAST APRIL. MOST PEOPLE FIND IT ALL PRETTY BORING, I GUESS...
...MEANWHILE, INVESTIGATIONS INTO CAPTURED VIGILANTE RORSCHACH ARE CONTINUING...
USUALLY, AS SOON AS I MENTION ORNITHOLOGY, FOLKS SORT OF SWITCH OFF AND...
SHHHH!
TODAY, POLICE ALLOWED NEWS CAMERAMEN INTO THE APARTMENT USED BY RORSCHACH, REAL NAME WALTER JOSEPH KOVACS.
HIS LANDLADY, MS. DOLORES SHAIRP, DESCRIBED KOVACS AS 'A NAZI PERVERT' AND SAID THAT HE'D FREQUENTLY PROPOSITIONED HER SEXUALLY...
HA! I KNEW IT!
THE END
SHE POINTED OUT STACKS OF RIGHT WING LITERATURE INCLUDING BACK ISSUES OF THE NEW FRONTIERSMAN.
11

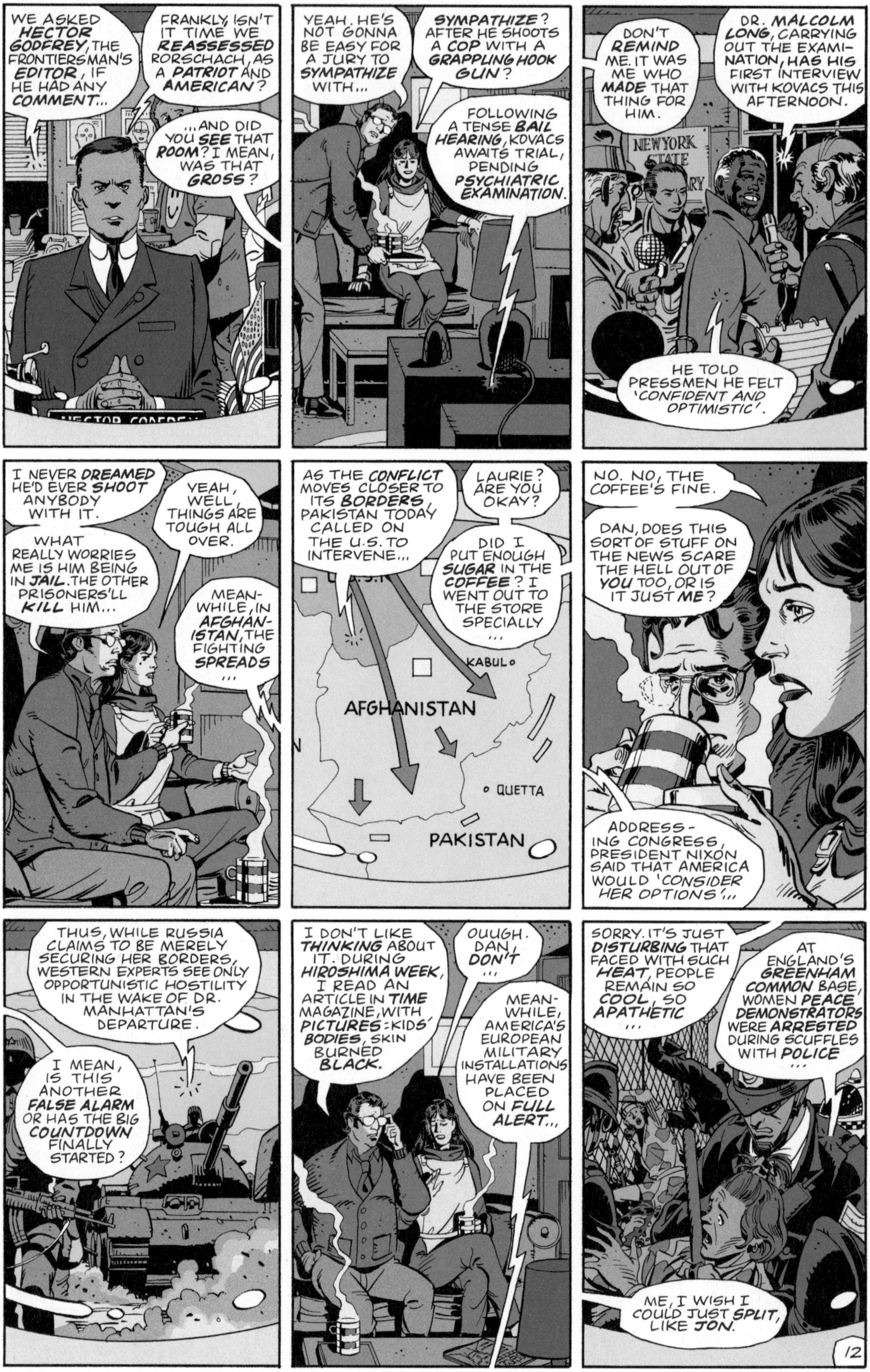
WE ASKED HECTOR GODFREY, THE FRONTIERSMAN'S EDITOR, IF HE HAD ANY COMMENT...
FRANKLY, ISN'T IT TIME WE REASSESSED RORSCHACH, AS A PATRIOT AND AMERICAN?
...AND DID YOU SEE THAT ROOM? I MEAN, WAS THAT GROSS?
YEAH. HE'S NOT GONNA BE EASY FOR A JURY TO SYMPATHIZE WITH...
SYMPATHIZE? AFTER HE SHOOTS A COP WITH A GRAPPLING HOOK GUN?
FOLLOWING A TENSE BAIL HEARING, KOVACS AWAITS TRIAL, PENDING PSYCHIATRIC EXAMINATION.
DON'T REMIND ME. IT WAS ME WHO MADE THAT THING FOR HIM.
DR. MALCOLM LONG, CARRYING OUT THE EXAMINATION, HAS HIS FIRST INTERVIEW WITH KOVACS THIS AFTERNOON.
NEW YORK
HE TOLD PRESSMEN HE FELT 'CONFIDENT AND OPTIMISTIC'.
I NEVER DREAMED HE'D EVER SHOOT ANYBODY WITH IT.
YEAH, WELL, THINGS ARE TOUGH ALL OVER.
WHAT REALLY WORRIES ME IS HIM BEING IN JAIL. THE OTHER PRISONERS'LL KILL HIM...
MEAN-WHILE, IN AFGHAN-ISTAN, THE FIGHTING SPREADS...
AS THE CONFLICT MOVES CLOSER TO ITS BORDERS, PAKISTAN TODAY CALLED ON THE U.S. TO INTERVENE...
LAURIE? ARE YOU OKAY?
DID I PUT ENOUGH SUGAR IN THE COFFEE? I WENT OUT TO THE STORE SPECIALLY...
KABUL
AFGHANISTAN
QUETTA
PAKISTAN
NO. NO, THE COFFEE'S FINE.
DAN, DOES THIS SORT OF STUFF ON THE NEWS SCARE THE HELL OUT OF YOU TOO, OR IS IT JUST ME?
ADDRESS-ING CONGRESS, PRESIDENT NIXON SAID THAT AMERICA WOULD 'CONSIDER HER OPTIONS'...
THUS, WHILE RUSSIA CLAIMS TO BE MERELY SECURING HER BORDERS, WESTERN EXPERTS SEE ONLY OPPORTUNISTIC HOSTILITY IN THE WAKE OF DR. MANHATTAN'S DEPARTURE.
I MEAN, IS THIS ANOTHER FALSE ALARM OR HAS THE BIG COUNTDOWN FINALLY STARTED?
I DON'T LIKE THINKING ABOUT IT. DURING HIROSHIMA WEEK, I READ AN ARTICLE IN TIME MAGAZINE, WITH PICTURES: KIDS' BODIES, SKIN BURNED BLACK.
OUUGH. DAN, DON'T...
MEAN-WHILE, AMERICA'S EUROPEAN MILITARY INSTALLATIONS HAVE BEEN PLACED ON FULL ALERT...
SORRY. IT'S JUST DISTURBING THAT FACED WITH SUCH HEAT, PEOPLE REMAIN SO COOL, SO APATHETIC...
AT ENGLAND'S GREENHAM COMMON BASE, WOMEN PEACE DEMONSTRATORS WERE ARRESTED DURING SCUFFLES WITH POLICE...
ME, I WISH I COULD JUST SPLIT, LIKE JON.
12

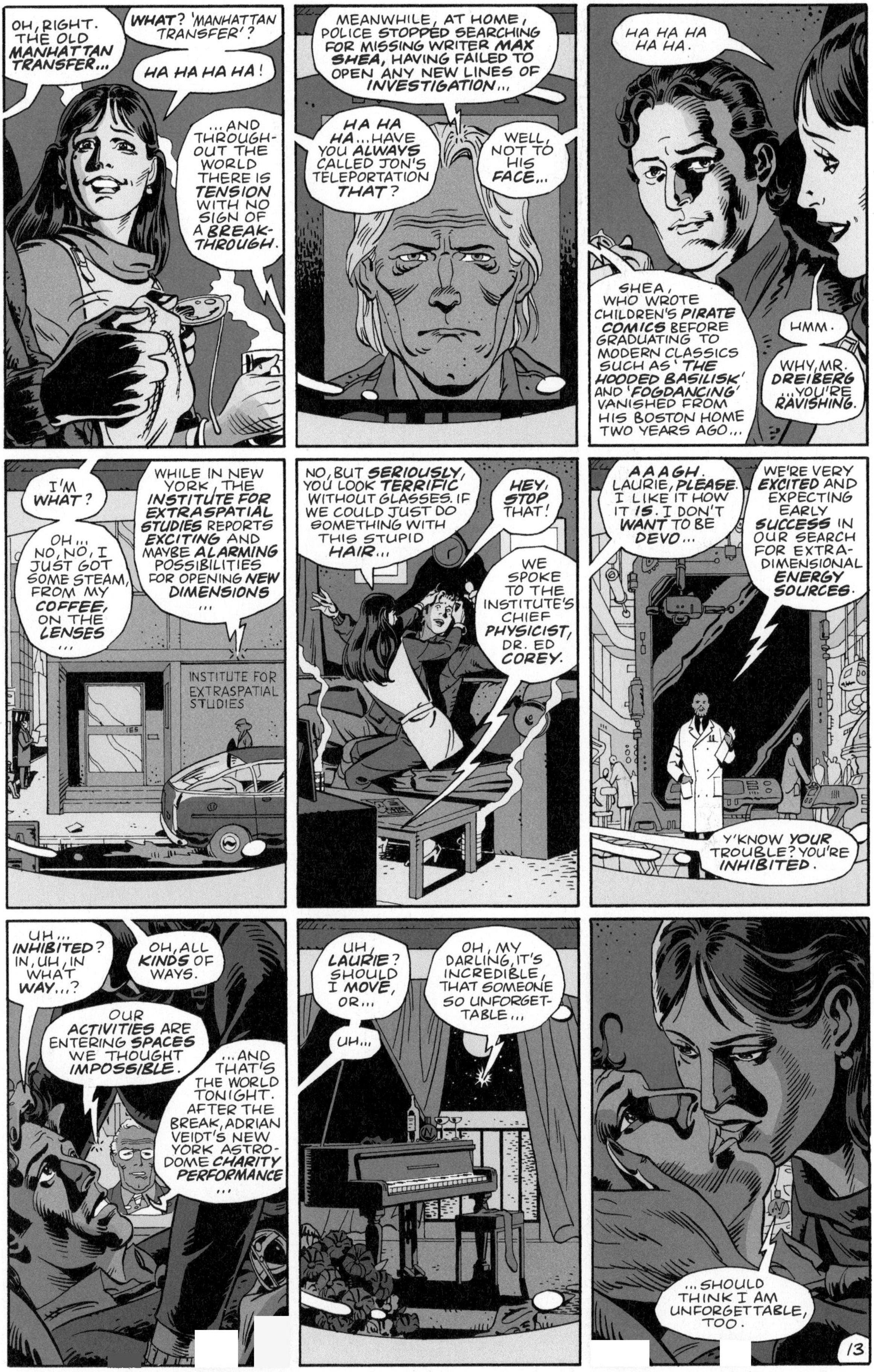

OH, RIGHT. THE OLD MANHATTAN TRANSFER...
WHAT? 'MANHATTAN TRANSFER'?
HA HA HA HA HA!
...AND THROUGHOUT THE WORLD THERE IS TENSION WITH NO SIGN OF A BREAKTHROUGH.
MEANWHILE, AT HOME, POLICE STOPPED SEARCHING FOR MISSING WRITER MAX SHEA, HAVING FAILED TO OPEN ANY NEW LINES OF INVESTIGATION...
HA HA HA... HAVE YOU ALWAYS CALLED JON'S TELEPORTATION THAT?
WELL, NOT TO HIS FACE...
HA HA HA HA HA.
SHEA, WHO WROTE CHILDREN'S PIRATE COMICS BEFORE GRADUATING TO MODERN CLASSICS SUCH AS 'THE HOODED BASILISK' AND 'FOGDANCING' VANISHED FROM HIS BOSTON HOME TWO YEARS AGO...
HMM.
WHY, MR. DREIBERG ...YOU'RE RAVISHING.
I'M WHAT?
OH... NO, NO, I JUST GOT SOME STEAM, FROM MY COFFEE, ON THE LENSES ...
WHILE IN NEW YORK, THE INSTITUTE FOR EXTRASPATIAL STUDIES REPORTS EXCITING AND MAYBE ALARMING POSSIBILITIES FOR OPENING NEW DIMENSIONS ...
INSTITUTE FOR EXTRASPATIAL STUDIES
IES
NO, BUT SERIOUSLY, YOU LOOK TERRIFIC WITHOUT GLASSES. IF WE COULD JUST DO SOMETHING WITH THIS STUPID HAIR...
HEY, STOP THAT!
WE SPOKE TO THE INSTITUTE'S CHIEF PHYSICIST, DR. ED COREY.
AAAGH. LAURIE, PLEASE. I LIKE IT HOW IT IS. I DON'T WANT TO BE DEVO...
WE'RE VERY EXCITED AND EXPECTING EARLY SUCCESS IN OUR SEARCH FOR EXTRA-DIMENSIONAL ENERGY SOURCES.
Y'KNOW YOUR TROUBLE? YOU'RE INHIBITED.
UH... INHIBITED? IN, UH, IN WHAT WAY...?
OH, ALL KINDS OF WAYS.
OUR ACTIVITIES ARE ENTERING SPACES WE THOUGHT IMPOSSIBLE.
...AND THAT'S THE WORLD TONIGHT. AFTER THE BREAK, ADRIAN VEIDT'S NEW YORK ASTRODOME CHARITY PERFORMANCE ...
UH, LAURIE? SHOULD I MOVE, OR...
UH...
OH, MY DARLING, IT'S INCREDIBLE, THAT SOMEONE SO UNFORGETTABLE...
...SHOULD THINK I AM UNFORGETTABLE, TOO.
13

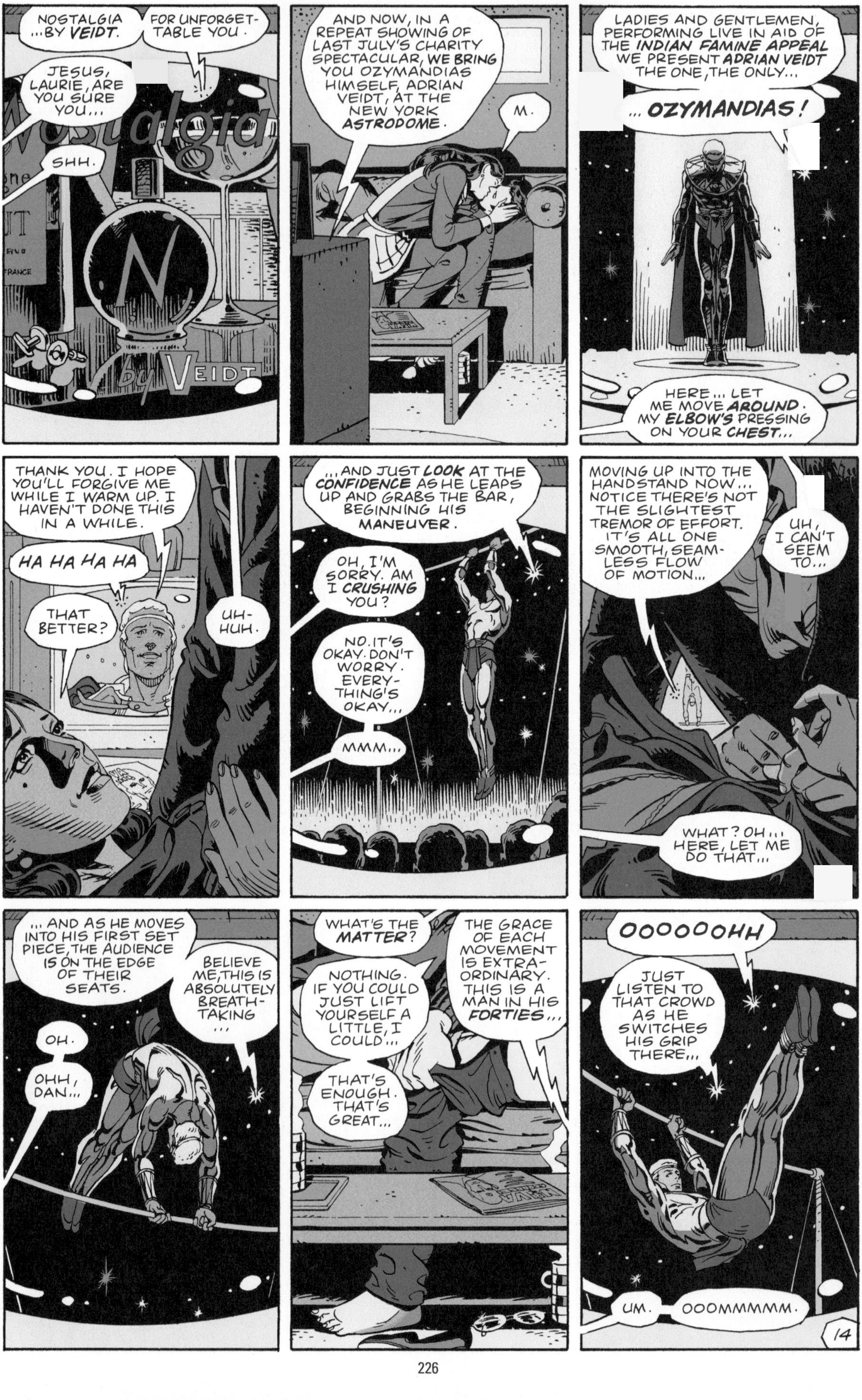
NOSTALGIA ...BY VEIDT.
FOR UNFORGET-TABLE YOU.
JESUS, LAURIE, ARE YOU SURE YOU...
SHH.
Nostalgia
by VEIDT
AND NOW, IN A REPEAT SHOWING OF LAST JULY'S CHARITY SPECTACULAR, WE BRING YOU OZYMANDIAS HIMSELF, ADRIAN VEIDT, AT THE NEW YORK ASTRODOME.
M.
LADIES AND GENTLEMEN, PERFORMING LIVE IN AID OF THE INDIAN FAMINE APPEAL WE PRESENT ADRIAN VEIDT THE ONE, THE ONLY...
... OZYMANDIAS!
HERE... LET ME MOVE AROUND. MY ELBOW'S PRESSING ON YOUR CHEST...
THANK YOU. I HOPE YOU'LL FORGIVE ME WHILE I WARM UP. I HAVEN'T DONE THIS IN A WHILE.
HA HA HA HA
THAT BETTER?
UH-HUH.
...AND JUST LOOK AT THE CONFIDENCE AS HE LEAPS UP AND GRABS THE BAR, BEGINNING HIS MANEUVER.
OH, I'M SORRY. AM I CRUSHING YOU?
NO. IT'S OKAY. DON'T WORRY. EVERY-THING'S OKAY...
MMM...
MOVING UP INTO THE HANDSTAND NOW... NOTICE THERE'S NOT THE SLIGHTEST TREMOR OF EFFORT. IT'S ALL ONE SMOOTH, SEAM-LESS FLOW OF MOTION...
UH, I CAN'T SEEM TO...
WHAT? OH... HERE, LET ME DO THAT...
... AND AS HE MOVES INTO HIS FIRST SET PIECE, THE AUDIENCE IS ON THE EDGE OF THEIR SEATS.
BELIEVE ME, THIS IS ABSOLUTELY BREATH-TAKING ...
OH.
OHH, DAN...
WHAT'S THE MATTER?
NOTHING. IF YOU COULD JUST LIFT YOURSELF A LITTLE, I COULD...
THE GRACE OF EACH MOVEMENT IS EXTRA-ORDINARY. THIS IS A MAN IN HIS FORTIES...
THAT'S ENOUGH. THAT'S GREAT...
OOOOOOHH
JUST LISTEN TO THAT CROWD AS HE SWITCHES HIS GRIP THERE...
UM.
OOOMMMMM.
14

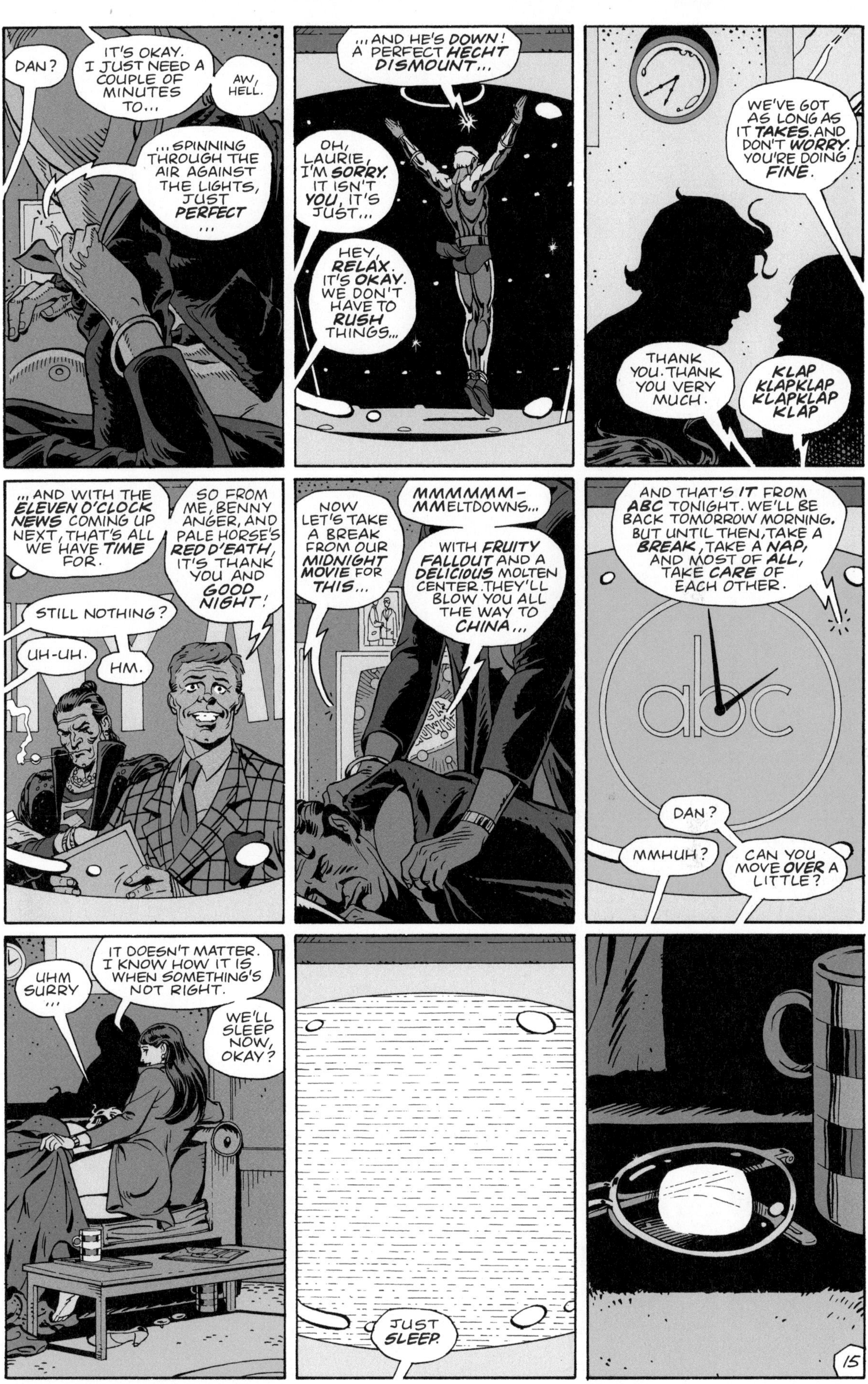

DAN?
IT'S OKAY. I JUST NEED A COUPLE OF MINUTES TO...
AW, HELL.
...SPINNING THROUGH THE AIR AGAINST THE LIGHTS, JUST PERFECT ...
...AND HE'S DOWN! A PERFECT HECHT DISMOUNT...
OH, LAURIE, I'M SORRY. IT ISN'T YOU, IT'S JUST...
HEY, RELAX. IT'S OKAY. WE DON'T HAVE TO RUSH THINGS...
WE'VE GOT AS LONG AS IT TAKES. AND DON'T WORRY. YOU'RE DOING FINE.
THANK YOU. THANK YOU VERY MUCH.
KLAP KLAPKLAP KLAPKLAP KLAP
...AND WITH THE ELEVEN O'CLOCK NEWS COMING UP NEXT, THAT'S ALL WE HAVE TIME FOR.
SO FROM ME, BENNY ANGER, AND PALE HORSE'S RED D'EATH, IT'S THANK YOU AND GOOD NIGHT!
STILL NOTHING?
UH-UH.
HM.
NOW LET'S TAKE A BREAK FROM OUR MIDNIGHT MOVIE FOR THIS...
MMMMMM-MMELTDOWNS...
WITH FRUITY FALLOUT AND A DELICIOUS MOLTEN CENTER. THEY'LL BLOW YOU ALL THE WAY TO CHINA...
AND THAT'S IT FROM ABC TONIGHT. WE'LL BE BACK TOMORROW MORNING. BUT UNTIL THEN, TAKE A BREAK, TAKE A NAP, AND MOST OF ALL, TAKE CARE OF EACH OTHER.
abc
DAN?
MMHUH?
CAN YOU MOVE OVER A LITTLE?
UHM SURRY ...
IT DOESN'T MATTER. I KNOW HOW IT IS WHEN SOMETHING'S NOT RIGHT.
WE'LL SLEEP NOW, OKAY?
JUST SLEEP.
15

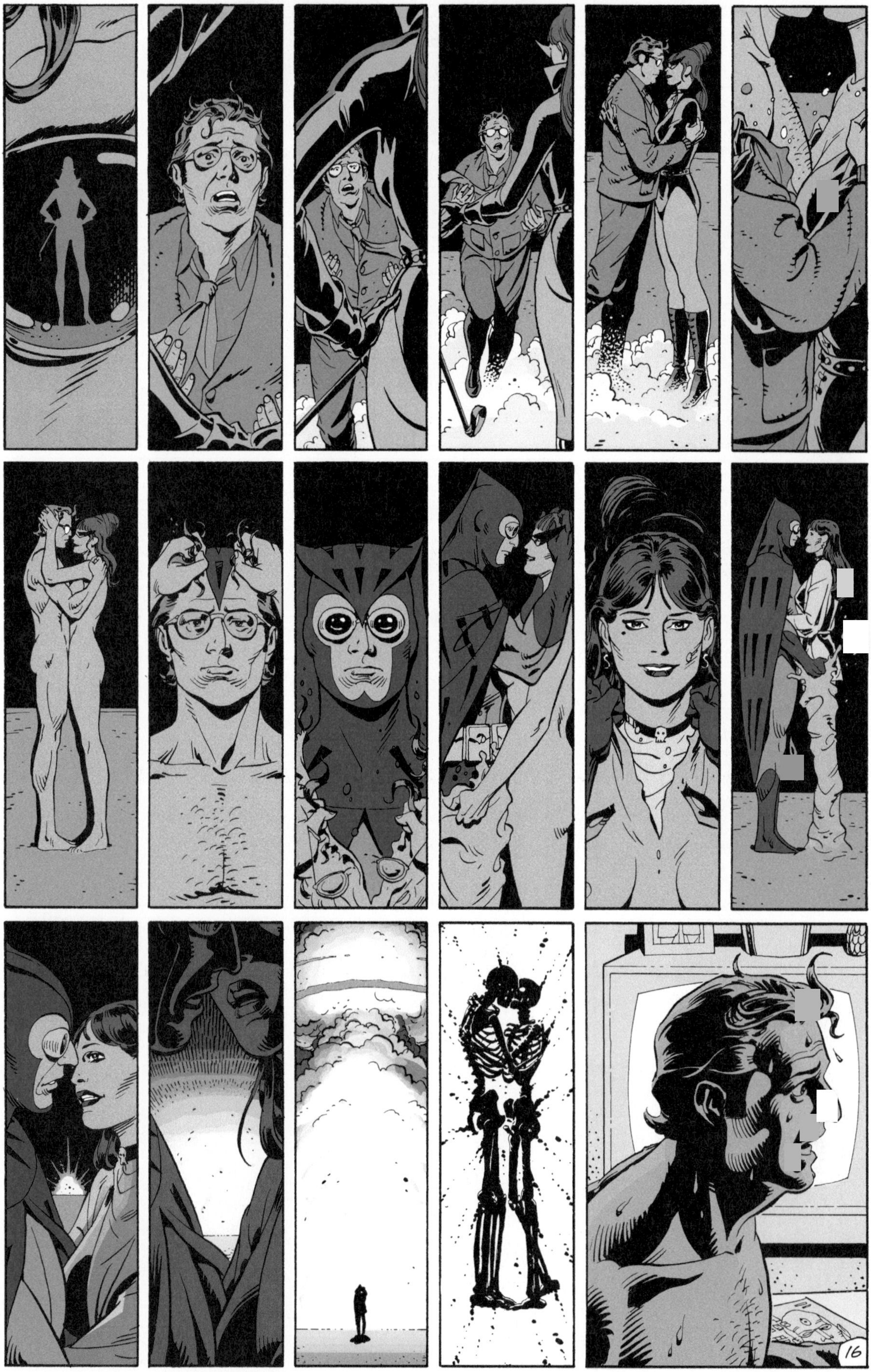
16

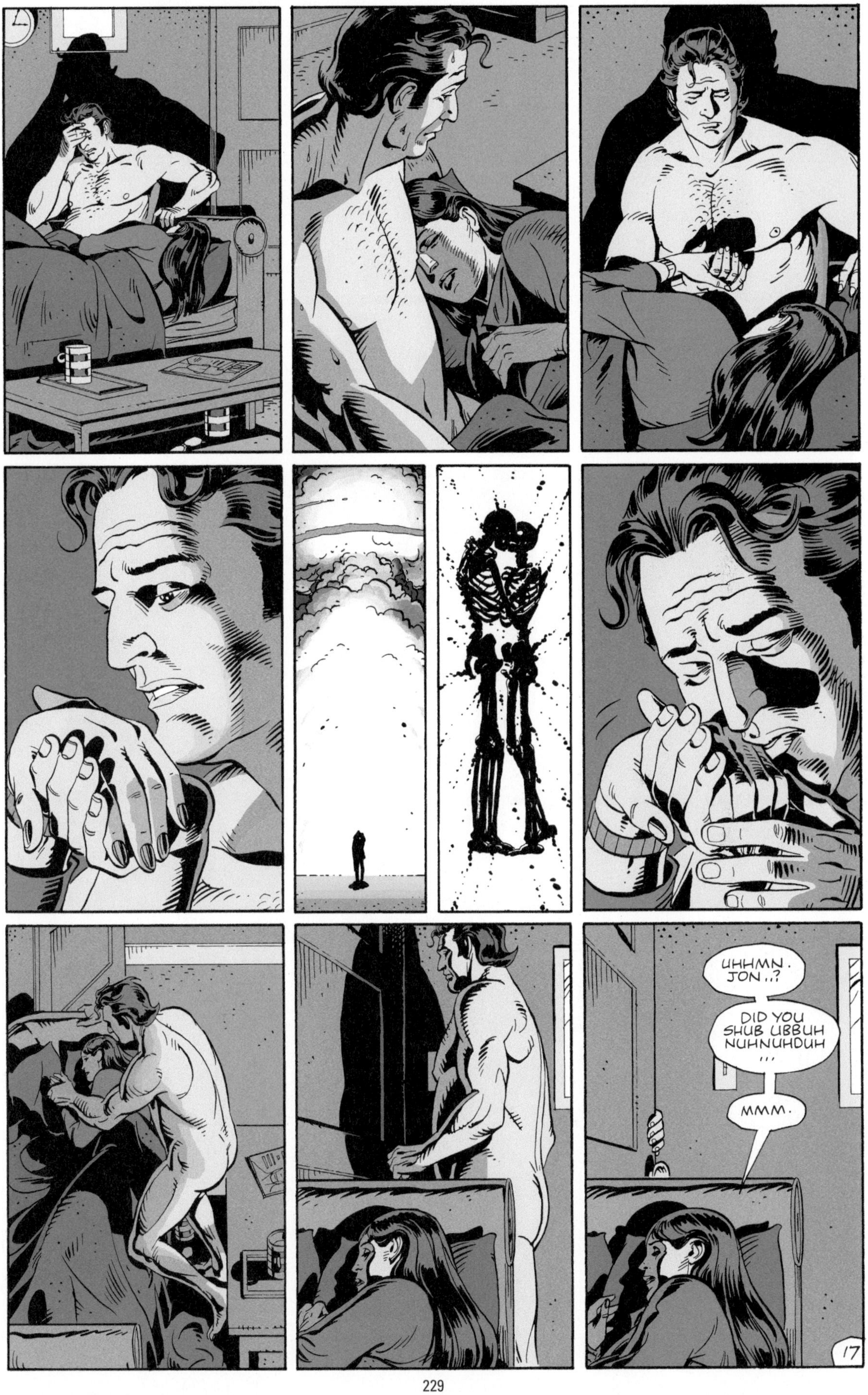
UHHMN. JON..?
DID YOU SHUB UBBUH NUHNUHDUH ...
MMM.
17

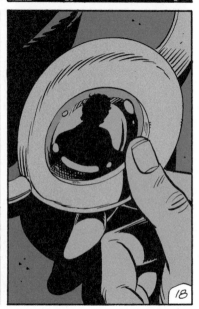

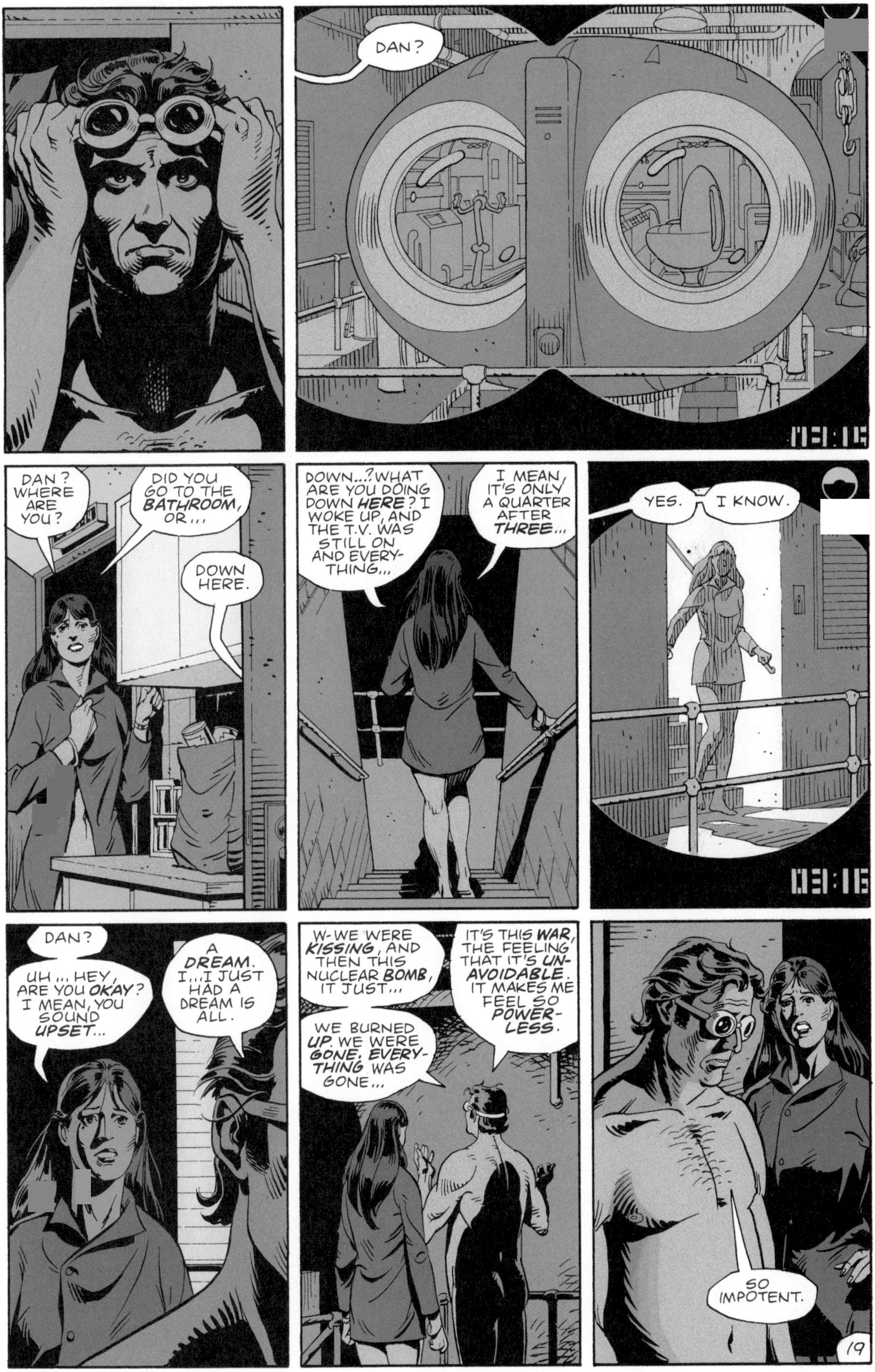
DAN?
03:15
DAN? WHERE ARE YOU?
DID YOU GO TO THE BATHROOM, OR...
DOWN HERE.
DOWN...? WHAT ARE YOU DOING DOWN HERE? I WOKE UP, AND THE T.V. WAS STILL ON AND EVERYTHING...
I MEAN, IT'S ONLY A QUARTER AFTER THREE...
YES.
I KNOW.
03:16
DAN?
UH... HEY, ARE YOU OKAY? I MEAN, YOU SOUND UPSET...
A DREAM. I... I JUST HAD A DREAM IS ALL.
W-WE WERE KISSING, AND THEN THIS NUCLEAR BOMB, IT JUST...
WE BURNED UP. WE WERE GONE. EVERYTHING WAS GONE...
IT'S THIS WAR, THE FEELING THAT IT'S UNAVOIDABLE. IT MAKES ME FEEL SO POWERLESS.
SO IMPOTENT.
19

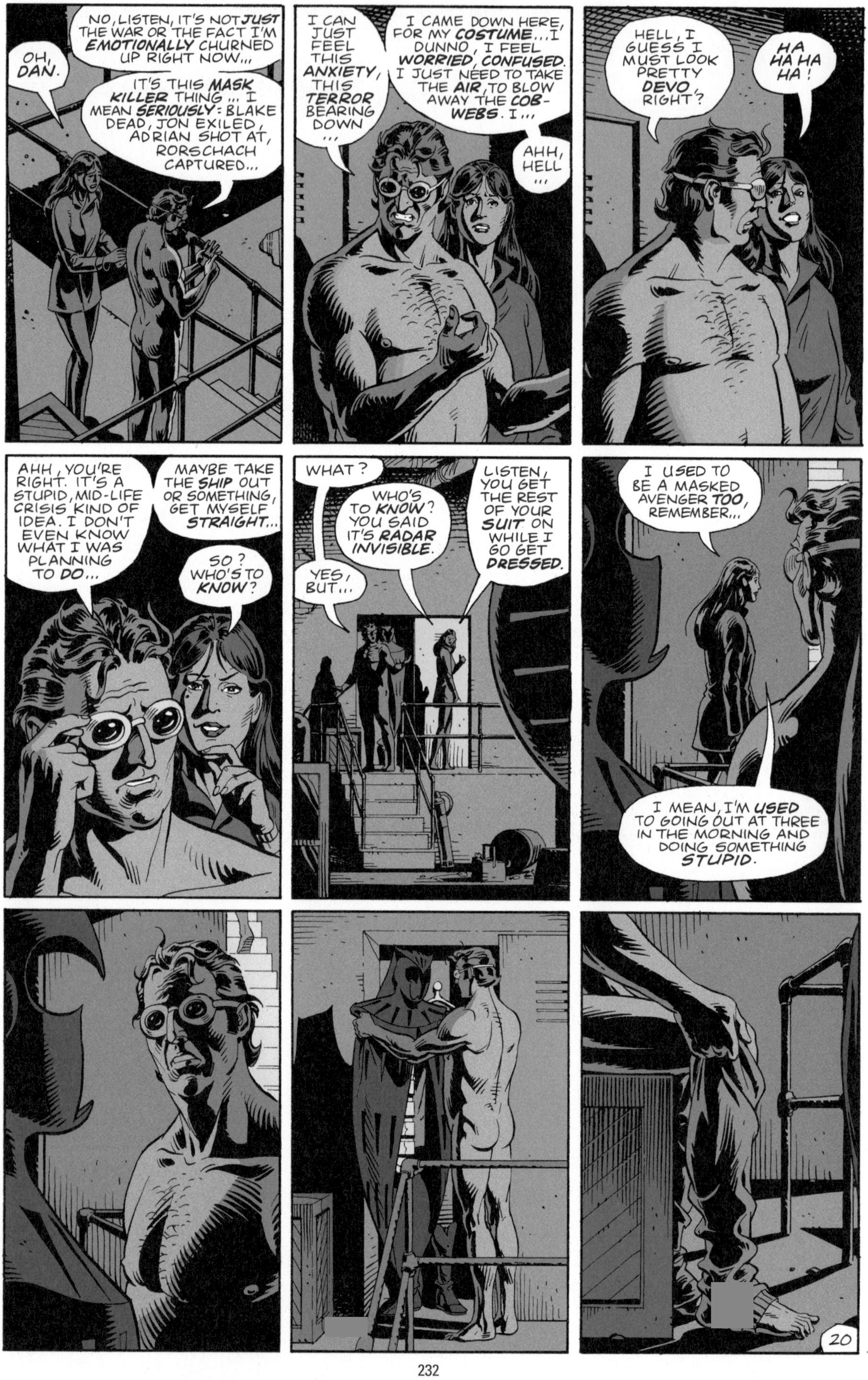

OH, DAN.
NO, LISTEN, IT'S NOT JUST THE WAR OR THE FACT I'M EMOTIONALLY CHURNED UP RIGHT NOW...
IT'S THIS MASK KILLER THING ... I MEAN SERIOUSLY: BLAKE DEAD, JON EXILED, ADRIAN SHOT AT, RORSCHACH CAPTURED...
I CAN JUST FEEL THIS ANXIETY, THIS TERROR BEARING DOWN ...
I CAME DOWN HERE, FOR MY COSTUME... I DUNNO, I FEEL WORRIED, CONFUSED. I JUST NEED TO TAKE THE AIR, TO BLOW AWAY THE COB-WEBS. I...,
AHH, HELL ...
HELL, I GUESS I MUST LOOK PRETTY DEVO, RIGHT?
HA HA HA HA!
AHH, YOU'RE RIGHT. IT'S A STUPID, MID-LIFE CRISIS KIND OF IDEA. I DON'T EVEN KNOW WHAT I WAS PLANNING TO DO...
MAYBE TAKE THE SHIP OUT OR SOMETHING, GET MYSELF STRAIGHT...
SO? WHO'S TO KNOW?
WHAT?
WHO'S TO KNOW? YOU SAID IT'S RADAR INVISIBLE.
YES, BUT...
LISTEN, YOU GET THE REST OF YOUR SUIT ON WHILE I GO GET DRESSED.
I USED TO BE A MASKED AVENGER TOO, REMEMBER...
I MEAN, I'M USED TO GOING OUT AT THREE IN THE MORNING AND DOING SOMETHING STUPID.
20

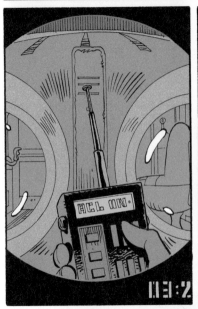

UH, DAN?

I'M READY.

ME TOO.

LET'S GO.

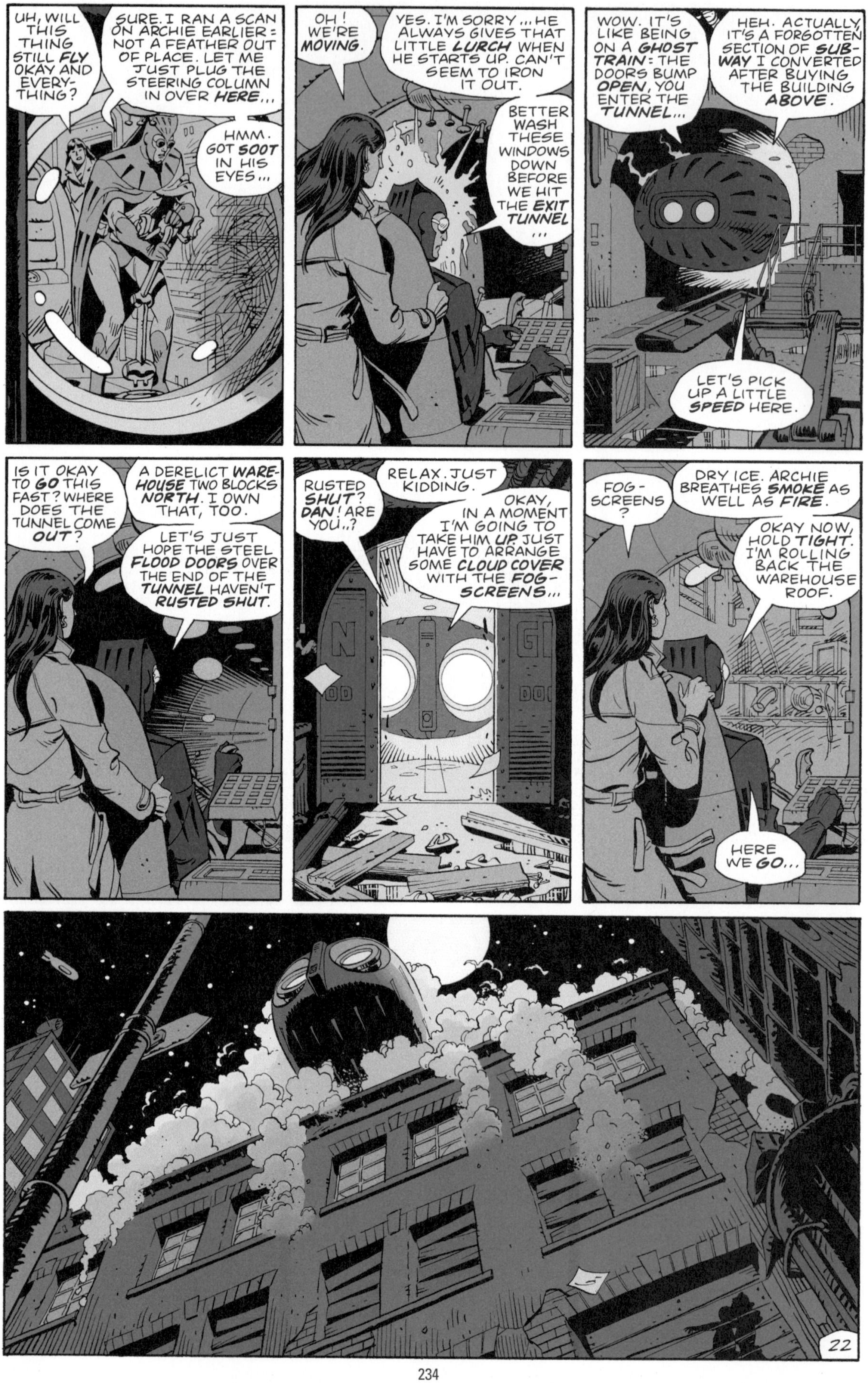
UH, WILL THIS THING STILL FLY OKAY AND EVERY-THING?
SURE. I RAN A SCAN ON ARCHIE EARLIER: NOT A FEATHER OUT OF PLACE. LET ME JUST PLUG THE STEERING COLUMN IN OVER HERE...
HMM. GOT SOOT IN HIS EYES...
OH! WE'RE MOVING.
YES. I'M SORRY... HE ALWAYS GIVES THAT LITTLE LURCH WHEN HE STARTS UP. CAN'T SEEM TO IRON IT OUT.
BETTER WASH THESE WINDOWS DOWN BEFORE WE HIT THE EXIT TUNNEL...
WOW. IT'S LIKE BEING ON A GHOST TRAIN: THE DOORS BUMP OPEN, YOU ENTER THE TUNNEL...
HEH. ACTUALLY, IT'S A FORGOTTEN SECTION OF SUBWAY I CONVERTED AFTER BUYING THE BUILDING ABOVE.
LET'S PICK UP A LITTLE SPEED HERE.
IS IT OKAY TO GO THIS FAST? WHERE DOES THE TUNNEL COME OUT?
A DERELICT WAREHOUSE TWO BLOCKS NORTH. I OWN THAT, TOO.
LET'S JUST HOPE THE STEEL FLOOD DOORS OVER THE END OF THE TUNNEL HAVEN'T RUSTED SHUT.
RUSTED SHUT? DAN! ARE YOU..?
RELAX. JUST KIDDING.
OKAY, IN A MOMENT I'M GOING TO TAKE HIM UP. JUST HAVE TO ARRANGE SOME CLOUD COVER WITH THE FOG-SCREENS...
FOG-SCREENS?
DRY ICE. ARCHIE BREATHES SMOKE AS WELL AS FIRE.
OKAY NOW, HOLD TIGHT. I'M ROLLING BACK THE WAREHOUSE ROOF.
HERE WE GO...
22

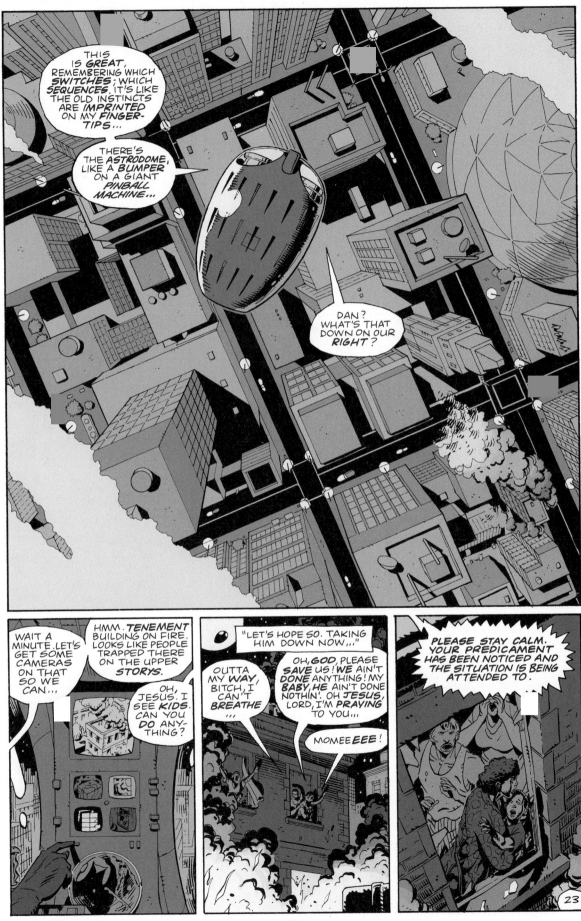

THIS IS *GREAT*, REMEMBERING WHICH *SWITCHES*; WHICH *SEQUENCES*. IT'S LIKE THE OLD INSTINCTS ARE *IMPRINTED* ON MY *FINGER-TIPS*...

THERE'S THE *ASTRODOME*, LIKE A *BUMPER* ON A GIANT *PINBALL MACHINE*...

DAN? WHAT'S THAT DOWN ON OUR *RIGHT*?

WAIT A MINUTE. LET'S GET SOME CAMERAS ON THAT SO WE CAN...

HMM. *TENEMENT* BUILDING ON FIRE. LOOKS LIKE PEOPLE TRAPPED THERE ON THE UPPER *STORYS.*

OH, *JESUS*. I SEE *KIDS*. CAN YOU DO ANY-THING?

"LET'S HOPE SO. TAKING HIM DOWN NOW..."

OH, *GOD*, PLEASE SAVE US! *WE* AIN'T *DONE* ANYTHING! MY *BABY*, HE AIN'T *DONE* NOTHIN'. OH *JESUS*, LORD, I'M *PRAYING* TO YOU...

OUTTA MY *WAY*, BITCH, I' CAN'T *BREATHE* ...

MOMEE *EEE* !

PLEASE STAY CALM. YOUR PREDICAMENT HAS BEEN *NOTICED* AND THE SITUATION IS BEING *ATTENDED* TO.

23

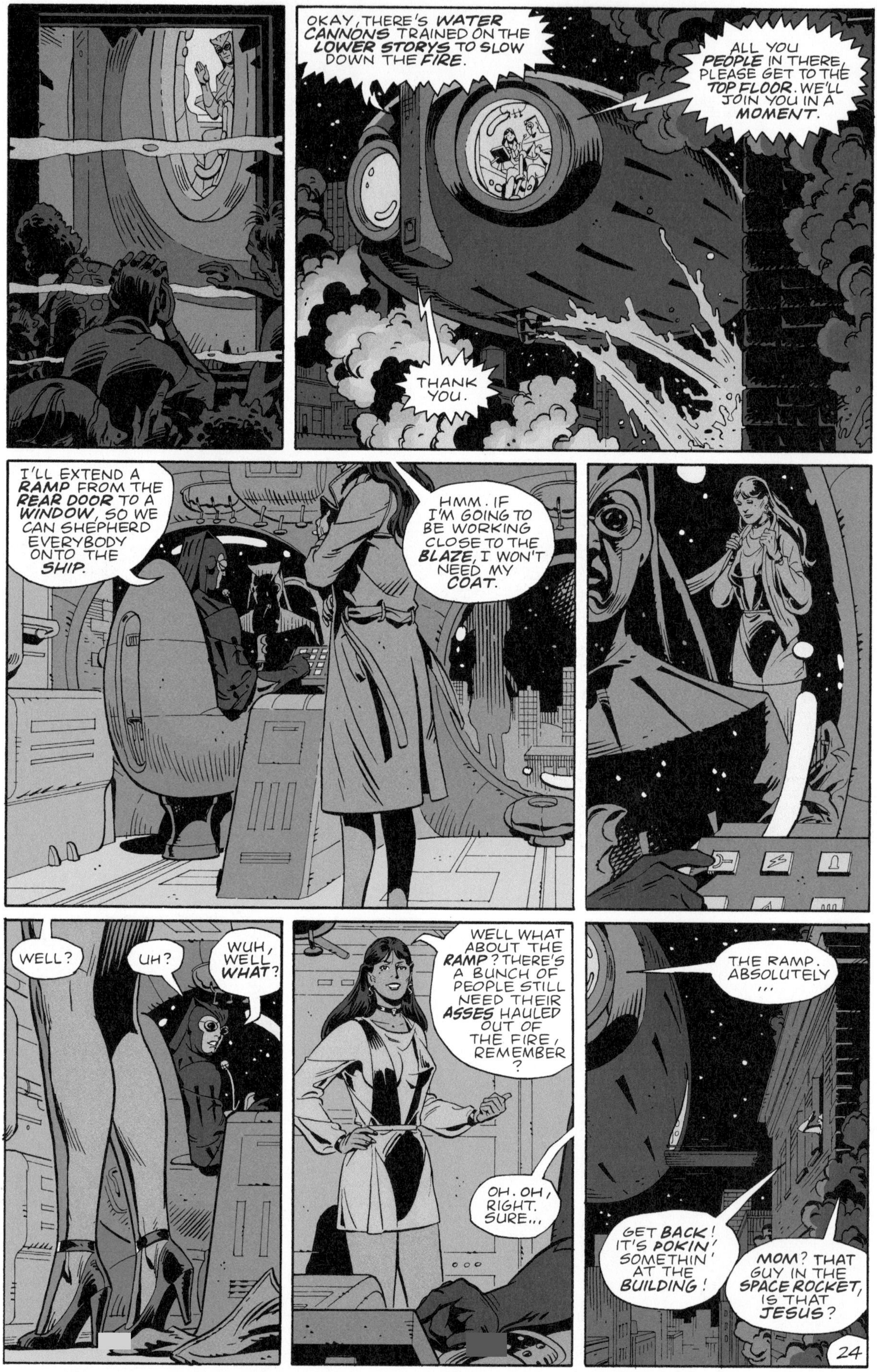
OKAY, THERE'S WATER CANNONS TRAINED ON THE LOWER STORYS TO SLOW DOWN THE FIRE.
ALL YOU PEOPLE IN THERE, PLEASE GET TO THE TOP FLOOR. WE'LL JOIN YOU IN A MOMENT.
THANK YOU.
I'LL EXTEND A RAMP FROM THE REAR DOOR TO A WINDOW, SO WE CAN SHEPHERD EVERYBODY ONTO THE SHIP.
HMM. IF I'M GOING TO BE WORKING CLOSE TO THE BLAZE, I WON'T NEED MY COAT.
WELL?
UH?
WUH, WELL WHAT?
WELL WHAT ABOUT THE RAMP? THERE'S A BUNCH OF PEOPLE STILL NEED THEIR ASSES HAULED OUT OF THE FIRE, REMEMBER?
OH. OH, RIGHT. SURE...
THE RAMP. ABSOLUTELY...
GET BACK! IT'S POKIN' SOMETHIN' AT THE BUILDING!
MOM? THAT GUY IN THE SPACE ROCKET, IS THAT JESUS?
24

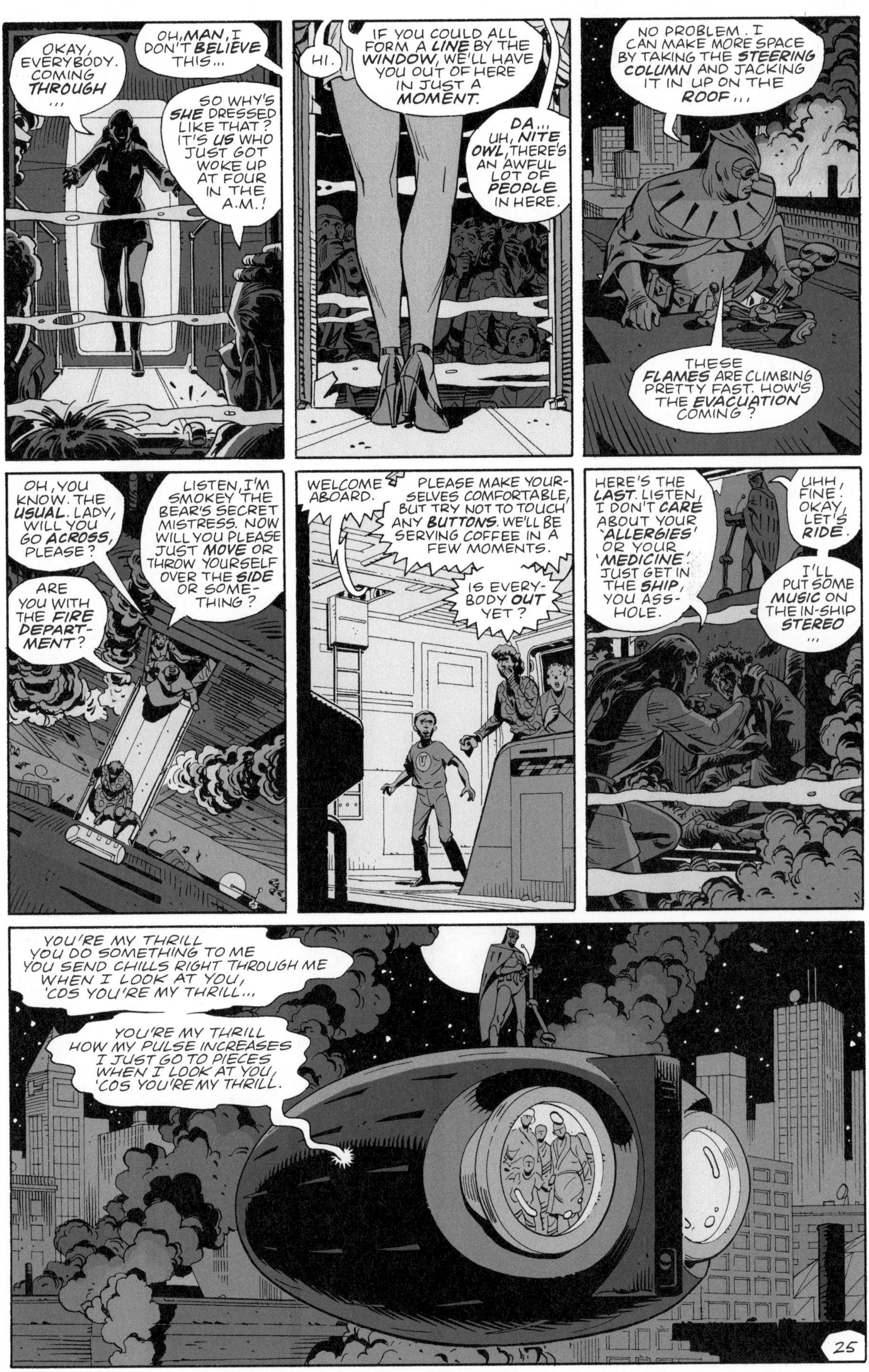

OKAY, EVERYBODY. COMING THROUGH ...
OH, MAN, I DON'T BELIEVE THIS...
SO WHY'S SHE DRESSED LIKE THAT? IT'S US WHO JUST GOT WOKE UP AT FOUR IN THE A.M.!
HI.
IF YOU COULD ALL FORM A LINE BY THE WINDOW, WE'LL HAVE YOU OUT OF HERE IN JUST A MOMENT.
DA... UH, NITE OWL, THERE'S AN AWFUL LOT OF PEOPLE IN HERE.
NO PROBLEM. I CAN MAKE MORE SPACE BY TAKING THE STEERING COLUMN AND JACKING IT IN UP ON THE ROOF...
THESE FLAMES ARE CLIMBING PRETTY FAST. HOW'S THE EVACUATION COMING?
OH, YOU KNOW. THE USUAL. LADY, WILL YOU GO ACROSS, PLEASE?
ARE YOU WITH THE FIRE DEPARTMENT?
LISTEN, I'M SMOKEY THE BEAR'S SECRET MISTRESS. NOW WILL YOU PLEASE JUST MOVE OR THROW YOURSELF OVER THE SIDE OR SOMETHING?
WELCOME ABOARD.
PLEASE MAKE YOURSELVES COMFORTABLE, BUT TRY NOT TO TOUCH ANY BUTTONS. WE'LL BE SERVING COFFEE IN A FEW MOMENTS.
IS EVERYBODY OUT YET?
HERE'S THE LAST. LISTEN, I DON'T CARE ABOUT YOUR 'ALLERGIES' OR YOUR 'MEDICINE'. JUST GET IN THE SHIP, YOU ASSHOLE.
UHH, FINE. OKAY, LET'S RIDE.
I'LL PUT SOME MUSIC ON THE IN-SHIP STEREO ...
YOU'RE MY THRILL
YOU DO SOMETHING TO ME
YOU SEND CHILLS RIGHT THROUGH ME
WHEN I LOOK AT YOU,
'COS YOU'RE MY THRILL...
YOU'RE MY THRILL
HOW MY PULSE INCREASES
I JUST GO TO PIECES
WHEN I LOOK AT YOU,
'COS YOU'RE MY THRILL.
25

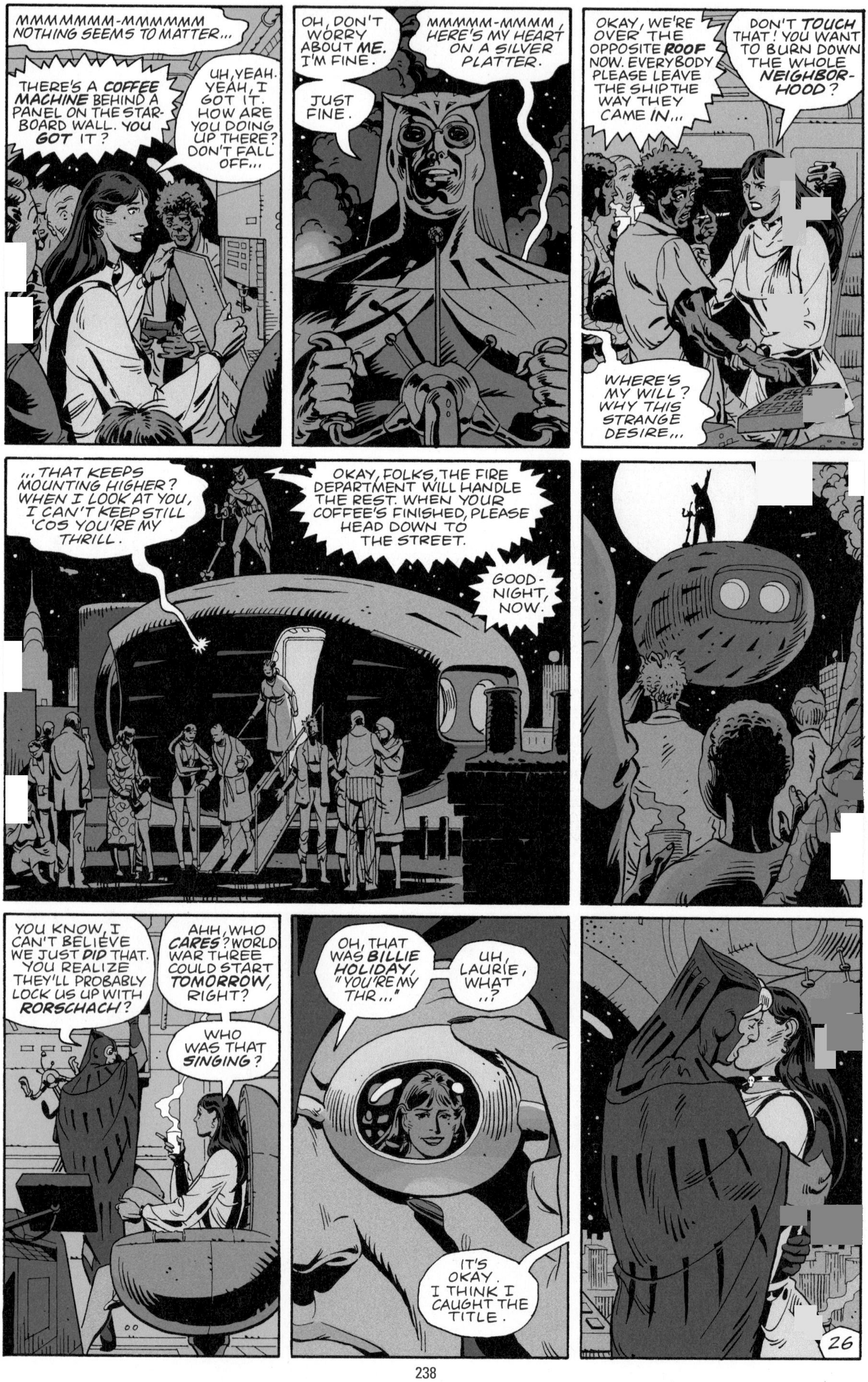
MMMMMMM-MMMMMM NOTHING SEEMS TO MATTER...
THERE'S A COFFEE MACHINE BEHIND A PANEL ON THE STARBOARD WALL. YOU GOT IT?
UH, YEAH. YEAH, I GOT IT. HOW ARE YOU DOING UP THERE? DON'T FALL OFF...
OH, DON'T WORRY ABOUT ME. I'M FINE.
JUST FINE.
MMMMMM-MMMM, HERE'S MY HEART ON A SILVER PLATTER.
OKAY, WE'RE OVER THE OPPOSITE ROOF NOW. EVERYBODY PLEASE LEAVE THE SHIP THE WAY THEY CAME IN...
DON'T TOUCH THAT! YOU WANT TO BURN DOWN THE WHOLE NEIGHBORHOOD?
WHERE'S MY WILL? WHY THIS STRANGE DESIRE...
...THAT KEEPS MOUNTING HIGHER? WHEN I LOOK AT YOU, I CAN'T KEEP STILL 'COS YOU'RE MY THRILL.
OKAY, FOLKS, THE FIRE DEPARTMENT WILL HANDLE THE REST. WHEN YOUR COFFEE'S FINISHED, PLEASE HEAD DOWN TO THE STREET.
GOOD-NIGHT, NOW.
YOU KNOW, I CAN'T BELIEVE WE JUST DID THAT. YOU REALIZE THEY'LL PROBABLY LOCK US UP WITH RORSCHACH?
AHH, WHO CARES? WORLD WAR THREE COULD START TOMORROW, RIGHT?
WHO WAS THAT SINGING?
OH, THAT WAS BILLIE HOLIDAY, "YOU'RE MY THR..."
UH, LAURIE, WHAT ...?
IT'S OKAY. I THINK I CAUGHT THE TITLE.
26

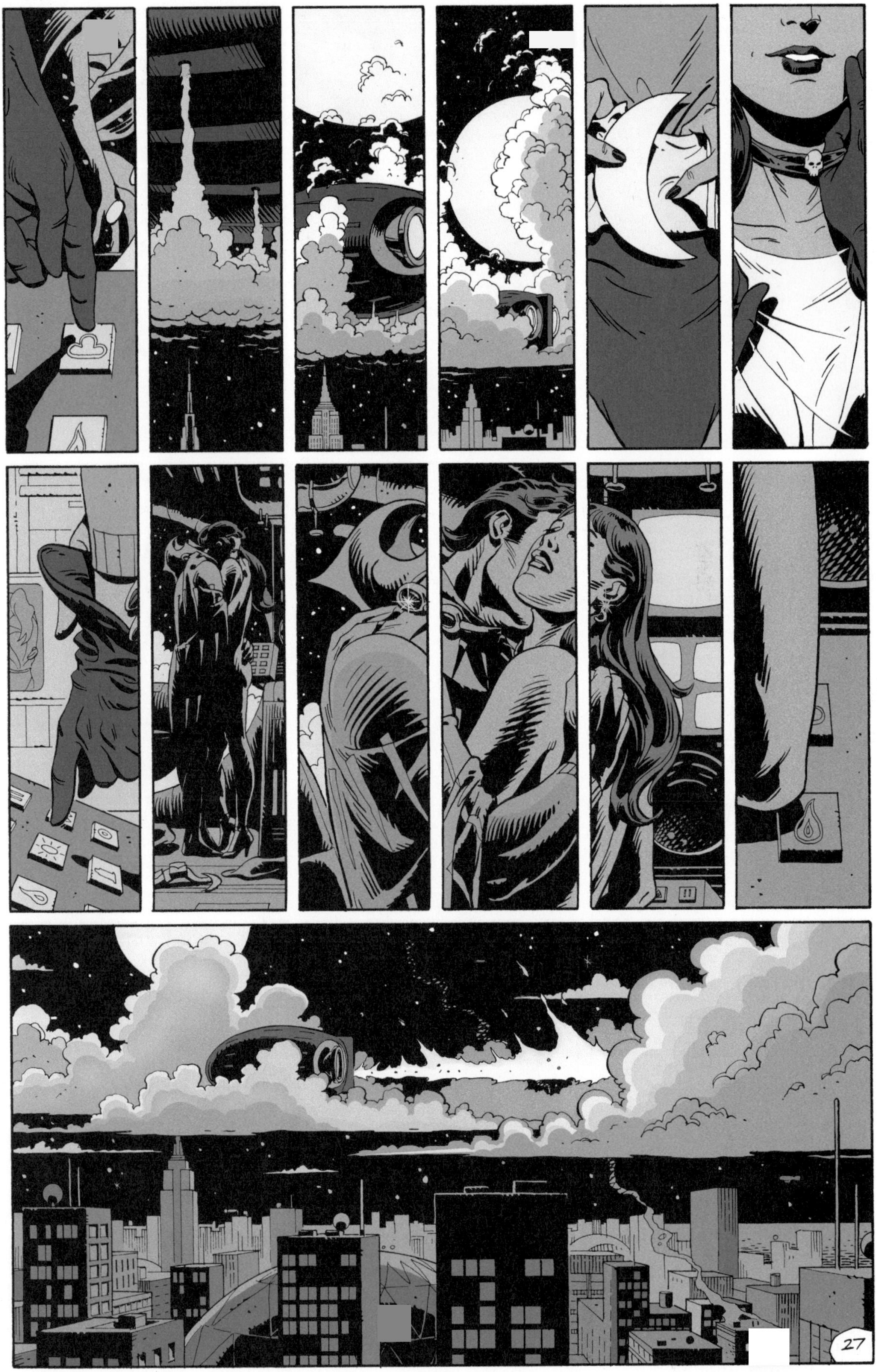
27

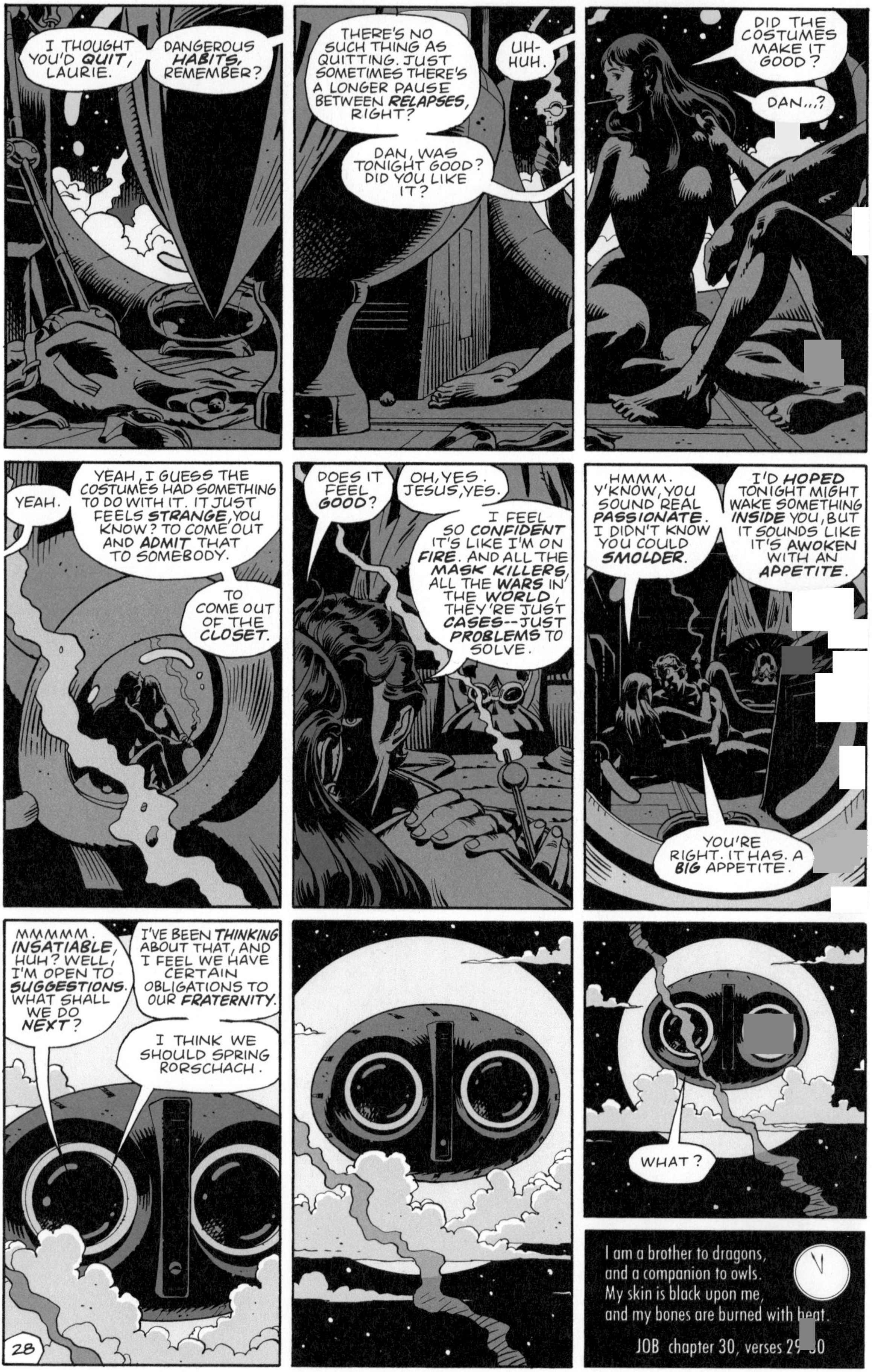
I THOUGHT YOU'D QUIT, LAURIE.
DANGEROUS HABITS, REMEMBER?
THERE'S NO SUCH THING AS QUITTING. JUST SOMETIMES THERE'S A LONGER PAUSE BETWEEN RELAPSES, RIGHT?
UH-HUH.
DAN, WAS TONIGHT GOOD? DID YOU LIKE IT?
DID THE COSTUMES MAKE IT GOOD?
DAN...?
YEAH.
YEAH, I GUESS THE COSTUMES HAD SOMETHING TO DO WITH IT. IT JUST FEELS STRANGE, YOU KNOW? TO COME OUT AND ADMIT THAT TO SOMEBODY.
TO COME OUT OF THE CLOSET.
DOES IT FEEL GOOD?
OH, YES. JESUS, YES.
I FEEL SO CONFIDENT IT'S LIKE I'M ON FIRE. AND ALL THE MASK KILLERS, ALL THE WARS IN THE WORLD, THEY'RE JUST CASES--JUST PROBLEMS TO SOLVE.
HMMM. Y'KNOW, YOU SOUND REAL PASSIONATE. I DIDN'T KNOW YOU COULD SMOLDER.
I'D HOPED TONIGHT MIGHT WAKE SOMETHING INSIDE YOU, BUT IT SOUNDS LIKE IT'S AWOKEN WITH AN APPETITE.
YOU'RE RIGHT. IT HAS. A BIG APPETITE.
MMMMM. INSATIABLE, HUH? WELL, I'M OPEN TO SUGGESTIONS. WHAT SHALL WE DO NEXT?
I'VE BEEN THINKING ABOUT THAT, AND I FEEL WE HAVE CERTAIN OBLIGATIONS TO OUR FRATERNITY.
I THINK WE SHOULD SPRING RORSCHACH.
28
WHAT?
I am a brother to dragons,
and a companion to owls.
My skin is black upon me,
and my bones are burned with heat.
JOB chapter 30, verses 29-30

The following text is reprinted from the Journal of The American Ornithological Society, Fall 1983.

BLOOD·FROM·THE SHOULDER·OF·PALLAS

🔲🔲🔲🔲🔲🔲🔲🔲🔲 BY DANIEL DREIBERG 🔲🔲🔲🔲🔲🔲🔲🔲🔲

Is it possible, I wonder, to study a bird so closely, to observe and catalogue its peculiarities in such minute detail, that it becomes invisible? Is it possible that while fastidiously calibrating the span of its wings or the length of its tarsus, we somehow lose sight of its poetry? That in our pedestrian descriptions of a

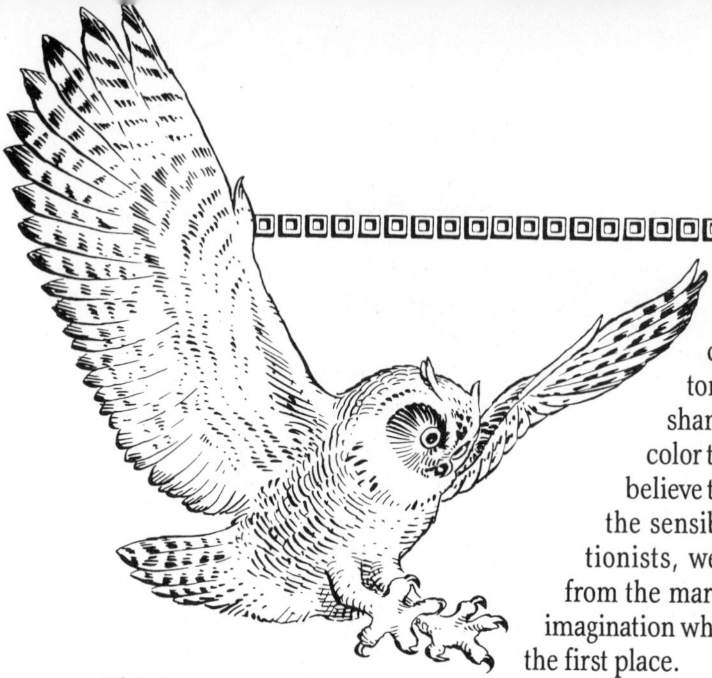

marbled or vermiculated plumage we forfeit a glimpse of living canvases, cascades of carefully toned browns and golds that would shame Kandinsky, misty explosions of color to rival Monet? I believe that we do. I believe that in approaching our subject with the sensibilities of statisticians and dissectionists, we distance ourselves increasingly from the marvelous and spell-binding planet of imagination whose gravity drew us to our studies in the first place.

This is not to say that we should cease to establish facts and to verify our information, but merely to suggest that unless those facts can be imbued with the flash of poetic insight then they remain dull gems; semi-precious stones scarcely worth the collecting.

When we stare into the catatonic black bead of a Parakeet's eye we must teach ourselves to glimpse the cold, alien madness that Max Ernst perceived when he chose to robe his naked brides in confections of scarlet feather and the transplanted monstrous heads of exotic birds. When some ocean-going Kite or Tern is captured in the sharp blue gaze of our Zeiss lenses, we must be able to see the stop motion flight of sepia gulls through the early kinetic photographs of Muybridge, beating white wings tracing a slow oscilloscope line through space and time.

Looking at a hawk, we see the minute differences in width of the shaft lines on the underfeathers where the Egyptians once saw Horus and the burning eye of holy vengeance incarnate. Until we transform our mere sightings into genuine visions; until our ear is mature enough to order a symphony from the shrill pandemonium of the aviary; until then we may have a hobby, but we shall not have a passion.

When I was a boy, my passion was for owls. During the long summers of the early fifties, while the rest of the country was apparently watching the skies for incoming flying saucers or Soviet missiles, I would hare across the New England fields in the heart of the night, sneakers munching through the dried grass and bracken towards my watch, where I would sit peering upwards in hope of a different sort of spectacle, ears straining for the weird scream that meant an old bird was out combing the dark for sustenance, a mad hermit screech, glaringly distinct from the snoring hiss of a younger owl.

Somewhere over the years; sometime during the yawning expanse between those snug years in the afterglow of a war well won and these current times, huddled in the looming shadow of a war unwinnable; someplace along the line my passion got lost, unwittingly refined from the original gleaming ore down to a banal and lusterless filing system. This gradual tarnishing had gone unnoticed, unchecked, finally calcifying into unthinking habit. It was not until comparatively recently that I managed to catch a dazzling glimpse of the motherlode through the accumulated dust of methodical study and academia: visiting a sick acquaintance at a hospital in Maine on behalf of a mutual friend, walking back across the shadowy parking lot with my mind reduced to blankness by the various concerns of the day, I suddenly and unexpectedly heard the cry of a hunting owl.

It was a bird advanced in years, its shriek that of a deranged old man, wheeling madly through the dark and freezing sky against the ragged night clouds, and the sound halted me in my footsteps. It is a fallacy to suppose that owls screech to startle their prey from hiding, as some have suggested; the cry of the hunting owl is a voice from Hell, and it turns the scrabbling voles to statues, roots the weasel to the soil. In my instant of paralysis there on the glistening macadam, between the sleeping automobiles, I understood the purpose behind the cry with a biting clarity, the way I'd understood it as a boy, belly flat against the warm summer earth. In that extended and timeless moment, I felt the kinship of simple animal fear along with all those other creatures much smaller and more vulnerable than I who had heard the scream as I had heard it, were struck motionless as I was. The owl was not attempting to frighten his food into revealing itself. Perched with disconcerting stillness upon its branch for hours, drinking in the darkness through dilated and thirsty pupils, the owl had already spotted its dinner. The screech served merely to transfix the chosen morsel, pinning it to the ground with a shrill nail of blind, helpless terror. Not knowing which of us had been selected, I stood frozen along with the rodents of the field, my heart hammering as it waited for the sudden clutch of sharpened steel fingers that would provide my first and only indication that I was the predetermined victim. The feathers of owls are soft and downy; they make no sound at all as they drop through the dark stratas of the sky. The silence before an owl swoops is a V-Bomb silence, and you never hear the one that hits you.

Somewhere away in the crepuscular gloom beyond the yellow-lit hospital grounds I thought I heard something small emit its ultimate squeal. The moment had passed. I could move again, along with all the relieved, invisible denizens of the tall grass. We were safe. It wasn't screaming for us, not this time. We could continue with our nocturnal business, with our lives, searching for a meal or a mate. We were not twitching nervelessly in stifling, stinking darkness, head first down the gullet of the swooping horror, our tails dangling pathetically from that vicious scimitar beak for hours before finally our hind legs and pelvic girdle are disgorged, our empty, matted skin curiously inverted by the process.

Although I had recovered my motor abilities in the aftermath of the owl's shriek, I found that my equilibrium was not so easily regained. Some facet of the experience had struck a chord in me, forged a connection between my dulled and jaded adult self and the child who sprawled in faint starlight while the great night hunters staged dramas full of hunger and death in the opaque jet air above me. An urge to experience rather than merely record had been rekindled within me, prompting the thought processes, the self-evaluation that has led to this current article.

As I remarked earlier, this is not to suggest that I immediately foreswore all academic endeavor and research pertaining to the field in order to run away and eke out some naked and primordial existence in the woods. Quite the contrary: I hurled myself into the study of my subject with renewed fervor, able to see the dry facts and arid descriptions in the same transforming magical light that had

favored them when I was younger. A scientific understanding of the beautifully synchronized and articulated motion of an owl's individual feathers during flight does not impede a poetic appreciation of the same phenomenon. Rather, the two enhance each other, a more lyrical eye lending the cold data a romance from which it has long been divorced.

Immersing myself avidly in dusty and long untouched reference books I came across forgotten passages that would make me almost breathless, dreary-looking tomes that would reveal themselves to be treasure houses of iridescent wonder. I rediscovered many long-lost gems amongst the cobwebs, antique and functional stretches of descriptive prose which nonetheless conveyed the violent and terrible essence of their subject matter effortlessly.

I stumbled once more across T.A. Coward's engrossing account on an encounter with an Eagle Owl: "In Norway I saw a bird that had been taken when in down from the nest, but it not only assumed the typical terrifying attitude, but made frequent dashes at the wire, striking with its feet. It puffed its feathers out, framed its head in its wings, and fired off a volley of loud cracks from its snapping beak, but what struck me most was the scintillating flash of its great orange eyes."

Then of course there is Hudson's account of the Magellanic Eagle-Owl which he wounded in Patagonia: "The irides were of a bright orange color, but every time I attempted to approach the bird they kindled into great globes of quivering yellow flame, the black pupils being surrounded by a scintillating crimson light which threw out minute yellow sparks into the air." In long-buried words such as the foregoing I caught some of the searing, apocalyptic intensity that I had felt in that wet hospital parking lot in Maine.

Nowadays, when I observe some specimen of *Carine noctua*, I try to look past the fine grey down on the toes, to see beyond the white spots arranged in neat lines, like a firework display across its brow. Instead, I try to see the bird whose image the Greeks carved into their coins, sitting patiently at the ear of the Goddess Pallas Athene, silently sharing her immortal wisdom.

Perhaps, instead of measuring the feathered tufts surmounting its ears, we should speculate on what those ears may have heard. Perhaps when considering the manner in which it grips its branch, with two toes in front and the reversible outer toe clutching from behind, we should allow ourselves to pause for a moment, and acknowledge that these same claws must once have drawn blood from the shoulder of Pallas.

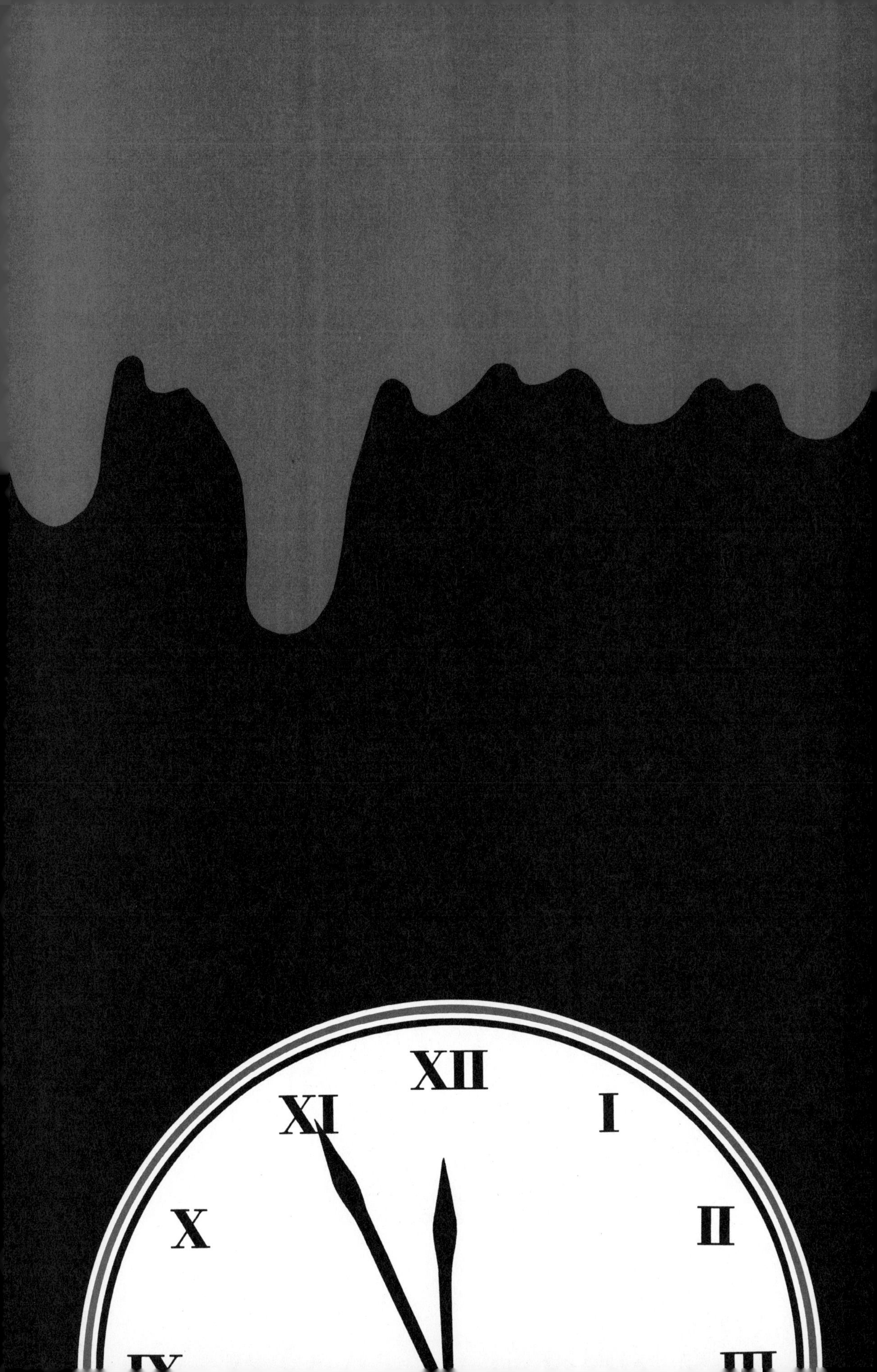
XII
XI
I
X
II

CHAPTER VIII

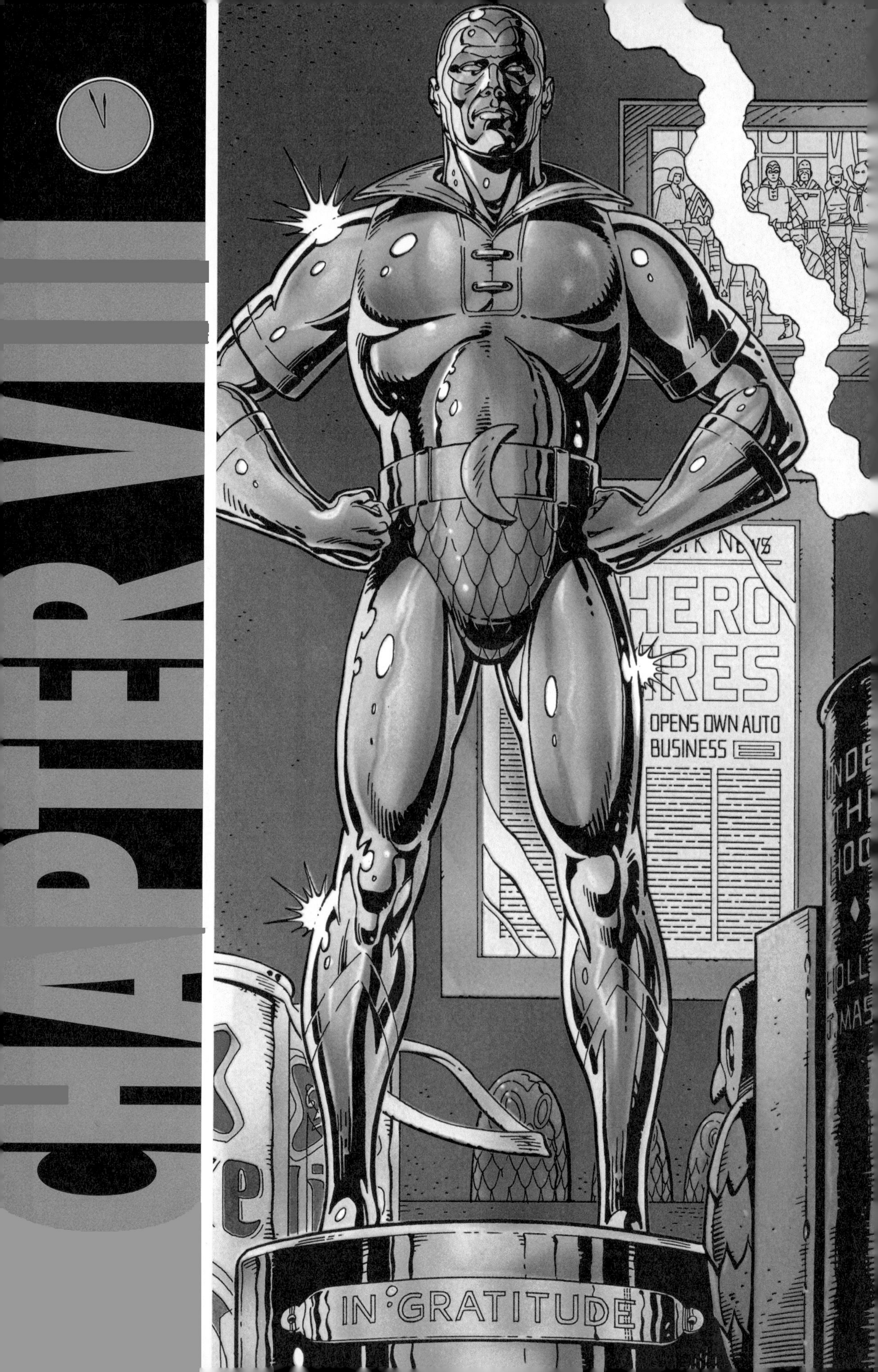

HERO
OPENS OWN AUTO BUSINESS
IN GRATITUDE

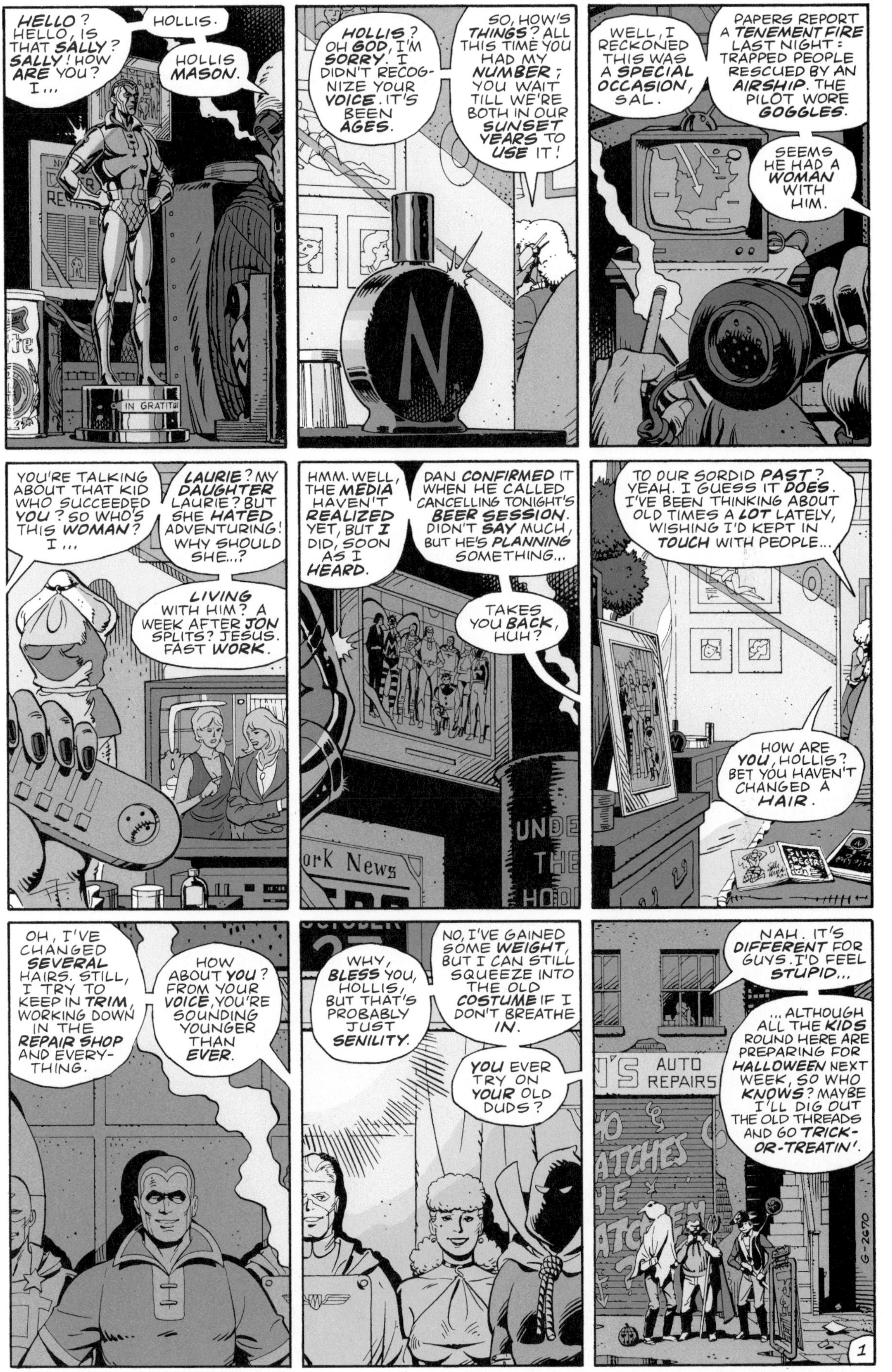
HELLO? HELLO, IS THAT SALLY? SALLY! HOW ARE YOU? I...
HOLLIS.
HOLLIS MASON.
IN GRATITU
HOLLIS? OH GOD, I'M SORRY. I DIDN'T RECOGNIZE YOUR VOICE. IT'S BEEN AGES.
SO, HOW'S THINGS? ALL THIS TIME YOU HAD MY NUMBER; YOU WAIT TILL WE'RE BOTH IN OUR SUNSET YEARS TO USE IT!
WELL, I RECKONED THIS WAS A SPECIAL OCCASION, SAL.
PAPERS REPORT A TENEMENT FIRE LAST NIGHT: TRAPPED PEOPLE RESCUED BY AN AIRSHIP. THE PILOT WORE GOGGLES.
SEEMS HE HAD A WOMAN WITH HIM.
YOU'RE TALKING ABOUT THAT KID WHO SUCCEEDED YOU? SO WHO'S THIS WOMAN? I...
LAURIE? MY DAUGHTER LAURIE? BUT SHE HATED ADVENTURING! WHY SHOULD SHE...?
LIVING WITH HIM? A WEEK AFTER JON SPLITS? JESUS. FAST WORK.
HMM. WELL, THE MEDIA HAVEN'T REALIZED YET, BUT I DID, SOON AS I HEARD.
DAN CONFIRMED IT WHEN HE CALLED CANCELLING TONIGHT'S BEER SESSION. DIDN'T SAY MUCH, BUT HE'S PLANNING SOMETHING...
TAKES YOU BACK, HUH?
ork News
UNDER THE HOO
TO OUR SORDID PAST? YEAH. I GUESS IT DOES. I'VE BEEN THINKING ABOUT OLD TIMES A LOT LATELY, WISHING I'D KEPT IN TOUCH WITH PEOPLE...
HOW ARE YOU, HOLLIS? BET YOU HAVEN'T CHANGED A HAIR.
OH, I'VE CHANGED SEVERAL HAIRS. STILL, I TRY TO KEEP IN TRIM, WORKING DOWN IN THE REPAIR SHOP AND EVERYTHING.
HOW ABOUT YOU? FROM YOUR VOICE, YOU'RE SOUNDING YOUNGER THAN EVER.
WHY, BLESS YOU, HOLLIS, BUT THAT'S PROBABLY JUST SENILITY.
NO, I'VE GAINED SOME WEIGHT, BUT I CAN STILL SQUEEZE INTO THE OLD COSTUME IF I DON'T BREATHE IN.
YOU EVER TRY ON YOUR OLD DUDS?
NAH. IT'S DIFFERENT FOR GUYS. I'D FEEL STUPID...
...ALTHOUGH ALL THE KIDS ROUND HERE ARE PREPARING FOR HALLOWEEN NEXT WEEK, SO WHO KNOWS? MAYBE I'LL DIG OUT THE OLD THREADS AND GO TRICK-OR-TREATIN'.
N'S AUTO REPAIRS
G-2670
1

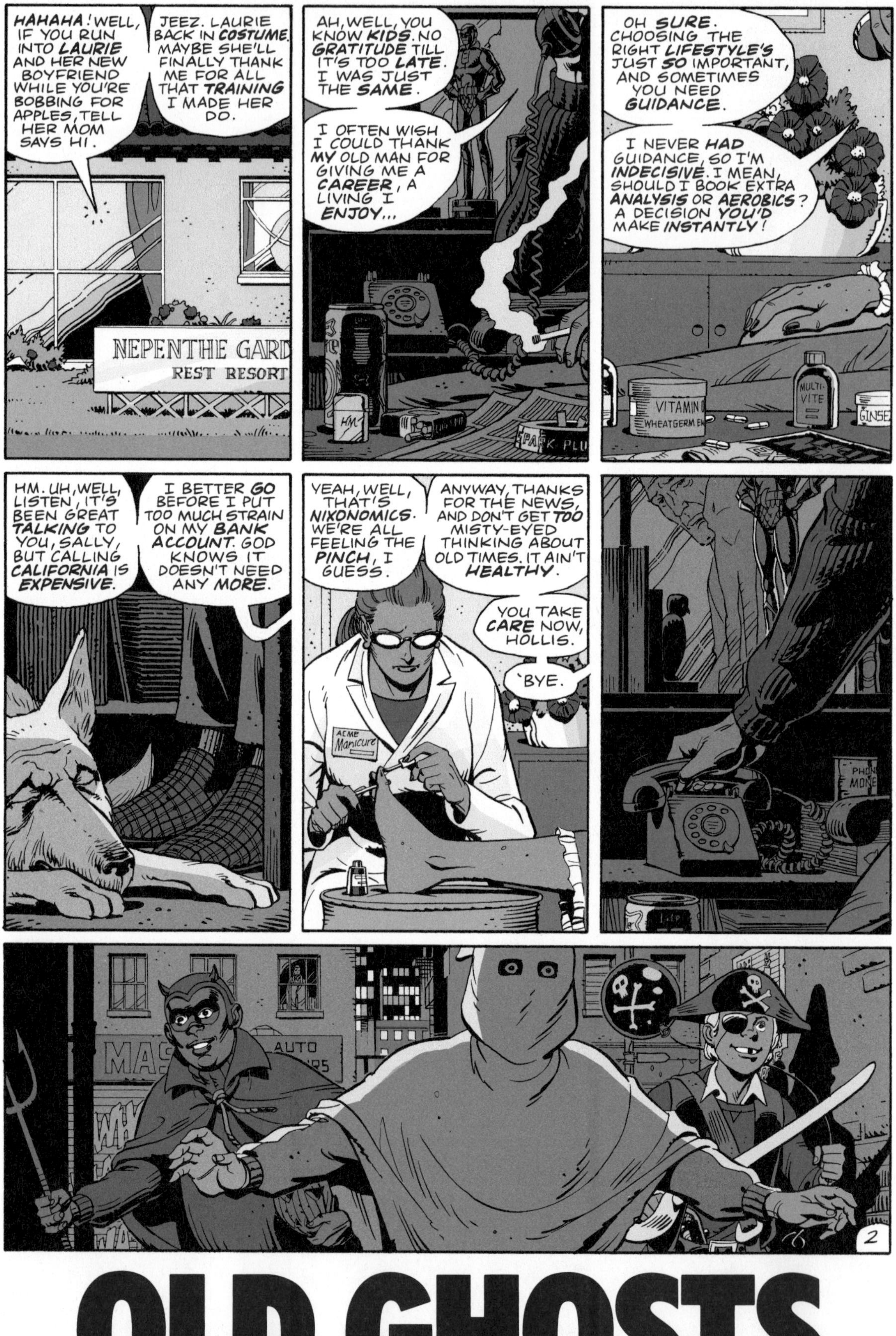
HAHAHA! WELL, IF YOU RUN INTO LAURIE AND HER NEW BOYFRIEND WHILE YOU'RE BOBBING FOR APPLES, TELL HER MOM SAYS HI.
JEEZ. LAURIE BACK IN COSTUME. MAYBE SHE'LL FINALLY THANK ME FOR ALL THAT TRAINING I MADE HER DO.
NEPENTHE GARD
REST RESORT
AH, WELL, YOU KNOW KIDS. NO GRATITUDE TILL IT'S TOO LATE. I WAS JUST THE SAME.
I OFTEN WISH I COULD THANK MY OLD MAN FOR GIVING ME A CAREER, A LIVING I ENJOY...
OH SURE. CHOOSING THE RIGHT LIFESTYLE'S JUST SO IMPORTANT, AND SOMETIMES YOU NEED GUIDANCE.
I NEVER HAD GUIDANCE, SO I'M INDECISIVE. I MEAN, SHOULD I BOOK EXTRA ANALYSIS OR AEROBICS? A DECISION YOU'D MAKE INSTANTLY!
VITAMIN
WHEATGERM
MULTI-VITE
HM. UH, WELL, LISTEN, IT'S BEEN GREAT TALKING TO YOU, SALLY, BUT CALLING CALIFORNIA IS EXPENSIVE.
I BETTER GO BEFORE I PUT TOO MUCH STRAIN ON MY BANK ACCOUNT. GOD KNOWS IT DOESN'T NEED ANY MORE.
YEAH, WELL, THAT'S NIXONOMICS. WE'RE ALL FEELING THE PINCH, I GUESS.
ANYWAY, THANKS FOR THE NEWS, AND DON'T GET TOO MISTY-EYED THINKING ABOUT OLD TIMES. IT AIN'T HEALTHY.
YOU TAKE CARE NOW, HOLLIS.
`BYE.
ACME Manicure
AUTO
2

OLD GHOSTS

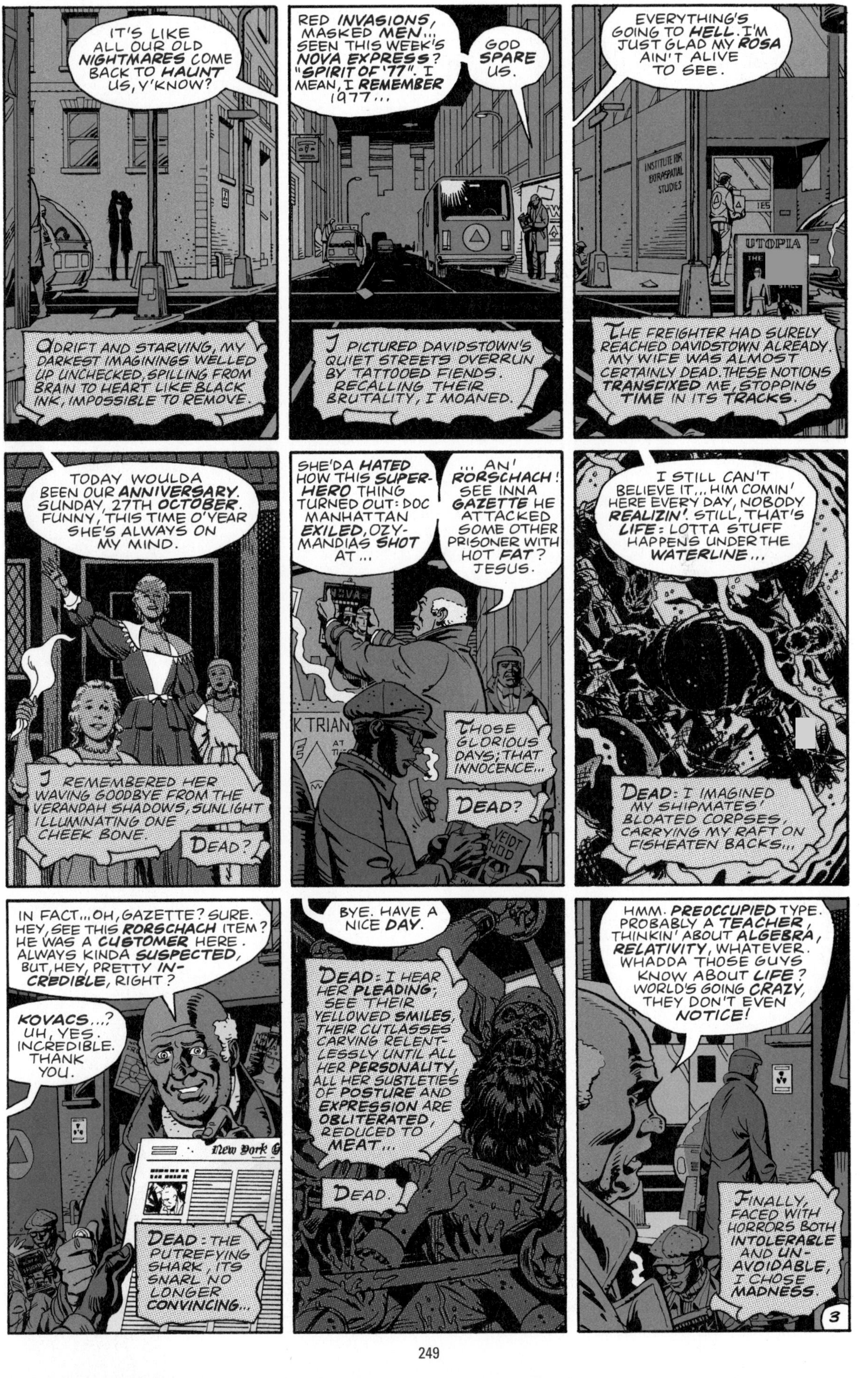
IT'S LIKE ALL OUR OLD NIGHTMARES COME BACK TO HAUNT US, Y'KNOW?
ADRIFT AND STARVING, MY DARKEST IMAGININGS WELLED UP UNCHECKED, SPILLING FROM BRAIN TO HEART LIKE BLACK INK, IMPOSSIBLE TO REMOVE.
RED INVASIONS, MASKED MEN... SEEN THIS WEEK'S NOVA EXPRESS? "SPIRIT OF '77". I MEAN, I REMEMBER 1977...
GOD SPARE US.
I PICTURED DAVIDSTOWN'S QUIET STREETS OVERRUN BY TATTOOED FIENDS. RECALLING THEIR BRUTALITY, I MOANED.
EVERYTHING'S GOING TO HELL. I'M JUST GLAD MY ROSA AIN'T ALIVE TO SEE.
INSTITUTE FOR EXTRASPATIAL STUDIES
UTOPIA
THE FREIGHTER HAD SURELY REACHED DAVIDSTOWN ALREADY. MY WIFE WAS ALMOST CERTAINLY DEAD. THESE NOTIONS TRANSFIXED ME, STOPPING TIME IN ITS TRACKS.
TODAY WOULDA BEEN OUR ANNIVERSARY. SUNDAY, 27TH OCTOBER. FUNNY, THIS TIME O'YEAR SHE'S ALWAYS ON MY MIND.
I REMEMBERED HER WAVING GOODBYE FROM THE VERANDAH SHADOWS, SUNLIGHT ILLUMINATING ONE CHEEK BONE.
DEAD?
SHE'DA HATED HOW THIS SUPER-HERO THING TURNED OUT: DOC MANHATTAN EXILED, OZY-MANDIAS SHOT AT...
... AN' RORSCHACH! SEE INNA GAZETTE HE ATTACKED SOME OTHER PRISONER WITH HOT FAT? JESUS.
THOSE GLORIOUS DAYS; THAT INNOCENCE...
DEAD?
I STILL CAN'T BELIEVE IT... HIM COMIN' HERE EVERY DAY, NOBODY REALIZIN'. STILL, THAT'S LIFE: LOTTA STUFF HAPPENS UNDER THE WATERLINE...
DEAD: I IMAGINED MY SHIPMATES' BLOATED CORPSES, CARRYING MY RAFT ON FISHEATEN BACKS...
IN FACT... OH, GAZETTE? SURE. HEY, SEE THIS RORSCHACH ITEM? HE WAS A CUSTOMER HERE. ALWAYS KINDA SUSPECTED, BUT, HEY, PRETTY IN-CREDIBLE, RIGHT?
KOVACS...? UH, YES. INCREDIBLE. THANK YOU.
DEAD: THE PUTREFYING SHARK, ITS SNARL NO LONGER CONVINCING...
BYE. HAVE A NICE DAY.
DEAD: I HEAR HER PLEADING; SEE THEIR YELLOWED SMILES, THEIR CUTLASSES CARVING RELENT-LESSLY UNTIL ALL HER PERSONALITY, ALL HER SUBTLETIES OF POSTURE AND EXPRESSION ARE OBLITERATED, REDUCED TO MEAT...
DEAD.
HMM. PREOCCUPIED TYPE. PROBABLY A TEACHER, THINKIN' ABOUT ALGEBRA, RELATIVITY, WHATEVER. WHADDA THOSE GUYS KNOW ABOUT LIFE? WORLD'S GOING CRAZY, THEY DON'T EVEN NOTICE!
FINALLY, FACED WITH HORRORS BOTH INTOLERABLE AND UN-AVOIDABLE, I CHOSE MADNESS.
3

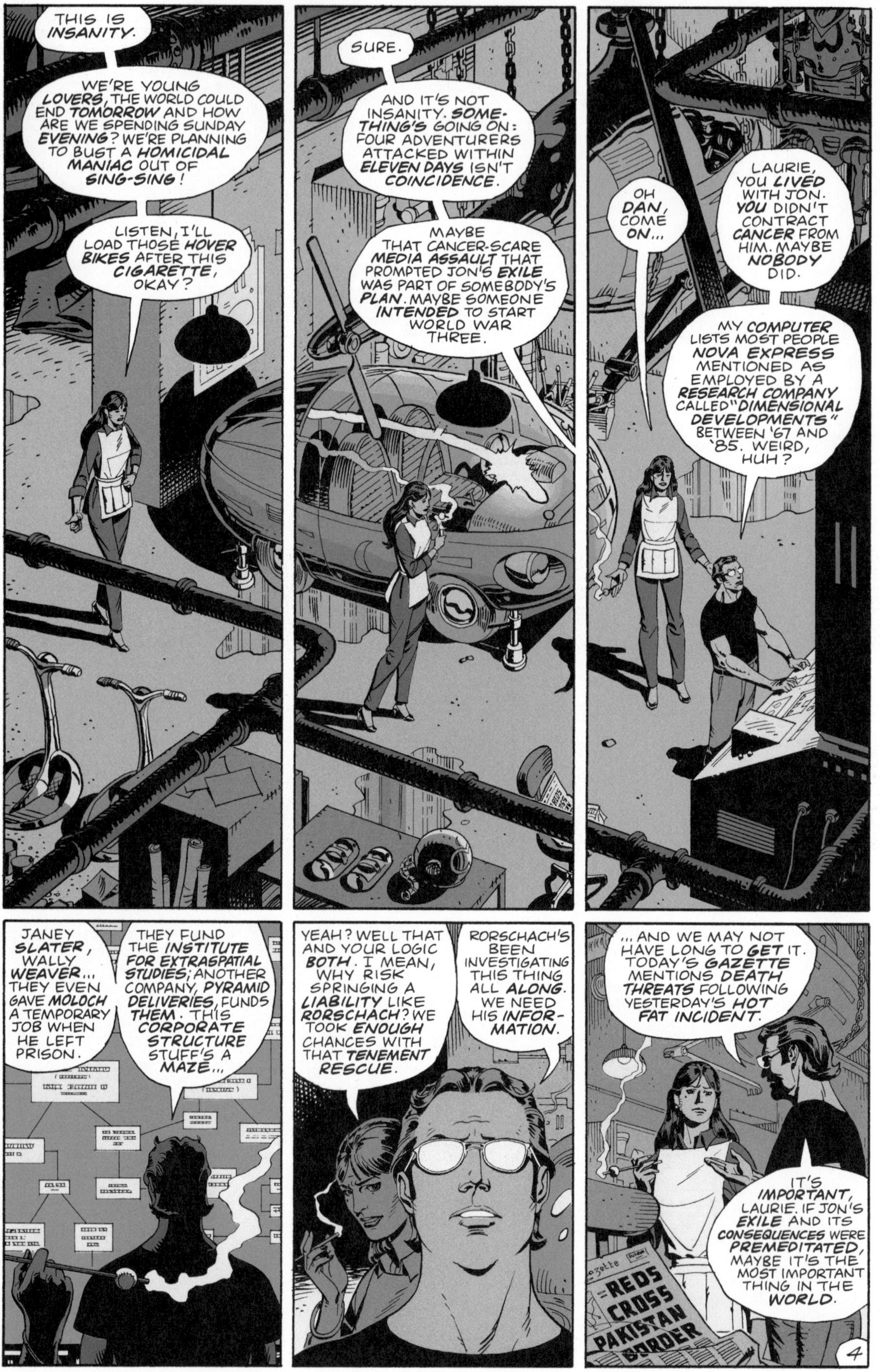

THIS IS INSANITY.
WE'RE YOUNG LOVERS, THE WORLD COULD END TOMORROW AND HOW ARE WE SPENDING SUNDAY EVENING? WE'RE PLANNING TO BUST A HOMICIDAL MANIAC OUT OF SING-SING!
LISTEN, I'LL LOAD THOSE HOVER BIKES AFTER THIS CIGARETTE, OKAY?
SURE.
AND IT'S NOT INSANITY. SOMETHING'S GOING ON: FOUR ADVENTURERS ATTACKED WITHIN ELEVEN DAYS ISN'T COINCIDENCE.
MAYBE THAT CANCER-SCARE MEDIA ASSAULT THAT PROMPTED JON'S EXILE WAS PART OF SOMEBODY'S PLAN. MAYBE SOMEONE INTENDED TO START WORLD WAR THREE.
OH DAN, COME ON...
LAURIE, YOU LIVED WITH JON. YOU DIDN'T CONTRACT CANCER FROM HIM. MAYBE NOBODY DID.
MY COMPUTER LISTS MOST PEOPLE NOVA EXPRESS MENTIONED AS EMPLOYED BY A RESEARCH COMPANY CALLED "DIMENSIONAL DEVELOPMENTS" BETWEEN '67 AND '85. WEIRD, HUH?
JANEY SLATER, WALLY WEAVER... THEY EVEN GAVE MOLOCH A TEMPORARY JOB WHEN HE LEFT PRISON.
THEY FUND THE INSTITUTE FOR EXTRASPATIAL STUDIES; ANOTHER COMPANY, PYRAMID DELIVERIES, FUNDS THEM. THIS CORPORATE STRUCTURE STUFF'S A MAZE...
YEAH? WELL THAT AND YOUR LOGIC BOTH. I MEAN, WHY RISK SPRINGING A LIABILITY LIKE RORSCHACH? WE TOOK ENOUGH CHANCES WITH THAT TENEMENT RESCUE.
RORSCHACH'S BEEN INVESTIGATING THIS THING ALL ALONG. WE NEED HIS INFORMATION.
...AND WE MAY NOT HAVE LONG TO GET IT. TODAY'S GAZETTE MENTIONS DEATH THREATS FOLLOWING YESTERDAY'S HOT FAT INCIDENT.
IT'S IMPORTANT, LAURIE. IF JON'S EXILE AND ITS CONSEQUENCES WERE PREMEDITATED, MAYBE IT'S THE MOST IMPORTANT THING IN THE WORLD.
Gazette
REDS CROSS PAKISTAN BORDER
4

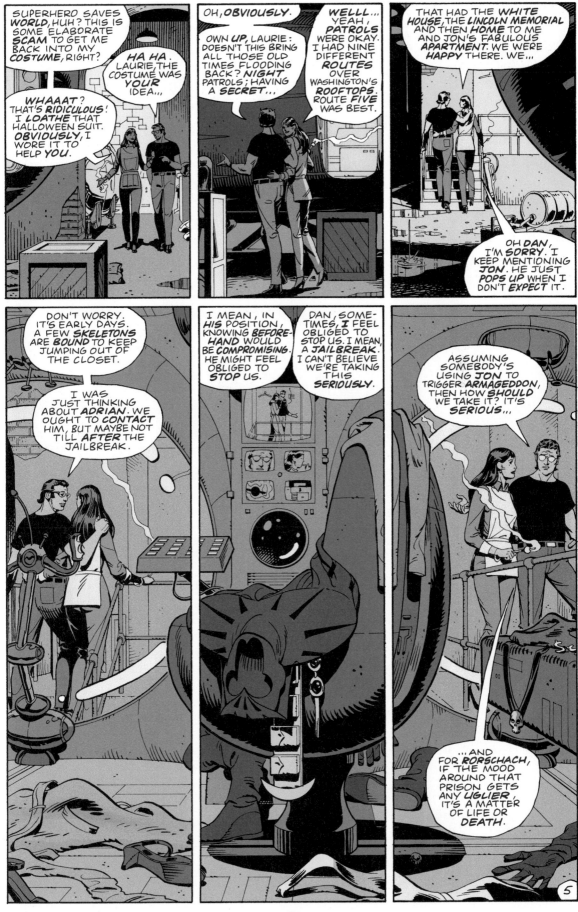

SUPERHERO SAVES **WORLD,** HUH? THIS IS SOME ELABORATE **SCAM** TO GET ME BACK INTO MY **COSTUME,** RIGHT?

HA HA. LAURIE, THE COSTUME WAS **YOUR** IDEA...

WHAAAT? THAT'S **RIDICULOUS!** I **LOATHE** THAT HALLOWEEN SUIT. **OBVIOUSLY,** I WORE IT TO HELP **YOU.**

OH, **OBVIOUSLY.**

OWN **UP,** LAURIE: DOESN'T THIS BRING ALL THOSE OLD TIMES FLOODING BACK? **NIGHT** PATROLS; HAVING A **SECRET...**

WELLL... YEAH, **PATROLS** WERE OKAY. I HAD NINE DIFFERENT **ROUTES** OVER WASHINGTON'S **ROOFTOPS.** ROUTE **FIVE** WAS BEST.

THAT HAD THE **WHITE HOUSE,** THE **LINCOLN MEMORIAL** AND THEN **HOME** TO ME AND JON'S FABULOUS **APARTMENT.** WE WERE **HAPPY** THERE. WE...

OH **DAN,** I'M **SORRY.** I KEEP MENTIONING **JON.** HE JUST **POPS UP** WHEN I DON'T **EXPECT** IT.

DON'T WORRY. IT'S EARLY DAYS. A FEW **SKELETONS** ARE **BOUND** TO KEEP JUMPING OUT OF THE CLOSET.

I WAS JUST THINKING ABOUT **ADRIAN.** WE OUGHT TO **CONTACT** HIM, BUT MAYBE NOT TILL **AFTER** THE JAILBREAK.

I MEAN, IN **HIS** POSITION, KNOWING **BEFOREHAND** WOULD BE **COMPROMISING.** HE MIGHT FEEL OBLIGED TO **STOP** US.

DAN, SOMETIMES, **I** FEEL OBLIGED TO STOP US. I MEAN, A **JAILBREAK.** I CAN'T BELIEVE WE'RE TAKING THIS **SERIOUSLY.**

ASSUMING SOMEBODY'S USING **JON** TO TRIGGER **ARMAGEDDON,** THEN HOW **SHOULD** WE TAKE IT? IT'S **SERIOUS...**

...AND FOR **RORSCHACH,** IF THE MOOD AROUND THAT PRISON GETS ANY **UGLIER,** IT'S A MATTER OF LIFE OR **DEATH.**

5

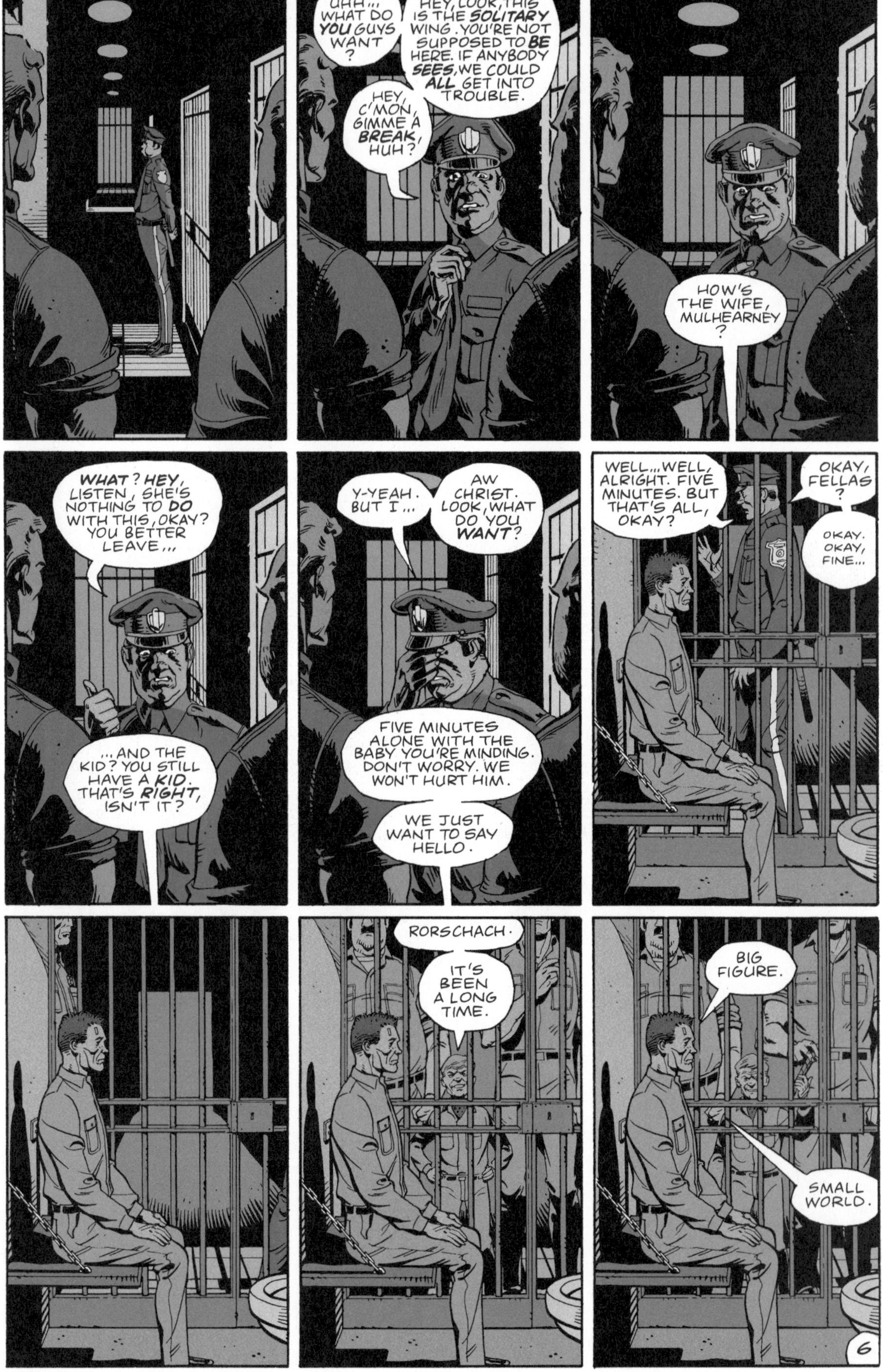
UHH... WHAT DO YOU GUYS WANT?
HEY, LOOK, THIS IS THE SOLITARY WING. YOU'RE NOT SUPPOSED TO BE HERE. IF ANYBODY SEES, WE COULD ALL GET INTO TROUBLE.
HEY, C'MON, GIMME A BREAK, HUH?
HOW'S THE WIFE, MULHEARNEY?
WHAT? HEY, LISTEN, SHE'S NOTHING TO DO WITH THIS, OKAY? YOU BETTER LEAVE...
...AND THE KID? YOU STILL HAVE A KID. THAT'S RIGHT, ISN'T IT?
Y-YEAH. BUT I...
AW CHRIST. LOOK, WHAT DO YOU WANT?
FIVE MINUTES ALONE WITH THE BABY YOU'RE MINDING. DON'T WORRY. WE WON'T HURT HIM.
WE JUST WANT TO SAY HELLO.
WELL... WELL, ALRIGHT. FIVE MINUTES. BUT THAT'S ALL, OKAY?
OKAY, FELLAS?
OKAY. OKAY, FINE...
RORSCHACH.
IT'S BEEN A LONG TIME.
BIG FIGURE.
SMALL WORLD.
6

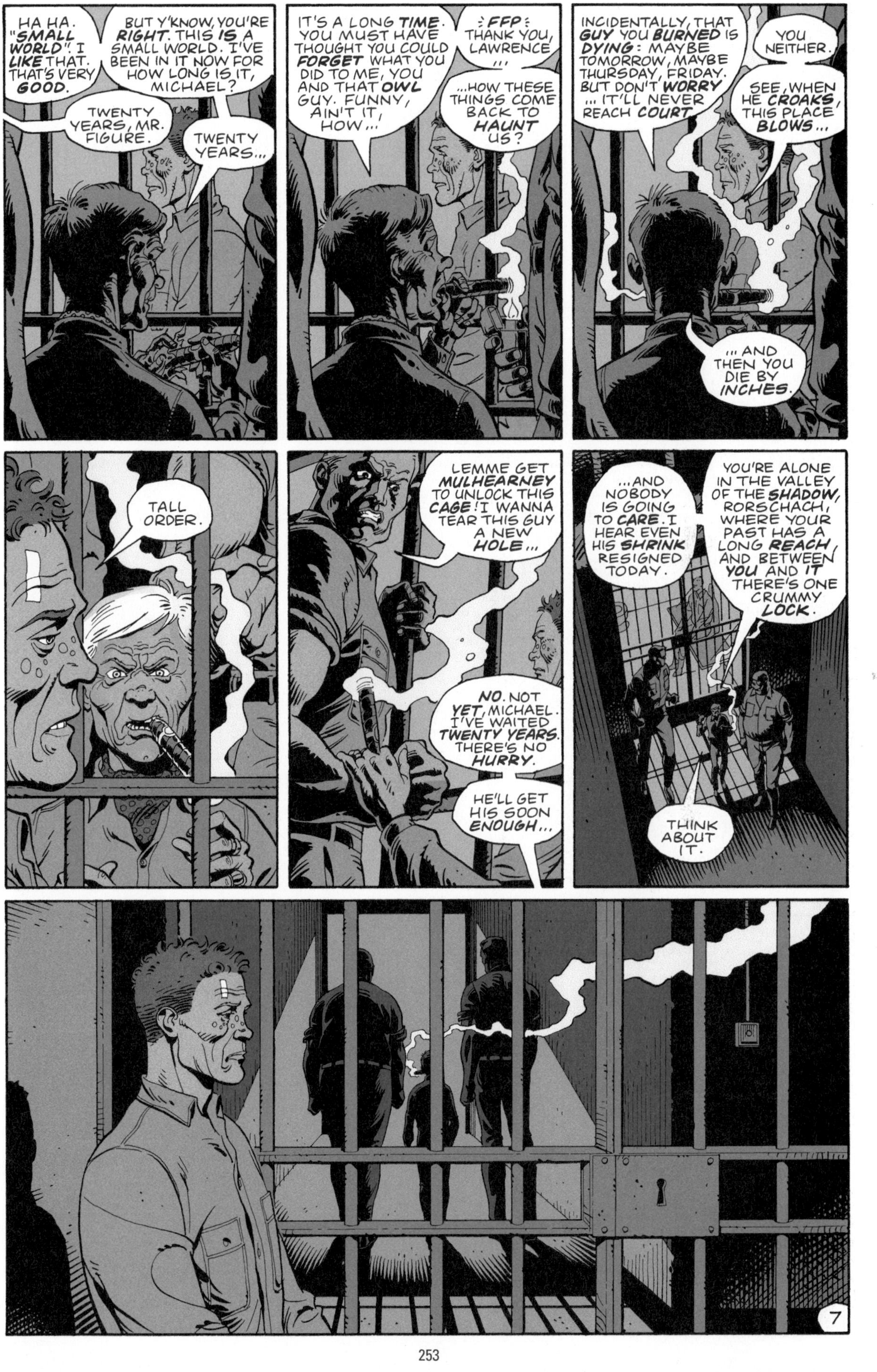
HA HA. "SMALL WORLD". I LIKE THAT. THAT'S VERY GOOD.
BUT Y'KNOW, YOU'RE RIGHT. THIS IS A SMALL WORLD. I'VE BEEN IN IT NOW FOR HOW LONG IS IT, MICHAEL?
TWENTY YEARS, MR. FIGURE.
TWENTY YEARS...
IT'S A LONG TIME. YOU MUST HAVE THOUGHT YOU COULD FORGET WHAT YOU DID TO ME, YOU AND THAT OWL GUY. FUNNY, AIN'T IT, HOW...
FFP
THANK YOU, LAWRENCE...
...HOW THESE THINGS COME BACK TO HAUNT US?
INCIDENTALLY, THAT GUY YOU BURNED IS DYING: MAYBE TOMORROW, MAYBE THURSDAY, FRIDAY. BUT DON'T WORRY... IT'LL NEVER REACH COURT.
YOU NEITHER.
SEE, WHEN HE CROAKS, THIS PLACE BLOWS...
...AND THEN YOU DIE BY INCHES.
TALL ORDER.
LEMME GET MULHEARNEY TO UNLOCK THIS CAGE! I WANNA TEAR THIS GUY A NEW HOLE...
NO. NOT YET, MICHAEL. I'VE WAITED TWENTY YEARS. THERE'S NO HURRY.
HE'LL GET HIS SOON ENOUGH...
...AND NOBODY IS GOING TO CARE. I HEAR EVEN HIS SHRINK RESIGNED TODAY.
YOU'RE ALONE IN THE VALLEY OF THE SHADOW, RORSCHACH, WHERE YOUR PAST HAS A LONG REACH, AND BETWEEN YOU AND IT THERE'S ONE CRUMMY LOCK.
THINK ABOUT IT.
7

EXCUSE ME? MY NAME'S DETECTIVE STEVEN *FINE*, I'M LOOKING FOR A DANIEL *DREIBERG*.

I'M DAN DREIBERG.

UH, YOU BETTER COME IN...

ALMOST *THROUGH* HERE, MR. *DREIBERG.* THIS BABY'LL HOLD OFF AN *ARMY*. SORRY WE KEPT YOU *WAITING* FOR THE *INSTALLATION*.

THAT'S OKAY. WELL, DETECTIVE, HOW CAN I *HELP* YOU?

EDWARD *BLAKE*. HOMICIDE VICTIM. YOU *KNEW* HIM.

UH, YES. VAGUELY.

YOU KNEW HIM WELL ENOUGH TO ATTEND HIS *FUNERAL*. I SAW THE *PHOTOGRAPHS*: YOU, ADRIAN *VEIDT*, DOC *MANHATTAN*.

YOU KEEP HEAVY COMPANY, MR. DREIBERG.

I MET BLAKE THROUGH *VEIDT*. I, UH, ONCE DONATED SOME *MONEY* TO ONE OF *VEIDT'S CHARITIES*.

BIG *GUY*, THAT *BLAKE*. FOR A *DIPLOMAT*. QUITE A *HEROIC FIGURE*. MAYBE HE WORKED *OUT*, HUH?

UH-HUH.

FUNNY... THERE'S BEEN A *LOT* OF "*HEROIC FIGURES*" IN THE NEWS LATELY: *RORSCHACH* CAPTURED, *VEIDT* SHOT AT, DOC MANHATTAN LEAVES *EARTH*, DAMN NEAR KICKING OFF WORLD WAR *THREE*...

CIGARETTE, MR. DREIBERG?

NO. THANKS. I DON'T.

New York Ga...

TANKS MASS [?]
EASTERN EUR[O...]

'PURELY DEFENSIVE' SAY REDS. | CALIFORNIA: GOVER... REAGAN URGES HARD LINE

VERY WISE.

...AND THEN THERE WAS THAT THING LAST *WEEKEND*. YOU READ ABOUT THAT? THAT *TENEMENT FIRE*?

ALL FINISHED, MR. DREIBERG. YOU GOT *MAXIMUM SECURITY*.

GORDIAN KNOT

UH, *RIGHT*. RIGHT. *THANKS*! I'LL SETTLE BY *CHECK*...

CRAZIEST STORY... THIS *AIRSHIP* RESCUES ALL THESE *PEOPLE*, HOVERING DOWN BETWEEN THE *BUILDINGS*. AIN'T MANY AIRSHIPS CAN DO *THAT*.

NO. INTERVIEWED SOME *WITNESSES*, BUT THE *DETAILS* WERE GARBLED: PILOT WORE *GOGGLES*; HAD A FEMALE *ACCOMPLICE*; PLAYED *MUSIC*; SERVED *COFFEE*...

HEY... "*SWEET CHARIOT*" *SUGAR* CUBES! ONLY COME IN *CATERING PACKS*, RIGHT?

UH, YES. I BELIEVE SO. WHY?

NO?

[SWEET CHAR...] SUGAR [...ATERING PACK] [COFFEE]

NO REASON.

Y'KNOW, THE ONLY SHIP I EVER HEARD OF COULD MANEUVER BETWEEN *BUILDINGS* BELONGED TO ONE OF THOSE MASKED *ADVENTURERS* THEY OUTLAWED IN '77.

COULDN'T HAVE *BEEN* HIM, NATURALLY... HE'D BE IN HIS *FORTIES* NOW.

8

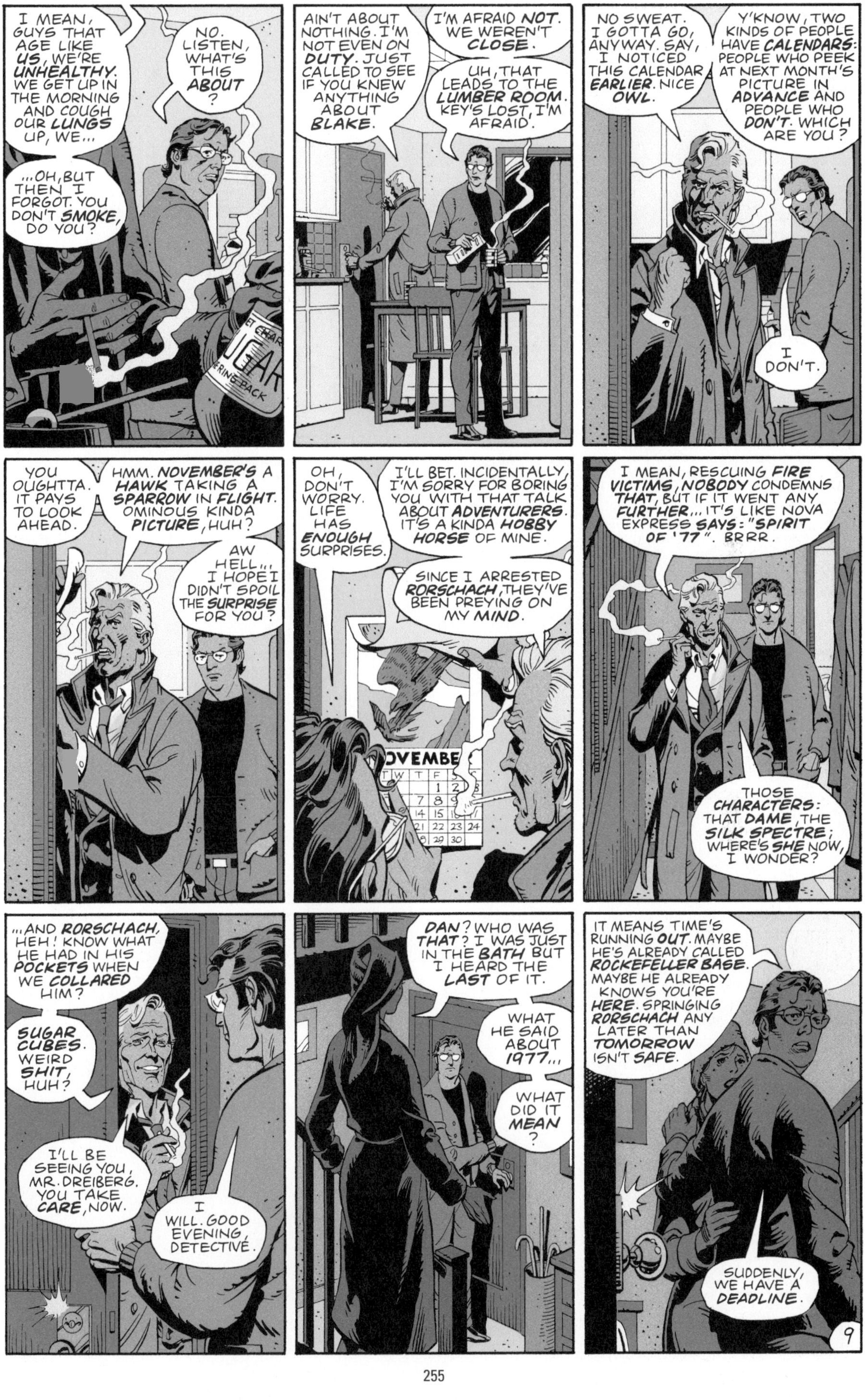

I MEAN, GUYS THAT AGE LIKE US, WE'RE UNHEALTHY. WE GET UP IN THE MORNING AND COUGH OUR LUNGS UP, WE...
NO. LISTEN, WHAT'S THIS ABOUT?
...OH, BUT THEN I FORGOT. YOU DON'T SMOKE, DO YOU?
AIN'T ABOUT NOTHING. I'M NOT EVEN ON DUTY. JUST CALLED TO SEE IF YOU KNEW ANYTHING ABOUT BLAKE.
I'M AFRAID NOT. WE WEREN'T CLOSE.
UH, THAT LEADS TO THE LUMBER ROOM. KEY'S LOST, I'M AFRAID.
NO SWEAT. I GOTTA GO, ANYWAY. SAY, I NOTICED THIS CALENDAR EARLIER. NICE OWL.
Y'KNOW, TWO KINDS OF PEOPLE HAVE CALENDARS: PEOPLE WHO PEEK AT NEXT MONTH'S PICTURE IN ADVANCE AND PEOPLE WHO DON'T. WHICH ARE YOU?
I DON'T.
YOU OUGHTTA. IT PAYS TO LOOK AHEAD.
HMM. NOVEMBER'S A HAWK TAKING A SPARROW IN FLIGHT. OMINOUS KINDA PICTURE, HUH?
AW HELL... I HOPE I DIDN'T SPOIL THE SURPRISE FOR YOU?
OH, DON'T WORRY. LIFE HAS ENOUGH SURPRISES.
I'LL BET. INCIDENTALLY, I'M SORRY FOR BORING YOU WITH THAT TALK ABOUT ADVENTURERS. IT'S A KINDA HOBBY HORSE OF MINE.
SINCE I ARRESTED RORSCHACH, THEY'VE BEEN PREYING ON MY MIND.
I MEAN, RESCUING FIRE VICTIMS, NOBODY CONDEMNS THAT, BUT IF IT WENT ANY FURTHER... IT'S LIKE NOVA EXPRESS SAYS: "SPIRIT OF '77". BRRR.
THOSE CHARACTERS: THAT DAME, THE SILK SPECTRE; WHERE'S SHE NOW, I WONDER?
...AND RORSCHACH, HEH! KNOW WHAT HE HAD IN HIS POCKETS WHEN WE COLLARED HIM?
SUGAR CUBES. WEIRD SHIT, HUH?
I'LL BE SEEING YOU, MR. DREIBERG. YOU TAKE CARE, NOW.
I WILL. GOOD EVENING, DETECTIVE.
DAN? WHO WAS THAT? I WAS JUST IN THE BATH BUT I HEARD THE LAST OF IT.
WHAT HE SAID ABOUT 1977...
WHAT DID IT MEAN?
IT MEANS TIME'S RUNNING OUT. MAYBE HE'S ALREADY CALLED ROCKEFELLER BASE. MAYBE HE ALREADY KNOWS YOU'RE HERE. SPRINGING RORSCHACH ANY LATER THAN TOMORROW ISN'T SAFE.
SUDDENLY, WE HAVE A DEADLINE.
9

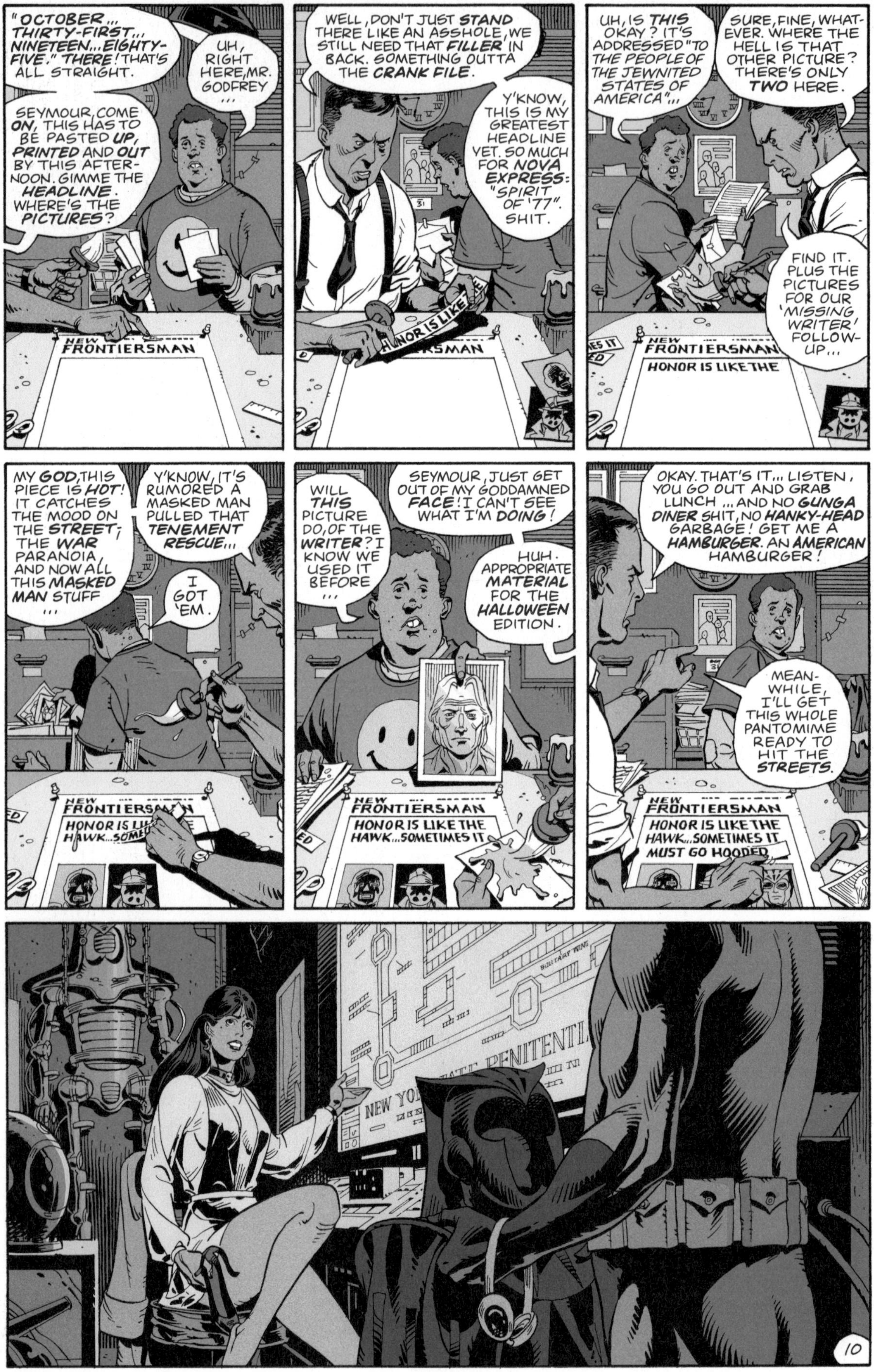
"OCTOBER... THIRTY-FIRST... NINETEEN... EIGHTY-FIVE." THERE! THAT'S ALL STRAIGHT.
UH, RIGHT HERE, MR. GODFREY...
SEYMOUR, COME ON, THIS HAS TO BE PASTED UP, PRINTED AND OUT BY THIS AFTERNOON. GIMME THE HEADLINE. WHERE'S THE PICTURES?
NEW FRONTIERSMAN
WELL, DON'T JUST STAND THERE LIKE AN ASSHOLE, WE STILL NEED THAT FILLER IN BACK. SOMETHING OUTTA THE CRANK FILE.
Y'KNOW, THIS IS MY GREATEST HEADLINE YET. SO MUCH FOR NOVA EXPRESS: "SPIRIT OF '77". SHIT.
UH, IS THIS OKAY? IT'S ADDRESSED "TO THE PEOPLE OF THE JEWNITED STATES OF AMERICA"...
SURE, FINE, WHATEVER. WHERE THE HELL IS THAT OTHER PICTURE? THERE'S ONLY TWO HERE.
FIND IT. PLUS THE PICTURES FOR OUR 'MISSING WRITER' FOLLOW-UP...
NEW FRONTIERSMAN
HONOR IS LIKE THE
MY GOD, THIS PIECE IS HOT! IT CATCHES THE MOOD ON THE STREET; THE WAR PARANOIA, AND NOW ALL THIS MASKED MAN STUFF...
Y'KNOW, IT'S RUMORED A MASKED MAN PULLED THAT TENEMENT RESCUE...
I GOT 'EM.
WILL THIS PICTURE DO, OF THE WRITER? I KNOW WE USED IT BEFORE...
SEYMOUR, JUST GET OUT OF MY GODDAMNED FACE! I CAN'T SEE WHAT I'M DOING!
HUH. APPROPRIATE MATERIAL FOR THE HALLOWEEN EDITION.
NEW FRONTIERSMAN
HONOR IS LIKE THE HAWK... SOMETIMES IT
OKAY. THAT'S IT... LISTEN, YOU GO OUT AND GRAB LUNCH... AND NO GUNGA DINER SHIT, NO HANKY-HEAD GARBAGE! GET ME A HAMBURGER. AN AMERICAN HAMBURGER!
MEANWHILE, I'LL GET THIS WHOLE PANTOMIME READY TO HIT THE STREETS.
NEW FRONTIERSMAN
HONOR IS LIKE THE HAWK... SOMETIMES IT MUST GO HOODED.
10

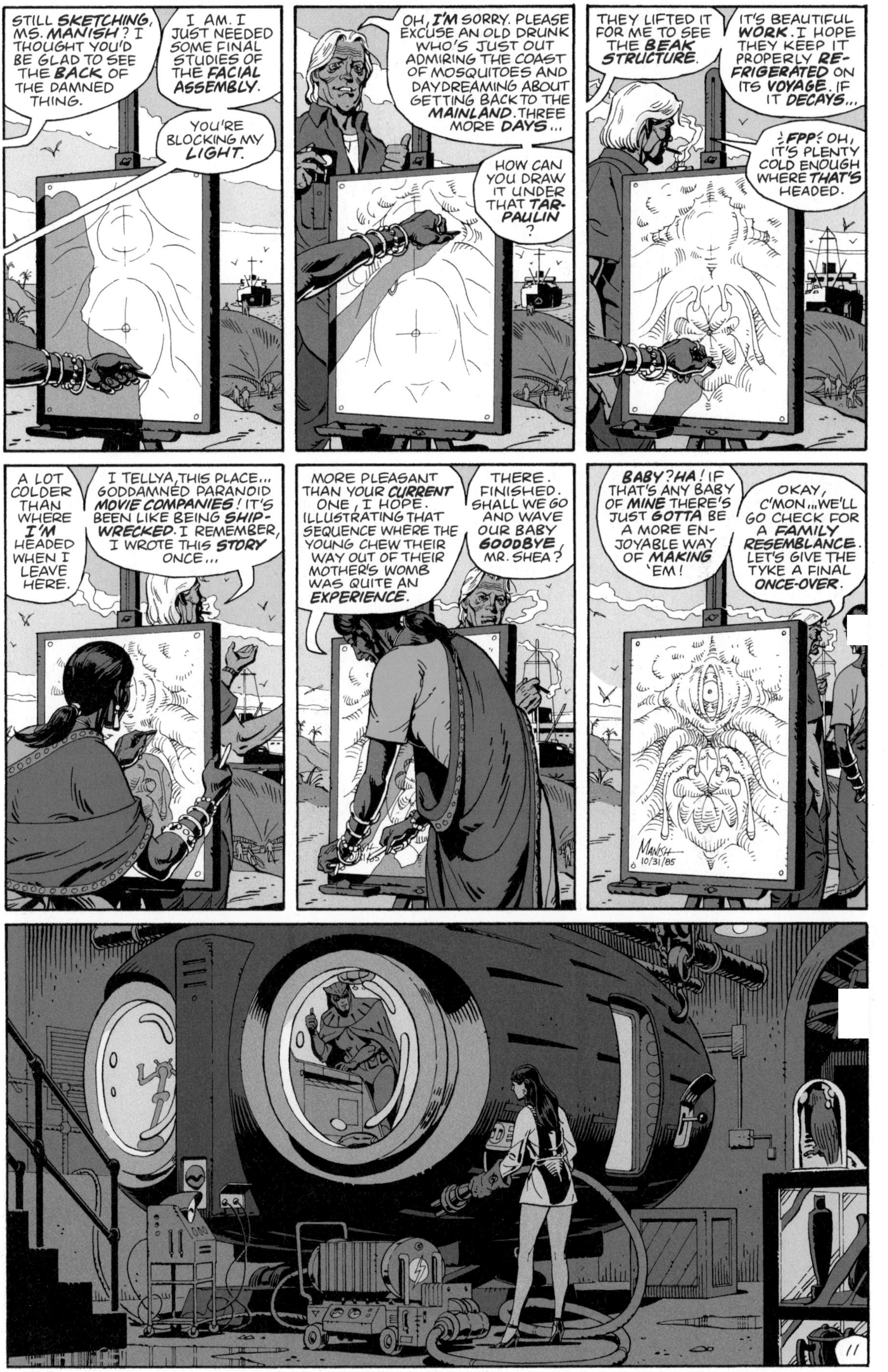
STILL SKETCHING, MS. MANISH? I THOUGHT YOU'D BE GLAD TO SEE THE BACK OF THE DAMNED THING.
I AM. I JUST NEEDED SOME FINAL STUDIES OF THE FACIAL ASSEMBLY.
YOU'RE BLOCKING MY LIGHT.
OH, I'M SORRY. PLEASE EXCUSE AN OLD DRUNK WHO'S JUST OUT ADMIRING THE COAST OF MOSQUITOES AND DAYDREAMING ABOUT GETTING BACK TO THE MAINLAND. THREE MORE DAYS...
HOW CAN YOU DRAW IT UNDER THAT TAR-PAULIN?
THEY LIFTED IT FOR ME TO SEE THE BEAK STRUCTURE.
IT'S BEAUTIFUL WORK. I HOPE THEY KEEP IT PROPERLY RE-FRIGERATED ON ITS VOYAGE. IF IT DECAYS...
FPP OH, IT'S PLENTY COLD ENOUGH WHERE THAT'S HEADED.
A LOT COLDER THAN WHERE I'M HEADED WHEN I LEAVE HERE.
I TELLYA, THIS PLACE... GODDAMNED PARANOID MOVIE COMPANIES! IT'S BEEN LIKE BEING SHIP-WRECKED. I REMEMBER, I WROTE THIS STORY ONCE...
MORE PLEASANT THAN YOUR CURRENT ONE, I HOPE. ILLUSTRATING THAT SEQUENCE WHERE THE YOUNG CHEW THEIR WAY OUT OF THEIR MOTHER'S WOMB WAS QUITE AN EXPERIENCE.
THERE. FINISHED. SHALL WE GO AND WAVE OUR BABY GOODBYE, MR. SHEA?
BABY? HA! IF THAT'S ANY BABY OF MINE THERE'S JUST GOTTA BE A MORE EN-JOYABLE WAY OF MAKING 'EM!
OKAY, C'MON...WE'LL GO CHECK FOR A FAMILY RESEMBLANCE. LET'S GIVE THE TYKE A FINAL ONCE-OVER.
MANISH
10/31/85
11

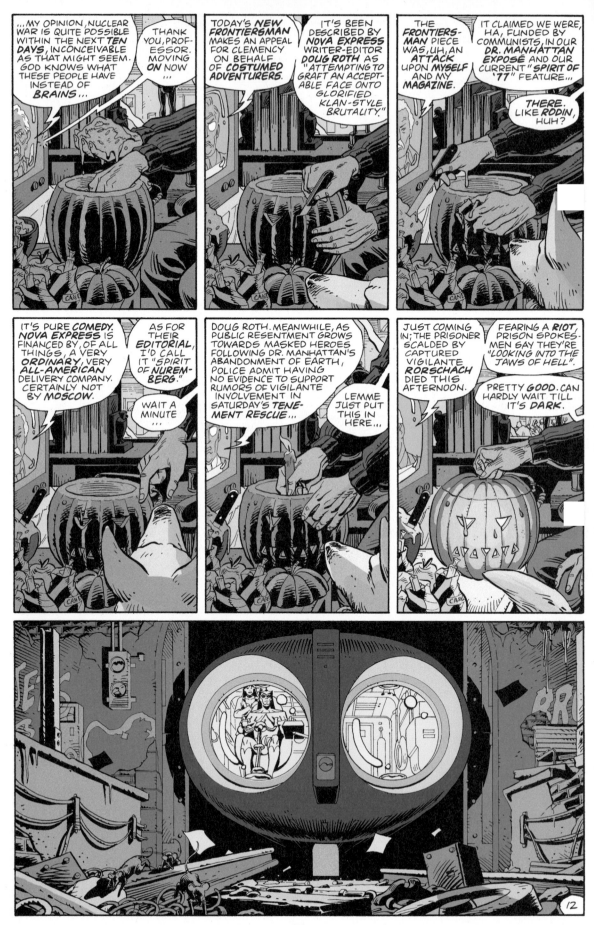

...MY OPINION, NUCLEAR WAR IS QUITE POSSIBLE WITHIN THE NEXT *TEN DAYS*, INCONCEIVABLE AS THAT MIGHT SEEM. GOD KNOWS WHAT THESE PEOPLE HAVE INSTEAD OF *BRAINS*...

THANK YOU, PROFESSOR. MOVING *ON* NOW ...

TODAY'S *NEW FRONTIERSMAN* MAKES AN APPEAL FOR CLEMENCY ON BEHALF OF *COSTUMED ADVENTURERS*.

IT'S BEEN DESCRIBED BY *NOVA EXPRESS* WRITER-EDITOR *DOUG ROTH* AS "ATTEMPTING TO GRAFT AN ACCEPTABLE FACE ONTO GLORIFIED KLAN-STYLE BRUTALITY."

THE *FRONTIERS-MAN* PIECE WAS, UH, AN *ATTACK* UPON *MYSELF* AND MY *MAGAZINE*.

IT CLAIMED WE WERE, HA, FUNDED BY COMMUNISTS, IN OUR *DR. MANHATTAN EXPOSÉ* AND OUR CURRENT *"SPIRIT OF '77"* FEATURE...

THERE. LIKE *RODIN*, HUH?

IT'S PURE *COMEDY*. *NOVA EXPRESS* IS FINANCED BY, OF ALL THINGS, A VERY *ORDINARY*, VERY *ALL-AMERICAN* DELIVERY COMPANY. CERTAINLY NOT BY *MOSCOW*.

AS FOR THEIR *EDITORIAL*, I'D CALL IT "SPIRIT OF *NUREMBERG*."

WAIT A MINUTE ...

DOUG ROTH. MEANWHILE, AS PUBLIC RESENTMENT GROWS TOWARDS MASKED HEROES FOLLOWING DR. MANHATTAN'S ABANDONMENT OF EARTH, POLICE ADMIT HAVING NO EVIDENCE TO SUPPORT RUMORS OF VIGILANTE INVOLVEMENT IN SATURDAY'S *TENE-MENT RESCUE*...

LEMME JUST PUT THIS IN HERE...

JUST COMING IN; THE PRISONER SCALDED BY CAPTURED VIGILANTE *RORSCHACH* DIED THIS AFTERNOON.

FEARING A *RIOT*, PRISON SPOKES-MEN SAY THEY'RE *"LOOKING INTO THE JAWS OF HELL"*.

PRETTY *GOOD*. CAN HARDLY WAIT TILL IT'S *DARK*.

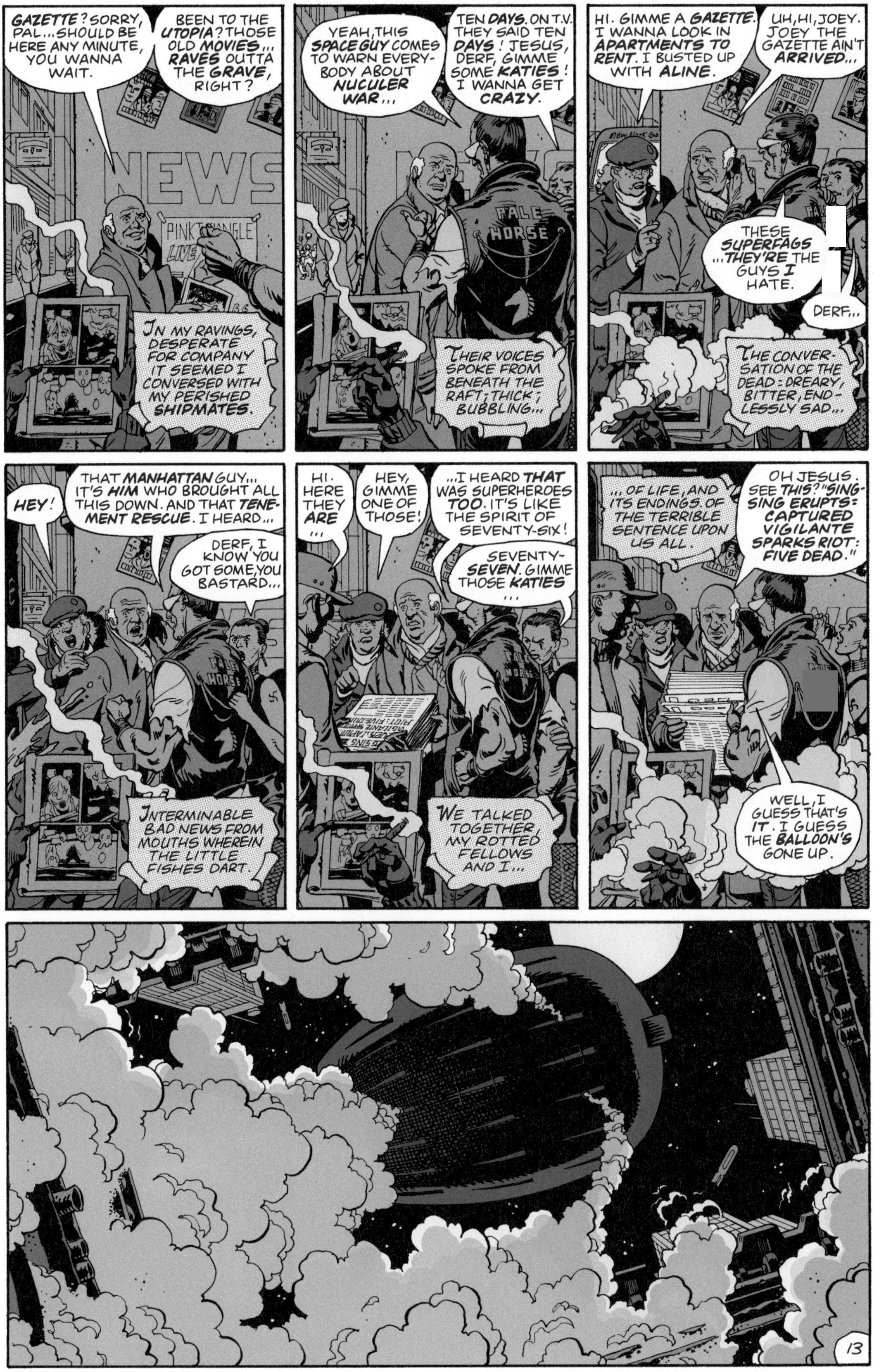
GAZETTE? SORRY, PAL...SHOULD BE HERE ANY MINUTE, YOU WANNA WAIT.
BEEN TO THE UTOPIA? THOSE OLD MOVIES... RAVES OUTTA THE GRAVE, RIGHT?
NEWS
PINK TRIANGLE LIVE
IN MY RAVINGS, DESPERATE FOR COMPANY IT SEEMED I CONVERSED WITH MY PERISHED SHIPMATES.
YEAH, THIS SPACE GUY COMES TO WARN EVERYBODY ABOUT NUCULER WAR...
TEN DAYS. ON T.V. THEY SAID TEN DAYS! JESUS, DERF, GIMME SOME KATIES! I WANNA GET CRAZY.
PALE HORSE
THEIR VOICES SPOKE FROM BENEATH THE RAFT; THICK; BUBBLING...
HI. GIMME A GAZETTE. I WANNA LOOK IN APARTMENTS TO RENT. I BUSTED UP WITH ALINE.
UH, HI, JOEY. JOEY THE GAZETTE AIN'T ARRIVED...
THESE SUPERFAGS ...THEY'RE THE GUYS I HATE.
DERF...
THE CONVERSATION OF THE DEAD: DREARY, BITTER, ENDLESSLY SAD...
HEY!
THAT MANHATTAN GUY... IT'S HIM WHO BROUGHT ALL THIS DOWN. AND THAT TENEMENT RESCUE. I HEARD...
DERF, I KNOW YOU GOT SOME, YOU BASTARD...
INTERMINABLE BAD NEWS FROM MOUTHS WHEREIN THE LITTLE FISHES DART.
HI. HERE THEY ARE...
HEY, GIMME ONE OF THOSE!
...I HEARD THAT WAS SUPERHEROES TOO. IT'S LIKE THE SPIRIT OF SEVENTY-SIX!
SEVENTY-SEVEN. GIMME THOSE KATIES...
WE TALKED TOGETHER, MY ROTTED FELLOWS AND I...
...OF LIFE, AND ITS ENDINGS. OF THE TERRIBLE SENTENCE UPON US ALL.
OH JESUS. SEE THIS? "SING-SING ERUPTS: CAPTURED VIGILANTE SPARKS RIOT: FIVE DEAD."
WELL, I GUESS THAT'S IT. I GUESS THE BALLOON'S GONE UP.
13

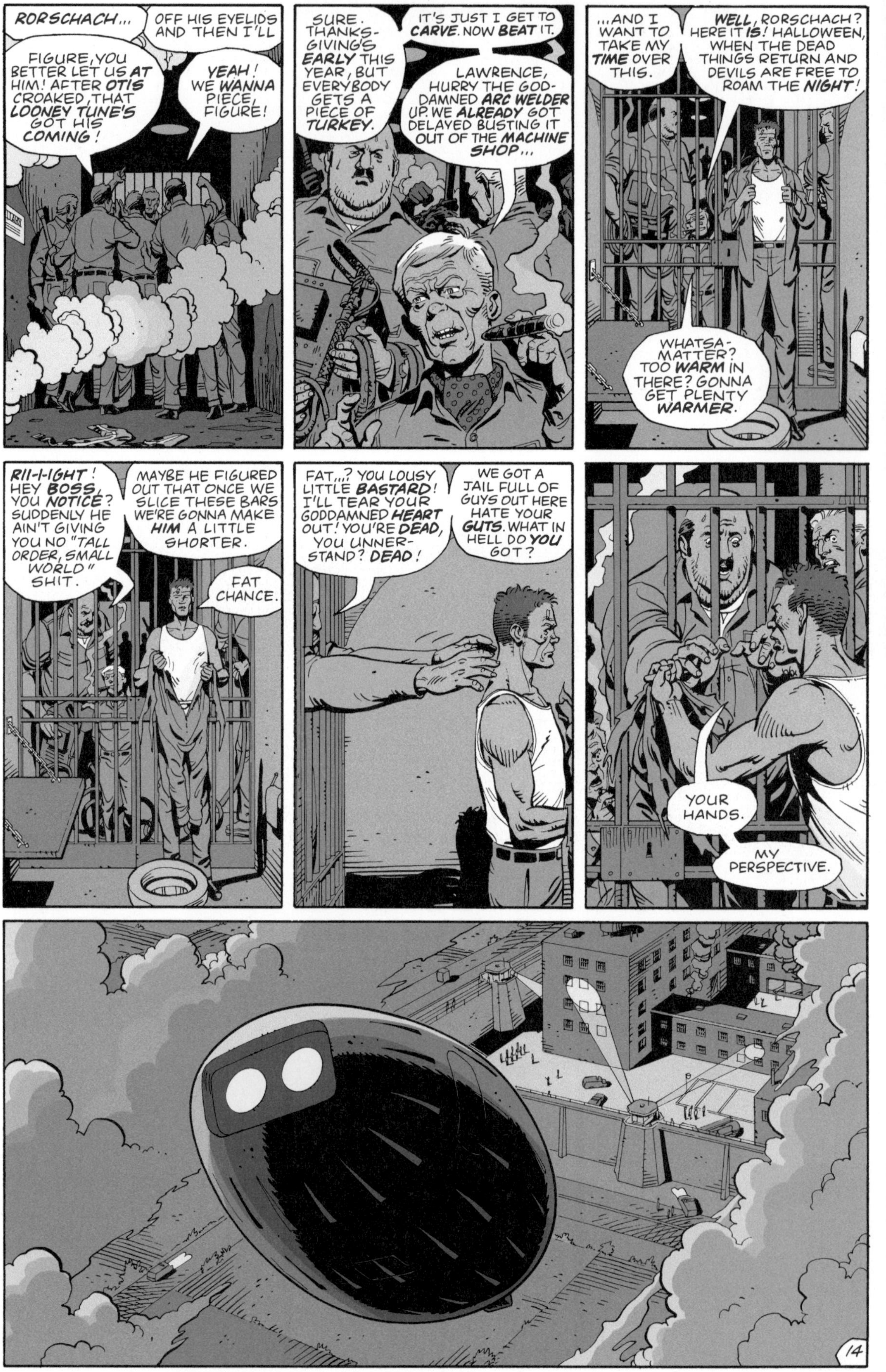

RORSCHACH...
FIGURE, YOU BETTER LET US AT HIM! AFTER OTIS CROAKED, THAT LOONEY TUNE'S GOT HIS COMING!
OFF HIS EYELIDS AND THEN I'LL
YEAH! WE WANNA PIECE, FIGURE!
SURE. THANKSGIVING'S EARLY THIS YEAR, BUT EVERYBODY GETS A PIECE OF TURKEY.
IT'S JUST I GET TO CARVE. NOW BEAT IT.
LAWRENCE, HURRY THE GODDAMNED ARC WELDER UP. WE ALREADY GOT DELAYED BUSTING IT OUT OF THE MACHINE SHOP...
...AND I WANT TO TAKE MY TIME OVER THIS.
WELL, RORSCHACH? HERE IT IS! HALLOWEEN, WHEN THE DEAD THINGS RETURN AND DEVILS ARE FREE TO ROAM THE NIGHT!
WHATSA-MATTER? TOO WARM IN THERE? GONNA GET PLENTY WARMER.
RII-I-IGHT! HEY BOSS, YOU NOTICE? SUDDENLY HE AIN'T GIVING YOU NO "TALL ORDER, SMALL WORLD" SHIT.
MAYBE HE FIGURED OUT THAT ONCE WE SLICE THESE BARS WE'RE GONNA MAKE HIM A LITTLE SHORTER.
FAT CHANCE.
FAT...? YOU LOUSY LITTLE BASTARD! I'LL TEAR YOUR GODDAMNED HEART OUT! YOU'RE DEAD, YOU UNNERSTAND? DEAD!
WE GOT A JAIL FULL OF GUYS OUT HERE HATE YOUR GUTS. WHAT IN HELL DO YOU GOT?
YOUR HANDS.
MY PERSPECTIVE.
14

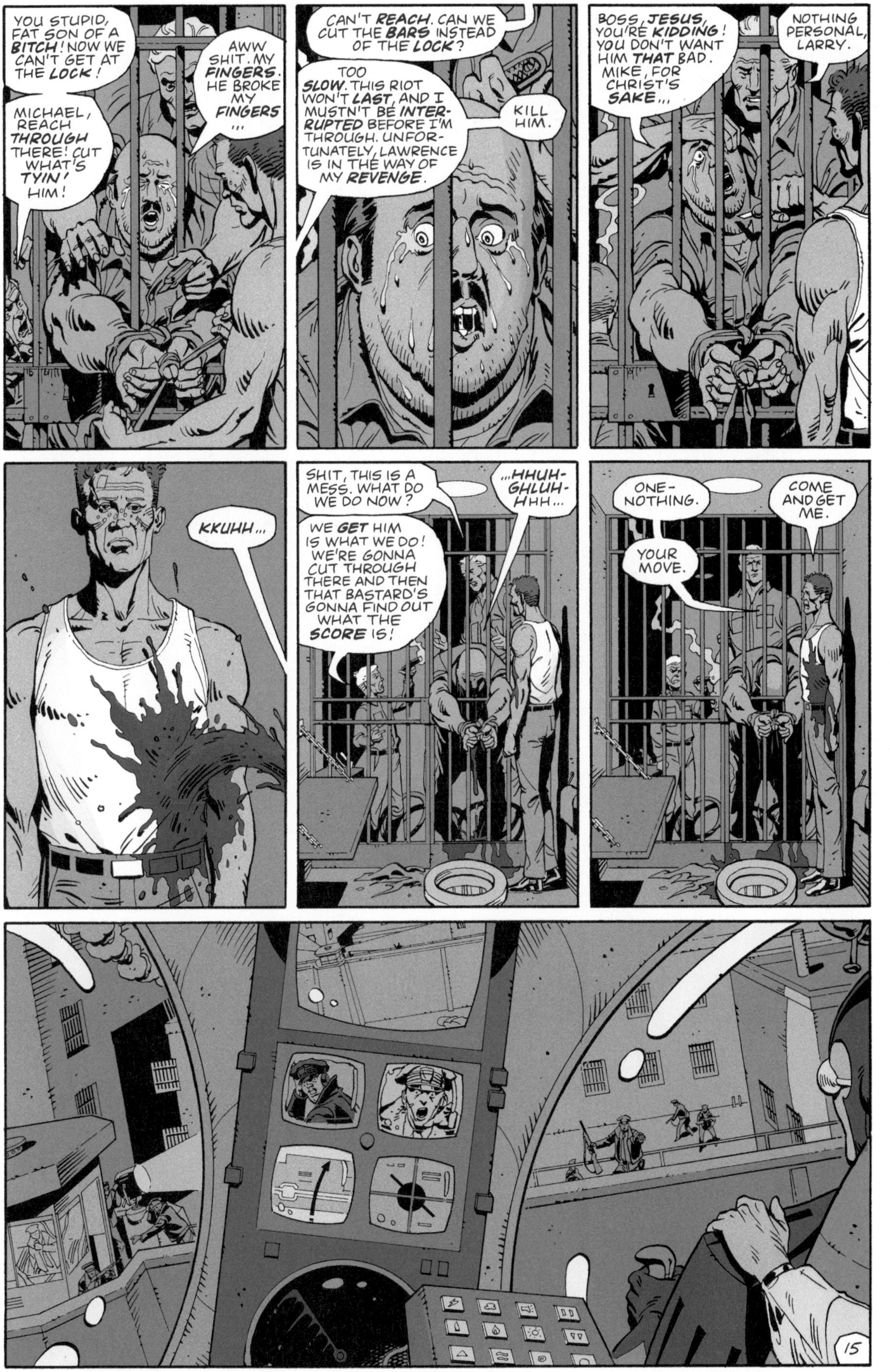
YOU STUPID, FAT SON OF A BITCH! NOW WE CAN'T GET AT THE LOCK!
MICHAEL, REACH THROUGH THERE! CUT WHAT'S TYIN' HIM!
AWW SHIT. MY FINGERS. HE BROKE MY FINGERS...
CAN'T REACH. CAN WE CUT THE BARS INSTEAD OF THE LOCK?
TOO SLOW. THIS RIOT WON'T LAST, AND I MUSTN'T BE INTERRUPTED BEFORE I'M THROUGH. UNFORTUNATELY, LAWRENCE IS IN THE WAY OF MY REVENGE.
KILL HIM.
BOSS, JESUS, YOU'RE KIDDING! YOU DON'T WANT HIM THAT BAD. MIKE, FOR CHRIST'S SAKE...
NOTHING PERSONAL, LARRY.
KKUHH...
SHIT, THIS IS A MESS. WHAT DO WE DO NOW?
...HHUH-GHLUH-HHH...
WE GET HIM IS WHAT WE DO! WE'RE GONNA CUT THROUGH THERE AND THEN THAT BASTARD'S GONNA FIND OUT WHAT THE SCORE IS!
ONE-NOTHING.
YOUR MOVE.
COME AND GET ME.
15

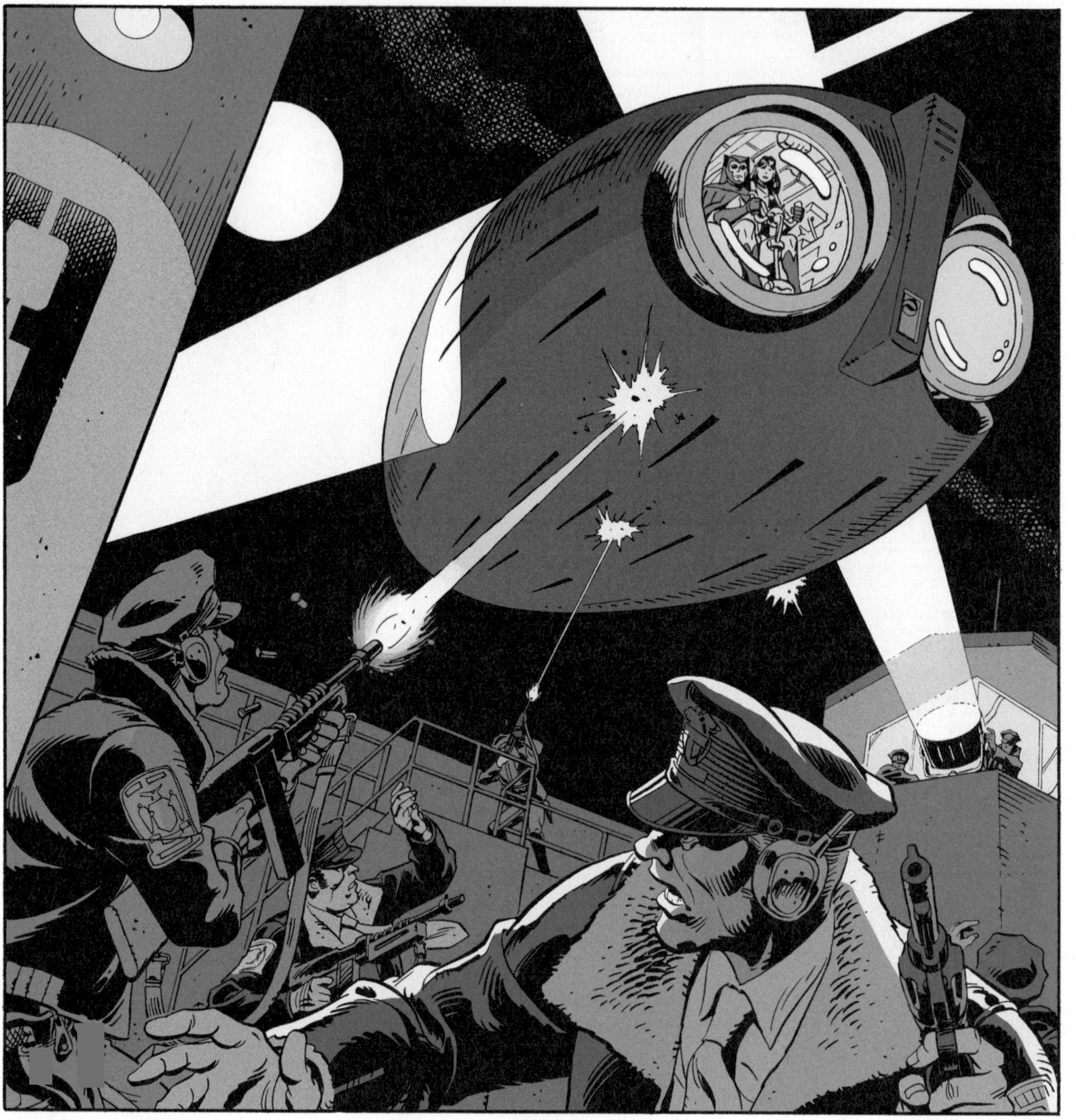

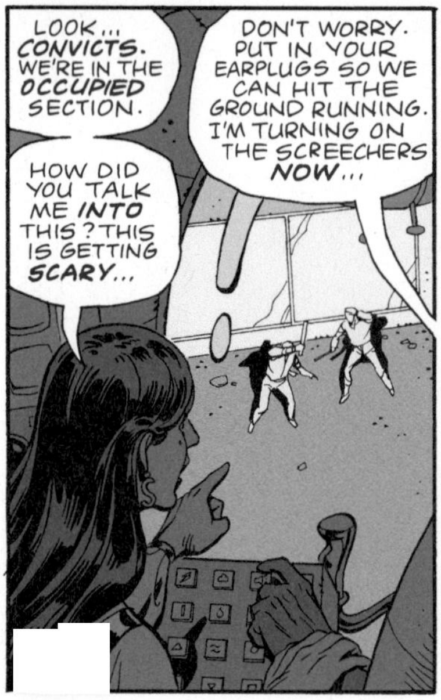
LOOK... CONVICTS. WE'RE IN THE OCCUPIED SECTION.
DON'T WORRY. PUT IN YOUR EARPLUGS SO WE CAN HIT THE GROUND RUNNING. I'M TURNING ON THE SCREECHERS NOW...
HOW DID YOU TALK ME INTO THIS? THIS IS GETTING SCARY...

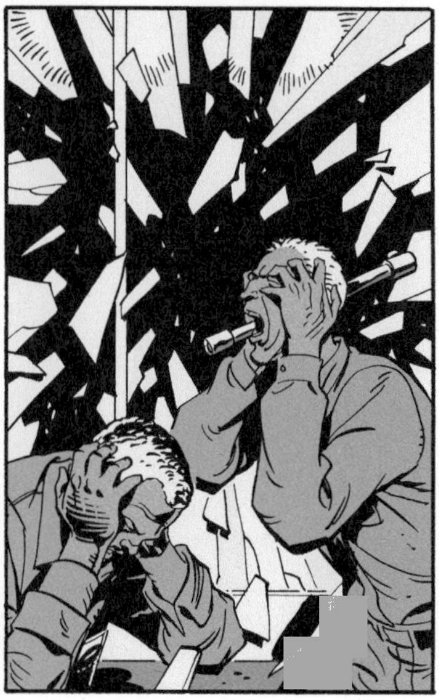

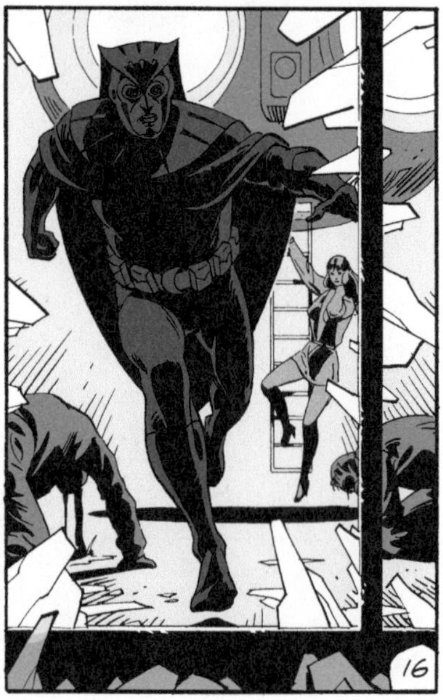
16

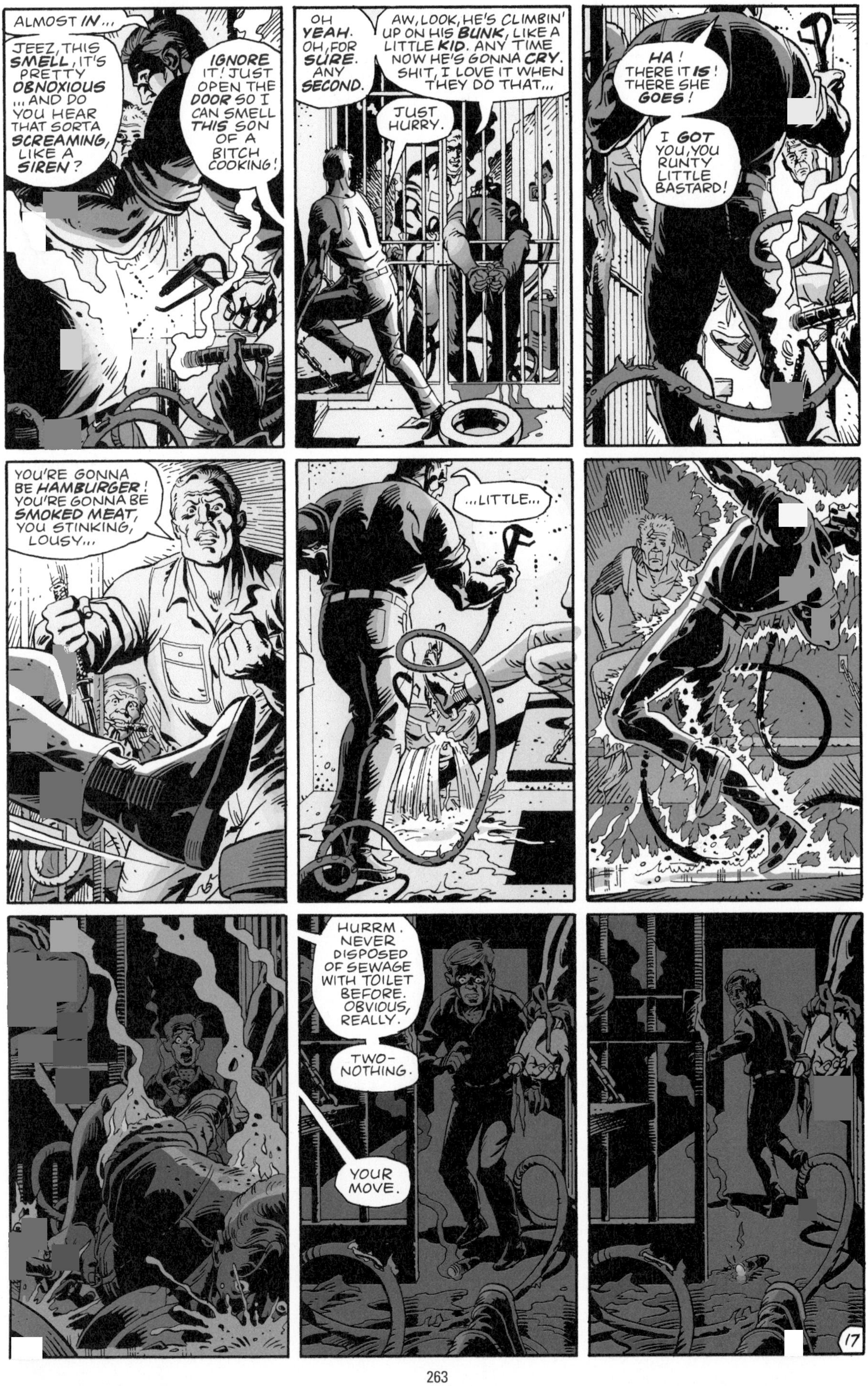
ALMOST IN...
JEEZ, THIS SMELL, IT'S PRETTY OBNOXIOUS ...AND DO YOU HEAR THAT SORTA SCREAMING, LIKE A SIREN?
IGNORE IT! JUST OPEN THE DOOR SO I CAN SMELL THIS SON OF A BITCH COOKING!
OH YEAH. OH, FOR SURE. ANY SECOND.
AW, LOOK, HE'S CLIMBIN' UP ON HIS BUNK, LIKE A LITTLE KID. ANY TIME NOW HE'S GONNA CRY. SHIT, I LOVE IT WHEN THEY DO THAT...
JUST HURRY.
HA! THERE IT IS! THERE SHE GOES!
I GOT YOU, YOU RUNTY LITTLE BASTARD!
YOU'RE GONNA BE HAMBURGER! YOU'RE GONNA BE SMOKED MEAT, YOU STINKING, LOUSY...
...LITTLE...
HURRM. NEVER DISPOSED OF SEWAGE WITH TOILET BEFORE. OBVIOUS, REALLY.
TWO-NOTHING.
YOUR MOVE.
17

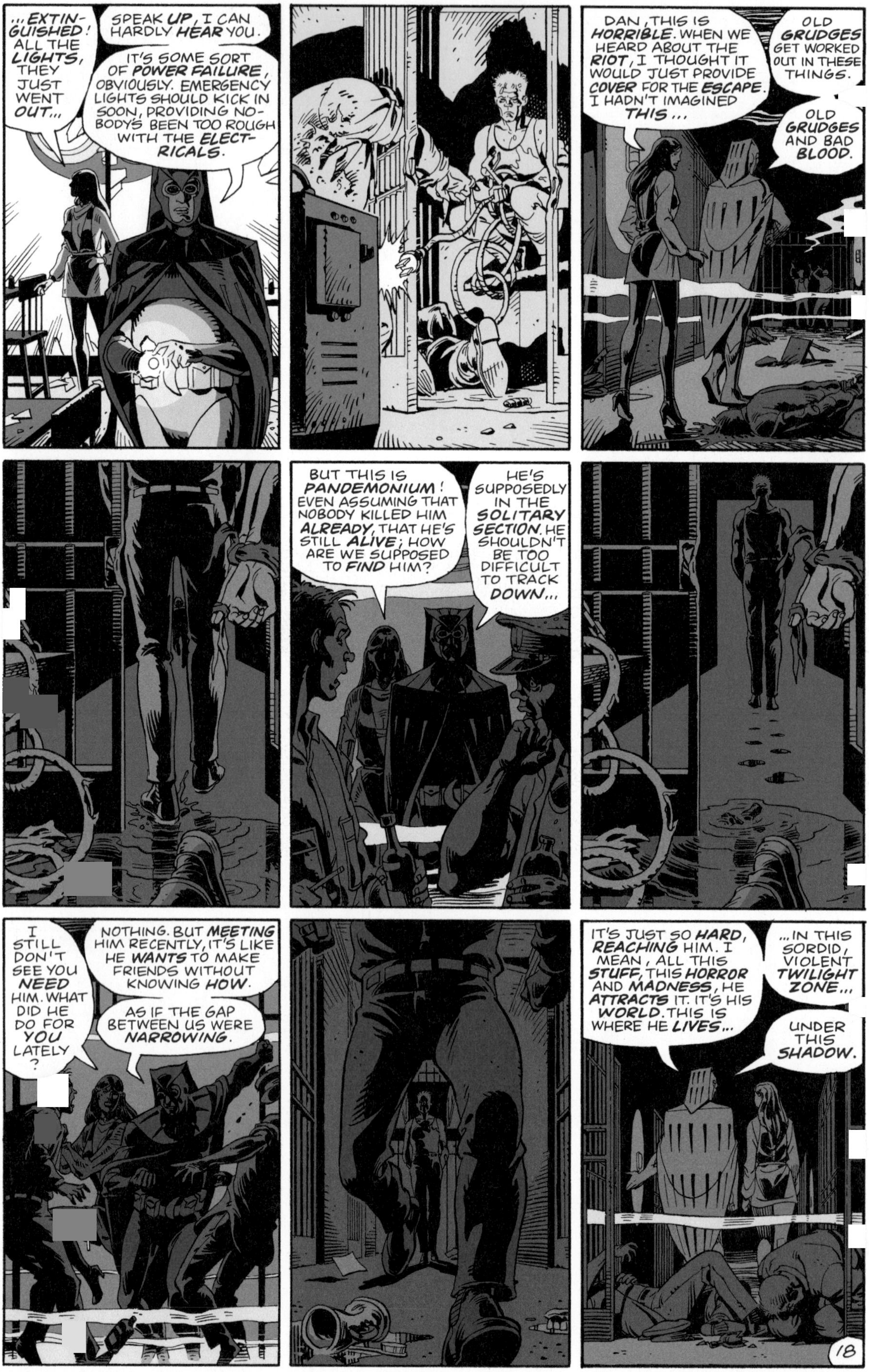
...EXTINGUISHED! ALL THE LIGHTS, THEY JUST WENT OUT...
SPEAK UP, I CAN HARDLY HEAR YOU.
IT'S SOME SORT OF POWER FAILURE, OBVIOUSLY. EMERGENCY LIGHTS SHOULD KICK IN SOON, PROVIDING NOBODY'S BEEN TOO ROUGH WITH THE ELECTRICALS.
DAN, THIS IS HORRIBLE. WHEN WE HEARD ABOUT THE RIOT, I THOUGHT IT WOULD JUST PROVIDE COVER FOR THE ESCAPE. I HADN'T IMAGINED THIS...
OLD GRUDGES GET WORKED OUT IN THESE THINGS.
OLD GRUDGES AND BAD BLOOD.
BUT THIS IS PANDEMONIUM! EVEN ASSUMING THAT NOBODY KILLED HIM ALREADY, THAT HE'S STILL ALIVE; HOW ARE WE SUPPOSED TO FIND HIM?
HE'S SUPPOSEDLY IN THE SOLITARY SECTION. HE SHOULDN'T BE TOO DIFFICULT TO TRACK DOWN...
I STILL DON'T SEE YOU NEED HIM. WHAT DID HE DO FOR YOU LATELY?
NOTHING. BUT MEETING HIM RECENTLY, IT'S LIKE HE WANTS TO MAKE FRIENDS WITHOUT KNOWING HOW.
AS IF THE GAP BETWEEN US WERE NARROWING.
IT'S JUST SO HARD, REACHING HIM. I MEAN, ALL THIS STUFF, THIS HORROR AND MADNESS, HE ATTRACTS IT. IT'S HIS WORLD. THIS IS WHERE HE LIVES...
...IN THIS SORDID, VIOLENT TWILIGHT ZONE...
UNDER THIS SHADOW.
18

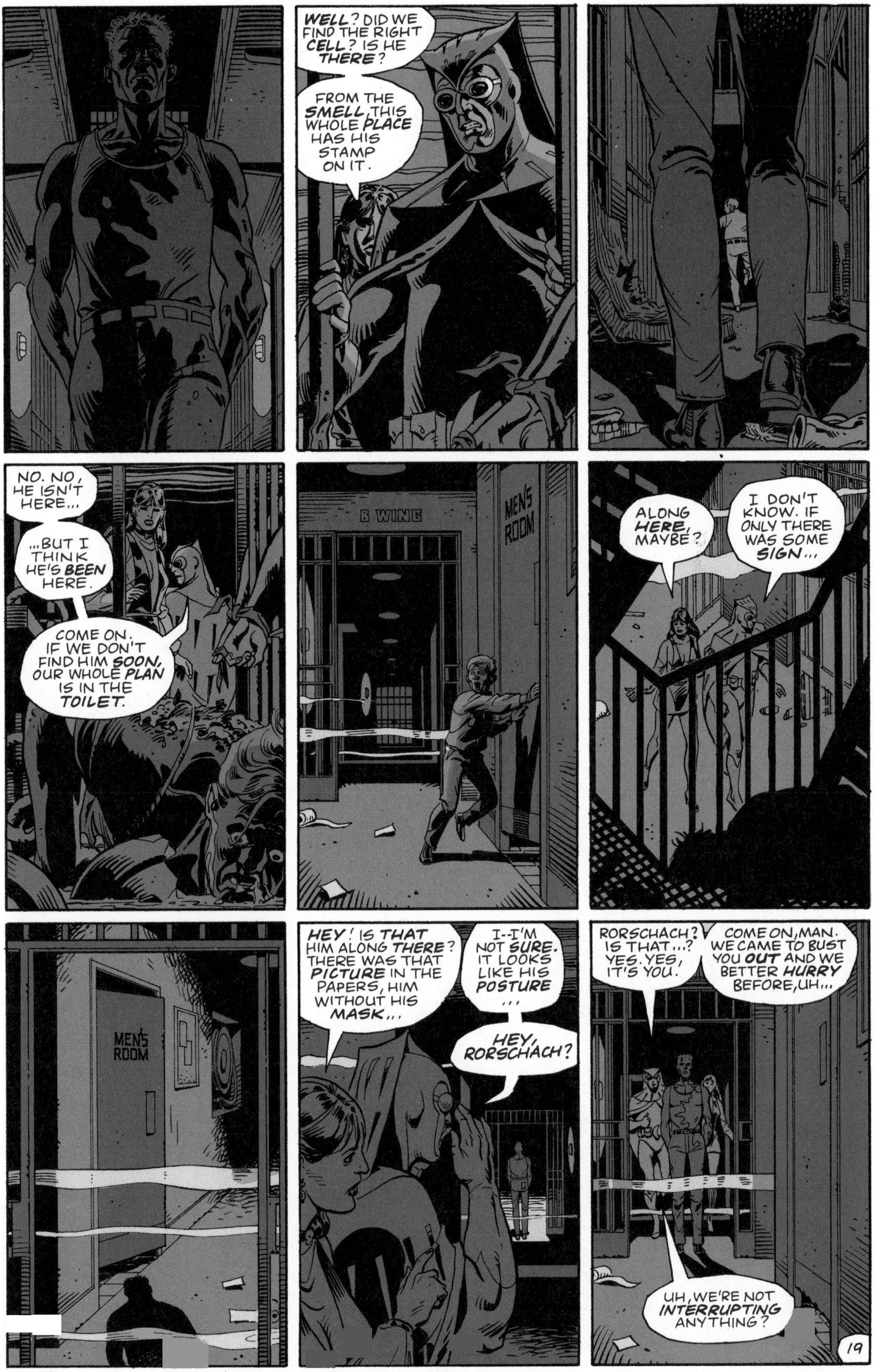
WELL? DID WE FIND THE RIGHT CELL? IS HE THERE?
FROM THE SMELL, THIS WHOLE PLACE HAS HIS STAMP ON IT.
NO. NO, HE ISN'T HERE...
...BUT I THINK HE'S BEEN HERE.
COME ON. IF WE DON'T FIND HIM SOON, OUR WHOLE PLAN IS IN THE TOILET.
B WING
MEN'S ROOM
ALONG HERE, MAYBE?
I DON'T KNOW. IF ONLY THERE WAS SOME SIGN...
MEN'S ROOM
HEY! IS THAT HIM ALONG THERE? THERE WAS THAT PICTURE IN THE PAPERS, HIM WITHOUT HIS MASK...
I--I'M NOT SURE. IT LOOKS LIKE HIS POSTURE...
HEY, RORSCHACH?
RORSCHACH? IS THAT...? YES. YES, IT'S YOU.
COME ON, MAN. WE CAME TO BUST YOU OUT AND WE BETTER HURRY BEFORE, UH...
UH, WE'RE NOT INTERRUPTING ANYTHING?
19

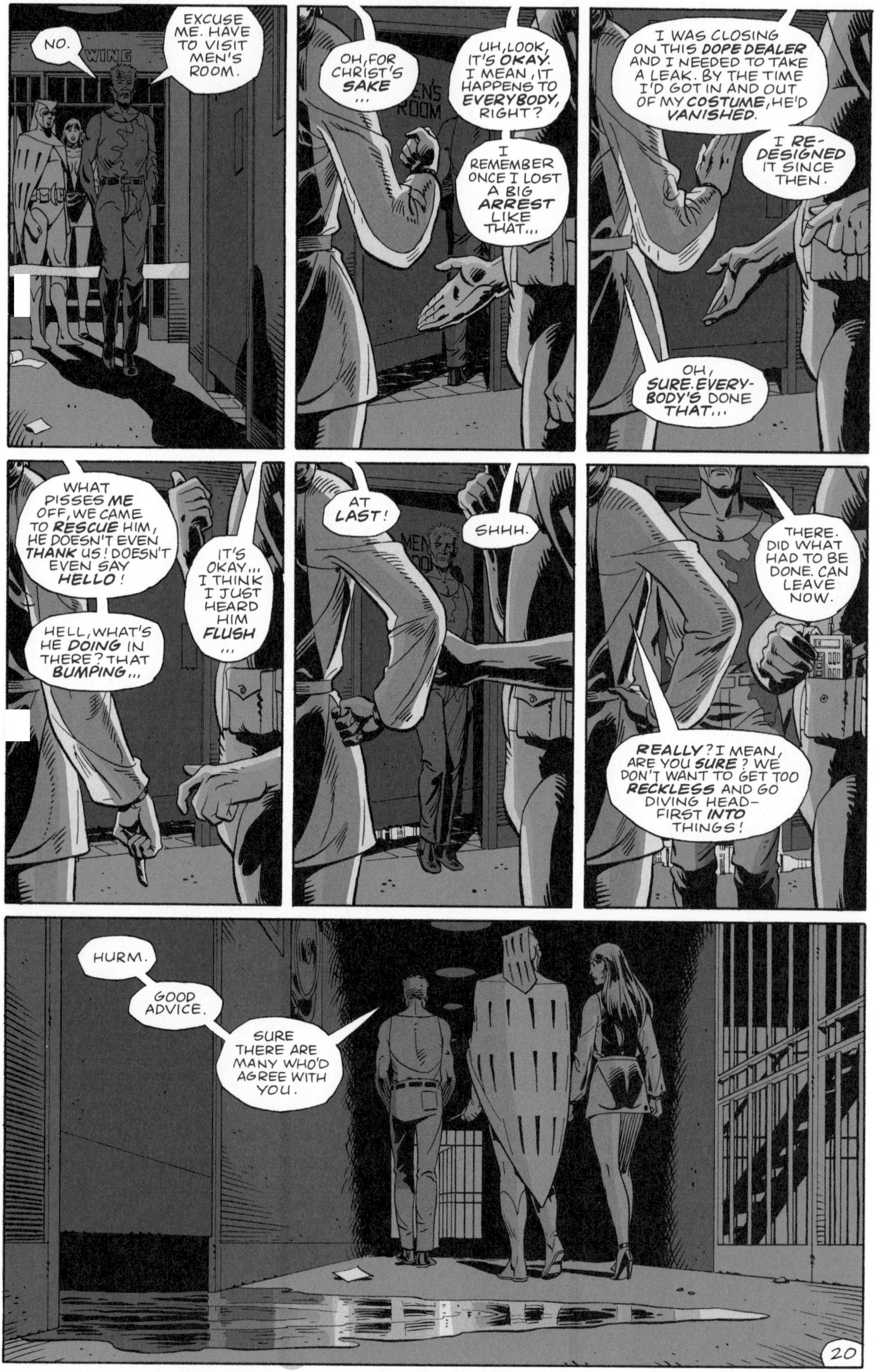

WING
NO.
EXCUSE ME. HAVE TO VISIT MEN'S ROOM.
OH, FOR CHRIST'S SAKE ...
UH, LOOK, IT'S OKAY. I MEAN, IT HAPPENS TO EVERYBODY, RIGHT?
I REMEMBER ONCE I LOST A BIG ARREST LIKE THAT...
I WAS CLOSING ON THIS DOPE DEALER AND I NEEDED TO TAKE A LEAK. BY THE TIME I'D GOT IN AND OUT OF MY COSTUME, HE'D VANISHED.
I RE-DESIGNED IT SINCE THEN.
OH, SURE. EVERYBODY'S DONE THAT...
WHAT PISSES ME OFF, WE CAME TO RESCUE HIM, HE DOESN'T EVEN THANK US! DOESN'T EVEN SAY HELLO!
HELL, WHAT'S HE DOING IN THERE? THAT BUMPING...
IT'S OKAY... I THINK I JUST HEARD HIM FLUSH ...
AT LAST!
SHHH.
THERE. DID WHAT HAD TO BE DONE. CAN LEAVE NOW.
REALLY? I MEAN, ARE YOU SURE? WE DON'T WANT TO GET TOO RECKLESS AND GO DIVING HEAD-FIRST INTO THINGS!
HURM.
GOOD ADVICE.
SURE THERE ARE MANY WHO'D AGREE WITH YOU.
20

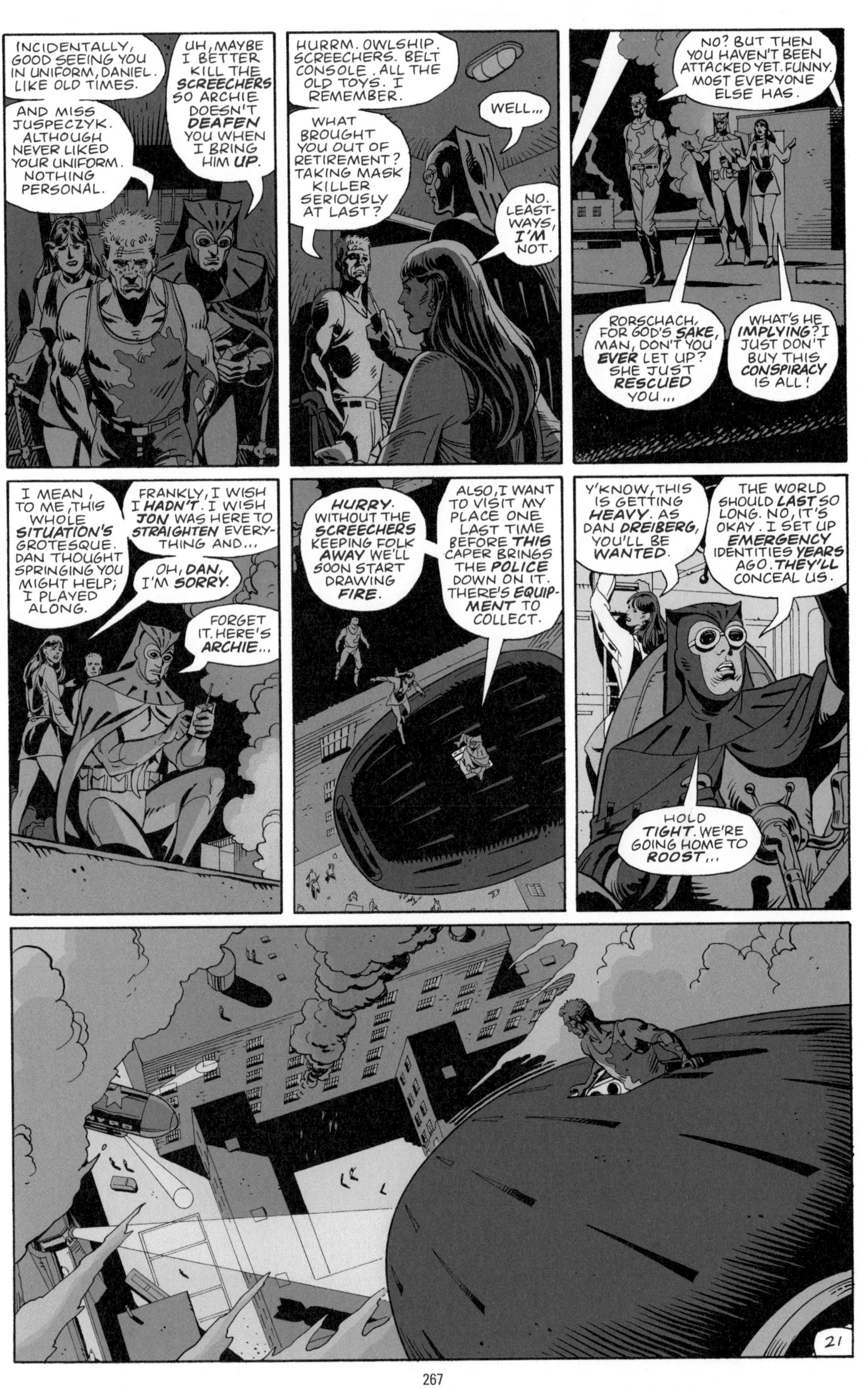
INCIDENTALLY, GOOD SEEING YOU IN UNIFORM, DANIEL. LIKE OLD TIMES.
AND MISS JUSPECZYK. ALTHOUGH NEVER LIKED YOUR UNIFORM. NOTHING PERSONAL.
UH, MAYBE I BETTER KILL THE SCREECHERS SO ARCHIE DOESN'T DEAFEN YOU WHEN I BRING HIM UP.
HURRM. OWLSHIP. SCREECHERS. BELT CONSOLE. ALL THE OLD TOYS. I REMEMBER.
WHAT BROUGHT YOU OUT OF RETIREMENT? TAKING MASK KILLER SERIOUSLY AT LAST?
WELL...
NO. LEAST-WAYS, I'M NOT.
NO? BUT THEN YOU HAVEN'T BEEN ATTACKED YET. FUNNY. MOST EVERYONE ELSE HAS.
RORSCHACH, FOR GOD'S SAKE, MAN, DON'T YOU EVER LET UP? SHE JUST RESCUED YOU...
WHAT'S HE IMPLYING? I JUST DON'T BUY THIS CONSPIRACY IS ALL!
I MEAN, TO ME, THIS WHOLE SITUATION'S GROTESQUE. DAN THOUGHT SPRINGING YOU MIGHT HELP; I PLAYED ALONG.
FRANKLY, I WISH I HADN'T. I WISH JON WAS HERE TO STRAIGHTEN EVERY-THING AND...
OH, DAN, I'M SORRY.
FORGET IT. HERE'S ARCHIE...
HURRY. WITHOUT THE SCREECHERS KEEPING FOLK AWAY WE'LL SOON START DRAWING FIRE.
ALSO, I WANT TO VISIT MY PLACE ONE LAST TIME BEFORE THIS CAPER BRINGS THE POLICE DOWN ON IT. THERE'S EQUIP-MENT TO COLLECT.
Y'KNOW, THIS IS GETTING HEAVY. AS DAN DREIBERG, YOU'LL BE WANTED.
THE WORLD SHOULD LAST SO LONG. NO, IT'S OKAY. I SET UP EMERGENCY IDENTITIES YEARS AGO. THEY'LL CONCEAL US.
HOLD TIGHT. WE'RE GOING HOME TO ROOST...
21

NOVEMBER

M	T	W	T	F	S	S
				1	2	3
4	5	6	7	8	9	
11	12	13	14	15	16	
18	19	20	21	22	23	2
25	26	27	28	29	30	

OKAY, THAT'S EVERYTHING FROM UP *HERE*, BUT I HAVE SOME STUFF TO LOAD DOWN IN THE *BASE-MENT*, SO...

UH, *LAURIE*? WHAT ARE YOU *DOING*?

CHANGING YOUR *CALENDAR*. ANOTHER *HOUR*, IT'LL BE *NOVEMBER*.

YOU SOUND *UPSET*. IS EVERYTHING *OKAY*?

YEAH. IT'S JUST STUFF CATCHING *UP* WITH ME ...THE *JAIL-BREAK*, THIS *WAR* THING ...EVERYTHING'S JUST SO SHITTY.

GUESS I WANT SOMEBODY TO WAVE A *WAND* AND MAKE IT ALL *BETTER*, Y'KNOW?

...BUT THERE'S NOBODY WHO CAN DO THAT, IS THERE?

LISTEN, I HAVE TO COLLECT SOME JUNK FROM THE *LIVING ROOM*...STUFF MY *MOTHER* INSISTED I HAVE, PERSONAL EFFECTS AND LIKE THAT...

BE RIGHT WITH YOU.

HELLO.

22

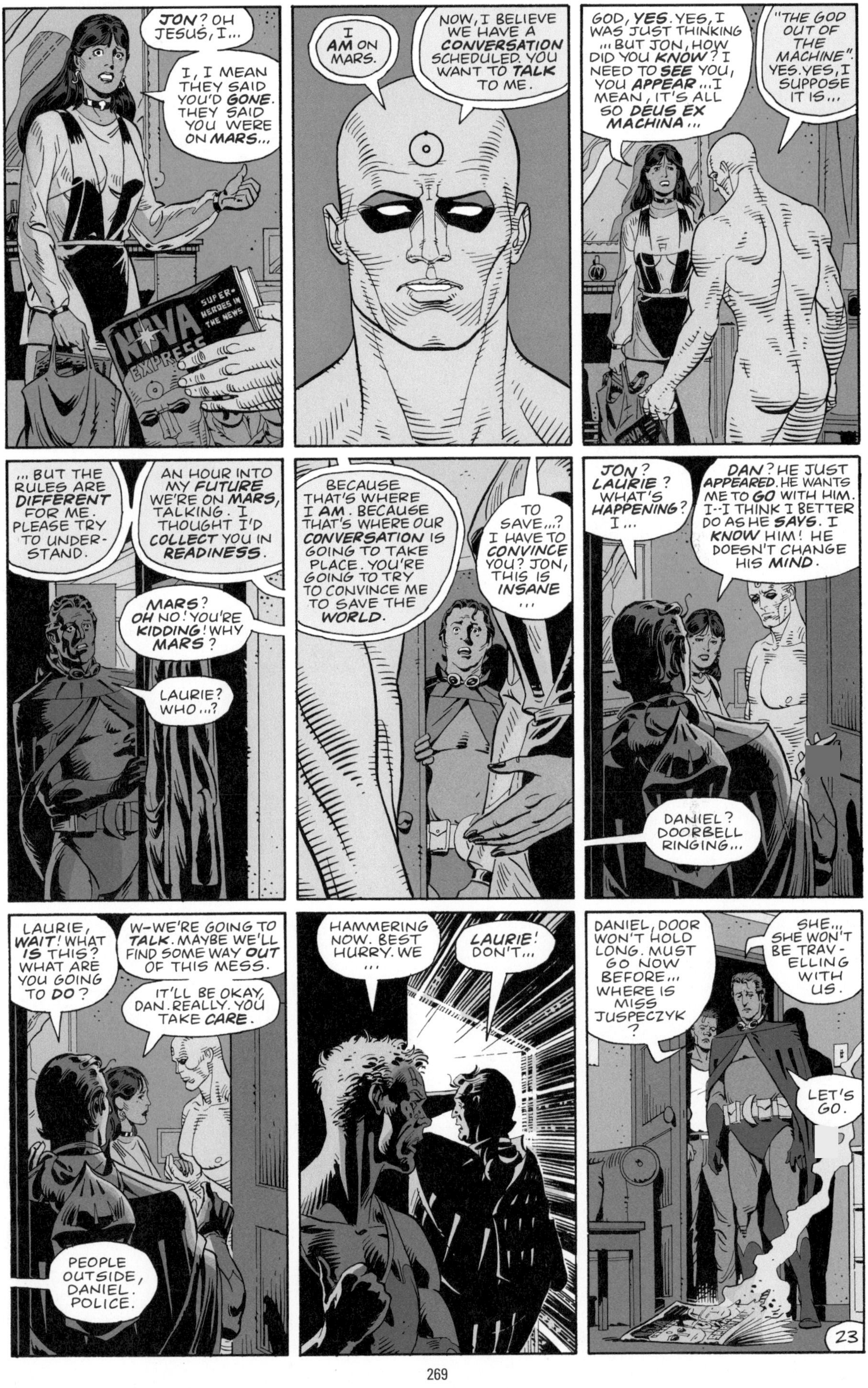
JON? OH JESUS, I...
I, I MEAN THEY SAID YOU'D GONE. THEY SAID YOU WERE ON MARS...
SUPER-HEROES IN THE NEWS
NOVA EXPRESS
I AM ON MARS.
NOW, I BELIEVE WE HAVE A CONVERSATION SCHEDULED. YOU WANT TO TALK TO ME.
GOD, YES. YES, I WAS JUST THINKING ...BUT JON, HOW DID YOU KNOW? I NEED TO SEE YOU, YOU APPEAR...I MEAN, IT'S ALL SO DEUS EX MACHINA...
"THE GOD OUT OF THE MACHINE". YES. YES, I SUPPOSE IT IS...
...BUT THE RULES ARE DIFFERENT FOR ME. PLEASE TRY TO UNDERSTAND.
AN HOUR INTO MY FUTURE WE'RE ON MARS, TALKING. I THOUGHT I'D COLLECT YOU IN READINESS.
MARS? OH NO! YOU'RE KIDDING! WHY MARS?
LAURIE? WHO...?
BECAUSE THAT'S WHERE I AM. BECAUSE THAT'S WHERE OUR CONVERSATION IS GOING TO TAKE PLACE. YOU'RE GOING TO TRY TO CONVINCE ME TO SAVE THE WORLD.
TO SAVE...? I HAVE TO CONVINCE YOU? JON, THIS IS INSANE...
JON? LAURIE? WHAT'S HAPPENING? I...
DAN? HE JUST APPEARED. HE WANTS ME TO GO WITH HIM. I--I THINK I BETTER DO AS HE SAYS. I KNOW HIM! HE DOESN'T CHANGE HIS MIND.
DANIEL? DOORBELL RINGING...
LAURIE, WAIT! WHAT IS THIS? WHAT ARE YOU GOING TO DO?
W-WE'RE GOING TO TALK. MAYBE WE'LL FIND SOME WAY OUT OF THIS MESS.
IT'LL BE OKAY, DAN. REALLY. YOU TAKE CARE.
PEOPLE OUTSIDE, DANIEL. POLICE.
HAMMERING NOW. BEST HURRY. WE...
LAURIE! DON'T...
DANIEL, DOOR WON'T HOLD LONG. MUST GO NOW BEFORE... WHERE IS MISS JUSPECZYK?
SHE... SHE WON'T BE TRAVELLING WITH US.
LET'S GO.
23

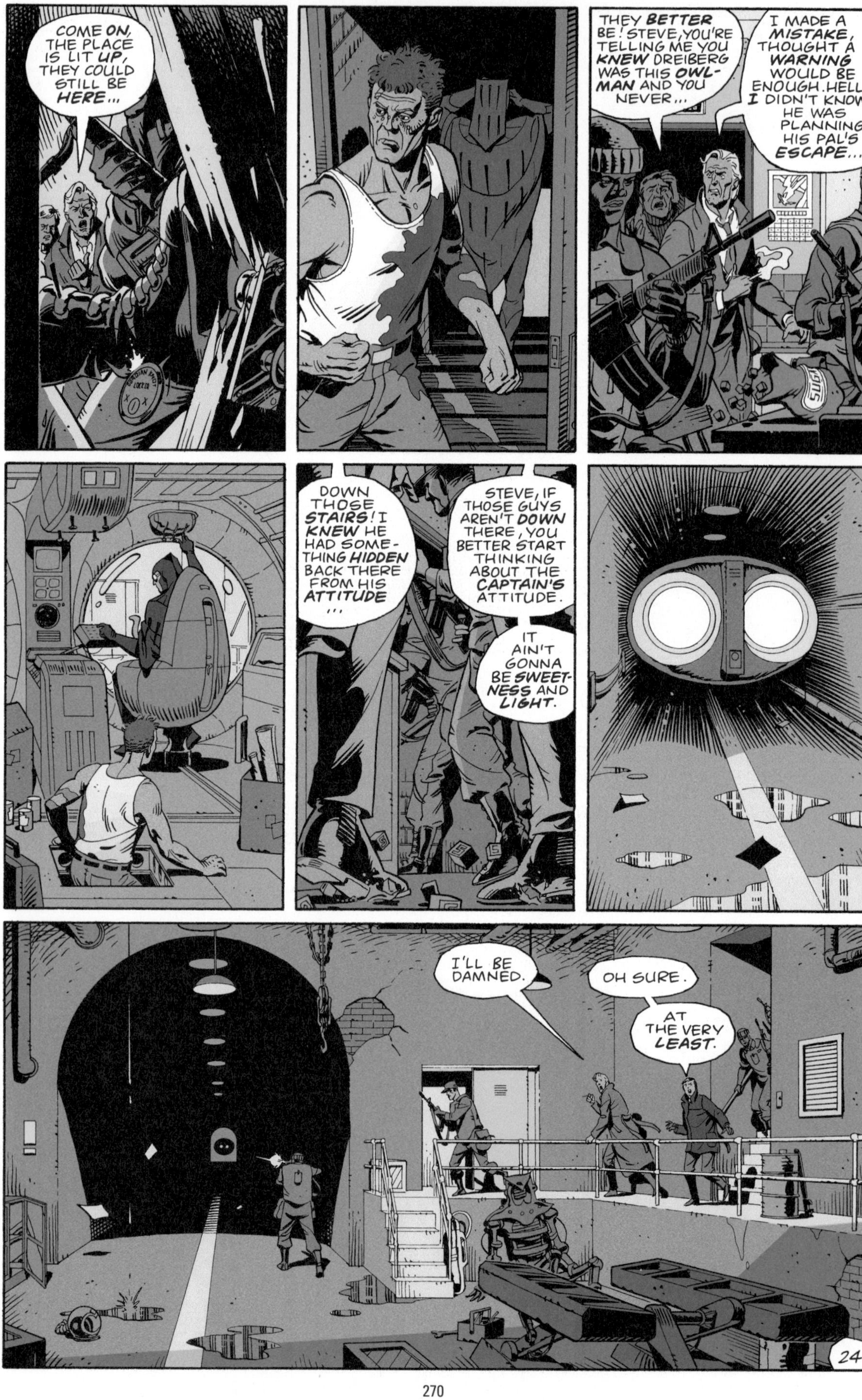
COME ON, THE PLACE IS LIT UP, THEY COULD STILL BE HERE...
THEY BETTER BE! STEVE, YOU'RE TELLING ME YOU KNEW DREIBERG WAS THIS OWL-MAN AND YOU NEVER...
I MADE A MISTAKE, THOUGHT A WARNING WOULD BE ENOUGH. HELL, I DIDN'T KNOW HE WAS PLANNING HIS PAL'S ESCAPE...
DOWN THOSE STAIRS! I KNEW HE HAD SOMETHING HIDDEN BACK THERE FROM HIS ATTITUDE...
STEVE, IF THOSE GUYS AREN'T DOWN THERE, YOU BETTER START THINKING ABOUT THE CAPTAIN'S ATTITUDE.
IT AIN'T GONNA BE SWEETNESS AND LIGHT.
I'LL BE DAMNED.
OH SURE.
AT THE VERY LEAST.
24

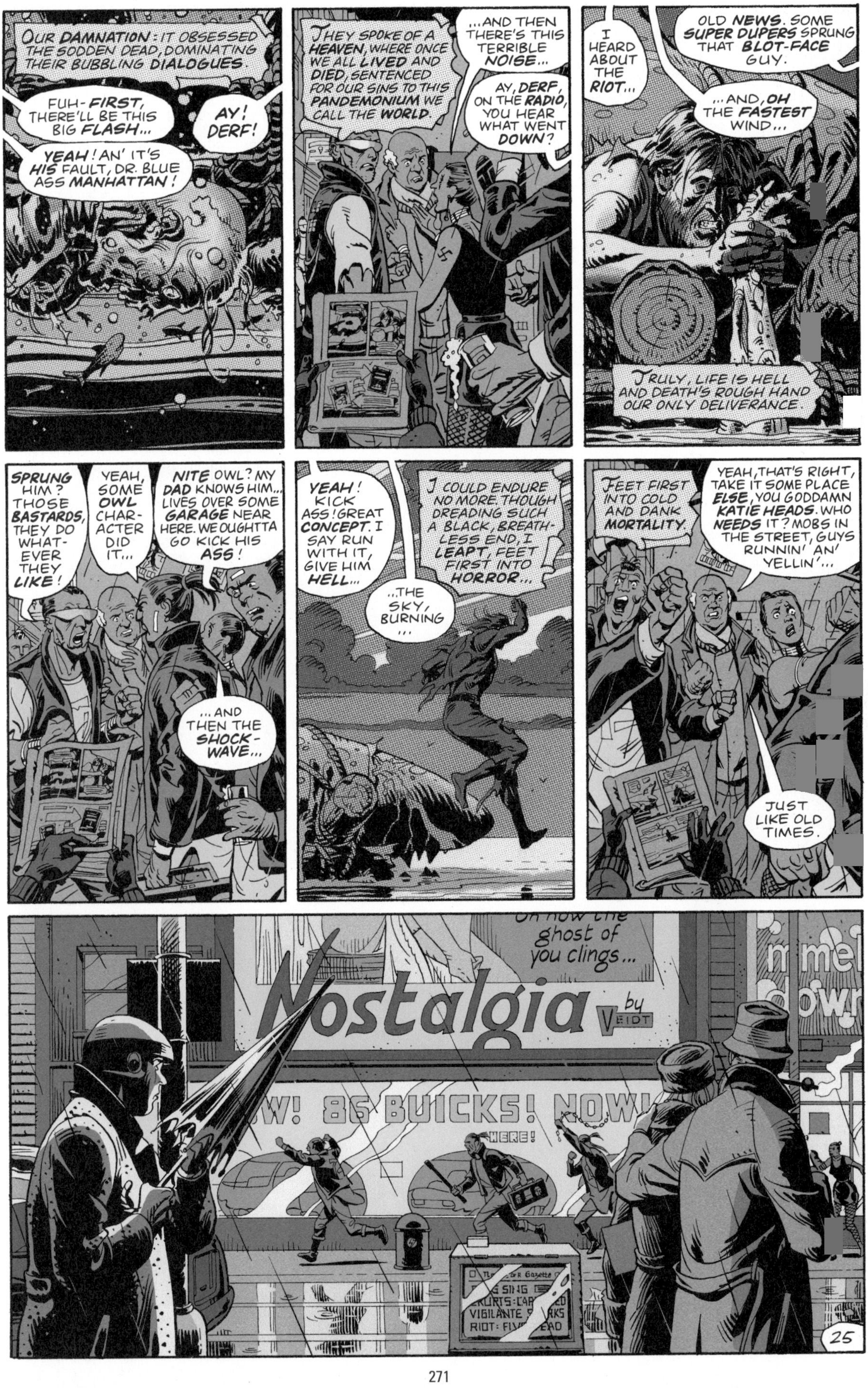
OUR DAMNATION: IT OBSESSED THE SODDEN DEAD, DOMINATING THEIR BUBBLING DIALOGUES.
FUH-FIRST, THERE'LL BE THIS BIG FLASH...
AY! DERF!
YEAH! AN' IT'S HIS FAULT, DR. BLUE ASS MANHATTAN!
THEY SPOKE OF A HEAVEN, WHERE ONCE WE ALL LIVED AND DIED, SENTENCED FOR OUR SINS TO THIS PANDEMONIUM WE CALL THE WORLD.
...AND THEN THERE'S THIS TERRIBLE NOISE...
AY, DERF, ON THE RADIO, YOU HEAR WHAT WENT DOWN?
I HEARD ABOUT THE RIOT...
OLD NEWS. SOME SUPER DUPERS SPRUNG THAT BLOT-FACE GUY.
...AND, OH THE FASTEST WIND...
TRULY, LIFE IS HELL AND DEATH'S ROUGH HAND OUR ONLY DELIVERANCE.
SPRUNG HIM? THOSE BASTARDS, THEY DO WHAT-EVER THEY LIKE!
YEAH, SOME OWL CHAR-ACTER DID IT...
NITE OWL? MY DAD KNOWS HIM... LIVES OVER SOME GARAGE NEAR HERE. WE OUGHTTA GO KICK HIS ASS!
...AND THEN THE SHOCK-WAVE...
YEAH! KICK ASS! GREAT CONCEPT. I SAY RUN WITH IT, GIVE HIM HELL...
I COULD ENDURE NO MORE. THOUGH DREADING SUCH A BLACK, BREATH-LESS END, I LEAPT, FEET FIRST INTO HORROR...
...THE SKY, BURNING...
FEET FIRST INTO COLD AND DANK MORTALITY.
YEAH, THAT'S RIGHT, TAKE IT SOME PLACE ELSE, YOU GODDAMN KATIE HEADS. WHO NEEDS IT? MOBS IN THE STREET, GUYS RUNNIN' AN' YELLIN'...
JUST LIKE OLD TIMES.
ghost of you clings...
Nostalgia by VEIDT
86 BUICKS! NOW!
HERE!
VIGILANTE
25

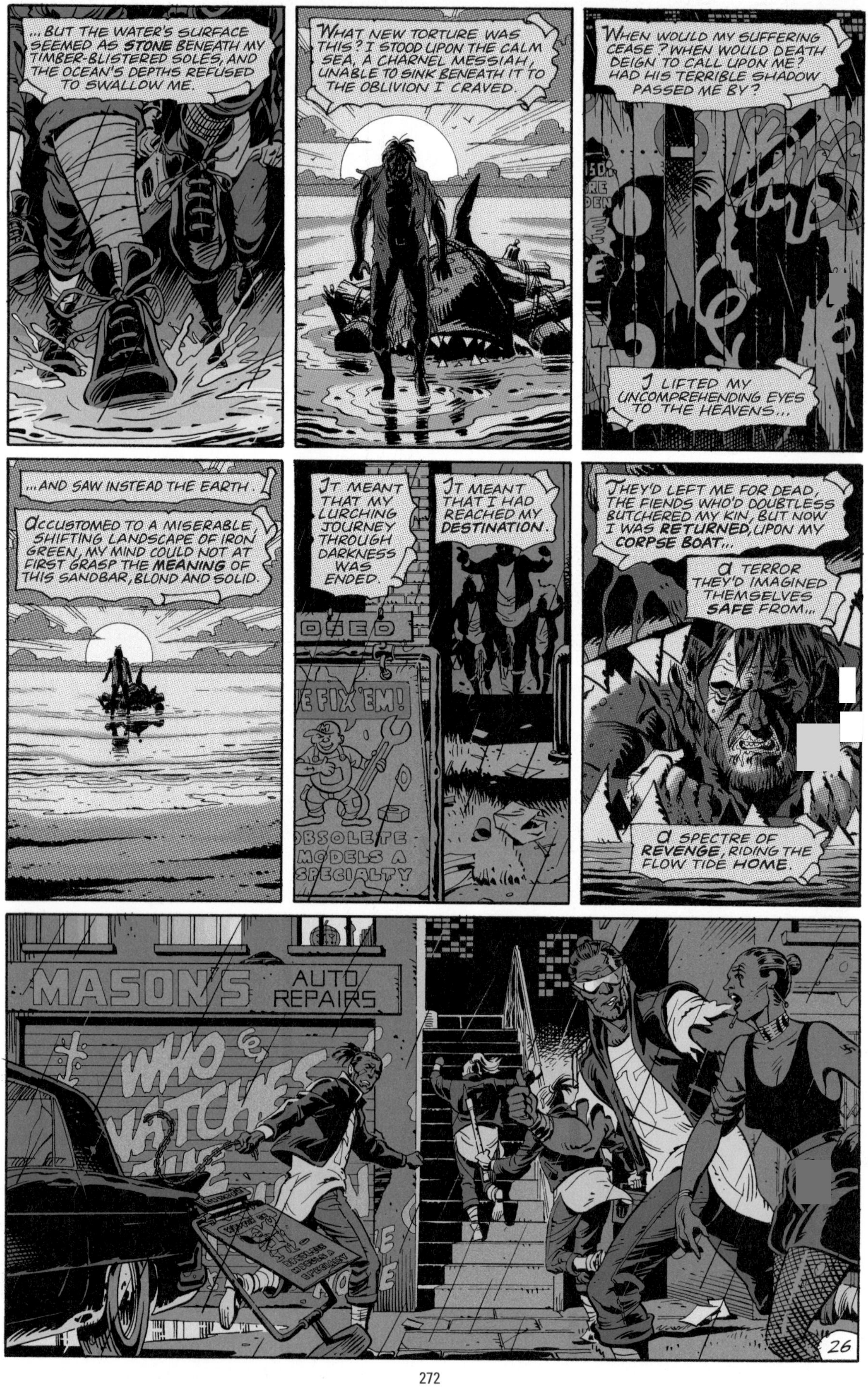
...BUT THE WATER'S SURFACE SEEMED AS STONE BENEATH MY TIMBER-BLISTERED SOLES, AND THE OCEAN'S DEPTHS REFUSED TO SWALLOW ME.
WHAT NEW TORTURE WAS THIS? I STOOD UPON THE CALM SEA, A CHARNEL MESSIAH, UNABLE TO SINK BENEATH IT TO THE OBLIVION I CRAVED.
WHEN WOULD MY SUFFERING CEASE? WHEN WOULD DEATH DEIGN TO CALL UPON ME? HAD HIS TERRIBLE SHADOW PASSED ME BY?
I LIFTED MY UNCOMPREHENDING EYES TO THE HEAVENS...
...AND SAW INSTEAD THE EARTH.
ACCUSTOMED TO A MISERABLE, SHIFTING LANDSCAPE OF IRON GREEN, MY MIND COULD NOT AT FIRST GRASP THE MEANING OF THIS SANDBAR, BLOND AND SOLID.
IT MEANT THAT MY LURCHING JOURNEY THROUGH DARKNESS WAS ENDED.
IT MEANT THAT I HAD REACHED MY DESTINATION.
OSED
E FIX 'EM!
OBSOLETE MODELS A SPECIALTY
THEY'D LEFT ME FOR DEAD, THE FIENDS WHO'D DOUBTLESS BUTCHERED MY KIN, BUT NOW I WAS RETURNED, UPON MY CORPSE BOAT...
A TERROR THEY'D IMAGINED THEMSELVES SAFE FROM...
A SPECTRE OF REVENGE, RIDING THE FLOW TIDE HOME.
MASON'S AUTO REPAIRS
WHO WATCHES
26

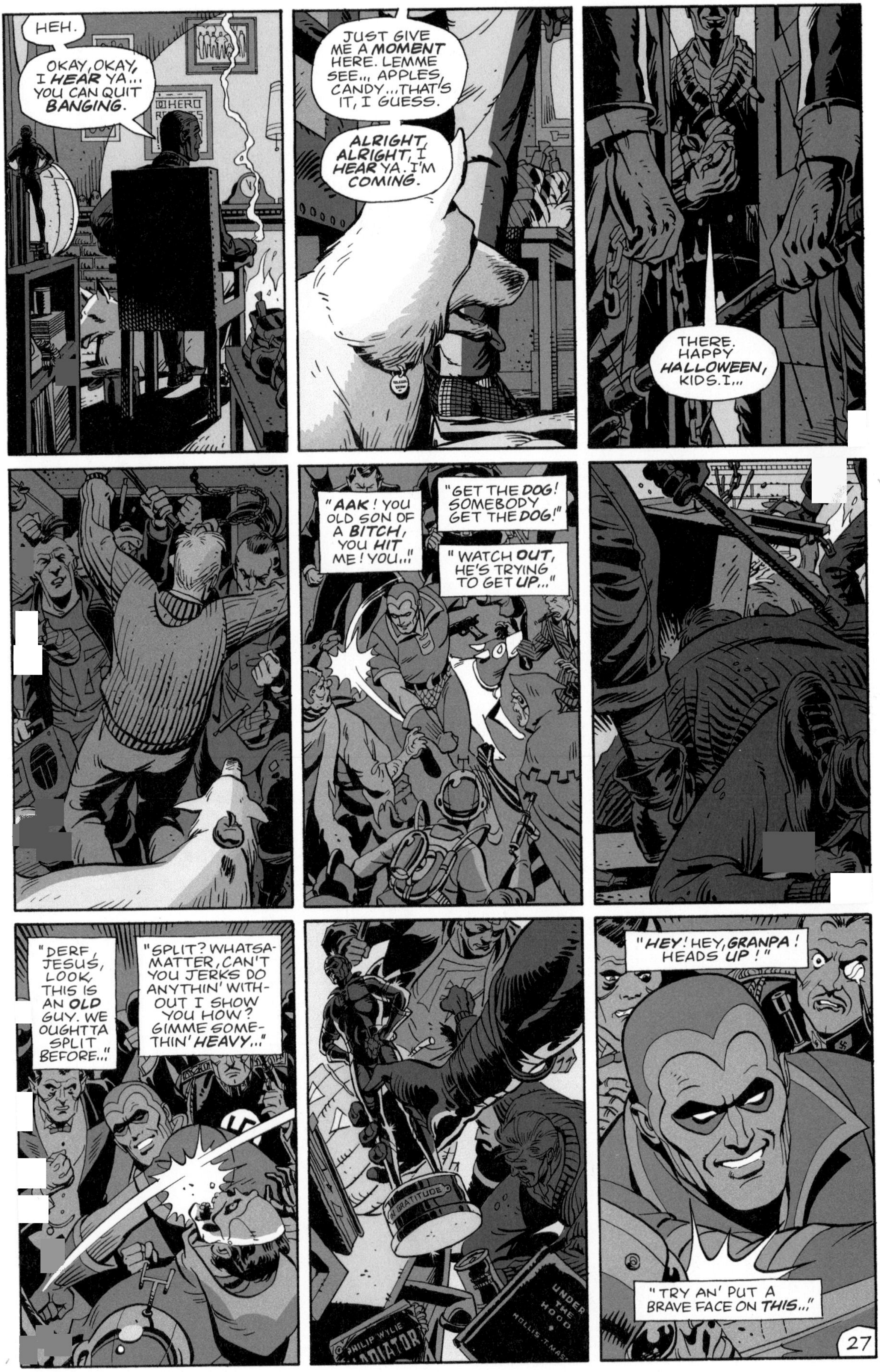
HEH.
OKAY, OKAY, I HEAR YA... YOU CAN QUIT BANGING.
JUST GIVE ME A MOMENT HERE. LEMME SEE... APPLES, CANDY... THAT'S IT, I GUESS.
ALRIGHT, ALRIGHT, I HEAR YA. I'M COMING.
THERE. HAPPY HALLOWEEN, KIDS. I...
"AAK! YOU OLD SON OF A BITCH, YOU HIT ME! YOU..."
"GET THE DOG! SOMEBODY GET THE DOG!"
"WATCH OUT, HE'S TRYING TO GET UP..."
"DERF, JESUS, LOOK, THIS IS AN OLD GUY. WE OUGHTTA SPLIT BEFORE..."
"SPLIT? WHATSAMATTER, CAN'T YOU JERKS DO ANYTHIN' WITHOUT I SHOW YOU HOW? GIMME SOMETHIN' HEAVY..."
IN GRATITUDE
PHILIP WYLIE
GLADIATOR
UNDER THE HOOD
HOLLIS T. MAS
"HEY! HEY, GRANPA! HEADS UP!"
"TRY AN' PUT A BRAVE FACE ON THIS..."
27

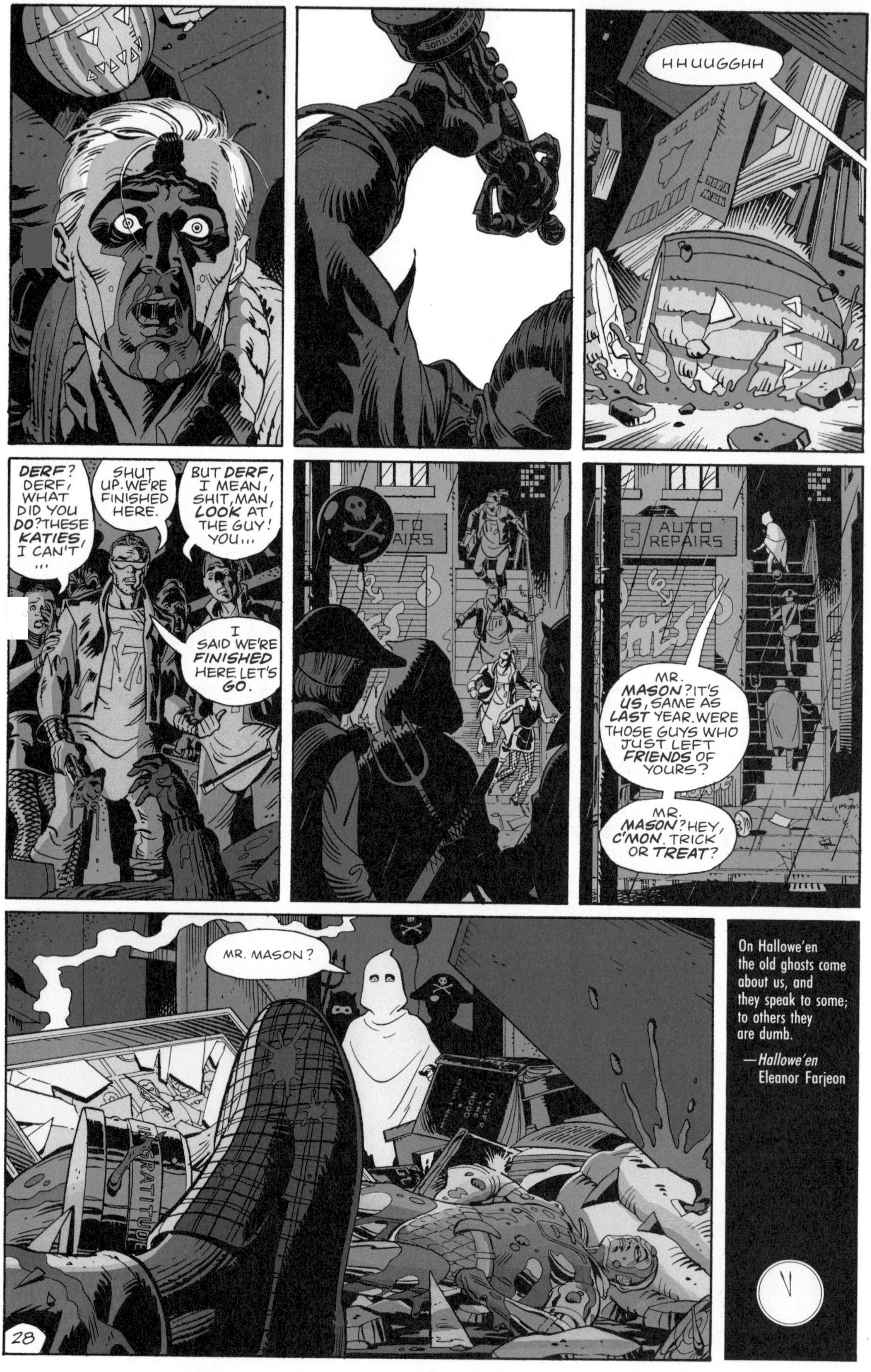
HHUUGGHH
DERF? DERF, WHAT DID YOU DO? THESE KATIES, I CAN'T ...
SHUT UP. WE'RE FINISHED HERE.
BUT DERF, I MEAN, SHIT, MAN, LOOK AT THE GUY! YOU...
I SAID WE'RE FINISHED HERE. LET'S GO.
AUTO REPAIRS
MR. MASON? IT'S US, SAME AS LAST YEAR. WERE THOSE GUYS WHO JUST LEFT FRIENDS OF YOURS?
MR. MASON? HEY, C'MON. TRICK OR TREAT?
MR. MASON?
On Hallowe'en the old ghosts come about us, and they speak to some; to others they are dumb.
—*Hallowe'en* Eleanor Farjeon
28

TRIM ON LEFT SPREAD

SAFETY

BANNER

Thursday, October 31st, 1985

50 cents

NEW FRONTIERSMAN

Issue IVII
No. 21

HONOR IS LIKE THE HAWK: SOMETIMES IT MUST GO HOODED

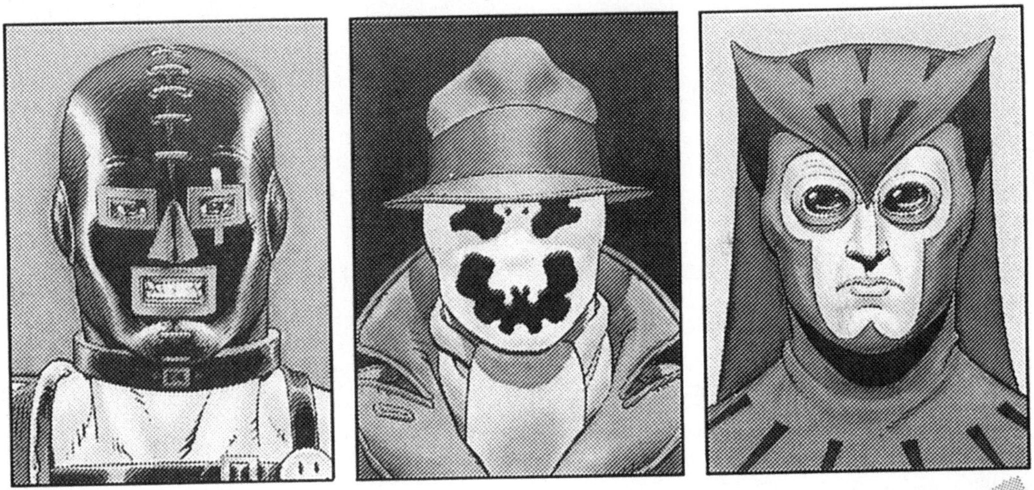

Hector Godfrey, Editor

RED ARMAGEDDON!

In this, the eleventh hour, with the world poised on the brink of Red Armageddon, it is vital that we, as a nation, should rally around those symbols that are closest to the great, warm, red-white-and-blue beating heart of this beleaguered country. They are our hope and our inspiration, the legends that urge our people onward even in times of deepest crisis.

Would our sense of national identity, our pride, our sense of honor; would these things be so enduring were it not for such great symbols of freedom as Paul Revere's midnight ride, or the Alamo, or the Gettysburg address? I think not. And yet, it seems there are those who, even in the dire adversity that besets us, see fit to ridicule and deride the very notions that have made America what she is today!

cont. on pg. 2

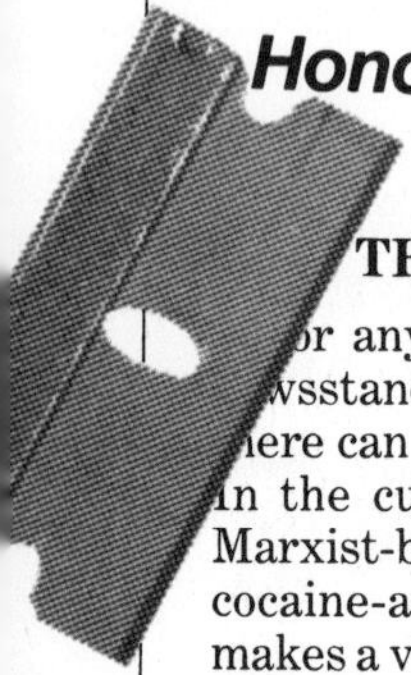

Honor is like . . . (cont.)

WHO THE HELL DO THEY THINK THEY ARE?

r any citizen who has been watching the wsstands over this last, unbearable month, ere can be little doubt who I am referring to. n the current edition of pseudo-intellectual Marxist-brat rock-star monthly *Nova Express*, cocaine-advocating editor DOUGLAS ROTH makes a vitriolic and unfounded attack upon the tradition of the masked lawman in our culture and attempts to stir up old prejudices and hatreds into a bloody wave of civil disorder.

It is hardly necessary for me to remind readers that in a previous edition of his inflammatory publication, Roth had spearheaded the cancer-smear character assassination of Dr. Manhattan. This wild and hysterical attack led to our country's greatest tactical asset leaving this world for self-imposed exile upon another. Ultimately, it may lead to searing nuclear apocalypse or our subjugation as a nation beneath the cossack boot of the U.S.S.R.

Nova Express, heaping libel upon libel, has followed up this potentially catastrophic feature with an article in its current edition that attempts to draw tenuous links between recent news items involving former masked adventurers and work them into some wild-eyed conspiracy theory, apparently forgetting that most of the "news items" involved were generated as a direct result of *Nova Express* and its irresponsible scaremongering! Roth refers gloatingly in his article to the fact that back copies of the *New Frontiersman* were found in the rented apartment of captured vigilante Rorschach after his arrest, citing this as "proof" of the aforementioned hero's poor character. He seems to suggest, with typical pothead disregard for logic, that Rorschach must be bad if he reads the *New Frontiersman*, while simultaneously implying that the *New Frontiersman* must be slightly disreputable if someone like Rorschach reads it! The overall effect of the piece is that of a snotty-nosed and unsubstantiated attack not only upon this paper and upon the individual costumed adventurers themselves, but also upon a whole American institution! Who the hell do Roth and his cringing staff of pinko sycophants think they are???

RIPPED OUT GUTS

The institution that Roth and his cronies are so casually ripping the guts out of is that of hooded justice, of a force for righteousness that dares to tread where the wimpy and useless laws laid down by the spineless dupes and fellow travellers in our judiciary forbid it to.

What about the Boston Tea Party? What about the spirit of the Lone Ranger? What about all those occasions when men have found it necessary to go masked in order to preserve justice above the letter of the law? *Nova Express* makes many sneering references to costumed heroes as direct descendants of the Ku Klux Klan, but might I point out that despite what some might view as their later excesses, the Klan originally came into being because decent people had perfectly reasonable fears for the safety of their persons and belongings when forced into proximity with people from a culture far less morally advanced.

No, the Klan were not strictly legal, but they did work voluntarily to preserve American culture in areas where there were very real dangers of that culture being overrun and mongrelized. Similarly, during our perfectly justified retaliatory bombing of Beirut in 1979, there were many of our so-called fair-weather-friend European allies who were bleating about supposed infringements of international law. Yet what are laws made for, if not to serve mankind? And if those laws through unforeseen circumstance become no longer applicable, is it not more noble to follow the course of right and justice; to serve the spirit of the law rather than its every dot and comma? In my book, anyone answering that question in the negative is someone without the moral backbone necessary to call himself an American. In the case of the *Nova Express* articles and their perpetrators, I would go so far as to call such a denial of time-tested patriotic virtues as being most definitely ANTI-American.

COKED-OUT COMMIE COWARDS

I've had it up to here with those coked-out commie cowards, and I think it's time we started to ask ourselves just who stands to benefit most from *Nova Express*' ridiculing of American legends and the subsequent subversion and undermining of our national morale? Can there be any doubt that the only beneficiary is the cause of international communism? Should we not perhaps call upon our authorities to take a closer look at exactly who is funding this pernicious piece of propaganda in pop star's

cont. on pg. 3

open up para. #

As we see it . . .

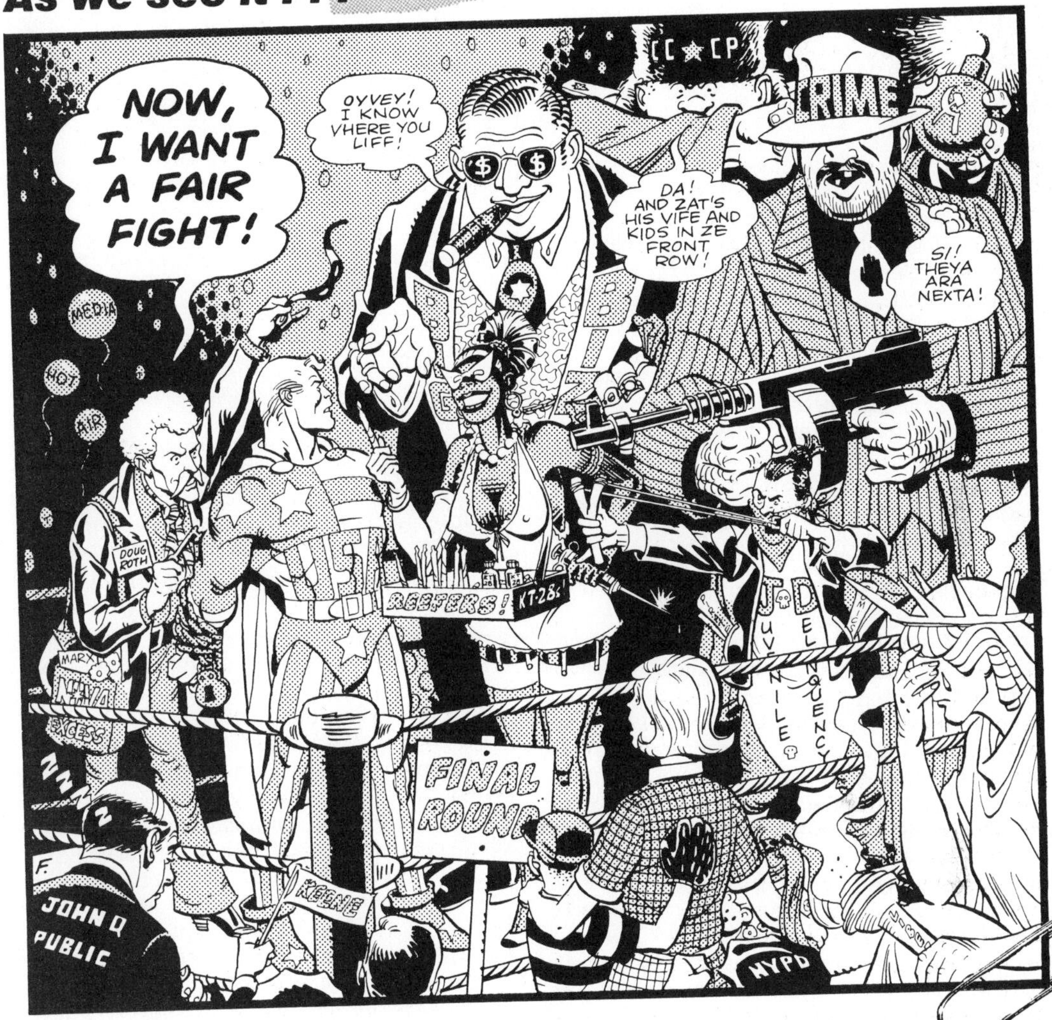
NOW, I WANT A FAIR FIGHT!
OYVEY! I KNOW VHERE YOU LIFF!
DA! AND ZAT'S HIS VIFE AND KIDS IN ZE FRONT ROW!
SI! THEYA ARA NEXTA!
CCCP
CRIME
MEDIA
HOT
AIR
DOUG ROTH
REEFERS!
KT-28
JD
JUVENILE DELINQUENCY
FINAL ROUND
JOHN Q PUBLIC
NYPD

Honor is like . . . (cont.)

clothing that finds its way onto our newsstands each week? Regular readers will know that I have already voiced my suspicions concerning a red hand in the denunciation and subsequent exile of Dr. Manhattan (see *N.F.*, Sunday 20th October: "Our country's protector smeared by the Kremlin") and will no doubt join me in perceiving this renewed assault by *Nova Express* upon our traditions and values as further proof of where that magazine's interests lie: Due East, and don't you forget it.

Hector Godfrey, Editor

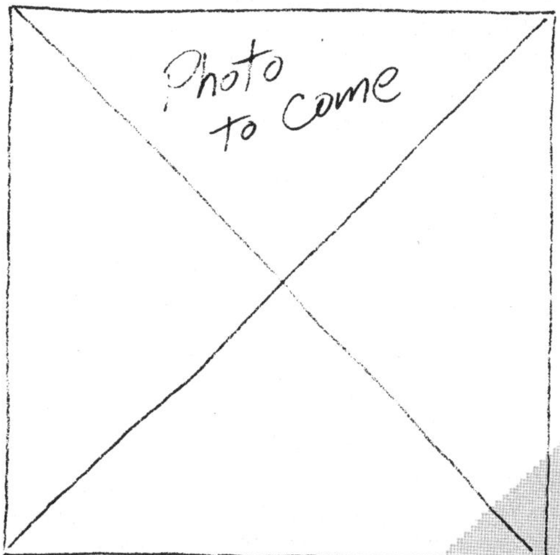
Photo to come

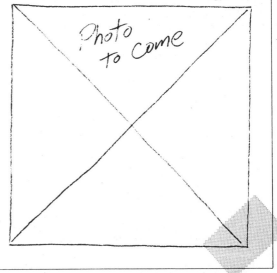

MISSING WRITER
VANISHED PERSONS LIST GROWS AS HUNT CALLED OFF

Earlier this week, police called off their inquiry into the mysterious disappearance of author Max Shea, citing lack of evidence as a principal contributing factor in their decision. *New Frontiersman* would like to remind both the authorities concerned and our readers of the overwhelming evidence already tabulated by this paper to suggest that Shea's disappearance was part of a carefully orchestrated conspiracy, the roots of which may yet be traced back to sinister Cuban interests.

Although it is true to say that Shea did indeed vanish without trace, leaving no clue whatsoever as to his destination, by considering the extraordinary amount of similar disappearances reported at approximately the same time, it is possible to glimpse a larger and more frightening picture as it emerges. In the two months leading up to Shea's disappearance, no less than four prominent creative figures also seemingly dropped from the face of the earth. These included radical architect Norman Leith, surrealist painter Hira Manish, and respected "hard" science fiction author James Trafford March. Admittedly, the circumstances in each case are wildly different and seem to allow for a simple, meaningless coincidence of human destinies . . . Manish was apparently suffering profound difficulties with her marriage, making her apparent abandonment of her husband and two sons somewhat less than surprising. March owed massive debts to the IRS, who had frozen his earnings. Leith was reportedly depressed and even suicidal during the run-up to his disappearance, as was fellow missing person, avant-garde composer Linette Paley. As reasons for disappearance, these each seem individually credible enough to make any notion of conspiracy unnecessary, and yet a doubt still remains: Can *four* such prominent people simply dematerialize in the space of half as many months, leaving such bright and promising careers and reputations behind them?

Added to this, we must consider those prominent people in other fields, who, although less prominent and thus less easy to gauge numerically, have also apparently melted into thin air during this period. I have on record an unusually high number of disappearances from amongst the scientific community, which, although consisting largely of semi-skilled menial workers, does include such notable names as that of Dr. Whittaker Furnesse, the brilliant eugenics specialist who according to his wife left the family home one evening to walk the family dog and quite simply never returned.

Odder still, and quite probably entirely unconnected, there is the disappearance of *part* of a person after his death, recorded on the same week Shea's vanishing act reached the public awareness. Parents and relatives of so-called psychic and clairvoyant Robert Deschaines, attending his funeral following the young medium's fatal stroke, were horrified to learn that ghoulish vandals or practical jokers had stolen the corpse's head from its body while it lay unattended upon a mortuary slab. Police voiced a few tenuous opinions concerning possible involvement by black magic cultists, but since then no further evidence has come to light.

Even discounting this last curiosity, is there nobody who is prepared to look into this bizarre glut of disappearances and see what emerges? Can it be that our increasingly shrill and nervous judiciary are actually afraid to look too far under this particular rug for fear of what they might find hidden there? The *New Frontiersman* repeats it warning: Talented and prominent Americans are being spirited away from under our noses.

Isn't it time somebody found out just where they are going?

Photo to Come

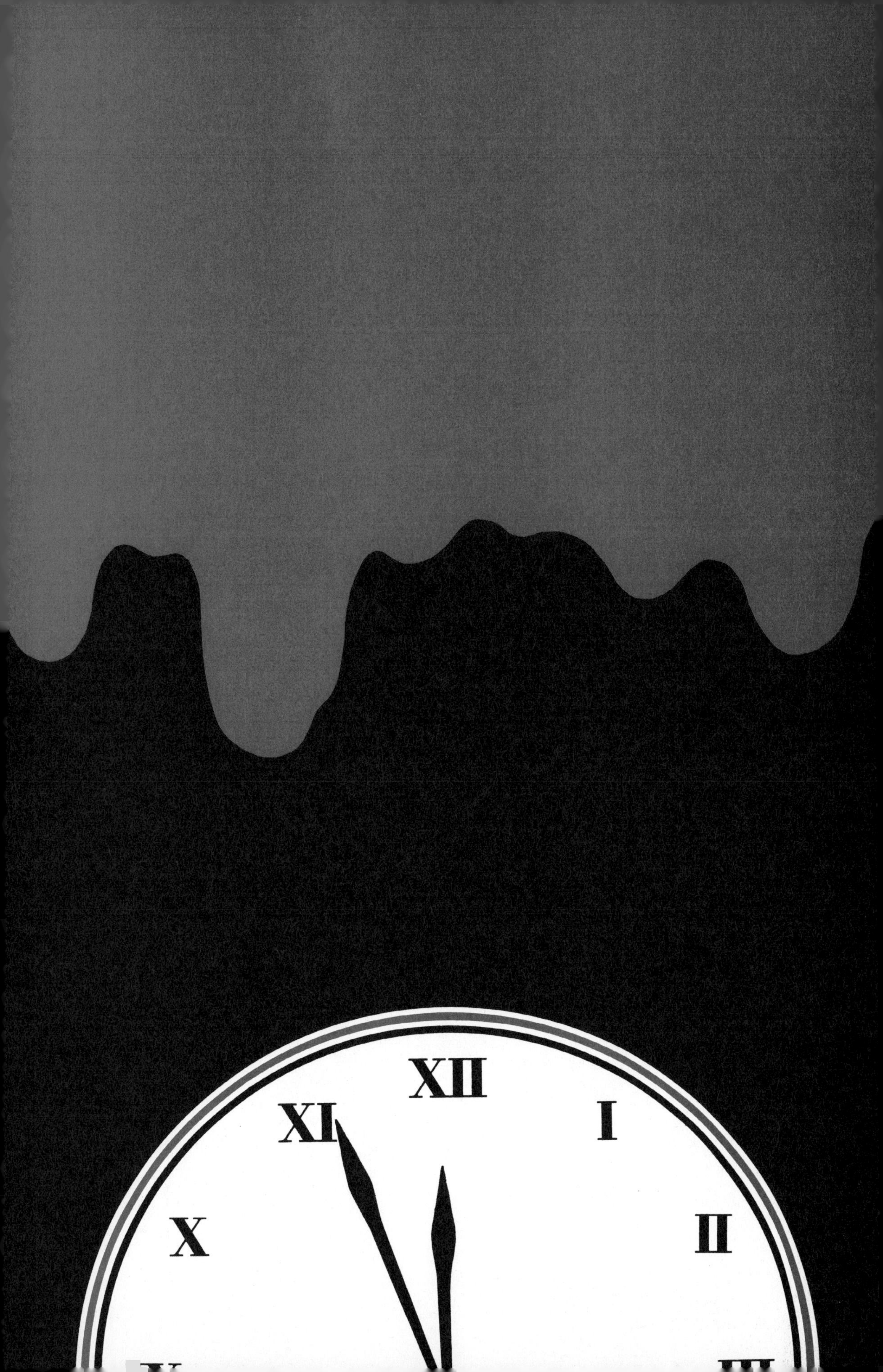

CHAPTER IX

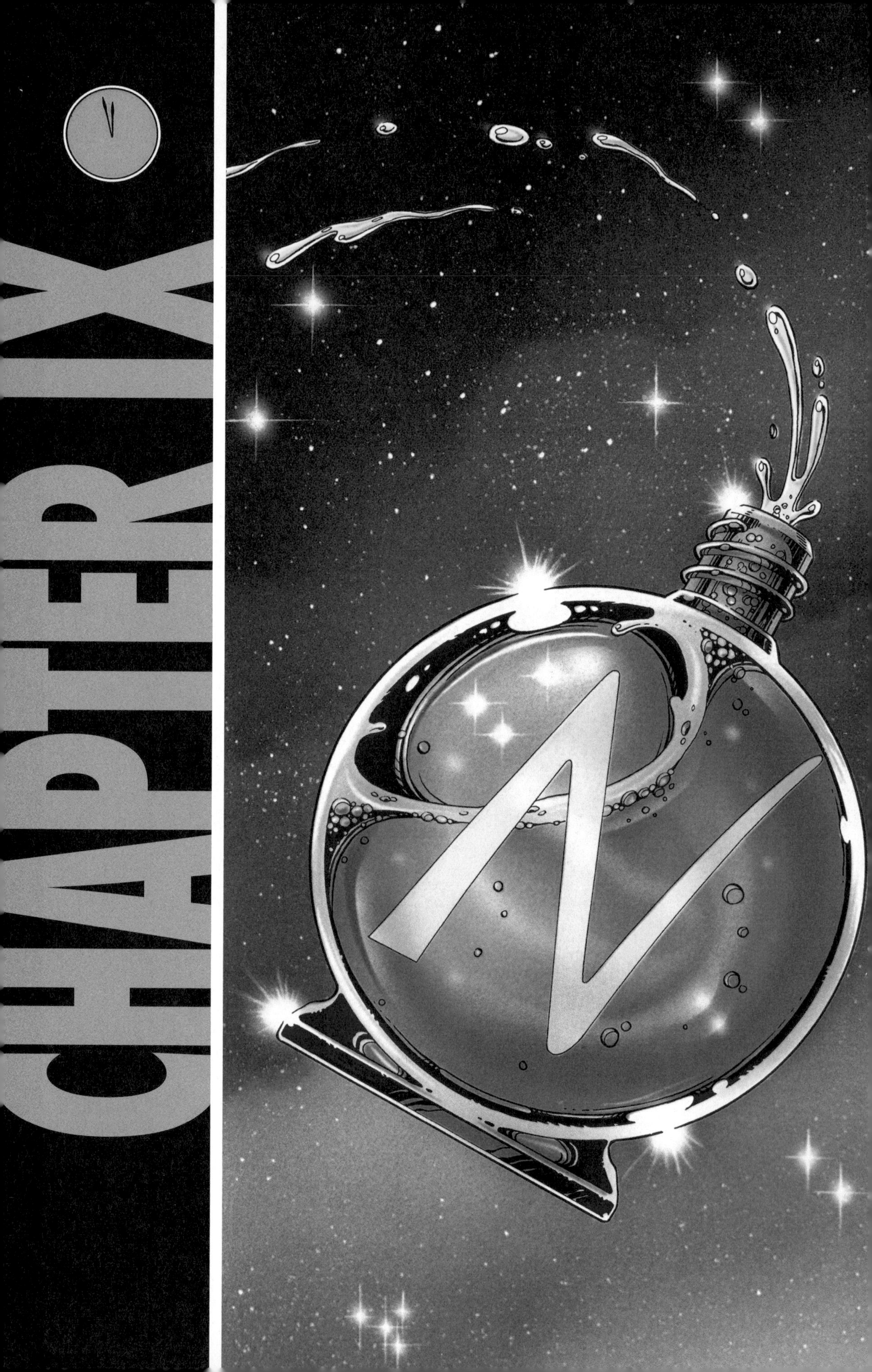

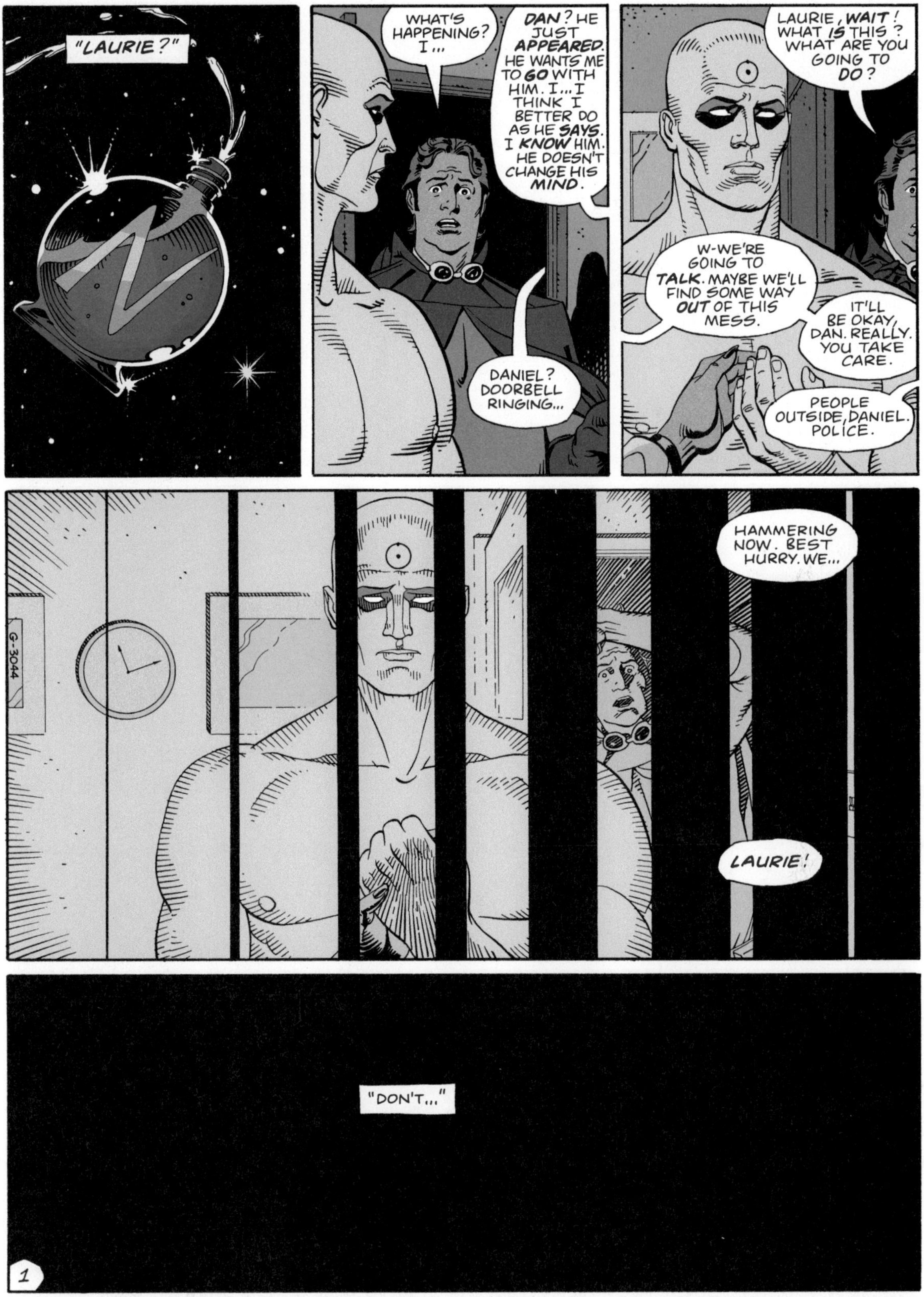
"LAURIE?"
WHAT'S HAPPENING? I...
DAN? HE JUST APPEARED. HE WANTS ME TO GO WITH HIM. I... I THINK I BETTER DO AS HE SAYS. I KNOW HIM. HE DOESN'T CHANGE HIS MIND.
DANIEL? DOORBELL RINGING...
LAURIE, WAIT! WHAT IS THIS? WHAT ARE YOU GOING TO DO?
W-WE'RE GOING TO TALK. MAYBE WE'LL FIND SOME WAY OUT OF THIS MESS.
IT'LL BE OKAY, DAN. REALLY. YOU TAKE CARE.
PEOPLE OUTSIDE, DANIEL. POLICE.
G-3044
HAMMERING NOW. BEST HURRY. WE...
LAURIE!
"DON'T..."
1

THE DARKNESS OF MERE BEING

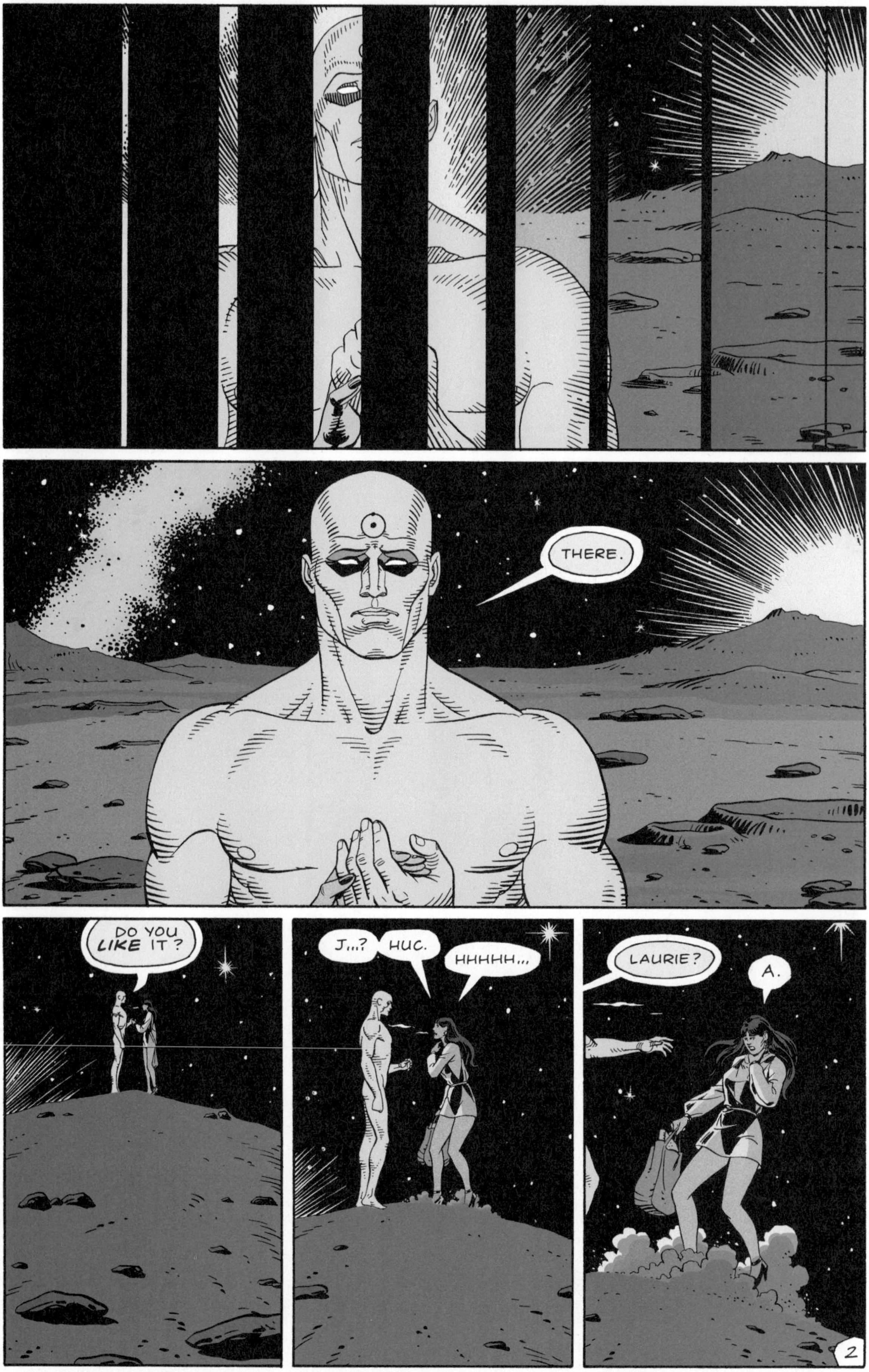
THERE.
DO YOU LIKE IT?
J...?
HUC.
HHHHH...
LAURIE?
A.
2

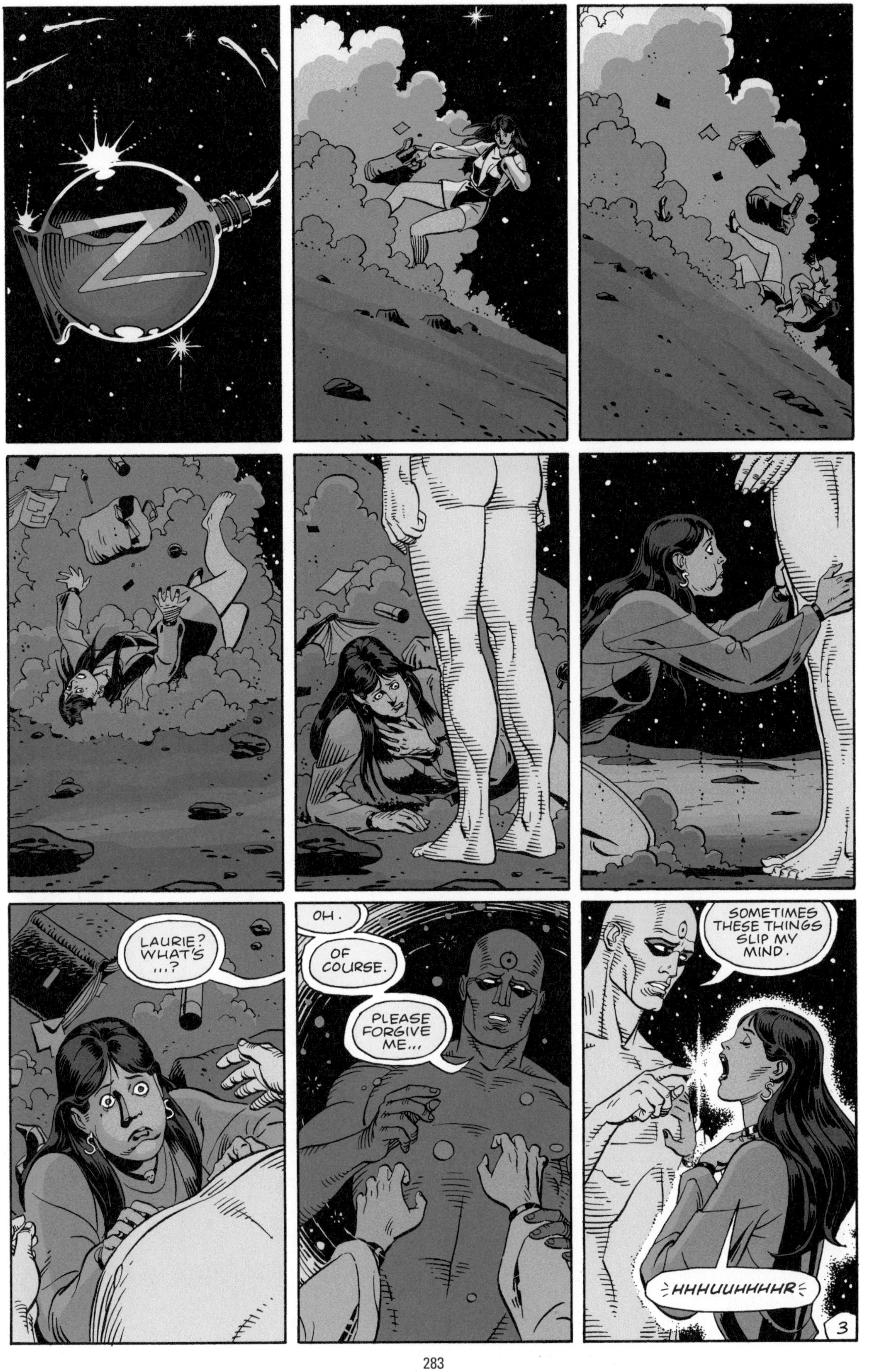
LAURIE? WHAT'S ...?
OH.
OF COURSE.
PLEASE FORGIVE ME...
SOMETIMES THESE THINGS SLIP MY MIND.
HHHUUHHHHR
3

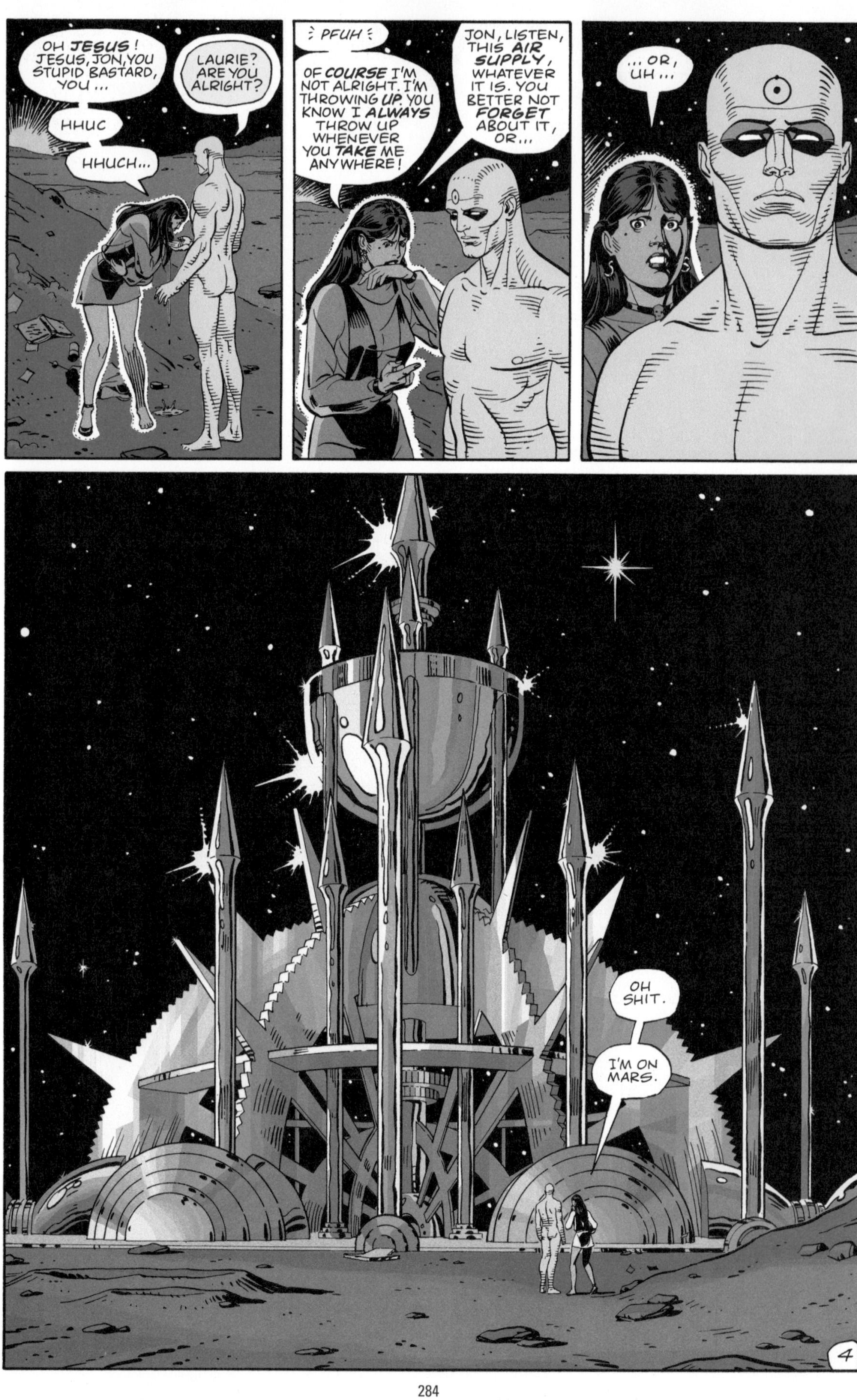
OH JESUS! JESUS, JON, YOU STUPID BASTARD, YOU...
LAURIE? ARE YOU ALRIGHT?
HHUC
HHUCH...
PFUH
OF COURSE I'M NOT ALRIGHT. I'M THROWING UP. YOU KNOW I ALWAYS THROW UP WHENEVER YOU TAKE ME ANYWHERE!
JON, LISTEN, THIS AIR SUPPLY, WHATEVER IT IS. YOU BETTER NOT FORGET ABOUT IT, OR...
...OR, UH...
OH SHIT.
I'M ON MARS.
4

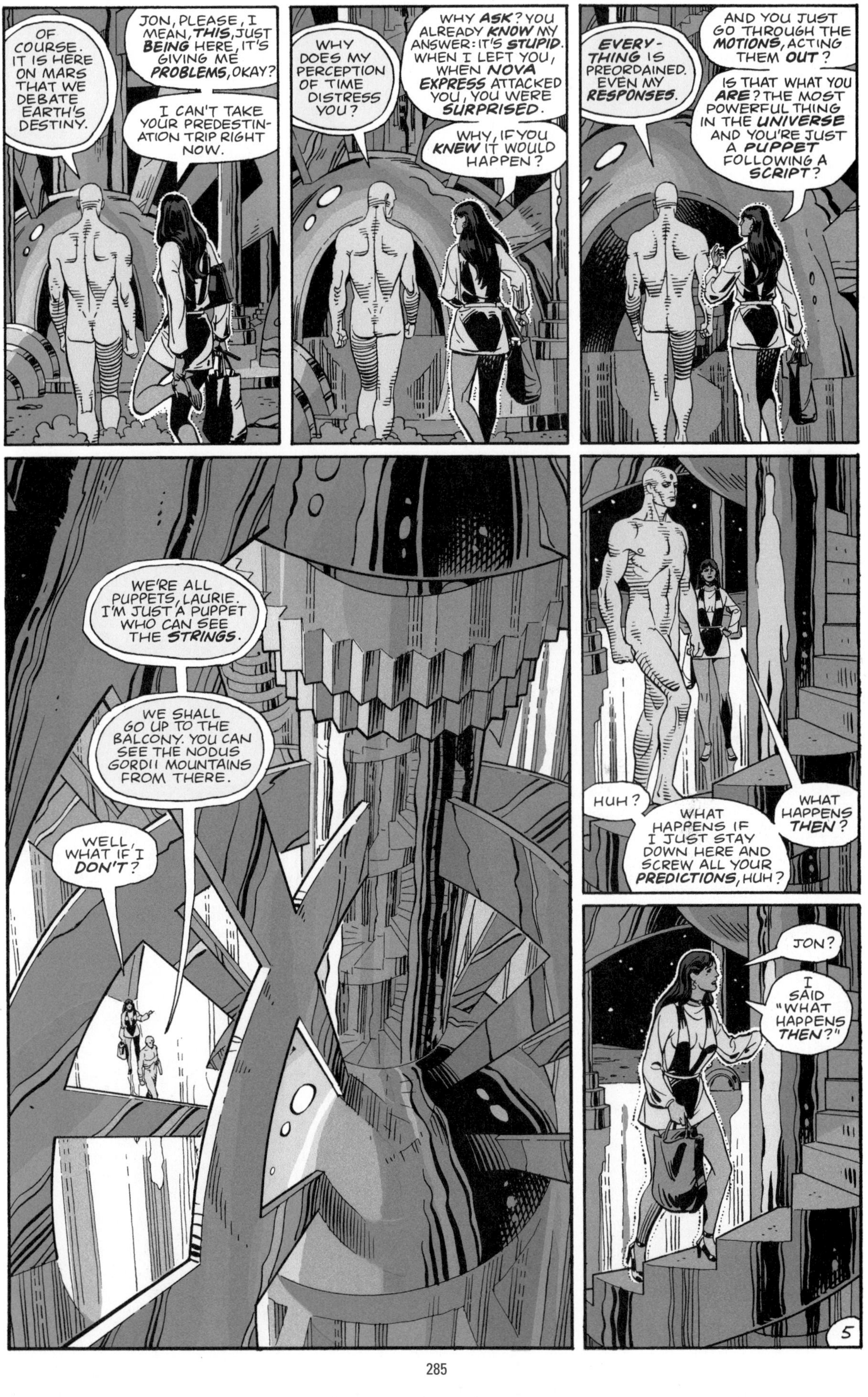

OF COURSE. IT IS HERE ON MARS THAT WE DEBATE EARTH'S DESTINY.
JON, PLEASE, I MEAN, THIS, JUST BEING HERE, IT'S GIVING ME PROBLEMS, OKAY?
I CAN'T TAKE YOUR PREDESTINATION TRIP RIGHT NOW.
WHY DOES MY PERCEPTION OF TIME DISTRESS YOU?
WHY ASK? YOU ALREADY KNOW MY ANSWER: IT'S STUPID. WHEN I LEFT YOU, WHEN NOVA EXPRESS ATTACKED YOU, YOU WERE SURPRISED.
WHY, IF YOU KNEW IT WOULD HAPPEN?
EVERYTHING IS PREORDAINED. EVEN MY RESPONSES.
AND YOU JUST GO THROUGH THE MOTIONS, ACTING THEM OUT?
IS THAT WHAT YOU ARE? THE MOST POWERFUL THING IN THE UNIVERSE AND YOU'RE JUST A PUPPET FOLLOWING A SCRIPT?
WE'RE ALL PUPPETS, LAURIE. I'M JUST A PUPPET WHO CAN SEE THE STRINGS.
WE SHALL GO UP TO THE BALCONY. YOU CAN SEE THE NODUS GORDII MOUNTAINS FROM THERE.
WELL, WHAT IF I DON'T?
HUH?
WHAT HAPPENS IF I JUST STAY DOWN HERE AND SCREW ALL YOUR PREDICTIONS, HUH?
WHAT HAPPENS THEN?
JON?
I SAID "WHAT HAPPENS THEN?"
5

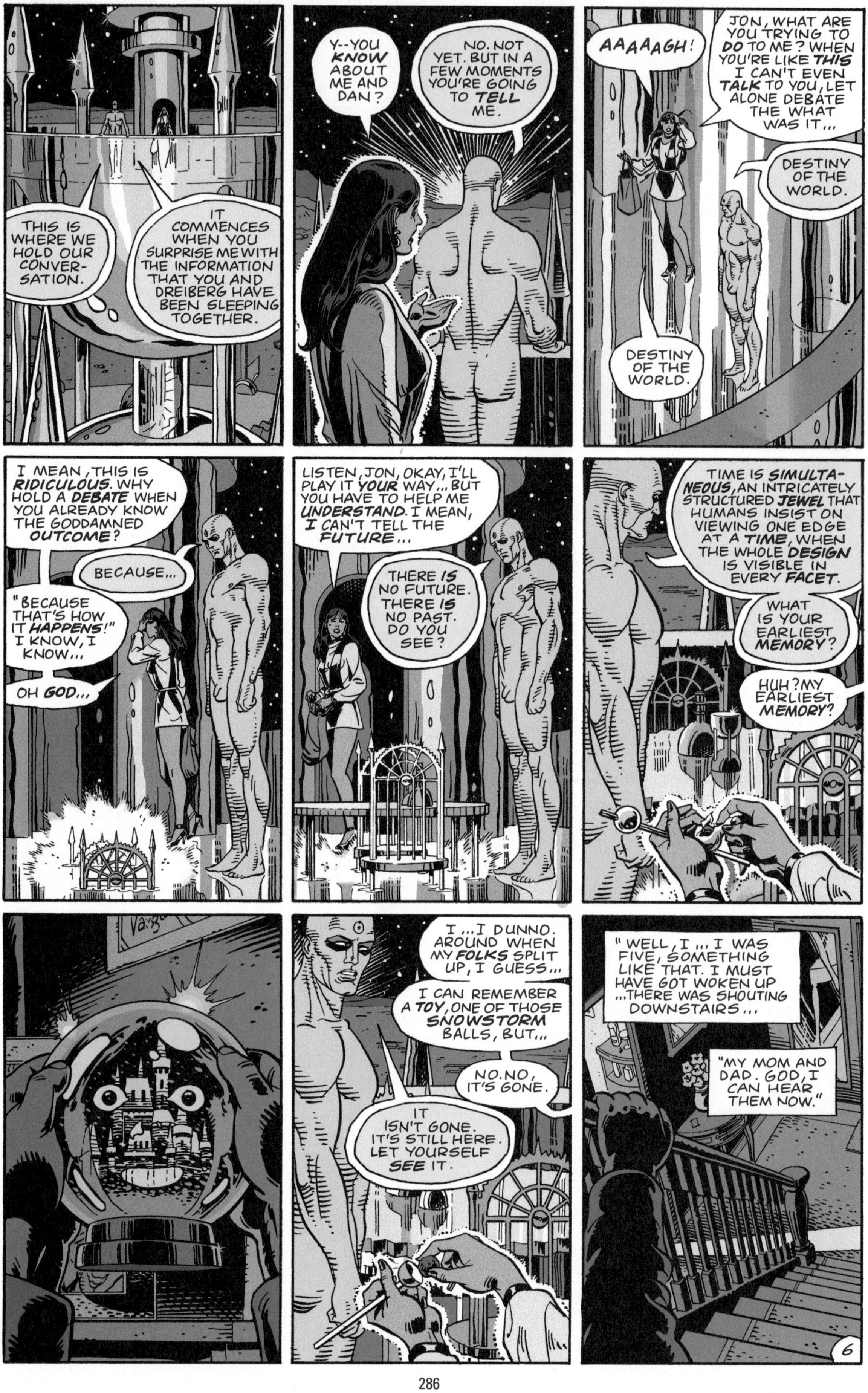
THIS IS WHERE WE HOLD OUR CONVER-SATION.
IT COMMENCES WHEN YOU SURPRISE ME WITH THE INFORMATION THAT YOU AND DREIBERG HAVE BEEN SLEEPING TOGETHER.
Y--YOU KNOW ABOUT ME AND DAN?
NO. NOT YET. BUT IN A FEW MOMENTS YOU'RE GOING TO TELL ME.
AAAAAAGH!
JON, WHAT ARE YOU TRYING TO DO TO ME? WHEN YOU'RE LIKE THIS I CAN'T EVEN TALK TO YOU, LET ALONE DEBATE THE WHAT WAS IT...
DESTINY OF THE WORLD.
DESTINY OF THE WORLD.
I MEAN, THIS IS RIDICULOUS. WHY HOLD A DEBATE WHEN YOU ALREADY KNOW THE GODDAMNED OUTCOME?
BECAUSE...
"BECAUSE THAT'S HOW IT HAPPENS!" I KNOW, I KNOW...
OH GOD...
LISTEN, JON, OKAY, I'LL PLAY IT YOUR WAY... BUT YOU HAVE TO HELP ME UNDERSTAND. I MEAN, I CAN'T TELL THE FUTURE...
THERE IS NO FUTURE. THERE IS NO PAST. DO YOU SEE?
TIME IS SIMULTA-NEOUS, AN INTRICATELY STRUCTURED JEWEL THAT HUMANS INSIST ON VIEWING ONE EDGE AT A TIME, WHEN THE WHOLE DESIGN IS VISIBLE IN EVERY FACET.
WHAT IS YOUR EARLIEST MEMORY?
HUH? MY EARLIEST MEMORY?
I... I DUNNO. AROUND WHEN MY FOLKS SPLIT UP, I GUESS...
I CAN REMEMBER A TOY, ONE OF THOSE SNOWSTORM BALLS, BUT...
NO. NO, IT'S GONE.
IT ISN'T GONE. IT'S STILL HERE. LET YOURSELF SEE IT.
"WELL, I... I WAS FIVE, SOMETHING LIKE THAT. I MUST HAVE GOT WOKEN UP ...THERE WAS SHOUTING DOWNSTAIRS...
"MY MOM AND DAD. GOD, I CAN HEAR THEM NOW."
6

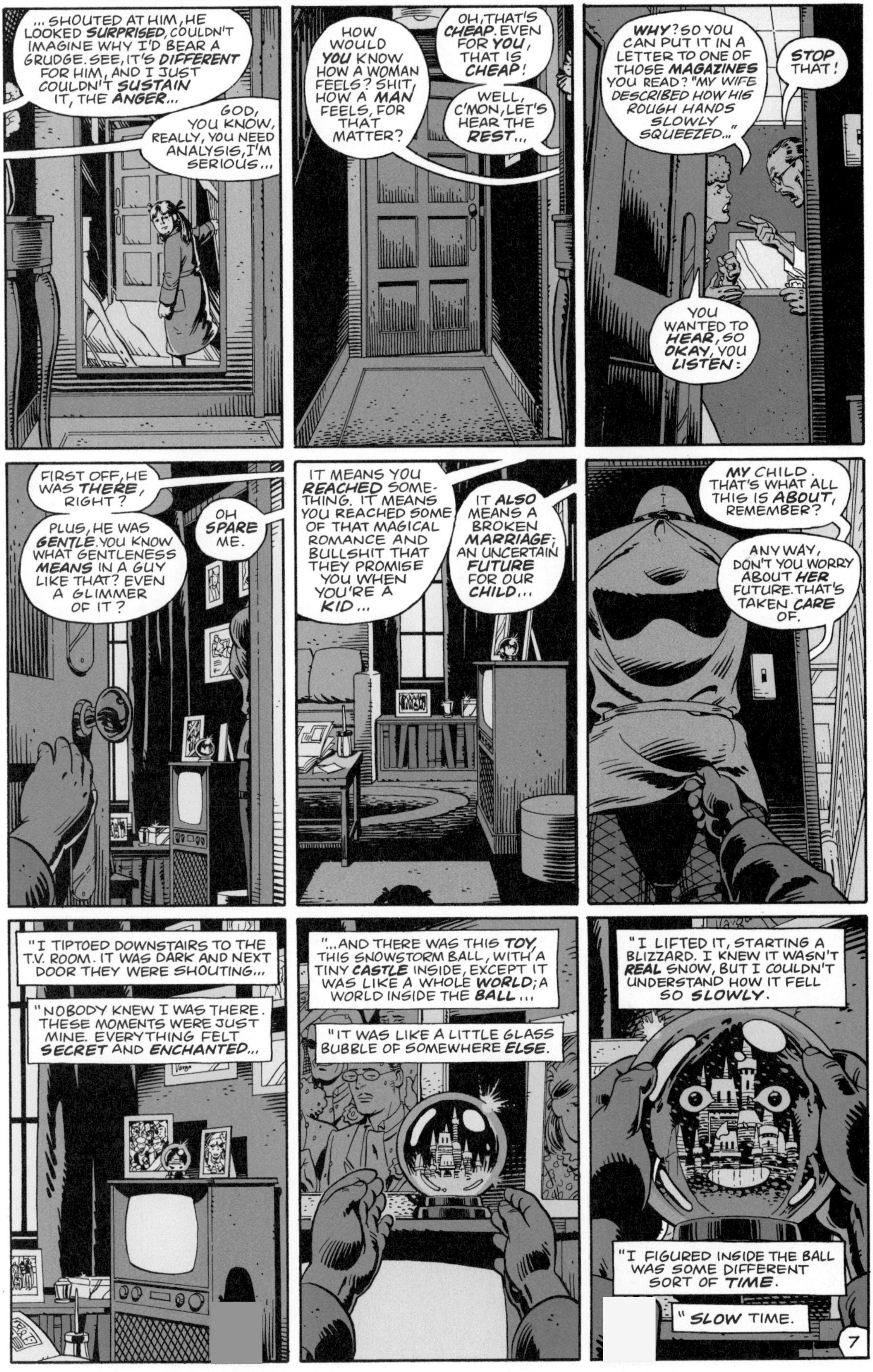
...SHOUTED AT HIM, HE LOOKED SURPRISED, COULDN'T IMAGINE WHY I'D BEAR A GRUDGE. SEE, IT'S DIFFERENT FOR HIM, AND I JUST COULDN'T SUSTAIN IT, THE ANGER...
GOD, YOU KNOW, REALLY, YOU NEED ANALYSIS, I'M SERIOUS...
HOW WOULD YOU KNOW HOW A WOMAN FEELS? SHIT, HOW A MAN FEELS, FOR THAT MATTER?
OH, THAT'S CHEAP. EVEN FOR YOU, THAT IS CHEAP!
WELL, C'MON, LET'S HEAR THE REST...
WHY? SO YOU CAN PUT IT IN A LETTER TO ONE OF THOSE MAGAZINES YOU READ? "MY WIFE DESCRIBED HOW HIS ROUGH HANDS SLOWLY SQUEEZED..."
STOP THAT!
YOU WANTED TO HEAR, SO OKAY, YOU LISTEN:
FIRST OFF, HE WAS THERE, RIGHT?
PLUS, HE WAS GENTLE. YOU KNOW WHAT GENTLENESS MEANS IN A GUY LIKE THAT? EVEN A GLIMMER OF IT?
OH SPARE ME.
IT MEANS YOU REACHED SOMETHING. IT MEANS YOU REACHED SOME OF THAT MAGICAL ROMANCE AND BULLSHIT THAT THEY PROMISE YOU WHEN YOU'RE A KID...
IT ALSO MEANS A BROKEN MARRIAGE; AN UNCERTAIN FUTURE FOR OUR CHILD...
MY CHILD. THAT'S WHAT ALL THIS IS ABOUT, REMEMBER?
ANYWAY, DON'T YOU WORRY ABOUT HER FUTURE. THAT'S TAKEN CARE OF.
"I TIPTOED DOWNSTAIRS TO THE T.V. ROOM. IT WAS DARK AND NEXT DOOR THEY WERE SHOUTING...
"NOBODY KNEW I WAS THERE. THESE MOMENTS WERE JUST MINE. EVERYTHING FELT SECRET AND ENCHANTED...
"...AND THERE WAS THIS TOY, THIS SNOWSTORM BALL, WITH A TINY CASTLE INSIDE, EXCEPT IT WAS LIKE A WHOLE WORLD; A WORLD INSIDE THE BALL...
"IT WAS LIKE A LITTLE GLASS BUBBLE OF SOMEWHERE ELSE.
"I LIFTED IT, STARTING A BLIZZARD. I KNEW IT WASN'T REAL SNOW, BUT I COULDN'T UNDERSTAND HOW IT FELL SO SLOWLY.
"I FIGURED INSIDE THE BALL WAS SOME DIFFERENT SORT OF TIME.
"SLOW TIME.
7

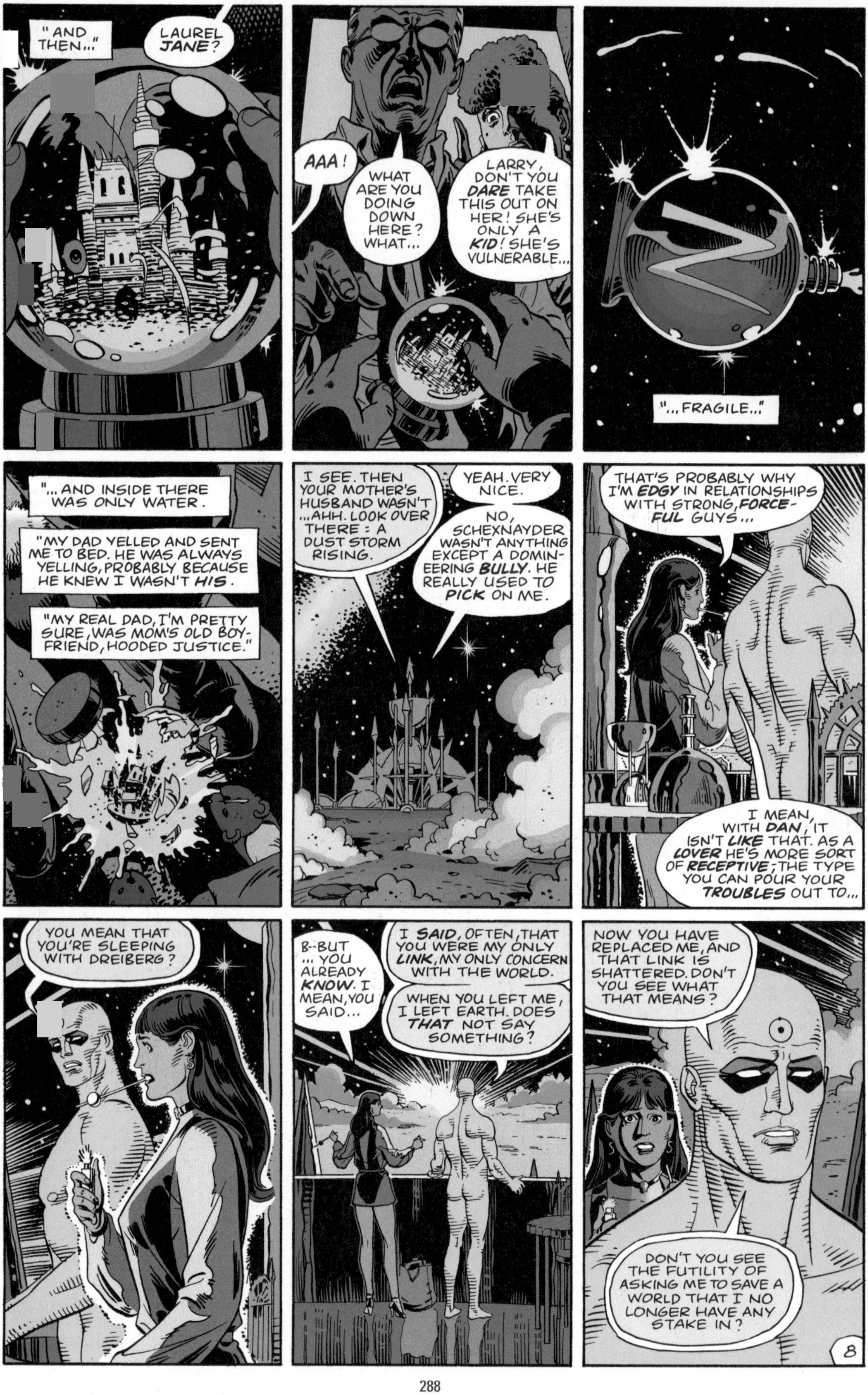
"AND THEN..."
LAUREL JANE?
AAA!
WHAT ARE YOU DOING DOWN HERE? WHAT...
LARRY, DON'T YOU DARE TAKE THIS OUT ON HER! SHE'S ONLY A KID! SHE'S VULNERABLE...
"...FRAGILE..."
"...AND INSIDE THERE WAS ONLY WATER.
"MY DAD YELLED AND SENT ME TO BED. HE WAS ALWAYS YELLING, PROBABLY BECAUSE HE KNEW I WASN'T HIS.
"MY REAL DAD, I'M PRETTY SURE, WAS MOM'S OLD BOY-FRIEND, HOODED JUSTICE."
I SEE. THEN YOUR MOTHER'S HUSBAND WASN'T ...AHH. LOOK OVER THERE: A DUST STORM RISING.
YEAH. VERY NICE.
NO, SCHEXNAYDER WASN'T ANYTHING EXCEPT A DOMIN-EERING BULLY. HE REALLY USED TO PICK ON ME.
THAT'S PROBABLY WHY I'M EDGY IN RELATIONSHIPS WITH STRONG, FORCE-FUL GUYS...
I MEAN, WITH DAN, IT ISN'T LIKE THAT. AS A LOVER HE'S MORE SORT OF RECEPTIVE; THE TYPE YOU CAN POUR YOUR TROUBLES OUT TO...
YOU MEAN THAT YOU'RE SLEEPING WITH DREIBERG?
B--BUT ... YOU ALREADY KNOW. I MEAN, YOU SAID...
I SAID, OFTEN, THAT YOU WERE MY ONLY LINK, MY ONLY CONCERN WITH THE WORLD.
WHEN YOU LEFT ME, I LEFT EARTH. DOES THAT NOT SAY SOMETHING?
NOW YOU HAVE REPLACED ME, AND THAT LINK IS SHATTERED. DON'T YOU SEE WHAT THAT MEANS?
DON'T YOU SEE THE FUTILITY OF ASKING ME TO SAVE A WORLD THAT I NO LONGER HAVE ANY STAKE IN?
8

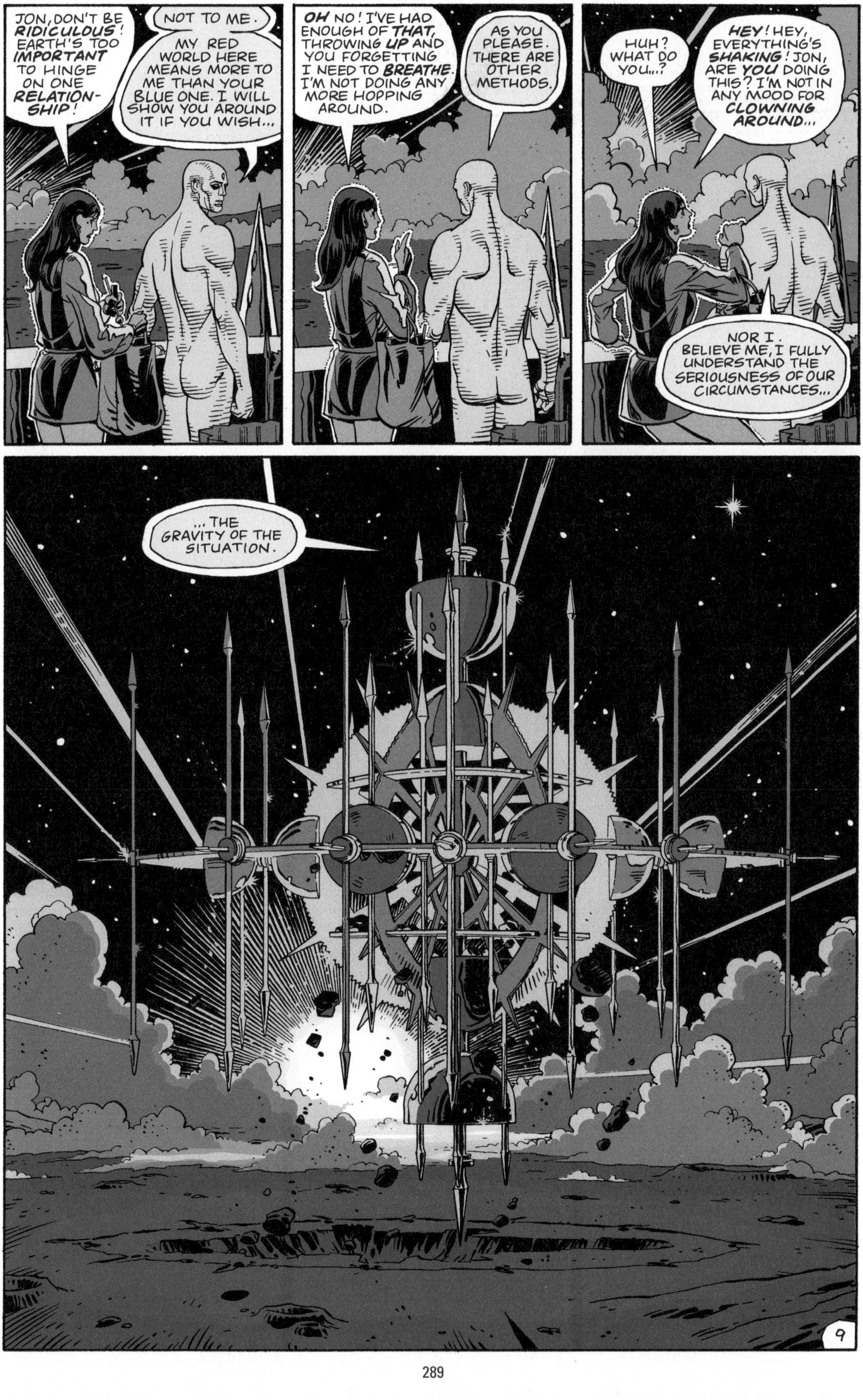
JON, DON'T BE RIDICULOUS! EARTH'S TOO IMPORTANT TO HINGE ON ONE RELATION-SHIP!
NOT TO ME.
MY RED WORLD HERE MEANS MORE TO ME THAN YOUR BLUE ONE. I WILL SHOW YOU AROUND IT IF YOU WISH...
OH NO! I'VE HAD ENOUGH OF THAT, THROWING UP AND YOU FORGETTING I NEED TO BREATHE. I'M NOT DOING ANY MORE HOPPING AROUND.
AS YOU PLEASE. THERE ARE OTHER METHODS.
HUH? WHAT DO YOU...?
HEY! HEY, EVERYTHING'S SHAKING! JON, ARE YOU DOING THIS? I'M NOT IN ANY MOOD FOR CLOWNING AROUND...
NOR I. BELIEVE ME, I FULLY UNDERSTAND THE SERIOUSNESS OF OUR CIRCUMSTANCES...
...THE GRAVITY OF THE SITUATION.
9

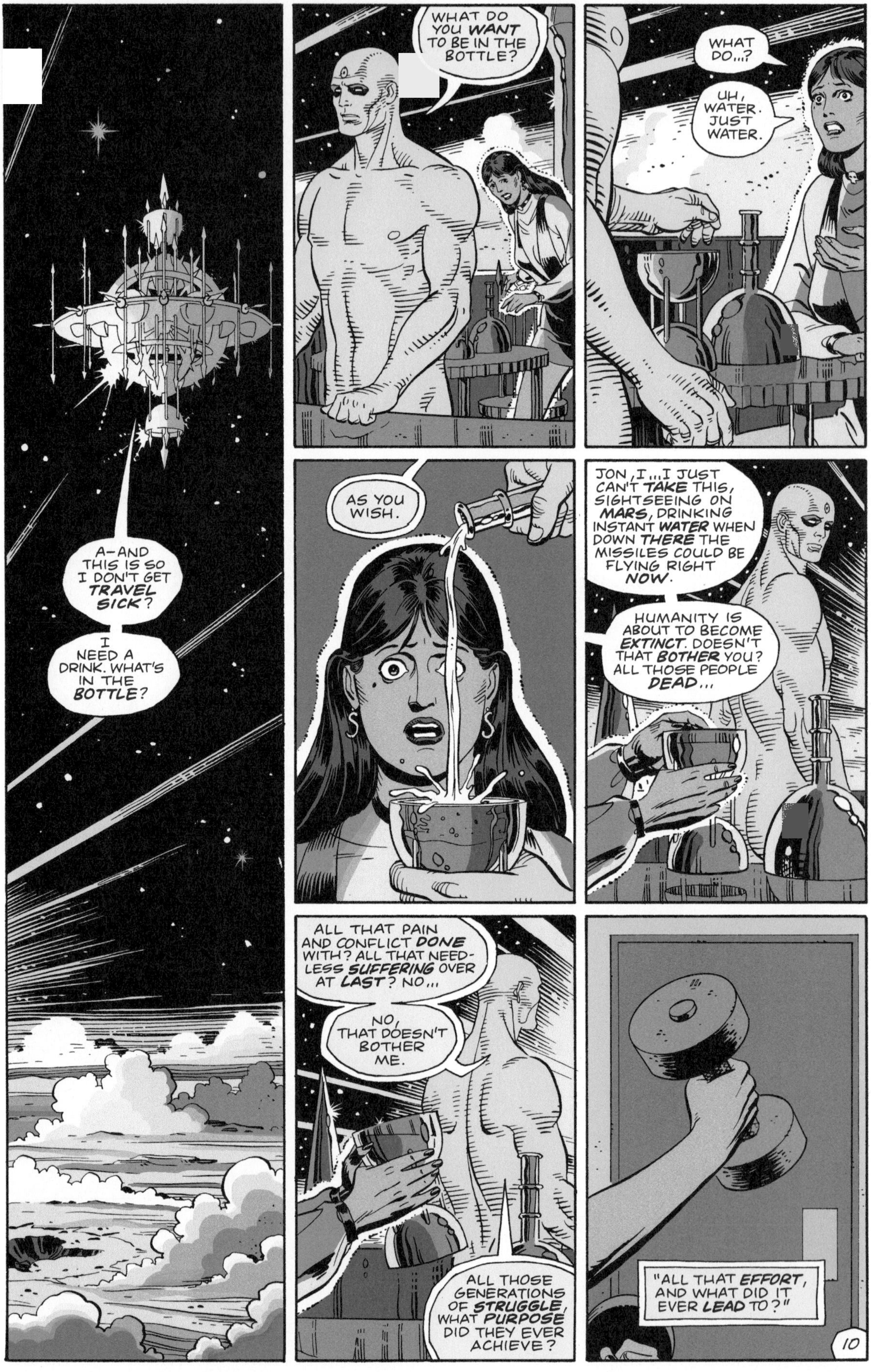
A-AND THIS IS SO I DON'T GET TRAVEL SICK?
I NEED A DRINK. WHAT'S IN THE BOTTLE?
WHAT DO YOU WANT TO BE IN THE BOTTLE?
WHAT DO...?
UH, WATER. JUST WATER.
AS YOU WISH.
JON, I...I JUST CAN'T TAKE THIS, SIGHTSEEING ON MARS, DRINKING INSTANT WATER WHEN DOWN THERE THE MISSILES COULD BE FLYING RIGHT NOW.
HUMANITY IS ABOUT TO BECOME EXTINCT. DOESN'T THAT BOTHER YOU? ALL THOSE PEOPLE DEAD...
ALL THAT PAIN AND CONFLICT DONE WITH? ALL THAT NEEDLESS SUFFERING OVER AT LAST? NO...
NO, THAT DOESN'T BOTHER ME.
ALL THOSE GENERATIONS OF STRUGGLE, WHAT PURPOSE DID THEY EVER ACHIEVE?
"ALL THAT EFFORT, AND WHAT DID IT EVER LEAD TO?"
10

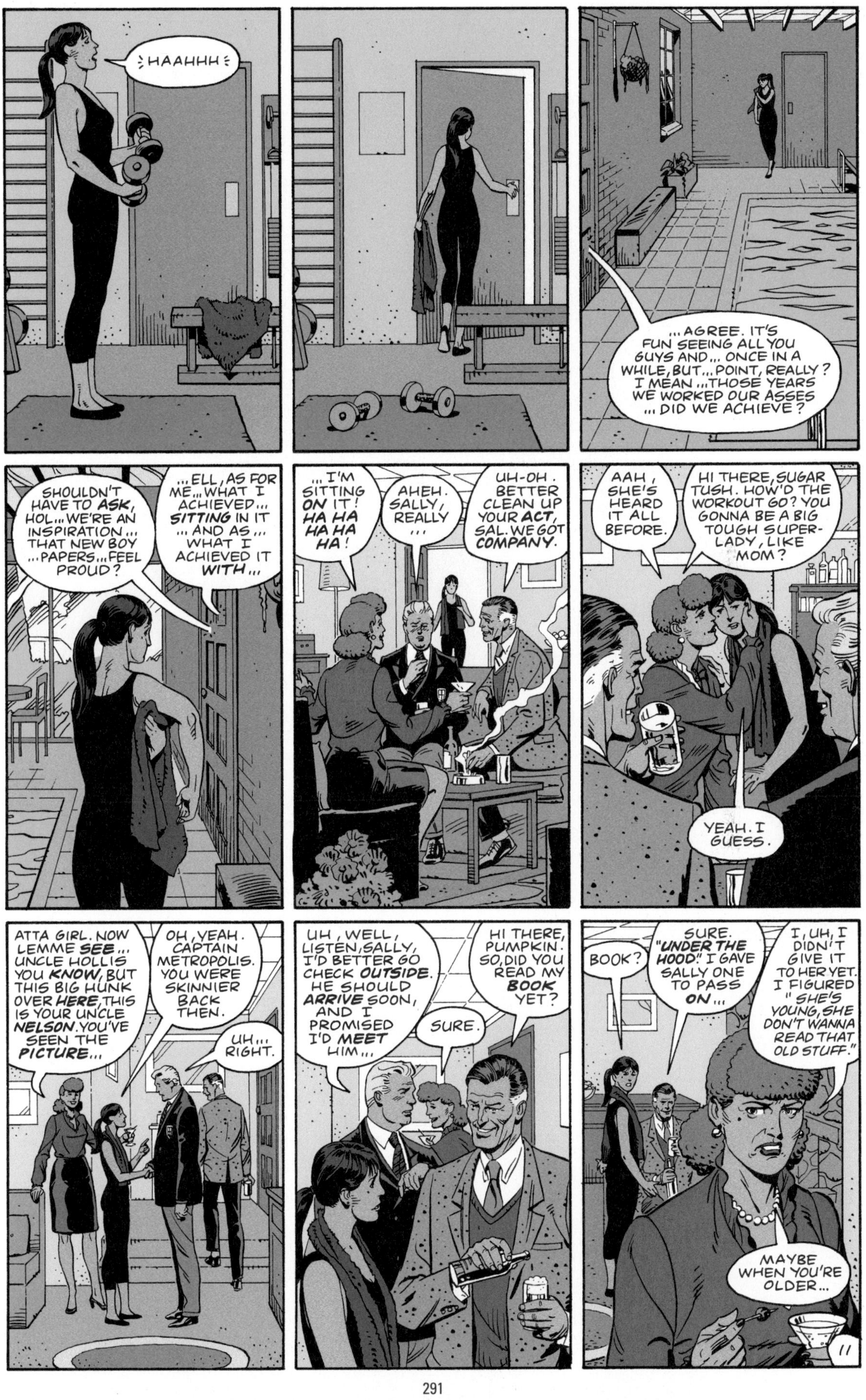
HAAHHH
...AGREE. IT'S FUN SEEING ALL YOU GUYS AND... ONCE IN A WHILE, BUT... POINT, REALLY? I MEAN ...THOSE YEARS WE WORKED OUR ASSES ... DID WE ACHIEVE?
SHOULDN'T HAVE TO ASK, HOL... WE'RE AN INSPIRATION... THAT NEW BOY ...PAPERS... FEEL PROUD?
...ELL, AS FOR ME... WHAT I ACHIEVED... SITTING IN IT ...AND AS... WHAT I ACHIEVED IT WITH...
... I'M SITTING ON IT! HA HA HA HA HA!
AHEH. SALLY, REALLY ...
UH-OH. BETTER CLEAN UP YOUR ACT, SAL. WE GOT COMPANY.
AAH, SHE'S HEARD IT ALL BEFORE.
HI THERE, SUGAR TUSH. HOW'D THE WORKOUT GO? YOU GONNA BE A BIG TOUGH SUPER-LADY, LIKE MOM?
YEAH. I GUESS.
ATTA GIRL. NOW LEMME SEE... UNCLE HOLLIS YOU KNOW, BUT THIS BIG HUNK OVER HERE, THIS IS YOUR UNCLE NELSON. YOU'VE SEEN THE PICTURE...
OH, YEAH. CAPTAIN METROPOLIS. YOU WERE SKINNIER BACK THEN.
UH... RIGHT.
UH, WELL, LISTEN, SALLY, I'D BETTER GO CHECK OUTSIDE. HE SHOULD ARRIVE SOON, AND I PROMISED I'D MEET HIM...
HI THERE, PUMPKIN. SO, DID YOU READ MY BOOK YET?
SURE.
BOOK?
SURE. "UNDER THE HOOD." I GAVE SALLY ONE TO PASS ON...
I, UH, I DIDN'T GIVE IT TO HER YET. I FIGURED "SHE'S YOUNG, SHE DON'T WANNA READ THAT OLD STUFF."
MAYBE WHEN YOU'RE OLDER...
11

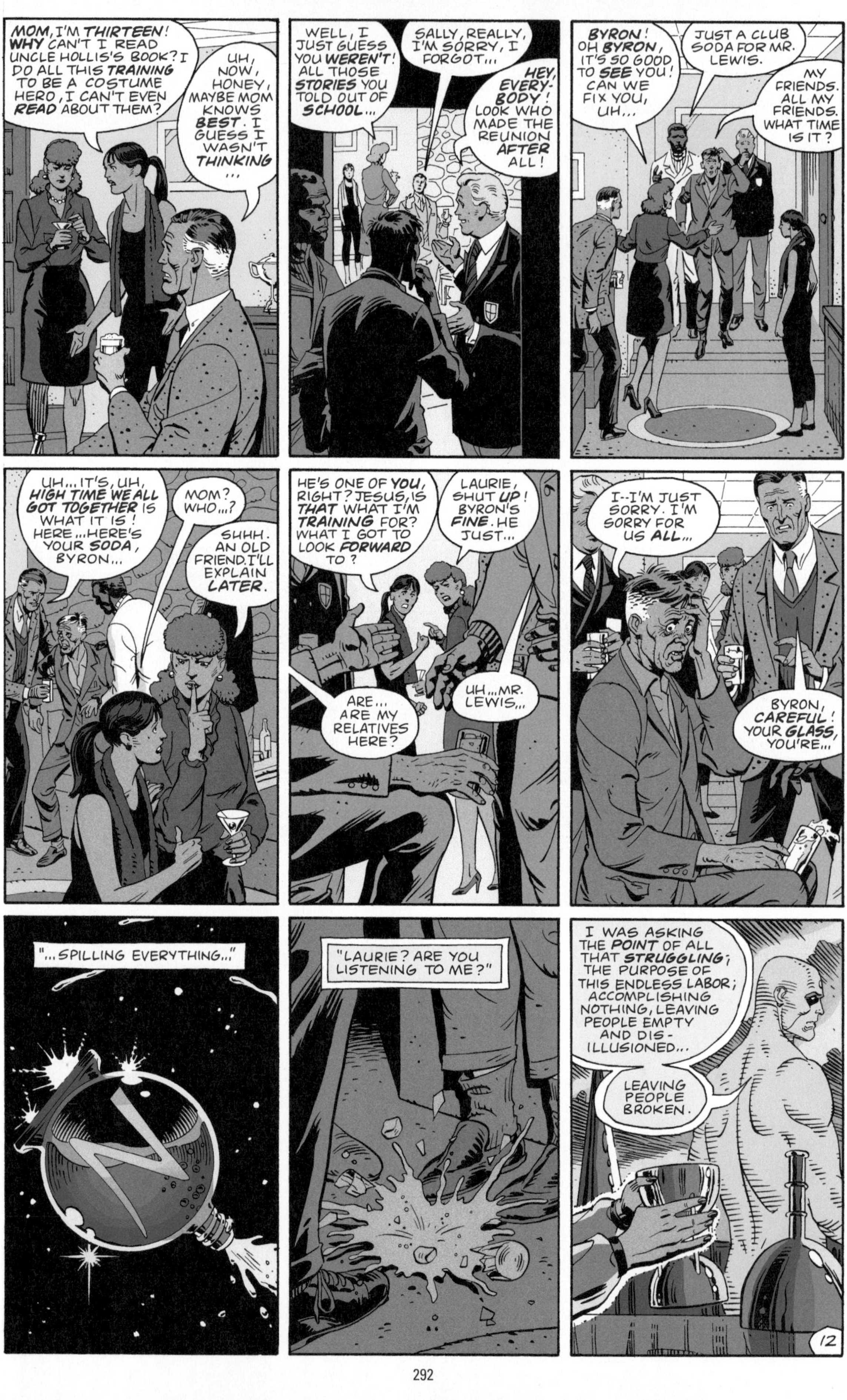
MOM, I'M THIRTEEN! WHY CAN'T I READ UNCLE HOLLIS'S BOOK? I DO ALL THIS TRAINING TO BE A COSTUME HERO, I CAN'T EVEN READ ABOUT THEM?
UH, NOW, HONEY, MAYBE MOM KNOWS BEST. I GUESS I WASN'T THINKING...
WELL, I JUST GUESS YOU WEREN'T! ALL THOSE STORIES YOU TOLD OUT OF SCHOOL...
SALLY, REALLY, I'M SORRY, I FORGOT...
HEY, EVERYBODY! LOOK WHO MADE THE REUNION AFTER ALL!
BYRON! OH BYRON, IT'S SO GOOD TO SEE YOU! CAN WE FIX YOU, UH...
JUST A CLUB SODA FOR MR. LEWIS.
MY FRIENDS. ALL MY FRIENDS. WHAT TIME IS IT?
UH... IT'S, UH, HIGH TIME WE ALL GOT TOGETHER IS WHAT IT IS! HERE... HERE'S YOUR SODA, BYRON...
MOM? WHO...?
SHHH. AN OLD FRIEND. I'LL EXPLAIN LATER.
HE'S ONE OF YOU, RIGHT? JESUS, IS THAT WHAT I'M TRAINING FOR? WHAT I GOT TO LOOK FORWARD TO?
LAURIE, SHUT UP! BYRON'S FINE. HE JUST...
ARE... ARE MY RELATIVES HERE?
UH... MR. LEWIS...
I--I'M JUST SORRY. I'M SORRY FOR US ALL...
BYRON, CAREFUL! YOUR GLASS, YOU'RE...
"...SPILLING EVERYTHING..."
"LAURIE? ARE YOU LISTENING TO ME?"
I WAS ASKING THE POINT OF ALL THAT STRUGGLING; THE PURPOSE OF THIS ENDLESS LABOR; ACCOMPLISHING NOTHING, LEAVING PEOPLE EMPTY AND DISILLUSIONED...
LEAVING PEOPLE BROKEN.
12

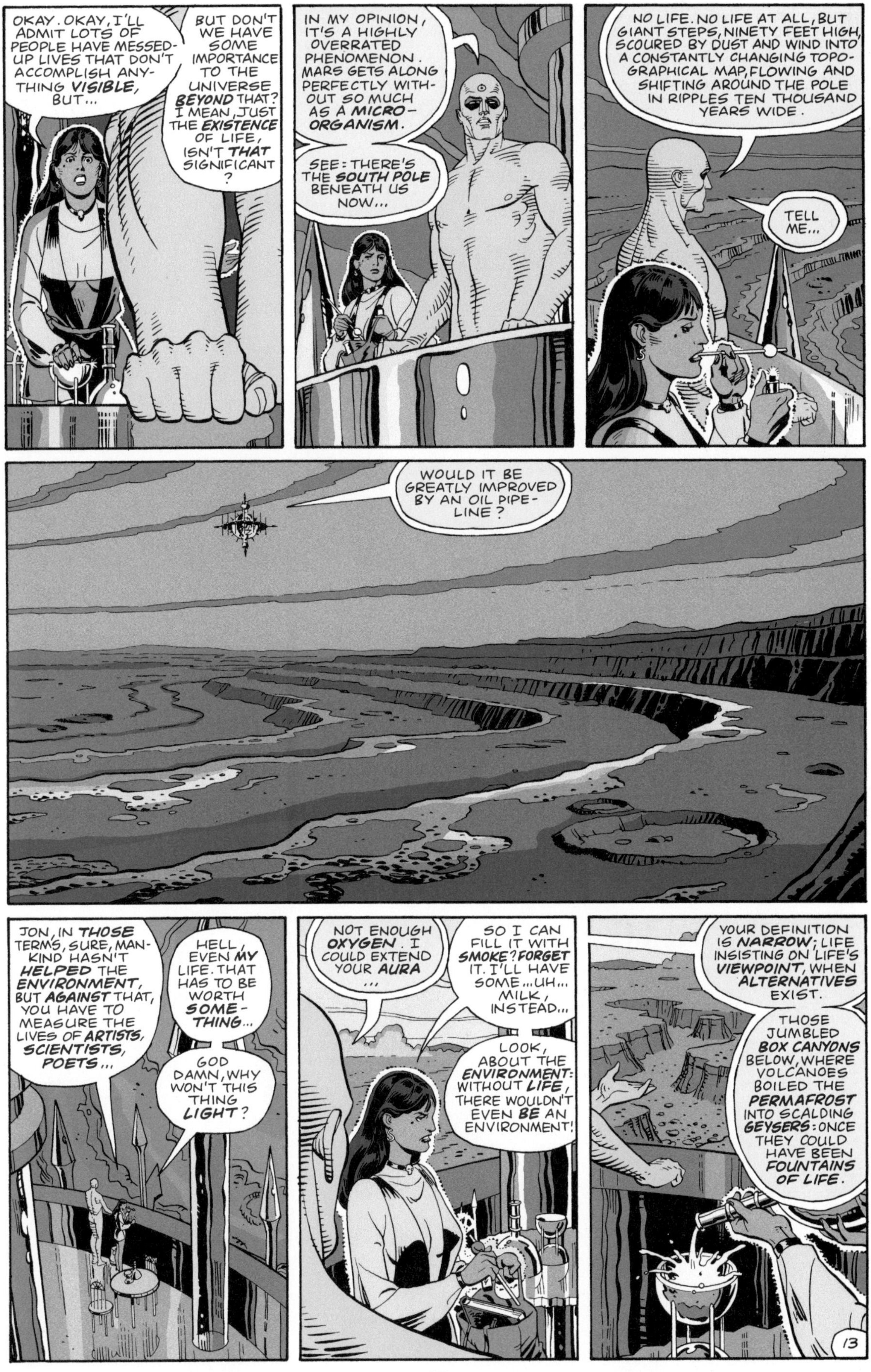
OKAY. OKAY, I'LL ADMIT LOTS OF PEOPLE HAVE MESSED-UP LIVES THAT DON'T ACCOMPLISH ANYTHING **VISIBLE**, BUT...
BUT DON'T WE HAVE SOME IMPORTANCE TO THE UNIVERSE **BEYOND** THAT? I MEAN, JUST THE **EXISTENCE** OF LIFE, ISN'T **THAT** SIGNIFICANT?
IN MY OPINION, IT'S A HIGHLY OVERRATED PHENOMENON. MARS GETS ALONG PERFECTLY WITHOUT SO MUCH AS A **MICRO-ORGANISM**.
SEE: THERE'S THE **SOUTH POLE** BENEATH US NOW...
NO LIFE. NO LIFE AT ALL, BUT GIANT STEPS, NINETY FEET HIGH, SCOURED BY DUST AND WIND INTO A CONSTANTLY CHANGING TOPOGRAPHICAL MAP, FLOWING AND SHIFTING AROUND THE POLE IN RIPPLES TEN THOUSAND YEARS WIDE.
TELL ME...
WOULD IT BE GREATLY IMPROVED BY AN OIL PIPELINE?
JON, IN **THOSE** TERMS, SURE, MANKIND HASN'T **HELPED** THE **ENVIRONMENT**, BUT **AGAINST** THAT, YOU HAVE TO MEASURE THE LIVES OF **ARTISTS**, **SCIENTISTS**, **POETS**...
HELL, EVEN **MY** LIFE. THAT HAS TO BE WORTH **SOMETHING**...
GOD DAMN, WHY WON'T THIS THING **LIGHT**?
NOT ENOUGH **OXYGEN**. I COULD EXTEND YOUR **AURA**...
SO I CAN FILL IT WITH **SMOKE**? **FORGET** IT. I'LL HAVE SOME... UH... MILK, INSTEAD...
LOOK, ABOUT THE **ENVIRONMENT**: WITHOUT **LIFE**, THERE WOULDN'T EVEN **BE** AN ENVIRONMENT!
YOUR DEFINITION IS **NARROW**; LIFE INSISTING ON LIFE'S **VIEWPOINT**, WHEN **ALTERNATIVES** EXIST.
THOSE JUMBLED **BOX CANYONS** BELOW, WHERE VOLCANOES BOILED THE **PERMAFROST** INTO SCALDING **GEYSERS**: ONCE THEY COULD HAVE BEEN **FOUNTAINS OF LIFE**.
13

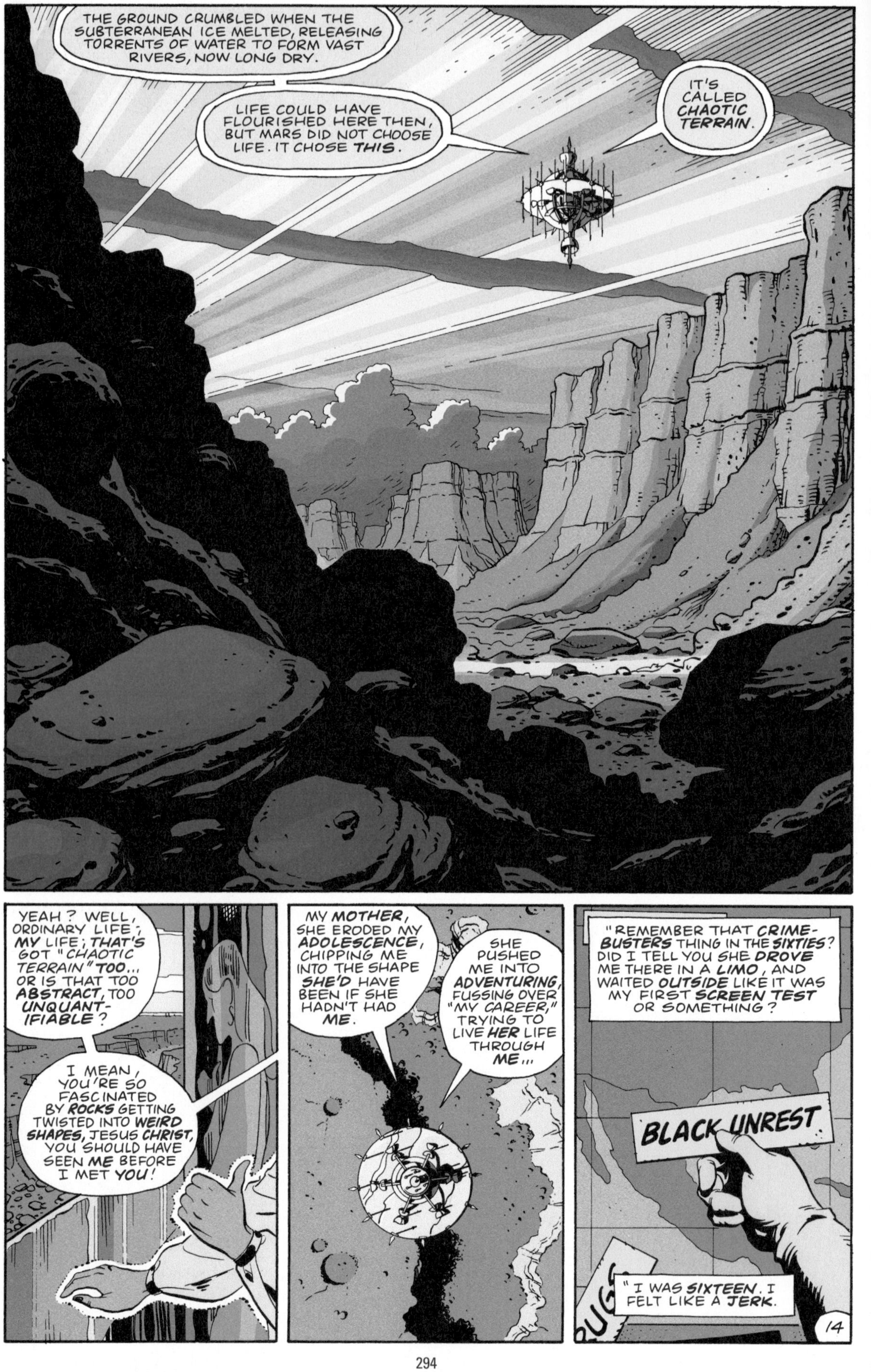
THE GROUND CRUMBLED WHEN THE SUBTERRANEAN ICE MELTED, RELEASING TORRENTS OF WATER TO FORM VAST RIVERS, NOW LONG DRY.
LIFE COULD HAVE FLOURISHED HERE THEN, BUT MARS DID NOT CHOOSE LIFE. IT CHOSE THIS.
IT'S CALLED CHAOTIC TERRAIN.
YEAH? WELL, ORDINARY LIFE; MY LIFE; THAT'S GOT "CHAOTIC TERRAIN" TOO... OR IS THAT TOO ABSTRACT, TOO UNQUANTIFIABLE?
I MEAN, YOU'RE SO FASCINATED BY ROCKS GETTING TWISTED INTO WEIRD SHAPES, JESUS CHRIST, YOU SHOULD HAVE SEEN ME BEFORE I MET YOU!
MY MOTHER, SHE ERODED MY ADOLESCENCE, CHIPPING ME INTO THE SHAPE SHE'D HAVE BEEN IF SHE HADN'T HAD ME.
SHE PUSHED ME INTO ADVENTURING, FUSSING OVER "MY CAREER," TRYING TO LIVE HER LIFE THROUGH ME...
"REMEMBER THAT CRIME-BUSTERS THING IN THE SIXTIES? DID I TELL YOU SHE DROVE ME THERE IN A LIMO, AND WAITED OUTSIDE LIKE IT WAS MY FIRST SCREEN TEST OR SOMETHING?
BLACK UNREST
"I WAS SIXTEEN. I FELT LIKE A JERK.
14

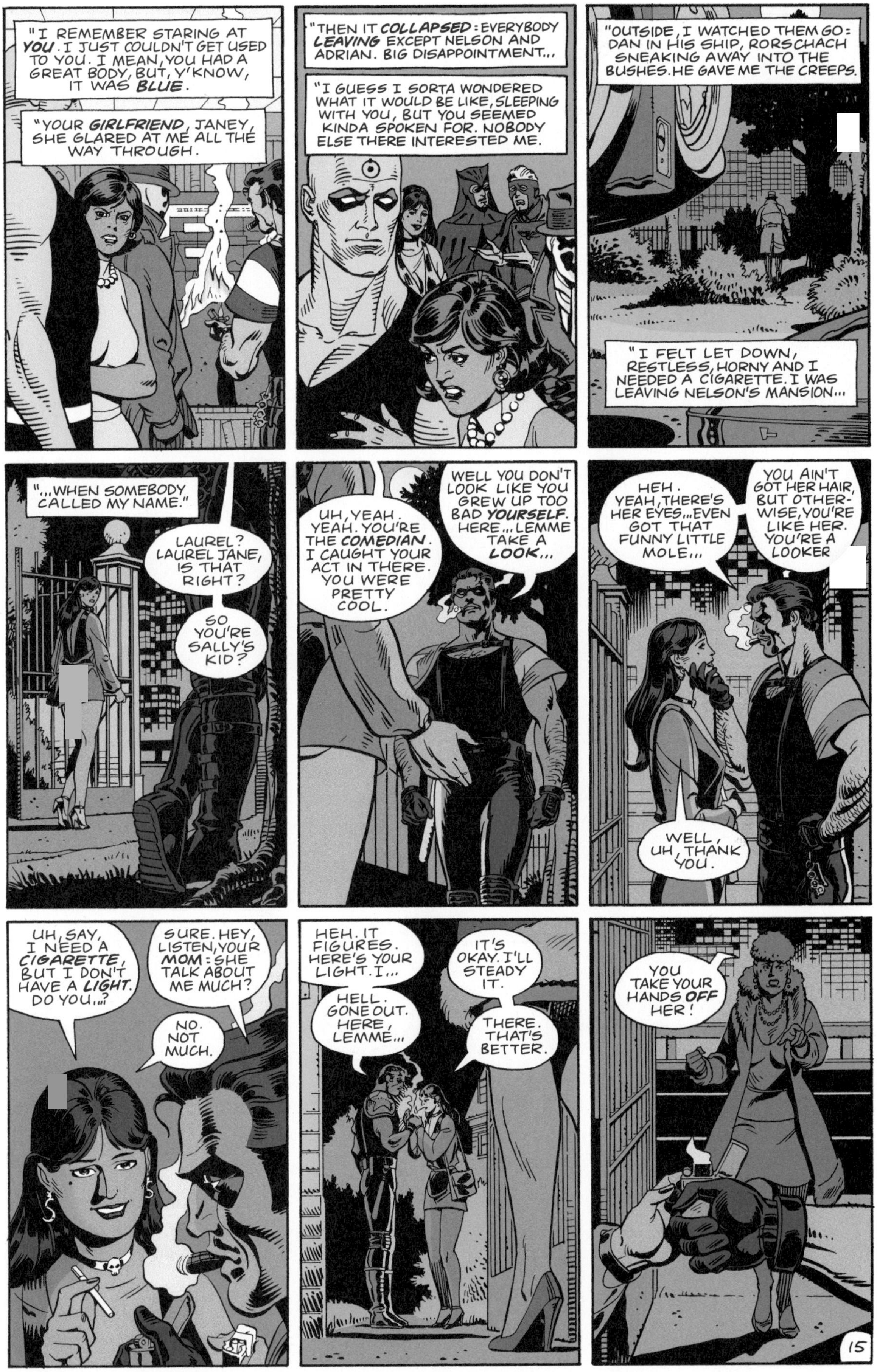
"I REMEMBER STARING AT YOU. I JUST COULDN'T GET USED TO YOU. I MEAN, YOU HAD A GREAT BODY, BUT, Y'KNOW, IT WAS BLUE.
"YOUR GIRLFRIEND, JANEY, SHE GLARED AT ME ALL THE WAY THROUGH.
"THEN IT COLLAPSED: EVERYBODY LEAVING EXCEPT NELSON AND ADRIAN. BIG DISAPPOINTMENT...
"I GUESS I SORTA WONDERED WHAT IT WOULD BE LIKE, SLEEPING WITH YOU, BUT YOU SEEMED KINDA SPOKEN FOR. NOBODY ELSE THERE INTERESTED ME.
"OUTSIDE, I WATCHED THEM GO: DAN IN HIS SHIP, RORSCHACH SNEAKING AWAY INTO THE BUSHES. HE GAVE ME THE CREEPS.
"I FELT LET DOWN, RESTLESS, HORNY AND I NEEDED A CIGARETTE. I WAS LEAVING NELSON'S MANSION...
"...WHEN SOMEBODY CALLED MY NAME."
LAUREL? LAUREL JANE, IS THAT RIGHT?
SO YOU'RE SALLY'S KID?
UH, YEAH. YEAH. YOU'RE THE COMEDIAN. I CAUGHT YOUR ACT IN THERE. YOU WERE PRETTY COOL.
WELL YOU DON'T LOOK LIKE YOU GREW UP TOO BAD YOURSELF. HERE... LEMME TAKE A LOOK...
HEH. YEAH, THERE'S HER EYES... EVEN GOT THAT FUNNY LITTLE MOLE...
YOU AIN'T GOT HER HAIR, BUT OTHERWISE, YOU'RE LIKE HER. YOU'RE A LOOKER
WELL, UH, THANK YOU.
UH, SAY, I NEED A CIGARETTE, BUT I DON'T HAVE A LIGHT. DO YOU...?
SURE. HEY, LISTEN, YOUR MOM: SHE TALK ABOUT ME MUCH?
NO. NOT MUCH.
HEH. IT FIGURES. HERE'S YOUR LIGHT. I...
HELL. GONE OUT. HERE, LEMME...
IT'S OKAY. I'LL STEADY IT.
THERE. THAT'S BETTER.
YOU TAKE YOUR HANDS OFF HER!
15

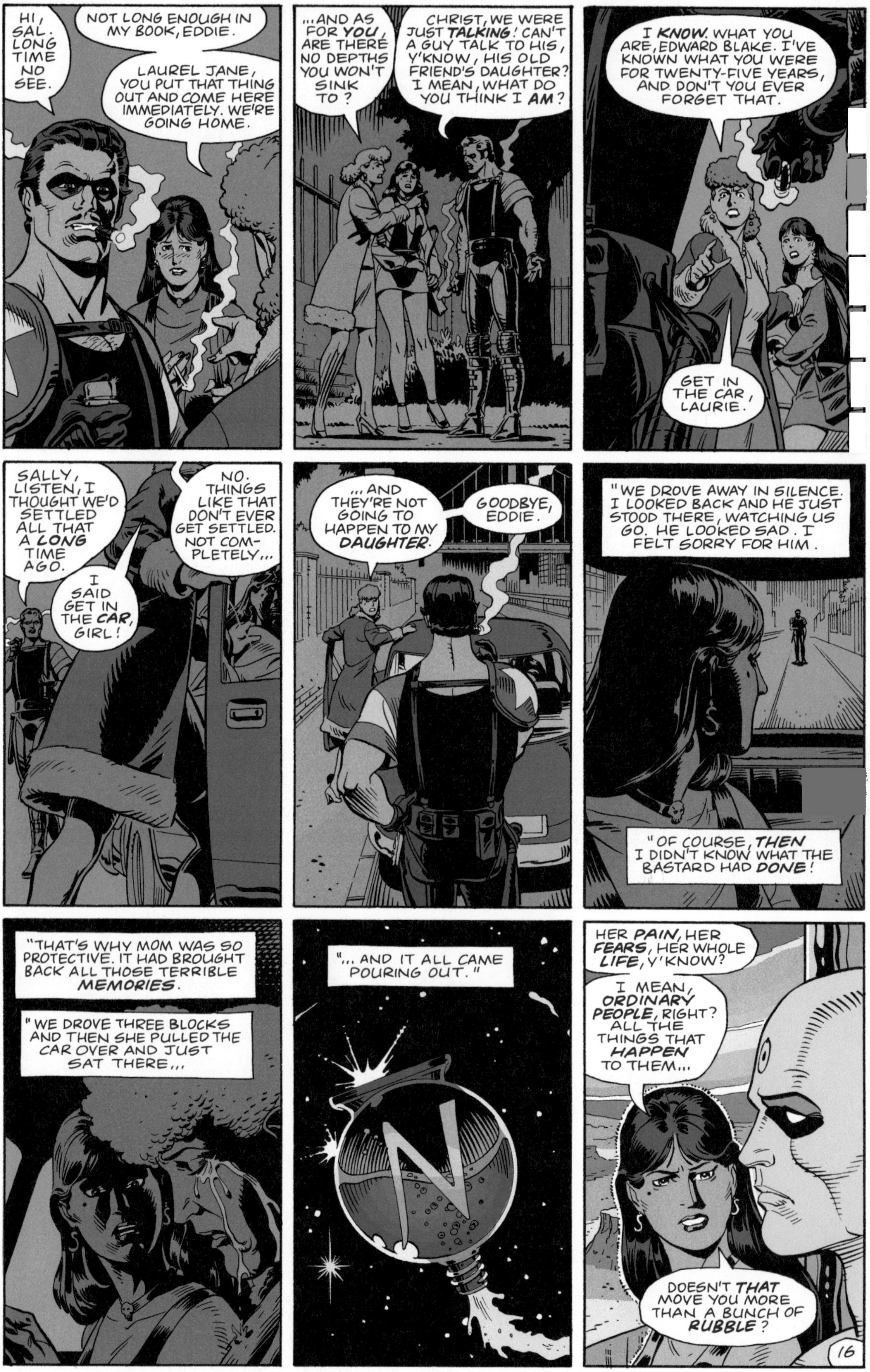
HI, SAL. LONG TIME NO SEE.
NOT LONG ENOUGH IN MY BOOK, EDDIE.
LAUREL JANE, YOU PUT THAT THING OUT AND COME HERE IMMEDIATELY. WE'RE GOING HOME.
...AND AS FOR YOU, ARE THERE NO DEPTHS YOU WON'T SINK TO?
CHRIST, WE WERE JUST TALKING! CAN'T A GUY TALK TO HIS, Y'KNOW, HIS OLD FRIEND'S DAUGHTER? I MEAN, WHAT DO YOU THINK I AM?
I KNOW WHAT YOU ARE, EDWARD BLAKE. I'VE KNOWN WHAT YOU WERE FOR TWENTY-FIVE YEARS, AND DON'T YOU EVER FORGET THAT.
GET IN THE CAR, LAURIE.
SALLY, LISTEN, I THOUGHT WE'D SETTLED ALL THAT A LONG TIME AGO.
NO. THINGS LIKE THAT DON'T EVER GET SETTLED. NOT COMPLETELY...
I SAID GET IN THE CAR, GIRL!
...AND THEY'RE NOT GOING TO HAPPEN TO MY DAUGHTER.
GOODBYE, EDDIE.
"WE DROVE AWAY IN SILENCE. I LOOKED BACK AND HE JUST STOOD THERE, WATCHING US GO. HE LOOKED SAD. I FELT SORRY FOR HIM.
"OF COURSE, THEN I DIDN'T KNOW WHAT THE BASTARD HAD DONE!
"THAT'S WHY MOM WAS SO PROTECTIVE. IT HAD BROUGHT BACK ALL THOSE TERRIBLE MEMORIES.
"WE DROVE THREE BLOCKS AND THEN SHE PULLED THE CAR OVER AND JUST SAT THERE...
"...AND IT ALL CAME POURING OUT."
HER PAIN, HER FEARS, HER WHOLE LIFE, Y'KNOW?
I MEAN, ORDINARY PEOPLE, RIGHT? ALL THE THINGS THAT HAPPEN TO THEM...
DOESN'T THAT MOVE YOU MORE THAN A BUNCH OF RUBBLE?
16

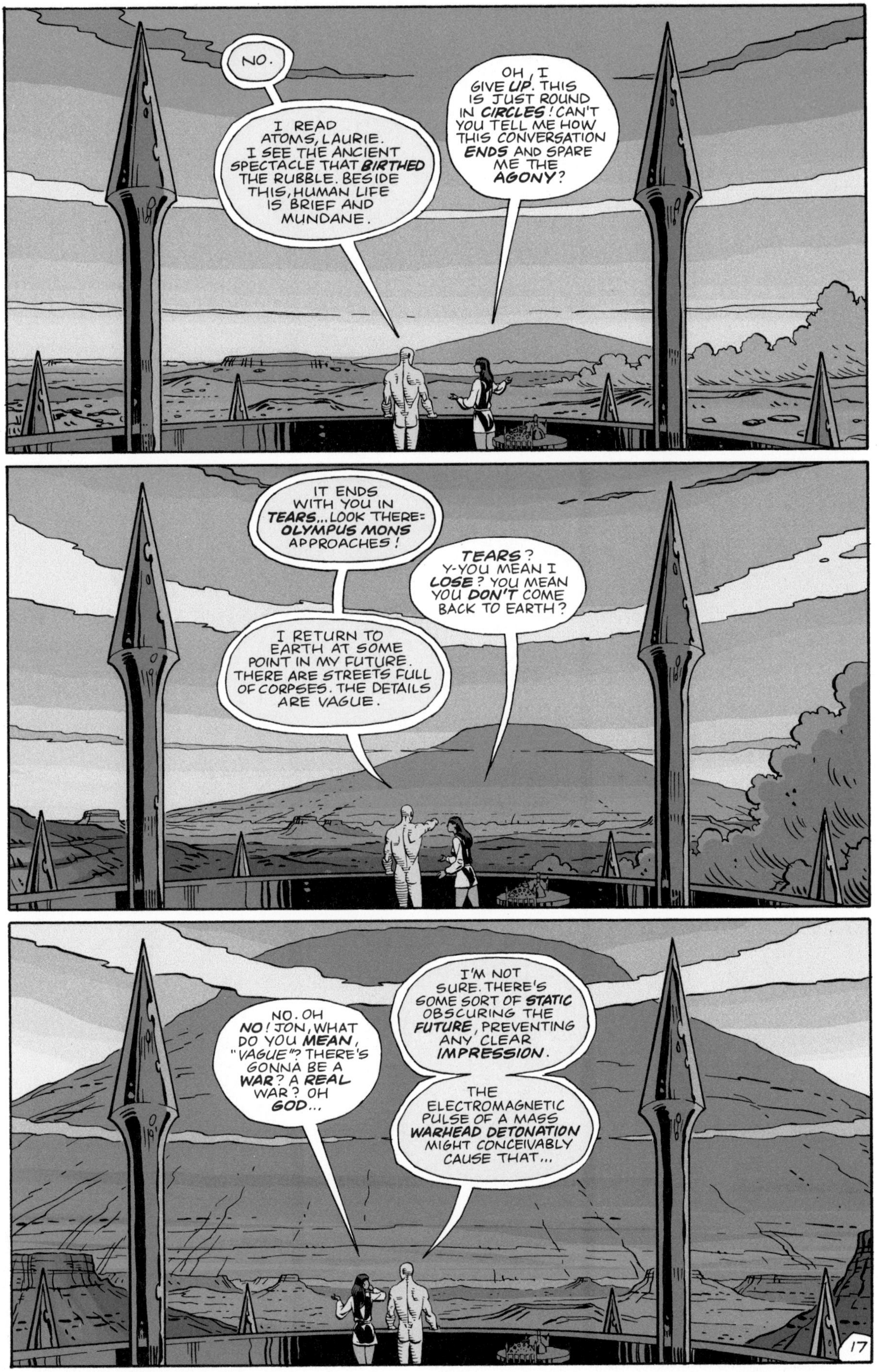
NO.
I READ ATOMS, LAURIE. I SEE THE ANCIENT SPECTACLE THAT BIRTHED THE RUBBLE. BESIDE THIS, HUMAN LIFE IS BRIEF AND MUNDANE.
OH, I GIVE UP. THIS IS JUST ROUND IN CIRCLES! CAN'T YOU TELL ME HOW THIS CONVERSATION ENDS AND SPARE ME THE AGONY?
IT ENDS WITH YOU IN TEARS... LOOK THERE: OLYMPUS MONS APPROACHES!
TEARS? Y-YOU MEAN I LOSE? YOU MEAN YOU DON'T COME BACK TO EARTH?
I RETURN TO EARTH AT SOME POINT IN MY FUTURE. THERE ARE STREETS FULL OF CORPSES. THE DETAILS ARE VAGUE.
NO. OH NO! JON, WHAT DO YOU MEAN, "VAGUE"? THERE'S GONNA BE A WAR? A REAL WAR? OH GOD...
I'M NOT SURE. THERE'S SOME SORT OF STATIC OBSCURING THE FUTURE, PREVENTING ANY CLEAR IMPRESSION.
THE ELECTROMAGNETIC PULSE OF A MASS WARHEAD DETONATION MIGHT CONCEIVABLY CAUSE THAT...
17

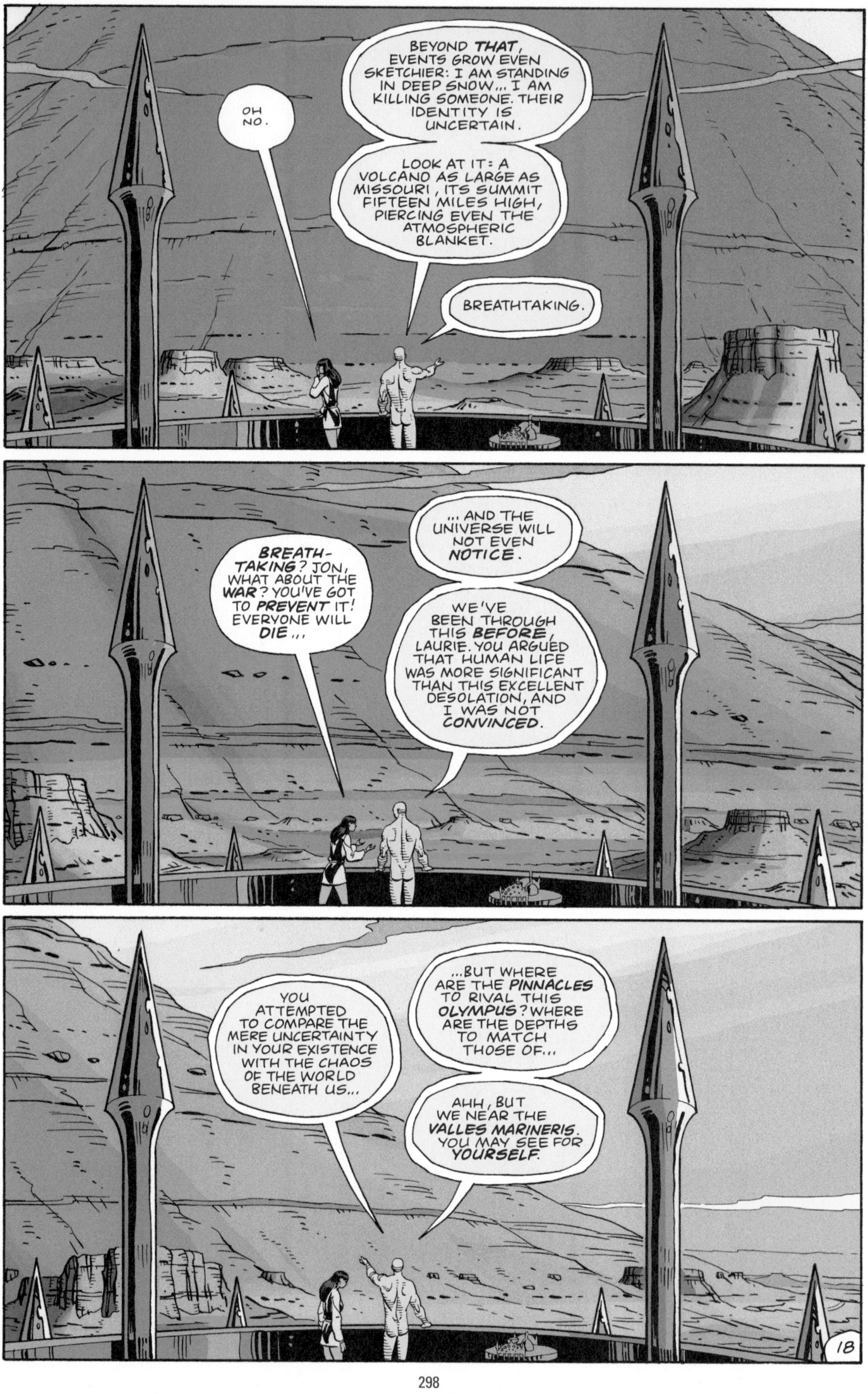
BEYOND THAT, EVENTS GROW EVEN SKETCHIER: I AM STANDING IN DEEP SNOW... I AM KILLING SOMEONE. THEIR IDENTITY IS UNCERTAIN.
OH NO.
LOOK AT IT: A VOLCANO AS LARGE AS MISSOURI, ITS SUMMIT FIFTEEN MILES HIGH, PIERCING EVEN THE ATMOSPHERIC BLANKET.
BREATHTAKING.
BREATHTAKING? JON, WHAT ABOUT THE WAR? YOU'VE GOT TO PREVENT IT! EVERYONE WILL DIE...
... AND THE UNIVERSE WILL NOT EVEN NOTICE.
WE'VE BEEN THROUGH THIS BEFORE, LAURIE. YOU ARGUED THAT HUMAN LIFE WAS MORE SIGNIFICANT THAN THIS EXCELLENT DESOLATION, AND I WAS NOT CONVINCED.
YOU ATTEMPTED TO COMPARE THE MERE UNCERTAINTY IN YOUR EXISTENCE WITH THE CHAOS OF THE WORLD BENEATH US...
...BUT WHERE ARE THE PINNACLES TO RIVAL THIS OLYMPUS? WHERE ARE THE DEPTHS TO MATCH THOSE OF...
AHH, BUT WE NEAR THE VALLES MARINERIS. YOU MAY SEE FOR YOURSELF.
18

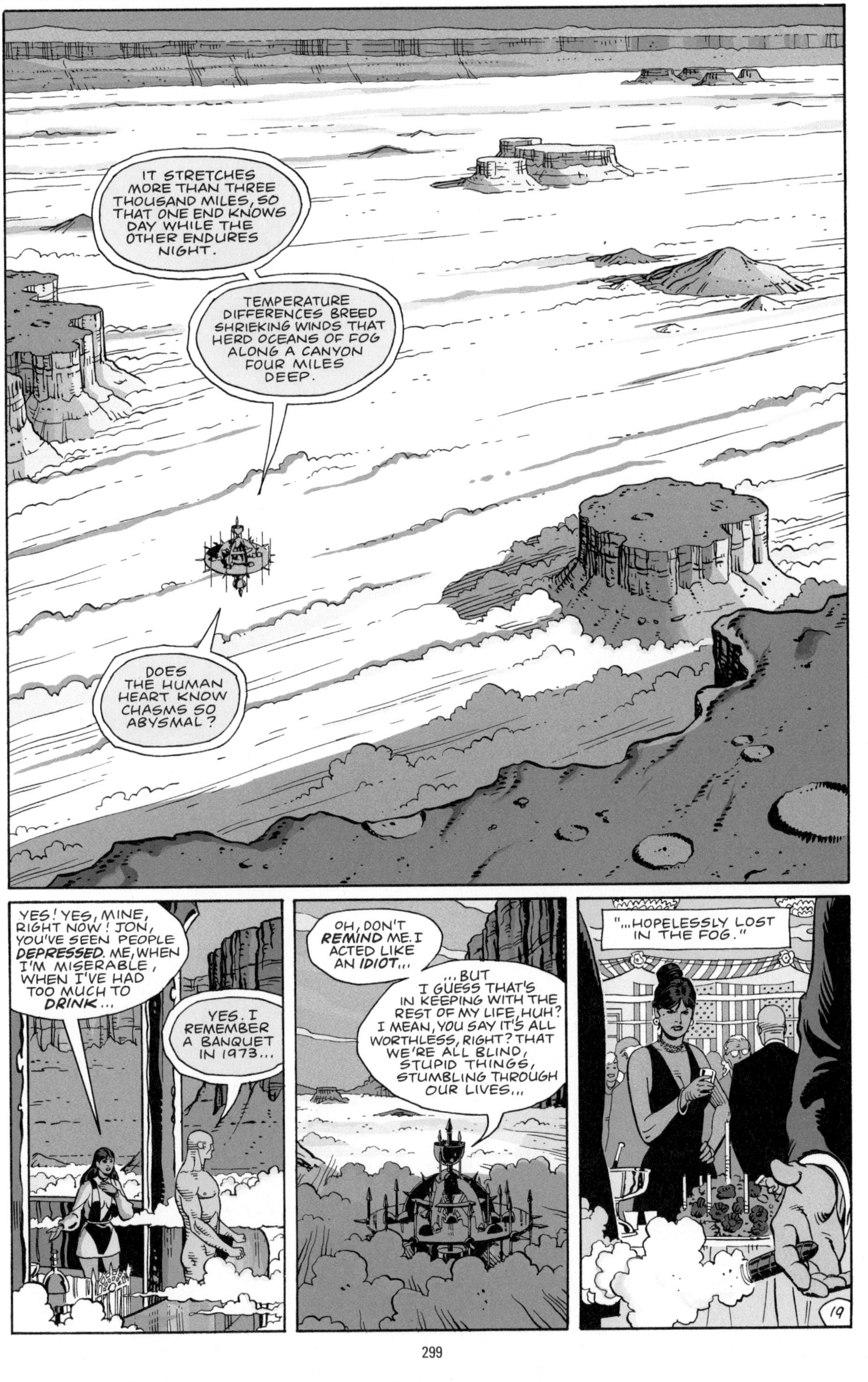
IT STRETCHES MORE THAN THREE THOUSAND MILES, SO THAT ONE END KNOWS DAY WHILE THE OTHER ENDURES NIGHT.
TEMPERATURE DIFFERENCES BREED SHRIEKING WINDS THAT HERD OCEANS OF FOG ALONG A CANYON FOUR MILES DEEP.
DOES THE HUMAN HEART KNOW CHASMS SO ABYSMAL?
YES! YES, MINE, RIGHT NOW! JON, YOU'VE SEEN PEOPLE DEPRESSED. ME, WHEN I'M MISERABLE, WHEN I'VE HAD TOO MUCH TO DRINK...
YES. I REMEMBER A BANQUET IN 1973...
OH, DON'T REMIND ME. I ACTED LIKE AN IDIOT...
...BUT I GUESS THAT'S IN KEEPING WITH THE REST OF MY LIFE, HUH? I MEAN, YOU SAY IT'S ALL WORTHLESS, RIGHT? THAT WE'RE ALL BLIND, STUPID THINGS, STUMBLING THROUGH OUR LIVES...
"...HOPELESSLY LOST IN THE FOG."
19

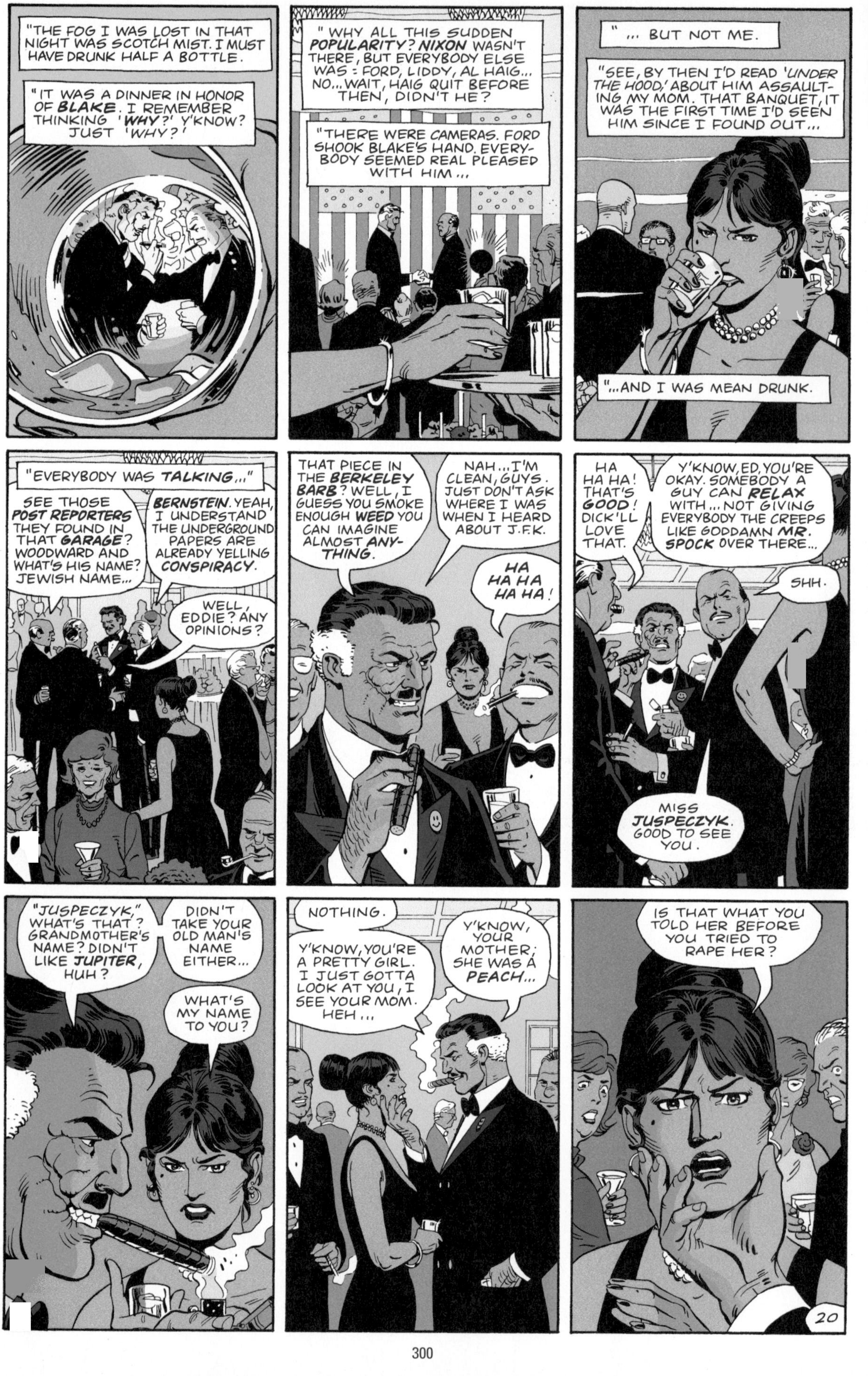
"THE FOG I WAS LOST IN THAT NIGHT WAS SCOTCH MIST. I MUST HAVE DRUNK HALF A BOTTLE.
"IT WAS A DINNER IN HONOR OF BLAKE. I REMEMBER THINKING 'WHY?' Y'KNOW? JUST 'WHY?'
" WHY ALL THIS SUDDEN POPULARITY? NIXON WASN'T THERE, BUT EVERYBODY ELSE WAS: FORD, LIDDY, AL HAIG... NO... WAIT, HAIG QUIT BEFORE THEN, DIDN'T HE?
"THERE WERE CAMERAS. FORD SHOOK BLAKE'S HAND. EVERYBODY SEEMED REAL PLEASED WITH HIM...
" ... BUT NOT ME.
"SEE, BY THEN I'D READ 'UNDER THE HOOD,' ABOUT HIM ASSAULTING MY MOM. THAT BANQUET, IT WAS THE FIRST TIME I'D SEEN HIM SINCE I FOUND OUT...
"...AND I WAS MEAN DRUNK.
"EVERYBODY WAS TALKING..."
SEE THOSE POST REPORTERS THEY FOUND IN THAT GARAGE? WOODWARD AND WHAT'S HIS NAME? JEWISH NAME...
BERNSTEIN. YEAH, I UNDERSTAND THE UNDERGROUND PAPERS ARE ALREADY YELLING CONSPIRACY.
WELL, EDDIE? ANY OPINIONS?
THAT PIECE IN THE BERKELEY BARB? WELL, I GUESS YOU SMOKE ENOUGH WEED YOU CAN IMAGINE ALMOST ANYTHING.
NAH... I'M CLEAN, GUYS. JUST DON'T ASK WHERE I WAS WHEN I HEARD ABOUT J.F.K.
HA HA HA HA HA!
HA HA HA! THAT'S GOOD! DICK'LL LOVE THAT.
Y'KNOW, ED, YOU'RE OKAY. SOMEBODY A GUY CAN RELAX WITH... NOT GIVING EVERYBODY THE CREEPS LIKE GODDAMN MR. SPOCK OVER THERE...
SHH.
MISS JUSPECZYK. GOOD TO SEE YOU.
"JUSPECZYK," WHAT'S THAT? GRANDMOTHER'S NAME? DIDN'T LIKE JUPITER, HUH?
DIDN'T TAKE YOUR OLD MAN'S NAME EITHER...
WHAT'S MY NAME TO YOU?
NOTHING.
Y'KNOW, YOU'RE A PRETTY GIRL. I JUST GOTTA LOOK AT YOU, I SEE YOUR MOM. HEH...
Y'KNOW, YOUR MOTHER, SHE WAS A PEACH...
IS THAT WHAT YOU TOLD HER BEFORE YOU TRIED TO RAPE HER?
20

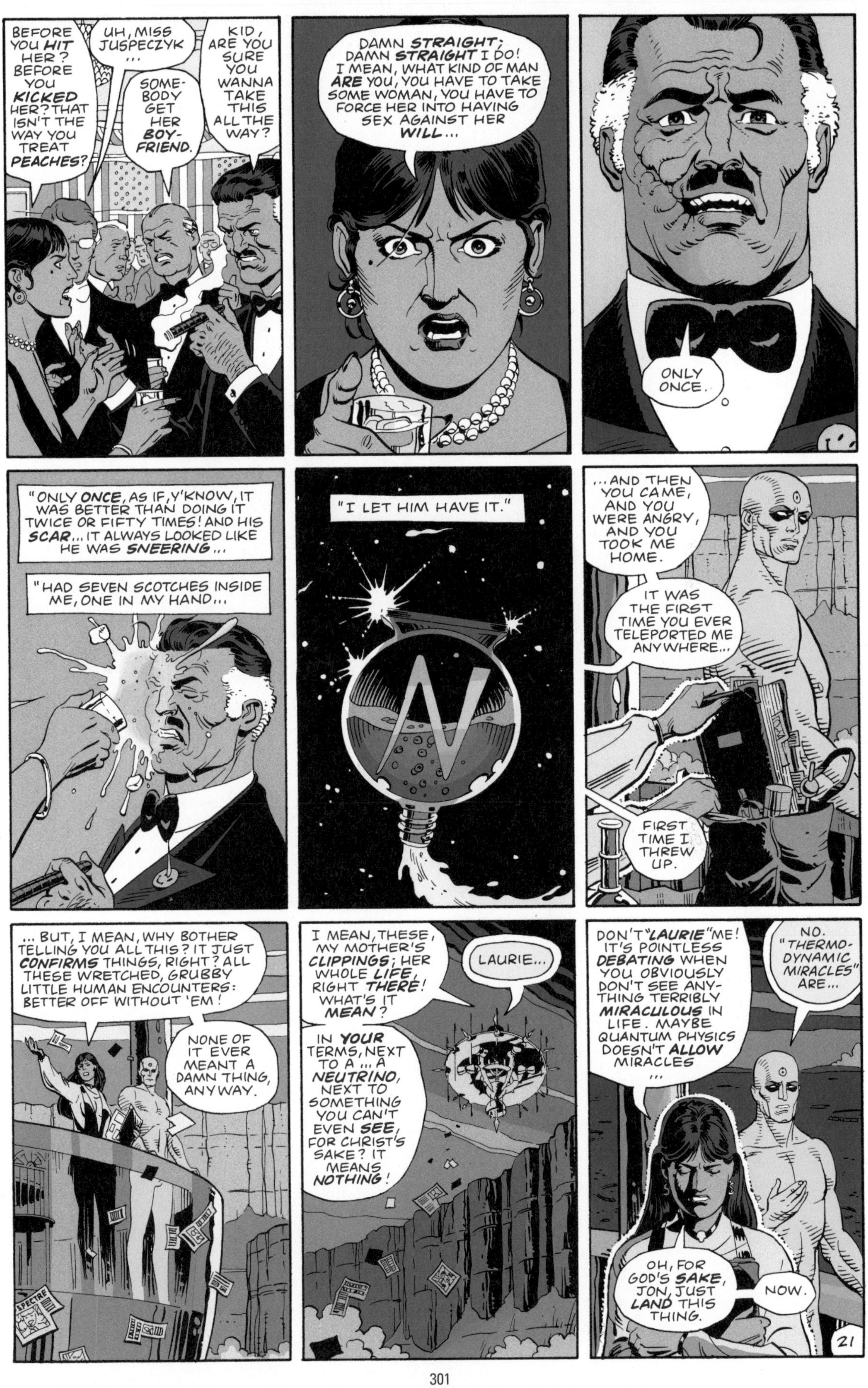
BEFORE YOU HIT HER? BEFORE YOU KICKED HER? THAT ISN'T THE WAY YOU TREAT PEACHES?
UH, MISS JUSPECZYK ...
SOMEBODY GET HER BOYFRIEND.
KID, ARE YOU SURE YOU WANNA TAKE THIS ALL THE WAY?
DAMN STRAIGHT; DAMN STRAIGHT I DO! I MEAN, WHAT KIND OF MAN ARE YOU, YOU HAVE TO TAKE SOME WOMAN, YOU HAVE TO FORCE HER INTO HAVING SEX AGAINST HER WILL...
ONLY ONCE.
"ONLY ONCE, AS IF, Y'KNOW, IT WAS BETTER THAN DOING IT TWICE OR FIFTY TIMES! AND HIS SCAR... IT ALWAYS LOOKED LIKE HE WAS SNEERING...
"HAD SEVEN SCOTCHES INSIDE ME, ONE IN MY HAND...
"I LET HIM HAVE IT."
...AND THEN YOU CAME, AND YOU WERE ANGRY, AND YOU TOOK ME HOME.
IT WAS THE FIRST TIME YOU EVER TELEPORTED ME ANYWHERE...
FIRST TIME I THREW UP.
... BUT, I MEAN, WHY BOTHER TELLING YOU ALL THIS? IT JUST CONFIRMS THINGS, RIGHT? ALL THESE WRETCHED, GRUBBY LITTLE HUMAN ENCOUNTERS: BETTER OFF WITHOUT 'EM!
NONE OF IT EVER MEANT A DAMN THING, ANYWAY.
SPECTRE
I MEAN, THESE, MY MOTHER'S CLIPPINGS; HER WHOLE LIFE, RIGHT THERE! WHAT'S IT MEAN?
LAURIE...
IN YOUR TERMS, NEXT TO A ... A NEUTRINO, NEXT TO SOMETHING YOU CAN'T EVEN SEE, FOR CHRIST'S SAKE? IT MEANS NOTHING!
DON'T "LAURIE" ME! IT'S POINTLESS DEBATING WHEN YOU OBVIOUSLY DON'T SEE ANYTHING TERRIBLY MIRACULOUS IN LIFE. MAYBE QUANTUM PHYSICS DOESN'T ALLOW MIRACLES ...
NO. "THERMODYNAMIC MIRACLES" ARE...
OH, FOR GOD'S SAKE, JON, JUST LAND THIS THING.
NOW.
21

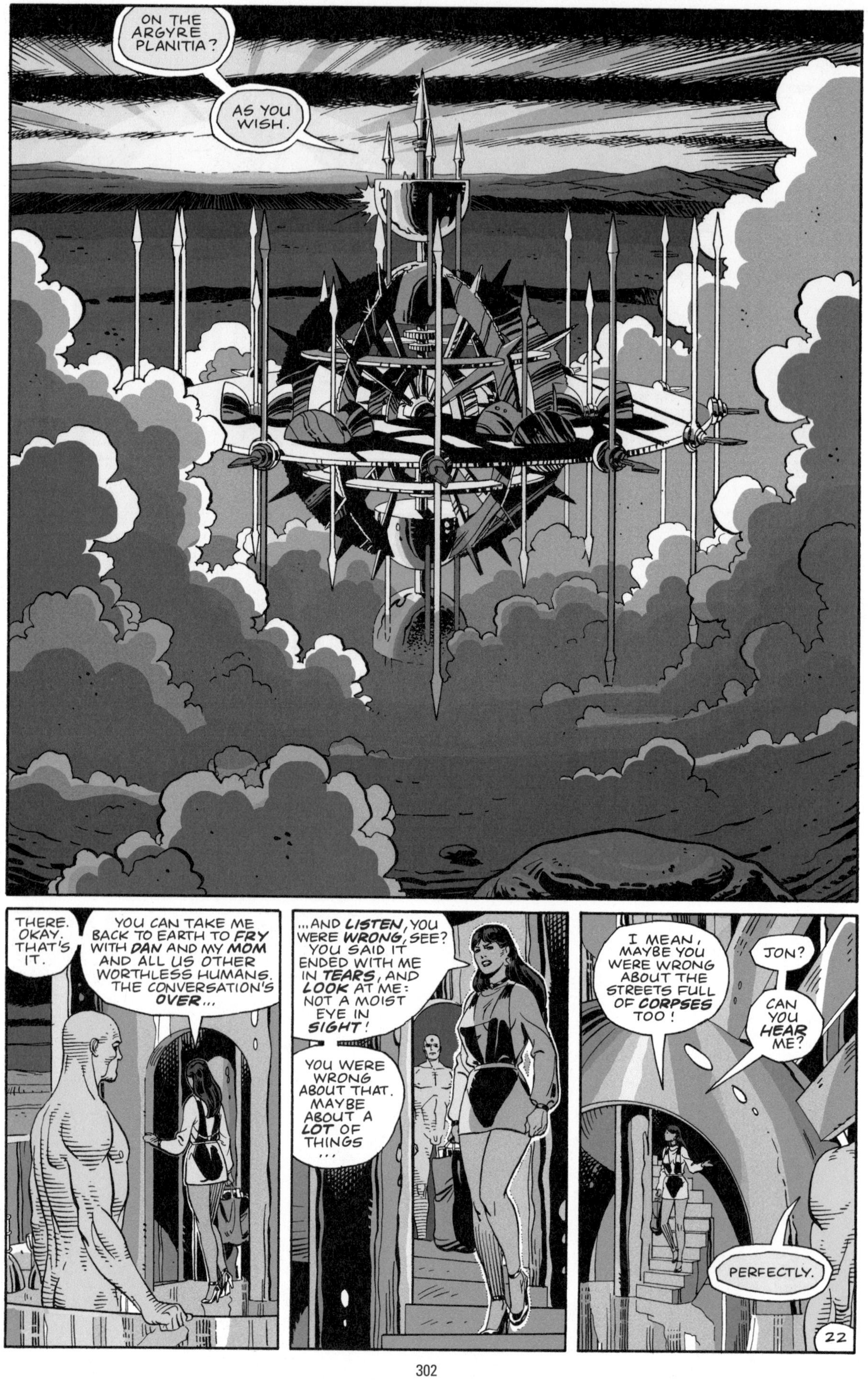
ON THE ARGYRE PLANITIA?
AS YOU WISH.
THERE. OKAY. THAT'S IT.
YOU CAN TAKE ME BACK TO EARTH TO FRY WITH DAN AND MY MOM AND ALL US OTHER WORTHLESS HUMANS. THE CONVERSATION'S OVER...
...AND LISTEN, YOU WERE WRONG, SEE? YOU SAID IT ENDED WITH ME IN TEARS, AND LOOK AT ME: NOT A MOIST EYE IN SIGHT!
YOU WERE WRONG ABOUT THAT. MAYBE ABOUT A LOT OF THINGS...
I MEAN, MAYBE YOU WERE WRONG ABOUT THE STREETS FULL OF CORPSES TOO!
JON?
CAN YOU HEAR ME?
PERFECTLY.
22

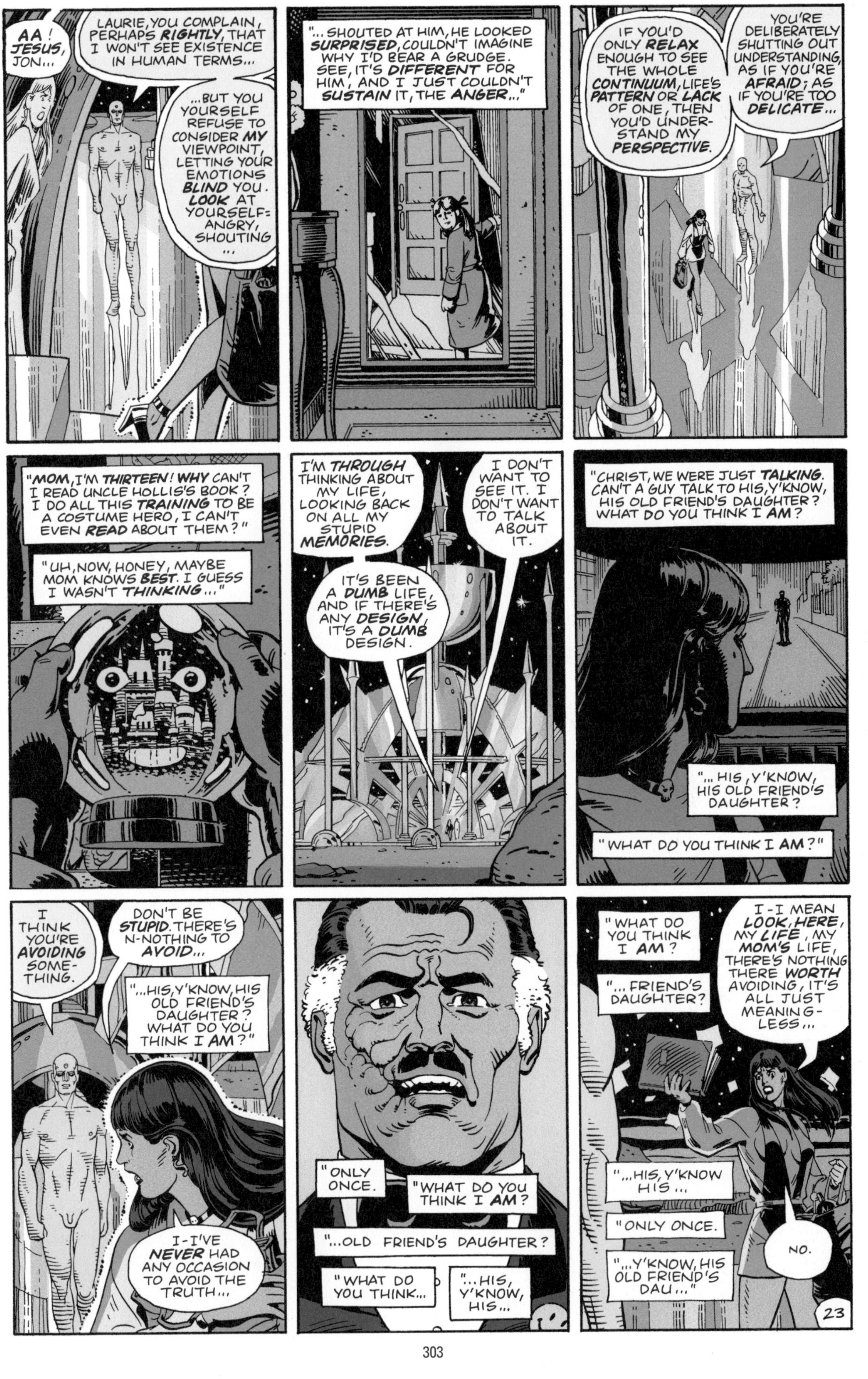
AA! JESUS, JON...
LAURIE, YOU COMPLAIN, PERHAPS RIGHTLY, THAT I WON'T SEE EXISTENCE IN HUMAN TERMS...
...BUT YOU YOURSELF REFUSE TO CONSIDER MY VIEWPOINT, LETTING YOUR EMOTIONS BLIND YOU. LOOK AT YOURSELF= ANGRY, SHOUTING ...
"...SHOUTED AT HIM, HE LOOKED SURPRISED, COULDN'T IMAGINE WHY I'D BEAR A GRUDGE. SEE, IT'S DIFFERENT FOR HIM, AND I JUST COULDN'T SUSTAIN IT, THE ANGER..."
IF YOU'D ONLY RELAX ENOUGH TO SEE THE WHOLE CONTINUUM, LIFE'S PATTERN OR LACK OF ONE, THEN YOU'D UNDERSTAND MY PERSPECTIVE.
YOU'RE DELIBERATELY SHUTTING OUT UNDERSTANDING, AS IF YOU'RE AFRAID; AS IF YOU'RE TOO DELICATE...
"MOM, I'M THIRTEEN! WHY CAN'T I READ UNCLE HOLLIS'S BOOK? I DO ALL THIS TRAINING TO BE A COSTUME HERO, I CAN'T EVEN READ ABOUT THEM?"
"UH, NOW, HONEY, MAYBE MOM KNOWS BEST. I GUESS I WASN'T THINKING..."
I'M THROUGH THINKING ABOUT MY LIFE, LOOKING BACK ON ALL MY STUPID MEMORIES.
IT'S BEEN A DUMB LIFE, AND IF THERE'S ANY DESIGN, IT'S A DUMB DESIGN.
I DON'T WANT TO SEE IT. I DON'T WANT TO TALK ABOUT IT.
"CHRIST, WE WERE JUST TALKING. CAN'T A GUY TALK TO HIS, Y'KNOW, HIS OLD FRIEND'S DAUGHTER? WHAT DO YOU THINK I AM?
"...HIS, Y'KNOW, HIS OLD FRIEND'S DAUGHTER?
"WHAT DO YOU THINK I AM?"
I THINK YOU'RE AVOIDING SOMETHING.
DON'T BE STUPID. THERE'S N-NOTHING TO AVOID...
"...HIS, Y'KNOW, HIS OLD FRIEND'S DAUGHTER? WHAT DO YOU THINK I AM?"
I-I'VE NEVER HAD ANY OCCASION TO AVOID THE TRUTH...
"ONLY ONCE.
"WHAT DO YOU THINK I AM?
"...OLD FRIEND'S DAUGHTER?
"WHAT DO YOU THINK...
"...HIS, Y'KNOW, HIS...
"WHAT DO YOU THINK I AM?
"...FRIEND'S DAUGHTER?
I-I MEAN LOOK, HERE, MY LIFE, MY MOM'S LIFE, THERE'S NOTHING THERE WORTH AVOIDING, IT'S ALL JUST MEANING-LESS...
"...HIS, Y'KNOW HIS...
"ONLY ONCE.
"...Y'KNOW, HIS OLD FRIEND'S DAU..."
NO.
23

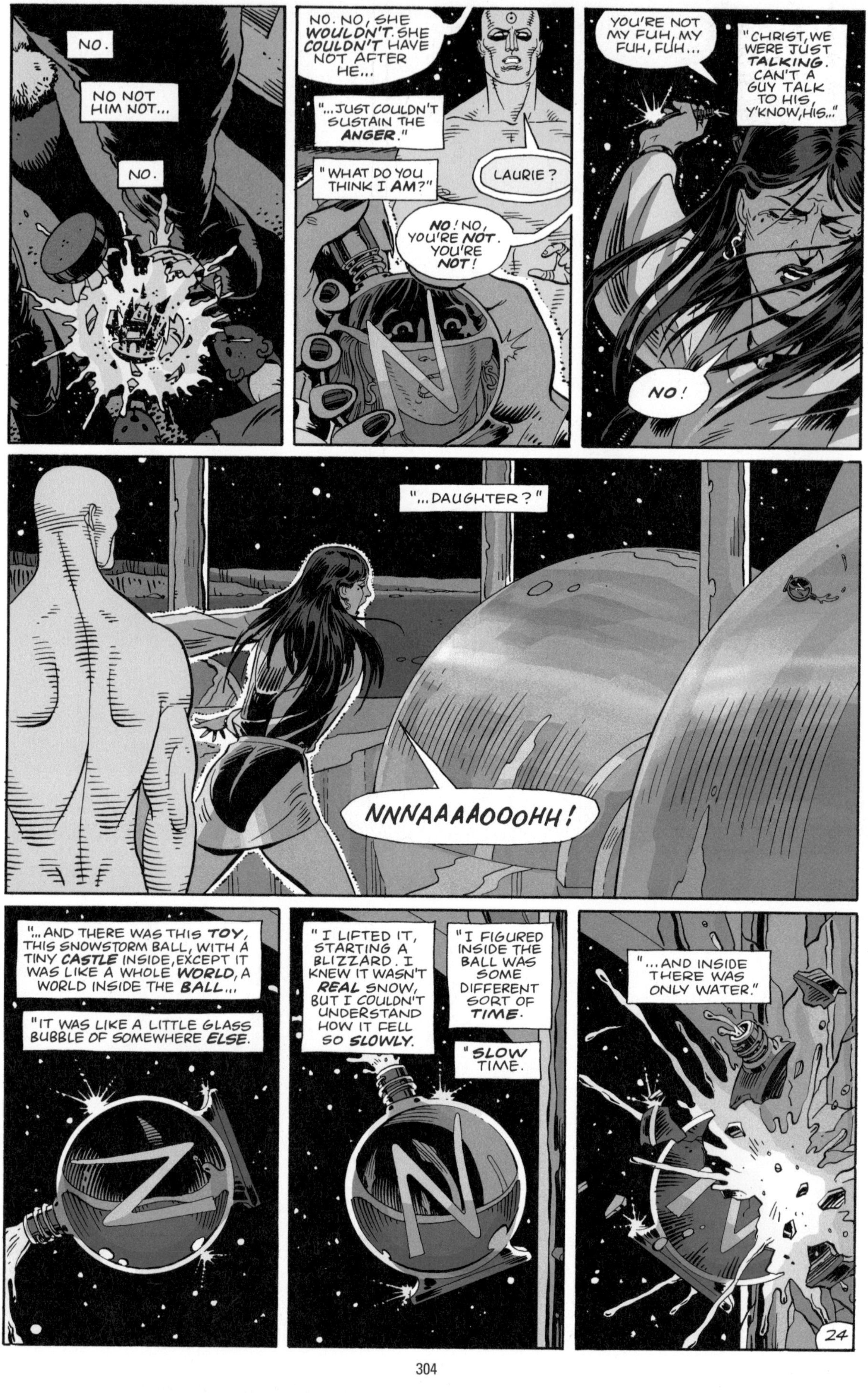
NO.
NO NOT HIM NOT...
NO.
NO. NO, SHE WOULDN'T. SHE COULDN'T HAVE NOT AFTER HE...
"...JUST COULDN'T SUSTAIN THE ANGER."
LAURIE?
"WHAT DO YOU THINK I AM?"
NO! NO, YOU'RE NOT. YOU'RE NOT!
YOU'RE NOT MY FUH, MY FUH, FUH...
"CHRIST, WE WERE JUST TALKING. CAN'T A GUY TALK TO HIS, Y'KNOW, HIS..."
NO!
"...DAUGHTER?"
NNNAAAAOOOHH!
"...AND THERE WAS THIS TOY, THIS SNOWSTORM BALL, WITH A TINY CASTLE INSIDE, EXCEPT IT WAS LIKE A WHOLE WORLD, A WORLD INSIDE THE BALL...
"IT WAS LIKE A LITTLE GLASS BUBBLE OF SOMEWHERE ELSE.
"I LIFTED IT, STARTING A BLIZZARD. I KNEW IT WASN'T REAL SNOW, BUT I COULDN'T UNDERSTAND HOW IT FELL SO SLOWLY.
"I FIGURED INSIDE THE BALL WAS SOME DIFFERENT SORT OF TIME.
"SLOW TIME.
"...AND INSIDE THERE WAS ONLY WATER."
24

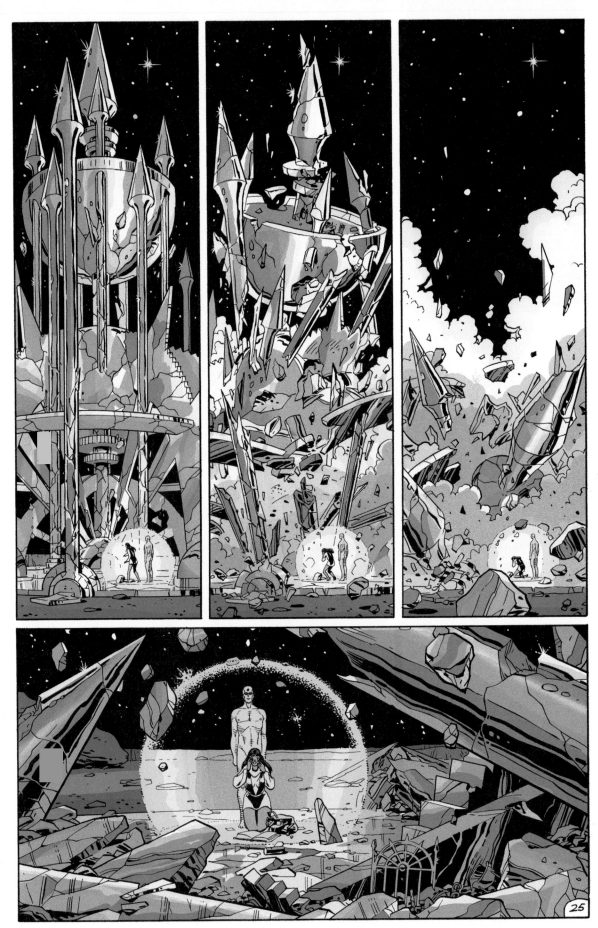

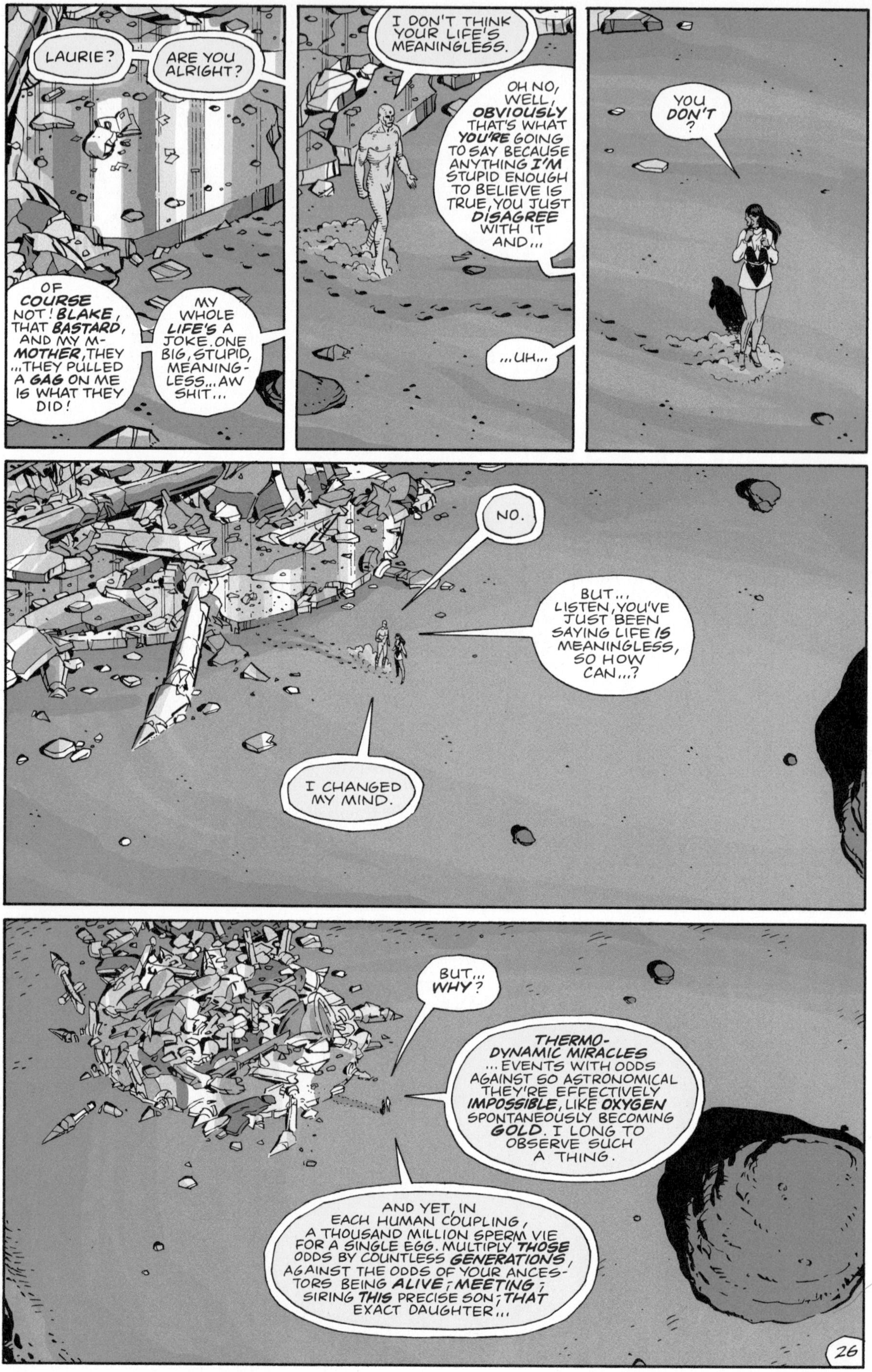
LAURIE?
ARE YOU ALRIGHT?
OF COURSE NOT! BLAKE, THAT BASTARD, AND MY M-MOTHER, THEY ...THEY PULLED A GAG ON ME IS WHAT THEY DID!
MY WHOLE LIFE'S A JOKE. ONE BIG, STUPID, MEANING-LESS... AW SHIT...
I DON'T THINK YOUR LIFE'S MEANINGLESS.
OH NO, WELL, OBVIOUSLY THAT'S WHAT YOU'RE GOING TO SAY BECAUSE ANYTHING I'M STUPID ENOUGH TO BELIEVE IS TRUE, YOU JUST DISAGREE WITH IT AND...
...UH...
YOU DON'T?
NO.
BUT... LISTEN, YOU'VE JUST BEEN SAYING LIFE IS MEANINGLESS, SO HOW CAN...?
I CHANGED MY MIND.
BUT... WHY?
THERMO-DYNAMIC MIRACLES ... EVENTS WITH ODDS AGAINST SO ASTRONOMICAL THEY'RE EFFECTIVELY IMPOSSIBLE, LIKE OXYGEN SPONTANEOUSLY BECOMING GOLD. I LONG TO OBSERVE SUCH A THING.
AND YET, IN EACH HUMAN COUPLING, A THOUSAND MILLION SPERM VIE FOR A SINGLE EGG. MULTIPLY THOSE ODDS BY COUNTLESS GENERATIONS, AGAINST THE ODDS OF YOUR ANCES-TORS BEING ALIVE; MEETING; SIRING THIS PRECISE SON; THAT EXACT DAUGHTER...
26

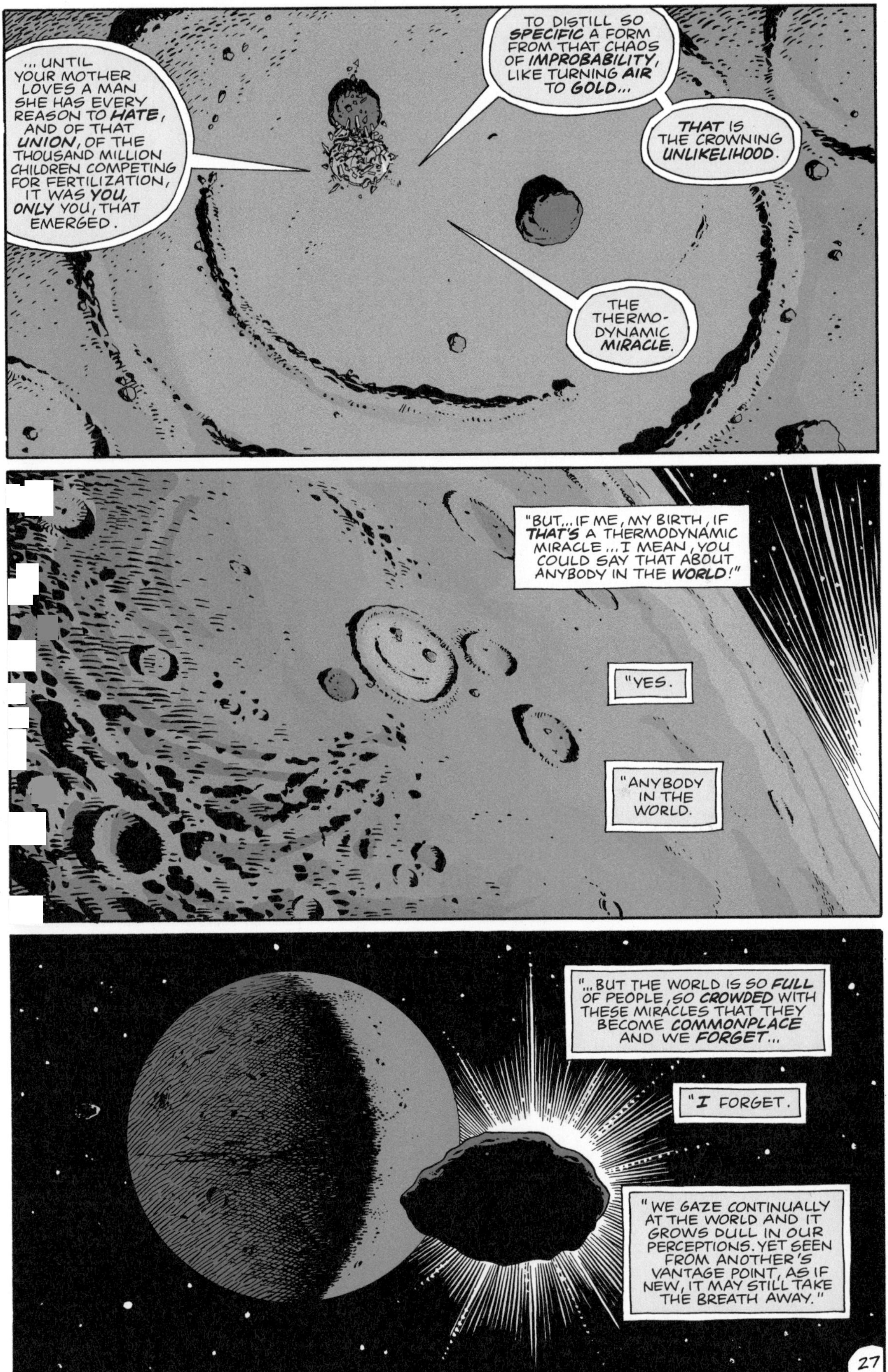
... UNTIL YOUR MOTHER LOVES A MAN SHE HAS EVERY REASON TO HATE, AND OF THAT UNION, OF THE THOUSAND MILLION CHILDREN COMPETING FOR FERTILIZATION, IT WAS YOU, ONLY YOU, THAT EMERGED.
TO DISTILL SO SPECIFIC A FORM FROM THAT CHAOS OF IMPROBABILITY, LIKE TURNING AIR TO GOLD...
THAT IS THE CROWNING UNLIKELIHOOD.
THE THERMO-DYNAMIC MIRACLE.
"BUT... IF ME, MY BIRTH, IF THAT'S A THERMODYNAMIC MIRACLE... I MEAN, YOU COULD SAY THAT ABOUT ANYBODY IN THE WORLD!"
"YES.
"ANYBODY IN THE WORLD.
"...BUT THE WORLD IS SO FULL OF PEOPLE, SO CROWDED WITH THESE MIRACLES THAT THEY BECOME COMMONPLACE AND WE FORGET...
"I FORGET.
"WE GAZE CONTINUALLY AT THE WORLD AND IT GROWS DULL IN OUR PERCEPTIONS. YET SEEN FROM ANOTHER'S VANTAGE POINT, AS IF NEW, IT MAY STILL TAKE THE BREATH AWAY."
27

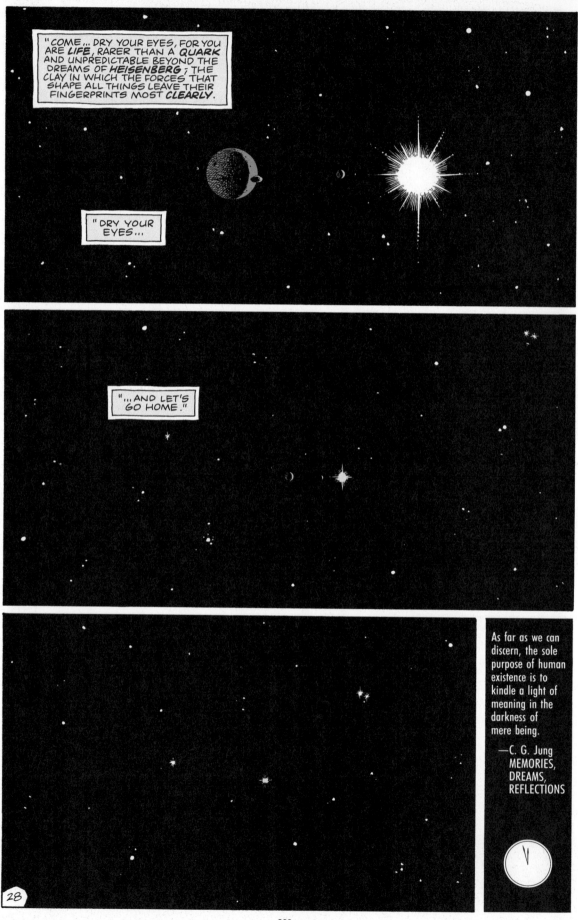

"COME... DRY YOUR EYES, FOR YOU ARE *LIFE*, RARER THAN A *QUARK* AND UNPREDICTABLE BEYOND THE DREAMS OF *HEISENBERG*; THE CLAY IN WHICH THE FORCES THAT SHAPE ALL THINGS LEAVE THEIR FINGERPRINTS MOST *CLEARLY*.

"DRY YOUR EYES...

"...AND LET'S GO HOME."

As far as we can discern, the sole purpose of human existence is to kindle a light of meaning in the darkness of mere being.

—C. G. Jung
MEMORIES, DREAMS, REFLECTIONS

28

Sal – thought you'd like this for your scrapbook

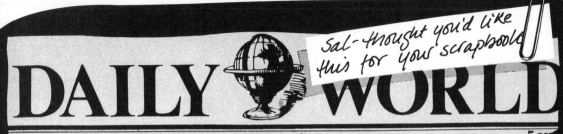

DAILY WORLD

January 12, 1939 — *More than news!* — 5c

VILLAINS VIE FOR VOLUPTUOUS VIGILANTE

Goons are going ga-ga over the latest do-gooder to pull on a tight costume and jump aboard the masked vigilante bandwagon. Why? Well, maybe it's because *this* costumed cutie is a *girl*! Shapely 18-year-old redhead Sally Jupiter (36-24-36) has taken the alluring and mysterious monicker of "Silk Spectre" as she dons the shortest long underwear yet and becomes the first feisty female to join the fight against felony.

Miss Jupiter's agent, Mr. Larry Schexnayder, says that former waitress and burlesque dancer Sally is such a hit with the hoods that they're practically tripping over each other in the rush to get nabbed by her! In testimony, he produced Mr. Claude Boke of no fixed address, currently out on parole after Sally, who happened to be on hand, arrested him during an attempted liquor store robbery.

"She beat me fair and square, but I don't hold no grudges. She's a pretty-looking young woman and I'd rather have her take me in than two fat old cops anytime," says Claude, who received a light fine and has since quit drinking and taken a job pumping gasoline.

Sally, who eventually hopes to move on to modeling work or movies, tells us that there is already a movie about her life in the works.

"It's called 'Silk Spectre: The Sally Jupiter Story,'" enthuses Sally, "and it's already in the planning stages. Larry and I have met with Mr. King Taylor of Hollywood, and everybody's very excited about it all."

I'm sure we all wish spunky Sal luck in her future endeavors, and if the above movie gets made, who knows? Maybe Sally will have to organize a special premiere . . . just for the criminal fraternity!

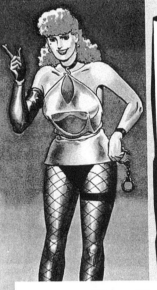

reports are true, she certainly has some explaining to do to her hubby and two kids back home on the ranch.

• • •

Meanwhile, over with the cape-and-mask crowd, lips are buzzing and tongues are wagging about cheesecake crime-crusher **Sally Jupiter**, alias the **SILK SPECTRE.** It seems that she and veteran vigilante **HOODED JUSTICE** are something of an item, and seldom out of each other's company. Can wedding bells be too far away? If you want evidence, just look whose arm our Sal is hanging onto in the recently released publicity photographs of that tights-and-trunk-clad team, **The Minutemen.** Between you and me, your Zelda wonders: Does he keep that hood and noose on *all* the time?

• • •

Spotted dancing cheek to cheek at a certain

King Taylor Productions

8-22-45

Sal and Larry

Hi, kids! I know, I know, it's been ages, but I think things are finally moving with "She Devils In Silk". (That's the latest title, by the way. Maurie dreamed it up. Hope you like it. We decided that "Sally Jupiter: Law In Its Lingerie" was too long after all.)

The latest version is looking good— we've retained a lot of the plot elements from the saturday morning Matinee approach we adopted after junking the documentary idea, and we've kept a lot of the footage we shot with you way back then. This new version has some added material to make it accessible to a more adult market, and I think you'll find it kinda fun. We have a young discovery named Cherry Dean that I'm very excited about, and she stands in for you in the new scenes. From the back, she's a dead ringer! It's phenomenal!

Anyway, I'll keep touching base with you as things progress.

Hugs and kisses,

King

MARINE LIEUTENANT USMC

NELSON GARDNER

KL5-2204

FREE-LANCE CONSULTANT

Dear Miss Jupiter,

Having seen you in the news lately, I wished to introduce myself. My name is Captain Metropolis, and I too am a costumed adventurer, with a keen interest in stamping out crime and injustice wheresoever it should rear its ugly head. I am delighted to find that you share these inclinations.

I note also from my perusal of the press that there are several other people of our persuasion stepping forward to join the struggle across America, and, being a military man by nature and career it struck me that it might be a distinct strategic advantage if we were to organize ourselves into some sort of battalion, ready to do our country's bidding at a moment's notice.

I suggest that such a group might be called 'The New Minute Men of America', and I have already devised such things as codes and passwords and strategic exercises that would serve us well in our war on infamy.

If you are interested in this proposal, please contact me through my representative, former Marine Lieutenant Nelson Gardner, whose card is enclosed.

I look forward very much to hearing from you.

Your costumed Comrade in the campaign against crime,

Captain Metropolis

Sally – thought there might be mileage in this – P.Rwise L.S.

Larry – Jesus Christ! Are you kidding –!

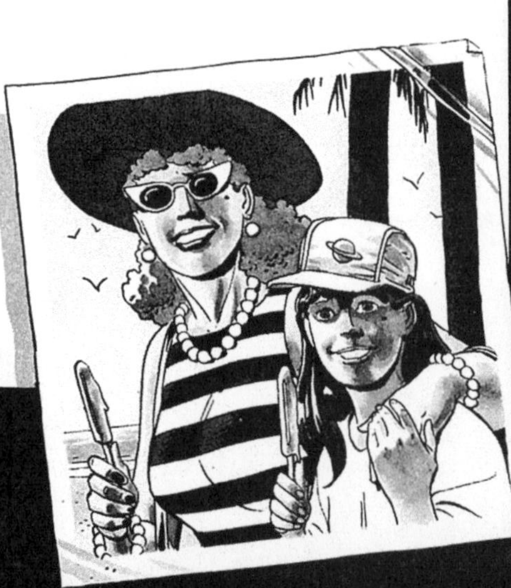

February 3rd, 1948

Dear Sally,

        Haven't been in touch lately because I thought you should have time to get over poor Bill's funeral. However, there's things that need talking over.

        Nelly called last night, upset over yet another tiff with H.J. Those two are getting worse. The more they row and act like an old married couple in public, the harder they are to cover for. I know that you've provided a pretty steady alibi for H.J. up to now, and that the publicity we got from that hasn't exactly hurt you either, but it can't last much longer. Nelly says he's always out when Nelly calls, out with boys, and apparently there's a lot of rough stuff going on. One of these punks only has to go to the cops with a convincing story and some convincing bruises to back it up and it would be the Silhouette fiasco all over again.

        I honestly wonder how long it can last. Lewis is drinking harder all the time, and has been very low since the thing with Bill. Mason is a big bouncy boy scout, same as ever, but with Nelly and H.J. acting up it's a pretty sorry spectacle at the meetings these days. Maybe now is the time to pull out and cut our losses. We've made quite a sum, you know, and I've often talked about a place out west somewhere; maybe now's the time we could take it on as a viable partnership proposition together? Anyways, at least think it over.

                     With fond regards,

Larry

nearest thing I ever got to a proposal

SCREEN REVIEWS

SILK SWINGERS OF SUBURBIA

DIR: Edmund "King" Taylor
STARRING: Cherry Dean, Rod Donovan, Dana Young, Lola Booker, Harry J. Peters, Sally Juniper.

If you like tasteful and sensually artistic modern cinema, then I recommend that this film be avoided at all costs. Cheaply made even by "B"-movie standards, this appears to have started life as a children's adventure serial, complete with unconvincing and dated footage of a stuntwoman in an antique chorus girl costume engaging in poorly staged fights with stock heavies. Edited into this unpromising and juvenile scenario with astonishing clumsiness, we have scenes of Miss Dean—similarly attired and being tied up, whipped and fondled by "Rod Donovan," who must surely be a relative of well-known hack director "King" Taylor, so close is the resemblance between the two men. Too awful even to be dignified with the term "pornography," the only real act of sadism in this film lies in releasing it; the only masochism in watching it.

PROBE PROFILE: SALLY JUPITER

an interview with a forties glamour girl and the seamier side of her crimefighting career.

PROBE: Sally, how much would you say that it's a sex thing, putting on a costume?

SALLY: No. I don't . . . Well, let me say this, for me, it was never a sex thing. It was a money thing. And I think for some people it was a fame thing, and for a tiny few, God bless 'em, I think it was a goodness thing. I mean, I'm not saying it wasn't a sex thing for some people, but, no, no, I wouldn't say that's what motivated the majority . . .

PROBE: There was Ursula Zandt, the Silhouette . . .

SALLY: Uh-huh. Well, sooner or later, okay, that's going to come up, so let me deal with that . . . First off, I didn't like her as a person. I mean, she was not an easy person to get along with. But, when the papers got hold of it, her being a—what is it—a gay woman they say nowadays, when that happened, I thought it was wrong. I mean, Laurence, who was my first husband, he got everybody to throw her out of the group to minimize the P.R. damage, but . . . I mean, I voted along with everybody else, but . . . well, it wasn't fair. It wasn't honest. I mean, she wasn't the only gay person in the Minutemen. Some professions, I don't know, they attract a certain type . . .

PROBE: Who else was gay?

SALLY: I'm not naming anybody. It was a couple of the guys, and they're both dead now. One died recently. I'm not saying who

it was, I'm just saying that we all knew, and we knew she wasn't the only one, and we slung her out just the same. When she got murdered like that . . . I mean, I never really liked her. Ursula. Was that her real name? I didn't know that. I didn't like her, but . . . throwing her out. We shouldn't have done that. I feel bad about that.

PROBE: On the subject of the Minutemen, in Hollis Mason's autobiography . . .

SALLY: Uh-oh! Here it comes.

PROBE: . . . he alleges that you were sexually assaulted by the Comedian, who, as you know, is still active. You've never said too much about this incident yourself . . .

SALLY: Well, why break a lifetime's habit?

PROBE: You won't comment upon that?

SALLY: I . . . Look, I don't bear any grudges. That's all. I know I should, everybody tells me I should but . . . look, I don't have to justify this, okay? It's just that nothing's that simple, not even things that are simply awful. You know, rape is rape and there's no excuses for it, absolutely none, but for me, I felt . . . I felt like I'd contributed in some way. Is that misplaced guilt, whatever my analyst said? I really felt that, that I was somehow as much to blame for . . . for letting myself be his victim not in a physical sense, but . . . but,

it's like what if, y'know? What if, just for a moment, maybe I really did want . . . I mean, that doesn't excuse him, doesn't excuse either of us, but with all that doubt, what it is to come to terms with it, I can't stay angry when I'm so uncertain about my own feelings . . .

PROBE: You're retired now, and it seems your daughter has been groomed to follow in your footsteps. Having seen the lifestyle for yourself, how do you feel about that?

SALLY: Mm. That's tough. I guess, in a lot of ways, it was me who pushed Laurie, that's my daughter, pushed her into this line of work . . . I know that when she's upset about something she always blames me for shoving her into such a weird career, but underneath somewhere, I think she secretly kinda likes it. She likes to bitch about it, but what else would she have done? Been a housewife? Got a job in a bank? So she didn't have a normal life! What's so great about normal life? Normal life stinks! You can ask anybody! No, no, of course, I'm her mother, I get worried about her. But in the end, I think she'll see what it was I gave her. I think she'll start to see her life next to the lives of other kids and she'll start thinking in terms of what I saved her from instead of what I condemned her to.

PROBE: You think so?

SALLY: I hope so.

"You know, rape is rape and there's no excuse for it, absolutely none, but for me, I felt . . . I felt like I'd contributed in some way."

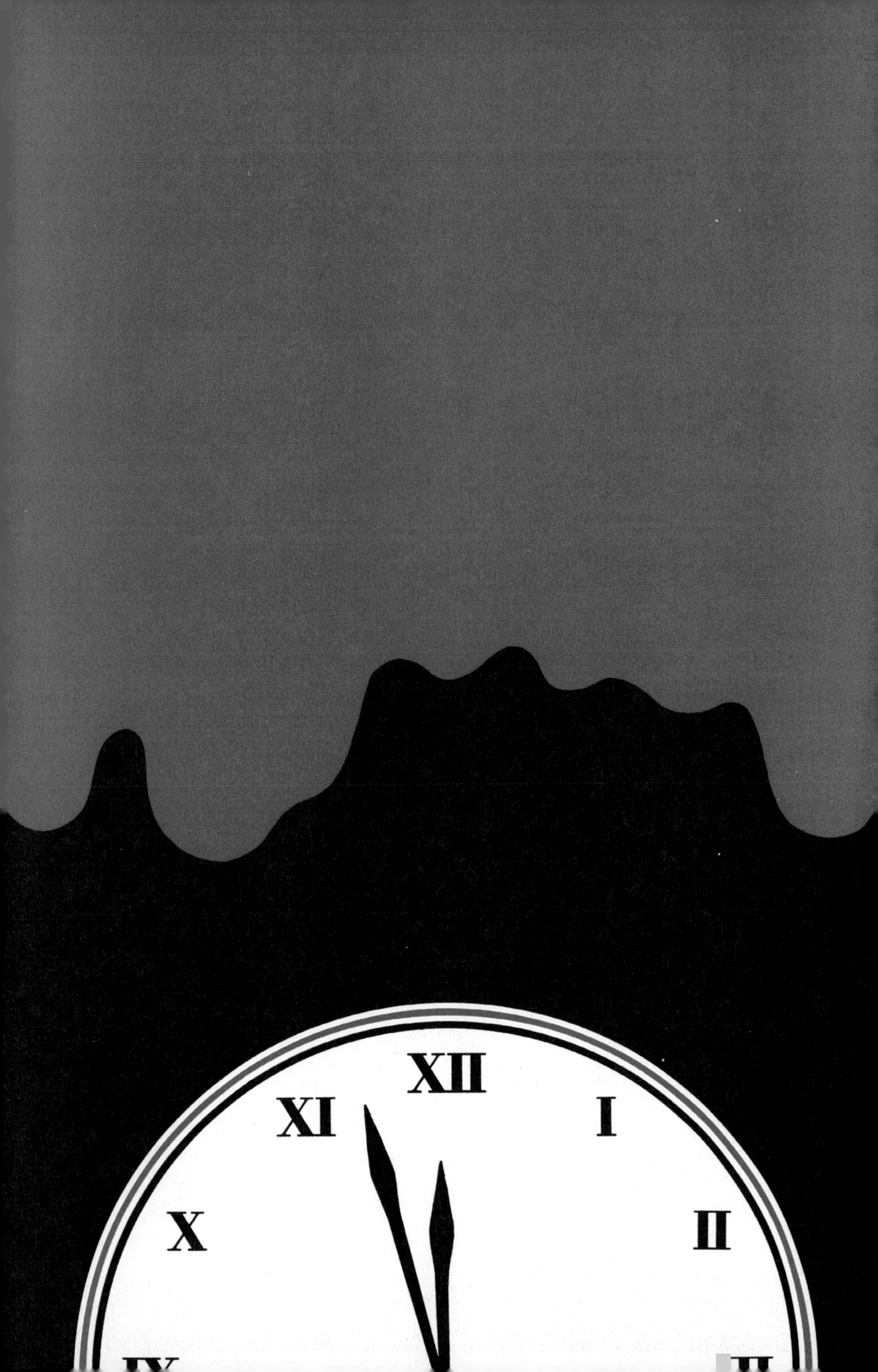
XII
XI
I
X
II

CHAPTER

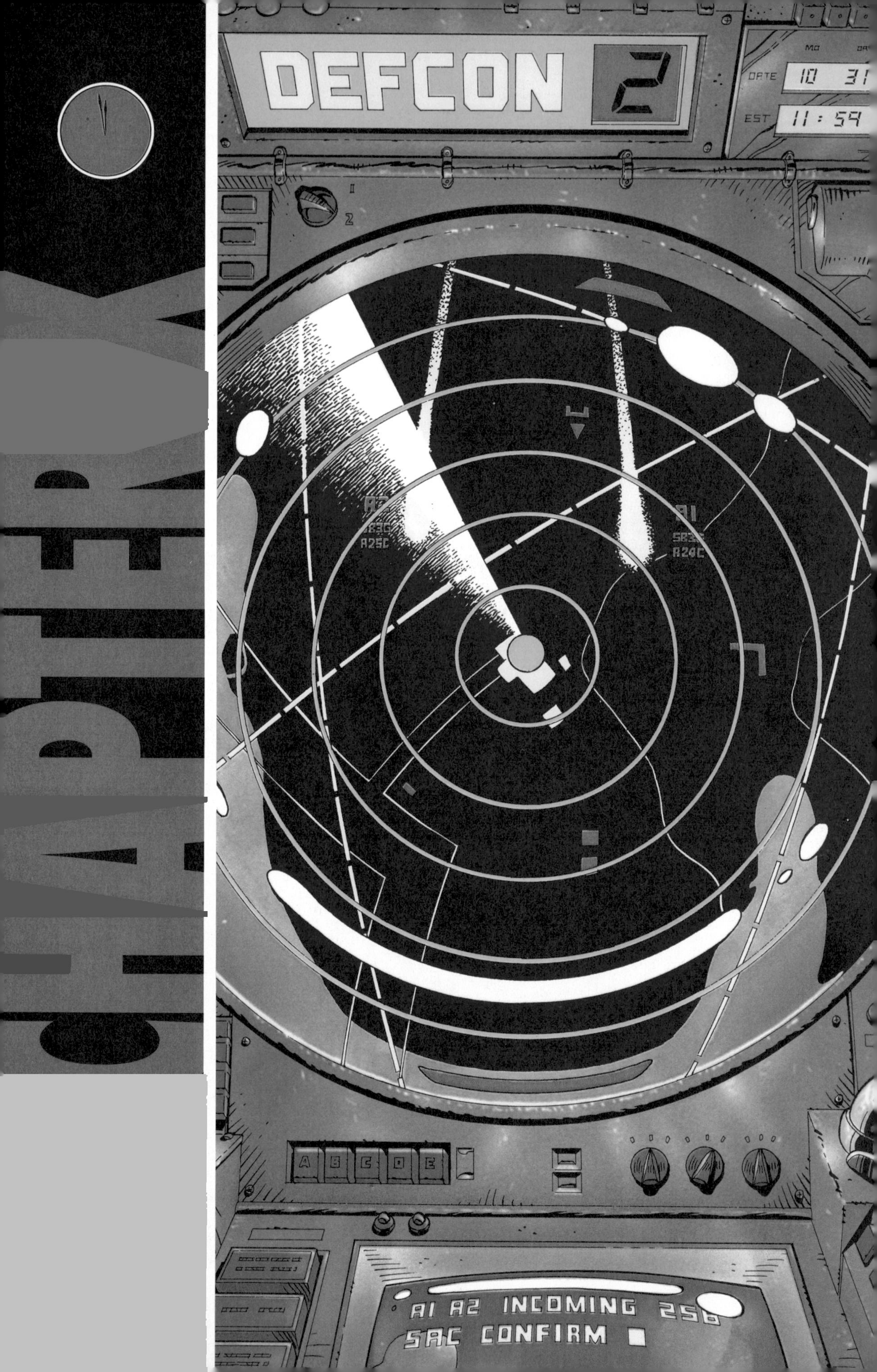
DEFCON 2
DATE 10 31
EST 11:59
A1
SB3G
A24C
A2
SB3G
A25C
A B C D E
A1 A2 INCOMING 256
SAC CONFIRM

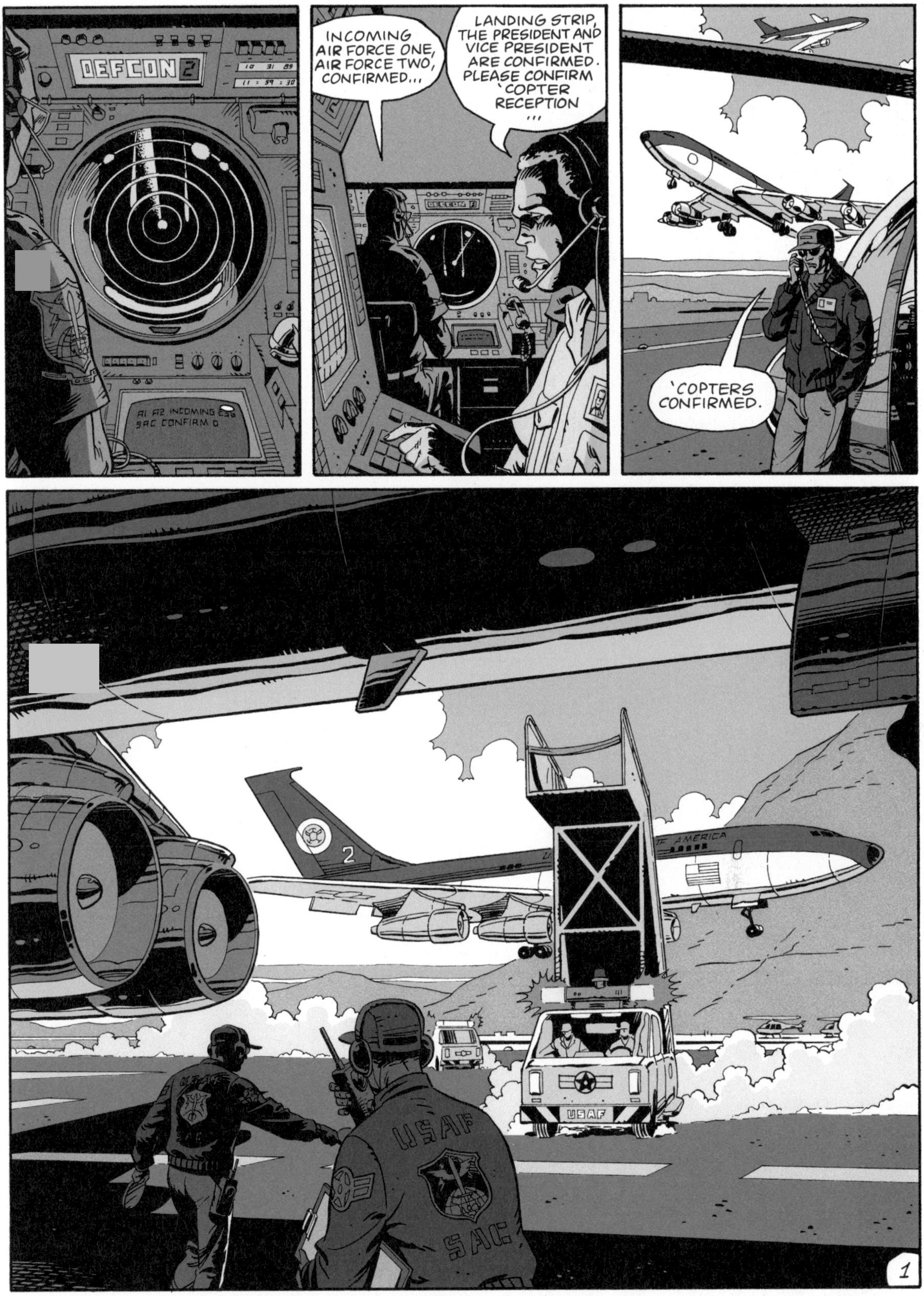
DEFCON 2
INCOMING AIR FORCE ONE, AIR FORCE TWO, CONFIRMED...
LANDING STRIP, THE PRESIDENT AND VICE PRESIDENT ARE CONFIRMED. PLEASE CONFIRM 'COPTER RECEPTION ...
'COPTERS CONFIRMED.
USAF
USAF
SAC
1

TWO RIDERS WERE APPROACHING...

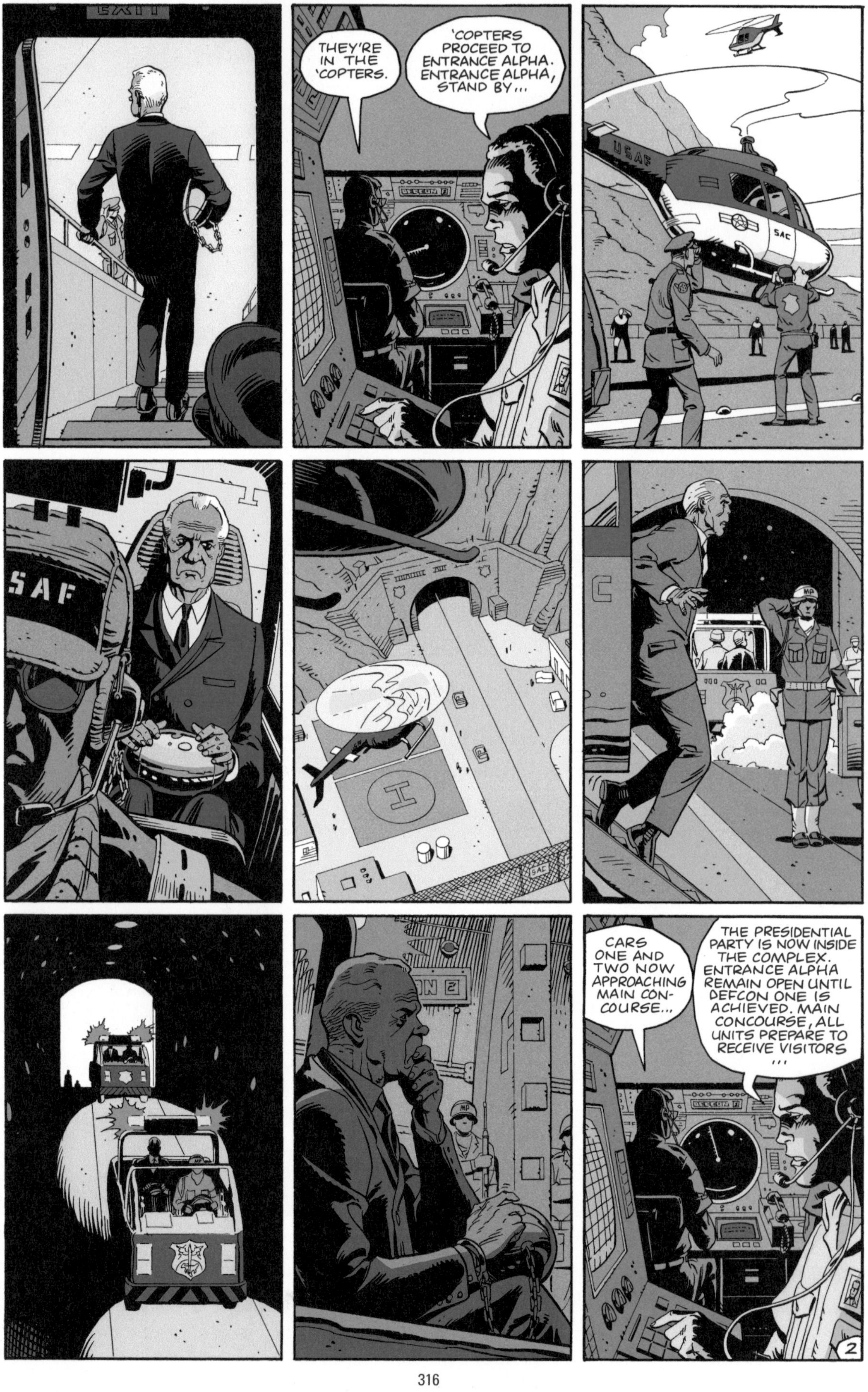
THEY'RE IN THE 'COPTERS.
'COPTERS PROCEED TO ENTRANCE ALPHA. ENTRANCE ALPHA, STAND BY...
CARS ONE AND TWO NOW APPROACHING MAIN CON- COURSE...
THE PRESIDENTIAL PARTY IS NOW INSIDE THE COMPLEX. ENTRANCE ALPHA REMAIN OPEN UNTIL DEFCON ONE IS ACHIEVED. MAIN CONCOURSE, ALL UNITS PREPARE TO RECEIVE VISITORS ...
2

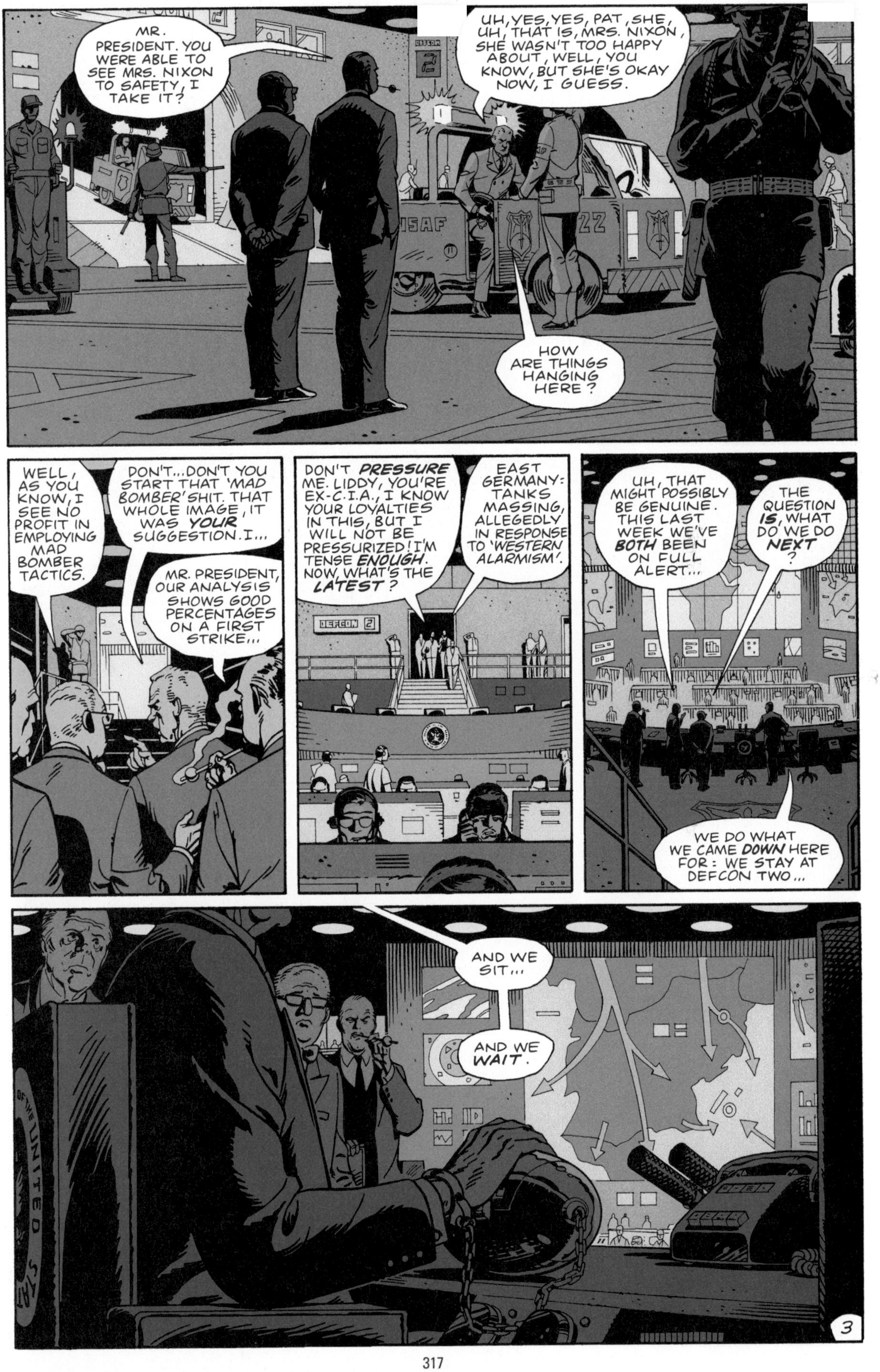
MR. PRESIDENT. YOU WERE ABLE TO SEE MRS. NIXON TO SAFETY, I TAKE IT?
UH, YES, YES, PAT, SHE, UH, THAT IS, MRS. NIXON, SHE WASN'T TOO HAPPY ABOUT, WELL, YOU KNOW, BUT SHE'S OKAY NOW, I GUESS.
HOW ARE THINGS HANGING HERE?
WELL, AS YOU KNOW, I SEE NO PROFIT IN EMPLOYING MAD BOMBER TACTICS.
DON'T... DON'T YOU START THAT 'MAD BOMBER' SHIT. THAT WHOLE IMAGE, IT WAS YOUR SUGGESTION. I...
MR. PRESIDENT, OUR ANALYSIS SHOWS GOOD PERCENTAGES ON A FIRST STRIKE...
DON'T PRESSURE ME. LIDDY, YOU'RE EX-C.I.A., I KNOW YOUR LOYALTIES IN THIS, BUT I WILL NOT BE PRESSURIZED! I'M TENSE ENOUGH. NOW, WHAT'S THE LATEST?
EAST GERMANY: TANKS MASSING, ALLEGEDLY IN RESPONSE TO 'WESTERN ALARMISM'.
DEFCON 2
UH, THAT MIGHT POSSIBLY BE GENUINE. THIS LAST WEEK WE'VE BOTH BEEN ON FULL ALERT...
THE QUESTION IS, WHAT DO WE DO NEXT?
WE DO WHAT WE CAME DOWN HERE FOR: WE STAY AT DEFCON TWO...
AND WE SIT...
AND WE WAIT.
3

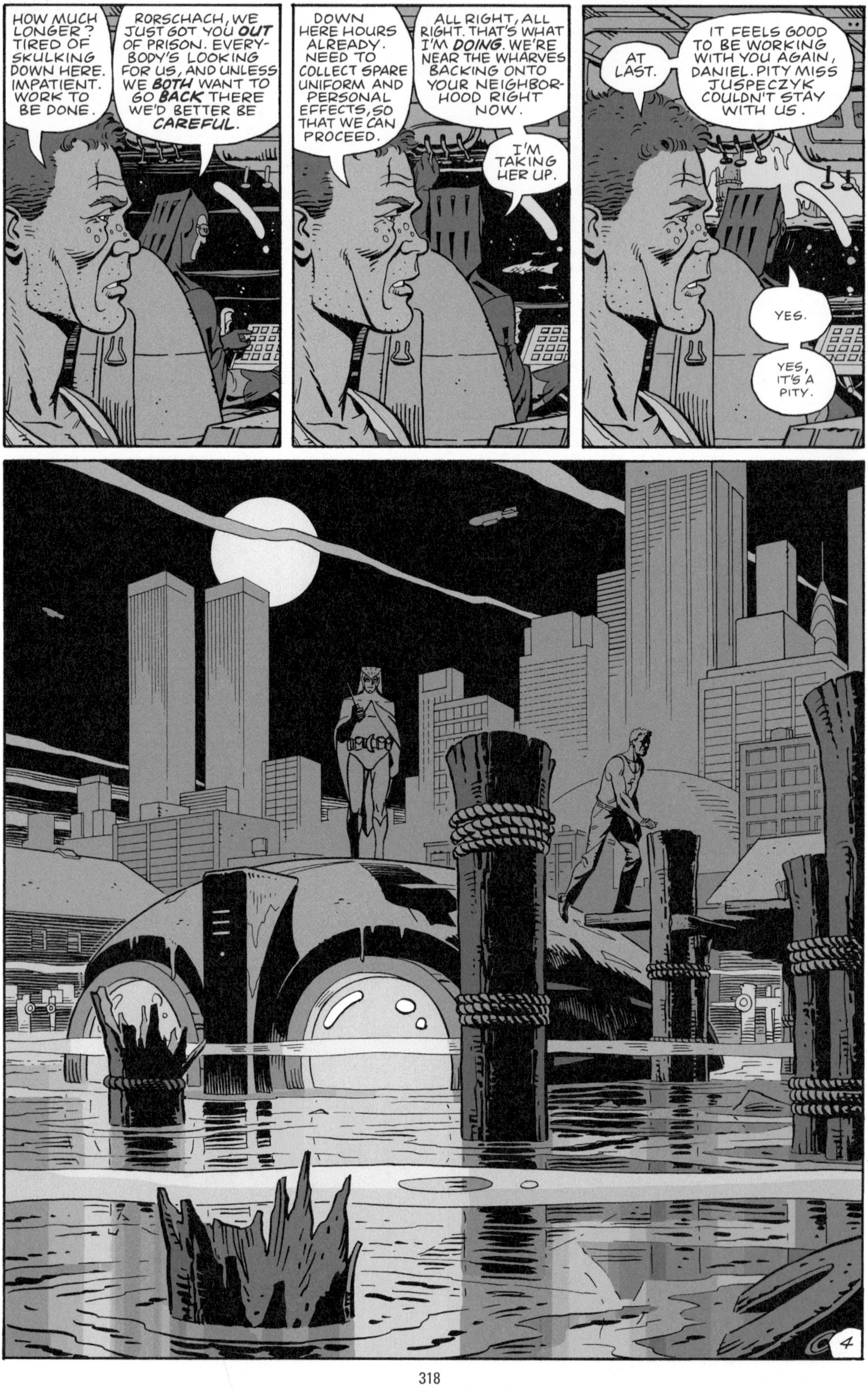

HOW MUCH LONGER? TIRED OF SKULKING DOWN HERE. IMPATIENT. WORK TO BE DONE.
RORSCHACH, WE JUST GOT YOU **OUT** OF PRISON. EVERYBODY'S LOOKING FOR US, AND UNLESS WE **BOTH** WANT TO GO **BACK** THERE WE'D BETTER BE **CAREFUL**.
DOWN HERE HOURS ALREADY. NEED TO COLLECT SPARE UNIFORM AND PERSONAL EFFECTS, SO THAT WE CAN PROCEED.
ALL RIGHT, ALL RIGHT. THAT'S WHAT I'M **DOING**. WE'RE NEAR THE WHARVES BACKING ONTO YOUR NEIGHBORHOOD RIGHT NOW.
I'M TAKING HER UP.
AT LAST.
IT FEELS GOOD TO BE WORKING WITH YOU AGAIN, DANIEL. PITY MISS JUSPECZYK COULDN'T STAY WITH US.
YES.
YES, IT'S A PITY.
4

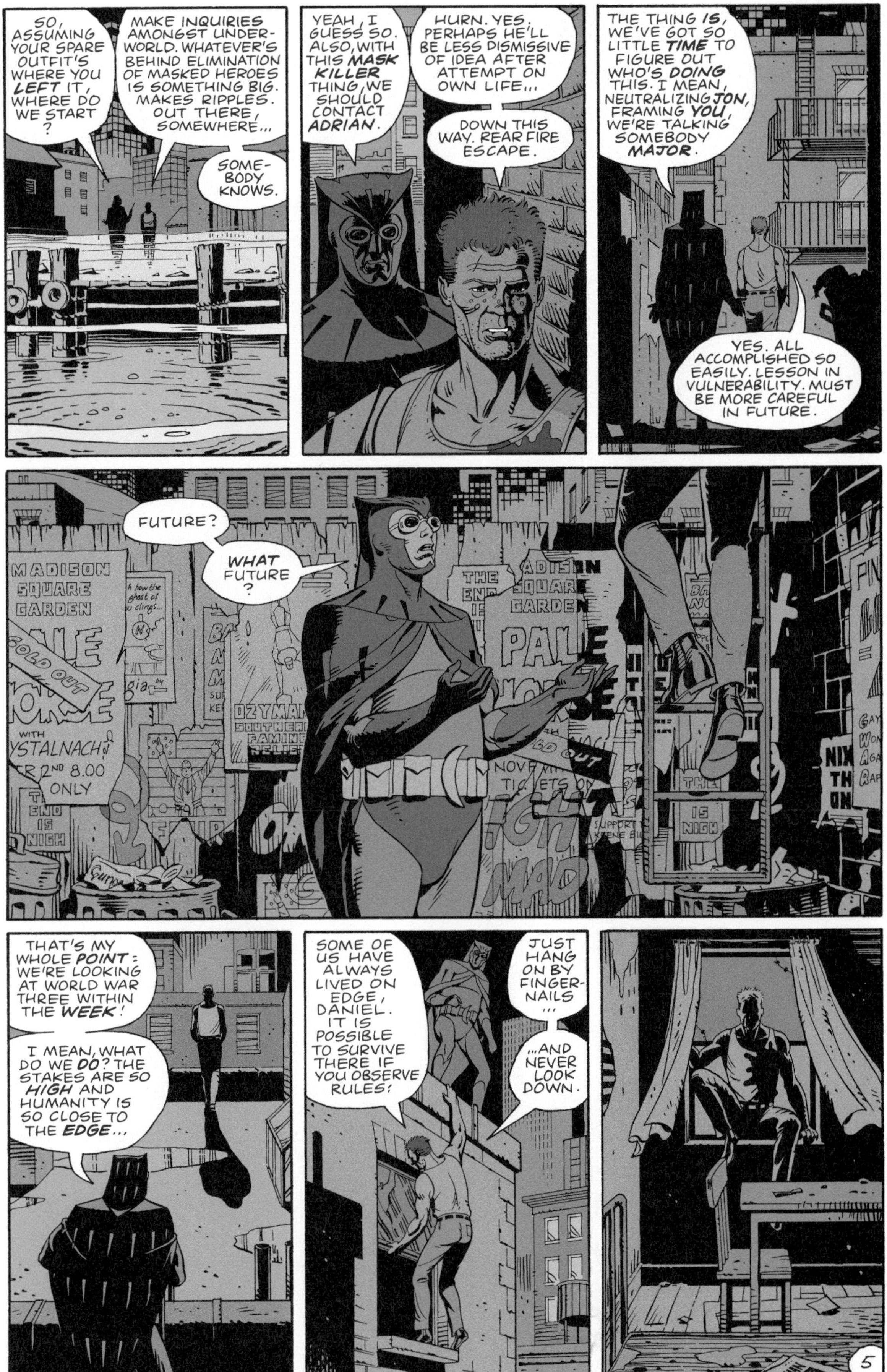

SO, ASSUMING YOUR SPARE OUTFIT'S WHERE YOU **LEFT** IT, WHERE DO WE START?
MAKE INQUIRIES AMONGST UNDER-WORLD. WHATEVER'S BEHIND ELIMINATION OF MASKED HEROES IS SOMETHING BIG. MAKES RIPPLES. OUT THERE, SOMEWHERE...
SOME-BODY KNOWS.
YEAH, I GUESS SO. ALSO, WITH THIS **MASK KILLER** THING, WE SHOULD CONTACT **ADRIAN**.
HURN. YES. PERHAPS HE'LL BE LESS DISMISSIVE OF IDEA AFTER ATTEMPT ON OWN LIFE...
DOWN THIS WAY. REAR FIRE ESCAPE.
THE THING **IS**, WE'VE GOT SO LITTLE **TIME** TO FIGURE OUT WHO'S **DOING** THIS. I MEAN, NEUTRALIZING **JON**, FRAMING **YOU**, WE'RE TALKING SOMEBODY **MAJOR**.
YES. ALL ACCOMPLISHED SO EASILY. LESSON IN VULNERABILITY. MUST BE MORE CAREFUL IN FUTURE.
FUTURE?
WHAT FUTURE?
MADISON SQUARE GARDEN
PALE HORSE
SOLD OUT
WITH
ONLY
THE END IS NIGH
THAT'S MY WHOLE **POINT**: WE'RE LOOKING AT WORLD WAR THREE WITHIN THE **WEEK**!
I MEAN, WHAT DO WE **DO**? THE STAKES ARE SO **HIGH** AND HUMANITY IS SO CLOSE TO THE **EDGE**...
SOME OF US HAVE ALWAYS LIVED ON EDGE, DANIEL. IT IS POSSIBLE TO SURVIVE THERE IF YOU OBSERVE RULES:
JUST HANG ON BY FINGER-NAILS...
...AND NEVER LOOK DOWN.
5

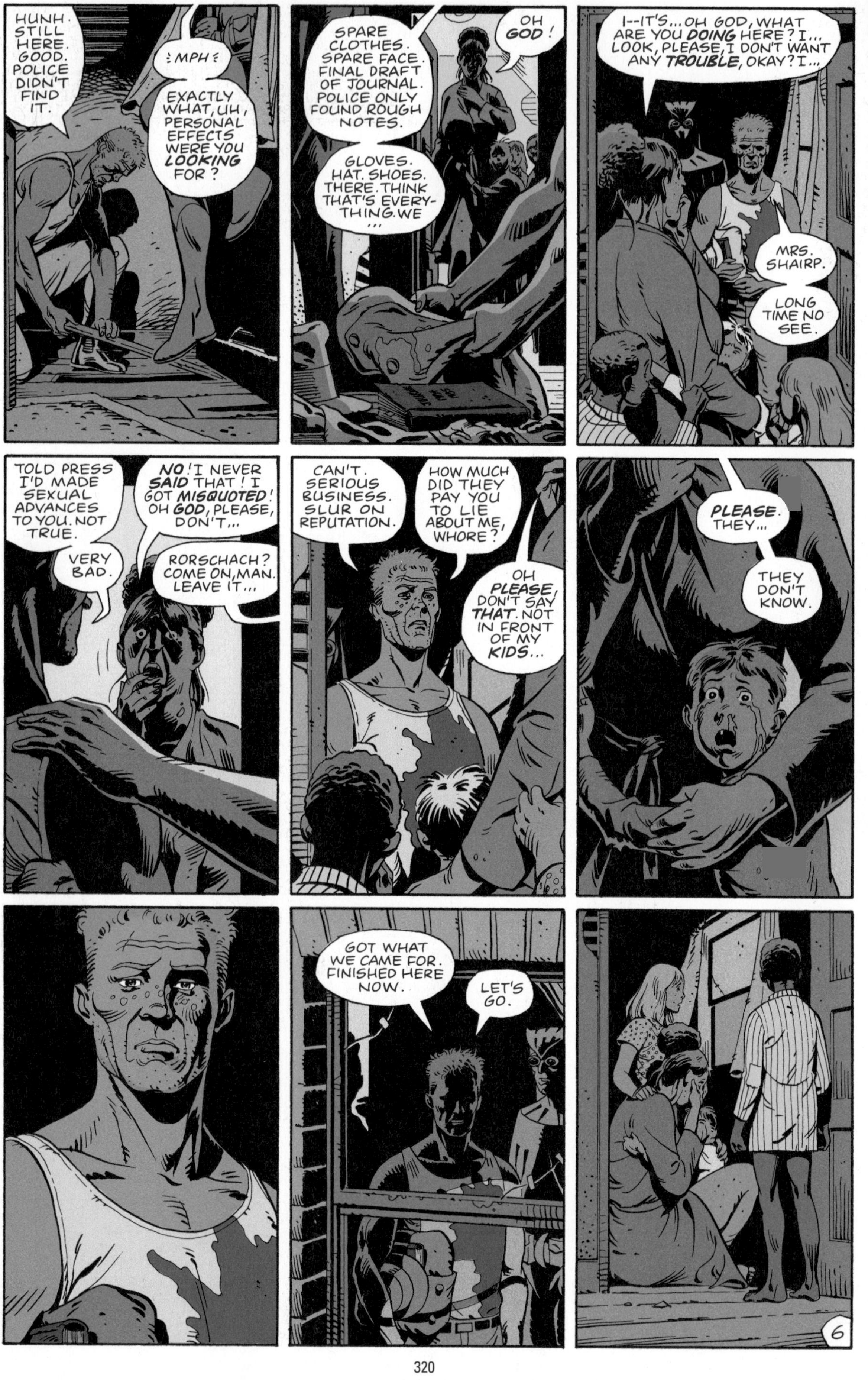
HUNH. STILL HERE. GOOD. POLICE DIDN'T FIND IT.
MPH
EXACTLY WHAT, UH, PERSONAL EFFECTS WERE YOU LOOKING FOR?
SPARE CLOTHES. SPARE FACE. FINAL DRAFT OF JOURNAL. POLICE ONLY FOUND ROUGH NOTES.
GLOVES. HAT. SHOES. THERE. THINK THAT'S EVERYTHING. WE ...
OH GOD!
I--IT'S... OH GOD, WHAT ARE YOU DOING HERE? I... LOOK, PLEASE, I DON'T WANT ANY TROUBLE, OKAY? I...
MRS. SHAIRP.
LONG TIME NO SEE.
TOLD PRESS I'D MADE SEXUAL ADVANCES TO YOU. NOT TRUE.
NO! I NEVER SAID THAT! I GOT MISQUOTED! OH GOD, PLEASE, DON'T...
VERY BAD.
RORSCHACH? COME ON, MAN. LEAVE IT...
CAN'T. SERIOUS BUSINESS. SLUR ON REPUTATION.
HOW MUCH DID THEY PAY YOU TO LIE ABOUT ME, WHORE?
OH PLEASE, DON'T SAY THAT. NOT IN FRONT OF MY KIDS...
PLEASE. THEY...
THEY DON'T KNOW.
GOT WHAT WE CAME FOR. FINISHED HERE NOW.
LET'S GO.
6

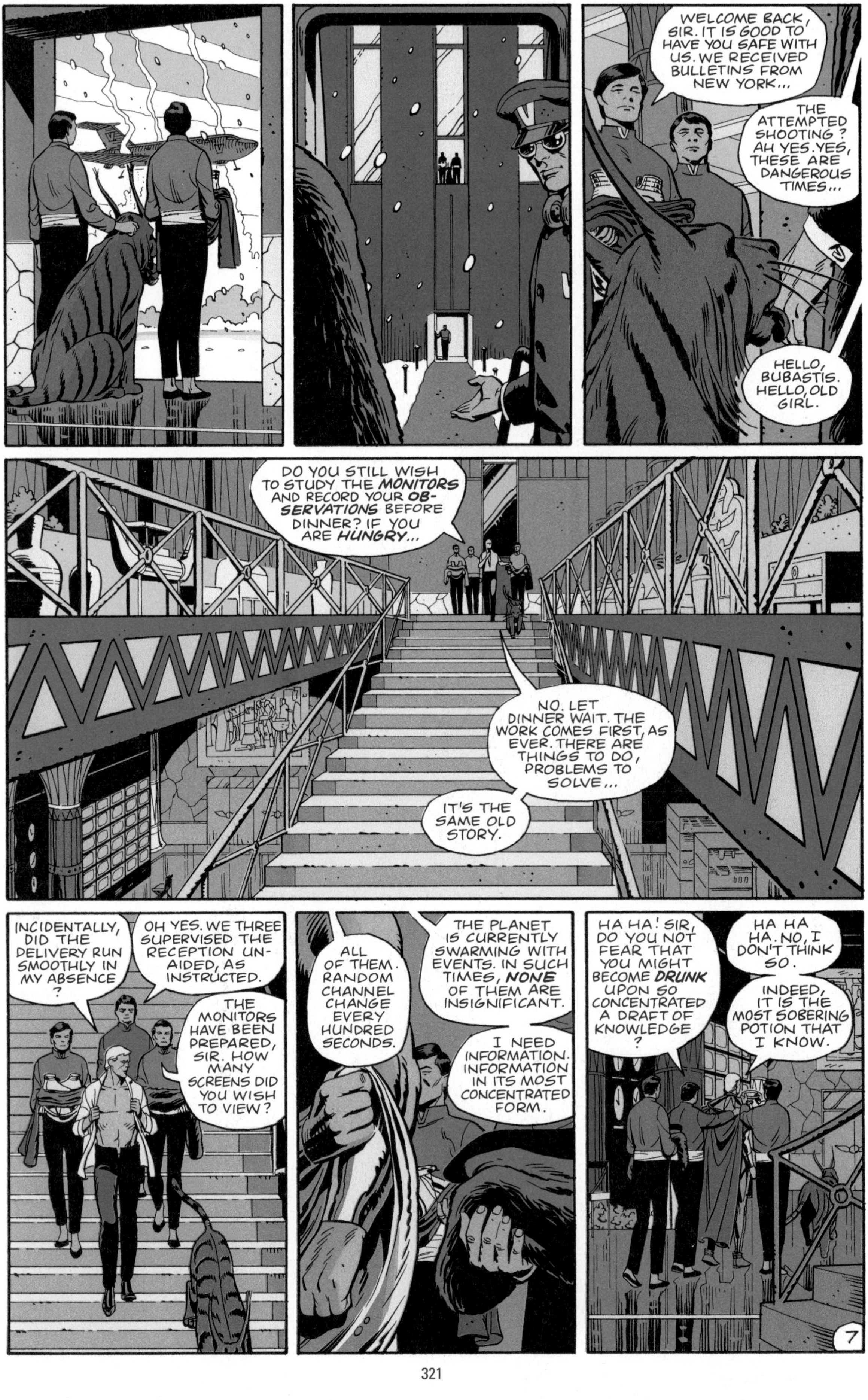
WELCOME BACK, SIR. IT IS GOOD TO HAVE YOU SAFE WITH US. WE RECEIVED BULLETINS FROM NEW YORK...
THE ATTEMPTED SHOOTING? AH YES. YES, THESE ARE DANGEROUS TIMES...
HELLO, BUBASTIS. HELLO, OLD GIRL.
DO YOU STILL WISH TO STUDY THE MONITORS AND RECORD YOUR OBSERVATIONS BEFORE DINNER? IF YOU ARE HUNGRY...
NO. LET DINNER WAIT. THE WORK COMES FIRST, AS EVER. THERE ARE THINGS TO DO, PROBLEMS TO SOLVE...
IT'S THE SAME OLD STORY.
INCIDENTALLY, DID THE DELIVERY RUN SMOOTHLY IN MY ABSENCE?
OH YES. WE THREE SUPERVISED THE RECEPTION UNAIDED, AS INSTRUCTED.
THE MONITORS HAVE BEEN PREPARED, SIR. HOW MANY SCREENS DID YOU WISH TO VIEW?
ALL OF THEM. RANDOM CHANNEL CHANGE EVERY HUNDRED SECONDS.
THE PLANET IS CURRENTLY SWARMING WITH EVENTS. IN SUCH TIMES, NONE OF THEM ARE INSIGNIFICANT.
I NEED INFORMATION. INFORMATION IN ITS MOST CONCENTRATED FORM.
HA HA! SIR, DO YOU NOT FEAR THAT YOU MIGHT BECOME DRUNK UPON SO CONCENTRATED A DRAFT OF KNOWLEDGE?
HA HA HA. NO, I DON'T THINK SO.
INDEED, IT IS THE MOST SOBERING POTION THAT I KNOW.
7

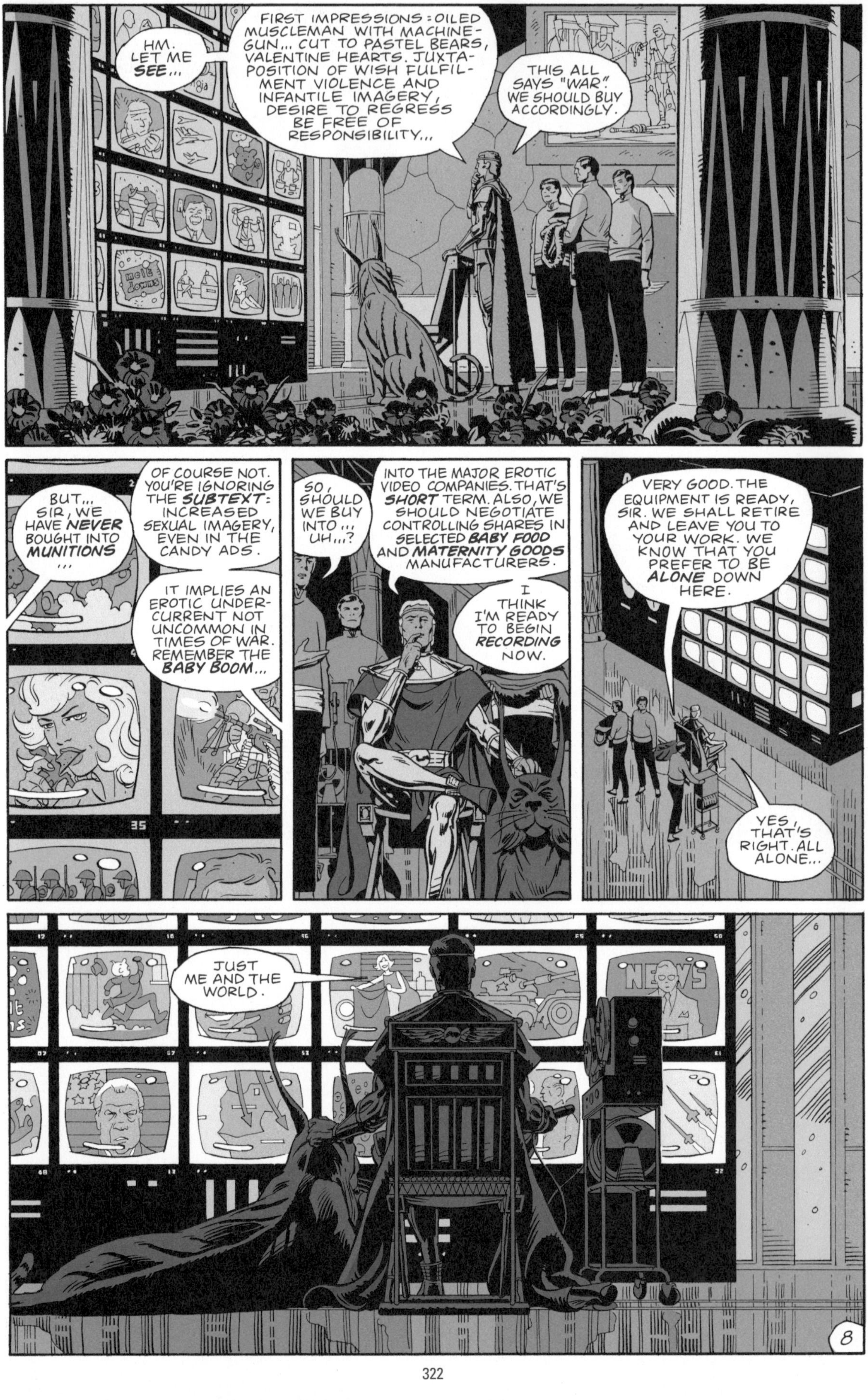
HM. LET ME **SEE**...
FIRST IMPRESSIONS: OILED MUSCLEMAN WITH MACHINE-GUN... CUT TO PASTEL BEARS, VALENTINE HEARTS. JUXTAPOSITION OF WISH FULFILMENT VIOLENCE AND INFANTILE IMAGERY, DESIRE TO REGRESS BE FREE OF RESPONSIBILITY...
THIS ALL SAYS "WAR". WE SHOULD BUY ACCORDINGLY.
BUT... SIR, WE HAVE **NEVER** BOUGHT INTO **MUNITIONS**...
OF COURSE NOT. YOU'RE IGNORING THE **SUBTEXT**: INCREASED SEXUAL IMAGERY, EVEN IN THE CANDY ADS.
IT IMPLIES AN EROTIC UNDERCURRENT NOT UNCOMMON IN TIMES OF WAR. REMEMBER THE **BABY BOOM**...
SO, SHOULD WE BUY INTO... UH...?
INTO THE MAJOR EROTIC VIDEO COMPANIES. THAT'S **SHORT** TERM. ALSO, WE SHOULD NEGOTIATE CONTROLLING SHARES IN SELECTED **BABY FOOD** AND **MATERNITY GOODS** MANUFACTURERS.
I THINK I'M READY TO BEGIN **RECORDING** NOW.
VERY GOOD. THE EQUIPMENT IS READY, SIR. WE SHALL RETIRE AND LEAVE YOU TO YOUR WORK. WE KNOW THAT YOU PREFER TO BE **ALONE** DOWN HERE.
YES, THAT'S RIGHT. ALL ALONE...
JUST ME AND THE WORLD.
NEWS
8

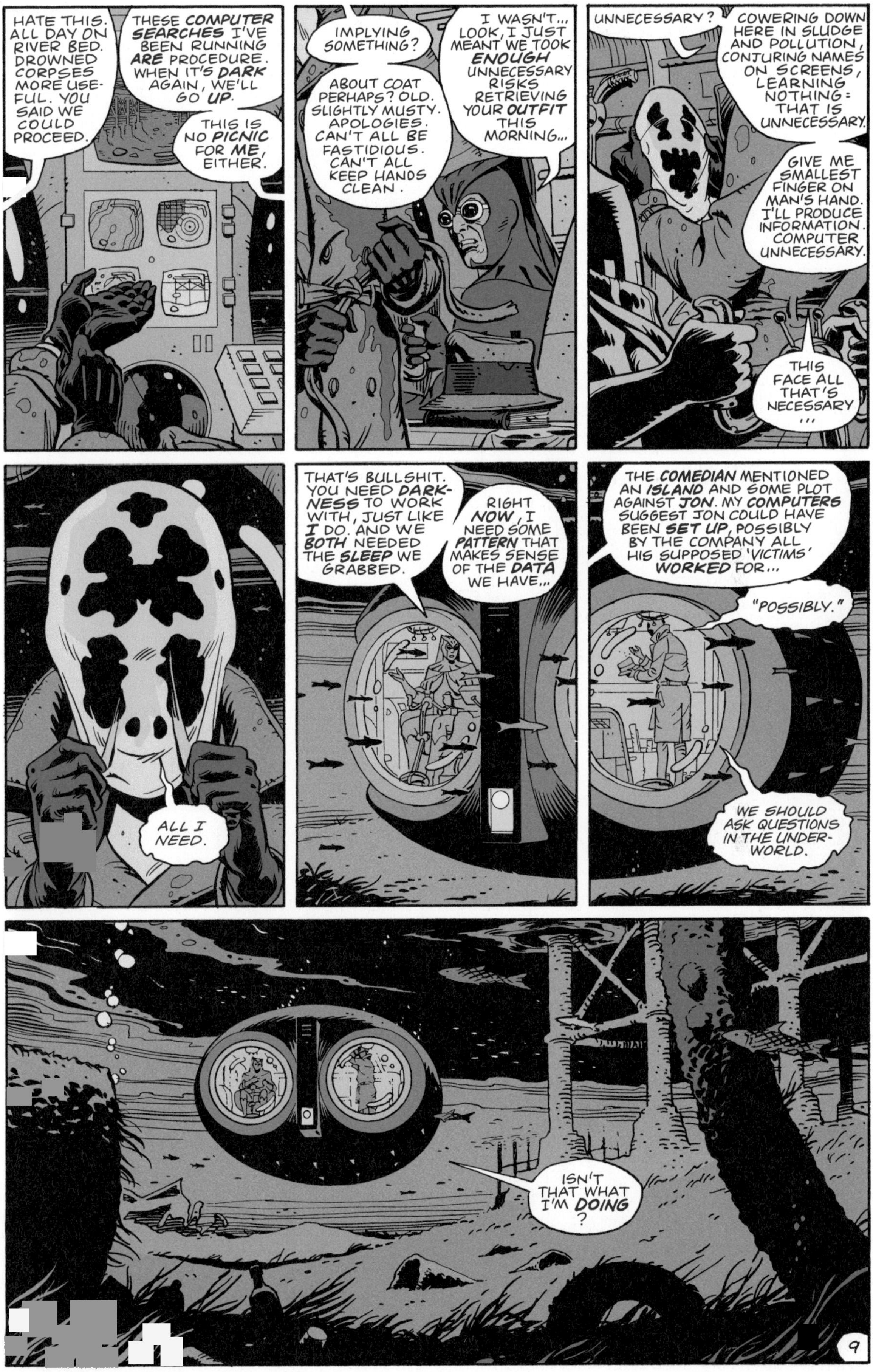
HATE THIS. ALL DAY ON RIVER BED. DROWNED CORPSES MORE USEFUL. YOU SAID WE COULD PROCEED.
THESE COMPUTER SEARCHES I'VE BEEN RUNNING ARE PROCEDURE. WHEN IT'S DARK AGAIN, WE'LL GO UP.
THIS IS NO PICNIC FOR ME, EITHER.
IMPLYING SOMETHING?
ABOUT COAT PERHAPS? OLD. SLIGHTLY MUSTY. APOLOGIES. CAN'T ALL BE FASTIDIOUS. CAN'T ALL KEEP HANDS CLEAN.
I WASN'T... LOOK, I JUST MEANT WE TOOK ENOUGH UNNECESSARY RISKS RETRIEVING YOUR OUTFIT THIS MORNING...
UNNECESSARY?
COWERING DOWN HERE IN SLUDGE AND POLLUTION, CONJURING NAMES ON SCREENS, LEARNING NOTHING: THAT IS UNNECESSARY.
GIVE ME SMALLEST FINGER ON MAN'S HAND. I'LL PRODUCE INFORMATION. COMPUTER UNNECESSARY.
THIS FACE ALL THAT'S NECESSARY...
ALL I NEED.
THAT'S BULLSHIT. YOU NEED DARKNESS TO WORK WITH, JUST LIKE I DO. AND WE BOTH NEEDED THE SLEEP WE GRABBED.
RIGHT NOW, I NEED SOME PATTERN THAT MAKES SENSE OF THE DATA WE HAVE...
THE COMEDIAN MENTIONED AN ISLAND AND SOME PLOT AGAINST JON. MY COMPUTERS SUGGEST JON COULD HAVE BEEN SET UP, POSSIBLY BY THE COMPANY ALL HIS SUPPOSED 'VICTIMS' WORKED FOR...
"POSSIBLY."
WE SHOULD ASK QUESTIONS IN THE UNDERWORLD.
ISN'T THAT WHAT I'M DOING?
9

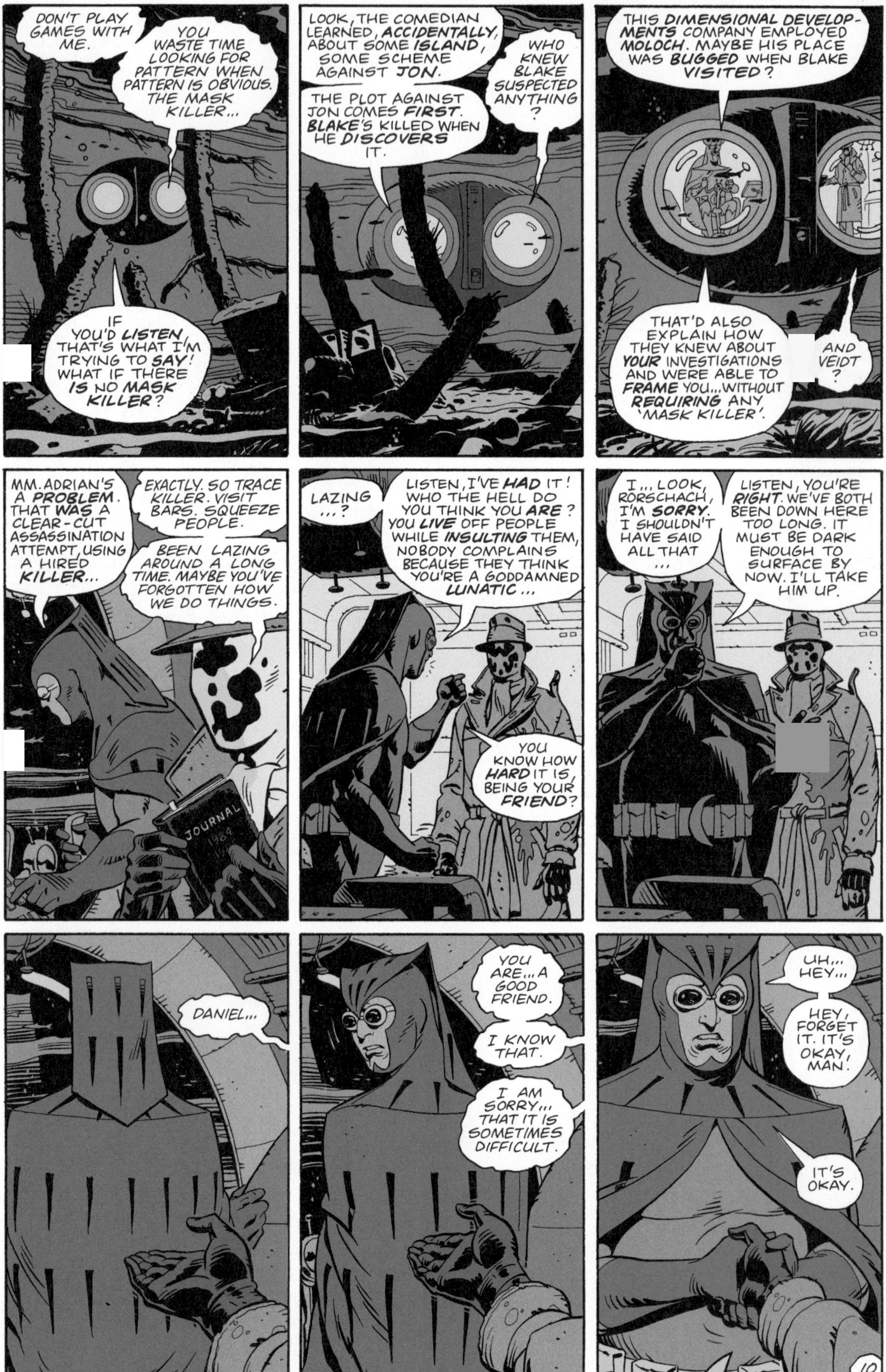
DON'T PLAY GAMES WITH ME.
YOU WASTE TIME LOOKING FOR PATTERN WHEN PATTERN IS OBVIOUS. THE MASK KILLER...
IF YOU'D LISTEN, THAT'S WHAT I'M TRYING TO SAY! WHAT IF THERE IS NO MASK KILLER?
LOOK, THE COMEDIAN LEARNED, ACCIDENTALLY, ABOUT SOME ISLAND, SOME SCHEME AGAINST JON.
THE PLOT AGAINST JON COMES FIRST. BLAKE'S KILLED WHEN HE DISCOVERS IT.
WHO KNEW BLAKE SUSPECTED ANYTHING?
THIS DIMENSIONAL DEVELOPMENTS COMPANY EMPLOYED MOLOCH. MAYBE HIS PLACE WAS BUGGED WHEN BLAKE VISITED?
THAT'D ALSO EXPLAIN HOW THEY KNEW ABOUT YOUR INVESTIGATIONS AND WERE ABLE TO FRAME YOU...WITHOUT REQUIRING ANY 'MASK KILLER'.
AND VEIDT?
MM. ADRIAN'S A PROBLEM. THAT WAS A CLEAR-CUT ASSASSINATION ATTEMPT, USING A HIRED KILLER...
EXACTLY. SO TRACE KILLER. VISIT BARS. SQUEEZE PEOPLE.
BEEN LAZING AROUND A LONG TIME. MAYBE YOU'VE FORGOTTEN HOW WE DO THINGS.
JOURNAL 1984 19
LAZING...?
LISTEN, I'VE HAD IT! WHO THE HELL DO YOU THINK YOU ARE? YOU LIVE OFF PEOPLE WHILE INSULTING THEM, NOBODY COMPLAINS BECAUSE THEY THINK YOU'RE A GODDAMNED LUNATIC...
YOU KNOW HOW HARD IT IS, BEING YOUR FRIEND?
I... LOOK, RORSCHACH, I'M SORRY. I SHOULDN'T HAVE SAID ALL THAT...
LISTEN, YOU'RE RIGHT. WE'VE BOTH BEEN DOWN HERE TOO LONG. IT MUST BE DARK ENOUGH TO SURFACE BY NOW. I'LL TAKE HIM UP.
DANIEL...
YOU ARE... A GOOD FRIEND.
I KNOW THAT.
I AM SORRY... THAT IT IS SOMETIMES DIFFICULT.
UH... HEY...
HEY, FORGET IT. IT'S OKAY, MAN.
IT'S OKAY.
10

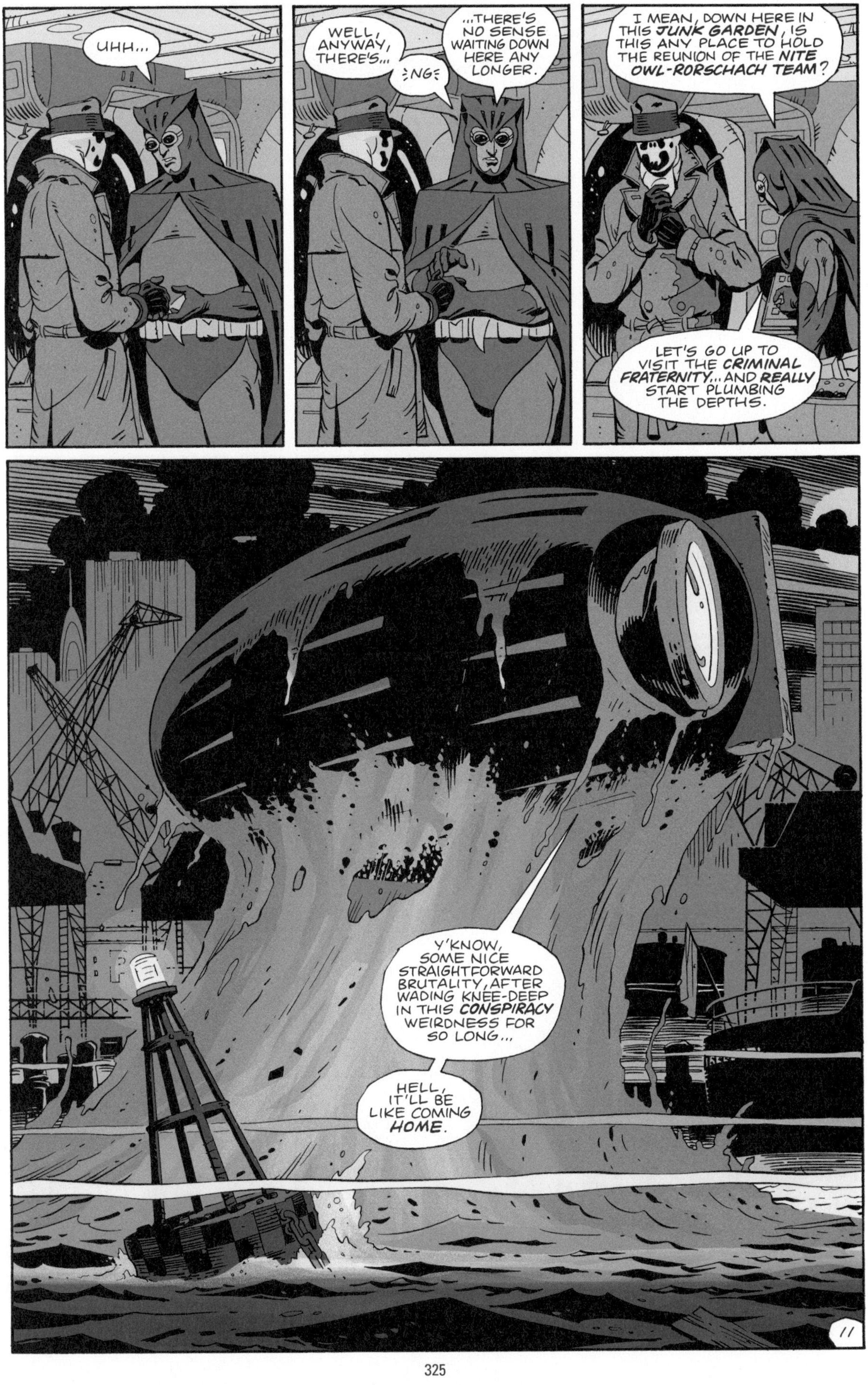
UHH...
WELL, ANYWAY, THERE'S...
NG
...THERE'S NO SENSE WAITING DOWN HERE ANY LONGER.
I MEAN, DOWN HERE IN THIS JUNK GARDEN, IS THIS ANY PLACE TO HOLD THE REUNION OF THE NITE OWL-RORSCHACH TEAM?
LET'S GO UP TO VISIT THE CRIMINAL FRATERNITY... AND REALLY START PLUMBING THE DEPTHS.
Y'KNOW, SOME NICE STRAIGHTFORWARD BRUTALITY, AFTER WADING KNEE-DEEP IN THIS CONSPIRACY WEIRDNESS FOR SO LONG...
HELL, IT'LL BE LIKE COMING HOME.
11

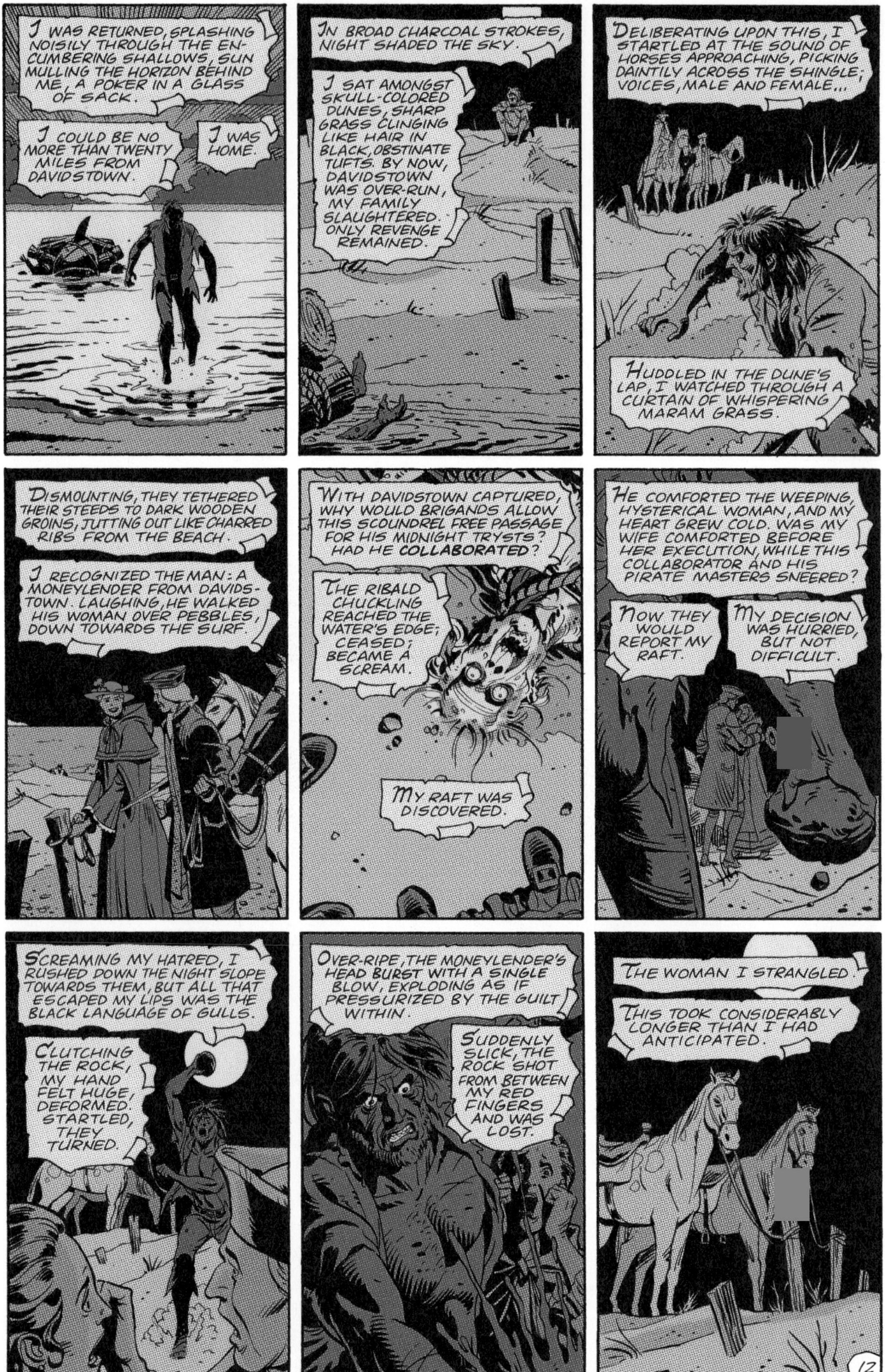
I WAS RETURNED, SPLASHING NOISILY THROUGH THE ENCUMBERING SHALLOWS, SUN MULLING THE HORIZON BEHIND ME, A POKER IN A GLASS OF SACK.
I COULD BE NO MORE THAN TWENTY MILES FROM DAVIDSTOWN.
I WAS HOME.
IN BROAD CHARCOAL STROKES, NIGHT SHADED THE SKY.
I SAT AMONGST SKULL-COLORED DUNES, SHARP GRASS CLINGING LIKE HAIR IN BLACK, OBSTINATE TUFTS. BY NOW, DAVIDSTOWN WAS OVER-RUN, MY FAMILY SLAUGHTERED. ONLY REVENGE REMAINED.
DELIBERATING UPON THIS, I STARTLED AT THE SOUND OF HORSES APPROACHING, PICKING DAINTILY ACROSS THE SHINGLE; VOICES, MALE AND FEMALE...
HUDDLED IN THE DUNE'S LAP, I WATCHED THROUGH A CURTAIN OF WHISPERING MARAM GRASS.
DISMOUNTING, THEY TETHERED THEIR STEEDS TO DARK WOODEN GROINS, JUTTING OUT LIKE CHARRED RIBS FROM THE BEACH.
I RECOGNIZED THE MAN: A MONEYLENDER FROM DAVIDSTOWN. LAUGHING, HE WALKED HIS WOMAN OVER PEBBLES, DOWN TOWARDS THE SURF.
WITH DAVIDSTOWN CAPTURED, WHY WOULD BRIGANDS ALLOW THIS SCOUNDREL FREE PASSAGE FOR HIS MIDNIGHT TRYSTS? HAD HE COLLABORATED?
THE RIBALD CHUCKLING REACHED THE WATER'S EDGE; CEASED; BECAME A SCREAM.
MY RAFT WAS DISCOVERED.
HE COMFORTED THE WEEPING, HYSTERICAL WOMAN, AND MY HEART GREW COLD. WAS MY WIFE COMFORTED BEFORE HER EXECUTION, WHILE THIS COLLABORATOR AND HIS PIRATE MASTERS SNEERED?
NOW THEY WOULD REPORT MY RAFT.
MY DECISION WAS HURRIED, BUT NOT DIFFICULT.
SCREAMING MY HATRED, I RUSHED DOWN THE NIGHT SLOPE TOWARDS THEM, BUT ALL THAT ESCAPED MY LIPS WAS THE BLACK LANGUAGE OF GULLS.
CLUTCHING THE ROCK, MY HAND FELT HUGE, DEFORMED. STARTLED, THEY TURNED.
OVER-RIPE, THE MONEYLENDER'S HEAD BURST WITH A SINGLE BLOW, EXPLODING AS IF PRESSURIZED BY THE GUILT WITHIN.
SUDDENLY SLICK, THE ROCK SHOT FROM BETWEEN MY RED FINGERS AND WAS LOST.
THE WOMAN I STRANGLED.
THIS TOOK CONSIDERABLY LONGER THAN I HAD ANTICIPATED.
12

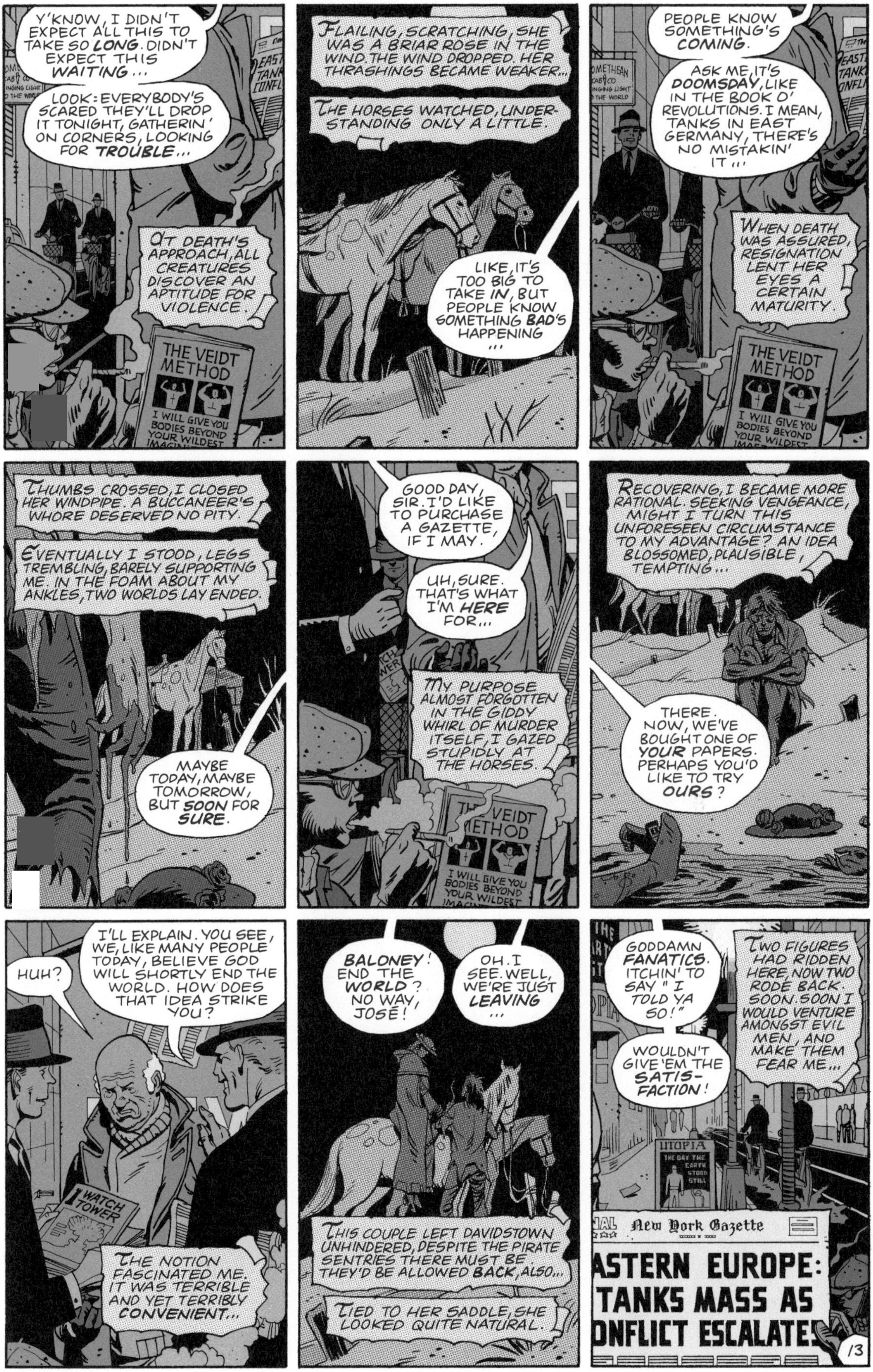
Y'KNOW, I DIDN'T EXPECT ALL THIS TO TAKE SO LONG. DIDN'T EXPECT THIS WAITING...
LOOK: EVERYBODY'S SCARED THEY'LL DROP IT TONIGHT, GATHERIN' ON CORNERS, LOOKING FOR TROUBLE...
AT DEATH'S APPROACH, ALL CREATURES DISCOVER AN APTITUDE FOR VIOLENCE.
THE VEIDT METHOD
I WILL GIVE YOU BODIES BEYOND YOUR WILDEST
FLAILING, SCRATCHING, SHE WAS A BRIAR ROSE IN THE WIND. THE WIND DROPPED. HER THRASHINGS BECAME WEAKER...
THE HORSES WATCHED, UNDERSTANDING ONLY A LITTLE.
LIKE, IT'S TOO BIG TO TAKE IN, BUT PEOPLE KNOW SOMETHING BAD'S HAPPENING...
PEOPLE KNOW SOMETHING'S COMING.
ASK ME, IT'S DOOMSDAY, LIKE IN THE BOOK O' REVOLUTIONS. I MEAN, TANKS IN EAST GERMANY, THERE'S NO MISTAKIN' IT...
WHEN DEATH WAS ASSURED, RESIGNATION LENT HER EYES A CERTAIN MATURITY.
THE VEIDT METHOD
I WILL GIVE YOU BODIES BEYOND YOUR WILDEST
THUMBS CROSSED, I CLOSED HER WINDPIPE. A BUCCANEER'S WHORE DESERVED NO PITY.
EVENTUALLY I STOOD, LEGS TREMBLING, BARELY SUPPORTING ME. IN THE FOAM ABOUT MY ANKLES, TWO WORLDS LAY ENDED.
MAYBE TODAY, MAYBE TOMORROW, BUT SOON FOR SURE.
GOOD DAY, SIR. I'D LIKE TO PURCHASE A GAZETTE, IF I MAY.
UH, SURE. THAT'S WHAT I'M HERE FOR...
MY PURPOSE ALMOST FORGOTTEN IN THE GIDDY WHIRL OF MURDER ITSELF, I GAZED STUPIDLY AT THE HORSES.
VEIDT METHOD
I WILL GIVE YOU BODIES BEYOND YOUR WILDEST
RECOVERING, I BECAME MORE RATIONAL. SEEKING VENGEANCE, MIGHT I TURN THIS UNFORESEEN CIRCUMSTANCE TO MY ADVANTAGE? AN IDEA BLOSSOMED, PLAUSIBLE, TEMPTING...
THERE. NOW, WE'VE BOUGHT ONE OF YOUR PAPERS. PERHAPS YOU'D LIKE TO TRY OURS?
HUH?
I'LL EXPLAIN. YOU SEE, WE, LIKE MANY PEOPLE TODAY, BELIEVE GOD WILL SHORTLY END THE WORLD. HOW DOES THAT IDEA STRIKE YOU?
WATCH TOWER
THE NOTION FASCINATED ME. IT WAS TERRIBLE AND YET TERRIBLY CONVENIENT...
BALONEY! END THE WORLD? NO WAY, JOSÉ!
OH. I SEE. WELL, WE'RE JUST LEAVING...
THIS COUPLE LEFT DAVIDSTOWN UNHINDERED, DESPITE THE PIRATE SENTRIES THERE MUST BE. THEY'D BE ALLOWED BACK, ALSO...
TIED TO HER SADDLE, SHE LOOKED QUITE NATURAL.
GODDAMN FANATICS. ITCHIN' TO SAY "I TOLD YA SO!"
WOULDN'T GIVE 'EM THE SATISFACTION!
TWO FIGURES HAD RIDDEN HERE, NOW TWO RODE BACK. SOON. SOON I WOULD VENTURE AMONGST EVIL MEN, AND MAKE THEM FEAR ME...
UTOPIA
THE DAY THE EARTH STOOD STILL
New York Gazette
ASTERN EUROPE: TANKS MASS AS ONFLICT ESCALATES
13

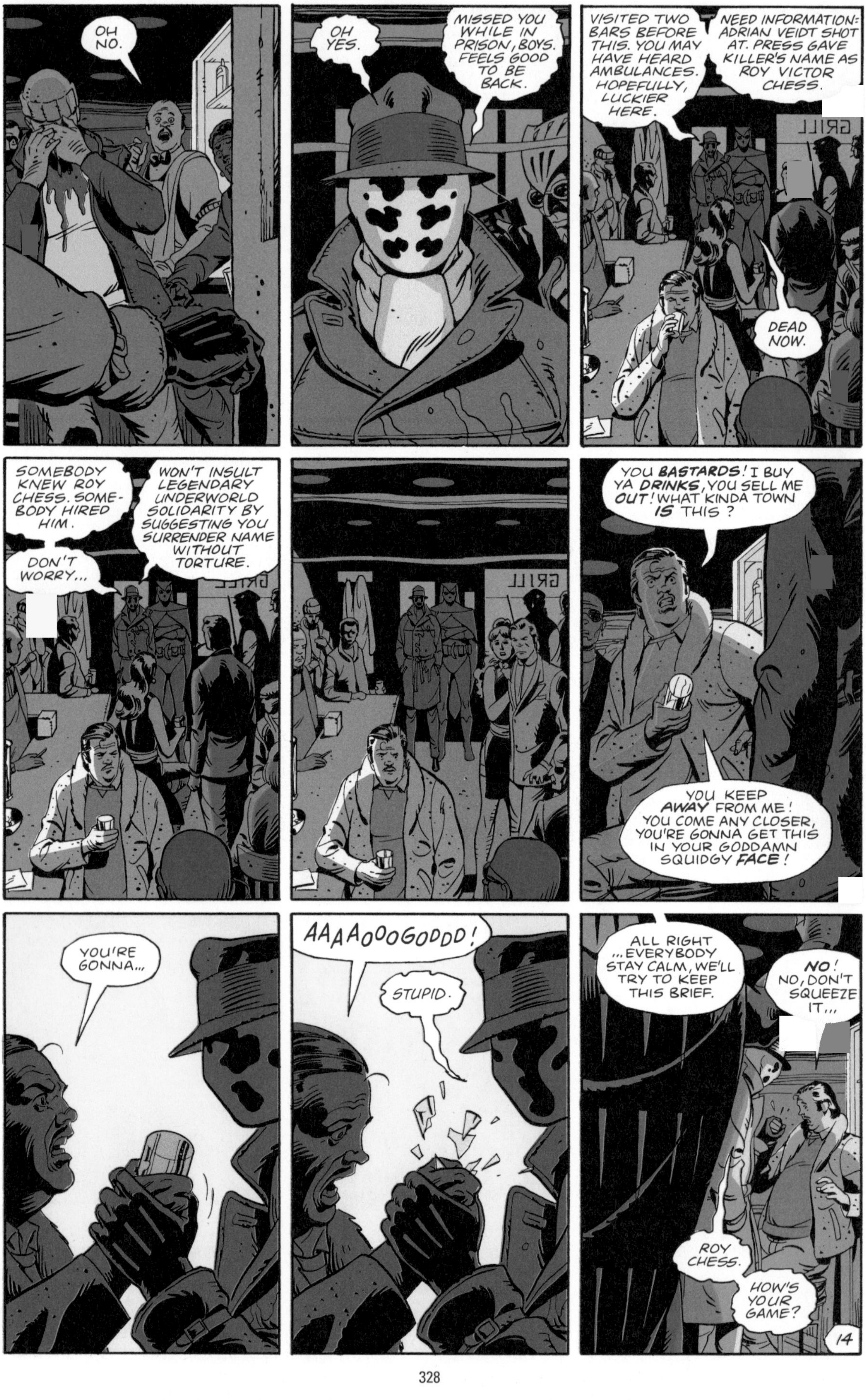
OH NO.
OH YES.
MISSED YOU WHILE IN PRISON, BOYS. FEELS GOOD TO BE BACK.
VISITED TWO BARS BEFORE THIS. YOU MAY HAVE HEARD AMBULANCES. HOPEFULLY, LUCKIER HERE.
NEED INFORMATION: ADRIAN VEIDT SHOT AT. PRESS GAVE KILLER'S NAME AS ROY VICTOR CHESS.
GRILL
DEAD NOW.
SOMEBODY KNEW ROY CHESS. SOMEBODY HIRED HIM.
DON'T WORRY...
WON'T INSULT LEGENDARY UNDERWORLD SOLIDARITY BY SUGGESTING YOU SURRENDER NAME WITHOUT TORTURE.
GRILL
GRILL
YOU BASTARDS! I BUY YA DRINKS, YOU SELL ME OUT! WHAT KINDA TOWN IS THIS?
YOU KEEP AWAY FROM ME! YOU COME ANY CLOSER, YOU'RE GONNA GET THIS IN YOUR GODDAMN SQUIDGY FACE!
YOU'RE GONNA...
AAAAOOOGODDD!
STUPID.
ALL RIGHT ...EVERYBODY STAY CALM, WE'LL TRY TO KEEP THIS BRIEF.
NO! NO, DON'T SQUEEZE IT...
ROY CHESS.
HOW'S YOUR GAME?
14

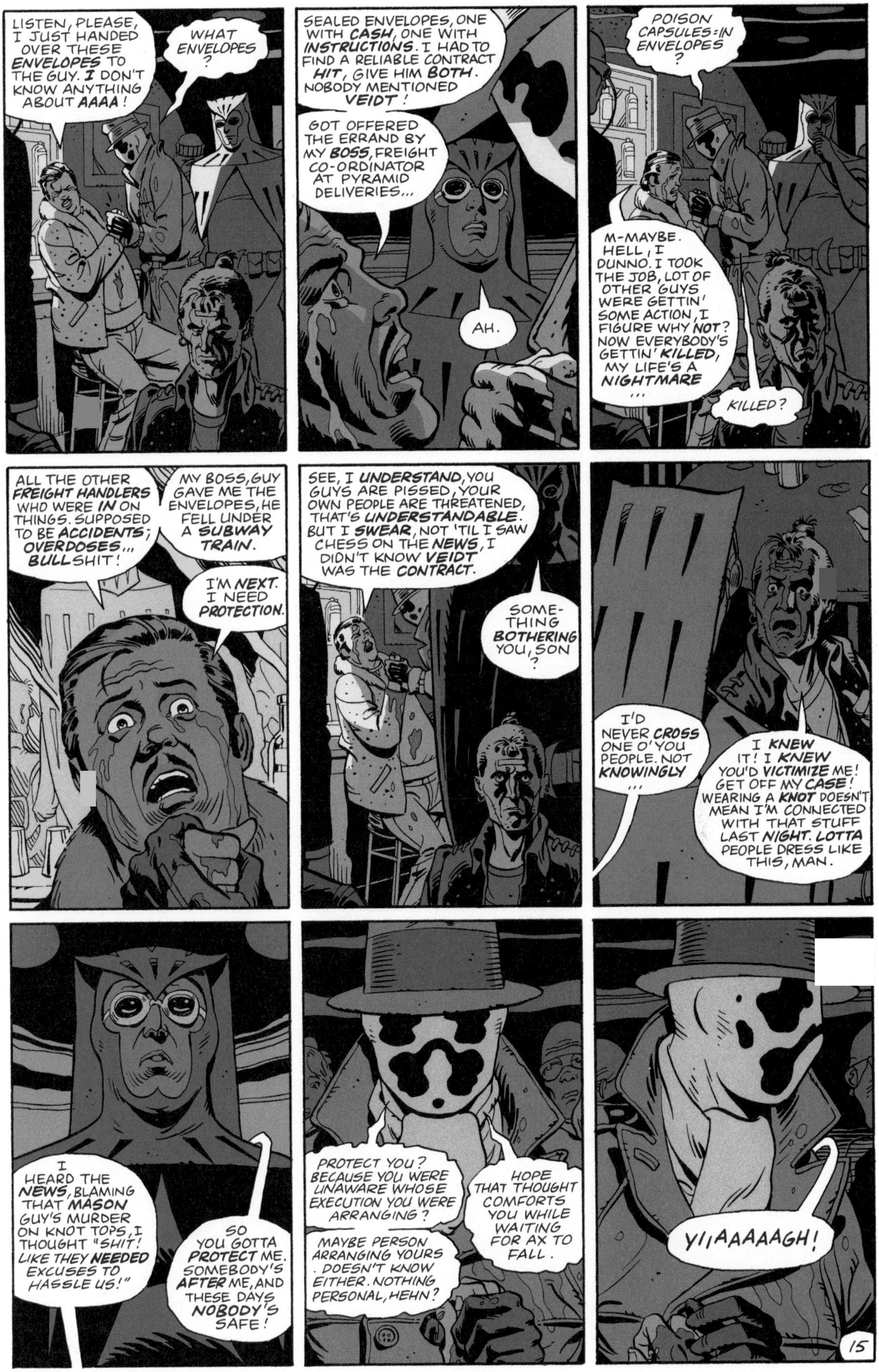
LISTEN, PLEASE, I JUST HANDED OVER THESE ENVELOPES TO THE GUY. I DON'T KNOW ANYTHING ABOUT AAAA!
WHAT ENVELOPES?
SEALED ENVELOPES, ONE WITH CASH, ONE WITH INSTRUCTIONS. I HAD TO FIND A RELIABLE CONTRACT HIT, GIVE HIM BOTH. NOBODY MENTIONED VEIDT!
GOT OFFERED THE ERRAND BY MY BOSS, FREIGHT CO-ORDINATOR AT PYRAMID DELIVERIES...
AH.
POISON CAPSULES=IN ENVELOPES?
M-MAYBE. HELL, I DUNNO. I TOOK THE JOB, LOT OF OTHER GUYS WERE GETTIN' SOME ACTION, I FIGURE WHY NOT? NOW EVERYBODY'S GETTIN' KILLED, MY LIFE'S A NIGHTMARE...
KILLED?
ALL THE OTHER FREIGHT HANDLERS WHO WERE IN ON THINGS. SUPPOSED TO BE ACCIDENTS; OVERDOSES... BULLSHIT!
MY BOSS, GUY GAVE ME THE ENVELOPES, HE FELL UNDER A SUBWAY TRAIN.
I'M NEXT. I NEED PROTECTION.
SEE, I UNDERSTAND, YOU GUYS ARE PISSED, YOUR OWN PEOPLE ARE THREATENED, THAT'S UNDERSTANDABLE. BUT I SWEAR, NOT 'TIL I SAW CHESS ON THE NEWS, I DIDN'T KNOW VEIDT WAS THE CONTRACT.
SOMETHING BOTHERING YOU, SON?
I'D NEVER CROSS ONE O'YOU PEOPLE. NOT KNOWINGLY...
I KNEW IT! I KNEW YOU'D VICTIMIZE ME! GET OFF MY CASE! WEARING A KNOT DOESN'T MEAN I'M CONNECTED WITH THAT STUFF LAST NIGHT. LOTTA PEOPLE DRESS LIKE THIS, MAN.
I HEARD THE NEWS, BLAMING THAT MASON GUY'S MURDER ON KNOT TOPS, I THOUGHT "SHIT! LIKE THEY NEEDED EXCUSES TO HASSLE US!"
SO YOU GOTTA PROTECT ME. SOMEBODY'S AFTER ME, AND THESE DAYS NOBODY'S SAFE!
PROTECT YOU? BECAUSE YOU WERE UNAWARE WHOSE EXECUTION YOU WERE ARRANGING?
MAYBE PERSON ARRANGING YOURS DOESN'T KNOW EITHER. NOTHING PERSONAL, HEHN?
HOPE THAT THOUGHT COMFORTS YOU WHILE WAITING FOR AX TO FALL.
YIIAAAAAGH!
15

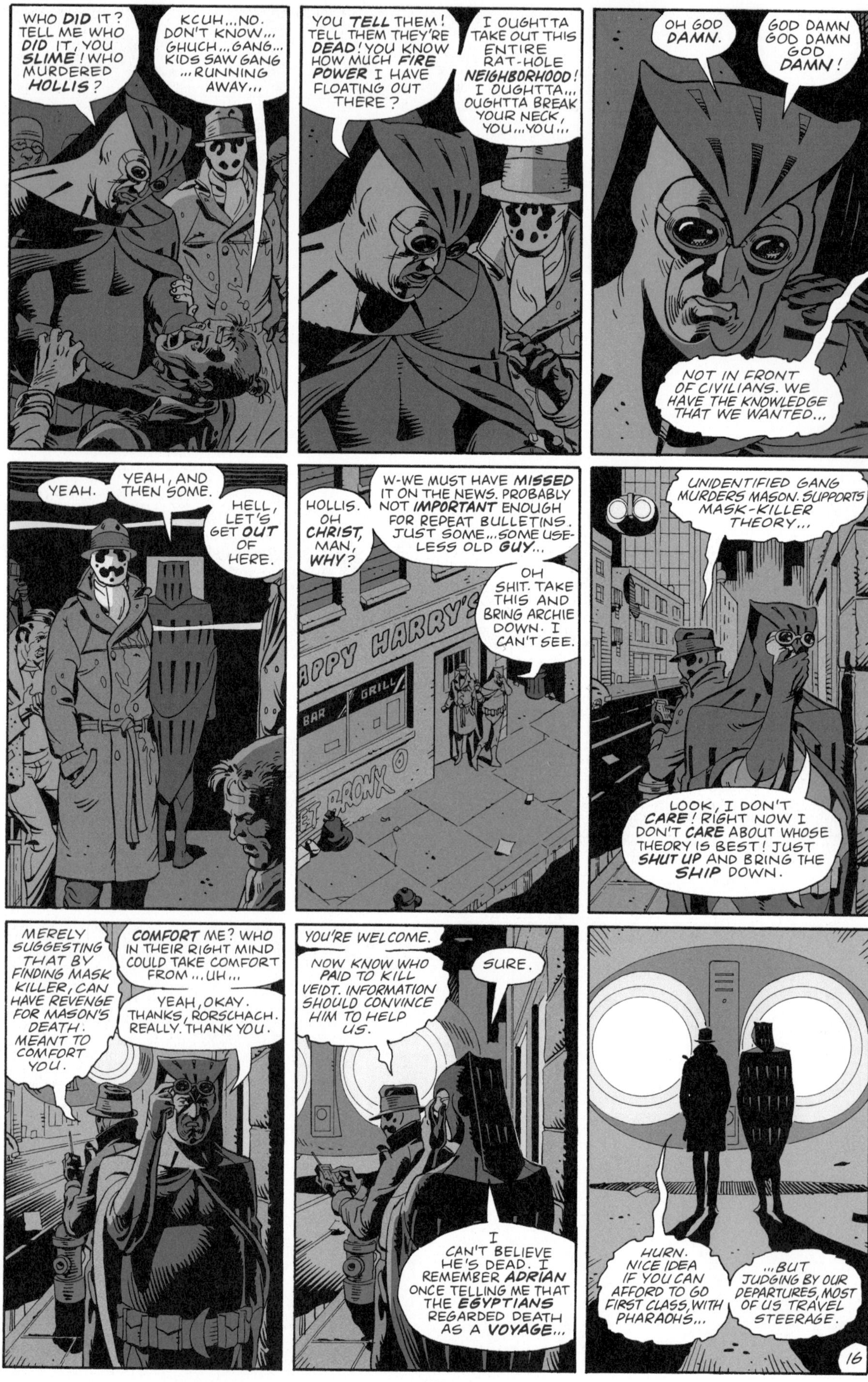
WHO DID IT? TELL ME WHO DID IT, YOU SLIME! WHO MURDERED HOLLIS?
KCUH...NO. DON'T KNOW... GHUCH...GANG... KIDS SAW GANG ...RUNNING AWAY...
YOU TELL THEM! TELL THEM THEY'RE DEAD! YOU KNOW HOW MUCH FIRE POWER I HAVE FLOATING OUT THERE?
I OUGHTTA TAKE OUT THIS ENTIRE RAT-HOLE NEIGHBORHOOD! I OUGHTTA... OUGHTTA BREAK YOUR NECK, YOU...YOU...
OH GOD DAMN.
GOD DAMN GOD DAMN GOD DAMN!
NOT IN FRONT OF CIVILIANS. WE HAVE THE KNOWLEDGE THAT WE WANTED...
YEAH.
YEAH, AND THEN SOME.
HELL, LET'S GET OUT OF HERE.
HOLLIS. OH CHRIST, MAN, WHY?
W-WE MUST HAVE MISSED IT ON THE NEWS. PROBABLY NOT IMPORTANT ENOUGH FOR REPEAT BULLETINS. JUST SOME...SOME USE-LESS OLD GUY...
OH SHIT. TAKE THIS AND BRING ARCHIE DOWN. I CAN'T SEE.
APPY HARRY'S
BAR
GRILL
UNIDENTIFIED GANG MURDERS MASON. SUPPORTS MASK-KILLER THEORY...
LOOK, I DON'T CARE! RIGHT NOW I DON'T CARE ABOUT WHOSE THEORY IS BEST! JUST SHUT UP AND BRING THE SHIP DOWN.
MERELY SUGGESTING THAT BY FINDING MASK KILLER, CAN HAVE REVENGE FOR MASON'S DEATH. MEANT TO COMFORT YOU.
COMFORT ME? WHO IN THEIR RIGHT MIND COULD TAKE COMFORT FROM...UH...
YEAH, OKAY. THANKS, RORSCHACH. REALLY. THANK YOU.
YOU'RE WELCOME.
NOW KNOW WHO PAID TO KILL VEIDT. INFORMATION SHOULD CONVINCE HIM TO HELP US.
SURE.
I CAN'T BELIEVE HE'S DEAD. I REMEMBER ADRIAN ONCE TELLING ME THAT THE EGYPTIANS REGARDED DEATH AS A VOYAGE...
HURN. NICE IDEA IF YOU CAN AFFORD TO GO FIRST CLASS, WITH PHARAOHS...
...BUT JUDGING BY OUR DEPARTURES, MOST OF US TRAVEL STEERAGE.
16

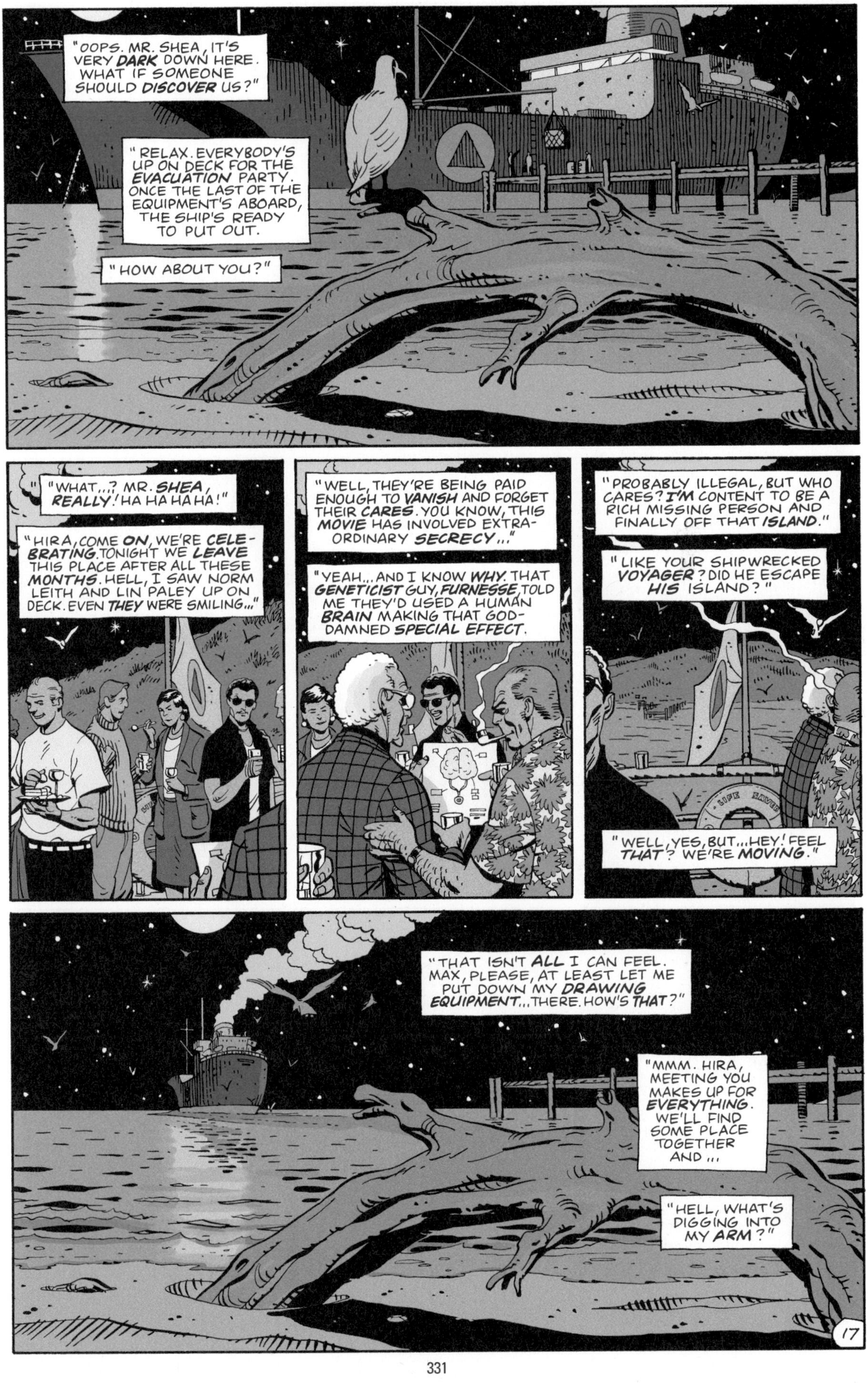
"OOPS. MR. SHEA, IT'S VERY DARK DOWN HERE. WHAT IF SOMEONE SHOULD DISCOVER US?"
"RELAX. EVERYBODY'S UP ON DECK FOR THE EVACUATION PARTY. ONCE THE LAST OF THE EQUIPMENT'S ABOARD, THE SHIP'S READY TO PUT OUT.
"HOW ABOUT YOU?"
"WHAT...? MR. SHEA, REALLY! HA HA HA HA!"
"HIRA, COME ON, WE'RE CELEBRATING. TONIGHT WE LEAVE THIS PLACE AFTER ALL THESE MONTHS. HELL, I SAW NORM LEITH AND LIN PALEY UP ON DECK. EVEN THEY WERE SMILING..."
"WELL, THEY'RE BEING PAID ENOUGH TO VANISH AND FORGET THEIR CARES. YOU KNOW, THIS MOVIE HAS INVOLVED EXTRAORDINARY SECRECY..."
"YEAH... AND I KNOW WHY. THAT GENETICIST GUY, FURNESSE, TOLD ME THEY'D USED A HUMAN BRAIN MAKING THAT GOD-DAMNED SPECIAL EFFECT.
"PROBABLY ILLEGAL, BUT WHO CARES? I'M CONTENT TO BE A RICH MISSING PERSON AND FINALLY OFF THAT ISLAND."
"LIKE YOUR SHIPWRECKED VOYAGER? DID HE ESCAPE HIS ISLAND?"
LIFE SAVER
"WELL, YES, BUT... HEY! FEEL THAT? WE'RE MOVING."
"THAT ISN'T ALL I CAN FEEL. MAX, PLEASE, AT LEAST LET ME PUT DOWN MY DRAWING EQUIPMENT... THERE. HOW'S THAT?"
"MMM. HIRA, MEETING YOU MAKES UP FOR EVERYTHING. WE'LL FIND SOME PLACE TOGETHER AND...
"HELL, WHAT'S DIGGING INTO MY ARM?"
17

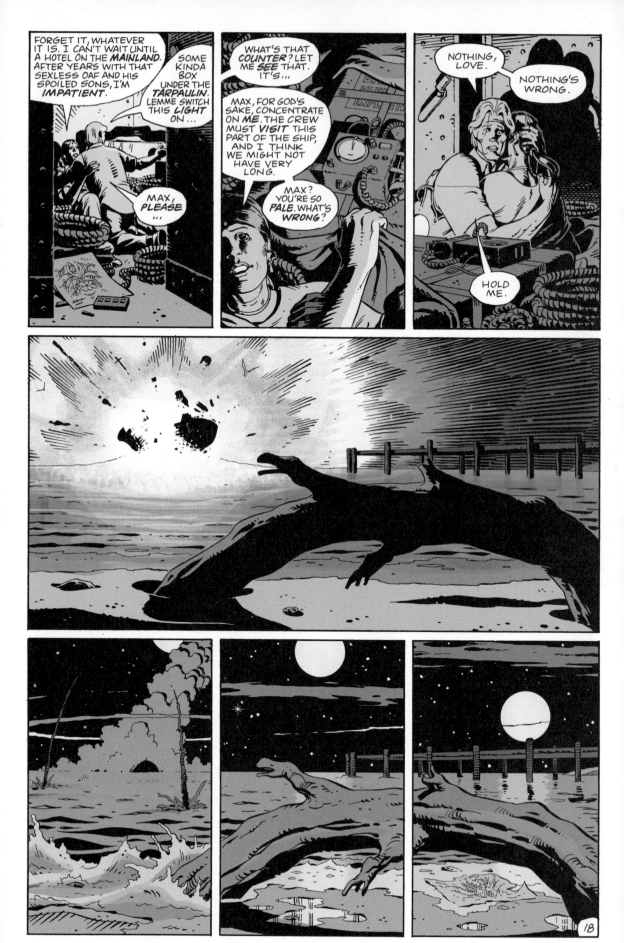

FORGET IT, WHATEVER IT IS. I CAN'T WAIT UNTIL A HOTEL ON THE *MAINLAND*. AFTER YEARS WITH THAT *SEXLESS OAF* AND HIS SPOILED SONS, I'M *IMPATIENT*.

SOME KINDA BOX UNDER THE *TARPAULIN*. LEMME SWITCH THIS *LIGHT* ON...

MAX, *PLEASE*...

WHAT'S THAT *COUNTER*? LET ME *SEE* THAT. IT'S...

MAX, FOR GOD'S SAKE, CONCENTRATE ON *ME*. THE CREW MUST *VISIT* THIS PART OF THE SHIP, AND I THINK WE MIGHT NOT HAVE VERY LONG.

MAX? YOU'RE SO *PALE*. WHAT'S *WRONG*?

NOTHING, LOVE.

NOTHING'S WRONG.

HOLD ME.

18

332

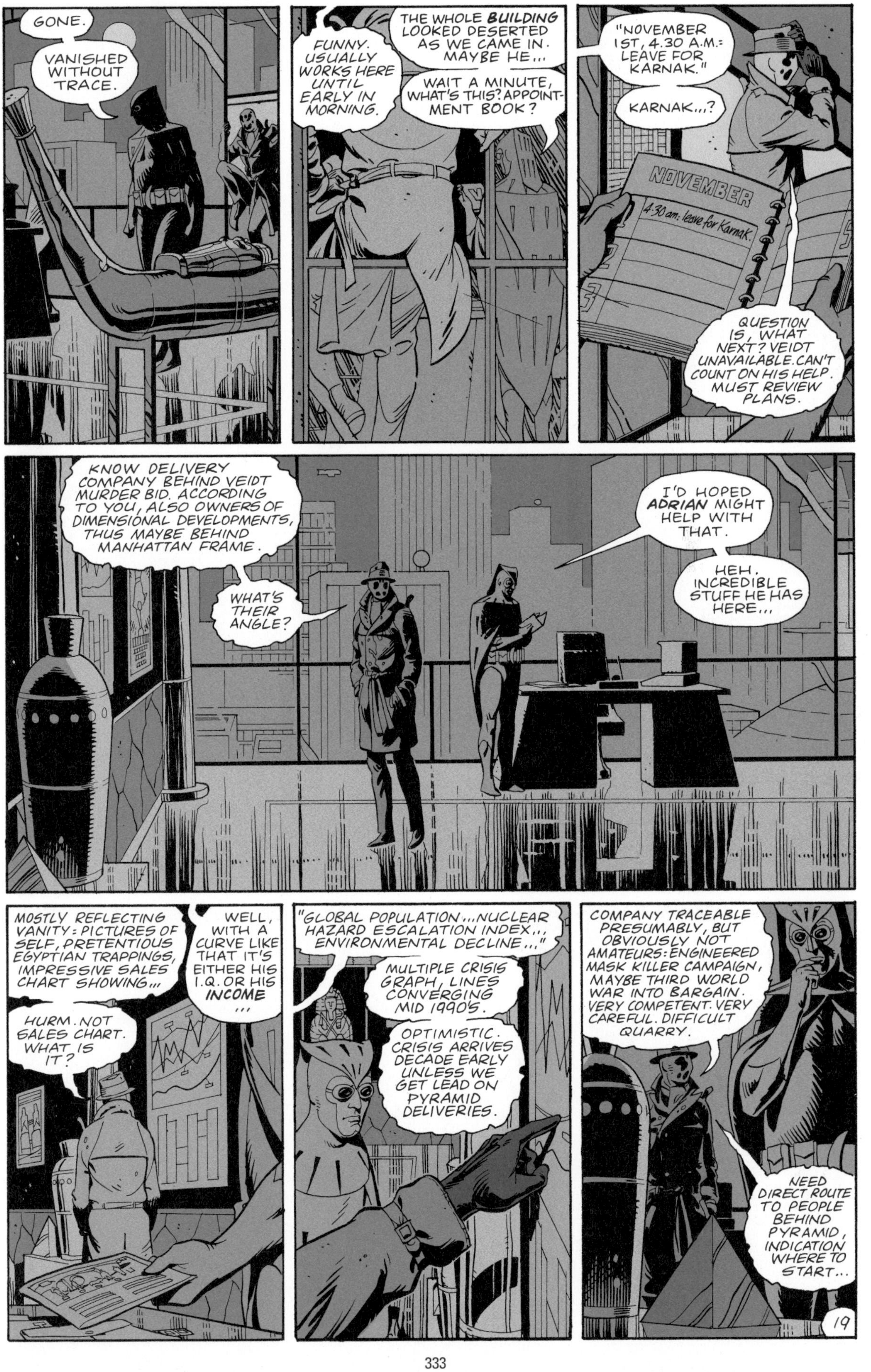
GONE.
VANISHED WITHOUT TRACE.
FUNNY. USUALLY WORKS HERE UNTIL EARLY IN MORNING.
THE WHOLE BUILDING LOOKED DESERTED AS WE CAME IN. MAYBE HE...
WAIT A MINUTE, WHAT'S THIS? APPOINTMENT BOOK?
"NOVEMBER 1ST, 4.30 A.M.: LEAVE FOR KARNAK."
KARNAK...?
NOVEMBER
4.30 am: leave for Karnak.
QUESTION IS, WHAT NEXT? VEIDT UNAVAILABLE. CAN'T COUNT ON HIS HELP. MUST REVIEW PLANS.
KNOW DELIVERY COMPANY BEHIND VEIDT MURDER BID. ACCORDING TO YOU, ALSO OWNERS OF DIMENSIONAL DEVELOPMENTS, THUS MAYBE BEHIND MANHATTAN FRAME.
WHAT'S THEIR ANGLE?
I'D HOPED ADRIAN MIGHT HELP WITH THAT.
HEH. INCREDIBLE STUFF HE HAS HERE...
MOSTLY REFLECTING VANITY: PICTURES OF SELF, PRETENTIOUS EGYPTIAN TRAPPINGS, IMPRESSIVE SALES CHART SHOWING...
WELL, WITH A CURVE LIKE THAT IT'S EITHER HIS I.Q. OR HIS INCOME...
HURM. NOT SALES CHART. WHAT IS IT?
"GLOBAL POPULATION... NUCLEAR HAZARD ESCALATION INDEX... ENVIRONMENTAL DECLINE..."
MULTIPLE CRISIS GRAPH, LINES CONVERGING MID 1990'S.
OPTIMISTIC. CRISIS ARRIVES DECADE EARLY UNLESS WE GET LEAD ON PYRAMID DELIVERIES.
COMPANY TRACEABLE PRESUMABLY, BUT OBVIOUSLY NOT AMATEURS: ENGINEERED MASK KILLER CAMPAIGN, MAYBE THIRD WORLD WAR INTO BARGAIN. VERY COMPETENT. VERY CAREFUL. DIFFICULT QUARRY.
NEED DIRECT ROUTE TO PEOPLE BEHIND PYRAMID, INDICATION WHERE TO START...
19

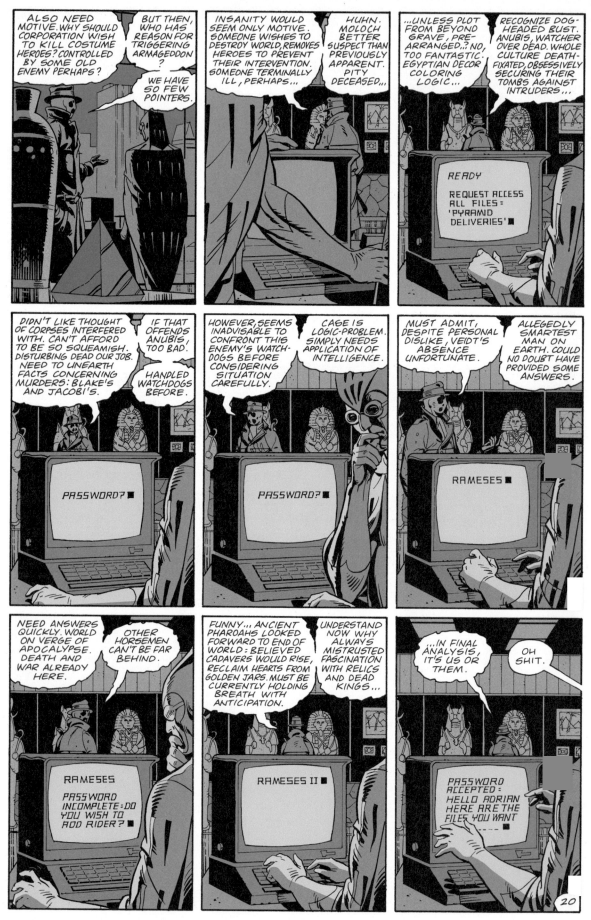

ALSO NEED MOTIVE. WHY SHOULD CORPORATION WISH TO KILL COSTUME HEROES? CONTROLLED BY SOME OLD ENEMY PERHAPS?

BUT THEN, WHO HAS REASON FOR TRIGGERING ARMAGEDDON? WE HAVE SO FEW POINTERS.

INSANITY WOULD SEEM ONLY MOTIVE. SOMEONE WISHES TO DESTROY WORLD, REMOVES HEROES TO PREVENT THEIR INTERVENTION. SOMEONE TERMINALLY ILL, PERHAPS...

HUHN. MOLOCH BETTER SUSPECT THAN PREVIOUSLY APPARENT. PITY DECEASED...

...UNLESS PLOT FROM BEYOND GRAVE, PRE-ARRANGED..? NO, TOO FANTASTIC. EGYPTIAN DECOR COLORING LOGIC...

RECOGNIZE DOG-HEADED BUST. ANUBIS, WATCHER OVER DEAD. WHOLE CULTURE DEATH-FIXATED, OBSESSIVELY SECURING THEIR TOMBS AGAINST INTRUDERS...

READY
REQUEST ACCESS ALL FILES = 'PYRAMID DELIVERIES' ▮

DIDN'T LIKE THOUGHT OF CORPSES INTERFERED WITH. CAN'T AFFORD TO BE SO SQUEAMISH. DISTURBING DEAD OUR JOB. NEED TO UNEARTH FACTS CONCERNING MURDERS: BLAKE'S AND JACOBI'S.

IF THAT OFFENDS ANUBIS, TOO BAD. HANDLED WATCHDOGS BEFORE.

HOWEVER, SEEMS INADVISABLE TO CONFRONT THIS ENEMY'S WATCH-DOGS BEFORE CONSIDERING SITUATION CAREFULLY.

CAGE IS LOGIC-PROBLEM. SIMPLY NEEDS APPLICATION OF INTELLIGENCE.

MUST ADMIT, DESPITE PERSONAL DISLIKE, VEIDT'S ABSENCE UNFORTUNATE.

ALLEGEDLY SMARTEST MAN ON EARTH. COULD NO DOUBT HAVE PROVIDED SOME ANSWERS.

PASSWORD? ▮

PASSWORD? ▮

RAMESES ▮

NEED ANSWERS QUICKLY. WORLD ON VERGE OF APOCALYPSE. DEATH AND WAR ALREADY HERE.

OTHER HORSEMEN CAN'T BE FAR BEHIND.

FUNNY... ANCIENT PHAROAHS LOOKED FORWARD TO END OF WORLD: BELIEVED CADAVERS WOULD RISE, RECLAIM HEARTS FROM GOLDEN JARS. MUST BE CURRENTLY HOLDING BREATH WITH ANTICIPATION.

UNDERSTAND NOW WHY ALWAYS MISTRUSTED FASCINATION WITH RELICS AND DEAD KINGS...

...IN FINAL ANALYSIS, IT'S US OR THEM.

OH SHIT.

RAMESES
PASSWORD INCOMPLETE: DO YOU WISH TO ADD RIDER? ▮

RAMESES II ▮

PASSWORD ACCEPTED = HELLO ADRIAN HERE ARE THE FILES YOU WANT ▮

20

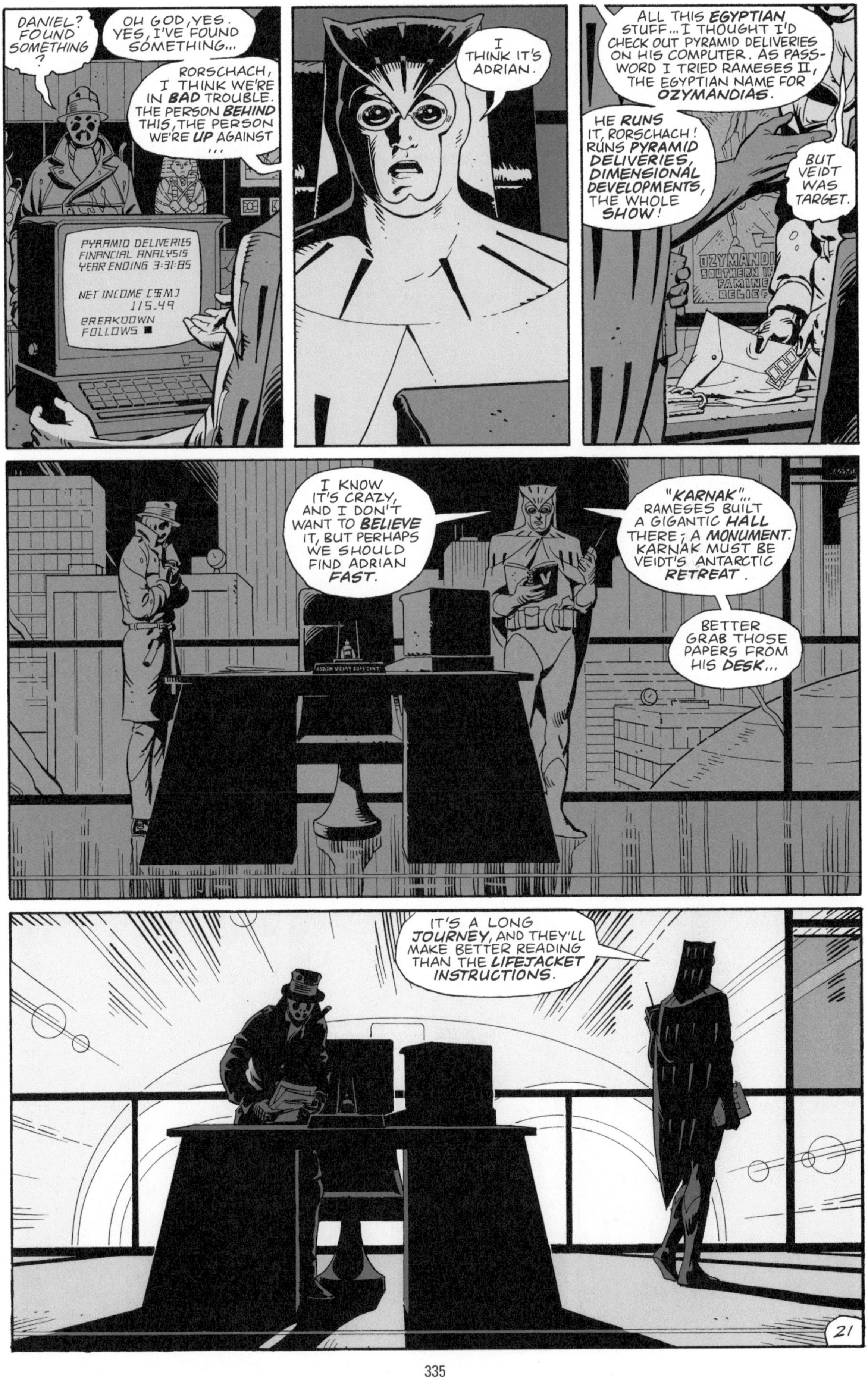
DANIEL? FOUND SOMETHING?
OH GOD, YES. YES, I'VE FOUND SOMETHING...
RORSCHACH, I THINK WE'RE IN BAD TROUBLE. THE PERSON BEHIND THIS, THE PERSON WE'RE UP AGAINST...
PYRAMID DELIVERIES FINANCIAL ANALYSIS YEAR ENDING 3:31:85
NET INCOME [$M] 115.49
BREAKDOWN FOLLOWS
I THINK IT'S ADRIAN.
ALL THIS EGYPTIAN STUFF... I THOUGHT I'D CHECK OUT PYRAMID DELIVERIES ON HIS COMPUTER. AS PASSWORD I TRIED RAMESES II, THE EGYPTIAN NAME FOR OZYMANDIAS.
HE RUNS IT, RORSCHACH! RUNS PYRAMID DELIVERIES, DIMENSIONAL DEVELOPMENTS, THE WHOLE SHOW!
BUT VEIDT WAS TARGET.
I KNOW IT'S CRAZY, AND I DON'T WANT TO BELIEVE IT, BUT PERHAPS WE SHOULD FIND ADRIAN FAST.
"KARNAK"... RAMESES BUILT A GIGANTIC HALL THERE; A MONUMENT. KARNAK MUST BE VEIDT'S ANTARCTIC RETREAT.
BETTER GRAB THOSE PAPERS FROM HIS DESK...
IT'S A LONG JOURNEY, AND THEY'LL MAKE BETTER READING THAN THE LIFEJACKET INSTRUCTIONS.
21

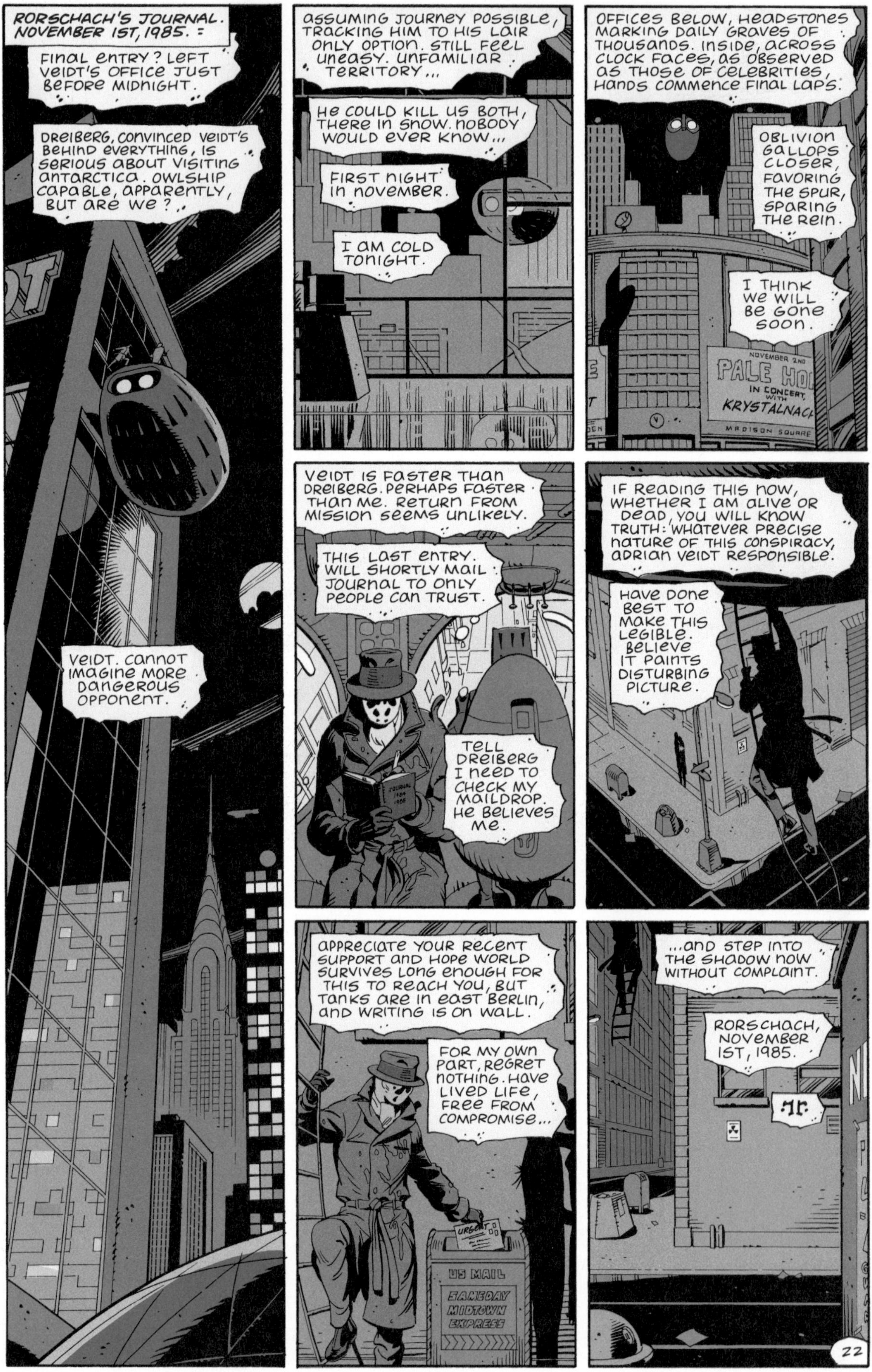
RORSCHACH'S JOURNAL. NOVEMBER 1ST, 1985. =
FINAL ENTRY? LEFT VEIDT'S OFFICE JUST BEFORE MIDNIGHT.
DREIBERG, CONVINCED VEIDT'S BEHIND EVERYTHING, IS SERIOUS ABOUT VISITING ANTARCTICA. OWLSHIP CAPABLE, APPARENTLY, BUT ARE WE?
VEIDT. CANNOT IMAGINE MORE DANGEROUS OPPONENT.
ASSUMING JOURNEY POSSIBLE, TRACKING HIM TO HIS LAIR ONLY OPTION. STILL FEEL UNEASY. UNFAMILIAR TERRITORY...
HE COULD KILL US BOTH, THERE IN SNOW. NOBODY WOULD EVER KNOW...
FIRST NIGHT IN NOVEMBER.
I AM COLD TONIGHT.
OFFICES BELOW, HEADSTONES MARKING DAILY GRAVES OF THOUSANDS. INSIDE, ACROSS CLOCK FACES, AS OBSERVED AS THOSE OF CELEBRITIES, HANDS COMMENCE FINAL LAPS.
OBLIVION GALLOPS CLOSER, FAVORING THE SPUR, SPARING THE REIN.
I THINK WE WILL BE GONE SOON.
NOVEMBER 2ND
IN CONCERT, WITH
MADISON SQUARE
VEIDT IS FASTER THAN DREIBERG. PERHAPS FASTER THAN ME. RETURN FROM MISSION SEEMS UNLIKELY.
THIS LAST ENTRY. WILL SHORTLY MAIL JOURNAL TO ONLY PEOPLE CAN TRUST.
TELL DREIBERG I NEED TO CHECK MY MAILDROP. HE BELIEVES ME.
IF READING THIS NOW, WHETHER I AM ALIVE OR DEAD, YOU WILL KNOW TRUTH: WHATEVER PRECISE NATURE OF THIS CONSPIRACY, ADRIAN VEIDT RESPONSIBLE.
HAVE DONE BEST TO MAKE THIS LEGIBLE. BELIEVE IT PAINTS DISTURBING PICTURE.
APPRECIATE YOUR RECENT SUPPORT AND HOPE WORLD SURVIVES LONG ENOUGH FOR THIS TO REACH YOU, BUT TANKS ARE IN EAST BERLIN, AND WRITING IS ON WALL.
FOR MY OWN PART, REGRET NOTHING. HAVE LIVED LIFE, FREE FROM COMPROMISE...
URGENT
US MAIL
SAMEDAY MIDTOWN EXPRESS
...AND STEP INTO THE SHADOW NOW WITHOUT COMPLAINT.
RORSCHACH, NOVEMBER 1ST, 1985.
22

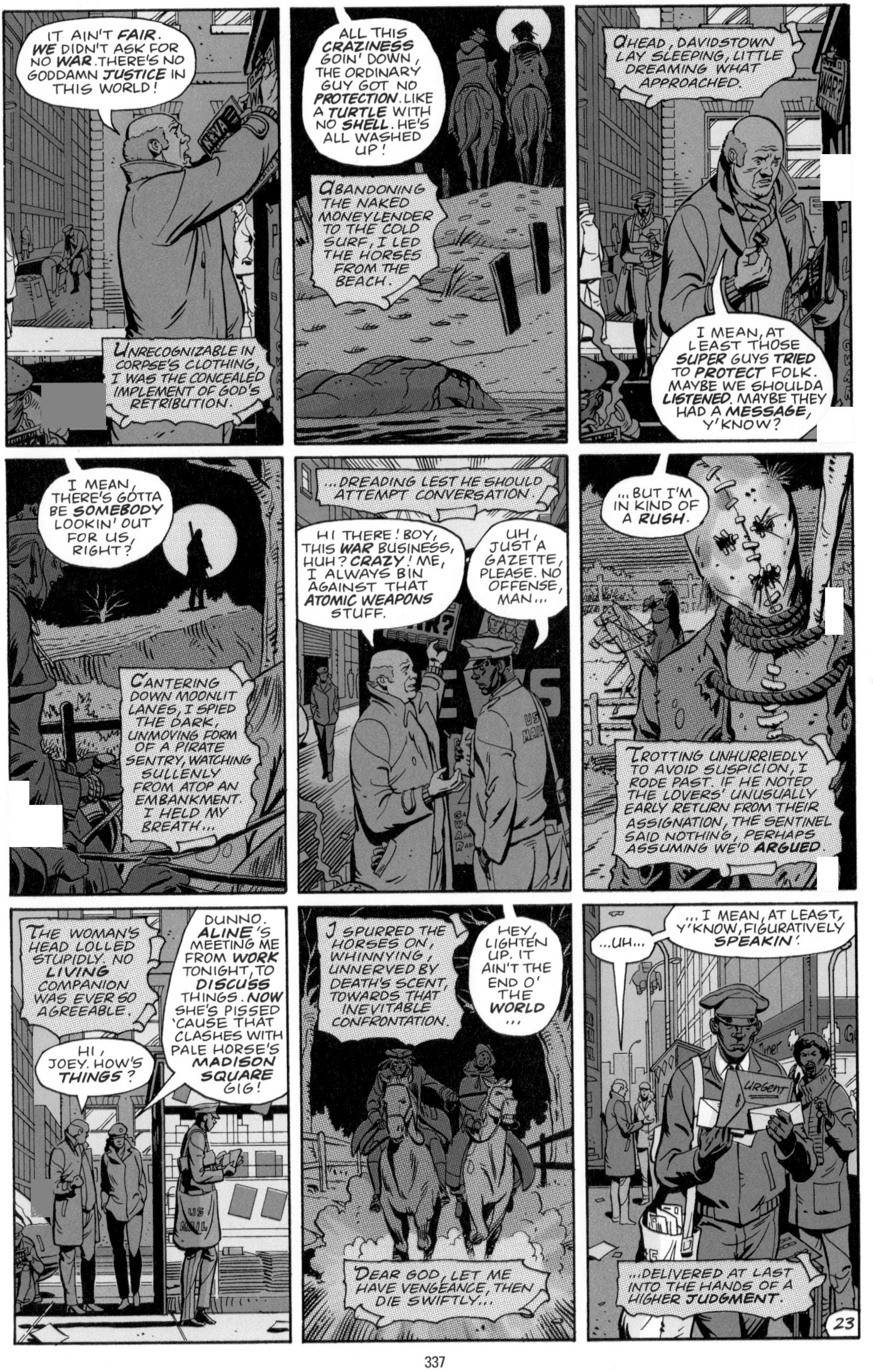

IT AIN'T FAIR. WE DIDN'T ASK FOR NO WAR. THERE'S NO GODDAMN JUSTICE IN THIS WORLD!
UNRECOGNIZABLE IN CORPSE'S CLOTHING, I WAS THE CONCEALED IMPLEMENT OF GOD'S RETRIBUTION.
ALL THIS CRAZINESS GOIN' DOWN, THE ORDINARY GUY GOT NO PROTECTION. LIKE A TURTLE WITH NO SHELL. HE'S ALL WASHED UP!
ABANDONING THE NAKED MONEYLENDER TO THE COLD SURF, I LED THE HORSES FROM THE BEACH.
AHEAD, DAVIDSTOWN LAY SLEEPING, LITTLE DREAMING WHAT APPROACHED.
I MEAN, AT LEAST THOSE SUPER GUYS TRIED TO PROTECT FOLK. MAYBE WE SHOULDA LISTENED. MAYBE THEY HAD A MESSAGE, Y'KNOW?
I MEAN, THERE'S GOTTA BE SOMEBODY LOOKIN' OUT FOR US, RIGHT?
CANTERING DOWN MOONLIT LANES, I SPIED THE DARK, UNMOVING FORM OF A PIRATE SENTRY, WATCHING SULLENLY FROM ATOP AN EMBANKMENT. I HELD MY BREATH...
...DREADING LEST HE SHOULD ATTEMPT CONVERSATION.
HI THERE! BOY, THIS WAR BUSINESS, HUH? CRAZY! ME, I ALWAYS BIN AGAINST THAT ATOMIC WEAPONS STUFF.
UH, JUST A GAZETTE, PLEASE. NO OFFENSE, MAN...
US MAIL
...BUT I'M IN KIND OF A RUSH.
TROTTING UNHURRIEDLY TO AVOID SUSPICION, I RODE PAST. IF HE NOTED THE LOVERS' UNUSUALLY EARLY RETURN FROM THEIR ASSIGNATION, THE SENTINEL SAID NOTHING, PERHAPS ASSUMING WE'D ARGUED.
THE WOMAN'S HEAD LOLLED STUPIDLY. NO LIVING COMPANION WAS EVER SO AGREEABLE.
HI, JOEY. HOW'S THINGS?
DUNNO. ALINE'S MEETING ME FROM WORK TONIGHT, TO DISCUSS THINGS. NOW SHE'S PISSED 'CAUSE THAT CLASHES WITH PALE HORSE'S MADISON SQUARE GIG!
US MAIL
I SPURRED THE HORSES ON, WHINNYING, UNNERVED BY DEATH'S SCENT, TOWARDS THAT INEVITABLE CONFRONTATION.
HEY, LIGHTEN UP. IT AIN'T THE END O' THE WORLD...
DEAR GOD, LET ME HAVE VENGEANCE, THEN DIE SWIFTLY...
...UH...
...I MEAN, AT LEAST, Y'KNOW, FIGURATIVELY SPEAKIN'.
URGENT
...DELIVERED AT LAST INTO THE HANDS OF A HIGHER JUDGMENT.
23

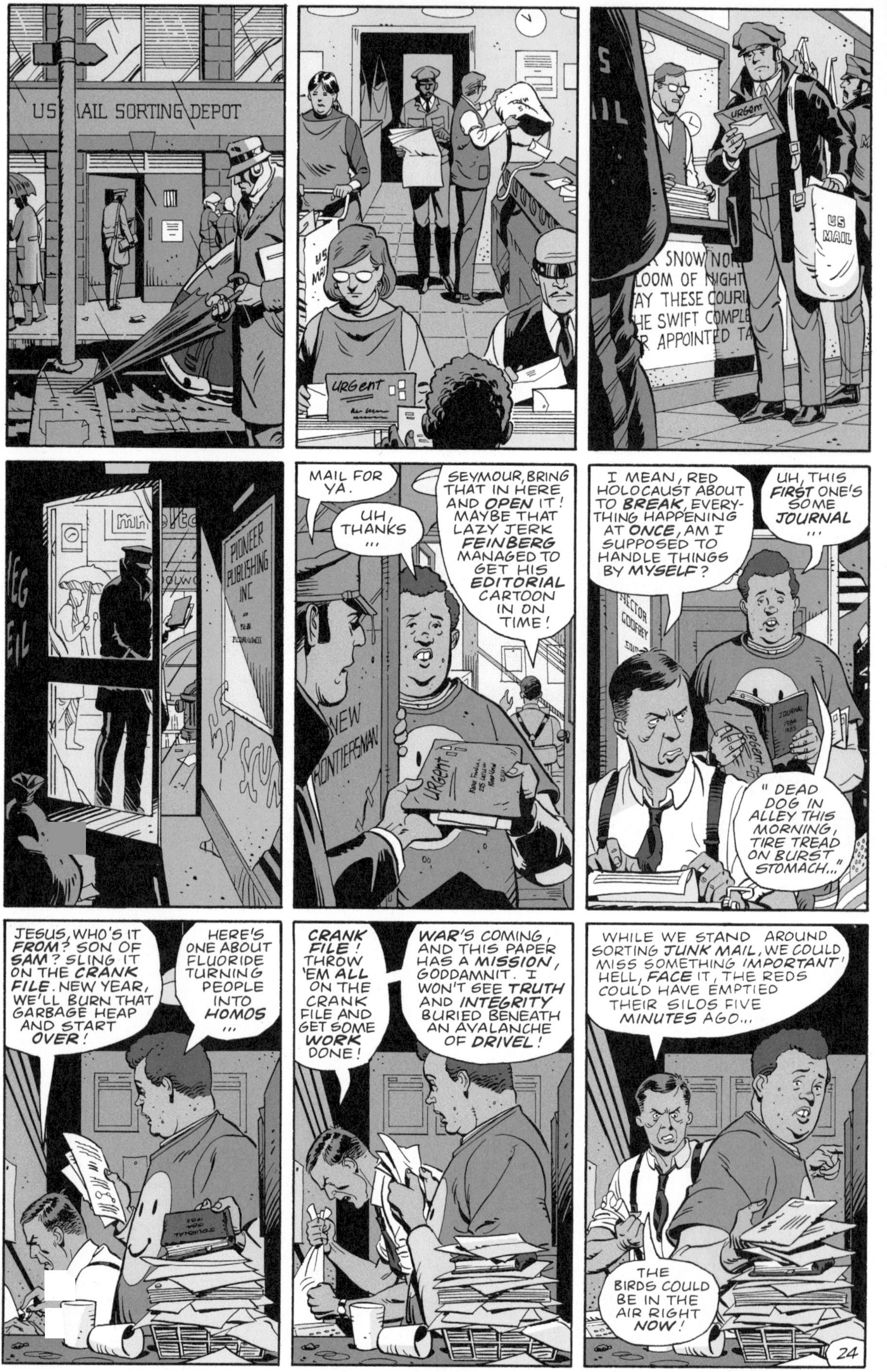
US MAIL SORTING DEPOT
URGENT
US MAIL
R SNOW NOR
LOOM OF NIGHT
AY THESE COURI
HE SWIFT COMPLE
R APPOINTED TA
PIONEER PUBLISHING INC
MAIL FOR YA.
UH, THANKS...
SEYMOUR, BRING THAT IN HERE AND OPEN IT! MAYBE THAT LAZY JERK FEINBERG MANAGED TO GET HIS EDITORIAL CARTOON IN ON TIME!
NEW FRONTIERSMAN
URGENT
I MEAN, RED HOLOCAUST ABOUT TO BREAK, EVERYTHING HAPPENING AT ONCE, AM I SUPPOSED TO HANDLE THINGS BY MYSELF?
UH, THIS FIRST ONE'S SOME JOURNAL...
HECTOR GODFREY
JOURNAL 1984 1985
"DEAD DOG IN ALLEY THIS MORNING, TIRE TREAD ON BURST STOMACH..."
JESUS, WHO'S IT FROM? SON OF SAM? SLING IT ON THE CRANK FILE. NEW YEAR, WE'LL BURN THAT GARBAGE HEAP AND START OVER!
HERE'S ONE ABOUT FLUORIDE TURNING PEOPLE INTO HOMOS...
CRANK FILE! THROW 'EM ALL ON THE CRANK FILE AND GET SOME WORK DONE!
WAR'S COMING, AND THIS PAPER HAS A MISSION, GODDAMNIT. I WON'T SEE TRUTH AND INTEGRITY BURIED BENEATH AN AVALANCHE OF DRIVEL!
WHILE WE STAND AROUND SORTING JUNK MAIL, WE COULD MISS SOMETHING IMPORTANT! HELL, FACE IT, THE REDS COULD HAVE EMPTIED THEIR SILOS FIVE MINUTES AGO...
THE BIRDS COULD BE IN THE AIR RIGHT NOW!
24

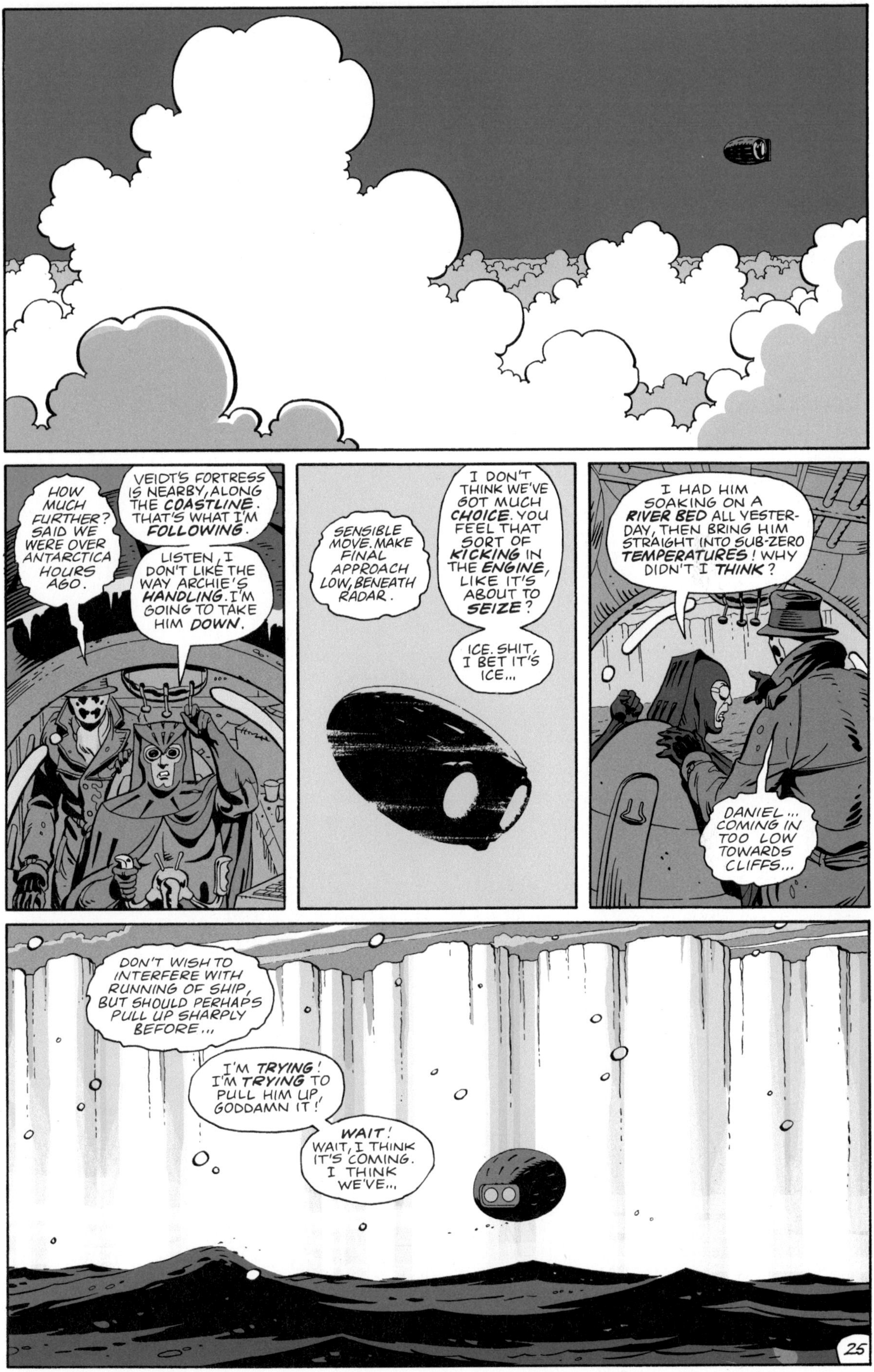
HOW MUCH FURTHER? SAID WE WERE OVER ANTARCTICA HOURS AGO.
VEIDT'S FORTRESS IS NEARBY, ALONG THE COASTLINE. THAT'S WHAT I'M FOLLOWING.
LISTEN, I DON'T LIKE THE WAY ARCHIE'S HANDLING. I'M GOING TO TAKE HIM DOWN.
SENSIBLE MOVE. MAKE FINAL APPROACH LOW, BENEATH RADAR.
I DON'T THINK WE'VE GOT MUCH CHOICE. YOU FEEL THAT SORT OF KICKING IN THE ENGINE, LIKE IT'S ABOUT TO SEIZE?
ICE. SHIT, I BET IT'S ICE...
I HAD HIM SOAKING ON A RIVER BED ALL YESTERDAY, THEN BRING HIM STRAIGHT INTO SUB-ZERO TEMPERATURES! WHY DIDN'T I THINK?
DANIEL... COMING IN TOO LOW TOWARDS CLIFFS...
DON'T WISH TO INTERFERE WITH RUNNING OF SHIP, BUT SHOULD PERHAPS PULL UP SHARPLY BEFORE...
I'M TRYING! I'M TRYING TO PULL HIM UP, GODDAMN IT!
WAIT! WAIT, I THINK IT'S COMING. I THINK WE'VE...
25

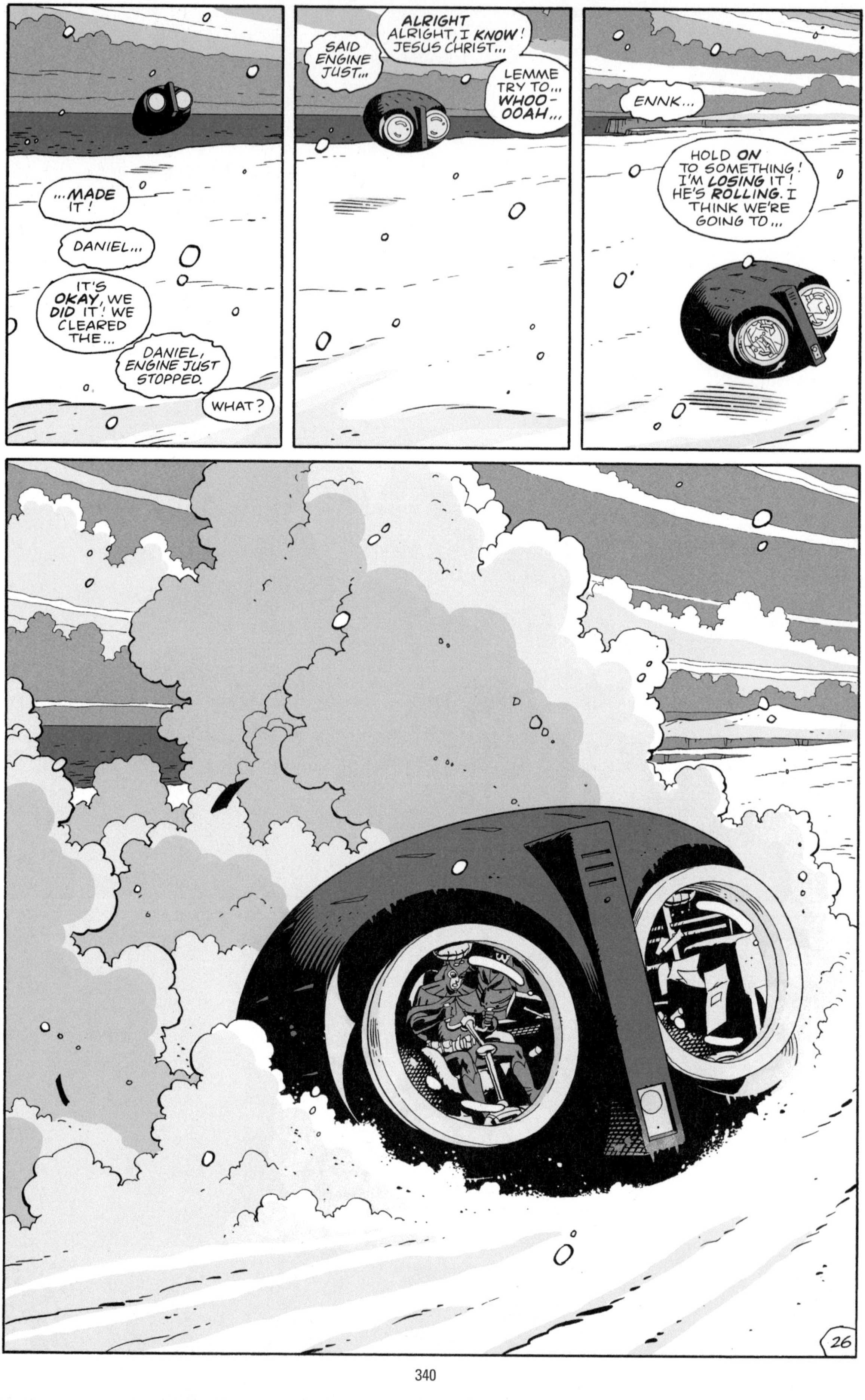
...MADE IT!
DANIEL...
IT'S OKAY, WE DID IT! WE CLEARED THE...
DANIEL, ENGINE JUST STOPPED.
WHAT?
SAID ENGINE JUST...
ALRIGHT ALRIGHT, I KNOW! JESUS CHRIST...
LEMME TRY TO... WHOO-OOAH...
ENNK...
HOLD ON TO SOMETHING! I'M LOSING IT! HE'S ROLLING. I THINK WE'RE GOING TO...
26

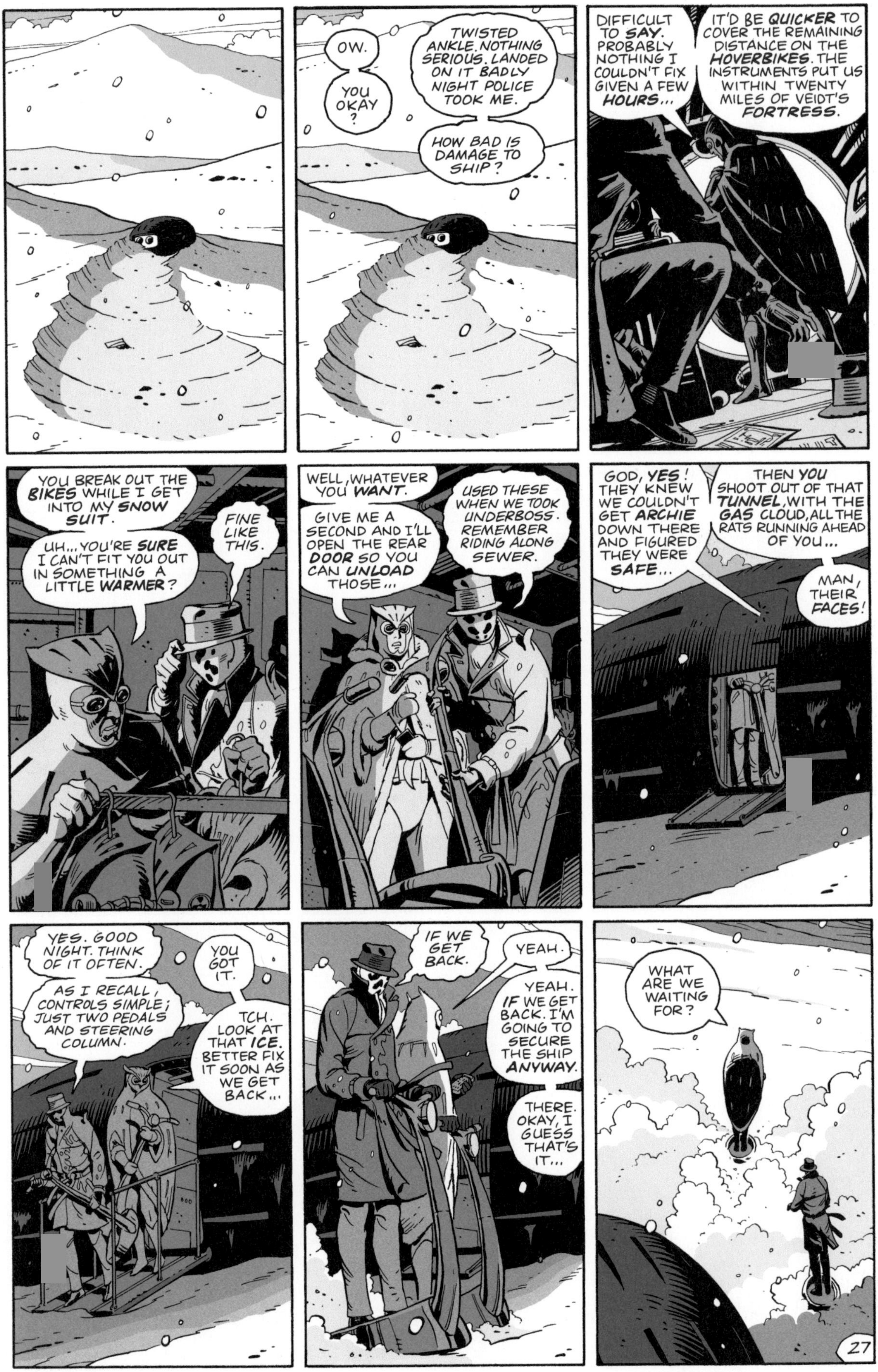
OW.
YOU OKAY?
TWISTED ANKLE. NOTHING SERIOUS. LANDED ON IT BADLY NIGHT POLICE TOOK ME.
HOW BAD IS DAMAGE TO SHIP?
DIFFICULT TO SAY. PROBABLY NOTHING I COULDN'T FIX GIVEN A FEW HOURS...
IT'D BE QUICKER TO COVER THE REMAINING DISTANCE ON THE HOVERBIKES. THE INSTRUMENTS PUT US WITHIN TWENTY MILES OF VEIDT'S FORTRESS.
YOU BREAK OUT THE BIKES WHILE I GET INTO MY SNOW SUIT.
UH... YOU'RE SURE I CAN'T FIT YOU OUT IN SOMETHING A LITTLE WARMER?
FINE LIKE THIS.
WELL, WHATEVER YOU WANT.
GIVE ME A SECOND AND I'LL OPEN THE REAR DOOR SO YOU CAN UNLOAD THOSE...
USED THESE WHEN WE TOOK UNDERBOSS. REMEMBER RIDING ALONG SEWER.
GOD, YES! THEY KNEW WE COULDN'T GET ARCHIE DOWN THERE AND FIGURED THEY WERE SAFE...
THEN YOU SHOOT OUT OF THAT TUNNEL, WITH THE GAS CLOUD, ALL THE RATS RUNNING AHEAD OF YOU...
MAN, THEIR FACES!
YES. GOOD NIGHT. THINK OF IT OFTEN.
YOU GOT IT.
AS I RECALL, CONTROLS SIMPLE; JUST TWO PEDALS AND STEERING COLUMN.
TCH. LOOK AT THAT ICE. BETTER FIX IT SOON AS WE GET BACK...
IF WE GET BACK.
YEAH.
YEAH. IF WE GET BACK. I'M GOING TO SECURE THE SHIP ANYWAY.
THERE. OKAY, I GUESS THAT'S IT...
WHAT ARE WE WAITING FOR?
27

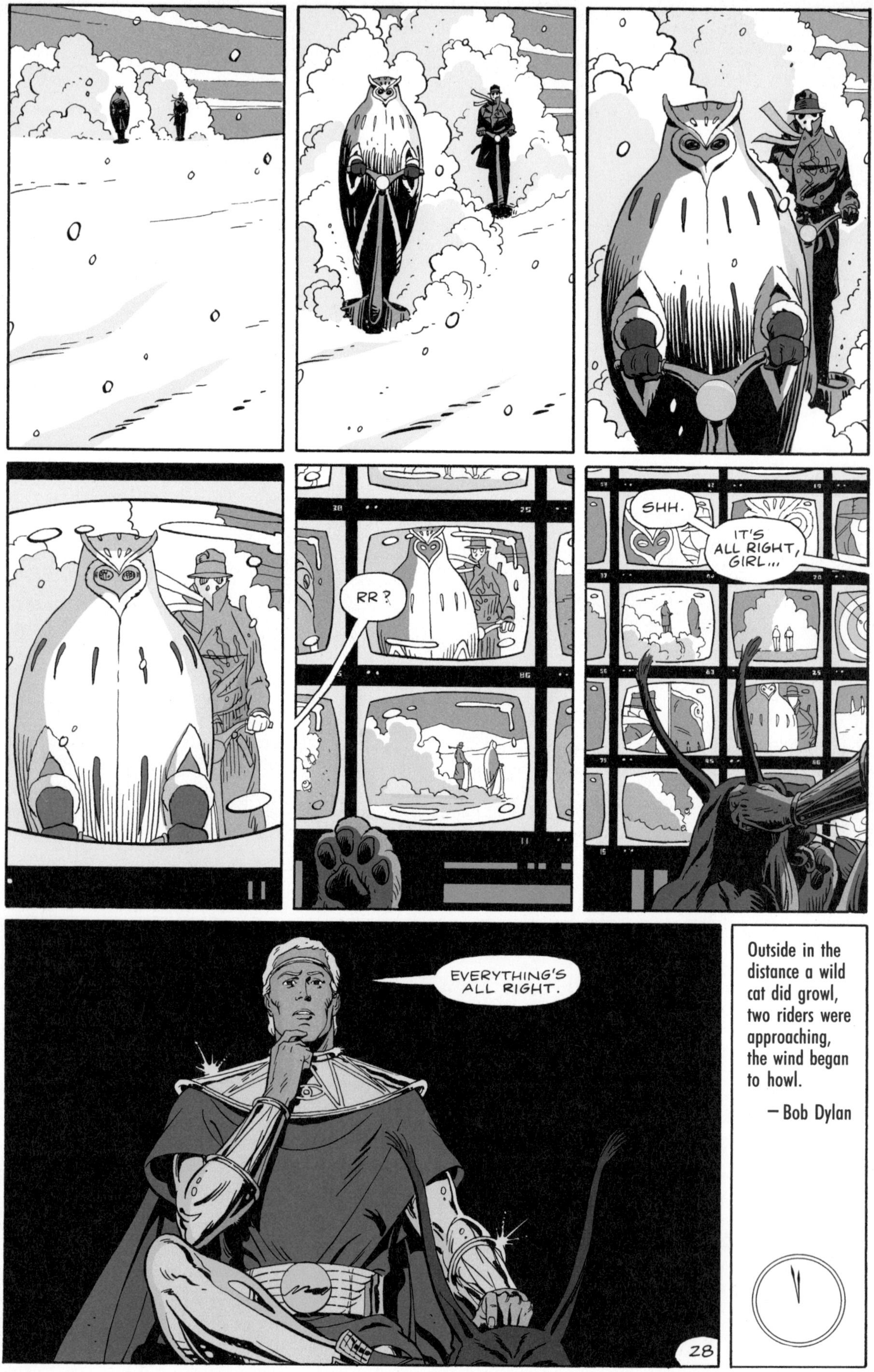
RR?
SHH.
IT'S ALL RIGHT, GIRL...
EVERYTHING'S ALL RIGHT.
28
Outside in the distance a wild cat did growl, two riders were approaching, the wind began to howl.
— Bob Dylan

day

Leo Winston
President
Marketing and Development

Dear Adrian,

Even though you vetoed an expanded range of dolls based upon former advesaries, I still feel that the Ozymandias action figure line needs to attain a higher profile on the marketplace, and that to me indicates an extended range of product. Several possibilities have ocurred to me, outlined below.

Firstly, figurines based upon Rorschach and Nite Owl seem to be viable. From a legal viewpoint, we're currently investigating the situation regarding the trademark and copyright laws. Our lawyers seem to think that since the costumed identities themselves are outlawed and illegal, there can be no legal claim to copyright upon their costumed images, leaving us free to register a copyright ourselves. This seems okay to me, but I'm advised that since you may have some personal connection with these individuals, there's a possibility that you'll feel differently.

Secondly, the Moloch figurine. Since Edgar Jacobi died recently, there may be a question of taste, but from what our lawyers can determine, Jacobi left no estate likely to oppose such a marketing move. Also, once again there can be no legal claim on Jacobi's part concerning infringement of an identitiy which is illegal in the first place.

Thirdly, and on a somewhat lighter note, I hope you will approve the inclusion of Bubastis. I know that she really didn't play any part in your exploits while you were an adventurer, but I understand that the people doing the Saturday morning Ozymandias cartoon show, scheduled for next fall, are keen that Bubastis should play a major role as a feline sidekick, making it therefore appropriate to play her up in our other merchandising.

Anyway, in anticipation of your approval concerning this expansion of the line and in the absence of any immediate legal difficulties, I had some of the boys in production put together this dummy promotional leaflet. Hope you get a kick out of it, and I'll be calling next week to discuss the "Ziggurat of Death" role playing game, so we can discuss all this then.

Best, as always,

Leo Winston

Leo Winston
Marketing and Development

26

27

28

VEIDT™
OWL SHIP™
NITE OWL™
MOLOCH THE MYSTIC™
RORSCHACH
BUBASTIS
OZYMANDIAS™

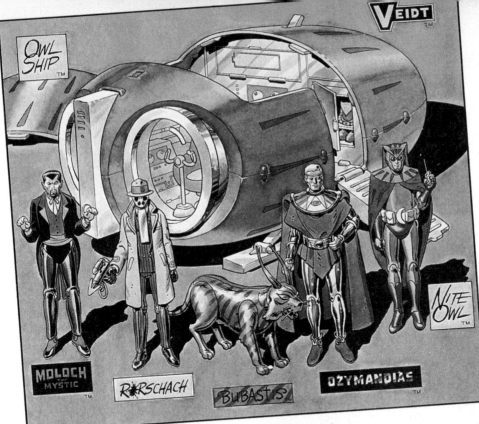

(OZ0001): Ozymandias:
This fully posable action doll, with removable cloak, tunic, and headband, is authentically molded to duplicate accurately the world-famous physique of athlete and former adventurer Adrian Veidt.

(OZ0002): Rorschach:
New Figure! Fully jointed and posable, this scale facsimile of the feared vigilante has a removable trenchcoat and hat.

(OZB001): Rorschach's Grappling Gun:
New Accessory! This scale model of the famous gas-powered grappling gun is spring loaded, and will fire a miniature hook, along with a length of line. Safe for children over five.

(OZ0003): Nite Owl:
New Figure! With removable cowl and belt, this fully posable model of the former nocturnal adventurer offers hours of exciting fun.

(OZB002): The Owlship:
New Accessory! Painstakingly assembled from existing photographs of this famous craft, our Owlship has an accessible and fully detailed cabin area, built to scale with **OZ0003.** Fully lighted cabin! Batteries not included.

(OZ0004): Moloch:
New Figure! With detachable handgun and stage magician's jacket, now you can thrill to the misdeeds of the infamous crown prince of the underworld in the safety of your own home.

(OZB003): Bubastis:
New Accessory! Fully posable, see the giant mutant Lynx of Ozymandias. Now she can help Adrian Veidt fight evil and help the innocent in *your* adventures, just like she does on TV.

Tues

Call
Laurie
75

VEIDT

Jeb –

Agree with you re: expansion of line. My study of recorded sales figures in a historical context suggests an increase in the sale of soldiers and action figures in times immediately prior to a period of anticipated war or bloodshed, and we should take advantage of this syndrome for as long as it lasts.

However, ethically very uncertain about Rorschach, Nite Owl and Moloch, plus accessories. Suggest instead we create costumed army of terrorists, introduce as main villains in Saturday cartoon, then duplicate here along with weapons, accessories and vehicles. More militaristic flavor will sell better. The American public has never really gone in for super-heroes in a big way. We'll discuss this next week.

Best,
Adrian Veidt

P.S. – Loved Bubastis. As soon as they're made, I must have one to give to her. Regards to Josephine and your children.

VEIDT Adrian Veidt
President and C.E.O.

THE VEIDT METHO

Hello. If you're reading
THAT, it's because you think you n
and magnetism? Advanced mental
we can offer you all these things
YOU! More than just a bodybuil
capable young men and women
difficult world that awaits in
understand, and if you follow i

Oh, how the ghost of you clings...
Nostalgia
by VEIDT

VEIDT Adrian Veidt
President and C.E.O.

Angela Neuberg
Director
Veidt Cosmetics & Toiletries

Dear Angela,

Enclosed you'll find a representative sample of our current magazine and billboard advertising, promoting Nostalgia.

The sexual imagery is obvious, the woman adjusting her stocking being overtly erotic, yet layered with enough romantic ambiance to avoid offense. In our choice of models for the Nostalgia ads I note that we have consistently chosen models with a slightly androgynous quality to their beauty, which I presume is to afford us a window into the gay marketplace, a tendency more pronounced in the ads for Nostalgia aftershave. This is all well and good, but it avoids the most significant element of the Nostalgia campaign:

In the soft focus imagery and romantic atmosphere, the advertisements conjure an idyllic picture of times past. It seems to me that the success of the campaign is directly linked to the state of global uncertainty that has endured for the past forty years or more. In an era of stress and anxiety, when the present seems unstable and the future unlikely, the natural response is to retreat and withdraw from reality, taking recourse either in fantasies of the future or in modified visions of a half-imagined past.

While this marketing strategy is certainly relevant and indeed successful in a context of social upheaval, I feel we must begin to take into account the fact that one way or another, such conditions cannot endure indefinitely. Simply put, the current circumstances out civilization finds itself immersed in will either lead to war, or they won't. If they lead to war, our best plans become irrelevant. If peace endures, I contend that a new surge of social optimism is likely, necessitating a new image for Veidt cosmetics, geared to a new consumer.

To this end, starting next year we will begin to phase out the Nostalgia line of ladies' and men's cosmetics, successful though they be, and replace them with a new line that better exemplifies the spirit of our anticipated target group. This new line is to be called the "Millenium" line. The imagery associated with it will be controversial and modern, projecting a vision of a technological Utopia, a whole new universe of sensations and pleasures that is just within reach.

I would like the new line to be ready for launch in the summer, and would appreciate it if some dummy ad copy and artwork could be assembled for my perusal and comment sometime before Christmas.

Anticipating your cooperation, and looking forward to working with you on this one. My fondest regards to Frank. We must have lunch soon.

Love,

Adrian Veidt

Adrian Veidt

Attached, manuscript for revised introduction updated "Veidt Method" self-improvement booklet. Please forward to relevant department.
— V.

VEIDT

Adrian Veidt
President and C.E.O.

THE VEIDT METHOD: AN INTRODUCTION

Hello. If you're reading this, it's because you sent away for my course, and if you did THAT, it's because you think you need a change in your life. A better body? Increased confidence and magnetism? Advanced mental techniques that will help you at home or in business? Well, yes, we can offer you all these things... but in order to have and enjoy them, there's got to be a new YOU! More than just a bodybuilding course, the Veidt Method is designed to produce bright and capable young men and women who will be fit to inherit the challenging, promising, and often difficult world that awaits in our future. The course is designed to be easy to read and to understand, and if you follow it through, I can assure you that you and your friends will quickly notice the results as a whole new realm of ability and experience is opened up to you. Below is a brief summary of what you can expect to find in the later chapters of this volume.

UNDERSTANDING THE SELF

Both the body and the mind are parts of a biological robot that our immaterial souls inhabit. Like any machines, they can be tuned, improved and made to run more efficiently, as long as one understands the process for doing so. Through meditation and intellectual exercise, we may come to use our minds in ways that we never thought possible. In this first chapter of our manual we will discuss lateral thinking, Zen meditation, and the power of dreaming and the subconscious, along with other useful techniques for the advancement of the mind and intellect. Though not a religion, there are powerful spiritual disciplines behind the Veidt Method that must be understood if the student is to proceed.

HEALTH AND THE BODY

In our second chapter, we explore the connection between body and mind, and learn how this helps us to conquer pain and illness without recourse to drugs and medicines. We will show you, step by step, a number of techniques for focusing the mind's healing power upon any ailing part of the body. In relation to this, we also examine how the actions of the body can be used to aid and focus the mind, taking into account Yogic doctrines and martial training.

CREATING A NEW YOU

Our third and longest chapter presents a carefully coordinated series of physical and

intellectual exercise systems which, if followed correctly, can turn YOU into a superhuman, fully in charge of your own destiny. All that is required is the desire for perfection and the will to achieve it. No special equipment or other hidden cash extras are necessary. The Veidt Method paves the way for a bright and hopeful future in which anyone can be a hero.

YOU AND THE WORLD

Just as you are a whole organic being, complete unto yourself, so are you also part of a larger social organism consisting of the people around you, the people you work with, and ultimately the whole world. When you yourself are strong and healthy in mind and body, you will want to react in a healthy and positive way to the world around you, changing it for the better if you are able, and improving the lot of both yourself and your fellow man. Our final chapter will help you to understand the organism that is the world, and your part in it. You will learn that one can either surrender responsibility for one's actions to the rest of the social organism, to be pulled this way and that by society's predominating tensions, or that one can take control by flexing the muscles of the will common to us all, affecting our environment positively and responsibly.

So, in conclusion, welcome to the Veidt Method for physical fitness and self-improvement, a step by step guide to realizing exciting potentials latent within every one of us. I hope that you'll be intrigued by what you find within, and I know that if you persevere you'll walk away from this book a different person.

There's a bright new world just around the corner. It's going to need heroes just as badly as this one does, and one of them could be YOU!

All best wishes and encouragement,

Adrian Veidt

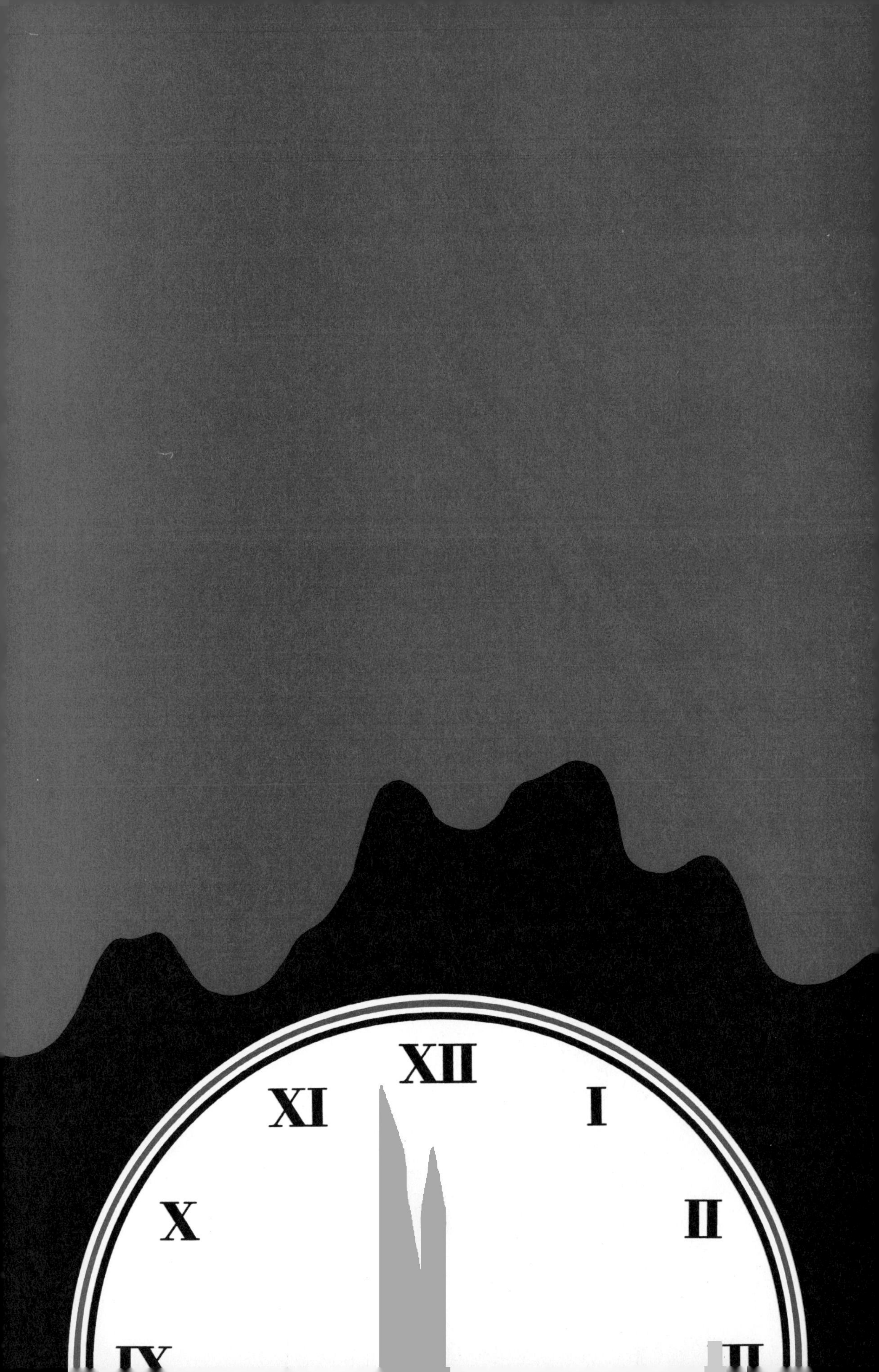

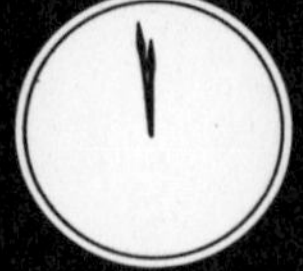

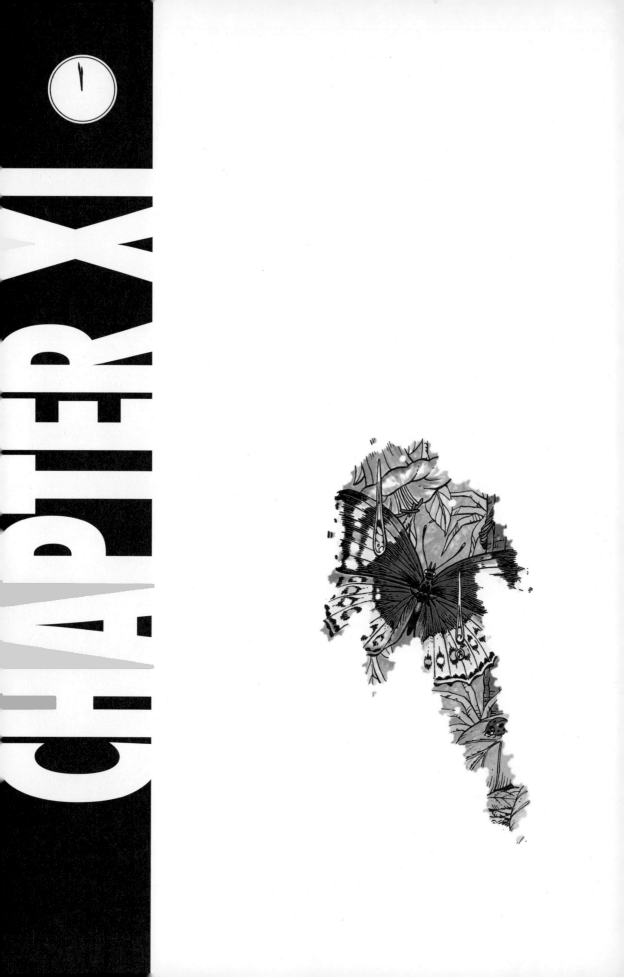

CHAPTER XI

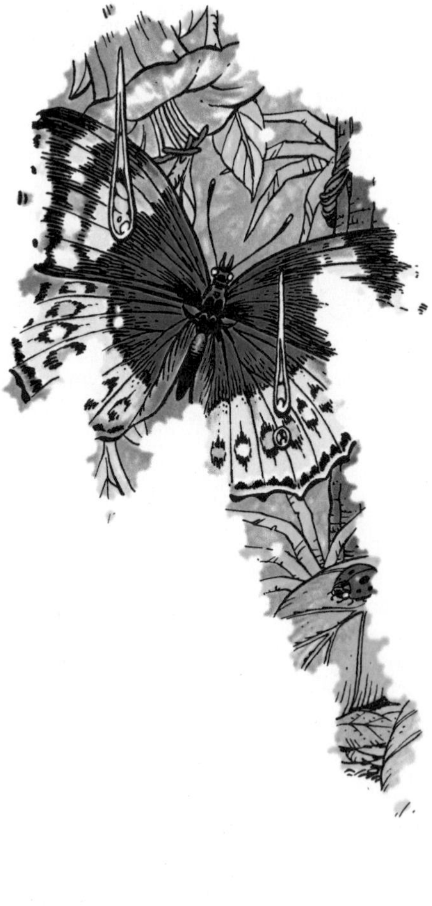

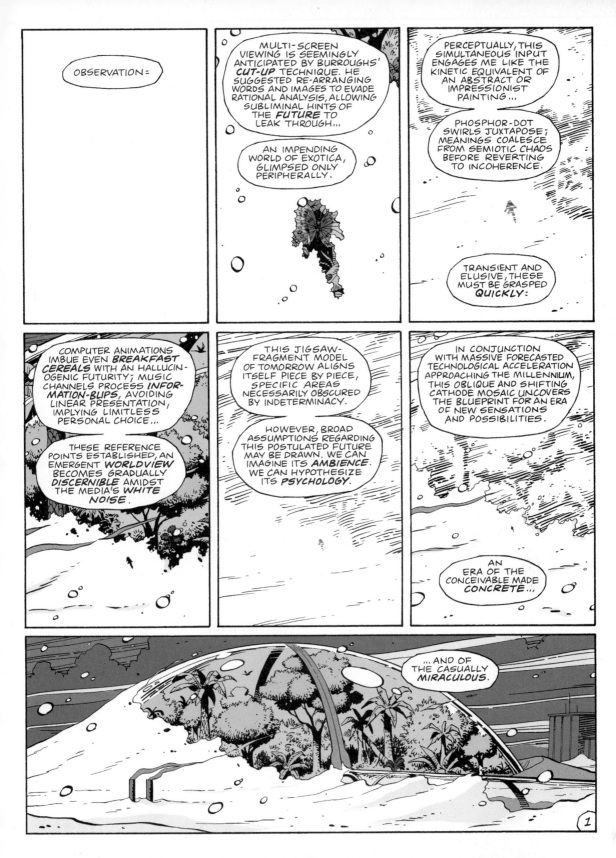

OBSERVATION=

MULTI-SCREEN VIEWING IS SEEMINGLY ANTICIPATED BY BURROUGHS' *CUT-UP* TECHNIQUE. HE SUGGESTED RE-ARRANGING WORDS AND IMAGES TO EVADE RATIONAL ANALYSIS, ALLOWING SUBLIMINAL HINTS OF THE *FUTURE* TO LEAK THROUGH...

AN IMPENDING WORLD OF EXOTICA, GLIMPSED ONLY PERIPHERALLY.

PERCEPTUALLY, THIS SIMULTANEOUS INPUT ENGAGES ME LIKE THE KINETIC EQUIVALENT OF AN ABSTRACT OR IMPRESSIONIST PAINTING...

PHOSPHOR-DOT SWIRLS JUXTAPOSE; MEANINGS COALESCE FROM SEMIOTIC CHAOS BEFORE REVERTING TO INCOHERENCE.

TRANSIENT AND ELUSIVE, THESE MUST BE GRASPED *QUICKLY*:

COMPUTER ANIMATIONS IMBUE EVEN *BREAKFAST CEREALS* WITH AN HALLUCIN-OGENIC FUTURITY; MUSIC CHANNELS PROCESS *INFOR-MATION-BLIPS*, AVOIDING LINEAR PRESENTATION, IMPLYING LIMITLESS PERSONAL CHOICE...

THESE REFERENCE POINTS ESTABLISHED, AN EMERGENT *WORLDVIEW* BECOMES GRADUALLY *DISCERNIBLE* AMIDST THE MEDIA'S *WHITE NOISE*.

THIS JIGSAW-FRAGMENT MODEL OF TOMORROW ALIGNS ITSELF PIECE BY PIECE, SPECIFIC AREAS NECESSARILY OBSCURED BY INDETERMINACY.

HOWEVER, BROAD ASSUMPTIONS REGARDING THIS POSTULATED FUTURE MAY BE DRAWN. WE CAN IMAGINE ITS *AMBIENCE*. WE CAN HYPOTHESIZE ITS *PSYCHOLOGY*.

IN CONJUNCTION WITH MASSIVE FORECASTED TECHNOLOGICAL ACCELERATION APPROACHING THE MILLENNIUM, THIS OBLIQUE AND SHIFTING CATHODE MOSAIC UNCOVERS THE BLUEPRINT FOR AN ERA OF NEW SENSATIONS AND POSSIBILITIES.

AN ERA OF THE CONCEIVABLE MADE *CONCRETE*...

...AND OF THE CASUALLY *MIRACULOUS*.

LOOK ON MY WORKS, YE MIGHTY...

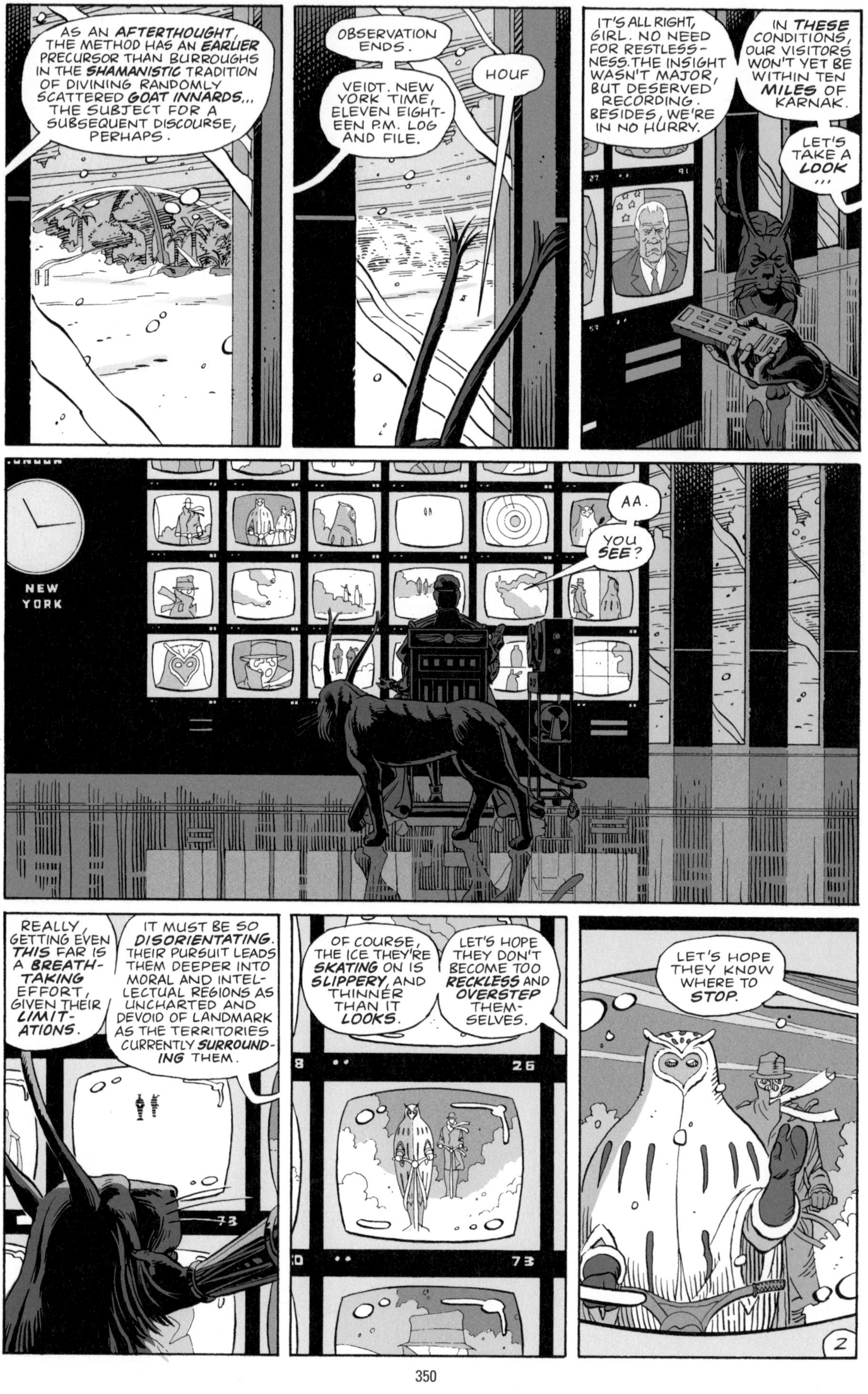

AS AN AFTERTHOUGHT, THE METHOD HAS AN EARLIER PRECURSOR THAN BURROUGHS IN THE SHAMANISTIC TRADITION OF DIVINING RANDOMLY SCATTERED GOAT INNARDS... THE SUBJECT FOR A SUBSEQUENT DISCOURSE, PERHAPS.
OBSERVATION ENDS.
VEIDT. NEW YORK TIME, ELEVEN EIGHTEEN P.M. LOG AND FILE.
HOUF
IT'S ALL RIGHT, GIRL. NO NEED FOR RESTLESSNESS. THE INSIGHT WASN'T MAJOR, BUT DESERVED RECORDING. BESIDES, WE'RE IN NO HURRY.
IN THESE CONDITIONS, OUR VISITORS WON'T YET BE WITHIN TEN MILES OF KARNAK.
LET'S TAKE A LOOK...
NEW YORK
AA.
YOU SEE?
REALLY, GETTING EVEN THIS FAR IS A BREATHTAKING EFFORT, GIVEN THEIR LIMITATIONS.
IT MUST BE SO DISORIENTATING. THEIR PURSUIT LEADS THEM DEEPER INTO MORAL AND INTELLECTUAL REGIONS AS UNCHARTED AND DEVOID OF LANDMARK AS THE TERRITORIES CURRENTLY SURROUNDING THEM.
OF COURSE, THE ICE THEY'RE SKATING ON IS SLIPPERY, AND THINNER THAN IT LOOKS.
LET'S HOPE THEY DON'T BECOME TOO RECKLESS AND OVERSTEP THEMSELVES.
LET'S HOPE THEY KNOW WHERE TO STOP.
2

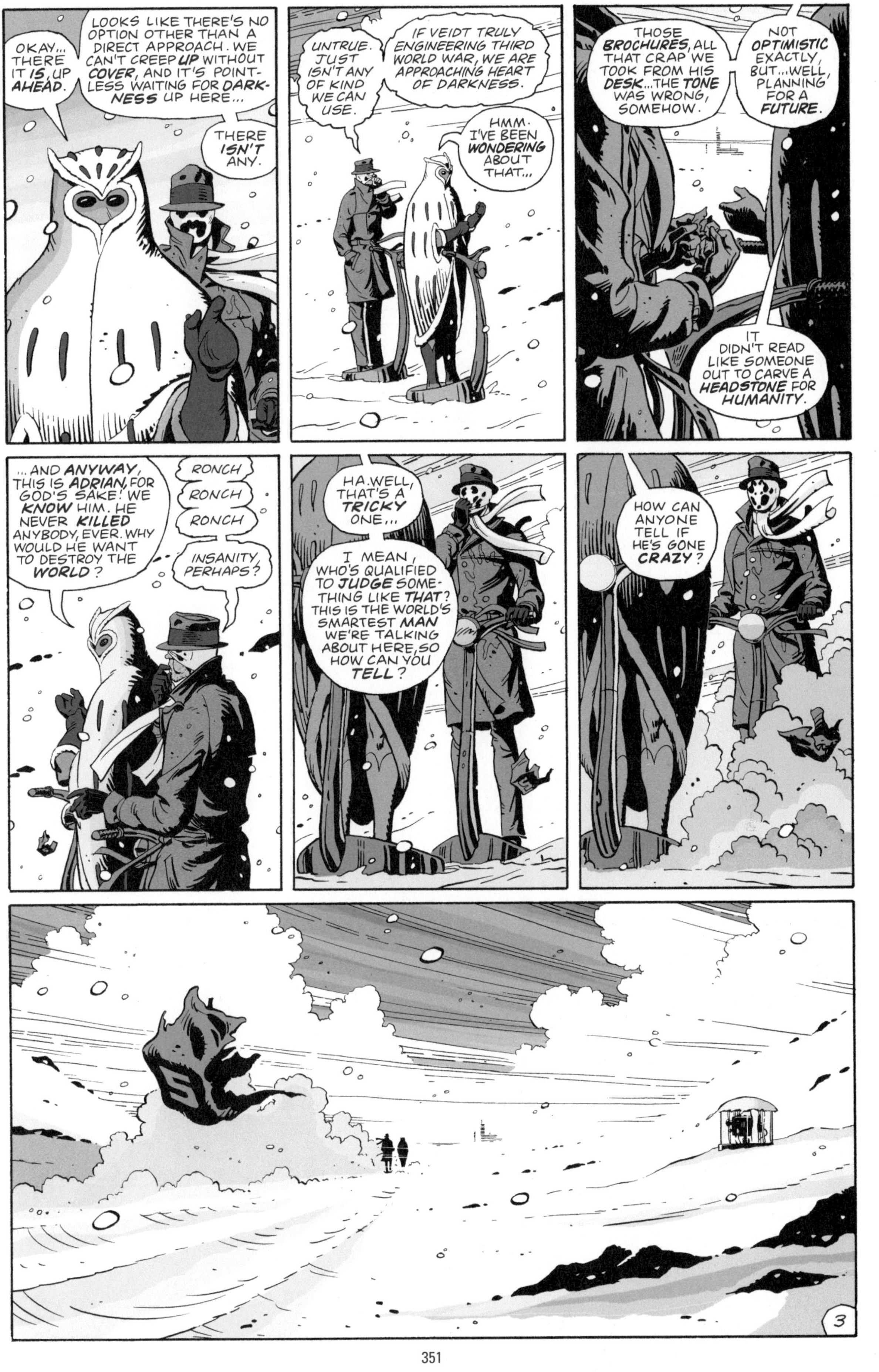
OKAY... THERE IT IS, UP AHEAD.
LOOKS LIKE THERE'S NO OPTION OTHER THAN A DIRECT APPROACH. WE CAN'T CREEP UP WITHOUT COVER, AND IT'S POINTLESS WAITING FOR DARKNESS UP HERE...
THERE ISN'T ANY.
UNTRUE. JUST ISN'T ANY OF KIND WE CAN USE.
IF VEIDT TRULY ENGINEERING THIRD WORLD WAR, WE ARE APPROACHING HEART OF DARKNESS.
HMM. I'VE BEEN WONDERING ABOUT THAT...
THOSE BROCHURES, ALL THAT CRAP WE TOOK FROM HIS DESK... THE TONE WAS WRONG, SOMEHOW.
NOT OPTIMISTIC EXACTLY, BUT... WELL, PLANNING FOR A FUTURE.
IT DIDN'T READ LIKE SOMEONE OUT TO CARVE A HEADSTONE FOR HUMANITY.
...AND ANYWAY, THIS IS ADRIAN, FOR GOD'S SAKE! WE KNOW HIM. HE NEVER KILLED ANYBODY, EVER. WHY WOULD HE WANT TO DESTROY THE WORLD?
RONCH
RONCH
RONCH
INSANITY, PERHAPS?
HA. WELL, THAT'S A TRICKY ONE...
I MEAN, WHO'S QUALIFIED TO JUDGE SOMETHING LIKE THAT? THIS IS THE WORLD'S SMARTEST MAN WE'RE TALKING ABOUT HERE, SO HOW CAN YOU TELL?
HOW CAN ANYONE TELL IF HE'S GONE CRAZY?
3

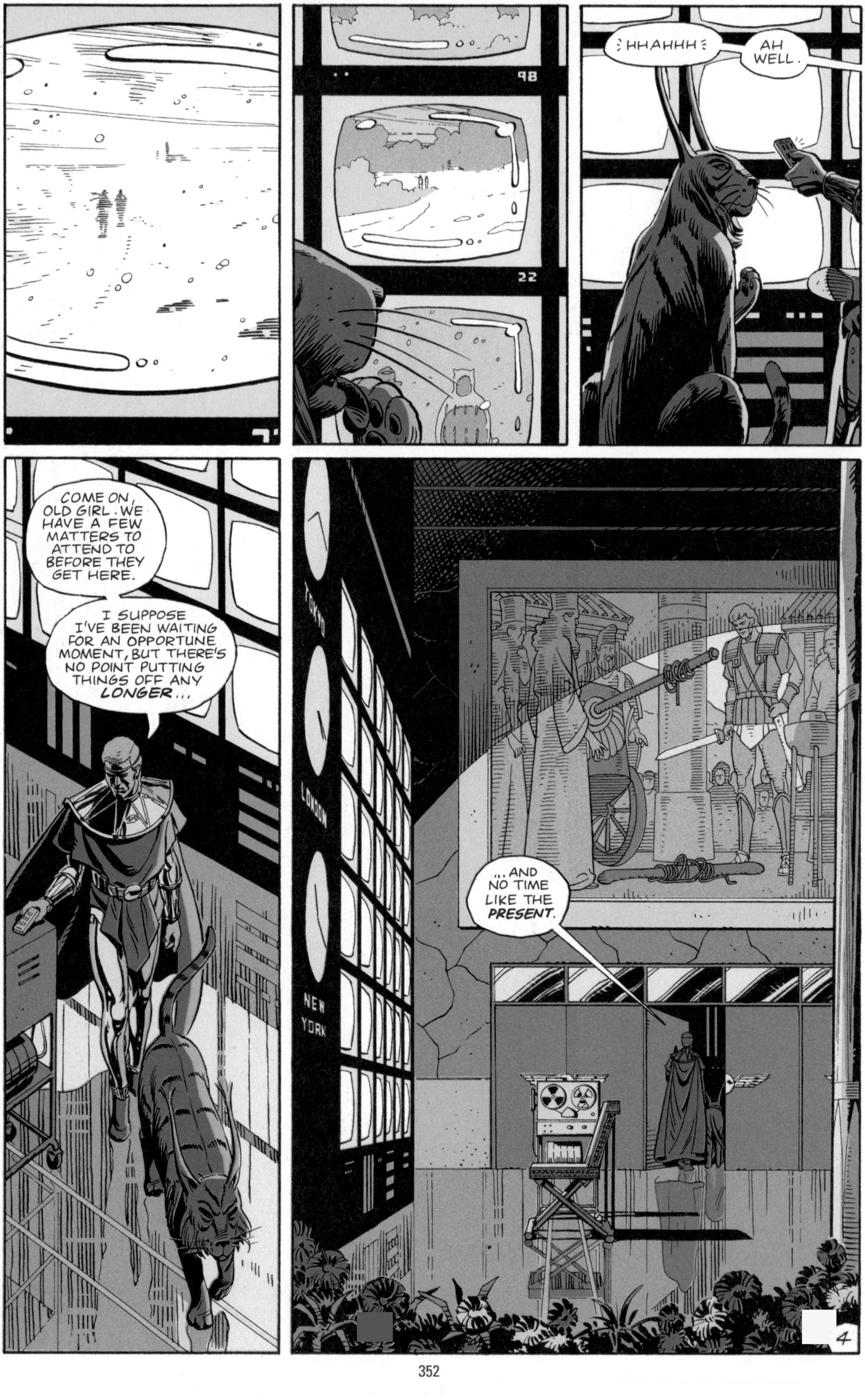

98
22
HHAHHH
AH WELL.
COME ON, OLD GIRL. WE HAVE A FEW MATTERS TO ATTEND TO BEFORE THEY GET HERE.
I SUPPOSE I'VE BEEN WAITING FOR AN OPPORTUNE MOMENT, BUT THERE'S NO POINT PUTTING THINGS OFF ANY **LONGER**...
TOKYO
LONDON
NEW YORK
...AND NO TIME LIKE THE **PRESENT**.
4

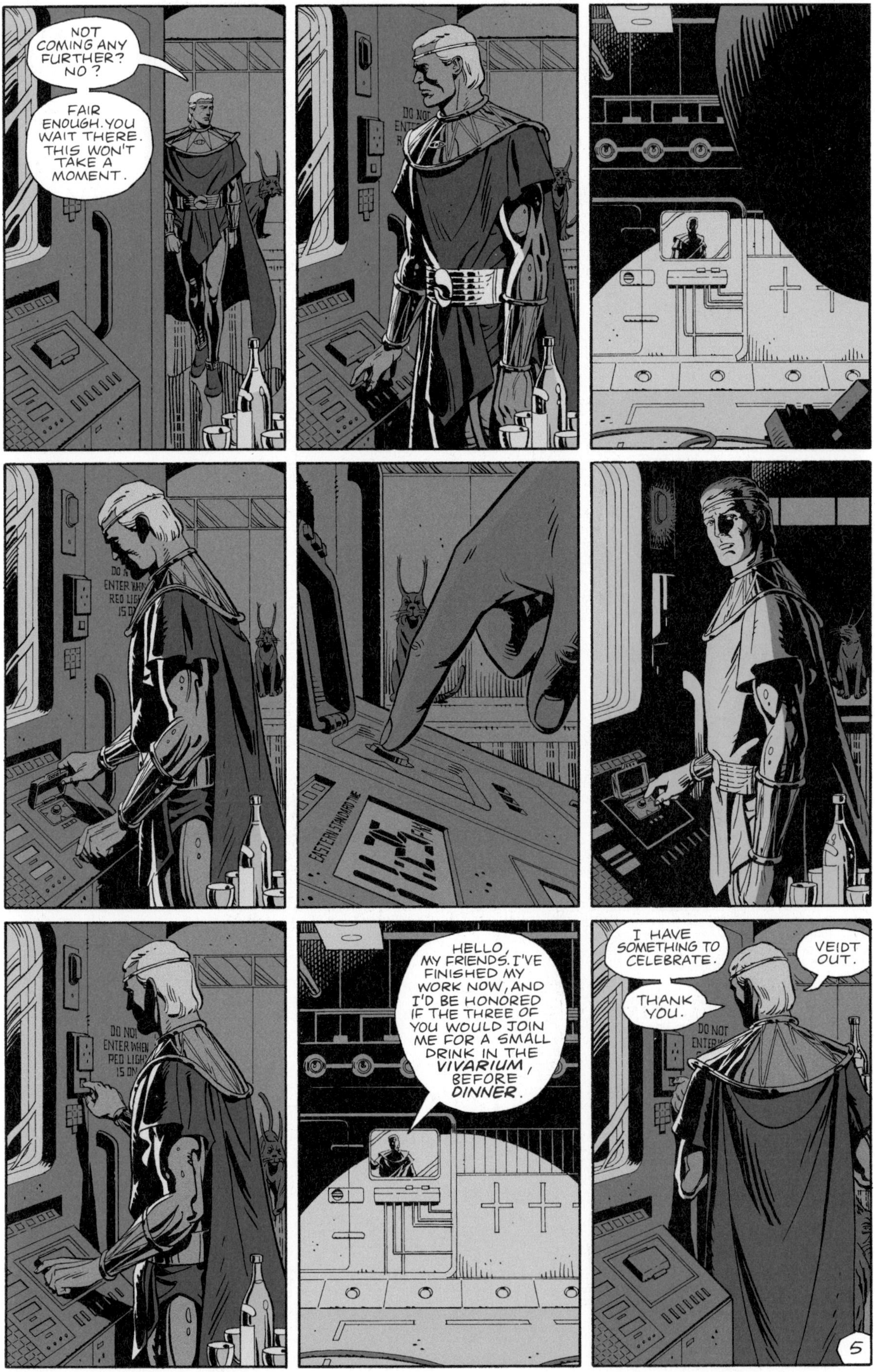
NOT COMING ANY FURTHER? NO?
FAIR ENOUGH. YOU WAIT THERE. THIS WON'T TAKE A MOMENT.
EASTERN STANDARD TIME
DO NOT ENTER WHEN RED LIGHT IS ON
HELLO, MY FRIENDS. I'VE FINISHED MY WORK NOW, AND I'D BE HONORED IF THE THREE OF YOU WOULD JOIN ME FOR A SMALL DRINK IN THE VIVARIUM, BEFORE DINNER.
I HAVE SOMETHING TO CELEBRATE.
THANK YOU.
VEIDT OUT.
5

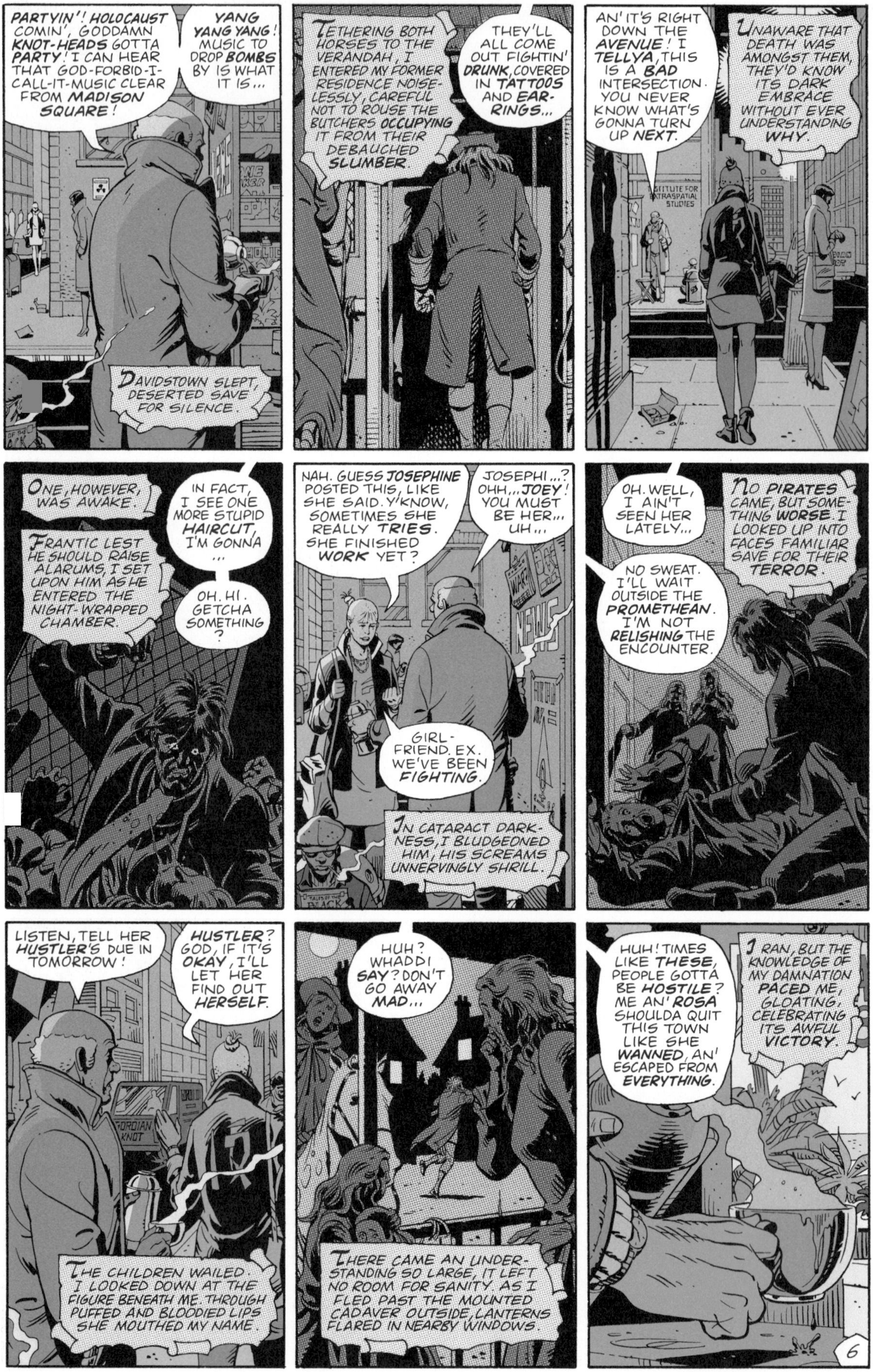
PARTYIN'! HOLOCAUST COMIN', GODDAMN KNOT-HEADS GOTTA PARTY! I CAN HEAR THAT GOD-FORBID-I-CALL-IT-MUSIC CLEAR FROM MADISON SQUARE!
YANG YANG YANG! MUSIC TO DROP BOMBS BY IS WHAT IT IS...
DAVIDSTOWN SLEPT, DESERTED SAVE FOR SILENCE.
TETHERING BOTH HORSES TO THE VERANDAH, I ENTERED MY FORMER RESIDENCE NOISELESSLY, CAREFUL NOT TO ROUSE THE BUTCHERS OCCUPYING IT FROM THEIR DEBAUCHED SLUMBER.
THEY'LL ALL COME OUT FIGHTIN' DRUNK, COVERED IN TATTOOS AND EARRINGS...
AN' IT'S RIGHT DOWN THE AVENUE! I TELLYA, THIS IS A BAD INTERSECTION. YOU NEVER KNOW WHAT'S GONNA TURN UP NEXT.
UNAWARE THAT DEATH WAS AMONGST THEM, THEY'D KNOW ITS DARK EMBRACE WITHOUT EVER UNDERSTANDING WHY.
EXTRASPATIAL STUDIES
ONE, HOWEVER, WAS AWAKE.
IN FACT, I SEE ONE MORE STUPID HAIRCUT, I'M GONNA ...
FRANTIC LEST HE SHOULD RAISE ALARUMS, I SET UPON HIM AS HE ENTERED THE NIGHT-WRAPPED CHAMBER.
OH. HI. GETCHA SOMETHING?
NAH. GUESS JOSEPHINE POSTED THIS, LIKE SHE SAID. Y'KNOW, SOMETIMES SHE REALLY TRIES. SHE FINISHED WORK YET?
JOSEPHI...? OHH,...JOEY! YOU MUST BE HER... UH...
GIRLFRIEND. EX. WE'VE BEEN FIGHTING.
IN CATARACT DARKNESS, I BLUDGEONED HIM, HIS SCREAMS UNNERVINGLY SHRILL.
OH. WELL, I AIN'T SEEN HER LATELY...
NO PIRATES CAME, BUT SOMETHING WORSE. I LOOKED UP INTO FACES FAMILIAR SAVE FOR THEIR TERROR.
NO SWEAT. I'LL WAIT OUTSIDE THE PROMETHEAN. I'M NOT RELISHING THE ENCOUNTER.
LISTEN, TELL HER HUSTLER'S DUE IN TOMORROW!
HUSTLER? GOD, IF IT'S OKAY, I'LL LET HER FIND OUT HERSELF.
GORDIAN KNOT
THE CHILDREN WAILED. I LOOKED DOWN AT THE FIGURE BENEATH ME. THROUGH PUFFED AND BLOODIED LIPS SHE MOUTHED MY NAME.
HUH? WHADDI SAY? DON'T GO AWAY MAD...
THERE CAME AN UNDERSTANDING SO LARGE, IT LEFT NO ROOM FOR SANITY AS I FLED PAST THE MOUNTED CADAVER OUTSIDE, LANTERNS FLARED IN NEARBY WINDOWS.
HUH! TIMES LIKE THESE, PEOPLE GOTTA BE HOSTILE? ME AN' ROSA SHOULDA QUIT THIS TOWN LIKE SHE WANNED, AN' ESCAPED FROM EVERYTHING.
I RAN, BUT THE KNOWLEDGE OF MY DAMNATION PACED ME, GLOATING, CELEBRATING ITS AWFUL VICTORY.
6

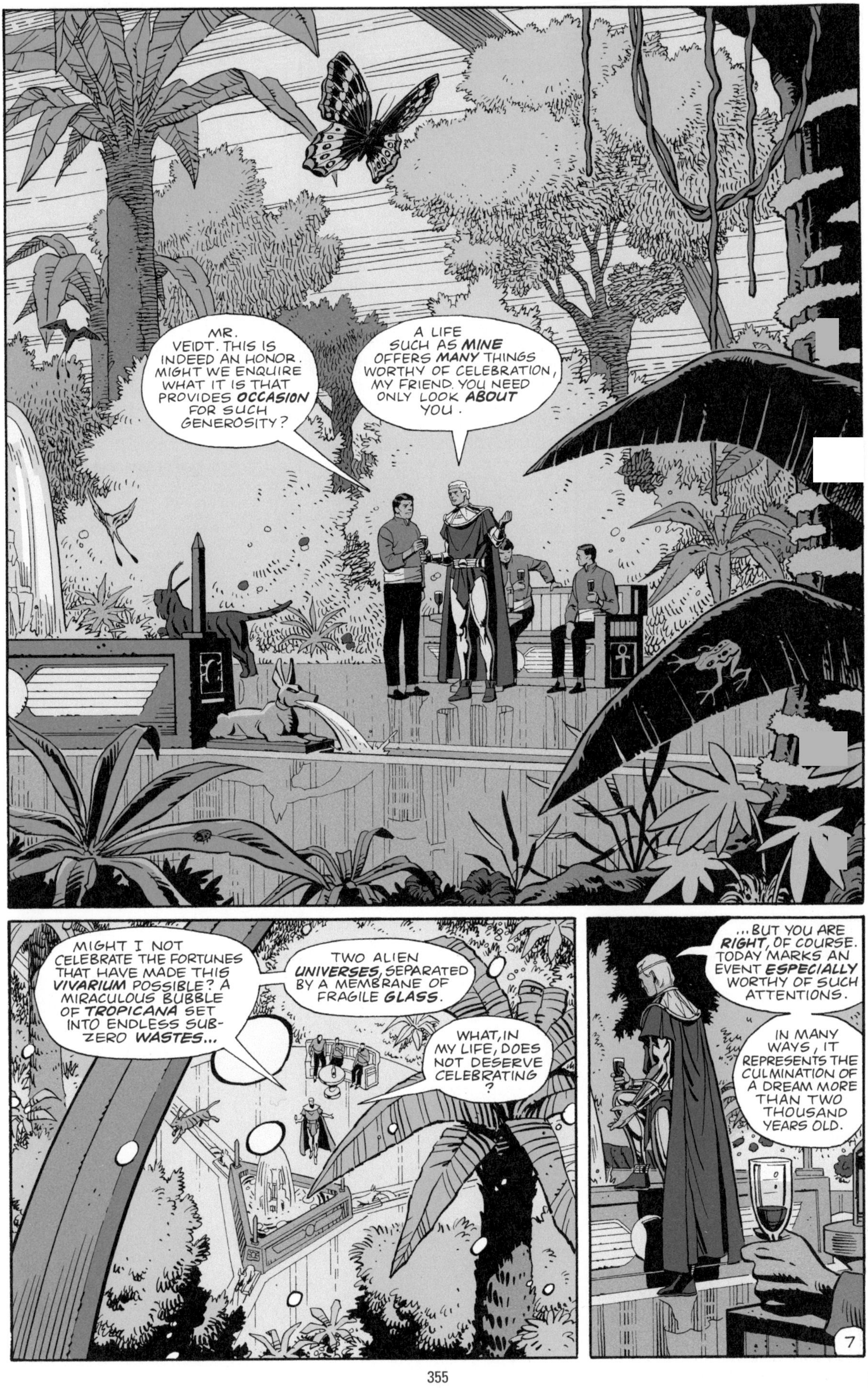
MR. VEIDT. THIS IS INDEED AN HONOR. MIGHT WE ENQUIRE WHAT IT IS THAT PROVIDES OCCASION FOR SUCH GENEROSITY?
A LIFE SUCH AS MINE OFFERS MANY THINGS WORTHY OF CELEBRATION, MY FRIEND. YOU NEED ONLY LOOK ABOUT YOU.
MIGHT I NOT CELEBRATE THE FORTUNES THAT HAVE MADE THIS VIVARIUM POSSIBLE? A MIRACULOUS BUBBLE OF TROPICANA SET INTO ENDLESS SUB-ZERO WASTES...
TWO ALIEN UNIVERSES, SEPARATED BY A MEMBRANE OF FRAGILE GLASS.
WHAT, IN MY LIFE, DOES NOT DESERVE CELEBRATING?
...BUT YOU ARE RIGHT, OF COURSE. TODAY MARKS AN EVENT ESPECIALLY WORTHY OF SUCH ATTENTIONS.
IN MANY WAYS, IT REPRESENTS THE CULMINATION OF A DREAM MORE THAN TWO THOUSAND YEARS OLD.
7

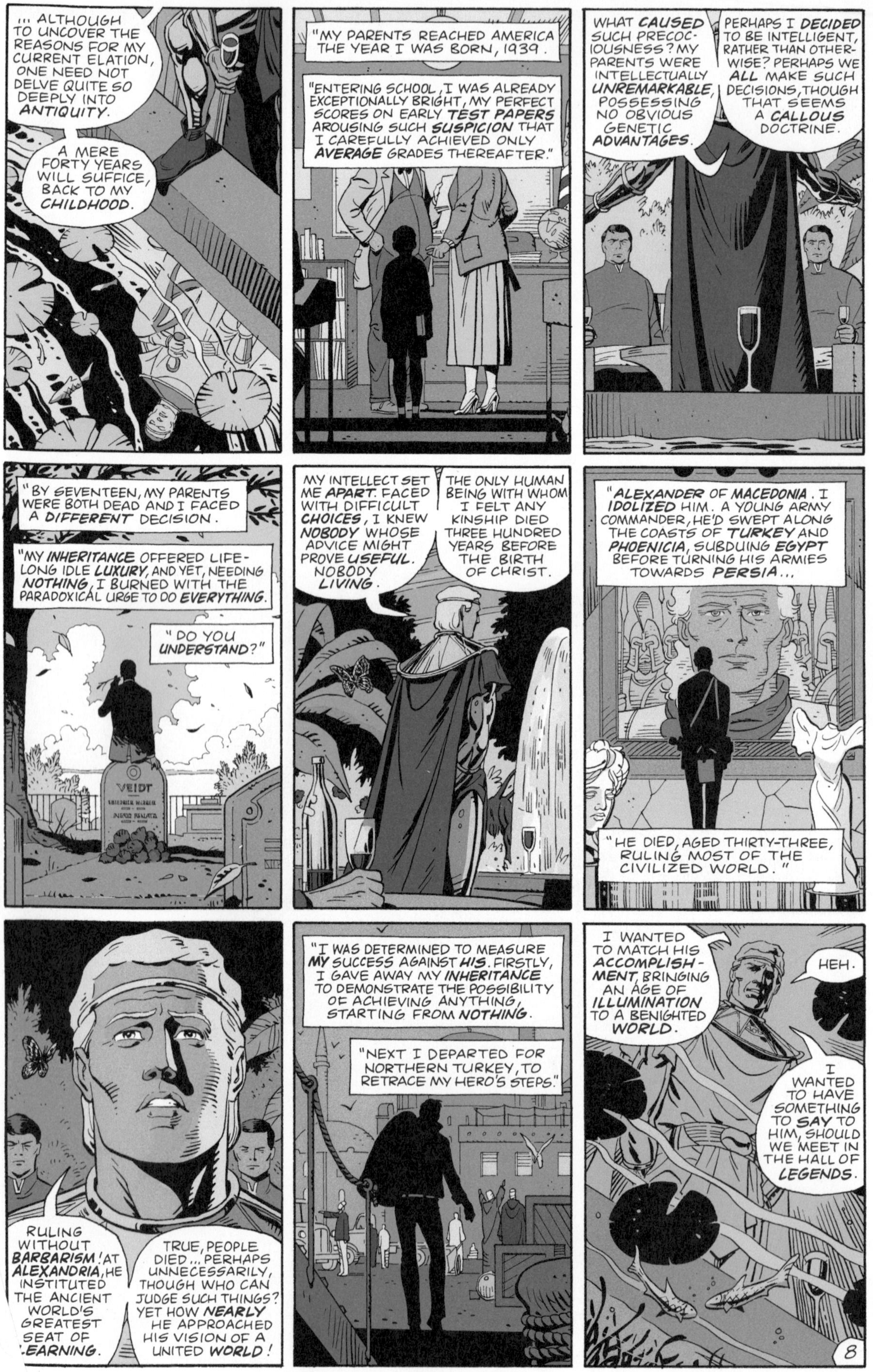
... ALTHOUGH TO UNCOVER THE REASONS FOR MY CURRENT ELATION, ONE NEED NOT DELVE QUITE SO DEEPLY INTO ANTIQUITY.
A MERE FORTY YEARS WILL SUFFICE, BACK TO MY CHILDHOOD.
"MY PARENTS REACHED AMERICA THE YEAR I WAS BORN, 1939.
"ENTERING SCHOOL, I WAS ALREADY EXCEPTIONALLY BRIGHT, MY PERFECT SCORES ON EARLY TEST PAPERS AROUSING SUCH SUSPICION THAT I CAREFULLY ACHIEVED ONLY AVERAGE GRADES THEREAFTER."
WHAT CAUSED SUCH PRECOCIOUSNESS? MY PARENTS WERE INTELLECTUALLY UNREMARKABLE, POSSESSING NO OBVIOUS GENETIC ADVANTAGES.
PERHAPS I DECIDED TO BE INTELLIGENT, RATHER THAN OTHERWISE? PERHAPS WE ALL MAKE SUCH DECISIONS, THOUGH THAT SEEMS A CALLOUS DOCTRINE.
"BY SEVENTEEN, MY PARENTS WERE BOTH DEAD AND I FACED A DIFFERENT DECISION.
"MY INHERITANCE OFFERED LIFE-LONG IDLE LUXURY, AND YET, NEEDING NOTHING, I BURNED WITH THE PARADOXICAL URGE TO DO EVERYTHING.
"DO YOU UNDERSTAND?"
VEIDT
MY INTELLECT SET ME APART. FACED WITH DIFFICULT CHOICES, I KNEW NOBODY WHOSE ADVICE MIGHT PROVE USEFUL. NOBODY LIVING.
THE ONLY HUMAN BEING WITH WHOM I FELT ANY KINSHIP DIED THREE HUNDRED YEARS BEFORE THE BIRTH OF CHRIST.
"ALEXANDER OF MACEDONIA. I IDOLIZED HIM. A YOUNG ARMY COMMANDER, HE'D SWEPT ALONG THE COASTS OF TURKEY AND PHOENICIA, SUBDUING EGYPT BEFORE TURNING HIS ARMIES TOWARDS PERSIA...
"HE DIED, AGED THIRTY-THREE, RULING MOST OF THE CIVILIZED WORLD."
RULING WITHOUT BARBARISM! AT ALEXANDRIA, HE INSTITUTED THE ANCIENT WORLD'S GREATEST SEAT OF LEARNING.
TRUE, PEOPLE DIED... PERHAPS UNNECESSARILY, THOUGH WHO CAN JUDGE SUCH THINGS? YET HOW NEARLY HE APPROACHED HIS VISION OF A UNITED WORLD!
"I WAS DETERMINED TO MEASURE MY SUCCESS AGAINST HIS. FIRSTLY, I GAVE AWAY MY INHERITANCE TO DEMONSTRATE THE POSSIBILITY OF ACHIEVING ANYTHING, STARTING FROM NOTHING.
"NEXT I DEPARTED FOR NORTHERN TURKEY, TO RETRACE MY HERO'S STEPS."
I WANTED TO MATCH HIS ACCOMPLISHMENT, BRINGING AN AGE OF ILLUMINATION TO A BENIGHTED WORLD.
HEH.
I WANTED TO HAVE SOMETHING TO SAY TO HIM, SHOULD WE MEET IN THE HALL OF LEGENDS.
8

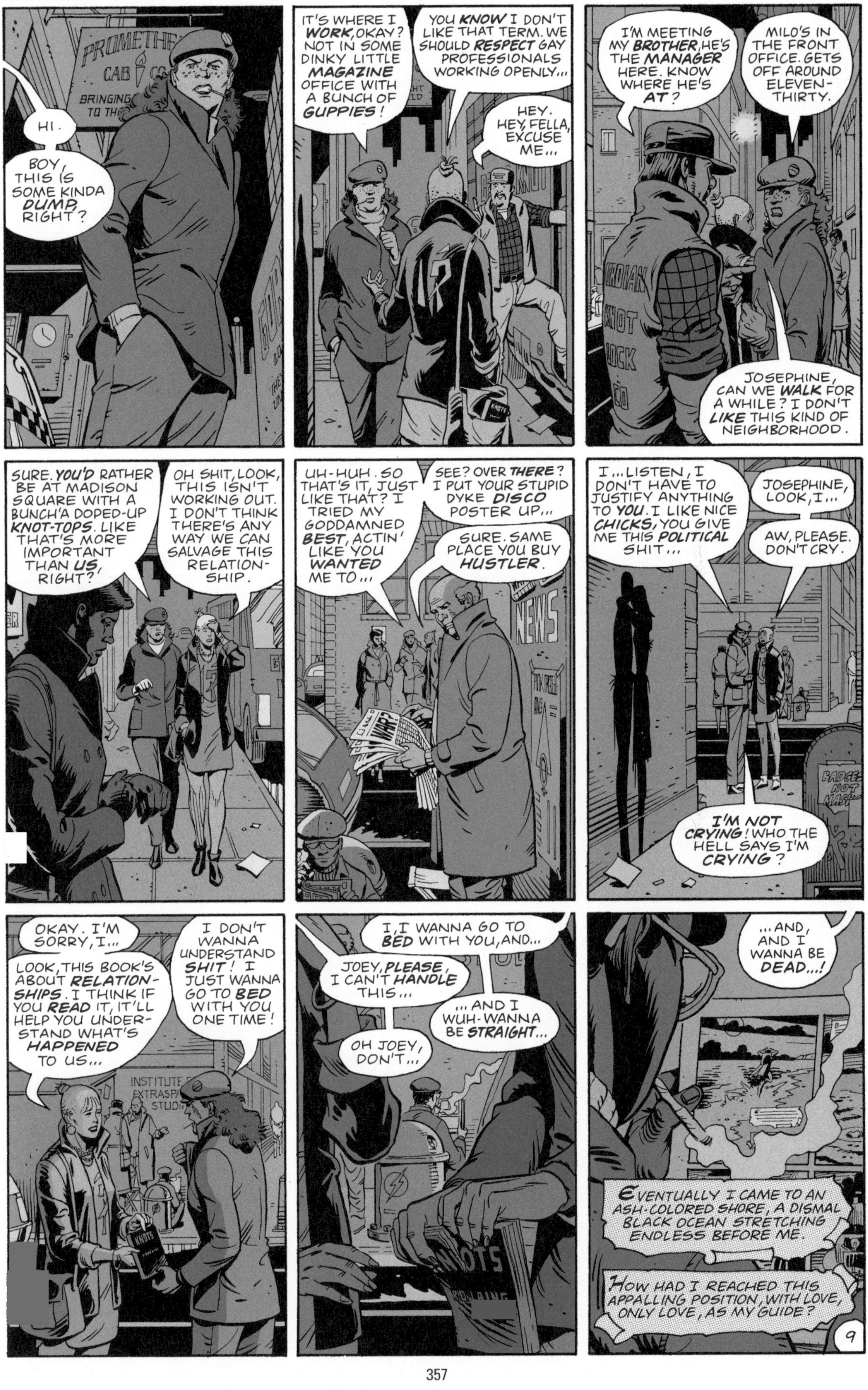
HI.
BOY, THIS IS SOME KINDA DUMP, RIGHT?
IT'S WHERE I WORK, OKAY? NOT IN SOME DINKY LITTLE MAGAZINE OFFICE WITH A BUNCH OF GUPPIES!
YOU KNOW I DON'T LIKE THAT TERM. WE SHOULD RESPECT GAY PROFESSIONALS WORKING OPENLY...
HEY. HEY, FELLA, EXCUSE ME...
I'M MEETING MY BROTHER, HE'S THE MANAGER HERE. KNOW WHERE HE'S AT?
MILO'S IN THE FRONT OFFICE. GETS OFF AROUND ELEVEN-THIRTY.
JOSEPHINE, CAN WE WALK FOR A WHILE? I DON'T LIKE THIS KIND OF NEIGHBORHOOD.
SURE. YOU'D RATHER BE AT MADISON SQUARE WITH A BUNCH'A DOPED-UP KNOT-TOPS. LIKE THAT'S MORE IMPORTANT THAN US, RIGHT?
OH SHIT, LOOK, THIS ISN'T WORKING OUT. I DON'T THINK THERE'S ANY WAY WE CAN SALVAGE THIS RELATION-SHIP.
UH-HUH. SO THAT'S IT, JUST LIKE THAT? I TRIED MY GODDAMNED BEST, ACTIN' LIKE YOU WANTED ME TO...
SEE? OVER THERE? I PUT YOUR STUPID DYKE DISCO POSTER UP...
SURE. SAME PLACE YOU BUY HUSTLER.
NEWS
I... LISTEN, I DON'T HAVE TO JUSTIFY ANYTHING TO YOU. I LIKE NICE CHICKS, YOU GIVE ME THIS POLITICAL SHIT...
JOSEPHINE, LOOK, I...
AW, PLEASE. DON'T CRY.
I'M NOT CRYING! WHO THE HELL SAYS I'M CRYING?
OKAY. I'M SORRY, I...
LOOK, THIS BOOK'S ABOUT RELATION-SHIPS. I THINK IF YOU READ IT, IT'LL HELP YOU UNDER-STAND WHAT'S HAPPENED TO US...
I DON'T WANNA UNDERSTAND SHIT! I JUST WANNA GO TO BED WITH YOU ONE TIME!
KNOTS
I, I WANNA GO TO BED WITH YOU, AND...
JOEY, PLEASE, I CAN'T HANDLE THIS...
...AND I WUH-WANNA BE STRAIGHT...
OH JOEY, DON'T...
...AND, AND I WANNA BE DEAD...!
EVENTUALLY I CAME TO AN ASH-COLORED SHORE, A DISMAL BLACK OCEAN STRETCHING ENDLESS BEFORE ME.
HOW HAD I REACHED THIS APPALLING POSITION, WITH LOVE, ONLY LOVE, AS MY GUIDE?
9

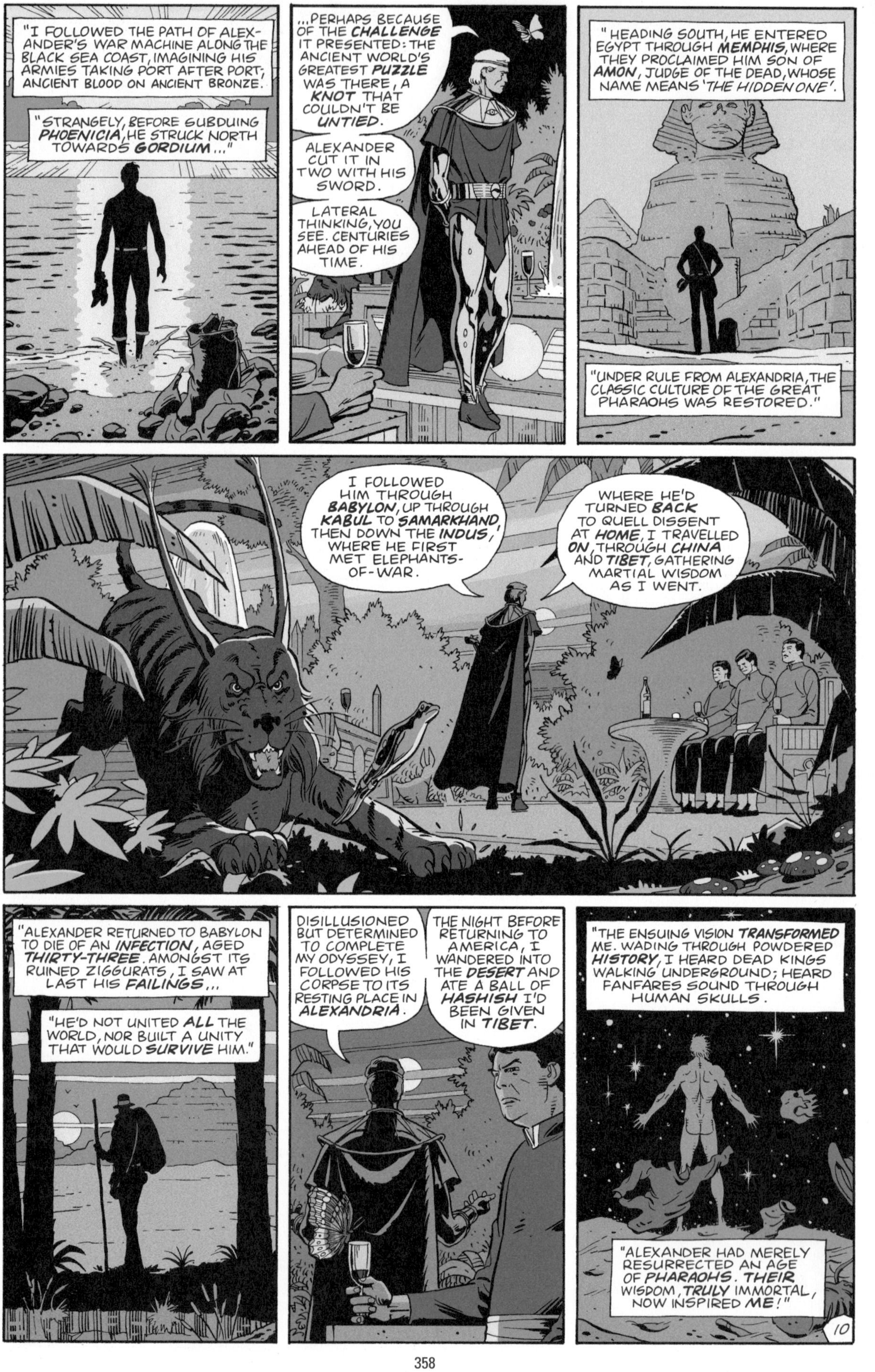
"I FOLLOWED THE PATH OF ALEXANDER'S WAR MACHINE ALONG THE BLACK SEA COAST, IMAGINING HIS ARMIES TAKING PORT AFTER PORT; ANCIENT BLOOD ON ANCIENT BRONZE.
"STRANGELY, BEFORE SUBDUING PHOENICIA, HE STRUCK NORTH TOWARDS GORDIUM..."
...PERHAPS BECAUSE OF THE CHALLENGE IT PRESENTED: THE ANCIENT WORLD'S GREATEST PUZZLE WAS THERE, A KNOT THAT COULDN'T BE UNTIED.
ALEXANDER CUT IT IN TWO WITH HIS SWORD.
LATERAL THINKING, YOU SEE. CENTURIES AHEAD OF HIS TIME.
"HEADING SOUTH, HE ENTERED EGYPT THROUGH MEMPHIS, WHERE THEY PROCLAIMED HIM SON OF AMON, JUDGE OF THE DEAD, WHOSE NAME MEANS 'THE HIDDEN ONE'.
"UNDER RULE FROM ALEXANDRIA, THE CLASSIC CULTURE OF THE GREAT PHARAOHS WAS RESTORED."
I FOLLOWED HIM THROUGH BABYLON, UP THROUGH KABUL TO SAMARKHAND, THEN DOWN THE INDUS, WHERE HE FIRST MET ELEPHANTS-OF-WAR.
WHERE HE'D TURNED BACK TO QUELL DISSENT AT HOME, I TRAVELLED ON, THROUGH CHINA AND TIBET, GATHERING MARTIAL WISDOM AS I WENT.
"ALEXANDER RETURNED TO BABYLON TO DIE OF AN INFECTION, AGED THIRTY-THREE. AMONGST ITS RUINED ZIGGURATS, I SAW AT LAST HIS FAILINGS...
"HE'D NOT UNITED ALL THE WORLD, NOR BUILT A UNITY THAT WOULD SURVIVE HIM."
DISILLUSIONED BUT DETERMINED TO COMPLETE MY ODYSSEY, I FOLLOWED HIS CORPSE TO ITS RESTING PLACE IN ALEXANDRIA.
THE NIGHT BEFORE RETURNING TO AMERICA, I WANDERED INTO THE DESERT AND ATE A BALL OF HASHISH I'D BEEN GIVEN IN TIBET.
"THE ENSUING VISION TRANSFORMED ME. WADING THROUGH POWDERED HISTORY, I HEARD DEAD KINGS WALKING UNDERGROUND; HEARD FANFARES SOUND THROUGH HUMAN SKULLS.
"ALEXANDER HAD MERELY RESURRECTED AN AGE OF PHARAOHS. THEIR WISDOM, TRULY IMMORTAL, NOW INSPIRED ME!"
10

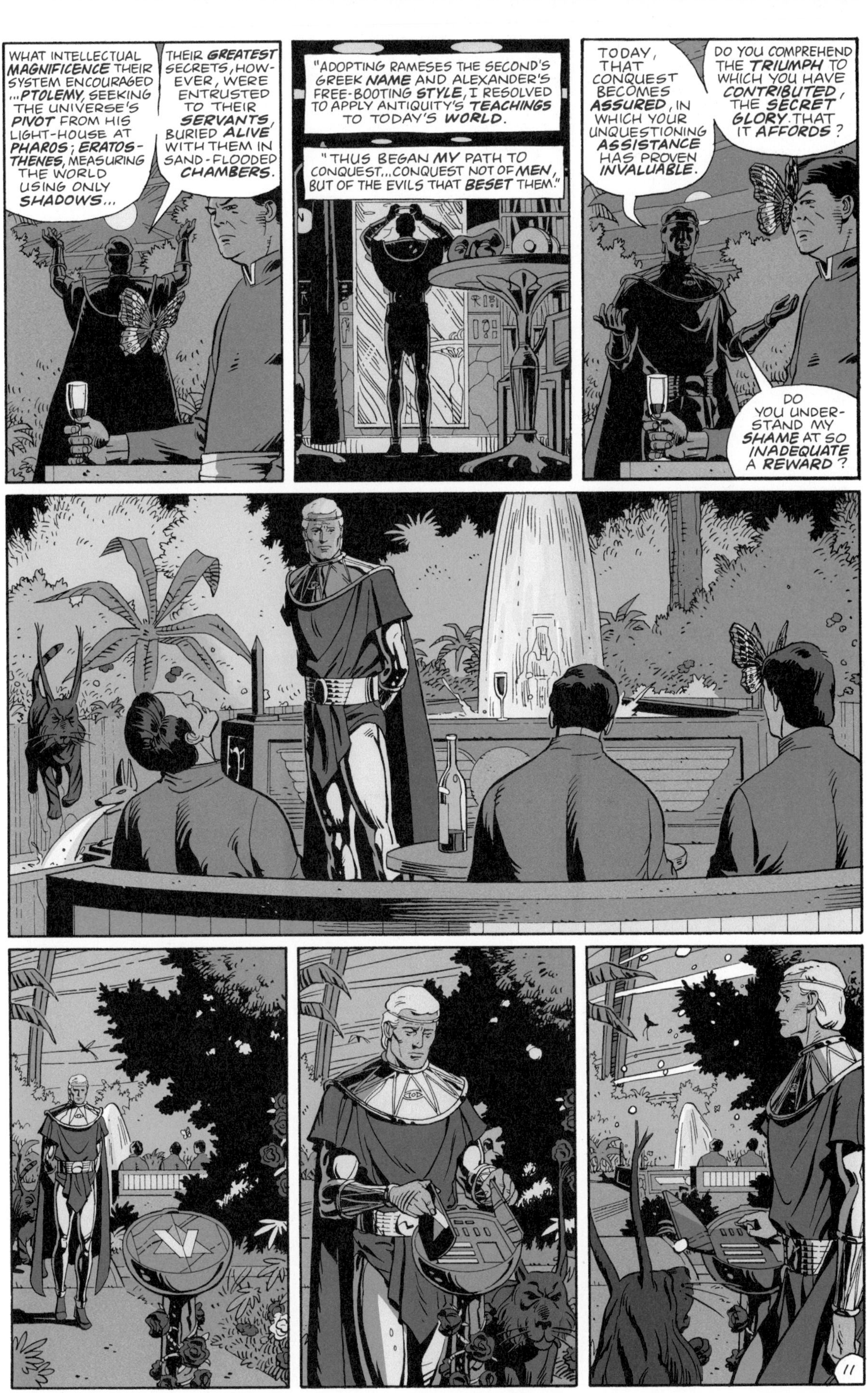
WHAT INTELLECTUAL MAGNIFICENCE THEIR SYSTEM ENCOURAGED ...PTOLEMY, SEEKING THE UNIVERSE'S PIVOT FROM HIS LIGHT-HOUSE AT PHAROS; ERATOSTHENES, MEASURING THE WORLD USING ONLY SHADOWS...
THEIR GREATEST SECRETS, HOWEVER, WERE ENTRUSTED TO THEIR SERVANTS, BURIED ALIVE WITH THEM IN SAND-FLOODED CHAMBERS.
"ADOPTING RAMESES THE SECOND'S GREEK NAME AND ALEXANDER'S FREE-BOOTING STYLE, I RESOLVED TO APPLY ANTIQUITY'S TEACHINGS TO TODAY'S WORLD.
"THUS BEGAN MY PATH TO CONQUEST...CONQUEST NOT OF MEN, BUT OF THE EVILS THAT BESET THEM."
TODAY, THAT CONQUEST BECOMES ASSURED, IN WHICH YOUR UNQUESTIONING ASSISTANCE HAS PROVEN INVALUABLE.
DO YOU COMPREHEND THE TRIUMPH TO WHICH YOU HAVE CONTRIBUTED, THE SECRET GLORY THAT IT AFFORDS?
DO YOU UNDERSTAND MY SHAME AT SO INADEQUATE A REWARD?
11

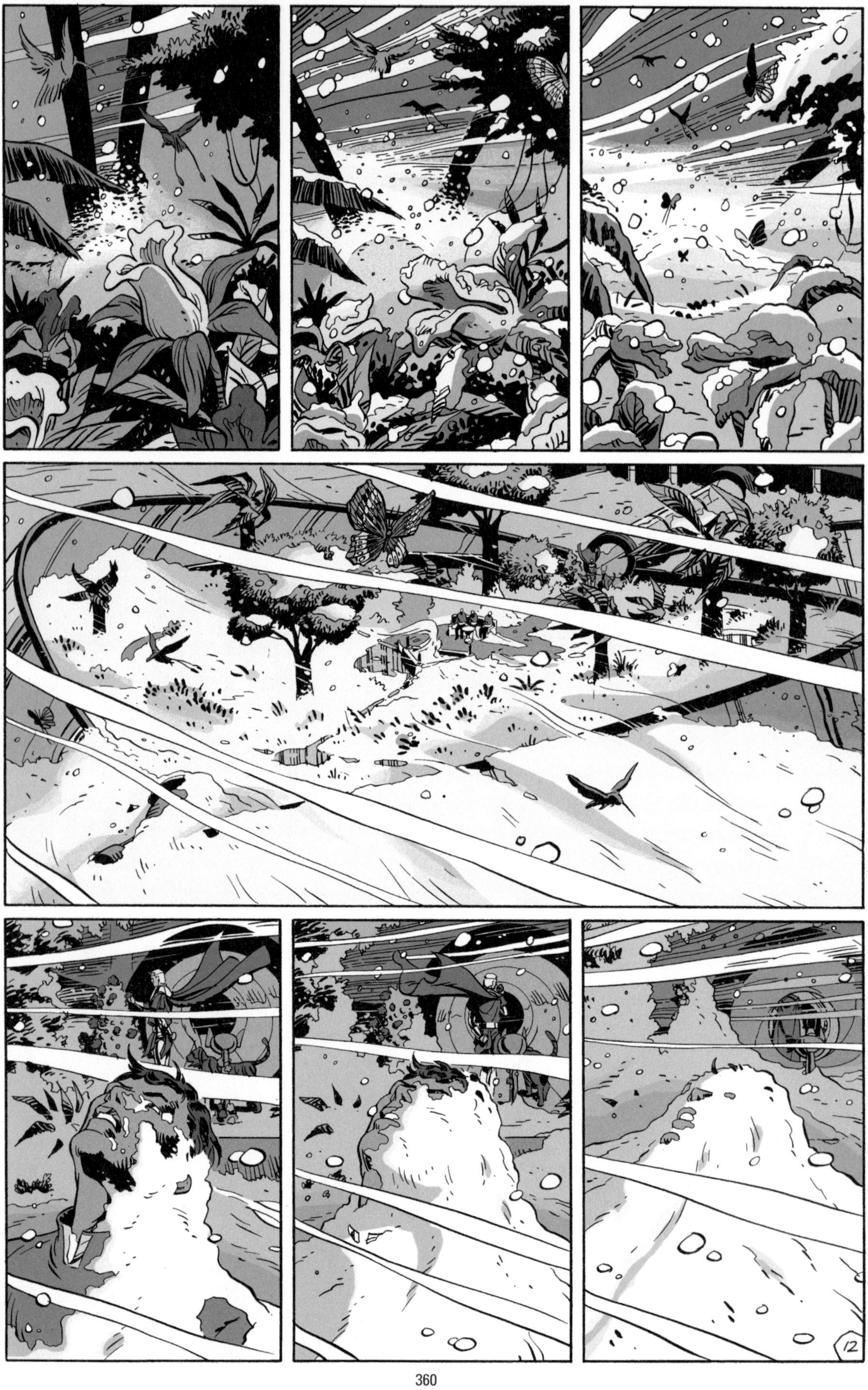
12

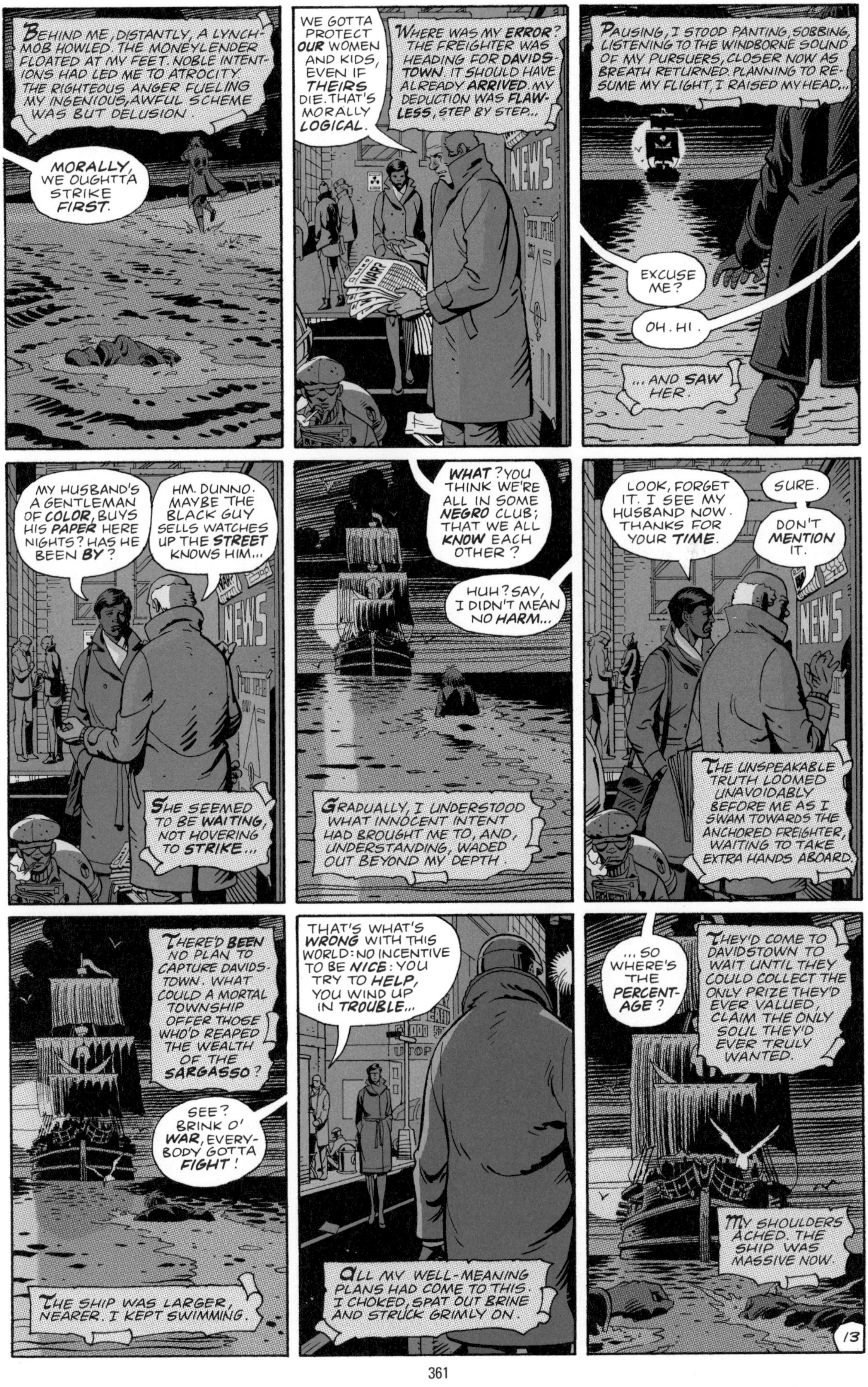

BEHIND ME, DISTANTLY, A LYNCH-MOB HOWLED. THE MONEYLENDER FLOATED AT MY FEET. NOBLE INTENTIONS HAD LED ME TO ATROCITY. THE RIGHTEOUS ANGER FUELING MY INGENIOUS, AWFUL SCHEME WAS BUT DELUSION.
MORALLY, WE OUGHTTA STRIKE FIRST.
WE GOTTA PROTECT OUR WOMEN AND KIDS, EVEN IF THEIRS DIE. THAT'S MORALLY LOGICAL.
WHERE WAS MY ERROR? THE FREIGHTER WAS HEADING FOR DAVIDSTOWN. IT SHOULD HAVE ALREADY ARRIVED. MY DEDUCTION WAS FLAWLESS, STEP BY STEP...
NEWS
WAR?
PAUSING, I STOOD PANTING, SOBBING, LISTENING TO THE WINDBORNE SOUND OF MY PURSUERS, CLOSER NOW AS BREATH RETURNED. PLANNING TO RESUME MY FLIGHT, I RAISED MY HEAD...
EXCUSE ME?
OH. HI.
...AND SAW HER.
MY HUSBAND'S A GENTLEMAN OF COLOR, BUYS HIS PAPER HERE NIGHTS? HAS HE BEEN BY?
HM. DUNNO. MAYBE THE BLACK GUY SELLS WATCHES UP THE STREET KNOWS HIM...
NEWS
SHE SEEMED TO BE WAITING, NOT HOVERING TO STRIKE...
WHAT? YOU THINK WE'RE ALL IN SOME NEGRO CLUB; THAT WE ALL KNOW EACH OTHER?
HUH? SAY, I DIDN'T MEAN NO HARM...
GRADUALLY, I UNDERSTOOD WHAT INNOCENT INTENT HAD BROUGHT ME TO, AND, UNDERSTANDING, WADED OUT BEYOND MY DEPTH.
LOOK, FORGET IT. I SEE MY HUSBAND NOW. THANKS FOR YOUR TIME.
SURE.
DON'T MENTION IT.
NEWS
THE UNSPEAKABLE TRUTH LOOMED UNAVOIDABLY BEFORE ME AS I SWAM TOWARDS THE ANCHORED FREIGHTER, WAITING TO TAKE EXTRA HANDS ABOARD.
THERE'D BEEN NO PLAN TO CAPTURE DAVIDSTOWN. WHAT COULD A MORTAL TOWNSHIP OFFER THOSE WHO'D REAPED THE WEALTH OF THE SARGASSO?
SEE? BRINK O' WAR, EVERYBODY GOTTA FIGHT!
THE SHIP WAS LARGER, NEARER. I KEPT SWIMMING.
THAT'S WHAT'S WRONG WITH THIS WORLD: NO INCENTIVE TO BE NICE: YOU TRY TO HELP, YOU WIND UP IN TROUBLE...
ALL MY WELL-MEANING PLANS HAD COME TO THIS. I CHOKED, SPAT OUT BRINE AND STRUCK GRIMLY ON.
...SO WHERE'S THE PERCENTAGE?
THEY'D COME TO DAVIDSTOWN TO WAIT UNTIL THEY COULD COLLECT THE ONLY PRIZE THEY'D EVER VALUED, CLAIM THE ONLY SOUL THEY'D EVER TRULY WANTED.
MY SHOULDERS ACHED. THE SHIP WAS MASSIVE NOW.
13

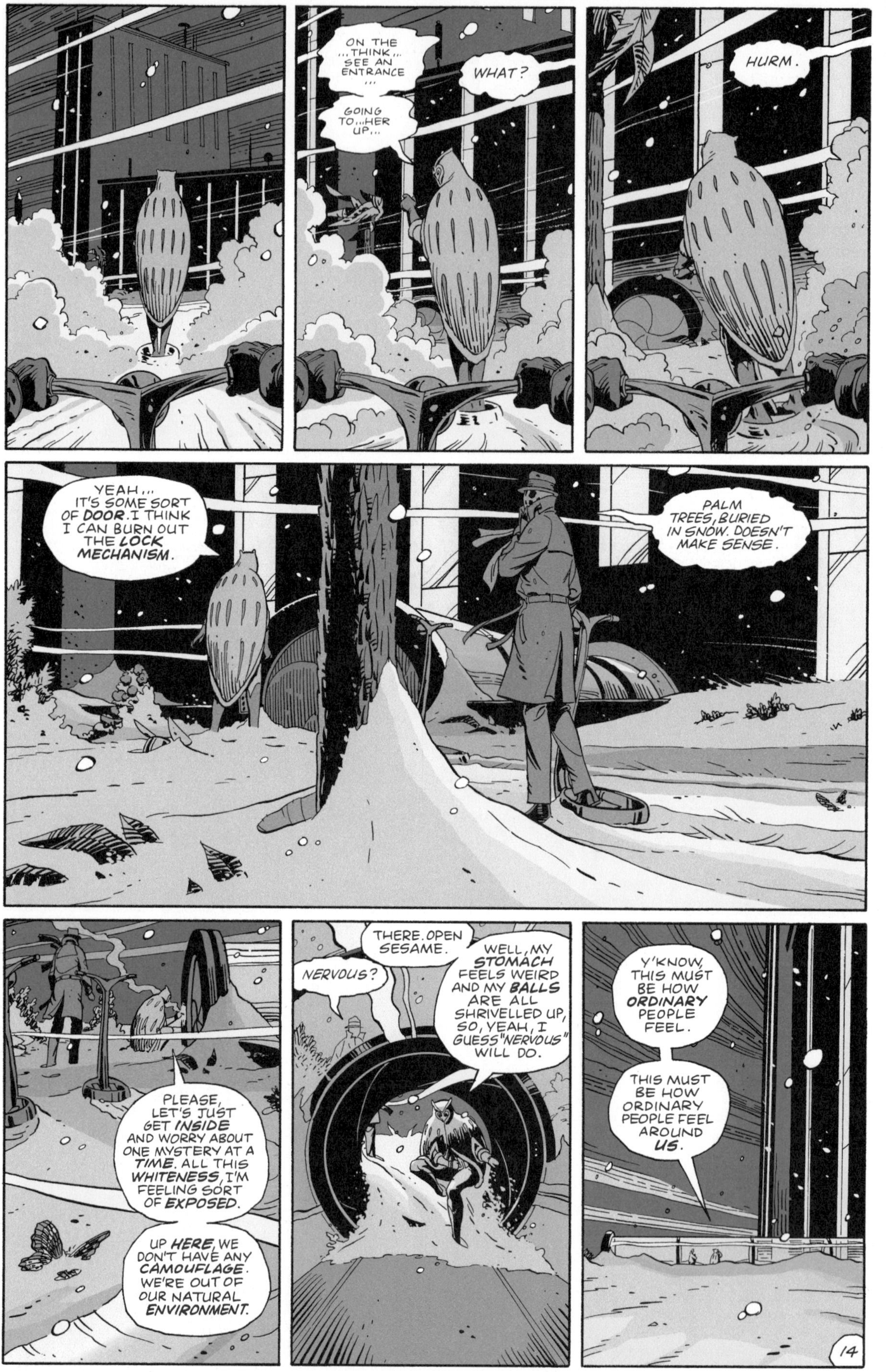
ON THE ...THINK... SEE AN ENTRANCE ...
GOING TO...HER UP...
WHAT?
HURM.
YEAH... IT'S SOME SORT OF DOOR. I THINK I CAN BURN OUT THE LOCK MECHANISM.
PALM TREES, BURIED IN SNOW. DOESN'T MAKE SENSE.
PLEASE, LET'S JUST GET INSIDE AND WORRY ABOUT ONE MYSTERY AT A TIME. ALL THIS WHITENESS, I'M FEELING SORT OF EXPOSED.
UP HERE, WE DON'T HAVE ANY CAMOUFLAGE. WE'RE OUT OF OUR NATURAL ENVIRONMENT.
THERE. OPEN SESAME.
NERVOUS?
WELL, MY STOMACH FEELS WEIRD AND MY BALLS ARE ALL SHRIVELLED UP, SO, YEAH, I GUESS "NERVOUS" WILL DO.
Y'KNOW, THIS MUST BE HOW ORDINARY PEOPLE FEEL.
THIS MUST BE HOW ORDINARY PEOPLE FEEL AROUND US.
14

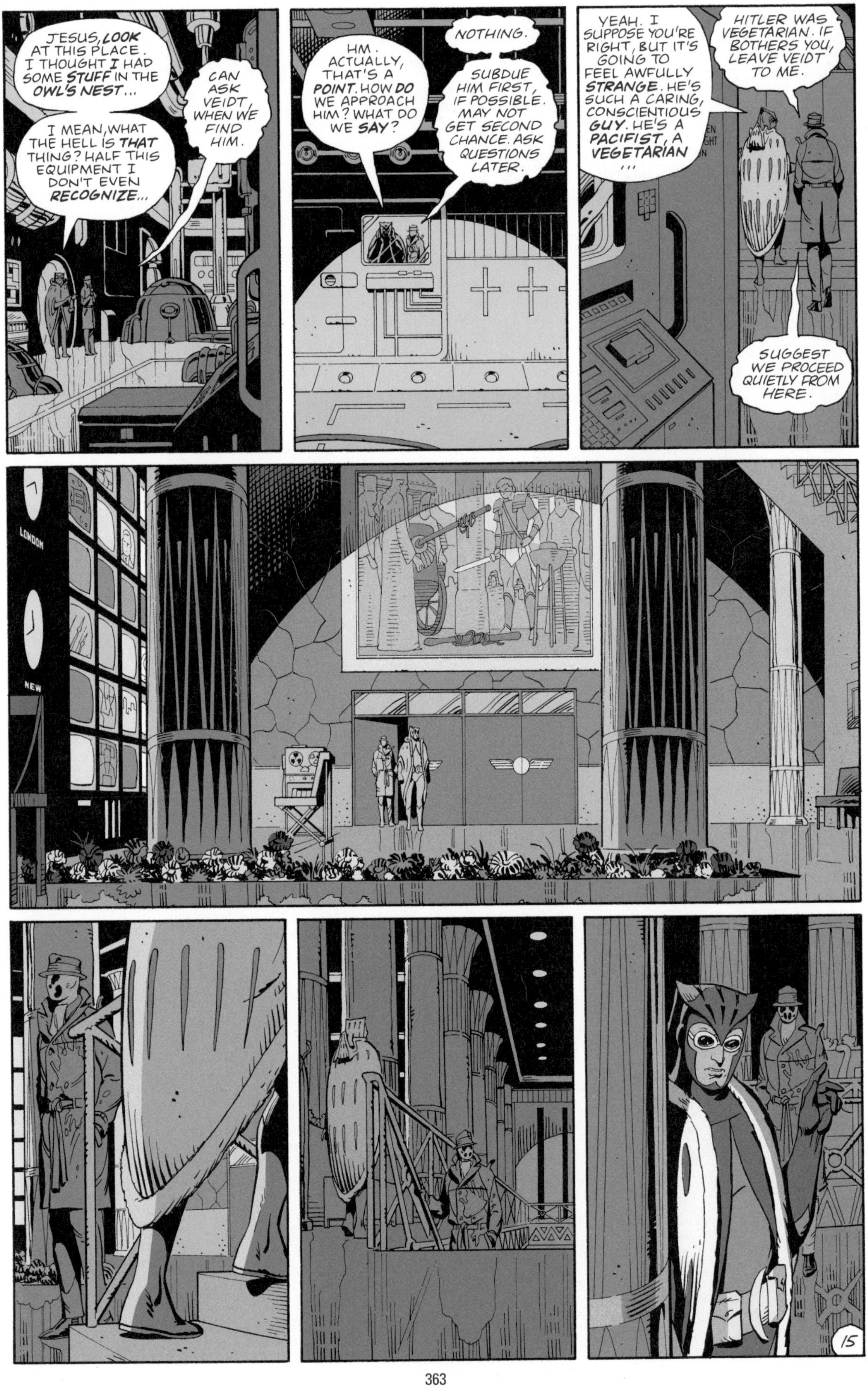
JESUS, LOOK AT THIS PLACE. I THOUGHT I HAD SOME STUFF IN THE OWL'S NEST...
I MEAN, WHAT THE HELL IS THAT THING? HALF THIS EQUIPMENT I DON'T EVEN RECOGNIZE...
CAN ASK VEIDT, WHEN WE FIND HIM.
HM. ACTUALLY, THAT'S A POINT. HOW DO WE APPROACH HIM? WHAT DO WE SAY?
NOTHING.
SUBDUE HIM FIRST, IF POSSIBLE. MAY NOT GET SECOND CHANCE. ASK QUESTIONS LATER.
YEAH. I SUPPOSE YOU'RE RIGHT, BUT IT'S GOING TO FEEL AWFULLY STRANGE. HE'S SUCH A CARING, CONSCIENTIOUS GUY. HE'S A PACIFIST, A VEGETARIAN...
HITLER WAS VEGETARIAN. IF BOTHERS YOU, LEAVE VEIDT TO ME.
SUGGEST WE PROCEED QUIETLY FROM HERE.
LONDON
NEW
15

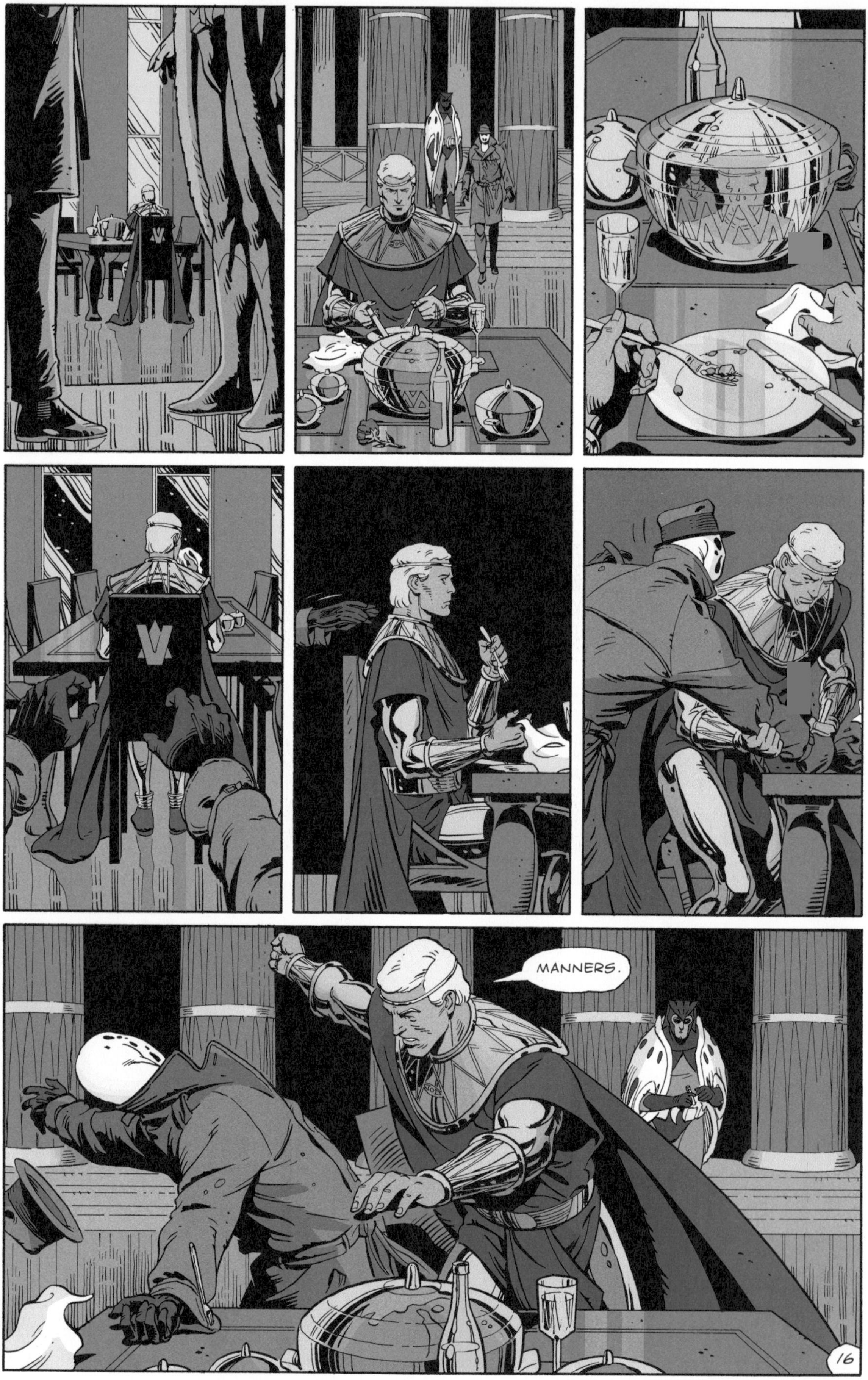
MANNERS.
16

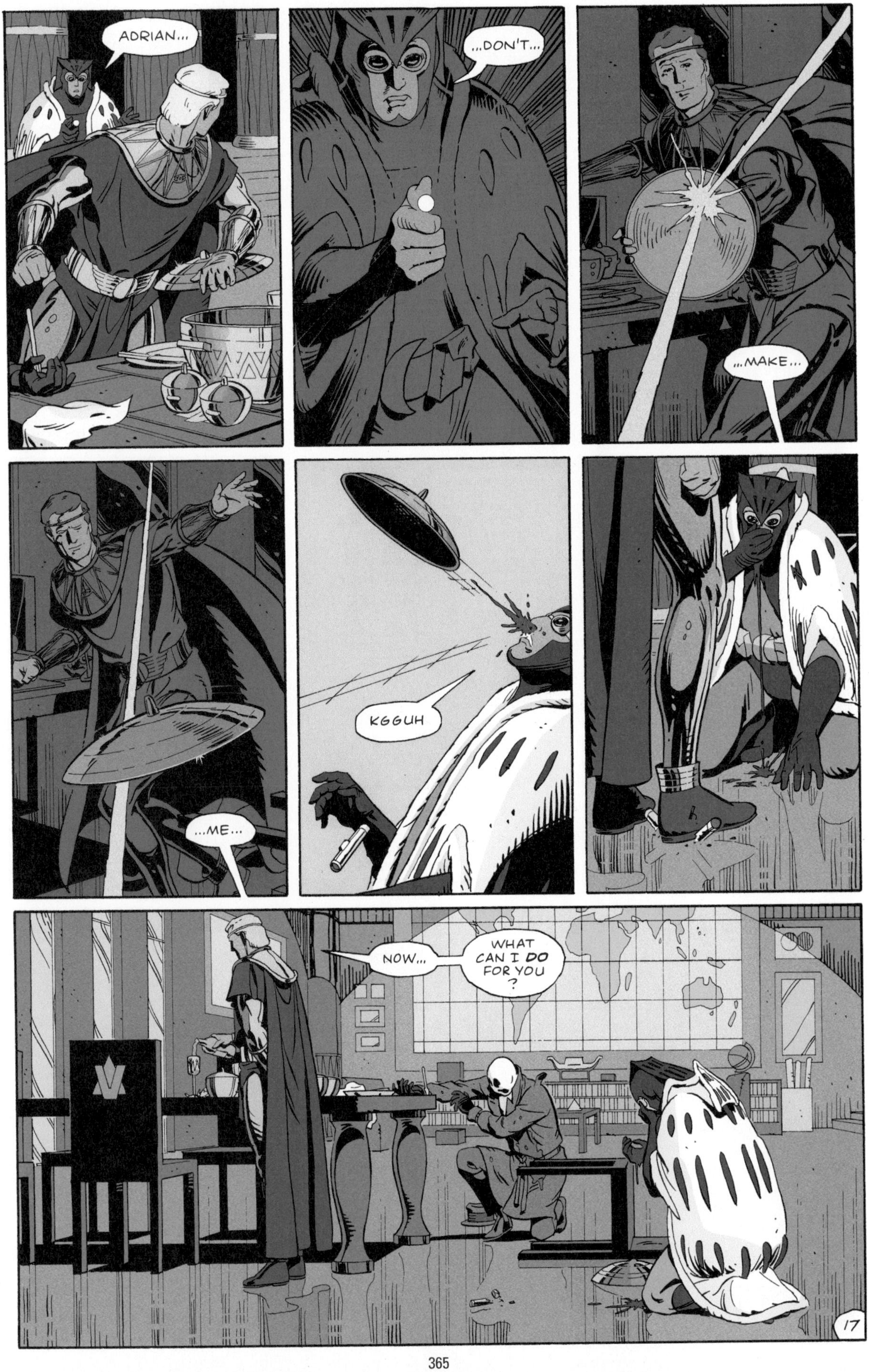
ADRIAN...
...DON'T...
...MAKE...
...ME...
KGGUH
NOW...
WHAT CAN I DO FOR YOU ?
17

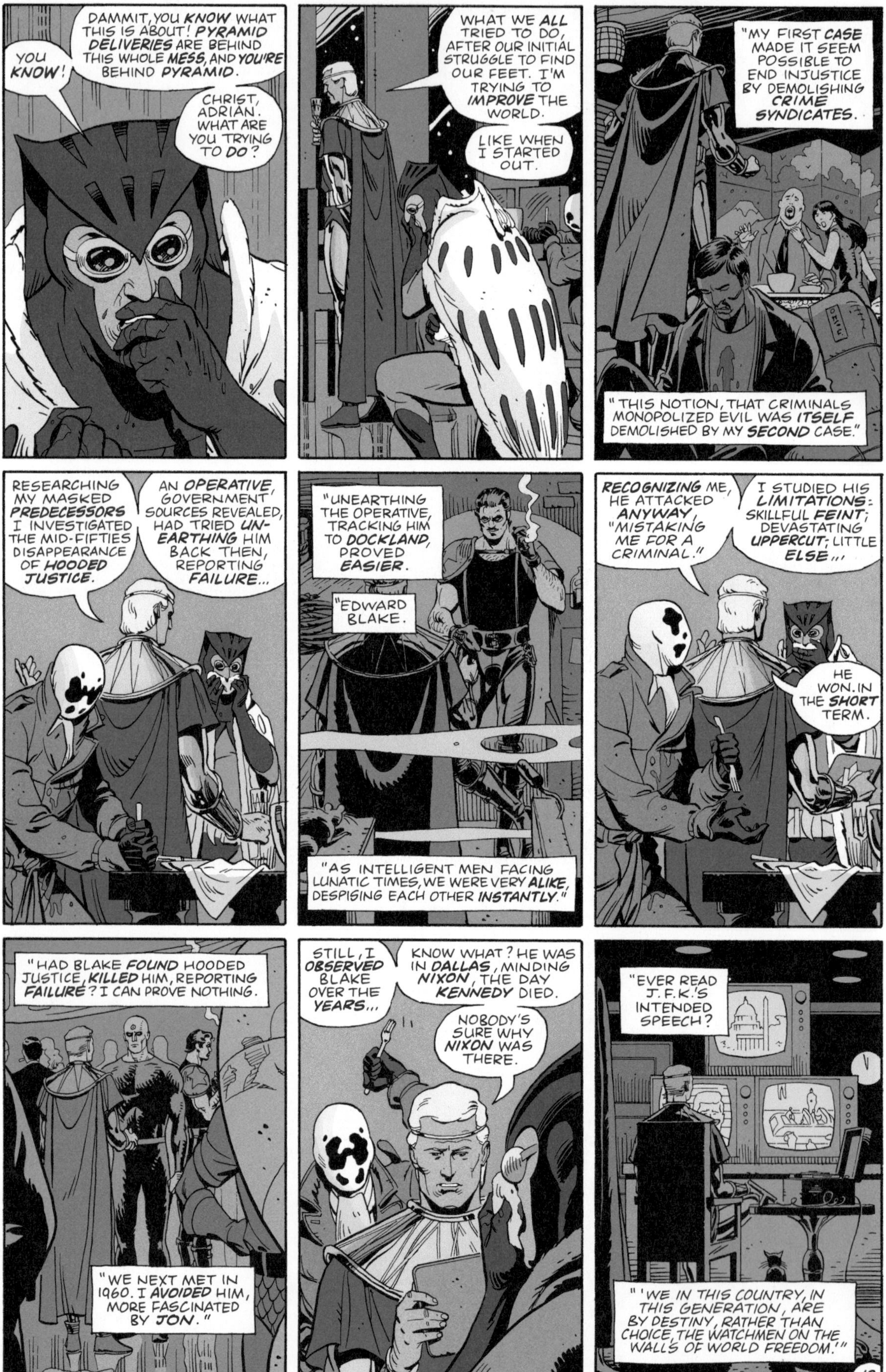
DAMMIT, YOU KNOW WHAT THIS IS ABOUT! PYRAMID DELIVERIES ARE BEHIND THIS WHOLE MESS, AND YOU'RE BEHIND PYRAMID.
YOU KNOW!
CHRIST, ADRIAN. WHAT ARE YOU TRYING TO DO?
WHAT WE ALL TRIED TO DO, AFTER OUR INITIAL STRUGGLE TO FIND OUR FEET. I'M TRYING TO IMPROVE THE WORLD.
LIKE WHEN I STARTED OUT.
"MY FIRST CASE MADE IT SEEM POSSIBLE TO END INJUSTICE BY DEMOLISHING CRIME SYNDICATES.
"THIS NOTION, THAT CRIMINALS MONOPOLIZED EVIL WAS ITSELF DEMOLISHED BY MY SECOND CASE."
RESEARCHING MY MASKED PREDECESSORS I INVESTIGATED THE MID-FIFTIES DISAPPEARANCE OF HOODED JUSTICE.
AN OPERATIVE, GOVERNMENT SOURCES REVEALED, HAD TRIED UN-EARTHING HIM BACK THEN, REPORTING FAILURE...
"UNEARTHING THE OPERATIVE, TRACKING HIM TO DOCKLAND, PROVED EASIER.
"EDWARD BLAKE.
"AS INTELLIGENT MEN FACING LUNATIC TIMES, WE WERE VERY ALIKE, DESPISING EACH OTHER INSTANTLY."
RECOGNIZING ME, HE ATTACKED ANYWAY, "MISTAKING ME FOR A CRIMINAL."
I STUDIED HIS LIMITATIONS: SKILLFUL FEINT; DEVASTATING UPPERCUT; LITTLE ELSE...
HE WON. IN THE SHORT TERM.
"HAD BLAKE FOUND HOODED JUSTICE, KILLED HIM, REPORTING FAILURE? I CAN PROVE NOTHING.
"WE NEXT MET IN 1960. I AVOIDED HIM, MORE FASCINATED BY JON."
STILL, I OBSERVED BLAKE OVER THE YEARS...
KNOW WHAT? HE WAS IN DALLAS, MINDING NIXON, THE DAY KENNEDY DIED.
NOBODY'S SURE WHY NIXON WAS THERE.
"EVER READ J.F.K.'S INTENDED SPEECH?
"'WE IN THIS COUNTRY, IN THIS GENERATION, ARE BY DESTINY, RATHER THAN CHOICE, THE WATCHMEN ON THE WALLS OF WORLD FREEDOM.'"
18

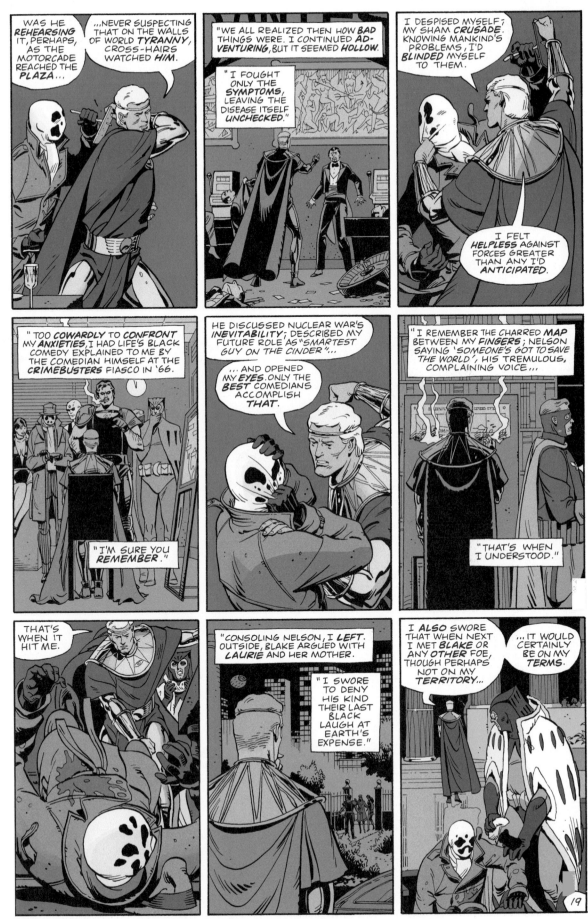

WAS HE **REHEARSING** IT, PERHAPS, AS THE MOTORCADE REACHED THE **PLAZA**...

...NEVER SUSPECTING THAT ON THE WALLS OF WORLD **TYRANNY**, CROSS-HAIRS WATCHED **HIM**.

"WE ALL REALIZED THEN HOW **BAD** THINGS WERE. I CONTINUED **AD-VENTURING**, BUT IT SEEMED **HOLLOW**.

"I FOUGHT ONLY THE **SYMPTOMS**, LEAVING THE DISEASE ITSELF **UNCHECKED**."

I DESPISED MYSELF; MY SHAM **CRUSADE**. KNOWING MANKIND'S PROBLEMS, I'D **BLINDED** MYSELF TO THEM.

I FELT **HELPLESS** AGAINST FORCES GREATER THAN ANY I'D **ANTICIPATED**.

"TOO **COWARDLY** TO **CONFRONT** MY **ANXIETIES**, I HAD LIFE'S BLACK COMEDY EXPLAINED TO ME BY THE COMEDIAN HIMSELF AT THE **CRIMEBUSTERS** FIASCO IN '66.

"I'M SURE YOU **REMEMBER**."

HE DISCUSSED NUCLEAR WAR'S **INEVITABILITY**; DESCRIBED MY FUTURE ROLE AS "SMARTEST GUY ON THE CINDER"...

... AND OPENED MY **EYES**. ONLY THE **BEST** COMEDIANS ACCOMPLISH **THAT**.

"I REMEMBER THE CHARRED **MAP** BETWEEN MY **FINGERS**; NELSON SAYING 'SOMEONE'S GOT TO SAVE THE WORLD', HIS TREMULOUS, COMPLAINING VOICE...

"THAT'S WHEN I UNDERSTOOD."

THAT'S WHEN IT HIT ME.

"CONSOLING NELSON, I **LEFT**. OUTSIDE, BLAKE ARGUED WITH **LAURIE** AND HER MOTHER.

"I SWORE TO DENY HIS KIND THEIR LAST BLACK LAUGH AT EARTH'S EXPENSE."

I **ALSO** SWORE THAT WHEN NEXT I MET **BLAKE** OR ANY **OTHER** FOE, THOUGH PERHAPS NOT ON MY **TERRITORY**...

...IT WOULD CERTAINLY BE ON MY **TERMS**.

19

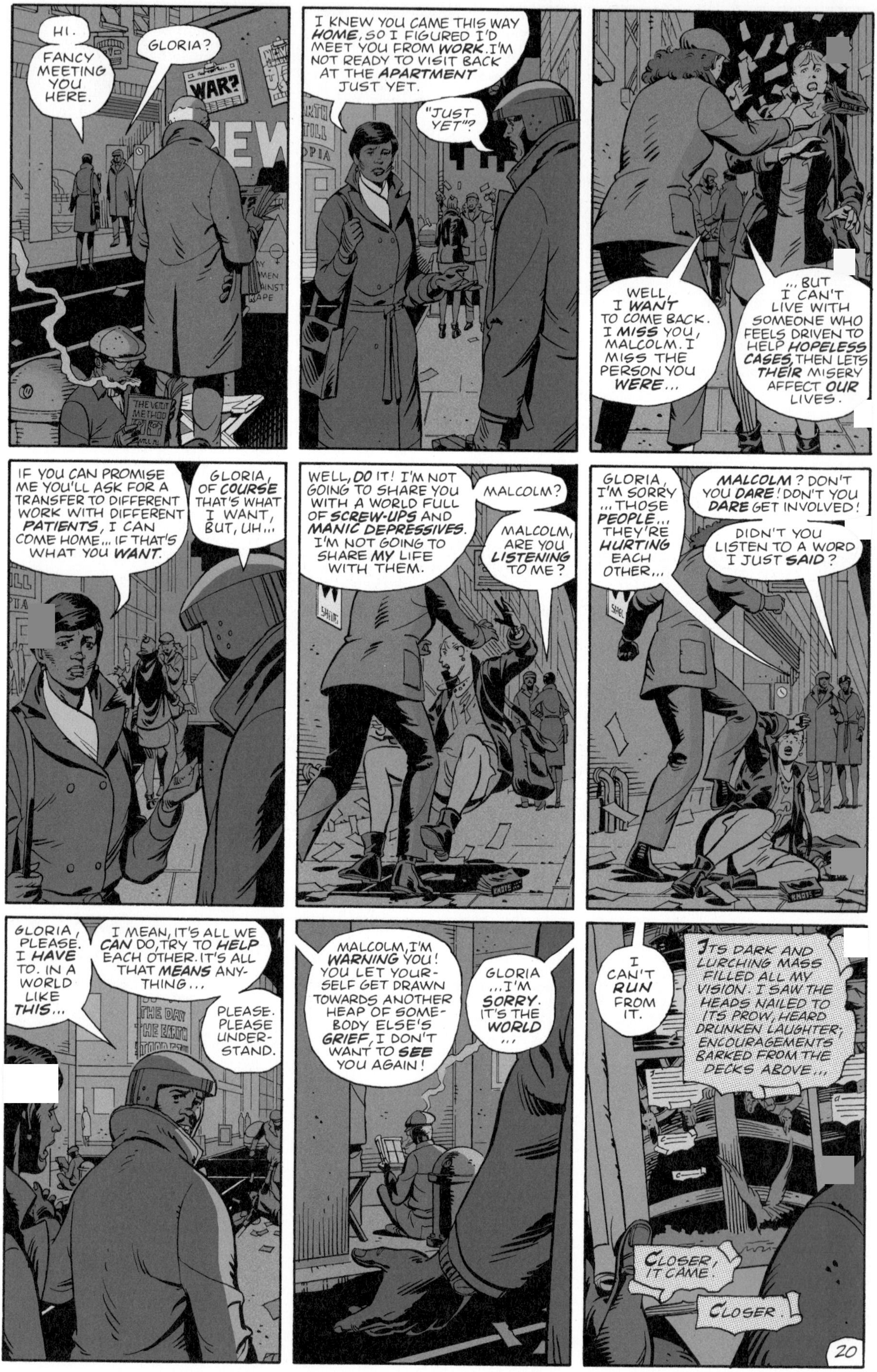

HI.
FANCY MEETING YOU HERE.
GLORIA?
WAR?
I KNEW YOU CAME THIS WAY **HOME**, SO I FIGURED I'D MEET YOU FROM **WORK**. I'M NOT READY TO VISIT BACK AT THE **APARTMENT** JUST YET.
"JUST YET"?
WELL, I **WANT** TO COME BACK. I **MISS** YOU, MALCOLM. I MISS THE PERSON YOU **WERE**...
...BUT I CAN'T LIVE WITH SOMEONE WHO FEELS DRIVEN TO HELP **HOPELESS CASES**, THEN LETS **THEIR** MISERY AFFECT **OUR** LIVES.
IF YOU CAN PROMISE ME YOU'LL ASK FOR A TRANSFER TO DIFFERENT WORK WITH DIFFERENT **PATIENTS**, I CAN COME HOME... IF THAT'S WHAT YOU **WANT**.
GLORIA, OF **COURSE** THAT'S WHAT I WANT, BUT, UH...
WELL, **DO** IT! I'M NOT GOING TO SHARE YOU WITH A WORLD FULL OF **SCREW-UPS** AND **MANIC DEPRESSIVES**. I'M NOT GOING TO SHARE **MY** LIFE WITH THEM.
MALCOLM?
MALCOLM, ARE YOU **LISTENING** TO ME?
GLORIA, I'M SORRY... THOSE **PEOPLE**... THEY'RE **HURTING** EACH OTHER...
MALCOLM? DON'T YOU **DARE**! DON'T YOU **DARE** GET INVOLVED!
DIDN'T YOU LISTEN TO A WORD I JUST **SAID**?
GLORIA, PLEASE. I **HAVE** TO. IN A WORLD LIKE **THIS**...
I MEAN, IT'S ALL WE **CAN** DO, TRY TO **HELP** EACH OTHER. IT'S ALL THAT **MEANS** ANY-THING...
PLEASE. PLEASE UNDER-STAND.
THE DAY THE EARTH
MALCOLM, I'M **WARNING** YOU! YOU LET YOUR-SELF GET DRAWN TOWARDS ANOTHER HEAP OF SOME-BODY ELSE'S **GRIEF**, I DON'T WANT TO **SEE** YOU AGAIN!
GLORIA ...I'M **SORRY**. IT'S THE **WORLD**...
I CAN'T **RUN** FROM IT.
ITS DARK AND LURCHING MASS FILLED ALL MY VISION. I SAW THE HEADS NAILED TO ITS PROW, HEARD DRUNKEN LAUGHTER; ENCOURAGEMENTS BARKED FROM THE DECKS ABOVE...
CLOSER, IT CAME.
CLOSER.
20

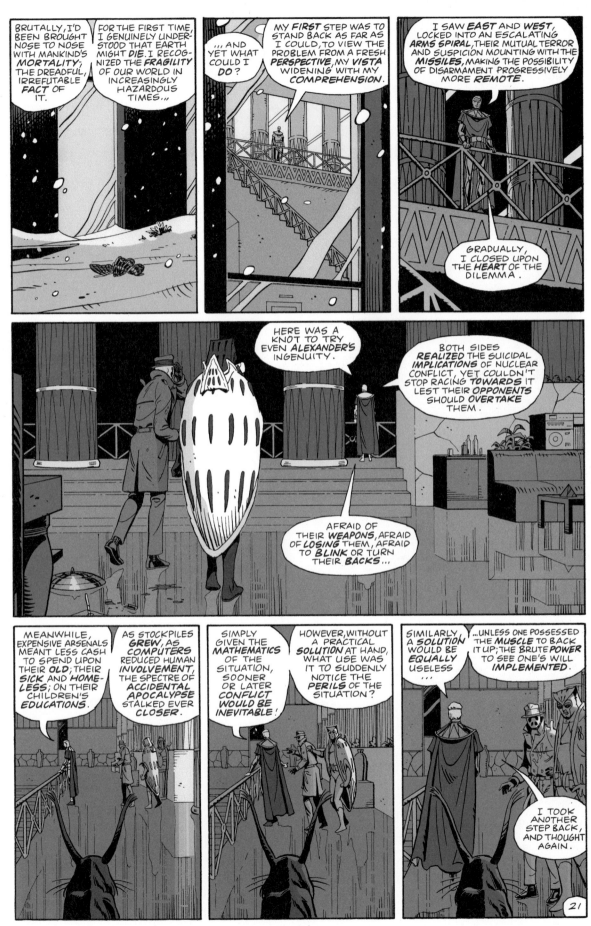

BRUTALLY, I'D BEEN BROUGHT NOSE TO NOSE WITH MANKIND'S *MORTALITY*; THE DREADFUL, IRREFUTABLE *FACT* OF IT.

FOR THE FIRST TIME, I GENUINELY UNDER-STOOD THAT EARTH MIGHT *DIE*. I RECOGNIZED THE *FRAGILITY* OF OUR WORLD IN INCREASINGLY HAZARDOUS TIMES...

..., AND YET WHAT COULD I *DO*?

MY *FIRST* STEP WAS TO STAND BACK AS FAR AS I COULD, TO VIEW THE PROBLEM FROM A FRESH *PERSPECTIVE*, MY *VISTA* WIDENING WITH MY *COMPREHENSION*.

I SAW *EAST* AND *WEST*, LOCKED INTO AN ESCALATING *ARMS SPIRAL*, THEIR MUTUAL TERROR AND SUSPICION MOUNTING WITH THE *MISSILES*, MAKING THE POSSIBILITY OF DISARMAMENT PROGRESSIVELY MORE *REMOTE*.

GRADUALLY, I CLOSED UPON THE *HEART* OF THE DILEMMA.

HERE WAS A KNOT TO TRY EVEN *ALEXANDER'S* INGENUITY.

BOTH SIDES *REALIZED* THE SUICIDAL *IMPLICATIONS* OF NUCLEAR CONFLICT, YET COULDN'T STOP RACING *TOWARDS* IT LEST THEIR *OPPONENTS* SHOULD *OVERTAKE* THEM.

AFRAID OF THEIR *WEAPONS*, AFRAID OF *LOSING* THEM, AFRAID TO *BLINK* OR TURN THEIR *BACKS*...

MEANWHILE, EXPENSIVE ARSENALS MEANT LESS CASH TO SPEND UPON THEIR *OLD*; THEIR *SICK* AND *HOME-LESS*; ON THEIR CHILDREN'S *EDUCATIONS*.

AS STOCKPILES *GREW*, AS *COMPUTERS* REDUCED HUMAN *INVOLVEMENT*, THE SPECTRE OF ACCIDENTAL *APOCALYPSE* STALKED EVER *CLOSER*.

SIMPLY GIVEN THE *MATHEMATICS* OF THE SITUATION, SOONER OR LATER *CONFLICT* WOULD BE INEVITABLE!

HOWEVER, WITHOUT A PRACTICAL *SOLUTION* AT HAND, WHAT USE WAS IT TO SUDDENLY NOTICE THE *PERILS* OF THE SITUATION?

SIMILARLY, A *SOLUTION* WOULD BE *EQUALLY* USELESS...

...UNLESS ONE POSSESSED THE *MUSCLE* TO BACK IT UP; THE BRUTE *POWER* TO SEE ONE'S WILL *IMPLEMENTED*.

I TOOK ANOTHER STEP BACK, AND THOUGHT AGAIN.

21

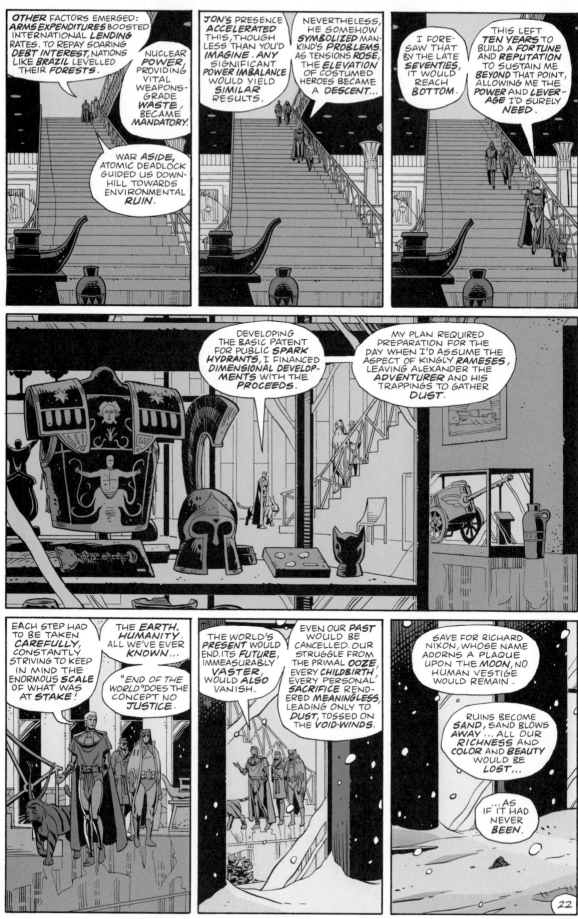

OTHER FACTORS EMERGED: ARMS EXPENDITURES BOOSTED INTERNATIONAL LENDING RATES. TO REPAY SOARING DEBT INTEREST, NATIONS LIKE BRAZIL LEVELLED THEIR FORESTS.

NUCLEAR POWER PROVIDING VITAL WEAPONS-GRADE WASTE, BECAME MANDATORY.

WAR ASIDE, ATOMIC DEADLOCK GUIDED US DOWNHILL TOWARDS ENVIRONMENTAL RUIN.

JON'S PRESENCE ACCELERATED THIS, THOUGH LESS THAN YOU'D IMAGINE. ANY SIGNIFICANT POWER IMBALANCE WOULD YIELD SIMILAR RESULTS.

NEVERTHELESS, HE SOMEHOW SYMBOLIZED MANKIND'S PROBLEMS. AS TENSIONS ROSE, THE ELEVATION OF COSTUMED HEROES BECAME A DESCENT...

I FORESAW THAT BY THE LATE SEVENTIES, IT WOULD REACH BOTTOM.

THIS LEFT TEN YEARS TO BUILD A FORTUNE AND REPUTATION TO SUSTAIN ME BEYOND THAT POINT, ALLOWING ME THE POWER AND LEVERAGE I'D SURELY NEED.

DEVELOPING THE BASIC PATENT FOR PUBLIC SPARK HYDRANTS, I FINANCED DIMENSIONAL DEVELOPMENTS WITH THE PROCEEDS.

MY PLAN REQUIRED PREPARATION FOR THE DAY WHEN I'D ASSUME THE ASPECT OF KINGLY RAMESES, LEAVING ALEXANDER THE ADVENTURER AND HIS TRAPPINGS TO GATHER DUST.

EACH STEP HAD TO BE TAKEN CAREFULLY, CONSTANTLY STRIVING TO KEEP IN MIND THE ENORMOUS SCALE OF WHAT WAS AT STAKE!

THE EARTH. HUMANITY. ALL WE'VE EVER KNOWN...

"END OF THE WORLD" DOES THE CONCEPT NO JUSTICE.

THE WORLD'S PRESENT WOULD END. ITS FUTURE, IMMEASURABLY VASTER, WOULD ALSO VANISH.

EVEN OUR PAST WOULD BE CANCELLED. OUR STRUGGLE FROM THE PRIMAL OOZE, EVERY CHILDBIRTH, EVERY PERSONAL SACRIFICE RENDERED MEANINGLESS, LEADING ONLY TO DUST, TOSSED ON THE VOID-WINDS.

SAVE FOR RICHARD NIXON, WHOSE NAME ADORNS A PLAQUE UPON THE MOON, NO HUMAN VESTIGE WOULD REMAIN.

RUINS BECOME SAND, SAND BLOWS AWAY... ALL OUR RICHNESS AND COLOR AND BEAUTY WOULD BE LOST...

...AS IF IT HAD NEVER BEEN.

22

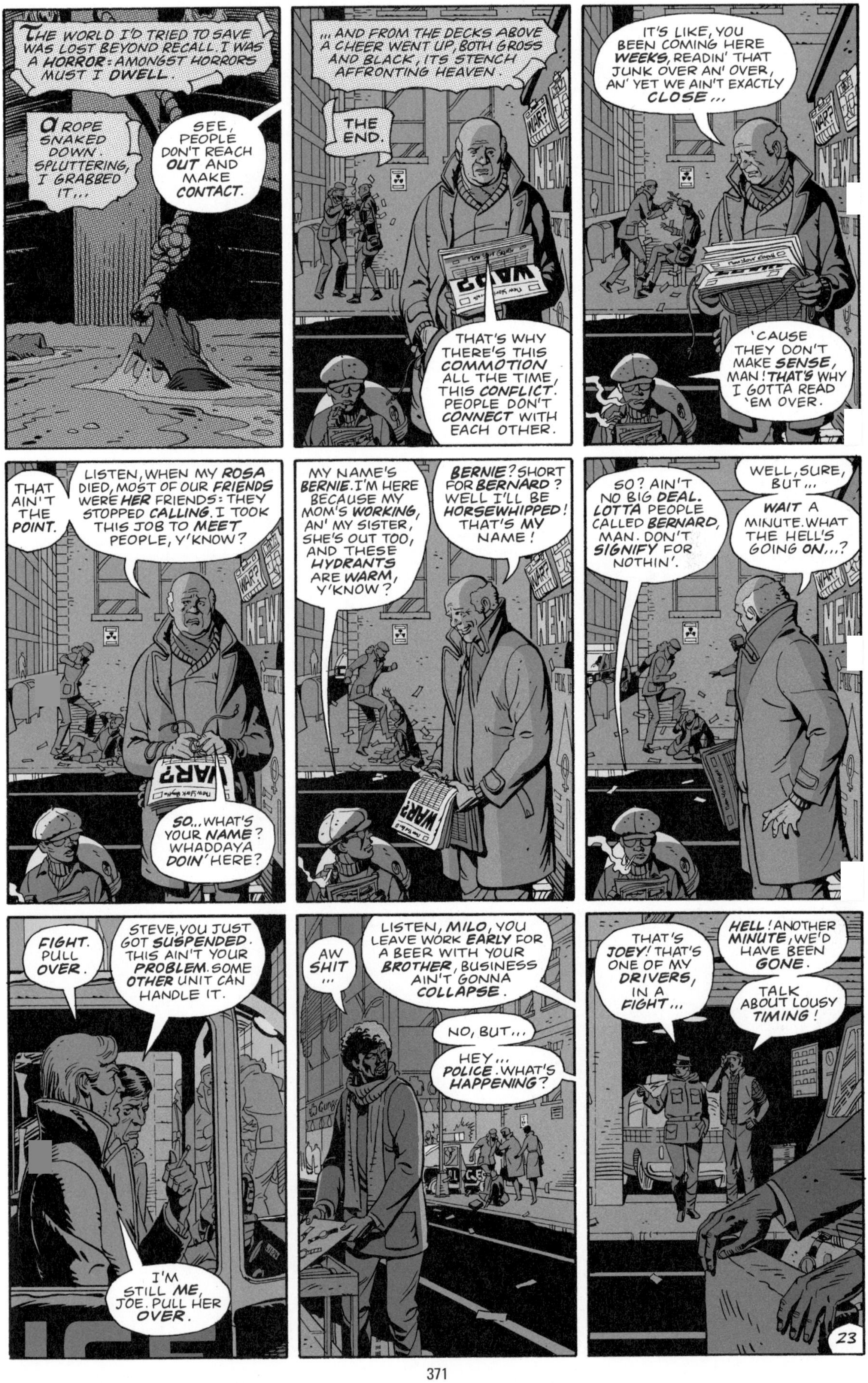
THE WORLD I'D TRIED TO SAVE WAS LOST BEYOND RECALL. I WAS A HORROR: AMONGST HORRORS MUST I DWELL.
A ROPE SNAKED DOWN. SPLUTTERING, I GRABBED IT...
SEE, PEOPLE DON'T REACH OUT AND MAKE CONTACT.
...AND FROM THE DECKS ABOVE A CHEER WENT UP, BOTH GROSS AND BLACK, ITS STENCH AFFRONTING HEAVEN.
THE END.
THAT'S WHY THERE'S THIS COMMOTION ALL THE TIME, THIS CONFLICT. PEOPLE DON'T CONNECT WITH EACH OTHER.
IT'S LIKE, YOU BEEN COMING HERE WEEKS, READIN' THAT JUNK OVER AN' OVER, AN' YET WE AIN'T EXACTLY CLOSE...
'CAUSE THEY DON'T MAKE SENSE, MAN! THAT'S WHY I GOTTA READ 'EM OVER.
THAT AIN'T THE POINT.
LISTEN, WHEN MY ROSA DIED, MOST OF OUR FRIENDS WERE HER FRIENDS: THEY STOPPED CALLING. I TOOK THIS JOB TO MEET PEOPLE, Y'KNOW?
SO... WHAT'S YOUR NAME? WHADDAYA DOIN' HERE?
MY NAME'S BERNIE. I'M HERE BECAUSE MY MOM'S WORKING, AN' MY SISTER, SHE'S OUT TOO, AND THESE HYDRANTS ARE WARM, Y'KNOW?
BERNIE? SHORT FOR BERNARD? WELL I'LL BE HORSEWHIPPED! THAT'S MY NAME!
SO? AIN'T NO BIG DEAL. LOTTA PEOPLE CALLED BERNARD, MAN. DON'T SIGNIFY FOR NOTHIN'.
WELL, SURE, BUT...
WAIT A MINUTE. WHAT THE HELL'S GOING ON...?
FIGHT. PULL OVER.
STEVE, YOU JUST GOT SUSPENDED. THIS AIN'T YOUR PROBLEM. SOME OTHER UNIT CAN HANDLE IT.
I'M STILL ME, JOE. PULL HER OVER.
AW SHIT...
LISTEN, MILO, YOU LEAVE WORK EARLY FOR A BEER WITH YOUR BROTHER, BUSINESS AIN'T GONNA COLLAPSE.
NO, BUT...
HEY... POLICE. WHAT'S HAPPENING?
THAT'S JOEY! THAT'S ONE OF MY DRIVERS, IN A FIGHT...
HELL! ANOTHER MINUTE, WE'D HAVE BEEN GONE.
TALK ABOUT LOUSY TIMING!
23

EACH STEP WAS SYNCHRONIZED.

JON, BEING TOO POWERFUL AND UNPREDICTABLE TO FIT MY PLANS, NEEDED REMOVING. THUS, DIMENSIONAL DEVELOPMENTS HIRED HIS PAST ASSOCIATES...

...AND GAVE THEM CANCER?

YES. WEAVER FIRST, SLATER AND MOLOCH LATER. UNWITTINGLY EXPOSED TO RADIATION, THEY WERE CLOSELY OBSERVED, CULTIVATED AS WEAPONS AGAINST JON.

MEANWHILE, TAKING ADVANTAGE OF NEW TECHNOLOGY, I RESEARCHED GENETICS... BUBASTIS WAS AN EARLY SUCCESS,...AND TELEPORTATION.

SINCE JON PROVED TELEPORTATION POSSIBLE, WHY DEVELOP ELECTRIC CARS? MY RESEARCHES WERE VITAL...LIKE MY ISLAND, SECRETLY PURCHASED IN 1970.

THE ONLY HERO RETAINING PUBLIC SYMPATHY, I QUIT TWO YEARS BEFORE THE KEENE ACT, CONCENTRATING ON MY PLAN.

"UNABLE TO UNITE THE WORLD BY CONQUEST... ALEXANDER'S METHOD ...I WOULD TRICK IT; FRIGHTEN IT TOWARDS SALVATION WITH HISTORY'S GREATEST PRACTICAL JOKE.

"THAT'S WHAT UPSET THE COMEDIAN, WHEN AWARENESS OF MY SCHEME CRASHED IN UPON HIM:

"PROFESSIONAL JEALOUSY."

BLAKE'S MURDER. YOU CONFESS?

CONFESSION IMPLIES PENITENCE. I MERELY REGRET HIS ACCIDENTAL INVOLVEMENT.

RETURNING FROM NICARAGUA BY AIR, HE SPOTTED A SHIP DOCKING AT AN UNCHARTED ISLAND. SUSPECTING SANDINISTA BASES, HE RESOLVED TO INVESTIGATE.

"I PICTURE HIM, SWIMMING TO THE ISLAND, DAGGER IN TEETH, PENETRATING ITS INSTALLATIONS. WHAT HE FOUND MUST HAVE COME AS A TERRIBLE BLOW.

"IMAGINE...THE PERFECT FIGHTING MAN DISCOVERING A PLOT TO PUT AN END TO WAR,...

"...AN END TO FIGHTING."

INSTITUTE FOR EXTRASPATIAL STUDIES

THE CAT
THE EARTH
ST

24

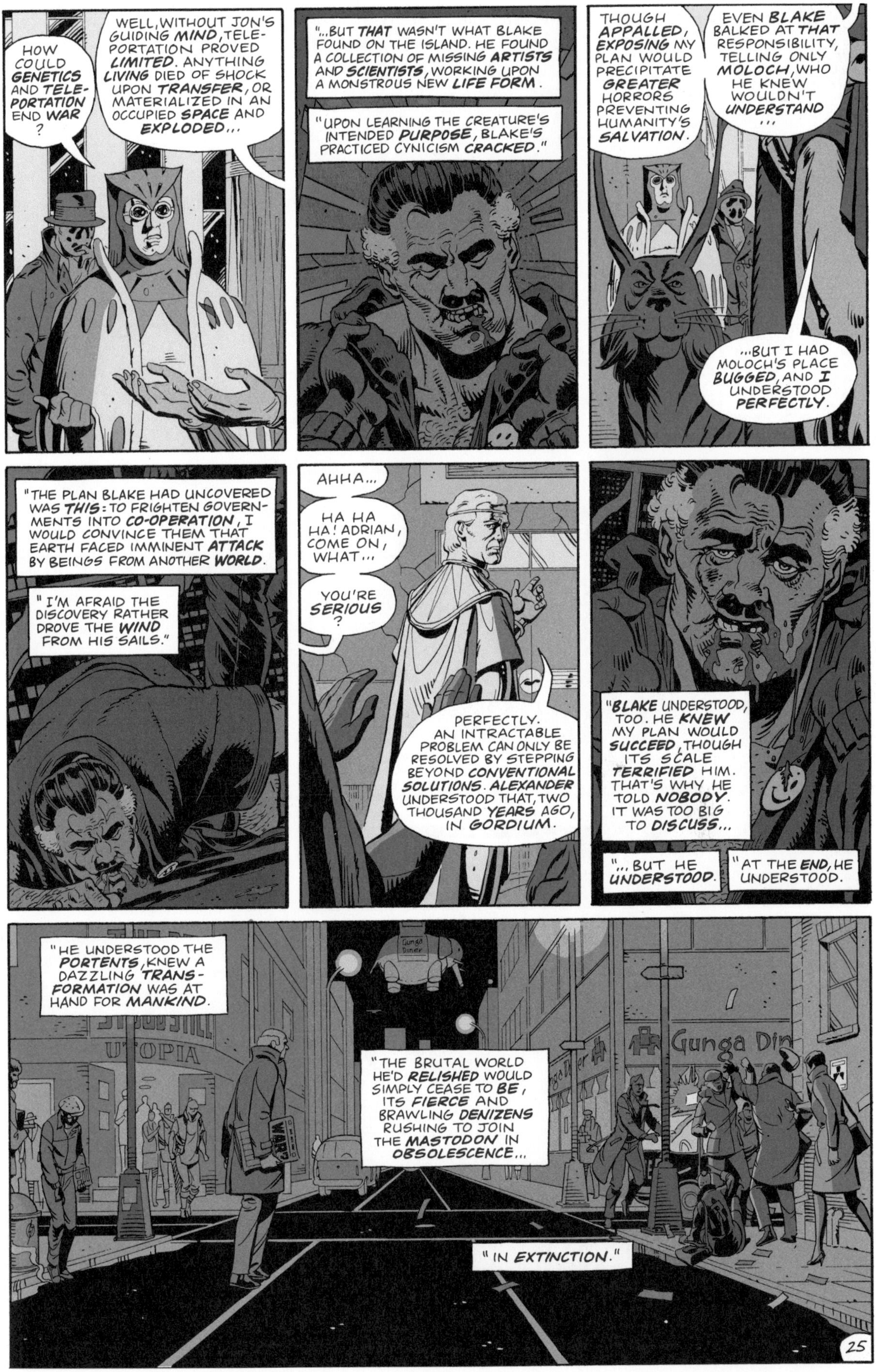
HOW COULD GENETICS AND TELEPORTATION END WAR?
WELL, WITHOUT JON'S GUIDING MIND, TELEPORTATION PROVED LIMITED. ANYTHING LIVING DIED OF SHOCK UPON TRANSFER, OR MATERIALIZED IN AN OCCUPIED SPACE AND EXPLODED...
"...BUT THAT WASN'T WHAT BLAKE FOUND ON THE ISLAND. HE FOUND A COLLECTION OF MISSING ARTISTS AND SCIENTISTS, WORKING UPON A MONSTROUS NEW LIFE FORM.
"UPON LEARNING THE CREATURE'S INTENDED PURPOSE, BLAKE'S PRACTICED CYNICISM CRACKED."
THOUGH APPALLED, EXPOSING MY PLAN WOULD PRECIPITATE GREATER HORRORS PREVENTING HUMANITY'S SALVATION.
EVEN BLAKE BALKED AT THAT RESPONSIBILITY, TELLING ONLY MOLOCH, WHO HE KNEW WOULDN'T UNDERSTAND...
...BUT I HAD MOLOCH'S PLACE BUGGED, AND I UNDERSTOOD PERFECTLY.
"THE PLAN BLAKE HAD UNCOVERED WAS THIS: TO FRIGHTEN GOVERNMENTS INTO CO-OPERATION, I WOULD CONVINCE THEM THAT EARTH FACED IMMINENT ATTACK BY BEINGS FROM ANOTHER WORLD.
"I'M AFRAID THE DISCOVERY RATHER DROVE THE WIND FROM HIS SAILS."
AHHA...
HA HA HA! ADRIAN, COME ON, WHAT...
YOU'RE SERIOUS?
PERFECTLY. AN INTRACTABLE PROBLEM CAN ONLY BE RESOLVED BY STEPPING BEYOND CONVENTIONAL SOLUTIONS. ALEXANDER UNDERSTOOD THAT, TWO THOUSAND YEARS AGO, IN GORDIUM.
"BLAKE UNDERSTOOD, TOO. HE KNEW MY PLAN WOULD SUCCEED, THOUGH ITS SCALE TERRIFIED HIM. THAT'S WHY HE TOLD NOBODY. IT WAS TOO BIG TO DISCUSS...
"...BUT HE UNDERSTOOD.
"AT THE END, HE UNDERSTOOD.
"HE UNDERSTOOD THE PORTENTS, KNEW A DAZZLING TRANSFORMATION WAS AT HAND FOR MANKIND.
UTOPIA
Gunga Diner
Gunga Din
WAR?
"THE BRUTAL WORLD HE'D RELISHED WOULD SIMPLY CEASE TO BE, ITS FIERCE AND BRAWLING DENIZENS RUSHING TO JOIN THE MASTODON IN OBSOLESCENCE...
"IN EXTINCTION."
25

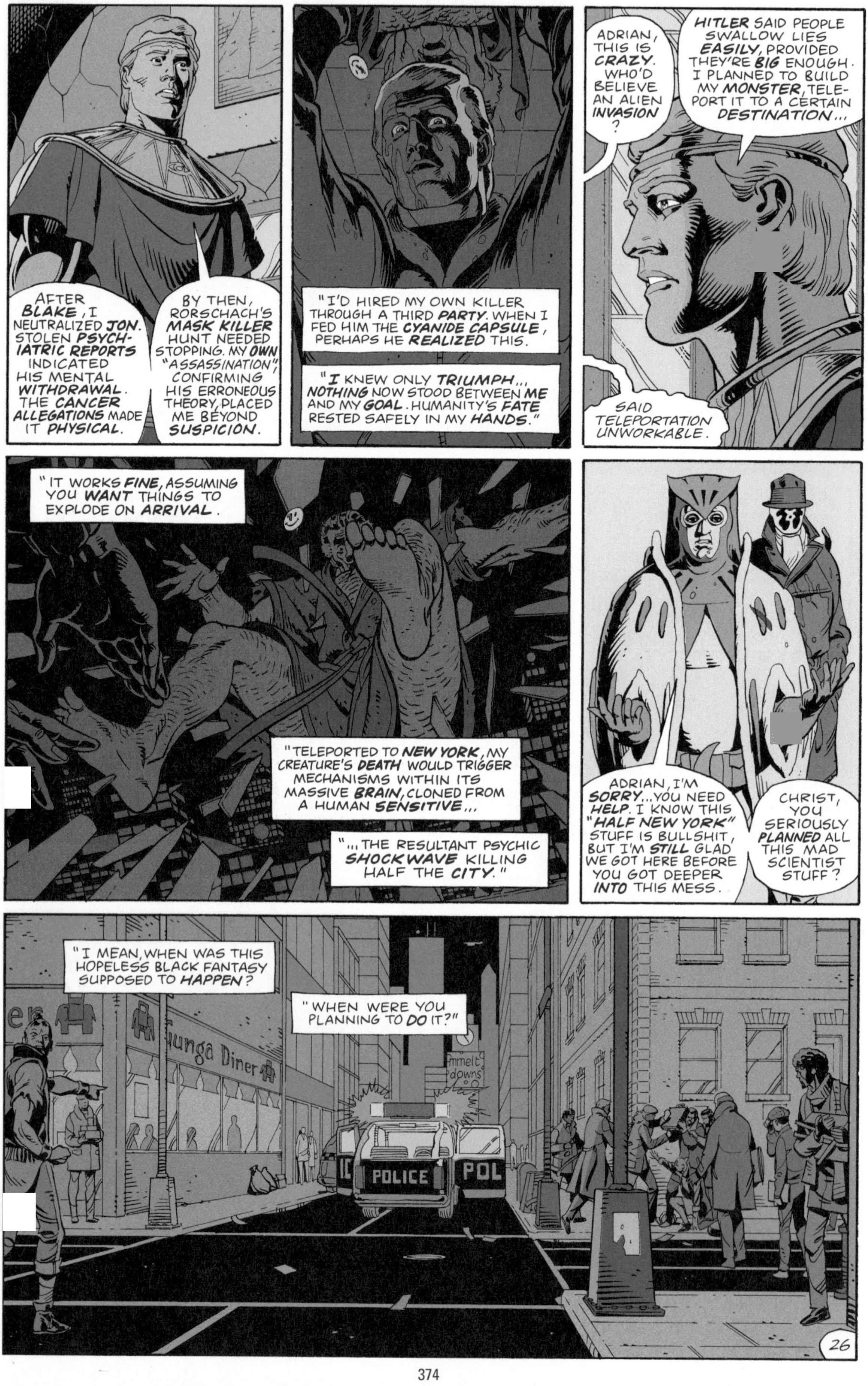

AFTER BLAKE, I NEUTRALIZED JON. STOLEN PSYCHIATRIC REPORTS INDICATED HIS MENTAL WITHDRAWAL. THE CANCER ALLEGATIONS MADE IT PHYSICAL.
BY THEN, RORSCHACH'S MASK KILLER HUNT NEEDED STOPPING. MY OWN "ASSASSINATION", CONFIRMING HIS ERRONEOUS THEORY, PLACED ME BEYOND SUSPICION.
"I'D HIRED MY OWN KILLER THROUGH A THIRD PARTY. WHEN I FED HIM THE CYANIDE CAPSULE, PERHAPS HE REALIZED THIS.
"I KNEW ONLY TRIUMPH... NOTHING NOW STOOD BETWEEN ME AND MY GOAL. HUMANITY'S FATE RESTED SAFELY IN MY HANDS."
ADRIAN, THIS IS CRAZY. WHO'D BELIEVE AN ALIEN INVASION?
HITLER SAID PEOPLE SWALLOW LIES EASILY, PROVIDED THEY'RE BIG ENOUGH. I PLANNED TO BUILD MY MONSTER, TELEPORT IT TO A CERTAIN DESTINATION...
SAID TELEPORTATION UNWORKABLE.
"IT WORKS FINE, ASSUMING YOU WANT THINGS TO EXPLODE ON ARRIVAL.
"TELEPORTED TO NEW YORK, MY CREATURE'S DEATH WOULD TRIGGER MECHANISMS WITHIN ITS MASSIVE BRAIN, CLONED FROM A HUMAN SENSITIVE...
"...THE RESULTANT PSYCHIC SHOCKWAVE KILLING HALF THE CITY."
ADRIAN, I'M SORRY... YOU NEED HELP. I KNOW THIS "HALF NEW YORK" STUFF IS BULLSHIT, BUT I'M STILL GLAD WE GOT HERE BEFORE YOU GOT DEEPER INTO THIS MESS.
CHRIST, YOU SERIOUSLY PLANNED ALL THIS MAD SCIENTIST STUFF?
"I MEAN, WHEN WAS THIS HOPELESS BLACK FANTASY SUPPOSED TO HAPPEN?
"WHEN WERE YOU PLANNING TO DO IT?"
Gunga Diner
POLICE
POL
26

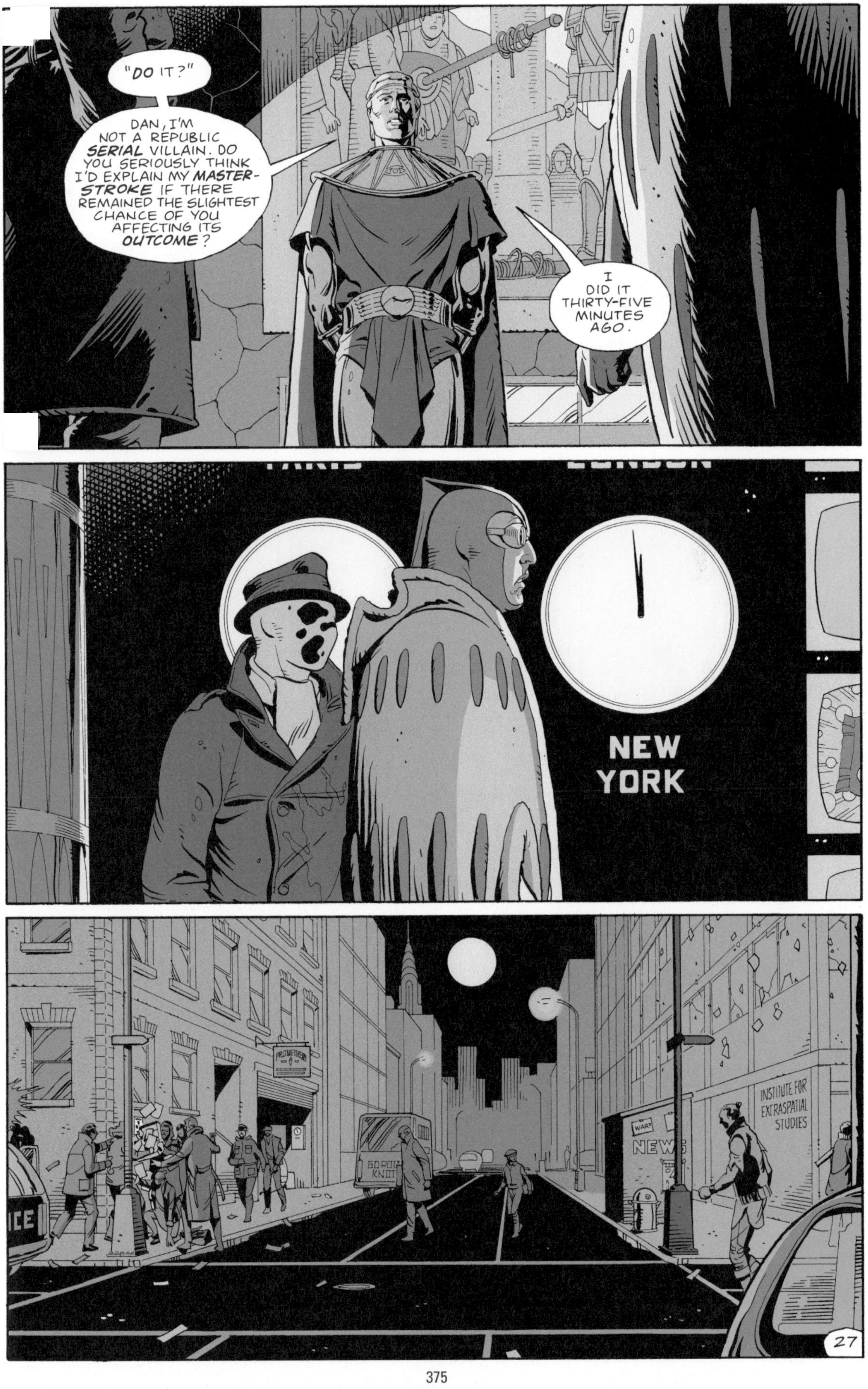
"DO IT?"
DAN, I'M NOT A REPUBLIC SERIAL VILLAIN. DO YOU SERIOUSLY THINK I'D EXPLAIN MY MASTER-STROKE IF THERE REMAINED THE SLIGHTEST CHANCE OF YOU AFFECTING ITS OUTCOME?
I DID IT THIRTY-FIVE MINUTES AGO.
NEW YORK
INSTITUTE FOR EXTRASPATIAL STUDIES
NEWS
27

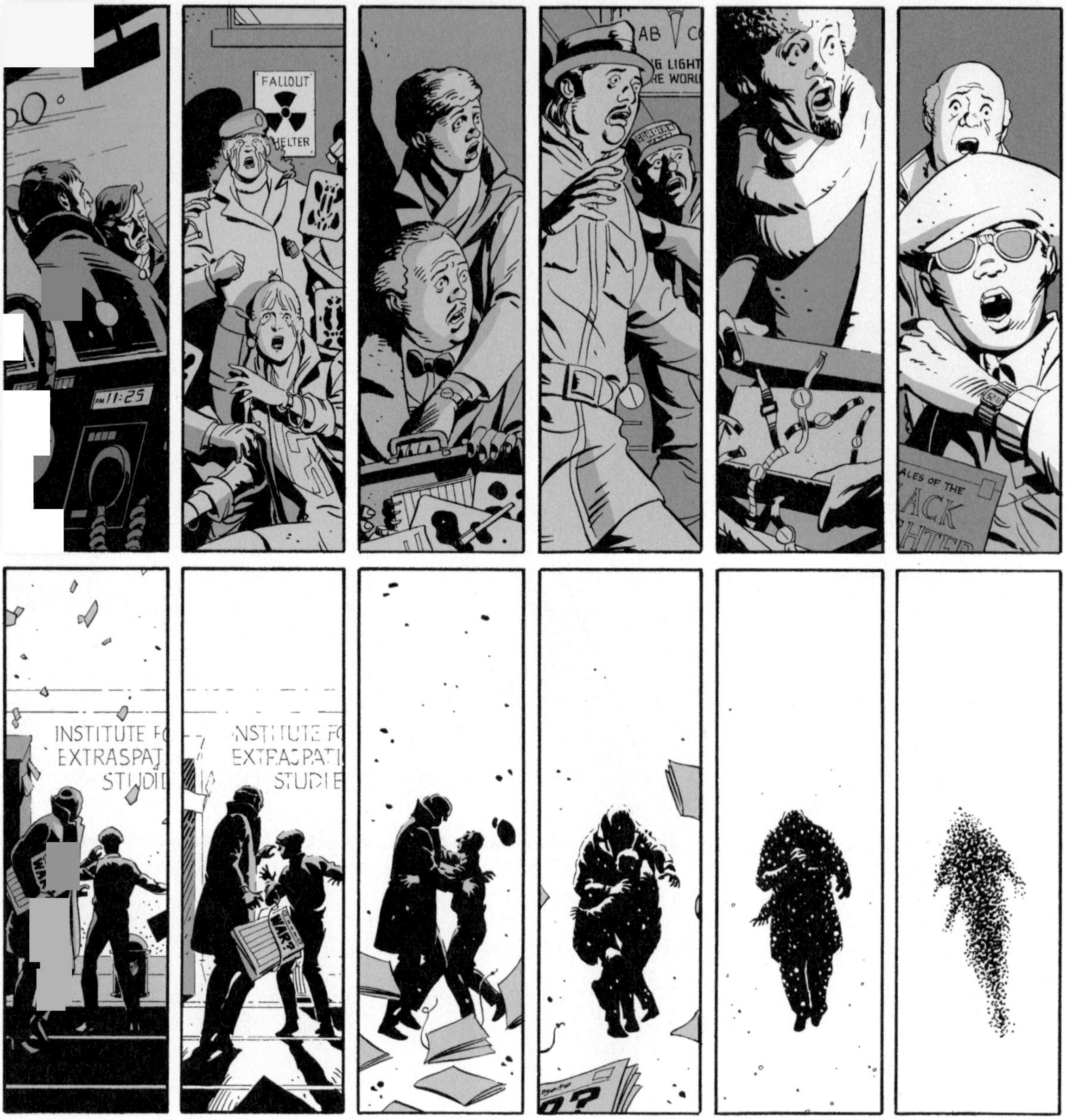
FALLOUT
HELTER
INSTITUTE FO
EXTRASPATI
WAR?

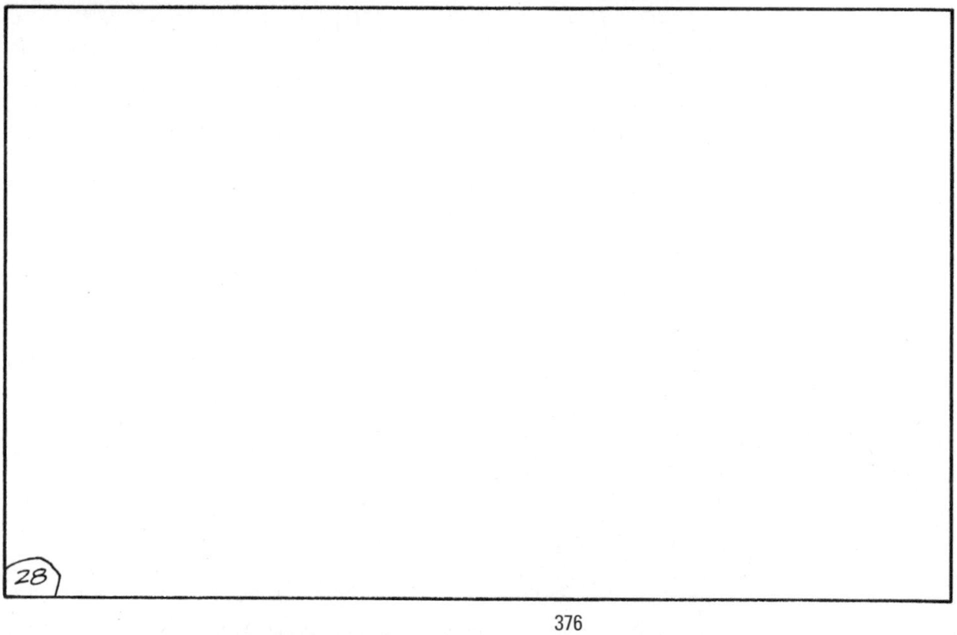
28

My name is
Ozymandias,
king of kings:
Look on my works,
ye mighty,
and despair!

—*Ozymandias*
Percy
Bysshe
Shelley

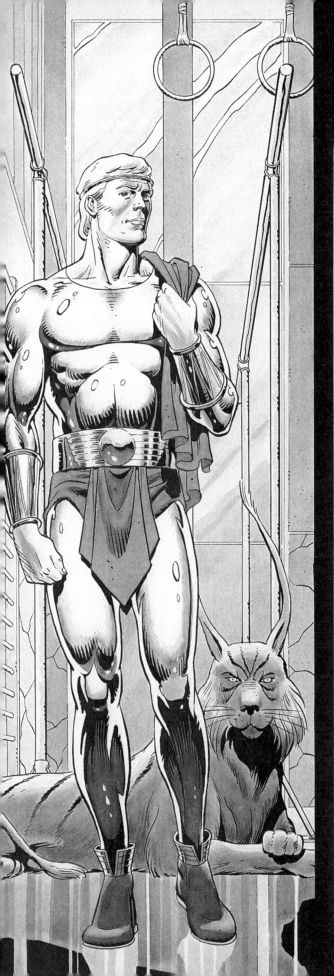

AFTER THE MASQUERADE:

Superstyle and the art of humanoid watching.

DOUG ROTH VISITS ANTARCTICA TO INTERVIEW ADRIAN VEIDT

VEIDT: "The frightening thing about the campaign to re-elect the president is that in the wake of the victory in Vietnam, I don't see how they can fail. C.R.E.E.P.! What a terrible acronym. I wonder who coined that one? Somebody who watched too many 'Man From U.N.C.L.E.' episodes in the sixties ... Liddy, or one of those other Washington humanoids."

"Humanoids." I'm sitting talking with a retired superhero in a glass dome filled with tropical flowers and hummingbirds, while outside the antarctic wind builds snowdrifts against the glass. I would imagine myself beyond surprise by this point, yet the sudden use of such an odd term is startling. Have I detected a hitherto unnoticed contempt for mere humans behind that eminently likable golden facade? Why "humanoids"? I put this to him, and he chuckles.

VEIDT: "I'm sorry, it's a sort of one-man private joke. I've been referring to Nixon's close subordinates as humanoids since I heard about the banquet ... and this is true, I promise ... where one of the presidential aides spilled a glass of water over Vice-President Ford. The aide was incredibly apologetic, obviously, but Ford just smiled and said 'Oh, that's okay. Nobody's human.' (*Laughter*) I've called 'em humanoids ever since."

Continued

The laughter of Adrian Veidt is deep and rich, filled with a warmth I hadn't anticipated as the jet he'd arranged lowered me gently from the blank white antarctic sky towards the dangerously small-looking black hyphen of the landing strip, set into the endless pack ice far below. The landscape was hard and cold, too big to get to grips with, and I expected much the same of any man who'd choose to live in it.

The plane was met at the landing strip by three enthusiastically friendly Vietnamese men who led me between obelisks of dark marble with rolling purple highlights towards the fortress dominating the nude white reaches beyond.

Servants? My liberal sensibilities recoiled at the concept with a predictable knee-jerk. Later, however, on learning that the men had been Vietcong refugees in danger of losing their lives in the purges following America's victory without Veidt's intervention, I wasn't so sure. Since Antarctica is owned by no nation, the men are theoretically safe from extradition, and their nominal boss seems to treat them more as respected friends than as lackeys. Certainly, they themselves seem deliriously happy with both their lot and their landlord.

"Mr. Veidt has made the effort to understand our culture. He talks to us often concerning our religious beliefs, asking many questions." The man who tells me this is sincere and heartfelt in his testimonial, showing an almost fatherly protective anxiety that this magazine should not misrepresent his employer:

"He is not one of your pop music stars. He does not inject drugs, or treat young women badly. Make sure that you say that."

When we reach the fortress, Veidt is still completing his daily workout in a gymnasium of vast, almost dreamlike proportions, where parallel bars meet at infinity. I'm cordially invited to watch while he finishes up, and as I observe that perfect swiss-watch of a body twirling and circling above me in easy defiance of gravity, all my earlier doubts concerning Veidt's accessibility return.

There he is, right up there above me: the man. Adrian Veidt. Ozyman . . . whoops. Uh-uh. We don't call him that anymore, do we? The mask is gone, but as he loops the high bar in slow, graceful centrifuge he still wears the golden leotard, and the headband. Every girlfriend I've had in the past four years has wanted to lay this guy, more than Jagger, more than Springsteen or D'Eath or any of those also-rans, and now here I am, squinting up at him, and yes, goddamn it, I have to goddamned admit that he looks like a goddamned god! I can't quite believe he'll submit to being interviewed by someone so obviously mired in the dregs of the gene pool as myself . . .

. . . but here he comes, dropping to the floor, picking up the purple towel that I realize later is actually the tunic of his costume, and wiping himself beneath the arms with it in a distinctly Homo sapiens fashion. He's walking towards me, his smile somewhere between Jackie Coogan and J.F.K., sticking out a hand that grips mine strongly enough to make me glad it's friendly. He glances towards the gymnasium windows, outside which a blizzard seems to be commencing and smiles again.

"Not the sort of snow you're used to in California, Mr. Roth."

A coke joke! Adrian Veidt, Ozy-freakin'-mandias himself has just told me a coke joke! Whoooo-ee! We fall easily into conversation from that point on, and after he's dressed he takes me for a tour of his fortress, opulent beyond the wildest dreams of Versailles. We end up in a large section of the main hall where one wall appears to be entirely covered with TV screens, all tuned to different channels. It is here that we hold our interview, and I notice his eyes often drifting across the riot of clashing images as we speak. It's only after I express worries concerning background noise and my recording equipment that he thinks to turn the sound of the multiple televisions down. They don't seem to affect _his_ concentration at all.

Before launching into my interview spiel, I take a breath and remember why I'm here. Almost lost in the cacophony surrounding the old Trickster's Constitutional amendment scam, one of America's best-respected and most consistently left-leaning superheroes quietly retired from crimefighting to pursue a career in business. When this magazine phoned him to ask why, he kindly offered to fly me up to his antarctic retreat where we could conduct the interview in comfort. Exhaling, I press the record button and begin.

NOVA: So, how do you get to be a superhero? Were your parents rich? I mean, did that give you advantages?

VEIDT: No more than I could help. My mother left me a lot of money when she died, but I gave it to charity when I was seventeen. I wanted to prove that I could accomplish anything I wanted starting from absolutely nothing. Also, I wanted to free myself of concern for money. Consequently, it's never been a problem for me. To answer your question, you get to be a superhero by believing in the hero within you and summoning him or her forth by an act of will. Believing in yourself and your own potential is the first step to realizing that potential. Alternatively, you could do as Jon did: Fall into a nuclear reactor and hope for the best. On the whole, I think I prefer to stick to my own methods. (_Laughter_)

NOVA: You'll forgive me for saying so, but isn't that philosophy a little Norman Vincent Peale? That self-realization stuff? How exactly do you exploit that potential to the degree that you obviously have?

VEIDT: The disciplines of physical exercise, meditation and study aren't terribly esoteric. The means to attain a capability far beyond that of the so-called ordinary person are within reach of

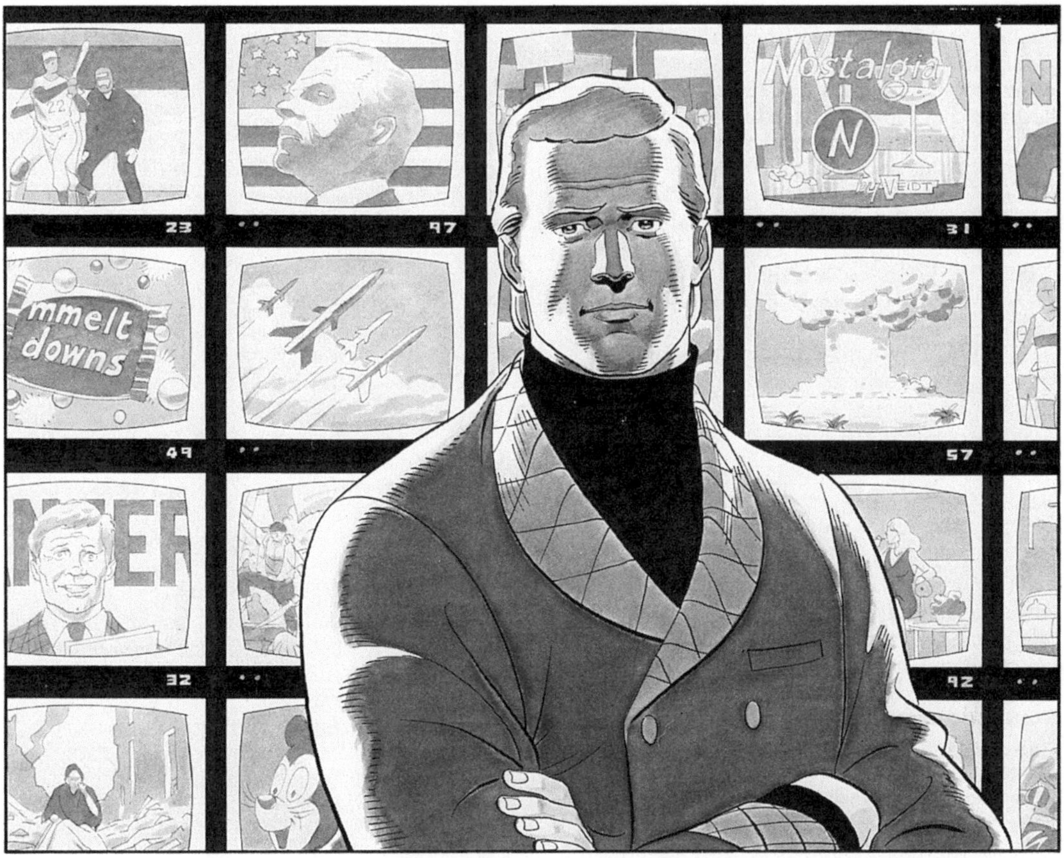
Nostalgia
N
mmelt downs

everyone, if their desire and their will are strong enough. I have studied science, art, religion and a hundred different philosophies. Anyone could do as much. By applying what you learn and ordering your thoughts in an intelligent manner it is possible to accomplish almost anything. Possible for the "ordinary person." There's a notion I'd like to see buried: the ordinary person. Ridiculous. There is no ordinary person.

NOVA: Returning to your costumed career, why did you quit?

VEIDT: There were a number of reasons, but I suppose basically it boiled down to my increasing uncertainty about the role of the costumed hero in the seventies. What does fighting crime mean, exactly? Does it mean upholding the law when a woman shoplifts to feed her children, or does it mean struggling to uncover the ones who, quite legally, have brought about her poverty? Yes, I've busted drug rings and been accused of being an establishment pawn for doing so . . . that happened a lot in the sixties. I've also uncovered plots by breakaway extremist factions within the Pentagon, for example the plot to release some unpleasantly specific diseases upon the population of Africa, the exposure of which led to the *New Frontiersman* denouncing me as a "Puppet of Peking" on the strength of my youthful travels through the East. I guess I've just reached a point where I've started to wonder whether all the grandstanding and fighting individual evils does much good for the world as a whole. Those evils are just symptoms of an overall sickness of the human spirit, and I don't believe you can cure a disease by suppressing its symptoms. That whole *Contac-400* approach to our society's problems, I despair of it. It doesn't work. Maybe as a businessman I can do more good, on a more meaningful scale.

NOVA: What sort of world do you see it being, in the future?

VEIDT: That depends upon us . . . each and every one of us. Futurology interests me perhaps more than any other single subject, and as such I devote a great deal of time to its study. Even so, technology is progressing at an ever-accelerating pace, and by early next century I would hesitate to predict *any* limitations upon what we might be capable of. I would say without hesitation that a new world is within our grasp, filled with unimaginable experiences and possibilities, if only we want it badly enough. Not a utopia . . . I don't believe that any species could continue to grow and keep from stagnation without *some* adversity . . . but a society with a more human basis, where the problems that beset us are at least *new* problems.

NOVA: You don't think there's a possibility we may have damaged the environment beyond repair, or that we might someday have a fatal nuclear showdown with the Soviets?

Continued

PHOTO COURTESY OF TRIANGLE INC. © 1975

Veidt cont.

VEIDT: Of course. Of course I do. I'd be ignoring the facts if I didn't accept those things as strong possibilities. As I said, it all depends on us, on whether we, individually, want Armageddon or a new world of fabulous, limitless potential. That's not such an obvious question as it seems. I believe there are some people who really do want, if only subconsciously, an end to the world. They want to be spared the responsibilities of maintaining that world, to be spared the effort of imagination needed to realize such a future. And of course, there are other people who want very much to live. I see twentieth century society as a sort of race between enlightenment and extinction. In one lane you have the four horsemen of the apocalypse . . .

NOVA: . . . and in the other?

VEIDT: The seventh cavalry. (*Laughter*)

NOVA: Changing the subject entirely, do you listen to much music? I wondered what your tastes might be, as a superhero . . .

VEIDT: I like electronic music. That's a very superhero-ey thing to like, I suppose, isn't it? I like avant-garde music in general. Cage, Stockhausen, Penderecki, Andrew Lang, Pierre Henry. Terry Riley is very good. Oh, and I've heard some interesting new music from Jamaica . . . a sort of hybrid between electronic music and reggae. It's a fascinating study in the new musical forms generated when a largely pre-technological culture is given access to modern recording techniques without the technological preconceptions that we've allowed to accumulate, limiting our vision. It's called dub music. You'd like it, I'm sure.

NOVA: How do you get on with the rest of the superhero fraternity? Some of them seem very right-wing in contrast with your own stance. I'm thinking of Rorschach, the Comedian, Dr. Manhattan . . .

VEIDT: *Jon*? Right-wing? (*Laughs*) If there's one thing in this cosmos that that man *isn't* capable of

doing it's having a political bias. Believe me . . . you have to meet him to understand. I mean, which do you prefer, red ants or black ants?

NOVA: Uh . . .? Well, I don't have any particular preference . . .

VEIDT: Exactly. Well, imagine how Jon feels. Rorschach, I don't know very well. I believe he's a man of great integrity, but he seems to see the world in very black and white, Manichean terms. I personally believe that to be an intellectual limitation.

NOVA: And the Comedian? I understand there's no love lost between you. I heard that he beat you in combat, back when you were just starting out . . .

VEIDT: Yes, well, that was a case of mistaken identity and general misunderstanding. For some reason it happens a lot when costumed crime-fighters meet for the first time. (*Laughter*)

NOVA: But you and the Comedian don't like each other?

VEIDT: My, but you're determined, aren't you? (*Laughs*) No, we're not great friends. It's largely a political difference. He sees me as an intellectual dilettante dabbling in national affairs that don't concern me. I see him as an amoral mercenary allying himself to whichever political faction seems likely to grant him the greatest license. The difference is as simple and as profound as that.

NOVA: There's no general sense of disillusionment with your fellow crimefighters, then?

VEIDT: Not at all. Some of my dearest friends are numbered amongst them. I wish them all nothing but luck in the years that lie ahead.

NOVA: In closing, you've often been referred to in the press as the world's smartest man. Is that true, and does it bother you?

VEIDT: No, that isn't true, but it's very flattering and I don't mind a bit. If somebody wants to call me the world's best-groomed man, then hey, that's okay too. (*Laughs*) No, no, I don't mind being the smartest man in the world. I just wish it wasn't this one. ★

THE TIMES THEY ARE A 'CHANGING

NOSTALGIA BY VEIDT

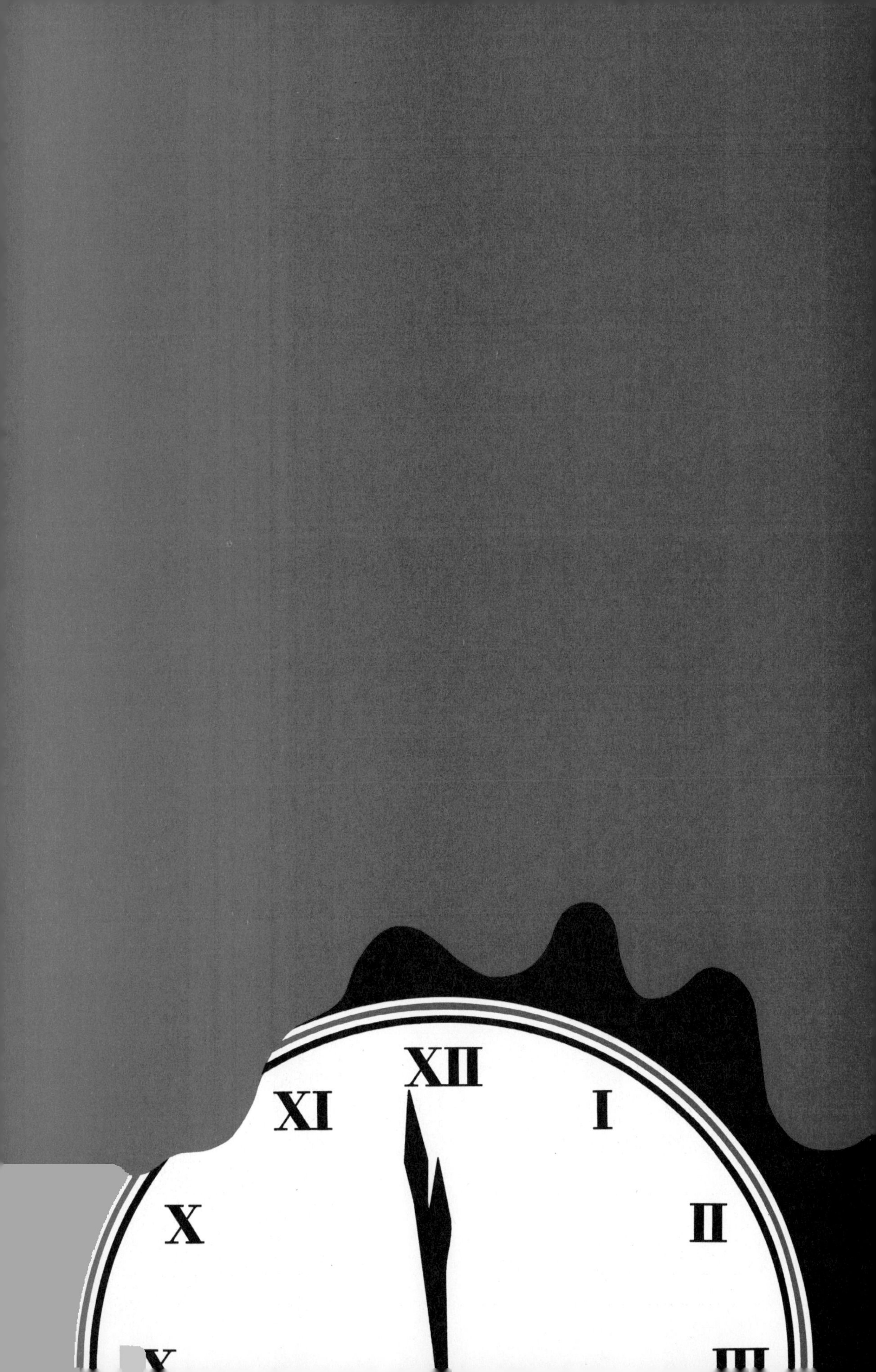
XII
XI
I
X
II

CHAPTER XII

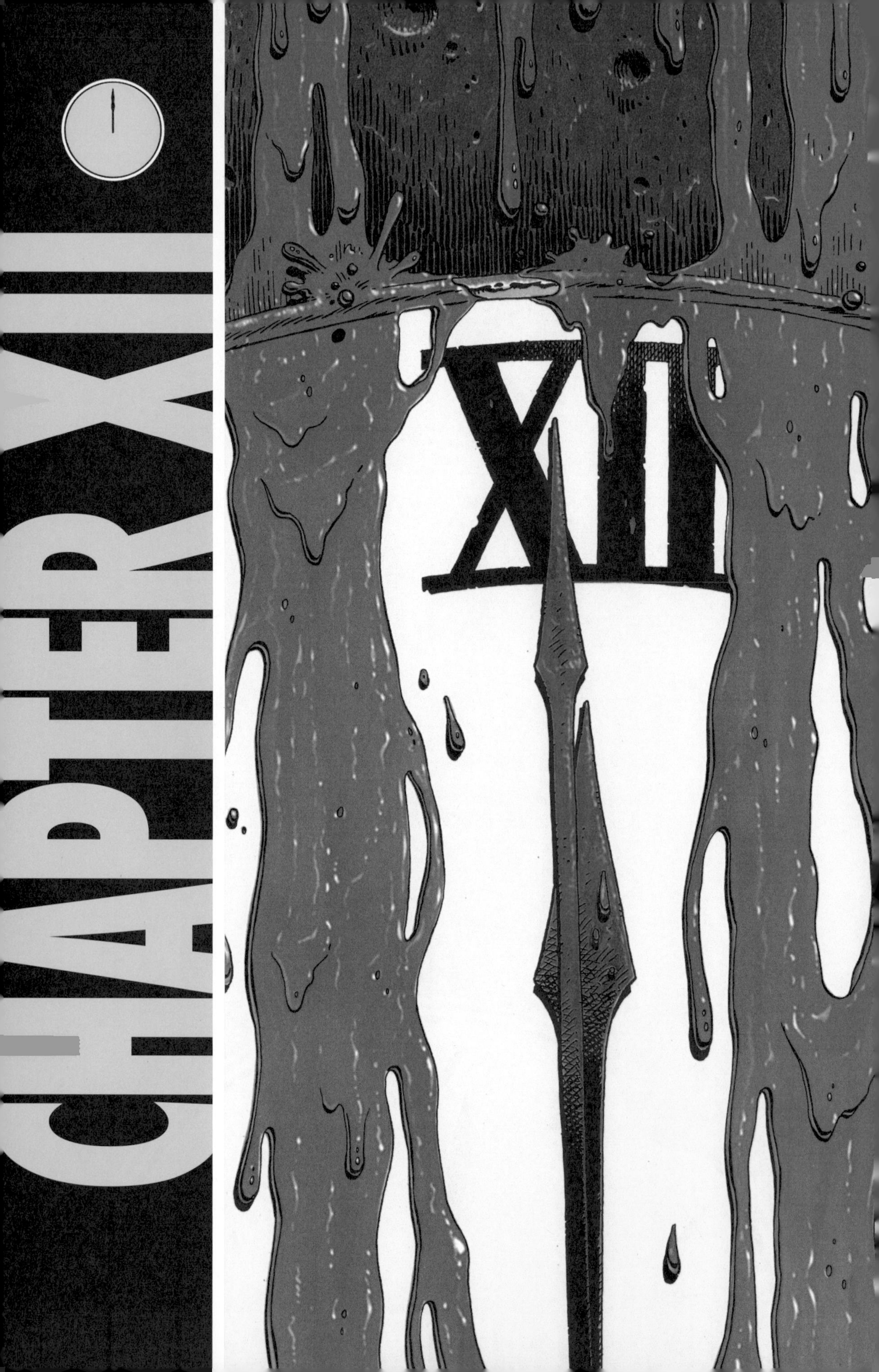

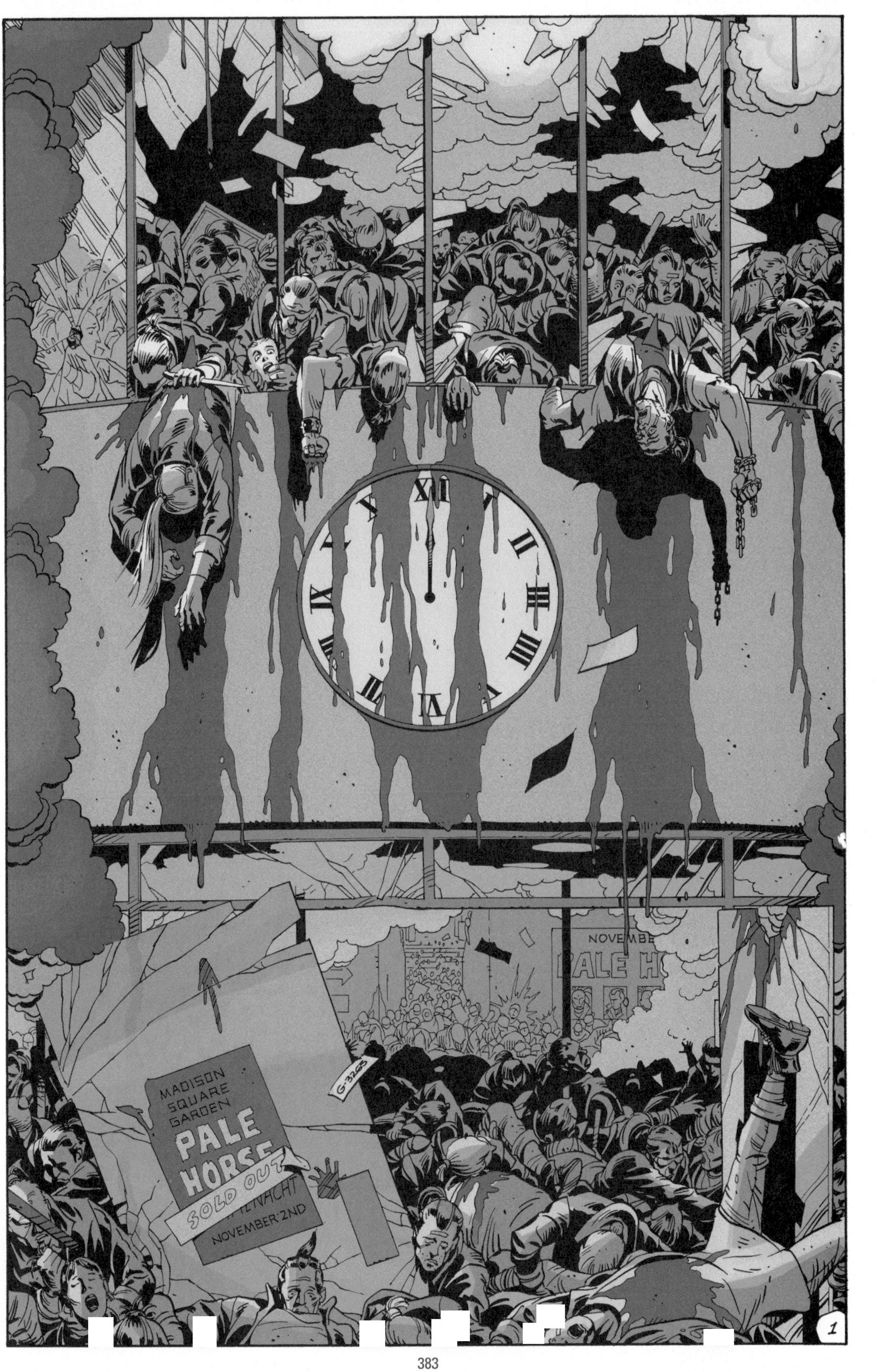
MADISON SQUARE GARDEN
PALE HORSE
SOLD OUT
NOVEMBER 2ND
G-3265
1

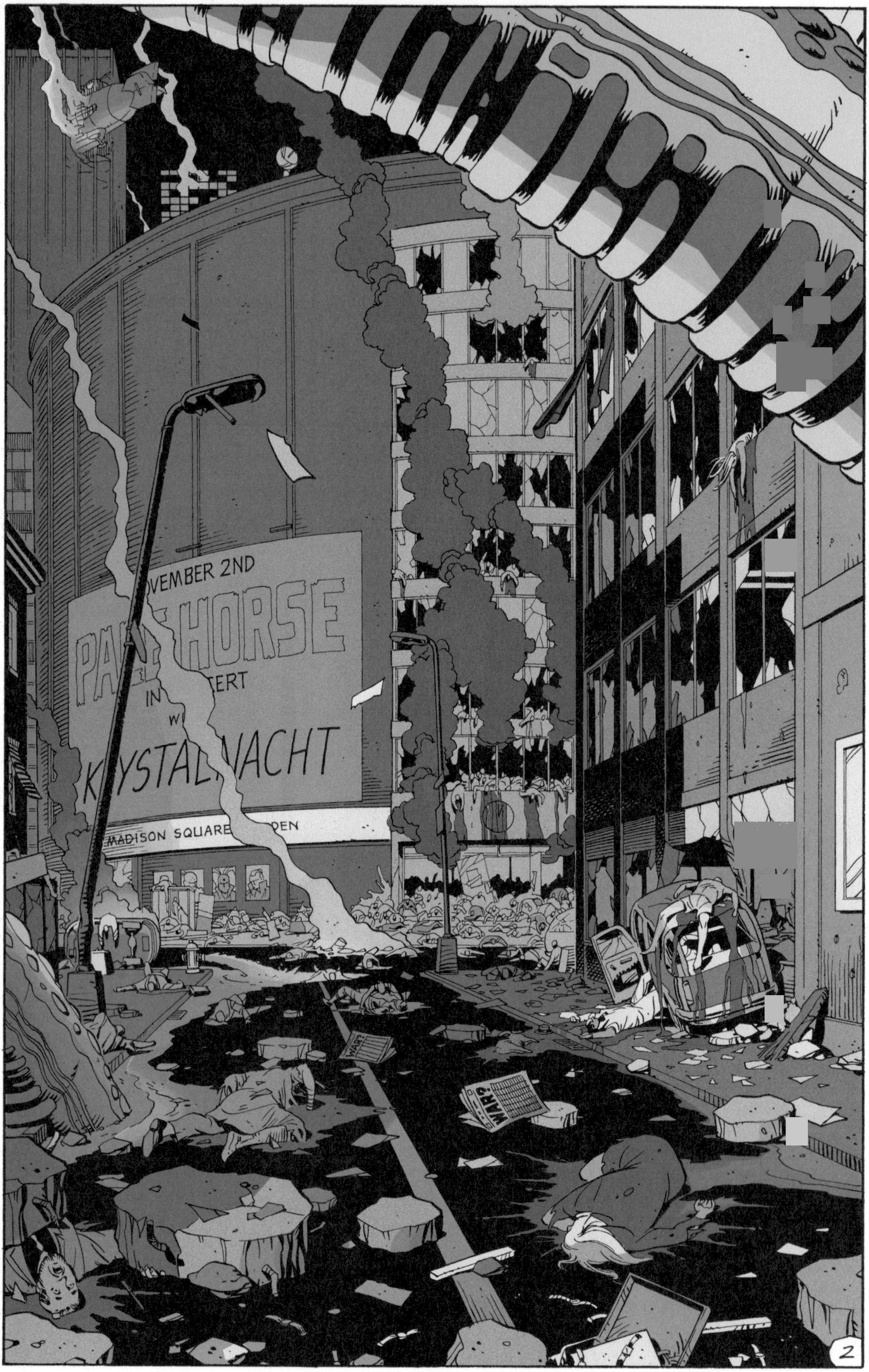
VEMBER 2ND
HORSE
ERT
ACHT
MADISON SQUARE
DEN
WAR?
2

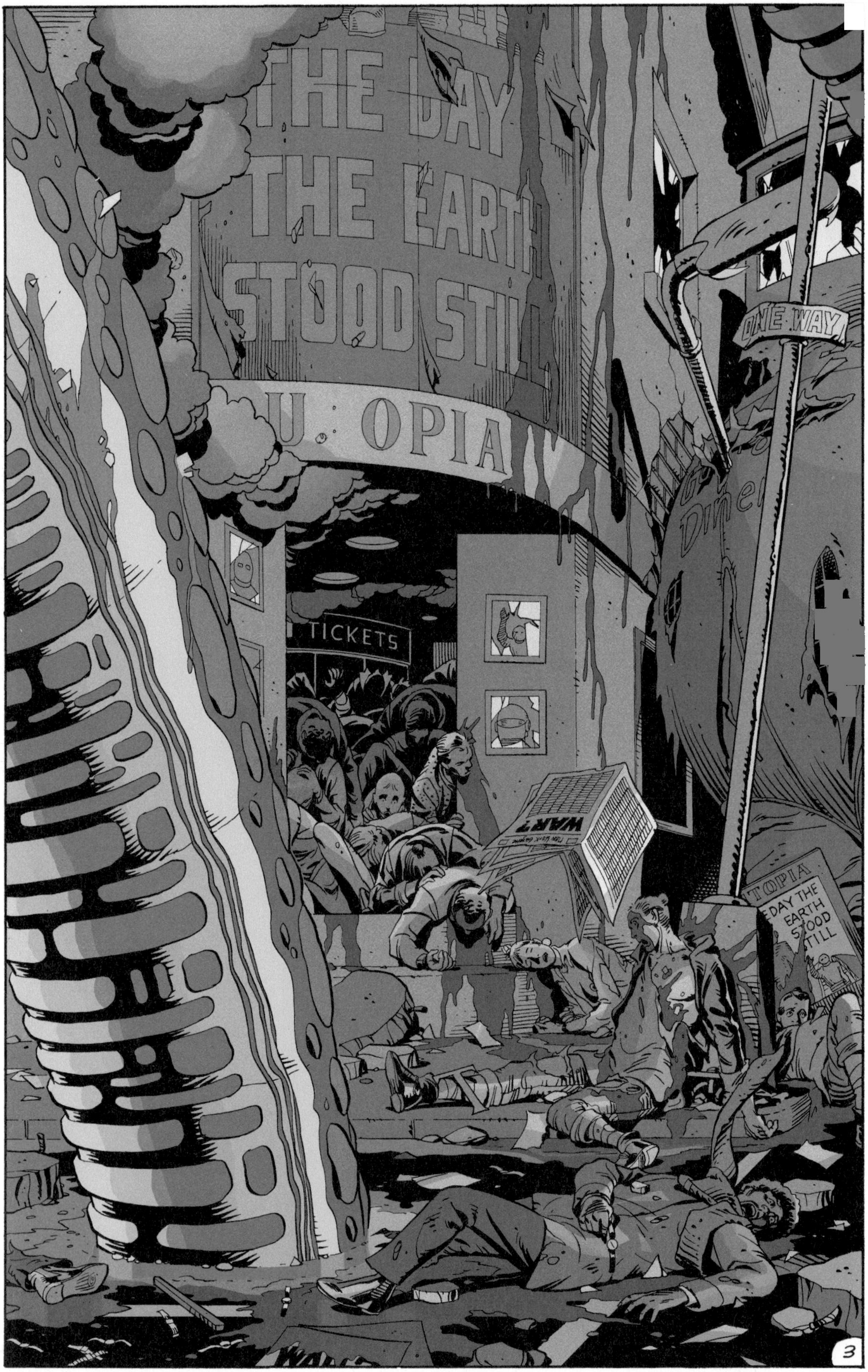
THE DAY THE EARTH STOOD STILL
U OPIA
TICKETS
ONE WAY
Diner
WAR?
TOPIA
DAY THE EARTH STOOD STILL
3

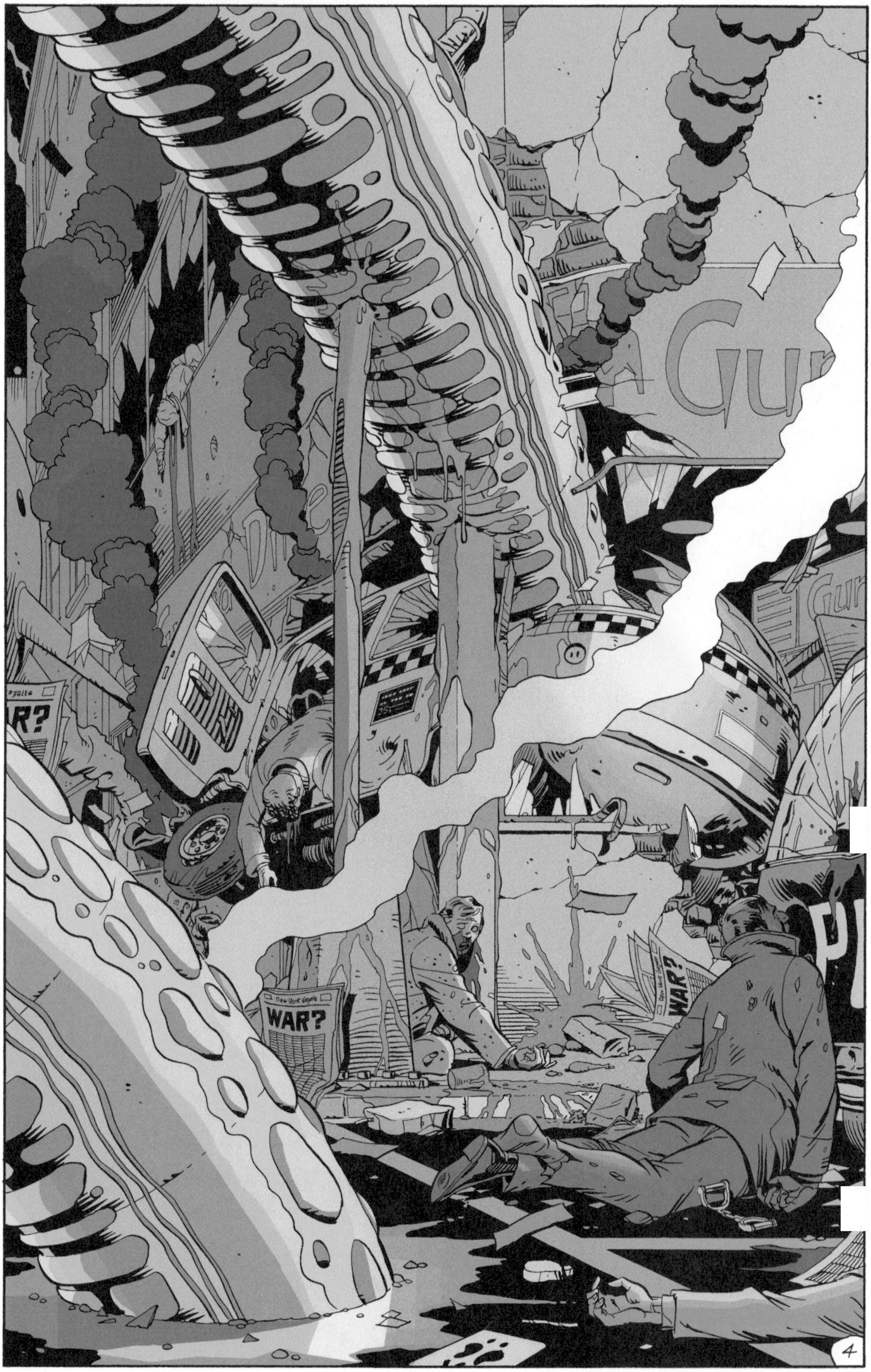
WAR?
WAR?

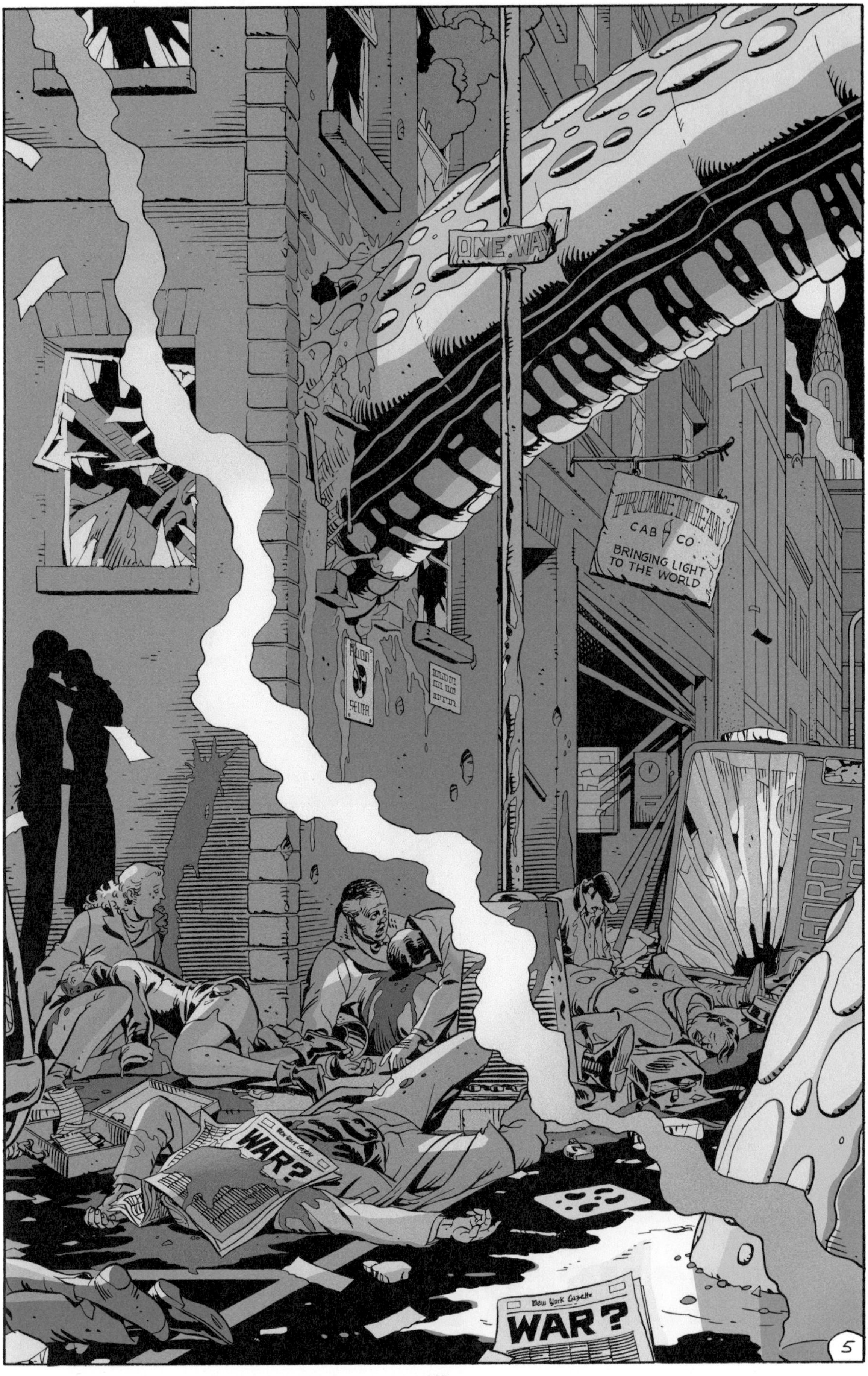
ONE WAY
PROMETHEAN
CAB CO
BRINGING LIGHT
TO THE WORLD
GORDIAN
WAR?
New York Gazette
WAR?
5

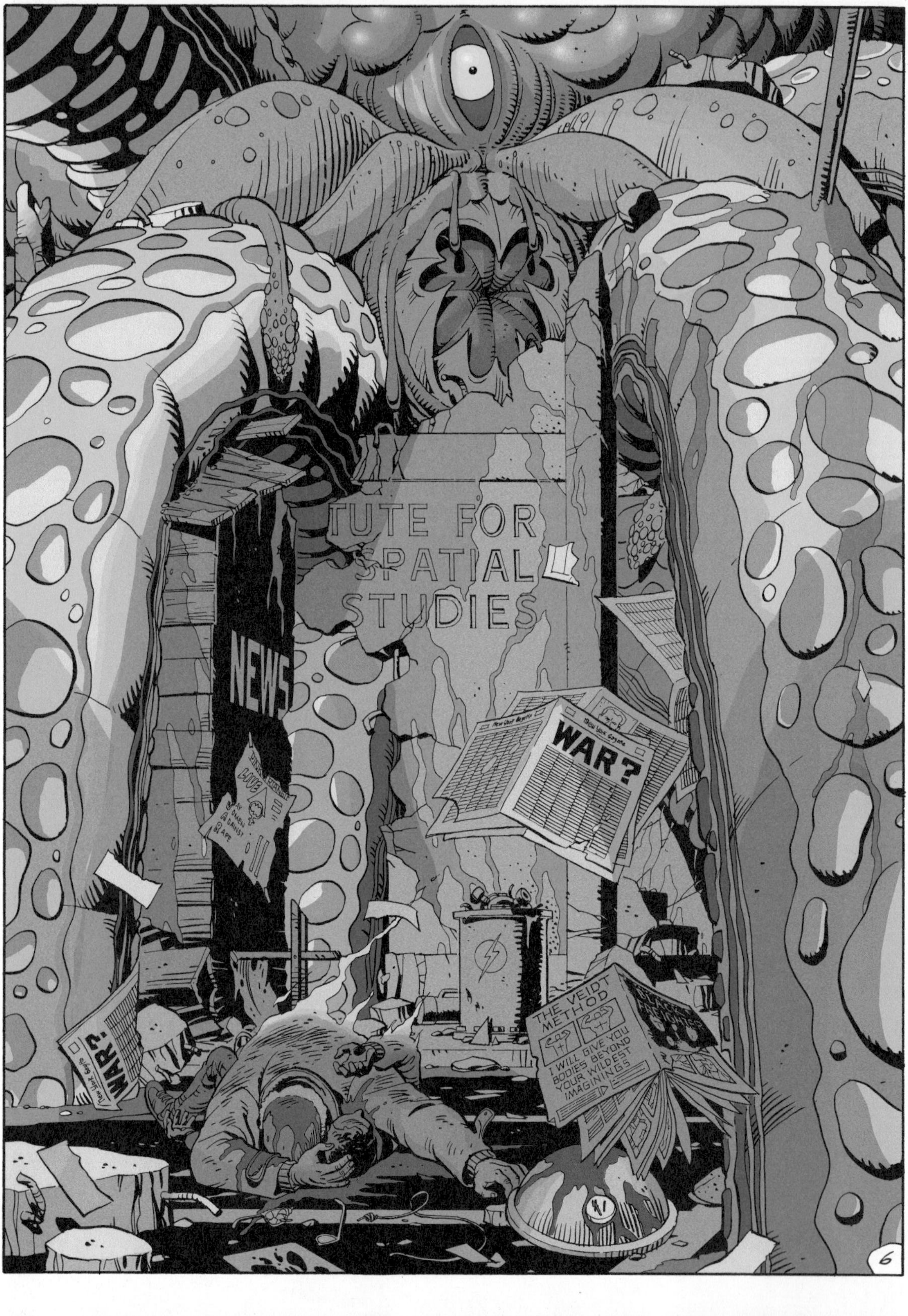
TUTE FOR
SPATIAL
STUDIES
NEWS
WAR?
THE VEIDT METHOD
I WILL GIVE YOU BODIES BEYOND YOUR WILDEST IMAGININGS
WAR?
6

A STRONGER LOVING WORLD

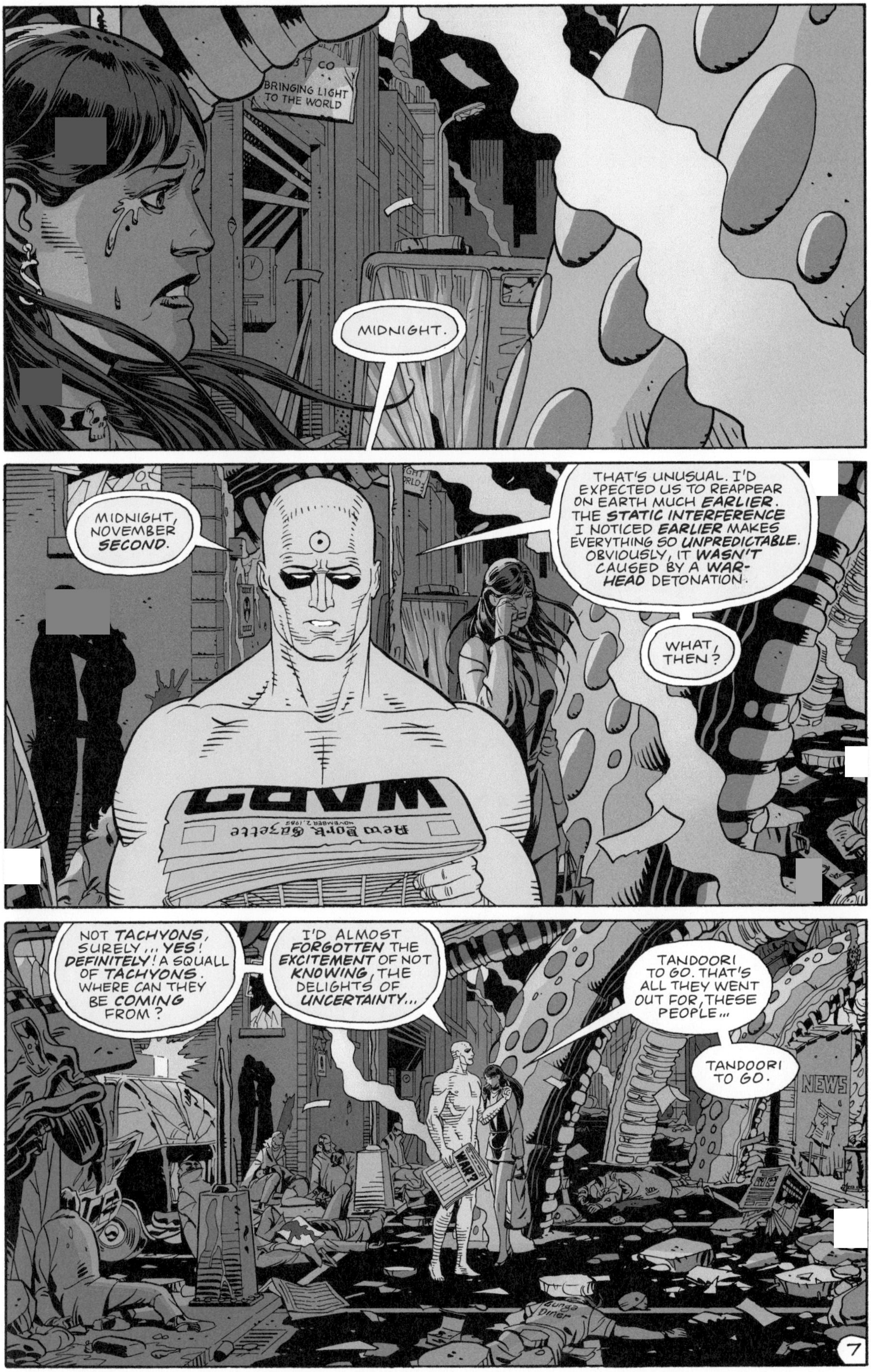
CO
BRINGING LIGHT TO THE WORLD
MIDNIGHT.
MIDNIGHT, NOVEMBER SECOND.
THAT'S UNUSUAL. I'D EXPECTED US TO REAPPEAR ON EARTH MUCH EARLIER. THE STATIC INTERFERENCE I NOTICED EARLIER MAKES EVERYTHING SO UNPREDICTABLE. OBVIOUSLY, IT WASN'T CAUSED BY A WAR-HEAD DETONATION.
WHAT, THEN?
NOT TACHYONS, SURELY... YES! DEFINITELY! A SQUALL OF TACHYONS. WHERE CAN THEY BE COMING FROM?
I'D ALMOST FORGOTTEN THE EXCITEMENT OF NOT KNOWING, THE DELIGHTS OF UNCERTAINTY...
TANDOORI TO GO. THAT'S ALL THEY WENT OUT FOR, THESE PEOPLE...
TANDOORI TO GO.
NEWS
Gunga Diner
7

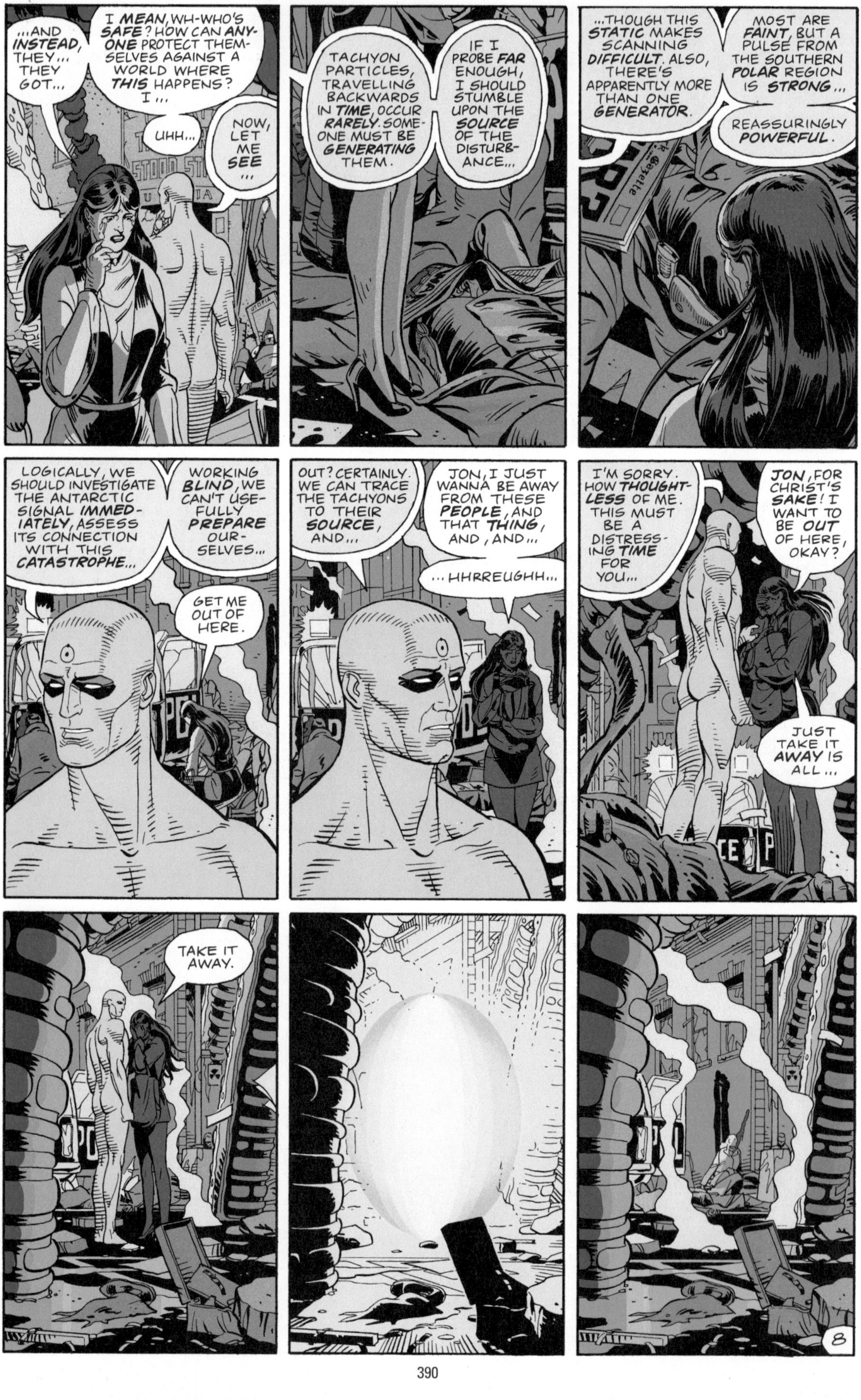
...AND INSTEAD, THEY... THEY GOT...
I MEAN, WH-WHO'S SAFE? HOW CAN ANYONE PROTECT THEMSELVES AGAINST A WORLD WHERE THIS HAPPENS? I...
UHH...
NOW, LET ME SEE...
TACHYON PARTICLES, TRAVELLING BACKWARDS IN TIME, OCCUR RARELY. SOMEONE MUST BE GENERATING THEM.
IF I PROBE FAR ENOUGH, I SHOULD STUMBLE UPON THE SOURCE OF THE DISTURBANCE...
...THOUGH THIS STATIC MAKES SCANNING DIFFICULT. ALSO, THERE'S APPARENTLY MORE THAN ONE GENERATOR.
MOST ARE FAINT, BUT A PULSE FROM THE SOUTHERN POLAR REGION IS STRONG...
REASSURINGLY POWERFUL.
LOGICALLY, WE SHOULD INVESTIGATE THE ANTARCTIC SIGNAL IMMEDIATELY, ASSESS ITS CONNECTION WITH THIS CATASTROPHE...
WORKING BLIND, WE CAN'T USEFULLY PREPARE OURSELVES...
GET ME OUT OF HERE.
OUT? CERTAINLY. WE CAN TRACE THE TACHYONS TO THEIR SOURCE, AND...
JON, I JUST WANNA BE AWAY FROM THESE PEOPLE, AND THAT THING, AND, AND...
...HHRREUGHH...
I'M SORRY. HOW THOUGHTLESS OF ME. THIS MUST BE A DISTRESSING TIME FOR YOU...
JON, FOR CHRIST'S SAKE! I WANT TO BE OUT OF HERE, OKAY?
JUST TAKE IT AWAY IS ALL...
TAKE IT AWAY.
8

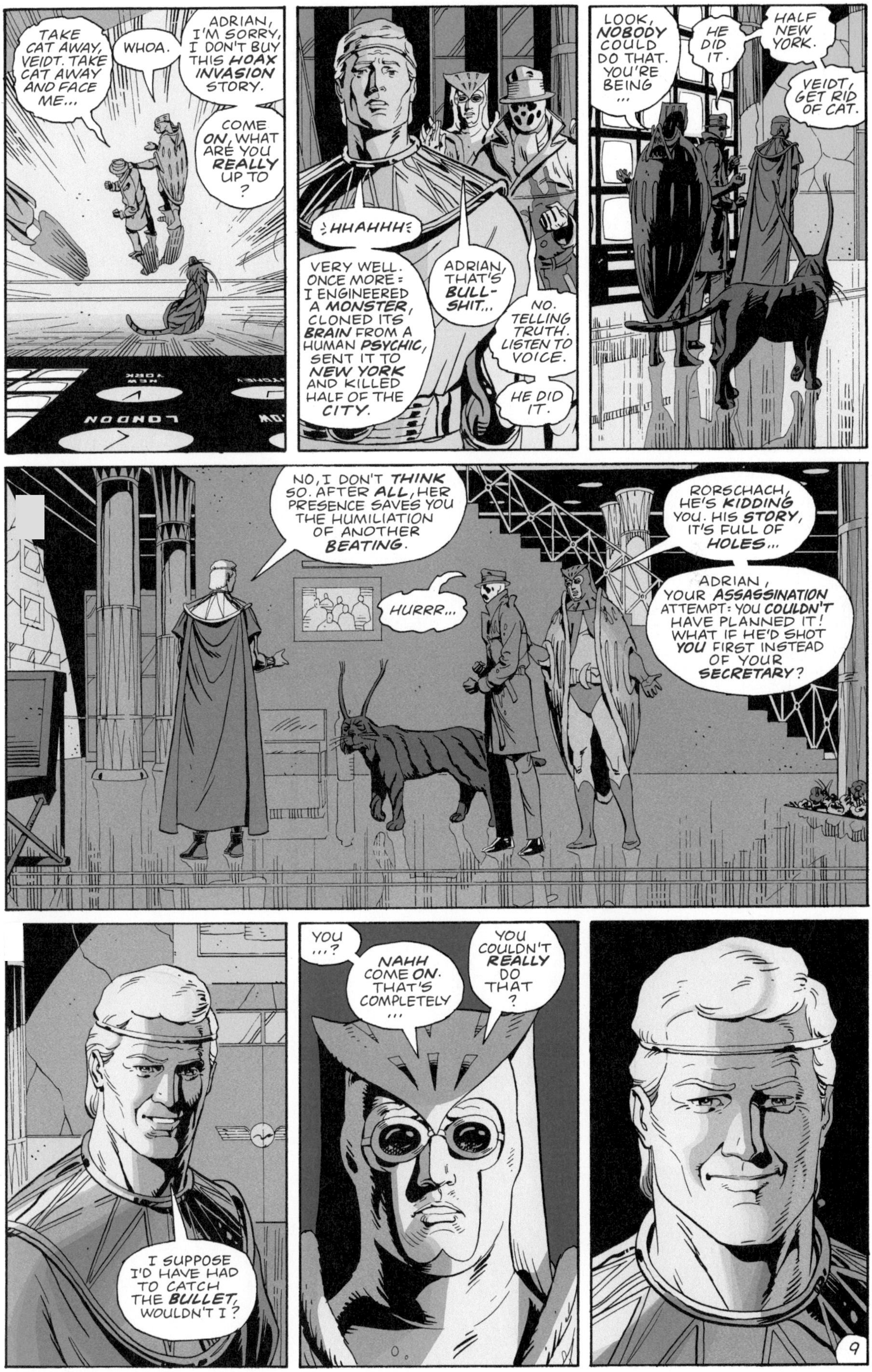
TAKE CAT AWAY, VEIDT. TAKE CAT AWAY AND FACE ME...
WHOA.
ADRIAN, I'M SORRY, I DON'T BUY THIS HOAX INVASION STORY.
COME ON, WHAT ARE YOU REALLY UP TO?
LONDON
NEW YORK
HHAHHH
VERY WELL. ONCE MORE: I ENGINEERED A MONSTER, CLONED ITS BRAIN FROM A HUMAN PSYCHIC, SENT IT TO NEW YORK AND KILLED HALF OF THE CITY.
ADRIAN, THAT'S BULL-SHIT...
NO. TELLING TRUTH. LISTEN TO VOICE.
HE DID IT.
LOOK, NOBODY COULD DO THAT. YOU'RE BEING...
HE DID IT.
HALF NEW YORK.
VEIDT, GET RID OF CAT.
NO, I DON'T THINK SO. AFTER ALL, HER PRESENCE SAVES YOU THE HUMILIATION OF ANOTHER BEATING.
HURRR...
RORSCHACH, HE'S KIDDING YOU. HIS STORY, IT'S FULL OF HOLES...
ADRIAN, YOUR ASSASSINATION ATTEMPT: YOU COULDN'T HAVE PLANNED IT! WHAT IF HE'D SHOT YOU FIRST INSTEAD OF YOUR SECRETARY?
I SUPPOSE I'D HAVE HAD TO CATCH THE BULLET, WOULDN'T I?
YOU ...?
NAHH COME ON. THAT'S COMPLETELY ...
YOU COULDN'T REALLY DO THAT?
9

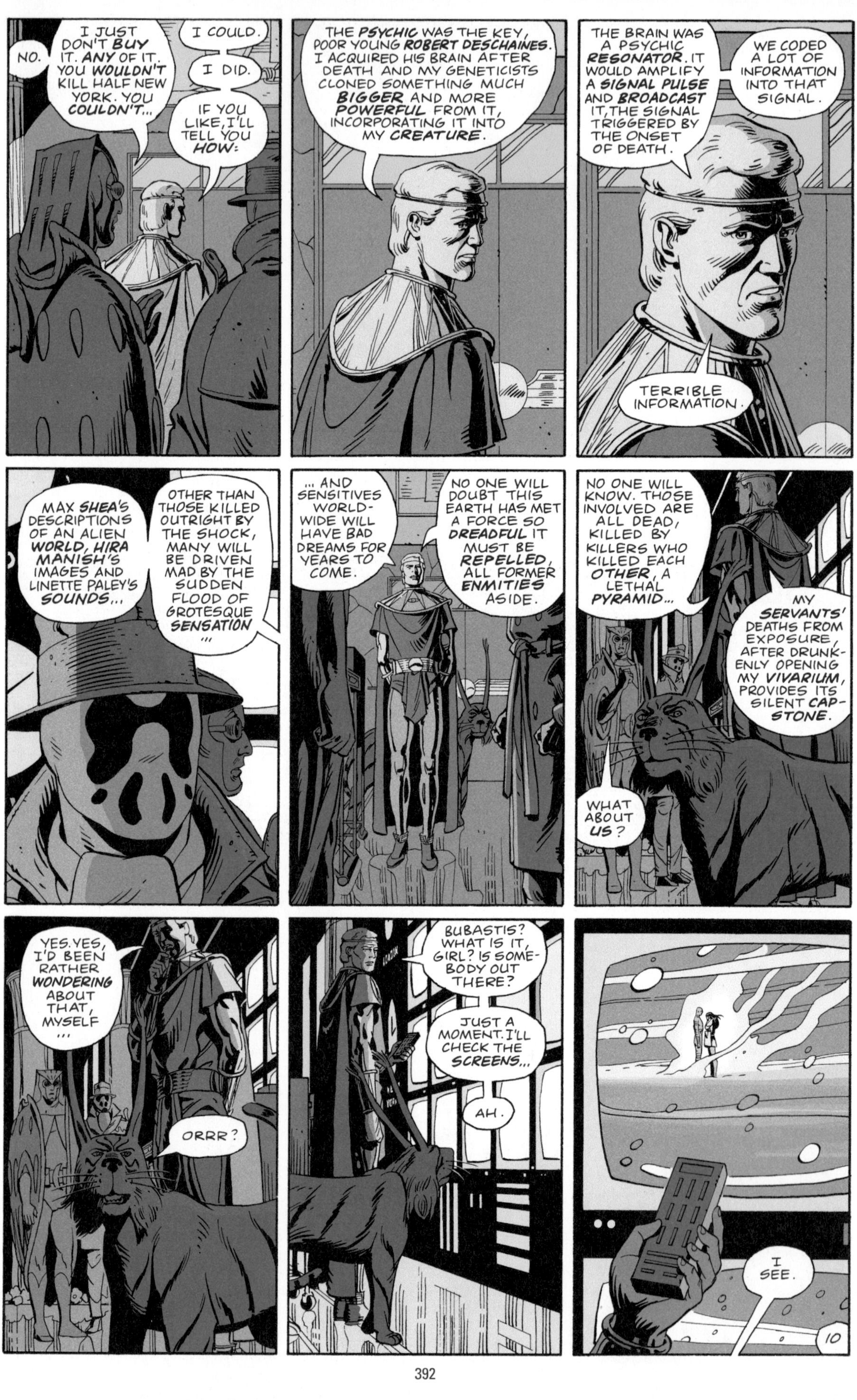
NO.
I JUST DON'T BUY IT. ANY OF IT. YOU WOULDN'T KILL HALF NEW YORK. YOU COULDN'T...
I COULD.
I DID.
IF YOU LIKE, I'LL TELL YOU HOW:
THE PSYCHIC WAS THE KEY, POOR YOUNG ROBERT DESCHAINES. I ACQUIRED HIS BRAIN AFTER DEATH AND MY GENETICISTS CLONED SOMETHING MUCH BIGGER AND MORE POWERFUL FROM IT, INCORPORATING IT INTO MY CREATURE.
THE BRAIN WAS A PSYCHIC RESONATOR. IT WOULD AMPLIFY A SIGNAL PULSE AND BROADCAST IT, THE SIGNAL TRIGGERED BY THE ONSET OF DEATH.
WE CODED A LOT OF INFORMATION INTO THAT SIGNAL.
TERRIBLE INFORMATION.
MAX SHEA'S DESCRIPTIONS OF AN ALIEN WORLD, HIRA MANISH'S IMAGES AND LINETTE PALEY'S SOUNDS...
OTHER THAN THOSE KILLED OUTRIGHT BY THE SHOCK, MANY WILL BE DRIVEN MAD BY THE SUDDEN FLOOD OF GROTESQUE SENSATION ...
... AND SENSITIVES WORLD-WIDE WILL HAVE BAD DREAMS FOR YEARS TO COME.
NO ONE WILL DOUBT THIS EARTH HAS MET A FORCE SO DREADFUL IT MUST BE REPELLED, ALL FORMER ENMITIES ASIDE.
NO ONE WILL KNOW. THOSE INVOLVED ARE ALL DEAD, KILLED BY KILLERS WHO KILLED EACH OTHER, A LETHAL PYRAMID...
MY SERVANTS' DEATHS FROM EXPOSURE, AFTER DRUNKENLY OPENING MY VIVARIUM, PROVIDES ITS SILENT CAPSTONE.
WHAT ABOUT US?
YES. YES, I'D BEEN RATHER WONDERING ABOUT THAT, MYSELF ...
ORRR?
BUBASTIS? WHAT IS IT, GIRL? IS SOMEBODY OUT THERE?
JUST A MOMENT. I'LL CHECK THE SCREENS...
AH.
I SEE.
10

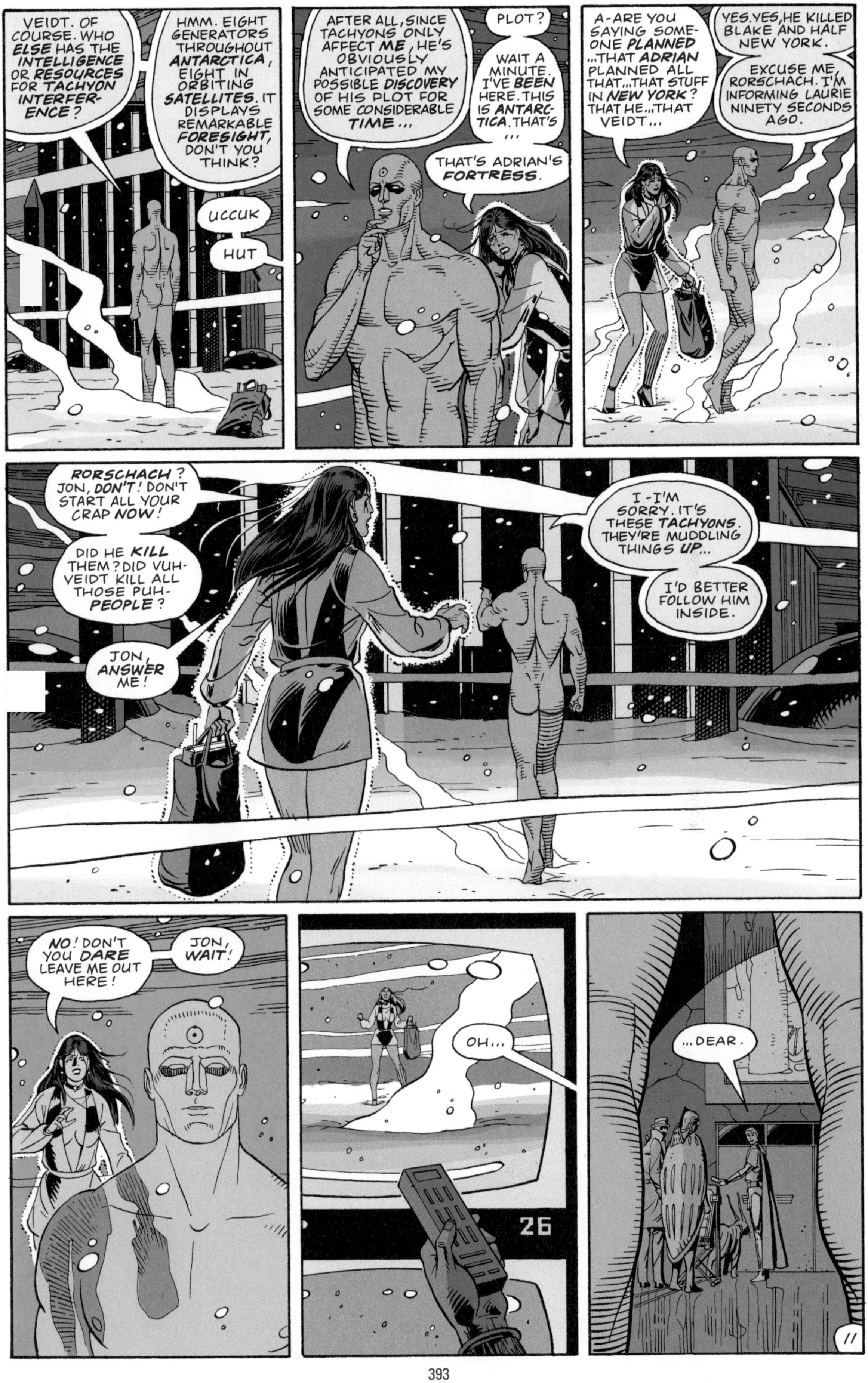
VEIDT. OF COURSE. WHO ELSE HAS THE INTELLIGENCE OR RESOURCES FOR TACHYON INTERFERENCE?
HMM. EIGHT GENERATORS THROUGHOUT ANTARCTICA, EIGHT IN ORBITING SATELLITES. IT DISPLAYS REMARKABLE FORESIGHT, DON'T YOU THINK?
UCCUK
HUT
AFTER ALL, SINCE TACHYONS ONLY AFFECT ME, HE'S OBVIOUSLY ANTICIPATED MY POSSIBLE DISCOVERY OF HIS PLOT FOR SOME CONSIDERABLE TIME...
PLOT?
WAIT A MINUTE. I'VE BEEN HERE. THIS IS ANTARCTICA. THAT'S ...
THAT'S ADRIAN'S FORTRESS.
A-ARE YOU SAYING SOMEONE PLANNED ...THAT ADRIAN PLANNED ALL THAT...THAT STUFF IN NEW YORK? THAT HE...THAT VEIDT...
YES. YES, HE KILLED BLAKE AND HALF NEW YORK.
EXCUSE ME, RORSCHACH. I'M INFORMING LAURIE NINETY SECONDS AGO.
RORSCHACH? JON, DON'T! DON'T START ALL YOUR CRAP NOW!
DID HE KILL THEM? DID VUH-VEIDT KILL ALL THOSE PUH-PEOPLE?
JON, ANSWER ME!
I-I'M SORRY. IT'S THESE TACHYONS. THEY'RE MUDDLING THINGS UP...
I'D BETTER FOLLOW HIM INSIDE.
JON, WAIT!
NO! DON'T YOU DARE LEAVE ME OUT HERE!
OH...
26
...DEAR.
11

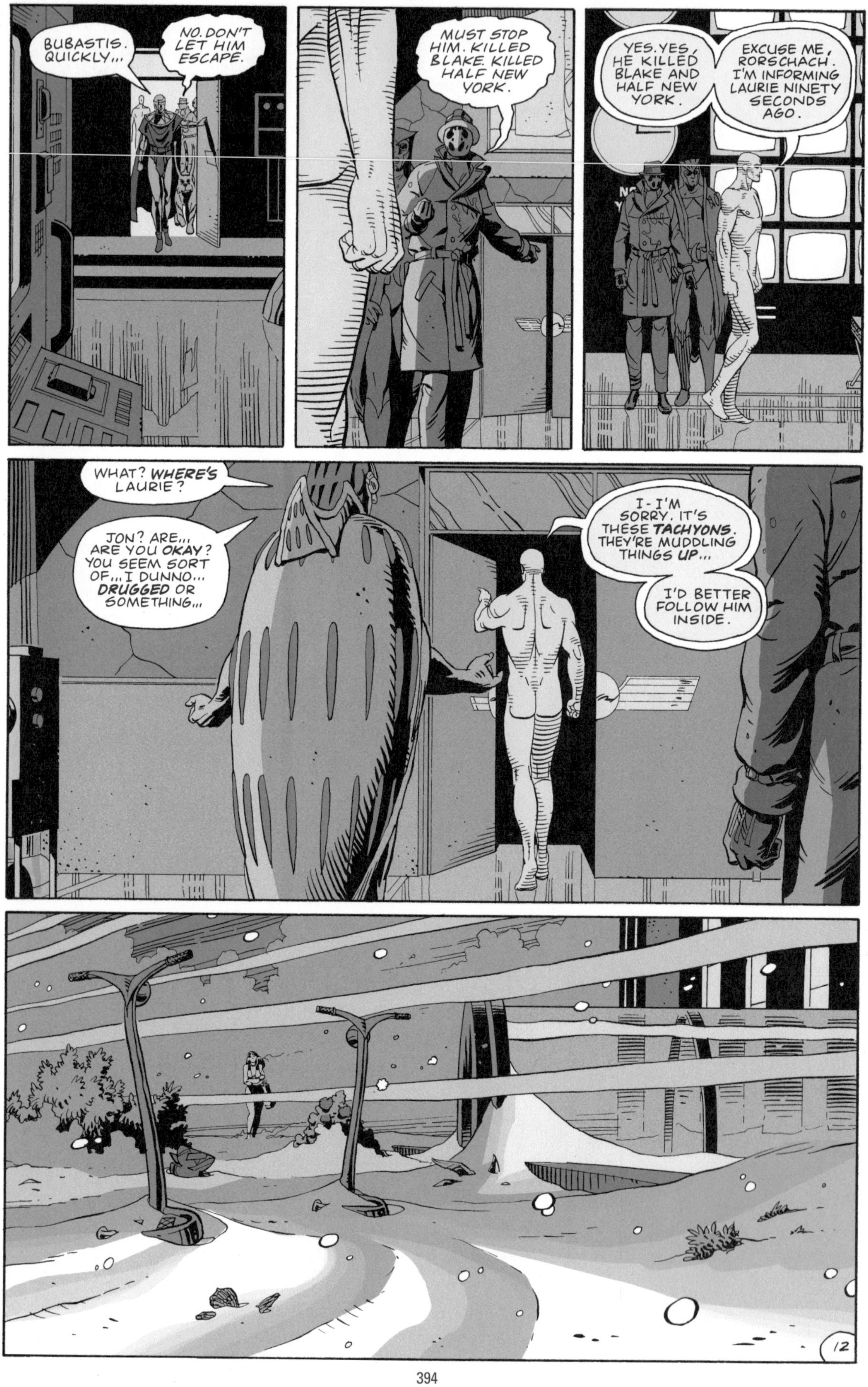
BUBASTIS. QUICKLY...
NO. DON'T LET HIM ESCAPE.
MUST STOP HIM. KILLED BLAKE. KILLED HALF NEW YORK.
YES. YES, HE KILLED BLAKE AND HALF NEW YORK.
EXCUSE ME, RORSCHACH. I'M INFORMING LAURIE NINETY SECONDS AGO.
WHAT? WHERE'S LAURIE?
JON? ARE... ARE YOU OKAY? YOU SEEM SORT OF... I DUNNO... DRUGGED OR SOMETHING...
I- I'M SORRY. IT'S THESE TACHYONS. THEY'RE MUDDLING THINGS UP...
I'D BETTER FOLLOW HIM INSIDE.
12

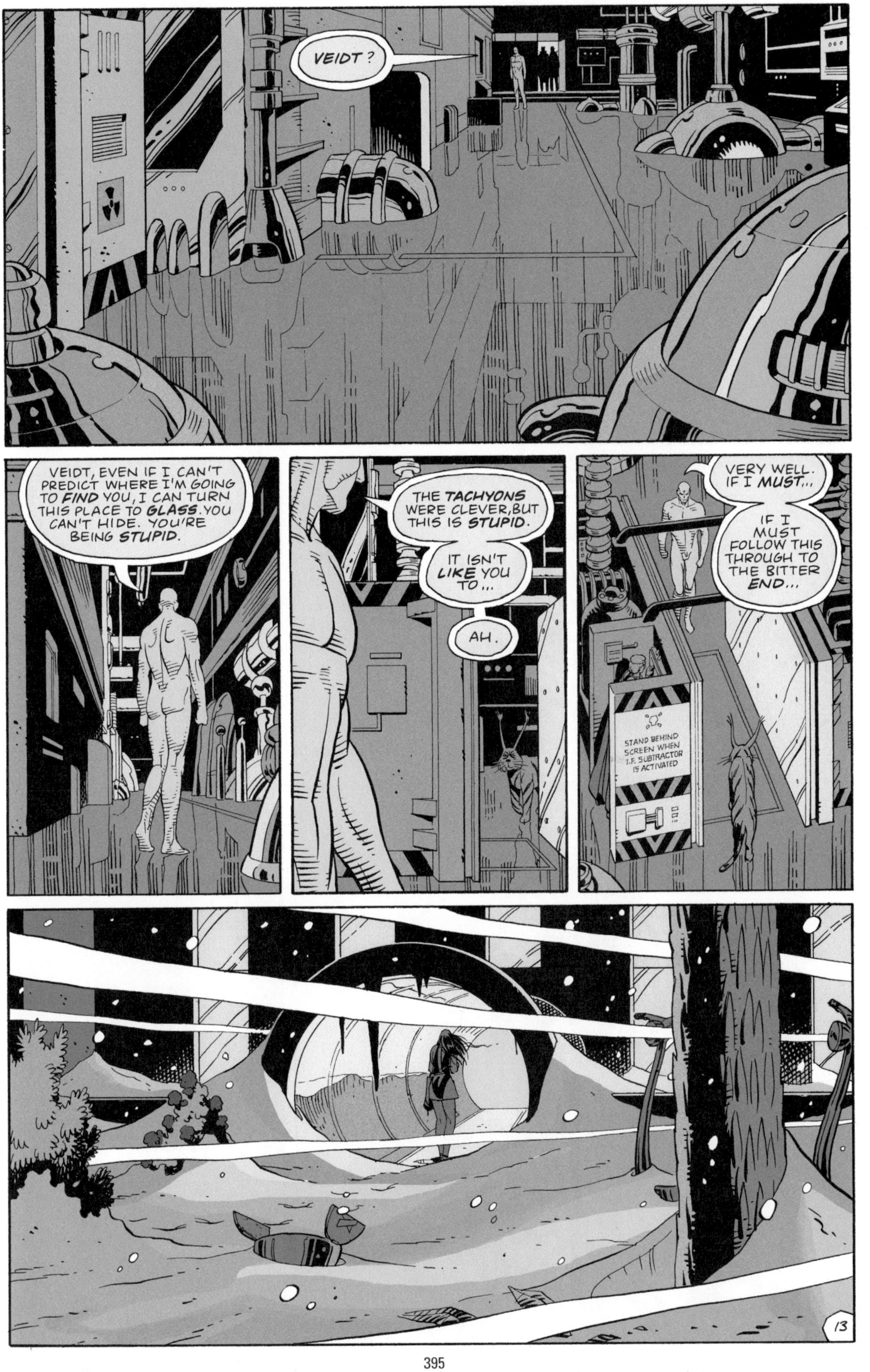
VEIDT ?
VEIDT, EVEN IF I CAN'T PREDICT WHERE I'M GOING TO FIND YOU, I CAN TURN THIS PLACE TO GLASS. YOU CAN'T HIDE. YOU'RE BEING STUPID.
THE TACHYONS WERE CLEVER, BUT THIS IS STUPID.
IT ISN'T LIKE YOU TO...
AH.
VERY WELL. IF I MUST...
IF I MUST FOLLOW THIS THROUGH TO THE BITTER END...
STAND BEHIND SCREEN WHEN I.F. SUBTRACTOR IS ACTIVATED
13

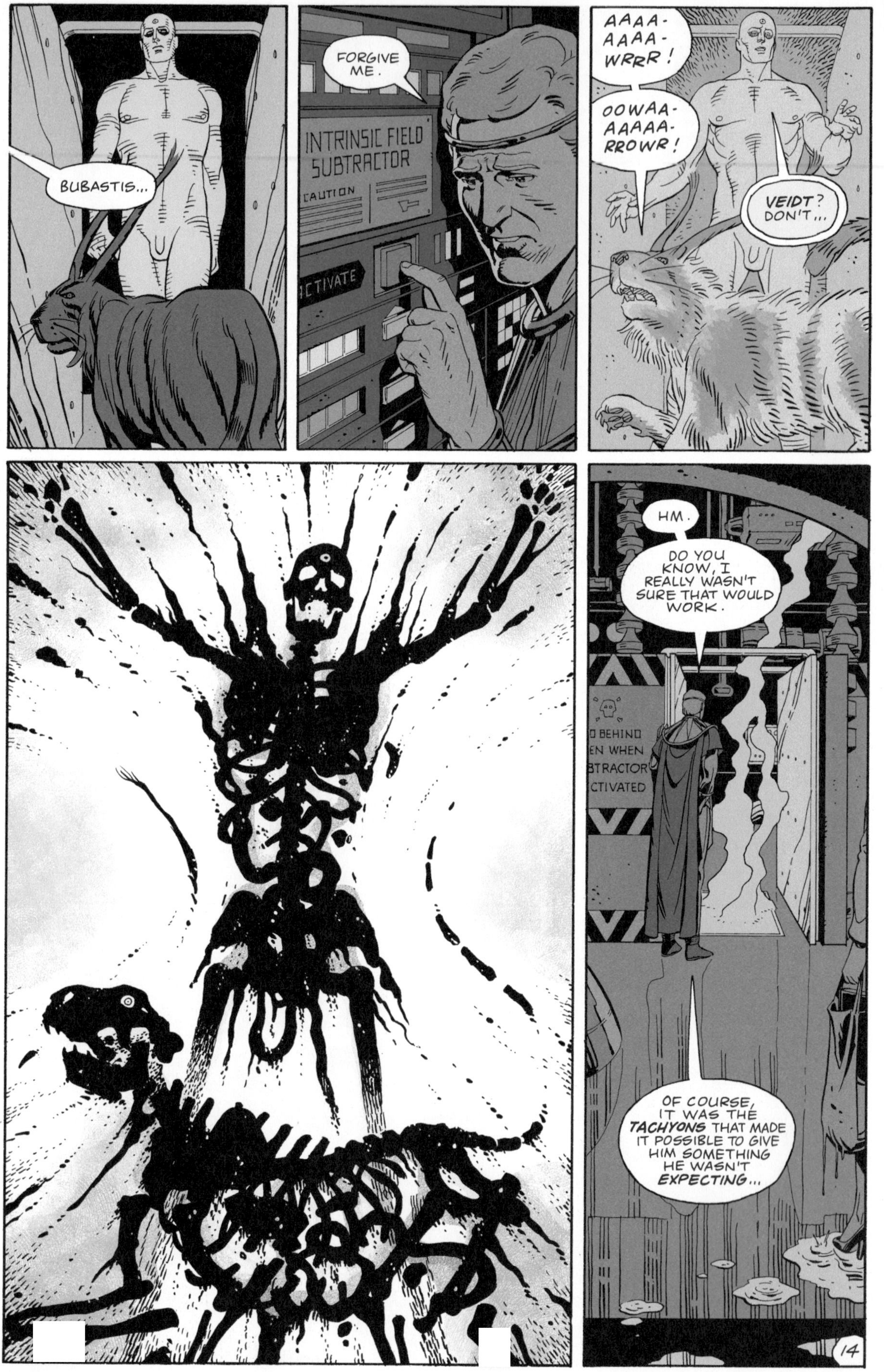
BUBASTIS...
FORGIVE ME.
INTRINSIC FIELD SUBTRACTOR
CAUTION
ACTIVATE
AAAA-AAAA-WRRR!
OOWAA-AAAAA-RROWR!
VEIDT? DON'T...
HM.
DO YOU KNOW, I REALLY WASN'T SURE THAT WOULD WORK.
O BEHIND EN WHEN BTRACTOR CTIVATED
OF COURSE, IT WAS THE TACHYONS THAT MADE IT POSSIBLE TO GIVE HIM SOMETHING HE WASN'T EXPECTING...
14

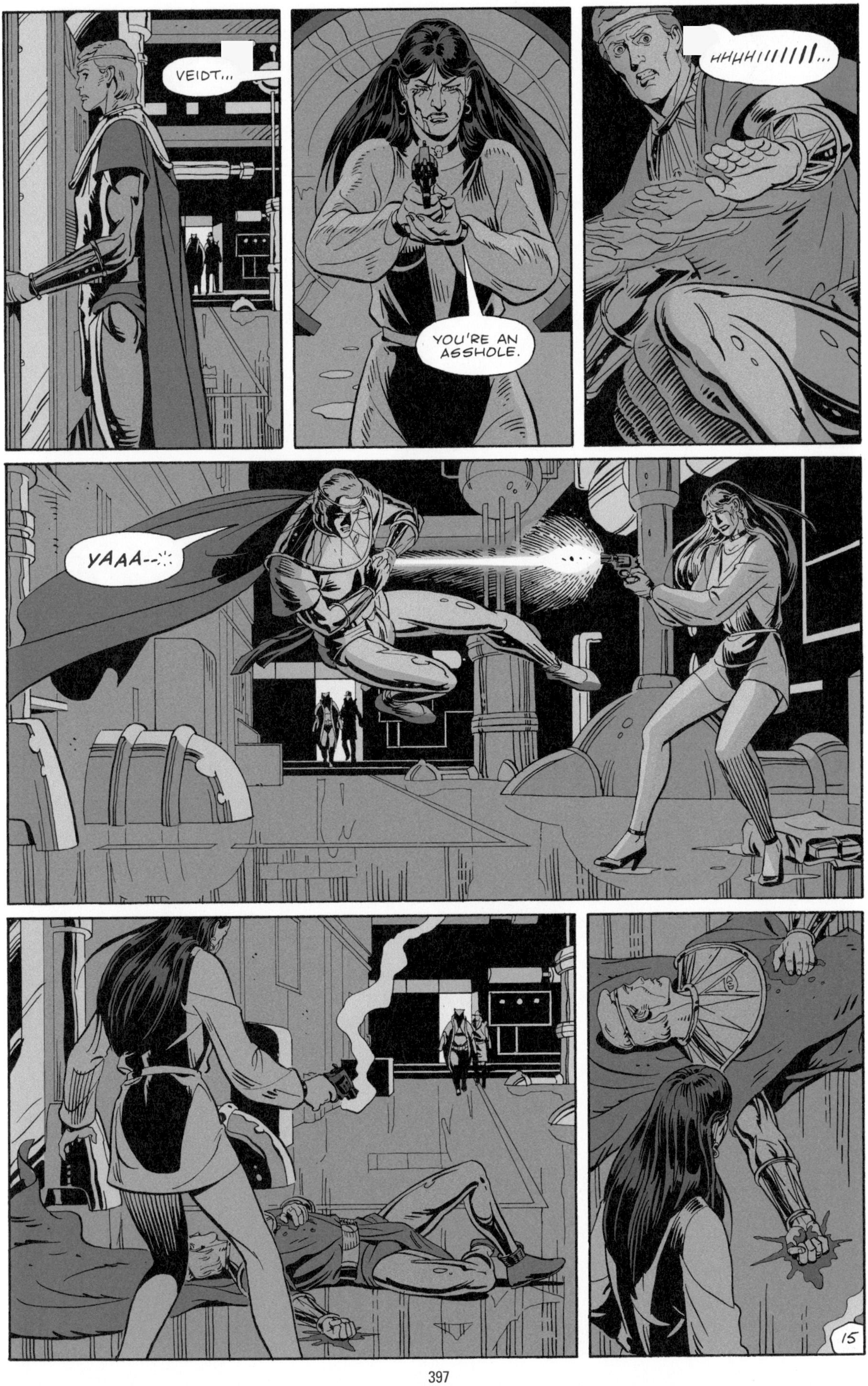

VEIDT...
YOU'RE AN ASSHOLE.
HHHHIIIIIII...
YAAA--
15

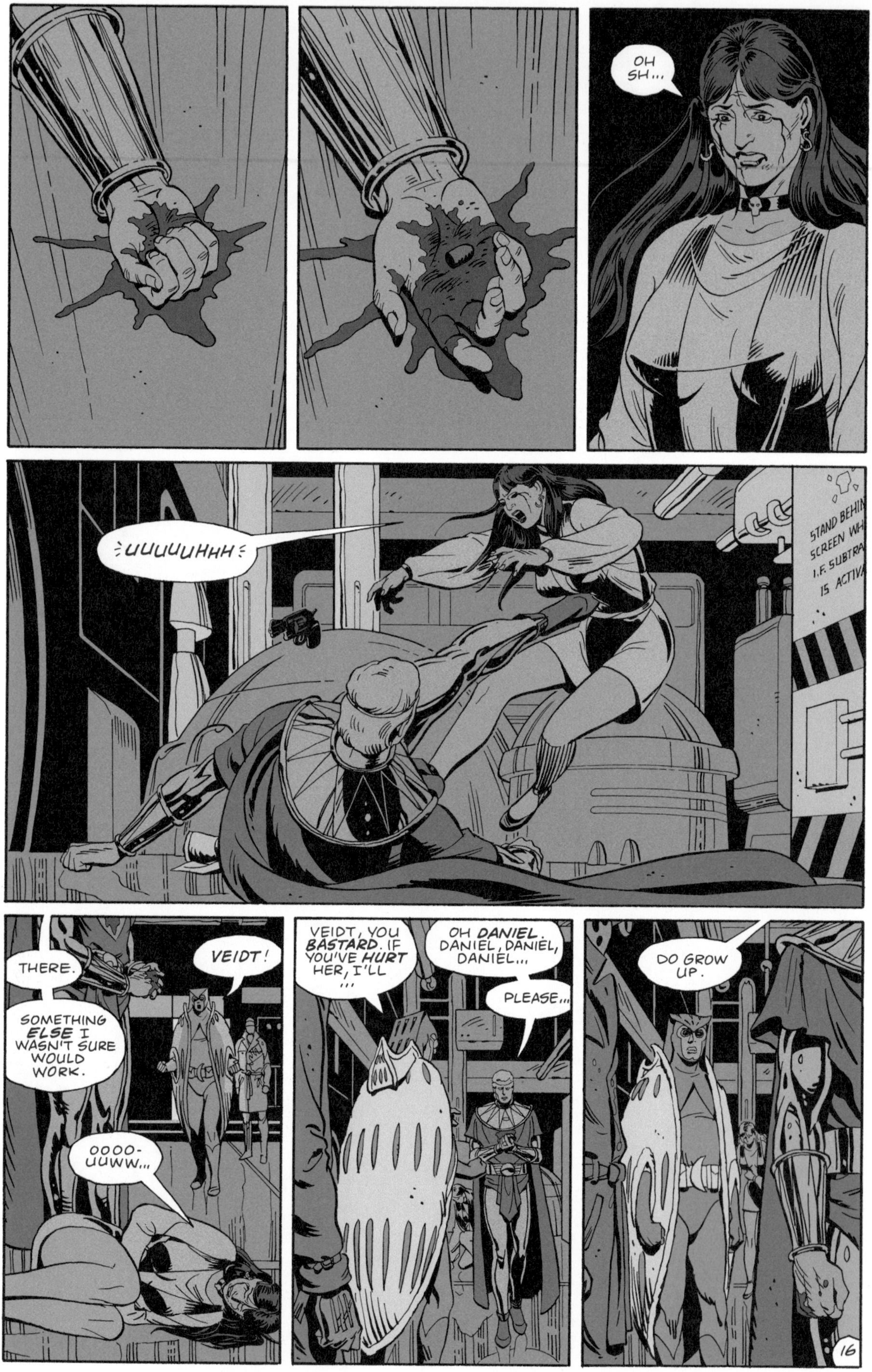

OH SH...
UUUUUHHH
STAND BEHIN
SCREEN WH
I.F. SUBTRA
IS ACTIVA
THERE.
SOMETHING ELSE I WASN'T SURE WOULD WORK.
VEIDT!
OOOO-UUWW...
VEIDT, YOU BASTARD. IF YOU'VE HURT HER, I'LL ...
OH DANIEL. DANIEL, DANIEL, DANIEL...
PLEASE...
DO GROW UP.
16

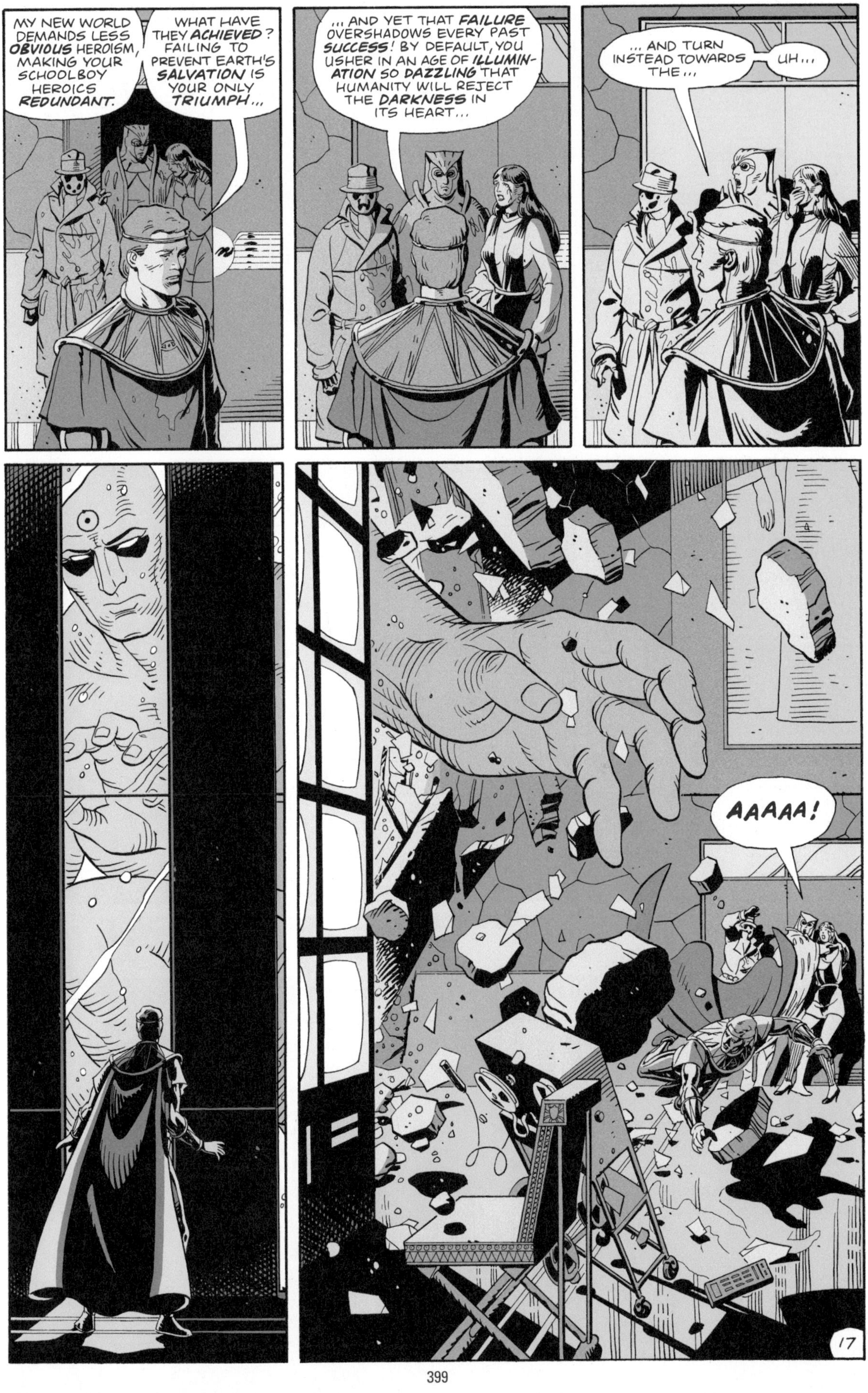
MY NEW WORLD DEMANDS LESS OBVIOUS HEROISM, MAKING YOUR SCHOOLBOY HEROICS REDUNDANT.
WHAT HAVE THEY ACHIEVED? FAILING TO PREVENT EARTH'S SALVATION IS YOUR ONLY TRIUMPH...
...AND YET THAT FAILURE OVERSHADOWS EVERY PAST SUCCESS! BY DEFAULT, YOU USHER IN AN AGE OF ILLUMINATION SO DAZZLING THAT HUMANITY WILL REJECT THE DARKNESS IN ITS HEART...
...AND TURN INSTEAD TOWARDS THE...
UH...
AAAAA!
17

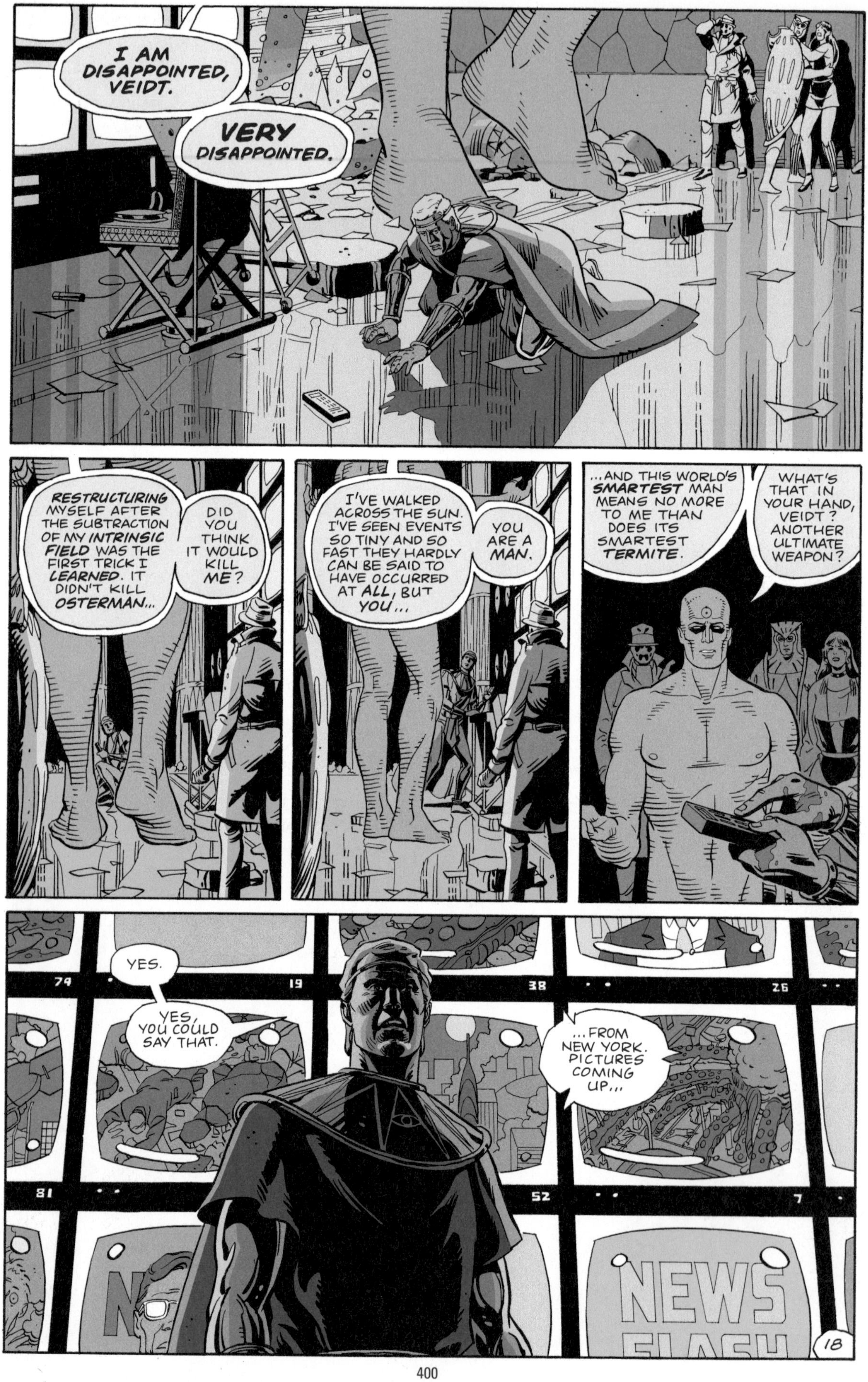
I AM DISAPPOINTED, VEIDT.
VERY DISAPPOINTED.
RESTRUCTURING MYSELF AFTER THE SUBTRACTION OF MY INTRINSIC FIELD WAS THE FIRST TRICK I LEARNED. IT DIDN'T KILL OSTERMAN...
DID YOU THINK IT WOULD KILL ME?
I'VE WALKED ACROSS THE SUN. I'VE SEEN EVENTS SO TINY AND SO FAST THEY HARDLY CAN BE SAID TO HAVE OCCURRED AT ALL, BUT YOU...
YOU ARE A MAN.
...AND THIS WORLD'S SMARTEST MAN MEANS NO MORE TO ME THAN DOES ITS SMARTEST TERMITE.
WHAT'S THAT IN YOUR HAND, VEIDT? ANOTHER ULTIMATE WEAPON?
YES.
YES, YOU COULD SAY THAT.
...FROM NEW YORK. PICTURES COMING UP...
NEWS
18

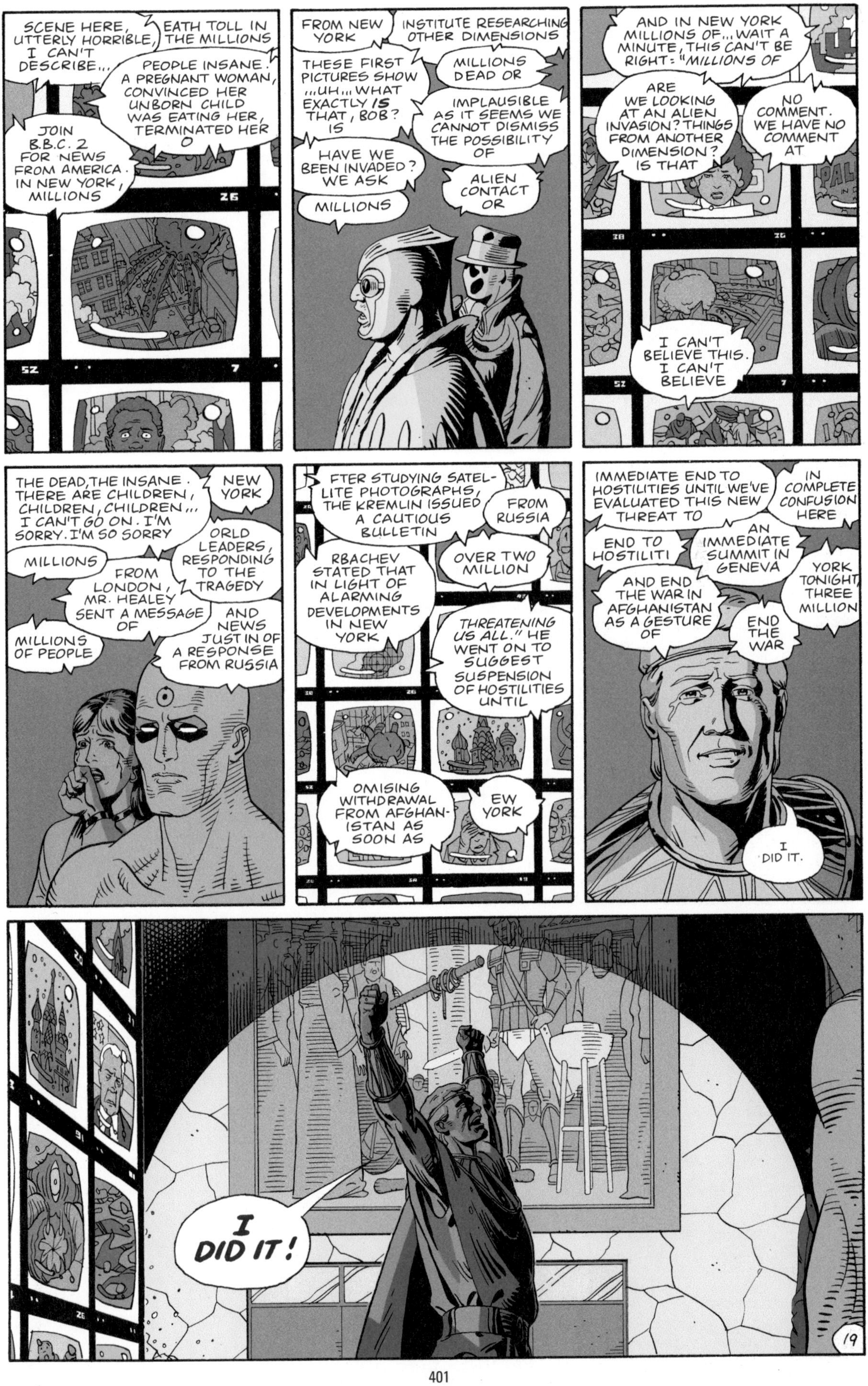
SCENE HERE, UTTERLY HORRIBLE, I CAN'T DESCRIBE...
EATH TOLL IN THE MILLIONS
PEOPLE INSANE. A PREGNANT WOMAN, CONVINCED HER UNBORN CHILD WAS EATING HER, TERMINATED HER O
JOIN B.B.C. 2 FOR NEWS FROM AMERICA. IN NEW YORK, MILLIONS
FROM NEW YORK
INSTITUTE RESEARCHING OTHER DIMENSIONS
THESE FIRST PICTURES SHOW ...UH... WHAT EXACTLY IS THAT, BOB? IS
MILLIONS DEAD OR
IMPLAUSIBLE AS IT SEEMS WE CANNOT DISMISS THE POSSIBILITY OF
HAVE WE BEEN INVADED? WE ASK
ALIEN CONTACT OR
MILLIONS
AND IN NEW YORK MILLIONS OF... WAIT A MINUTE, THIS CAN'T BE RIGHT: "MILLIONS OF
ARE WE LOOKING AT AN ALIEN INVASION? THINGS FROM ANOTHER DIMENSION? IS THAT
NO COMMENT. WE HAVE NO COMMENT AT
I CAN'T BELIEVE THIS. I CAN'T BELIEVE
THE DEAD, THE INSANE. THERE ARE CHILDREN, CHILDREN, CHILDREN... I CAN'T GO ON. I'M SORRY. I'M SO SORRY
NEW YORK
MILLIONS
ORLD LEADERS, RESPONDING TO THE TRAGEDY
FROM LONDON, MR. HEALEY SENT A MESSAGE OF
AND NEWS JUST IN OF A RESPONSE FROM RUSSIA
MILLIONS OF PEOPLE
FTER STUDYING SATELLITE PHOTOGRAPHS, THE KREMLIN ISSUED A CAUTIOUS BULLETIN
FROM RUSSIA
RBACHEV STATED THAT IN LIGHT OF ALARMING DEVELOPMENTS IN NEW YORK
OVER TWO MILLION
THREATENING US ALL." HE WENT ON TO SUGGEST SUSPENSION OF HOSTILITIES UNTIL
OMISING WITHDRAWAL FROM AFGHANISTAN AS SOON AS
EW YORK
IMMEDIATE END TO HOSTILITIES UNTIL WE'VE EVALUATED THIS NEW THREAT TO
IN COMPLETE CONFUSION HERE
END TO HOSTILITI
AN IMMEDIATE SUMMIT IN GENEVA
YORK TONIGHT, THREE MILLION
AND END THE WAR IN AFGHANISTAN AS A GESTURE OF
END THE WAR
I DID IT.
I DID IT!
19

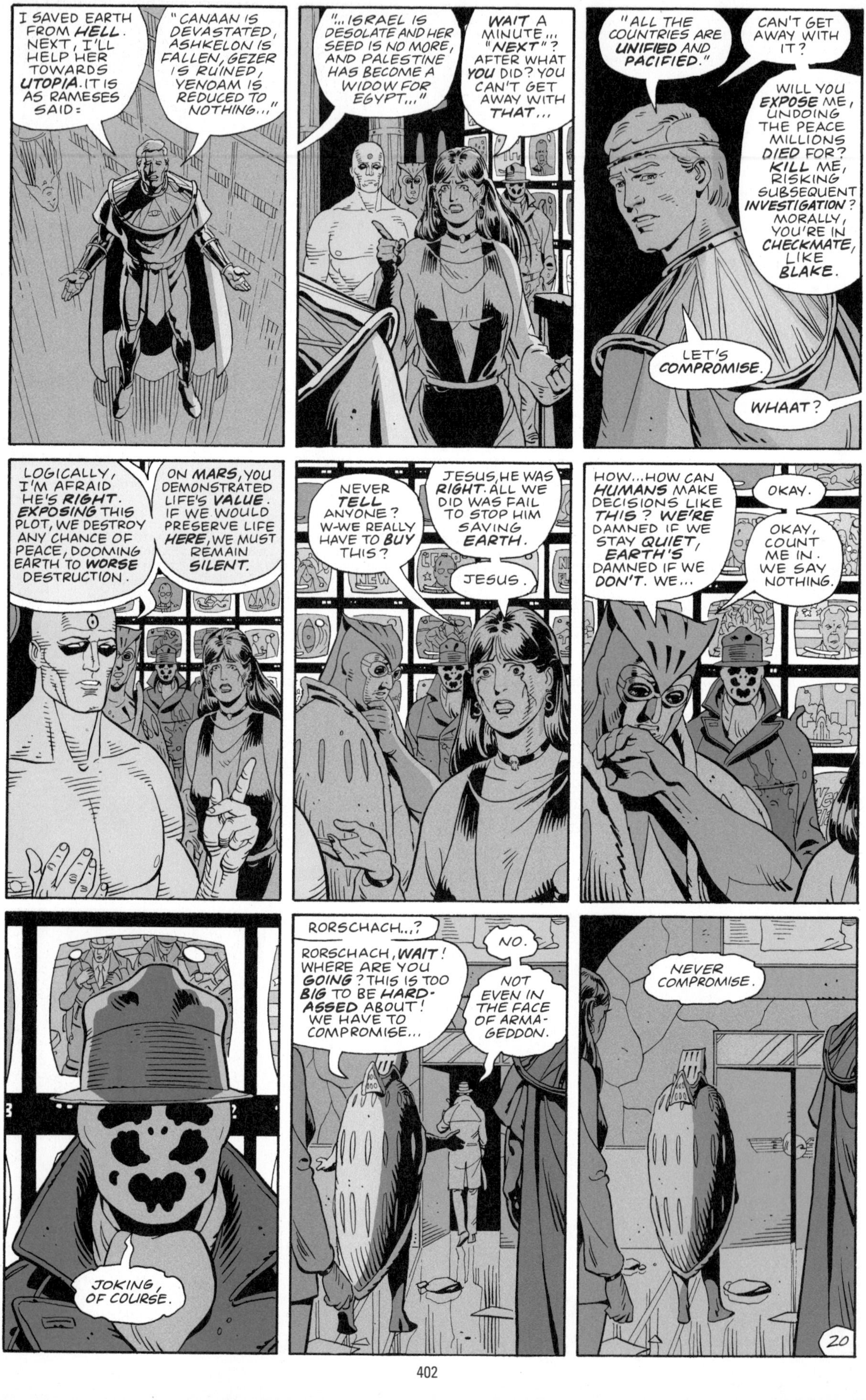
I SAVED EARTH FROM HELL. NEXT, I'LL HELP HER TOWARDS UTOPIA. IT IS AS RAMESES SAID:
"CANAAN IS DEVASTATED, ASHKELON IS FALLEN, GEZER IS RUINED, YENOAM IS REDUCED TO NOTHING..."
"...ISRAEL IS DESOLATE AND HER SEED IS NO MORE, AND PALESTINE HAS BECOME A WIDOW FOR EGYPT..."
WAIT A MINUTE... "NEXT"? AFTER WHAT YOU DID? YOU CAN'T GET AWAY WITH THAT...
"ALL THE COUNTRIES ARE UNIFIED AND PACIFIED."
CAN'T GET AWAY WITH IT?
WILL YOU EXPOSE ME, UNDOING THE PEACE MILLIONS DIED FOR? KILL ME, RISKING SUBSEQUENT INVESTIGATION? MORALLY, YOU'RE IN CHECKMATE, LIKE BLAKE.
LET'S COMPROMISE.
WHAAT?
LOGICALLY, I'M AFRAID HE'S RIGHT. EXPOSING THIS PLOT, WE DESTROY ANY CHANCE OF PEACE, DOOMING EARTH TO WORSE DESTRUCTION.
ON MARS, YOU DEMONSTRATED LIFE'S VALUE. IF WE WOULD PRESERVE LIFE HERE, WE MUST REMAIN SILENT.
NEVER TELL ANYONE? W-WE REALLY HAVE TO BUY THIS?
JESUS, HE WAS RIGHT. ALL WE DID WAS FAIL TO STOP HIM SAVING EARTH.
JESUS.
HOW...HOW CAN HUMANS MAKE DECISIONS LIKE THIS? WE'RE DAMNED IF WE STAY QUIET, EARTH'S DAMNED IF WE DON'T. WE...
OKAY.
OKAY, COUNT ME IN. WE SAY NOTHING.
JOKING, OF COURSE.
RORSCHACH...?
RORSCHACH, WAIT! WHERE ARE YOU GOING? THIS IS TOO BIG TO BE HARD-ASSED ABOUT! WE HAVE TO COMPROMISE...
NO.
NOT EVEN IN THE FACE OF ARMAGEDDON.
NEVER COMPROMISE.
20

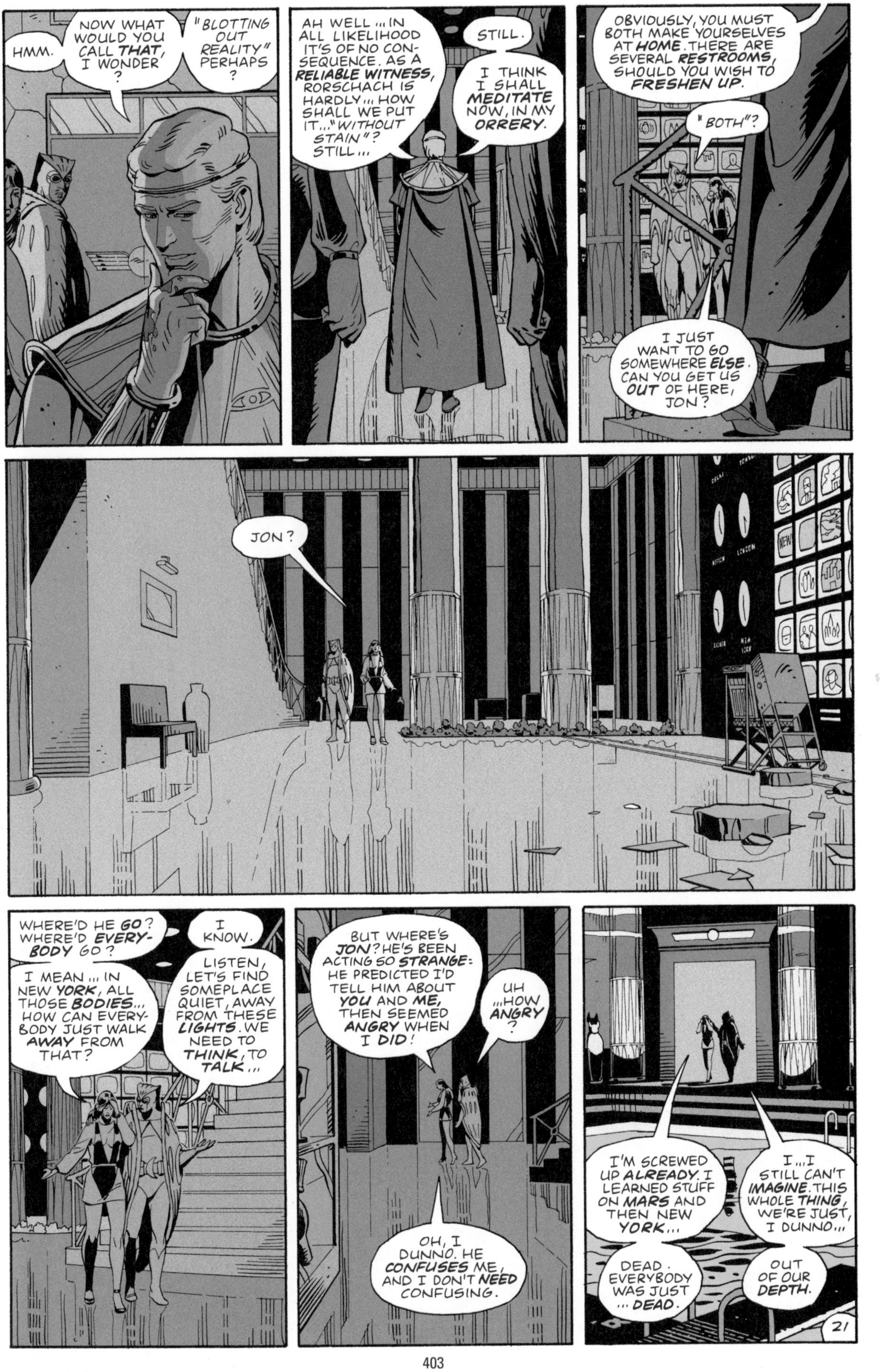
HMM.
NOW WHAT WOULD YOU CALL THAT, I WONDER?
"BLOTTING OUT REALITY" PERHAPS?
AH WELL ... IN ALL LIKELIHOOD IT'S OF NO CONSEQUENCE. AS A RELIABLE WITNESS, RORSCHACH IS HARDLY ... HOW SHALL WE PUT IT ... "WITHOUT STAIN"? STILL ...
STILL.
I THINK I SHALL MEDITATE NOW, IN MY ORRERY.
OBVIOUSLY, YOU MUST BOTH MAKE YOURSELVES AT HOME. THERE ARE SEVERAL RESTROOMS, SHOULD YOU WISH TO FRESHEN UP.
"BOTH"?
I JUST WANT TO GO SOMEWHERE ELSE. CAN YOU GET US OUT OF HERE, JON?
JON?
WHERE'D HE GO? WHERE'D EVERYBODY GO?
I MEAN ... IN NEW YORK, ALL THOSE BODIES ... HOW CAN EVERYBODY JUST WALK AWAY FROM THAT?
I KNOW.
LISTEN, LET'S FIND SOMEPLACE QUIET, AWAY FROM THESE LIGHTS. WE NEED TO THINK, TO TALK ...
BUT WHERE'S JON? HE'S BEEN ACTING SO STRANGE: HE PREDICTED I'D TELL HIM ABOUT YOU AND ME, THEN SEEMED ANGRY WHEN I DID!
UH ...HOW ANGRY?
OH, I DUNNO. HE CONFUSES ME, AND I DON'T NEED CONFUSING.
I'M SCREWED UP ALREADY. I LEARNED STUFF ON MARS AND THEN NEW YORK ...
DEAD. EVERYBODY WAS JUST ... DEAD.
I ... I STILL CAN'T IMAGINE. THIS WHOLE THING, WE'RE JUST, I DUNNO ...
OUT OF OUR DEPTH.
21

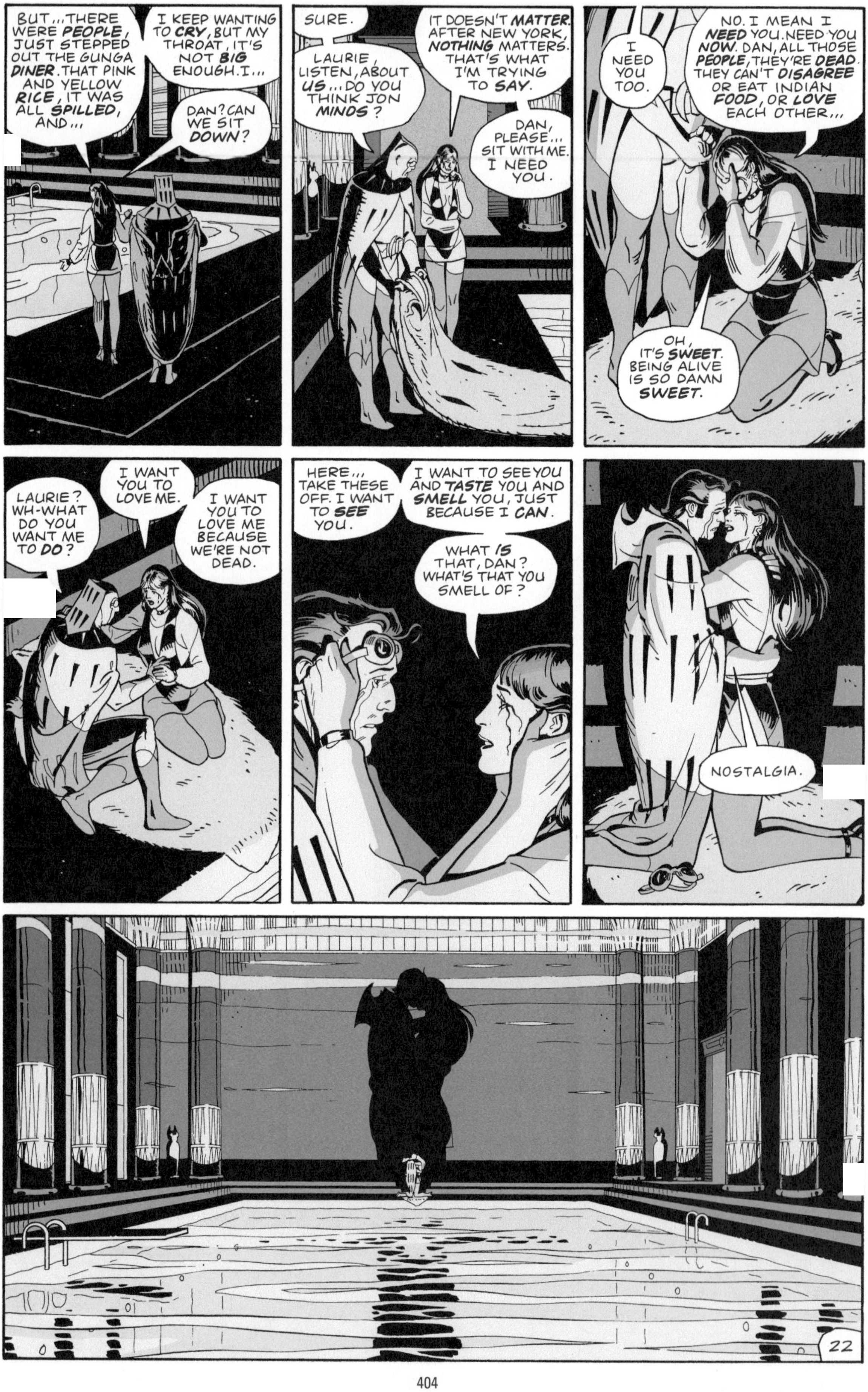

BUT... THERE WERE PEOPLE, JUST STEPPED OUT THE GUNGA DINER. THAT PINK AND YELLOW RICE, IT WAS ALL SPILLED, AND...
I KEEP WANTING TO CRY, BUT MY THROAT, IT'S NOT BIG ENOUGH. I...
DAN? CAN WE SIT DOWN?
SURE.
LAURIE, LISTEN, ABOUT US... DO YOU THINK JON MINDS?
IT DOESN'T MATTER. AFTER NEW YORK, NOTHING MATTERS. THAT'S WHAT I'M TRYING TO SAY.
DAN, PLEASE... SIT WITH ME. I NEED YOU.
I NEED YOU TOO.
NO. I MEAN I NEED YOU. NEED YOU NOW. DAN, ALL THOSE PEOPLE, THEY'RE DEAD. THEY CAN'T DISAGREE OR EAT INDIAN FOOD, OR LOVE EACH OTHER...
OH, IT'S SWEET. BEING ALIVE IS SO DAMN SWEET.
LAURIE? WH-WHAT DO YOU WANT ME TO DO?
I WANT YOU TO LOVE ME.
I WANT YOU TO LOVE ME BECAUSE WE'RE NOT DEAD.
HERE... TAKE THESE OFF. I WANT TO SEE YOU.
I WANT TO SEE YOU AND TASTE YOU AND SMELL YOU, JUST BECAUSE I CAN.
WHAT IS THAT, DAN? WHAT'S THAT YOU SMELL OF?
NOSTALGIA.
22

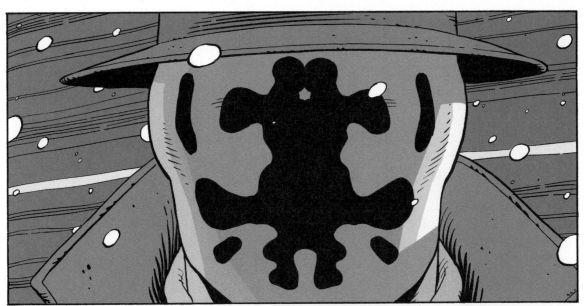

WHERE ARE YOU GOING?

BACK TO OWLSHIP. BACK TO AMERICA.

PEOPLE MUST BE TOLD.

EVIL MUST BE PUNISHED.

RORSCHACH...

YOU KNOW I CAN'T LET YOU DO THAT.

23

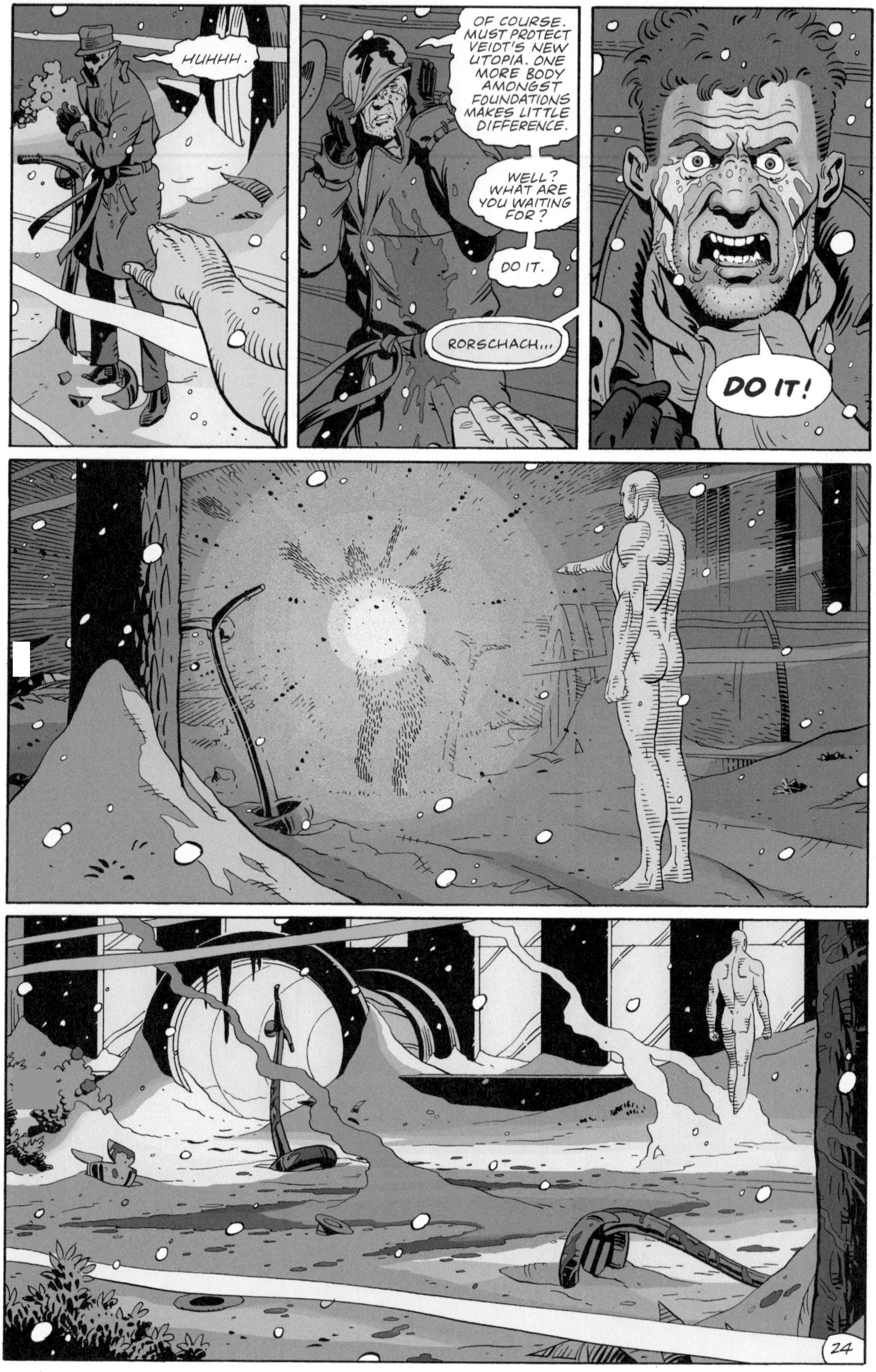
HUHHH.
OF COURSE. MUST PROTECT VEIDT'S NEW UTOPIA. ONE MORE BODY AMONGST FOUNDATIONS MAKES LITTLE DIFFERENCE.
WELL? WHAT ARE YOU WAITING FOR?
DO IT.
RORSCHACH...
DO IT!
24

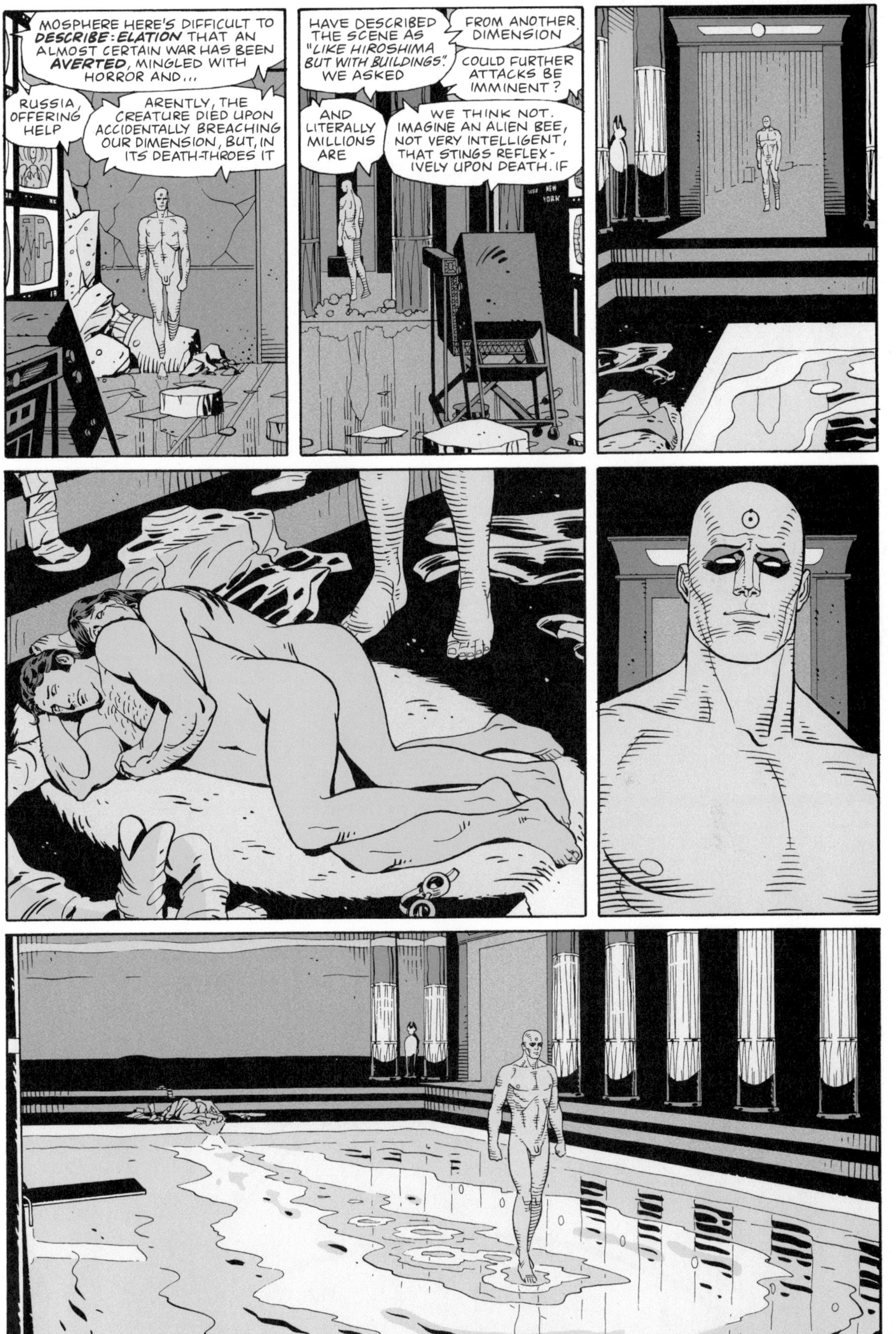
MOSPHERE HERE'S DIFFICULT TO DESCRIBE: ELATION THAT AN ALMOST CERTAIN WAR HAS BEEN AVERTED, MINGLED WITH HORROR AND...
RUSSIA, OFFERING HELP
ARENTLY, THE CREATURE DIED UPON ACCIDENTALLY BREACHING OUR DIMENSION, BUT, IN ITS DEATH-THROES IT
HAVE DESCRIBED THE SCENE AS "LIKE HIROSHIMA BUT WITH BUILDINGS." WE ASKED
FROM ANOTHER DIMENSION
COULD FURTHER ATTACKS BE IMMINENT?
AND LITERALLY MILLIONS ARE
WE THINK NOT. IMAGINE AN ALIEN BEE, NOT VERY INTELLIGENT, THAT STINGS REFLEX-IVELY UPON DEATH. IF
NEW YORK
25

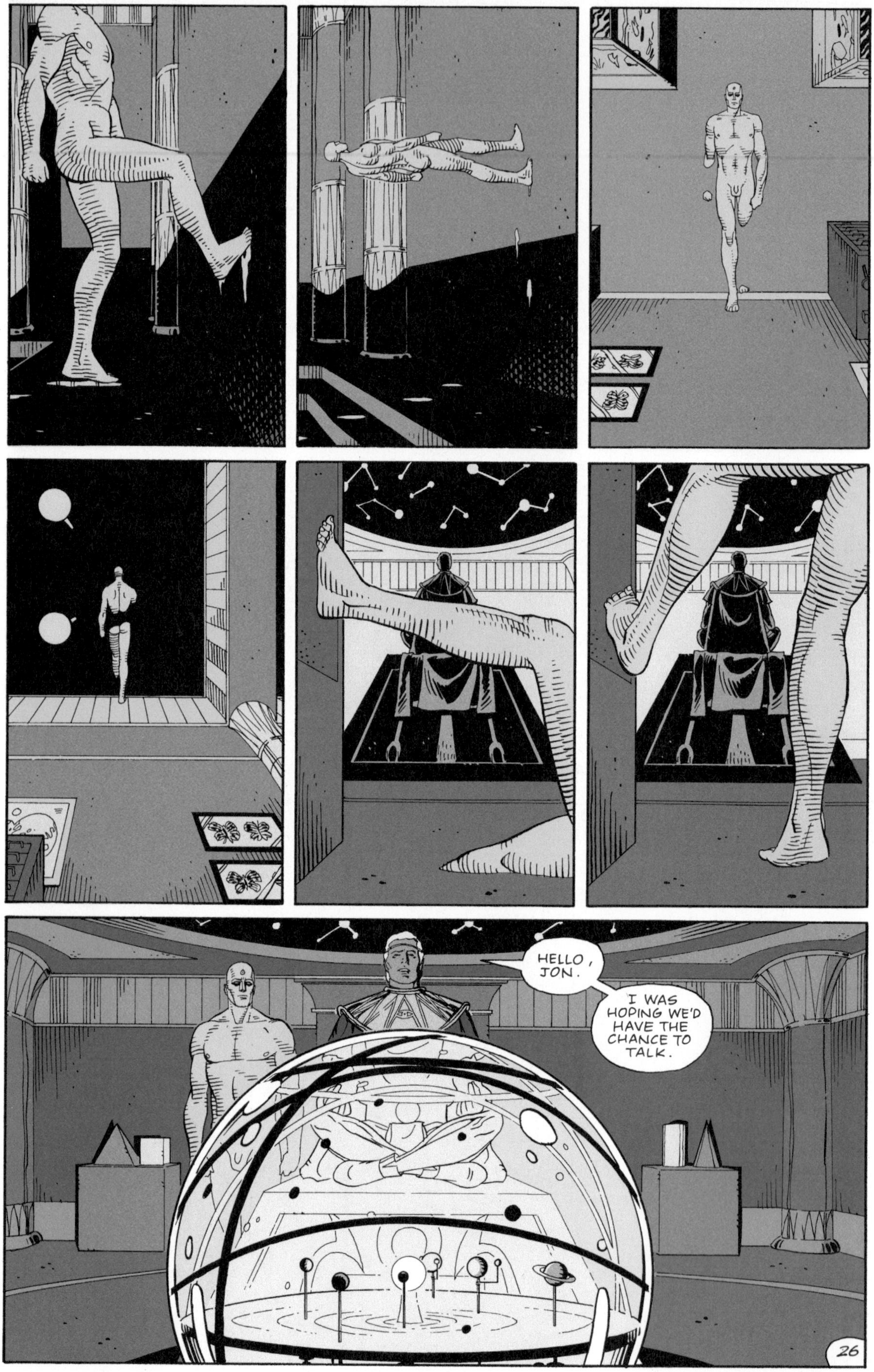
HELLO, JON.
I WAS HOPING WE'D HAVE THE CHANCE TO TALK.
26

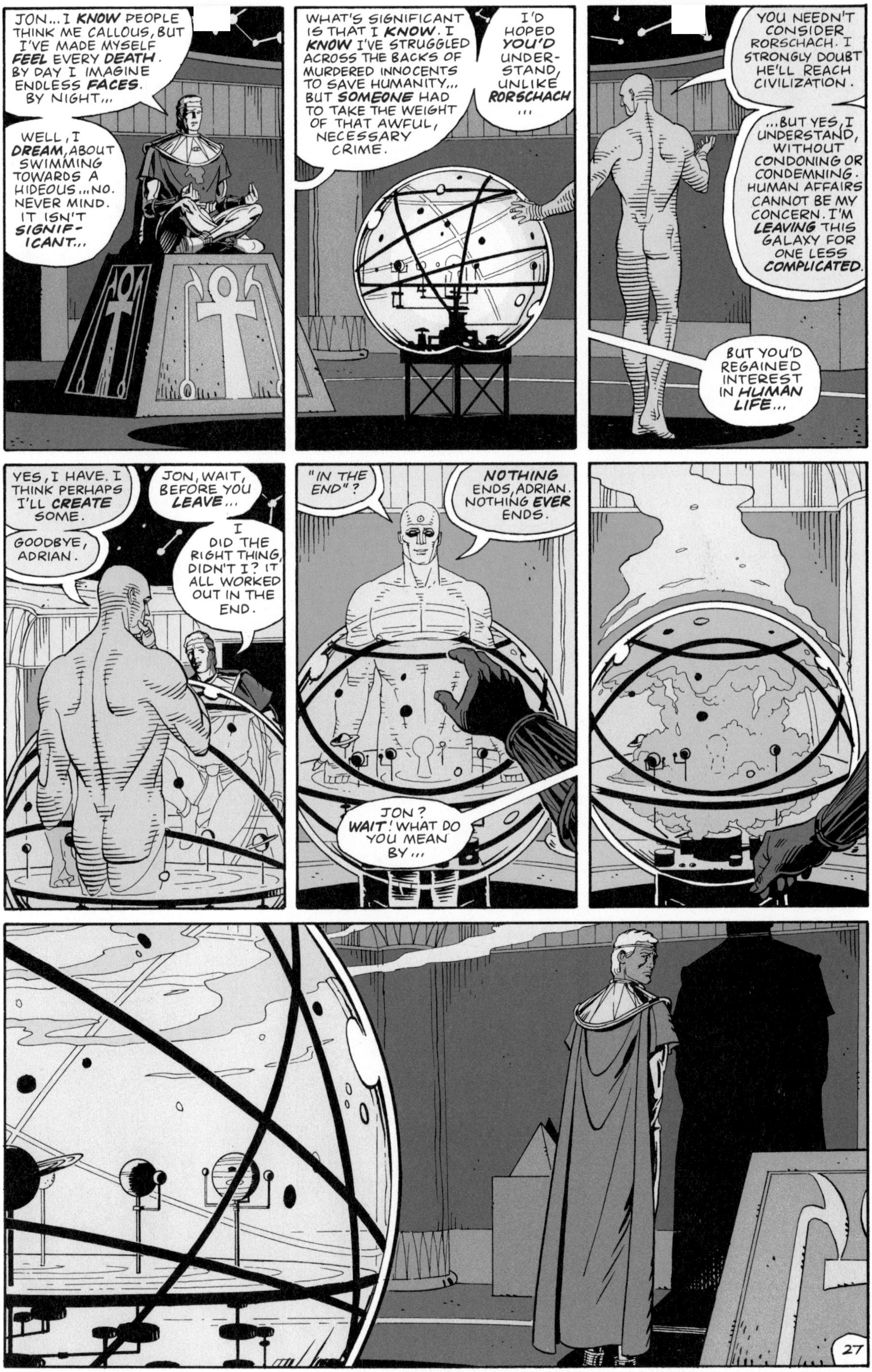

JON...I KNOW PEOPLE THINK ME CALLOUS, BUT I'VE MADE MYSELF FEEL EVERY DEATH. BY DAY I IMAGINE ENDLESS FACES. BY NIGHT...
WELL, I DREAM, ABOUT SWIMMING TOWARDS A HIDEOUS...NO. NEVER MIND. IT ISN'T SIGNIF-ICANT...
WHAT'S SIGNIFICANT IS THAT I KNOW. I KNOW I'VE STRUGGLED ACROSS THE BACKS OF MURDERED INNOCENTS TO SAVE HUMANITY... BUT SOMEONE HAD TO TAKE THE WEIGHT OF THAT AWFUL, NECESSARY CRIME.
I'D HOPED YOU'D UNDER-STAND, UNLIKE RORSCHACH...
YOU NEEDN'T CONSIDER RORSCHACH. I STRONGLY DOUBT HE'LL REACH CIVILIZATION.
...BUT YES, I UNDERSTAND, WITHOUT CONDONING OR CONDEMNING. HUMAN AFFAIRS CANNOT BE MY CONCERN. I'M LEAVING THIS GALAXY FOR ONE LESS COMPLICATED.
BUT YOU'D REGAINED INTEREST IN HUMAN LIFE...
YES, I HAVE. I THINK PERHAPS I'LL CREATE SOME.
GOODBYE, ADRIAN.
JON, WAIT, BEFORE YOU LEAVE...
I DID THE RIGHT THING, DIDN'T I? IT ALL WORKED OUT IN THE END.
"IN THE END"?
NOTHING ENDS, ADRIAN. NOTHING EVER ENDS.
JON? WAIT! WHAT DO YOU MEAN BY...
27

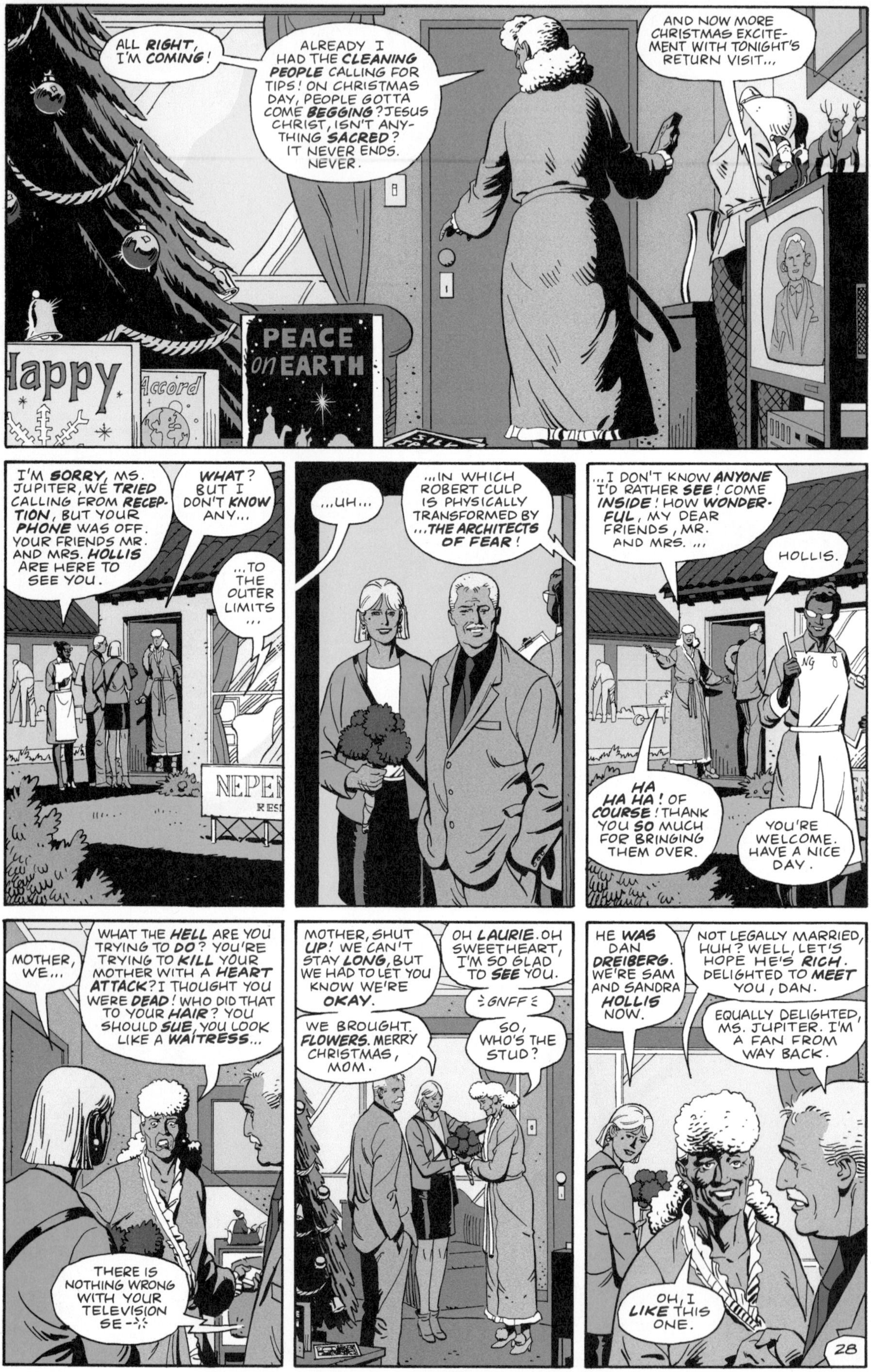
ALL RIGHT, I'M COMING!
ALREADY I HAD THE CLEANING PEOPLE CALLING FOR TIPS! ON CHRISTMAS DAY, PEOPLE GOTTA COME BEGGING? JESUS CHRIST, ISN'T ANYTHING SACRED? IT NEVER ENDS. NEVER.
AND NOW MORE CHRISTMAS EXCITEMENT WITH TONIGHT'S RETURN VISIT...
Happy
Accord
PEACE on EARTH
I'M SORRY, MS. JUPITER, WE TRIED CALLING FROM RECEPTION, BUT YOUR PHONE WAS OFF. YOUR FRIENDS MR. AND MRS. HOLLIS ARE HERE TO SEE YOU.
WHAT? BUT I DON'T KNOW ANY...
...TO THE OUTER LIMITS...
...UH...
...IN WHICH ROBERT CULP IS PHYSICALLY TRANSFORMED BY ...THE ARCHITECTS OF FEAR!
...I DON'T KNOW ANYONE I'D RATHER SEE! COME INSIDE! HOW WONDERFUL, MY DEAR FRIENDS, MR. AND MRS. ...
HOLLIS.
HA HA HA! OF COURSE! THANK YOU SO MUCH FOR BRINGING THEM OVER.
YOU'RE WELCOME. HAVE A NICE DAY.
MOTHER, WE...
WHAT THE HELL ARE YOU TRYING TO DO? YOU'RE TRYING TO KILL YOUR MOTHER WITH A HEART ATTACK? I THOUGHT YOU WERE DEAD! WHO DID THAT TO YOUR HAIR? YOU SHOULD SUE, YOU LOOK LIKE A WAITRESS...
THERE IS NOTHING WRONG WITH YOUR TELEVISION SE--
MOTHER, SHUT UP! WE CAN'T STAY LONG, BUT WE HAD TO LET YOU KNOW WE'RE OKAY.
OH LAURIE. OH SWEETHEART, I'M SO GLAD TO SEE YOU.
GNFF
WE BROUGHT FLOWERS. MERRY CHRISTMAS, MOM.
SO, WHO'S THE STUD?
HE WAS DAN DREIBERG. WE'RE SAM AND SANDRA HOLLIS NOW.
NOT LEGALLY MARRIED, HUH? WELL, LET'S HOPE HE'S RICH. DELIGHTED TO MEET YOU, DAN.
EQUALLY DELIGHTED, MS. JUPITER. I'M A FAN FROM WAY BACK.
OH, I LIKE THIS ONE.
28

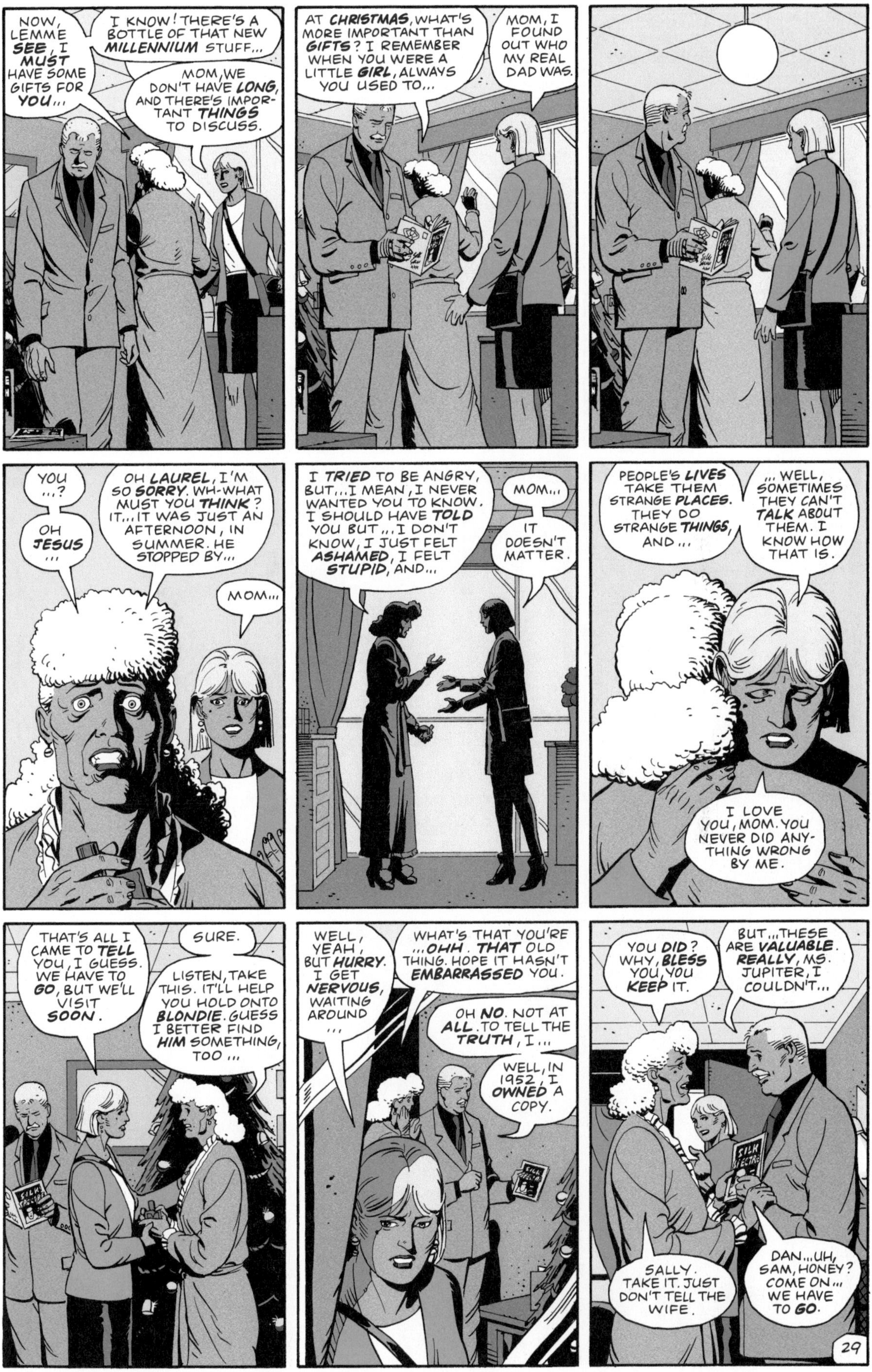
NOW, LEMME SEE, I MUST HAVE SOME GIFTS FOR YOU...
I KNOW! THERE'S A BOTTLE OF THAT NEW MILLENNIUM STUFF...
MOM, WE DON'T HAVE LONG, AND THERE'S IMPORTANT THINGS TO DISCUSS.
AT CHRISTMAS, WHAT'S MORE IMPORTANT THAN GIFTS? I REMEMBER WHEN YOU WERE A LITTLE GIRL, ALWAYS YOU USED TO...
MOM, I FOUND OUT WHO MY REAL DAD WAS.
YOU ...?
OH JESUS ...
OH LAUREL, I'M SO SORRY. WH-WHAT MUST YOU THINK? IT... IT WAS JUST AN AFTERNOON, IN SUMMER. HE STOPPED BY...
MOM...
I TRIED TO BE ANGRY, BUT... I MEAN, I NEVER WANTED YOU TO KNOW. I SHOULD HAVE TOLD YOU BUT... I DON'T KNOW, I JUST FELT ASHAMED, I FELT STUPID, AND...
MOM...
IT DOESN'T MATTER.
PEOPLE'S LIVES TAKE THEM STRANGE PLACES. THEY DO STRANGE THINGS, AND...
... WELL, SOMETIMES THEY CAN'T TALK ABOUT THEM. I KNOW HOW THAT IS.
I LOVE YOU, MOM. YOU NEVER DID ANYTHING WRONG BY ME.
THAT'S ALL I CAME TO TELL YOU, I GUESS. WE HAVE TO GO, BUT WE'LL VISIT SOON.
SURE.
LISTEN, TAKE THIS. IT'LL HELP YOU HOLD ONTO BLONDIE. GUESS I BETTER FIND HIM SOMETHING, TOO...
WELL, YEAH, BUT HURRY. I GET NERVOUS, WAITING AROUND ...
WHAT'S THAT YOU'RE ...OHH. THAT OLD THING. HOPE IT HASN'T EMBARRASSED YOU.
OH NO. NOT AT ALL. TO TELL THE TRUTH, I...
WELL, IN 1952, I OWNED A COPY.
YOU DID? WHY, BLESS YOU, YOU KEEP IT.
BUT... THESE ARE VALUABLE. REALLY, MS. JUPITER, I COULDN'T...
SALLY. TAKE IT. JUST DON'T TELL THE WIFE.
DAN... UH, SAM, HONEY? COME ON... WE HAVE TO GO.
29

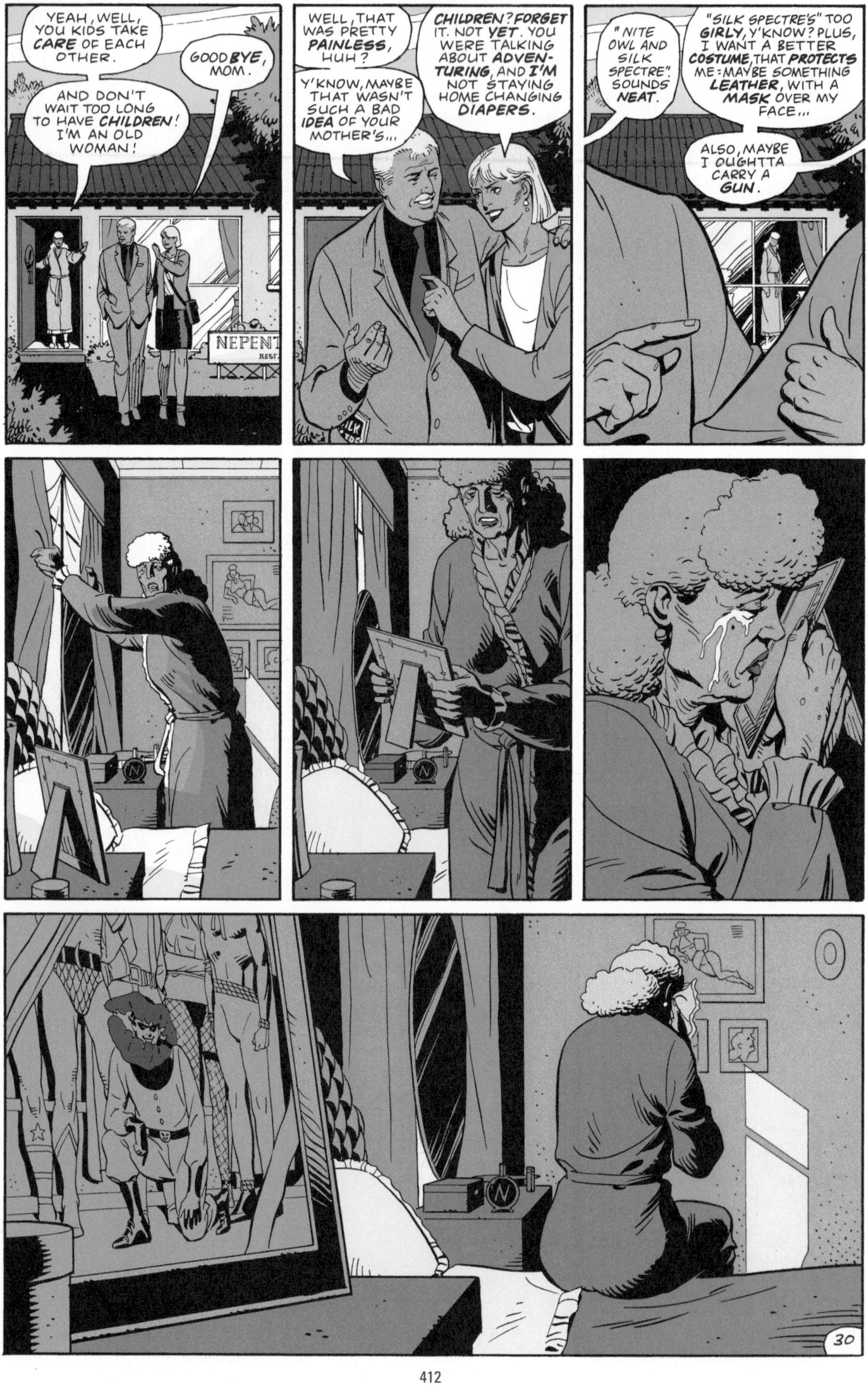
YEAH, WELL, YOU KIDS TAKE CARE OF EACH OTHER.
AND DON'T WAIT TOO LONG TO HAVE CHILDREN! I'M AN OLD WOMAN!
GOODBYE, MOM.
NEPENT
WELL, THAT WAS PRETTY PAINLESS, HUH?
Y'KNOW, MAYBE THAT WASN'T SUCH A BAD IDEA OF YOUR MOTHER'S...
CHILDREN? FORGET IT. NOT YET. YOU WERE TALKING ABOUT ADVENTURING, AND I'M NOT STAYING HOME CHANGING DIAPERS.
"NITE OWL AND SILK SPECTRE". SOUNDS NEAT.
"SILK SPECTRE'S" TOO GIRLY, Y'KNOW? PLUS, I WANT A BETTER COSTUME, THAT PROTECTS ME=MAYBE SOMETHING LEATHER, WITH A MASK OVER MY FACE...
ALSO, MAYBE I OUGHTTA CARRY A GUN.
30

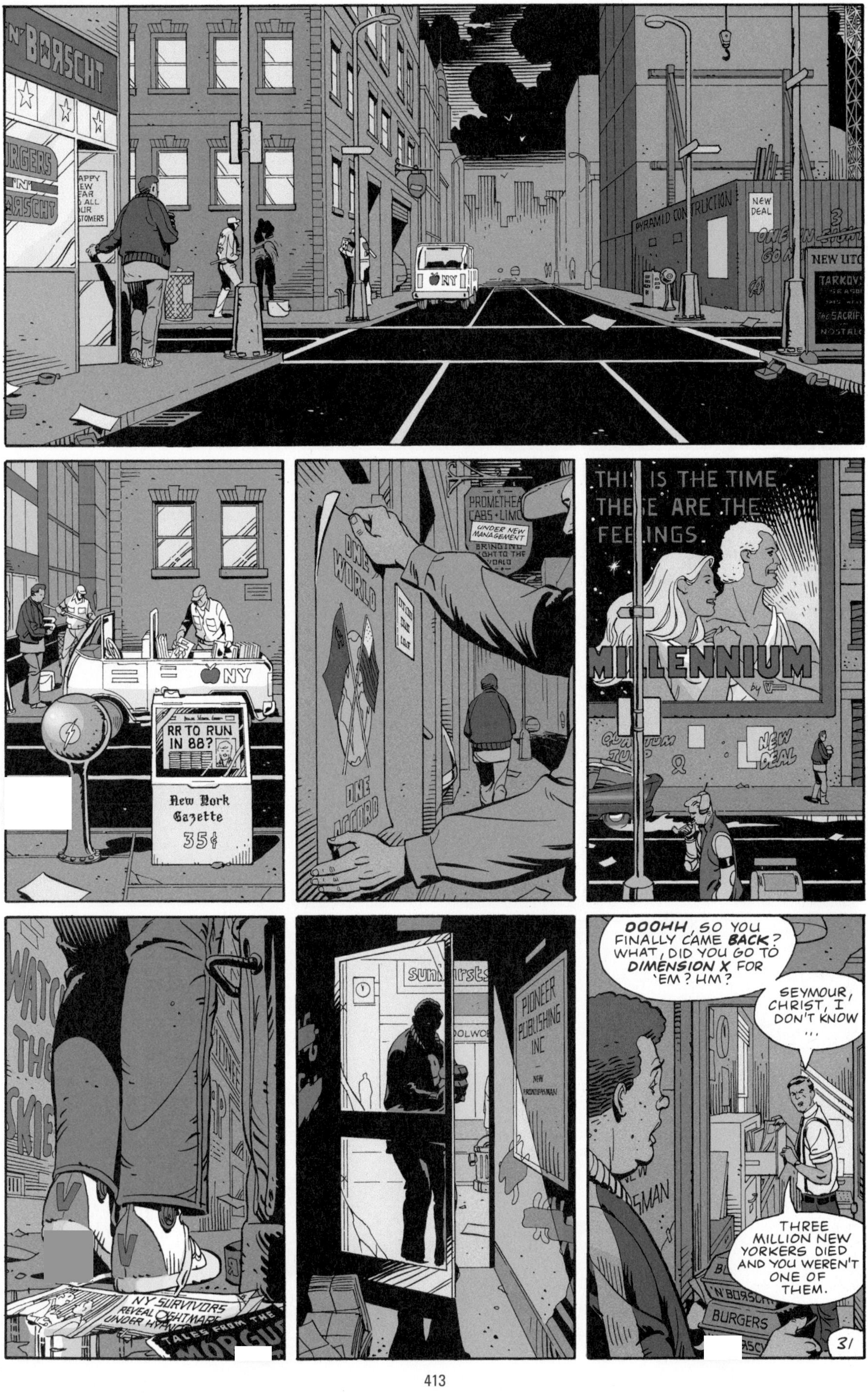
BORSCHT
PYRAMID CONTRUCTION
NEW DEAL
NY
RR TO RUN IN 88?
New York Gazette
35¢
PROMETHEAN CABS • LIMO
UNDER NEW MANAGEMENT
ONE WORLD
ONE ACCORD
THIS IS THE TIME
THESE ARE THE
FEELINGS
MILLENNIUM
NEW DEAL
PIONEER PUBLISHING INC
NEW FRONTIERSMAN
DOOHH, SO YOU FINALLY CAME BACK? WHAT, DID YOU GO TO DIMENSION X FOR 'EM? HM?
SEYMOUR, CHRIST, I DON'T KNOW ...
THREE MILLION NEW YORKERS DIED AND YOU WEREN'T ONE OF THEM.
'N' BORSCHT
BURGERS
31

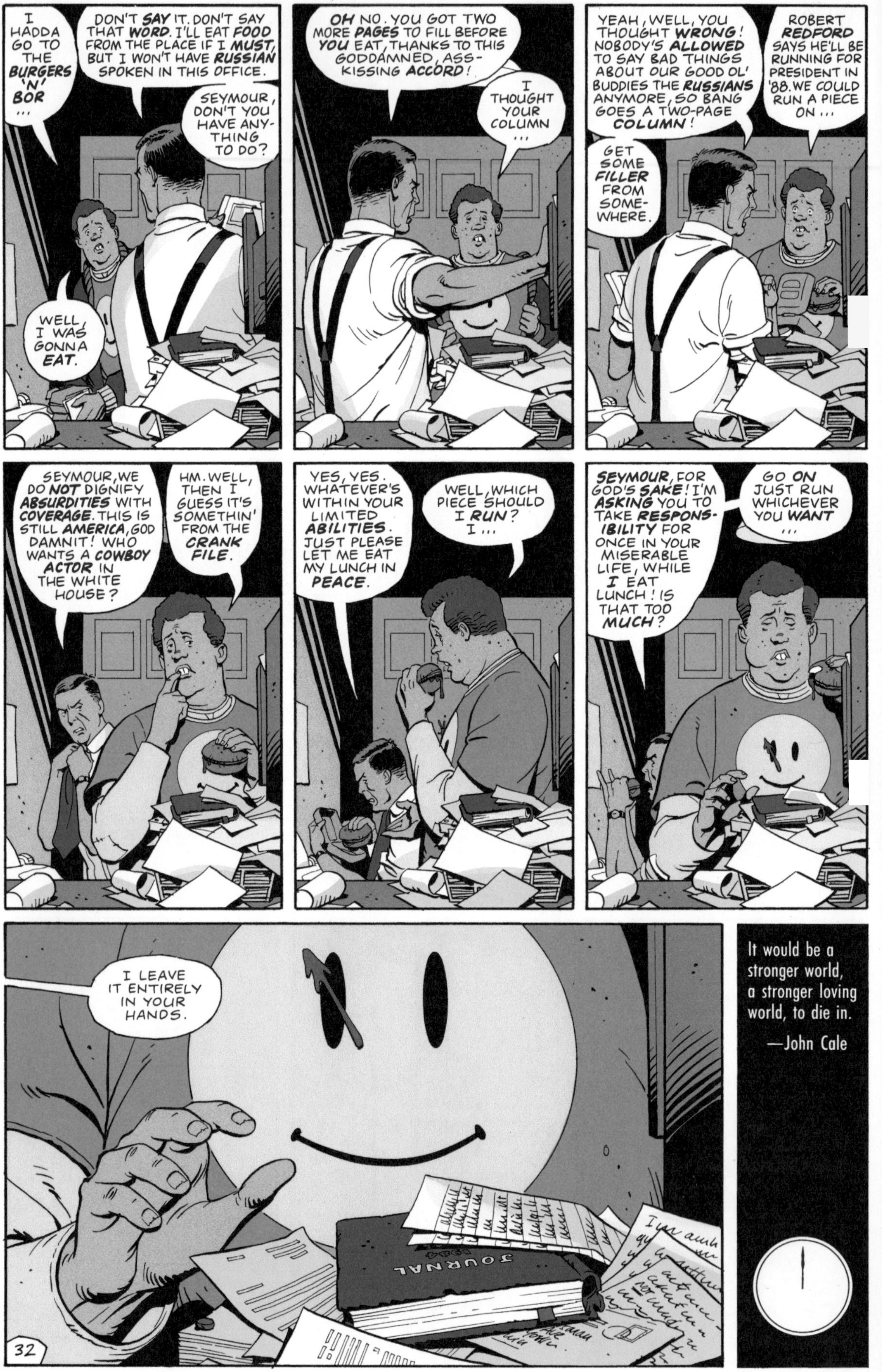
I HADDA GO TO THE BURGERS 'N' BOR ...
DON'T SAY IT. DON'T SAY THAT WORD. I'LL EAT FOOD FROM THE PLACE IF I MUST, BUT I WON'T HAVE RUSSIAN SPOKEN IN THIS OFFICE.
SEYMOUR, DON'T YOU HAVE ANYTHING TO DO?
WELL, I WAS GONNA EAT.
OH NO. YOU GOT TWO MORE PAGES TO FILL BEFORE YOU EAT, THANKS TO THIS GODDAMNED, ASS-KISSING ACCORD!
I THOUGHT YOUR COLUMN ...
YEAH, WELL, YOU THOUGHT WRONG! NOBODY'S ALLOWED TO SAY BAD THINGS ABOUT OUR GOOD OL' BUDDIES THE RUSSIANS ANYMORE, SO BANG GOES A TWO-PAGE COLUMN!
GET SOME FILLER FROM SOMEWHERE.
ROBERT REDFORD SAYS HE'LL BE RUNNING FOR PRESIDENT IN '88. WE COULD RUN A PIECE ON ...
SEYMOUR, WE DO NOT DIGNIFY ABSURDITIES WITH COVERAGE. THIS IS STILL AMERICA, GOD DAMNIT! WHO WANTS A COWBOY ACTOR IN THE WHITE HOUSE?
HM. WELL, THEN I GUESS IT'S SOMETHIN' FROM THE CRANK FILE.
YES, YES. WHATEVER'S WITHIN YOUR LIMITED ABILITIES. JUST PLEASE LET ME EAT MY LUNCH IN PEACE.
WELL, WHICH PIECE SHOULD I RUN? I ...
SEYMOUR, FOR GOD'S SAKE! I'M ASKING YOU TO TAKE RESPONSIBILITY FOR ONCE IN YOUR MISERABLE LIFE, WHILE I EAT LUNCH! IS THAT TOO MUCH?
GO ON JUST RUN WHICHEVER YOU WANT ...
I LEAVE IT ENTIRELY IN YOUR HANDS.
32
It would be a stronger world, a stronger loving world, to die in.
—John Cale

XII
II

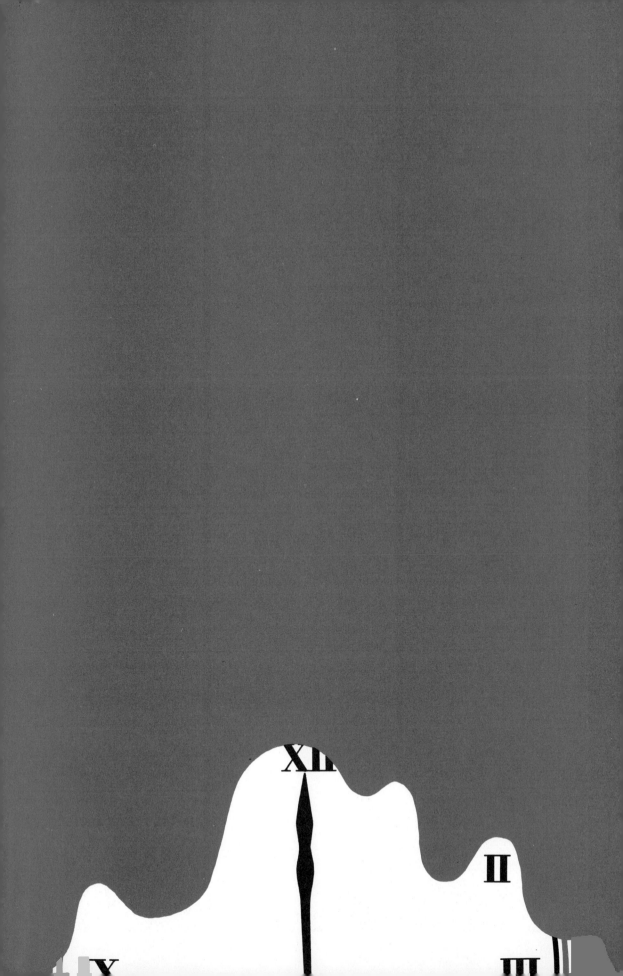

Quis custodiet
ipsos custodes.

Who watches the watchmen?

—Juvenal, *Satires,* VI, 347
Quoted as the epigraph of the Tower
Commission Report, 1987

GLIMPSES

Conceptual Sketches, Process, and Development

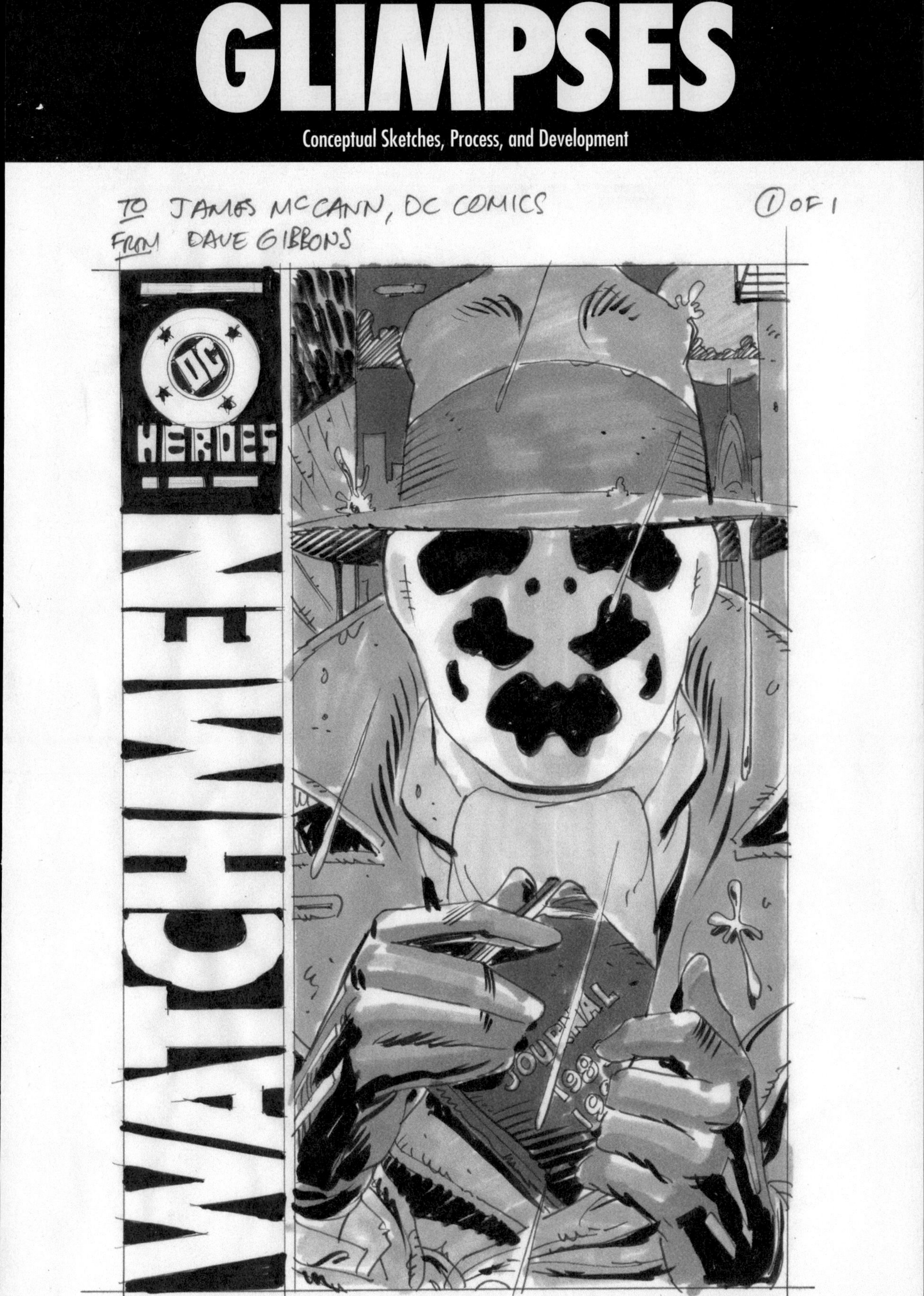
TO JAMES McCANN, DC COMICS
FROM DAVE GIBBONS
1 OF 1
DC
HEROES
WATCHMEN
JOURNAL

Marker rough for the third Mayfair Games role-playing module.

Dear Alan, Len, Ed, Richard, fellow Americans,

Here are the cover and ad sketches for your perusal.

The ads are open to re-arrangement -- perhaps the bottom line could be dropped and just have 'Who watches the Watchmen' more clearly seen in the picture. Or maybe just have the logo and 'Coming soon...' info.

I've done a whole batch of covers to show that there is some mileage in the basic idea of a semi-abstract non-figurative design. Hopefully, the stark simplicity of the covers will make them leap off the stands. Note that the cover leads into the story and also that there is at least a'face' in each, albeit a badge, a clock face or a chalked-up doodle.

As far as the treatment of the artwork goes, it could either be the usual line drawing with added color (perhaps on blue/grey line for more subtlety) or a full-blown tromp l'oeil painting. In this case, I would do the design and John Higgins could do the finished full-colour rendering. We did this on a recent DR WHO album cover and it worked well.

Looking forward to your comments,

Dave

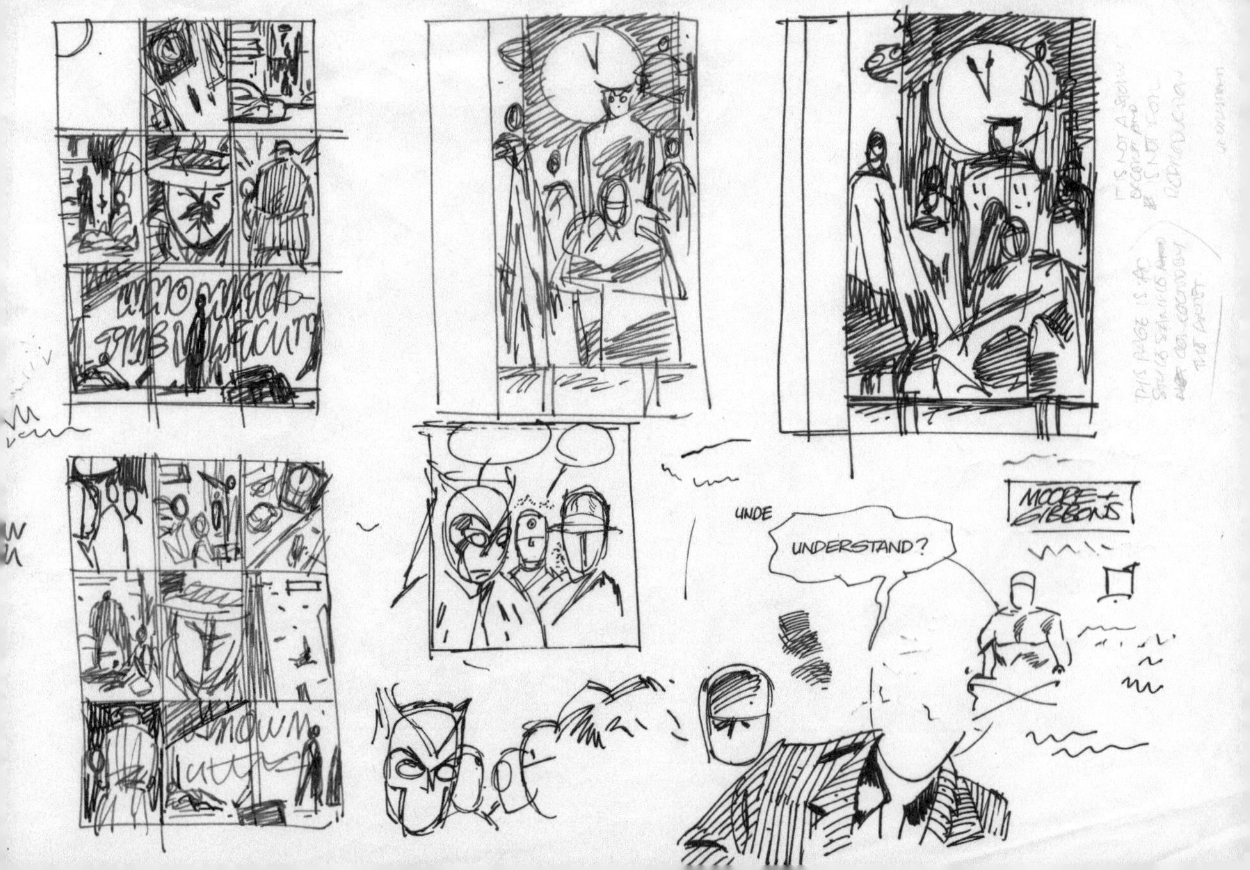
UNDE
UNDERSTAND?
MOORE + GIBBONS

Opposite top: Correspondence from Dave Gibbons to DC Comics editors and art directors concerning *Watchmen* promotional art.

Opposite bottom: Rough thumbnail sketches of the first group shot of the Watchmen.

Final inked illustration of the Watchman that appears in DC Comics Who's Who.

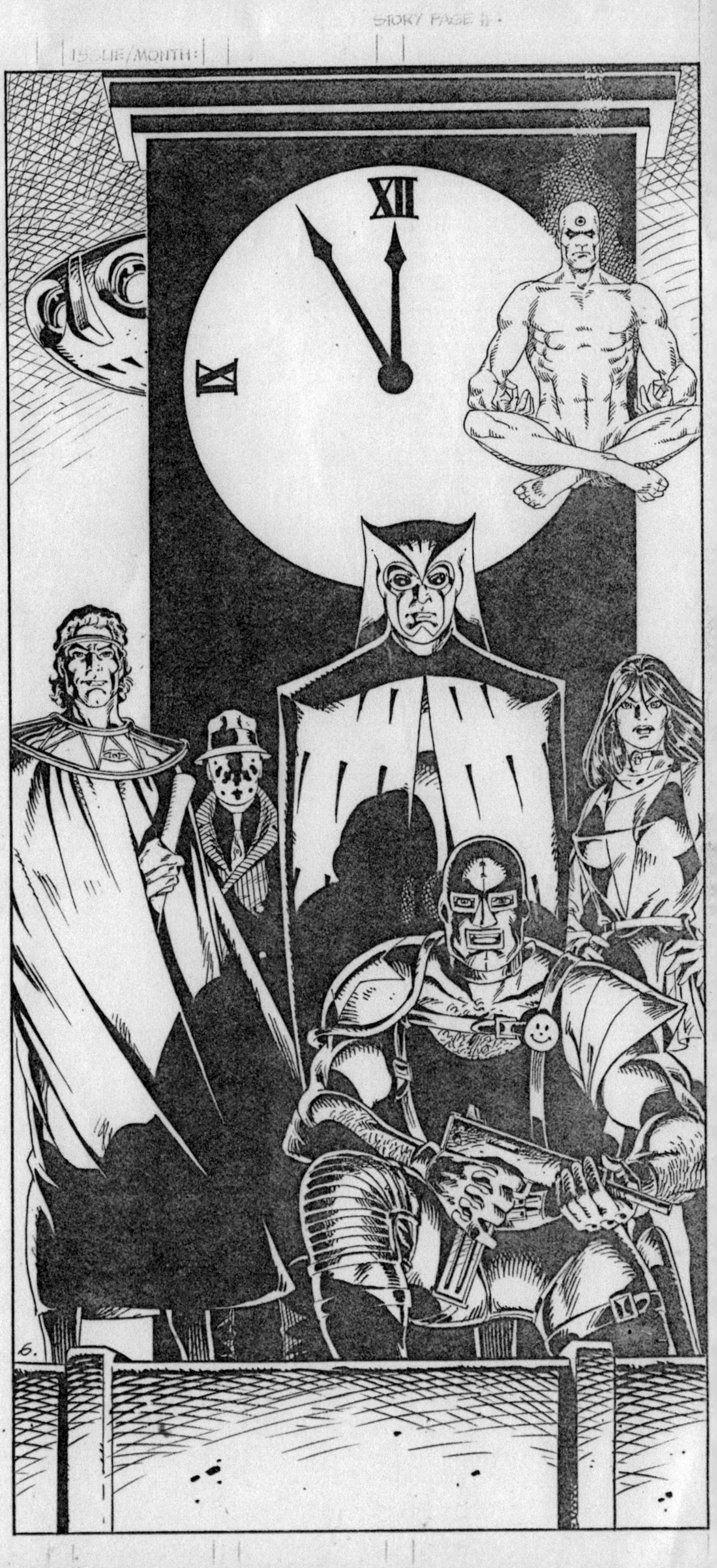

STORY PAGE #
ISSUE/MONTH:
XII
IX

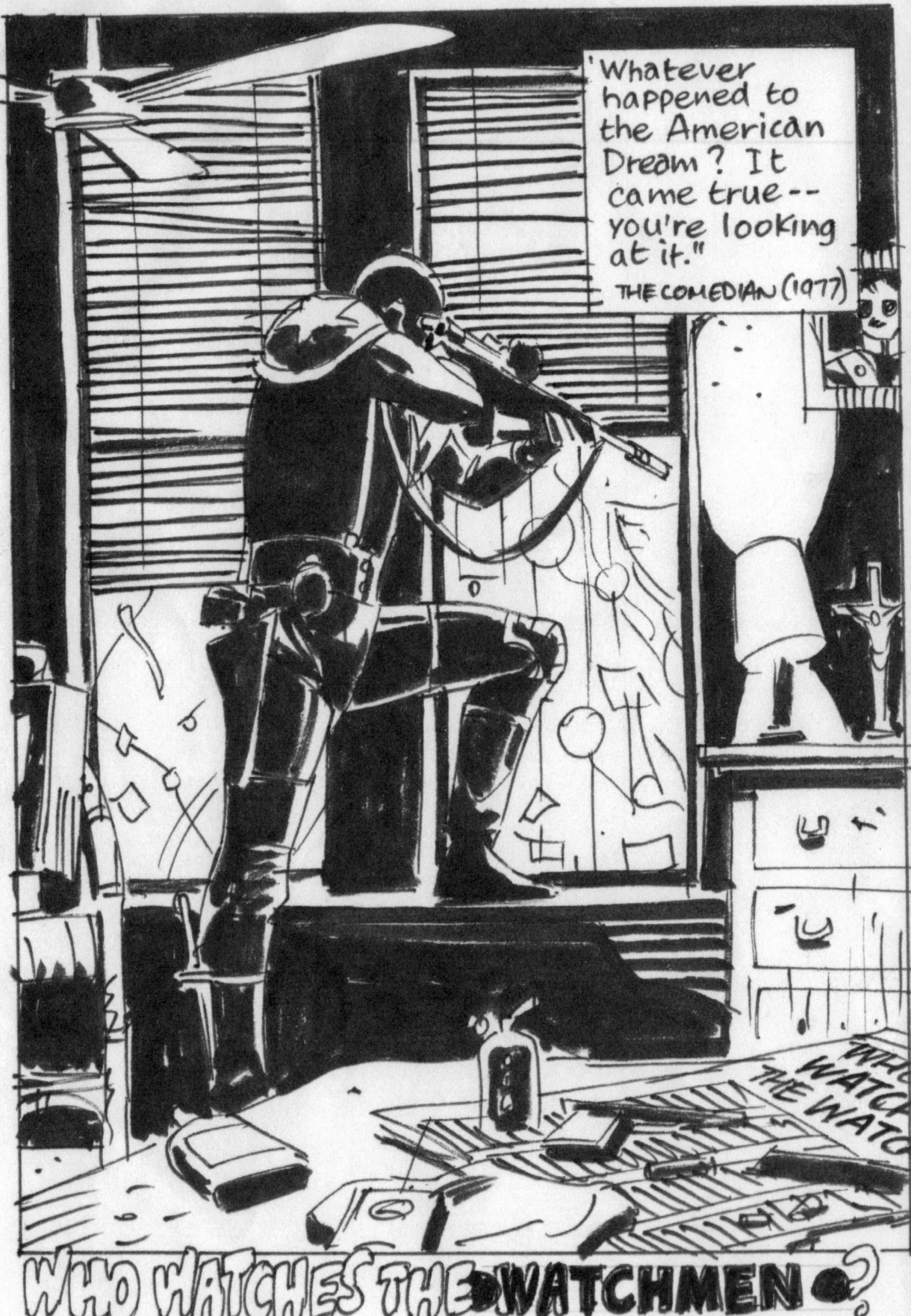
"Whatever happened to the American Dream? It came true-- you're looking at it."
THE COMEDIAN (1977)
WHO WATCHES THE WATCHMEN?

Preliminary sketches and inked roughs for three of the black and white character portraits featuring the Comedian, Nite Owl, and Silk Spectre which ran in the portfolio edition.

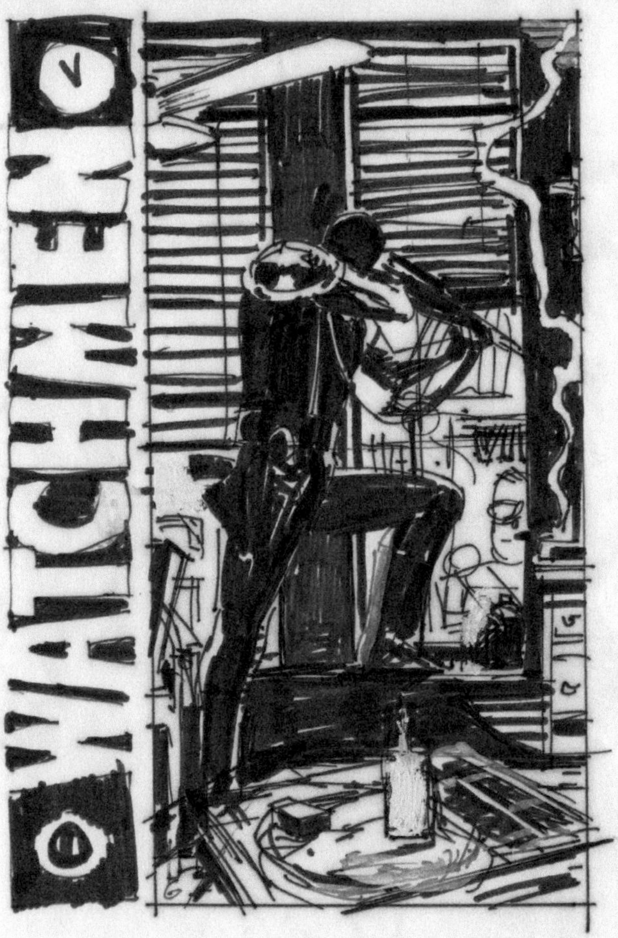
WATCHMEN

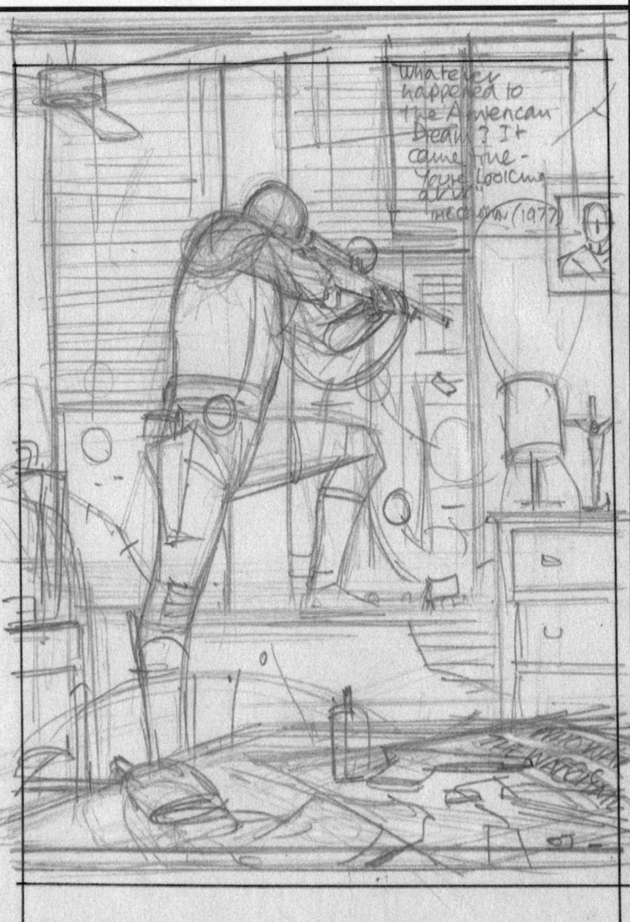
Whatever happened to the American Dream? It came true - you're looking
The Comedian (1977)

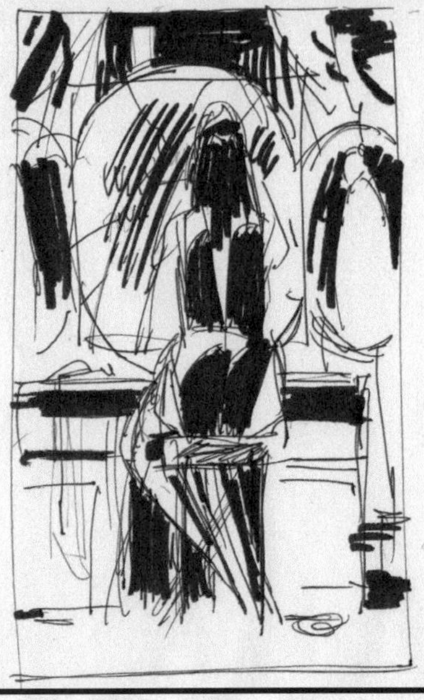

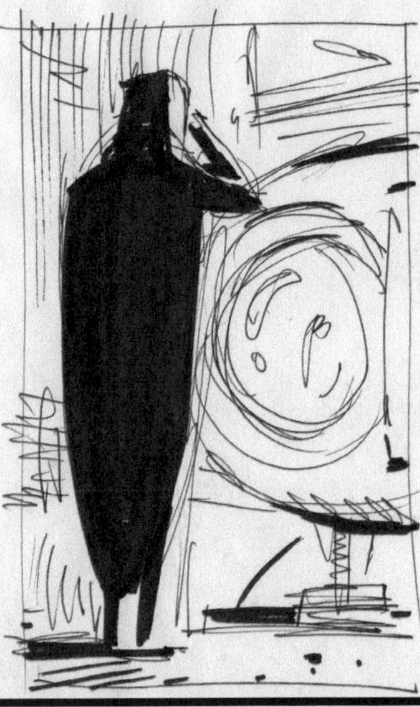

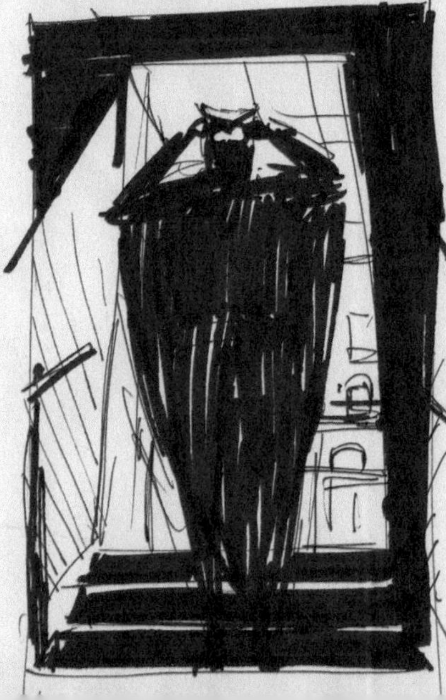

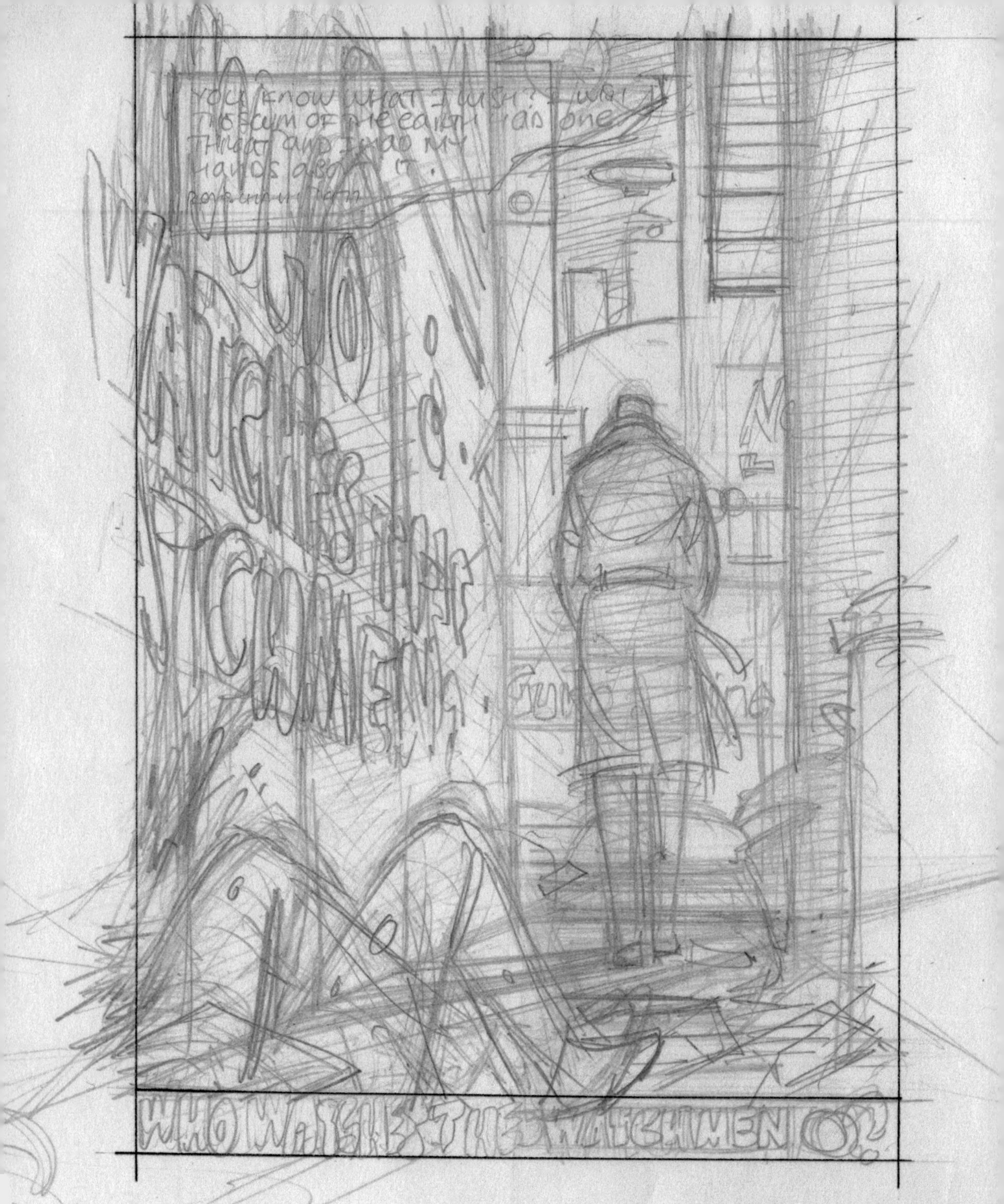
YOU KNOW WHAT I WISH?
THE SCUM OF THE EARTH HAD ONE
THROAT AND I HAD MY
HANDS
WHO WATCHES THE WATCHMEN

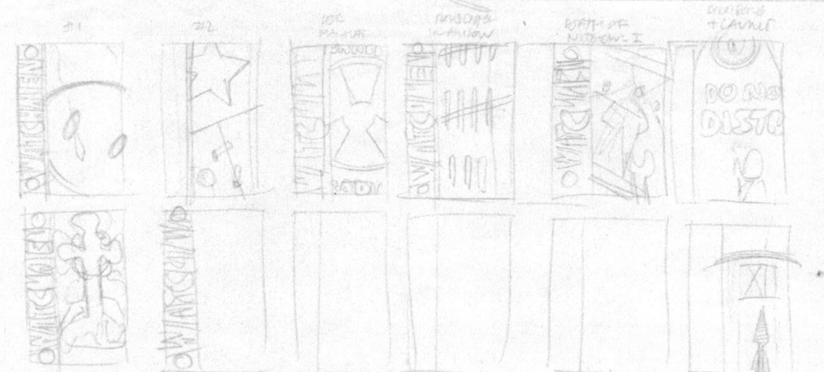

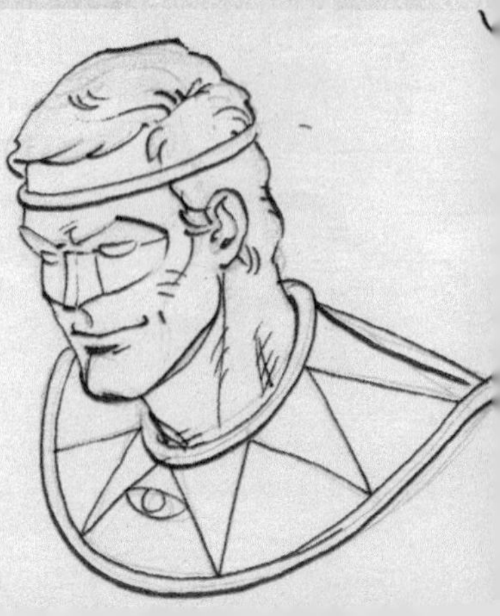

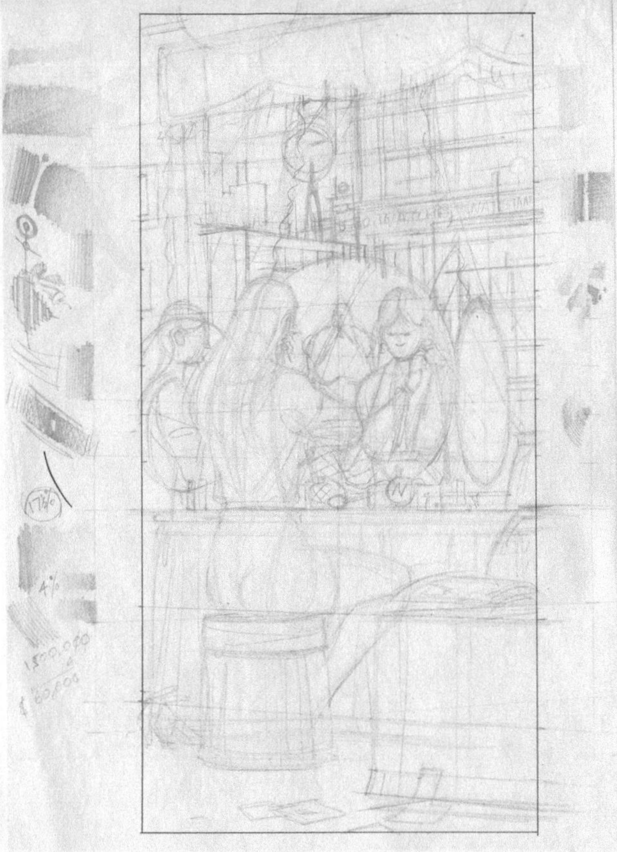

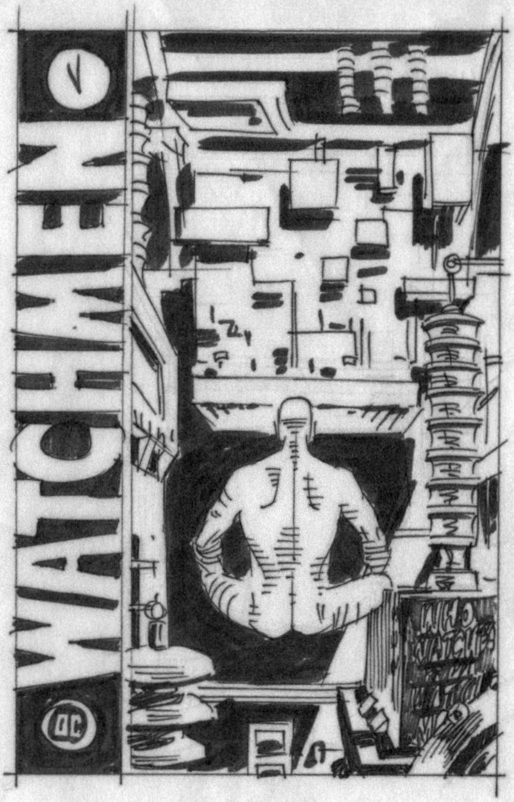
WATCHMEN

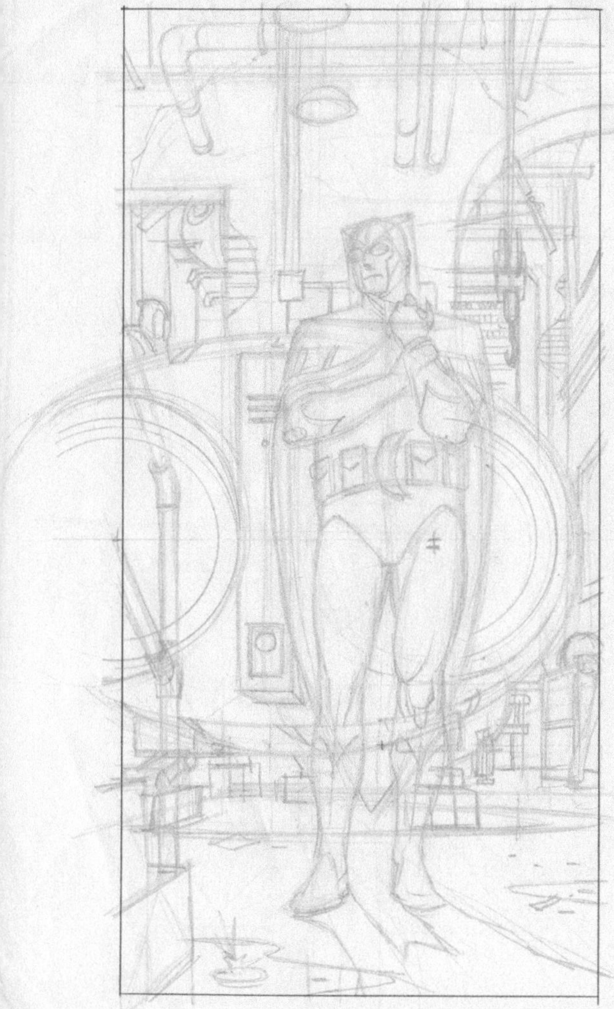

Progression of thumbnails, pencils, and inks of promotional Watchmen artwork.

Opposite bottom left: Unused cover designs.

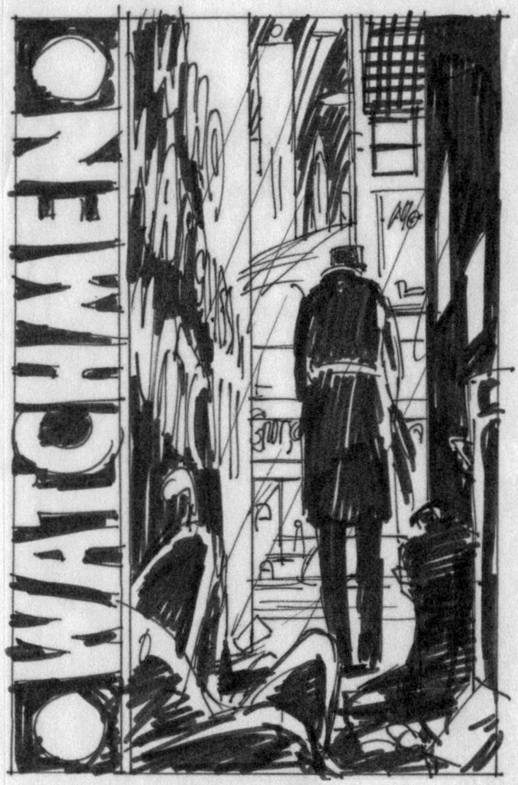
WATCHMEN

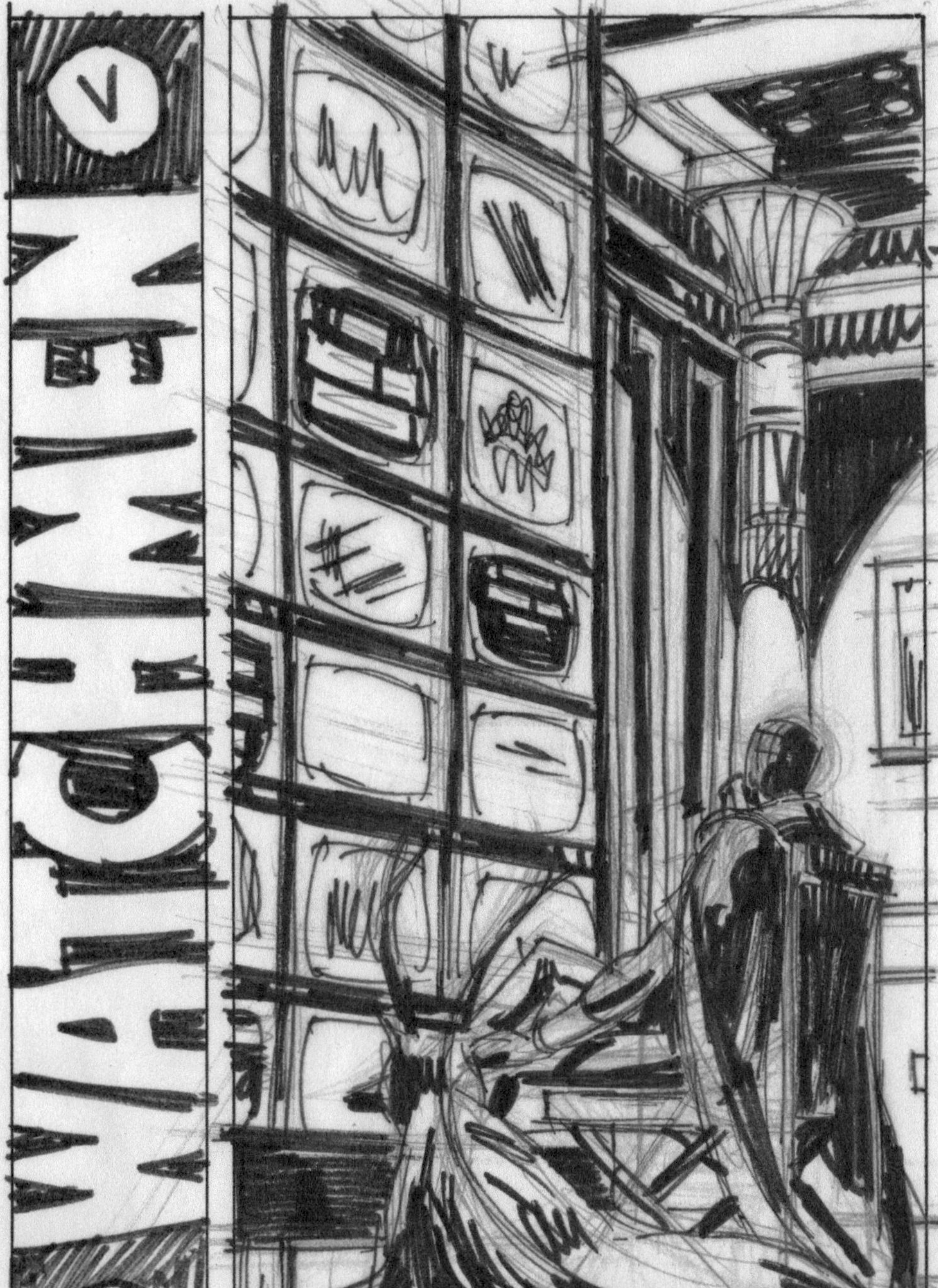
WATCHMEN

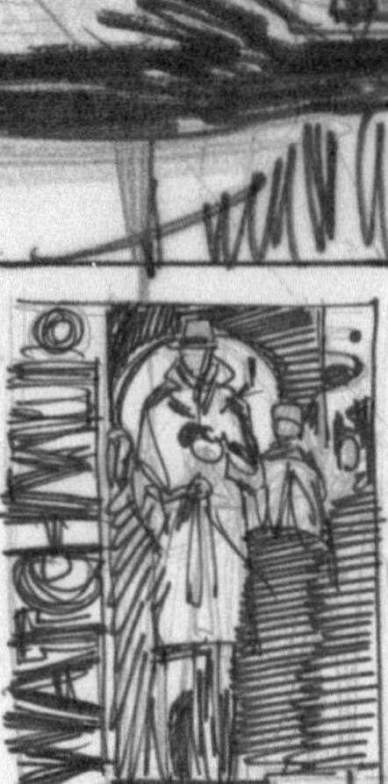
WATCHMEN

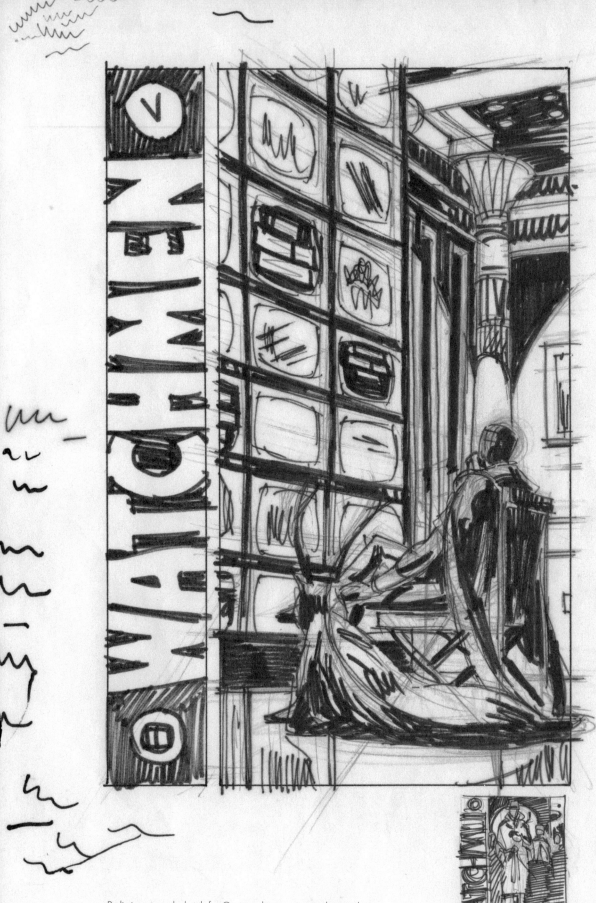

Preliminary rough sketch for Ozymandias promotional artwork.

Opposite: Character sketches of Laurie and Dan.

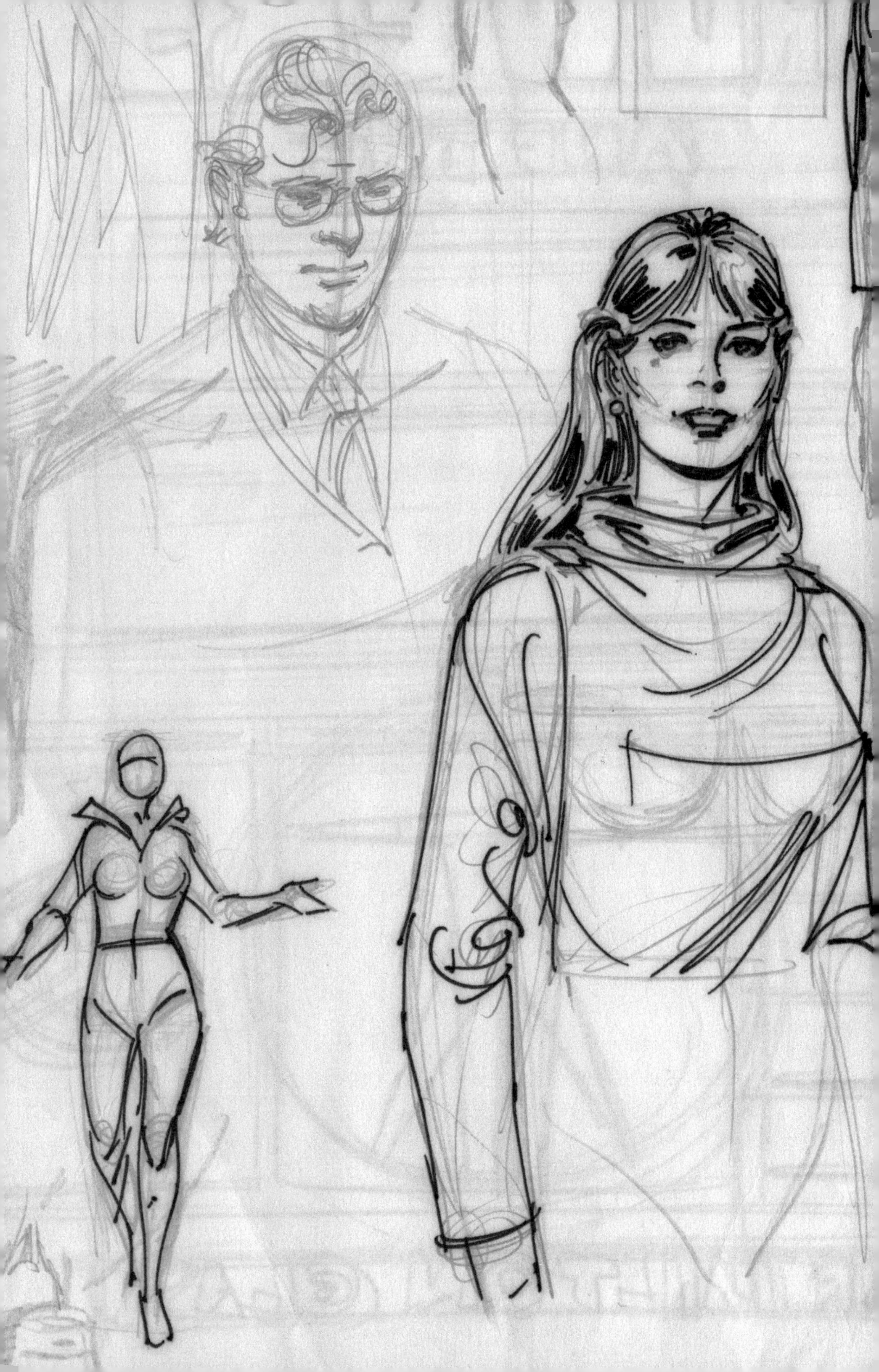

SPATIALLY GENERATED ENERGY RESEARCH PROJECT
S G E R P

CANNON 'DICTATES' MEMOIRS FOR POSTERITY
BIG SHOCK WHEN WE SEE CLOCK AT 00·01 (WE'VE SEEN SO
MUCH OF IT JUST BEFORE MIDNIGHT)

WHAT IF SILK SPECTRE'S MUM WAS ORIGINALLY DOC MANHATTAN'S
GIRLFRIEND + HAS BEEN REPLACED BY DAUGHTER? MUCH ANGUISH
ALL ROUND, EH?

STRICT FORMAT 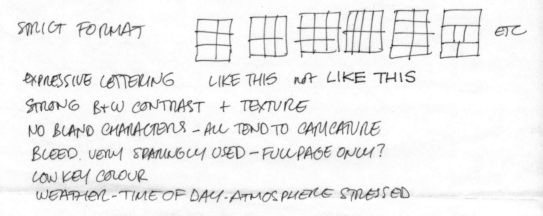 ETC

EXPRESSIVE LETTERING   LIKE THIS   not LIKE THIS
STRONG B+W CONTRAST + TEXTURE
NO BLAND CHARACTERS - ALL TEND TO CARICATURE
BLEED. VERY SPARINGLY USED - FULL PAGE ONLY?
LOW KEY COLOUR
WEATHER - TIME OF DAY · ATMOSPHERE STRESSED

Dave Gibbons' handrwritten notes concerning the look of Watchmen.

Opposite bottom: Pencilled headshots of Adrian Veidt, Edward Blake, and Dan Drieberg.

WORLD

GEODESIC DOMES
REAR ENGINED ELECTRIC CARS (LIGHTWEIGHT POLYACETYLENE BATTERIES
          REQUIRING RARE LITHIUM FOR MANUFACTURE)
DOUBLE BREASTED SUITS
UNUSUAL FAST FOODS
UNUSUAL FADS, ADDICTIONS
NO DISEASE
(NO POVERTY)
WIDESPREAD FEELINGS OF INADEQUACY, LACK OF MOTIVATION
PIRATE, MEDIAEVAL, WESTERN RATHER THAN S.F. MOVIES ETC?
LESS SEXUAL RESTRAINT
AIRSHIPS
SUBMARINE FREIGHTERS
EARTH ORBIT = ANTARCTICA
ANTARCTICA = RICH KIDS HOLIDAY PLAYGROUND (MAYBE OZ'S HQ HERE)
WEATHER CONTROL

CAPTAIN ATOM (DOC MANHATTAN)

    BOWIE
    ELRIC
    ALIENATED, ISOLATED
    MYSTICAL HERMIT
    PERMANENT 25 GOING ON 44

SEES WORLD AS
SUB-ATOMIC SYSTEM

THUNDERBOLT (OZYMANDIAS)

    10 × HUMAN INTELLIGENCE
    YOUNG 37 WILL LIVE TO 150
    REDFORD, KENNEDY
    POPULAR CELEBRITY
    RICH
    PERFECT
    LONER
    'PRESCIENT' THRU INTELLIGENCE

SEES WORLD AS
ORGANISM WITH HIM
AT CENTRE

BLUE BEETLE (NITE OWL)

    ORDINARY, FALLIBLE, HUMAN
    HEROIC, THO NOT NATURALLY COURAGEOUS
    SCIENTIST
    DEEP THINKING, CONCERNED, DOUBTING
    'VETERAN' HERO, MALADJUSTED
    SUBSTITUTE FOR ORIGINAL
    NEWMAN, FURILLO

DOESN'T KNOW
HOW HE SEES
WORLD

QUESTION (RORSHACH)

    MURDERER
    PSYCHOPATH OR SAINT?
    QUINTESSENTIAL 'DITKO'
    UTTERLY ALONE
    IMPLACABLE
    RUTHLESS
    UNPREDICTABLE
    'WILD CARD'
    BRONSON, 'LONELY'

SEES WORLD AS
IMMORAL + FLABBY +
IN NEED OF STRICT
MORAL CODE

PEACEMAKER (THE COMEDIAN)

    DIRTY FIGHTER, RETIRED
    ATHLETIC, ANIMAL
    (DIRTY HARRY?) (MEETS NICK FURY?)
    (MEETS HANNIBAL OF 'A-TEAM'?)
    'SERIOUS PEOPLE'
    WORKMANLIKE

HAS NO TIME
OR INTEREST FOR
'SEEING' WORLD

NIGHTSHADE (SILK SPECTRE) (?)

    DEPRIVED CHILDHOOD
    DUNAWAY, STREEP

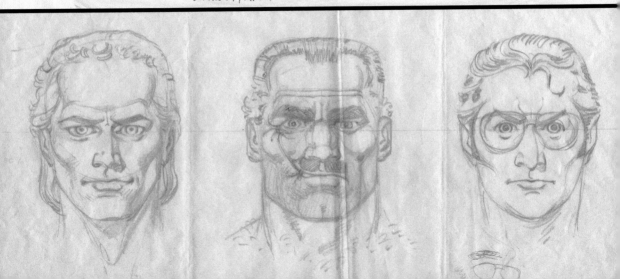

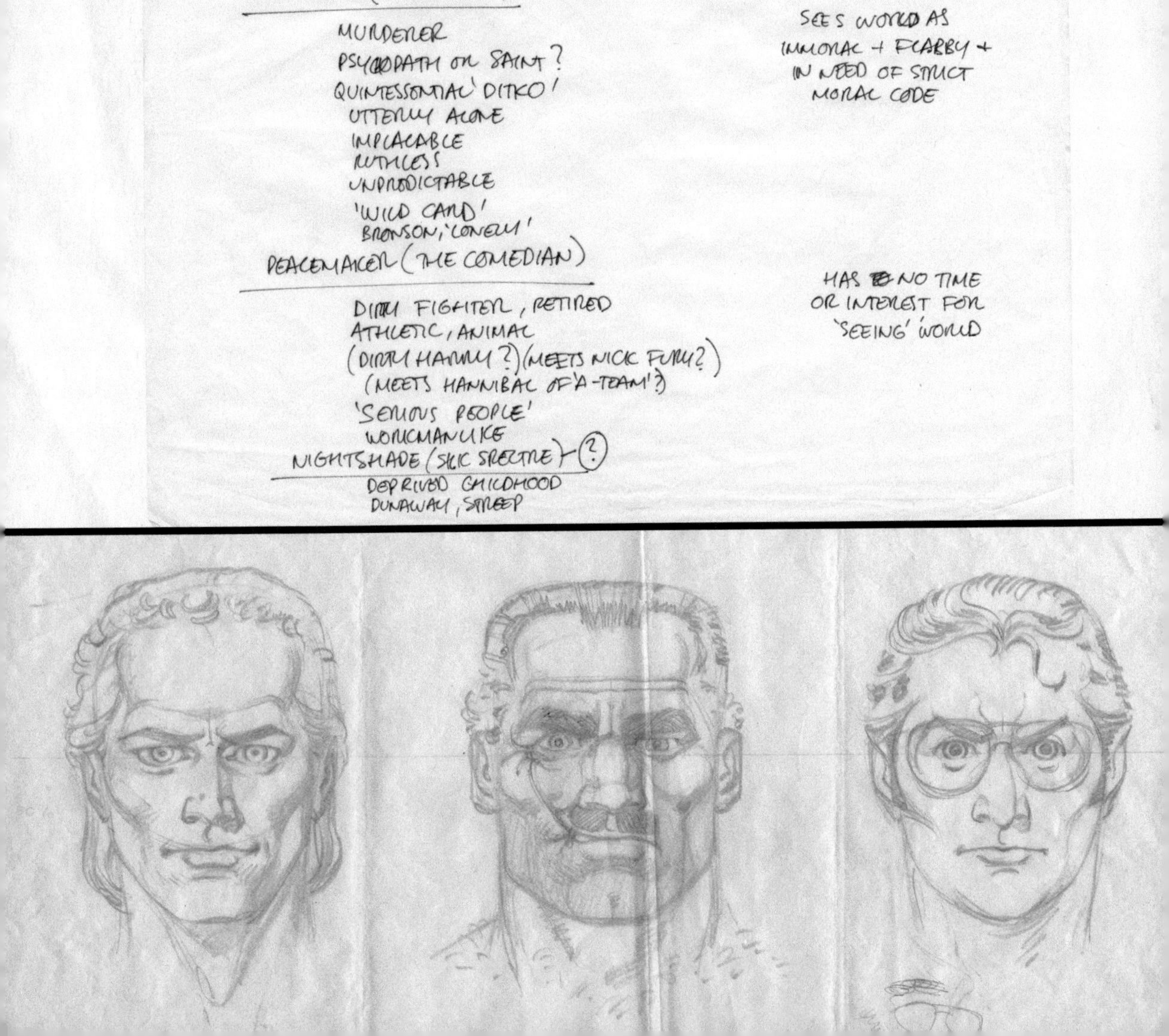

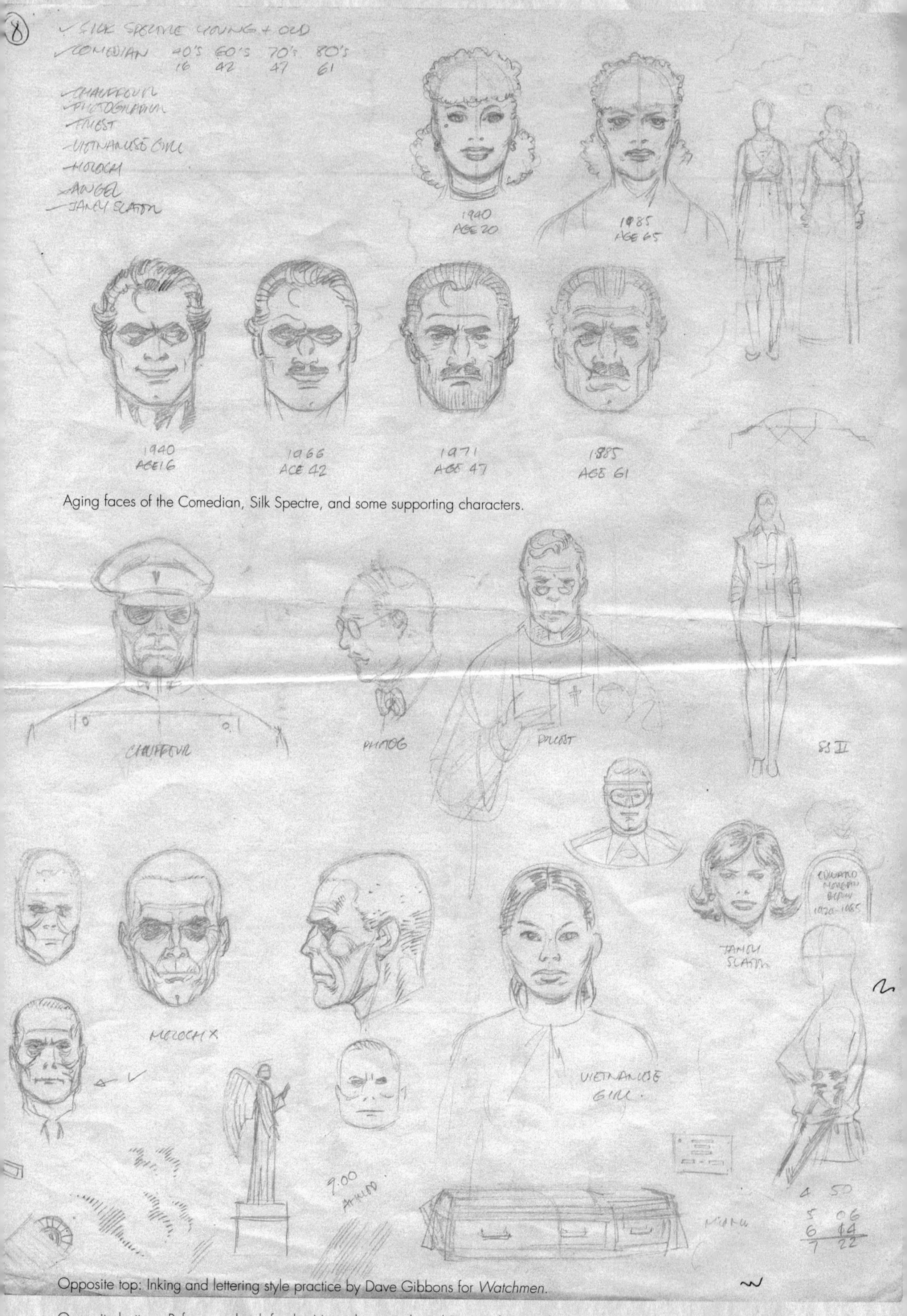
SILK SPECTRE YOUNG + OLD
COMEDIAN 40'S 60'S 70'S 80'S
16 42 47 61
1940
AGE 20
1985
AGE 65
1966
AGE 42
1971
AGE 47
AGE 61
CHAUFFEUR
PHOTOG
MOLOCH
VIETNAMESE GIRL

Aging faces of the Comedian, Silk Spectre, and some supporting characters.

Opposite top: Inking and lettering style practice by Dave Gibbons for *Watchmen*.

Opposite bottom: Reference sketch for the Mars photograph and Dr. Manhattan's hydrogen symbol featured in Chapter 9. The mapping allowed for consistency in its many appearances throughout the issue.

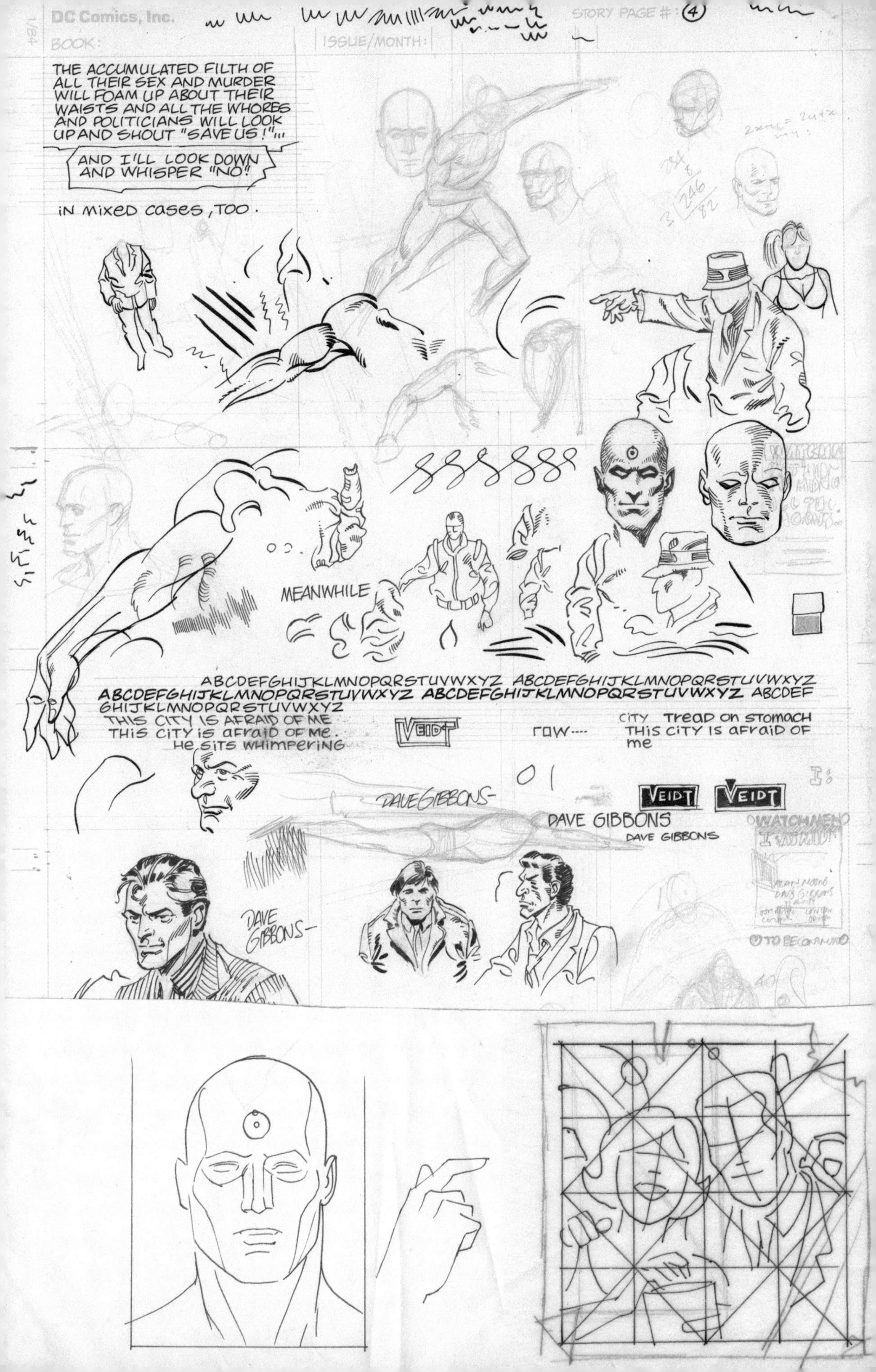
DC Comics, Inc.
BOOK:
ISSUE/MONTH:
STORY PAGE #: 4
THE ACCUMULATED FILTH OF ALL THEIR SEX AND MURDER WILL FOAM UP ABOUT THEIR WAISTS AND ALL THE WHORES AND POLITICIANS WILL LOOK UP AND SHOUT "SAVE US!"...
AND I'LL LOOK DOWN AND WHISPER "NO!"
in mixed cases, too.
MEANWHILE
ABCDEFGHIJKLMNOPQRSTUVWXYZ ABCDEFGHIJKLMNOPQRSTUVWXYZ
ABCDEFGHIJKLMNOPQRSTUVWXYZ ABCDEFGHIJKLMNOPQRSTUVWXYZ ABCDEF
GHIJKLMNOPQRSTUVWXYZ
THIS CITY IS AFRAID OF ME
THIS CITY is afraid of me.
He sits whimpering
VEIDT
row----
CITY Tread on stomach
THIS CITY is afraid of me
DAVE GIBBONS-
VEIDT
VEIDT
DAVE GIBBONS
DAVE GIBBONS
DAVE GIBBONS-

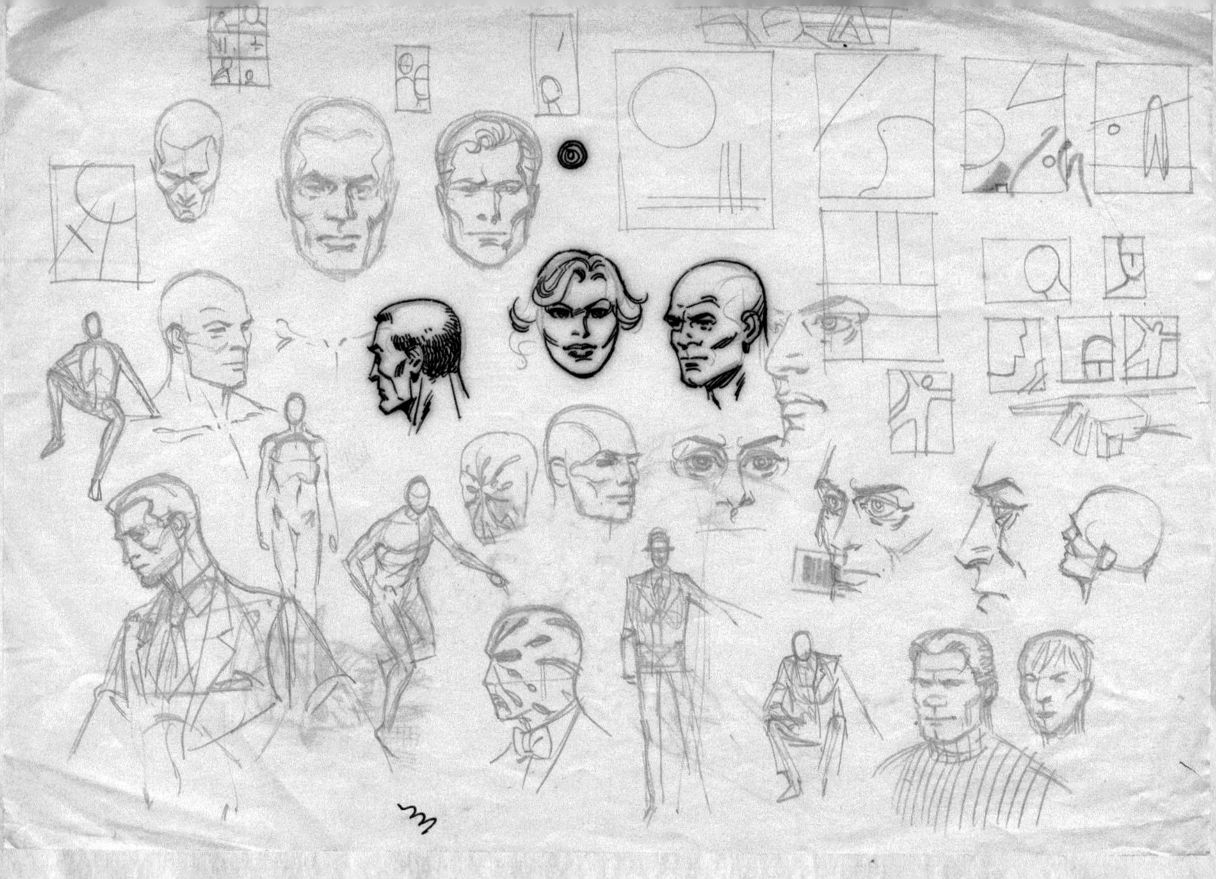

Above and below: Character sketches featuring Walter Kovacs and his psychiatrist, Malcolm Long.

Opposite: Inking tryouts of Rorschach, the Comedian, the detective, and a generic tough guy.

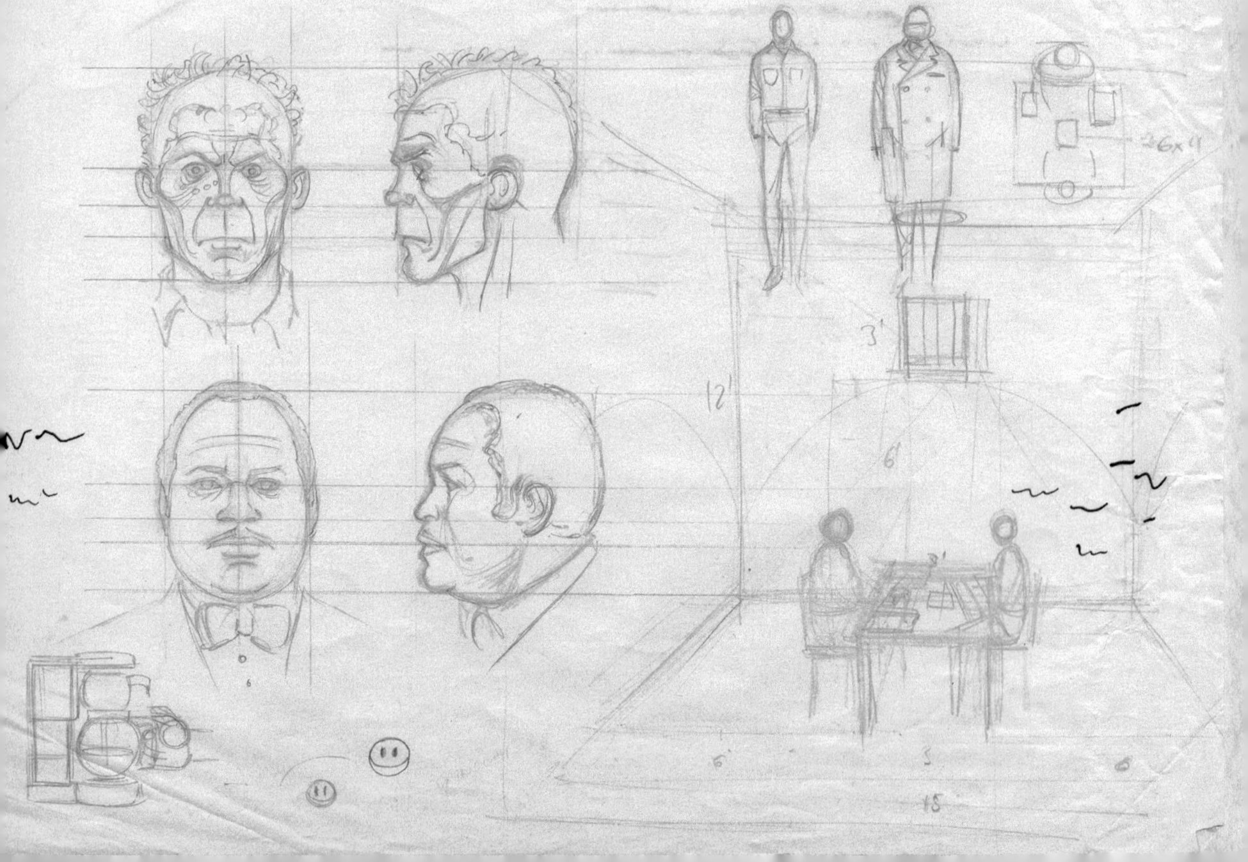

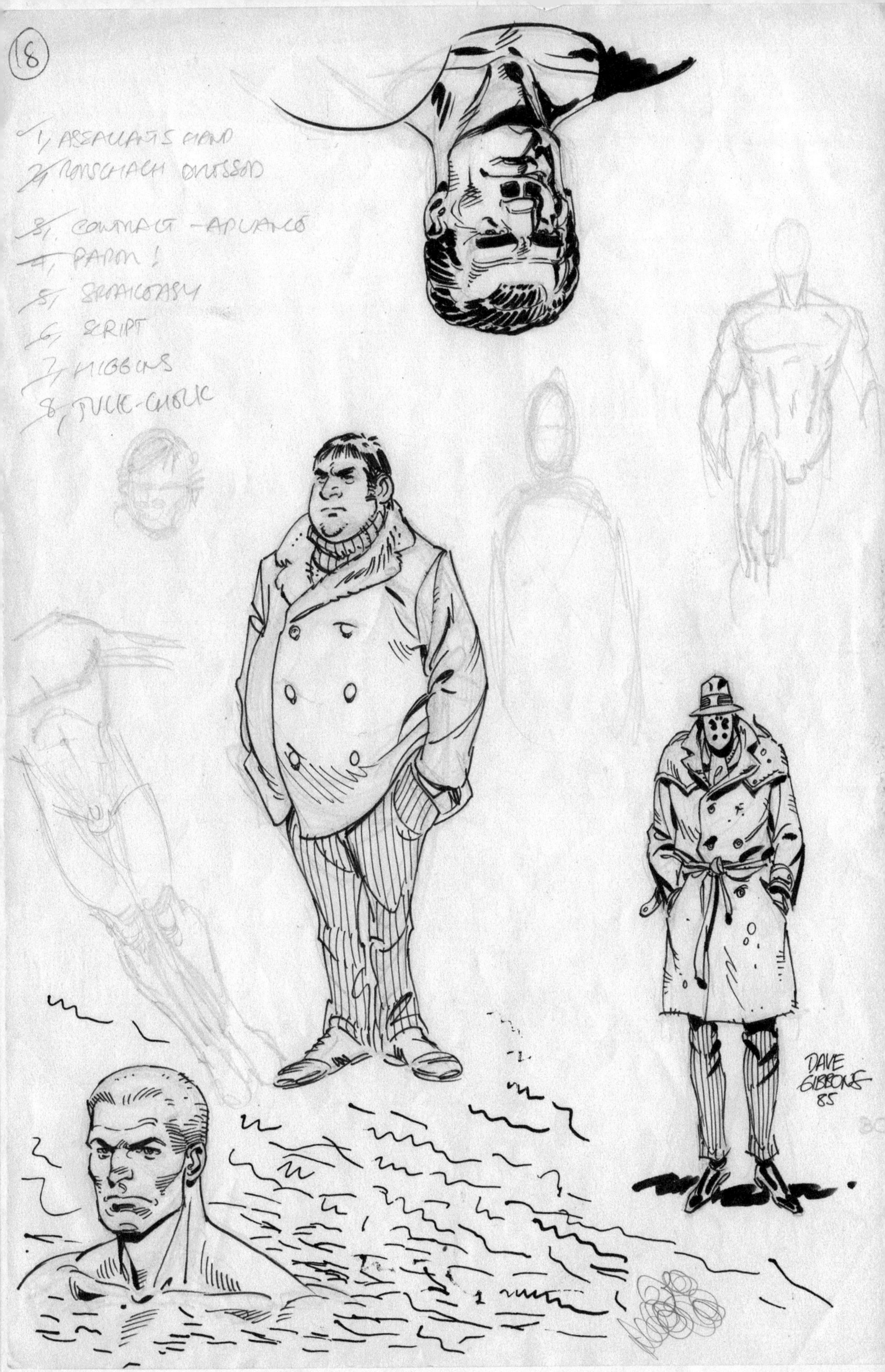
18
6, SCRIPT
DAVE GIBBONS 85

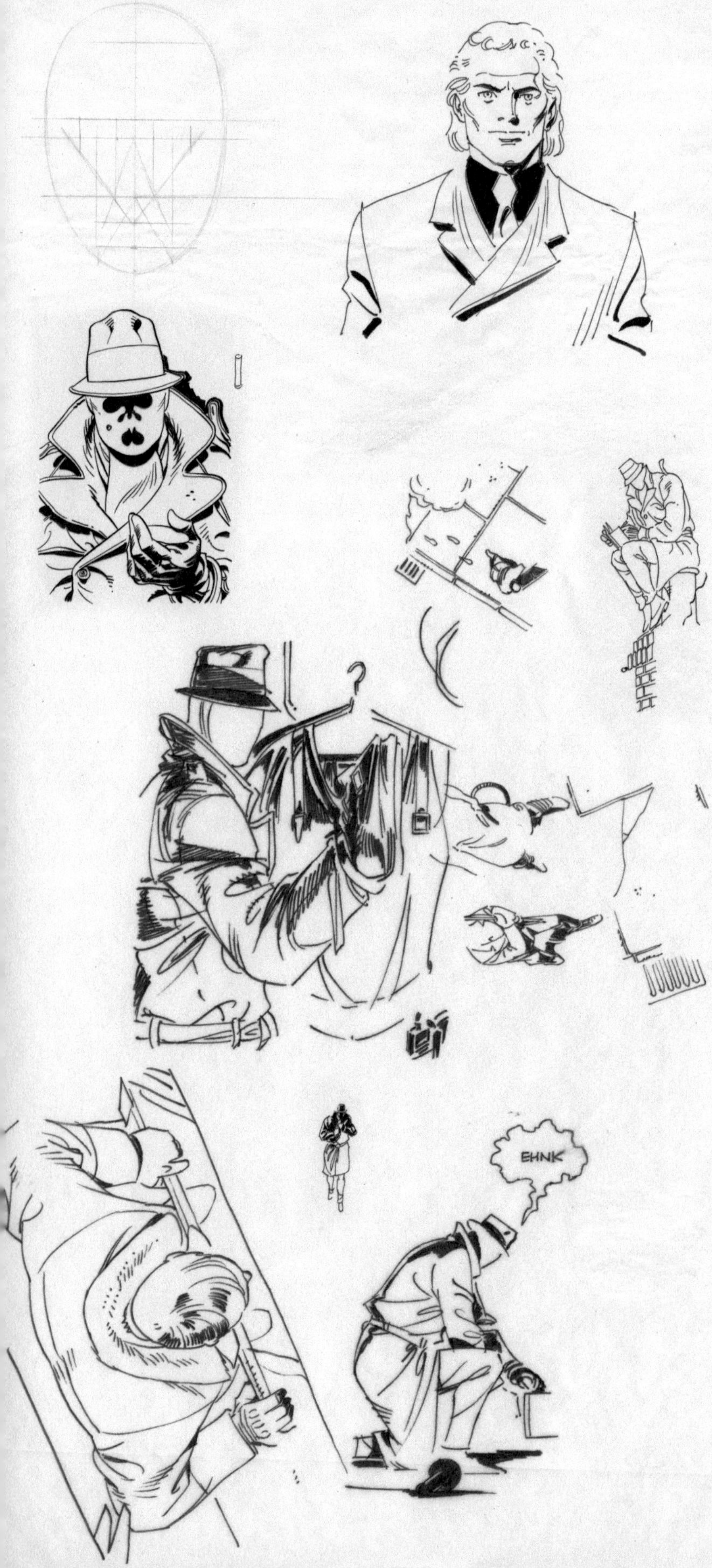
EHNK

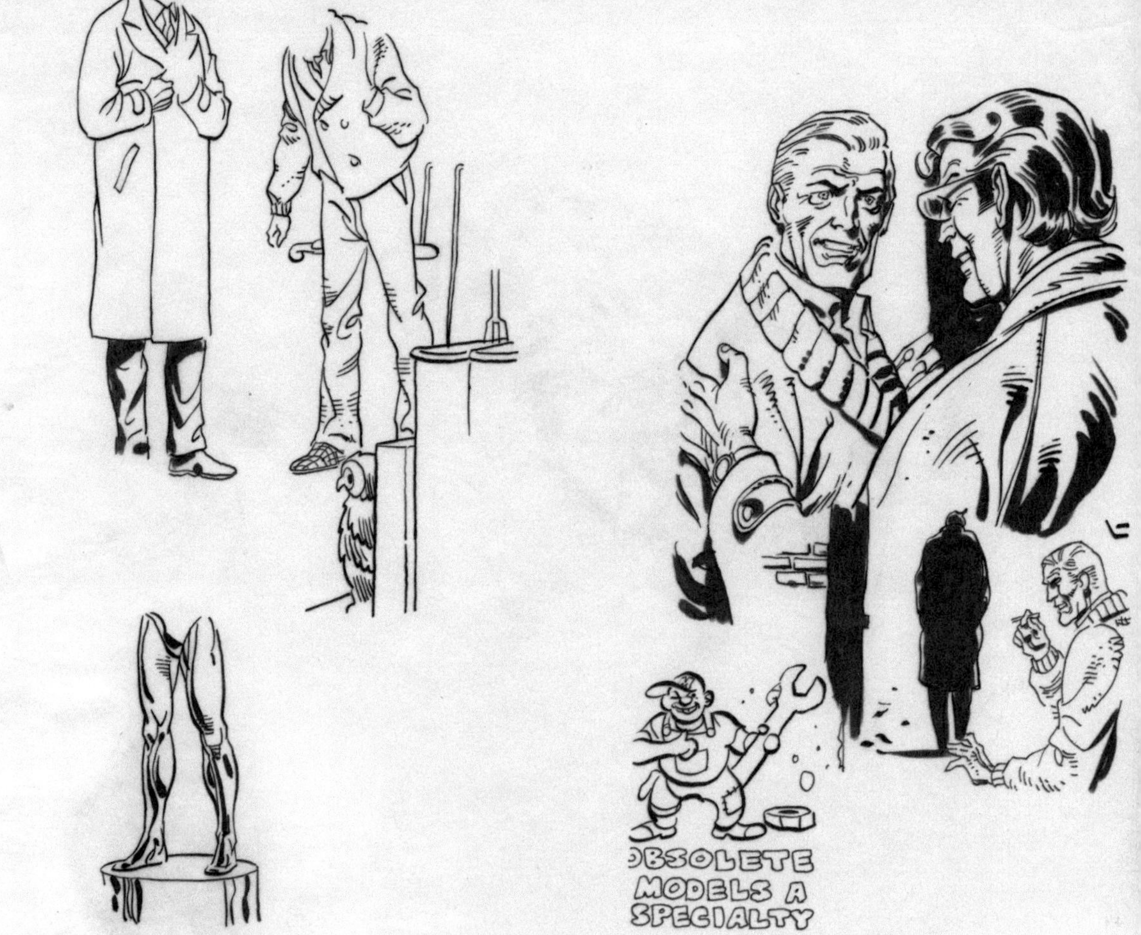
OBSOLETE
MODELS A
SPECIALTY

Above and opposite: Inking warm-ups on tracing vellum.

Below: Alternate blood-spattered smiley version and character studies of young Walter and his mom.

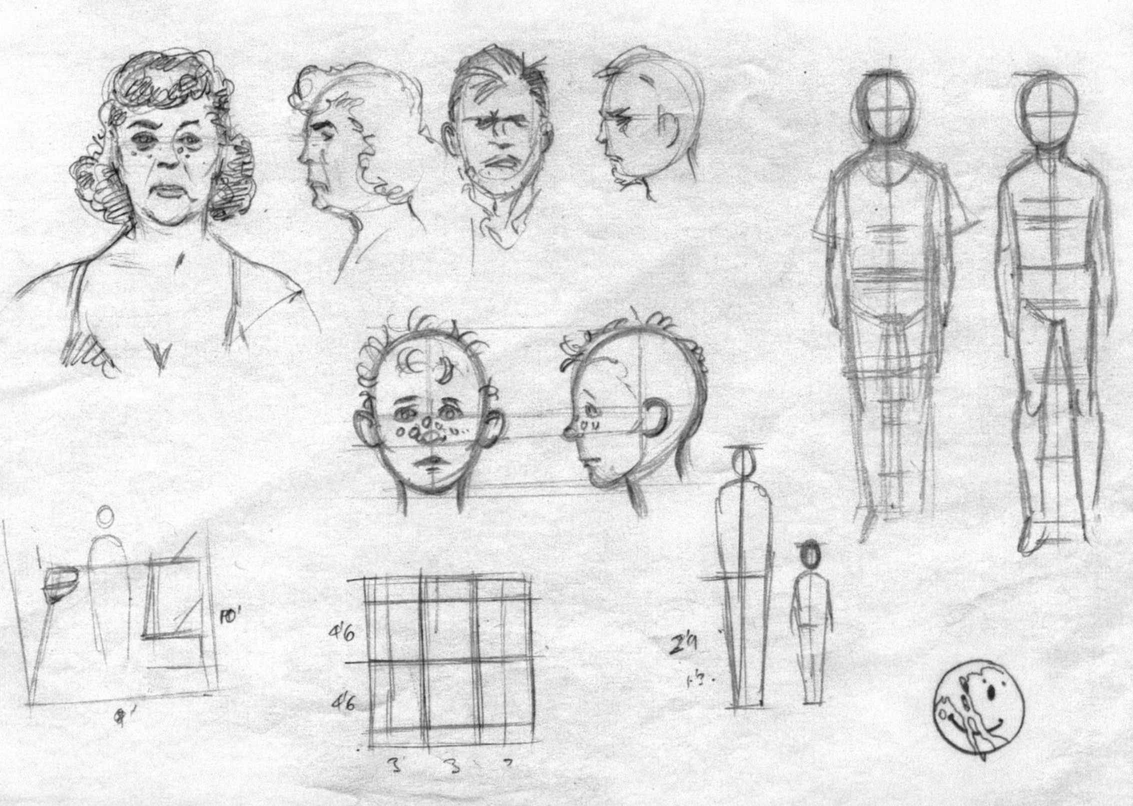

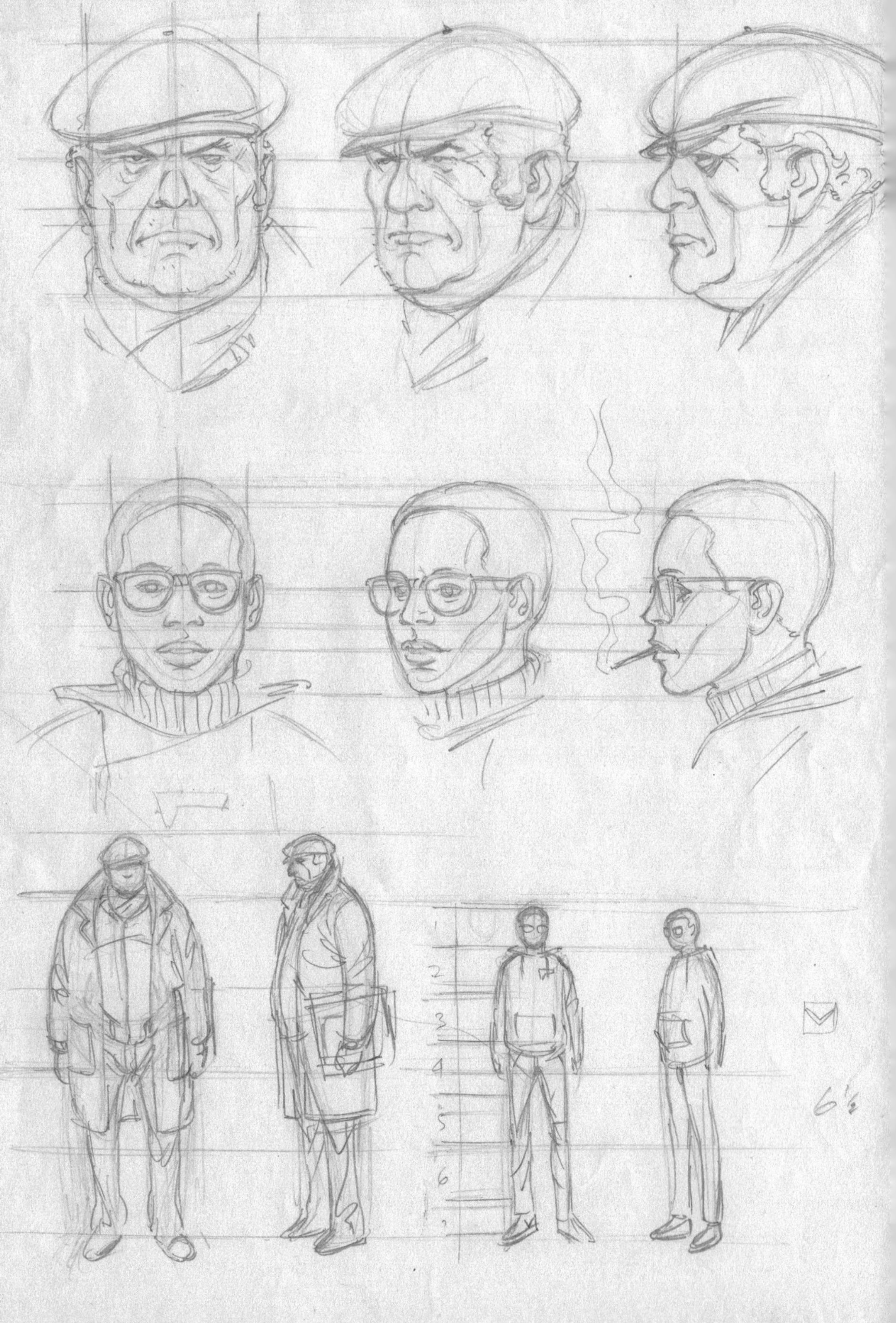

Model sheet for the two Bernies.

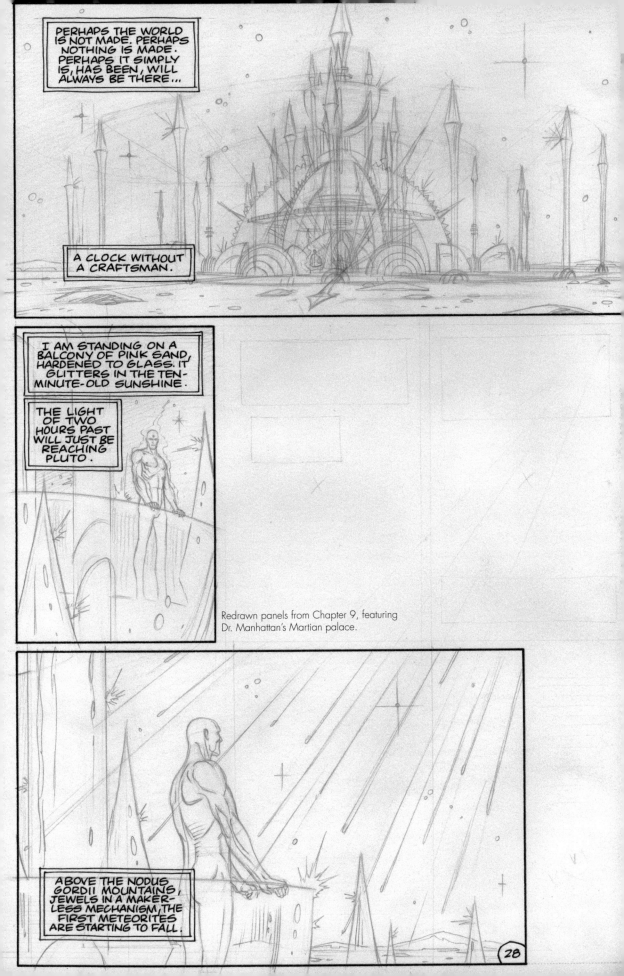

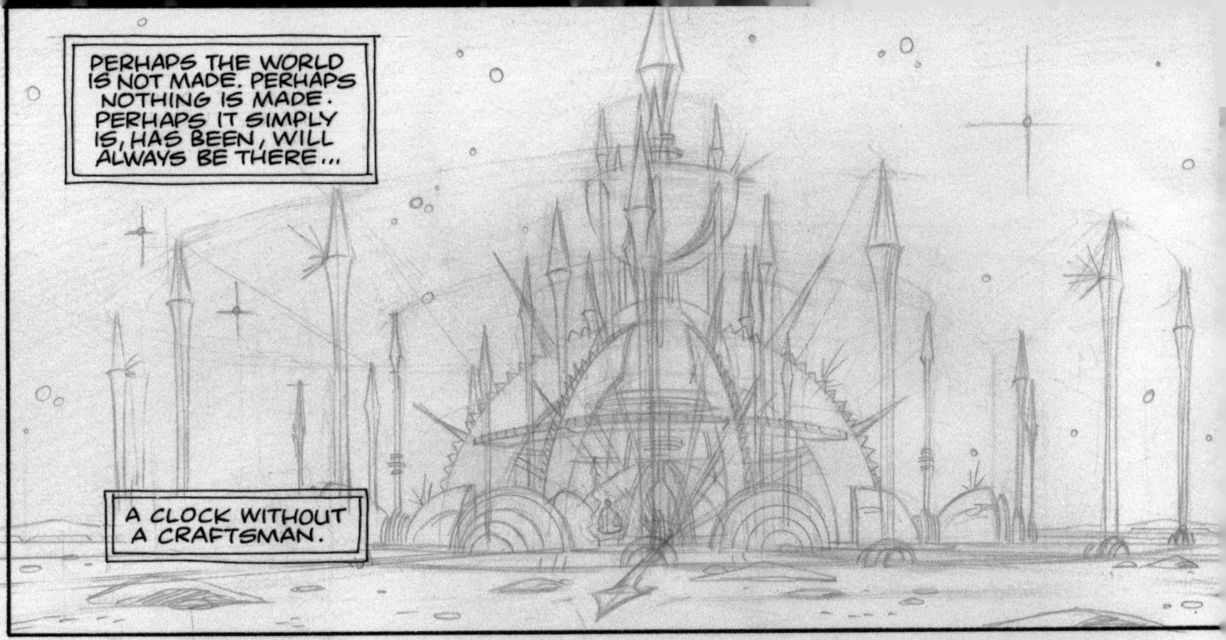
PERHAPS THE WORLD IS NOT MADE. PERHAPS NOTHING IS MADE. PERHAPS IT SIMPLY IS, HAS BEEN, WILL ALWAYS BE THERE...
A CLOCK WITHOUT A CRAFTSMAN.

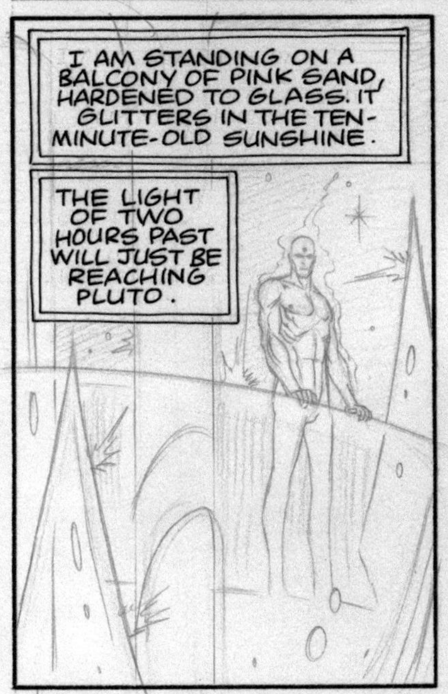
I AM STANDING ON A BALCONY OF PINK SAND, HARDENED TO GLASS. IT GLITTERS IN THE TEN-MINUTE-OLD SUNSHINE.
THE LIGHT OF TWO HOURS PAST WILL JUST BE REACHING PLUTO.

Redrawn panels from Chapter 9, featuring Dr. Manhattan's Martian palace.

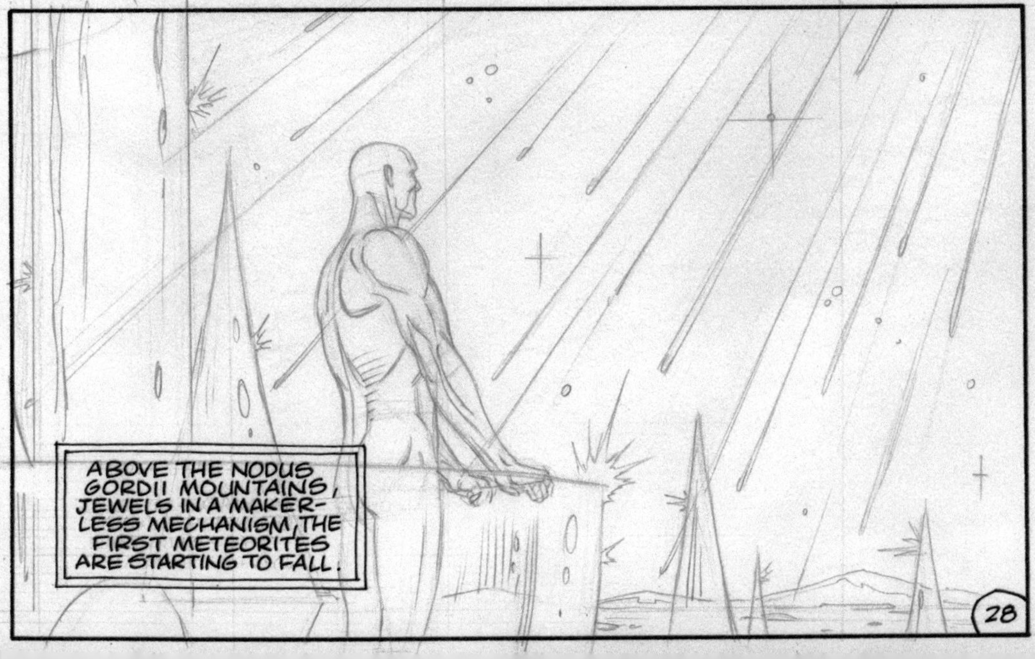
ABOVE THE NODUS GORDII MOUNTAINS, JEWELS IN A MAKER-LESS MECHANISM, THE FIRST METEORITES ARE STARTING TO FALL.
28

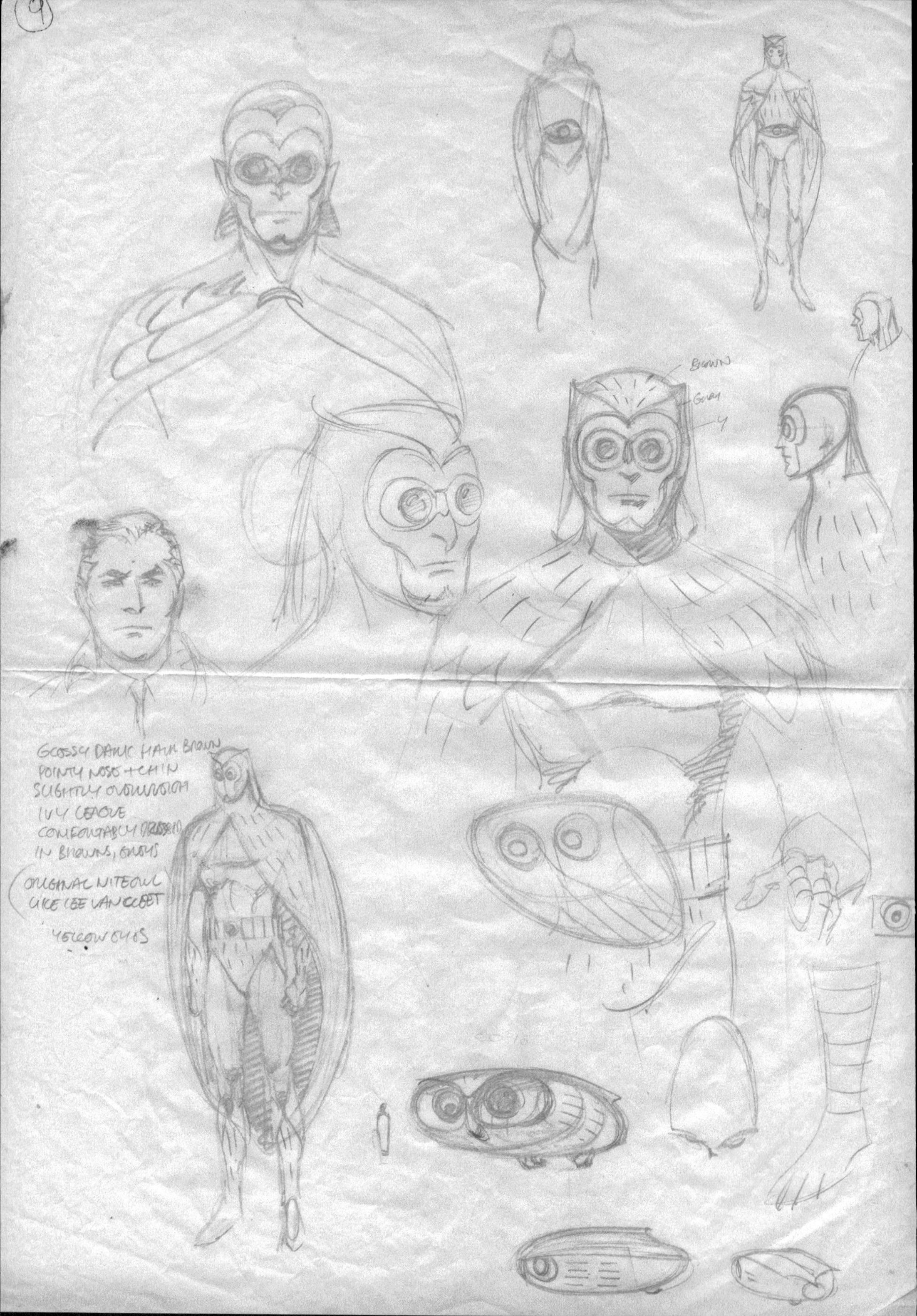
9
BROWN
GRAY
Y
GLOSSY DARK HAIR BROWN
POINTY NOSE + CHIN
SLIGHTLY OVERWEIGHT
IVY LEAGUE
COMFORTABLY DRESSED
IN BROWNS, GREYS
(ORIGINAL NITE OWL
LIKE LEE VAN CLEEF
YELLOW EYES

Above: Character sketches of Nite Owl.

Opposite: Redrawn panel from Chapter 9.

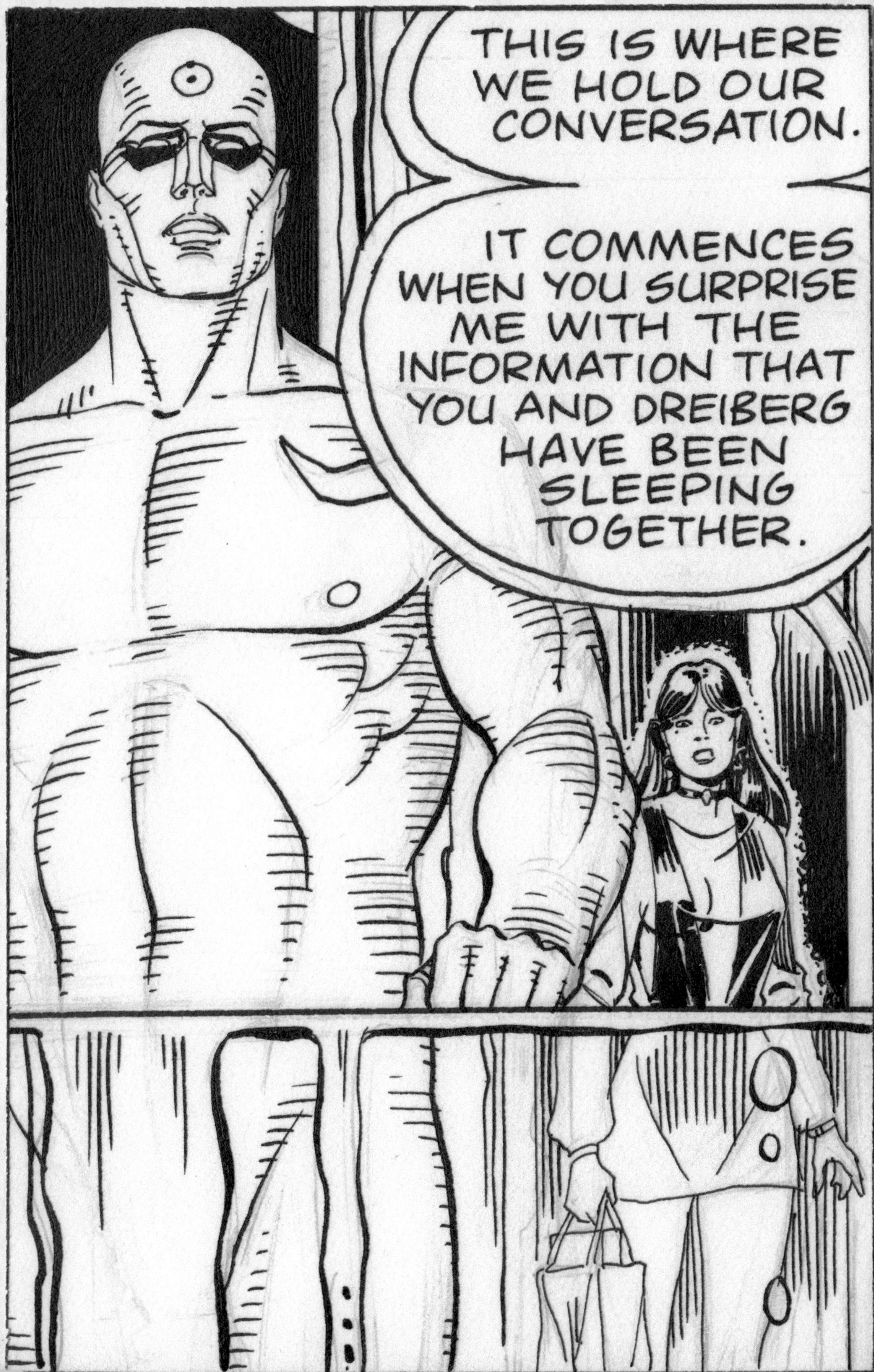
THIS IS WHERE WE HOLD OUR CONVERSATION.
IT COMMENCES WHEN YOU SURPRISE ME WITH THE INFORMATION THAT YOU AND DREIBERG HAVE BEEN SLEEPING TOGETHER.

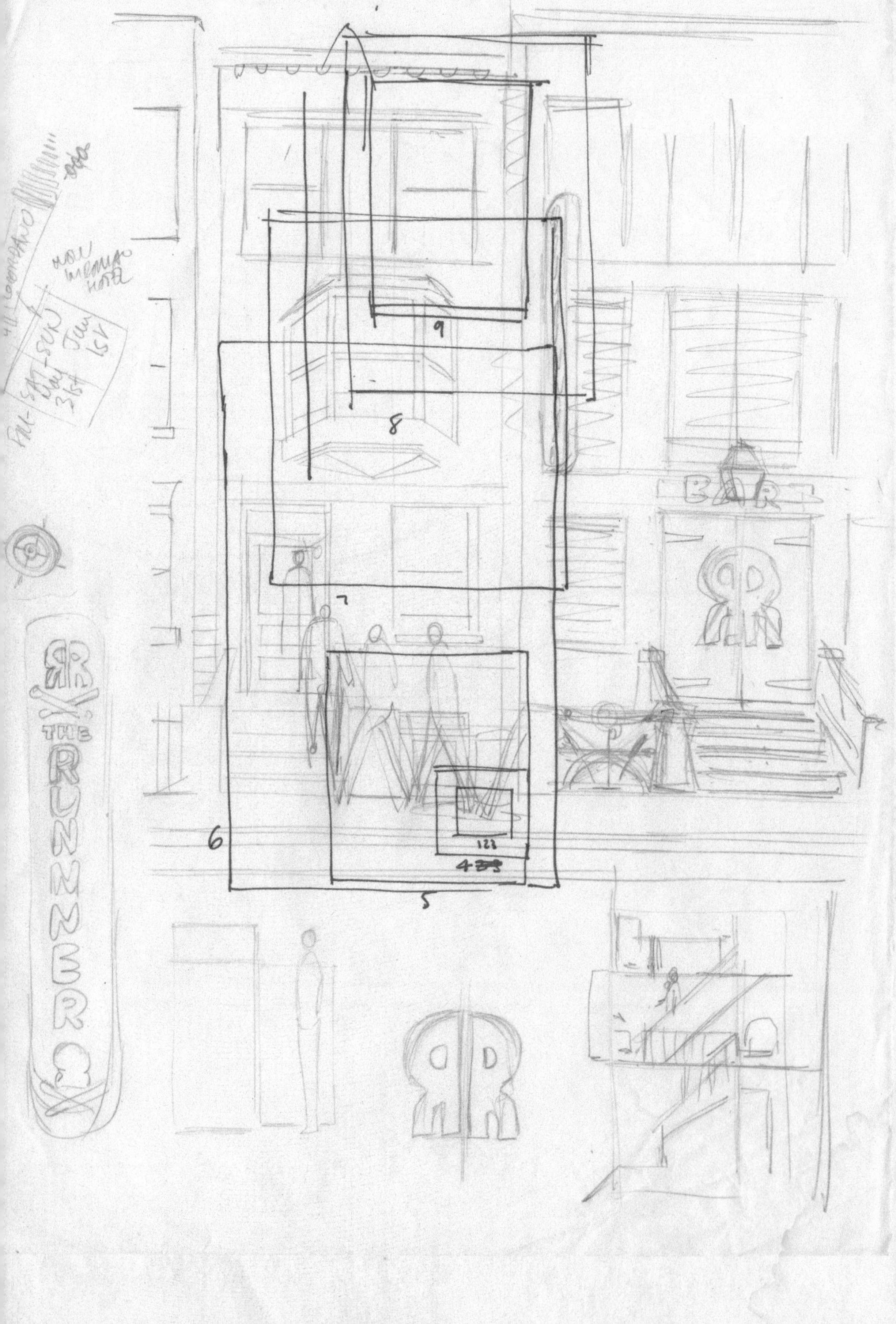

BAR
THE
RUNNER
9
8
7
6
5
123

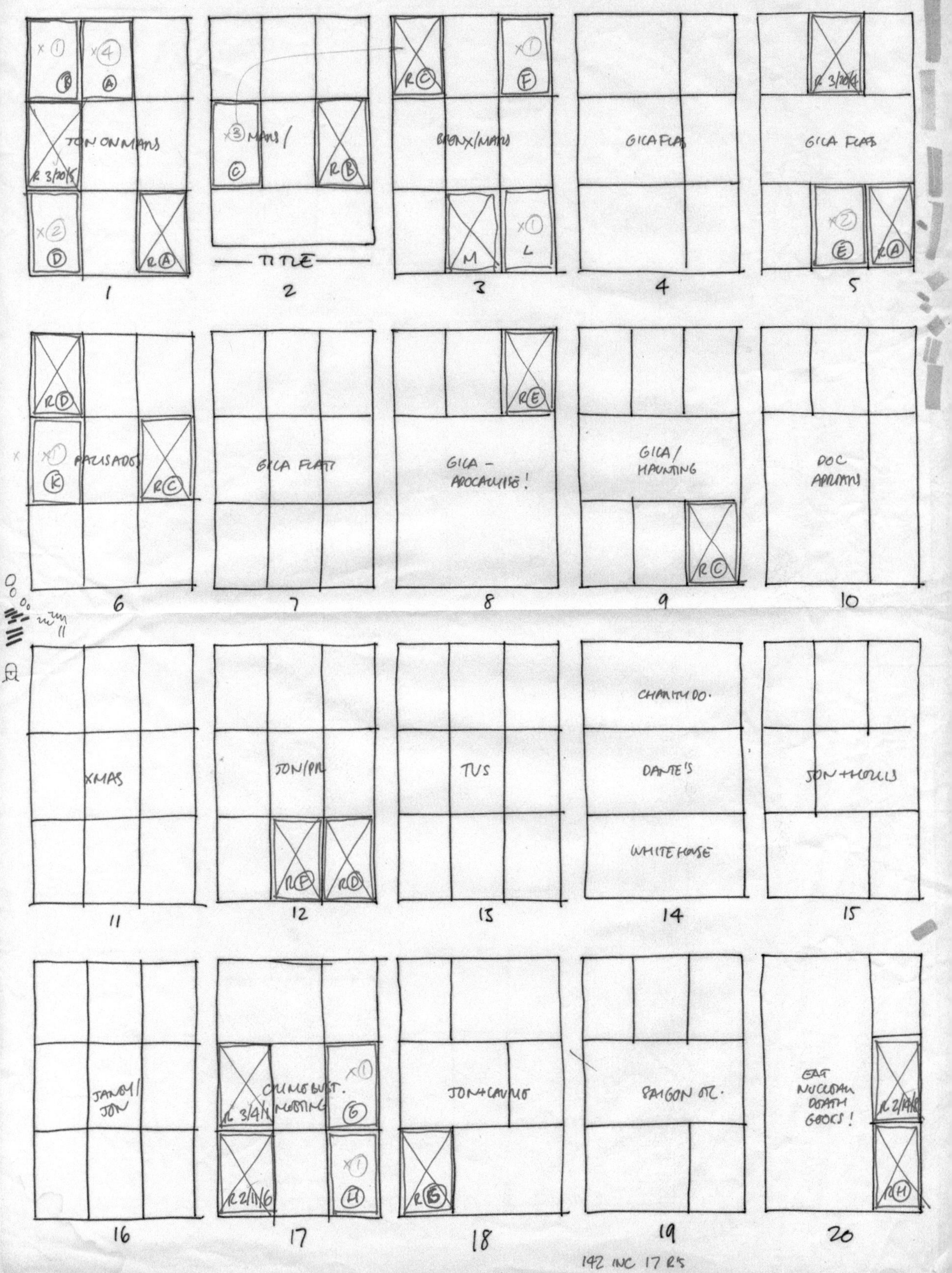
JON ON MARS
MARS /
TITLE
BRONX/MARS
GILA FLATS
GILA FLATS
PALISADES
GILA FLATS
GILA – APOCALYPSE!
GILA / HAUNTING
XMAS
TVS
CHARITY DO.
DANTE'S
WHITE HOUSE
JON + HOLLIS
JANEY / JON
CRIMEBUST. MEETING
JON + LAURIE
SAIGON ETC.
EAT NUCLEAR DEATH GEEKS!
1
2
3
4
5
6
7
8
9
10
11
12
13
14
15
16
17
18
19
20
142 INC 17 R'S

Opposite: Schematic for Moloch's house, showing "camera movement" for Rorschach's approach and interior architecture.

Above: Partial issue plan, showing division of pages and scene lengths.

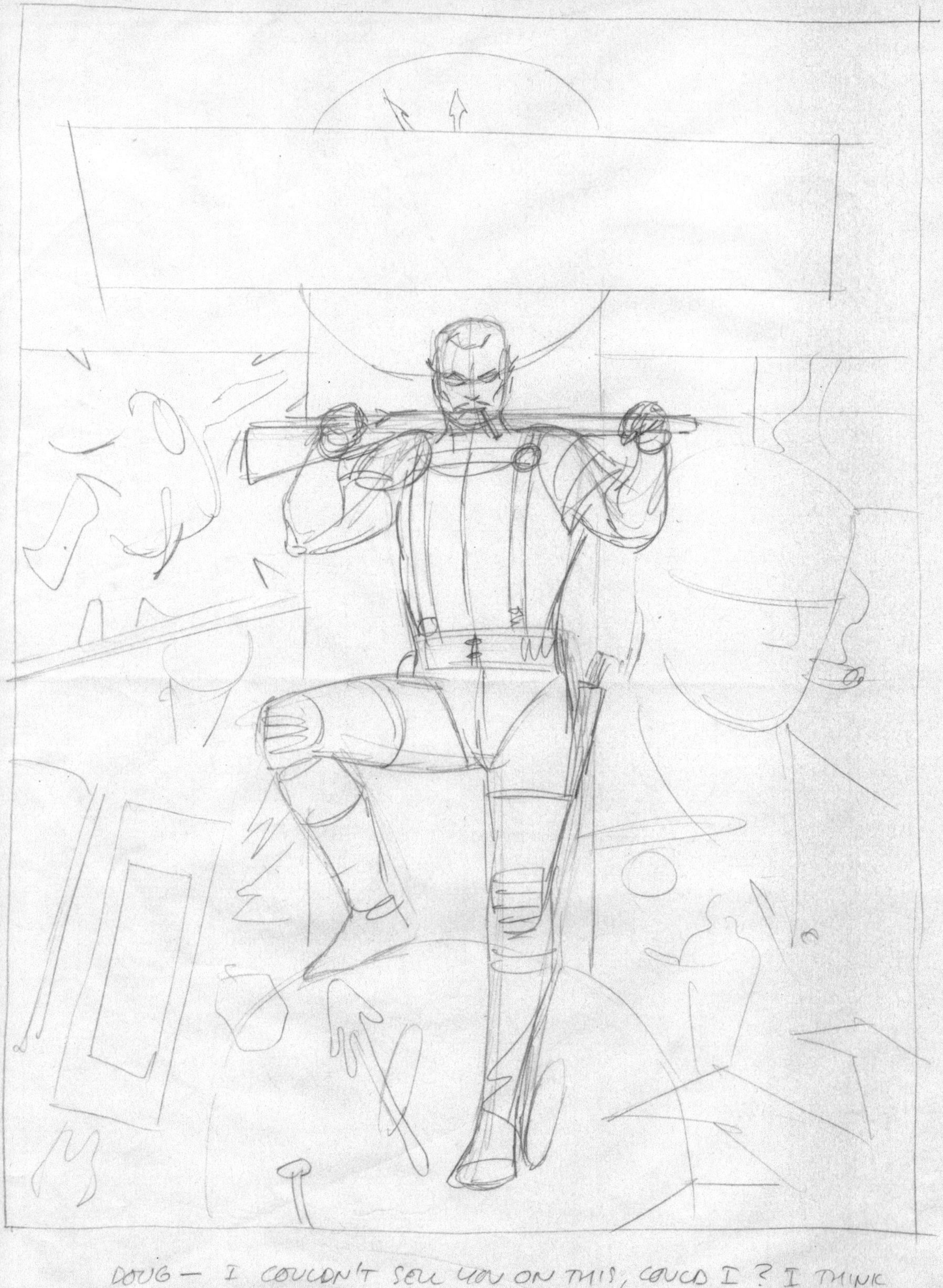

DOUG — I COULDN'T SELL YOU ON THIS, COULD I? I THINK A POSE LIKE THIS HAS MENACE, WHEREAS A RUNNING POSE LOOKS LIKE 'ACTION MAN' OR 'GI JOE' AND IS A LITTLE OUT OF CHARACTER WITH THE SERIES

Dave

(CALL ME LATE WEDNESDAY OR EARLY THURSDAY!)

Preliminary roughs for the first volume of the French album edition featuring the Comedian.

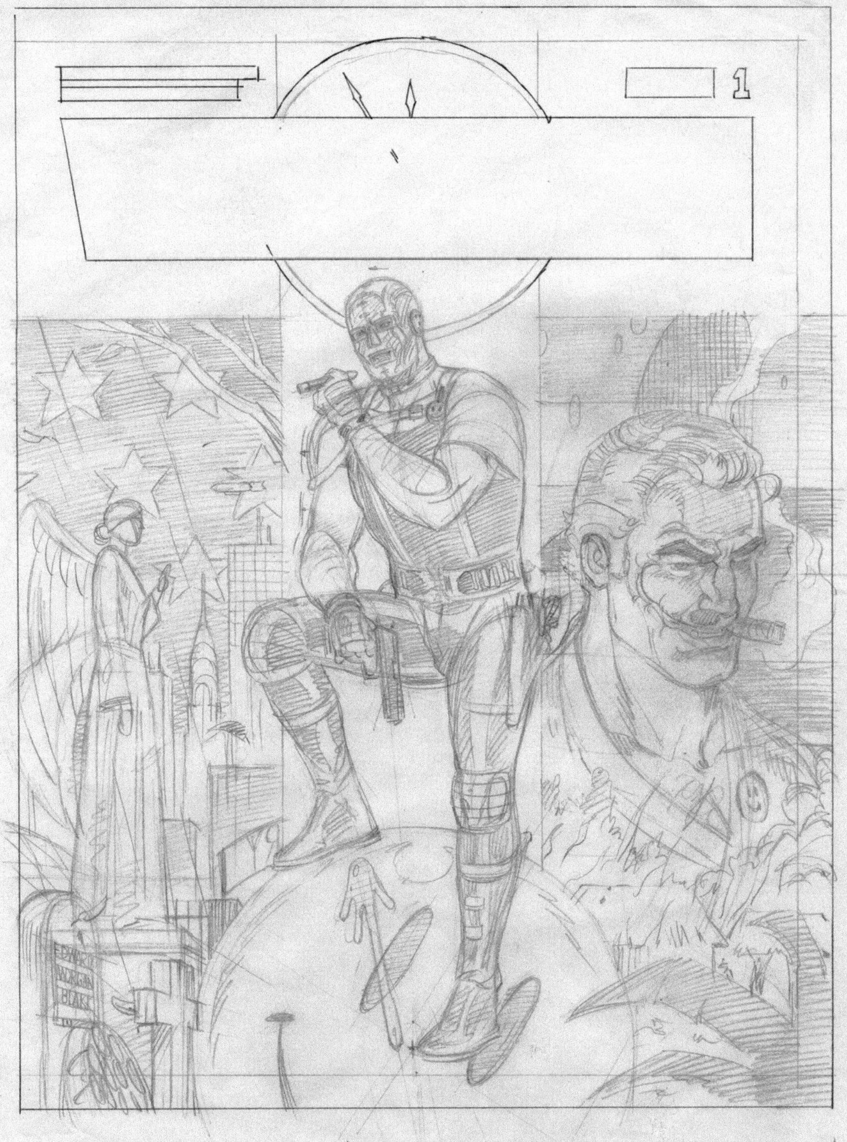
1
EDWARD MORGAN BLAKE

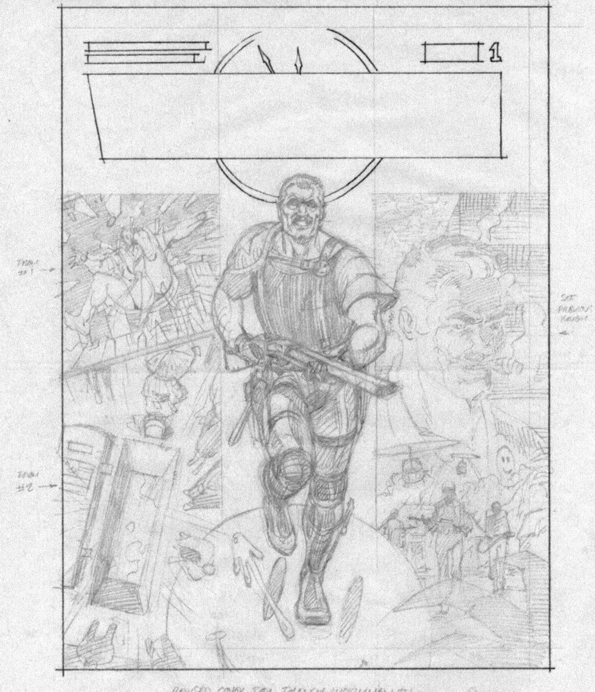
1
REVISED COVER FOR FRENCH WATCHMEN #1

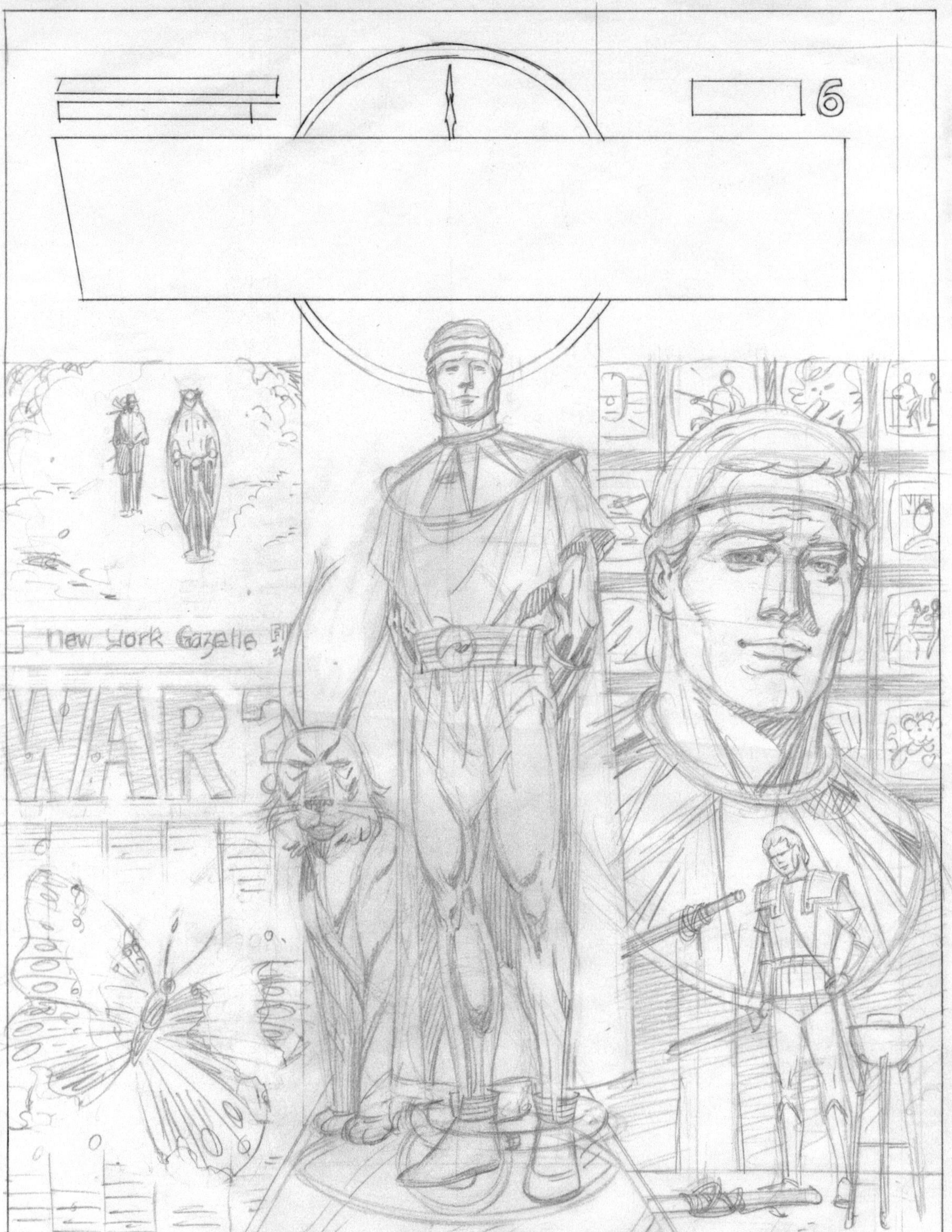
6
New York Gazette
WAR

Preliminary and finished pencilled covers for the French album editions featuring Ozymandias, Silk Spectre, Nite Owl, and Dr. Manhattan.

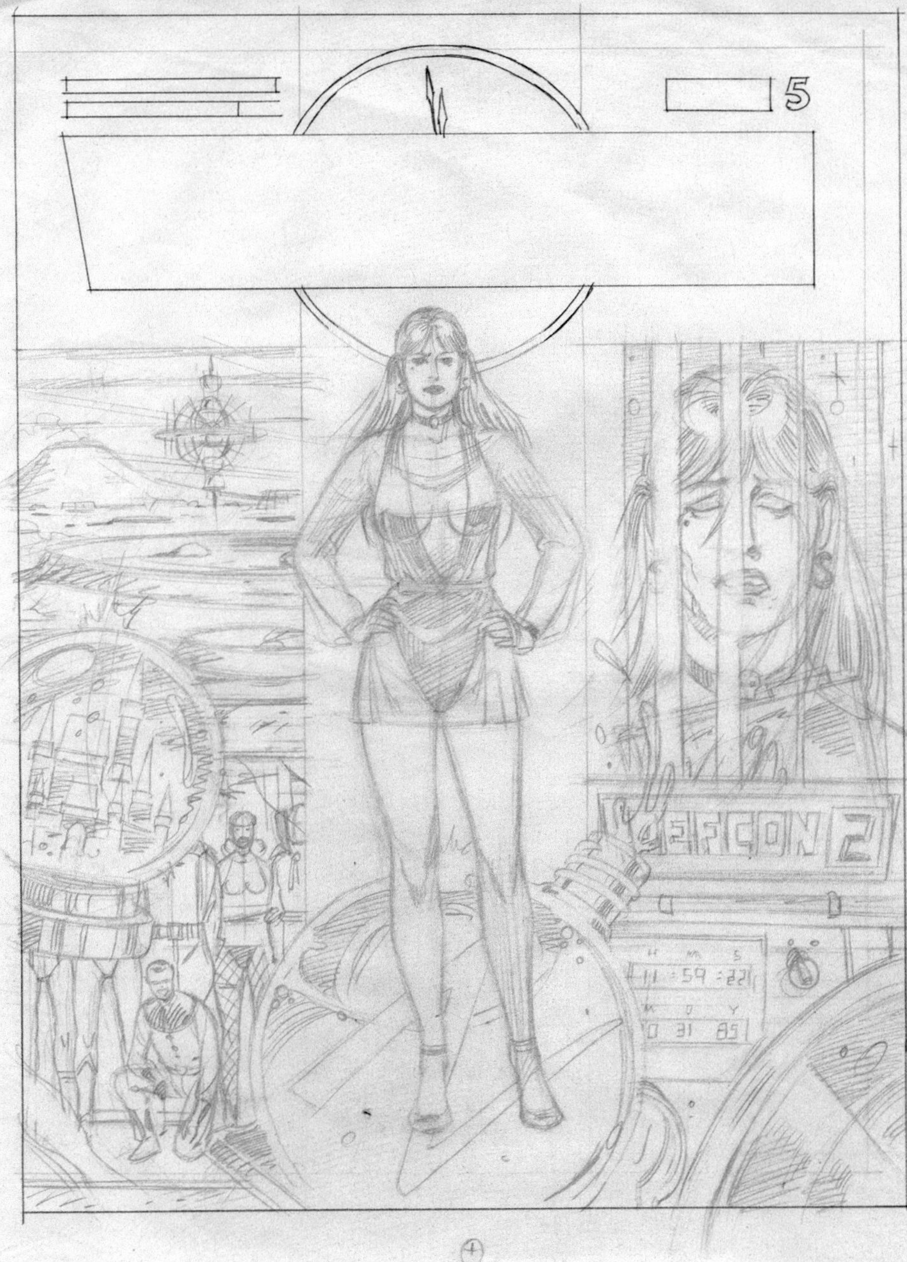
5
EFCON 2
H M S
11 : 59 : 22
M D Y
0 31 85

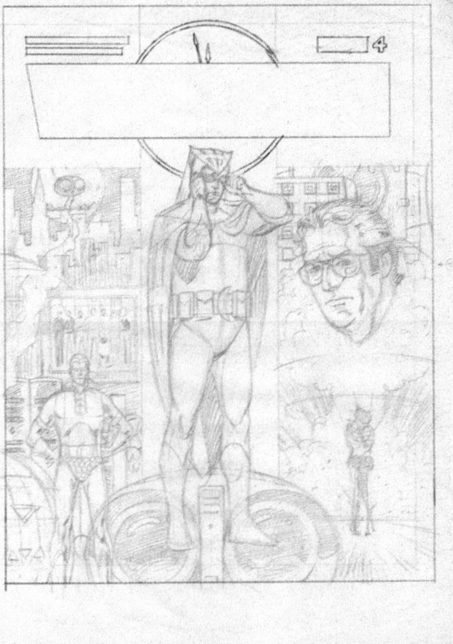
4

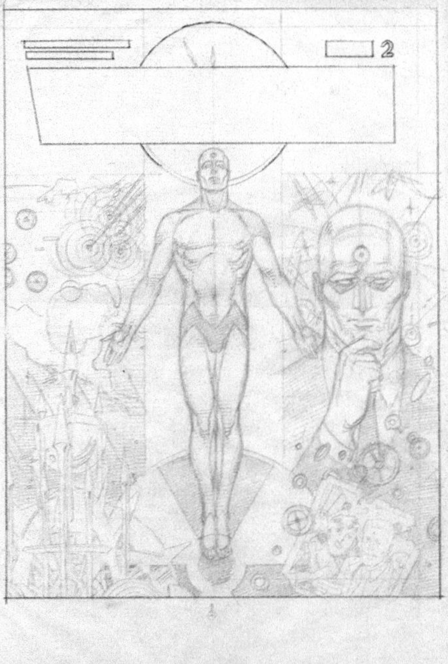
2

Cover illustrations for the French album edition. John Higgins painted over pencils, then Dave Gibbons added detail.

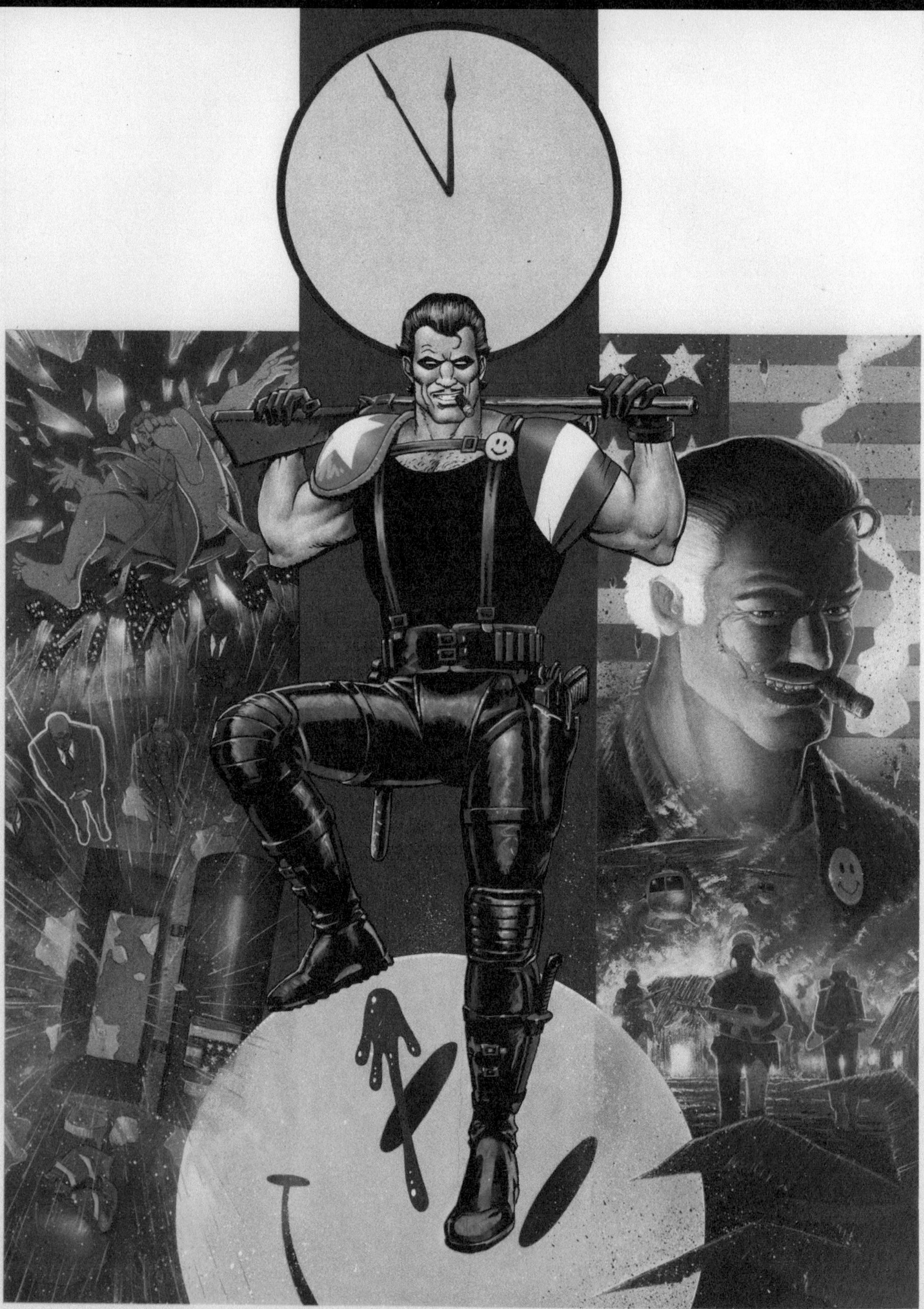

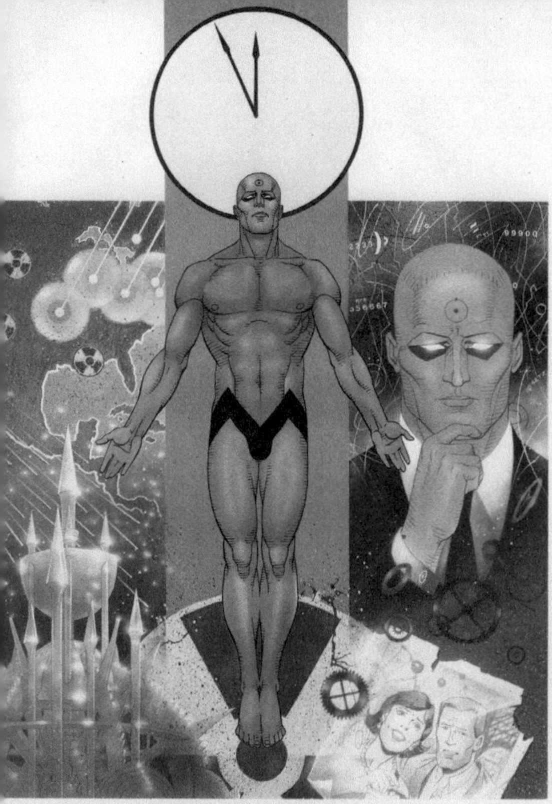

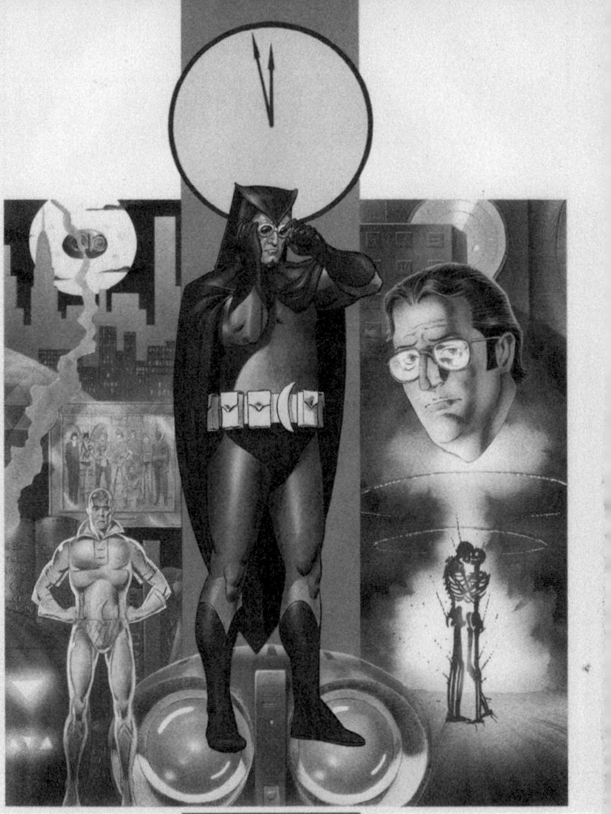

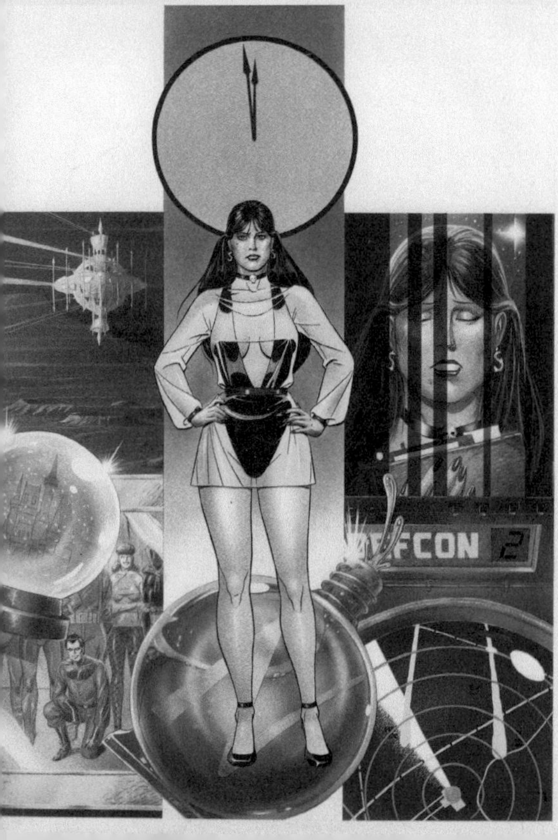

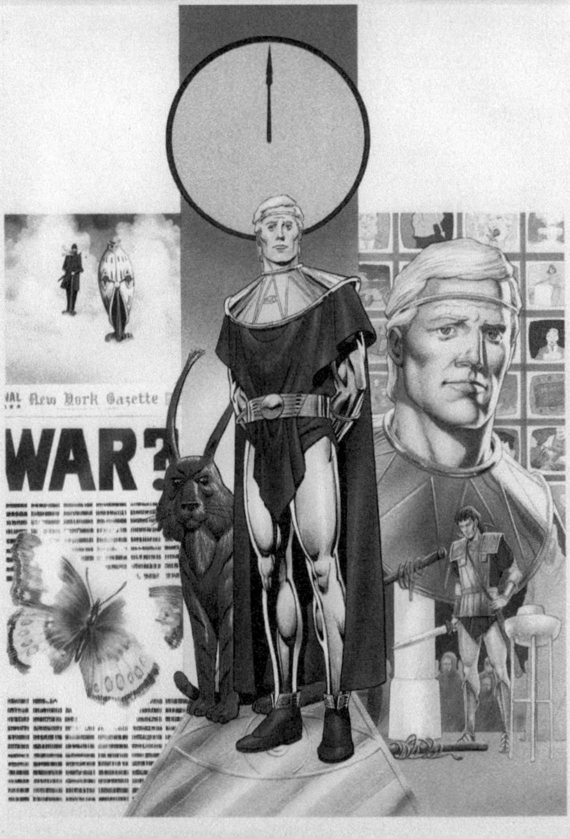
New York Gazette
WAR?

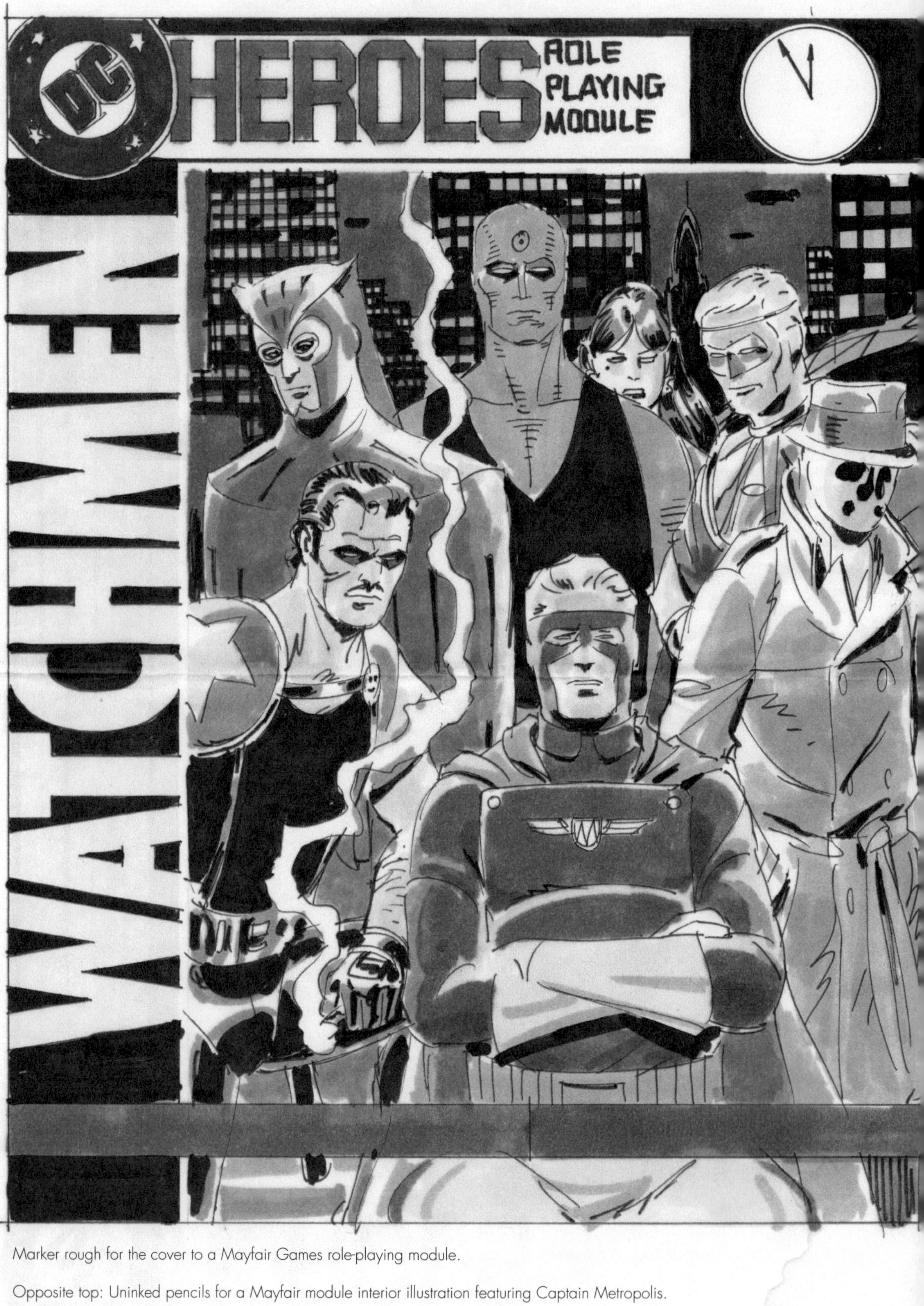
DC
HEROES
ROLE
PLAYING
MODULE
WATCHMEN

Marker rough for the cover to a Mayfair Games role-playing module.

Opposite top: Uninked pencils for a Mayfair module interior illustration featuring Captain Metropolis.

Opposite bottom: Inked interior illustrations of character headshots from the Mayfair role-playing module.

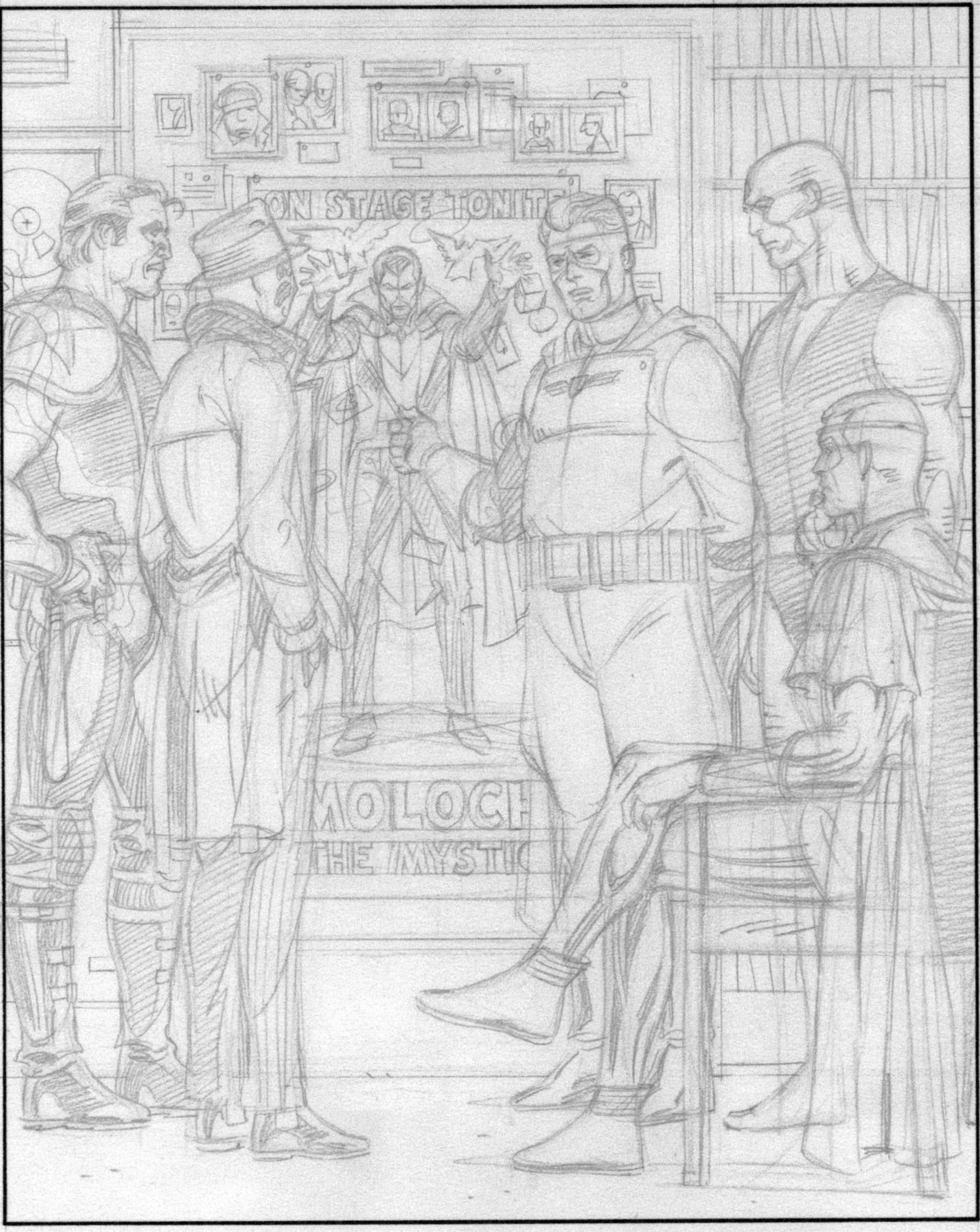
ON STAGE TONIT
MOLOCH
HE MYSTIC

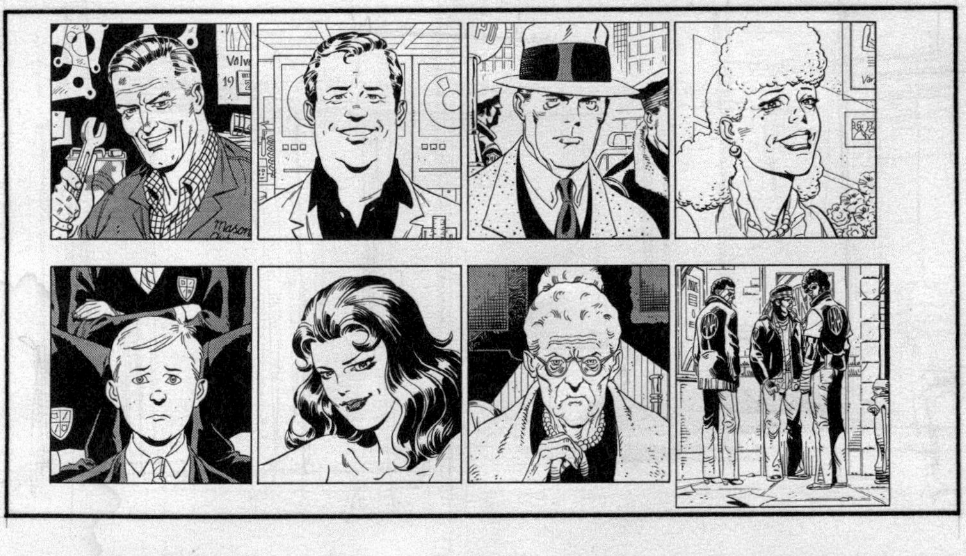

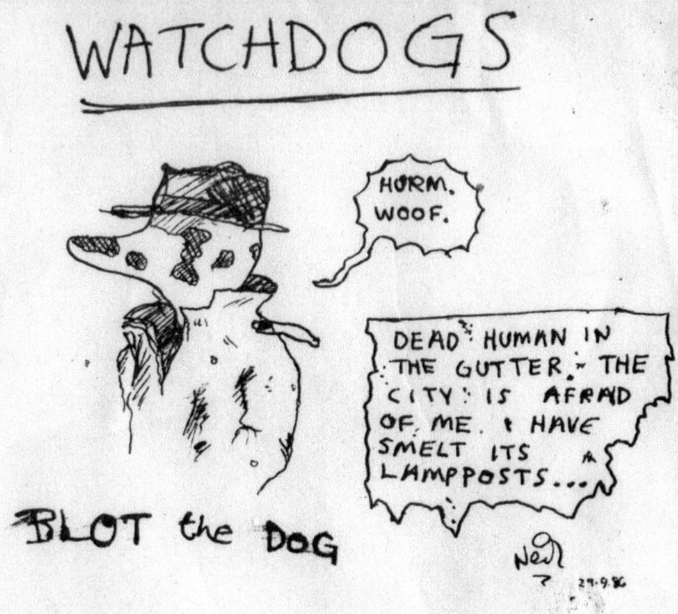
WATCHDOGS
HURM. WOOF.
DEAD HUMAN IN THE GUTTER. THE CITY IS AFRAID OF ME. I HAVE SMELT ITS LAMPPOSTS...
BLOT the DOG
Neil
29.9.86

Sketch of a Watchmen spin off suggestion by a young Neil Gaiman.

Dear Dave —

I'm down at an SF writer's conference near Bournemouth.

Doodled the above, following our panel discussion at UKAKKCN.

Hope life is fine & fun

Neil Gaiman